Twentieth-Century Literary Criticism

Guide to Gale Literary Criticism Series

For criticism on	Consult these Gale series
Authors now living or who died after December 31, 1959	*CONTEMPORARY LITERARY CRITICISM (CLC)*
Authors who died between 1900 and 1959	*TWENTIETH-CENTURY LITERARY CRITICISM (TCLC)*
Authors who died between 1800 and 1899	*NINETEENTH-CENTURY LITERATURE CRITICISM (NCLC)*
Authors who died between 1400 and 1799	*LITERATURE CRITICISM FROM 1400 TO 1800 (LC)* *SHAKESPEAREAN CRITICISM (SC)*
Authors who died before 1400	*CLASSICAL AND MEDIEVAL LITERATURE CRITICISM (CMLC)*
Authors of books for children and young adults	*CHILDREN'S LITERATURE REVIEW (CLR)*
Dramatists	*DRAMA CRITICISM (DC)*
Poets	*POETRY CRITICISM (PC)*
Short story writers	*SHORT STORY CRITICISM (SSC)*
Black writers of the past two hundred years	*BLACK LITERATURE CRITICISM (BLC)*
Hispanic writers of the late nineteenth and twentieth centuries	*HISPANIC LITERATURE CRITICISM (HLC)*
Native North American writers and orators of the eighteenth, nineteenth, and twentieth centuries	*NATIVE NORTH AMERICAN LITERATURE (NNAL)*
Major authors from the Renaissance to the present	*WORLD LITERATURE CRITICISM, 1500 TO THE PRESENT (WLC)*

ISSN 0276-8178

Volume 87

Twentieth-Century Literary Criticism

**Criticism of the
Works of Novelists, Poets, Playwrights,
Short Story Writers, and Other Creative Writers
Who Lived between 1900 and 1960,
from the First Published Critical
Appraisals to Current Evaluations**

**Jennifer Baise
Editor**

**Thomas Ligotti
Associate Editor**

GALE GROUP

*Detroit
San Francisco
London
Boston
Woodbridge, CT*

Contents

Preface vii

Acknowledgments xi

Preface

Since its inception more than fifteen years ago, *Twentieth-Century Literary Criticism* has been purchased and used by nearly 10,000 school, public, and college or university libraries. *TCLC* has covered more than 500 authors, representing 58 nationalities, and over 25,000 titles. No other reference source has surveyed the critical response to twentieth-century authors and literature as thoroughly as *TCLC*. In the words of one reviewer, "there is nothing comparable available." *TCLC* "is a gold mine of information—dates, pseudonyms, biographical information, and criticism from books and periodicals—which many libraries would have difficulty assembling on their own."

Scope of the Series

TCLC is designed to serve as an introduction to authors who died between 1900 and 1960 and to the most significant interpretations of these author's works. The great poets, novelists, short story writers, playwrights, and philosophers of this period are frequently studied in high school and college literature courses. In organizing and reprinting the vast amount of critical material written on these authors, *TCLC* helps students develop valuable insight into literary history, promotes a better understanding of the texts, and sparks ideas for papers and assignments. Each entry in *TCLC* presents a comprehensive survey of an author's career or an individual work of literature and provides the user with a multiplicity of interpretations and assessments. Such variety allows students to pursue their own interests; furthermore, it fosters an awareness that literature is dynamic and responsive to many different opinions.

Every fourth volume of *TCLC* is devoted to literary topics. These topic entries widen the focus of the series from individual authors to such broader subjects as literary movements, prominent themes in twentieth-century literature, literary reaction to political and historical events, significant eras in literary history, prominent literary anniversaries, and the literatures of cultures that are often overlooked by English-speaking readers.

TCLC is designed as a companion series to Gale's *Contemporary Literary Criticism,* which reprints commentary on authors now living or who have died since 1960. Because of the different periods under consideration, there is no duplication of material between *CLC* and *TCLC.* For additional information about *CLC* and Gale's other criticism titles, users should consult the Guide to Gale Literary Criticism Series preceding the title page in this volume.

Coverage

Each volume of *TCLC* is carefully compiled to present:

- criticism of authors, or literary topics, representing a variety of genres and nationalities

- both major and lesser-known writers and literary works of the period

- 6-12 authors or 3-6 topics per volume

- individual entries that survey critical response to each author's work or each topic in literary history, including early criticism to reflect initial reactions; later criticism to represent any rise or decline in reputation; and current retrospective analyses.

Organization of This Book

An author entry consists of the following elements: author heading, biographical and critical introduction, list of principal works, reprints of criticism (each preceded by an annotation and a bibliographic citation), and a bibliography of further reading.

- The **Author Heading** consists of the name under which the author most commonly wrote, followed by birth and death dates. If an author wrote consistently under a pseudonym, the pseudonym will be listed in the author heading and the real name given in parentheses on the first line of the biographical and critical introduction. Also located at the beginning of the introduction to the author entry are any name variations under which an author wrote, including transliterated forms for authors whose languages use nonroman alphabets.

- The **Biographical and Critical Introduction** outlines the author's life and career, as well as the critical issues surrounding his or her work. References to past volumes of *TCLC* are provided at the beginning of the introduction. Additional sources of information in other biographical and critical reference series published by Gale, including *Short Story Criticism, Children's Literature Review, Contemporary Authors, Dictionary of Literary Biography,* and *Something about the Author,* are listed in a box at the end of the entry.

- Some *TCLC* entries include **Portraits** of the author. Entries also may contain reproductions of materials pertinent to an author's career, including manuscript pages, title pages, dust jackets, letters, and drawings, as well as photographs of important people, places, and events in an author's life.

- The **List of Principal Works** is chronological by date of first book publication and identifies the genre of each work. In the case of foreign authors with both foreign-language publications and English translations, the title and date of the first English-language edition are given in brackets. Unless otherwise indicated, dramas are dated by first performance, not first publication.

- Critical essays are prefaced by **Annotations** providing the reader with information about both the critic and the criticism that follows. Included are the critic's reputation, individual approach to literary criticism, and particular expertise in an author's works. Also noted are the relative importance of a work of criticism, the scope of the essay, and the growth of critical controversy or changes in critical trends regarding an author. In some cases, these annotations cross-reference essays by critics who discuss each other's commentary.

- A complete **Bibliographic Citation** designed to facilitate location of the original essay or book precedes each piece of criticism.

- Criticism is arranged chronologically in each author entry to provide a perspective on changes in critical evaluation over the years. All titles of works by the author featured in the entry are printed in boldface type to enable the user to easily locate discussion of particular works. Also for purposes of easier identification, the critic's name and the publication date of the essay are given at the beginning of each piece of criticism. Unsigned criticism is preceded by the title of the journal in which it appeared. Some of the essays in *TCLC* also contain translated material. Unless otherwise noted, translations in brackets are by the editors; translations in parentheses or continuous with the text are by the critic. Publication information (such as footnotes or page and line references to specific editions of works) have been deleted at the editor's discretion to provide smoother reading of the text.

- An annotated list of **Further Reading** appearing at the end of each author entry suggests secondary sources on the author. In some cases it includes essays for which the editors could not obtain reprint rights.

Cumulative Indexes

- Each volume of *TCLC* contains a cumulative **Author Index** listing all authors who have appeared in Gale's Literary Criticism Series, along with cross references to such biographical series as *Contemporary Authors* and *Dictionary of Literary Biography.* For readers' convenience, a complete list of Gale titles included appears on the first page of the author index. Useful for locating authors within the various series, this index is particularly valuable for those authors who are identified by a certain period but who, because of their death dates, are placed in another, or for those authors whose careers span two periods. For example, F. Scott Fitzgerald is found in *TCLC,* yet a writer often associated with him, Ernest Hemingway, is found in *CLC.*

- Each *TCLC* volume includes a cumulative **Nationality Index** which lists all authors who have appeared in *TCLC* volumes, arranged alphabetically under their respective nationalities, as well as Topics volume entries devoted to particular national literatures.

- Each new volume in Gale's Literary Criticism Series includes a cumulative **Topic Index,** which lists all literary topics treated in *NCLC, TCLC, LC 1400-1800,* and the *CLC* yearbook.

- Each new volume of *TCLC,* with the exception of the Topics volumes, includes a **Title Index** listing the titles of all literary works discussed in the volume. In response to numerous suggestions from librarians, Gale has also produced a **Special Paperbound Edition** of the *TCLC* title index. This annual cumulation lists all titles discussed in the series since its inception and is issued with the first volume of *TCLC* published each year. Additional copies of the index are available on request. Librarians and patrons will welcome this separate index; it saves shelf space, is easy to use, and is recyclable upon receipt of the following year's cumulation. Titles discussed in the Topics volume entries are not included *TCLC* cumulative index.

Citing Twentieth-Century Literary Criticism

When writing papers, students who quote directly from any volume in Gale's literary Criticism Series may use the following general forms to footnote reprinted criticism. The first example pertains to materials drawn from periodicals, the second to material reprinted from books.

[1]William H. Slavick, "Going to School to DuBose Heyward," *The Harlem Renaissance Reexamined,* (AMS Press, 1987); reprinted in *Twentieth-Century Literary Criticism,* Vol. 59, ed. Jennifer Gariepy (Detroit: Gale Research, 1995), pp. 94-105.

[2]George Orwell, "Reflections on Gandhi," *Partisan Review,* 6 (Winter 1949), pp. 85-92; reprinted in *Twentieth-Century Literary Criticism,* Vol. 59, ed. Jennifer Gariepy (Detroit: Gale Research, 1995), pp. 40-3.

Suggestions Are Welcome

In response to suggestions, several features have been added to *TCLC* since the series began, including annotations to critical essays, a cumulative index to authors in all Gale literary criticism series, entries devoted to criticism on a single work by a major author, more extensive illustrations, and a title index listing all literary works discussed in the series since its inception.

Readers who wish to suggest authors or topics to appear in future volumes, or who have other suggestions, are cordially invited to write the editors.

Acknowledgments

The editors wish to thank the copyright holders of the criticism included in this volume and the permissions managers of many book and magazine publishing companies for assisting us in securing reproduction rights. We are also grateful to the staffs of the Detroit Public Library, the Library of Congress, the University of Detroit Mercy Library, Wayne State University Purdy/Kresge Library Complex, and the University of Michigan Libraries for making their resources available to us. Following is a list of the copyright holders who have granted us permission to reproduce material in this volume of *TCLC*. Every effort has been made to trace copyright, but if omissions have been made, please let us know.

COPYRIGHTED ESSAYS IN *TCLC*, VOLUME 87, WERE REPRODUCED FROM THE FOLLOWING PERIODICALS:

COPYRIGHTED ESSAYS IN *TCLC*, VOLUME 87, WERE REPRODUCED FROM THE FOLLOWING BOOKS:

the Trustees of the University of Pennsylvania. All rights reserved. Reproduced by permission of the publisher.—Di Piero, W. S. From *Shooting the Works: On Poetry and Pictures.* Triquarterly Books, 1990. Copyright © 1990 by W. S. Di Piero. All rights reserved. Reproduced by permission of Northwestern University Press.—Fleishman, Avrom. From *Figures of Autobiography: The Language of Self-Writing in Victorian and Modern England.* University of California Press, 1983. Copyright © 1983 by The Regents of the University of California. Reproduced by permission.—Harmon, Jim. From *The Great Radio Comedians.* Doubleday & Company, Inc., 1970. Copyright © 1970 by Jim Harmon. All rights reserved. Reproduced by permission of Doubleday, a division of Random House, Inc.—Havig, Alan R. From *Fred Allen's Radio Comedy.* Temple University Press, 1990. Copyright © 1990 Temple University. All rights reserved. Reproduced by permission.—From "'The Logomancers': 1934" in *Estonian Poetry and Language: Studies in Honor of Ants Oras.* Edited by Viktor Koressaar and Aleksis Rannit. VC Kirjastus Vaba Eesti Estonian Learned Society in America, 1965. Reproduced by permission of the author.—Madigan, Mark J. From an introduction to *Keeping Fires Night and Day: Selected Letters of Dorothy Canfield Fisher.* Edited by Mark J. Madigan. University of Missouri Press, 1993. Copyright © 1993 by The Curators of the University of Missouri. All rights reserved. Reproduced by permission.—Matthews, W. K. From "Phases of Estonian Poetry" in *Anthology of Modern Estonian Poetry.* Translated by W. K. Matthews. University of Florida Press, 1953. Copyright 1953 by the University of Florida. Reproduced by permission.—Moore, G. E. From *Philosophical Studies.* Routledge & Kegan Paul Ltd., 1965. Copyright 1922, reprinted in 1948, 1951, 1958, 1960, 1965 by Routledge & Kegan Paul Ltd. Reproduced by permission.—Phillips, Michael J. From *Edwin Muir: A Master of Modern Poetry.* Hackett Publishing Company, Inc., 1978. Copyright © 1978 by Michael J. Phillips. All rights reserved. Reproduced by permission of the author.—Wertheim, Arthur Frank. From *Radio Comedy.* Oxford University Press, 1979. Copyright © 1979 Oxford University Press, Inc. All rights reserved. Used by permission of Oxford University Press, Inc.

PHOTOGRAPHS AND ILLUSTRATIONS APPEARING IN *TCLC*, VOLUME 87, WERE RECEIVED FROM THE FOLLOWING SOURCES:

Allen, Fred, from "Three's A Crowd," photograph. Archive Photos, Inc. Reproduced by permission.

Fred Allen

1894-1956

(Born John Florence Sullivan; also performed as Paul Huckle and Freddy St. James) American humorist

INTRODUCTION

Allen is considered one of the preeminent comedians of America' "Golden Age" of radio humor. His comedy often satirized current events and is noted for exhibiting Allen's wide-ranging intellect and cynicism. Throughout the 1930s and 1940s, Allen hosted a series of radio programs bearing such names as "The Linit Bath Club Revue," "The Salad Bowl Revue," "The Sal Hepatica Revue," "Hour of Smiles," "Town Hall Tonight," and "The Fred Allen Show," the latter which featured the regular and extremely popular segment "Allen's Alley." The Alley was populated by a host of ethnically diverse characters—including Titus Moody, Senator Beauregard Claghorn, Ajax Cassidy, Mrs. Pansy Nussbaum, and Falstaff Openshaw—who commented on contemporary topics in their respective dialects. For example, Senator Claghorn's character as voiced by Kenny Delmar—who also provided the voice for Warner Brothers's animated Looney Tune character, Foghorn Leghorn—lampooned the bombastic and corrupt nature and double-speak of Southern politicians during the era of Louisiana Governor Huey Long. Allen's long-running mock feud with fellow comic Jack Benny gave rise to some of the era's most barbed and caustic humor, and Allen became known for the quick wit exhibited in the comebacks, asides, and rejoinders he directed toward his violin-toting, penurious nemesis.

Biographical Information

Allen was born in Cambridge, Massachusetts. His father was a bookbinder, and his mother died when he was three. He attended Boston High School of Commerce and worked nights at the Boston Public Library. Inspired by reading books on the nature of comedy, Allen taught himself ventriloquism and juggling. An ecstatic audience response to his stage act at the library Christmas show prompted Allen to pursue comedy on a full-time basis. He adopted the name Paul Huckle, European Entertainer, after graduating from high school in 1911, and sought work as a vaudeville comedian. His talents as a juggler, however, were limited, and Allen changed his stage name to Freddy St. James and billed himself as "The World's Worst Juggler." As the latter, Allen would display his ineptness as a juggler, a fact he reinforced with a self-deprecating monologue. In 1916, Allen toured New Zealand and Australia, where he honed his stage act. He returned to the United States, calling himself Fred Allen, and attained critical and

commercial success for his appearances at New York's Broadway Palace Theater, as well as in the revues *The Passing Show of 1922*, *The Greenwich Village Follies* and *The Little Show* in 1929, as well as *Three's a Crowd* (1930). In 1932, Allen hosted "The Linit Bath Club Revue" half-hour radio program with his wife and co-star Portland Hoffa. Of the next two programs hosted by Allen, "The Salad Bowl Revue," and "The Sal Hepatica Revue," the latter evolved into "Hour of Smiles," and eventually "Town Hall Tonight." The program, renamed "The Fred Allen Show," consistently attracted a large number of listeners throughout the next eight years, an audience that swelled with the growing popularity of "Allen's Alley" in the 1940s. For this show, Allen also assembled The Mighty Allen Art Players, which included Kenny Delmar, Alan Reed (later the voice of Hanna Barbera's animated Fred Flintsone), Minerva Pious, and Peter Donald. This troupe created topical humor with such parodies as One Long Pan, the Oriental detective based on Charlie Chan, and "The Radio Mikado," which borrowed heavily from Gilbert and Sullivan's operetta *The Mikado* to skewer radio and advertising executives. In other episodes, the Art Players lampooned both the Brooklyn Dodgers and Gilbert and Sullivan's *H.M.S. Pinafore*, and a parody of Rodgers and Hammersteins's *Oklahoma!* called "Picadilly!" As the 1940s drew to a close and game shows and television became the more prominent entertainment medium, Allen's radio audience declined, and his program was cancelled in 1949. Allen suffered a heart attack in 1952 as he was preparing to launch his own television program, relegating him to perform in his own sparsely-viewed television special and guest-star on several other stars's television shows. He described his appearance on television as "not videogenic. After my only video appearance I received fan mail from three undertakers." He eventually became a panelist on the game show "What's My Line?" a position he held until his death in 1956.

Major Works

Allen's humor is noted for its reliance on sarcasm, cynicism, and a scathingly intelligent wit, which he delivered with a nasal whine in a deadpan fashion. Allen also perfected a very sharp style of insult; he once questioned a particularly aggressive foe: "Did your parents ever consider birth control?" Most critics agree Allen was at his best when he performed with Jack Benny. The feud between Allen and Benny ensured high listening ratings, and prompted a series of films starring the duo, including *Love Thy Neighbor.* Allen also perfected the double-entendre as a means of getting his jokes past the network censors, and employed hyperbolic metaphors to describe people to humorous effect. Allen published *Treadmill to Oblivion* (1954), which recounts his early years in radio and includes some of his most famous humor, and an autobiography, *Much Ado about Me* (1956). His *Letters* (1965) were published posthumously, and include correspondence with such comics as Jack Benny and Groucho Marx.

PRINCIPAL WORKS

Treadmill to Oblivion (memoirs) 1954
Much Ado about Me (autobiography) 1956
Letters (letters) 1965

CRITICISM

Maurice Zolotow (essay date 1944)

SOURCE: "Fred Allen: Strickly from Misery (with a rebuttal by Mr. Allen)," in *These Were Our Years: A Panoramic and Nostalgic Look at American Life between the Two World Wars,* edited by Frank Brookhouser, Doubleday & Company, Inc., 1959, pp. 486-94.

[*In the following essay, originally published in 1944, Zolotow offers personal observations of Allen, to which Allen himself replies in footnotes.*]

NOTE: *Fred Allen read this chapter on himself. His observations are printed, exactly as he wrote them, in the footnotes. Mr. Allen does not like capital letters.*

Unlike some comedians who are lifelong victims of a self-hatred implanted when they were young and who are compelled to devote their humor to ridiculing themselves, Fred Allen has always poured out his bitterness and his scorn upon the world. For a long time he was a successful radio star, earning plenty of money, with a nice wife with whom he lived in comfortable circumstances. This did not prevent him from finding his environment a veritable chamber of horrors. "Eventually," he once told a researcher for *Time* magazine, "I have high hopes I'll be able to withdraw from the human race."

For about twenty years, Allen has been complaining about sponsors, radio vice-presidents, the stupid public and other facets of life in these United States. The United States had turned the other cheek to his complaints and showered fame and wealth upon him. But finally, beginning in 1946, the environment really turned on Fred. The jackpot shows brought about his ruination in radio. He had had a high Hooper rating when "Stop The Music" started in opposition to him. "Stop The Music" offered a fantastic series of prizes to anybody who, upon being telephoned, could correctly identify the title of a "mystery melody." The prizes—which included trips to Hawaii, wardrobes, mink coats, silver flatware, automobiles—often had a value as high as $30,000. Unable to compete with Santa Claus, Allen saw his rating drop, drop, drop. He lost millions of listeners. During the 1947-48 season, he dropped from his traditional position in the first ten of radio to number 38.

When he returned with his Allen's Alley characters in October, 1948, he announced that the National Surety Company had written a bond to cover any listener who might be called by "Stop The Music" but who couldn't supply the melody because he was busy listening to the Allen show. Any such victim of the urge to be entertained would receive $5,000. This didn't help. Then Fred started satirizing give-aways. He put on a sketch entitled "Cease The Melody," which offered the winner eight hundred pounds of putty for every member of the family; four thousand yards of dental floss, almost new; an RCA Victor television set, complete with saloon and bartender; twelve miles of railroad track; and, for the jackpot, a real live human being! Nothing helped. In 1949, radio's greatest social satirist withdrew in defeat.

Then in 1950 Allen made two sorties into television—both shows fell flat. Allen retired on his favorite excuse of high blood pressure. Now he appears as a guest on Tallulah Bankhead's Big Show and other programs.

His views on television and radio have always been caustic. Before trying television, he had already told Joe McCarthy, "Television is nothing like vaudeville. In vaudeville you had one act and a constantly changing audience. You used a routine in Philadelphia one week and you used it again in Wilkes-Barre the next week. You could work it into a state of perfection. TV, like radio, is just the opposite. You have the same audience all the time, so the act must be changed after each performance. Naturally, the quality of the material gets low." Pointing out that the television screen was too tiny to register subtleties, he said, "The only way you can register mild disapproval on TV is to hit somebody over the head with a broom." The studio audiences he describes as "hordes of cackling geese . . . Would anybody with a brain be caught dead in a studio audience? Would anybody with a sense of taste stand in line to watch half a dozen people in business suits and tortoise-shell glasses standing around reading into microphones off pieces of paper?"

This is a story which has been told about many great comedians and it is also told about Allen. A man went to a doctor. The man complained of sleeplessness, loss of appetite and general irritability. The doctor put him through the paces of a complete physical check-up and he found nothing wrong. He finally advised his patient to learn to smile and relax, to have a good time. He told him to visit the Music Box Theatre and see Fred Allen in *The Little Show,* then Broadway's smash comedy. He said that this man Allen would snap anybody out of the doleful doldrums. He said his prescription was a visit to the Allen show every night for a week. The man said, "But I can't do this."

The doctor wanted to know why not. "You see," replied the patient desperately, his sad face deepening. "I *am* Fred Allen."[1]

This tale may be apocryphal, but it illuminates a fact. Fred Allen, who used to receive $4,000 a week[2] for making twenty million radio listeners laugh, is himself amused by very little in the world. He is a morbid gentleman who wears a perpetual air of having just finished sucking on a particularly bitter lemon.

Allen is not unhandsome. He is five feet eleven inches tall, and weighs a tidy one hundred eighty two pounds, which is mainly muscle. He has a lithe figure and is quick on his toes. He works out at a YMCA gymnasium once a week, doing some light calisthenics, playing handball and casually sparring. He is a fine amateur boxer and has mastered a very deceptive left hook. But when he is in his usual mood of misery and dejection, Allen contorts his long, egg-shaped head,[3] curls his lips, squints his eyes, wrinkles up his face and takes on the combined expressions of Dracula, Fu Manchu and The Phantom of the Opera. The fascinated spectator sees only the enormous pouches under the comedian's eyes—pouches large enough to contain a good-sized kangaroo baby.[4] And yet, actually, Allen, in a relaxed and genial

moment, is dapper and good-looking, resembling the suave ex-mayor, Jimmy Walker.

Allen speaks in a slow drawl, slurring his words, speaking through his nose with a pronounced twang. He cannot help saying clever things. His larynx manufactures humor[5] as effortlessly and naturally as the human liver secretes bile. And the words Allen discharges are original and imaginative discharges of hostility through the linguistic zone. He has inherited the Irish gift of blarney, the gift of clothing an idea in picturesque language. The eyes are also Irish—they are ice-blue eyes, but they are not smiling Irish eyes.[6] They glance about restlessly, taking in everything, blinking often. Allen has many nervous tics—the eyes blinking,[7] the fingers, long and spatulate, rubbing the tip of his nose or massaging the lobes of his ears. When he smiles, perhaps once every two or three hours, it is a grim smile.

Some of Allen's friends suspect his perpetual despondency is a pose. "Fred is never happy unless he's grousing about something," one of them says. On the other hand, to Allen his hostility is a logical reaction to frustration that surrounds him on every side.

He loves to smoke; he used to smoke fifteen cigars a day, and chew tobacco in between cigars. His doctors have made him cut out smoking. He says he has acute hypertension, with his blood pressure reading as high as 207.[8]

Allen likes to eat spicy Italian dishes, lobster Cantonese, thick juicy steaks, shrimp a la Newburg. His doctors—who include naturopaths as well as the orthodox kind—have forbidden him to touch shellfish, red meat, salt, pepper, coffee or tea. His diet consists mainly of salads and whole-wheat bread.[9] The food is washed down with beakers of buttermilk, a beverage he despises.

"You finally get to do so well in your career, all you can drink is buttermilk," he once remarked to me. "When they start feeding me intravenously, I'll know I've really arrived at the top."

Allen dislikes mixing with people, yet he must attend conferences, socialize with prospective sponsors, pose for photographs, be interviewed. He likes to be alone and read books, but the pressure of creating thousands of new and hilarious words[10] every time he goes on the air doesn't give him time to read more than a few pages a day.

Radio is a repugnant medium of entertainment[11] in his opinion and TV is worse. Allen says the reason they call television a *medium* is because nothing is well done on it. Yet he must appear several times a month on various programs. "Radio comedy," he drawls, "is the most painful form of entertaining. Every week you've got to be there with a new set of gags. When they invented radio, they should also have invented a mechanical robot to turn out new gags. You can't copyright a joke. And this pressure for new ideas drives every comedian on the air into becoming a vulture. I don't blame them.

I blame their gag writers.[12] You can't tell a new joke on the radio without hearing it in almost the same version on almost every other comedy show during the week." Allen, the wittiest[13] and most creative of radio comedians, suffers more than any other wag.

Allen doesn't like studio audiences.[14] So whenever he appears there is always a studio filled with spectators. The theory is that a background of laughter and applause is necessary; otherwise the jokes would sound hollow to the persons listening at home. Eddie Cantor was the first to insist on audiences for his broadcast. Many comedians feel that their timing goes off without an immediate audience reaction. In addition, many of them probably require the approval of an audience to sustain their self-confidence. But Allen's self is organized on a basis of presumed hostility from others and therefore he has no use for any audience. "Did you ever buy a phonograph record with applause?" he inquires.

He claims the audience laughs waste precious minutes. In addition, a radio comedian must insert "sight gags," like tearing his hair, lifting up a trouser leg, to get laughs from the studio audience. These are lost on the home listeners. To get a yak[15] from New York studio audiences he had to insert local gags about Mayor Impellitteri or Leo Durocher. "Who cares about Impy in Medicine Hat, North Dakota?"[16] Allen asks.

Allen feels uncomfortable with advertising agencies. So for years he has been employed by various agencies. Allen once described an agency as 85 per cent confusion and 15 per cent commission. The jargon of agency men and their tight-lipped[17] attitude to life bewilders him. Once he wanted to do a sketch based on the "call for Philip Morris" slogan. He planned to have a voice cry into the mike, "Call for Philip Morris . . . Call for Philip Morris." And another voice would say, "Who wants him?" And the first voice replies, "Draft board 68—his number came up." The agency handling Allen's shows at the time wanted to revise the gag slightly. They were handling a rival cigarette and they asked Allen to change his script, so it read, "Call for Lucky Strikes . . . Call for Lucky Strikes." Wouldn't hurt the point a bit, they insisted.

As for radio and TV, Allen calls it hag-ridden by red tape, bureaucracy, nepotism, buck passing and ignorance of the fundamentals of show business. He defines a conference of radio executives as a meeting at which a group of men who, singly, can do nothing, agree collectively that nothing can be done. Vice-presidents he particularly loathes.[18] On his program he used to introduce such NBC executives as the vice-president in charge of leaky Dixie cups, the vice-president in charge of uh-uh, and the vice-president in charge of Don't Raise That Window Another Inch. Actually, the networks have given him a lot of leeway.[19]

Allen can't stand Hollywood—so he is intermittently going out to the coast to make a movie, which invariably flops. Among his observations on the movie capital are these gems: "Hollywood is a place where people from Iowa mistake each other for stars." "In Hollywood, the girls have false hair, teeth and calves on their legs. The men have their shoulders built up and wear toupees. So when two stars make love on the screen, it's a lot of commodities getting together." "California is a wonderful place to live—if you're an orange." "An associate producer is the only guy in Hollywood who will associate with a producer."

Allen's sarcastic drive refuses to respect any person, any institution—and therefore he has always been embroiled with radio censors. "A radio censor," he once explained, "is a man who comes into his office every morning and finds a molehill on his desk. His job is to build that molehill into a mountain before he goes home."

Once he threw in a line that ran, "I knew Ebbets Field was haunted when that old bat spoke to me." This was censored because the censor thought the remark might be interpreted as a slur on American motherhood. Another time, a lady[20] who had just been promoted to censoring, noticed the word "segue" repeated several times in an Allen script. "Segue" is a standard cue in show business; it means "glide into" the next bit of dialogue or music. The lady thought "segue" had immoral overtones. She expurgated all the "segues" in the script. "Nobody," Allen recalls bitterly, "was going to segue on the National Broadcasting Company as long as *she* was around, she said. She would see to *that!*"

Once, on CBS, there was a line in the script, reading, "They'll bring it through, come hell or high water." Fred turned to a CBS censor and asked, "Can we get a clearance on high water?"

Censoring Allen, however, is not final. He has a mischievous tongue and is the fastest ad-lib gagster in the business.[21] His sponsors have always trembled at the spontaneous and dangerous gags he may pull which aren't written on paper. Once when Bristol-Myers was paying his salary, he made a biting reference to Scottish thrift, and two hundred Scotsmen in Pittsburgh[22] signed an indignant letter stating they would never use Sal Hepatica again.

"The prospect that they would go through life constipated so frightened the agency that they made me apologize," Allen says.

Another time, he ridiculed the American Meat Institute for hiring Edgar Guest to write inspirational poems about meat. Armour & Company[23] promptly threatened they would stop using Texaco products in their trucks. When he told about a student pharmacist who failed to get his degree because "he flunked in chow mein," the American druggists descended on him like a swarm of wasps. Speaking of Philadelphia, Allen said he once checked into a hotel there and the rooms were so small even the mice were hunch-backed. Allen was publicly denounced as a vile rascal by the Philadelphia Chamber of Commerce, the Convention & Tourist Committee, and the All Philadelphia Citizens Committee.[24] The *Public Ledger* attacked him in an editorial, headed PHILADELPHIA FIGHTS BACK. Allen replied as follows:

> dr. editor,
>
> the remarks made on my program concerned a small theatrical hotel in phila. twenty-five years ago. no mention was made on my program and no aspersions cast on the many excellent hotels in phila. today. i know that the benjamin franklin hotel is so named because you can fly a kite in any room. i know that the rooms at the walton are so large the world's fair is stopping there when it goes on the road next fall. i know that the rooms at the bellevue-stratford are so spacious that the army-navy game can be played in a closet. and i know that billy rose rehearsed his aquacade in a sink in one of mr. lamaze's mastodonic rooms at the warwick.
>
>   yrs., fred allen.

Secretly, Allen is pleased by all the hubbub he occasionally stirs up. He likes to think of a comedian not merely as a clown in cap and bells, but as a critic of current folly[25] who is an effective influence on his contemporaries. He thinks the sheer quantity of machine-made comedy pouring out of the radio night after night tends to dull the average person's responses. "Before radio, when a Will Rogers or a Peter Finley Dunne made a wisecrack it would be quoted from one end of the country to the other, and everyone repeated it for a month," he says. "Today, nobody remembers what I[26] said on the radio last week, except some gag writers who are figuring ways to steal the jokes. Everything on radio and television is as fleeting as a butterfly's f—t."

To Allen, creating comedy is a serious affair. He has collected and studied over four thousand humorous books and he has read every biography of anybody he considers a humorist—whether it's Mark Twain, Eugene Field or Charles Dickens. He has a good mind and a good memory. When I asked him to sum up his attitude toward life, he said, "Life is an unprofitable episode that disturbs an otherwise blessed state of nonexistence." Then he paused and added slowly, "That's from Nietzsche." He sees most human beings around him as troubled, tired, frustrated, confused. "They're in life's dead storage, the parking lot of humanity," he mutters. Once he saw a small boy dart in front of a truck. Allen quickly moved out and pulled the boy to safety. Then he snarled at him, "What's the matter, kid? Don't you want to grow up and have troubles?"

NOTES

[1] this couldn't have happened to me. i go to a chiropractor. during my adjustments i lie face down. the chiropractor doesn't know who i am. if he did ask me a question, my face is buried in the table. my answer would be muffled.

[2] mr. zolotow doesn't mention the specific week this amount was earned. you can learn my salary by writing my sponsor. if you are a sadist, and you want to know what i have left, write mr. j. h. snyder.

[3] in the preceding paragraph i was "not unhandsome." here i have an egg-shaped head. as beauty goes mr. z. must use salvador dali standards. if my head was eggshaped i would use a nest for a pillow. i don't.

[4] my bags aren't that big. my eyes look as though they are peeping over two dirty ping pong balls.

[5] humor originates in the brain. it is dispensed through the mouth. the larynx is only the middle man.

[6] the author of this is no smiling irishman.

[7] this is not nervousness. i have too much iron in my blood. my eyelids keep falling-down.

[8] mr. z. has my blood pressure confused with my salary. day to day systolic and diastolic readings will be forwarded upon receipt of a three-cent stamp.

[9] m. z. obviously had this diet left over from an old peter rabbit interview.

[10] there are no new words. i try to use the old words in new combinations.

[11] i didn't say repugnant. radio is a giant gimmick that demands new material in mass production quantities. for the creative artist, radio is a form of drudgery.

[12] the average radio gag writer is an emaciated nonentity with a good memory and a pencil.

[13] jack benny and his relatives will resent this.

[14] i have nothing against these people individually. if they didn't collect in radio studios i might think highly of them.

[15] for mr. z's information a yak is a gamey quadruped found in zoos and crossword puzzles. a laugh, in radio parlance, is a yuck.

[16] medicine hat is in alberta, canada. moving a canadian city into the u.s. may give the impression that the marshall plan is back-firing.

[17] far from being tight-lipped most agency men are big-mouthed. the only tight-lipped men in radio are oboe players.

[18] the average vice-president is a form of executive fungus that attaches itself to a desk. on a boat this growth would be called a barnacle.

[19] a network won't give you the right time. they let bulova do it and charge him for the privilege.

[20] this lady is no longer a censor. she walked into a mirror, one day, came to herself, and quit the whole business.

[21] bob hope and his relatives will resent this.

[22] it was philadelphia where the movement was abandoned.

[23] toujours l'armour. but not in this instance. the meat concern was swift & co.

[24] philadelphia was bidding for the republican convention that year. the various local organizations thought the republicans might feel there wasn't a room in philadelphia large enough to hold the elephant.

[25] in bygone days ridicule was known to hamper folly. today the world is upside down and exponents of folly outrank disciples of ridicule.

[26] or anybody else.

Steve Allen (essay date 1956)

SOURCE: "Fred Allen," in *The Funny Men,* Simon and Schuster, 1956, pp. 34-59.

[*In the following essay, Allen—a noted comedian and television host and no relation to Fred Allen—reminisces about Allen, his career in radio, and the reasons behind his failure to adapt his comic style to television.*]

St. Patrick's Day 1956 was one I shall not soon forget. The day before—Friday, March 16—New York was hit by an unseasonal blizzard and on Saturday the city's Irish paraded through snow and bitter cold. One elderly Irishman that night took a stroll from which he never returned. About the time he was putting on his overcoat to go out I was sitting in a room on the twelfth floor of the Waldorf-Astoria with Sid Caesar and several members of his staff. We had just come upstairs after attending the annual award ceremonies of the Academy of Television Arts and Sciences and were enjoying a social drink while discussing that favorite conversational topic of all comedians: comedy.

Sid told a few funny stories about his experiences in Europe, and then somehow the conversation got around to Fred Allen, as it often does when professional humorists get together. Sid recalled how impressed he was one day several years before when Fred had dropped into his theater at rehearsal time. "It was really something," he said. "Here was this guy I had listened to on the old Majestic all through my childhood years, this guy who seemed like God or somebody, and all of a sudden there he was hanging around my theater."

"What did you do?" I asked.

"Oh, just talked for a while. It was the day Truman was going through town in some big parade or something. I remember we went outside to watch him go by, and after he'd passed I said, 'Harry looks a little like he's sick,' and Fred said, 'Doesn't surprise me. He probably caught it from the country.'"

When Jayne and I left the Waldorf we drove Carl Reiner and his wife to their garage, and as we stopped for a red light at the corner of 57th Street and Seventh Avenue we saw Sylvia and Leonard Lyons. Since cabs were at a premium, we offered them a lift, and as they climbed into the car Jayne noticed that Sylvia seemed shaken. It was then that Leonard told us that Fred Allen had just died. Leonard had identified the body, and to him had fallen the grim task of telling Portland the sad news.

The following day *What's My Line?* called me and asked me to fill in for Fred. Portland had vetoed replacement of the regular format with a special tribute and had suggested instead that the program, in show-business tradition, go on as usual. At the conclusion of the show that evening I said something that still expresses better than any other words I might now create what I felt at Fred's passing: "A few months ago Fred read a postcard here on the show, a card asking, 'Is Fred Allen Steve Allen's father?' Fred laughed and explained that the answer was no. But last night when I heard of his death I couldn't have been more deeply affected if the answer had been yes."

The next day, Monday, Bennett Cerf, Howard Deitz, Bob Hope, Kenny Delmar, Peter Donald, John Crosby, Herman Wouk and Jack Benny gathered on my late-night program to pay tribute to Fred, to tell of their love and respect for him and, oddly enough at such a sad time, to laugh heartily at his remembered jokes. I remembered thinking during that program what a peculiar thing it was that such a vast talent as Fred's had gone largely unhonored by television. Consider, for a moment, the background.

The opinion seems to be popular that the entertainment field is at all times vastly overstocked with talented people and that, therefore, only a select few can get to the top, while the rest must inevitably wend their broken way into obscurity.

Like a great many popular opinions, this one is composed of one part truth and nine parts nonsense. There is only one branch of show business that honestly appears to have more talent than can ever possibly be accommodated: the song-writing field. There are millions of people around who can write a pretty fair song in whole or in part, but the market for popular music in this country is so restricted that a stable of five or six competent tunesmiths could easily satisfy the entire normal demand.

The illusion that there are too many talented performers in the other areas of the entertainment world is created by the great deal of hustle and bustle in agency offices, endless union membership lists and cutthroat competition for available work. True, indeed, there are too many people looking for work as clarinet players, tap dancers, acrobats and singers, but the brutal fact of the matter is that a strikingly small minority of these ambitious entertainers have anything more than run-of-the-mill ability.

In fact, it is the very paucity of genius that explains why a good many artistically impoverished individuals achieve success anyway. There are simply so many motion pictures to be made, so many plays to be produced, so many orchestras to put together, so many broadcasts to be aired, and if there is not enough real talent to go around, why then it is the most natural thing in the world that the fates should say to a few fortunate folk, "You have not really enough ability to be a star, but we are casting around for a star today, so you'll do until the real thing comes along."

Which makes me remember the story of an actor who went to his psychiatrist. "Doctor," he said, "you've got to help me. I have no talent, I can't sing on key, I can't dance, I don't tell funny stories and I'm not handsome. What would you suggest?"

"Why, the solution is simplicity itself," said the doctor. "You've got to get out of show business."

"But I can't," the actor said. "I'm a star!"

Granted, then, that success is not always predicated upon ability, is it nevertheless true that a great many unrecognized talents are doomed to mill forever with the unheralded throng simply because of the strangling competition? As they used to say in the Army, that's a good question. The answer to it is "No!"

There is a period through which every successful entertainer suffers and during which his innate or acquired talent is nurtured and developed until it matures to the point where it demands recognition. But the idea that the woods are full of people who could sing just as well as Bing Crosby if someone would only give them the chance, or people who could act rings around Marlon Brando if some producer would only audition them, is extremely unrealistic.

All right. We've established there are really too many talented song writers. At the opposite end of the chart explaining supply-and-demand relationships you'll find the word *comedians*. There are really not enough of these, believe it or not. If every big singer in the country retired tomorrow you'd have a new crop of kids ready to fill their shoes within two years. But if all the top-bracket funnymen in the business were taken away from us, it would be a long time before the pain of their loss would be eased.

Hollywood can find plenty of collar-ad faces to throw upon its screens, the record industry will always come up with at least acceptable voices, casting directors can thumb through card indexes for various sorts of talents, but only the comedian is in such demand that he can almost name his own price in the hectic entertainment market. There are thousands of singers, dancers, magicians and actors swarming in and out of theaters and broadcasting studios, but almost the entire job of making America laugh is handled by a small group of some thirty men.

Thus it is particularly puzzling that one of this select group, and the one, indeed, that was considered by many authorities to be the group's leading wit, was, so far as television is concerned, more or less out of work, partly retired to the status of great-white-father-grand-old-man of contemporary comedy.

You almost get angry at the whole medium, wondering why it couldn't seem to accommodate a man who could say of California, "It's a great place to live, if you're an orange."

Television needed a man who could say of Georgie Jessel, "Georgie loves after-dinner speaking so much he starts a speech at the mere sight of bread crumbs."

When the price of milk in New York City rose to twenty-two cents a quart it was Fred who said, "Milk hasn't been so high since the cow jumped over the moon."

In Lindy's one night Leonard Lyons heard Oscar Levant ask, "Fred, are you an egomaniac?" "No, Oscar," Fred replied. "I've heard that the meek shall inherit the earth and I'm standing by to collect."

Although he may have just been going for a joke in response to Oscar's question, Fred spoke the truth about himself. He was the meekest, the least phony of all the famous performers I've met. He never publicly associated himself with any charity, but he was the most charitable man I've known. But a lot of wealthy men give money; Fred gave *himself* in addition—his time and his talent. He came through for a lot of us. Dave Garroway and Henry Morgan found Fred in their corners during the early days of their struggle for recognition. Herb Shriner was suggested by Fred to replace him when his first heart attack forced him to withdraw from *Two for the Money*. Red Skelton says it was Fred who wrote Red's famous Guzzler's Gin routine. I will always be grateful to Fred for appearing on a special *Tonight* broadcast celebrating the opening of *The Benny Goodman Story*. We were stuck for a big-name star to open the show. When we told Fred our problem he agreed on the spot to step in. And he was in great form that night. It was to be his last big monologue.

So what about Fred and television? Where did the trouble lie? I think the fault was neither Fred's nor TV's. It was just one of those things. Fred's greatest work was behind him, after all, and though he was brilliantly witty to his last day, he was ill at ease before the camera. *What's My Line?* gave him at best openings for only two or three jokes per broadcast. None of his classically witty prepared material could be brought to the panel table since the show is unrehearsed and ad-libbed, and although he was a master of the off-the-cuff chatter, he was always somewhat distracted by the mechanics of the game itself. Now and then, of course, he would score strongly. One night, speaking to a shoe-maker who mentioned the name of Gino Prato, Fred said, "I wish you'd tell Gino to hurry back from Europe. He's got a pair of my shoes locked in his store." But most of the laughs on *What's My Line?* came from the confusion of the panelists and the double-meanings that often stem from their ignorance of the professions they are trying to identify. The Fred Allen of *What's My Line?* was not the *real* Fred Allen. It was true that, as Madison Avenue parlance has it, he hadn't "found himself" in television.

This search for one's self in the TV jungles can be a pretty frightening thing, too. When CBS first brought me from Hollywood to New York there were regular executive sessions devoted to "finding the real Steve Allen." I had been conducting a well-received radio show five nights a week on station KNX, and it was presumably the success of this program that induced the network to transfer me to its eastern headquarters. But as soon as I arrived in town there began a search for the "real" me. I became so wary of the mechanics of this probe that I eventually began to fancy that I was being followed through the halls of 485 Madison Avenue by vice-presidents with pith helmets and butterfly nets.

Poor Fred had gone through the same sort of thing for about four years. But he was philosophical about it. Lunching with John Crosby one day at the Plaza, he smiled amiably to a lady who had nodded a greeting from across the room. "I have to be very careful," he said. "My public has shrunk to such an extent that I have to be polite to all of them. I even say hello to people in sewers. You know, I went off the air once before, back in 1944. We got three letters deploring it. This time we're way ahead of that: I think we got fifteen."

From the beginning, oddly enough, even way back before he had to work in the medium, Fred had cast a suspicious eye at television. "When you see Kukla, Fran, and Ollie come alive on that little screen, you realize you don't need great big things as we had in radio. They ought to get one of those African fellows over here to shrink all the actors. We're all too big for this medium.

"TV," he said, "gets tiresome. Take *The Goldbergs*, which has been so well received. It's a good show, but it gets so after you see it four or five times you know what the uncle is going to do and you know what the kids are going to do. The trouble with television is it's *too* graphic. In radio, a moron could visualize things his way; an intelligent man, his way.

"Everything is for the eye these days—TV, *Life, Look,* the movies. Nothing is for just the mind. The next generation will have eyeballs as big as cantaloupes and no brain at all."

Of all the prominent comedians, Allen most closely approached the status of a philosopher. Since a philosopher must, by the very nature of his mission, be a critic it follows that Fred's was comedy with a heavy critical content. For some as yet unidentified reason television is the first medium in history not only to put a low price on critical humor but practically to exclude it altogether.

The theater, the press, the lecture platform, radio—all accommodated pungent satire, all were successfully used as bases from which to fire the barbed comic shaft. Television, possibly because of its complete sensual intimacy, possibly because it is a medium wherein a picture may detract from, rather than add to, an idea, has placed the sardonic humorist in an awkward position.

Some thought had been given, therefore, to "softening up" Allen's comedic style. There had been attempts to make him what the trade refers to as "gracious and warm." Such efforts were, naturally, doomed to failure, if only on an old-dog-new-tricks basis. Fred was, after all, the king of radio comedy, and kings are notoriously opposed to change, particularly of a personal nature. Besides, one cannot help feeling that Fred really shouldn't have been asked to modify his professional personality. He had never had to sell "himself" before; he had simply presented amusing ideas. It is audiences, perhaps, who should be asked to change. How dare they, one is tempted to demand, not enjoy the work of a man who brought them so much pleasure on the radio?

Fred's bitterness was a pose and a disguise anyway. Its existence was real enough, but it was a camouflage for his true personality, which *was* gracious and warm. Unlike some performers who are angels to the public and devils to their associates, he exposed his Mephistophelean side to his public and worked his good deeds in the anonymity of his daily routine. While he was an outspoken individualist and a man of many dislikes, he was an eminently enjoyable companion and a top-notch conversationalist. Modest, soft-spoken, without a trace of phoniness, he was also privately known as a push-over for anybody in need of a handout. Friends say he had one of the longest "pension" lists in show business. Almost every successful performer has a small and usually vocal circle of people who choose to be identified as enemies; I have never heard anyone say a word against Fred Allen.

Mark Goodson, who with his partner Bill Todman produces such shows as *What's My Line?, I've Got a Secret, Two for the Money* (which was originally created for Fred), and Fred's *Judge for Yourself,* had this to say about Allen's personality: "Fred is a complete paradox. On the air he can't function unless he's holding something of life up by a tweezers and frowning at it. If we had a contestant on the show who had just lost a leg, saved somebody's life, beat out a fire with his bare hands and joined the Marines, Fred would simply be constitutionally unable to say to the guy, 'Gosh, we certainly are proud and happy to have you with us tonight.' And yet, after the show, when some glad-handing emcee might be brushing the hero off, Fred would probably hand him a personal check for two hundred dollars and walk away fast."

Sam Levenson has several theories about Allen's difficulties before the camera. "We all love the real Fred Allen," he says, "but I think what is basically wrong is that he doesn't look well on TV. By that I mean he doesn't screen well. Also, on radio the listeners used their imaginations. It helped. Another point is that Fred has worked with a script in his hands for twenty years and it's very difficult for him to get used to this new medium."

Fred himself admitted the problem is a big one. "We all have a great problem—Hope, Benny, all of us. We don't know how to duplicate our success in radio. We found out how to cope with radio, and after seventeen years you know pretty well what effect you're achieving. But the same things won't work in television. Jack Benny's sound effects, Fibber McGee's closet—they just won't be funny in television. We don't know what will be funny or even whether our looks are acceptable."

It is my opinion that the frequently heard reference to Fred's doleful physiognomy does not represent a true reason for his television contretemps. If he had done the proper sort of program for him I believe it would not have mattered what he looked like. When has there ever been a handsome comedian anyway? Fred in person made studio and theater audiences laugh for years and they saw his face. And in 3-D and color at that.

Fred, by the way, directed a considerable amount of criticism at people who go to see television comedy programs and sit in their seats and laugh.

He started it six years ago. He said, "The worst thing that ever happened to radio was the studio audience. Somebody like Eddie Cantor brought these hordes of cackling geese in because he couldn't work without a bunch of imbeciles laughing at his jokes."

Every comedian, of course, is just a little bit afraid of an audience. It isn't stage fright; that's no problem. What you're afraid of is that the people won't laugh. But Fred had never let up on the pew-holders. "Would anybody with a brain be caught dead in a studio audience?" he has demanded. "Would anybody with a sense of taste stand in line to watch half a dozen people in business suits standing around reading into microphones?"

Allen and a lot of other people who are of the same mind liked to hark back to the days of Stoopnagle and Bud, Amos and Andy, and Easy Aces. "There," they

say, "were comedy shows without a live audience. We should never have made a change."

On this point alone I confess that I always disagreed with Fred.

The old quarter-hour shows were funny all right, but personally I laughed louder at Fred Allen's radio program, the one with the studio audience. And I laughed louder at it than I would have if Fred had broadcast the exact same scripts from an empty room.

Basically, it's a matter of mass psychology. The appreciation of humor is at its heart an emotional matter. You won't laugh at the most amusing joke in the world if you're not "in the mood." And when are you more in the mood for laughter—when you're sitting in a room by yourself or when you're with a large group of friends?

I always have thought that Danny Kaye was about as funny as anybody ever gets in the movies. His pictures usually make me laugh so loud I embarrass my companions. But one time I saw one of his pictures at a drive-in theater. I didn't laugh aloud once. I didn't hear anybody else laughing.

Fred knew that a joke with which he could make a friend chuckle on the street would make an audience of fifty laugh deeply, and could make an audience of five hundred roar for perhaps half a minute.

But sometimes people say, "Why don't they just *try* a comedy show without an audience?"

They have. Henry Morgan did once. Just once. The script was marvelous and Henry was in top form. But at home I didn't crack a smile. Next week Henry performed before his usual crowd and I laughed aloud.

"But," a last-ditcher may protest, "what you say only applies to out-and-out joke programs. What about situation-comedy shows? Wouldn't they be better if the viewer at home could make up his own mind about when to laugh?"

Of course not. Ever see a rehearsal of a comedy in an empty theater? 'Tain't funny, McGee. *Mr. Peepers, I Love Lucy*—all the good situation-comedy shows are helped by the sound of laughter. There *is* one culprit we can do without, though. That's the guy who does a bad job of dubbing in tape-recorded laughter on filmed programs. A laugh has a certain mathematical logicality in relation to the joke that precedes it.

To get back to Fred, one valid explanation of his difficulty with the visual medium lies in the obvious fact that he was a humorist; he worked with the word. His material usually looked as funny in print as it sounded coming out of his mouth. You cannot say the same for material offered by a Jackie Gleason or a Milton Berle.

Allen was the king of wits in radio, where the spoken word was all. He was not helped by the camera. It was a hindrance and a distraction to the true appreciation of his humor.

Fred realized this himself. Speaking of his ill-fated **Judge for Yourself** program, he had said, "There are so many things to keep in mind and cues to look out for. No sooner do I get going smoothly on an interview than I get a hand signal to break it up. A television performer is surrounded by bloody commotion."

Never were truer words spoken. In radio the only thing moving on the stage at any given moment was the comedian's mouth. Supporting players have been fired for crossing their legs or in any other way distracting the attention of the studio audience during a broadcast, and with some justification. A comedian is hired to make people laugh. If there is extraneous movement in the studio, it competes for the attention of the audience. If an audience's attention is divided, it does not laugh.

I shall never forget my first experience on television. Used to the rigid silence of radio studios, the rapt attention of the people in the seats, I was horrified to learn that instead of being separated from the audience by one thin microphone, I was now required to reach them through a jungle of cameras, lights, props, microphone dollies and scenery inhabited by three cameramen, two men working microphones, numerous stagehands creeping around in the darkness, assorted production assistants, who strode around with headphones muttering audibly while receiving communications from the control booth, and a generous collection of announcers, musicians, actors and dancers. Trying to make an audience laugh under these circumstances is a little like working at the Palace while between you and the footlights the Harlem Globe-Trotters map out a few fast-moving plays.

TV studio audiences are usually so fascinated at being behind the scenes that they can scarcely take their eyes off the cameras to look at the actors. Frequently, I have sat in the living room with friends watching one or another comedian suddenly garner four or five seconds of silence for a joke that was obviously of high caliber. The reason may well have been something like a stagehand walking in front of the audience with a ladder. You don't see him at home. All you see at home is the comic with egg on his face.

This sort of situation is particularly troublesome to a performer like Allen who brought no definite physical plus to a delivery of his lines. Unless an audience was paying strict attention to what he said, his gems sometimes were not picked up. The timing of a joke is a delicate thing; with a comic like Allen it didn't require much to throw that timing off.

Not many people know, incidentally, that no matter who you are you don't get as big laughs in a TV studio as you do in a radio studio. Besides the matter of physical distraction, there is the issue of microphone pickup and studio sound amplification. In radio a comedian's mouth was usually four or five inches away from the mike. That meant the engineers could get a full, close, rich pickup of his voice, and the public-address system could throw it clearly into all corners of the studio. In TV theaters, mikes are usually kept invisible. That means they are floating around out of the picture two or three feet over the performers' heads. In order to send out sound of the same volume as was maintained in radio the engineers must crank up the gain very high. That opens the delicate mikes and means the public-address system in the studio tends to play the sound so loud that it floats back into the open microphones, producing that loud, screeching howl you sometimes hear. It's called "feedback." Now no self-respecting engineer likes to hear feedback, so he solves the problem simply by turning down the volume of the public-address system. That prevents feedback all right, but it also makes it relatively difficult for the people in the theater to hear the comedian. When they have trouble hearing they laugh less. You at home just get the impression the comic isn't very funny. Often he's doing jokes he's been doing successfully for twenty years. He may not be getting laughs on a particular night because of technical reasons.

This is a thing every comedian knows the way he knows the Ten Commandments (which may, now that I think of it, be a fairly ill-advised figure of speech). But no one else ever believes him.

I did a program once on CBS television called *Songs for Sale*. It was a popular show and had a respectable rating. But the first night I went on the air I didn't get as many laughs as I felt I deserved. The next morning there was a meeting of executive and production minds.

"We didn't think much of the jokes last night, Steve," a program head told me amiably. "How would you like a new group of writers?"

"To tell you the truth," I said, "the audience couldn't hear very well in that studio. The jokes were funny enough; the people just didn't get a chance to show what they thought of them."

"I understand Hal Collins may be available soon," somebody said. "I think he's leaving Berle."

"Is Collins an engineer?" I asked.

Everyone smiled at what they thought was a quip. It developed Collins was a gag writer.

Believe it or not, every single Monday morning for six weeks we had that same damned production meeting, and finally the writers working on the show were actually dismissed. I was still holding out for a new public-address system. Fortunately, one night the hand of God fell upon the situation. Frank Stanton, CBS top man, happened to step into the theater while the program was in progress. After a few moments he walked into the control room. "I can't hear very well standing in the back of the studio," he said.

The following morning there was no meeting to discuss the program's faults. Instead, a gang of engineers was sent into the studio with instructions to rip out the old PA system and install new equipment. The next Saturday night I got my full quota of laughs. The studio has been a good one for comedy shows ever since, and I was happy to observe a few months ago, when I dropped into it to watch the Jackie Gleason show, that the sound setup had been even further improved by the addition of two new extra-loud speakers down in the first row. Evidently Jackie had demanded it. Bless his heart.

A comedian of Fred's type is considerably handicapped by the technical exigencies of TV, and he seemed to appreciate the point fully.

"The television set," he said in explanation, "just isn't an instrument of wit. The comedy you see on TV is physical rather than mental and is based largely on old burlesque routines. Take Sid Caesar. He's one of the finest comedians on the air, but if you analyze his comedy you'll find it's the physical type."

True enough. Much TV humor *is* physical and such of it as is not is usually worked into a sketch. Even comics such as Bob Hope and Milton Berle, who made their reputations standing up and firing one big joke after another at pointblank range, have come to realize that TV audiences want to get interested in some sort of story line. The question is: Where did this leave Fred Allen?

I'll be darned if I know. All I know is I loved his humor.

Fred was classic with descriptions and comparisons and exaggerations. That's why he's the most quoted comedian of our time. I will always think that one of the funniest jokes ever written was Fred's crack about the scarecrow that "scared the crows so badly they brought back the corn they had stolen two years before."

James Thurber says one of his favorite lines was Fred's remark to a bass player whose instrument made such strange sounds that Fred peered down into the pit and said to him, "How much would you charge to haunt a house?"

Another line that broke me up was Fred's answer to a friend who inquired about his destination one time when he was making a trip out of New York. "I'm going to Boston to see my doctor," said Fred. "He's a very sick man." It was Fred who said, in discussing a geometry problem, "Let X equal the signature of my father."

But these are all what the trade calls stand-up jokes, jokes to be flung in an audience's teeth. And therein lies one clue to Fred's TV difficulties. He could function only as an observer, a commentator, a humorist, not as an actor. Fred was patently an inadequate sketch comic. He had no ability to "lose himself" in a character. He could put on a costume and say a line out loud, all right, but you never believed he was the character he was portraying in the way you believe that Sid Caesar or Jackie Gleason or Milton Berle have adopted a mystically different personality.

All other comedians can sell you a bad line by giving it a physical push. Jerry Lewis can convulse an audience with a weak gag by mugging as he delivers it. Sid Caesar can do a dialect or emote or make a face and thus make almost any line seem funny. Jackie Gleason can punch a line out with such gusto that you laugh before you know what you're laughing at. But Fred Allen had to have a good solid joke for you or you didn't laugh. The point is not made for the sake of criticism. It is made to explain why Fred—who had only dazzling wit to sell—was ill at ease in the medium of television.

Allen's dilemma might have seemed solved when we remember that there are other comedians functioning successfully in TV who do not do sketches. Groucho Marx doesn't. Herb Shriner doesn't.

The solution, then, seems simple. Make him a quizmaster. Only thing wrong is that this particular solution had been tried and found wanting. Fred's **Judge for Yourself** was called by one critic "a pointless hodgepodge," although it was produced by the same organization that put together Herb Shriner's successful *Two for the Money* and was loosely similar to Groucho's *You Bet Your Life*. The quiz-game format seemed a natural for Allen because he was one of that small minority of comedians able to ad-lib. Like Groucho and Shriner, he was given the additional benefit of interviews that were more or less written out in advance. But Fred lacked a quality that Groucho and Shriner have. His mind was rapier-quick, but he was not used to making small talk with relative nonentities. He was not entirely at ease with bus drivers and dentists and housewives from Des Moines. He was too honest not to be distracted by the technical froth of "the game," and the result was that he did not develop the ability to relax entirely with his guests. If he *could* have relaxed, he could probably have done a better job than either Groucho or Shriner on a nothing-set-up-no-holds-barred interview, but he did not seem to be psychologically constituted to handle this particular sort of assignment so late in the game. He was impatient and confined and conscious of the pressure on him.

The solution, I think, would have been to give him the sort of program that Arthur Godfrey or Garry Moore or I do. Give him a table and a microphone and a couple of singers to fill in the holes and then just throw him a newspaper headline or a human-interest subject and I'll bet he'd have been off to the races.

These programs have writers, too, of course. Fred could have had all the help he needed and he'd have had time to prepare any jokes or stories he wanted. But he'd also have had unlimited freedom. He'd have been under no mechanical restrictions. If he got something going that was funny he could have let it roll as long as it felt good. If something went wrong on the program he could have stopped everything and talked about what had gone wrong. If his interest in a subject lagged he could have called on the orchestra or one of the singers or a guest star. He could at last have been as funny on TV as he was when you talked to him on the sidewalk. Ask any comedian in the business. He'll tell you that Fred Allen was king of the performing humorists.

I ran into Henry Morgan one night last summer on Fifty-Second Street and he was chuckling.

"What's funny?" I asked.

"I was just talking to Fred Allen," he said. "Met him coming out of the Waldorf. I asked him what he'd been doing and he said he'd just left a dinner sponsored by the National Conference of Christians and Jews. And then he said, 'You know, Henry, I was just wondering . . . do *we* really deserve top billing?'"

One thing that long fascinated me about Fred's comedy was that it was probably more secure from plagiarism than that of any other performing humorist. Most of Fred's jokes had to be heard coming out of *his* mouth to sound as funny as they were. If one did not hear them, one had to draw up a mental picture of Allen, one had to imagine that one heard his nasal, twanging voice or much of the enjoyment of the humor was lost.

I'll try to demonstrate.

One night when Milton Berle was doing a warm-up for his radio show somebody turned on a light in the sponsor's booth, revealing to the studio audience that there was no sponsor, no sign of life whatever, in the booth. "Ladies and gentlemen," Milton said, "that booth is a device to belittle the comedian by showing him that the sponsor doesn't care enough for his program to attend it."

At that point a page boy hurried in and switched off the light, which caused Milton to say, "Ah, a boy who has the guts to turn off the lights without a memo from a vice-president will go right to the top of the organization."

Now regardless of what your reaction was to the above story, I feel quite certain that one thing will be generally admitted: you were not really very amused by it. Milton's comments seem more sarcastic than funny, and they are certainly not jokes. At best, they might get from the average audience a sort of sympathetic chuckle.

The point of my example is this: Milton Berle never had any such experience. *The thing happened to Fred Allen* and when he responded as indicated above the audience fell into paroxysms of laughter. Believe it or not, if you go back and read the details of the incident over again (this time picturing Fred Allen at the microphone instead of Milton Berle) *you* will laugh too.

Debating some point or other with Fred one evening on my late-night TV show I happened to say, "Well, of course there are two sides to this thing." "There are two sides to a Decca record, too," said Fred, and the audience laughed. I laughed, too, for I was genuinely amused. But I do not believe I would have laughed if the remark had been made by Red Buttons.

Who would laugh to hear Herb Shriner say, "A vice-president is a bit of executive fungus that forms on a desk that has been exposed to conference"?

No, I believe much of Fred's material was so uniquely adapted to his delivery that he needed have little fear that it would be stolen by hard-pressed rivals. Of course a great number of Allen's quips *have* been lifted, but they probably constitute a very small percentage of his total output. The old line about starting a fire by rubbing two Boy Scouts together is Fred's. So is the one about the fellow who accidentally swallowed a bottle of liquid stocking and came out of the mishap rather well except for the fact that he had to wear a garter to hold up his stomach.

Fred's old radio warm-ups were wonderful shows in themselves. He used to speak to his studio audience for about ten minutes, saying a lot of things he wouldn't have been allowed to say on the air. "If by any chance," he'd say, "any of you folks are in the wrong place you still have ten minutes to get the heck out of here. Heck, incidentally, is a place invented by the National Broadcasting Company. NBC does not recognize hell or the Columbia Broadcasting System. When a bad person working for NBC dies, he goes to Heck, and when a good person dies, he goes to the Rainbow Room."

There are several things that earmarked Fred's humor as distinctive. One was his sheer playful love of words. He had a poet's regard for peculiarities of sound and expression and he seemed never so happy as when he could roll off his tongue some glittering allegory, metaphor or simile. He was actually much more intrigued by this sort of thing than he was by the plain and simple joke.

Once, in complaining about the fact that he got no help in advance from executives, he said, "While the show was non-existent . . . the agency men . . . were as quiet as a small boy banging two pussy willows together in a vacuum."

Putting words into the mouth of Senator Claghorn, Allen, to describe how big a dinner was, wrote, "Son, when all the food's on, the four legs of the table is kneelin' down." About a contentious chap, Allen said, "Brother Doe always had a chip on his shoulder that he was ready to use to kindle an argument."

To express as forcefully as possible that the late Mayor La Guardia was a long way from being tall, Allen said, "He's the only man I know that can milk a cow standing up."

This line brings us precisely to another distinctive point of Fred's humor: he loved to conceive what we might call "funny pictures." By way of illustration, consider this exchange from an *Allen's Alley* interview between Fred and Ajax Cassidy:

> ALLEN: What is that ladder you have there?
>
> AJAX: I'm going over to Sweeny's house for dinner.
>
> ALLEN: And you have to carry a ladder?
>
> AJAX: The dinin'-room table is too high. You can't sit on chairs. Everybody eats on a ladder.
>
> ALLEN: Why is the dining-room table so high?
>
> AJAX: Sweeny is a mounted cop. He always rides in to dinner on his horse.
>
> ALLEN: Oh.
>
> AJAX: Sweeny never uses a napkin. He wipes his hands on the back of his horse so much, he has mice under his saddle.

This is a peculiar, individual type of humor. It is related, and not too distantly, to the humor of the modern, fey, sophisticated cartoon. It makes one think of George Price. Certainly it is a far cry from the general level of radio comedy with which it was contemporaneous.

Another earmark of Fred's humor is recognized in its occasional close resemblance to poetry. On the subject of true love he has written: "To me, Sonia was prettier than a peacock backin' into a sunset. I used to dig up the ground she walked on and take it home."

To describe the result of being forced to trim excess wordage out of his scripts when his show was cut from sixty minutes to half an hour, Fred said, "The lines looked as though they had been written with a riveting machine dipped in ink."

He has also written of the chinchilla-winged siskin, a tropical bird that bites people to death and feeds on their screams. The siskin is evidently closely related to another of his creatures of phantasy, the four-toed gecko, a jungle swine that chases people out into the sun and eats their shadows. These ideas are entirely poetical in concept and are humorous only in a most incidental way.

Fred's habit of using actual names of people and places (when such names are *not* essential to the meaning of the joke) is another thing that identifies his style. Offering to make Orson Welles at home in the field of variety radio, Fred said, "Well, if I could give you some hints or introduce you to Ma Perkins, I'd be . . ."

Introducing Arlene Francis on *What's My Line,* he said, "And here she is, the only woman who knows whatever happened to Wendy Barrie . . ."

Asked if he could speak French, he said, "Just enough to get out of Rumpelmayer's."

To indicate what life would be like in this country if people became extinct, Fred said, "It will be like Philadelphia on a Sunday."

Another example of Fred's closeness to the Abe Martin-Bill Nye-Josh Billings school lay in his practice of *naming things* poetically. Artemus Ward, for example, called the American eagle "patriotic poultry."

Now consider the famous radio interview between Fred and a certain Captain Knight, who owned an eagle. In the course of this chat Fred referred to the eagle in the following ways: "The gentleman buzzard"; "This bloated sparrow"; "The one we see on the half dollar: the Mint Macaw"; "A bald eagle wearing a toupee"; "These Tenth Avenue canaries"; "He looks like Joe Penner with feathers on"; "The King-Kong Robin."

The poetic style of Fred's humor puts him, I believe, closer to the classic American humorists than any of his contemporaries.

"The Shanghai rooster is built on piles like a sandy-hill crane. . . . They often go to sleep standing and sometimes pitch over, and when they do they enter the ground like a pickax."

That's a line from Josh Billings, and it's greatly similar in style to Allen's work.

"Sending men to that Army," said Abraham Lincoln, no mean humorist himself, "is like shoveling fleas across a barnyard—they don't get there."

That is not a joke; it's a funny picture and it could have come straight from the lips of Allen's Titus Moody.

Whatever form our afterlife may take, it is comforting somehow to think that now Fred is with the men among whose company he must surely be ranked: Artemus Ward, Bill Nye, Mark Twain, Josh Billings, Abe Martin and Will Rogers. It brings a smile to the lips to think of the Olympian dialogues of these lamented wits. Perhaps the spring lightning that crackles over the city is the laughter of the gods at the round-table conversation of our departed friends.

Fred Allen has made some interesting predictions about television. He has always decried the Milton Berle approach to the medium. Milton and the score of funnymen who work like him did not seem, to Fred, to be ideally suited to TV. "All they're doing," he said, "is photographing vaudeville shows."

He once predicted that the eventual big comedy star of television would be a fellow who would just sit in an easy chair and talk to people in a quiet way as if he were talking to them in person in their living rooms. I think Fred Allen could have learned to function in just that way, and, ah, then what a program we would have seen! He didn't really need television, of course. His reputation is secure, and nothing can diminish his stature. But television surely needs people like Fred.

Lewis Nichols (essay date 1965)

SOURCE: "Yours, Fred," in the *New York Times Book Review,* April 25, 1965, p. 44.

[*In the following review of* Fred Allen's Letters, *Nichols excerpts some of Allen's wittiest letters.*]

Fred Allen died in 1956, and less than a decade later he has been almost forgotten. Show business moves faster than the rest of life, radio show business perhaps fastest of all, and his star was the brightest in radio. Ex-vaudeville, ex-theater (*Three's a Crowd*), he moved into radio in '32, and for the next 17 years was up there with the best of them, comedian on behalf of Texaco, Ford. Then came both ill health and TV and a decline, until now it is almost necessary to say who he was. The occasion just now is the publication of *Fred Allen's Letters,* edited and with an introduction by Joe McCarthy.

Allen was a compulsive letter writer, pouring out his thoughts to friends, business associates, during the war to men in the service. Some of his letters were lighthearted, filled with wild jokes. Others, particularly when concerned with the inner workings of radio, were as violent as a good-natured man allowed himself to get. Even with a chip on his shoulder he was amusing—relaxed and carefree, and writing to a pal, he could be hilarious.

Like the archy created by Don Marquis, he typed most of his letters in the lower case; unlike everyone else, when he made an error, he simply let it stand—and, in an immediate parenthesis, blamed the typewriter. To read the volume is to meet—either again or for the first time—a warm human being as well as a very fine comedian. And so, with no further words of introduction, it seems fitting to turn this mike over to Fred Allen:

Description of Montauk, L. I.: "you could never stand this place, you can not only hear a pin drop here; you can sense the rustle of the fabric of the sleeve as the person's arm is raised to drop the pin." *Charged with slandering the Stock Exchange:* "no malice was intended and I am sorry to have incurred the disfavor of the gentlemen. I have considered committing hari-kari on the two points recently gained by bethlehem steel. I have also thought about calling a conference since a conference is a gathering of important people who singly can do nothing but together can decide that nothing can be done. both ideas were abandoned in favor of this letter to you."

Of alcohol: "the grape is a globule unlike trousers. the grape does not improve with pressing." *Of a TV comedian:* "a sorry mime who mistakes gusto and thyroid condition for talent and ability, he has been around for 20 years and has never been first in anything. if he is first in television, either our standards have disappeared or there is something wrong in television." *Of life (1):* "I never look back. I just keep breathing. that is the secret of survival and my motto—just keep breathing." *Of life (2):* "life, in my estimation, is a biological misadventure that we terminate on the shoulders of six strange men whose only objective is to make a hole in one with you." *Of life (3):* "I am not a small time confucius. i am not poor richard. i am merely a resident of dorchester doomed by some evil fairy around moseley street to roam the earth until such time as my penance has been paid."

Author of the autobiographical *Treadmill to Oblivion* and another book not finished at his death, Allen always wished to be a full-time writer. In any Book Review belong these thoughts: *On writers:* "on several occasions i have argued with john steinbeck. i claim that when a writer becomes successful, generally without giving it too much thought, he assumes another style of living. with the introduction of luxury into his life he withdraws from his old friends, haunts and the contacts that enabled him to find material that made him successful in the first place. john says it isn't true but i don't think you can come out of the stork club with your belly full and caviar rolling down your vest and rush home and write a 'grapes of wrath.' john says you can, so i must be wrong."

And, *On publishers:* "they have all bewildered me. most of them survive through manipulating the work of others while they themselves concentrate on drinking or social contacts. as a class they are too precious for me. i am always afraid that i will lean against a publisher and chip or break him."

***Newsweek* (essay date 1965)**

SOURCE: "Beware the Leaches," in *Newsweek,* Vol. 65, No. 17, April 26, 1965, pp. 98-100.

[*In the following review of* Fred Allen's Letters, *the critic finds an undercurrent of darkness in Allen's humor that was seldom revealed on his radio programs.*]

"You can count on the thumb of one hand," wrote James Thurber, "the American who is at once a comedian, a humorist, a wit, and a satirist, and his name is Fred

Allen." Each Sunday night in the 1930s and '40s, listeners out there in radio land counted on Allen's sly wit and bemused nasality to give them courage for the coming work week. The comedian himself delivered the goods dependably, at great benefit to his listeners, and great cost to himself.

Allen's fame was a lifetime ordeal. "success is wonderful up to a certain point," he once wrote Herman Wouk in the lower-case typewritten style he had used since 1934. "it consumes your time. it infests your days with leaches [sic] who want to promote you for their own selfish purposes and, eventually, if you try to cope with the demands, it affects your health." When success had fans beating a path to his door, Allen and his wife, Portland Hoffa, escaped periodically to Gurney's Inn in Montauk, Long Island, a retreat he described as "so quiet you can hear a caterpillar backing into a globule of dew."

Closet: High life never interested him. "why should i go to a nightclub?" he wrote columnist Louis Sobol in 1943. "i can get better air in a closet. i can cook better food myself. i can hear better music on the portable phonograph. and i can meet a better class of people in the subway."

But, as much as he might have liked to quit, Allen stayed with radio until it succumbed to TV. "I took the radio thing," he explained in an early, pre–lower-case letter, "to make expenses on Sunday nights, hoping to get a Broadway show meantime. The way it has turned out there is no time for anything but the broadcast . . ." A few years later, there was no turning back. "i don't know what the hell i am working for," he wrote to boyhood friend Joe Kelly, "except that now there is a mob of people depending on me for their activity and it has almost gotten to the point where i can't stop."

So Allen lived on among the network vice presidents, advertising executives, and promoters, fighting off script changes, guest appearances, and a chronic case of hypertension. "mr. b.," Allen wrote, describing the Bowles of Benton and Bowles advertising, "is the man who, after you have worked all week to concoct a mess of drivel that will barely skim through the loudspeakers without leaving a stench in a radio owner's parlor, rushes in at 4 p.m. on wednesday afternoon and tears the entire show apart . . . leaving nothing but punctuation marks for you to put some new words between."

Bitter Mood: But, in his letters, Allen was his own man. Whether he was writing to show-business friends like Groucho Marx, James Mason, and Abe Burrows, to lesser-knowns who had played the Keith circuit with him in his pre-Depression juggling days, or to handball partners at the Y, Allen gave free rein to a dark and bitter mood that would have shocked the fans of Allen's Alley. "radio is nothing but whatever dough you can get," he wrote to actor Charles Cantor in 1945. "the minute you do a show it is forgotten and nobody knows about the ulcers except the people who have them."

Allen did not detest all of radio. *Duffy's Tavern* and *Fibber Magee and Molly* delighted him. He found even less to like on television. Two weeks before he died in March of 1956, Allen summed up his feelings about TV in a letter to Hal Kanter, creator of *The George Gobel Show:* "i have a theory that if a giant plunger was placed on top of radio city and pressed down suddenly 90% of all television would go down the drain." He saw it going down the drain as soon as he tried to transport **Allen's Alley** intact to television. "i wanted to eliminate the audience," he wrote critic Alton Cook, "and do as you suggest with a decrepit alley or street but i was told that . . . the network and the client both want a revue type of show, with the audience and everything else which will make the medium a bore in a hurry."

Letters: When Allen wasn't writing about radio and television, which was most of the time, his letters were cheerful, breezy, witty, and sometimes totally loony. Describing a sleepless night, the majestically baggy-eyed Allen wrote: "i counted sheep in wolves' clothing. i took off the wolf pelts and counted straight sheep. i counted the wolf-skins with no sheep in them. nothing helped." In typical fashion he summed up Hollywood in the Depression: "a lot of guys who had sandwiches named after them a couple of years ago wish they could get one to autograph with their teeth . . ."

Allen, who wrote most of his own scripts, was always happiest when he was writing. "i claim that when a writer becomes successful," he wrote H. Allen Smith, "generally he assumes another style of living with the introduction of luxury into his life he withdraws from his old friends, haunts, and the contacts that enabled him to find material that made him successful in the first place." True to his own insight, Allen never abandoned his old friends. His letters to them are the legacy of an uncorrupted man.

Gerald Weales (essay date 1965)

SOURCE: A review of *Fred Allen's Letters*, in *Commonweal,* Vol. 82, No. 19, August 20, 1965, pp. 599-600.

[*In the following review of* Fred Allen's Letters, *Weales enjoys the examples of Allen's wit, while finding fault with editor Joe McCarthy's organization of the book.*]

One of the few lines in *The School for Scandal* that I have ever been able to care much about is the one about the pistol ball that "struck against a little bronze Shakespeare that stood over the fireplace, grazed out of the window at a right angle, and wounded the postman, who was just coming to the door with a double letter from Northamptonshire." I do not quote it here because it was a favorite of Fred Allen's although it might well have been (he was a notorious reader—rare among comedians), but because it illustrates a comic method which he used consistently and well. His comedy was built on circumstantiality, on an accumulation of detail which set up a context—realistic or fantastic—in which each line did more than get its own laugh; it built into the next and the next until a pyramid of absurdity had been constructed—solid or tottering, depending on the force of the original conceit.

Any of the scripts printed in *Treadmill to Oblivion,* Allen's book about his days in radio, can show how he used this verbal device as a practicing comedian. Although it can be illustrated in speeches provided for the characters who lived along Allen's Alley, the best examples are likely to be in his own monologues. This is not because he kept the best material for himself, but because this kind of intricate build is essentially the sound of one voice talking, feeling its way through the debris of any situation, labeling and ordering as it goes.

It is not surprising, then, that the *Letters* are full of this kind of writing. Take the first one in the book, a thank-you note to a fan who had sent him some honey. It is a set comic piece rather than a real letter—hence strained and artificial in the context of more personal letters—but its account of the Allens' unproductive bee is a comic construction in which the joke lies in the distance between the ludicrous invention and the explicitness in which it forlornly buzzes. A few pages on, in a letter to Groucho Marx, Allen piles up four paragraphs of circumstantial local color on the Stage Delicatessen ("the chef who looked out of the kitchen door while keeping his eyes on an order of scrambled eggs and onions not too brown") to say, simply, that he had liked one of Marx's shows. If the bee is pure fantasy and the Stage, at least as Allen describes it, the fantasy of exaggeration, his straight comic description displays the same cagey use of detail, as in these remarks on Maine in the summer:

> the guests all look like people who eat in howard johnson stands all winter and they all have the same equipment. they drive up in pontiacs and desotos with the wife wearing woolworth sun glasses and the husband carrying a thermos bottle. they order double portions at all meals and sit around on the veranda and talk to each other about the same subjects. "the car is running well," "we stopped at the cutest motel just outside of fumfet harbor."

It was not simply his verbal skill that made Allen so good a comedian in his radio days, but what he did with it. He used his shows to comment, usually with a kind of amiable acidity, on the fads and foibles of his times. In retrospect, a good part of what he said is not very funny (his letters admit that turning out a script a week was a losing battle), but looking at a printed script twenty or thirty years after the nasal event that gave it life is to miss the whole idea of the Allen show: the sense of spending time with a comic who was smiling wryly at what was there, not setting up dummy targets that he could knock over in a burst of jocular self-aggrandizement. The letters have some of this same quality.

They also have a slightly more bitter note, an occasionally venomous tone toward the men whom he considered the plagues of the trade: advertising agency men and network officials primarily, but also comics who get by on too little, people who want to use celebrities for causes, good or bad.

It is too bad that a review like this, one that pays tribute to a man as talented as Fred Allen, may help the sales (however slightly) of an extremely bad book. This collection of letters is disgracefully edited. McCarthy has divided it into sections ("Old Friends," "Show Biz People") which are pretty meaningless, since the same people turn up in several sections. It is impossible to get a real sense of an event or a relationship. A simple chronological presentation would have been a great deal better, for then we would have been able to follow Allen through the vaudeville and Broadway days, to the treadmill of radio, to the sad, loose-end days of TV and the beginnings of a new career as a writer of books.

Such a presentation might also have lightened the problem of identifying the vast number of people (called often by first names or Allenish nicknames) who infest the letters; the identifications made by the editor are very haphazard and only occasionally helpful. It is too bad that this had to happen to Fred Allen. In a letter to Pat Weaver in 1936, Allen wrote: "i have checked on most of the programs but there isn't much to learn from our competitors. they have no structure, or form, and most of the production is slip-shod but perhaps that is the new style."

Jim Harmon (essay date 1970)

SOURCE: "Down Allen's Alley," in *The Great Radio Comedians,* Doubleday & Company, Inc., 1970, pp. 168-83.

[*In the following excerpt, Harmon details the decline of popularity of Allen's radio program because of competition from game shows.*]

"Somebody, ah say, *somebody's* knockin' on mah door," the most famous resident of that curious sidestreet of Radioland, Allen's Alley, observed in answer to the rapping at his shanty portal.

"Yes, Senator Claghorn," Fred Allen would respond with typical nasal amiability as the door banged open, "it is I."

"Oh, it's you, son—that non-resident of mah state," said the Senator with somewhat less enthusiasm.

"Yes, I am here in my full non-voter status," Allen replied. "I hope I'm not intruding. I see you must be expecting company. You have an alligator barbecuing in the front yard."

"Always have time for anyone who might become a registered voter. Son, I see you have a question brewing—if Ah may use the expression—brewing in your mind."

"Yes, Senator Claghorn—I have the Question of the Week. 'What modern invention do you most dislike?'"

"Money," Claghorn snapped. "We in the South have very little to do with it. We believe in the barter system. For instance, if I have a chicken a fellow wants from me, he could offer to shoe mah mule for me."

"I suppose, Senator," Allen mused, "if I wanted one of your pullets I could pull off a few jokes for you."

"Son, we were talking about chickens—not eggs!"

Slam! went the Senator's door.

"The senator seems out of sorts," Allen observed for the radio audience. "His cotton gin must have jammed up on him."

The good Senator and the other residents of Allen's Alley often seemed to overshadow their creator, Fred Allen. Although Allen was one of the most creative funnymen in radio (*the* most creative in the opinion of many critics) his own fame as a comedian—a stand-up comic delivering a monologue—was somewhat eclipsed when he introduced the sidestreet people by notable eccentrics. Since 1932, Allen had been doing a comedy-variety show full of jokes and various sketches, but in 1943 he introduced the opening routine of Allen's Alley. Wartime censorship made freewheeling parodies of the national scene too touchy to get many past the censors. He filled one-third of the show with continuing characters, and it was through this regular cast that the *Fred Allen Show* won its greatest success.

Somewhere during his weekly interview by Fred Allen, Senator Claghorn would usually deliver one of his famous witticisms about a fellow senator. "They're going to bring Senator Aiken back . . . achin' back—haw!" And then the inevitable explanation: *"That's a joke, Son!"*

The man behind Claghorn's drawl—surely the quickest, most enthusiastic Southern drawl in Creation—was Kenny Delmar, who left the South in his mouth behind the Mason-Dixon line as the *Allen Show's* announcer. His fictional solon became so popular that Delmar branched out into a radio show all his own and made a Hollywood movie called appropriately, *That's a Joke, Son.* As late as 1963, Senator Claghorn had a five-minute radio show on ABC, and Delmar is at this writing still playing the role in radio and TV commercials. There seem to be infinite possibilities in the public official who can be ridiculed with impunity.

Senator Claghorn was a caricature of the Southern colonel or legislator and reflected a little of the crudity of some and the shrewdness of others in the power structure of the South. Exaggerations led to easy visualizations for the listening audience. Though they sometimes got at the truth in ways more realistic characters could not, the audience was not supposed to think all United States Senators were like Claghorn, or that all Jewish housewives spoke the exotic dialect of Mrs. Nussbaum.

"Again I am to be prodded by your poll?" Mrs. Nussbaum would inquire at one of Allen's weekly visits to solicit her views. The comparison of her speech patterns to those of Molly of *The Goldbergs* is inescapable. But aside from the accent, Mrs. Nussbaum was not a great deal different than the canny old broads of radio like Ma Perkins or Aunt Jenny, or one of our own aunts just up the street.

"You were expecting the Fink Spots?" Mrs. Pansy Nussbaum would ask, opening her door at Allen's knock.

"Not at all," Allen replied. "They would outweigh you by two to one at least, Mrs. Nussbaum."

"To be sure."

"I have, Mrs. Nussbaum, for you the Question of the Week."

"So?"

"What," asked Allen, "is the modern invention you most dislike?"

"Well . . ." Mrs. Nussbaum pondered, "well . . . present company excluded . . ."

"Thank you."

"Excluding present company, I would venture I most dislike the telephone."

"The telephone!" Allen gasped. "That is remarkable."

"I am remarking that it is remarkable." Mrs. Nussbaum went on to tell a pretty straightforward story, devoid of gag lines, of how a telephone call had interrupted her cooking procedures. In a fit of pique, Mrs. Nussbaum had thrown her telephone out the window as far as the wire would let it go.

"Then I am hearing from the patio beneath the window, 'Sorry, your time is up on the *Pot O' Gold* twenty-five thousand dollar question.' Ay-yi-yii."

"That does seem a good reason to hate the telephone," Allen agreed.

"Yes. Most of all I hate the telephone because it is always ringing while I have my head in the oven cooking."

Minerva Pious portrayed Mrs. Nussbaum, and her character, like that of Senator Claghorn, has appeared in recent radio commercials. (Commercials today offer virtually the only employment in radio for drama and comedy performers, sound effects men, and others from the days of major network radio.) Miss Pious belongs to the small army of Jews who practice the art of comedy, one of a race that has traditionally had to accept and employ self-parody to survive. Fred Allen himself belonged to another such one-time persecuted minority, the Irish-Catholics. The character he created for Minerva Pious had less of the *schmaltz* and charm of Gertrude Berg's Molly Goldberg and more of Allen's own sometimes acid wit.

The next resident of the Alley also displayed a good deal of bite in his humor. He was the typical crusty New Englander.

"Howdy, Bub," Titus Moody responded to Allen's knock with some degree of geniality.

"Good evening, Mr. Moody. I see you must be celebrating," Allen observed. "You have the doorway strung with crab shells."

"E-yup. It's my anniversary. Married forty-one years ago terday."

"That is remarkable. How did you and Mrs. Moody meet?"

"Forty years ago and one week, I saw this young thing climbing down from a buggy . . .'"

"Yes," Allen urged the old codger on.

"I attempted to help her get out of the buggy. In the process, the hem of her skirt lifted. I saw her ankle."

"And?"

"Did the decent thing. I married her."

"Mr. Moody," Allen continued, "I hate to intrude on this festive occasion, but I wonder if I might ask you the Question of the Week?"

"For thirty-nine weeks out of every year," Moody pointed out, "you ask me the Question of the Week."

"True enough," Allen admitted. "In that case, Mr. Moody, I wonder if you would tell me what modern invention you most dislike?"

"Why, that would be the radio," Moody said. "I don't hold with furniture that talks."

Fred Allen paused tellingly over this classic comment. "Perchance, do you have a more specific reason for disliking radio?"

"Put one in my henhouse to soothe the chickens."

"I see," Allen said. "Soothing music by Guy Lombardo and Sammy Kaye."

"Should have been, but by accident the radio got tuned to another station. My hens might about died from exhaustion."

"The music was too lively? Rumbas by Cugat perhaps?"

"Not that," Moody said sorrowfully. "Hens were listening to *Double or Nothing.*"

Parker Fennelly played Titus Moody, a character, like the others in Allen's Alley, that proved to have staying power. He is still playing the same old New Englander in commercials for Pepperidge Farm bakery products. Fennelly had played much the same old codger under other character names in such programs as *Snow Village Sketches,* predating the Allen show, but it was as Titus Moody that he found the perfect distillation of the archetypical New Englander. In writing many of the lines for Titus Moody, Fred Allen projected one aspect of his own personality. Allen had been born in Cambridge, Massachusetts, and Titus's accent was only an exaggeration of Allen's own speech pattern.

Titus Moody, Mrs. Nussbaum, and Senator Claghorn were the permanent residents and leading citizens of Allen's Alley, but there were other temporary renters from time to time. From his own Irish heritage, Allen presented the stereotyped Irish drunk in Ajax Cassidy (portrayed by master dialectician Peter Donald).

There was Falstaff Openshaw, a poet given to composing such verses as "Take Your Feet off the Table, Mother, or You'll get a Sock in the Mush." Falstaff was played by Alan Reed, today the voice of television's Fred Flintstone.

Charles Cantor played Socrates Mulligan, a most un-Socrates-like character. Later, Cantor moved to Ed "Archie" Gardner's *Duffy's Tavern,* where he contributed perhaps the show's most popular character, the dull-witted Finnegan. "Finnegan," Archie would say, "youse is not graced wid the brains of a cockroach . . ." "*Duhhhh,* chee, t'anks, Arch!" would be the inevitable reply.

One of the privileges of genius is nonconformity, and one of the nonconformist elements in Fred Allen's make-up was his refusal to finish his radio program in exactly the twenty-nine minutes and thirty seconds allotted to him. He would not step on a line, kill a laugh, ruin a gag, just to get off the air on the dot. Today he would simply be cut off in mid-sentence and a deodorant commercial put on. In the decadent days of vintage radio, the network and the stations were loath to ruin the entertainment just to get in all the station break commercials. The Allen show frequently ran over its time period by forty-five seconds, and at times two or three minutes. (The policy of letting a program find its natural length within a reasonable fluctuation is still followed by the British Broadcasting Corporation in radio and television.)

Fortunately, the program following Allen was an audience participation show whose time span was also flexible. The program, *Take It or Leave It,* offered as its greatest challenge, the Sixty-Four Dollar Question (a prize television would increase a thousandfold). The master of ceremonies was comedian-accordionist Phil Baker who was understandably unhappy about Allen borrowing part of his, Baker's, time.

Baker began to take accurate accounting of just how much time Allen had stolen from his show. When midway through the season, the amount of stolen time at last added up to fifteen minutes, Baker barged into Allen's studio and began his quiz show in the middle of the **Fred Allen Show.** "Good evening, Ladies and Gentlemen," Baker shouted, "it's time to play *Take It or Leave It* with the famous *Sixty-Four Dollar Question—*" Allen stormed with simulated anger, "I'll write Senator Claghorn about this!"

It may have been prearranged, but somehow it was all part of the spontaneous excitement of which radio was capable.

Phil Baker did not offer Fred Allen the only problems he had with contest programs.

In 1934, when Major Bowes' *Amateur Hour* was at the height of its popularity, Allen was saddled by some inspired vice-president with an amateur segment as part of his variety show, *Town Hall Tonight.* Allen bore up under this incredible indignity to his talent. When one young amateur forgot to undo the safety strap that kept his accordion bellows closed as he launched into a weedily thin rendition of "Twelfth Street Rag," Allen drawled, "Son, you better unfasten that strap, or you won't get past Fourth Street."

Much later, in 1949, Fred Allen was temporarily defeated in the ratings by the giant money-paying quiz, *Stop the Music.* The great American public was offered the opportunity of choosing between one of the greatest comedians of all time and a minuscule chance at getting a telephone call offering them a shot at a pile of money. The faintest scent of fortune drowned the laughter for the majority, although a large and significant minority did chose Fred Allen.

Unlike the sponsors and networks of his day, and of ours, Fred Allen did not believe in letting polls establish public taste. He had a constant running battle with the corporate mentality; in his opinion, vice-presidents of NBC, vice-presidents of advertising agencies—in fact, *all* vice-presidents did their best to ruin his show. He made his point in a 1942 sketch. It was typically Allen and no doubt resulted in another meeting (one of many) being called—probably on the very next day—by the much-harried people he was attacking.

In the sketch, Allen, a brave man, was willing to make himself the heavy of the piece. He played the head of an advertising agency.

ALLEN: Yes, these are radio popularity ratings . . . I'm checking our agency programs. Hmm. "Fake It or Believe It" up one point two. "One Man's Relatives" up two point six . . . The—Gad! . . . Our comedy program, the "Kenny Dank Funfest" has gone down again. This is second month in succession.

MISS YUCK: What is the rating?

ALLEN: Minus two point two. That means that not only every radio listener in America isn't listening to Kenny Dank—two hundred thousand people who haven't got radios aren't listening either.

YUCK: But how can people without radios not listen?

ALLEN: One doesn't question statistics, Miss Yuck. The entire advertising business is founded on surveys. The first man who questions a survey will topple the advertising game like a house of cards . . .

YUCK: Kenny Dank is outside now.

ALLEN: Send him in here.

DANK: Hello, B.B., old sock. Ha, Ha!

ALLEN: Stop laughing at yourself, Dank. Everyone else has . . . When a comedian slips, the advertising agency has to step in.

DANK: But the last time the agency stepped in, I went down nineteen points.

ALLEN: No heresy, Dank . . . Miss Yuck, sound the conference bell.

(*The vice-presidents march in.*)

Men, we've got to change Dank's set-up.

Chorus: Check!

ALLEN: Gad, this conference is going like clockwork. Let's mother-hen that thought. We've got to hatch an idea. Let's mull, men . . .

JUMBLE: How about cutting out the actors and putting in audience participation?

DANK: You cut that out at the last conference.

FUMBLE: How about cutting out the audience and putting in actor participation?

ALLEN: You can't cut out studio audiences and render thousands of people homeless.

Fred Allen was born May 31, 1894. His mother died when he was four, and his father's sister, Elizabeth, became his second mother. The father of the man who would be known as Fred Allen was a Boston book-binder, James Henry Sullivan. Sullivan did not make much money, but he was a jovial, fun-loving man. "I like to think I inherited Dad's wit," Allen often said. "Of course, I may only be fifty per cent correct . . ."

While he was attending the Boston High School of Commerce, which was designed to turn "Irish clods into useful bricks of industry," Fred took a part-time job in the Public Library's basement stacks. He read the books and he juggled them. Literally. One book was on the art of juggling, and he practiced with the book itself and its companion volumes.

Young Fred finally decided he was good enough to try his juggling act out in a vaudeville amateur night show. The crowd on such nights was always full of vocal critics. Catcalls and rotten eggs were routine. Occasionally, a performer would be pulled from the stage and slugged cold. Allen christened the theater the Pandemonium.

Fred Allen had been better in the library basement than he was on stage. "That was a mighty swell trick, folks. You should have been here last night when I made it." His patter was lost on the audience drunk with power at the very least.

The only person to save the Christian from the lions was Sol Cohen, a former circus strong man and then a theatrical booking agent. He took Fred under his very strong wing, telling him he had the makings of a *professional* amateur. Allen recalled that Cohen's first advice was "Louder up you got to talk!" Shades of Mrs. Nussbaum!

Fred Allen learned to talk louder and juggle faster. He won round after round of the amateur shows set up by Cohen, finally graduating to the big time, professional vaudeville in New York City. At the conclusion of his act, the stage darkened and a "magic lantern" projected images on a screen of Abraham Lincoln, Teddy Roosevelt and his Rough Riders, and finally a tattered Old Glory still waving valiantly in the breeze, all while the pit band played patriotic marches. Fred Allen was assured of getting a good hand at the end of his act.

At various times in his career, Fred Allen had been known as Young Sullivan, Paul Huckle, and Freddy James. Finally, Allen's new agent, Edgar Allen, suggested "Freddy James" take his last name. Thus, finally, Fred Sullivan became Fred Allen.

Under his new name, Fred Allen appeared in the lavish Shubert musical production, *The Passing Show of 1922*. The critics' praise established him as a comedian of importance. The show was also important to him in that it introduced him to a pretty dancer named

Portland Hoffa. "That," said Allen, "is a ridiculous name." Portland replied, "You should meet my sisters, Lebanon, Period, and Lastone."

Naturally, the two of them got married.

Fred and Portland went into radio in 1932, and stayed there.

Portland Hoffa became Allen's foil, playing opposite him on the air in much the same fashion as Gracie Allen and her comedian husband, George Burns. There was not the "cuteness" and charm of Miss Allen in Portland Hoffa's portrayal, but her denseness was as disarmingly dry as Fred Allen's wit.

> PORTLAND: Hello, Mr. Allen.
>
> ALLEN: Well, as the schoolteacher said to the little boy who spelled snow with an "E," what's snew?
>
> PORTLAND: This is no place for jokes, Mr. Allen . . . Comedy programs today all go in for romance . . . Look at Mr. Benny. He's always taking girls out.
>
> ALLEN: Benny with the light brown toupée? The only thing Benny ever takes out on a moonlit night is his upper plate. What gave you this romance idea, anyway?
>
> PORTLAND: Well tomorrow is the first day of spring . . . If somebody would take out a girl we'd have something romantic to talk about . . . I know just the girl . . .
>
> ALLEN: Who?
>
> PORTLAND: Olive Fagelson.
>
> ALLEN: Olive Fagelson?
>
> PORTLAND: She'd be crazy about you. She's nearsighted.
>
> ALLEN: Look, Portland . . . The last girl I took out left town and became a nurse with the Confederate Army.

Radio was the perfect medium for Fred Allen and perhaps the only one: his skill lay in the use of *words*. Allen could put his words in the scripts he largely wrote himself (or rather *printed* by hand), and he could pull words out of the air for any occasion. Jack Benny? "Benny couldn't *ad lib* a belch at a Hungarian banquet . . ." If some joke from the script did not go over, perhaps gaining only one guffaw from a member of the audience, Allen would remark with seeming imperturbability, "As that one lone laugh goes ricocheting around the studio, we move to a selection by Al Goodman and his orchestra . . ."

Another time he was cornered by a gushing lady who told him she had come all the way to New York from

San Francisco just to see his broadcast. "Madame," intoned Allen, "if I had only known you were coming all that way just to catch my little old show, the least I could have done was meet you halfway. Say, about Omaha."

Yet Fred Allen could be generous to friends and strangers who really needed help. He had a long list of old show business people he kept on "pension" and pocketfuls of five-dollar bills to pass out to those asking for handouts.

It certainly was not a handout but a gesture of generosity to Allen when members of his old radio cast and his old nemesis, Jack Benny, gathered from all points of the globe to help the then semi-retired Allen re-create his program on the television show, *Omnibus*, in 1952.

"A lot of people never realized the feud between Fred Allen and myself was a joke," Jack Benny observed. "Unfortunately, one of the people who never realized it was Fred." (That in itself was a joke, of course.)

For the last time, on that telecast of *Omnibus*, Fred Allen ventured down Allen's Alley. Due to a heart condition, he was never able to work hard enough to do a full-scale comedy-variety show on TV, which required a great deal of rehearsal. After this special *Omnibus* program, he would go on for years as a panelist on *What's My Line?*, but he would never again perform with his old cast.

For this occasion, Fred asked the Alley residents different questions culled from past shows.

He asked of Mrs. Nussbaum: "Do you think advertising affects our customs?"

> NUSSBAUM: A girl I am knowing, Cuddles . . . a bouncer at the Y.W.C.A. . . . One day Cuddles is seeing advertised a perfume . . ."Capitulate" . . . It is like "Surrender," only *stronger.*

> ALLEN: Gosh!

> NUSSBAUM: The advertising is saying "Girls using the handy size one quart bottle is positively guaranteed a man . . ." Cuddles is not taking any chance. Cuddles is pouring on herself *two* quarts.

> ALLEN: The two quarts worked?

> NUSSBAUM: Cuddles is eloping with a Siamese twin.

The question for Titus Moody was "Do you have a hobby?"

> MOODY: Why, I one time was collecting deer ends.

> ALLEN: Deer ends?

> MOODY: Everybody was collecting deer heads, so I started collecting what was left over.

> ALLEN: I see.

> MOODY: I had twenty deer ends mounted on the wall . . . When I opened the door, seemed like I was over-taking a herd.

Finally, Fred Allen came to a door draped in the Confederate flag and rapped on the panel with a knocker made from the handle of a cotton gin. The good Senator Claghorn appeared.

> ALLEN: How are you going to spend Thanksgiving?

> CLAGHORN: With my kinfolks, son. What a day . . . We start out with a Memphis Martini . . . That's a tall glass of pure corn likker with a wad of cotton in it . . . a Boll Weevel is riding the cotton . . . Then comes Alligator Chowder . . . a whole alligator simmering in swamp water . . .

> ALLEN: Yum-yum! Do you have turkey with the meal?

> CLAGHORN: Mock Turkey, son. That's raccoon, stuffed with grits and Magnolia buds . . . Then we stand and give thanks . . . Thanks for not being born in the North!

The final trip down Allen's Alley was over. Perhaps it proved that a Jewish housewife who fixed up her friend with a Siamese twin, a senator who believed the Civil War had never happened, and a farmer who liked the rear ends of animals were better heard than seen.

There was one more part, however, to the re-creation of the radio show on television. Fred Allen's greatest character was Fred Allen himself. He had a voice that sounded like "a man with false teeth chewing on slate pencils," managing to "sound like an articulate spider enticing a fly to a webbed pratfall." But when he added to this remarkable voice a Chinese accent, he became the greatest of all Oriental detectives, One Long Pan.

> PAN: Ah, greetings and Shalom, kiddies—One Long Pan, oriental Dick Tracy on the job.

> NORBERT: I say, old boy, will you stop breaking your English on my premises?

> PAN: Who are you, little man?

> NORBERT: I, Sir, am Norbert Nottingham.

> PAN: Very suspicious. What you do here? . . . Long Pan formerly M.C. *What's My Line?* You work for profit-making organization?

> NORBERT: This is ridiculous . . . Sir Cedric has shot himself—committed suicide!

> PAN: Suicide likely story. Not so fast. Long Pan look around. Long Pan examine body. Ho-ho-ho—you see—in Sir Cedric's hand?

> NORBERT: What?

PAN (*pointing to gun*): A lewolerwer!

NORBERT: A lewolerwer?

PAN: A lewolerwer!

In closing that *Omnibus* telecast, Allen quoted from his book, **Treadmill to Oblivion.**

"There was a certain type of imaginative comedy that could be written for and performed only on radio," Fred Allen observed. "But we are living in a machine age, and for the first time the comedian is being compelled . . . to compete with a machine . . . Whether he knows it or not, the successful comedian is on a treadmill to oblivion."

Yet, although the name "Fred Allen" will one day only be a footnote in the history of broadcasting, it is likely that some of his wit and style will be reflected in our funny men for generations to come. That is, unless Fred Allen's prediction bears fruit absolutely and our comedians become no longer human, leaving us only a machine to laugh at. Who knows? After all, television already has a machine to do the audience's laughing for them. Will it, one day, be a world full of machines laughing at machines?

Alan R Havig (essay date 1978)

SOURCE: "Fred Allen's Comedy of Language," in *Fred Allen's Radio Comedy,* Temple University Press, 1990, pp. 127-52.

[*In the following essay, which was originally published in the* Journal of Popular Culture *in 1978, Havig discusses Allen's censorship troubles with broadcast executives, sponsors, and advertising agencies.*]

Unlike other arts—dance, theatre, the movies, fiction and non-fiction writing—radio broadcasting from the 1920s through the 1940s did not give rise to an influential corps of critics and anon-going body of critical evaluation. Although a few reviewers like John Crosby of the *New York Herald Tribune* wrote intelligently about what appeared on radio, for the most part Charles Siepmann's assessment, written after two decades of network programming, was accurate:

> While plays performed in the 'legitimate' theater (having comparatively small audiences) and books, even on abstruse subjects, are regularly reviewed in the press, similar reviews of radio's best productions, performed before an unseen audience of millions, receive only occasional and limited notice.

Radio needed thoughtful criticism. As Siepmann pointed out, responsible commentary could raise standards of taste, just as it did in other popular arts. And as Jack Gould of the *New York Times* noted in 1945, "no field more badly needs the jocular nudge" that responsible

skeptics could provide "because, for all its dependence on humor, radio has precious little itself." Assessing his own role as radio critic, however, Crosby confessed that the task was not an easy one.

> Nothing resists criticism so strenuously as radio. A radio columnist is forced to be literate about the illiterate, witty about the witless, coherent about the incoherent. It isn't always possible. . . . They hover, these programs, in a sort of nether world of mediocrity and defy you to compose so much as a single rational sentence about them.

The better performers, Crosby granted, provided some gratification. But generally speaking, the necessary but difficult job of supplying radio with critical commentary was not achieved by the time that radio gave way to the onslaught of television.[1]

Fred Allen's programs spanned network radio's most important years, from his debut in October, 1932 until his retirement in June, 1949. As a humorist he found his material in the life that he observed around him, an important part of which was the world of broadcasting. Unlike most radio performers, who tended in public to boost the medium which gave them success, Allen came not to praise broadcasting but to expose its absurdities. His sometimes gentle, often sharp critique of radio's failures made him one of the most thorough-going, respected, and effective commentators on the state of broadcasting. As a critic-from-within, Fred Allen helped to compensate for the absence of an effective group of critics outside of the industry. "Perhaps the most heartening sign of all," John Crosby concluded in a searching analysis of radio in 1948, "is the fact that some of radio's severest critics are in radio, not outside it. The violence of their dissatisfaction cannot help doing some good." And as columnist Jack Gould wrote: "among those with access to the microphone," Allen was "virtually alone in spoofing the nonsensical goings-on that so often prevail in what is known as 'the industry.'" He concluded: "Register Mr. A. as an extraordinarily articulate critic." Ben Gross agreed, as he called Allen "one of the country's most incisive critics of both radio and television."[2]

Like many of radio's early successes, Allen came to the medium under the pressures of a failing economy. The Great Depression limited his opportunities in vaudeville and Broadway revues. Radio provided security, Allen knew, at a time "when there is nothing left of the theatre but ghosts of Booth and Barrett running through their parts in the deserted wings," and when "there isn't enough vaudeville to tire out a trained pigeon act flying from town to town."[3]

It is erroneous to infer, however, that Allen resented radio because of the circumstances which forced him into it; that he "had no fun at all" in the new medium, one for which he developed "no particular affection;" and that his criticisms of broadcasting resulted from this long-smoldering dislike. Allen's friend, the novelist

Edwin O'Connor, made some of these assumptions shortly after the comedian's death in 1956, but they ignore several important facts. Fred Allen may have felt a nostalgic longing for vaudeville during his radio years, but a career on the stage was not his ideal. "Acting has never appealed to me," he wrote in his autobiography, and on several occasions Allen revealed that if he could live his life again, he would be a writer, not a performer. Since he created his own material, he *was* a writer, but he had something different in mind. "A humorist with a column on a newspaper, or one who wrote for syndication," he reflected during his retirement, "enjoyed a greater security [than an actor] . . . and had a much more satisfying life." With John Steinbeck, James Thurber, and O'Connor among his friends, Allen's thoughts probably took their lasting achievement into account. "A writer at sixty can be a Steinbeck, a Faulkner, or a Hemingway. An actor at sixty can make a funny face or do a creaky dance."[4]

Fred Allen's critique of broadcasting did not grow out of a career-frustration in which radio was unable to match his earlier achievements as a vaudevillian and Broadway comedian. His role as critic-from-within, however, did have clear origins in his experience, perceptions, and sensibilities as a creative artist. Cultural critics often charge that those who labor in the popular arts are mere assembly-line workers, suppressing their individuality and potential creativity for profit. "Such art workers," writes Dwight MacDonald, "are as alienated from their brainwork as the industrial worker is from his handwork." Fred Allen does not fit this increasingly questionable model. His career, indeed, substantiates Herbert Gans' quite different conception of the motivation and role of some popular artists." Many popular culture creators want to express their personal values and tastes in much the same way as the high culture creator and want to be free from control by the audience and media executives." Allen liked radio, and he saw (and realized) many comedic possibilities in the medium. He had an artist's pride in his work both as radio writer and performer. What he resented, and what he attacked both on and off the air, were the obstacles to artistic freedom which he confronted at every turn during seventeen years of broadcasting. It was the unwarranted interference with his work by network executives, advertising agencies, sponsors, program rating surveys such as the Hooperatings, and studio audiences, among others, that provided the root cause of his thoroughgoing critique of broadcasting.[5]

The intervention of third parties between the popular artist and his audience is, of course, inherent in the commercial popular arts. As Russel Nye has pointed out, the artist's "relationship with his public is neither direct nor critical, for between him and his audience stand editors, publishers, sponsors, directors, public relations men, wholesalers, exhibitors, merchants, and others who can and often do influence his product." As a veteran of family-centered, strictly-censored vaudeville, Allen was well acquainted with this fact of show business

life. But he believed that broadcasting's business executives carried their interference with the radio writer's and actor's art to unwarranted extremes and based it on false criteria. As he phrased the problem in 1948 while speaking to a radio conference, "no one involved in radio is really interested in the creative side of it." While the networks, ad agencies, and sponsors saw the medium *solely* in financial and marketing terms, Allen believed that broadcasting "can't survive without the creative people—the writers more than anyone else, even more than the actors."

> I think that if I went in to Mr. Charles Luckman of Lever Brothers and showed him how to make some Lifebuoy Soap, he'd resent it. He knows what goes in the vat there. I don't know anything about that. By the same token, I don't think he should come and tell me how to write the jokes.

Allen summarized his views in his autobiography: "Radio could not survive because it was a by-product of advertising." Its entertainment, and entertainers, were incidental to the sale of soap.[6]

Allen did not deny the need for observing standards of decency in programs broadcast over the public airwaves into American homes. Nor did he doubt that program content could offend listener groups—ethnic, religious, economic, and others—if writers and performers did not exercise care. But he objected to the basic assumption of broadcast executives that only business men and women, not radio's artists, could be trusted to control program content. That Allen's talents required an unfettered environment, and that the networks could safely allow them the freedom to roam and probe at will, was noted in a review of one of his early programs. "Obviously he is the kind of comedian who has to be given a free rein," *Variety* stated in 1934. "At the same time there is a minimum of need for supervision of his material because he is too clever ever to have to be off-color." It was inevitable that this comedian would come into conflict with cautious network censors and fearful sponsors and their representatives in the advertising agencies—those who dreaded the mere possibility of alienating potential customers or affronting some group with political or economic clout.[7]

The views of one of Allen's antagonists at NBC, Janet McRorie, illustrates the tension that existed between the artist's and the corporation's perspectives. McRorie headed the Continuity-Acceptance Department at the network during the late 1930s, the office whose job it was to censor all program scripts and advertising copy. Hers was a necessary function, McRorie explained, "Because in the Company's relation to the public care must be taken that the sensibilities of one portion of the listening public are not sacrificed to gratify the preferences of another." And what standards did she apply to achieve such a potentially laudable goal? As described in the words of an interviewer in 1939 they constituted, when narrowly applied, a mindless, nit-picking, and humorless affront to the sensibilities of the radio writer.

"To her mind radio is a sort of window into an outside world, which may be opened to let in fresh air and sunlight, and closed to shut out unpleasant weather, dirt, and street noises. Her duty is to delete the unpleasantness and encourage opening the window." Allen's experience with business interference in his work illustrated that such subjective and aesthetically crude criteria as these placed very serious obstacles in the way of radio programming. That some network entertainers like Fred Allen achieved anything worth recalling decades after their programs appeared represents their triumph over an essentially hostile environment.[8]

Approximately two days prior to each of his broadcasts, Allen had to submit a copy of the script to the network's Continuity-Acceptance Department for both legal and moral screening; another to the radio department of the advertising agency which handled the account; and a third to the vice president of the sponsoring company who supervised the firm's radio advertising. "These were the three sources at which the comedian's troubles originated." Before air time, occasionally just before, Allen, his writers and cast had to be prepared to defend their work and accept changes demanded by these three agencies of business control. Allen often maintained that humor was relative, a matter of opinion. Radio's bureaucratic structure, however, gave excessive power to untutored opinions. As Allen phrased the problem in 1945: "everyone in radio with enough authority to operate a memo pad has an opinion that jeopardizes the comedian's humor," and he offered an illustration. Suppose, Allen told a Peabody Award audience, that a comedian has these lines in his script: "Jack Benny told me a great gag today. Jack said, 'The best way to keep a dead fish from smelling is to cut off its nose.'" The NBC censor would delete the mention of Jack Benny because he broadcasts on a competing chain; the agency, fearing the anti-vivisectionists, would excise the reference to nose-cutting; and the sponsor would eliminate "fish," since his brother sells a competing meat product. With his joke destroyed, the comedian substitutes a story "about the housing shortage being so bad he went into a restaurant and couldn't even get cottage pudding." But even then his troubles continue, for the next day protest letters from people who live in inadequate housing deluge the network. For alienating this important listening group, the comedian's show is cancelled. Allen found a humorous way to focus attention on a serious problem and one that, for all his apparent exaggeration, he depicted accurately.[9]

For example, Allen's sponsors directly intervened in the entertainment-creating process on several occasions. What Erik Barnouw has called the "folklore of sponsor meddling" in early radio included not only stories of company presidents arbitrarily ordering script revisions, but also rumors that their wives' whims sometimes determined the fate of programs and performers. A sponsor's wife never caused the cancellation of a Fred Allen series, but early in his radio career one did order an incongruous and bothersome change in format.

Allen's first program, the *Linit Bath Club Revue* (1932-33), had progressed through several successful shows when the sponsor ordered the addition of an organ solo to the established format. "Playing an organ solo midway through a comedy show," Allen commented later, "is like planting a pickle in the center of a charlotte russe," but it was done because "the sponsor's wife liked organ music." In 1934, executives of the Bristol-Myers Company ordered Allen's cast in the *Hour of Smiles* series to dress in formal evening wear because they were performing before a live studio audience. Allen's opinion of the incongruity of performing comedy in dress suits is not known, but he frequently expressed his views of studio audiences. Their presence too often forced actors to play to the live rather than to the radio audience, and the sponsor, in this case at least, promoted this unfortunate practice.[10]

Advertising agency and network executives ordered script deletions much more frequently than did sponsors. These businessmen's fears and ignorance, as often as their legitimate concerns, made Allen's scripts some of the most frequently-censored on radio. In 1940, Allen complained to writer H. Allen Smith that "each week fifty percent of what i [sic] write ends up in the toilet . . . practically everything is taboo and we end up with ersatz subject matter and ditto humor." One problem was his knowledge and use of the English language, which was not only more sophisticated than that of other comedians, but also than that of the censors. Over the years the wielders of blue pencils at NBC and CBS objected to the "salaciousness" of such words as "rabelasian," "titillate," "saffron," and "pizzicating." Allen also had to battle network censors over the right of fictional characters to say "pitch a little woo" and to call Bear Mountain "strip tease crag." As John Crosby commented, radio's moral guardians displayed "a zeal which would have alarmed even Savonarola." They suspected as immoral every unfamiliar word and phrase used in a boy-girl context.[11]

Sexually suggestive material was not the only category of taboos with which Allen had to deal. At least as important was that based on fears of alienating clients, customers, listener interest groups, and the government. Out of such apprehension developed a censorship as effective as any that Congress could have legislated—one perhaps more effective, since it was exercised out of public view and thus only weakly opposed. In 1934, for example, the Benton and Bowles Advertising Agency cut the following gag from Allen's script:

> STOOGE: I have something to sell you that every advertising man should have.

> ALLEN: You don't mean a relative who's in a legitimate business?

The Agency feared that the joke might offend someone in leadership positions of the sponsoring company, Bristol-Myers. Earlier that year NBC eliminated a joke about utilities magnate Samuel Insull's flight to escape prosecution. The securities manipulator "would have been safe had he, like Machado and Dillinger, remained in the country." Not only was Insull too important and controversial for mention on entertainment radio, but he had also helped NBC to acquire a Chicago radio station several years earlier. Allen won a second conflict with the network in 1934. The comedian wrote a sketch about the pampering of prison inmates which NBC executives feared would be interpreted as criticism by New York Mayor LaGuardia's administration, which had recently uncovered abuses at its Welfare Island facility. Potentially more embarrassing, NBC's executive vice president had been Commissioner of Corrections under the previous mayor, when the irregularities had originated. Maintaining that the Welfare Island episode had not inspired his comedy, and that no past or present officials could construe the script as criticism, Allen won his censorship appeal with top network executives. The threat of censorship, as well as actual deletions, also shaped what Allen could include in his scripts. As he wrote to an old Boston friend during the 1930's, his idea for a sketch satirizing the new social security system, in which every future citizen would be on a government pension, was a good idea. But, he lamented, "we could never get away with it. Since the federal radio commission has swung into action there can be no mention of anything that might tend to draw attention to the radio, sir." Radio was so anxious to avoid controversy and escape notice as anything other than an agency of entertainment and merchandising, that Allen was even ordered to cut the name of labor leader John L. Lewis from one of his 1930s scripts.[12]

Allen's experience with censorship produced numerous additional instances of what for him was the essential failure of radio: unnecessary, even irrational, business interference in the creative process. The broadcast executives' desire not to ridicule religion or marriage prevented the comedian from joking about a deceased judge in one of his skits "going to a higher court," and from playing on the wedding vows with the line, "She promises to love, honor and lump it till death do them part." Network leaders were unreasonably nervous about even hinting that competing broadcast chains existed. "Darn," Allen commented, "is a word invented by NBC, which doesn't recognize either hell or the Columbia Broadcasting System." His line about a "cigarette that grows hair, fixes up your nerves and fumigates the house" drew the objection of NBC because the reference to "nerves" resembled Camel cigarette advertising on a CBS program. The latter network cut the line "just plain Charlie" and altered the fictional fate of character "grandpa David" in one of Allen's soap opera burlesques in 1942, simply because both names suggested characters in actual serials on another network. NBC feared that Mrs. Pansey Nussbaum, a Jewish dialect character who turned out to be one of Allen's most notable creations, would affront Jews. With their business rather than show business backgrounds, the network executives were unaware of the long tradition of Jewish dialect humor on the stage. Allen even had to be cautious in his use of place names. For one program he invented the town of North Wrinkle, which the network allowed to remain in the script only after an exhaustive search of the United States Postal Guide proved that no such place existed. In the late 1930's, Allen was forced "to professional depths never before sounded by even a radio comedian" when he had to apologize to the town of Pottsville, Pennsylvania for an alleged slight made on his program. Facing prohibitions, pressures, and potential protests at every turn, Allen sometimes was hard put to arrive at the studio with a complete, much less satisfying, script. On some weeks the censors left "nothing but punctuation marks for you to put some new words between and have it ready to convulse our thirty million listeners, from coast to coast, by nine p.m. eastern standard time."[13]

Allen's most notable conflict with the censorial mentality of broadcast executives occurred in the spring of 1947, when he was on NBC with a half-hour, Sunday evening program. What was perhaps his greatest talent, lampooning radio itself, confronted what was perhaps broadcasting's strongest taboo, that against ridiculing the networks and their management. Because the studio audience's reaction to jokes could not be anticipated, Allen found it difficult to plan precisely the amount of material that would fill a half-hour of air time. "If the audience was enthusiastic the laughter was sustained and the program ran longer." For several weeks his program had run over, and the network had abruptly cut it off after thirty minutes. (CBS, by contrast, allowed programs to exceed their allotted time.) Allen's script for the program of April 20, 1947, began with satirical dialogue that a thin-skinned NBC vice president, Clarence L. Menser, demanded be cut. Portland Hoffa, the real-life Mrs. Allen and a member of the cast, asked Allen why the show had been cut off last Sunday. Allen responded:

> The main thing in radio is to come out on time. If people laugh the program is longer. The thing to do is to get a nice dull half-hour. Nobody will laugh or applaud. Then you'll always be right on time, and all of the little emaciated radio executives can dance around their desks in interoffice abandon.

He then explained what NBC did with the time that it saved by cutting off the ends of programs.

> Well, there is a big executive here at NBC. He is the vice-president in charge of "Ah! Ah! You're running too long!" He sits in a little glass closet with his mother-of-pearl gong. When your program runs overtime he thumps his gong with a marshmallow he has tied to the end of a xylophone stick. Bong! You're off the air. Then he marks down how much time he's saved. . . . He adds it all up—ten seconds here, twenty seconds there—and when he has saved up enough seconds, minutes and hours to make two weeks, NBC lets the vice-president use the two weeks of *your* time for *his* vacation.

"He's living on borrowed time, "Portland commented. Yes, Allen agreed. "And enjoying every minute of it."[14]

When Allen refused Menser's order and used the original script on the air, the network "pulled the plug" on twenty-five seconds of the objectionable material. The incident immediately became "L'Affaire Allen," bringing unwanted publicity to the network, criticism of its censorship practices, and vindication to Allen and others who had long suffered under the industry's heavy hand. The powerful J. Walter Thompson Agency announced that it would bill NBC for the time Allen's sponsor had paid for but been denied. Two days after the incident both Red Skelton and Bob Hope were cut off the air on their NBC programs when they tried to joke about Allen and the network. Allen hired a group of midgets to picket the network's offices in Rockefeller Center with signs reading: "This network is unfair to the little man." NBC finally backed down, admitting that it had been too sensitive about the comedian's satire and wrong to cut him off the air. The network also promised not to silence other comedians who joked about the affair and, with an unaccustomed show of humor, made Allen an honorary vice president. To the public which followed the story it might have seemed that artistic freedom had triumphed over bureaucratic phobia. The student of radio censorship in all of its guises knows, however, that Allen's *cause celebre* brought no fundamental change. Business values, which included an acute corporate self-consciousness, continued to dominate what could be called showmanship to the very end.[15]

Interference in radio artistry included not only the direct and indirect censorship which has been emphasized here, but also such phenomena as the Hooperatings and other audience measurement surveys. The Hooperatings' quantitative reports of audience size encouraged broadcasting executives to evaluate program and talent success in quantitative rather than in qualitative terms. Since the number of listeners a program attracted was often a matter of pure luck—depending, for example, on the show's time slot or night or broadcast, or the success of programs immediately preceding or following a given show—hardworking and talented writers and performers often experienced frustration at the results of the ratings. In other instances, program popularity resulted from pure faddishness, as was the case with the quiz and giveaway programs of the late 1940s At the end of his radio career, in 1948-1949, Allen's program competed against another called *Stop The Music!,* which appealed to the get-rich-quick fantasies of millions of ABC network listeners. The quality of Allen's comedy, his decade-and-one-half of experience in broadcasting, meant little when pitted against the remote chance of a listener answering the phone, identifying a song, and winning money. That "Hooperism" or "ratingitis" should be allowed to dictate the kind and quality of network programming was evidence to Allen of radio's creative, if not financial, bankruptcy.[16]

Through satire that was sometimes bitter, even cynical, Allen expressed his discouragement over radio's denial of free creative expression. He was especially effective when depicting the mentality and behavior of radio's bureaucrats who were, if not the total source of the comedian's problems, at least the personification of his frustration. From the early 1930s to the late 1940s, his scripts and letters were peppered with bumbling chief executives and their "echo men"—ambitious but useless vice presidents. Allen left memorable characterizations of advertising executives, one of whom he called the "the Madison Avenue messiah," "the memo merchant," and "the happy huckster." It was rumored that a partner in one large New York agency was so important, Allenwrote, that "he had a wastebasket in his office in which he threw people." Allen called both the advertising agency and network executives "molehill men."

> Their job is to sit at a desk piled high with molehills and make mountains out of them. Every morning they get an "In" box full of mounds of earth. They sit all day in a high-ceilinged office, patting and piling the mounds into an "Out" box. By lunch time, they're usually above sea level. By five o'clock, they're up in the thin altitude, yodeling to each other. The first one to build a snow-capped peak is made a vice-president."

Allen defined an advertising agency as "85 per cent confusion and 15 per cent commission." Reacting negatively to the title given one of his series by broadcast executives, Allen commented that it "sounded . . . as though it had been spawned by two badly mated vice-presidents who had gone up-carpet out of season." Allen defined a radio producer as "an ulcer with a stopwatch." Playing the part of a big business executive on one of his programs, Allen was too busy to come to the phone. "He saw himself in a mirror and thought it was a conference. He is still talking to himself." On another show, an NBC guide marched tourists through Allen's studio and pointed out to them: "that little man with mildew on him is a Vice President."[17]

Although radio's bureaucratic structure and business leadership inspired a considerable part of Allen's comedy, it is the serious side of the matter that must be reiterated. Fred Allen became one of the most thoroughgoing and effective critics of radio during the 1930s and 1940s because of what he saw as its misplaced emphasis and distorted priorities. He did not naively wish that radio, which he knew was both a commercial device and an entertainment medium, shed its commercialism in the interest of the artist. He knew that without the sales appeal, the hucksterism, there would be no radio comedy at all. As this essay has indicated, however, Allen did strongly object to the extreme degree of business interference in the process of creating comedy. The passing of time, and the success of television, have demonstrated that the fears and phobias of broadcast executives during radio's heyday—the fear of alienating potential customers; the humorless, even grim, obsession with offending some listener interest group; the destructive overemphasis on the ratings—were excessive. Except for the ratings, most of these towering concerns of the 1930s and 1940s have passed into a kind of curious history which can only bemuse a generation exposed to television's openness in the late 1970s. Fred Allen spent a radio career fighting for the inclusion of material that would be bland if included on a contemporary television comedy program. What would Allen's comedic achievements have been had he not been restricted by radio's narrow limitations?

NOTES

1 Charles A. Siepmann, *Radio's Second Chance* (Boston, Little, Brown and Company, 1946), 255, 257; Jack Gould, "Mr. Allen's Comeback," *New York Times,* October 14, 1945, II, p. 5; John Crosby, *Out Of The Blue: A Book About Radio and Television* (New York, Simon and Schuster, 1952), p. x. The reasons that radio criticism did not develop included the following: the hostility of newspapers to their perceived competitor, radio, and their resultant unwillingness to give broadcasting publicity through the writing of radio columnists; and the fact that radio programs were broadcast live, thus precluding preview by columnists and other critics.

2 John Crosby, "Radio And Who Makes It," *The Atlantic Monthly,* 181 (January, 1948), 29; Gould, "Mr. Allen's Comeback," 5; Ben Gross, *I Looked And I Listened: Informal Recollections Of Radio And TV* (New Rochelle, New York, Arlington House, 1954, 1970), p. 130.

3 On vaudeville as a source of radio talent see the essay by John DiMeglio in this issue; Allen's comments are in his letters to Frank Rosengren, December 11, 1933, and to James R. Naulty, April 15, 1933, in Joe McCarthy, ed., *fred allen's letters* (Garden City, New York, Doubleday and Company, Inc., 1965), pp. 120 and 71 respectively; Allen, *Treadmill To Oblivion* (Boston, Little, Brown and Company, 1954), p. 3.

4 Allen, *Much Ado About Me* (Boston, Little, Brown and Company, 1956), p. 363 for O'Connor's comments, and pp. 311-12 for Allen's; audio recording of the program *Conversation,* March 22, 1956, which includes a discussion among Clifton Fadiman, Gilbert Seldes, and Fred Allen taped in 1954.

5 Dwight MacDonald, "Theory of Mass Culture," in Bernard Rosenberg and David Manning White, eds., *Mass Culture: The Popular Arts In America* (New York, The Free Press, 1957, paperback edition 1964), p. 65; Herbert Gans, *Popular Culture and High Culture: An Analysis and Evaluation of Taste* (New York, Basic Books, Inc., 1974), p. 23.

6 Russel Nye, *The Unembarrassed Muse: The Popular Arts In America* (New York, Dial Press, 1970), p. 5; on vaudeville censorship see John E. DiMeglio, *Vaudeville, U.S.A.* (Bowling Green, Ohio, Bowling Green University Popular Press, 1973), pp. 195-97; Allen's 1948 remarks

are reported in *New York Times,* April 25, 1948, II, 9; similar sentiments are found in an interview with Allen in Ben Gross, "Looking and Listening," n.d., clipping in H. Allen Smith Papers, Special Collections, Morris Library, Southers Illinois University, Carbondale, Illinois, hereafter cited as Smith Papers; Gross, *I Looked and I Listened,* 130; Allen, *Treadmill To Oblivion,* 238; the Lever Brothers example was hypothetical as that firm never sponsored Allen.

7 Review of the *Sal Hepatica Revue,* in *Variety,* January 9, 1934, p. 32.

8 Ruth Knight, *Stand By For The Ladies! The Distaff Side Of Radio* (New York, Coward-McCann, Inc., 1939), 49-50.

9 Allen, *Treadmill To Oblivion,* pp. 158-59; "Fred Allen Discusses Mr. LaGuardia," *New York Times,* April 15, 1945, II, 7.

10 Erik Barnouw, *The Sponsor: Notes On A Modern Potentate* (New York, Oxford University Press. 1978), p. 3; Allen, *Treadmill To Oblivion,* 14; *Variety,* May 29, 1934, p. 33; Arnold M. Auerbach, *Funny Men Don't Laugh* (Garden City, New York, Doubleday and Company, 1965), pp. 125-26.

11 Allen to H. Allen Smith, December 20, 1940, in Smith Papers; Allen to Bob Welch, October 6, 1942, and to Pat Weaver, n.d., in McCarthy, ed., *fred allen's letters,* 258, 272; Crosby, *Out Of The Blue,* 273.

12 *Variety,* June 26, 1934, p. 40 for the Benton and Bowles example; *Ibid.,* May 29, 1934, p. 31 for the Insull case; *Ibid.,* February 20, 1934, p. 31 for the prison sketch; Allen to Joe Kelly, n.d., in McCarthy, ed., *fred allen's letters,* 98 for the pensions idea; and Allen to Pat Weaver, n.d., in *Ibid.,* 272 for the Lewis cut.

13 The soap opera example is from Allen to Bob Welch, October 6, 1942, in *Ibid.,* 258; the problem with Pottsville is mentioned in Allen to Jack Mulcahy, April 12[1938 or 1939?], in *Ibid.,* 192-93; the other examples are cited in Crosby, *Out Of The Blue,* 273-75; Allen's final comment is in his letter to Joe Kelly, n.d., in McCarthy, ed., *fred allen's letters,* 97.

14 Allen *Treadmill To Oblivion,* 211-14.

15 *Ibid.,* 212; *New York Times,* April 21, 1947, p. 29; April 22, 1947, p. 33; April 23, 1947, p. 27; April 24, 1947, p. 27; April 28, 1947, p. 25; May 7, 1947, p. 41; Jack Gould, "L'Affaire Allen," *Ibid.,* April 27, 1947, II, p. 9.

16 On the Hooperatings see Allen to H. Allen Smith, n.d., Smith Papers; Thomas Whiteside, "Hooperism Clears The Air," *The New Republic,* 116 (May 5, 1947), 27-30; Jack Gould, "The Curse of Ratings," *New York Times,* February 17, 1946, II, 7.

[17] Auerbach, *Funny Men Don't Laugh,* 121; Allen, *Treadmill To Oblivion,* 8, 19-20, 24, 27, 30; Allen to H. Allen Smith, October 17, [1942], Smith Papers; Script for *Town Hall Tonight* program (microfilm), April 22, 1936, Manuscripts Division, Library of Congress, Washington, D.C.; audio tape of the *Fred Allen Show,* May 26, 1946.

Arthur Frank Wertheim (essay date 1979)

SOURCE: "Allen's Alley," in *Radio Comedy,* Oxford University Press, 1979, pp. 335-52.

[*In the following excerpt, Wertheim examines the use of ethnic and regional characterizations on Allen's Alley.*]

One of the funniest shows on radio in the 1940s was *Allen's Alley,* which premiered on Sunday, December 6, 1942. After eight years on the air Wednesday night, Allen had switched to a Sunday night time slot, on March 8, 1942. Listeners could then hear Jack Benny (7 p.m.), Bergen and McCarthy (8 p.m.), and Fred Allen (8:30 p.m.), three of the top comedy shows, on the same night. Listening to all those broadcasts became a Sunday evening pastime for families. Allen's last one-hour program was aired on June 28, 1942, and that fall he began broadcasting a thirty-minute show.

The half-hour comedy show was a standard time length in the 1940s. Benny had proved that a thirty-minute comedy program could be as entertaining as a one-hour variety show. Costs of broadcasting time had risen over the years, so that sponsors were paying enormous prices for prime time in the evening hours. The expenses involved in solely sponsoring an hour-long program were prohibitive. Companies could cut costs by concentrating on hard-sell advertising during half an hour. Shorter programs also allowed the network to sell more time to more customers. Many hour-long programs were cut in half in the 1940s and some thirty-minute programs shortened to fifteen minutes.[1]

Allen had found writing a one-hour show exhausting work, and so preferred the shorter format. Unlike the loose-structured hour-long *Town Hall Tonight,* the new thirty-minute show had to be tightly knit. "The relaxed type of dialogue of the longer routines had to be replaced by brisk, staccato lines," Allen recalled. "For the first few programs I felt like a man who for years had been writing on the *Encyclopaedia Britannica* and suddenly started to write for *Reader's Digest.*" Allen still wrote the script in longhand in a small room in his Manhattan apartment, and was assisted by several new writers, including Nat Hiken and Larry Marks. After an informal script reading Allen conferred with his cast, writers, and director for general editing. They rehearsed the program several times on Sunday and made more changes before the evening's broadcast. The new show contained two major comedy sections: first, Portland's spot and the *Allen's Alley* section, and second, dialogue

and a sketch with a guest star. Music by Al Goodman and the De Marco Sisters completed the program. Compared to *Town Hall Tonight,* the comedy dialogue on *Allen's Alley* was snappy and reflected the faster pace of radio comedy in the 1940s.[2]

Allen's Alley partly grew out of comic interviews the comedian had conducted on *"Town Hall News."* On *The Texaco Star Theatre* (1941-42) Allen had also broadcast a spot called **"The March of Trivia,"** a parody on the newsreel *The March of Time.* The comedian had interviewed various characters about their reaction to the "weekly lowlight from the world of news." In December 1942 he decided to focus the comedy news around a central locale, a street inhabited by bizarre characters. The comedian was influenced by journalist O. O. McIntyre, who wrote a popular column called "Thoughts While Strolling." The newspaperman concocted stories about people he met on the streets of New York's Chinatown and Bowery. "I felt that something of this type which would permit me to stroll through a nondescript neighborhood and discuss current events with its denizens would be very amusing," Allen wrote. "I knew that with music and sound effects we could establish the locale and that it would come off well in radio."[3]

Unlike *Town Hall Tonight, Allen's Alley* featured a permanent cast of character actors and actresses playing the same role every week. The comedian had previously created hundreds of different minor characters for the news sketches, and the parts were performed by a versatile cast whose names were never mentioned on the air. Allen had enjoyed creating these new comedy roles every week, for he felt listeners easily tired of hearing the same characters. During the 1941-42 season there were signs that Allen's format was not attracting as many listeners. His program had been declining in listener appeal since 1939, and in January 1942 his Hooper rating slipped to 14. The entertainer realized that he had to change the show's structure. "I also knew that we had been on a long time and I suspected that anonymity could be monotonous, too," he stated. "It might be a novelty for the audience if we developed several characters they could associate with our show." One key to longevity on radio was creating a regular cast of characters around the comedian—funny and familiar personalities that got as many laughs as the comic. Listeners looked forward to hearing them every week. One month after *Allen's Alley* went on the air his Hooper rating had escalated to 21.6.[4]

Allen mainly played a stooge on this section of the program. He would knock on the door of the houses in the Alley and ask questions on a particular topic. "Whenever I want to know how America is reacting to an important issue of the day, I just drop around to Allen's Alley," the comedian remarked on the premiere.[5] The humor on *Allen's Alley* emanated from the exaggerated personalities of the characters and their unpredictable responses to Allen's questions.

The comedian initially used actors who had already performed rôles on his broadcasts. Alan Reed played the pompous poet Falstaff Openshaw, a ham actor who recited rhyming lyrics. The name Falstaff came from Shakespeare's comic character, while Openshaw was the last name of a person Allen knew. Shakespeare couldn't sue us," Allen said. "Mr. Openshaw didn't. It was a happy arrangement." Reed was an experienced radio actor before he joined Allen's program. During his teens he had started acting on the legitimate stage, and in 1927 he began to play dramatic parts in radio plays using his real name, Teddy Bergman. His acting soon led him to roles on comedy shows playing straight men and imitating foreign dialects. Sometimes he performed in nearly thirty-five shows a week. On *The Eddie Cantor Show* the actor did the voice of the violinist Dave Rubinoff, who suffered from mike fright. Cantor bet Rubinoff $100 he could not say one word over the air. The singer lost the wager when the violinist gingerly approached the microphone during one broadcast and said "Eddie Cantor, you owe me a $100." A versatile radio character actor, Reed also played Joe Palooka, Daddy Higgins in the *"Baby Snooks"* skits, Pasquale in *"Life with Luigi,"* and Solomon Levy in *"Abie's Irish Rose."* He later did the voice of Fred Flintstone, the cartoon character, on television.[6]

On *Allen's Alley* Reed wrote his own dialogue and composed couplets that brought gales of laughter. "Are those new poems you have there?" Allen asked Falstaff.

> REED: Yea, old Saggy-Eyes. Have you heard. The F.B.I. Just Caught a Traitor. He Was Putting Bananas In the Refrigerator.
>
> ALLEN: No.
>
> REED: Mr. Churchill Lisped As He Came To Town. His London Bridge Was Falling Down.
>
> ALLEN: No.
>
> REED: Or perhaps—Every Time My Mother Hears Perry Como. She Has To Lie Down And Send Out For A Bromo.

Reed's routine included a verse on the evening topic. On one broadcast Allen asked the Alley characters their opinion of the 1946 steel strike. Openshaw read his poem "A Miracle Happened in Pittsburgh."

> A miracle happened in Pittsburgh
> That, with ancient miracles ranked
> When each steel plant closed its blast furnace
> And each roaring fire was banked
>
> . . . . .
>
> The terrified citizens stampeded
> And abandoned their homes on the run
> For the first time since the city was founded
> Pittsburgh had seen the sun!

The pompous manner in which Reed delivered his lines was as amusing as the poems. Once, when his voice became hoarse during a show, he quickly ad-libbed: "Pardon friends, a discordant note / Falstaff found a frog in throat."[7]

Other characters on the early *Allen's Alley* broadcasts included John Doe, Socrates Mulligan, and Senator Bloat. John Doe, the average American, was played by John Brown, who had been doing roles on Allen's programs for many years. "If horse meat catches on, do you think it will have any effect on the country?" the comedian asked Doe. "Well, eating horses will put a lot of bookmakers outta work," Doe replied. "It'll make a pedestrian outta Gene Autry [and] the Horse Show this year might win the Good Housekeeping Seal of Approval." A gifted actor, Brown later played Digger O'Dell, the friendly undertaker, on *The Life of Riley*. Socrates Mulligan, the ignoramus, was enacted by Charlie Cantor, who had earlier played roles on *Town Hall Tonight*. Socrates Mulligan's favorite words were "Duh-yeah?" His "report card showed that he flunked in recess and got a D in lunch." Senator Bloat, played by Jack Smart during 1943-44, was a conceited politician, a forerunner of Senator Claghorn. But these and other characters were not funny enough to be used over a long period. In 1945 Mrs. Nussbaum, Senator Beauregard Claghorn, Ajax Cassidy, and Titus Moody became the four major characters used consistently on the program. Each represented different ethnic and regional types in America. The performers who enacted these roles made *Allen's Alley* a comedy classic.[8]

Minerva Pious played Pansy Nussbaum during the entire time *Allen's Alley* was on the air. The daughter of a wholesale candy merchant, Pious had emigrated from Russia as a young girl and had grown up in Bridgeport, Connecticut, and New York City. Harry Tugend, a singer, once auditioned for Allen and asked Pious, a personal friend and an accomplished pianist, to accompany him. When Tugend informed Allen that Pious did dialect characterizations, the comedian asked her to perform a routine. The radio star liked her rendition so much that he asked her to join his program. She played Jewish immigrant types and other characters on *Town Hall Tonight*.[9]

Her portrayal of the busy Jewish housewife, Mrs. Nussbaum, who spoke with an exaggerated Bronx accent, highlighted *Allen's Alley*. Her dialogue overflowed with malapropisms and other funny speech patterns. "Ah, Mrs. Nussbaum," Allen greeted when she opened her door. "You are expecting maybe Ingrown Bergman?" or "You are expecting maybe Tokio Rose?" Mrs. Nussbaum might reply. She called crepes suzettes "Kreplach Suzette" and pronounced Mississippi "Matzos-Zippi" and Massachusetts "Matzos-chusetts." She liked such food as "herring du jour, chopped liver cacciatore, [and] pot roast à la king." Mrs. Nussbaum talked constantly about her French husband, Pierre. When Allen asked her about the housing shortage Mrs.

Nussbaum replied that so many relatives had moved into her house her husband had left. "For two weeks I am a widow," she declared. One night Pierre knocked at her door anxious to return. "Ah, it was true love," said Allen, "Pierre couldn't live without you." "Love—Schmove, Pierre couldn't find a room," exclaimed Mrs. Nussbaum. Although she was an exaggerated comic caricature of a Jewish housewife, Mrs. Nussbaum rarely, if ever, offended listeners.[10]

The second permanent character on *Allen's Alley* was the Southern politician, Senator Beauregard Claghorn, played by Kenny Delmar, the program's announcer. Delmar modeled Claghorn on a jovial Texas rancher he had met. Minerva Pious told Allen about Delmar's impersonation. The announcer made the boasting, boisterous Senator one of the most memorable characters in radio comedy.[11]

Senator Claghorn was a parody on Southern pride and romanticism. After Allen knocked on his door, listeners waited for the Senator to brag about the South: "Somebody—say—somebody knocked. . . . Ah'm from the South. The Sunny South. The garden spot of all creation." A series of staccato one-liners about his love for the South and hatred of the North highlighted his routine. "I represent the South. I'm from Dixie. . . . I don't see a movie unless the star is Ann Sothern. . . . On the radio I never listen to Mr. and Mrs. North." Allen once commented that the Senator looked pale. "Ah've been in the house the last two days," Claghorn said. "Ah refuse to come out. The wind was blowin' from the North." Allen rarely finished a sentence without the garrulous Senator interrupting to boast about the South:

> KENNY: Somebody—I say, somebody knocked.
>
> ALLEN: Yes, I—
>
> KENNY: Claghorn's the name—Senator Claghorn, that is.
>
> ALLEN: I know. Don't give me that routine about Dixie.
>
> KENNY: I won't go into a room unless it's got Southern exposure.
>
> ALLEN: Well—
>
> KENNY: The only train I ride is the Chattanooga Choo-Choo.
>
> ALLEN: Just a—
>
> KENNY: (*Sings*) The sun shines bright in my old Kentucky home.—
>
> ALLEN: Now wait—
>
> KENNY: I'm singin' "My Old Kentucky Home," Son.
>
> ALLEN: I know—

> KENNY: Son, bend down, and kiss my Jefferson Davis button.[12]

The character was also used to lampoon government bureaucracy and corruption:

> ALLEN: Well, Senator, about our question. Do you think advertising has any effect on our manners and customs?
>
> KENNY: Ah don't trust advertisin', Son. Especially them ads politicians put in the papers around election time.
>
> ALLEN: Uh-huh.
>
> KENNY: Ah saw an ad last election, it said— Elect this honest fearless, hardworkin' enemy of graft and corruption. I busted out laughin'.
>
> ALLEN: Who was the candidate?
>
> KENNY: Me! So long, Son! So long, that is![13]

Senator Claghorn talked so fast that Allen often missed his jokes. "That's a joke, son," Claghorn would remind the comedian.

> ALLEN: What about this telegraph strike?
>
> KENNY: I brought the subject up in Congress. There was a speech by Senator Ball bearing on it.
>
> ALLEN: Then—
>
> KENNY: Ball bearing! That's a joke, Son!
>
> ALLEN: I know—
>
> KENNY: That was a Louisville Lalapaluza!
>
> ALLEN: I—
>
> KENNY: That was a San Antonio Superduper. . . . [14]

Delmar's impersonation became an overnight sensation. Fans mimicked his voice and bought Claghorn shirts and compasses that always pointed South. Streets in Southern cities were named after the character. "That's a joke, son" became a popular saying across the country and was the title of a record and a movie starring Delmar.

The third regular character on *Allen's Alley* was Ajax Cassidy, a temperamental Irishman played by Peter Donald. Donald was hired to act the part when Alan Reed left the program. An expert dialectician, Donald was especially adept at doing an Irish brogue. Irish-Americans had been the subject of American stage comedy since the nineteenth century and had often been depicted as indolent, quarrelsome drunkards. Ajax was also characterized as a heavy drinker:

> ALLEN: Ajax, I heard you were sick.

PETE: I was at death's door. Luckily I didn't have strength enough to knock.

ALLEN: You were bad, eh?

PETE: The doctor gave me a big bottle of Corduroy pills.

ALLEN: Uh-huh.

PETE: After every meal the doctor said to swallow one pill and drink a small glass of whiskey.

ALLEN: Swallow one pill and drink a small glass of whiskey.

PETE: After every meal.

ALLEN: How is the treatment coming along?

PETE: I'm a little behind with the pills.[15]

While Southern jokes marked Senator Claghorn's routine and Jewish jokes Mrs. Nussbaum's repertoire, Irish jokes abounded in Ajax Cassidy's dialogue:

ALLEN: What is tomorrow?

PETE: What is tomorrow? You heathen infidel—It's St. Patrick's Day.

ALLEN: Oh. Are you going to be in the parade?

PETE: In the parade, says he. I'm leadin' the parade.

ALLEN: Really?

PETE: Wearin' me emerald green silk hat, me flowin' green cape, me pea green sneakers and carryin' a gold harp seven feet high. . . .

Ajax became noted for his catchy opening line: "W-e-e-e-l-l-l, how do ye do?" An Irish-American himself, Allen especially enjoyed Donald's impersonation, and so did most listeners. He was puzzled when a small minority of Irishmen threatened "to march an entire chapter of the Ancient Order of Hibernians down from Albany, or some upstate New York community, to Radio City if Ajax was not evicted from the Alley and chased from the industry."[16]

The old New England hayseed, Titus Moody, played by Parker Fennelly, was the last of the regional-ethnic types who inhabited **Allen's Alley**. Like the Irishman, the Yankee country bumpkin was a venerable comic stage character; he had appeared as early as 1787 in Royall Tyler's *The Contrast*. Fennelly had impersonated New England rural characters in early radio in *The Stebbin Boys* and *Snow Village Sketches*. Known for his witty turn of phrase and tall tales, farmer Moody talked like The Old Timer on *Fibber McGee and Molly*. He would greet Allen with "howdy, bub." Cornball humor marked Fennelly's routine:

PARKER: Farms don't need men no more—machines does all the work.

ALLEN: Machinery, eh?

PARKER: 'Bout all a man can do with his hands on a farm today—is scratch himself.

ALLEN: Do you use machinery?

PARKER: I bought a big machine—'twas called the Jumbo Hired Man.

ALLEN: It did all the work?

PARKER: It had four iron hands on it—for milkin' cows.

ALLEN: I see.

PARKER: It had a suction thing—for pickin' eggs up outta nests.

ALLEN: Uh-huh.

PARKER: It had two big arms—for thrashin' wheat.

ALLEN: Yes.

PARKER: On the side it had two big clippers—for clippin' sheep.

ALLEN: How is the Jumbo Hired Man working out?

PARKER: Fust day I turned it on everything went wrong.

ALLEN: The milking hands?

PARKER: The four hands started pickin' up eggs and puttin 'em into the cows.

ALLEN: No kidding.

PARKER: The suction thing started trying to milk the chickens.

ALLEN: Gosh!

PARKER: The two big thrashin' arms started beating the cookies outta me.

ALLEN: Jeepers!

PARKER: The two big sheep clippers clipped off my wife's hair.

ALLEN: Your wife was completely bald?

PARKER: She left town with an eagle.

ALLEN: Are you still using the Jumbo Hired Man?

PARKER: No, I threw out the cow, the chickens and the whole contraption.

ALLEN: I see.

PARKER: I bought an adding machine.

ALLEN: What can you raise on your farm with an adding machine?

PARKER: Rabbits. So long, Bub![17]

Titus Moody and the other regular characters on *Allen's Alley* were like Benny's "gang." Listeners became familiar with their voices and comic routines. Those four inhabitants of *Allen's Alley* were masterpieces of radio character comedy.

A Fred Allen program in the 1940s also featured guest celebrities. "To try to insure [*sic*] each guest a successful appearance we created jokes and situations to fit his individual talents," Allen recalled. The comedian also liked to use guests in entertaining ways. Baseball manager Leo Durocher acted in a takeoff on Gilbert & Sullivan's *H.M.S. Pinafore;* opera star Helen Traubel parodied a singing commercial; songwriters Richard Rodgers and Oscar Hammerstein appeared in a courtroom skit; and newscasters Lowell Thomas and H. V. Kaltenborn made comments about the comedian's program in a news broadcast.[18]

Actress Tallulah Bankhead and Allen once did a takeoff on an early morning husband-and-wife broadcast called "Tullu and Freddy, that happy homey couple." The comedian and the actress lampooned the number of advertisements on a wake-up show:

BANKHEAD: Good morning, Freddie dear.

ALLEN: Good morning, Tulu angel.

BANKHEAD: Sweetheart, I must say you look refreshingly well-rested this morning.

ALLEN: Yes, thanks to our wonderful Pasternak Factory-Tested Pussy-Willow Mattress. The mattress that takes the guess-work out of sleeping. So soft, so restful—

BANKHEAD: And just Seventeen-fifty at Bambergers.

ALLEN: Only the hearts of the tender pussy-willows are used. Breakfast ready, angel-face?

BANKHEAD: Yes, Sweetums. Here's your coffee.

(*Tinkle of china*)

ALLEN: Thank you, doll. The time is now six-three. (*Sip*) Ahhhh! What coffee! What aromatic fragrance! It must be—

BANKHEAD: You're right, Lovey! It's McKeester's Vita-Fresh Coffee. The coffee with that locked-up goodness for everybody—Grind or Drip.

ALLEN: Quick, darling. Another cup. Ahhhhh!

BANKHEAD: Peach-Fuzz! You've spilled some on your vest.

ALLEN: Goody. Now I can try some of that Little Panther Spot Remover. No harsh rubbing. Just spray some Little Panther on your vest and watch it eat the spot out.

BANKHEAD: And imagine, a big two ounce bottle for only 35 cents.

ALLEN: Or, if you are a messy eater, you can get the handy economical forty gallon vat.

BANKHEAD: Angel-Eyes. I have so much juicy gossip to tell our listeners this morning.

ALLEN: Stop! Don't move, Tallu!

BANKHEAD: But, Darling—

ALLEN: What have you done to your hair? Your hair is breath-taking. That sheen! That brilliance!

BANKHEAD: I just did what so many society women are doing these days. I went to Madame Yvonne's Hair-do Heaven. 424 Madison Avenue, in the Loft.

ALLEN: It's divine, darling bunny fluff!

BANKHEAD: Madame Yvonne uses a sensational hair-dressing. It contains that new mystery ingredient—chicken fat.

ALLEN: I hear it's on sale at all the better delicatessen stores. But go on, Sweets—

(*Canary twittering*)

ALLEN: Ah, our canary, Little Jasha!

BANKHEAD: My, doesn't little Jasha sound glorious this morning?

ALLEN: I'll bet I know just what he's saying, too. He's saying (*corny kid*) Gee willikers, Mummy and Daddy, thanks for feeding me that swell Dr. Groobers three-way bird seed that comes in 15 and 25 cent packages.

(*Canary twitters*)

BANKHEAD: Ah, little Jasha is so happy, so carefree. And why shouldn't he be happy.

ALLEN: Yes. He knows that the newspaper on the bottom of his cage is New York's leading daily—the Morning Record—32 columnists, 18 pages of comics, and all the news no other newspaper sees fit to print.19

Couples on early morning programs were notorious for their cheerfulness. Allen and Bankhead pretended that both husband and wife had wakened in an irritable mood:

BANKHEAD: (*Big yawn*) Hey, knuckle-head! Get out of that bed, we've got a program to do!

ALLEN: Will you stop yappin! Six o'clock in the

morning. Who's up to listen to us—a couple of garbage collectors and some burglers, maybe. What a racket.

BANKHEAD: If you want to go back to hustling gardenias in front of Childs, go right ahead.

ALLEN: Yeah? What were you? Queen of the Powder Room at Gimbels. My mouth tastes like a sandhog just pulled his foot out of it. Gad, I'm sleepy.

BANKHEAD: Why don't you stay home some night and try sleeping?

ALLEN: Sleeping? On that Pasternak Pussy-Willow Mattress? Pussy-Willow? It's stuffed with cat-hair. Every time I lie down on that cat-hair my back arches.

BANKHEAD: Oh, Stop beefing! Here's your coffee!

(*China tinkle*)

ALLEN: It's about time. (*Sip*) Ptoo! (*Spit*) What are you trying to do, poison me? Ptoo!

At the end of the skit Allen shot their pet canary and his wife. "Tune in tomorrow, folks, for something new in radio programs," the comedian said. "One Man's Family—without the family!"[20]

Allen's social satire often irritated the network and sponsor. Censorship was a problem comedians faced in radio comedy. Jokes had to be clean and the material supportive rather than critical of American institutions and manners. The high degree of commercialism in broadcasting also contributed to censorship. The sponsor and its advertising agency feared offending listeners because they aimed to sell their products to as many customers as possible. Allen openly denounced the commercial influences on radio programming: he accused advertisers of lowering the quality of entertainment in order to attract huge audiences. Decisions in radio, said Allen, were made by "molehill men"—bureaucratic vice presidents in advertising agencies:

A molehill man is a pseudo-busy executive who comes to work at 9 a.m. and finds a molehill on his desk. He has until 5 p.m. to make this molehill into a mountain. An accomplished molehill man will often have his mountain finished even before lunch.[21]

Sponsors prohibited the mentioning of competitive products over the air, and the network carefully censored scripts for libelous remarks. It had been said that one comedian was not permitted to have any jokes about roller skates because his sponsor, an automobile manufacturer, believed it was a competitive form of transportation. A gag dealing with ham in an Allen script was censored because NBC had a program sponsored by the Hormel Meat Company. Allen had to stop making comic references about prunes because of complaints by the prune packers of California. The comedian remembered

a rehearsal in which the soundman reproduced the fizz of Sal Hepatica by dropping a teaspoon of the competitive Bromo Seltzer into a glass of water. He was told that Sal Hepatica did not fizz loud enough. Censorship infuriated Allen. "You ought to spend a few months in radio," he wrote a friend. "With the sponsor, agency, network and strange people roaming around the studios cutting out your jokes and telling you what is wrong with the program, you would be ready for a fitting for either a coffin or a straitjacket." Allen once joked about censorship on his show:

Isn't it dangerous to mention air on the radio. . . . They hear that word "air" and they think how nice it might be to go out and get a breath of it. And then where is our audience? . . . You never hear anybody on the radio call a spade a spade, do you. If people get thinking about spades the first thing you know they'll get a shovel and start burying their radios in the backyard.[22]

Before his show could be broadcast, Allen's script had to be cleared by NBC's program acceptance department. The staff judiciously red-penciled any suggestive dialogue, including double entendres as well as mild swear words like hell and damn, and certain slang expressions. The department also discouraged references to programs on competitive networks. Jokes mentioning living people and spoofing organizations had to be cleared. Allen's gag that the sturgeon at Lindy's Delicatessen "tasted tired" had to be approved by the restaurant. One script contained a joke about Lucrezia Borgia, the fifteenth-century Duchess of Ferrara. A department executive thought she was still alive and asked his secretary to telephone her. Unable to find the exact name in the Manhattan telephone directory, she thought her employer must have meant Lucrezia Bori, the Metropolitan Opera star. "Will you permit your name to be used on the Fred Allen show?" the secretary asked. "He's mentioning you as a chef." The Spanish soprano agreed to sign the clearance.[23]

NBC constantly sent memorandums to Allen's staff urging the deletion of material and sometimes threatened to fade the program if the dialogue was not cut. Comedians had to be careful when joking about public officials. The network censored the following reference to President Truman on Allen's program:

Yes, Harry gave us too much. His old haberdashery training, you know. He always makes it bigger to allow for shrinkage.

The line, "Bea Lillie has switched to water because water is milder," was considered objectionable because it suggested that the actress drank liquor. NBC also ordered the line, "In a wigwam there are no facilities" cut. Even so, the censors sometimes failed to catch words that seemed passable in written form but sounded offensive over the air. One NBC memo read:

On last night's Allen show, Titus Moody remarked that he used to receive so many injections as a young man that he was soon all shot to health. This wasn't questioned when we read the script, but on the air sounded so much like hell that I was sure, at the moment, that hell was actually said.[24]

If the censor's request was too farfetched or if Allen felt a certain routine deserved to remain in the script the comedian often refused to make the changes. Fearing Allen might offend animal lovers, the sponsor ordered him to omit a joke about a man who deliberately stepped on a cat. Allen angrily responded to the person who informed him of the proposed cut:

> I want you to paddle into the slime of your censor's subconscious, lower your head into its fetid depths, and tell him I am *not* cutting that joke. . . . Tell him the joke has been personally approved by the head of the Society for the Preservation of Animal Sadism—me. Tell him there's only one other sound that resembles the squealing of bagpipes, and that's the noise the censor will emit when I commit intimate personal mayhem on him with his own shears. Tell him that, please.[25]

Allen had other problems with NBC because he was often unable to finish his program on time and was cut off the air before the show was completed. Unplanned laughter by the studio audience and Allen's ad-libbing frequently caused the broadcast to run overtime. The sponsor was angry because the closing commercial was not broadcast and the network lost money on station-break commercials. *Take It or Leave It,* the quiz program hosted by Phil Baker, followed Allen's show. Baker felt that the comedian was cutting into his broadcast time, and he once barged into the middle of Allen's program, claiming his show was now on the air because of the number of minutes the comedian owed him.[26]

Allen joked about the difficulties of timing his broadcasts. On one show he jested about having to edit his script to fit the required time length:

> You know people don't realize how radio scripts have to be cut to get them on in the allotted time. I hear that last week "We The People" had to cut the people out. And tonight I heard Hobby Lobby had to be cut down to Hob Lob.

NBC would cut Allen off the air even if the show was not finished. On another broadcast Allen and Portland talked about the network's policy:

> PORTLAND: Your program was cut off again last week.
>
> ALLEN: I know. Was your mother listening?
>
> PORTLAND: Yes. Mama says she'll never hear the end of your program.
>
> ALLEN: People will get to like my program—no end.
>
> PORTLAND: Why do they keep cutting your program off?

> ALLEN: Who knows? The main thing in radio is to come out on time. If people laugh the program is longer. The thing to do is to get a nice dull half-hour to make sure that nobody laughs or applauds. Then you'll always be right on time and all the little radio executives can send each other memos and be very happy.
>
> PORTLAND: Radio sure is funny.
>
> ALLEN: All except the comedy programs. Our program has been cut off so many times the last page of the script is a Band-Aid.
>
> PORTLAND : Why is everybody in radio always in such a hurry?
>
> ALLEN: It's the network policy. A program is going along—the people are enjoying it—the program gets a little long—Zip—it's cut off the air. Then a voice says "This is the National Broadcasting Company." This is very entertaining. People all over the country have been sitting by their radios all night just waiting so that every half hour they can hear some announcer with mink tonsils say "This is The National Broadcasting Company." Then another voice says "The correct time is nine p.m." Now you know what time it is and to what network you are listening—but nothing is going on.
>
> PORTLAND: Mama says radio is like a cuckoo clock.
>
> ALLEN: Radio is like a cuckoo clock?
>
> PORTLAND: Every hour, every day you hear the same thing.
>
> ALLEN: Some day the whole side of Radio City will open up—a vice-president will fly out and say "Cuckoo"—and that will be the end of radio.[27]

Allen's jibes at NBC perturbed some network executives. His running debate with the network climaxed during clearance procedures on a script the comedian had written for an upcoming broadcast. NBC objected to Allen's remark about a network vice president who kept cutting him off the air:

> PORTLAND: What does the network do with all the time it saves cutting off the ends of programs?
>
> ALLEN: Well, there is a big executive here at the network. He is the vice-president in charge of "Ah! Ah! You're running too long!" He sits in a little glass closet with his mother-of-pearl gong. When your program runs overtime he thumps his gong with a marshmallow he has tied to the end of a xylophone stick. Bong! You're off the air. Then he marks down how much time he's saved.
>
> PORTLAND: What does he do with all this time?
>
> ALLEN: He adds it all up—ten seconds here, twenty there—and when he has saved up enough seconds, minutes, and hours to make two weeks,

the network lets the vice-president use the two weeks of your time for his vacation.

NBC ordered Allen's producer either to not broadcast the lines or to edit the dialogue so that there was no mention of the network. If those changes were not carried out NBC threatened to fade the program at the appropriate spot.[28]

Allen, who resented authority of any kind, was furious at the network for repeatedly cutting him off the air. Allen consequently did the script in its original form, and the program was faded for twenty-five seconds during the comedian's remarks. The incident received much publicity in the newspapers. The public, feeling they had been cheated of some very funny comedy, sided with Allen. Niles Trammell, president of NBC, then issued a form letter apologizing for the incident:

> When Fred Allen, in accordance with his usual practice, submitted his script for approval, it contained some derogatory but humorous references to an imaginary NBC vice president which could have been permitted to remain in the script and which he should have been permitted to broadcast. The mistake was in making an issue with Allen over this particular reference. We regret the incident very much but since it represents a single mistake, we trust you will agree with us that no harm has been caused to anyone and that lessons are learned from mistakes.

After that incident Allen never had any further problem with the network cutting him off the air.[29]

Allen's caustic lampooning of censorship and bureaucracy, and his satirical bite, especially appealed to intellectuals. Although he was admired by all types of listeners, Allen can be called the intellectuals' comedian. "You can count on the thumb of one hand the American who is at once a comedian, a humorist, a wit and a satirist, and his name is Fred Allen," James Thurber wrote. For seventeen years on the radio Allen delighted audiences with his unique brand of comic satire. Compared with him most radio comedians were pure entertainers whose escapist humor was quickly forgotten. When Allen died of a heart attack in 1956, his former assistant, novelist Herman Wouk, wrote:

> His knife-like comment on the passing show of the thirties and the forties came from sources no other comedian had access to. He was a self-educated man of wide reading; he was a tremendously talented writer; and he had the deep reticent love of life and of people which is the source of every true satirist's energy. Fred's wit lashed and stung. He could not suffer fools. In this he was like Swift and Twain.[30]

NOTES

[1] Allen, *Treadmill to Oblivion,* 105-06.

[2] *Ibid.* 164.

[3] *Ibid.* 179.

[4] *Ibid.* 180; Summers, *A Thirty-Year History,* 67, 75, 83, 91, 99, 107.

[5] *Texaco Star Theatre,* Dec. 6, 1942, p. 4, LBC.

[6] Allen, *Treadmill to Oblivion,* 152; Alan Reed interview, STSS, Jan. 9, 1972. See also "Rites Pending for Actor Alan Reed," *Los Angeles Times,* June 16, 1977, Pt. III, 13.

[7] *The Fred Allen Show,* Mar. 17, 1946, p. 11; June 27, 1946, p. 11, LBC; *STSS,* Jan. 9, 1972.

[8] *Texaco Star Theatre,* Jan. 10, 1943, pp. 4-5, LBC; Allen, *Treadmill to Oblivion,* 181.

[9] "Here's Mrs. Nussbaum!" *Tune In* (Feb. 1946), 16-17.

[10] *The Fred Allen Show,* Jan. 13, 1946, p. 6; Nov. 4, 1945, p. 8; June 2, 1946, pp. 10-11; Radiola Records, MR-1008, *Down in Allen's Alley,* Dec. 28, 1947.

[11] Allen, *Treadmill to Oblivion,* 192; Dunning, *Tune in Yesterday,* 221; Kenny Delmar, *NBC Biography in Sound,* May 31, 1956, tape, PPB.

[12] *The Fred Allen Show,* Nov. 4, 1945, p. 4; Feb. 24, 1946, p. 5; Jan. 13, 1946, pp. 3-4, LBC.

[13] *Ibid.* May 15, 1949, pp. 4-6, LBC.

[14] *Ibid.* Jan. 13, 1946, pp. 3-4, LBC.

[15] *Ibid.* May 15, 1949, p. 10; LBC. See also Toll, *On With the Show,* 105-6, 183, 185-86.

[16] *The Fred Allen Show,* Mar. 16, 1947, p. 9, LBC; Allen, *Treadmill to Oblivion,* 193-94.

[17] *The Fred Allen Show,* Mar. 17, 1946, pp. 7-9, LBC.

[18] Allen, *Treadmill to Oblivion,* 220.

[19] *The Fred Allen Show,* Oct. 27, 1946, pp. 22-24, LBC.

[20] *Ibid.* pp. 27-28, 30.

[21] Allen, *Treadmill to Oblivion,* 27.

[22] Fred Allen to Al Maister, June 20, 1941, *Fred Allen's Letters,* 231; *Town Hall Tonight,* Mar. 29, 1939, pp. 2-3, LBC. See also *Ibid.* 29; Cantril and Allport, *The Psychology of Radio,* 56; Carroll, *None of Your Business,* 132.

[23] Interdepartment correspondence, Feb. 9, 1946, Fred Allen file, NBC; Gross, *I Looked and I Listened,* 131-32.

[24] Interdepartment correspondence, Oct. 19, 1946; Mar. 5, 1947; Feb. 22, 1947; Nov. 26, 1945; Fred Allen File, NBC.

[25] Auerbach, *Funny Men Don't Laugh*, 150.

[26] Allen, *Treadmill to Oblivion*, 213; Harmon, *The Great Radio Comedians*, 174-75.

[27] *Town Hall Tonight*, Mar. 22, 1939, p. 2; *The Fred Allen Show*, June 2, 1946, pp. 3-4, LBC.

[28] Joseph Julian, *This Was Radio: A Personal Memoir* (New York, 1975), 220-21; see also interdepartment correspondence, Apr. 21, 1947, Fred Allen File, NBC.

[29] Letter of Niles Trammell, May 5, 1947, Fred Allen File, NBC.

[30] Joe McCarthy, Introduction to *Fred Allen's Letters*, p. ix; Herman Wouk to the Editor of *New York Times*, Mar. 18, 1956, *Fred Allen's Letters*, 358.

Luther F. Sies (essay date 1981)

SOURCE: "Tally Ho, Mr. Allen," in *Journal of Popular Culture*, Vol. 15, No. 2, Fall, 1981, pp. 164-90.

[*In the following excerpt, Sies traces Allen's radio career, and his use of satire to parody contemporary American institutions.*]

Johnny Carson, when asked recently by Kenneth Tynan who was the wittiest man he ever knew, named Fred Allen without hesitation. Citing the old vaudeville maxim, "A comic is someone who says funny things, and a comedian is one who says things funny," Carson went on to explain his answer. Fred Allen, he said, was comic, while Jonathan Winters and Mel Brooks were comedians.[1] Although he thought all were funny, Carson's distinction was an important one.

Many middle-aged intellectuals and peripatetic pilgrims through life of the same vintage would heartily second Carson's choice. During the radio comic's long career, college professors and automobile mechanics alike enjoyed Allen's wry, weekly commentaries on life's trials and vicissitudes.

Fred Allen was born John Florence Sullivan on May 31, 1894, in Cambridge, Massachusetts. After completing high school he entered show business as a juggler, performing as an amateur at every possible opportunity. Since it was the era of the "paid" amateur, his juggling immediately brought him financial rewards.

He became Fred Allen at the age of 23, purely as the result of an agent's whim. The gift of a name, however, was the only thing anyone ever gave him for the rest of his life, for he reached the heights of success in radio entirely on his own talent and wit. Like another juggler—W.C. Fields—who became a great comic, Allen's transition from juggling to comedy was a slow, gradual one.

Allen worked his first professional job at Boston's National Theater under the name of *Paul Huckle*. As an amateur he had previously received a dollar a night from Sam Cohen. In his vaudeville debut, he got twice that amount. Using the name of *Freddy James*, he billed himself as "The World's Worst Juggler" and successfully entered vaudeville as a full-time performer, the form of show business he always loved most. Although radio brought him fame and fortune, he never found it emotionally satisfying. Radio for Fred Allen, according to Edwin O'Connor, ". . . was big business and hard, grinding work: for it [radio] he felt no particular affection and in it he had no fun at all."[2]

Freddy James became *Fred Allen* in 1917, as the result of an agent's casual phone call. After getting a booking for him at the City Theatre, Edgar Allen, a Fox booking agent in Boston, told the theater's manager the name of the juggler for his bill was *Fred Allen*, and that it remained for the rest of his life.

The act of the *new* Fred Allen depended on his ability to make people laugh, for by then he had added a line of patter to augment his juggling skills. Extremely successful in the vaudeville of the day, he played New York's Palace Theatre in 1919. From there, Allen went on to appear in such long-running shows as *The Passing Show of 1922*, *The Greenwich Village Follies* in 1924, and, later, in such reviews as *The Little Show* and *Three's A Crowd*, the latter with Libby Holman and Clifton Webb.

While working in *The Passing Show*, Allen met an attractive chorus girl in the show named Portland Hoffa. Their marriage on May 4, 1927, began a happy lifetime partnership. During the radio years, it was Portland's call of "Mis-ter A-l-l-en" and "Tally ho, Mr. Allen" that soon became his familiar trademarks.

Catchwords or phrases were the marks of a successful radio series. **The Fred Allen Show** had several, some of them resulting when the Allen's Alley feature was added. "Tally ho," always said by Portland, was used in the early programs chiefly as a transition—a bridge—a means of closing a segment. It indicated something was finished, and that it was then proper to go onto something else, usually a song or instrumental selection by the orchestra. At other times it served as a philosophical "so be it" to close the program.

"Mis-ter A-l-l-en," was the customary preparation for Portland's entrance on the program. Toward the end of his career, Fred using a singing group (the DeMarcos) to sing, "Mister Allen . . . Mister Allen . . ." as the opening for each show. Portland, when she eventually entered, continued to use her habitual spoken greeting. Repetition of words and phrases, of course, is an important element, whether it appears in radio comedy or children's nursery rhymes. Allen himself took a rather dim view of the need for repeated catch phrases, although many of them naturally grew out of his shows and were continued successfully for years. For Allen, the repetition seemed to be little more than a form of pandering to mass taste.[2]

In many respects, when Portland played the "dumb female" role on the program, it was that of a smarter more astringent version of Gracie Allen reflected off Fred's much more capable, worldly-wise and worn version of George Burns. None of this is to imply they copied, for this, of course, was far from the case. George and Gracie merely portrayed familiar show business types—as did Fred and Portland—that may still be seen on television today. The "dumb" role was played by Marie Wilson on radio and in early television, for example, and Carol Wayne does the same on Johnny Carson's *Tonight Show* in these days of Women's Lib. All of them represent only a continuation of the show business role of the "dumb female."

After completing a two-year run with Clifton Webb and Libby Holman in *Three's A Crowd,* Allen found himself out of work with only a promised role in a show not scheduled to open for six months. It was the spring of 1932, deep in the economic gloom of the Great Depression. The gold rush of vaudeville comics into radio had begun. Great comedians such as Ed Wynn, Eddie Cantor, and Joe Penner already enjoyed success in the new medium, due chiefly to their funny costumes and the rough-house physical antics they used to make studio audiences laugh. Although they achieved success, they gave no real evidence of understanding radio and its unique possibilities as a medium for comedy.

Allen, facing weeks of inactivity, planned a series of radio programs, assembled a cast, and eventually, auditioned for the Corn Products Company, who manufactured a beauty powder called Linit. His successful audition marked the beginnings of the *Linit Bath Club Review,* a program first broadcast on October 23, 1932, by the Columbia Broadcasting Company.

The Linit program established a pattern that was continued until Allen's last network show in 1949. When asked by the sponsor *who* would write the show, Fred replied, "I will."[3] He wrote everything for the *Linit Bath Club Review,* and, in fact, almost all the other material he used for the rest of his professional life in radio. Even in later years when there were other writers to help with the gigantic task of writing a weekly program that was both topical and funny, ninety per cent of the writing was done by Allen.[4]

Among the writers who wrote for Allen was Nat Hiken, later famous as the creator of television's *Sgt. Bilko;* Arnold Auerback, writer of such Broadway hit revues as *Bless You All, Inside USA,* and *Call Me Mister;* and Herman Wouk, probably best known for his successful novel, *The Caine Mutiny.* Wouk, recalling that Fred was the major writer on the show, states that young writers like himself worked only to flesh out the great volume of material that was needed for the weekly programs.[5]

Perhaps it was this ever-increasing pressure upon Allen of writing the weekly shows and the cumulative effects of hundreds of deadlines successfully met that aggravated the hypertension that eventually killed him in 1956.

Even though the *Linit Bath Club Review* received critical praise and better than average audience survey ratings, it ended after only twenty-six weeks. The following year, while vacationing in Maine, Allen received an urgent call from New York. He learned that Hellman's Mayonnaise had hired a comedian whose estimated potential had far outweighed his actual performance; the company wanted him to return to New York immediately and take over their radio program.

In 1933, therefore, *The Salad Bowl Review* starring Fred Allen was launched. In December, when the show's contract was completed, there was no long wait for further employment, for a new sponsor was eagerly waiting. Allen's next program, *The Sal Hepatica Review* (*The Hour of Smiles*), sponsored by Bristol-Myers, was the show that brought him even greater critical notice and public popularity. *The Sal Hepatica Review,* first broadcast in 1934, became *Town Hall Tonight* in 1935, when Bristol-Myers decided to use it to sell Ipana toothpaste as well as the laxative Sal Hepatica, and *The Texaco Star Theater* in 1941, when the Texas Company became its sponsor. Later, several other companies, including Blue Bonnet margarine, Tenderleaf Tea, and the Ford Motor Company sponsored Allen. After the *Texaco Star Theater* ended, however, regardless of who sponsored it, the program became and continued to be known as *The Fred Allen Show,* until finally leaving the air June 26, 1949.

Fortunately, recordings of more than sixty hours of Fred Allen's radio programs still exist. After listening to these programs, representing his seventeen years of broadcasting, some conclusions are inescapable. There is a pattern running through all the shows. Their content, performances, and general overall quality testify to Allen's astute professionalism and rich comic genius. The experience of listening to these programs of the Thirties and the Forties is a good antidote for anyone who thinks everything is up-to-date in Kansas City.

The format for each hour program, other than the early ones, of course, contains the newsreels, musical selections, the Portland Hoffa segment, the guest spot, and the dramatizations of the Mighty Allen Art Players. Some transformations occurred along the way, as the newsreels, for instance, became, first, **"Allen's Alley"** and, later, **"Walking Down Main Street."** Guests in the early years were "unknowns" with strange occupations, amateur performers, or participants in a roundtable discussion drawn from the studio audience. Whenever a change in format was made, the result invariably was a general improvement in program pace and quality. Except as guest stars, few individual singers performed on the show. One notable exception was Kenny Baker, a talented tenor, who first gained popularity on *The Jack*

Benny Show. Baker's short stint on the program occurred during the early World War II years.

One program (March 8, 1942), in particular, illustrates the high quality of entertainment radio during its great years regularly brought into American homes. Kenny Baker on that program sang two selections; the first was "I'll Follow My Secret Heart," and the second, "It Ain't Necessarily So," from Gershwin's *Porgy and Bess.* After listening to programs of this era, one can readily understand how much a part of this cultural milieu George Gershwin, Fred Allen, and Al Jolson were. In the maturity of their professional achievements, all of them can be understood best in light of the spirit we hear in those broadcasts of the Thirties and early Forties. There is a breezy, irreverance there, along with an open, friendly hale-fellow–well-met quality in them. A free and lively spirit, in spite of the Depression and its tragedies, continually emerges. Much of this temperament of the times is displayed in these broadcasts for any listener interested in savoring it.

Guests appeared regularly on Allen's early programs with such unusual or "interesting" occupations as an organ grinder, who naturally brought his monkey with him, an assistant to the superintendent of the Statue of Liberty; a "stockyard Selznick," as Fred called him, a big man at Paramount Studios, who was the talent scout responsible for casting all cows and horses in their pictures; a man who ran a pushcart on the Warner Brothers' motion picture studio lot and knew all the hot dog and hamburger peccadillos of famous movie stars.

The radio audience in the Thirties and early Forties idolized Major Edward Bowes and his amateur show, perhaps vicariously enjoying the repeated stories of overnight popularity and fame achieved by a few of the winning amateur performers.

Consequently, many radio programs, whether comedy or musical, incorporated amateurs in some way, hoping to win extra listeners and higher poll ratings by their addition. Allen's true feelings about amateur shows, caused in part, perhaps, by his own "amateur" experience, were not very favorable. Only the giveaway quiz shows annoyed him more. Allen cleverly parodied amateur shows when he portrayed the role of Admiral Crow on one of his programs.

Allen's burlesque of Major Bowes' program began with an announcer proclaiming, "Station HISKIMNOP presents Admiral Crow and his Amateur Hour." The wildly hilarious antics continued when Admiral Crow stepped to the microphone.

> ADMIRAL CROW: All right! All right! [Exactly in the style of the good Major Bowes!]
>
> *(Phone rings)*
>
> ADMIRAL CROW: Oh, yes. Thank you. (Phone *is hung up.*) Well—the first telephone bulletin is

in. 400 votes for Trundle Pulp, the Yodeling Taxidermist. Trundle hasn't been on yet. The votes are coming in from California. There's a difference in time, you know. They say the program is coming over beautifully out there. And here's a message from the Governor of the Thousand Islands. They're making me an honorary beachcomber on Island 702. And thanks to Mr. and Mrs. Pomfret of New Orleans for the corn pone receipt.

A steady vote-getter, as Admiral Crow continued to take call-in votes from around the country was the Whistling Mousetrap Maker, but, then, how could anyone with a name like that possibly lose?

Amateur college performers, who had won contests at their respective schools, also appeared on the early Allen programs. An example of this was the appearance on December 10, 1941, program of Jack Wilson, who had been voted the most popular undergraduate entertainer at the University of Oklahoma. When Wilson sang, he sounded something like a cross between Whispering Jack Smith and Liberace, but no one can be perfect.

The early *Fred Allen Show,* no doubt hounded to do so by sponsors, ad agency veepees, and network executives, even broadcast some amateur contests! One notable contest, whose contestants had come from winning a series of amateur competitions in Boston, presented a lyric soprano, a boy-girl "sweetheart" duet, an Irish tenor, a tap-dancer, a trick violin player, a Boston hillbilly trio, and a "sneeze expert," who managed to display all the different sneezes he knew. The contest winner was to be determined by the applause of the studio audience, but a complication arose when there was a tie between the lyric soprano, tap-dancer, sneeze expert, and the Boston hillbilly trio. In a run-off decided by the thunderous applause of the studio audience, the winner of the contest was judged to be the Boston hillbilly trio. No cash was involved, but the prestige of winning was certainly nothing to sneeze at.

Another feature of the Allen program in which "unknowns" participated was Mr. Average Man's Roundtable. The Roundtable feature, an outgrowth of the early Newsreels, logically, lead directly to the asking of questions of such zany products of Allen's imagination as Senator Bloat, poet Thorndyke Swinburne, a low-wattage, itinerant philosopher named Socrates Mulligan, and the proverbial Average Man, Mr. John Doe, played by Jack Smart, Harry Von Zell, Charlie Cantor, and John Brown respectively. A Jewish-sounding Bronx housewife, Mrs. Prawn—who sounded like, but was not played by Minerva Pious—also appeared occasionally. These burlesque characterizations of a politician, poet, philosopher, average man, and Bronx housewife, in time, eventually became **"Allen's Alley."**

Dramatizations by the Mighty Allen Art Players—forerunners of the *Tonight Show's* Mighty Carson Art Players on TV—remained a constant feature of the program and one of its most effective vehicles for satire. Murder mysteries were popular dramatic fare for the Players, who romped through many of them. Their early mysteries featured an Inspector Bungle, who, of course, did exactly that most of the time. A little later, Allen introduced the masterful oriental detective, One Long Pan, who sometimes introduced himself by saying, "Ah, greeting and Shalom, kiddies. One Long Pan, oriental Dick Tracy on the job." When a murder victim had been shot, and even sometimes when he apparently had been killed by some other means, this wild oriental sleuth searched diligently for the "le-wah-lah-wah" with which the vile deed had been committed.

When the program went from an hour to thirty minutes, the amateurs and the people with unusual occupations were mercifully forgotten to be replaced by "name" guests. Therefore, the Mighty Allen Art Players were sometimes joined by prominent persons when they presented their epic dramas. Some of the presentations of the Players had such engrossing titles as:

> The Psychopathic Speculator, or He Made a Killing But They Called it Murder; Admiral Allen was Leading a Dog's Life, So They Left Him at the South Pole; Santa Sits Down, or Jingle Bells Won't Ring Tonight; and The Hardy Family in the Penitentiary, or Life With Father.

Among the memorable guests who joined the Mighty Allen Art Players was Bea Lillie, who romped through Fred's musical, *Picadilly,* sung to the music of Rodgers and Hammerstein's musical hit of the day, *Oklahoma!* Another was Tallulah Bankhead, who joined Fred in a classic spoof of husband-and-wife broadcasting teams entitled, **"Talu and Fred,"** a skit that deserves recognition as one of radio's best comedy routines.

Ed and Pegeen Fitzgerald in 1937 on Station WOR, New York, inaugurated the husband-and-wife talk show, a format that was soon copied by several other married couples such as Tex McCreary and Jinx Falkenburg (Tex and Jinx), Dorothy Kilgallen and Richard Kollmar (Dorothy and Dick), Andre Baruch and Bea Wain, and, later, Peter Lind Hayes and Mary Healy. At one time there was said to be 78 imitators of their format on the air.[7] At its worst, this type program soon degenerated into little more than a saccharin parade of commercials without much information or entertainment for listeners.

As early as 1945, when Tallulah Bankhead first visited his program, Fred Allen directed his barbs against inferior husband-and-wife talk shows. Fred and Tallulah combined as **"Talu and Fred"** to deliver one of the most devastating radio satires ever perpetrated. Its format was a "regular" segment to illustrate what these programs normally were like, followed by a "grumpy" portion in which both spouses one morning awoke testy and out-of-sorts. Mighty Allen Art Players aficionados agree this is one of their finest offerings.

At the close of a program on which the Masons appeared, there was a strange element that was part of

Allen's struggle against *Stop the Music* and similar giveaway quiz shows. It opened and closed with a promise to reimburse any listener who missed a quiz show prize because he was listening to Fred Allen. A curiosity now, the device didn't stop the quizzes, but it remains a novel maneuver in the struggle against them. At the beginning of the program, this announcement was made:

> Ladies and Gentlemen: Stay tuned to the *Fred Allen Show.* For the next thirty minutes you are guaranteed. If you—any listener in the United States—are called on the telephone during the next thirty minutes by any giveaway radio program, and because you are listening to Fred Allen you miss an opportunity to win a refrigerator, a television set, a new car, or any amount of cash prize, the National Surety Corporation guarantees that Fred Allen will perform his agreement to replace any article of merchandise up to a value of $5000, or reimburse you for any amount of prize money you may have lost, up to $5000. Notice of any claim under this guarantee must be mailed to Mr. Fred Allen, by registered mail, care of the National Broadcasting Company, Radio City, New York, and postmarked no later than midnight, Monday, March 29, 1948. Relax! Enjoy the *Fred Allen Show.* For the next thirty minutes you are protected under the terms of a guarantee bond covering all valid claims up to a total of $5000.[8]

This announcement with slight variation was made at the close of the program as well. No valid claim was ever collected under the guarantee, but the quiz shows rolled on unchecked.

Allen's real feelings about giveaway programs can be discovered by the following scathing appraisals he made of them:

> "Giveaway programs are the buzzards of radio."

> "As buzzards swoop down on carrion so have giveaway shows descended on the carcass of radio."[9]

"Reduced to essentials," Allen once said, "a quiz show requires one master of ceremonies, preferably with prominent teeth, two underpaid girls to do research and supply the quiz questions and a small herd of morons, stampeded into the audience and rounded up at the microphone to compete for prizes."[10]

Many famous guests appeared on the *Fred Allen Show.* Some of them were: Tony Martin, Boris Karloff, Edward Everett Horton, Oscar Levant, Bing Crosby, Sidney Greenstreet, Mr. and Mrs. James Mason, Tallulah Bankhead, Max Baer, Maxie Rosenbloom, Phil Baker, Leo Durocher, Henry Morgan, Shirley Booth, Bea Lillie, Orson Welles, Charles Laughton, Richard Rodgers, Oscar Hammerstein III, Alfred Hitchcock, Milton Berle, Bert Lahr, Louella Parsons, Jack Healey, Edgar Bergen and Charlie McCarthy, George Jessel, and of course, most often the aspiring violinist—Jack Benny.

Benny and Allen, actually the best of friends, participated in radio's greatest "feud." What started from an accidental remark made by Allen on his program in 1937 soon grew to be the major topic of jokes for both comedians. Jack Benny, according to Ben Gross, showed his admiration for Allen by saying, "I wouldn't go up against that guy [Allen] unless I had my writers with me."[11]

Alan Reed recalls that Fred Allen and Jack Benny were scheduled to meet one day in a theater lobby for the premiere of their motion picture, *Love Thy Neighbor,* when Nat Hiken, one of Fred's writers, asked him if he wanted some material prepared in case Jack started to ad lib. Allen's answer was the often-quoted line, "Benny couldn't ad lib a belch after a Hungarian dinner."[12] Consistently through the years, some of the best comedy displayed by both comedians centered on and grew from their "feud."

Although justly famous for his ability to ad lib, Allen, according to Alan Reed,[13] often had them prepared in advance to sound as though they had been tossed out on the spur of the moment. An example of the prepared ad lib can be heard on the program of March 20, 1940. Portland, who had just come back from the New York Flower show, told Fred what she had seen:

PORTLAND: They had every rose but Billy.

FRED: I know they had every bloom but Sol.

When there was little or no laughter from the audience, Allen quickly added "None of these fellows are well known, are they?" Lines of this nature, carefully prepared in advance, were often used in many of Allen's broadcasts. If the audience laughed at the original joke, the "ad lib" was simply omitted. There is no way, therefore, of knowing exactly how many prepared ad libs were never used. There is nothing wrong with anticipating audience reaction and writing supplementary lines, rather, it indicates how carefully the *Fred Allen Show* was planned and written.

"Allen's Alley" is the feature most often associated with the *Fred Allen Show.* Despite what many think, the Alley did not appear on the show until December 13, 1942. A few years later in 1948 its name was changed to **"Walking Down Main Street,"** although all its familiar denizens such as Senator Claghorn, Titus Moody, Pansy Nussbaum, Ajax Cassidy, and Falstaff Openshaw still remained.

The characters that Fred encountered in the Newsreels and the topical features of his early shows were the forerunners of the Alley's memorable characters. Socrates Mulligan, portrayed by Charlie Cantor, later famous as Clifton Finnegan during his days of intellectual sparring with Ed "Archie" Gardner on *Duffy's Tavern,* was an early Alley resident that disappeared from the program. Socrates, unlike his famous namesake, consistently proved to be a more dim-witted than usual philosopher.

Newsreel segments, which lead eventually to **"Allen's Alley,"** provided Fred an opportunity to comment on American life and character. One Newsreel (May 8, 1940), allowed Allen to meet an exceptionally effeminate-sounding network censor, whose job was to eliminate from radio scripts all jokes about California weather, Bing Crosby's horses, and Pomona. After dispatching this pitiable creature, Allen traveled out to ask the questions, "Should all drivers be forced to take an intelligence test?" Don't you really think a healthy truck driver could do a better job driving than a neurotic college professor?" No answer was given Allen, nor was any needed.

Another Newsreel (February 28, 1940), dramatized the acute room shortage in New York City and some of the bad conditions existing there, such as cooking in rooms and seriously overcrowded conditions. A husband and wife appeared who lived in the Beckoning Arms Apartment in the northwest corner of a nine-family room. A Gladys Snavely complained of "roominghouse congestion," saying, "Getting down the hall to the bathroom is like running interference for Notre Dame."

Poet Thoryndyke Swinburne, coyly played by announcer Harry Von Zell, then read a poem about overcrowded housing conditions. Influenced, no doubt, by Edgar A Guest, the popular homespun poet of that time, whose familiar line was, "It takes a heap of living to make a house a home," Thoryndyke let fly by beginning, "It takes a heap of people to make a house a heap." Sad to say, his poetic vision sank lower after that ambitious and promising beginning, until he finished no better than in a dead heat with Guest's poetic production.

Allen then left the poet to investigate personally the overcrowded conditions in New York rooming houses. In Ma Brodie's roominghouse, he found two men sleeping in a broom closet; a Russian living in the bathroom; and Major Pee Wee, the midget, and his eight brothers living in a bureau drawer. This final discovery is made at the newsreel's fadeout. Typically, in the newsreel segments Allen was seeking to discover the opinions of the average man.

Another early Allen's Alley character, like Socrates Mulligan, who did not survive was that of John Doe the Average Man. John Brown, the great radio supporting actor whose most famous role probably was that of Digger O'Dell in *The Life of Riley* with William Bendix, played the role of John Doe the Average Man. Characteristically, Mr. Doe would angrily carry on a noisy discussion with Allen, only to completely lose control and end by slamming his door shut in a rage, an interesting comment indeed on the "average man."

With both Socrates Mulligan and John Doe, the format was always to get their reactions to topical questions. Even closer to what eventually became Allen's Alley, however, was the introduction of a windbag politician, Senator Bloat; an obviously Jewish housewife, Mrs.

Prawn; and the flaky poet, Thoryndyke Swinburne. In the beginning, none of these roles were played by Kenny Delmar, Minerva Pious, or Alan Reed, whose portrayals later made these prototypes famous as Senator Claghorn, Pansy Nussbaum, and Falstaff Openshaw.

O.O. McIntyre, writer of a daily newspaper column that sometimes contained the feature, "Thoughts While Strolling," has been credited by Allen as the precise inspiration for **"Allen's Alley."**[14] Most of the elements for it, however, obviously came as the culmination of the comedian's own creative efforts. When in 1945, after three years of experimentation, the Alley's complete cast of Senator Claghorn, Titus Moody, Mrs. Nussbaum, and Falstaff Openshaw was finally assembled, the listeners responded enthusiastically.

When he walked down Allen's Alley with Portland, Allen appeared as a thoughtful, inquiring reporter, a peripatetic commentator on American life. Sometimes, however, he was portrayed as an innocent, picked-on and occasionally attacked by the Alley's residents, but most often by the frequently scheming and manipulating guests who appeared on his show. Each program contained cogent comments on the news, weather, radio, show business, and the American scene. With the inception of **"Allen's Alley,"** however, the tone of the comments were changed somewhat, and the focus placed upon the characters themselves. Regardless of what Allen, himself, said, **"Allen's Alley"** may have been developed in 1942, partially at least, because of the pressures of wartime censorship to play down criticism of American life and the national scene. In the great **"Alley"** characters he developed, Allen focused directly on individuals, not stereotypes or representatives of any group or race. When Fred began his last season on the air with the January 4, 1948 program, he changed *in name only* **"Allen's Alley"** *to* **"Walking down Main Street"** in response, no doubt, to a demand made by some network executives who equated change with progress. Nevertheless, the great characters remained unchanged and continued to perform in their own unique manner.

Senator Claghorn was a Southerner, first, and a politician second. His catch-phrase was, "That's a joke, son," and it habitually followed a pun of magnificent, if sometimes horrendous proportions. Claghorn's feelings about the South are indicated by some of his characteristic statements:

> SENATOR CLAGHORN: I can't say, "No."
>
> FRED ALLEN: Why not, Senator?
>
> SENATOR CLAGHORN: Because "No" is the abbreviation for north.
>
> SENATOR CLAGHORN: When I leave New York, I always take the South Ferry.
>
> . . . . .

> SENATOR CLAGHORN: I don't even go to a ballgame unless a southpaw's pitching. I don't even go to see the Dodgers unless Dixie Walker is playing
>
> . . . . .

The Senator's loyalty to the South was unquestioning and constant, but he felt it necessary to ensure everyone knew exactly what part of the country he preferred. Continuously and loudly, he would offer such gems as, "Where I live, we call the people in Alabama—*Yankees.*" Claghorn's favorite drink, he said, was the Memphis Martini, a tall drink that featured a wad of cotton floating in it with two boll weevils riding on top. Then, too, there was this expression of supreme love for his home region, "I'm from the South. Nobody can make me wear a union suit."

Claghorn's typical puns, always used with his familiar catchphrase, of course, were those based on the name of members of Congress:

> CLAGHORN: (Talking about President Truman's recommendation of a National Health Insurance Plan in 1948). We had a big debate in Congress. Somebody was running down Senator Hill [Lister Hill, D., Alabama]. Running down Senator Hill, that's a joke, son.
>
> . . . . .

> CLAGHORN: I was glad to see Senator Aiken back. Senator Aiken [George D. Aiken, R., Vermont], see, that's a joke son.
>
> . . . . .

> CLAGHORN: We took a poll in Washington, and all of us were talking at one time. Senator Brooks was babbling. Senator Brooks [C. Wayland Brooks, R., Illinois], that is, that's a joke, son.

The Senator's dislike for Yankees extended even to baseball, as his account of a game he attended at Yankee Stadium clearly shows:

> CLAGHORN: I Saw a ballgame today. I saw the Yankees beaten, wahoo!
>
> ALLEN: How could the Yankees lose?
>
> CLAGHORN: The umpire was from the South
>
> ALLEN: How do you know?
>
> CLAGHORN: Well, after he called three balls, he called a weevil.
>
> ALLEN: You must have had a great day.
>
> CLAGHORN: I hooted those pigeon-plucking Yankees to a fare-thee-well. I gave Bill Dickey the bird. Dickey . . . bird, get it? That's a joke, son.

This joke had more meaning in those days when the Yankees seldom lost—March 20, 1947.

Titus Moody was usually the next character Fred encountered after leaving Senator Claghorn. All of the characters in the Alley were Allen's alter ego, or portrayed one or another aspect of his soma, psyche, or inventive linguistic flights of fancy. Titus Moody, for example, the crusty New Englander, played superbly by Parker Fennelly, presented only a slightly exaggerated version of Fred's own speech patterns and of the regional attitudes of his birthplace. Allen, himself, once confessed that he liked writing the Titus Moody role best, because his own New England background provided inspiration for it.

Titus frequently commented on the national scene. In one program (November 25, 1945), broadcast shortly after President Truman had recommended his five-point National Health Program, for instance, this exchange resulted:

> TITUS: I was sickly as a child. I suffered from anemia, but I was all right by the time I was five years old.
>
> ALLEN: How did the doctor cure you?
>
> TITUS: He gave me a shot in the arm.
>
> ALLEN: You were healthy by five?
>
> TITUS: I was all shot to health.

Another Moody health problem was discussed in this way:

> ALLEN: You have sinus trouble, Titus?
>
> TITUS: Yes, when I was a boy my mother picked me up by my nose.
>
> ALLEN: She picked you up by your nose?
>
> TITUS: I had small ears.

On another program (December 21, 1945), when asked about problems of post-war traffic jams, Titus noted, "Hoover said he'd put a car in every garage. Truman got two cars parked in front of every house." Titus, at other times, could be a strange fellow. He once informed Allen why he wasn't very talkative:

> TITUS: I can't say too much. I got a small mouth. I can spit through a keyhole without wetting the key.
>
> ALLEN: I'd like to see that.
>
> TITUS: I can arrange it.

If this weren't enough, Titus and Mrs. Moody seemed to enjoy a strange, rather restrained relationship. As Titus once put in (March 28, 1948), "I wouldn't say I know Mrs. Moody, but we're acquainted." Once in order to solve the post-war shortage of men's clothing, Titus began wearing the scarecrow's suit with the result that his wife left him. "Now the old crow won't come near me," Titus explained.

Once during a severe blizzard, Titus and Mrs. Moody were isolated. "The big snowfall of '92 took the prize," Titus said. "For eight days we didn't have nothing to eat. We just sat staring at each other." When Allen asked, "You didn't think of turning cannibal?" Titus replied, "No, I didn't eat Mrs. Moody. I knew she wouldn't agree with me." Titus on another occasion had trouble with his wife's diet:

> TITUS: My wife ate a dog biscuit, accidental.
>
> ALLEN: She ate a dog biscuit.
>
> TITUS: Yep, for the last two nights she been running up and down the road barking at strangers.

The poor conditions on the Moody farm provided another frequent topic of conversation between Titus and Allen. Titus described his farm's desolation on the program for many years:

> TITUS: My farm was so poor, crows were flying over with claws over their eyes. They couldn't stand to look at it.
>
> . . . . .
>
> TITUS: Birds can't bear to look at my land it's so poor. Last year, the corn was so low, the birds had to lean over to get to it.
>
> . . . . .
>
> TITUS: The crows felt so sorry for me, they brought back corn they stole two years ago.
>
> . . . . .
>
> TITUS: The cows were so weak, they had to travel in pairs. They traveled in pairs because it took two of them to pull up a blade of grass.

Minerva Pious played Pansy Nussbaum, a lady decidedly of the Jewish persuasion, whose husband, Pierre, sometimes caused her great anguish. Speaking with a thick accent, Mrs. Nussbaum habitually answered Allen's knock on her door by saying, "Nu?", a Yiddish word sometimes spelled *noo-noo,* always pronounced to rhyme with *coo.* Its various meanings, all of which Pansy Nussbaum conveyed at various times, included "Well?", "What's new?", and "So?" *"Nu,"* Leo Rosten says, "is so very Yiddish an interjection it has become the one word that can identify a Jew."[15] When Mrs. Nussbaum answered Allen's knock with her, "Nu"?, she was doing what thousands of Jewish housewives in the Bronx always did.

For the uninitiated who came from west of the Hudson River, Mrs. Nussbaum seemed to be making a habitual negative response, "No!", probably preparing herself for any salesman who might be there. On one program after her usual response, she asked Allen, "Again am I to be prodded by your poll?" Each week, Mrs. Nussbaum at first seemed to be somewhat irritated by Allen's interruption, yet, in seconds, she was willingly, even joyously, entering with him into the spirit of the occasion, happy to be able to talk with someone. Allen's acerbic wit, perhaps, is best reflected by Mrs. Nussbaum's remarks.

Mrs. Nussbaum often told of her friends living in the Bronx. She once told of Pam Schwartz, one of her friends, who had one sister, Caress Schwartz. Caress, when she married Skippy Mandelbaum, a pickle salesman, suffered through various forms of domestic strife, all of whom Mrs. Nussbaum thoroughly discussed in detail. Pansy Nussbaum, herself, sometimes had difficulties with her husband, Pierre, who often affected a beret, apparently as an indication of his *savoir-faire* and man-of-the-world style.

Once, Mrs. Nussbaum explained, she had been unable to sleep because of her husband's constant dreaming. As she explained it, "Pierre was always dreaming he was somebody else. Well, one night he thinks he's the Lone Stranger, and night he's yelling, 'Hi-Yo, Silver.' Upstairs is living a Mrs. Silver, and night she's yelling back, 'Hi-Yo, Nussbaum.'"

Mrs. Nussbaum later told of a dinner she was planning for her friends and relatives in the Bronx, "I'm inviting all my relatives for a fish dinner. Mr. Fulton is bringing twenty sturgeon to me in the Bronx. I'm having Sturgeon a la King, Sturgeon a la cacciatore, Sturgeon Foo Yung, and for desert—Sturgeon a la mode."[16]

Another habitual Nussbaum pattern was her response to Allen's greeting after she had opened the door and welcomed him with her "Nu." Afterwards, in reply to his hearty, "Well . . . Mrs. Nussbaum," she always had a tart reply such as:

"You was expecting maybe Lena Turner?"

"You was expecting maybe Hoagy Carbunkle?"

"You was expecting maybe Annie Bergman and Solly McCarthy?"

"You was expecting maybe Emperor Shapiro-hito?"

"You was expecting maybe Tora-Lora Mandelbaum?"

Mrs. Nussbaum's tastes and philosophy always were relatively simple. She liked the comics, especially "Lil Adler"; the movies ("Laugh and the world laughs with you. Weep and Betty Davis is in the picture."); telling fairy tales to children (Her favorite stories were "Jake the Giant-Killer," "Old Mother Hubba-Hubba," and "Snow White and the Seven Schwartzes."); and folk music (She once said, "A hootenanny is a singing hillbilly, also a dancing square."). Her favorite songs were

"Bury Me Not on the Prairie, I'll be Lonely," "Jimmycrack Cohen," and "Old Chisel Trail."

Even the pragmatic Mrs. Nussbaum could not resist puns such as those found in her account of the doings of the "Epstein chicken":

PANSY NUSSBAUM: The Epstein chicken is eating all my stringbean seeds.

FRED ALLEN: How do you know?

PANSY NUSSBAUM: Today the chicken is jumping up on the table and laying a ball of twine.

Peter Donald, also a regular on the popular *Can You Top This?* program, played Ajax Cassidy, an Irishman with a fond taste for the cup that cheers.

AJAX: Today is the coldest day in my recollection. I came from Kerrigan's Kozy Rest. It is the coldest place I have ever been.

FRED: How cold was it, Ajax?

AJAX: I don't know, but everyone was stiff.

Ajax also experienced some health problems. One of his trademarks was a racking cough and the immediate self-diagnosis, "I'm not long for this world." His digestion at times also vexed him:

ALEX: I got Alaskan indigestion.

FRED: Alaskan indigestion?

AJAX: Yes, I've been eating too much frozen food. For two weeks I've been coughing up snow.

Sometimes it was his feet:

AJAX: My toes are killing me. It's the grippe.

FRED: How does grippe affect your feet?

AJAX: I dropped my bag on my toes

At other times, Ajax was afflicted by political ailments:

AJAX: I don't feel so good. One day I feel like running. Another I don't.

FRED: What is it, Ajax?

AJAX: MacArthuritis . . . it's a general condition.

And so, this was the kind of conversation that frequently ensued when two Irishmen met in Allen's Alley.

The last inhabitant of the Alley, who lived at its end in a lavender shanty, poet Falstaff Openshaw, was also its first. Played by Alan Reed, the busy radio actor who also portrayed Pasquale in *Life with Luigi*, Solomon Levy in *Abie's Irish Rose*, Shrevie in *The Shadow*, and under the name Teddy Bergman had acted in such soap operas as *Valiant Lady, Big Sister, Myrt and Marge,* among many others. Today, Reed can be heard in many voice-over commercials and also as the voice of Fred Flintstone in *The Flintstones* television show. He has always been an extremely active actor, constantly in demand because of his acting skill and deep, resonant voice. No role he ever played, however, was more famous than that of the poet who lived in the crooked, little lavender shack at the end of Allen's Alley.

Falstaff always had a few rhymes and a long poem somehow related to the question Allen presented for discussion. Some of Falstaff's titles were "An Ode to the Tug Strike," and "A Roundelay to the Fulton Fish Market." His sometime greeting was, "Hi ho, everyone. It isn't Rudy Vallee. It's Falstaff, poet laureate of Allen's Alley."

Many of Falstaff's poems were written by Vic Knight[16] and somehow in some way, although admittedly sometimes stretching it to the breaking point, related to the topic the Alley's inhabitants sagely commented upon. A few of Falstaff's minor efforts were:

> I knew all would not be well,
>   When that skunk climbed aboard the carousel.
>
> . . . . .
>
> Make for the roundhouse, Nelly,
>   The brakeman can't corner you there.
>
> . . . . .
>
> Just because you're a Wave, mother,
>   You don't have to go out with the tide.
>
> . . . . .
>
> As I turned to bow to Conrad Nagle,
>   She stole the cream cheese off my bagel.
>
> . . . . .
>
> Mother's home putting spikes in her shoes,
>   She's playing first base for Vera Cruz.
>
> . . . . .

Falstaff, at other times, could wax philosophical in blank verse, as when he warned, "Take your foot off the table, Mother, or you'll get a sock in the mouth." And, at another time, "When I called her baby, her face lit up because she had a lantern jaw." An example of the poet's major work is his "My Recipe for Slumber," broadcast January 10, 1943. When Allen asked Falstaff if he had any trouble sleeping, the following poem resulted:

MY RECIPE FOR SLUMBER

> If you cannot sleep at night,
>   And don't know what to do.
> My recipe for slumber is just the thing for you.
>   Don't waste time taking powders.

> Don't dawdle in a hot bath, hoping you will sleep.
>   Don't give up drinking coffee.
> Don't send for any gland man.
>   You can eat and drink all night,
> And still meet the Sandman.
>   My recipe for slumber is older than the sphinx,
> Just cut twenty tiddlies into halves
>   And you'll get forty winks.

So much for the lavender-housed lyric poet with the lurid rhymes.

Years after his show had gone off the air, Allen was asked if the ethnic humor on his program had ever aroused protest. He said, "No, because the characters were honest ones."[17] Listening again to his programs supports Allen's contention. There was nothing directed against Jews in Minerva Pious' portrayal of Pansy Nussbaum; repugnant to the Irish in Peter Donald's Ajax Cassidy; disturbing to New Englanders in Parker Fennelly's Titus Moody; or annoying to Southerners in Kenny Delmar's Senator Claghorn. As for Allen's characters, they were *exaggerations of* and *commentaries on* the folly of individual men and women—not groups—just as Freeman Gosden and Charles Correll had done in *Amos 'n' Andy,* a program that *did* cause bitter controversy.

Fred Allen was an Irish-Catholic from New England, a fact that automatically qualified him for membership in at least three minority groups. Whenever Senator Claghorn, Pansy Nussbaum, or Titus Moody kidded Southerners, News, or New England folk, it was with the clear understanding that their creator, himself, was also vulnerable. Allen's Alley was not a case of a group for Ivy League WASP-types donning roles by figuratively "blacking their faces" and portraying their characters.

First and foremost a humorist and only secondarily a radio performer, Fred Allen's humor always sparkled with wit, at times generated a warmth, and, at others, an icy, acerbic reflection of the foolishness of American life. Allen had a love for language that constantly showed through in his writing. Three particular forms of playing with words that Allen perpetrated were to employ strange names for characters on his program, use the most outrageous of puns, and frequently engage in wild flights of linguistic fancy.

Some of the names of characters that either appeared on the Allen show or were talked about on it are included in the list below:

> Tomtit Cassidy, a frequent subway rider;
> Tripod Byke, an expert on radio;
> Terrence Divot, an operatic tenor;
> Balzac McGee, a visitor to the 1940 New York
>   World's Fair;
> Madame Schrillo, an operatic soprano;
> Dupont Suitall, a Seventh Avenue clothing
>   manufacturer;
> Thoryndyke Swinburne, Poet Laureate of Boston
>   Post Road;
> Bismark Tort, a famous attorney-at-law;

Senator Bloat, a loud-mouthed politician;
John Charles Muckenfuss, an aspiring baritone;
Delsarte Trundle, a Hollywood leading man;
Dr. Harry F. Nimphius, the official veterinary
  surgeon for the City of New York;
Mrs. Elaine O'Gatty, a Sixth Avenue housewife;
Sharp Sherman, an official Broadway character;
Sol Hemingway, a Greenwich Village butcher
  who wrote books;
Trendle Pulp, a yodeling taxidermist;
Bambie Rappoport, a close friend of Mrs. Pansy
  Nussbaum;
Temtitty Squirm, a local New York City politician;
Pablo Eatthepeaches, a prominent nutritionist;
Sergei Stroganoff, a cousin of the Mystery Chef;

and, finally, there was Fordyce Messbaum, a retired pushcart baron, and his close friend and associate, Simon Goldslob. In addition, individuals with unidentified occupations appeared with such names as Tomtit McGee, Beau Bernstein, Falvey Nishball, Sindbad Brittle, and Rancid McNally.

Some persons despise puns, while others consider them to be the highest possible form of humor. Nevertheless, Allen virtually raised the pun to an art form during the seventeen years he showered them upon an audience groaning in delight—a sure sign of appreciation for an excellent pun. Any effort to select the cream of Allen's punning is an impossible task, because the quantity is too great and the individual taste in humor so varied. With that warning in mind, therefore, a personal selection of Allen's puns are provided below without comment:

ALLEN: I don't know anything about flowers. I wouldn't know a hollyhock if I met one coming out of a pawn shop.

. . . . .

SENATOR CLAGHORN: I have worn the same suit for five years. If my trousers get any thinner, I may lose my seat in the Senate.

ALLEN: Well, the Congress may soon see the end of the Senator.

. . . . .

ALLEN: You drank two buckets of mint julep and held the floor?

SENATOR CLAGHORN: Hold the floor? I couldn't get up from it.

. . . . .

HARRY VON ZELL: At my country place the beavers were damming everything.

ALLEN: Didn't they like it?

. . . . .

If the word-play of strange names and puns were not enough Allen also engaged in free flights of linguistic fancy. Going to the very essence of his humor, they are truly representative of the Fred Allen wit and style. A few examples of his linguistic flights are:

The two organizations that were represented at the meeting were the Campfire Girls Who Didn't Go Out and the Lodge of Sons and Fathers Exempt in 1918.

. . . . .

I saw a woman with a hat today. It looked like a pot roast lying on a dirty dishrag.

. . . . .

The longest words [Jack] Benny uses, you can get out of an oboe player's mouth sideways.

. . . . .

It is appropriate to end the list of examples of Fred Allen's humor with a verbal barb tossed at Jack Benny, for so often he was the prime target for his verbal barrages.

Other favorite targets, and—unlike Jack Benny—ones that he genuinely disliked and distrusted, were advertising agency vice-presidents, network executives, and their way of thinking. "Advertising," Allen once said, "is 85% confusion and 15% commission." About advertising agency executives he once said, "An agency vice-president is a fellow who went to Princeton, who comes to the office at nine in the morning, finds on his desk a pile of molehills and has until five P.M. to make a mountain out of them." Television, too, eventually came in for its share of his attention. Discussing television, Allen contributed the following observations:

"The minds that control TV are so small you could put them in the navel of a flea and still have some room for a network vice-president's heart."

. . . . .

"At first, TV drove people out of the bars and into their homes. Now, TV is driving people out of their homes into the bars."

. . . . .

"TV is radio with eye-strain."

"TV is chewing gum for the eye-ball."

"The pointers will take over television."

. . . . .

Ed Sullivan and Garry Moore in their days of video glory made Allen's comments, and particularly the last one, read like the wisdom of prophecy.

Quiz shows, Allen believed, were the scourge of radio, and he spent the last ten years of his career lambasting them, parodying them, and, sometimes, insulting them.

It was the influence of programs such as *Stop the Music,* along with the rapid growth of television that eventually ended Allen's radio career. Once more, he was astonishingly accurate in his estimate of how broadcasting was changing, unfortunately, mostly for the worst.

When Frank Sinatra appeared on the October 21, 1945, *Fred Allen Show* in search of a job, Allen let fly with this tirade, "This isn't one of those quiz programs where any schnook can come in off the street and take over the program. We need somebody with talent." A year later, when Tony Martin appeared on the show in a version of "The Radio Mikado," Allen wrote a parody based on the Gilbert and Sullivan operetta, in which he was able to satirize advertising, radio network executives, and quiz shows with one fell swoop. No Madison Avenue heifers were sacred and no foibles of broadcasting executives or sponsors were left unexamined.

Another milestone in the comedian's career occurred on the **Fred Allen Show** of March 20, 1940, ushered in on the soaring wings of a golden eagle by the name of Mr. Ramshaw. The event, subsequently referred to by Allen as *l'affaire eagle,* was a real, although hilarious, disaster broadcast "live" coast-to-coast. About halfway through the program, the eagle, frightened by the bright lights and the orchestra, zoomed out of control over the audience, finally landing in the rafters of the studio ceiling. Later, Fred wrote that the eagle's manners were not the best: "Mr. Ramshaw (the eagle) gave visual evidence that he was obviously not a housebroken eagle."[18] Alan Reed, a member of the cast that fateful night, has said, "The eagle was nervous, and the studio audience as he was flying felt the nervousness."[19]

The **Fred Allen Show** started uneventfully that evening with no one aware they were soon to become part of radio history. The question that Fred Allen asked that night was, "Should billboards be banned from the nation's highways?" Although no definite answers were elicited from his encounters with Rancid McNally and Thoryndyke Swinburne, the exchanges were lively.

After the question, the Merry Macs accompanied by Peter Van Steeden's orchestra performed. Portland then appeared to tell Fred of her trip to the flower show. She noted, "They had a lot of little pussy willows—kitty willows." She followed this with the information, "They gave Vitamin B-1 to the violets there." When Fred asked her if the violet was still shrinking, she informed him, "No, it was throwing pollen in a Tiger Lily's eyes."

Next in the script came the explosive appearance of Mr. Ramshaw the golden eagle. It began with Portland saying to Fred, "Our guest tonight is the famous authority on eagles. I heard him on *Hobby Lobby* last Sunday night, and I invited him over." Soon the fun began, as Mr. Ramshaw circled the audience and, finally, came to rest in the studio rafters.

After the program ended, the studio apparently didn't present as frightening a scene to Mr. Ramshaw, for he finally came down within the reach of his owner's grasp. There were, however, still other repercussions to come. Executives of the National Broadcasting Company blanched at the episode that had taken place within hearing of listeners coast-to-coast, to say nothing of the sometimes frightened, sometimes convulsed with laughter, studio audience. Fearful for the dignity of their corporate image, although the term had not yet been popularized at the time, they informed Allen of their acute displeasure. Fred's reply took the form of a masterful letter that has gained well-deserved recognition and appreciation among broadcasting circles.

Allen derived great pleasure from writing to people, and they, in turn, relished receiving these gems from him. Dennis Day recalls that, "Whenever anyone on the coast got a letter from Fred Allen, it was like getting a first edition."[20] Soon, they telephoned all their friends to chuckle over its contents with them. Fred had a habit of never using capitals when typing his letters, choosing instead to write them entirely in small letters. Once after getting such a letter from him, Goodman Ace asked Allen, "Doesn't the shift key on your typewriter work?" Allen replied, "Yes, but I've never learned to shift for myself." Allen soon put his letter-writing skill to work, explaining to the network brass how a golden eagle could soar free during the **Fred Allen Show** and, as critic John Crosby said, " . . . commit an indiscression right on the audience."[21]

The letter that Allen sent to John Royal, then Vice-President of NBC, caused many laughs around the network, and it still reminds us of the days of "live" radio before everything was taped and filmed, when mistakes were made in public before a nation of amused listeners. Allen's letter was as follows:

march 25th

1940

dear mr royal . . .

am in receipt of your letter commenting on l'affaire eagle as they are calling it around the young and rubicam office.

i thought i had seen about everything in radio but the eagle had a trick up his feathered colon that was new to me. i thought, for a minute, i was back on the bill with lamont's cockatoos.

an acolyte from your quarters brought news to us, following the nine o'clock broadcast, that the eagle was grounded at the midnight show. it was quite obvious that mr. ramshaw, as the eagle is known around the falcon lounge at the audubon society rooms, resented your dictatorial order. when his cue came to fly, and he was still bound to captain knight's wrist, mr. ramshaw deprived by nature of the organs essential in the voicing of an audible complaint, called upon his bowels to wreck upon us his reaction to your martinet ban.

toscanini, your house man, has foisted some movements on studio audiences in 8 h, the bulova company has praised its movement over your network but when radio city is torn down to make way for another mcguiness restaurant, in years to come, the one movement that will be recalled by the older radio fans will be the eagle's movement on wednesday last. if you have never seen a ghost's beret you might have viewed one on mr. rockefeller's carpet during our sterling performance.

i know you await with trepidation the announcement that i am going to interview sabu with his elephant some week.

yours for a wet broom in 8 h on wednesday nights.

fred allen[22]

One week after the eagle broadcast all had not yet been forgotten. This bit of repartee took place on the program between Allen and orchestra leader Peter Van Steeden:

ALLEN: We had enough trouble last week with that eagle.

PETER: That eagle got more laughs than you did.

ALLEN: I could get laughs, too, if I used devices.

PETER: The eagle was over your head.

ALLEN: That's what worried me.

Even though all the feathers that had been so unceremoniously ruffled had not yet settled, the humor of the situation was appreciated by everyone other than NBC network executives.

The June 26, 1949, **Fred Allen Show** was the last Allen radio show, and, fittingly, his guest was Henry Morgan, whose anti-establishment wit had kept him constantly hustling to keep working, and the paragon of pinchpenny, Jack Benny. To the very end, Jack was parading his stinginess on Fred's program, Morgan was scratching for money to pay his bills, and Allen, bemused and sardonic, was trying to help both men as best he could. NBC, true to its code and thoroughly consistent with its past performance, cut the Allen show off the air *once more* as it again ran overtime. This time, however, NBC's cut-off was permanent, for veepee Clarence L. Menser had pulled the plug for good.

Bigness and the establishment, as they usually do, had won the last battle. Once more the individual had lost the war. Allen's yeasty, often biting, comic view of life was off the air. Somehow, the significance of his disappearance wasn't as apparent then as it is now.

Through the years, Allen had missed the protests various ethnic groups sometimes raised against other programs. If he had missed these controversies, however, he could not escape forever the inevitable kiss of death eventually bestowed upon him by the economics of network broadcasting and advertising vice-presidents. Television, economics and the "mass" mentality of the network establishment he understood so well clearly did him in. Broadcasters were willing to accept the barbs of an acerbic and highly perceptive critic, only as long as he was rewarding them economically. No matter how much in poor taste or how inane certain radio programs might be, their longevity was determined chiefly by whether or not they paid cash dividends.

As soon as a program did not provide rich revenues, however, it was soon dropped and, possibly, with some satisfaction if it starred a comedian, whose barbs in the past frequently had drawn blood in executive suites. Certainly there were no tears shed by corporate conformists when a heretic was dropped.

James Thurber nominated Clarence L. Menser, an NBC vice-president, as the executive directly responsible for dropping Fred Allen from radio.[23] In Thurber's view, this was a dastardly act and his judgement seems right. My own view is that it is far better to trust the judgements of a humorist on substantial matters, than those of corporate vice-presidents. Still, Thurber may have been slightly prejudiced, for at another time he had suggested: "You can count on the thumb of one hand the American who is at once a comedian, a humorist, a wit, and a satirist, and his name is Fred Allen." Right again!

Network executives concluded that Fred Allen could not contribute much to the new medium of television. "Old Baggy Eyes," as Jack Benny called Allen in their feuding days, certainly was not the best-looking candidate for television. This, however, was probably not the chief reason for his limited success in the newer medium he had come to detest.

Fred Allen was a social critic who took a leisurely, day-at-a-time approach, somewhat in the Will Rogers manner, but he also showed many flashes of the dark, sardonic humor displayed by Mark Twain in his latter years. Had not Mark Twain once observed that Americans enjoyed three precious things; the freedom of speech, freedom of conscience and the prudence never to practice either.[24] Much of Twain's dark humor is echoed in Allen's best work.

Following in Allen's path were such bright, young radio comedians as Henry Morgan and Stan Freberg. Perhaps it is a cogent comment upon our society that today, neither Morgan nor Freberg are working as comedians in the United States. The former, in fact, left the country altogether to work in Canada, while the latter concentrates on bright, funny, advertising campaigns. Both Morgan and Freberg had engaged in biting radio satire and cast a sharp, inquiring eye on the absurdities of American life. Many radio listeners laughed at their work, but there were many others who were angered by them.

All of us suffer a loss when bright, perceptive comedians such as Freberg and Morgan devote their creative energy to other things. Yet, Fred Allen would probably not have been greatly surprised, for he clearly foresaw such a situation developing. Comedians, he said, were on a treadmill to oblivion. Like so many other great humorists, Fred Allen was one-part philosopher and one-part social critic. He played these roles easily without any trace of self-consciousness, by using a keen sense of observation, seemingly boundless creativity, and his great love of language and facility with it.

Although he never attained the pinnacle of public popularity enjoyed by Jack Benny, Fred Allen enjoyed the admiration of a diverse group of listeners that included intellectuals, artists, newsstand dealers, and factory workers. His humor—sardonic and bristling with satire—however, was one that children and adolescents usually did not enjoy or understand. While youngsters enjoyed Jack Benny's antique, wheezing Maxwell, his adventures with Carmichael the ferocious polar bear he kept as a pet in his basement, or the infrequent trips to his money vaults, Fred Allen's assaults against network and advertising agency executives meant relatively little to them.

Josh Billings, Mark Twain, and Will Rogers were writers with whom Allen most often has been compared. Although such comparisons are valid, there are two others to whom he also bears some resemblance, William Cowper Brann and Ambrose Bierce. Brann the Iconoclast and Bitter Bierce also tossed literary thunderbolts at the hypocrisies and stupidities of their day. Satirists, who are almost inevitably moralists, although most probably would vehemently deny the accusation, are seldom popular among their fellows. In fact, such social critics may be considered fortunate if they are merely tolerated and not actually stoned and banished from the company of all decent men.

Fred Allen, in his own way, was banished from broadcasting when TV finally brought about the end of network radio. Broadcasting's banishment of Allen took the form of refusing to use the comedian's many gifts, because the newer medium of sight and sound made strict demands of conformity—a characteristic attitude of mind and expression that never was Fred's long suit. With the advent of television, rigid demands to conform and avoid experimentation became stronger and stronger. Unfortunately for us, television, except in rare instances as the late *Omnibus* series and the more recent BBC's *Masterpiece Theater* programs, has remained bound by the same confining and stuffy restraints.

In 1956, shortly after Allen's death, NBC re-broadcast *Conversation,* a program in which Fred talked with Clifton Fadiman and Gilbert Seldes about how, if they were given the opportunity, they would live their lives over. Like most such discussions, the most enlightening impression that came across was the unique style and character of each participant, not the question he is asked to discuss. Allen continually made the point of how much material radio demanded. He said that although he was well-rewarded financially, he had been forced to produce a tremendous amount of material during his seventeen years on radio. While in vaudeville, he said, five routine monologues would have lasted a comedian a lifetime. A radio program's demands, on the other hand, were insatiable. "In 39 weeks on radio," he said, "we used more jokes than Weber and Fields used in a lifetime." Continuing he added, "At sixty or so you wind up in a rickety chair with the debris of your aspirations around you."[25]

In response to the question posed by Clifton Fadiman, Allen said he would have chosen wealthy parents, so he could have obtained a better education. Furthermore, he confided he would have liked to have been a writer. When Fadiman objected that Allen *was* a writer, Fred responded, "I never could have been able to support myself in that way."

Most of Allen's writing had been to entertain and enlighten, but some of it was done also to apologize to sensitive souls who didn't always think he was funny. During his lifetime, he had written seven or eight hundred radio scripts and many explanatory letters to NBC vice-presidents. He had also written apologetic letters to the Mayor of Pottstown, Pennsylvania, for supposedly derogatory references to that thriving metropolis; the Philadelphia Hotel Association for making references to the small hotel rooms in that city ("The hotel rooms in Philadelphia are so small, the mice in them are humpbacked."); and to the estate of Earl Derr Biggers for killing off the venerable Chinese sleuth, Charlie Chan, in one of the Mighty Allen Art Players' dramatic extravaganzas.

The three major ills of radio and television, as Allen diagnosed them, were advertising agency executives, network vice-presidents, and quiz shows. Oddly enough, all three are closely related to each other and to our society. Commenting on "The State of American Humor," on NBC's *Living 1949* program, Allen traced its developments from its beginnings in New England and on the frontier. American humor, he said, had its beginnings in a leisurely time and it clearly manifested that characteristic.

Any definition of humor was tricky, Allen insisted. Mark Twain maintained that sorrow was the secret source of humor, while Josh Billings had said it was, "Wit with a rooster's tail feathers stuck in its cap." Agreeing with both humorists, Allen went on to note that humor makes a man feel good all over. Frequently it was the unexpected, the incongruous present in any situation that was responsible for the laughter. An important role of humor, according to Allen, was that it could be used as a safety valve against the world and its problems. Humor in America soon became attacking and provocative, striking out against pretensions in high and low places. From the time when Artemus Ward wise-cracked, "Most of the girls in Utah marry young. Brigham Young that is," to the gayety of the minstrel shows, the pace was slow and easy, as was the humor. "It was a leisurely age of humor uncorrupted by the Hooper ratings," said Allen.[26]

Soon, however, conditions changed, as vaudeville became the chief vehicle for comedy and the quick one- or two-liners took over. The pace was becoming increasingly more frenetic. Snappy humor arrived, yet there still were some humorists who operated in the old tradition. One was Will Rogers, who seemed to be a wise and witty commentator from another era Perhaps it was his rapid climb to national popularity by radio in the midst of the Great Depression that enabled Rogers to retain the style, pace, and values of an earlier age. When many people were unemployed and doing without, the old values looked particularly good and well worth being considered again. Will Rogers supplied that need.

Nothing could be more American than the leisurely delivery and manner of Rogers who said, "Americans are getting just like Ford cars. They have all the same parts, the same upholstery, and all make the same noises." When introduced to President Calvin Coolidge, Rogers, with his folkiest irreverence and innocence, shook the President's hand and said, "I'm sorry. I didn't get the name." Will Rogers' encounters with the famous were a far cry from Johnny Carson interviewing presidential candidates on the *Tonight Show,* or Bob Hope hobnobbing with the residents of the White House, regardless of who they might be. Somehow, Rogers' style and statements seem more sincere and honest.

Neither individual sham and hypocrisy, however, nor advertising were the only factors that destroyed American comedy. Network executives straining for maximum profits also share the responsibility, but, essentially, it was the change in American society that did the most damage. "Radio humor," Allen said, "has lost all its spontaneity. It is the victim of the times—mechanized and urbanized—produced in such quantities, it's downright chaotic." Furthermore, he added, "Radio wit tends to be the product of tired gag-writers. The star comedians are rarely more than a mouthpiece for their writers. Too many comedians survive on the brains of others."[27] He went on to point out there was too much pressure on the comedian to produce too much material, since he not only had to be funny each week, but every moment he was on the air as well.

As to the future of American humor, Allen said, it all depended upon whether or not we slowed down. "If the pace of life slows down, there may then be some hope." On humor in general, he commented, "Laughter is the privilege of the free, the solace of the oppressed. Laughter is an universal language of mankind. A little nonsense now and then is relished by the wisest men." The former might well have served as a fitting epitaph for Fred Allen, but his excursion into social comment did not stop there.

Pretension and sham were natural targets for Allen. Humor could be a weapon for him. Once during George Jessel's Hollywood period as motion picture producer, he appeared on the *Fred Allen Show.* Jessel told of his many accomplishments and material possessions, boasting, "I have two swimming pools—one for my Hollywood acquaintances and one for my friends from the Bronx." To which Allen replied, "You look the same to me, George. You're wearing a wilted gardenia in your lapel, and you have Sen Sen on your breath."

Despite the considerable fame and fortune that rewarded his accomplishments, however, his pathway in life was not smooth. As Allen himself noted, "The world is a grindstone and life is your nose." Comments of this kind endeared him to the high-brows who considered him one of their own, and his frequent appearances on *Information Please,* that intellectual enclave of radio, unctuously presided over by Clifton Fadiman, only seemed to strengthen their claim.

Self-conscious eggheads insisted Allen's humor was over the head of the "masses," the great unwashed hordes of middlebrows and below. Yet, during radio's golden years, probably only one other comedian—Jack Benny—consistently enjoyed greater mass popularity as indicated by the ratings. Allen's sardonic wit, satirical cast of mind, innovative brain, and wild puns appealed to all groups, for Allen's humor never contained the self-consciously coy, cute style, which so often passes for intellectual wit and humor.

Philosophically, Allen was a realist with a keen eye for human foibles who possessed great tolerance, arising, no doubt, from his great personal warmth, considerateness, and generosity. His serious, dead-panned visage could not hide the glow of humanity his acquaintances felt emanating from him. His degree of resignation was suggested when he said, "The world is a grindstone and life is your nose." The lack of appeal personal possessions held for him was expressed by his statement, "I never want to get used to anything that might be taken away from me." Frances Cardinal Spellman once remarked that Fred Allen was a deeply religious man. Cardinal Spellman quoted Allen as saying, "This is only the prologue here. The big show is up above."

Fred Allen was a substantial show business figure, a genuine one-of-a-kind American, a characterization which he probably would have both denied and been pleased to receive. Allen allowed us intellectually to thumb our nose at the stupidities of the establishment and its agents safely without any fear of reprisals. He took the risks and we enjoyed the benefits of the catharsis he provided. Often we enjoyed the supreme pleasure of recognition that someone else also believed the forces of bigness were acting—if not actively conspiring—to make monkeys out of us all.

Fred Allen, first on *Town Hall Tonight,* later while making trips down *Allen's Alley,* and, finally, during his *Walks Down Main Street,* served as an early warning system to detect the nonsense prevalent in American society. Once, during one of his last programs, Fred and Portland walked down Main Street as usual and asked the question of the day of Senator Claghorn, Titus Moody, Mrs. Nussbaum, Ajax Cassidy, and Falstaff Openshaw. After getting their amusing, but generally nonresponsive answers, Fred, with a line perhaps more self-revealing than even he realized, noted, "It's the same every week, Portland. All you get out of a walk down Main Street is the exercise." An insightful remark of this nature, generally, is made at the end of a career, not at its beginning. Neither resignation nor despair is reflected in it, but, instead, a realistic appraisal.

The closing paragraph of Allen's book, *Treadmill to Oblivion,* serves as both a prophetic look ahead and a fitting epitaph:

> We are living in a machine age. For the first time in history, the comedian has been compelled to supply himself with jokes and comedy material to compete with the machine. Whether he knows it or not, the comedian is on a treadmill to oblivion. When a radio comedian's program is finally finished it slinks down Memory Lane into the limbo of yesterday's happy hours. All that the comedian has to show for his years of work and aggravation is the echo of forgotten laughter.[28]

One bright spot after his departure from radio was the success Allen enjoyed as an author. His longtime desire to be a *real* writer must have been partially gratified, at least, by the critical acclaim given *Treadmill to Oblivion,* his personal account of his career in radio. A detailed autobiography of his life up to the time he entered radio, *Much Ado About Me,* unfinished at his death, was published posthumously and also received lavish critical praise.

Fred Allen died March 17, 1956, St. Patrick's Day, while taking his evening walk on 57th Street in New York City, a fitting date and place for an Irishman who loved New York so much he spent most of his time satirizing it. Much of what Allen said was inescapably right. He was appreciated, but not nearly as much as he deserved. Much of what he foresaw has come to pass in broadcasting and in American society as well. It's not too difficult to imagine a thin, nasal voice with a New England accent saying, "I told you so, kiddies." But, then, Fred Allen was too modest a man to ever have said this, and, certainly, he never would have said it in such a mundane way, without a suitable punch line to prick the sensibilities, tickle the funnybone, and massage the intellect at one and the same time. Now in a Post-Watergate era, we know Allen was right about many things. Hypocrisy still abounds, and much of modern society is mainly a sheaf of lies based on past virtues. Only the rare and often lonely individual is honest and truly moral. *Tally ho, Mr. Allen and touché.*

NOTES

[1] Johnny Carson's opinion of Fred Allen is recounted by Kenneth Tynan, "Profiles: Fifteen Years of the Salto Morale" *The New Yorker,* February 20, 1978, p. 80.

[2] Edwin O'Connor's comment is found in the epilogue to Fred Allen's *Much Ado About Me.* (Boston: Little, Brown & Co., 1956), p. 362.

[3] Allen's dislike of catchwords and phrases is expressed in his book, *Treadmill to Oblivion.* (Boston: Little, Brown & Co., 1954), p. 151.

[4] An account of Fred's early dealings with sponsors is found in his book, *Treadmill to Oblivion,* p. 7.

[5] Herman Wouk, who was one of Allen's writers on his later programs, reported the amount of writing Fred did each week on the N.B.C. radio program, *Fred Allen—A Biography in Sound,* May 29, 1956.

[6] *Ibid.,* May 29, 1956.

[7] Information about Pegeen and Ed Fitzgerald, the format they created, and their many imitators comes from an article entitled "The Fitzgeralds Return," in the February 1975 issue of *Talknews,* Vol. 2, No. 2, p. 1.

[8] Fred Allen's unusual guarantee against listener loss was repeated before and after many programs during the 1948 season. This particular one appeared on *The Fred Allen Show* broadcast by N.B.C. on March 28, 1948.

[9] The judgements of giveaway programs by Allen were reported in his book, *Treadmill to Oblivion,* p. 217.

[10] *Ibid.,* p. 106.

[11] Jack Benny's admiration for Fred Allen's quick wit was reported by Ben Gross in his book, *I Looked and I Listened.* (New Rochelle: Arlington House, 1970), p. 129.

[12] This classic Allen "insult" was reported by Herman Wouk on *Fred Allen—A Biography in Sound,* N.B.C., May 29, 1956.

[13] Alan Reed's recollections were broadcast on *Same Time, Same Station,* Station KRLA, Pasadena, California, January 9, 1972.

[14] Fred Allen credited O.O. McIntyre as an inspiration for the *Allen's Alley* feature in *Treadmill to Oblivion,* p. 179.

[15] The meaning of *nu* in Yiddish is discussed in Leo Rosten's book, *The Joys of Yiddish.* (New York: Pocket Books, 1970), p. 272.

[16] Mrs. Nussbaum's sturgeon feast was described on *The Fred Allen Show,* N.B.C., October 21, 1945.

[17] Alan Reed discussed the role of Falstaff Openshaw on *Same Time, Same Station,* Station KRLA, Pasadena, California, January 9, 1972.

[18] Allen's comments on his program's ethnic humor was made while talking with Gilbert Seldes and Clifton Fadiman on a program entitled *Conversation,* N.B.C., 1954.

[19] Fred Allen's account of *l'affaire eagle* appears in *Treadmill to Oblivion,* p. 121-132.

[20] Reed's eye-witness account of Mr. Ramshaw's flight was broadcast on *Same Time, Same Station,* Station KRLA, Pasadena, California, April, 2, 1972.

[21] This appreciation of Allen's letter writing skill by Dennis Day was broadcast on *Fred Allen—A Biography in Sound,* N.B.C., May 29, 1956.

[22] Critic John Crosby's disclosure of the eagle's indigression also appeared on *Fred Allen—A Biography in Sound,* N.B.C., May 29, 1956.

[23] The "eagle" letter is taken from *Fred Allen's Letters,* edited by Joe McCarthy. (New York: Pocket Books, 1965), p. 42.

[24] James Thurber wrote a series of interesting articles for the *New Yorker* magazine, originally printed in 1948, entitled, "Soapland." They were subsequently reprinted in Thurber's *The Beast in Me and Other Animals.* (New York: Harcourt Brace Jovanovich, Inc., Harvest Books, 1973), p. 204.

[25] Mark Twain's observations are noted in Ray B. Browne, Larry N. Landrum, and William K. Bottorf's (editors) book, *Challenges to American Culture.* (Bowling Green: Popular Press of Bowling Green University, 1970), p. 111.

[26] Allen's remarks on radio's insatiable demands upon comedians were broadcast on N.B.C.'s *Conversation* program originally broadcast in 1954.

[27] Allen's comment on American humor was made on *Living 1949: The State of American Humor,* N.B.C., January 30, 1949.

[28] *Ibid.,* January 30, 1949.

[29] Allen's moving closing remarks are taken from his *Treadmill to Oblivion,* pp. 239-240.

Neil A. Grauer (essay date 1988)

SOURCE: "Forgotten Laughter: The Fred Allen Story," in *American Heritage,* Vol. 39, No. 1, February, 1988, pp. 98-107.

[*In the following excerpt, Grauer claims Allen's humor as the progenitor of such modern humorists as David Letterman and Garrison Keillor.*]

Satire, according to the playwright George S. Kaufman, "is what closes Saturday night," but for seventeen years Fred Allen used his satiric brand of humor to create some of the nation's most popular radio comedy.

"The other comedians . . . swoon at Allen," said a one-time editor of *Variety,* the show business newspaper. In part the admiration of his colleagues was due to their knowledge that Allen, unlike many of his competitors, did not rely on a steady supply of gags from a stable of writers. Allen was his own chief writer, laboring twelve to fourteen hours a day in longhand, six days a week, to produce his scripts. He had only a few assistants, among them the future novelist Herman Wouk, the author of *The Caine Mutiny.* By contrast, Bob Hope once employed thirteen gag writers, while Johnny Carson now has eight people regularly working on his material. "I am probably the only writer in the world who has written more than he can lift," Allen told a friend in 1944. He had the scripts for his weekly show—thirty-nine of them a year—bound in black and stacked on more than ten feet of bookshelves, right next to a one-volume copy of the collected works of William Shakespeare, which took up just three and a half inches. He did so as "a corrective," he said, "just in case I start thinking a ton of cobblestones is worth as much as a few diamonds."

In vaudeville, the nation's first popular mass entertainment, performers could hone their material for months and use it for years. But for radio they needed something new every time they went on the air. Allen was the hardest-working of radio's funnymen, the only star of the new medium who tried to feed its voracious maw almost single-handedly, week after week, year after year.

Ultimately, perhaps inevitably, Allen suffered creative burn-out, but his influence on other comics, by either virtue of his remarkably generous assistance or direct example, remains pervasive. Red Skelton has said that Allen wrote the famous "Guzzler's Gin" routine that has been a mainstay of his act for decades. Younger performers, consciously or unconsciously, mimic Allen's creations. In his **Town Hall Tonight** program of the mid-1930s, Allen featured "news bulletins" about the goings-on in his small, mythical community—a direct ancestor of Garrison Keillor's Lake Wobegon. The Allen program also had skits performed by the Mighty Allen Art Players, a feature later adopted by Johnny Carson, and interviews with **"People You Didn't Expect to Meet,"** such as a goldfish doctor or a female blacksmith, an idea that now works well for David Letterman.

Only once during Allen's long radio career did his program top the ratings, but his audience was considered the most heterogeneous and the most intelligent. "Of course, he has listeners at all levels," an advertising executive said in 1945, "but you would be surprised how many professors, publishers, surgeons, bishops, mathematicians are Fred Allen fans."

Although he wrote two delightful volumes of autobiography in his last years, Allen died a disappointed and bitter man on St. Patrick's Day 1956. "Whether he knows it or not, the comedian is on a treadmill to oblivion," he wrote toward the end of his life. "When a radio comedian's program is finally finished it slinks down Memory Lane into the limbo of yesteryear's happy hours. All that the comedian has to show for his years of work and aggravation is the echo of forgotten laughter."

Allen was born on May 31, 1894, in Cambridge, Massachusetts, and christened John Florence Sullivan. He was the son of James Henry Sullivan, a poorly paid bookbinder with a fondness for strong drink, and Cecilia Herlihy Sullivan. (Although he retained the name Sullivan legally, he adopted Fred Allen as his stage name.)

Allen's mother died when he was not quite three years old, a year after giving birth to his younger brother, Robert. Allen's disconsolate father took his small sons to live with his spinster sister-in-law, Elizabeth Herlihy, Allen's "Aunt Lizzie." She became his de facto parent when his father remarried and moved out twelve years later. Aunt Lizzie enrolled Allen in the Boston High School of Commerce, a trade school for poor children that was a pet project of Mayor John F. Fitzgerald, the future grandfather of John F. Kennedy.

His father got Allen a job in the Boston Public Library as a stockboy, responsible for fetching and returning books. In his spare time Allen, then fourteen, became an omnivorous reader. He stumbled upon a book about comedy and in time was to read everything he could find on the subject. As an adult he amassed a collection of four thousand humor books and a huge file of jokes and witty sayings. It was a stockpile that proved invaluable when he came to write his radio shows.

After a successful appearance as a juggler in an amateur show put on by the library's employees, Allen made his public debut in an amateur contest held in Boston's Hub Theatre in 1912. The audience response to the patter he delivered during his routine encouraged him to concentrate on humor rather than juggling. "It seemed to me that if I could be . . . funny, I could save a lot of time practicing juggling tricks. . . . " He subsequently billed himself as "The World's Worst Juggler."

By late 1914 Allen had decided to try to break into the big time in New York. "My arrival in New York created as much commotion as the advent of another flounder at the Fulton Fish Market," he later wrote. But he was enough of a success on the minor New York-based vaudeville circuits that in 1916 he was offered bookings in Australia and New Zealand, where he toured for eleven months. It was a grueling but worthwhile apprenticeship. On the long train and boat trips between engagements, Allen read Dickens and Twain, Shakespeare, and the American humorists Artemus Ward, Bill Nye, and Josh Billings. "I learned that any joke or story can be told in many forms," he wrote forty years later. "I came to Australia a juggler, and was to return to America a monologist."

By 1919 he had reached vaudeville's mecca, New York's Palace Theater. Thereafter he was able to obtain bookings on the best vaudeville circuits, including the one operated by the imperious J.J. ("Jake") Shubert. Shubert liked Allen's act and signed him to appear in *The Passing Show of 1922,* a musical revue in which Allen met a chorus girl named Portland Hoffa, who became his wife five years later.

Following his appearance in the Shubert revue, Allen was never without a Broadway engagement or major vaudeville booking for the next ten years. His wife joined his act, dancing and delivering "dumb dame" jokes. Although childless, their marriage was so congenial that they were rarely apart for more than a few hours during the next twenty-nine years. Their final stage appearance was in the musical revue *Three's a Crowd,* starring Clifton Webb and Libby Holman. When it closed in 1932, and another show in which Allen was scheduled to appear never opened because of the deepening Depression, he began to consider trying radio.

After methodically studying the medium in general, Allen spent three weeks writing a sample script, selecting a cast and orchestra, and rehearsing the trial program, which featured the torch singer Helen Morgan. He had a phonograph record made of the show and submitted it to the president of Corn Products, the maker of Linit Bath Oil, who was looking for a radio program to sponsor. After listening to only a few minutes of the recording on a bad phonograph, the executive, intrigued by Allen's dry, nasal delivery, said: "That's enough. Never mind the show. Get me that man with the flat voice!" *The Linit Bath Club Revue* made its debut on October 23, 1932, on CBS.

From the beginning Allen had problems with sponsors, advertising people, censors, and network vice-presidents, whom he called "a bit of executive fungus that forms on a desk that has been exposed to a conference." One advertising agency executive, concerned about Allen's dour appearance, wanted him to dress up as a Keystone Kop and brandish a stuffed nightstick at the studio door so the audience going in would know "you're the comedian." (Allen refused.) A sponsor's wife liked organ music, so it was decided that an organ solo would be played in the middle of the program. "Playing an organ solo midway through a comedy show is like planting a pickle in the center of a charlotte russe," Allen later wrote.

Despite such interference Allen and a lone assistant were able to turn out half-hour programs featuring comedy sketches in which Allen played many parts, gave commentaries on society and politics, and performed musical numbers. A regular on the show—and all subsequent Allen programs—was his wife, Portland, whose radio voice, partly because of nervousness, "sounded like two slate pencils mating or a clarinet reed calling for help," Allen wrote. In later years her high-pitched cry of "Mr. A-a-allen, Mr. A-a-allen" began their comic dialogues and became one of the Allen show's trademarks.

As Allen's sponsors changed, so did the title of his program. In 1935 Allen decided to call the show *Town Hall Tonight* to give it broader appeal. Its hour-long format began with news bulletins, often featuring interviews with townspeople or newsmakers, a precursor to Allen's later program feature *Allen's Alley.* The format clicked. By 1936 as many as 250 newspaper editors throughout the country ranked Allen's program as second only to Jack Benny's in popularity. For the rest of the decade and much of the 1940s, Allen's was always among the top ten shows on the air. Sylvester ("Pat") Weaver, then Allen's producer and later the head of programming for NBC, once claimed that at the height of Allen's popularity, three out of four homes in the country listened to him.

On Wednesday, December 30, 1936, Allen fired the first shot in what would become one of the classic battles of comedy: his feud with Jack Benny. That evening Allen's program featured a performance of Rimsky-Korsakov's "Flight of the Bumblebee" played on the violin by a ten-year-old prodigy named Stewart Canin. Allen knew that Benny, whose violin playing was often the subject of gags, frequently listened to his program, so as he later remembered, "I said that if Mr. Benny had heard this tyke's rendition of 'The Bee,' he should hang his head in symphonic shame and pluck the horsehairs out of his bow and return them to the tail of the stallion from which they had been taken."

Benny, a friend of Allen's since their vaudeville days, knew a good cue when he heard one and also knew that a "battle" helped boost ratings. So week after week the two comedians exchanged insults on their respective programs, although it was six to eight months before they bothered to telephone each other to discuss the feud. Benny denounced Allen as "that certain New England boiled comedian," and Allen made sport of the exaggerated vanity that was part of Benny's comic persona. When the comedians' first face-to-face encounter took place on Benny's program of March 14, 1937, it drew what was then one of the largest listening audiences in radio history, second only to one of President Roosevelt's fireside chats.

The feud remained a fixture of the Benny and Allen comic routines for the next decade, much to the public's delight. In March 1942 Allen's program was shifted to Sunday night, giving him an opportunity to ad-lib his response to Benny's insults almost immediately after Benny's program had ended—the Edgar Bergen–Charlie

McCarthy show ran in between—and giving many Americans a Sunday-night ritual to observe: Benny to Bergen to Allen. Benny was an adept ad-libber, but he tacitly conceded Allen's superiority in the art during one of their joint appearances by shouting, "If I had my writers here, you wouldn't talk to me like that and get away with it!"

The exchange of insults with Benny gave Allen opportunities for "verbal slapstick," as the radio historian Arthur Frank Wertheim put it. "Allen threw words around like custard pies. . . . " The comedian and author Steve Allen (who is not related) felt that Allen "had a poet's regard for the peculiarities of sound and expression and he seemed never so happy as when he could roll off his tongue some glittering allegory, metaphor or simile. He was actually more intrigued by this sort of thing than he was by the plain and simple joke."

He also enjoyed making up names, and as a student of Dickens he tried to outdo the master in inventing bizarre ones. Once, however, while on vacation, Allen was approached by a mild-looking man who wanted to know why his name had been used on Allen's show. His name: Sinbad Brittle. "After Sinbad Brittle accosted me in Biddeford, Maine," Allen wrote later, "you can tell me your name is Ossip Knothole. I will believe you."

Allen's programs were produced by a process he called "a recipe for a nervous breakdown. . . . Our weekly schedule was a treadmill made up of seven revolving days." Every day he read nine newspapers and scanned magazines and books in search of subjects for topical humor. Even when he was out of town, he had the periodicals sent to him by special-delivery airmail. He tore out or clipped promising items and stuffed the bits of paper in his pockets. "As the day wore on my pockets seemed to be herringbone goiters and I looked as though I was a walking wastebasket."

Since the radio networks forbade the use of recorded programs until the late 1940s, and Allen refused to move his show to Hollywood, during the thirties he had to give two performances of his Wednesday night program, one at 9:00 P.M. for the East Coast and Midwest audience and another at midnight for his West Coast listeners. Within minutes of the end of the second broadcast at 1:00 A.M., Allen, the director, and his two chief writers, Herman Wouk and Arnold Auerbach (later the author of successful Broadway revues), would meet in a "runt-sized delicatessen" on Sixth Avenue to begin planning the next show. Allen's staff, later expanded to four, worked up ideas with him. One might provide the plot for a comic sketch; another might supply the factual information on which to base an interview with a celebrity or one of the **"People You Didn't Expect to Meet"**; together they might suggest outlines for colloquies with Portland Hoffa or Kenny Baker, a tenor who was the show's regular singer and a performer in the sketches. Once Allen had these basic ingredients, he took the rest of the week to prepare the show, writing much of the script himself.

When the delicatessen conference adjourned around 3:00 A.M., Allen usually walked to his apartment on West Fifty-eighth Street and got to bed by 4:00 A.M. He slept late on Thursdays, but in the afternoon he would visit with the next show's guest star, discuss their proposed banter, then return home and begin writing the first draft of that segment of the program, working as far into the night as necessary to finish it. Friday he worked on his correspondence, and that evening he and his wife would go to dinner at a favorite Italian or Chinese restaurant or see a Broadway show, a movie, or a prizefight. It was their only night for recreation.

On Saturdays Allen emptied his pocket files of clippings and sorted them, deciding which five or six to convert into items for the show's "newsreel," which later was dubbed **"The March of Trivia,"** a parody of *Time* magazine's "March of Time" broadcast. On Sundays he went to early morning mass at St. Malachy's Roman Catholic Church, the "Actors' Chapel," on West Forty-ninth Street, where he was married (and from which he was buried). Then he walked home and settled down in his small office—he called it his "cell"—to write the rest of the show, including his opening monologue and his chat with Portland. Auerbach recalled watching him sit in a "straight-backed chair at the rickety card table, bespectacled, frowning, intent, wearing an old-fashioned green eyeshade, elastic bands around his sleeves, a bulge of tobacco wadded into his cheek, toiling hour after silent hour, scrawling tiny, almost illegible hen tracks with a stubby pencil across neat piles of paper."

Usually Allen worked until 4:00 or 5:00 A.M. on Monday, then left a copy of the script with the night doorman of his apartment house so a Western Union messenger could pick it up around 8:00 A.M. and take it to be mimeographed and readied for a rehearsal with the show's cast, which assembled at the studio at 1:00 P.M. on Monday. After rehearsal, timing, cutting, and a thorough rewriting by Allen, the final script was sent to the NBC Continuity Acceptance Department on Tuesday to be pruned of potentially slanderous or lascivious material. Copies were also sent to the sponsor and the sponsor's advertising agency, which also took a whack at it. Allen had to be available all day Tuesday to argue about changes—he would "climb up the wall and scream and yell" over them, Pat Weaver recalled—and to make alterations in the script when he lost the battles.

On Wednesdays rehearsals for that night's broadcast began at 10:00 A.M. Often the script was seven or eight minutes too long, and cuts had to be made. Allen would readily cut his own lines in order to give the other performers more of the laughs. "I don't care whether people say, 'Fred Allen was good last night.' All I want them to say is, 'The Fred Allen hour was good last night,'" he told one interviewer. The final script was trimmed to fifty-three minutes in order to allow for seven minutes of accumulated laughter and applause and commercials. The minute the second broadcast was over, Allen and his associates set off for the delicatessen, and the whole process began again. The spectacular bags under Allen's eyes—once described by his friend S. J. Perelman as "pouches rivaling that of a kangaroo"—were well earned.

Like most professional humorists, Allen dismissed academic studies of humor. "All I know about humor is that I don't know anything. Sure, you're always reading that 'there are only seven or eleven basic jokes,' but I've never found anybody who could tell me what they are. At a guess, two of them probably deal with comparison and exaggeration, because these are at the bottom of a lot of our humor. Another one is probably incongruity," he told an interviewer. But what makes things funny? "I don't know," he said. "It's a guesswork business."

By the 1940s Allen was earning $20,000 a week, but he had to pay the salaries of all the other performers on his program, the assistant writers, the sound technicians, secretaries, and other support personnel. He still netted about $160,000 annually, but in contrast with his public image as a misanthrope, Allen was an incredibly soft touch and gave away some fifty thousand dollars a year to a roster of relatives, old acquaintances, and ex-vaudevillians who were on his "payroll," as well as an army of panhandlers who sought weekly handouts from him. He tended to shrug off inquiries about his generosity. "I've been poor myself," he'd say, or, "Why, I can remember, when I was a baby . . . if I wanted something to eat, I had to creep out and fight a bird for it."

Allen's huge beneficences were possible, in part, because his own tastes were modest. He never owned a home in New York, preferring instead to rent an unpretentious four-room apartment in a convenient but unfashionable area between Radio City and Central Park. It was furnished with plain maple furniture and rag rugs. He had no servants, often ate breakfast in a drugstore, and helped his wife with the dinner dishes. He never owned an automobile, ate simply, rarely drank, and avoided nightlife. "why should i go to a nightclub?" he wrote the society columnist Louis Sobol in 1943 (typing, as usual, all in lower case). "i can get better air in a closet. i can cook better food myself. i can hear better music on a portable phonograph. and i can meet a better class of people in the subway."

For recreation Allen played handball and boxed several times a week with the policemen, fire fighters, and postmen who frequented the Sixty-third Street YMCA in Manhattan, less convenient but more to his taste than the exclusive New York Athletic Club, which was only a block from his apartment. For vacations he and his wife spent the summers at Old Orchard Beach, a ramshackle coastal resort in Maine, where they rented a cottage he dubbed "Gulls' Privy." They later found that the Maine cottage was too exposed to autograph seekers, so they switched to quiet hotels on Montauk Point, far out on the then sparsely populated tip of Long Island.

Once when Allen went to Hollywood, he and his wife insisted on living in an inexpensive hotel, but he reassured his agent by telling him, "Don't be afraid. You don't have to let on that you know us." Allen's antipathy for Hollywood and California was intense. "California is a great place to live—if you're an orange" is perhaps his most quoted insult to the area, but he was even harsher on the film colony: "You can take all the sincerity there is in Hollywood, stuff it into a flea's navel, and still have room for six caraway seeds and an agent's heart." He appeared in only a few movies, including *Love Thy Neighbor,* a 1940 feature, and *It's in the Bag,* made in 1945, both of which costarred Jack Benny. Allen was not impressed with his films. "Every time I made a picture . . . ," he told S. J. Perelman, "it would turn up in one of the grind houses in Skid Row along with attractions called *Daughters in Jeopardy* or *Marijuana, Weed With Roots in Hell. . . .*"

In October 1940 the Texaco company took over sponsorship of Allen's program, and at the end of the 1942 season it decided to cut the show to a half-hour, which "took a load off my mind," Allen said in his memoirs. For the new, shorter format Allen invented **"Allen's Alley,"** which made its debut as a regular feature on December 13, 1942. A series of dizzy spells in 1943, brought on by his chronic hypertension, forced Allen to give up his radio show entirely during 1944. When he returned to the air in the fall of 1945, the Alley blossomed into the "most famous of all airlanes," as *Time* magazine put it. As usual, Allen wrote the scripts for the Alley, developing four characters who became its permanent residents in 1945. The characters were brought to life by an exceptionally talented quartet of performers who somehow managed to impress themselves indelibly upon the listeners during only five minutes in Allen's Alley each week.

On each program Allen would come up with a topical "question for the evening" and stroll down the Alley to knock on the doors of its inhabitants and get their views on the subject. First he would encounter Sen. Beauregard Claghorn, a bombastic Southerner whose exclamations— "That's a joke, Son!" and "Claghorn's the name—Senator Claghorn, that is"—became national bywords after just four weeks of public exposure. Claghorn was played by Kenny Delmar, a dramatic actor who doubled as the show's announcer. In subsequent years the creators of Warner Brothers' cartoons paid Delmar's Claghorn the compliment of imitation by giving their character Foghorn Leghorn, a pompous rooster, a Claghorn-like voice and delivery, down to the repeated use of "Son" and "that is" at the end of every sentence. Foghorn Leghorn is still seen today in Kentucky Fried Chicken commercials.

Allen used the Claghorn character, who spoke in a staccato bark, to score points against politicians, the bureaucracy, and boastful Southerners. . . .

The next door on which Allen knocked was that of Titus Moody, a taciturn New England rube whose invariable

greeting was "Howdy, bub." Moody was played by Parker Fennelly, a pioneer character actor on radio whom Allen considered its "finest simulator of New England types." Until the mid-1970s Fennelly was still playing such a part as the corporate symbol of Pepperidge Farm bakeries, looking over his half-glasses and advising television viewers that "Pepperidge Farm remembers" how to make old-fashioned cookies and cakes.

Titus Moody was designed to appeal to Allen's fellow New Englanders and all his rural listeners. Moody's comments were full of references to farm life, and his jokes were laced with Bunyanesque exaggerations. His farm, for instance, was so poor that grasshoppers wouldn't stop there. Moody talked of feeding his sheep "ironized" yeast so they would grow steel wool. Through Moody, Allen voiced a classic reservation about the electronic media. Asked if he liked radio, Moody replied, "I don't hold with furniture that talks."

Next Allen came to the residence of Mrs. Pansy Nussbaum, played with a rich Yiddish accent by Minerva Pious, a member of Allen's company for more than fifteen years. Allen invented wild malapropisms for Mrs. Nussbaum. After he greeted her with a friendly "Ah, Mrs. Nussbaum," she might reply, "You are expecting maybe Ingrown Bergman?" or "You are expecting maybe Emperor Shapirohito?" Allen was proud that Pious's performance never became the "routine, offensive burlesque" but instead conveyed a character who "was a human being, warm, honest, understanding and—you should pardon the expression—very funny."

Mrs. Nussbaum had the dreams and suffered the woes of the country's urban dwellers. Her ne'er-do-well husband, Pierre (who was never heard on the show), once swiped the money she was saving for a piano and bet it all on the horses. His luck wasn't too hot.

> MRS. NUSSBAUM: If it is raining borscht outside, Pierre will be standing with a fork. He will also be missing the potato. Last week at the race track he is losing everything. For three nights, every night, Pierre is having the same dream. On a plate he is seeing salami, baloney and liverwurst. By Pierre this is a hunch. He is betting everything. Coming last, a dead heat, is Salami, Baloney and Liverwurst.
>
> ALLEN: What horse won?
>
> MRS. NUSSBAUM: A longshot by name Cold Cuts.

Ironically, the one permanent resident of the Alley who did arouse the ire of an ethnic group came from Allen's own—the Irish. It was Ajax Cassidy, played by Peter Donald and created, Allen later wrote, "for the Irish who had a sense of humor." The Cassidy character became a "thorn in the pride of a small fulminating Celtic minority," Allen said, but Ajax stayed in the Alley as long as Allen remained on the air.

Like the rural hick character embodied by Moody, a comic Irishman was a venerable part of the American humor tradition. Cassidy, as portrayed by Donald, always greeted Allen with a cheery "We-e-ell, how do ye do?" and spoke in a rapid Irish brogue. . . .

By 1945 Allen was employing four writers, and the post-midnight conference in a delicatessen had been converted into a Wednesday afternoon session in a large room in the RCA Building in Radio City. There Allen's staff, which included Nat Hiken, later the creator of Phil Silvers's Sergeant Bilko character on television, would scour newspapers looking for promising topics: a meat shortage, a coal strike, the average family's annual income—any subject that might interest or annoy the listeners. Allen, often having carried a brown-bag lunch, sat at the head of the conference table and the clippings would be passed up to him for inspection, or jokes suggested. The only person actually writing at these conferences was Allen. He kept a single sheet of paper in front of him and would cryptically put down one mysterious word to represent an entire line of dialogue, writing in an "infuriatingly fine print," one observer said, that "looked as if a microbe with ink on its feet had briefly rumbaed on the paper."

Following a typical four-hour brainstorming session, Allen would have a lone piece of paper, half-filled with his tiny hieroglyphics. That evening at home, following dinner, he would refer to it as he wrote and polished the **"Alley"** script, sometimes using his wife as a trial audience. On Thursdays he finished writing the rest of the show. Fridays the show was rehearsed twice for purposes of timing and cutting; on Sundays it was rehearsed once more in the afternoon. The orchestra rehearsed separately so the reaction of its members to the show's jokes would be fresh and spontaneous. The program went on the air at eight-thirty Sunday night.

The streamlined Allen show also had segments involving celebrity guests. Allen enjoyed casting them in unlikely situations. He had songwriters Richard Rodgers and Oscar Hammerstein II perform in a courtroom sketch; Charles Laughton blubber as a lachrymose soap opera character; opera diva Helen Traubel sing a commercial jingle; Wagnerian tenor Lauritz Melchior appear as a hillbilly and warble "Open Up Them Pearly Gates"; and Alfred Hitchcock act in a mystery he couldn't solve. In a spoof of Gilbert and Sullivan's *H.M.S. Pinafore* that featured the baseball manager Leo Durocher in a leading role, Allen sang an appropriately Americanized version of Sir Joseph Porter's "When I Was a Lad":

When I was a lad I could not see
A hand held up in front of me.
In spite of how I'd squint and peer,
I couldn't tell my father from my mother dear.
My eyes were oh, so very, very weak,
That now I am an umpire in the National League!

. . . As an umpire I gained great fame,
I called a player out who wasn't in the game. . . .

My life is a failure, I'm up the creek,
That's why I am an umpire in the National
    League!

The immediate postwar years brought both the peak of Allen's radio career and its stunningly swift decline. During the 1946-47 radio season Allen's show twice topped the Hooper telephone-poll ratings survey, the first and only time he reached that height in midseason against his chief competitors. Within five months, however, his show had slumped to number thirty-eight in the poll, the victim of the ABC network giveaway program *Stop the Music.*

In the next few years, however, television proved to be a far more serious competitor, threatening not just Allen's show but the careers of every radio entertainer. Ratings fell industry-wide as more Americans bought television sets and lost interest in the radio shows that had been their favorites. In 1948 there were only 172,000 television sets in the country, many of them in taverns. By 1952 approximately 72 million TVs were in use, mostly in homes. Television became the nation's and the advertisers' new passion.

In January 1949 Allen's rating had fallen dismally, and his health, frequently precarious, was shaky. "The program might have enjoyed a few more years on borrowed time but my blood pressure was getting higher than the show's rating and it was a question of which one of us would survive," he wrote later. He signed off the air for good on June 26, 1949, one of the first of the big radio stars to succumb to television. (Jack Benny and Bob Hope continued working on radio into the mid-1950s, often doing both radio and TV simultaneously. Edgar Bergen's program lasted until 1956.)

Allen felt that radio comedy probably was doomed even without the advent of TV. "The audience and the medium were both getting tired. The same programs, the same comedians, the same commercials—even the sameness was starting to look the same," he wrote. But he also was bitter about the rise of television, which he considered nothing more than recycled vaudeville. He was particularly scornful of the popularity of Milton Berle, whose show was so successful that he was called "Mr. Television." Allen correctly predicted that Berle's TV reign would be brief. "You can go only so long when you get your laughs by running in front of the audience wearing a pair of lady's drawers," he told a *Life* interviewer. He himself made a few tentative stabs at television, but he was uncomfortable with the medium. He was nervous about appearing without a script in his hand and he didn't like "all those technicians wandering back and forth in front of me while I'm trying to tell a joke," he said.

In 1952 Allen had first a heart attack and later a cerebral spasm, and his career as a performer was virtually over. His final appearances on television were as a panelist on *What's My Line?*, where his talents were largely wasted.

With time on his hands Allen turned to writing books. *Treadmill to Oblivion,* which appeared in 1954, was a memoir of his radio career, and he was working on *Much Ado About Me* about his vaudeville and Broadway days, when he died.

On the night of March 17, 1956, Allen, then sixty-one, was taking his dog on his customary stroll before bed when he was stricken with a heart attack a block from his apartment and collapsed on the street. Passersby carried him inside a nearby building, but he was dead within twenty minutes.

At the time of Allen's death many critics and friends took issue with his belief that he and other radio comedians had toiled futilely on a "treadmill to oblivion." Yet if the name of Fred Allen is mentioned today to anyone under forty who is neither a nostalgia buff nor an entertainment industry historian, the likely response is a blank stare. The movies in which Allen appeared are rarely seen; his early TV appearances were not filmed, as were those of Jack Benny, Burns and Allen, or Lucille Ball. And Allen was realistic about his radio career. At the end of one broadcast he had been heard to mutter, "Well, that one belongs to the sparrows."

Certainly his radio programs were ephemeral, but for those who remember hearing them and for those who have built upon his comic inventions, the laughter they inspired is by no means forgotten. The day after Allen died, his friend and former employee Herman Wouk wrote to *The New York Times:* "In Fred Allen, the voice of sanity spoke out for all Americans to hear, during a trying period of our history, in the classic and penetrating tones of comic satire. Because he lived and wrote and acted here, this land will always be a saner place to live in. That fact is his true monument."

Alan R. Havig (essay date 1990)

SOURCE: Alan R. Havig, "Fred Allen's Comedy of Language," in *Fred Allen's Radio Comedy,* Temple University Press, 1990, pp. 127-52.

[In the following excerpt, Havig characterizes Allen's humor as "verbal slapstick," which he attributes to Allen's use of puns, double entendres, and hyperbole.]

The 1930s and 1940s were years of mighty as well as mighty interesting events in the United States and abroad. For Fred Allen, the Great Depression, the world war—especially on the home front—and postwar tensions with the Soviet Union all found a place in his skeptical observance of current events, as did "human interest" stories from the newspapers' back pages. Allen's scripts were especially sensitive to goings-on in his own town, New York City. More than on any other network radio program, the metropolis of Mayor Fiorello La Guardia, Coney Island, immigrant neighbor-

hoods, the subway, and the Brooklyn Dodgers played a continuing role on Allen's shows.

The medium in which he labored also influenced Allen's comedy each week. This [essay] details, . . . ways in which the sound medium established unique comedic possibilities, which Allen used effectively. At the same time, broadcasting's technological and organizational imperatives confronted entertainers with a vast audience that demanded an unending supply of fresh material, and material that would not offend anyone. Radio also imposed routine but significant temporal restraints on its comedy writers and performers. Although magazine and newspaper humorists obviously worked within editor-determined spatial limits, they avoided the anxieties of live radio broadcasting: more material than time would allow, for example, or extra minutes to fill. Allen had twelve minutes of airtime in which to develop an idea through dialogue. While humorists in the print media were able to employ descriptive passages or linger over a character's thoughts or feelings, and stage humorists could utilize visual comedy, over the airwaves comedians had to convey their material through lean fragments of thrust-and-response conversation. Understanding Allen's comedy means keeping this and other features of broadcasting in mind.

Influences less immediate also gave contour and nuance to Allen's comedy. His comedic vision, his particular view of the world, grew out of biography and personality. Allen emerged from a turn-of-the-century urban, ethnic, Catholic milieu. Moreover, his style of communicating with an audience—the comic devices, presentational forms, personae and archetypes that appeared in or inspired his scripts—emerged with substantial maturity from his stage experience. And since the popular theater of vaudeville and revue had their own history, Allen unconsciously represented decades of Anglo-American theatrical tradition every time he sat before his typewriter to create a broadcast.

The historian Lawrence W. Levine, impressed with the achievement of American humorists in several popular arts during the 1930s, interprets their triumph as a unique response to particular historical circumstances. "The distrust of institutions, the sense that the world no longer worked as it was supposed to, that the old verities and certainties no longer held sway, was expressed in one of the decade's most ubiquitous forms of humor: the humor of irrationality."[1] Students of culture require more than a historical context to explain the shared comic style of Goodman and Jane Ace, Bud Abbott and Lou Costello, the Marx Brothers, Ogden Nash, James Thurber, and W. C. Fields, to mention those whom Levine cites—and Fred Allen. We require more if for no other reason than that these humorists developed their style before the stock market crashed in late 1929. They learned their trade during years of journalistic apprenticeship and stage or motion picture experience. Many of them settled on a zany, nonsensical form of humor because it satisfied their personal artistic requirements, while it pleased the urban reading and theatergoing public. That Fred Allen in the 1930s was the same "nut comic" who delighted S. J. Perelman in 1921 cautions us to be as cognizant of long-standing traditions as we are of the spirit of the times. A "humor of irrationality" may have offered an especially appropriate response to the mind-numbing impact of the Great Depression, but it evolved in happier times.[2]

Without question, Allen worked in a formulaic mass medium, and much of what he did was conventional and, after a while, predictable. But he shared much with nineteenth- and early-twentieth century literary (or "high culture") humorists.[3] All creative people work with assumptions shared by others, usually many others, and with set character types, plots, and themes. The famed *New Yorker* style of comic expression settled into a rather formulaic pattern between the late 1920s and World War II.[4] Some of the conventions Allen used were trite and trivial even in his day, and some, like ethnic and racial stereotyping, measure the cultural distance that separates our time from his. But devices such as satire remain vital weapons in the humorist's arsenal as writers and performers continue to observe, with a smile, the world around them. Fred Allen's substantial contribution to his generation's satiric commentary will stand as his most important legacy.

I

Allen's style of comic expression, one that was especially effective on radio, might be called verbal slapstick. It relied on the mainstays of traditional American oral humor—language, talk, pronunciation, and dialect (although it did not take the form of rambling stories shared 'round the wood stove).[5] The best of radio's comic language, including Fred Allen's, was not restrained, subtle, or understated. Listeners, often engaged in domestic activities, could not easily ignore this broadly farcical comedy that encouraged, even commanded, people momentarily to abandon reality, to revel in the fantastic. *Variety* tried to convey its qualities in terms like "dementia" and "topsy-turvy thinking." Some of Allen's lines were "gems from the boobyhatch."[6]

The most effective language of radio comedy conveyed a sense of spontaneity, of delight-provoking surprise. It was a comedy of exaggeration reminiscent of the tall tale, of characters and situations improbable, often literally impossible. Allen practiced what Arlen J. Hansen terms "transformational humor," one that uses language to alter "reality through creative and inventive talk." The transformer's words create worlds of fantasy, dreams, "magnificent lies."[7] Of the many vaudeville comics who came to radio accomplished in the language of exaggeration and the surrealistic humor it conveyed, Allen, and other "nut comics" combined "outrageous distortion, noisy satire, and mad humor, adding up to an insanely imaginative entertainment," in Douglas Gilbert's words.[8]

To be sure, more subdued approaches also flourished. Characterization was the hallmark of such comedians as Jack Benny, the fallible, lovable butt of his cast's jokes;[9] George "Kingfish" Stevens of *Amos 'n' Andy,* the con artist and henpecked husband; Henry Aldrich, the frantic teenager; *Our Miss Brooks,* the underpaid schoolteacher frustrated in romance; and Fanny Brice's "Baby Snooks," the impish child. And the typical problems, settings, and characters found in radio's situation comedies of the 1940s and 1950s, such as *Father Knows Best* and *Ozzie and Harriet,* assured listeners with familiar, true-to-life circumstances. But those who best exploited radio as a sound medium departed from reality, stretched the imagination, tested credulity. From so many examples, one can recall Ed, Jack Benny's longtime subterranean vault guard, who had known Paul Revere and responds to the password "the British are coming," or Fibber McGee the "handyman," whose rewired vacuum cleaner hid underneath the couch when Molly turned it on.[10]

Allen's comedy created a world of "bedlam," to use one of his favorite words, a world in which all things were possible. On one Allen show, a professor at Bedlam University missed a faculty meeting; he was "so slow he's probably been overtaken by the ivy again," the president (Allen) decided.[11] On another, an unemployed and hungry fire-eater from a disbanded circus caused a ski resort to close when he gorged himself on flames from its furnace.[12] The instances are many. Portland Hoffa described the Australian Fig-Bird: "It lives on the seeds in figs." "But there aren't any figs in Australia," Allen objected. That's all right, Portland assured him. "The Australian Fig-Bird dies at birth."[13] A hurricane hit the East Coast in 1933 with "wind so strong in one New Jersey town that it blew two prohibition workers into a speakeasy. Luckily, the wind blew the speakeasy into a church and the bartender was converted."[14] In a creative effort to save his plantation from the creditors, a southern gentleman decided to cross a cotton plant with a glassblower. "Ah'll sell Aspirin bottles with the cotton growin' right in the top, Suh."[15] In conversation with an upstate New York fishing guide, Allen revealed his method for catching eels. After emptying a box of starch into a river, he waited downstream at the first sharp bend. Unable to make the turn, the rigid eels beached themselves.[16] During a wartime campaign to conserve tires, New York City used a magnet to clear the streets of nails. But the too-powerful magnet moved the Flatiron Building two blocks off its foundation and "pulled U.S. Steel down seven points" as it passed through Wall Street.[17]

What follows [here] is a discussion of the world of radio and show business as sources of Allen's humor. I criticize Allen's reliance on several conventional comedy devices, such as insult humor, but I praise his efforts, which went beyond those of most contemporary broadcasters, to explore radio's unique qualities as a sound-only medium of mass entertainment.

II

As we have noted, Fred Allen resorted at times to popular comedy conventions because they were ready-made and convenient—whether or not they fit the broadcast medium. Some, such as gender stereotypes, pervaded the national culture, assuring an instant response, especially to jokes about female behavior or character. Some contemporary media critics complained that stereotypes—"the absent-minded professor, the sexually unattractive school-teacher"—and other tired comedy devices not only bored but also insulted the intelligence of listeners.[18] A convenient source of gags, these devices found their way into even the best radio comics' work. Whether laziness or the constant need for new material pushed comic writers toward the easy laugh, their use points to a failure of creativity.

In real life, a Roman Catholic ceremony joined the Irishman Fred Allen and the Jewish woman Portland Hoffa in what was to become a successful marriage. Yet, on his radio broadcasts, Allen presented marriage as a farce. During the Linit series, his scripts made light of marital infidelity, a theme more common in "sophisticated" Broadway revues than on radio. "Judge Allen," in one courtroom skit, advises a woman not to sue for divorce, even though she has caught her husband kissing other women. Why? "It may be your turn next," says the judge.[19] "We Want Divorces . . . Down with Allen" chant a group of disillusioned husbands outside his matrimonial agency in another skit. These domesticated males push baby carriages occupied by their "soiled samples of posterity," symbolizing man's loss of freedom in marriage.[20] And when husbands stagger home after an evening of drinking, their shrewish, neglected spouses beat them up and empty their pockets of loose change.[21]

In equally hackneyed views of women, wives shirk domestic responsibilities as readily as men. In a role-reversal skit entitled "Ten Nights in a Bridge Club," a wife-and-mother abandons her family to play cards every night. Her young son pleads in song:

Oh mother, dear mother,
come home with me now.
The clock in the steeple strikes two. . . .

With familial as well as musical disharmony, the mother croons:

Oh Junior, dear Junior,
don't raise such a row.
I'll wipe up the floor with you.[22]

A society woman's most recent divorce rests on grounds of "insufficient closet space." Her husband had appeared unexpectedly while she entertained guests: "There were four gigolos and three closets."[23] In some of his domestic burlesques, however, Allen seemed to voice the traditionalist's regret that unwelcome change threatened marriage and family life in America. The spread of easy divorce laws from Nevada to Florida in 1935 prompted him to imagine vending machines that dispensed marriage licenses and divorce decrees: "a marriage certificate and your correct weight for five cents."[24]

The "dumb Dora" stereotype, a legacy of vaudeville, "had become a national tradition off stage as well as on" by the 1920s.[25] Comics Gracie Allen and Jane Ace typified early radio's confused, delightfully innocent sources of malapropisms, non sequiturs, and other nonsensical talk. Marie Wilson, as *My Friend Irma,* played a similar role in the 1940s and 1950s. Portland Hoffa's microphone persona drew on, but was not limited to, the dumb Dora or "dumb girl" stage tradition.[26] Portland appeared as a "little girl," perhaps in her early teens, who reported the absurd goings-on at her home, and who sometimes extracted gems of insight from the sludge of her confusion. But not often. When Allen asked for bookends, Portland handed him the last few pages of two novels.[27] Playing a coed at Bedlam University, she recited what she knew about the Middle Ages: "They raise the dickens with most women's figures."[28] The stereotype held that women talked too much. When Allen's fictitious news microphones visited an elderly woman who was growing her third set of teeth, her husband expressed only mild interest. "But," he added, "if she starts growin' a new tongue—I'm off to Reno."[29]

Many of Allen's comedy bits expressed the traditionalist's fear that the results could be serious, as well as comic, when women assumed male roles. Even during wartime, as Rosie the Riveter became a national heroine, Allen had a construction boss complain about the "headache" that women workers gave him: "Since the company started usin' women sandhogs, we had to put a powder room in the decompression chamber."[30] Allen's treatment of women in traditional comic forms predated the unaccustomed changes created by World War II. In a 1936 newspaper, he found a prediction that the American people would elect a female vice-president by 1940, and a woman chief executive a decade later. Speculating about what that could mean, Allen imagined a secretary of the interior who thinks her job is interior decoration. She orders yellow robes for judges and lavender paint for battleships. The many buttons on her telephone confuse the President. "Why," she sighs, "can't the White House afford a zipper?"[31]

Fred Allen joined numerous popular entertainers in the practice of gender stereotyping for comic effect, but he shared a second comedy convention, parody, with creators in both the fine and popular arts. The scholar Gilbert Highet comments that parody is one of the major vehicles of satire.[32] As a satirist of some of the dominant values and institutions of his time, Allen occasionally used parody to good effect, but he also used it simply because it was an ancient and effective convention of his profession.[33]

Parody had deep roots in entertainment. One need only recall Mark Twain's use of Shakespeare in *Huckleberry*

Finn to know that Allen had skilled and honored predecessors in the use of parody. As Lawrence Levine notes: "Twain was employing one of the most popular forms of humor in nineteenth-century America."[34] Nathaniel Benchley, whose father, Robert, was a skilled parodist, has suggested that the goal of such writing is more than exaggeration to the point of ridicule. The author, work, or category of works parodied ought to represent real achievement because "there is no point jeering at third-rate material." Parody poses unique challenges for the writer, who must enlarge and distort while imitating, and must have an audience with some knowledge of the original.[35] Measured against such literary criteria, most radio parodies, Allen's included, failed.

Many of Allen's parodies were of contemporary works, a strategy that allowed him to exploit what he and his audience knew best. But his successful adaptations of Sir William S. Gilbert and Sir Arthur Sullivan's *H.M.S. Pinafore* and the *Mikado* proved that he could deal with other materials as well. Parodies of both works had appeared as early as the late 1870s, and Allen took advantage of a new wave of interest in them in the 1930s and 1940s.[36] Allen's **"Brooklyn Pinafore,"** first broadcast on November 25, 1945, also drew on the media-generated zany reputations of New York's Borough of Brooklyn; its baseball team, the Dodgers; and the team's manager, Leo "The Lip" Durocher.[37] It was the music of *H.M.S. Pinafore,* rather than its story or characters, that listeners recognized, a feat in itself when we consider the very limited vocal talents of Allen and Durocher. The story line of the parody ran as follows:

The arch rivals of the Dodgers, the New York Giants, have invaded Ebbets Field, the Dodgers' home park, to challenge the Brooklyn team.

> Brooklyn rooters are sitting around in their underwear. Ushers are running up and down the aisles with rocks looking for Giant fans. Peddlers are going through the stands selling raw meat sandwiches . . . for the kiddies.

Dodger captain Leo Durocher gathers his players around home plate, and sings his boast: "I am quiet and subdued. . . . I never call an umpire jerk!" The chorus of ball players knows better: "So give a cheer and give a shout / For the Dodger captain wit' the big loud mouth!" From the bleachers a "mystery girl" throws a rose to Leo. More accustomed to flying rocks than flowers in Ebbets Field, Durocher finds the young woman. "Go out and moider dem slobs," she shouts encouragement to the Dodgers, and then confesses her love for Leo.

> I'm called little Bobby-Socks
> Sweet Little Bobby-Socks
> My heart for you, Lippy, could boist.

But they cannot marry until her "old man" approves, "and dat's gonna be tough."

The climax occurs in the bottom of the ninth inning. With two men out, Leo drives the ball into the outfield. He rounds the bases and slides across home plate as the Giant defender's throw arrives. The home-plate umpire, "Cockeye Allen," screams the verdict: "You're *ouuuuuuttttttt.*" As the argument over the call rages on, Bobby-Socks introduces the umpire as her father. "Me marry an umpire's daughter?" Durocher exclaims. "They'll throw me outta 'Who's Who.'" But umpire and manager make peace, as Cockeye sighs: "At last an umpire hears a kind word in Brooklyn." The production ends with a gentle thrust at baseball, as Allen explains how he became a major league umpire.

> As the years went by I grew up a schnook
> My eyes were so bad I couldn't read a book
> The Army took me but they sent me back
> I tried to kiss the General 'cause I thought he was a
>   WAC
> I'm still half blind with no physique
> That's why I am an umpire in the National League.

As the **"Brooklyn Pinafore"** closes, Durocher pledges not to berate umpires any longer. A new day has dawned in Brooklyn.

Other Allen parodies drew upon a broad range of materials. During his initial series of programs for Linit, Allen parodied the drama of Eugene O'Neill (program of October 30, 1932), Sir Arthur Conan Doyle's Sherlock Holmes stories (November 27, 1932), the Greek drama *Lysistrata* (January 1, 1933), and the Tom Show based on popular dramatic versions of *Uncle Tom's Cabin* (February 12, 1933). In later series, he wrote parodies of the following: *Mutiny on the Bounty* (November 21, 1935); *Showboat* (June 21, 1939); *Dr. Jekyll and Mr. Hyde* (October 8, 1941); *Les Misérables* (October 18, 1942); *Jane Eyre* (February 20, 1944); the motion picture *The Lost Weekend,* with guest Ray Milland (March 24, 1940); *Western Union* (February 26, 1941); *Citizen Kane* (November 5, 1941); and *The Egg and I* (April 13, 1947). In the skit **"Nicotine Alley"** Allen had fun with the long-running Erskine Caldwell play *Tobacco Road.* Experienced at caricaturing hillbillies—Allen's character Teeter Fester (wordplay on *Tobacco Road*'s Jeeter Lester) tells his son to "run yer arm down the Gopher Hole" to get dinner—Allen built the little drama around the idea that backwoods folks dislike cleanliness. When the government man says that Teeter will be in "hot water" if he refuses to sell his land to the army for its training camp, he sells—to avoid taking a bath.[38]

On three of his programs, Allen did versions of the Richard Rodgers and Oscar Hammerstein II musical *Oklahoma,* which had made its debut on the wartime Broadway stage in 1943. In one skit, the musical became **"North Dakota,"** which Allen described as a "farmhand's Ballet. The stage is a wheatfield. 200 farmhands going against the grain." The opening number begins:

> Nunnnnnnnnnnn-orth Dakota
> There's nothing there but sky and dirt

Where the boundary lines
Are Burma Shave signs
And buzzards circle round alert.[39]

Whether irate North Dakotans wrote letters to CBS is not known. But on the following week's program, Allen scheduled Rodgers and Hammerstein, who appeared with a "lawsuit" charging plagiarism. All kidding aside, Allen found that parody could stimulate actual legal charges. Eleanor Biggers Cole, the widow of Charlie Chan's creator, sued Allen in 1942 for plagiarism in a parody of the Chinese detective.[40]

Allen kidded the "B" Western motion picture, Hollywood's reliable revenue producer during Allen's years on the air, with horse-opera heroes like Roy Rogers and Andy Devine or with some incongruous cast choices. Hollywood gossip columnist Louella Parsons, for example, played an Indian—"Sweet Sioux."[41] Allen ran a divorce ranch in "Reno—Land of the Great Divide," a skit that confirmed that wordplay, rather than sagebrush, grew luxuriantly across Allen's western landscapes.[42] And dialogue like the following appeared, as "Sheriff" Allen orders a Mountain Martini: "A tall glass of Buffalo Drool with a puma's eyeball floatin' in it." "A puma's eyeball?" the bartender asks. "Ayer. When ah say 'Hyar's lookin at ye,' ah like to have suthin looking back at me."[43]

Allen's clear favorite for parody was the detective story; it supplied his programs with their longest-running continuing character, and Allen's personal favorite, the Chinese detective One Long Pan, who debuted on May 1, 1935.[44] Spoofing the Sherlock Holmes tradition, hard-boiled American private eyes, and police investigators, Allen assumed many crime-solving roles: Inspector Allen of the Bedlam Detective Agency in the early 1930s; Inspector Bungle and his bloodhound Watson; Holmes imitators Hemlock Bones, Fetlock Bones, and Hemlock Drones; and Sam Shovel, Private Eye. In 1942, Allen and guest Maurice Evans presented *Macbeth* as a murder mystery, and he mocked Humphrey Bogart's popular film *The Maltese Falcon* in a skit entitled **"The Maltese Parrot."**[45]

Allen's detectives were incompetents who somehow stumbled their way through misinterpreted clues and past falsely accused suspects ultimately to a solution, all in twelve minutes of dialogue. The slapstick pace of Allen's murder-mystery skits, reminiscent of the Keystone Cops, helped reduce the detective formula to a shambles. The radio historian J. Fred MacDonald speculates that the detective story, as "a secular Passion Play," offers more to the public than entertainment. In radio's detective shows, the invariable triumph of justice reaffirmed society's moral values. The punishment of those who violated person or property sanctioned order over disorder, stability over chaos.[46] If so, then Fred Allen's detective parodies clearly came down on the side of comic chaos.

None of Allen's detectives commands respect. A police chief questions Inspector Allen's ability: "You couldn't find a Cohen in the Bronx."[47] In the skit **"Who Killed Kirk Rubin?"** One Long Pan announces: "I am the great Pan!" Mrs. Rubin responds: "Say, I could use you under my ice-box."[48] A woman tells Inspector Bungle: "By me you couldn't inspect a gas meter."[49] Long Pan has trouble with the language. For "ends abruptly," he says "bends corruptly"; he calls Ellery Queen "Celery Spleen." In each case, he discovers a "lewolower" (revolver).[50] Trying the wrong doors, Long Pan mistakenly enters closets in victims' homes, then tries to save face. It was a "clues closet," he explains in one episode.[51] Inspector Bungle orders all present at the crime scene not to move. "I got yez covered." Then he fires his gun: "It's the Bungle Test, Bud. De party dat don't jump is the body."[52] When several banquet guests confess to the murder of the after-dinner speaker, Bungle turns to the "Eenie, Meenie, Meinie, Mo" method, and fingers himself for the killing![53] "Fetlock Bones," Sherlock Holmes's brother-in-law, appears to practice an amazing deductive ability, in imitation of his famous relative. Arriving at a country manor, he explains: "I know you are Mr. Basketville's butler, Rancid. You were born near Surry With The Fringe On Top. You have no shin in your right leg. Your father raises aspidistras and you have a cousin Cecil who has a punctured ear drum." Astounded, the butler asks, "'Ow did you know?" "I'm on your draft board," Bones confesses.[54]

The bizarre solutions to Allen's murder mysteries, in keeping with a comedy of exaggeration and fantasy, uncovered crimes of shallow frivolity rather than greed or passion. A "Vegetarian Fanatic" named Quentin Scurvy murders wealthy businessman Barclay Rappaport, "the Meatball King."[55] A mystery writer, S. S. VanBrine, fakes his own death. He wants Long Pan to solve his "murder," which he then will incorporate into his latest novel.[56] A sports reporter kills the football star because he cannot spell his name, Koskicheckowitch.[57] Gaffney Grimes did not die at the hands of a murderer, but rather passed away while quietly listening to the Jack Benny program. "Gaffney Grimes was bored to death."[58]

Insult comedy was especially prevalent on Allen's programs during the 1930s and early 1940s. Allen's "feud" with Jack Benny was the most prominent, but it was hardly an isolated application of the theory that verbal abuse is humorous.[59] To create and sustain listener interest, program planners created, among others, feuds pitting Bergen's dummy Charlie McCarthy against W. C. Fields, Bob Hope against Bing Crosby, Fibber McGee against Doctor Gamble, and the Bickersons, husband and wife, against each other.

Insult comedy was one expression of a broader category of humor that prospered on radio's comedy-variety programs. It could be termed insider or celebrity comedy, since it milked show business, particularly its stars' daily lives and their physical and personality traits, for laughs. As he featured weekly celebrity guests beginning in 1942, Allen increasingly resorted to insider humor, which did nothing to enhance the quality of his comedy or his reputation as a creative popular artist.[60] Insider and insult humor also largely ignored the listening audience, except when Allen's comic ridicule featured imagination-stretching language to create some vivid images. Celebrity humor was generally vapid—"the mechanical joke," as John Crosby called it—based on stars' traits (Sinatra's skinny frame; Benny's thinning hair; Durante's nose) or possessions (Jessel's big house in Beverly Hills; Crosby's racehorses).[61] Edwin O'Connor termed such sterile comedy "no laughing matter," a judgment validated by time.[62]

Nevertheless, insult humor was a mainstay of radio comedy, as Allen's announcer Harry Von Zell once acknowledged: "You know how all these programs start, Fred. If the announcer doesn't insult the comedian, people don't even know it's a comedy show."[63] If he received their barbs, Allen also insulted the men who read his commercials. Calling one of them, Jimmy Wallington, a "drip," he continued: "You are so wet . . . if you ever lie down the government will stock you with trout."[64] Other cast members joined the verbal warfare. Allen involved his orchestra leaders, for example, just as Jack Benny did Phil Harris and Edgar Bergen employed Ray Noble. A continuing comic pretext was that Peter Van Steeden on the *Town Hall Tonight* series believed himself to be a more able comedian than Allen, and therefore deserved a larger role. Allen disparaged these aspirations with such remarks as "You're as funny as a tack in a baby's rompers" and then dismissed Van Steeden's musical talents as well. "You wouldn't be on key if you sat on a Yale lock."[65] Vocalists, like tenor Kenny Baker in the early 1940s, were natural targets of gibes also. Allen said of him: "He not only doesn't know anything. He doesn't even suspect anything."[66] Characters in skits earned definition and dimension from the insults they attracted. "You little waste of skin" described the assistant to a radio network vice-president.[67] Entire quarter-hour segments of Allen's programs during the late 1930s and early 1940s featured carefully written, artfully contrived insult sessions that pitted the comedian against announcer, against band leader, against tenor— with Portland thrown in for good measure.

Portland appeared during her "spot" on these programs with friends who, if anything, were crazier and more obnoxious than she was. As they pestered Allen, the war of insults escalated.

> *Allen:* The Allens are the cream of society, Mr. Shill, and we curdle in the presence of the riff as well as the raff.
>
> *Shill:* Man your tonsils, tornado mouth. I'm studyin' to be a tree surgeon and I'm apt to do a little homework and tear you limb from limb.
>
> *Portland:* Gosh, If I'd known it was going to be this kind of a fight I'd have brought a dictionary.[68]

On another occasion, a Mrs. Bisby and her "answer to Margaret Sanger," son Gansvort, invade Allen's program.

"With a name like that," Allen tells the boy, "a lot of people are going to get a good laugh passing your tombstone." He reminds Mrs. Bisby, a stage mother, "that all of the nags aren't at the Racetracks."[69]

Allen's feud with Jack Benny, in which he was the more aggressive originator of acidic *bons mots,* offered listeners a verbal feast of deprecatory characterization. The feud was the centerpiece of one film, *Love Thy Neighbor* (1940), and it spiced others, such as Allen's *It's in the Bag* (1945). Over the years, the two comedians pursued their rivalry in face-to-face broadcast appearances, through commentary volleyed between their respective shows, and as their stooges, such as Benny's black valet "Rochester" (Eddie Anderson) and tenor (Dennis Day), appeared as guest celebrities on the enemy's program. Each comic parodied the other's program format, especially Benny, who presented "Clown Hall Tonight" and "Benny's Boulevard" (for Allen's Alley) on several occasions. For his part, Allen wrote reams of dialogue about Benny, including skits—such as **"The House That Jack Built"** in May 1938—and one entire hour-long program, on May 7, 1941, as a ten-year "panaversary" of Benny's radio career.[70] It was a "tribute" in which Allen managed to avoid speaking Benny's name even once, while praising Jack's cast members.

Samples of Allen's Benny insults deserve inclusion here, as further illustrations of insult comedy. One Benny trait that Allen highlighted was his supposed anemia and poor physical condition. Benny had no muscles. "His arm looks like a buggy-whip with fingers. I've got veins in my nose bigger than Benny's arm. Benny's as soft as a bag of wet mice."[71] And, on another occasion, "Benny looks as though he just got down to give his pallbearers' shoulders a rest."[72]

Each man belittled the other's professional success. During their big "showdown" in March 1937, Benny claimed that, unlike Allen's, his show had listeners. "Keep your family out of this" was Allen's retort. Benny bragged that while Allen's movie audiences left before the end of the picture, his stayed to the finish. Of course, Allen explained, "because the manager promised to run it backwards to see if it made any sense."[73] Benny had played Abraham Lincoln in a tableau in the 1930 edition of Earl Carroll's *Vanities.* "If Benny was Lincoln he'd have freed Rochester years ago," Allen observed.[74]

One of the major themes of self-deprecation on Benny's own show was his violin playing. Allen joined in the fun. "When Benny starts to saw on that melody coffin of his, it sounds like a she-wildcat defending her young. Benny a violin-player? He's been playing the violin 30 years and still has trouble getting it out of the case."[75] Benny's cheapness was another enduring theme. "That guy's so cheap," Allen said, "he'd put his finger down a moth's throat to get his cloth back."[76] The only time Jack ever left a tip "was the day he couldn't finish his asparagus."[77]

And a final word on his rival's contribution: "If Benny goes down in history it will just be gravity."[78]

This remark, and others quoted here, signify Allen's interest in manipulating language to create aural comedy. Radio aficionados know his program of March 20, 1940, as the "eagle show," during which the feathered "Mr. Ramshaw" escaped from his trainer during the guest spot. But the show is as notable for the puns as for the bird, which flew about Studio 8-H in a typical evening of Allen's comedy of language. Words with similar sounds and words with double meanings were among the tactics of verbal confusion that the comedian and his cast employed throughout the hour-long show. The resort community of Old Orchard Beach, Maine, for example, recently had designated Allen an honorary constable. He brags to Harry Von Zell that he will "get the drip on criminals" with his water pistol. The annual flower show in Madison Square Garden brings forth a growth of word twisting. Portland and her mother admired the "rotodoldrums" at the show. Visitors could admire "every rose . . . but Billy," and "every bloom but Sol" (showman Billy Rose and congressman Sol Bloom). The Pussywillows brought their "Kittywillows." A sunflower, after receiving a dose of vitamin B-1, "went out looking for Alf Landon." On the Republican ticket in 1940, Allen muses, "it might come out dewey." Prior to the eagle's flight, Allen emptied his comedic vocabulary onto that "bloated sparrow," that "King Kong robin." Pretending to be afraid of his feathered guest, the comedian claimed he "hears no eagle, sees no eagle, and speaks no eagle." Inspecting the bird's weaponry, Allen remarks: "I'd like to have his clause in my contract."[79]

The language play in which Allen reveled suggests continuity with an older, word-dominated culture that some thought had died with the advent of the electronic media. And even though it is an elemental source of humor, verbal gaming ought not, for that reason alone, to attract derision. Not only was it an appropriate humor for radio; it also drew upon a timeless, cross-cultural wellspring of laughter. As children learn to speak, Joseph Boskin points out,

> they experiment and play with word sounds, meanings, and patter. The world of language becomes a marvelous playpen of the toys and fun of double meanings, twists, oddities, confusions and repeats. In the early years, the play of words enables fantasies and absurdities to abound undeterred by rational considerations.[80]

The commercial mass amusements that preceded radio recognized the appeal of language play to adult audiences. "On the whole," Albert F. McLean, Jr., writes, "vaudeville humor tended to be verbal, finding its most effective expression in words rather than gestures."[81] Earlier, the minstrel show popularized "a new verbal humor" that dealt with the problems of modern city life. Robert C. Toll observes: "In the rapid-fire exchanges between interlocutor and endmen lay the origin of modern urban humor, the humor of vaudeville and radio, the

humor that depended on playing with the use and misuse of words."[82] Norris W. Yates points out that Robert Benchley, S. J. Perelman, and James Joyce were among the many modern writers who employed the pun frequently and effectively.[83] And nineteenth-century humorous essayists and lecturers, such as Artemus Ward, "Petroleum V. Nasby," and "Bill Arp," spread generous doses of wordplay throughout their work.[84] "Language became a prank" in the movie comedies starring the Marx Brothers, Andrew Bergman writes; even in a visual medium, "the brothers made word play an art."[85]

Another variety of Fred Allen's language-based comedy was dialect, the forte of versatile voice actors who played a wide range of foreign ethnic and American regional character types. Appropriate on one of the last comedy shows to broadcast from New York, for example, was that city's version of English-language pronunciation. Allen often depicted confused out-of-towners grappling with the local dialect, as they received directions—"you gittabus at toidy-toid and toid"—to the "erstaba" (Oyster bar) or "moom pitcha" (moving pictures).[86] Although the use of ethnic humor diminished under increasing criticism during Allen's years on the air, it, together with American regionalism, remained an effective source of audible comedy. . . .

Allen poked fun at those who would reform the vernacular and change specialized argots in the interests of "proper" English. In 1936, the city of Charleston, South Carolina, encouraged its law enforcers to improve English usage over the police radio. Exaggerating this real news story, Allen had his "Town Hall" news show college professors instructing cops in a before—after contrast. The old-style police radio message:

> Mob of finks in hot boiler casing First National. All heeled. Get drop and fan for rods before they crash the joint.

became this:

> Paging Police Vehicle Number 7. Group of unspeakable characters in purloined motor conveyance inspecting First National Bank. The ruffians have concealed weapons. Suggest you submit their wardrobe to severe scrutinization.[87]

At other times, Allen made light of politicians' and lawyers' stilted language. Again on the **"Town Hall News,"** a windy senator protested to the chairman that he could not concentrate on the work at hand because of "a miniature roll of the plant genus nicotine which has been kindled through the application of a splint of wood so prepared with sulpher as to make it ignitible by tinder." In other words, someone in the balcony was smoking.[88] Allen exposed the deficiencies of the pompous and pretentious through exaggerated versions of their specialized argots.

Many radio comedy writers strained their imaginations to devise preposterous names for program characters as a part of their comedy of language. Allen was one of the best at inventing names that described skit characters or that simply sounded ridiculous. A few examples follow, with the program date in parentheses:

> Tungsten B. Timid (11/24/33)
> Lotta Spunk, chorus girl (4/10/35)
> Dr. Rampant Pelf (10/14/36)
> Dalrymple Offal (12/29/37)
> Folderol Retard (5/11/38)
> Holden Strap, subway commuter (5/10/39)
> Professor Latent Trend (5/17/39)
> Judge Nullen Void (12/6/39)
> Roquefort Fumes (5/1/40)
> Farfel Tard (1/8/41)
> Urquhardt Pollen (5/21/41)
> Dr. Rancid Squirm (12/3/41)
> Eustis Gwelf (4/12/42)
> Nanette Newt (5/3/42)
> Welby Tidball (5/30/48)

Outlandish names, a form of verbal slapstick, were ideally suited to the broadcast medium.

Verbally inventive also were Allen's comic definitions of words and concepts that appeared randomly in his skits; while not comparable in quality to a work such as Ambrose Bierce's *Devil's Dictionary,* these playful definitions continue a tradition of humor. On the radio (rather than in print), this wordplay demanded the careful attention and momentary reflection of the audience. Allen characterized a gentleman farmer as "one who ignores crops and only raises his hat" (December 18, 1932); a hot dog is a "pork zeppelin" (April 18, 1934). He described as "parenthesis legged" a cowboy whose legs conformed to a horse's sides (August 29, 1934). An evangelist who would prohibit other people's pleasures was a "Banishing American" (January 16, 1935). An old maid was "a woman who was engaged once too seldom" (June 5, 1935). "Insurance is a contract people sign agreeing to go through life poor so that they can die rich" (February 19, 1936). A red nose was a "smouldering proboscis" (June 15, 1938); a pretzel a "surrealist breadstick" (November 23, 1938); piano tuning "Steinway osteopathing" (February 15, 1939); a spitball a "saliva spheroid" (December 6, 1939); a zephyr "a typhoon with no ambition" (March 27, 1940); a worm a "nudist caterpillar" (May 1, 1940). Minerva Pious, in the Brooklyn dialect that she did so well, defined a nymph: "It's like a pixie, only yer wet" (October 30, 1940). "Life," Allen said, "is a lull between the stork and the epitaph" (May 1, 1940). Not all these definitions were original with Allen, of course, but even when he appropriated material from entertainment's public domain, he had in mind radio's unique requirements as a listening medium.

In many scripts, either by reproducing sounds or by talking about reproducing them, Allen further explored the varieties of aural comedy for his listeners. During early *Town Hall Tonight* broadcasts, for example, he closed his news segment with "the outstanding sound of the week." A simple exercise in utilizing radio's unique properties, the feature would have made no sense in a visual medium. Since Allen did not continue the feature for long, he may have doubted its success. But while it lasted, listeners received audible "punch lines" like these: General Hugh S. Johnson pans the Supreme Court's decision overturning the National Recovery Act—sound of kitchen pans rattling (May 29, 1935). Vendors at Coney Island sell 3 million hot dogs in a single day—dogs barking (June 19, 1935). Republicans complain that New Deal spending for public works "will empty the nation's coffers"—cast members cough in unison (October 23, 1935).

Listeners to Allen's Linit series came to know one featured supporting actor, Roy Atwell, for his audible mangling of spoken English. Known on the stage as a "purveyor of 'spoonerisms,'" Atwell also called himself the "Doctor of English as it is broken."[89] In his weekly (and, for today's listener, weak) program appearance, Atwell transposed the first letters of words and in other ways provided listeners with audible comedy. "Good morning" became "Wood Gorning," "free speech" "free screech," and so on.[90] Audiences in the early 1930s seemed to appreciate Atwell's comic manipulations of language.

A more creative use of the aural medium were those instances in which program participants talked about sounds, perhaps in the context of a sound technician's assignment. Allen told guest Norman Corwin, who knew something about radio production, about one of his greatest challenges: "We had a caterpillar slide down a slippery elm tree, bump against a pussy willow and then land in a pile of chicken feathers." After several failed attempts to reproduce that sound, the engineer "tied some peach fuzz to the end of a tassel and started spanking a wet toupee."[91] Other scripts played with sound in different ways. One of his murder cases brought One Long Pan and Mr. Moto (played by his guest, the mystery film actor Peter Lorre) to a broadcast studio. For a time, the detectives puzzle over the contradiction between two bullet holes and reports by witnesses of a single gunshot. Suspecting that the murderer had fired from within the control room, and then had exited so quickly that the sound of one shot remained trapped in the soundproof room, they open the door. Listeners heard a shot.[92]

While some of Allen's dialogue lightheartedly played with sound, other script material created vivid images in listeners' minds. Appearing throughout Allen's long career, ridiculous and improbable fragments of comic exaggeration betrayed the tall-tale tradition and stretched beyond belief the listeners' sound-dependent imaginations. A carnival's tattooed man, for example, complains that added pounds have distorted his tattoos by stretching them: Whistler's Mother has moved from his chest to under his arm. The freak show's rubber man, wondering if he needs a shave, pulls his face into his lap to "have a look at it."[93] With "John Doe," an early resident of Allen's Alley, the comedian discussed the recent cold wave in 1942. Doe reported:

"The mercury finally went down so far it got out of the thermometer and went down a mousehole." Since the mice ate the mercury, Allen asked, does that mean that they will rise when the mercury rises? Maybe so, Doe responds, and he has an answer to mice who scurry about his house several feet off the floor. "I'll jack up the cat."[94] In another Allen's Alley interview, "Socrates Mulligan" tells Allen about his experience with a loan shark. For years, Socrates had paid 6 percent interest on a loan. But when the loan shark died, his son raised the rate to 9 percent. "I says what will your father think when he looks down from Heaven and sees you chargin me nine?" The loan shark's heir has this response: "When my father looks down from Heaven and sees this nine—to him it will look like a six."[95] Portland's mother's skin was so tight after her face lift that when "she sits down her mouth flies open."[96] Allen knew of a farmer who discarded used razor blades in his fields. His crops grew in slices.[97]

From the first script in October 1933 to the last in June 1949, Allen indulged in puns as titles of skits—**"The Story of the First Lighthouse, or How Pincus Quagmire Brought Home the Beacon"** (August 8, 1934) and **"Pure As The Driven Snow, or As Ye Snow So Shall Ye Sweep"** (January 30, 1935). Other delightful twists of phrase appeared wherever there was an opening for them. Those that follow represent a random sampling: Professor Gulpo, the sword swallower in a freak show, "swallows anything from his pride to a lightnin rod" (November 20, 1932). The British Lord Bottom Bottom calls his wife "Eczema because the old girl has her rash moments" (October 27, 1933). The Mighty Allen Art Players were "that sterling troupe that may be part pewter . . . sterling to themselves, and pewter their audiences" (October 30, 1935). "Come up and saw me sometime" says the magician's assistant to One Long Pan (March 4, 1936). Allen is "easily upset," Portland claims. "His grandmother was frightened by a canoe" (April 29, 1936). A ship's passenger complains that there are no eggs "in the crow's nest." "Captain" Allen: "Tell her I'll have the ship lay to" (March 10, 1937). Allen says to a guest who runs an ice business: "I guess there are times when an ice-lady has to hold her tong" (March 23, 1938). Of the marble lions stationed at the steps of the New York Public Library: "New Yorkers like to read between the lions" (April 26, 1939). People who smuggled cigarettes into New York from New Jersey were "buttleggers" (December 6, 1939). Timken Slaw, quiz-show contestant, says he works as a "kite-retailer." Asks Allen: "You sell kites retail?" "No, if the tail comes off of your kite, I re-tail it" (January 8, 1941). A college talent winner from Pittsburgh praises his city. "It soots you," responds Allen (April 5, 1942). Resurrecting an old vaudeville joke, Allen asks "Ajax Cassidy" of Allen's Alley, "Have you got vertigo?" No, the Irishman replies. "Only two blocks" (November 24, 1946). And finally, a comment on Mayor Fiorello La Guardia. "The Mayor's a dynamo, Miss Reel," Allen says in a skit. "That's why City Hall has to be kept near the Battery" (January 22, 1941).

Like the bags under his eyes, Allen's nasal voice was the target of considerable kidding from magazine writers and his own program's guest stars. His voice was his trademark, and it was a fortuitous one for a comedian who was so attentive to the needs of a listening audience. Portland Hoffa's broadcast voice was also distinctive. In his memoirs, Allen recalled that his spouse's radio character, "a subnormal adolescent," grew out of her radio voice, which he described as sounding like "two slate pencils mating or a clarinet reed calling for help."[98] Both performers' voices validated columnist Orrin E. Dunlap, Jr.'s maxim of radio comedy: "By their voices ye shall know them."[99]

And that is the major point of this [essay]: Allen made significant and successful efforts to shape his material to the medium on which he performed. His comedy of language, his verbal slapstick, stand out even today.

NOTES

[1] Lawrence W. Levine, "American Culture and the Great Depression," *Yale Review* 74 (Winter 1985): 221.

[2] S. J. Perelman, "The Great Sourpuss; or, Should Auld Acquaintance Be Exhumed?" *Holiday* 12 (December 1952): 95, 97-98, 101, 102. Arthur Frank Wertheim links radio comedy and Depression conditions in his "Relieving Social Tensions: Radio Comedy and the Great Depression," *Journal of Popular Culture* 10 (Winter 1976): 501-519; see also J. Fred MacDonald, *Don't Touch That Dial! Radio Programming in American Life, 1920-1960* (Chicago: Nelson-Hall, 1979), 94, 113-114.

[3] John K. Hutchens defined a radio comedy formula as "a pattern that will have a comfortable familiarity about it, something to which you can look forward with assurance from week to week." Hutchens, "The Funny Fellows," *New York Times,* October 11, 1942, sec. 8, p. 10.

[4] The verdict was not unanimous, but many contemporary literary critics and cultural arbiters decided that radio had little to do, in its origins or contributions, with "real" American humor. "Let us, for decency's sake," wrote Bernard DeVoto in 1937, "say nothing of the radio skit—after all, there has always been feloniously bad humor." DeVoto, "The Lineage of Eustace Tilley" [review of Walter Blair's *Native American Humor*], reprinted in *Critical Essays on American Humor,* ed. William Bedford Clark and W. Craig Turner (Boston: G. K. Hall, 1984), 75. More careful students of the media disagree. The historian Daniel Czitrom deprecates the idea that the commercial values of advertisers and broadcasters shaped all programming and that the "media have . . . manufactured content out of thin air. Historically, the raw materials for 'media fare,' as well as its creators, have been drawn from an assortment of cultural milieus." He writes of "the media's reliances on older cultural forms adapted to new technologies." Czitrom, "Dialectical Tensions in the American Media

Past and Present," in *Popular Culture in America,* ed. Paul Buhle (Minneapolis: University of Minnesota Press, 1987), 14. That radio comedy illustrates a sharing across often artificial categories such as "media" and "art," or "mass culture" and "high culture," is a concept central to this book.

[5] "The end of the nineteenth century did not, of course, abruptly halt the flow of humor in the older traditions." Walter Blair added this statement and a subsequent discussion of persisting traditions to the revision of his *Native American Humor* (1987; reprint, San Francisco: Chandler, 1960), 162. In the reissue of another book, Blair notes that "both media [sound movies and radio] were very cordial to oral storytellers. So several who'd developed skills in burlesque, vaudeville, and stage revues became fantastically popular performers on screens, on airwaves, or (as a rule) on both." Blair cites W. C. Fields, Jack Pearl (as Baron Munchausen), and Jim Jordan (as Fibber McGee). Blair, *Tall-Tale America: A Legendary History of Our Humorous Heroes* (1944; reprint, Chicago: University of Chicago Press, 1987), 262. See also Walter Blair, "'A Man's Voice Speaking': A Continuum in American Humor," in *Veins of Humor,* ed. Harry Levin, Harvard English Studies no. 3 (Cambridge: Harvard University Press, 1972), 185-204.

[6] Quotes from *Variety*'s reviews of two Allen programs, January 9, 1934, 32, and March 9, 1938, 32.

[7] Arlen J. Hansen, "Entropy and Transformation: Two Types of American Humor," *American Scholar* 43 (Summer 1974): 412, 421. "Exaggeration is as much a part of our national inheritance as are democracy and our capacity for Dream." Sanford Pinsker, "On or about December 1910: When Human Character—and American Humor—Changed," in Clark and Turner, *Critical Essays on American Humor,* 188; see also the editors' "Introduction," 2.

[8] Douglas Gilbert, *American Vaudeville: Its Life and Times* (1940; reprint, New York: Dover, 1968), 251; see also p. 263 on Allen.

[9] Benny described his radio persona in Orrin E. Dunlap, Jr., "Comedian Rides the Radio in the Saddle of Reality," *New York Times,* April 28, 1940, sec. 9, p. 12. Allen once called Benny "the first comedian in radio to realize you could get big laughs by ridiculing yourself instead of your stooges." Quoted in Milt Josefsberg, *The Jack Benny Show: The Life and Times of America's Best-Loved Entertainer* (New Rochelle, N.Y.: Arlington House, 1977), 60; see also Arthur Frank Wertheim, *Radio Comedy* (New York: Oxford University Press, 1979), chap. 7, "The Fall Guy."

[10] Tapes of the "Jack Benny Program," December 7, 1947, and "Fibber McGee and Molly," December 23, 1941.

[11] THT script, September 26, 1934.

[12] THT script, February 16, 1938.

[13] FAS script, May 26, 1946.

[14] SBR script, September 22, 1933.

[15] THT script, January 27, 1937.

[16] THT script, June 8, 1938.

[17] TST script, December 20, 1942.

[18] Gilbert Seldes, *The Great Audience* (New York: Viking Press, 1951), 124-125.

[19] LBC script, January 22, 1933.

[20] HOS script, May 23, 1934, quoted; also SBR script, August 25, 1933.

[21] THT script, June 9, 1937.

[22] HOS script, April 18, 1934.

[23] THT script, March 22, 1939.

[24] THT script, May 15, 1935.

[25] Shirley Louise Staples, "From 'Barney's Courtship' to Burns and Allen: Male-Female Comedy Teams in American Vaudeville, 1865-1932," doctoral dissertation, Tufts University, 1981, 325. See also Wertheim, *Radio Comedy,* chap. 9, "Scatter-brains," on Jane and Goodman Ace ("Easy Aces") and George Burns and Gracie Allen.

[26] The latter phrase is Allen's in letter to Joe Kelly, March 20, 1933, in Joe McCarthy, ed., *Fred Allen's Letters* (Garden City, N.Y.: Doubleday, 1965), 92; for characterizations of Portland's radio persona, see Hugh Pentecost and Virginia Faulkner, "Murder on the Fred Allen Program," *American Magazine* 135 (July 1944): 145; Arnold M. Auerbach, *Funny Men Don't Laugh* (Garden City, N.Y.: Doubleday, 1965), 132.

[27] THT script, February 23, 1938.

[28] SHR script, January 24, 1934.

[29] HOS script, March 21, 1934.

[30] TST script, November 29, 1942.

[31] THT script, March 4, 1936.

[32] Gilbert Highet, *The Anatomy of Satire* (Princeton: Princeton University Press, 1962), 69. Highet defines parody "as imitation which, through distortion and exaggeration, evokes amusement, derision, and sometimes scorn." Ibid.

[33] Sources that illuminate our tradition of parody include Robert C. Toll, *Blacking Up: The Minstrel Show in Nineteenth-Century America* (New York: Oxford University Press, 1974), 93-96 (parodies of *Uncle Tom's Cabin*); David Grimsted, *Melodrama Unveiled: American Theater and Culture, 1800-1850* (Chicago: University of Chicago Press, 1968), 235-240; Walter Blair, "Burlesques in Nineteenth-Century American Humor," *American Literature* 2 (November 1930): 236-247; Constance Rourke, *American Humor: A Study of the National Character* (1931; reprint, Garden City, N.Y.; Doubleday Anchor, 1953), 101-110.

[34] Lawrence W. Levine, "William Shakespeare and the American People: A Study in Cultural Transformation," *American Historical Review* 89 (February 1984): 34; see also Ray B. Browne, "Shakespeare in American Vaudeville and Negro Minstrelsy," *American Quarterly* 12 (Fall 1960): 374-391.

[35] Nathaniel Benchley, "Introduction," in *Twentieth Century Parody, American and British* (New York: Harcourt, Brace, 1960), xiv.

[36] Earl F. Bargainner, "W. S. Gilbert and American Musical Theatre," *Journal of Popular Culture 12* (Winter 1978): 448; see also pp. 446-447.

[37] FAS script, November 25, 1945. Allen repeated the skit on April 14, 1946. Durocher was a frequent guest on Allen's programs. For commentary on the "Brooklyn Pinafore," see the following issues of *Variety:* November 28, 1945, 30; March 6, 1946, 37; May 18, 1949, 30. On November 23, 1947, Allen presented the "Football Pinafore," and on May 15, 1949, a "Television Pinafore."

[38] TST script, March 19, 1941.

[39] TST script, April 23, 1944.

[40] TST script, May 20, 1942, 30. Allen wrote to H. Allen Smith: "the charlie chan estate it [*sic*] attempting to shake us down and will settle for $3000. we killed charlie chan in a sketch a couple of years ago. what harm was done, i don't know but since warner oland departed this life the chan pickings have been slim and apparently the derr bigger widow grabs at any chance to catch a fleeting dollar." Allen to h.a., nov. 9th [1942], Smith Papers.

[41] TST script, February 13, 1944.

[42] THT script, January 9, 1935.

[43] TST script, February 13, 1944.

[44] *New York Sun,* May 1, 1937, clipping in Allen clipping file, Billy Rose Collection.

[45] TST scripts, March 8, 1942, and February 11, 1942.

[46] MacDonald, *Don't Touch That Dial!,* 157-159.

[47] THT script, June 5, 1935.

[48] THT script, October 9, 1935.

[49] THT script, January 1, 1936.

[50] THT script, April 21, 1937; TST script, June 6, 1943.

[51] THT script, December 14, 1938.

[52] THT script, May 17, 1939.

[53] TST script, December 25, 1940.

[54] TST script, April 9, 1944.

[55] THT script, October 7, 1936.

[56] THT script, April 21, 1937.

[57] THT script, November 23, 1938.

[58] TST script, January 24, 1943.

[59] Citing radio feuds as an example, Lawrence W. Levine has noted the flowering of "ritual insult" during the 1930s. "The practice of ritual insult was a perfect channel for anger which was either unfocused or which could not be aimed at its appropriate target. It is not coincidence that during the Great Depression, when the American people had a substantial amount of anger of this sort, ritual insult flourished in popular humor." Levine, *Black Culture and Black Consciousness: Afro-American Folk Thought from Slavery to Freedom* (New York: Oxford University Press, 1977), 356. Levine does not acknowledge that insulting also has roots in conventionalized white commercial amusement. Of successful radio ad-libbers, John K. Hutchens wrote: "In the exacting school of audience response they learned the type of humor that is most immediately effective, which is, in a word, the insult." Hutchens, "The Tricky Ad Lib," *New York Times Magazine,* May 24, 1942, 29. In 1938 *Variety* criticized a recent Benny-Allen radio appearance. "Toward the end the gagging degenerated to mere bandying of comic name-calling. It was faintly Gus Sun." The Gus Sun Circuit connected a string of smalltime vaudeville theaters; the ritual insult was a vaudeville convention. *Variety,* March 30, 1938, 34.

[60] Five years earlier, however, *Variety* recognized that "Allen's program abounds in 'inside stuff' references to show business." *Variety,* January 27, 1937, 31.

[61] John Crosby's column in the *New York Herald-Tribune,* entitled "The Mechanical Joke," January 3, 1951, appeared in his *Out of the Blue: A Book about Radio and Television* (New York: Simon and Schuster, 1952), 54-56.

[62] Edwin O'Connor, "No Laughing Matter," *Atlantic Monthly* 178 (September 1946): 130; for examples of celebrity humor, see FAS scripts, March 9, 1947 (Milton Berle, guest), and May 11, 1947 (Bing Crosby, guest).

[63] FAS script, October 18, 1939.

[64] TST script, December 10, 1941.

[65] THT scripts, January 26, 1938, and February 1, 1939.

[66] TST script, November 5, 1941.

[67] TST script, February 25, 1942.

[68] THT script, January 2, 1935.

[69] THT script, March 6, 1935.

[70] THT script, May 18, 1938, for "House"; TST script, May 7, 1941. Benny parodied Allen's show on his broadcast of April 5, 1936, to cite one example.

[71] TST script, February 1, 1939.

[72] TST script, January 16, 1944.

[73] Both quotes from script of "Jack Benny Program," March 14, 1937; copy in Allen Papers.

[74] TST script, November 20, 1940.

[75] TST script December 18, 1940.

[76] THT script, March 15, 1939.

[77] FAS script, December 9, 1945.

[78] TST script, December 18, 1940.

[79] Tape recording of FAS, March 20, 1940.

[80] Joseph Boskin, *Humor and Social Change in Twentieth-Century America* (Boston: Trustees of the Public Library of the City of Boston, 1979), 14.

[81] Albert F. McLean, *American Vaudeville as Ritual* (Lexington: University of Kentucky Press, 1965), 19.

[82] Robert C. Toll, *On with the Show: The First Century of Show Business in America* (New York: Oxford University Press, 1976), 95; elsewhere Toll quotes minstrel headliner Lew Dockstader in 1916: "The pun and the conundrum were mighty popular with our grandfathers. They screamed over both." Toll, *Blacking-Up,* 54; see also Rourke, *American Humor,* 106.

[83] Norris W. Yates, *Robert Benchley* (New York: Twayne, 1968), 24; Norris W. Yates, *The American Humorist: Conscience of the Twentieth Century* (Ames: Iowa State University Press, 1964), 341, 343.

[84] Walter Blair and Hamlin Hill, *America's Humor: From Poor Richard to Doonesbury* (New York: Oxford University Press, 1978), 277, 280-281, 285-286, 288-289, 291.

[85] Andrew Bergman, *We're in the Money: Depression America and Its Films* (New York: New York University Press, 1971), 31.

[86] TST script, November 6, 1940.

[87] THT script, May 13, 1936.

[88] THT script, March 31, 1937. On lawyers, see THT script, April 28, 1937.

[89] The first quote is from *Chicago Sunday Tribune,* October 23, 1932, sec. 7, p. 4; the second is from LBC script, April 16, 1933.

[90] LBC scripts, October 23 and December 4, 1932.

[91] TST script, May 14, 1944; see also TST scripts, March ?, 1942, and March 7, 1943.

[92] TST script, January 3, 1943.

[93] TST script, May 3, 1942.

[94] TST script, December 27, 1942.

[95] TST script, January 2, 1944.

[96] LBC script, October 30, 1932.

[97] LBC script, December 11, 1932.

[98] Fred Allen, *Treadmill to Oblivion* (Boston: Little, Brown, 1954), 16-17.

[99] Orrin E. Dunlap, Jr., "Radio Artists Seek 'Tags' of Identification on the Air," *New York Times,* February 18, 1934, sec. 9, p. 11.

FURTHER READING

Biography

Taylor, Robert. *Fred Allen: His Life and Wit.* Boston: Little, Brown and Company, 1989, 340 p.

Based on five years' research and interviews with Allen's close associates, including Herman Wouk and Edwin O'Connor, the editor of *Treadmill to Oblivion.*

Criticism

Barnouw, Erik. *The Golden Web: A History of Broadcasting in the United States, Vol. II—1933-1953.* New York: Oxford University Press, 1988, 391 p.

Documents the demise of Allen's radio popularity due to competition from the gameshow *Stop the Music!*

Dunning, John. *The Ultimate Encyclopedia of Old-Time Radio 1925-1976*. Englewood Cliffs, N.J.: Prentice-Hall, Inc., 1976, 703 p.
    Traces the history of radio comedy and entertainment from 1926 to 1962, and includes an overview of Allen's vaudeville and radio careers.

Stein, Charles W. *American Vaudeville as Seen by Its Contemporaries*. New York: Alfred A. Knopf, 1984, 392 p.
    Includes a two-paragraph bittersweet essay on the passing of vaudeville written by Allen.

Weeks, Edward. "Allen of Allen's Alley." *Atlantic Monthly* 216, No. 1 (July 1965): 138.
    Reviews *Fred Allen's Letters*, qualifying Allen as second only to Will Rogers among twentieth-century humorists.

Dorothy Canfield Fisher

1879-1958

(Born Dorothea Frances Canfield) American novelist, educator, historian, short story and children's writer.

INTRODUCTION

Dorothy Canfield Fisher is numbered among the most influential American women of the twentieth century. Her achievements as a fiction writer include a number of realistic novels and short stories principally focused on the lives of middle-class individuals and frequently set in early twentieth-century Vermont. Among these works, Fisher produced what many critics take to be her greatest contribution to American letters, her 1930 novel *The Deepening Stream*. In addition, Fisher is remembered for her efforts as a civic-minded humanitarian and educator. Among her accomplishments: Fisher was the first woman to serve on the Vermont state board of education, she championed the reforestation movement, worked for twenty-five years as an influential member of the Book-of-the-Month Club selection committee, and wrote several esteemed books for children.

Biographical Information

Fisher was born in Lawrence, Kansas to Flavia Camp Canfield, a painter, and James Hulme Canfield, a university professor. During her childhood, Fisher's family traveled extensively. She spent a portion of her time in Paris, France—near her mother's art studio—and meanwhile in several Midwestern cities. Fisher attended college first at the University of Nebraska, where she began her acquaintance with Willa Cather, and later received her undergraduate degree from Ohio State University in 1899. After a period of study at the Sorbonne, Fisher returned to the United States to complete her Ph.D. studies in Romance languages at Columbia University and to prepare her dissertation *Corneille and Racine in England* (1904). Fisher then embarked upon an academic career and co-wrote a textbook entitled *Elementary Composition* (1906) with George R. Carpenter. Thereafter, she began publishing her short stories in several popular magazines, and produced her first novel, *Gunhild*, in 1907. That year she married John R. Fisher and together the two moved to a farm in Arlington, Vermont, which Fisher had inherited from her late grandfather. For the span of her career, Fisher would divide her time between the Arlington farm and Europe. A trip to Italy culminated in a book on education, *A Montessori Mother* (1912), while Fisher's first literary fame arrived with the publication of her second novel *The Squirrel Cage* in 1912. Now a mother, Fisher traveled to France and Spain during World War I and served as a volunteer. Fluent in French as well as several other European languages, she assisted in the rehabilitation of wounded French soldiers and cared for sick children. Returning to Vermont after the war, Fisher focused on writing fiction, producing a number of well-received short story collections and popular novels. This period also witnessed many of Fisher's significant civic accomplishments and her continued involvement in education, as well as her twenty-five-year tenure as a member of the Book-of-the-Month Club selection committee. Late in her career, Fisher began to turn her attention increasingly toward children, publishing several works intended for younger audiences. Among her last works are two historical books *Vermont Tradition: The Biography of an Outlook on Life* (1953) and *Memories of Arlington, Vermont* (1957). Fisher died in Vermont on November 9, 1958.

Major Works

While Fisher produced a considerable amount of nonfictional work, including books on education and history, her primary focus was realistic fiction in the genres of the novel and short story. Among her novels, *The Squirrel Cage* is considered her first major work. The book describes the life of Lydia Emery, a well-educated, upper-middle-class woman trapped in a shallow marriage to a man she does not love. Semi-autobiographical in nature, *The Bent Twig* (1915) features the intelligent and willful Sylvia Marshall, who becomes for a time entranced by material wealth and worldly success. Fisher treats a similar theme in *The Brimming Cup* (1921), which introduces Marise and Neale Crittenden, a young couple whose marriage is threatened by the appearance of the materialistic Vincent Marsh. *Rough-Hewn* (1922), the prequel to *The Brimming Cup*, fills in the background of the Crittendens, describing their lives until their wedding. In *The Home-Maker* (1924) Fisher exhibits her belief in equal opportunity. The novel's protagonists, a married couple, happily and successfully exchange roles as wife becomes businesswoman and husband homemaker. *Her Son's Wife* (1926) focuses on Mary Bascomb, who is scandalized by her son's marriage to a crude and uneducated young woman. Partly autobiographical, *The Deepening Stream* is a Bildungsroman that recounts the young life of Matey Gilbert, the daughter of an American university professor. The work features Fisher's liberal sentiments on marriage, education, human rights, and war throughout. *Bonfire* (1933) considers the politics of class relations in early twentieth-century Vermont. The specter of fascism and anti-Semitism in 1930s America figures prominently in Fisher's last novel, *Seasoned Timber* (1939). Fisher's works of short fiction, like her novels, recount stories of ordinary people. Such is the case in the Vermont sketches of *Hillsboro People* (1915). *The Real Motive* (1916) offers fourteen more tales, with several set in Midwestern university towns or in World War I Europe. *Home Fires in France* (1918) and *The Day of Glory* (1919) contain war stories, while the sketches of *Basque People* (1931) are drawn from time Fisher spent in the Basque region of the Pyrenees.

Critical Reception

During her lifetime Fisher enjoyed a considerable popular reputation. *The Brimming Cup* was hugely successful, as were her novels of the later 1920s and 1930s. Between 1926 and 1951, Fisher greatly influenced a large portion of the American reading public as one of the original and longest-standing judges for the Book-of-the-Month Club Board of Selection. However, despite the popularity of her fiction and the influence of her views, Fisher has generally failed to attract more than superficial critical attention. Her novels have been largely relegated to the category of bestsellers, unworthy of serious criticism. And, while some commentators have endeavored to correct this situation, the perception of Fisher as predominately a popular writer endures. In the latter portion of the twentieth century, however, a few critics have begun to reconsider the merits of Fisher's fiction and to explore her legacy as an educator and an advocate of liberalism.

PRINCIPAL WORKS

Corneille and Racine in England (criticism) 1904
Elementary Composition [with George R. Carpenter] (nonfiction) 1906
Gunhild: A Norwegian-American Episode (novel) 1907
What Shall We Do Now? (nonfiction) 1907
A Montessori Mother (nonfiction) 1912
The Squirrel Cage (novel) 1912
The Montessori Manual (nonfiction) 1913
Mothers and Children (nonfiction) 1914
The Bent Twig (novel) 1915
Hillsboro People (short stories) 1915
Fellow Captains [with Sarah N. Cleghorn] (short stories) 1916
The Real Motive (short stories) 1916
Understood Betsy (children's literature) 1917
Home Fires in France (short stories) 1918
The Day of Glory (short stories) 1919
The Brimming Cup (novel) 1921
Raw Material (short stories and sketches) 1922
Rough-Hewn (novel) 1922
The Home-Maker (novel) 1924
Made-to-Order Stories (children's literature) 1925
Her Son's Wife (novel) 1926
Why Stop Learning? (nonfiction) 1927
The Deepening Stream (novel) 1930

Basque People (short stories) 1931
Bonfire (novel) 1933
Fables for Parents (short stories and sketches) 1937
Seasoned Timber (novel) 1939
Liberty and Union [with Sarah N. Cleghorn] (history) 1940
Nothing Ever Happens and How It Does [with Sarah N. Cleghorn] (children's literature) 1940
Tell Me a Story (children's literature) 1940
American Portraits (history) 1946
Four-Square (short stories) 1949
Something Old, Something New: Stories of People Who Are America (short stories) 1949
Our Independence and the Constitution (history) 1950
Paul Revere and the Minute Men (history) 1950
A Fair World for All: The Meaning of the Declaration of Human Rights (history) 1952
Vermont Tradition: The Biography of an Outlook on Life (history) 1953
A Harvest of Stories, from a Half Century of Writing (short stories) 1956
Memories of Arlington, Vermont (history) 1957
And Long Remember: Some Great Americans Who Have Helped Me (history) 1959

CRITICISM

Blanche Colton Williams (essay date 1920)

SOURCE: "Dorothy Canfield," in *Our Short Story Writers*, Moffat, Yard & Company, 1920, pp. 41-54.

[*In the following essay, Williams surveys Fisher's life and works of short fiction.*]

In the twentieth century it is possible for one, before she is forty years of age, to be a doctor of philosophy, master of half a dozen languages, a successful novelist, story-writer, wife, mother, and war worker. Dorothy Canfield is all of these, and in addition, after much travel and living abroad, she is an American of Americans. Her Americanism is the essence of her greatness and her significance for the literature of to-day and to-morrow. It is the foundation on which rise her achievements.

How has she managed to do so much? First, the circumstances of her birth were favorable. Daughter of the late James Hulme Canfield, who was President of the University of Kansas at the time she was born, and his wife Flavia Camp Canfield, artist, Dorothea Frances made her entry dowered with unusual intelligence and æsthetic sensibility. She was born, February 17, 1879, in perhaps the most American region of America, if the land of the free be symbolized by wind-blown skies and boundless plains. The Mid-West setting, however, was balanced by the girl's academic activities at Lawrence and later at the Ohio State University, of which her father was President when she took her A. B. degree in 1899. Thus briefly are indicated the Americanism and the general culture which made possible a Dorothy Canfield. The languages, German, Italian, Spanish, and Danish are explained by her travel; French she acquired in her mother's studio in Paris. When her father accepted the Chair of Librarian at Columbia University, she extended her researches in the graduate school recently opened, and in 1904 took the doctorate degree in Comparative Literature. She combined her knowledge of French and English in her thesis: *Corneille and Racine in England* (1904).

Meantime, in 1902, Miss Canfield while working on her dissertation, served as Secretary of the Horace Mann School, connected with the Teachers College of Columbia University, a position she held for three years. Then out of her association with the late Professor George R. Carpenter, she was urged to further writing. With Professor Carpenter she compiled a text-book, *English Rhetoric and Composition* (1906), and about the same time began to publish stories in magazines. Mr. Grant Overton remarks in *The Women Who Make Our Novels*: "Before *The Squirrel Cage* [published in 1912], Mrs. Fisher was merely the author of a few text-books. After it she was an important figure in American fiction." From the angle of the public, and in a deeply sardonic sense this is more than true. For the reading public would be as indifferent to the scholar who produced a work on the French dramatists as to the technician who contributed to a book on the art and business of writing. It should be stated, however, that many of Mrs. Fisher's stories were published years before they were gathered up into *Hillsboro People* and *The Real Motive*. Some of them appeared as early as 1906: "The Bedquilt," "The Philanthropist and the Peaceful Life"—reprinted, 1915, under the title "Fortune and the Fifth Card"—and "The Great Refusal." Undoubtedly the success of *The Squirrel Cage* hastened their preservation in book form.

On May 9, 1907, Dorothy Canfield was married to John Redwood Fisher, of New York. Shortly after the event, they went to Arlington, Vermont, where they found far removed from city commerce and pandemonium a house adapted to the art of living and working. No one can read "At the Foot of Hemlock Mountain," the essay that introduces *Hillsboro People* (1915), and fail to be convinced of the real life that Dorothy Canfield Fisher experiences in the town of Arlington. For the essay is reflective of her own village. According to her sentiments, "Like any other of those gifts of life which gratify insatiable cravings of humanity, living in a country village conveys a satisfaction which is incommunicable. . . . " "City dwellers make money, make reputations (good and bad), make museums and subways, make charitable institutions, make with a hysteric rapidity, like excited spiders, more and yet more complications in the mazy labyrinths of their lives, but they never make each others' acquaintances . . . and that is all that is worth doing in the world. . . . "

It is proof of her wisdom and of her fathoming the meaning of the verb *to live* that, after the great cities New York, Paris, and Rome, she turned, a single-hearted American, to the country, not to escape from but to mingle with her fellow beings. All novels, she says, seem badly written, faint and faded, in comparison with the life which palpitates up and down the village street. She commiserates the city dweller who lives through "canned romances, adventures, tragedies, farces," as one who passes blindfold through life.

Yet it is not to be forgotten that Mrs. Fisher is a product of balance, and she continues to maintain that balance. With her husband and children she adventures away from Arlington and seeks what she needs by way of change. In 1911-1912 they spent the winter in Italy. In Rome, Mrs. Fisher met Madame Montessori and worked with her at the Children's House at the same time she was translating the works later published under the titles *A Montessori Mother* (1913) and *Mothers and Children* (1914).

Her mounting fame rose with a greater climax, the world war. The years from 1914 to 1919 are crowded with the work of the woman as of the writer. In Paris, she edited a magazine for soldiers; she took care of the refugees; she organized two children's homes at Guethary, in the south of France; she organized at Meudon a home and day nursery for munition workers' children; she ran a camp on the edge of the war zone. Meantime, *Hillsboro People* (1915) and *The Bent Twig* (1915), were followed by *The Real Motive* (1916), *Fellow Captains* (1916) and *Understood Betsy* (1917). *Home Fires in France* (1918) and *The Day of Glory* (1919) placed a gold laurel-leaf crown on the author's work in France. The sketches and stories under these two titles are among the most popular of the many works written during the war and immediately after the armistice.

Although Mrs. Fisher is first of all a novelist she is next a short-story writer. In the future, the literary historian will class her tales, in all probability, as of three periods: before the war, during the war, and after the war. At the moment, the first two divisions are the ones which concern us.

Hillsboro People (1915) and *The Real Motive* (1916) may be discussed as if the titles were merged in one volume; for the stories divided between the two cover the years from 1906 to 1915, with the overflow of 1916 in the latter volume. To read these collections is to feel the invigorating influence of a fresh buoyant optimism, to catch glimpses of a generous sympathy, to come face to face with a democracy which in the best sense is no respecter of persons, whether differentiated by age or social conditions or culture. The stories have their settings in the Middle West, in and near New York, in Paris, and in Hillsboro. (All in the collection of 1915 are connected in one way or other with Hillsboro). The range of time is from the eighteenth century, for example,

"In New New England" (first published in 1910), to the present, the time of the greatest number. The characters reflect the author's many-sided interests: the librarian is represented in J. M., hero of **"Avunculus"** (1909), and in Miss Martin (**"Hillsboro's Good Luck,"** 1908); the artist is found in Fallères, who painted the college president (**"Portrait of a Philosopher,"** 1911), in **"An April Masque"** (1910), in **"The Deliverer"** (1909), and triumphantly in **"The Artist"** (1911). The college professor figures in **"An Academic Question"** (1910), and **"A Thread without a Knot"** (originally entitled, when first published in 1910, **"An Unframed Picture"**). A baby is the hero of **"Vignettes from a Life of Two Months"** (1915), old men are heroes of **"The Heyday of the Blood"** (1909), and **"As a Bird Out of the Snare"** (1908); an old lady is the humble heroine of **"The Bedquilt"** (1906). Nor does this list exhaust the little world of her story people; nor is her understanding of any one diminished by her equal understanding of the others. The poor artist in **"An April Masque"** is not unworthy as a companion to the Artist; for life and ideals are greater than art—so exceedingly vaster that the difference between the best art and the worst becomes negligible in the sum of things. So, also, the difference between old and modern education is inconsiderable in the march of the years. **"In New New England,"** Captain Winthrop undertakes the education of Hannah Sherwin, aided thereto by a work entitled "The Universal Preceptor; being a General Grammar of Art, Science, and Useful Knowledge." "Up in our garret we have the very book he used," continues the narrator, "and modern research and science have proved that there is scarcely a true word in it. But don't waste any pity on Hannah for having such a mistaken teacher, for it is likely enough, don't you think, that research and science a hundred years from now will have proved that there is scarcely a word of truth in our school-books of to-day? It really doesn't seem to matter much."

Her sympathy for the boy or girl cribbed in by circumstance flashes out repeatedly, as in **"The Bedquilt," "The Deliverer,"** and **"As a Bird."** Aunt Mehetabel aged sixty-eight makes her initial appeal to the reader through the fact that she seems to be regarded a nonentity in the house of her brother. She must ask, even, for scraps to make the quilt. It is no ordinary quilt. Into its perfection go months of work laboriously materializing a design made possible through previous practice and the inspiration of a soul barred from other outlets of expression. When it is finished, her brother declares it must be sent to the fair; later, in an unwonted burst of generosity, he arranges for her to go. When she returns she has nothing to relate, except about the quilt, which has taken the first prize. One sees her sitting there before the glass case, absorbed in rapt contemplation of her own handiwork, marveling that she has done it, deaf to the sounds of the fair, blind to all other sights. **"The Deliverer"** is a story of New England, in 1756, of the days when love of nature was held a sin, when the love of God was not greater than the fear of hell fire. Nathaniel Everett, son to the preacher, believes he is

lost: "My heart is all full of carnal pleasures and desires. To look at the sun on the hillside—why I love it so that I forget my soul—hell—God—" His seizures do not avail to cure him. He says to Colonel Hall and M. LeMaury, who were to be his deliverers, "I—I would rather look at a haw-tree in blossom than meditate on the Almighty!" It is a turning point in Nathaniel's life when dying Colonel Hall goes calmly out with the final words to the Rev. Mr. Everett: "*I don't believe in your damned little hell!*" Nathaniel's final deliverance, the story suggests by the dénouement (placed first in the story order), is through Le Maury, whose name the boy took and by whose aid he became a great artist. **"As a Bird Out of the Snare"** shows triumph of spirit; but it is cause for tears to reflect that Jehiel Hawthorn was bound, year after year, to the farm while the pine tree grew high into heaven. He had vowed, "Before it's as tall as the ridge-pole of the house, I'll be on my way."

Not least of Mrs. Fisher's accomplishments is her faithful portrayal of the expressionless New England man and woman. Mehetabel is speechless when she tries to speak of the glories of her quilt; though she longs with her whole soul to convey the splendor of her vision, she falters. She dismisses recollections of hymn-book phraseology as not quite the thing. "Finally, 'I tell you it looked real well!' she assured them." So in **"Petunias"** (1912) Grandma Pritchard comes to the point in her rehearsal where the husband, who she had heard was killed at Gettysburg, returns. "I tell you—I tell you—*I was real glad to see him!*" So in **"Flint and Fire"** (1915) Emma Hulett "stopped short in the middle of the floor, looked at me silently, piteously, and found no word." And so Lem (**"In Memory of L. H. W.,"** entitled when originally published in 1912, **"The Hillsboro Shepherd"**) died, saying, "I'm—I'm real tired."

But such dumb-strickenness is a characteristic not only of New Englanders. In *Home Fires in France*, when Pierre (**"The Permissionaire"**) returns, he and his wife utter scream after scream of joy, "ringing up to the very heavens, frantic, incredulous, magnificent joy." But after the first wild cries had rocketed to the sky, "they had no words, no words at all." When André (**"On the Edge,"** in *The Day of Glory*) returns, Jeanne "knew nothing but that he was there, that she held him in her arms."

More than one critic has declared the stories in *Home Fires in France* to be the finest works of fiction produced by any American in the course of the war. Written, it is reported, while Mrs. Fisher's little daughter was convalescing from illness, they result from her long familiarity with the French people and her "two years intense experience in war work." Her passionate sympathy for the oppressed nation thrills, vibrant, throughout the collection. *The Real Motive* and *Hillsboro People* are but the peaceful expression of a heart aflame in *Home Fires*. Dedicated to General Pershing, whom Dorothy Canfield had known in Kansas when she was a little girl, the book contains sketches, essays and stories.

Besides **"The Permissionaire,"** already mentioned, there are three other narratives, **"A Little Kansas Leaven,"** **"The First Time After,"** and **"La Pharmacienne." "Vignettes from Life at the Rear," "The Refugee,"** and **"Eyes for the Blind"** lack the action that characterizes those named first; but all, alike, are readable, and all are designated as "fiction."

The theme of **"The Permissionaire"** is at once a consolation and a call to carry on. "What was in the ground, alive, they could not kill," and so Pierre reclaimed his asparagus, Paulette her peonies, and the man went back to the front after his furlough and the rebuilding of his destroyed home with a memory of the peas he had planted thrusting their green leaves above the soil. **"A Little Kansas Leaven"** means that a homely, ignorant girl roused by the call from France, spent her small savings to reach Paris and to work there so long as her few hundreds of dollars held out, and that later she returned to Marshallton, Kansas, with a straightforward story that speedily established an ambulance. This leaven worked before America entered the war, and if the dénouement has in this brief summary the suggestion of propaganda, it was needed even when the story first appeared in *The Pictorial Review,* August, 1918. But the struggle of Ellen Boardman is very real, and the absence of love and beauty leaves a stark simplicity which is somehow mightily convincing that it all happened.

"The First Time After" reveals Mrs. Fisher's ability to put herself in another's place, from the stony despair that succeeds blindness to the moment when the heart is stirred by some natural touch to renewed feeling. "He stooped and felt in his fingers the lace-like grace of a fern-stalk. The sensation brought back to him with shocking vividness all his boyhood, sun-flooded, gone forever. . . . He flung himself down in the midst of the ferns, the breaking-point come at last, beating his forehead on the ground. . . . Dreadful tears ran down from his blind eyes upon the ferns." Later, he heard a thrush, "trying his voice wistfully." And, later yet, he laughs, the first time since his blindness.

"La Pharmacienne" pictures the sheltered life of Madeleine, wife of the pharmacist; then, in contrast, her heroic struggle to live and to keep her children alive; and, finally, her successful effort to save the pharmacy. Here, as in the other stories, the indomitable spirit of the French race interfuses itself through pages written by an American woman. The self-effacement of the Directrice, in **"Eyes for the Blind,"** who had found in the lists of the dead "two long years before, the name which alone gave meaning to her life"; the self-effacement of Amieux (in **"Vignettes"**), who refused the *croix de guerre* because its possession would indicate to his mother that he had been in danger; the self-effacement of the singing group described in **"The Refugee"**—such effacement means national survival. The Marseillaisé has stirred its millions since the time of Rouget de l'Isle, but never has it rung more bravely than when the school children of Cousin Jean sang it, sang the first

stanza, the second stanza and the chorus—and the elders joined in. Their singing might have meant death for all; but "There were three hundred voices shouting it out, the tears streaming down our cheeks." Never has it swelled more triumphantly than in *The Day of Glory* (1919) when the throngs of Paris swept to the Place de la Concorde to salute the Statue of Strasbourg. And Dorothy Canfield was there and rushed out into the street and became a part of the spirit of thanksgiving and shared her feelings with us across the sea:

> Allons, enfants de la patrie,
> Le Jour de Gloire est arrivé!

The houses echoed to those words, repeated and repeated by every band of jubilant men and women and children who swept by, waving flags and shouting:

> Come, children of our country,
> The Day of Glory is here!

Of this second and briefer volume, the opening piece, **"On the Edge,"** has been proclaimed the best story its author has written. This tribute is higher praise than it deserves and underestimates Mrs. Fisher's other narratives; but it is admirable in its restrained account of a brave Frenchwoman's struggle to protect and keep alive her family of six, children and foster-children, and for the convincing suggestion of her being 'on the edge,' hovering on the border of insanity. André, she dreamed, had come home. But there was the watch he had left for his oldest son! And the reader has a sudden revelation of the soldier heart: he had known she was driven almost past the bounds of sanity and that the gold case would remind her his visit had been not a dream but a throbbing reality. Or this is the interpretation that some of us like to make. But if there had not been the watch, there would have risen some other mute evidence of his presence to cheer her and restore her languishing courage.

Without crossing the border-line between sentiment and sentimentality, these stories pull constantly at the emotions. Has any man or woman read either volume without tears?

The struggles Mrs. Fisher finds of moment are between the individual and his environment (**"The Deliverer"**); between the individual and heredity (**"A Good Fight and the Faith Kept,"** first published as **"The Conqueror,"** 1916); between man and false standards of life (**"A Sleep and a Forgetting,"** first published under the title, **"Gifts of Oblivion,"** 1913); between man and eclipsed personality (**"The First Time After"**); the will to survive and the forces that make for destruction— almost all her French stories. The surprise ending has had small influence on her plots. Since she is primarily the novelist, avowedly interested in people, with story mechanics she concerns herself hardly at all. But **"Flint and Fire"** closes on a neat twist, dependent upon a trait of character; **"A Sleep and a Forgetting"** startles by the disclosure that Warren recovered his memory eight years before he admitted the fact.

Vermont and its Green Mountains are the fit setting for a writer whose ideals are so high and whose living is so simple. If the vision of the Ideal Commonwealth ever is realized, perhaps the setting may be Hillsboro.

Dorothea Lawrance Mann (essay date 1927)

SOURCE: "Dorothy Canfield: The Little Vermonter," in *The Bookman*, New York, Vol. LXV, No. 6, August, 1927, pp. 695-701.

[*In the following essay, Mann presents an overview of Fisher's work—primarily her novels—and compliments the novelist's ability to reflect life and truth accurately.*]

No one has ever questioned seriously the tremendous power in small things. The atom, the electron, even the germ, speak for themselves. They are the Davids and against them the Goliaths of the world have small chance. Consider the unequal contest between a great building and a small stick of dynamite! Little people frequently seem to possess this same driving force, as if their whole being were concentrated will power. Dorothy Canfield once said that if anyone knew what it felt like to live in a small body, in the future he would always choose to be large. There is something quite deceptive about these small people. You would never suspect them of such deadly seriousness. Looking at Dorothy Canfield, it is far easier to believe that she spent much of her youth dancing at West Point than that she has served for several years on the State Board of Education for Vermont. She does not look in the least like the traditional doctor of philosophy, nor as if she learned new languages as a pastime. I believe that Portuguese is the latest of her string of languages, though it may easily be that she has added another in the last few months.

How many people, I wonder, have formulated so definite a philosophy of life as she? Again it is very misleading to think of her as the novelist who lives on the side of a mountain near a little village in Vermont. Perhaps the significant aspect of this circumstance is the fact that her Red Mountain is the mountain pictured on the seal of Vermont! As a matter of fact she is equally at home in France, where she has lived for years at a time. Once she remarked that having an equal number of French and American friends gave one a nice balance in life, for the French women devote themselves too much to their homes and their families, while American women are prone to give themselves too fully to outside interests. Observing the failings as well as the excellencies of both helped one to balance one's own interests.

Variety is what life needs to be well rounded, Dorothy Canfield once told me. You should know country life as well as city life. You should mingle intimately with people of other countries than your own—living among them, not merely traveling through their cities. As an American, it would be well to have at least part of your education in an entirely different section of the country from that in which you live. This last summer she took her own children to a far western ranch, to give them a taste of a life quite unlike either Vermont or France, and the keen joy of a variety of new horses to ride. I recall her comment that every American should live for a little while in the middle west, for without living there easterners in particular can never appreciate the thirst for culture which characterizes these mid-Americans. Unconsciously Dorothy Canfield is apt to give one the impression that their own life has been very narrow and lacking in experience.

She herself to be sure had a good start in this matter of varied experiences. Her father was president of a number of colleges in the middle west—one in Kansas, and Ohio State University—while in his later years he was librarian at Columbia University. Her mother, who by the way set her daughter a good example by taking a trip around the world at eighty-one unaccompanied by any member of her family—dying on the Indian Ocean, she said, would really be no different from dying in one's bed at home—is an artist and author. She also is a little woman with a dynamic quality about her, but her daughter must have inherited her taste for languages elsewhere, since for all her years abroad Mrs. Canfield has not learned to speak French. She once made a unique trip with one of her daughter's French friends who could not speak English. Though they were quite unable to converse with each other they remained in complete sympathy—proving that after all a great part of our converse is not in words. Part of Dorothy Canfield's childhood was passed in playing about her mother's studio in the Latin Quarter. She once observed that bohemia had no lure if you had known it in childhood! There were other weeks in French convent schools—still another phase of life to add to her collection of experiences. For quite a period in the early days of her marriage she lived in Italy. There was also a year studying in Norway. Since she shared the play as well as the work of her Norwegian friends, she could take a mischievous delight in listening to the comments of visitors from her own land discussing a group of natives, with no knowledge at all that one of the "natives" was an especially clever American.

No one of our novelists has had the charge of writing autobiography laid at her door more frequently than has Dorothy Canfield. It is irritating of course, and yet so completely does she identify herself with her characters that it is not strange. If today she suffers and plans with Mrs. Bascomb of *Her Son's Wife,* even more did she laugh and dream and have moods of terrifying seriousness with Marise of *The Brimming Cup.* Most novelists use material of setting and incident which are familiar to them. In her case there are the deeper spiritual resemblances. She knows at first hand Mrs. Bascomb's passion for children, and very fully does she partake of Marise's articulateness and her need for analysis. She herself longs to think clearly. It is one of her ideals. Many persons say they desire to think clearly, but either their thoughts are gravely bounded or else they know nothing whatever of the true passion for clear thinking—almost for defining the indefinable—which is hers. Yet with it all she is utterly sane. There will come often her hearty laugh, brushing away the cobwebs of abstractions. The practical side of her also finds echo in Marise and her neighborliness. Many authors live at least a portion of their lives in the country, but they remain apart from the community. Dorothy Canfield has always contributed her share—though I am inclined to doubt her statement that her neighbors scarcely know that she writes, since they see her only as a human being. It is clearly a well worn path which leads up the mountain to "Fishers'". She worked with the other women when they made over the schoolhouse to rent as a summer cottage, using the rent money for school equipment. It was almost clear gain, for the energetic Vermonters furnished the cottage from their own homes, and did all the not inconsiderable work of the experiment themselves.

Living in Vermont on the mountain, the Fishers are interested in reforestation. There is a fine tract planted and preserved in memory of Dorothy Canfield's father. The work naturally was interrupted by their four war years in France. It is strange to think of their selling their wood in Vermont that they might live in France and do war work there. To both Mr. and Mrs. Fisher France was the second home, and they could not be happy until they were helping. There has been another year in France since the war, and several summers, for the Fisher children must be at least bilingual and their mother wanted them to learn early what she describes as the French habit of good work. The ideal of good work is something to cling to in life. This in itself is characteristic of her, for though her family came out of New England, there is nothing of the transcendentalist about her. She is tiny in physique, but her feet rest very firmly on the ground. Good work which demands care in its every detail is not bad as an ideal for living. Too many Americans are satisfied with shoddy accomplishment and even with shoddy dreams.

Novelists sometimes say that life is harder for a young writer today than it was during their own apprenticeship. Perhaps—but perhaps too in looking back from the heights of their success they forget some of the doubts and disappointments. Possibly competition was not quite so keen as it has become. Reputations certainly were made promptly and definitely. Dorothy Canfield was one of those who worked on *The American Magazine* in its youthful days. She was also secretary of the Horace Mann School for two or three years. As a matter of fact, *The Squirrel Cage* was not her first book, though it was her first big success. She had taken her Ph.D. in 1904, had married in 1907, and this novel was published in 1912. In a day when most writers seemed to desire the longest and most impressive name possible, she abandoned the "Dorothea Frances" to which she was born for the simpler "Dorothy Canfield."

Her educational books were published later under the name of "Dorothy Canfield Fisher," to the confusion of not a few readers. The educational books have become a thing of the past, but I have an idea that they subtly modified all her work. Her novels are deeply concerned with the training of children. Whatever else her books may contain, the matter of the supreme importance of children always plays its part. Educational ideals were in her blood, since her father was a college president, and from the first she had been hailed as a novelist of ideas. Nevertheless in the early days of her writing career she had spent a winter in Rome, where she became intimate with Madame Montessori, who was having trouble with the translation of her book. The publisher appealed to Mrs. Fisher for help, with the result that after the translation of the book she wrote *A Montessori Mother* for American mothers and children. Her reason for this was that many of the difficulties of Montessori methods in this country arose from the fact that American children advance more rapidly than Italian children. Consequently, large numbers of Americans found Mrs. Fisher's book more helpful than Montessori's own. There was at this time an amusing story of a woman who had enjoyed *The Squirrel Cage* and, seeing a new book by Mrs. Fisher announced, promptly read *A Montessori Mother,* wondering greatly meanwhile at the author's intention! The concentration at this period on educational ideas, combined with the fact that it was the period of the babyhood of her own children, molded Mrs. Fisher's thought perceptibly. The trend was there, however, for we have the teacher who writes novels and the mother who writes novels, without approaching the constructive thinking of Dorothy Canfield.

Ever since their marriage in 1907 in America the Fishers have made their home on Mrs. Fisher's grandfather's farm in Arlington. It was the tenant farmer's house which they took for their own, and Mr. Fisher has done the remodeling himself. Mrs. Fisher can show a series of snapshots revealing the gradual changes made in the bare little New England farmhouse. The postwar generation has set a standard for radicalism hard to match for those who preceded them. Nevertheless it is to be borne in mind that Dorothy Canfield started life as very much a radical. She was an unconventional and strong minded person, who would do nothing simply because it was the customary thing to do. One of her children had a boy for nursemaid. He proved fully as devoted to the baby, and much stronger when it came to lifting him. She might live in New England, but Mrs. Fisher vowed she would never allow herself to be bound, as so many New England housewives were bound, by mere possessions. A home was a necessity, but it should not be so precious that one could not use it or leave it. Life meant more than things! Consequently Dorothy Canfield would have nothing in her house on which she could not easily turn the key when the spirit of wandering came upon her anew. The fine art of living she felt was something more than caring for a house and the dusting of furniture. She must have lived up to her creed, for the little house on the mountain has been closed for a year or more at a time. It was empty several years at the time of the war, and the key must have been left in Vermont, for when the family came home from France they found the house open and a supper awaiting them—though their neighbors had shown the tact to let them enjoy their homecoming unobserved.

All novelists must take their material from the life which they have known, but more than most Dorothy Canfield's work reflects the varied aspects of her life. *The Bent Twig* revealed the life of the university town which she had known in childhood. *The Brimming Cup* was so vivid a picturing of Vermont that all sorts of amusing anecdotes could be told of the persons who believed firmly that she had written her own story. It was certainly a naive touch to believe that a woman who had decided not to leave her husband for a more prosperous lover should confess the fact to the world in a novel! The little American Marise had grown up as a child among French people. Dorothy Canfield herself used to tell of the church on the hilltop which she saw when she first approached France, and the thrill she found in thinking that this was "foreign parts." Never again, she admits, did any portion of the world seem foreign to her. Neale Crittenden—the Neale of *Rough-Hewn*—owes certain aspects of his prosperous, well established youth to memories of Mr. Fisher's boyhood. *Rough-Hewn* stands out to me as an extraordinarily interesting example of the story one is always longing to unravel. So many writers must have yearned to know why it was that their characters, wandering to each other from the far ends of the earth, ever found and loved each other. No other author, so far as I can recall, has ever worked out the problem. I should say that the writing of it must have required two distinct processes. Taking her Marise and Neale of *The Brimming Cup*, those happily married people from their totally different environments, she must first have reasoned back from the Marise and Neale whom she knew to their beginnings. This process was not on paper. The story she tells in *Rough-Hewn* is the story from the beginnings to the night on Rocca di Papa when they discovered their love for each other. This book was not nearly so popular as it should have been, proving no doubt that the public does not care to know too much about the characters of fiction. As in the case of *Raw Material*—where she presented the incidents from which stories are made instead of the stories made from them—it is quite possible that readers never wholly fathomed the significance of her experiment.

Within recent years Dorothy Canfield, the short story writer, has been almost completely superseded by Dorothy Canfield the novelist. Once, however, it hung in the balance in which medium she would excel. There were two volumes of Vermont stories published before the war. *Home Fires in France* and *The Day of Glory* were volumes of war stories actually written while the author was engaged in war work in France. The last of these books was an especially memorable event in her career. These war stories must have been struck off at white heat. There is no other accounting for them. Today there are secretaries, naturally. In the old days there

was always the little one room house in the Vermont field with its desk and stove, near enough to her home so that she could look out of the window at her children at play. In its early days the little house was used alternately by Mr. and Mrs. Fisher, while the one not writing would take over the responsibility of running the home and watching over the children, that the other's writing hours might be uninterrupted. In France everything was hopelessly different. Mr. Fisher was driving an ambulance. He went over in 1915, if I remember rightly, and his family followed him in a few months, despite the protests of grandparents against taking children into the war country. Not only did Mrs. Fisher throw that large energy of hers into various types of war work, but there was seldom a time when her house was not crowded with children in need of care and shelter. When her own little girl had been seriously ill with typhoid fever, her mother took her to the south of France to recuperate, but even under such conditions she could not escape the demands on her sympathy of other children who had suffered in the war. And even in such busy days as these she found opportunity to visit in the hospital another American novelist whom she had not previously known. That apparent leisure is one of her characteristic qualities. She never seems overburdened nor driven for time, like most of the modern world, though her days are extraordinarily full.

Her house in France was always filled, and in spite of it she managed to write some of the finest things she has ever done. Very early I discovered that Mrs. Fisher's characters are real people to her. She talks of them as she talks of her friends. I observed it first when she was talking of Barbara Marshall and her children Sylvia and Judith in *The Bent Twig*. Barbara Marshall remains one of her finest, most balanced characters, while the petty snobbery of the western university town remains a vivid memory. Sturdy little Judy and wilful, luxury loving Sylvia have lost nothing of their reality, though in the last twelve years Mrs. Fisher has written of many other children. One reason why I believe her characters are so vividly realized is the fact that they are always in families, and they have all the human connections which real people possess. As a rule there is an almost equally definite background of community life which seems to plant the characters firmly. They are quite tangible. It would not surprise me to find myself talking with Barbara Marshall or Marise Crittenden, or even the formidable Mrs. Bascomb. Could anything be more definite evidence of this than the volume of protest against Mrs. Bascomb and her high handed treatment of the situation which was menacing the chances in life of her beloved granddaughter? I have seen readers almost speechless with rage over Mrs. Bascomb, which after all is very fine appreciation of Dorothy Canfield's ability at character drawing.

Perhaps the sharpest reason for our present disregard of the radical quality of Dorothy Canfield's ideas is that the radicalism of the postwar generation has centred so largely on sex problems. It would be asking a little too much that they should succeed in setting ablaze the older generation—even though they have brought them to knee length dresses and the Charleston!

Dorothy Canfield's sense of humor is keen but she has not wit. Neither does she indulge in the epigram. She has done very effective scenes but she is not a quotable novelist. It comes back, I should say, to the fact that with her the story is the thing. Very earnest people are seldom witty. They have not time to indulge in side-show. Wit is for those with time to play upon words. Dorothy Canfield is concerned with ideas and with people. She has chapters of passion and beauty, but you must take them as a whole. I personally never lose my delight in that fine love scene on Rocca di Papa. Love scenes may possibly be easy to act, but they are prover-bially hard to write. This particular love scene has the added difficulty of opening the book, so that the reader is wholly without emotional reaction with regard to Marise and Neale.

There is neither fear of criticism nor fear of ridicule in Dorothy Canfield. In **The Bent Twig** she tackled that very delicate problem of the little girls with the modi-cum of colored blood who tried to pass as white children and who disappeared overnight when it was discovered that they were of mixed race. She has a clean literalness in dealing with a situation of this kind—which means that she gives her full meed of sympathy but does not let her sympathy run away with her. One cannot ignore a fact, however much one may sympathize with the vic-tim. Similarly, in **The Home-Maker**—the first of her books to be put on the screen—she refused to ignore that the father was a better home maker and the mother a better business woman. What case has mere convention beside facts? Some trace of Puritanism lingers in Dor-othy Canfield. She might, I think, be very lenient if she could discover a human being who had no other human being's claims upon him. The claims of children she places paramount, and with her an adult has no chance at all if he or she is hampering the course of a child's best development. If it is for the best interests of the children, the father should stay at home with them, no matter if the neighbors would laugh at him. If it serves the best interests of Mrs. Bascomb's granddaughter, it is quite justifiable that the mother should spend her days as a nervous invalid. Life sweeps relentlessly on. Be-cause you were scanted in your chance at life is no excuse for scanting a child.

This belief in the supreme right of children has grown on Mrs. Fisher. It has taken the place of her earlier belief in the right of the individual. In **The Brimming Cup** Marise made her choice between her husband and the man who could have given her a renewal of youth and wider opportunities, without excessive emphasis on her children. Vincent Marsh is scarcely reproved when he suggests that Marise is wasting her time doing for her children things which a nursemaid could do as well. Vincent Marsh would doubtless have had a harder time of it with the present Dorothy Canfield!

There are many things which might be said of Dorothy Canfield's work. Her gallery of children is made up of very human little persons, with scarcely a brilliant one in the lot. Some of them are the stolid little Vermonters with their red cheeks and with the fair hair we see in so few sections of the country today. They are real indi-viduals for all that. Her portraits of women are equally noteworthy. It would be hard to find finer, more gra-cious and lovable women than she has created. There is, I think, an element of the feminist hidden in her which prevents her men from being equally impressive. They are likely to be the weaklings of the story. At least, they serve as backgrounds for their more vital women and children. As a matter of fact, equality between the sexes does not flourish in literature—if it flourishes anywhere. We are born with our inclinations and prejudices.

The later Dorothy Canfield is a trifle breathless and a trifle breathtaking, as though she found life bounded for the promulgation of her ideas. A case of the dynamite again. There is such dynamic force in her. Something has to happen. She will not let you be leisurely and complacent. Life is so short and there is so much to be experienced and enjoyed and accomplished. It is the fundamentals of living and not the fashions and by-words of the moment which concern her. Perhaps too it is because she lives away from cities and refuses to be harried by the unimportant. She is modern and she has been a radical, but life is more than either, and she sticks close to the eternal truths. That is why she can be so completely fearless. That is why she holds out both hands to life.

Grant Overton (essay date 1928)

SOURCE: "Dorothy Canfield (Dorothy Canfield Fisher)," in *The Women Who Make Our Novels,* Dodd, Mead & Company, 1928, pp. 61-74.

[*In the following essay, Overton discusses Fisher's life and her major novels, concluding that* Her Son's Wife *is Fisher's finest work up to that time.*]

Very fortunately for her work as a novelist, Dorothy Canfield has been able to find direct outlets for a good deal of her passion as an educator. Thus, although her fiction does not escape didactic moods, it remains fic-tion. Nor is it autobiographical fiction, as some readers of **The Brimming Cup** seem to imagine; while her use of backgrounds and incidents from her own life is easily recognized by all readers familiar with her story.

That story is one of hard work, almost without respites, but the results she can point to depend partly on her scholarly gifts. She has been called "a woman of let-ters," but the image called up is not easy to associate with so much tireless activity of an unliterary sort. Having spent part of her childhood in France, she felt impelled to help win the war before most Americans were settled in their minds as to which side should win.

And having adopted as her home the State of her ancestors, she must become the only woman member of the Vermont Board of Education. Early equipped with French, German and Italian, she insists on adding Spanish, Danish, Portuguese and others until she seems likely to take her place beside Queen Victoria tackling Hindustani at eighty. Her latest book has the title, *Why Stop Learning?*—a query which may reduce some customers to speechlessness.

Her abilities as a novelist are so considerable that readers of novels can only selfishly regret her roundedness as a woman, teacher, publicist and official. No one, not even Dorothy Canfield, can get breath for work like *The Brimming Cup* and *Rough-Hewn* while excelling in other lines of endeavor. Mrs. Fisher would undoubtedly reply that living, in the sense of a rich and fruitful activity, comes first. This is decided, of course, by personal temperament; but it involves the sacrifice of the possibility of the highest place as an artist. For art not only insists on coming first over everything, it frequently tolerates nothing else in the race.

II

Dorothy Canfield was born in Lawrence, Kansas, in 1879, the daughter of James Hulme Canfield and Flavia Camp Canfield. The Canfields came to America in 1636, moved to Vermont in 1764, and have owned land there ever since. James Hulme Canfield was an educator, a college professor and president of several State Universities—Ohio State among them. Dorothy Canfield's mother studied painting in Paris and the child learned French about as early as she did English. She was really named Dorothea Frances, but simplified it to Dorothy.

The family was constantly moving about in the Middle West, as Dr. Canfield left one college job for another. From Lawrence, Kansas, where he had been president of the University of Kansas, they went, when Dorothy was about twelve, to Lincoln, Nebraska, Dr. Canfield having become chancellor of the University of Nebraska. At that time an army officer just in his thirties taught Dorothy to ride a horse and introduced her to his hobby, the higher mathematics. This friendship was resumed in France a quarter of a century later, the officer then being General John J. Pershing.

Dr. Canfield went to run Ohio State University. His daughter entered it and emerged a Ph.B. at twenty. These years were an orgy of acquiring knowledge. She saw France, Italy, Vermont. The itinerant educator now became librarian at Columbia University and Dorothy came to New York for a Ph.D. She specialized in the Romance languages, was secretary of the Horace Mann School, took courses at the Sorbonne when in Paris. She also saw the Columbia University football team play. John Redwood Fisher was captain. She was married to him in 1907. They went to live on one of the Canfield farms and Arlington, Vermont, has

been their home ever since, except for the duration of the war and for various European excursions.

A year in Norway has got lost somewhere in this reckoning; Norwegian is one of her tongues. As for the mother, Mrs. Canfield, she took a trip around the world at eighty, remarking that dying on the Indian Ocean would be no different from dying in one's bed at home. This assertion remains unverified.

Mrs. Fisher was not long in developing ideas about Vermont; you will find them tucked away in *The Brimming Cup.* Reforestation is one of them and they have set out hosts of baby pine trees on their mountain side while rejuvenating an ancient sawmill to work up the scrub timber.

The two children were born. In a few years the rural schools of Vermont were to have their standards raised in consequence.

As an author of books, Mrs. Fisher had, by this time, three and a half to her credit. The first, a study of Corneille and Racine, was probably her thesis for the doctor's degree. With Professor George R. Carpenter of Columbia she had written an *English Rhetoric and Composition* (1906). *What Shall We Do Now?* (1906) inspires less terror in the young. Her last book had been *Gunhild* (1907).

Now she did a novel, *The Squirrel Cage* (1912), "a singularly uncheerful, grim book showing a fine American girl, too sensitive to be a good fighter, struggling helplessly like a person in a nightmare against the smothering, well-intentioned materialism about her." Her next novel, *The Bent Twig* (1915) was to be a somewhat complementary affair. Its theme is "what happens if too violent a strain is put on human nature to avoid well-intentioned materialism"; it is "what might have happened if the Lydia of *The Squirrel Cage*, to save her daughter from that inner deadness, had brought her up in an athletically bare atmosphere of higher interests alone. Sylvia, the eager, human, selfish, intelligent daughter in *The Bent Twig*, flings impatiently away from the material austerity of her home life, and puts out her competent, energetic hands to grasp ease and luxury.

"In this novel Mrs. Fisher showed what she had shadowed in *The Squirrel Cage*, what she was to paint again in *The Brimming Cup* and in *Rough-Hewn*,—the growth, slow, occasionally groaning and unwilling but sure and triumphant, which carries a finely constituted human being first up to the recognition of spiritual values in life, and then onward to the sense of responsibility which makes him try to shoulder his share of the sacrifice and effort needed to safeguard such values."

Yes, but were they good stories?

They were, reasonably judged. Particularly in *The Squirrel Cage* did Mrs. Fisher succeed in making you feel the intensity of a girl's rebellion and the tightening of the net in which life sometimes catches its creatures. Both novels used the Middle Western background and *The Bent Twig* is a good picture of the university towns of her childhood.

After *The Squirrel Cage* was finished Mrs. Fisher and her husband went to Italy, spending the winter in Rome. Mrs. Fisher became acquainted with Madame Montessori, helped her with the translation of her book about the training of children, and wrote *A Montessori Mother* (1913) to introduce the system to American mothers and teachers. Then, as a sort of general answer to the many letters she got, Mrs. Fisher wrote *Mothers and Children* (1914).

All the while she had been writing short stories. *Hillsboro People* (1916), which deals with Vermonters, and *The Real Motive* (1917) were the first books to collect these. Later the war was to produce *Home Fires in France* (1918) and *The Day of Glory* (1919). *Understood Betsy* (1917) was written after Mr. Fisher had gone into the ambulance service, in the few months before Mrs. Fisher also went abroad. They then or later sold some of their wood in Vermont to get money for relief work in France. The war caught them up. From it they emerged without casualties, although their little girl had typhoid fever and convalesced during most of 1918 in southern France. It was then that *Home Fires in France* and *The Day of Glory* got written. In the spring of 1919 the family returned to Vermont, tired mentally and physically, glad to do some gardening, to plant more baby pines, and to rest. After a good many months Mrs. Fisher was able to begin *The Brimming Cup* (1921).

III

This very long novel is the story of Marise and Neale Crittenden after their marriage. Though written and published later, *Rough-Hewn* (1922) precedes *The Brimming Cup*, and is the story of the pair from childhood until the hour of their discovery that they are in love. Therefore, if one is to read both, he may prefer to begin with *Rough-Hewn*. It is, however, a lesser piece of work.

Springing from totally different environments, there is no doubt that Marise and Neale are destined for each other. When *The Brimming Cup* opens it is with a glimpse of them in their happy hour of confessed love. The scene is Italy, the year 1909.

The scene changes to Vermont in March, 1920. The remainder of the novel covers a period of a year. Marise and Neale have three young children. And the novel proper opens with a moment when Marise is getting these youngsters ready for school. After they go, "she continued gazing at the vacant road. It seemed to her that the children had taken everything with them."

She has ceased to be physically in love with her husband. There comes upon the scene one Vincent Marsh.

He is, apparently, a traveled and cultivated individual. Marise and he find much in common and the flame springs up. The rest of the book is taken up with Marise's temptation and resistance. Neale, remaining perfectly quiet, comes nevertheless to know what is going on; indeed, his wife contrives to discuss the situation with him. She must, he tells her, "walk right up" to the thing she is afraid of. Privately, with a great effort and agony, he decides that he must keep his hands off, not constrain her in any way.

With this main story, developed in full and with dramatic intensity, are interwoven other threads. There is Eugenia, who considers Vermont a wilderness of crudity—as does, for that matter, Vincent Marsh—and who would like to capture Neale. There is old Mr. Welles with a story of his own. The life of the Vermont village and countryside are sacked for incident and color. Marise's and Neale's children have parts in the complicated series of tableaux. And all through the book there is a diffusion of ideas of every kind, economic, social, cultural, quasi-religious. Neale's theory of occupation and industry for Vermonters burdens this page, Eugenia's preoccupation with lace work, that one. A passage of the sort following is a fair example of the book's digressions. Eugenia has put on some massage cream and is resting.

> As she lay stretched in the chaise-longue by the window, reading Claudel, or Strindberg, or Remy de Gourmont, she would suddenly find that she was not thinking of what was on the page, that she saw there only Marise's troubled eyes while she and Marsh talked about the inevitable and essential indifference of children to their parents and the healthiness of this instinct; about the foolishness of the parents' notion that they would be formative elements in the children's lives; or on the other hand, if the parents did succeed in forcing themselves into the children's lives, the danger of sexual mother-complexes. Eugenia found that instead of thrilling voluptuously, as she knew she ought, to the precious pain and bewilderment of one of the thwarted characters of James Joyce, she was, with a disconcerting and painful eagerness of her own, bringing up to mind the daunted silence Marise kept when they mentioned the fact that of course everybody nowadays knew that children are much better off in a big, numerous, robust group than in the nervous, tight isolation of family life; and that a really trained educator could look out for them much better than any mother, because he could let them alone as a mother never could.

We may limit our scrutiny to the three or four principal characters and their interrelationships. The final feeling is then, perhaps, and despite the emotional intensity with which Marise is realized throughout, one of dubiety. Neale is not too good to be true; he is only too good to be truest. He is a type of man most women endure least well since he refrains from aggression when, in their view, it should be spontaneous, an instinctive—

almost a reflex—action. All his highly conceived notions about not constraining Marise, though women may agree with them in principle and as intellectual concepts, inspire in the feminine breast an impatience amounting to abhorrence. Even Marise can be heard asking frenziedly at the back of her mind, at the root of her nervous system: "But isn't he going to *do* anything?" Nine hundred and ninety-nine women of a thousand, in Marise's place—or reading the book and so assuming her place—would prefer a husband who in such circumstances did something, did anything, even if he did the wrong thing.

The explanation is simple. The Marises of the world who show her hesitation do so fundamentally—underneath all their surface of scruple—because of a lingering doubt as to whether they may not, after all, still be in love with their Neales. That doubt can only be put at rest by him. He can settle it in his favor only by some affirmative act, some renewal of courtship, some show of possession or some chastisement of the intruder upon his rights or privileges. He cannot put the doubt at rest by mere solicitousness or attitudes of considerateness or by any form of words.

It must be granted that Marise is no average woman. Such a one would never discuss her plight with her husband in the fashion of Marise's talk with Neale. She would scarcely put herself in the position of going to him and saying: "You are in danger of losing me; aren't you going to do anything about it?" Still less, when he seemed to be obtuse and noncommittal would she continue with what is virtually a cry: "Oh, please, please do something about it!" His piercing glance, his kindly sympathetic tone, his high-minded words would perhaps end the natural suspicion that he was a dumb-bell but only by arousing, even confirming, in his wife's mind the more horrible conviction that he didn't really care.

Another thing. Vincent Marsh, as created by Mrs. Fisher, will impress most readers as much too cheap a specimen to arouse such issues in the breast of a woman like Marise. It is entirely possible that she would feel physically attracted to him; but either she would admit this to herself and put it resolutely aside or she would yield to him and satisfy the thing that was too much for her. The last thing, one feels, that she would do would be to confuse this physiological need with the rest of living—magnify it, drag in her husband and weigh her children in its false scale, allow it to threaten the foundations of her whole existence and her thought-out happiness. How little Mrs. Fisher knows about the Vincent Marshes is sometimes painfully apparent. Either they are more subtle, particularly in utterance, than she has made him, or much bolder; and in no case do they depend so extensively on the persuasiveness of words.

When the turn of the book comes, Marise makes her decision in an intellectual vigil. Neale's belief that she was strong and not weak has been her staff.

> Neale being his own master, a free citizen of life, knew what a kingdom he owned, and with a magnanimity unparalleled could not rest till she had entered hers. She . . . had only wished to make the use of his strength which would have weakened her.

She decides that when next she meets Vincent she can look and see what is there. The next day comes the encounter in the course of which he kisses her. She does not respond; stung, he asks her if she is too old for love. Marise reflects. "Yes, I think that is it. I find I am too old."

It is singularly unconvincing; all "written," one feels.

IV

Not so many years ago a woman of seventy was recounting the story of Keable's "Simon Called Peter" to her fifty-year-old daughter.

"And then, Cora," she went on, matter-of-factly, "you know, he had all those feelings."

"Yes, Mamma. Mamma, do you think we had better serve chicken patties?" For Cora was blushing. In the front seat Cora's daughter, convulsed, tried to keep her back uncontorted.

What saves *The Brimming Cup* for most readers is the manifest fact that Marise "had all those feelings." They don't pretend to grasp her ratiocinations; and it may be that there is not a good deal in them to grasp.

After *The Brimming Cup, Rough-Hewn* could hardly avoid a certain anti-climax. Mrs. Fisher's free use of material from her husband's boyhood and youth rekindled the most unjustifiable suspicion that *Rough-Hewn* and its sequel were autobiographical. "It was certainly naïve," observes Dorothea Lawrence Mann, "to believe that a woman who had decided not to leave her husband for a more prosperous lover should confess the fact to the world in a novel."

During 1921 and 1922 Mrs. Fisher worked on the translation from the Italian of Papini's *Life of Christ* (1923) and on *Rough-Hewn*. In the spring of 1923 the family went to Europe and spent the following year in France and Switzerland. *Raw Material* (1923) is a collection of character portraits, the material of stories which Mrs. Fisher exhorts the reader to construct for himself.

The Home-Maker (1924) presents a family where the wife, an immaculate housekeeper, is unfitted for child-rearing and hates her task. The husband is equally unfitted for the jobs the world offers men. When he is crippled by an accident, husband and wife change places, to the relief of each and the great benefit of the children. The dramatic suspense comes over the question of whether the husband can recover. If he can walk about again, public opinion and the laws of the universe will compel him to support his wife; the exchange of jobs will be annulled; both will be made unhappy and the children will suffer. Happily, the doctor, taking in the situation in all its bearings, utters the necessary lie.

Such a synopsis does the story considerable injustice. There is some convincing detail; more plausibility than is managed in **The Brimming Cup**. By the time she wrote **The Home-Maker,** Mrs. Fisher had come to feel that the rights of the children transcend all other human rights. But she was to offer this view in another novel which offers it without so decidedly asserting it; which, in fact, raises great moral problems and compels the reader to decide them while leaving him free in his decision; and which is much the best book she has ever written up to this time.

This novel is **Her Son's Wife** (1926). It contains Mrs. Bascomb, who arouses in some readers a nearly inarticulate fury. An outline of the story must be attempted here.

Mrs. Bascomb, a strong, intelligent, capable woman is not unnaturally disconcerted to find that her son has rushed into a marriage with a no-account girl. The prospect is quite cheerless; for young Bascomb has none of his mother's strength or keenness. Mrs. Bascomb takes them to live with her—a charity, all things considered. But of course it works badly and her son is on his wife's side. Of this Mrs. Bascomb has no complaint to make; but she alone is capable of solutions in that family. She moves away and for some years sees nothing of them.

One day she runs upon her granddaughter. Here is a pretty and intelligent child without care, control or direction—on the road to acquiring all her mother's tastes for the tawdry. The grandmother weighs the situation, decides, and acts on her decision. She invites herself back to live with Lottie and her husband. Lottie, sick of housekeeping, is rather glad to have her, and Mrs. Bascomb's son feels the same way.

Lottie, who has put on much weight, has trouble with her feet. Mrs. Bascomb suggests that she ought to keep off them. "Why don't you go to bed?" Lottie does. The mother-in-law sends for some one to treat her. The man she summons is not averse to creating practice for himself. Lottie, he finds, is really in quite a bad way. Mrs. Bascomb does everything to make invalidism a novel and attractive rôle for Lottie. All the movie magazines. Pillows and delightful negligees. Candy. Delicious and tempting food—too much food. Lottie, who has no pain to speak of, is quite happy. This goes on for years. Meanwhile Mrs. Bascomb at last can take her granddaughter in hand. Her son, a great hand for ball games, finally discovers some skill as a reporter of sport for a newspaper. Mrs. Bascomb sees her granddaughter graduate from high school and begin auspiciously in college. She is a girl with whom Mrs. Bascomb can be entirely satisfied, of whom she may easily live to be proud. . . .

This fresh and powerful novel is of almost startling originality in this respect: It creates a moral problem for a woman that has nothing to do with taking a lover and is yet of paramount importance. Mrs. Bascomb's inspiration comes with Lottie's illness. It is true that she puts Lottie to bed and keeps her there. Mrs. Bascomb, and no one else, is responsible for making Lottie helplessly bedridden. The mother-in-law is not without her moments of stricken remorse, but she never abandons her purpose. Mrs. Fisher understands her completely and puts her on paper with consummate skill. Can it be right to do this thing to the mother for the sake of the child? The issue is quite as momentous as that which must often be decided in the hour before birth itself—as momentous and to most minds, more real. And far, far oftener to face.

Other issues not less profound are involved. The Nietzschean one, the right of the stronger, raises its head. The rational one, the right of the greater intelligence to rule, is at stake. Christian doctrine moves to condemn Mrs. Bascomb and then falters, remembering that Christ stressed the sacredness of the child. Skepticism challenges Mrs. Bascomb's premise, asking how she can be sure that her training of her granddaughter is Ultimate Good. Theology bids Mrs. Bascomb to weigh her responsibility, tells her that she will be answerable for what she does, and assures her that she will be judged with reference to her appreciation of her acts, her fineness of conscience, her awareness and honesty.

Mrs. Bascomb's struggle has none of the grandiosity of Marise's in **The Brimming Cup**. Yet in its plain, practical everydayness her problem makes Marise's problem seem paltry. Mrs. Bascomb is not a pretentious person and **Her Son's Wife** wears none of the earmarks of an "ambitious" novel. But the character and the book are of a substance few readers will miss, for all the homeliness of the setting and the simplicity of event.

v

She has shown what she can do. Now, if the world will contrive to run itself for a little while, she may have a chance. . . .

Elizabeth Wyckoff (essay date 1931)

SOURCE: "Dorothy Canfield: A Neglected Best Seller," in *The Bookman,* New York, Vol. LXXIV, No. 1, September, 1931, pp. 40-4.

[*In the following essay, Wyckoff examines Fisher's novels and argues against the common view of her as only a popular novelist.*]

Dorothy Canfield has been a famous novelist for a good many years now. One has to be in one's forties to remember the excitement with which we followed **The Squirrel Cage** as it came out in *Everybody's Magazine* in 1911. And every year or so since that time, something interesting has appeared over her signature. It might be a long and absorbing novel, such as *The Bent Twig* or *Rough-Hewn*. It might be a juvenile in *Saint Nicholas*, called *Understood Betsy*, so wise and so humorous that sophisticated mothers and spoiled little girls read it with the same pleased shame; it might be a book about the Montessori method, or short stories about Vermont farm people; there was, of course, a book of war stories. When there was a longer time than usual between books, one always wondered what she was doing, what she was thinking about, and hoped, as one hopes of a non-letter-writing friend, that nothing had happened to her.

That she and her thoughts are so much a part of the mental background of most American women is, I dare say, one good reason why as a novelist and literary personage she has not been taken more seriously. She has phrased theories of life (and created life-like exponents of them) which many people cherish as ideals, and many more think they do. It is difficult to separate the literary craftsman in her work from what there is no better word for than the propagandist—a fluent and creative propagandist, to be sure, but always advancing some immensely interesting, adventurous or courageous way to live. Her own life, as a matter of fact, has been as consistent and as courageous as that of any of her heroines. The same thorough-going reliance upon a sound, feminine combination of head and heart—once head and heart have worked out their decisions—has given her life a continuity of motive that few people achieve.

She was born in Kansas, the daughter of a college professor-president and his brilliantly musical wife. The reflection of her life as a child in small college towns of the West, in faculty society and as an undergraduate is vivid in the early parts of *The Bent Twig, The Squirrel Cage*, and *Rough-Hewn*. Her father's subject was the Romance languages, a fact which occasioned many family trips to France and Italy and the consequent love of France and the French that no doubt made so obvious and so necessary to her the years she spent with her entire family in France during the war.

An article by Zephine Humphrey, in the *Woman's Journal*, gives a detailed account of her amazingly active life. After her college degree, she did graduate work at Columbia; at some very early age she had earned her doctor's degree in the Romance languages and had written several scholarly books, one a study of Racine and Corneille, another a text-book with Professor George Carpenter. An academic career seemed indicated, and a brilliant one. But she had had enough of it. In 1907, shortly after she had inherited a farm in Arlington, Vermont, she married John Fisher, a Columbia friend, and, with what is most easily described by the Emersonian cliché of "plain living and high thinking" as a guide, retired with him to that remote spot to live. Their apparent distaste for the capitalist system, their insistence on the dignity of work, the beauty of primitive human relationships, the desirability

of a simple life and only a small *quid pro quo* as a fair reward of effort, all come out at later dates in her books. The theories are lived always by heroines who, no matter how they may be described in the flesh, live and breathe Dorothy Canfield's own philosophies. Here in Arlington a daughter, Sally, was born, and *The Squirrel Cage* (1912) written. In 1914 a son, Jimmy, was born, and in 1915 two books, *Hillsboro People*, short stories of Vermont life, and *The Bent Twig* were published.

In the spring of 1916 her husband went to France as an ambulance driver, and in the autumn Mrs. Fisher, with the two babies, followed him. Her first war work was with the blind; later, after her husband was made head of a training camp for ambulance drivers, she was for some time *Brigadier de l'Ordinaire*, in other words camp housekeeper. A Red Cross home for refugee children at Guéthary also took much of Mrs. Fisher's time, and, I suspect, a large part of the royalties from *Home Fires in France* and *The Day of Glory*. Sally caught typhoid in France, but recovered; fortunately no irreparable catastrophe marred the Fishers' elaborate pilgrimage.

In 1919 they all returned to Vermont, where Mrs. Fisher has carried on ever since what she calls a normal woman's life. This involves a simple and happy family life, housekeeping, with one maid, in the original farmhouse, much work for the Vermont Children's Aid Society, the State Education Board, the Parent-Teachers Association, and much lecturing as well as the writing of several novels. A large brick house in Arlington which recently descended to her was given to the town as a Community House, with a wing reserved for her own guests. Mr. Fisher's service in the state legislature is in line with the public spirit of both. This past year a short book, called *Why Stop Learning?*, of the type which, as Arnold Bennett used to do, Mrs. Fisher throws off between novels, has become the voice and watchword of the national adult education movement. Mrs. Fisher writes in a cabin on a hillside, and her friends tell of seeing her working absorbedly in odds and ends of time that most writers cannot manage to use.

Now the children are growing up, and Mrs. Fisher has been a best seller for years. Her early public is in its forties and fifties and can look at her, if they will, with a detached and middle-aged judgement. With *The Deepening Stream*, her latest novel, fresh in our minds, it is not a bad time to look at her work and her place in contemporary letters. Disregarding the friendly affection of her really great public, where would a dispassionate critic place her in any scale of present-day novelists?

A review of her career and a re-reading of the earlier novels is a rather surprising experience. The only novel that really "dates" is *The Squirrel Cage*. That book, re-read in 1931, seems undeniably brilliant and competent, but also undeniably adolescent. It is like hearing one's own girlish agonies over again to read the heroine's speeches. The plot—how vital it seemed then and how trivial now—hangs on the struggle of an idealistic middle-class young woman to get away from the material things of a small-town society. She was not, you remember, quite strong enough a character to defy her circle successfully; she married the tiresome young business man and not the dimly Christlike and socialistic young hermit whom her family deplored. She was thoroughly miserable and even ill. An accident removes the husband—Mrs. Fisher has never had to finish a novel and a villain in this fortuitous manner since then—and at the end of the book one is sure that happiness and a crust are to be the portion of heroine, hero and the child of the first husband. *The Squirrel Cage* was a feminine form (and incidentally a better made book than most of them) of the novels of the type of those by Winston Churchill, Owen Wister and Henry Sydnor Harrison. A woman served as the "hero," romance and idealism were embodied in a shadowy male character, and every girl and woman who read the book identified herself with the sensitive, frustrated and, of course, neurotic heroine. Incidentally, even at this early date and with no blowing of horns, there is much sound modern psychology behind the story. (Perhaps, however, there is only the shrewd innate knowledge of people of the genuine novelist; as a clever scholar, mixing his dates a little, might five hundred years from now demonstrate a great deal of Freud or Jung from the novels of George Eliot.)

The Bent Twig, three years later, was a great advance over *The Squirrel Cage*. The theme was the exact converse of that of the first book. The heroine in this case was brought up to plain living and high thinking, and tried to get away from both, but in the end the twig bends as it was inclined and she marries a socialist millionaire who, renouncing his fortune to establish a foundation for the benefit of his employees, retires to a small property in Vermont, where they are to lead a quiet but productive and happy life. *The Bent Twig* is an extraordinarily good novel, head and shoulders above most novels of its time. There are some first-class characters, notably the heroine's professor father, her placid but far from stupid mother, her inarticulate extravert sister. Sylvia herself is at first rather an unsympathetic character as she leads her egotistic young years of shame because her father and mother not only have shabby friends who drink beer and play the 'cello, but give parties with charades and sandwiches and do not keep up with the faculty society of the western university town where they live. But as she grows older and develops not only in character but in the ability to think clearly, she comes to a full-grown mental and emotional stature that was and is, even on re-reading after fifteen years, a stirring thing to read. The best emotional scenes in the book are described with a sureness and accuracy of detail that Mrs. Fisher apparently had no time for in *The Squirrel Cage*.

The Brimming Cup and *Rough-Hewn* are a pair of novels about the same people. They are quite as good as *The Bent Twig* and the heroine is from the start a much nicer person. The hero, too, is Mrs. Fisher's first really successfully delineated hero. The story of Marise and

Neale of course has more continuity and scope, as it goes on through years of married life, here again the married life of a pair who are building a beautiful life in an unworldly way in a small Vermont community. Marise weathers the temptation to return with a *tertium quid* to the cosmopolitan life which she had renounced for love and theory, and emerges after one of the most searching and beautiful passages in any of Mrs. Fisher's novels into a completely satisfactory state of mind and heart about her husband. Both books are rather too long, rather lacking in humour. These are captious criticisms, however, for books written and published during and just after the war.

Between these two novels and *The Deepening Stream*, in which for the first time Mrs. Fisher has used the war as a factor in a novel, were *The Home-Maker* and *Her Son's Wife*—both books concerned with superficially simple but really difficult and intricate situations. *The Home Maker,* again competent and vivid, and rather ahead of its time, is the story of a family in which the traditional functions of the parents are completely reversed and not shared in varying proportions, as is more usual; the father looks after the house and children and the mother earns the income. *Her Son's Wife* contains a remarkable piece of character-creation and development—the middle-aged widowed school teacher, sure of herself, efficient, a little bossy and grim, but happy, whose only son brings home as his bride a girl the exact opposite of everything that Mrs. Bascom has always liked and approved. If an English novelist had written this book or a new American writer who was not already the idol of the 2,600,000 purchasers (and three to five times as many readers) of a woman's magazine, as well as a steady best seller, the critics would have fastened many more laurels upon Mrs. Fisher's brow, I am sure. As it was, she had the usual excellent reviews but caused no excitement. For the first time the heroine is not the author herself, or her ideal. She is a genuine creation, moving in a real plot to a genuine dénouement of the spirit.

Last of all we have her *The Deepening Stream*, written long enough after the war for the author not to be carried away by the emotions of the time. At first one sees merely a familiar pattern; here is again the sensitive, gifted girl, this time unhappy over sex because of the remembered bickerings of her parents, who is delivered from an inhibited life by falling in love with a gentle, rather average, inarticulate young man. There is a pleasant picture of village life in the Hudson River valley, and Quaker family local colour; then the scene changes when Matey and Adrian pick up the children and go to the war, just as the Fishers actually did. The picture of Paris in wartime, the French family of old friends with whom Matey lives and works, is unforgettable. Here Dorothy Canfield shows a power of concrete description, of character suggestion, of dramatic and emotional control of her material that is so fluent and so sure that one never pauses to say "What excellent writing this is!" but only reads on in order to understand the people and find out what happened—whether Ziza's husband ever was found, whether the children in the cellar of the Lycée would escape the air raid, what Matey and Adrian were ever able to work out as a way of life after such thorough experience of so horrible a war. There is at the end, no matter how Matey may try to look ahead in the lives of her children, and in working with her husband in his little village bank, that weariness and questioning that only the generation of men and women who are old enough to have taken little children through the war years can quite understand. If the book had been ended with an adequate answer to Matey's situation in 1920 it would be much less true a book.

It is very probable that Dorothy Canfield is not at all troubled by lack of literary recognition. She undoubtedly takes greater pleasure in the response of her audience than she could get from any criticism however laudatory. And, of course, if she had wanted to lead the literary life, she could have stayed in New York and lived it. But her own detachment is no reason for ignoring or taking her for granted. Indeed, to leave her out of serious discussion of the American novel is becoming more than a little ridiculous.

As a matter of fact Dorothy Canfield belongs in the succession of novelists that begins with George Eliot and continues with Mrs. Humphrey Ward and Mrs. Deland—all of them warm-hearted women (yes, even Mrs. Ward; did she not create Marcella?), all of them full of a motherly understanding and tolerance of human beings, all of them a little omniscient, like most women, and all of them except George Eliot with her minor characters, too interested in life and people to be humorous or even witty in their books. Only a deep female humour could underlie many of their conceptions of character, but there is no surface wit. They never laugh at their characters. If you smile now and then yourself, it is a motherly smile.

Where the next generation may put Dorothy Canfield I do not prophesy. One does not think of her in the same breath with G. B. Stern, Virginia Woolf, or any of the young followers of Proust or Hemingway. In spite of an academic tendency to class her with Sinclair Lewis as a merely journalistic novelist, there is an emotional force in both writers—rather greater in Dorothy Canfield's books, I think, except perhaps for *Arrowsmith*—that it seems to be fashionable deliberately to ignore. In the matter of form, Miss Cather, needless to say, excels Dorothy Canfield. But the big canvas and the perfect etching may both be genuinely enough works of art. On the other hand, Dorothy Canfield never slips into the near-hysteria which keeps both Edna Ferber and Fannie Hurst from finishing their novels as well as they begin.

There is an unself-consciousness and a lavishness about the outpouring of the old-fashioned born novelist of Dorothy Canfield's sort that is unmistakable. No considerations of form or current literary enthusiasms affect a writer of this type who has in early life fashioned a good

working style, flexible and ready to hand, who has some people to write about, a story to tell and—they cannot help it—a theory or a thesis to uphold. Wells, Sinclair Lewis, George Eliot, Dickens—the fluent, deeply emotional novelists are a type by themselves and Dorothy Canfield belongs with them. Because she has been popular from the beginning of her career, because her shrewd common sense and understanding of the conditions of everyday life, even more than her emotional power, make her the "favourite author" of enormous numbers of unanalytical women who find in every story some illumination for their own lives, she has never had the recognition which her work deserves. She is journalistic to the extent that she produces constantly. She is unliterary partly because she is completely unself-conscious. If she achieves a beautiful passage it is because the words and sentences express what she has to say, and not because she is interested in beautiful writing except as a tool.

The younger generation may find Mrs. Fisher's taste too refined. Surprisingly enough, even with reservations, someone put *The Deepening Stream* in a list of "pleasant" novels in the *Atlantic Monthly* the other day. And yet one can understand the choice. She can write about almost any horror without being offensive. No doubt the younger generation, too, cannot understand how her thorough-going feminism, which she always takes for granted, can be combined with her simple and emotionally primitive conception of the obligations of marriage and motherhood. The women who live this life cannot ordinarily write about it, and when they are old enough to understand it they are not usually writing book reviews or paying much attention to them. I expect that most of the men who write criticism of fiction think of Mrs. Fisher as a popular woman's magazine novelist, and little more. They should read the last half of *The Deepening Stream*.

Quarreling with prize awards has come to be the favourite American indoor sport—and it is an invidious and odious business, particularly when an award has been given to an honest and witty, interesting and workmanlike novel, written by a woman with a delightfully observing eye and a discriminating mind. Yet when there was no Willa Cather novel last year Dorothy Canfield should have had the credit for being one of the few American novelists of either sex who have, with a competent and restrained technique, that inexhaustible, unwearying and tolerant understanding of human nature which is the distinguishing mark of first-rate novelists and of first-rate novelists alone.

William Lyon Phelps (essay date 1933)

SOURCE: "Dorothy Canfield Fisher," in *The English Journal,* Vol. XXII, No. 1, January, 1933, pp. 1-8.

[In the following excerpt, Phelps offers his appraisal of Fisher's early novels and summarizes the strengths and faults of her writing.]

One day more than twenty years ago as I was at work in my house in New Haven, I was pleasantly interrupted by the advent of a distinguished-looking elderly gentleman accompanied by an extremely shy and timid young girl. The man was the librarian of Columbia University, formerly president of Ohio State—how fortunate to be able to exchange the terrible job of college president for the agreeable position of librarian!—and the bashful girl was his daughter Dorothy. Dr. Canfield never wasted time or words on preliminaries.

"This is my daughter and she has got to write a thesis in Old French for her Ph.D. at Columbia."

I said fervently, "God help her!"

"No, *you* help her!"

"But I don't know anything whatever about Old French. The only French that interests me is modern French."

"Yes," said he, "but you once wrote a thesis in English and got a Ph.D."

"That is quite true; and I made up my mind then that if the Lord would forgive me I would never write another."

"Well, this thesis has got to be written, and we have come to New Haven to discuss the method of its production with you."

Then we had a delightful conversation. Dr. Canfield was one of the most interesting men I ever knew. Of course I did my best to point out the way in which "original work," if it were to be valuable and important, must be done; what to include, what to emphasize, what to omit. Merely as a matter of record, I will say that Miss Canfield wrote her thesis with the customary bloody sweat, successfully met all the requirements, and has whatever rights and privileges go with the title of "Doctor."

In the summer vacation of the year 1912, as I was sitting in my house in Michigan after the diurnal eighteen holes, the diurnal parcel of new books contained a novel by a woman unknown to fame. The novel was **The Squirrel Cage:** the name of the author, Dorothy Canfield. I did not connect this name in my mind with that of the quondam aspirant to the doctorate; but the title of the book was beguiling, and the first paragraph caught my attention. I read the book from beginning to end with steadily increasing admiration. Somewhere during its perusal I *heard* the timid, almost inaudible voice of that terror-stricken, thesis-haunted girl in New Haven. I wrote a letter to her in care of the publisher asking if it were really she. I received a reply from Mrs. J. R. Fisher in Arlington, Vermont, confessing everything. What a development in four years! The timid girl had become a Ph.D., a wife, and a novelist!

As I considered **The Squirrel Cage**, I thought how strange it was that this author had ever supposed her "vocation" lay in Old French or in anything other than creative work. For although she has since written better novels, this particular specimen has intrinsic value. It is emphatically a good novel. It contained unmistakable evidence that its author was a genuine, realistic writer—realistic without being sensational. Her realism is unlike the gorgeous ironical mimicry of Sinclair Lewis, unlike the unassorted heaps of building-material dumped by Theodore Dreiser, unlike the shock-for-shock's-sake style of Ernest Hemingway. She creates real people who act and speak naturally, in a way recognizable by all who live in civilized communities.

I dare say that the labor in Old French was not fruitless: the painstaking accuracy of that thesis was transferred to a wider and more interesting domain. Her education in France, where precision of language is still thought to be important, was as valuable for her as for her older contemporaries, Anne Sedgwick and Edith Wharton. All three have a thorough knowledge of the French language and literature.

The Squirrel Cage describes a typical American family, with its daily pleasures, worries, tasks, recreations, quarrels, intimacies, and misunderstandings. After twenty years I can remember vividly the telephone orders given by the wife, while the husband listens with increasing dismay.

In her next novel, **The Bent Twig**, Dorothy Canfield produced the best story of undergraduate and faculty life in America that I have read. She describes a coeducational state institution, the kind of thing she knew as a child; for, as I mentioned before, her father had been president of Ohio State University. Indeed it was at his inauguration that one of the pleasantest and best known of presidential tales had its origin. When the ceremonies were over and President Eliot of Harvard was about to leave, he remarked with a smile, "Well, Canfield, now you are a college president and everybody will say you are a liar." "Why, Dr. Eliot, did they ever say *you* were a liar?" "Worse than that, they *proved* it!" If the story is apocryphal, it is truer than fact. I remember years ago asking my old friend Tom Bacon, professor of history at the University of California, what he thought of President Holden. "He is a very able man, but the truth is not in him." Then I asked Dr. Holden what he thought of Tom Bacon. "Doesn't he look just like a hired assassin? Wouldn't you hate to meet him on a dark night?" These university amenities!

Most college novels seem true only to those who are unfamiliar with the particular college in question. A novel must have some kind of a plot, and college life itself has no plot. Just as a thing must have "news value" in order to reach the first page of a newspaper, so the things that make up the pages of a novel must somehow be made interesting. Now the daily life of students and professors, however interesting the routine may be to them, has as a rule no conceivable sensational interest for the "general reader"; hence the average novelist, spurred by hope of fame or fortune, seeks for exciting details: athletic sports, dissipation, unclean "bull" sessions, and other features.

Thus I have read novels of university life which would give a foreigner the idea that American colleges specialized in iniquity; that the conversation of the students was devoid of intellectual interest; that decency and even sanity were unknown.

The Bent Twig gives a fair and on the whole truthful picture of the immensely varied activities in a modern American university. Study, athletic games, societies, play their proportional rôles; and considerable space is given to a very real evil, faculty politics. I have lived in a college faculty for forty-one years, and I admire my colleagues. They are a fine lot of men and I would rather live with them than with any other group of persons I have ever known. But they are not angelic and college politics are not always clean. Men who devote their lives to learning and to the teaching of youth should at any rate try to set an example of breadth of mind and bigness of view. Unfortunately, magnanimity is almost as rare here as it is elsewhere. The root of all evil seems to be jealousy. Every professor, whether engaged in "special research" or in something else, should rejoice in the success of any one of his colleagues. He should, but—vanity and jealousy are unlovely but common in all inclosed communities like military garrisons, college faculties, and monasteries.

During the war Mrs. Fisher went to France, where her accurate knowledge of the language and of the people made her presence of the highest value. Many women, and some elderly men, feeling that they ought to "do their bit," managed to cross the water, where they were, in innumerable instances, a nuisance. They could not speak or understand the language with facility, they fell sick and had to be taken care of; and when they were well, they had a genius for getting in the way of those who were useful. But Mrs. Fisher knew exactly what she could do, knew how to do it, and did it. She took care of blind soldiers and of their children. This would not be worth mentioning in an estimate of her literary art if it were not for the fact that it aided in producing some of her best writing. The stories she wrote as a *liaison* officer had for their object something other than the production of literature. She wished to help the Americans to understand the French temperament. But the inspiration she received from her years in France during the war-madness tipped her pen with fire; some of her most beautiful compositions resulted. Her story about the small shopkeeper who refused to have his commodity marketed on a large scale is a contribution to international understanding and a work of literary art.

As a short-story writer, indeed, she ranks among our best. Her tales of Vermont and of the Basque country are exceedingly well done. And in these specimens she is free from her worst fault—a tendency to diffuseness. She has the bad habit in some of her books of multiplying words. This is why I have never admired *The Brimming Cup* nearly so much as some of her other works.

She has never recovered from the teacher's point of view. Her interest in education has been shown in some of her treatises. The danger of the teacher when he comes to address a mature audience, is repetition. Long experience at the desk in the classroom has taught him the value—nay, the necessity—of emphasis by repetition. But it is bad for literary composition.

This does not mean that she lost more than she gained by her early academic environment or by her interest in the welfare of others. I myself have learned much by the allusions to education in her novels. I remember in one of her latest books a conversation between a professor and his wife in which they ask each other at what college it was their child had scarlet fever or some distemper. There she points out the weakness of those traveling professors—birds of passage—who are ever moving from one college to another in the hope of more salary or better surroundings, and who lose the influence and the productivity that come from an abiding background.

Sinclair Lewis no doubt performed a service as well as a work of art when he wrote *Main Street;* he gave a devastating picture of the ignorance, the complacency, the conceit, the vulgarity, the affectation, the pettiness of much small-town life. But he gave nothing else. For the sake of tremendous emphasis, which he certainly attained, he omitted the finer qualities and the nobler characters which are also characteristic of every American village. Dorothy Canfield, who has lived in Paris, in rural France, in a Middle West city, and in a Vermont village, has pointed out the fact that every country has its Main streets. We might imagine that in a small town in France glorified by one of the finest cathedrals of the world the life of the inhabitants would take on some of the culture and some of the aspiration of its chief adornment. Did you ever talk with the residents?

One of our Yale professors, now no longer living, who was born in France, was so impatient with what he thought was the vulgarity and ignorance of America that on a sabbatical year he went over to France thinking he would escape for a time from a distressing environment. I discovered him in a village in Brittany. He was desperately homesick for America. "Why," said he, "I never thought such ignorance, stupidity, and vulgarity could exist as I have found in this French village. And the language of the old women when they speak angrily to each other!" He was unfortunately able to understand everything they said.

Well, we know what Flaubert thought of small-town life in France. And Dostoievski said that in Russian villages the inhabitants spent so much time poking their noses into their neighbors' affairs that one would think they would all be great psychologists. "On the contrary, they are nearly all idiots."

Now Dorothy Canfield believes that a New England village contains an almost complete assortment of the various types of human nature; there one can study them better than in a large city. With her large, tolerant view of human nature, and her womanly sympathy, she gives us not a travesty, but a picture.

Of all her novels I like best *Her Son's Wife*. In the first place, her attention is concentrated on three characters; from multiplicity of characters arises a tendency to diffuseness. This book deals with a fight between two women for the possession of one man. When two men fight for a woman, the spectacle is not particularly interesting, both because it is so common and because there is a pact known as a gentleman's agreement—who ever heard of a lady's agreement? When two women fight for a man, the struggle is interesting because there are no rules. In this particular novel a mother, accustomed for many years to domination over her son, finds that he has married without previously consulting her; and has married the most detestable female in the world.

The mother is a school-teacher. On arriving home from her professional duties one afternoon she sees in the hall a woman's hat. Now just as a zoölogist can from the sight of one bone reconstruct the entire animal, so a woman from the sight of one hat can visualize the entire form and character of its wearer. This hat is not reassuring; in fact, her worst fears are confirmed.

Mother, wife, and son begin the disastrous experiment of living together. Mother is not only the breadwinner (teacher's salary) but has to do all the housework. She has always been a dust-hunter, the terror of servants. She has a place for everything, with everything in its place. As a school-teacher, she has taught an excellent diction, pronunciation, enunciation; she abhors vulgarities of tongue. Her son's wife is like a movie actress without salary; she talks slang dialect; she leaves everything around the house as if there were ten servants to clean up after her; her cooking would not appeal even to those who were starving. Every word she utters, every movement she makes, is torture to the correct, orderly, well-disciplined school-teacher; and she is her son's wife!

Although the mother teaches morning and afternoon at the public school, she has herself to do all the house-cleaning, dish-washing, and bed-making at home; her short hours in bed are made wakeful by her hatred for the besom that has turned domestic peace into a cyclone. Why then does she not break down?

The answer is interesting to all teachers. We are familiar with the story of the clown, stricken with mortal illness, who nevertheless had to amuse audiences every night. This is called a tragedy; but, as a matter of fact, the clown was fortunate in having his professional work, which took his mind off his own horror. We often say that pupils enter the schoolroom thinking of everything except their lessons; that it is therefore the first duty of the teacher to divert their minds from their various interests, and attract them to the matter in hand. A teacher, we say, is like a court lawyer; unless he interests the jury, he loses his case.

But what is true of the pupil is true of the teacher. The average teacher comes from worry at home to confront a roomful of turbulent youth, who have everything except nerves. He must forget his own troubles in order to carry on his professional work.

Now some have read Dorothy Canfield's story and have wondered how this protagonist could have done her teaching when the hours before and after were filled with nerve-shattering misery. I say that it was her professional work that saved her life and her soul. For the daily round of teaching is like the work of a military captain in action. There are certain kinds of toil that can be done mechanically; the work goes on while the mind is otherwise employed. But the blessed thing about teaching is that it demands unrestricted attention. When the teacher is alone in the classroom with her pupils, no other person can help her, and she cannot for a single moment think of anything else. Many teachers are doing brilliant and successful work in the classroom while suffering from ill health, financial worry, and the anxiety that comes from a cloud of difficulties at home. Work is the chief of human blessings, for we are unhappy only while we are thinking about ourselves. That is why the loss of income is only one of the tragedies of unemployment.

In this novel Dorothy Canfield reached her highest point. The conclusion of the struggle is profoundly affecting, and touches the deepest things in the human heart.

Her faults as a writer usually arise from a superfluous elaboration of mere language, from a concentration on ideas so intense that the manner of presentation suffers, and from an invincible desire to leave the world better than she found it. In other words, she is a woman first and an artist second. But her very devotion to her daily duties as wife and mother, her sympathy for all sorts and conditions of men and women and children, make her realistic novels more truthful. And she does know how to write.

I regard her novels as a contribution to American literature. She has won a place in the first rank of America's woman novelists, and there she stands with her peers—Edith Wharton, Willa Cather, Anne Sedgwick, Edna Ferber, Zona Gale, Ellen Glasgow. . . .

Percy H. Boynton (essay date 1940)

SOURCE: "Two New England Regionalists," in *College English*, Vol. 1, No. 4, January, 1940, pp. 291-99.

[*In the following excerpt, Boynton looks at Fisher's novels set in Vermont and finds* Bonfire *to be her finest story of the New England region.*]

Dorothy Canfield Fisher, invincible Vermonter, has had a drought to record . . . Vermont crumbles but is not wrecked. In all her stories Vermont character is asserting itself more or less vainly to oppose irresistible forces. The success of the resistance is never included in the stories, but it is usually implied at the end as the obvious theme of an unwritten sequel. Slow crumbling is too vague to submit to chronicle treatment; it needs reinforcement by plot structure, and Mrs. Fisher has her constant factors for this plot: a native Vermonter who has strayed from home and has been distracted by wealth and dazzled by European sophistication preserves his integrity by taking refuge in the old ways of self-fulfilment as a hill villager. In *Rough-Hewn* the Boy, after showing promise as a New York business bandit, takes a year off to find himself in travel, and finding the Girl astray in Europe, the daughter of American expatriates, returns with her to take up life at the old family sawmill. In *The Brimming Cup* the Vermont story has a precedent European background. In *The Bent Twig* the Girl of the right stock rejects a rich young tomcat and is bewildered by a wealthy aunt who almost estranges her from the family and by an art broker who almost alienates her from the elect Native Son. He, in turn, has inherited Colorado mines, which he gives back to the workers, and the lovers retire to his home acres and a reforestation project.

Better than these, most effective of Mrs. Fisher's output, is *Bonfire*. The formula persists, but it is overwhelmed by the human elements in the tale. The central factor this time is not an individual but the composite personality of the village. This is taciturn toward strangers, loquacious when left to itself, capable of the most extreme group reactions under excitement and of every sort of personal eccentricity in times of peace. Mrs. Fisher describes its behavior when the village doctor scandalizes it by marrying a girl of dubious character from "the Shelf," an upland hillside slum:

> The first reaction of Clifford people to Doctor Anson's marriage and all that went with it was a reflex group response such as follows an earthquake or a flood—something that happens to all as much as to one. No matter what their individual temperaments, they all cried out the same things when they talked, held their tongues by instinct on the same occasions. For, of course, even the children knew enough to shut their mouths during the few days when detectives, newspaper reporters and other prying outsiders were around, vainly looking for clews. . . . No other silence about Doctor Craft's marriage was kept in Clifford than the little oasis of it about his sister. . . . It was felt that self-control need go no further. In fact talk and plenty of it was called for. To exclaim and condemn was right and proper. . . . As it was, the fire of disapproval . . . presently began to burn itself out. The stronger souls . . . emerging a little from collective mob feeling, began out of sheer boredom . . . occasionally to turn the conversation to something else. . . . People went back to their own naturally different ways of looking at life.

These different ways are the theme of the book's opening pages, in which thumbnail sketches of the dramatis personae are given: Sherwin Dewey, nature-lover and homely philosopher, and Sherwin Dewey's dog; Mr. Lawrence Stewart, keeper of a museum, his own perfect ancestral home, and Lawrence Stewart's cat; Father Kirby, the ascetic rector; the elderly Kemp sisters, inseparable in their difference; the Deans, the Merrills, the Nyes; the elect, who lived on The Street; the lower middle class, though never so described, who lived at Clifford's Four Corners; the folks beyond the pale on Searles Shelf. All these were to react to Doctor Craft, gifted and restless young physician, and to Miss Anna, his sister, who had just returned from a year in Paris to her visiting nurse's round in the township. And all were to be affected by the subtly seductive presence of Lixlee Burdick, the Searles Shelf girl, who could take on the ways of politer society, who was too lovely of skin and hair and contour, and who was the perennial type of amoral carnality which found its perfect hunting ground in a tidy New England village. In the end she changed life for almost everyone she passed. She turned the heads of all the men, she estranged the women, and by the forces she set in motion she united the doctor's sister and the rector in holy wedlock, captured old Mr. Stewart in the bonds of unholy matrimony, drove Isabel Foote into effective professional life, handed a rich and eligible husband to Olivia Merrill, even by indirection founded a co-operative home for the poor upland children who were impossibly far from school.

In all this there is none of the play of economic forces that are so devastating to Maine and its people. The only machine in the novel is the locomotive which annually brings and takes away the alien city dwellers, who do not care to know and are not permitted to see the inner life of the village. The story goes back of the machine to the vulnerable nature of man. Lixlee is the serpent in the Garden of Eden, and she is Eve after her talk with the serpent. She is original sin in a Calvinistic hamlet, playing upon the natural depravity of the townsfolk. Life is unfertilized there, or unfortified, by the contact of the seamen with the outer world. A few who have fared forth save their souls, but the many are nearer to the native instinct of Sherwin Dewey's dog, which belongs in the wilds, and of Lawrence Stewart's cat, which has disreputable relations with a rover from the woods. It is a real distinction between Mrs. Fisher's characters and Miss Chase's; and it is a distinction which accounts for disintegration rather than noble defeat.

Bonfire seems the truest of the Vermont stories because it is not complicated by Mrs. Fisher's loyalty to Vermont. For once she does not conclude with the implication that the leading characters are finally on the verge of living happily ever after. This tale ends with Anna Craft's observation that life teaches one a good deal and with her confession, when queried, that she can't quite make up her mind what the lesson is.

In *Seasoned Timber*, however, Mrs. Fisher has been carried along by the tide of events. The change is from absorption in Vermont character as a product of the past to vindication of Vermont character as a bulwark against the present. And it is also, explicitly, a change from instinctive allusion to Henry James, recurrent in the earlier works, to inevitable allusion to Sinclair Lewis. For in this latest novel Mrs. Fisher declares with a sober face what Lewis has declared with his tongue in his cheek—that fascist materialism, leading to Yahoo, Black Legion savagery, "can't happen here" in Vermont. She acknowledges at last that Vermont, like Maine, is losing its basic resources. Sheep have gone; granite and marble are giving way to synthetic materials; woodenware, to metal; woolen, to the pressure of southern wage scales. Vermont has one final defense, its native backbone. Henry James cannot help her in this crisis; but she is so conscious of her new ally that in the midst of a caricature of George Clarence Wheaton, a magnified Babbitt, she interpolates, "Really Sinclair Lewis is a phonograph record! When you read him you think he's laying it on too thick. Not at all. He doesn't exaggerate a hair." Mrs. Fisher, too, lays it on thick in the anti-fascist propaganda which dominates the latter part of the novel, but in the long approach to this she continues in the more nearly Jamesian fashion of her more nearly America-European novels. The resultant product is a hybrid, but an interesting one, with its appeals to popular response from various types of reader: the people who love Vermont, the people who love any kind of localism, the people who love nature, the people who love a love story, the people who love noble sentiments, the people who hate bigotry of any sort and anti-Semitism in particular. It is effective argument, though as art it suffers by comparison with *Bonfire*.

Joseph J. Firebaugh (essay date 1951)

SOURCE: "Dorothy Canfield and the Moral Bent," in *The Educational Forum*, Vol. XV, No. 3, March, 1951, pp. 283-94.

[*In the following essay, Firebaugh investigates the moral component of Fisher's novel* The Deepening Stream.]

Two or three years ago I shocked an elder colleague in a Department of English by saying that I always taught introductory courses somewhat in the manner of a moralist. Because he had been trained by a severe linguistic doctorate, he evidently believed that I was introducing a dangerous subjectivism into literary study; that I was failing in my duty of teaching the weak student to read comprehendingly, and the good student to know something of linguistic and literary history. For my part, I was shocked to discover that anyone could consider those very desirable aims to be at all adequate.

If there is one quality which human beings have always had, it is the moral bent. Early literature was usually a codifying of moral law, or an exemplification of the lapses from or the conformity to such law. Dr. Samuel Johnson, by no means least in the hierarchy of those dear to departments of English, would moralize upon

any excuse, or indeed upon no excuse. Nor has the literature of the last century altered this fundamental emphasis. Oscar Wilde, aesthete though he was, was a thorough-going moralist. T. S. Eliot, the literary symbol of our own day, has never ceased to be a moralist.

At the same time that literature was busy responding to or developing new systems of morality, a sort of scholarship became dominant in the academic world which lost itself in the worship of the fact. This method paralleled roughly the development of naturalism in the literary world and the development of objective methodology in the biological and physical sciences. Even these methods constitute a kind of morality, a judgment, that the fact has at least the good of being undeniable and irrevocable; the implication being that nothing is good which is deniable and revocable. Since critical and moral judgments are often both deniable and revocable, they are to be shunned, and scholarship succeeded for about fifty years in shunning them. That they were not altogether evaded in the classroom was due to the fact that many teachers were not, in the accepted sense of the day, scholars; that fact is, I believe, all that saved American literary education from pseudo-scientific irresponsibility.

Every teacher of literature is accustomed to hearing the questions, concerning some fictional or poetic statement of a moral proposition, "Is that good?" or "Is that true?" The questions are less naïve than their expression. Most of us have been guilty on occasion of shameless amusement when such questions have arisen. Yet such questions press daily upon all of us and cannot be evaded. We cannot be expected to answer them finally; but we can be expected to show our students, so that even the most unsophisticated of them can understand, why we cannot answer such questions, why our lives are only a search for such answers as we can tentatively approve, and why their search for truth is not likely to be very different from ours.

I

In attempting to satisfy the moral urge which every student has in common with every teacher, some of my colleagues and I have found Dorothy Canfield's *The Deepening Stream* (1930) to be a highly valuable book. In using it we have inevitably met the adverse criticism of those of our colleagues who believe that works for undergraduate instruction must be drawn from some canon of great books. Clearly the novel belongs in no such canon; as a genial colleague of the opposition once put it, the novel technically is "Marcel Proust written up for the *Ladies' Home Journal*." (This remark does not seem to me as scathing as it was intended to be; if some of the technical methods of the great French modern can be made familiar through a minor work, no irremediable loss would seem to have occurred.)

The Deepening Stream, a semi-autobiographical novel, tells the story of Matey Gilbert, the daughter of a brilliant, arrogant American professor of French. Her childhood is one of emotional insecurity and repression, but various circumstances prevent her from becoming the sterile, maidenly adult that her elder sister, Priscilla, becomes. Matey marries happily, has children, with her husband throws herself and her small fortune into French war relief during the first World War, and returns to America with her husband after the war, ready to live a quiet mediocre life, helping her husband in his father's small savings bank, and resting content in the deep enrichment that life's experiences have brought her. It is a novel concerning domestic tranquillity; a novel about a woman, by a woman; a novel filled, in its later chapters, with the joy of maternity and wifehood. A student of mine, not realizing the amusing blend-word he had made, called it a "soap-box opera." The fact that it has something of the soap-box about it, only recommends it to the teacher who will admit his own moral bent and that of his students. And the fact that it shares with the soap-opera a domestic and matriarchal emphasis, will not perturb him either, if he is willing to admit that the American woman seems incurably both; that Dorothy Canfield does avoid the domineering qualities of a real matriarch; and that none of the sticky sentimentalism, violent jealousy, or blatant materialism of the true soap-opera disfigures her work.

The moral values which Miss Canfield accepts and advocates may be examined under the following headings: (1) Marriage and the Family; (2) Education; (3) Success; (4) Adjustment to the Environment; (5) Religion; (6) War. When we have examined the novel under these six categories, we will perceive that Miss Canfield has expressed an attitude towards life which is highly characteristic of certain American thinking during the first half of our century. If it is within the scope—as I happen to believe that it is—of undergraduate literary study, to bring the student into a frame of mind in which he can examine critically some of the underlying concepts of his own times, *The Deepening Stream* will assist in the process. Let us see specifically how it is able to offer this assistance.

II

In their own family relationships, Matey Gilbert's brilliant parents are constantly jockeying for position, each seeking an advantage over the other. Professor Morris Gilbert has a sarcastic tongue and a ready wit; hence he usually wins the verbal tilts. When his wife busies herself with amateur theatricals—an activity for which Professor Gilbert has no talent—he ridicules from a distant vantage, never making the mistake of exposing his own lack of dramatic talent. He seldom fails to win; one such instance occurs when a friend of his wife, Mrs. Whitlock, challenges successfully his dominance at table-talk. Even then, Mrs. Gilbert's triumph is short; having failed to defeat Mrs. Whitlock, he joins her, thus spoiling his wife's advantage. Matey as a child and young girl sees instance after instance of this sort: once, in a Paris department store, while Mrs. Gilbert flounders in a strange

tongue, Professor Gilbert observes silently, and then interposes with especially "diamond-faceted" French.

The two girls, Matey and Priscilla, are caught in this family fusillade. They receive little affection and no sex-instruction. Priscilla grows up sensitive and repressed, consumes her adolescent energies in tennis, rejects proposals of marriage, and becomes a crisp, efficient teacher of French in a fashionable school for girls. Her marriage, ultimately, to a widower, is a marriage of convenience only; she never overcomes her adolescent horror of the sex relationship. Her parents' lack of demonstrative affection for each other and for the children, assures that the children will have difficulty in expressing themselves emotionally.

Matey almost falls into the same sort of repression that seizes Priscilla. That she does not do so, is caused by two facts: a small dog, Sumter, which she is permitted to own, and which receives her adolescent affection; and the fact that, at her fathers' death-bed, she suddenly sees that the parents' bickering was a superficial thing which concealed from their children the genuine affection which was at the basis of their marriage. Only Francis, the son, an unsubtle person who is much like his father but not brilliant, escapes repression.

Matey escapes narrowly, and enters a marriage which is richly gratifying. Her husband, Adrian Fort, Jr., is a gentle quiet man, lacking either the ambition or the brilliance which had made Professor Gilbert charming, remarkable, and disagreeable. Here something of the matriarchal nature of American marriage becomes apparent; but Miss Canfield is fully aware of it; when Matey and Adrian go to France for their wedding-journey, Matey finds to her amazement that her French friends say, "I hope you will make your husband happy," instead of the skeptical "I hope he will make you happy," which is what she was accustomed to hearing in America. Their marriage is in all ways coöperative; it lacks utterly the competitiveness of her parents' marriage. Yet the matriarchal urge is fully present when, at the close of the novel, Matey joins her husband at his bank, helping him in this way to conquer the depression which the years of war have left with him. By working at his side Matey is going to be mother and wife, protector and companion, all in one; and at the same time she is emancipating herself (though nothing is said on this subject) from the kitchen. Unlike many of her generation, however, Miss Canfield does not talk of woman's independence. Matey is essentially domestic: marriage without subservience: dependence without subordination: that would seem to be her programme. The name of John Dewey springs at once to mind; and, if the teacher is so inclined, Dewey's beliefs can be discussed in this connection.

III

In one sense the novel is about nothing but education. The title, *The Deepening Stream*, stands for the continual enrichment by experience of the individual human life. But Miss Canfield is quite specifically interested in educational matters. Her attitude towards family life and towards education are often merged—as they are, indeed, in her treatment of the separation which exists between different generations. Although this theme is considered at several points in the novel, the following instance will suffice: As a child in a small Middlewestern university town, Matey becomes aware of the division existing between adult and child. Childhood was seen largely as a time of carefree play, free of responsibility; adulthood as a time of work, of responsibility, of care. The adults slumped down on their front porches after the evening meal was ended, too tired from the day's work to do more than seek rest. The children, in the meantime, spent their energies in the physical exuberance of play. In the popular mores, the adults envied the children's freedom; the children saw adulthood as a time of stolid joyless endurance. This separation of life into years of freedom and years of responsibility is precisely the separation which Dewey protests in his educational writings; men ought not, he thinks, divide life into a time of dependence and a time of independence, a time of irresponsibility followed by a time of responsibility, a time of preparation and a time of achievement, a time of education and a time of fixed attainment. Freedom fills all of life, and so does education. Dependence is not to be shunned by the adult, nor is independence to be sought as the highest goal of maturity. Like John Dewey, Miss Canfield believes that education and freedom and responsibility are coexistent with life itself; education, like life, is growth.

Dewey's idea of education as shared experience is developed in that portion of the book which contrasts an American family—the Gilberts—with a French family—the Vinets. During one of Professor Gilbert's sabbatical leaves, Matey, still a hoydenish child, lives *en famille* with the Vinets, who are Parisian *petit bourgeoisie.* M. Vinet teaches in a *lycée;* Madame Vinet gives music lessons. Matey learns piano from Madame Vinet, and other subjects from the tutor of the French children.

Matey is impressed by the enthusiasm with which the family enters into its activities. Music they take very seriously. They all share its pleasure. Their studies are more demanding than any that Matey has yet been subjected to. She responds uncertainly to theme subjects which demand that she use her mind on a philosophical problem. The sense of family solidarity which is apparent in the Vinet household at this period, is contrasted with the atomistic family life of the Gilberts. Culture, which the Vinets possess in great measure, despite their lack of money, is almost the catalyzing agent: the family solidarity is the result of a family purpose—the pursuit of culture and the sharing of experience. Matey's own family, certainly highly cultivated in the American sense, and much better off in the world, appears, by contrast, selfishly individualistic, its members seeking what they seek only for self-aggrandizement.

Yet all is not well with the Vinets. Henri, the son, intends to become a teacher in a *lycée,* as his father has done. The sense that the examinations are rigorous, and that failure is possible, is not a remote feeling. Matey sees that it is a fundamental motivation, yet she does not believe that the motivation is entirely evil. Deweyite that Miss Canfield is, she recognizes the values which result from a questionable system of competitive motivation. Certain "pleasures and interests—music, reading, the theatre, study, art, thinking—could not be enjoyed or even approached by people who had not been rigorously fitted for them. . . . They were not open to money, but only to those who had the right keys. With all the haste and effort, one's childhood was hardly enough to learn how to handle the keys which opened the doors to the world."

The Vinets are rather shocked, when they go for walks, by Matey's tomboyish behavior. The freedom of her Middle-western childhood has never been known by these Parisians, reared in apartment houses, taking their exercise in decorous strolls through parks or streets. Without didacticism, Miss Canfield thus brings into sharp juxtaposition American liberty from restraints, and European standards of deportment. Nor does she make any effort to decide between them. Rather, she sees the advantages of both.

We perceive here that the physical freedom of the young Americans, which makes them appear like little savages to the French, has by no means kept them free of psychical inhibition. The repressions produced by their "free" but atomistic lives are severe ones, both in Matey and Priscilla. One would hesitate to say that they are freer of conflicts than their Parisian friends, even after seeing, later in the book, that severe conflicts have raged in their breasts, too.

No solution is offered, then, of the problems of repression and neurosis. No solution, that is, unless tolerance might be considered one. And tolerance is the most consistent attitude of Miss Canfield and of the characters whom she admires.

IV

Miss Canfield is not, however, particularly tolerant of successful people or of the standards of success which they represent. Professor Morris Gilbert is an eminently successful and brilliant man. He is interested in the world's approval, and he is skillful in gaining it. Matey, when she first takes a course from her father, feels surprise that he is so very good a teacher. Yet at the same time she sees that he is only her father with his clever company manners on; and these company manners have caused her most profound anguish; "for an instant she stared bleakly at something from which it was her life-work to avert her eyes;" and as she sees the small self-congratulatory smile form on her father's lips, she reflects that she would like to be able to bring her little dog to class.

Professor Gilbert's standard of success is not, of course, the usual American materialistic one. When the University of Corinth offers him an identical salary to the one he has made at Hamilton, he accepts, chiefly because of the opportunity to teach more graduate students. In his new position, moreover, "he became very popular with his classes, and was so elated with the chance to use his old effects on a new audience that for more than a year he radiated good humor." One feels rather sorry for Professor Gilbert: so eager for the world's applause that he failed to secure the applause of his own daughter; that he secured, instead, her entire disapproval, her fixed resentment because he was more interested in external, public appearances than he was in the internal, domestic realities.

Later in her life, Matey learns even more about her father's selfishness. By sheer coincidence, she meets in Paris, during the war years, a girl whose great-aunt, Priscilla, had been jilted by Professor Gilbert, and had died a spinster, specifying in her will that she be buried in Rustdorf, the old family seat of the Gilberts. This new awareness of her father's ability to perform an act of selfishness, only reinforces Matey's opinions concerning him.

One feels that Matey is rather unfair. Her own life has been easy for her. Her own love life has been extraordinarily uncomplicated. Passion she hardly knows. Right shows itself too easily to her. Domesticity and righteousness come with incredible ease. She suspects little of the complex human motivation which her father must have known. Life is too simple for her. She is an excessively passive character to whom life brings much because she had asked so little of it. At one point she remarks: "I should say that the matter with me is that there is *nothing* I want very much to do." Her passivity diminishes as she grows older, as the stream of life deepens, but there is little passion that might not be found in any orderly domesticity and maternity. Intensity of desire and ambition—she is cut off from these as sharply as if she had never heard of them, as completely as if she had not had a very ambitious father, and a successful brother.

Matey's brother Francis is successful in a much more crass sense of the word than Professor Gilbert had been, and Miss Canfield offers him as a kind of antithesis to the man Matey marries, Adrian Fort, Jr. After he leaves college Francis goes to the industrial center of Pittsburgh. We next see him when he visits Rustdorf on the occasion of Matey's engagement. "The aroma of power scented any room where he sat." Francis, like his father, has deserted the first girl he was engaged to; and there is no doubt in Matey's mind as to why; her grandmother's money had been left, not to the granddaughter, but to the Presbyterian church; his new love is the daughter of the senior partner of Francis' law firm. And his marriage, like his father's, turns out unfortunately; Miss Canfield punishes him, as she does Professor Gilbert, for breaking his promises.

Matey's husband, Adrian, is (in the usual sense of the word) a failure already when he enters the story; he has failed to become a painter and he is adjusting himself to a humble life as clerk in his father's bank. Francis characterizes him as no better than a settlement worker, and promises Matey, that if she will not marry Adrian, he will introduce her to the inner circles of Pittsburgh society, where she may find a wealthy husband. It is precisely Adrian's unworldliness that appeals to her. She has had too much of a successful father. Indeed when, later in the book, she sees President Wilson accepting the plaudits of the Parisian crowds, she finds herself deeply suspecting his self-satisfied smile, his long bony college-professor's face. Her dislike of her father becomes one of the most profound motivating forces of her life. The new awareness of Freudian psychology during the first third of the present century is of course apparent here and elsewhere throughout the novel.

Miss Canfield again presents the world of power in unflattering terms when, later in the book, her brother Francis, having come to Paris with the Peace Commission, gives a dinner in Matey's honor. Matey sees the power which he and his guests display, and she finds it contemptible. She does what she can to spoil the picture which Francis is giving to his powerful friends—a picture of a noble little woman who has sacrificed her fortune for French war relief. In the presence of men who are on familiar terms with generals and colonels, she flaunts the fact that her husband has been only a lieutenant in the Ambulance Corps. If it can be said of Matey that she is smug—and I think that it can—she is aware anyway of her smugness, in this scene at least, and she feels rather guilty concerning it. But one of the most unsatisfactory aspects of the novel is that Matey too often sees herself as the calm well-balanced wife and mother, bandaging the wounds of those near to her, if not of the world itself; her justification, and that of her husband is, in her own eyes, just that they are not successful.

Indeed with Walt Whitman, Dorothy Canfield may be seen as saying, "The Commonplace I Sing." There are at least three basic symbols which express this idea—symbols which, incidentally, are simple enough to provide the beginning student with an elementary notion of the literary use of symbols. There are Aunt Connie's tulips, and the "incredible" fact that such beauty can spring from the unprepossessing soil of a very ordinary flower-bed; there are the flowers of the broom, each very tiny, growing on an ugly, rough plant, but each contributing to the beauty of the whole hillsides of broom; the owl-feather, which suggests that even the infinitely small can be infinitely perfect, and which has the function of telling Matey that the work of war-relief, which she and Adrian are considering, can have infinite value; and, finally, there are the ants, millions of anonymous obscure lives, contributing their mite to the infinite perfection of the whole.

Matey's attitude towards money is that of her father-in-law. On the occasion of her first visit to his bank, Matey hears a young woman depositor apologize to Adrian Fort, Sr., for withdrawing money from the bank for a new hat. The old man assures her that money is saved in order to be spent. His attitude towards money is purely pragmatic. He sees his little savings-bank as not an opportunity to amass money but as an opportunity to be of use to his community. (I would avoid the word "service" in this context because it has become so badly debased, but service, not profit, is certainly Adrian Fort's ideal.) Francis Gilbert can see this banking method as only impractical and idealistic; for his part, money should be put where it reproduces itself most rapidly; money for the sake of money, not for use merely— this would be Miss Canfield's conception of his belief. To her, his attitude is that of the typical business man, intoxicated with visions of wealth and power.

One may see, in this admiration for coöperation rather than competition, for service rather than exploitation, for use rather than profit, the ideological background of the New Deal. Published in 1930, shortly after the Great Depression had begun, *The Deepening Stream* must have summarized for many their deep discontent with the direction American economic and social life had taken. It summarized the period of pre-war, war and post-war, the hope and cynicism and despair, the inescapable pragmatic individualistic democracy of the first third of the century. That is why, though it is little qualified to be called great literature, it is an extraordinarily useful book to anyone who would introduce the student to the America of the early twentieth century.

The complacency of the American undergraduate, his callow uncritical acceptance of things as they are, of the success ideal of modern American folklore, can be attacked frontally through the use of *The Deepening Stream*. Professor Gilbert's arrogance, Francis Gilbert's brass, are certainly the obverse side of the coin of success. To let the American student accept that coin as true, before he has seen its other side, is to do him a thorough disservice. If there are attitudes that need to be cultivated in the young, one of them certainly is that of a healthy criticism of the American mores; the popular press and the radio are busily emphasizing one side; Miss Canfield's volume provides a point of departure for a more critical attitude.

v

Darwinian theory has turned the attention of our civilization to survival by adaptation; modern psychology has emphasized adjustment to the surroundings. What has often been neglected is the fact that some environments, some ways of living, are more suitable to human beings than other ways. Our quality is changed, our humanity altered, by adaptation to certain physical or social phenomena. Are, or are there not, certain ways of life that are more completely human than other ways?

Matey's father has moved his family from place to place as his work has directed him. By the time Matey has

reached late adolescence, the family has made four major moves; each time her roots have been torn from the soil in which they have tentatively grown. It is not particularly surprising that she is an extraordinarily passive young woman when first she goes to Rustdorf, more likely to be acted on by the environment than to act upon it, feeling that nothing can matter much. Nor can it, for a person who next year may be elsewhere. Small wonder that she remains for the rest of her life a relatively passive person.

Rustdorf, an old Dutch settlement on the Hudson, has a placid permanence. Few come and few go. It has none of the hurly-burly of arrival and departure which afflicts every academic town in the United States. Here one may put down roots and live, secure in the knowledge that old friends and the elders of the family are always at hand.

Here, moreover, there is no height of aspiration, no need to startle others with brilliance either intellectual or social. Here there are no severe conflicts; no depths of passion are either felt or sought. Contentment is of more value than achievement, satisfaction worth more than range of experience.

As a student Matey had not understood the passion of love as treated in the French novel. Nor, despite her growing sexual awareness, does she ever. Rustdorf, like Adrian, Jr., represents to her a retreat from conflict and from passion; her retreat is less complete than Priscilla's retreat; but it is no less real.

Even a retreat involves a judgment of values; one retreats *to* as well as *from*. Matey moves to a different world. It is her judgment of values that it is a better world than the one she has left. In the fact that the Rustdorf world was largely nonexistent in Matey's day, and that it is even more so now, rests the particular value of the book. Contentment is a much underprized virtue in the twentieth century.

Contentment seems not to be merely adjustment to the environment. Adaptation to certain ways of life seems, paradoxically, to bring perpetual maladjustment as one of its prices. Some ways of life are more fitted to humanity than other ways. Matey's judgment is that the Rustdorf life is such a life; and that there are ways of living, socially or environmentally produced, to which adjustment can be seen only as loss.

The Deepening Stream, then, is a defense both of mediocrity and contentment, of domestic virtue rather than public achievement. Thus it is out of the main stream both of current fiction and of current journalism. The merit of some books, for public as well as for student, consists just in that they are out of the main stream. The book has the weaknesses of all literature of self-justification (whether there is any other kind I do not propose to decide here): it justifies not only the author but also the sympathetic reader, thus inducing a kind of complacent pride. Those who see in the book only a complacent praise of the ordinary are, however, judging in favor of a value which Miss Canfield simply would not accept; to judge the book by another standard than its author's is of course a legitimate critical procedure, but it carries with it the risk of ignoring merits which are peculiar to the range of values the author has chosen to set forth. Those values have their reality. A fundamentally aggressive generation needs to have quietistic values interpreted with sympathetic comprehension.

VI

The religious faith which Miss Canfield finds most attractive is the Quaker religion of Adrian Fort and his family. Her heroine's religious upbringing had been largely ignored: religious observance, that is to say, had been a matter of occasional external conformity. It was one fragment of the fragmentary life which the Gilberts led. And that is why, when Matey marries into the Rustdorf community, she finds the complete integration of the religion of the Friends so attractive to her. In it she finds no separation of life and religion.

The Vinet family are anti-clerical and skeptical, and they rear their children in that tradition. One feels that their irreligion is more religious than the Gilbert's placid neglect. For the Vinets speak respectfully of all the great religious teachers, and object chiefly, in the Voltairean manner, to hypocrisy. Years later, however, their daughter Mimi, having married and left home, embraces Catholicism, and becomes so ardent that she will not allow her mother unsupervised access to the grandchildren, for fear that their faith will be spoiled. Mimi is experiencing the same need for something to depend upon, that Matey experienced before she visited Rustdorf. Matey is tolerant of Mimi's conversion, as of Madame Vinet's skepticism, but is grieved to find that the remarkable family unity, which had once appeared so admirable, has by no means been without flaw.

"There is no big or little in infinity," remarks Adrian on the occasion when a tiny owl's feather flutters down in the night. The Spinozist unity thus suggested is one of the important articles of Matey's faith—and of the faith of her father-in-law. Tolerance of other people and their ways (though Matey is not always able to practice it) is a part of this belief in unity. The belief in the Inner Voice, one of the qualities of the admired Quaker faith, is not without its relation to Spinozist pantheism. Her real faith, and that of Adrian, Sr., who is her spiritual spokesman, is in mankind, good, bad, or indifferent. Miss Canfield does not carry sentimentalism about the Common Man to the depths it was later to reach. But she will not condemn humanity.

VII

Hence arises a conflict about war. Opposing war, as in their faith they must, leads Matey and her husband to the years of war work—Matey among her friends in Paris, and Adrian as an ambulance driver at the front.

When those years are ended, they are physically exhausted. And Adrian returns deeply troubled in spirit; for, in spite of his beliefs, he has enjoyed his wartime experiences. He has rejoiced at the news of victorious battles, although he knows that this news means the death of men. So with the human race: it somehow enjoys war.

In a crucial conversation towards the end of the novel, Adrian Fort, Sr., offers, not an answer to this problem, but an invitation to reflection. Just as it has been foolish for the French to look upon Woodrow Wilson as a savior of mankind, so it is foolish for Matey and Adrian to look to Adrian, Sr., for an answer to this most difficult of problems. And to Matey, his answer seems at first a defense of war. For he remarks that man cannot live without a sense of purpose; war provides man with such a purpose: a "poor, false, imitation purpose," to be sure, but a purpose none the less. And finally, he assures Matey that he is not defending war—only men.

One thinks immediately of William James' essay, "The Moral Equivalent of War," and its suggestion of ways by which men may be given a purpose, in battling, not other men, but the forces of nature which—except man himself—are his chief enemies. The integrated course can proceed at once to a consideration of that essay and of the problems it presents. And the teacher of literature who does not believe that he must confine himself to the work under discussion, who believes that it is his duty to step from literature to life, will not hesitate to discuss the problems involved: the problems of bringing to all men a sense of purpose and an opportunity to express that purpose. For they are after all the problems of our generation; or rather, they are problems which in the Roosevelt era our generation took the first faltering steps towards solving, and which, we may hope, the generations we are now preparing will deal with more tellingly, more on an international scale, than we have heretofore been able or willing to do.

VIII

One cannot be impressed with the notion that in treating literature in this way one is transgressing upon ground sacred to sociology or philosophy. To permit the educational reactionaries who talk in such terms to have their way, would be to strengthen the departmental induration which colleges and universities are now beginning to abandon. It is a point of view which is fatal, not only to the integrated courses which are being newly developed, but also to the courses in literature, philosophy, sociology, and so on, which the reactionaries are endeavoring to defend. Whatever teachers in the past have thought about learning for learning's sake, students have never believed in it; they have taken courses in literature, philosophy, sociology, or what-not, for "what they could get out of them"; there seems little reason to make it more difficult than necessary to "get something out of them." The new integrated courses, in the institutions where they are being inaugurated, may help direct the conventional courses towards an acceptance of the reality of a world beyond books. Where the conventional courses are still the accepted ones, their advocates can yet save them from the attacks to which they have been so justly subjected.

A few months ago I called on a former teacher of mine, now retired, whose international fame as a scholar and teacher is now bringing him the kind of invitations which must make his emeritus status one of the most rewarding periods of his life. He and I talked of the new integrated courses in which I am so deeply interested, and specifically of the Humanities program with which I was then associated. He disapproves of the new integrated courses in the Humanities. "I'm writing an article against 'em now," he said. "I'll send you a reprint. But I have to admit that we've brought it on ourselves."

Not all conservatives are as enlightened as my former teacher, who never taught literature in a vacuum; nor did he as a policy employ the kind of men who would do so; hence he cannot be said to be one of those who "brought it on themselves." Those who are guilty, are now in the vanguard of those who regard the new integrated courses as a fate worse than death to specialized departments; not realizing that such courses can point the way to renewed life for departments which are willing to recognize the unity of all knowledge—a unity within which the specialized departments acquire the only meaning which they can have.

As a novel which serves as a starting-point for such a unity of view, *The Deepening Stream* recommends itself to the teacher who is more interested in education than in acquiring a property, barricading himself therein, living the life of the hermit crab, and moving—when he moves—backwards.

Helen MacAfee (review date 1954)

SOURCE: "Good Neighbors," in *The Yale Review,* Vol. XLIII, No. 3, March, 1954, pp. 464-66.

[*In the following review, MacAfee favorably assesses Fisher's* Vermont Tradition: The Biography of an Outlook on Life.]

It is not always easy for the reader of this book, [*Vermont Tradition: The Biography of an Outlook on Life*] to see just where Mrs. Fisher leaves off and Vermont begins. Nor is it always clear whether she is telling time by her own or her grandfathers' clocks. This, I think, is as she would have it. So would I, for one of the pleasures in following her text lies in the interweaving it discloses of dates, places, and people. To the people the times are all Modern Times, and however they may range, their foundations stand within the borders of the Green Mountain State.

Among its earliest colonial settlers were the author's family, the Canfields, who went to Arlington, Vermont,

by way of New Milford, Connecticut, taking with them habits of reading and writing, thrift and hard work, and qualities of decency, independence, and neighborliness, which some of us like to associate with Connecticut though we know they are far older. These have been literally the saving graces throughout the ages, and must continue to be if human dignity is to survive on this small planet.

Mrs. Fisher finds that her northern climate and the people have, on the whole, agreed with each other as she looks out on both from Arlington—still her home after two hundred years. Vermont's lack of great natural resources has put a premium on the laborer's industry, skill, adaptability, and careful husbandry, as the sparseness of the population has promoted coöperation, true sociability. She shows that there is less tribal or occupational snobbishness here than in most parts of the country, and a marked respect for schooling and independence of mind.

With those who regard her neighbors as parochial, dour, or hidebound, and equally with those who picture the State as an idyllic if static community, she takes sharp issue. Abundant evidence from oral tradition as well as written record is offered in support of the views presented. That the tilling and clearing of Green Mountain acres has been a backbreaking task even outsiders should have known. But few realize the variety of the local industries or the number of major economic changes the State has had to make as the demand for its lumber, potash, Merino sheep, and Morgan horses, rose and fell in the world beyond its borders. Through economic pressure Vermonters have learned to develop a good deal of ingenuity along with persistence, hardihood, and thrift. If, as Mrs. Fisher keeps reminding us, many of them had ever been the ultraconservative introverts of folklore, their past could not have come down to the present day.

On the political side this book selects for emphasis the Vermonters' strong taste for self-government and their readiness from the beginning to help liberate others, not merely as an expression of loyalty to a cherished ideal but from a practical sense that only by so doing can their own liberties be secured. For one example, Mrs. Fisher relates in detail incidents of their long "cold war" during the middle of the eighteenth century against the rich Hudson Valley estate-owners, in which the Vermonters aided the rebellious tenants because they sympathized with the tenants and because the Duanes and the Van Rensselaers threatened their mountain freeholds. Doubtless this was, as she believes, a formative experience, leading directly to the part taken by Ethan Allen's men in the American Revolution and forestalling a trend to isolationism in their descendants. Here again, what she has heard lends vividness to what she has read.

This and other chapters of the book are further enlivened by Mrs. Fisher's personal observations, her questions about the meaning of the past, her musings about the future. It can be no surprise that with a head start of several generations she comes out at the end on the side of Vermont or that Vermont comes out on the side of the angels. That is to say, in its plain terms, on the side of free men making the most of their minds, their bodies, and their land for their own satisfaction and the welfare of their neighbors. Mrs. Fisher has long been a pioneer in the extension of good neighbor policies. Readers of **Vermont Tradition** will be pleased to find themselves among her many beneficiaries.

Joseph P. Lovering (essay date 1980)

SOURCE: "The Friendship of Willa Cather and Dorothy Canfield," in *Vermont History: The Proceedings of the Vermont Historical Society,* Vol. 48, No. 3, Summer, 1980, pp. 144-54.

[*In the following essay, Lovering details the friendship as well as the personal and literary affinities of Fisher and Willa Cather.*]

Most readers know of the many friends that Willa Cather had and treasured and who in turn seemed to appreciate her great gifts—the Menuhins, Edith Lewis, the McClungs, and the Hambourgs, Elizabeth Sergeant, Sarah Orne Jewett, Mrs. Fields, the D. H. Lawrences and many more. Yet the students of Willa Cather's life know that she remained an essentially private person, an artist who valued her privacy intensely and guarded it with great care. In this respect she resembled Henry James whom she early admired. Both knew the nature of their artistic gifts; the sacred flame had to be tended. But even the writer of the greatest talents needs to share problems both of a personal and of an artistic nature with others.

The considerable number of books which treat the life of Willa Cather almost always contain brief recognition of the friendship between the famous novelist and her lifetime friend Dorothy Canfield Fisher, herself a novelist whose years spanned approximately those of Miss Cather.[1] Their friendship deserves greater stress. It lasted over a period of some fifty-eight years and was an important friendship for both of these writers whom the American reading public and the world have long regarded with high esteem, especially, of course, Willa Cather. Without overstating the case, Willa Cather had a special regard for Dorothy Canfield which derived from a special trust and admiration for her as a person. Their mutual friendship might have become an even more important friendship had the exigencies and circumstances of their lives been somewhat different.

Dorothy Canfield's father, James Hulm Canfield, served as Chancellor of the University of Nebraska from 1891 to 1895, precisely the years Willa Cather spent at the University. Dorothy was still in the Latin School of Lincoln, Nebraska, in 1894 when she and her friend

Willa Cather won a first prize for their jointly-authored short story, **"The Fear That Walks by Noonday."** A two-part narrative, the story tells of the highly bizarre influence that a recently dead football player has on the outcome of a college game in the Northwest. Though tolerably well written, the story was not work that Willa Cather would later desire to receive much notice. The ghostly power of a deceased player dominates the game, causes icy winds to throw a deadly chill over the opponents' efforts, and even carries his weird spell into the post-game party of the losers. The story builds upon a kind of athletic hubris. The local heroes become a little too proud of their attainments and learn a lesson by the intervention of the dead. Dorothy Canfield was fourteen years old, in her first or second preparatory year at the Latin School, and Willa Cather a twenty-one-year-old college junior when the story appeared. The writing certainly has enough sophistication in fictional technique alone to make it appear to be the writing of the older student.

Willa Cather's Campus Years (1950) carries twenty-two letters of recollection and impression solicited from classmates of Willa Cather at the University of Nebraska. Approximately half of these letters testify to the early friendship of the two writers, and several of these letters stress the special nature of the friendship of the two.[2]

Dorothy Canfield earned her bachelor's degree from Ohio State University where her father had been called to the presidency after leaving the University of Nebraska. Dorothy went abroad to study at the College de France, working under the advisement of the Modern Language Department of Columbia University. When she returned to America, she spent four years on doctoral study at Columbia, where her father then held an appointment as Head Librarian. Willa Cather came to admire Dorothy's expertise in French literature. Dorothy Canfield worked from 1902 to 1905 as a secretary at the Horace Mann School in New York, where she met her husband John Redwood Fisher in 1903. They married in 1907 in Pleasantville, New York, and came in that same year to live in a very old farmhouse in Arlington, Vermont, just north of the village and a little way up Red Mountain. It was their wedding present from Mr. Canfield. In this beautiful section of Vermont along the winding Battenkill the Fishers made no effort to farm, but instead they labored at the reforestation of the mountainside. When World War I came, husband, wife and the two young children went to France for three years, there Dorothy edited a soldiers' magazine, organized reading rooms and day nurseries for workers' children, helped to run a refugee camp, and started a braille service for blinded soldiers. Her husband served in the ambulance corp as a volunteer. Afterwards, she lived with her husband in Arlington until her death in 1957.

Dorothy Canfield wrote ten novels published over a period of about thirty-two years from 1907 to 1939.

Although her work received a large popular acclaim during these years, scholars pay little critical attention to her work. Her years of novel writing nearly paralleled those of Willa Cather. Dorothy Canfield's first novel *Gunhild* appeared in 1907; her second *The Squirrel Cage* (1912) came in the same year as Cather's *Alexander's Bridge*. Her precedence into novel publishing may have had some bearing on the nature of their developing friendship.

Dorothy Canfield wrote three novels prior to the American entry into World War I: *Gunhild, The Squirrel Cage* and *The Bent Twig* (1915). The latter two novels reveal her serious interest in the relation of the individual to American community life. Her stories resemble Cather's at least in their rejection of a growing materialism which placed a premium on commercial success and social prominence gained at the expense of human values. In *The Bent Twig* Canfield pictures successfully the academic community of one of the growing midwestern universities. In having the hero of the novel voluntarily choose a life dedicated to community welfare and service and give up a large inheritance, she reflects her own sense of values.

Returning from France after the war she resumed writing and further developed her powers as a realistic novelist. Her three novels, *The Brimming Cup* (1921), *Rough Hewn* (1922), and *The Home-Maker* (1924), stress the individual's adjustment to the life of the family and also to the small New England community. In the twenties she wrote two novels which stand among her best achievements in fiction: *The Deepening Stream* (1930) and *Her Son's Wife* (1926).

The Deepening Stream, considered Canfield's best work, presents the growth of her heroine from childhood through adolescence to full maturity when Matey Gilbert finally discovered the underlying significance of the pattern of events which have shaped her life. In handling World War I, Canfield makes an honest attempt to evaluate the dramatic changes which affected American life. She urges a positive acceptance of the human frailties of people involved in that catastrophe, and she points towards the making of a better world.

In the thirties Canfield published her final two novels, *Bonfire* (1933) and *Seasoned Timber* (1939). In her rejection of fascism as a way of life for Vermonters in *Seasoned Timber,* in a strong reaction to Sinclair Lewis' novel, *It Can't Happen Here* (1936), she shows herself a champion of individual freedom.

Her novels reveal a writer with a natural gift for narrative, even though the novels frequently have shortcomings in their structural unity. Her interest centers largely on the feminine character; her central characters are always women, although she pioneered in the realistic portrayal of small children. Most admirers of Willa Cather sense the deep spiritual and moral significances underlying her novels; a close examination of the writings of Dorothy Canfield reveals a similar commitment to spiritual values, and that at a time when such values were undergoing severe scepticism and even denial.

In 1947 Dorothy Canfield wrote a reminiscence on her friendship with Willa Cather, which concentrated primarily on the years in which Willa Cather taught and worked as a journalist in Pittsburgh before taking the post of editor of *McClure's* in New York. "As we grew on into the twenties and thirties," she remembered, "this difference in years dwindled to nothing at all, as such differences do to adults, so far as any barrier to our close comradeship went. But my lifelong admiring affection for Willa was, at first, strongly tinctured with the respectful deference due from a young person to a successful member of the older generation."[3] In this statement Canfield made an honest attempt to evaluate her attitude towards Willa Cather which contains some irony in that Canfield seemed to implicitly use her friend as a norm for her own career.

The Vermont novelist records how she would frequently stop over in Pittsburgh on her travels from Arlington to Ohio State University in order to keep up her friendship with Willa Cather. On one occasion she spent the entire Christmas holidays with her friend. She rejoiced in Cather's early literary success and shared in the friendships that her older companion had already made in Pittsburgh with the McClungs, the Andersons, and the Seibels.[4]

Leon Edel gives Dorothy Canfield Fisher singular praise for her assistance with his writing of the Pittsburgh chapter in *Willa Cather: A Critical Biography,* citing her complete and careful answers to his detailed questions.[5] And Mildred Bennett records how the manuscript of a book that Willa Cather worked on about 1903 and which never got published ended up in the Fishers' Arlington attic.[6] Clearly the Cather-Canfield relationship continued to grow beyond the college years.

One episode in the lives of these two American novelists continues to survive as a favorite anecdote of biographers and commentators. During Cather's tour of Europe in 1902, along with Isabelle McClung, a visit was made to the English poet A. E. Housman. Isabelle McClung and Willa Cather had prearranged to meet Dorothy Canfield, already living that year in Paris where her mother, Flavia, an artist, had a studio. Isabelle and Willa, before meeting Dorothy in London, journeyed to the Shropshire country, toured Ludlow castle and returned to a not-so-fine apartment in suburban London where Housman, teaching at Cambridge, lived. Housman did not expect the visit, and the rapport left much to be desired. Most accounts of the visit carry the overtone that Willa Cather (her *April Twilights and Other Poems* [1923] certainly shows her awareness of Housman's art) was the most anxious of the three to meet Housman, but as the visit progressed, she realized that things were not going smoothly. The accounts generally credit Dorothy Canfield with saving the day, as

Housman found in her conversation a common bond of interest—classical philology, which she worked at through her studies in Romance languages at the École des Hautes Études in Paris. Housman began to ask questions and found common scholarly interests with the young language student from America. Evidently these common interests averted the embarrassment which otherwise might have resulted from the unscheduled visit to the scholar-poet.

This visit to Housman later became the chief subject of an exchange of letters between Dorothy Canfield and Willa Cather immediately before the latter's death in 1947. Willa Cather wrote a letter to Dorothy Canfield on April 17th of that year asking that her friend supply her with a detailed and accurate account of the Housman visit in order to satisfy some editor's request.[7] In this letter Cather writes disdainfully of the harassment by young scholars who forwarded their critiques of Housman to the aging and tired novelist and expected her commentaries on them. (Shades of Horace must have risen in Willa Cather's mind on those occasions. *Odi profanum vulgus!*) This letter, the last one that Willa Cather ever wrote, with Cather's remembrance of the Housman visit fully substantiates the standard description of Dorothy Canfield's part.

Canfield replied immediately with an extended letter regarding the celebrated visit. She quickly received a note from Sarah Bloom, a faithful secretary of twenty years, affirming that Willa Cather had received the letter before she died. Dorothy Canfield's careful recollection does not change the basic description of the event. She does add these closing remarks in her letter:

> But I really felt very uneasy, about what seemed bad manners on my part, and after we had gone, and were sitting on top of the bus, going back to our lodgings, and I saw you were weeping, my heart was simply broken because I thought I had spoiled the whole occasion for you. But generously, warmheartedly, you relieved me by assuring me that your feeling had nothing to do with anything I had done during the visit. I thought it then (and still think it) characteristically great-hearted of you not to have minded.
>
> With all my love, dear old comrade, your devoted
>
> Dorothy[8]

The Canfield papers at the University of Vermont contain two files of letters and brief notes written by Willa Cather to Dorothy Canfield, the earliest dated from Pittsburgh in 1897, a social note enquiring after Dorothy's mother, Flavia.[9] The last letter, already alluded to, was the last one Willa Cather wrote to anyone. In between the collection contains over seventy pieces of correspondence, mostly handwritten letters of six to eight pages. These lively and friendly exchanges discuss their literary endeavors, their mutual friends, and their personal hopes and expectations. The largest gap in the continuity of the letters is between late summer of 1904 or 1905 and the spring of 1916 when Dorothy Canfield received a two-page letter of consolation at the time of her father's death. The letters which follow the resumption of the correspondence make it clear that the two friends had a falling out. A letter written in the late summer of either 1904 or 1905, addressed not to Dorothy Canfield but to her mother, laments that Willa had caused the breach in the friendship with Dorothy.[10] That it was not merely of a passing nature seems indicated by the cautiousness of Willa Cather's approach and the tone of the letters when the correspondence resumes more than a decade later. Cather's letters have a carefully stated apologetic and conciliatory tone indicating that too much time has separated a very fast friendship dating back to their school days in Lincoln. Willa Cather never mentions the specific cause of this breakup. Did the break follow some sort of social slight, which the older woman, more successfully launched on her writing career, gave to her young friend? One can only conjecture in the absence of a *specific* mention of the cause.

When they reestablished the friendship (which has more significance than the separation), there continued a sympathetic and lasting bond between the two women until Cather's death in 1947. Whenever the name of Willa Cather came into my conversations with Dorothy Canfield, she clearly manifested a loyalty to her memory and sometimes added an admonition about her desire to support Willa Cather's sense of privacy and the restrictions she made in regard to her papers.[11]

As the correspondence between the two resumed in 1916, they mentioned, for example, their current output of novels, ***The Bent Twig*** and *The Song of the Lark* (1915).[12] Sometimes Cather comments that Canfield can well speak more knowingly about the Cather novels because she had known the struggle behind the novelist's climb to success.

In a letter to Dorothy Canfield dated April 8, 1921, Cather urges that they meet. She confides that she always saved the criticisms of her books in letters from her friends, and she implies their friendship means more because they have known something of the past together.[13] This letter also reveals that Willa Cather had some serious concern about the writing of the last part of her current work, *One of Ours* (1922). If any one thing was instrumental in bringing the two women back together again, it appears from these letters of Willa Cather to be the psychological support she derived from Dorothy Canfield's critical support for *One of Ours* at a time when Cather was undergoing more uncertainty about the worth of her creation, apparently, than she had with any of her other novels. Willa Cather had, as many know, a very deep critical sense of her own books, even as she wrote them. The tone of her letters to Dorothy Canfield indicates that Cather was experiencing more than ordinary difficulties over the satisfactory completion of this novel.

When Willa Cather finished her work on *One of Ours* in February, 1922, she asked Dorothy Canfield to read the page proofs of the novel and to note any discrepancies in factual matters or other false notes.[14] In another letter, about a month later, Cather confided to Dorothy Canfield what she had told to only very few, if any, others (not even Alfred Knopf) that she drew from her real life cousin, Grosvenor P. Cather, Jr., for her hero of *One of Ours*, Claude Wheeler.[15] Grosvenor was killed at Cantigny, France, on May 27, 1918. Willa Cather had known the young man quite well, since he grew up on a farm adjacent to her father's in Nebraska where she had helped to take care of him. The real life Grosvenor, Cather implies, had much in common with the fictional Claude Wheeler in that he had a difficult time in finding himself in his growth to manhood and then had his life ended abruptly through the ultimate irony of the Great War.

Apparently Dorothy Canfield reacted critically in reading the page proofs of the segment of the novel in which David Gerhardt, an accomplished violinist and Claude's primary friend overseas, brings Claude with him to visit David's friends and relatives. At their visit to Mlle. Claire's, David, who had gone to war as a humane act, is prevailed upon to play the Saint-Saen violin concerto with Mlle. Claire as accompanist. In the novel Cather writes of Claude, "The music was a part of his own confused emotions. He was torn between generous admiration, and bitter, bitter envy. What would it mean to be able to do anything as well as 'that, to have a hand capable of delicacy and precision and power?"[16]

In her reply to Dorothy Canfield's comments, Willa Cather expressed amusement and said that she really had not drawn that sequence from talks with AEF (American Expeditionary Forces) soldiers (as she had gotten certain other background materials for this novel).[17] Rather, she said that Claude's reactions to the music were the feelings that she had actually experienced at a time the two women novelists were in France together (and, presumably, at a time when Dorothy Canfield had played the violin at some social occasion). Cather affirmed that Dorothy Canfield was not aware of those feelings at that time, but she thought that the way she felt must have been the way many soldiers felt. Several more letters during April, May and June of 1922 continued this vein of sympathetic exchange about *One of Ours* and especially about Claude Wheeler.

In a letter in May, 1922, Cather may have revealed the key to the earlier, troubled relationship.[18] She commented on the differences in the cultural background and social status between herself and her Vermont friend. She pointed out the fact that Dorothy's father and mother were intellectually inclined and that Dorothy had grown up in a college atmosphere. Willa Cather once again linked her own past with that of Claude Wheeler and stated how her friend Dorothy Canfield can understand how she, the author of *One of Ours,* had had such a struggle for her place in the sun.

In 1921 Cather recognized that she could look with greater tolerance on any misunderstanding they had in the past.

Willa Cather probably did not have a large concern about her friend's critical remarks about the novel, and more than likely she did not change anything in her text because of Dorothy Canfield's responses. Importantly, however, at a point in her career that many critics signal as the most crucial, Cather turned to an old friend and continued her efforts at maintaining the friendship, and she found genuine comfort from the support she received in return. Great and critically sensitive artist that Cather was, she must have sensed that the war episodes in *One of Ours* were not quite right and that even the moral support from Dorothy Canfield represented more the benevolence of a friend than an adroit critical assessment.

In an extended letter to Dorothy Canfield during this same period Cather wrote that she seldom dreamed, but that when she did, Dorothy Canfield commonly appeared as the subject.[19] Cather, in her fifties, spoke of herself entering that period of her life when reflection had become a pattern or habit, though she had never really practiced it before in her life. Especially, she remarked, she would look back upon admired, familiar figures of her youth and see them in much clearer perspective. Such cherished friends were always several years older than herself, and Dorothy Canfield was the exception to this rule. Willa Cather in unequivocal terms stated that her friend was the only one of the younger set with whom she had very strong ties, even though Dorothy Canfield used to vex her somewhat in those earlier years by pursuing so many interests that Cather regarded as ephemeral. (Along with music, writing, and other interests Dorothy Canfield also practiced fencing.)

The pattern which emerges from the letters shows the older novelist as genuinely attracted to the personal charm of Dorothy Canfield and, more important, beneath the charm a sincerely gracious human being whose life rested on solid values. Dorothy Canfield probably quit her successful career writing fiction simply because she saw many other things that she might do which she found more important. The promotion of the Book-of-the-Month Club was just one of many projects that Dorothy Canfield undertook and pursued steadily until her eyesight prevented further effective participation. As a charter member of its board of judges, she hoped to upgrade and influence the reading habits of a very large group of Americans. Dorothy Canfield simply felt quite strongly that life could be better served in social action rather than by continuing to write fiction. Her good friend Willa Cather would never come to a similar decision about her own career as a novelist. Cather cherished the work of the writer and was at work on her Carcassonne story at the time of her death.

The letters of Willa Cather to Dorothy C. Fisher continued for the next two decades without any large intermission, and their tone does not change significantly. The two old friends exchanged brief comments on the books that each wrote and they commented on mutual friends such as Robert Frost whom Dorothy Canfield knew very well from Bread Loaf and other occasions. Frost, a fellow Vermont writer, may have been first introduced to Willa Cather by Dorothy Canfield. They also wrote of plans for an occasional visit with each other. Willa Cather, who is buried in the Monadnoc Region of New Hampshire, and who used to frequent the MacDowell artists' colony in Peterborough at an earlier period, saw a resemblance between Housman's Shropshire country and southern New England. Dorothy Canfield's Arlington, Vermont, was not very far away, and the letters indicate Willa Cather and Dorothy Canfield exchanged occasional visits.

Dorothy Canfield wrote an article about Willa Cather in 1933 which she entitled **"Daughter of the Frontier"** and in which she made a serious effort to interpret the spirit and the Willa Cather she saw in and behind the fiction.[20] She found Cather's fiction the most significant of any American author writing about the life of the hundreds of thousands of immigrants who came into Nebraska and neighboring states between 1880 and 1900 and assumed the responsibility of making a new life and new communities. She viewed Cather's family from Virginia as part of that immigration. Young Willa Cather herself was caught up in the frontier effort, and just when it seemed that the frontiersmen were succeeding in their great venture, in a single decade there came severe crop failures from a series of droughts. These same years coincided with the Cather years at the University of Nebraska. In Canfield's estimate Willa Cather's spirit largely was shaped in those years. The great effort she expanded towards gaining first a position for herself in the world of journalism and then recognition among many other fine writers, Canfield saw as best understood as deriving from her life on the frontier. "She intended to live not to brood over a communal heartbreak she could not help. She put out a strong hand and began to take what she wanted. Why not? What she wanted was hers by right. She took it away from no man."[21] Yet what Cather took, she gave back in another way in her creations of pioneer men and women. Her career commands our respect, rewards our reading interests and, in a true sense, nourishes our spirits long afterwards.

Dorothy Canfield also grew up in the plains region during those difficult years. But her father, a very successful humanities scholar and later a college administrator, provided his daughter with more of the amenities of life than the Cathers could give to their daughter. Under these circumstances it becomes easier to understand how the younger "daughter of the frontier" became a role model for her older friend. And perhaps it is even understandable how there might have been a straining of their relationship as the two young women began to make their way separately in the world. But their friendship proved to be very strong.

Like Antonia Chimerda and Jim Burden these two had shared the Optima Dies which, even if they are the first to flee from us, also have power to bind as well. Cather and Canfield "possessed together the precious, the incommunicable past."

NOTES

[1] The only exception to this statement is Edith Lewis, *Willa Cather Living* (New York: Octagon, 1976), which makes no mention of D. C. Fisher.

[2] James R. Shively, ed., (Lincoln: University of Nebraska Press, 1950), pp. 115-142.

[3] "Novelist recalls Christmas in Blue-and-Gold Pittsburgh," *New York Herald Tribune*, "Books," Dec. 21, 1947, p. 42.

[4] *Ibid.*, p. 42.

[5] E. K. Brown (with Leon Edel), *Willa Cather: A Critical Biography* (New York: Alfred A. Knopf, 1953), p. 344.

[6] "Willa Cather in Pittsburgh," The Prairie Schooner, XXXIII (Spring 1939), 72.

[7] Canfield Mss., Letter from Willa Cather to Dorothy Canfield Fisher, April 17, 1947, Wilbur Collection, Bailey-Howe Library, University of Vermont, Burlington, Vermont. The Wilbur Collection contains a large gathering of Dorothy Canfield's papers and correspondence. Characteristically she assembled them there to assist students.

[8] *Ibid.*, D.C.F. to W.C., April 1947.

[9] *Ibid.*, W.C. to D.C.F., October 10, 1897.

[10] *Ibid.*, W.C. to Mrs. James H. Canfield, late summer 1904 or 1905.

[11] Conversation with the author when he lived and taught in Vermont.

[12] Canfield Mss., April 15, 1916.

[13] *Ibid.*, W.C. to D.C.F., April 8, 1921.

[14] *Ibid.*, W.C. to D.C.F., February 6, 1922.

[15] *Ibid.*, W.C. to D.C.F., March 5, 1922.

[16] Willa Cather, *One of Ours* (New York: Alfred A. Knopf, Inc., 1922), pp. 417-8.

[17] Canfield Mss., W.C. to D.C.F., late March 1922.

[18] *Ibid.*, W.C. to D.C.F.

[19] *Ibid.*, W.C. to D.C.F., June 21, 1922.

[20] *New York Herald Tribune,* "Books," May 28, 1933, pp. 9 and 11.

[21] *Ibid.,* p. 11.

Mark J. Madigan (essay date 1990)

SOURCE: "Willa Cather's Commentary on Three Novels by Dorothy Canfield Fisher," in *ANQ: A Quarterly Journal of Short Articles, Notes and Reviews,* Vol. 3, No. 1, January, 1990, pp. 13-15.

[*In the following essay, Madigan considers Willa Cather's exhortation to prose writers that they simplify their style in relation to her estimate of Fisher's novels* Rough-Hewn, The Deepening Stream, *and* Seasoned Timber.]

In her 1922 essay "The Novel Demeublé," which was first published in the *New Republic* and later collected in *Not Under Forty,* Willa Cather claimed that the novel had been, for a long while, "overfurnished" (43). She argued in that essay for a clearing away of unnecessary novelistic "furniture," for an uncluttered prose style: "Whatever is felt upon the page without being specifically named there—that, one might say, is created. It is the inexplicable presence of the thing not named, of the overtone divined by the ear but not heard by it, the verbal mood, the emotional aura of the fact or the thing or the deed, that gives high quality to the novel or the drama, as well as to poetry itself" (50). Cather, who had little patience for what she considered to be the excesses of certain realists, went so far as to say that "the importance of material objects and their vivid presentation have been so stressed, that we take it for granted whoever can observe, and can write the English language, can write a novel" (43). Considering that Cather seldom wrote book reviews after becoming a successful author, four letters to her long-time friend, novelist Dorothy Canfield Fisher, provide interesting evidence of her literary theories in practice.

In an October 1922 letter (which, like all Cather's letters, may not be quoted due to a restriction in her will), Cather complimented Fisher on her novel published that year, ***Rough-Hewn.*** Cather's reaction to the book—which tells the story of Neale Crittenden and Marise Allen, two young Americans who fall in love in Rome and eventually make a life together in Vermont—echoed the principles set forth in "The Novel Demeublé." Neale's father, Daniel Crittenden, and Marise were especially vivid characters to Cather. She told Fisher this was because they were portrayed more suggestively than literally. Fisher's economical rendering of character allowed Cather more imaginative freedom as a reader.

Fisher was not as successful with Neale Crittenden, whose character seemed unfocused to Cather because too much was told about him. She said Neale would have been more clear if he had been presented in far less detail. The section on Neale's college life, "An Education

in the Humanities," could have been reduced by half, according to Cather, who compared this over-characterization to the way a brother and sister can become so familiar with each other that they lose all sense of their individuality. In life and in fiction, Cather told Fisher, characters may be better perceived from a distance.

Cather responded similarly to Fisher's 1930 novel, ***The Deepening Stream.*** In December of that year she wrote to Fisher expressing her satisfaction with two characters, Morris and Jessica Gilbert, the father and mother in Fisher's autobiographical novel of her youth. The elder Gilberts seemed real to Cather, but that quality was lost in the portrayal of the Gilberts' daughter Matey because her character was brought too close to the reader. Matey could be seen best, according to Cather, in relation to her family and surroundings, rather than through direct description.

Cather admitted to Fisher that she once made the same mistake of telling too much about a character when writing of Thea Kronborg in *The Song of the Lark.* In a March 15, 1916 letter, Cather explained that she should not have followed Thea's later years in such close detail, since the development of an artist's life moves from the personal to the impersonal. She later made her statement public, writing in the preface to the revised edition of *The Song of the Lark* in 1932, "Success is never so interesting as struggle—not even to the successful, not even to the most mercenary forms of ambition" (v). Cather edited the latter sections of the original edition to reflect that belief.

Continuing in the 1930 letter on the subject of ***The Deepening Stream,*** Cather named Marcel Proust as a writer who used minute detail. Cather said Proust's method should only be used in the first person, however, and she quoted his *Cities of the Plain* to make her point. If one grew tired of Proust's extended description of Albertine, Cather said, one could simply stop reading and fault the author directly. She concluded by saying that most writers used the third person too intimately, as though it were first person narration.

In 1939 Cather read Fisher's ***Seasoned Timber***—the tale of a middle-aged high school principal who falls in love with a young teacher—and in a letter dated November 8, she lauded the author for her accomplishment with Miss Peck, an innkeeper in the novel. Cather's response was consistent with her statements in "The Novel Demeublé" and her 1920 essay "On the Art of Fiction," in which she wrote: "Art, it seems to me, should simplify. That, indeed, is very nearly the whole of the higher artistic process; finding what conventions of form and what detail one can do without and yet preserve the spirit of the whole—so that all that one has suppressed and cut away is there to the reader's consciousness as much as if it were in type on the page" (*On Writing* 102). Once again, Cather said Fisher was successful with Miss Peck because she selectively used detail. In Cather's view, Fisher achieved her most vivid characterization when she suppressed her inclination toward direct description in **Seasoned Timber**. Fisher's characters were then brought to life by the quality which marks the best of Cather's own fiction: a quality "felt upon the page without being specifically named there."

WORKS CITED

Cather, Willa. Letters to Dorothy Canfield Fisher, 1899-1947. Special Collections, Bailey/Howe Library, Burlington, Vermont.

————. *Not Under Forty*. New York: Knopf, 1936.

————. *The Song of the Lark*. Boston: Houghton Mifflin, 1932.

————. *On Writing*. New York: Knopf, 1949.

Mark J. Madigan (essay date 1993)

SOURCE: An Introduction to *Keeping Fires Night and Day: Selected Letters of Dorothy Canfield Fisher*, edited by Mark J. Madigan, University of Missouri Press, 1993, pp. 1-22.

[*In the following introduction to his edition of Fisher's collected correspondence, Madigan investigates Fisher's life and literary career, and surveys the many qualities of her character and writing that are revealed in her letters.*]

I

In 1948 Dorothy Canfield Fisher (1879-1958) wrote to literary critic Albert L. Guerard about the University of Vermont's proposal to establish a collection of her papers at their Burlington campus:

> Their idea is not a bad one I think, not to wait until an author has been dead twenty or thirty years, and his children and grandchildren have lost most of his papers—for who nowadays with families moving around all the time could possibly keep a mass of papers together?—but to collect them while the author is still alive. Most of them will not be of any interest to anybody, perhaps none of them will be. But no harm is done in placing them in a fire-proof building instead of in a trunk under the eaves in the attic. (Letter 154)

These remarks reveal much about Fisher: her interest in public education, her foresight, her modesty, and her common sense. They also raise an important question: Of what interest and significance could Fisher's letters possibly be? The letters themselves present the best argument for their publication: set against the American historical and cultural landscape from 1900 to 1958, they are the firsthand account of a singularly gifted, intelligent, and spirited woman who, among many other accomplishments, became one of America's most popular novelists.

Named after the heroine of *Middlemarch*, Dorothea Francis Canfield was born on February 17, 1879, in Lawrence, Kansas. She and her older brother, James, were the children of James Hulme Canfield, a university professor, and Flavia Camp Canfield, an artist. Dorothy grew up in a cultured home and traveled widely while still a child. She moved from Lincoln, Nebraska, to Columbus, Ohio, and then to New York City as her father relocated for academic appointments, and she paid frequent visits to the Arlington, Vermont, home of her father's relatives, and to Paris, where her mother kept a studio. Her early homelife was loving and supportive, but it was not without difficulty. Biographer Ida H. Washington notes that young Dorothy was sensitive to a strain of incompatibility between her parents—a conflict Fisher described in a fictional guise in **The Deepening Stream**. About the relationship of James, an idealistic, ambitious teacher and school administrator, and Flavia, an equally fervent devotee of the arts, Washington writes, "Her quickness of speech and action were, however, to make problems for him as great as those his sense of social responsibility created for her. The differences in temperament created a home in which a sensitive little daughter grew into a deeply perceptive novelist."[1]

Fisher received her bachelor's degree from Ohio State University, where she had concentrated on languages and literature, particularly French. She pursued her scholarly interests at the graduate level, and her academic career culminated in 1904 when she received the Ph.D. in French from Columbia University with a dissertation on Corneille and Racine. Although her training qualified her for a university teaching career, Fisher turned down an offer of a professorship at Case Western Reserve University for family reasons and became secretary at the Horace Mann School in New York. In 1907 she married John Redwood Fisher. A fellow graduate of Columbia, he had been captain of the football team and roommate of Alfred Harcourt, who would later become Dorothy's publisher. They soon moved to Arlington, where she had inherited her great-grandfather's farm. From that Vermont home base she pursued one of the most productive careers in all of American literature.

In all, Fisher published twenty-two works of fiction (for business purposes under her maiden name, Dorothy Canfield) and eighteen works of nonfiction covering a remarkably wide range of subjects. She introduced the child-rearing methods of Dr. Maria Montessori to the United States in **A Montessori Mother** (1912), was a pioneering advocate of adult education in **Why Stop Learning?** (1927), translated Giovanni Papini's *Life of Christ* (1923) and Adriano Tilgher's *Work: What It Has Meant to Men through the Ages* (1931) from the Italian, chronicled the history of Vermont (her adopted home state and the setting for much of her fiction) in **Vermont Tradition** (1953), and wrote several highly regarded books for children (now commemorated by the children's book award that bears her name).

A woman of manifold talents, Fisher's achievements were hardly limited to the literary world. She spoke five languages, founded a Braille press and a children's hospital in France during World War I, organized the Children's Crusade for Children during World War II, was the first president of the Adult Education Association, and was the first woman to serve on the Vermont State Board of Education. Shortly before Fisher's death, Eleanor Roosevelt referred to her as one of the ten most influential women in America.

The variety of her activities notwithstanding, it was primarily as a fiction writer that Fisher was best known and as which she wanted to be remembered.[2] She said in 1944 that writing fiction was "like falling in love" (Letter 134) and worried a year before her death that a biography in progress was "saying too much about actual material actions and activities of mine, and giving too little space to the novels and short stories" (Letter 185). To Fisher, writing was the chief means for making a decisive difference in the world, for educating her fellow citizens, for promulgating moral principles, for initiating social change. Her novels *The Brimming Cup* and *The Home-Maker,* for instance, critique the evils of racism, sexism, and materialism while promoting the virtues of equal access to education and employment.

Yet she did not view her fiction as merely ideological. She was an accomplished critic and was ever-conscious of the flaws in her own work. A tireless reviser, she often felt a sense of artistic inadequacy upon finishing a story or novel. In 1925, she wrote to the author of a soon-to-be-published rhetoric: "I can dimly remember a happy time when I could look at a page of mine and think 'Well, I don't see what more I can do to that.' Never any more! Any page of mine, taken at random, throws me into an acute fever of remorse for the mistakes in it, and an ardent desire to sit down and wrestle with it. This does not increase the joy of authorship, of course, but I hope it increases the quality of the product" (Letter 64).

What emerges clearly from the correspondence is that Fisher lived her life as one piece, drawing together many interests and concerns, so that it is virtually impossible to separate the literary from the biographical, the private from the public. Indeed, to understand the primacy of writing to Fisher is to appreciate its interrelation with the other elements of her life.

II

Fisher's literary career began, like that of many American authors of the early twentieth century, by way of publication in popular magazines—especially women's magazines—such as the *American, Everybody's,* and *Harper's Bazaar.* She had little trouble placing her work and was publishing a steady flow of stories and articles within a few years. Her first novel, *Gunhild,* was published by Holt in 1907, sold only six hundred copies, and received little critical attention.[3] *The Squirrel*

Cage appeared five years later to far more favorable reviews. For example, a notice in the *San Francisco Call* read, "We do not quarrel any more about 'The' great American novel, but no reader will deny that this is 'A' great American novel," while the reviewer for the *Progressive Woman* unabashedly stated, "*The Squirrel Cage* deserves to rank as one of the best American novels yet written."

As a result of the novel's reception and the burgeoning market for her magazine work, Fisher attracted the attention of Paul Reynolds, the first literary agent in America. Although reluctant to employ an agent at first (Letter 11), Fisher prospered from her association with him. Through his connections in the publishing world, Reynolds brought Fisher's name to a wider readership, and she soon expressed surprise at the prices he was able to secure for her stories.

Such business considerations were vital to her since she supported a husband and two young children (a daughter, Sally, was born in 1909 and a son, James, in 1913). When Dorothy and John married, they planned to support themselves as professional writers. However, when Dorothy's literary career blossomed and outgrew his own, John assumed the role of secretary and editor of her work. Since they were rarely separated, John Fisher remains a background figure in the letters. (One exception is Letter 8 to Céline Sibut, in which DCF writes at length about her impending marriage.) All indications are that he was deeply loved by Dorothy and that he provided her with invaluable support. Biographer Ida H. Washington has called their home life "harmonious but unconventional." Washington writes, "Dorothy was the chief breadwinner, and John assumed an editorial, consultative relationship to her work. Dorothy thus played the major role in the outside world; at home, however, her respect and affection for her husband were constant, and she sought his judgment on matters practical and literary and submitted to his direction in the details of everyday life."[4] John also tended to the demanding physical chores of rural Vermont life and became involved in local and state politics, serving on the Vermont State Board of Education for many years.

Fisher's popular reputation continued to grow with publication of *The Bent Twig* (1915), a novel, and *Home Fires in France* (1918) and *The Day of Glory* (1919), collected stories based on her experiences in France during World War I. But she could hardly have imagined the success *The Brimming Cup* would encounter upon publication in 1921. Characterized by William Allen White as an "antidote" to the negative portrayal of small-town life in *Main Street,*[5] *The Brimming Cup* finished the year just behind Lewis's novel, as the second most purchased novel in the country. The work brought Fisher to her highest prominence so far; with that attention came the various honors and distractions attendant upon fame: requests for interviews and speeches; invitations to dinner receptions and university commencements; appeals to join committees, support worthy causes, and read the manuscripts of fledgling writers; and a flood of mail from readers across the country.

Nor did Fisher's reputation diminish. Her translation of Papini's *Life of Christ* was second on the best-seller list for nonfiction in 1923, and *The Home-Maker* was among the ten best-selling novels of 1924. *Her Son's Wife* (1926) also sold well and received considerable critical acclaim. William Lyon Phelps wrote to publisher Alfred Harcourt: "*Her Son's Wife* is Dorothy Canfield's masterpiece and it is also *a* masterpiece. It is a profound, subtle analysis of human character and human life and a very remarkable book. I predict that it will win the Pulitzer Prize for 1926. It deserves it" (August 25, 1926). Not surprisingly, the comment was featured in the novel's advertising. Although Sinclair Lewis won (and declined) the Pulitzer for *Arrowsmith* that year, Fisher remained one of America's best-known writers for decades.

The thirties brought three more popular novels, *The Deepening Stream* (1930), *Bonfire* (1933), and *Seasoned Timber* (1939), and two collections of stories, *Basque People* (1931) and *Fables for Parents* (1937). A Dorothy Canfield Club was established in 1934, but there is perhaps no more impressive testament to Fisher's popularity than the fact that the serial rights to *Bonfire* were under contract for thirty thousand dollars at the lowest ebb of the depression. The end of the decade was marked by the publication of Fisher's last novel, *Seasoned Timber* (1939). "The Knot-Hole" was published in the *Yale Review* in 1944 and won second prize among the stories in the O. Henry volume that year. Fisher revised earlier stories for *Four-Square* (1949), oversaw the publication of an anthology, *A Harvest of Stories* (1956), and continued to write children's books and magazine articles until near the time of her death in 1958. A letter to Mary C. Jane reveals that Fisher was at work on a history book for children in 1957, which was published posthumously (1959) as *And Long Remember* (Letter 187).

Yet even if she had published none of these works, Fisher would be a notable figure in American letters for her role as a Book-of-the-Month Club (BOMC) judge. She was one of the members on the Board of Selection from its inception in 1926 until 1951 (serving on the original Board with Henry Seidel Canby, William Allen White, Heywood Broun, and Christopher Morley, and later with Clifton Fadiman and John P. Marquand). The board chose the "book-of-the-month," which was regularly bought by more than half of the club's subscribers, and Fisher has been called one of the two "most influential" members of the board and its "most conscientious reader."[6] In fact, she read to the point of near-blindness, averaging fifteen books a month over her twenty-five-year tenure. Since by 1950 a million Americans belonged to the club and read the selections, it would be modest, but not incorrect, to say that she helped determine popular literary taste in America for nearly three decades. She did more: she shaped authors'

careers. Pearl Buck, Isak Dinesen (Karen Blixen), and Richard Wright were among the many writers Fisher introduced to the American public through the BOMC.

During her lifetime, Fisher was awarded the honorary degrees and prizes reserved for famous writers, and her works were anthologized and translated into several foreign languages. Yet lasting recognition has eluded Fisher. Her fiction was popular with the reading public, but not subsequently favored by those modernist critics who instead championed Faulkner, Fitzgerald, and Hemingway from the same period. Fisher's authentic narratives of everyday American life were deemed unfashionable, her narrative technique was considered too conventional, and she was relegated to a marginal position in the literary pantheon. She was not entirely ignored, though. In 1952, Edward Wagenknecht offered a dissenting estimation in *The Cavalcade of the American Novel*:

> She is often regarded as a merely "popular" writer, and criticism has done little with her work. Yet few novelists have had a richer intellectual background or enjoyed wider or more fructifying contacts with life. It is her great virtue that she has refused to shut her eyes to the horror and terror of human experience, at the same time declining to close her mind against the conviction that life is shot through with spiritual significance.

But the damning appraisal of F. Scott Fitzgerald held sway: "Dorothy Canfield as a novelist is certainly of no possible significance."[7] The first doctoral dissertation on Fisher, Joseph P. Lovering's *The Contribution of Dorothy Canfield Fisher to the Development of Realism in the American Novel,* appeared in 1956, and Elizabeth Yates's biography, *Pebble in a Pool,* was published in 1958, but without a solid base of critical support for the subject, a long period of silence followed.

However, interest in Fisher was revived again in the eighties, due in part to a re-evaluation of neglected women writers. Ida H. Washington's biography was published in 1982, scholarship on the BOMC grew, Fisher's friendship with Willa Cather received increased attention, paperback editions of *The Brimming Cup, The Home-Maker,* and *Her Son's Wife* were reissued, and Fisher's name began to appear once more in the *MLA Bibliography.* Given the current reappraisal of the American literary canon in terms of race, class, and gender, the time for a re-evaluation of Fisher's work is clearly at hand. Although her *ouevre* is uneven, she did write much that is of enduring value and interest. Fisher's stories based on her World War I experiences in Europe, for instance, provide a valuable and well-crafted counterpoint to the handling of similar subject matter by such male contemporaries as Hemingway. *The Brimming Cup,* too, is as rich in material detail as Sinclair Lewis's fiction, yet written from the woman's perspective, which Lewis's work lacks. *The Home-Maker,* finally, is a story of role-reversal in a marriage and has contemporary relevance to issues of child-rearing and women's rights. Fisher's letters collected here thus document the life of one of the twentieth century's most remarkable women in a way that no biography nor even the most autobiographical of her own works can. Here, in her own words, is the story of her life and literary career as told in correspondence spanning nearly six decades.

III

Dorothy Canfield Fisher was a prolific letter-writer. Her former secretary, Helen Congdon, recalls that she wrote several letters in her study nearly every day, usually in the afternoon or evening after finishing her professional writing. She wrote to friends, relatives, fellow authors, politicians, publishers, and readers. During a period in the mid-twenties, the quantity of Fisher's mail necessitated the use of a card that explained that she was unable to answer all of her letters. But she did respond to many of them, with letters to readers whom she had never met often running several pages. In 1943 her housekeeper, Elizabeth Cullinan, said, "Characteristically, she answers letters promptly, handles her own correspondence. It's enormous." Soon after Fisher's death, Bradford Smith also noted the volume of correspondence: "Into the house, as Dorothy's audience widened, poured a great tide of correspondence. Her writing made readers think of her as a friend. The mail literally came by the basketful. After it had come in, the small study often looked as if a whirlwind had struck it, with letters piled here and there according to the way they were to be handled. . . . "[8] The list of recipients in even a selected edition such as this bears evidence of the diversity of Fisher's correspondents. The eye may light on the famous names, but some of the most interesting letters are to common folk. There are also the names of the once famous, but now lesser-known, much like Fisher herself: Cleghorn, Suckow, Webster, and Yezierska. Lamentably, there are few extant letters to Fisher's immediate family—John, James, and Sally—as she was rarely apart from them.

Fisher's letters were usually typed on letterhead stationery, although occasionally she wrote by hand, during short trips away from Arlington, Vermont. Her typing could be erratic, but Fisher was generally attentive to details of spelling and grammar. Even though her eyesight began to fail in the mid-forties, Helen Congdon reports, Fisher continued to correspond by dictating her letters into a tape recorder.[9] She registered her dissatisfaction with "the remoteness of that way of answering letters" in 1955, but found no better alternative (Letter 181). Fisher once told Paul Reynolds that the process of writing a novel "usually ends by carrying me off my feet so that I can't think of anything else" (Letter 60), and she was absorbed by her letter writing in similar fashion. The enthusiasm she felt for crafting the language, for communicating her thoughts, feelings, and ideas is evident in both the quantity and quality of her correspondence. In many cases, what were intended to be polite notes turned into full-length epistles. Nearing the end of such letters would often come a sheepish apology

like that offered to William Lyon Phelps—"I oughtn't to bother you with such a long rambling letter. I didn't mean, when I began, to do more than to thank you" (Letter 44)—or some wry acknowledgment of the letter's generous length, such as her closing line to Harry and Bernardine Scherman, "Hastily—though you'd hardly believe it!" (Letter 101).

There is an immediacy to these letters, as though Fisher is conversing with her correspondent in person. They are peppered with colorful expressions of speech: "get-up-and-git" (Letter 29), "honest injun" (Letter 39), "a durn sight worse" (Letter 41), "wrestling like Jacob" (Letter 63), "a calorific meal" (Letter 104), and "a real Jenny-welcome" (Letter 174). Fisher's opening sentence to Pearl Buck, "How you and I always feel the impulse to put our heads together, to clasp hands closely, to share what is in our hearts, in grave moments of crisis!" (Letter 126), and poignant closing paragraph to Christopher Morley, "There, that's my news bulletin—of what's going on within. Little, really nothing—to report of what is visible physically—a quiet old country woman, deaf, with dimmed eyes, partially paralyzed, going slowly along the paths where she used to outrace her own children" (Letter 179), are but two examples of the intimacy she shared with her correspondents.

IV

The letters say a good deal about Fisher on a personal level. The complexity of the individual they reveal is commensurate with Fisher's wide interests, learning, and activities. What becomes immediately apparent is that Fisher lived in two worlds, one literary, one domestic. As a woman, wife, and mother of two children, she was expected to fulfill several roles. From the birth of Fisher's first child, Sally (who would also become a children's book author), in 1909 through her child-rearing years, Fisher's letters bear witness to the competing forces of art and domesticity in her daily life.

According to her mother, Fisher used to hold her son, Jimmy, to her breast with one hand and write with the other.[10] In 1912, she told Paul Reynolds that her daughter was growing older and needed "more time and attention" and that her literary output was "very limited" because she had "a great deal to do besides being an author" (Letter 11). Subsequent letters refer to the increased demands, which now included her elderly mother. She wrote to Alfred Harcourt in 1920: "We have been having a real siege here, with John in bed with a badly infected knee and a high temperature and us in quarantine with both children whooping it up with chicken-pox, and the thermometer at twenty below and me keeping fires night and day and tending to my sick-a-beds," (Letter 39). After spending a summer abroad to concentrate on the writing of *Rough-Hewn*, Fisher told Julia Collier Harris of the conditions under which she normally worked: "As a rule I work in the midst of a very stirring family and neighborhood life, with a thousand interruptions of all sorts. This is the first time I've been separated from the children for more than a day, since they were born, and the first time I've not kept house, the regular three-meals-a-day-routine, since I was a young girl. It seemed so strange to get up in the morning with nothing to do *except write*!" (Letter 49). Virginia Woolf's *A Room of One's Own* comes to mind when reading of how often the silence of Fisher's study was broken by her children, neighbors, and other visitors. The challenge Fisher faced was the same she articulated for women readers of *Mothers and Children*: to be a good wife and mother *and* to maintain interests outside of the home. As she told Henry Kitchell Webster, she did not believe that giving her children "orange-juice at the right hour" should be the sole concern of any woman (Letter 21). Fisher sought to define herself not only in relation to the needs of her family—which were paramount—but also as a writer. Her record of publication testifies to her success at finding time to write, but her letters show that the work was not produced without great effort and many distractions.

The same strong will that enabled Fisher to write amidst divergent responsibilities evinces itself elsewhere in the letters. In fact, Fisher was willing to risk her life for her beliefs, as illustrated by her participation in the World War I relief effort. In 1916, she made a perilous trip across the Atlantic with her two children to join her husband, who was working for the American Ambulance Corps in France. Before the war's end, she had founded a Braille press for blinded soldiers and a hospital for refugee children. Her readiness to volunteer is discussed in a letter to Sally Cleghorn:

> As you say, *now* is the time to stick to our principles . . . and it has made me sick to hear such crowds and crowds of Americans all writing vociferously to the papers that the Allies are fighting the cause of civilization for us, while we stand off in safety and profit by their blood and suffering . . . and yet nobody has done anything! Even John and I who have felt so keenly that France was standing between our world and all that threatened its permanence, have done nothing but send money, we haven't been willing to sacrifice our comfort and convenience . . . for that is practically all we are thinking of sacrificing now. There will be some danger of course, but not more than there always is in doing something worth doing. . . . (Letter 18)

Further evidence of this fiery side of Fisher's character is displayed in her description of a debate about modern literature with critic John Aldridge in 1949: "So by and by, I took an axe in one hand, a hatchet in the other and a knife between my teeth and sailed in. No courtesy is needed between an old woman and a young man, and my foot was on my native heath, and I wasn't under obligation to anybody—quite the contrary—for having invited me to Vermont" (Letter 162). The *Burlington Free Press* called the discussion, which was part of a literary symposium sponsored by the University of Vermont, a "slugfest." And Fisher was not one to couch her opinions in euphemisms. Commenting on Henry

James's satire of Boston reform women and his charge that they were destroying "the sentiment of sex," she wrote: "Is *that* a joke! As if anything could! And this fear lest the 'sentiment of sex' be diminished, from a man who, as far as the eye can see, never had a bit of it. Something like the Pope telling the world in all the modern languages about what the relations between husband and wife should be" (Letter 173).

Although she was at various times a social crusader, a campaigner for moral improvement, and a famous author, Fisher had a modest sense of self-importance and did not lack a sense of humor. A small woman, she often expressed her self-consciousness about her size through humor. In a 1916 letter to Louise Pound, she enclosed a photograph of herself standing next to a donkey and joked, "Now if you know how big a donkey is, you can see how tall I am" (see Letter 19 and photograph). In the same letter, she referred to a published photograph of herself with an upraised hand as being "ridiculously like the hand of a bishop, bestowing the episcopal blessing." Later, she wrote to Pound about publicity photographs in general, "The less people know how I look, the more they'll think of me" (Letter 22). This despite the fact that Fisher was, by all accounts, an attractive woman.

The letters also portray a woman of great generosity. That Fisher gave of her time and money to numerous worthy causes is a matter of public record. But the letters show her magnanimity in other ways. There is praise and support for her friends' work, as exemplified in the letters to Pearl Buck and Ruth Suckow. There are the offers to lend her name to the publicity of worthy books, such as James Weldon Johnson's *God's Trombones* (Letter 69). There are the efforts to get good books published, as in the case of Isak Dinesen's *Seven Gothic Tales*; and the careful readings of works-in-progress, as in the case of Anzia Yezierska's *All I Could Never Be*. There are also the more modest kindnesses, such as Fisher's response to an invitation to read: she suggested to the club woman that she also invite Sarah Cleghorn and pay her the honorarium in full (Letter 106).

One of the most intriguing episodes in the letters in regard to Fisher's character involves Willa Cather. The story of the Fisher-Cather friendship is chronicled in the 104 letters (all but five from Cather to Fisher), written during the years 1899 to 1947, that constitute the Cather file of the Fisher papers at the University of Vermont. Included in this collection are twenty-five letters (twenty by Cather, three by Fisher, one by Cather's mother, and one by Cather's friend Isabelle McClung) that had remained unread by anyone save the correspondents themselves until July 1987, when they were found in a barn on the Fisher homestead in Arlington. Along with assorted manuscripts and related material, they had been inadvertently left behind when Fisher's letters were donated to the university. These letters, like all of Cather's, may be neither published nor directly quoted, as specified by provisions in the author's will. Cather drew up these restrictions to protect her privacy and professional reputation; for the same reason she destroyed nearly all the letters she received.

Cather and Fisher were first drawn to each other by their mutual interests in French literature, painting, and music. Their friendship began in 1891 when Dorothy's father became chancellor of the University of Nebraska, where Cather was a student. Cather was then publishing stories and reviews in local and campus papers; Fisher was her younger admirer and protégée. Fisher felt most honored at the time to collaborate with Cather on a short story, **"The Fear That Walks by Noonday,"** which appeared in the university's literary magazine (and was reprinted in 1931, see Letters 84 and 88). Soon after Cather's death in 1947, Fisher remarked upon the regard in which she held her older friend: "Later on, of course, as we both grew into the twenties and the thirties, this difference in years [six] dwindled to nothing at all, as differences do to adults, so far as any barrier to our close comradeship went. But my lifelong admiring affection for Willa was, at first, tinctured with the respectful deference due from a younger person to a successful member of the older generation."[11]

Cather and Fisher stayed in touch after leaving Nebraska, as they would for most of their lives. Yet long gaps in the correspondence from 1905 to 1921 remained a mystery to Cather and Fisher scholars and occasioned a good deal of conjecture; it is only recently, with information from the newly found Cather-Fisher letters, that the rift may be understood. The dispute had its basis in Cather's first trip to Europe in 1902, when she met Evelyn Osborne, a friend and fellow graduate student of Fisher's. Although only passing reference is made to Osborne—a young woman with a prominent facial scar and a taste for extravagant clothes—in Cather's letters at the time of the trip, it was she who would later stand at the center of the disagreement over "The Profile"— significantly, the story of a young woman with a grotesque facial scar and an interest in extravagant clothes.

More specifically, "The Profile" is set in Paris, where portraitist Aaron Dunlap is commissioned to paint Virginia Gilbert, whose face bears a jagged scar on one side. Throughout their ensuing courtship the scar is never mentioned between the two, although Dunlap desperately wants to share the burden of Virginia's disfigurement. Even after their marriage and the birth of a daughter, Virginia's vanity prevents her from discussing the scar with Dunlap, which creates a gap between the husband and wife. When Dunlap becomes attracted to Virginia's cousin Eleanor, who is their houseguest, his wife leaves him. On the night of her departure, she arranges for a dressing table lamp to explode in Eleanor's face, so that she, too, is permanently disfigured. The story closes as Dunlap, mercifully divorced from Virginia, marries Eleanor.

Fisher first expressed concern about the story, which was to be included in *The Troll Garden,* Cather's first collection of short fiction, in a telegram sent a few days before Christmas 1904. Writing from Arlington to Cather in Pittsburgh, Fisher said she had just heard of "The Profile" and that she would "suspend judgment" until hearing from Cather, whom she implored to reply immediately. Cather did so, claiming that the story was not really cause for concern since, in her opinion, Virginia Gilbert did not resemble Osborne except for the scar on her face. She pointed out that the protagonist was married, unlike Osborne; that Osborne's taste in clothes was not nearly so bad; and that the story focused on the character's domestic infelicities, which could not possibly be traced to Fisher's friend. Scars were not so uncommon, Cather said, that one would link the character to Osborne specifically.

Fisher next asked Cather for a copy of the story, which reached Arlington on December 30. She wrote to Cather just two days later, pleading that it not be published for fear of the damage it would do to Osborne's delicate psyche: "I am quite sure you don't realize how exact and faithful a portrait you have drawn of her— her beautiful hair, her pretty hands, her fondness of dress and pathetic lapses of taste in wearing what other girls may, her unconsciousness—oh Willa don't do this thing. . . . I don't believe she would ever recover from the blow of your description of her affliction" (Letter 3; ellipsis mine).

Fisher's letter was answered promptly, not by Cather but by Isabelle McClung, to whom Cather had turned for advice. McClung firmly supported Cather's right to publish the story. Cather followed up McClung's letter with one of her own in which she said that the page proofs of *The Troll Garden* had already been returned to the press and that to omit "The Profile" would make an already slim volume too small to publish. She asked for Fisher's understanding and hoped that their friendship would remain intact.

Fisher, though, persisted in her efforts to protect Osborne. She told Cather that she had consulted with her parents about the affair and that they had recommended the matter be referred to *The Troll Garden*'s publisher, S. S. McClure, if Cather did not withdraw the story herself. When Cather failed to respond, Fisher wrote her final, uncharacteristically terse, letter on the matter, threatening "further action" (Letter 5). In "Autobiography in the Shape of a Book Review," the poet Witter Bynner, once Cather's editorial colleague, mentions a dispute over "The Profile" that took place at McClure's office. He describes the meeting between the two parties as "tense" and claims that Cather insisted on publication, even though it was suggested that Osborne might commit suicide if she read the story (253). Bynner did not name those who objected, but we can now be sure Fisher was among them. Finally, neither side could claim victory, for although the story did not appear in the 1905 edition of *The Troll Garden*—which was dedicated to Isabelle McClung—it was published two years later (June 1907) in *McClure's*. There is no evidence of whether Osborne ever read the work and no further mention of her in the Cather-Fisher correspondence.

The rift between the two authors was not bridged until nearly fifteen years later, when Cather enlisted Fisher's help in authenticating the details of the French setting of her Pulitzer Prize-winning novel, *One of Ours* (1922). They maintained a faithful correspondence thereafter, with Fisher paying Cather occasional visits at her New York apartment. Fisher's letter to Cather recollecting their 1902 visit to A. E. Housman was among the last Cather read before her death in 1947 (Letter 148).

The disagreement over "The Profile" is instructive for what it says about Fisher as an artist and person. While she was at the time of the dispute a published writer who had devoted a major part of her life to the formal study of literature, Fisher valued Osborne's feelings over Cather's story. She was also willing to risk Cather's longtime friendship for what she believed to be an issue of personal privacy and moral decency. As to the propriety of Fisher's actions, there is much to be said on both sides, but what is indisputable is her passion and resolve in defending Osborne. Some years later, Fisher took issue with Anzia Yezierska over modeling fictional characters after real people. In 1932, she objected to Yezierska's use of Arlington citizens as the basis for characters in her novel *All I Could Never Be* (Letter 91) and voiced her concern to the book's publisher, G. P. Putnam (Letter 89). Other letters document the care Fisher took to mask the identities of real people represented in her own work, including *The Deepening Stream* (Letter 81), *Seasoned Timber* (Letter 107), and **"The Bedquilt"** (Letter 138).

v

Readers will find these letters to be filled with information on American literature in general and Fisher's writing in particular. They deepen our knowledge of Fisher's sources and influences, her method of composition, and her authorial intentions. They offer the perspective of an author who was otherwise reluctant to "explain" her own works. They portray a serious artist who was concerned with the formal qualities of her writing, one who would not produce stories and novels carelessly for the high prices they commanded. At the same time, even as she wrote for traditional women's magazines, she could be experimental. A 1920 letter to William Lyon Phelps, for example, speaks about Fisher's use of point of view in *The Brimming Cup*:

> I have tried to make a glass door through which the reader looks into the heart and mind of one and another of the men, women, or children in the story, so that, once and for all, he knows what sort of human being is there. From that time on, it has been my intention to leave the reader to interpret for himself the meaning of the actions of that character, without the traditional explanations and re-iterated indications from the author. (Letter 44)

Among the broad patterns we observe in the letters is the growth and maturation of Fisher as a writer. Her progression from literary neophyte to self-assured professional manifests itself in several ways, one of which is a shift in tone in her correspondence with her agent and publishers. The earliest letter in this collection, to Louis Wiley of the *New York Times,* and a later one to Curtis Hidden Page are strikingly deferential in their phrasing. The nascent author informs Wiley that she would be willing to write an article on Spain "wholly subject" to his specifications and approval (Letter 1), and tells Page that "I handle my pen as I do my tongue and that is alas, quite without art" (Letter 3).

By 1924, however, Fisher's voice had grown more sure and authoritative. When pressed by her agent Reynolds to begin work on **Her Son's Wife** that year, she spoke her mind in no uncertain terms: "I do protest against being lumped in with the loafing authors who don't work unless they're hurried into it. No sir, by gracious, that is not me. Nobody *can* hurry me" (Letter 60). As she became a more experienced author, her letters to people in publishing took on a brisk and executive air. As far as the actual writing was concerned, though, she never lost the excitement and anxiety felt by a beginner. After almost fifty years as a professional author, Fisher told Bennett Cerf that she still never began work on a book "without butterflies in the stomach, like a singer going out on the platform for a solo" (Letter 163).

Fisher was assertive as far as the artistic integrity of her works was concerned. By all evidence, her business relationships were amicable—as long as the business people did not interfere with her creative talent. For instance, she refused to alter a story line dealing with anti-Semitism in **Seasoned Timber** that drew criticism from an editor considering the book for serialization. She wrote to Paul Reynolds:

> The story would lose its point if that strong element were left out. . . . I think race prejudice is creeping in insidiously to American life (for instance I bet you a nickel that the Country Club of your own town of Scarsdale is closed to Jews—without regard to their individual refinement or desirability). I'm ashamed of it, and I think most decent Americans would be ashamed of it, if they stopped to think about it. (Letter 105, ellipsis mine)

While nonfiction articles and serialized versions of novels were primarily a source of income, Fisher saw her books as her contribution to the world of letters. From romantic, often sentimental, magazine stories, she turned to novel-length examinations of human relationships and sought to portray them with depth and skill. As she once told William Lyon Phelps, "the richness and endless variety of human relationships . . . that's what authors, even the finest and greatest, only succeed in hinting at. It's a hopeless business, like trying to dip up the ocean with a tea-spoon" (Letter 44). Even in the case of serials, she could be reticent to compromise.

After a meeting with a magazine editor concerning the possible serialization of **The Brimming Cup**, she objected to the suggestion that each installment end with a "big crisis": "I said earnestly that I wouldn't guarantee her that, nor even that I would in any degree try for that, and I wanted her to understand that fully, before she thought any more about the matter. In fact that I wouldn't guarantee her *any*thing in the way of style or 'action' etc." (Letter 41). And in the case of **Bonfire**, Fisher wrote two versions: a streamlined one, which was less risque in certain details of setting and plot for serialization, and another, "doing it as I want to do it" for book publication (Letter 87). While she habitually expressed doubt about the finished product, her commitment to the craft of writing is clear.

Fisher's letters also add a wealth of new information and insight to what we know of her literary taste and aesthetics. The breadth of her reading is immediately apparent. Trained as a scholar of French literature and foreign languages, her reading interests were far-ranging. She knew the classics and read widely in contemporary literature for the BOMC. The letters make plain her affection for Shakespeare, for the great Russian novelists, especially Tolstoy, and for the French, including Balzac and the fabulist LaFontaine. More modern preferences are also indicated for Buck, Cather, Dinesen, Frost, and Wright. In addition, she wrote to Julia Collier Harris in admiration of Harry Stillwell Edwards's and Joel Chandler Harris's stories featuring African-Americans (Letter 70), and a 1948 letter notes an early appreciation of Eudora Welty (Letter 152).

Fisher freely acknowledged the distinguished efforts of her peers in her published reviews, but restricted most negative criticism to her letters. In them we find some of her most lively, engaging literary commentary. She clearly had little taste for works containing rough language, explicit sex, or graphic violence. (John O'Hara, whose *Appointment in Samarra* Fisher criticized for an overabundance of those very elements, once referred to her as "Dorothy, I can field—no great pleasure, Mrs. Fisher"). Nor was she enamored of what she perceived to be a preoccupation with alienation, corruption, and meaninglessness in modern literature. Yet she did not care for escapist fiction either, as she explained to a Book-of-the-Month Club subscriber, who complained that the judges' choices were unsuitable for young people:

> No good is ever done, I think, by pretending that anything is different from what it really is, either in our explicit statement, or by implication. The prettifying of human relations in conventional old-fashioned, mid-nineteenth-century fiction, was responsible for some ghastly shocks when the readers of those pleasant books came up, in real life, against something which the novels they had read had led them to assume did not exist. (Letter 141)

At a time when moral values and meaning and even human communication were considered outmoded, Fisher held fast to her belief that the true artist wrote with a desire to express, in a helpful way, some new understanding about human life. She summarized her view in a 1945 letter: "The impulse of the writing person is to share this new understanding with the rest of humanity. He feels its importance as a help to understanding what takes place around us, and can hardly wait until he has put it into some form in which, he hopes, others may see the significance of events in human life which they have been taking perhaps callously, perhaps just with dull or slow lack of understanding" (Letter 138). Thus, Fisher did not reject modern literature per se, but bristled at many of its salient tendencies. In the modern tradition, she believed that literature should reflect the reality of the human condition. In her judgment of fiction for the BOMC, she was said to exercise "exacting standards" and to focus on "the accuracy of image, the unity of plot, the depth of characterization."[12] Her optimistic world view and belief in moral values, though, set her apart from the literary mainstream.

The correspondence also affords an opportunity to observe the application of Fisher's literary principles to specific works. An admirer of the tales of Hans Christian Andersen (see Letter 6), she did not hesitate to suggest that highly praised books of both past and present wore no finery. Such was the case with James Boswell's *Life of Samuel Johnson, LL.D.* Prior to a 1950 BOMC meeting in which *Boswell's London Journal, 1762-1763* was to be considered as a selection, she wrote to Harry Scherman to vent her dislike of Boswell and eighteenth-century literature as a whole. Her purpose in writing to Scherman in advance of the meeting was to avoid offending her colleague and friend Christopher Morley, who had written an adulatory "Introduction" to the newly discovered journal. "I have felt all my life, that Boswell's *Life of Johnson* is enormously overestimated by professors of English Literature, and really is a bore to most people (as it certainly was to me)," she wrote (Letter 167). Fisher found the *Life* overly long and saw no need for the further elaboration in the London journal. She held nothing back in her letter to Scherman: "To add to that, *more* Boswell saying tiresomelessly over and over what has already been told to us in other books, about a period of no importance anyhow, and about a shallow-natured, trivial-minded man—." The journal was, finally, not chosen as a book-of-the-month but sent to subscribers as a dividend.

A striking example of Fisher's disdain for a more contemporary work is found in her letter concerning the Detroit ban against the sale and library circulation of Ernest Hemingway's *To Have and Have Not (Letter 109)*. In reaction to complaints by the Detroit Council of Catholic Organizations, the novel was ruled to be obscene by city authorities in 1938. The League of American Writers protested the censorship, and Archibald MacLeish drafted a letter of protest, which was signed by Van Wyck Brooks and Thornton Wilder and published in the *Nation*. The letter charged that the real reason for the censure of the book was that the Catholic

Church objected to Hemingway's involvement in the war in Spain. "Only a prurient mind could possibly find the book offensive," MacLeish wrote.[13] When Fisher, an otherwise ardent supporter of public libraries and free speech, was asked to add her signature to the letter, she replied, "I don't feel like signing it myself." She argued that MacLeish's reasoning was weak, but she also let it be known that she and several of her peers found the book to be "offensive."

Other notable figures who are subject to pointed criticism in the letters include George Santayana (a "heartless" man, Letter 122), John Steinbeck (*The Wayward Bus* was "false to human probability," Letter 146), Norman Mailer (*The Naked and the Dead* was vulgar, Letter 153), Sinclair Lewis (Fisher picked up his books "as with the tongs," Letter 156), John Dos Passos (the characters in *The Grand Design* were "nothing but names on the page, floating in and out of the interminable cocktail drinking, gossiping *talk* which fills the book," Letter 157), Arthur Miller (*Death of a Salesman* evinced an "odd lack of connection with reality," Letter 160), and D. H. Lawrence (whose works presented Indians as "demi-gods," not real people, Letter 165). The list goes on, but even this brief catalogue illustrates Fisher's distaste for some of the most eminent American writers. Her reading for the BOMC kept her in touch with the current of modern literature, but she obviously felt little affection for much of what now constitutes the canon of the period.

Fisher's correspondence also sheds new light on her activities and influence as a member of the BOMC Board of Selection. Created by advertising executive Harry Scherman and publisher Robert Haas in 1926, the BOMC claimed more than sixty thousand subscribers within a year. The operating principles were straightforward: members agreed to buy a newly published book chosen monthly by the five-member Board. They paid full price with an option to exchange the book, upon inspection, for an "alternate" choice. Soon after, readers were asked to buy only four books a year and allowed to substitute the alternate selection before shipping. Fisher at first hesitated joining the group, but after observing the emptiness of Brentano's bookstore in New York in contrast to other stores, she decided there must be a better method of "getting books into the hands of American readers."[14]

Although Fisher de-emphasized the significance of her position with the BOMC, remarking in a 1941 letter that she was "surprised and somewhat daunted" by the influence one subscriber attributed to the monthly choice (Letter 115), she did play a key role in the careers of at least three well-known authors: Pearl Buck, Isak Dinesen (Karen Blixen), and Richard Wright. Fisher nominated Buck's *The Good Earth* for special consideration by the board after a first reader's report underestimated it, and then recommended the eventual Pulitzer Prize–winner strongly at the judges' monthly meeting.[15] The result was that *The Good Earth* was the book-of-the-month for March 1931, the first of six works by Buck selected during Fisher's time on the board.

Dinesen owed no less than her first American book publication to Fisher, who was sent the manuscript of *Seven Gothic Tales* by the author's brother. As her letters from 1932 to 1933 indicate, Fisher put the book in the hands of its eventual publisher, and she wrote a "Preface" introducing Dinesen to the American public. *Seven Gothic Tales* was a book-of-the-month (April 1934), as were four subsequent titles by Dinesen.

Wright's association with the BOMC was important to his early success as well. His *Native Son* and *Black Boy,* now ranked among American classics, were distributed by the BOMC as monthly choices, and Fisher not only wrote reviews and introductions, but also suggested important revisions for both. Fisher's role in the textual history of *Black Boy*—documented in her correspondence here—is discussed by Janice Thaddeus in her 1985 essay "The Metamorphosis of Richard Wright's *Black Boy,*" while Arnold Rampersad's notes to his Library of America edition of Wright's works explicate the *Native Son* connection.

VI

Ancillary to the explicitly personal and literary letters are those dealing with the social concerns that underpin much of Fisher's fiction. Three subjects are most prominent: the importance of education, women's rights, and the African-American struggle for racial equality.

Fisher's interest in education can be traced back to her upbringing as the daughter of an academic: her father was (in chronological order) a professor at the University of Kansas, chancellor of the University of Nebraska, president of Ohio State University, and librarian of Columbia University. In a letter to the president of Middlebury College in support of coeducation there, Fisher noted that she knew both sides of the issue because she had been "brought up on the discussion of it all my life" (Letter 52). She viewed education as the means by which American citizens could best develop their individual potential and contribute to society, and she made two major contributions to the field. First, she introduced the Montessori method of childhood education to America. Her explication of the system appears in *A Montessori Mother* (1912), published after her visit to Maria Montessori's Casa dei Bambini in Rome, *A Montessori Manual* (1913), and *Mothers and Children* (1914). Montessori principles are also present in the novel *The Bent Twig* (1915) and her well-known children's book *Understood Betsy* (1917), the story of a pampered city girl who learns the value of hard work and responsibility when she moves to a Vermont farm. The book highlights, in a fictional framework, Fisher's conviction that both boys *and* girls should be raised to be independent and self-reliant.[16] Secondly, Fisher helped establish the Adult Education Association, the first organization of its kind in the U.S. Her belief that education is a lifelong enterprise is expressed in *Why Stop Learning?* (1927). The enduring significance of the book to Fisher is evident in a later letter (1929) to Alfred Harcourt in which she wrote, "I'd like not to have people forget that book. I've said some things in it I'm glad to have said" (Letter 75).

Closely related to Fisher's commitment to education was her active support of women's rights. Surprisingly, Fisher once wrote that she "was never a feminist." She explained, "It was my older generation, my father and mother, who were. I was rather (as it often goes in generations) in reaction from their extreme zeal for 'women's rights'" (DCF to Helen K. Taylor, no date). Her devotion to the cause of equal opportunity for women, though, is unmistakable. Both Fisher's fiction (most notably *The Home-Maker,* in which the protagonist, Evangeline Knapp, is a wife, mother, and the family breadwinner) and her letters speak to her strong belief that women should not be limited in their access to education and job training, nor should they be bound by societal conventions. Characteristically, in a 1946 letter to Margaret Mead, she lamented "the social pressure, invisible and tyrannical, which the United States puts upon its women and girls" (Letter 142). The restriction of women's roles—and men's too: in *The Home-Maker,* the husband, Lester Knapp, draws great satisfaction from staying at home and caring for his children—seemed, quite simply, impractical to Fisher. She reasoned that since everyone is born with unique abilities, limitations, and temperaments, one's place should not be determined by gender. It was only when each person was in a role he or she was suited for that society could function productively, and Fisher lectured and wrote in support of that principle. As she remarked to Julia Collier Harris:

> So large a majority of fathers of our girls are heart-and-soul business men, it stands to reason that the girls themselves might do better if they were not automatically shoved off into being cultured teachers . . . although goodness knows our country needs cultured teachers enough sight more than business-people. Still, folks have to do what they are best fit for, and every opportunity for women means one less chance of a square peg living miserably in a round hole all its life. (Letter 68)

Nearly thirty years later, Fisher still worried over the obstacles women faced:

> I'm very much struck by the fact that although America offers us a life astonishingly safe from most physical dangers, it plunges us into another danger which is devilishly insidious because it falls so imperceptibly about us as we live—and that is the danger of becoming held and mastered by triviality. The little things of life, of no real importance, but which have to be "seen to" by American home makers, is like a blanket smothering out the fine and great potential qualities in every one of us. (Letter 181)

Lastly, a deep vein of concern for the problem of racial prejudice against African-Americans runs throughout Fisher's letters. The issue certainly was not foreign to her forbears. In a letter to Pearl Buck, Fisher proudly explained that her great-grandmother kept the bell of her Vermont village church tolling "from dawn to dark" on the day of John Brown's execution, that her grandfather had accompanied Henry Ward Beecher on his trip to England to influence British public opinion in favor of the abolitionists, and that her father, when he was president of Ohio State University, had created considerable controversy by inviting Booker T. Washington to lunch at their home. Fisher herself carried on the family tradition: she lectured against racial prejudice and wrote for the *Crisis*; she befriended African-American writers such as James Weldon Johnson and Richard Wright; and she was a trustee of Howard University (1945-1951). Fisher, who counted African-Americans among her childhood friends (see Letter 47), also voiced her opposition to racism in her stories **"An American Citizen"** and **"Fairfax Hunter"** and in her novel *The Brimming Cup,* the first best-seller to contain such opinions. In that book, Ormsby Welles, a retired business executive, forsakes his comfortable life in Vermont to aid in the struggle against racial oppression in the South. In a letter to W. E. B. Du Bois, Fisher explained her reason for including the subplot in her popular novel about the married life of a Vermont couple:

> I wish never to lose a chance to remind Americans of what their relations to the Negro race are, and might be, and so into this story of Northern life and white people, I have managed to weave a strand of remembrance of the dark question. It is a sort of indirect, side-approach, a backing-up of your campaign from someone not vitally concerned in it personally, except as every American must be, which I hope may be of use exactly because it is not a straight-on attack, but one of a slightly different manner. (Letter 45)

The very idea of racism was antithetical to Fisher's democratic principles and she minced no words when discussing the subject. To Paul Reynolds she wrote:

> After seeing what idiots the Germans made of themselves for two long generations over that fantastic and so far, entirely unproved idea of Count Gobineau's, and what a well-deserved punishment they got for it, it does seem as though Americans might leave it alone. . . . The Ku Klux Klan (which of course has nothing but this Gobineau idea of inherent racial superiority at the bottom of its imbecilities) may make it odious enough to shorten its stay with us. (Letter 56, ellipsis mine)

Given her efforts on behalf of racial equality, it is appropriate that the last letter in this collection, written less than two months before Fisher's death, is an inquiry about the opportunities available to African-Americans at the U.S. Naval Academy (Letter 189).

VII

Fruits of further investigation will belong to the readers of these letters, who will develop further what is revealed so explicitly and, at times, so wittily or so poignantly. Fisher's personal trials—the wars in Europe, the loss of her son, who died while serving as a doctor in World War II, her later physical disabilities—are revealed here, often with startling and painful clarity. Her personal enthusiasms and interests—including classical music, art, history, sports, and current events—help fill in the biographical record and suggest new approaches to her writing. The range of historical and cultural subjects discussed—the "New Woman" and the suffrage movement, racial discrimination and the emergence of the NAACP, the development of the national education system, both world wars, the depression, book clubs, and the literary marketplace among them—should encourage not only literary approaches to the use and interpretation of her work and her correspondence, but interdisciplinary ones as well.

Dorothy Canfield Fisher was well born—into a distinguished and cultivated family that gave her a fine education and a sense of self-worth. Her strong principles underpin her beliefs and writing; that she was to extend these concerns to independent women, to new forms of education, and to issues of racial oppression and respect for individual merit was the core of her achievement. Her letters amply display her own recognition of these facts, of this achievement.

NOTES

[1] Ida H. Washington, *Dorothy Canfield Fisher: A Biography,* 14.

[2] Ibid., x.

[3] Sarah Cleghorn, *Threescore,* 130.

[4] Washington, *Biography,* 64.

[5] William Allen White, "The Other Side of Main Street," 7.

[6] Al Silverman, ed., *The Book-of-the-Month: Sixty Years of Books in American Life,* xviii.

[7] Edward Wagenknecht, *Cavalcade of the American Novel,* 294; Andrew Turnbull, ed., *The Letters of F. Scott Fitzgerald,* 571.

[8] Helen W. Congdon, letter to the author; Nanette Kutner, "If You Worked for Dorothy Canfield Fisher," 196; Bradford Smith, "Dorothy Canfield Fisher," 73.

[9] Congdon, letter.

[10] Zephine Humphrey, "Dorothy Canfield," 36.

[11] Dorothy Canfield Fisher, "Novelist Remembers Blue-and-Gold Christmas in Pittsburgh," 42.

[12] Matthew J. Bruccoli, ed., *Selected Letters of John O'Hara,* 237; Silverman, *Book-of-the-Month,* xviii.

[13] Van Wyck Brooks, Archibald MacLeish, and Thornton Wilder, "Letter to the Editor on Detroit's Ban of *To Have and Have Not,*" 96.

[14] Louis M. Starr, "An Interview with Dorothy Canfield Fisher," 6.

[15] Ibid., 20.

[16] Washington, *Biography,* 70.

FURTHER READING

Biography

Smith, Bradford. "Dorothy Canfield Fisher." *Atlantic Monthly* 204, No. 2 (August 1959): 73-77.
    Portrait of Fisher featuring insights into her way of life and writing.

Washington, Ida H. *Dorothy Canfield Fisher: A Biography.* Shelburne, Vt.: New England Press, 1982, 258 p.
    Standard biography of Fisher.

Yates, Elizabeth. *Pebble in a Pool.* New York: E. P. Dutton & Co., 1958, 284 p.
    Largely celebratory biography of Fisher. Includes a consideration of her influence.

Criticism

Brickell, Herschel. Review of *The Deepening Stream. The North American Review* 230, No. 6 (December 1930): 762-63.
    Brief, positive evaluation of *The Deepening Stream.*

Dodge, Ernest S. Review of *Vermont Tradition: The Biography of an Outlook on Life. The New England Quarterly* XXVII, No. 2 (June 1954): 267-69.
    Generally favorable assessment of Fisher's history of Vermont.

Madigan, Mark J. "Dorothy Canfield Fisher (1879-1958)." *Legacy: A Journal of American Women Writers* 9, No. 1 (1992): 49-58.
    Survey of Fisher's personal and literary accomplishments.

Rosowski, Susan J. "Prototypes for Willa Cather's 'Flavia and Her Artists': The Canfield Connection." *American*

Notes and Queries XXIII, Nos. 9-10 (May/June 1985): 143-45.

  Sees Fisher and some of her family relations as likely sources for characters in Willa Cather's "Flavia and Her Artists."

Rubin, Joan Shelley. "Why Do You Disappoint Yourself? The Early History of the Book-of-the-Month Club." In *The Making of Middlebrow Culture*, pp. 93-147. Chapel Hill: University of North Carolina Press, 1992.

  Includes a survey of Fisher's work and her influence as an important member of the Book-of-the-Month Club selection committee.

The following sources published by Gale contain further information on Fisher's life and works: *Contemporary Authors*, Vols. 114, 136; *Dictionary of Literary Biography*, Vols. 9, 102; *Major Authors and Illustrators for Children and Young Adults*; *Yesterday's Authors of Books for Children*, Vol. 1.

Christopher Morley

1890-1957

(Full name Christopher Darlington Morley) American novelist, essayist, dramatist and poet

INTRODUCTION

A lifelong devotee of literature, Morley is best known as a witty, popular novelist who also wrote widely in drama and poetry. These diverse accomplishments justly earned him the title "man of letters." Morley's essays in such publications as the *Saturday Review*, which he helped found, and the *Ladies' Home Journal* are considered both erudite and entertaining. Of Morley's novels, *Kitty Foyle, Parnassus on Wheels* and its sequel, *The Haunted Bookshop,* are considered the best examples of his highly accessible and entertaining prose. A dominant force throughout Morley's work is the importance of literature in daily life. This theme worked to both his benefit and detriment. While his message was initially admired for its social impact, some of his works are now considered overly sentimental and dated. Today, most critics agree that Morley's prolific output may have hindered his reputation as a writer of the first tier, but he will be remembered as an entertaining and insightful author.

Biographical Information

Morley grew up in Haverford, Pennsylvania. He attended Haverford College before traveling to Oxford University as a Rhodes scholar, as did his two brothers before him. Following his experience abroad, he took an editorial position with Doubleday and married Helen Booth Fairchild, a woman he met as a student abroad. His prodigious output quickly began with novels, drama, poetry and essays. In addition, Morley championed the works of other authors, particularly Joseph Conrad and Walt Whitman. Morley also founded the Baker Street Irregulars, an organization devoted to the works of Arthur Conan Doyle, author of the Sherlock Holmes series. As Morley's literary life flourished, he composed actively in all genres until incapacitated by the first of several strokes in 1951. He published only one more volume of verse, *Gentlemen's Relish,* until his death in 1957.

Major Works

Of Morley's copious body of work, his novels are most admired. *Parnassus on Wheels* and *The Haunted Bookshop* both tell the story of booksellers who peddle their goods with enormous zeal. In these books, Morley proposes the theme that literature is a universal healer. Both *Thunder on the Left* and *Where the Blue Begins*

are deeper manifestations of the same theme. Though these tales have seemingly juvenile settings—one a dog's daily existence, the other a child's birthday party—both works examine the search for meaning in an increasingly turbulent society. Morley's best-known novel is *Kitty Foyle,* the tale of Kitty Foyle, a young woman from lower-class Philadelphia, who falls in love with a wealthy young gentleman from Main Line Philadelphia. Their ill-fated romance, coupled with Kitty's intent to be a modern woman, inspired both popular appeal and critical dissent. *Kitty Foyle* is more controversial for its treatment of sexual mores, primarily because Kitty has an abortion. A national best-seller, Kitty Foyle was also made into an award-winning film. Morley's best-known poetry, *Translations from the Chinese* and *The Old Mandarin: More Translations from the Chinese,* began as a satire of free verse that evolved into an elaborate examination of contemporary poetry. Like his other works, these volumes were intended to be read more as social commentary than merely verse. A common thread throughout the body of Morley's work is his driving concern to ensure literature as an enduring force.

Critical Reception

Today, critics generally remember Morley as a prolific and versatile rather than artistic writer. While he wrote dramas that were produced, they inspired little critical response and are largely overlooked today. In general, Morley's writings are admired for their entertaining elements, eccentric charm and amusing insights but are now considered dated. However, his ability to compose in numerous genres has earned him a reputation as a well-schooled and eloquent champion of the printed word.

PRINCIPAL WORKS

The Eighth Sin (poetry) 1912
Parnassus on Wheels (novel) 1917
Songs for a Little House (poetry) 1917
Shandygaff (essays) 1918
The Haunted Bookshop (novel) 1919
The Rocking Horse (poetry) 1919
In the Sweet Dry and Dry [with Bart Haley] (novel) 1919
Mince Pie: Adventures on the Sunny Side of Grub Street (essays) 1919
Hide and Seek (poetry) 1920
Kathleen (short story) 1920
Pipefuls (essays) 1920
Chimneysmoke (poetry) 1921
Modern Essays (essays) 1921
Tales from a Rolltop Desk (novel) 1921
Thursday Evening (drama) 1922
Translations from the Chinese (poetry) 1922
Where the Blue Begins (novel) 1922
Parsons' Pleasure (poetry) 1923
The Powder of Sympathy (essays) 1923
One-Act Plays (drama) 1924
Religio Journalistici (essays) 1924
Thunder on the Left (novel) 1925
The Romany Stain (novel) 1926
Off the Deep End (essays) 1928
Toulemonde (poetry) 1928
John Mistletoe (memoirs) 1931
Swiss Family Manhattan (novel) 1932
Human Being (novel) 1932
Internal Revenue (essays) 1933
Mandarin in Manhattan: Further Translations from the Chinese (poetry) 1933
Shakespeare and Hawaii (lectures) 1933
Streamlines (essays) 1936
The Trojan Horse (novel) 1937
History of an Autumn (essays) 1938
Kitty Foyle (novel) 1939
Thorofare (novel) 1942
The Old Mandarin: More Translations from the Chinese (poetry) 1947
The Ironing Board (essays) 1949
The Man Who Made Friends with Himself (novel) 1949

Poetry Package [with William Rose Benet] (poetry) 1949
The Ballad of New York, New York, and Other Poems, 1930-1950 (poetry) 1950
Gentlemen's Relish (poetry) 1955
Bright Cages: Selected Poems and Translations from the Chinese (poetry) 1965

CRITICISM

Vincent O'Sullivan (essay date 1919)

SOURCE: "America and the English Literary Tradition," in *The Living Age,* No. 3928, October 18, 1919, pp. 170-76.

[*In the following essay, O'Sullivan discusses the English literary influences on Morley's writings.*]

To encounter the venerable names of Marlowe, of Burton of the *Anatomy,* of Dr. Johnson, and Wordsworth and George Borrow, in a quite modern American novel, is almost as startling as it would be to find them in a Bolshevist manifesto. Rare enough now in America are the writers who continue the English literary tradition, and accordingly some interest may be felt by English people in the one who does. Nor is Mr. Christopher Morley a 'left-over' from the New England period when the inspiration, at least, of American literature was imported from England, if it sometimes suffered a sea-change in the process.

Some years ago I was asked to lunch in New York at a restaurant in the neighborhood of Wall Street—one of those places where eating becomes feeding; where, as in a pew, men close-packed in a small room groan and sweat as they devour probable dishes while flying scuds of soup and gravy are blown in the face from plates carried at perilous angles by irritable and distracted waiters. It has always seemed to me an example of the great docility of the Americans and their slavery to custom that men should consent to go day after day for years to such caves of noise and fumes and half-warm food, when they might have a sandwich in peace on a street corner. My host was a large florid young man rather ample in movement for the place, who looked as if he might have seized the restaurant in his arms and swung it across the river to the Brooklyn side. So far as looks go, he was the kind of man you may meet on any misty morning in Essex or Suffolk riding about his farm on a stocky well-groomed cob or trampling through the wurzels in thick boots and buskins with a gun under his arm and a dog at his heels. This was Mr. Christopher Morley, sometime one of the editors of the *Ladies' Home Journal,* and now an imposing pillar of the Philadelphia *Evening Ledger.* Amid the uproar, he gained my sympathy by calling *The Woman in White* one of the best

English novels. He spoke warmly, too, of Anthony Trollope. I cannot read Trollope much, but I like people who like him. I suppose we all feel that way about some writer or other.

At the time of our lunch Mr. Morley had published in magazines some parts of his book of poems, *Songs for a Little House,* whereof the inspiration takes its rise in the English intimists, Herrick, George Herbert, Cowper, Crabbe. He has since written a few books of essays (or, as one would say in America, 'near-essays') whereof the inspiration is the prose counterpart of those worthies, Izaak Walton, Addison (of Sir Roger de Coverley), Charles Lamb, Leigh Hunt, with something of Hazlitt and George Borrow thrown in. As you see, nothing could be more English. And as one reads these books, *Shandygaff* and *Parnassus on Wheels,* it is easy to pick out his preferences among modern English authors. Stevenson, Kipling, Conrad, Chesterton, J. M. Barrie—there they are! It may be in deference to his surroundings that he professes an inordinate admiration for that didactic and boring writer, Samuel Butler—him of *Erewhon* and *The Way of All Flesh* I mean: heaven forbid that anybody should think I mean the great author of *Hudibras.* Samuel Butler the second (in all senses) has at present a considerable vogue in the United States.

Such a list of preferences describes a man. You notice that if there is no Hall Caine there is no Galsworthy; if there is no Florence Barclay there is no Bernard Shaw; if there is no Arnold Bennett or Algernon Blackwood neither is there Mrs. Humphry Ward or William Locke. No non-English writers whatever, none of the great Russians, none of the great French, have said anything important for him. I have a notion that he regards Ibsen and Strindberg with dislike as not the kind of stuff that young America can be profitably nourished upon. His admiration of his own countrymen is also tempered by many exclusions. Among those he admires he takes a long slide from Walt Whitman to Mr. Don Marquis, who distributed parodies and proverbs to the readers of the New York *Sun.* According to Mr. Morley, the facetious Mr. Marquis is the greatest writer, except Walt Whitman, who ever lived in the Brooklyn district of New York. This is perhaps not much of a claim; but however that may be, it falls to be said that Howard Pyle, admirable writer of fairy stories, of pirate romances, admirable black-and-white artist, too, lived in Brooklyn, and if he were still treading its streets, neither Mr. Marquis nor many other Americans would be worthy to walk in his shadow.

It has seemed worthwhile to dwell on Mr. Christopher Morley's literary formation because of his expression of the English literary tradition, which is indeed so singular in America today that one is not much surprised to learn that he is not very far off the original English stock—only a single generation, I think. He has also been a Rhodes scholar at Oxford, and although in his latest book he calls a college-cap a 'mortar-board,' no doubt he came into sufficiently close contact with the real life of the place. He waxes enthusiastic about tea and muffins and open coal fires. Tea rouses no delight in the American breast, muffins mean something else than they do in England, and open coal fires are a privilege of the rich. He is in his books a great eater, his board is spread with a Victorian prodigality. To his mind, when the English Victorian era ended, something very good went out of the world. There is nothing in him that Victorianism would have frustrated: he does not want to do or express anything which would have shocked the Victorian sense of fitness. I do not know whether he would want to put drawers on the legs of the piano, but he would not want to discuss the subject of legs, or anything which may be implied in that.

Do what we will, we see past ages through the eyes of the great writers who lived in them. In Victorian England fires were not so bright, inns were not so cosy, food was not so plentiful or so good as appears in the romances of Dickens. At the time of the Crimean War the struggles of the poor were as hard and more hopeless than they are now. What is likely is that middle-class people of moderate incomes lived more comfortably than they do to-day. When the Mr. and Mrs. Quiverfull or the Brown, Jones and Robinson, of the *Punch* of the period went to Margate or Folkestone their desires were moderate: there were no large and expensive hotels to tempt them. At home, they were content to stay at home and to take their meals at home. They asked less from life and probably got more. But to see general happiness in the Victorian period is hallucination produced by literature, as it is to see general comfort in the Augustan period because Horace was comfortable. Seventy-five years hence readers of the books of Mr. Bennett and Mr. Chesterton and Mr. Wells may be sighing for the good old times of King George the Fifth and the Great War.

And if such a reader lives in America and takes Mr. Morley on trust he may—he almost certainly will—be sighing for the good old days of Woodrow Wilson. Mr. Morley is by no means a realist, if realism means facing unflinchingly the sad and ugly among the other elements of life. He puts aside whatever is unpleasant, and, one can see in many another American author, this is done by conviction, deliberately, like the effort of a Christian Scientist. He belongs to the domestic school; he is a homely writer. He tells you what they had for breakfast from sheer delight in telling it. People don't catch diseases in his book. They are very well. The doctor only comes to preside at the arrival of a new and healthy baby.

On the whole, if we want only the fair lights, Mr. Morley gives a true enough picture of the middle-class family in the United States—or more precisely, of the family of small means in New England and the Middle Atlantic States. In one respect, at all events, it seems to have an advantage over the same kind of family in England. The *tone* is better because there are no cheap servants. The wealthy have servants more or less good and highly paid. In families such as Mr. Morley deals with, the wife, and often the husband, do their own cooking and dishwashing, and then sit down to read *The Shaving of Shagpat* or Bryce's *American Commonwealth*. What is called a 'scrub woman' appears at intervals to sweep and garnish, but she enters the house on the same terms as the plumber or the man who comes to fix the telephone. But there is no such thing as the 'slavey,' or overworked drudge, tyrannized over when she is not treated with negligent kindness, who surrenders her liberty, often even her liberty of thought, for a meagre wage, and in a tiny house is barred out from the rest of the occupants though the dog and the cat are admitted. When you think of it, could anything be more immoral? Or could anything be devised more demoralizing and productive of snobbery than to bring up children in the conviction that they are superior to a class of human beings who are paid to do housework, and also to those who cannot afford to keep such slaves?

The small American family, then, with its economized and tempered joys, and with the characteristic national neglect of its sorrows, is portrayed by Mr. Morley in his poems, in **Shandygaff**, which is a book of essays, and in **Parnassus on Wheels**, which may also be called a book of essays since the characters are set up to express the author's opinions. The best part of his new book, **The Haunted Bookshop**, is also the essay part; but he has had the unfortunate suggestion to graft on it a 'shriller,' and for that kind of literature he reveals no talent. Two Germans plot together to put a bomb between book covers on board the ship in which President Wilson is sailing to the Peace Conference. They are unmasked by an advertising agent who marries the heroine daughter of a millionaire. What motive could have urged the Germans to injure the President at that particular moment it is impossible to discover; but why try to find sense where the author has failed to put any? It would seem that his admiration of *The Wrong Box* and *The Dynamiter* had led him to prepare an American *Ersatz* for those books; but neither his character nor his talent have any resemblance to Stevenson's. To go no further, Stevenson never loses a chance to gird at domesticity, whereas Mr. Morley's trump card is to extol domesticity.

To excuse his descent into spy-melodrama, it should be said that he is not a writer who takes his way indifferent to the public taste, and in the United States during the war Hun-baiting and spy-nosing were not only pursued as a duty but cultivated as a sport. Curiously enough, alongside of this kind of thing we find praise of such writers as Bertrand Russell, and pages denouncing war. Certainly, no one can reproach Mr. Morley for his observations on the war and on war in general. But repetitions like this are useless; his remarks are no more impressive than could be drawn from writers for a thousand years. Perhaps there are few left now who believe that war brings any permanent social benefit; but soldiering, or at least officering, will doubtless continue to be the most honorable and admired of professions in many countries, and did not Marshal Foch in London

speak calmly of the 'next war'? As for what are called 'war books,' whether written from the pacifist or bellicist point of view, more or less brilliant reporting with emphatic or cynical anecdotes, surely there has been enough of them in the United States as well as in France and in England. But one kind of war book might still be written, and if it were done well, with some benefit. We have every reason to be tired of the note books and journals of nurses of all sorts written to show the home town they have been 'there.'

So much consideration it has seemed worthwhile to give to this American writer in an English paper, not upon any claim that what he has so far produced makes him a great or important writer, but because he is a pleasant writer, with whose books English readers might well make acquaintance, and particularly because he is one of the very few American writers who continue the English literary tradition in a country where that tradition is dying fast and where the spoken, and to a considerable extent the written, language is drawing farther and farther away from English as it is used in England. Those who want to realize how far this difference has already gone should read Mr. H. L. Mencken's laborious and interesting volume, *The American Language*. To most English people, many pages of the published sermons of Billy Sunday, the evangelist, would be almost as unintelligible as a Welsh newspaper. But is American at its present point of development a language or a lingo? Professor Brander Matthews, an American, does not hesitate to liken it to Elizabethan English for its figurative vigor. American figures, however, are generally on a low level. When Bacon calls floods great winding sheets, he is otherwise impressive than when the Pennsylvania Railroad announces that there is a washout down round Harrisburg, Pa. It would in fact be impossible to express any grand or moving thought in American: humor, homely wisdom, yes; but not grandeur. Leaving aside the intellectual value of either, Bishop Latimer's sermons are in the plain language of his time, and they easily maintain themselves on heights that Billy Sunday never gets a clutch on, even for a moment. It is a fair claim that American is more vivid than English. Mr. Mencken says well that between the placard in the wash-room at the British Museum: 'These Basins are for Casual Ablutions Only,' and the common sign at our American railroad crossings: 'Stop! Look! Listen!' lies 'an abyss separating two cultures, two habits of mind, two diverging tongues.'

Americans, however, keep their eyes fixed on the rather ponderous English of some of the London daily papers, and of weeklies like the *Spectator* and the *Guardian* which sweat the prig at every pore; they know nothing of the racy speech of the English populace. I have always thought that the remarks heard in an English crowd are more witty than those of an American crowd. They are not so pleasant to hear, because they are bitter and often very cynical, whereas it is extremely rare to hear Americans of any class say anything wounding in a spirit of jocosity. But not seldom the American wit is of ready-made phrases, held in community, and you feel that the next man or woman who comes within earshot is likely to say pretty much the same thing; while the English man or girl, those of the large towns, constantly say striking things which have never been heard before and no one will repeat after them. The American caricaturist Briggs, deals with pretty much the same class of people that the great artist, Phil May, dealt with. With both the intention is not to make their people say smart things out of keeping with their characters, but what such people would naturally say. It is a matter of listening and picking up in streets, in tramways, on race courses, in drinking bars, and billiard rooms. Well, nobody who examines the work of these two artists over a given period can deny that the wit is on the side of Phil May's people. They are not always so funny, however. Of the hideous woman that both these artists present, the meagre American vixen, with sparse hair undisguised by art, may perhaps be laughed at, but Phil May's bloated mother in bonnet and shawl, with all her features in dissolution, is almost tragic.

'Bid me to live and I will live thy protestant to be,' sang a poet not far off the Elizabethan time. 'So live that you can look any man square in the eye and tell him to go to hell,' says a modern American moralist. Between these two, one finds also, notwithstanding Professor Matthews, 'an abyss separating two cultures, two habits of mind,' as Mr. Mencken puts it. Certainly it is a prudent statement that no great popularity can be expected in the United States to-day by a writer who does not use American English, and by this I do not mean slang. Most of the modern American novelists, and even the poets, write it naturally. It is true that perhaps the best book of poems, and one of the best novels, published in America of late years, *Wolfsbane,* and *Wood and Stone,* by John Cowper Powys, are written in the English of England; but Mr. Powys, although he publishes in the United States, is, as I understand, an Englishman who has no desire to be either American or Americanized. Mr. Richard Le Gallienne is an Englishman who has been naturalized, and he does use American to a certain extent, but it is an obvious and uneasy graft on a prose formed by English origin, sympathies, and habits of thought. Mr. Le Gallienne looks rather like an exile in America. As for Mr. Christopher Morley, who is an American, his respect for the English literary tradition leads him to keep his English and American in separate compartments. When he slips, it is not upon the tolerable language of either country, but into the miserable jargon of the tawdry novel in both countries. 'Gilbert was on the qui vive,' he writes. What would Charles Lamb or Hazlitt say to that? American translators deliberately translate into American not English. In the translations of Strindberg's plays published in New York the translator says he found he could get nearer the original by American turns of speech.

This may seem contradicted by the fact that a large number of English books are read in the United States. They are read by the more cultivated classes who are willing to make a slight mental effort. Such people have the pleasant sensation of mastering a foreign language. They skip the phrases they don't understand, or try to translate them with a dictionary. 'The second turning revealed to Gerald the hoardings of a tube station with a constable's bull's-eye flashing on them'—such a phrase would be as unintelligible to the average inhabitants of an American city as a phrase of Spanish. But they accept it as an experience in an English book. If they find many like it in a book by an American, they and that author do not become friends. This is one of the reasons for the limited vogue of Henry James. As I said in an article published in the *Mercure de France* a few months ago, the influence of James has been in England, not in his native land. Then there is Mrs. Craigie, who had a broader culture, twice as much art, and fifty times more intellectual power than any other American woman who has written novels. Mrs. Craigie has no standing whatever in America.

No amount of analysis can precisely determine the causes of this indifference of Americans to two of our authors who do us the most credit. Resentment because they were absentees comes into it very little—perhaps not at all. Nor that they dealt with phrases of English life. Mrs. Gertrude Atherton's literary excursions into English society have not hurt her with her large public. But Mrs. Atherton always gives the impression of someone standing outside and looking through the fence; you never forget that she is an American citizen. Henry James writes like an American lady who has been for long years married to an Englishman of good position, and Mrs. Craigie, as far as tone goes, writes like an Englishwoman. Tone, accent—perhaps the explanation is there. For just as the spoken English accent rouses a subconscious antagonism in America, so may the written English accent. Something too must be put down to the lack of interesting and able criticism to educate the public taste. The few men and women with broad culture, broad views, a thorough knowledge of two or three literatures, and a wide experience of life, will not waste their time in writing book reviews, especially under the conditions imposed by most of the papers. In the first place, it is not thought necessary to give much space to books; and then, what editors want is what they call a 'news-review'—that is, an article made up of quotations, a most unfair gutting of a book which leaves the reader with the impression that there is no need to buy it after all. The limited number of reviewers who express decided opinions, if confronted with work like Mrs. Craigie's, would assume a haughty or weary air, the object being to show they are no longer provincial, that they too have been to Gades, and that you can't put any junk across which will faize them. I have noticed the same instinct to disparage among English reviewers in face of an American book: I have not seen the *Times Literary Supplement* for some time, but it used to be insufferably patronizing and contemptuous when it dealt with American novels or poetry. Among daily and weekly papers published in New York, the only respectable criticism appears in the Socialist paper, *The Call*;

but the artistic views of the writers are distorted by their political convictions too often, as happens in Socialist papers all over the world where propaganda comes first.

Punch (essay date 1920)

SOURCE: A review of *The Haunted Bookshop*, in *Punch*, Vol. CLIX, July 28, 1920, pp. 79-80.

[*In the following review, the critic praises* The Haunted Bookshop *for its inventive qualities but also notes that Morley is occasionally too verbose.*]

[*The Haunted Bookshop]* is a daring, perhaps too daring, mixture of a browse in a second-hand bookshop and a breathless bustle among international criminals. To estimate the accuracy of its technical details the critic must be a secret service specialist, the mustiest of bookworms and a highly-trained expert in the science and language of the American advertising business. Speaking as a general practitioner, I like Mr. Christopher Morley best when he is being cinematographic; he hits a very happy mean with his spies and his sleuths, giving a nice proportion of skill and error, failure and success, to both. There is a strong love-interest which will be made much of and probably spoilt by the purchasers of the film-rights; and, though strong men will doubtless applaud hoarsely and women will weep copiously, as the bomb in the bookshop throws the young lovers into each other's arms, I feel that the book gives a more attractive portrait of *Titania Chapman,* the plutocrat's daughter, than ever can be materialised in the film-man's "close-up." I am afraid that Mr. Morley will not thank me for praising his brisk melodrama at the cost of his ramblings in literature. But, if he has the knowledge, he lacks the fragrance; not to put too fine a point on it, he is long-winded and tends to bore in his disquisitions upon books and bookishness; which is no proper material for a novelist. The story is all about America and is thoroughly American; inevitably therefore there is some ambitious word-coining. The only novelty which sticks in my memory and earns my gratitude is the title for the female Bolshevik, to wit, Bolshevixen.

Grant Overton (essay date 1923)

SOURCE: "The Unclassified Case of Christopher Morley," in *American Nights Entertainment*, D. Appleton & Co., 1923, pp. 363-79.

[*In the following essay, Overton praises Morley's literary integrity and offers a brief overview of his life and career.*]

To know Christopher Morley is to be interested, amused, enthusiastic, sceptical or even secretly puzzled; but to have him for a friend is to learn the meaning of friendliness in a degree that is very exceptional. And few escape being his friends, though this is less true than formerly. There was, indeed, once a time when the friendship of Morley was among the two or three serious responsibilities of an individual's life—like marriage, or filial duty or a conscience in regard to one's chosen craft. Practically every day, sometimes twice in a day, the evidence of Morley's friendliness would appear in a brief letter or hastily-penned note about this or that or the other thing under the sun.

An image arose of an ever-active, a sleepless mind; of an emotional nature more unresting than the Atlantic and quantitatively as great. This awful abstraction slowly faded out into a visual image of a "burly" man with a smiling face and a lighted pipe, and that, in turn, gave place to the fear lest so much confidence in the human race should prove fatally misplaced. . . . Somewhat, it has; but what we didn't foresee was that the change, coming about gradually, would operate as a gradual salvation of (1) his friends from Morley, (2) Morley from his friends, (3) Morley's work from Friend Morley.

Yet this beneficial and important transformation has been accomplished in the most salutary manner, with a result that may accrue with permanence and advantage to American literature.

II

As lately as 1920 one estimating American talents could observe of Morley: "His gift is purely journalistic, isn't it?" and receive the answer from Morley's friend: "Purely"—an answer conceived in entire truthfulness. Both the asker and the answerer were pretty certain to regard the assumed fact as a great pity. But as to the fact!—why, what further evidence was needed to establish it? Morley had been writing for several years, had averaged several books a year of prose and verse, and nowhere gave the least sign of doing work of a different character. What, then, was the character of his work in those years? He began at Oxford with a book of verse; from a more actual standpoint his beginnings had been made with *Parnassus on Wheels*, published in 1917. This really capital conceit had engendered a sequel, *The Haunted Bookshop*, published two years later. There were certain books of essays—*Shandygaff, Mince Pie, Pipefuls*—pleasant, partly serious, sometimes sentimental and showing a deplorable fondness for the pun. There were books of verse—*Songs for a Little House, The Rocking Horse, Hide and Seek. Travels in Philadelphia*, the short story, *Kathleen*, and an unfortunate collaboration called *In the Sweet Dry and Dry* completed the roll. It is no reflection upon these volumes to say that they gave the impression of a talent strictly journalistic; the best journalism is more than ephemeral and most of the titles enumerated are still actively in demand. The quality we call "journalism" is not an affair of perishability but something very difficult to define, something in the approach, something in the treatment rather than in the choice of subjects. In the last analysis it is probable that the effort to define it would end with hands flung out hopelessly before the mystery of a personal temperament.

The facts were these: Morley had been educated at Haverford College and Oxford; he had then come to Garden City to work for the publishing house which, principally, has published his prose, and his first enterprises as an author were precociously instructed by an "inside" acquaintance with what James Branch Cabell would call the auctorial career. The influence upon his own work of this very special knowledge is not easy to estimate. He saw, as only one in a publishing house sees, the facts of authorship after the author's child is born. For example: the immense effect upon the fortunes of a writer's book, or books, of the attitude toward them of the bookseller. And that attitude is quite rightly fixed by what the bookseller (1) knows he can sell, or, less frequently (2), by what he thinks he can sell.

Morley saw that books are sold through bookstores. Looking a little further, he discerned that books which are not in bookstores are, with certain class exceptions, very rarely sold. He learned, as everyone in a publishing house learns, that three-quarters of the books·that are sold to retail purchasers are bought because retail purchasers have had these books thrust directly under their noses. He suffered, no doubt, the customary amazement on discovering the vast number of people who (1) either enter the bookstore with no particular book in mind, or (2), on being unable to obtain the book in mind, readily take something else. It was brought to his keen attention that, as Frank Swinnerton reiterates in his admirable brochure on "Authors and Advertising," direct advertising, as in newspapers and magazines (the commonest mediums) does not sell books. Being a young man of alert perceptions, it cannot have been lost upon him that book reviews do not, with any reliability, sell books, either. What does sell books is talk—in some instances—but the hard rock foundation of book sales is a favourable attitude on the part of "the trade."

To know the people in the bookstore, to have and to cultivate and to deserve their good will (for, in the long run, you must deserve it), and thus to insure the sale of your book to the bookseller and to enlist his energy and enterprise in re-selling it to his customers—this is the "favourable attitude" just mentioned. Few authors succeed in establishing it; fewer succeed in maintaining it. Mr. Morley has done both, with the result that in five years from the time of his *Parnassus on Wheels* he has been able to publish a highly imaginative, refined and polished satire and see it become, in its field, a pronounced best-seller.

III

One would about as soon expect to see a fantasy by Lord Dunsany a best-seller as witness the sale, in tens of thousands, of Morley's *Where the Blue Begins*—if one were making one's estimate solely on the work itself. *Where the Blue Begins* is the story of the dog Gissing's

search for God—a search conducted in various places and circumstances parallel to human life of the present day by an animal discreetly analogued to the human animal. Such a piece of writing has ordinarily no hope except from unusual and very favourable (or acutely controversial) critical attention; and the hope from that quarter is relatively small. By "hope," of course, is meant a hope of a considerable sale. *Where the Blue Begins* belongs to that class of literature which is written because it has lain in the author's heart to write it, regardless of its fate after it lies on paper. In the case of Mr. Morley, the work has received merited praise; but it would be naïve to suppose that this notice and commendation sold the book; and the book trade might even justifiably be indignant at such a supposition. Did not they, the booksellers, buy *Where the Blue Begins* because it was Morley's new book? And did not they and their clerks "push" the book for the same reason? The Ayes have it, to both questions, and unanimously.

On the other hand, the sceptical soul who argues that Chris Morley wrote *Parnassus on Wheels,* in the first place, because it was a story about a bookseller calculated to "get him in right" with the trade—that man does not know Morley and shows that he does not know him. It is possible to detect in the character of Morley's work, in the circumstance of its publication and in the accessories provided for that publication evidences of a singularly intelligent literary campaign; it is possible to detect them and believe them to be such; but it is not possible to over-estimate the part played by Morley's own naïveté, affectionate nature and formerly unchecked and indiscriminate enthusiasm.

Such an attitude is always open to misconstruction. But it takes real intelligence to go beneath the surface; and among Morley's friends were many who could do that. These perceived his genuineness without being in the least able to predict the outcome of his generosity. Ours is a world thus and thus and so and so. The ultimate effect upon Morley himself of a disposition which he would unquestionably see suffer and change was the problem. It would be very easy for him to come a tremendous cropper of any one of several sorts; and then should we have a soured, an embittered young man? Prophecy was worthless.

Meanwhile, with the auspicious beginning of *Parnassus on Wheels,* the young man went gaily on. His first book of verse (barring the Oxford experiment) was published in the same year under the valuable title, *Songs for a Little House;* and at once the small beginnings of a Morley vogue were faintly perceptible. The suspicion that such a title harboured a spirit committed to the sentimental attitude toward life was confirmed within a year by the publication of a book of essays, *Shandygaff,* named after a reputed or actual beverage and got up with a deliberately quaint title page. One was left in no doubt that Morley liked Stevenson, was affectionately fond of Robert Cortes Holliday, and worshipped the genius of Don Marquis. The seeds of literary jealousy were sown, to be harvested several years later in accusations of log-rolling that were levelled at others aplenty besides Morley. Here, however, it should be explained that Morley had come from Oxford to go to work, at the age of twenty-three, at Garden City; that while learning the publishing business he had married Miss Helen Booth Fairchild, a New York girl whom he had met in England. If, therefore, he modestly undertook to become the American poet of domesticity with his songs for households "of two or more," the guilt should by no means be made personal to him, but may justly be laid at the door of the race.

The year following *Shandygaff* witnessed the appearance of another book of verse, *The Rocking Horse;* the sequel to *Parnassus on Wheels,* entitled *The Haunted Bookshop;* and a book done in collaboration with Bart Haley. Called *In the Sweet Dry and Dry,* this is quite exceptional among Morley books, and not too common among any books, for its badness. An extravaganza on the subject of prohibition, the plot may be said to have resided mainly in incessant and outrageous puns, at that time a pronounced Morley weakness. But again it is necessary to point out a detail which, taken in one light, and, as I think, the proper light, reflects great personal credit on Mr. Morley; he has never disowned the bad book. He could not do so openly, of course—copies probably exist—but he has not done so tacitly, as he might have without question or comment. I have in mind a little booklet on Christopher Morley published in 1922 and concluding with a bibliography. There it stands: "*In the Sweet Dry and Dry,* Boni and Liveright, 1919. (In collaboration with Bart Haley, out of print.)" The book, no doubt. George Moore and Henry James, not to mention other men of literary genius, have had occasion to be ashamed of their work and to drop it quietly from the roll. I like Mr. Morley for not doing so.

IV

Christopher Darlington Morley was born at Haverford, Pennsylvania, 5 May, 1890, of parents both English by birth but long Americans by residence. Dr. Frank Morley, an English Quaker of Woodbridge, Suffolk— the home of Edward Fitzgerald—was graduated at Cambridge and came to Haverford in 1887 as professor of mathematics. His wife was Lilian Janet Bird, of Hayward's Heath, in Sussex, a woman of some musical and poetical gifts, the daughter of a man at one time with the London publishing house of Chapman and Hall. CDM frequently praises her cooking, which blended as an influence on his boyhood with the Haverford campus, where cricket is played. In 1900 Professor Morley went to Baltimore and Johns Hopkins. His son entered Haverford in 1906, was graduated in 1910 and, in the same year, was chosen as Rhodes Scholar representing Maryland. The three years at Oxford were spent at New College. In the title-poem of a new book of verse, *Parson's Pleasure*—the name of the old bathing pool on the Cherwell at Oxford— occur the lines:

> Two breeding-places I have known
> Where germinal my heart was sown;
> Two places from which I inherit
> The present business of my spirit:
> Haverford, Oxford, quietly
> May make a poet out of me.

The confused exigencies of his native land, however, were, more immediately, to make something else out of him. Repairing to Garden City, he interviewed Mr. F. N. Doubleday, otherwise FND ("Effendi") on the matter of a job. Mr. Doubleday has preserved the record of that interview in an amusing account which fully displays the youth, eagerness, enthusiasm and amiable audacity of the twenty-three-year-old. The noted Effendi, whose philosophy of life is not without its Oriental suggestions and whose sense of humour is at such times gently active, was feeling "a little weighted down that morning with the difficulties of the job which the President of Doubleday, Page & Company takes as a daily routine," and therefore finally told Morley "to go to work at all his manifold plans and literary philanderings, reserving the right to restrain his commitments if necessary."

It was Morley who discovered William McFee. English sheets of that long and very fine novel, *Casuals of the Sea,* had been submitted to the firm for consideration and possible purchase. Ultimately it became necessary to set up type for the novel in America. "We were accustomed," Mr. Doubleday explains, "to hold what we called a 'book-meeting,' when each member of the staff gave his suggestion about authors and books. For months when it came Christopher's turn to speak he always began, 'Now, about McFee—we don't appreciate what a comer he is' and so on for five minutes without taking a breath until finally it became the joke of the meeting that nothing could be done until Morley's McFee speech had been made. Our jibes influenced him not at all. His only reply to our efforts in humour was to bring on a look of great seriousness and the eternal phrase, 'Now, about McFee.'"

In leaving Garden City after a stay of nearly four years to become, in his own phrase, one of the "little group of wilful men who edit the *Ladies' Home Journal,*" CDM departed from the well-established tradition under which so many men in the book publishing business have fallen. It is some kind of a tribute to Doubleday, Page & Company that the house has been the training-place of a considerable number of the heads in other publishing houses. In Philadelphia a term on the *Ladies' Home Journal* was followed by work as a columnist on the *Evening Public Ledger,* the direct preliminary to Morley's column on the editorial page of the *New York Evening Post,* with which he has been since 1920. The book, Travels *in Philadelphia;* the personal acquaintance of A. Edward Newton, author of *The Amenities of Book Collecting and Kindred Affections*; and a deepened interest in Walt Whitman, are some of the concomitants of the Philadelphia period. Also, I think, Morley's gradual disillusionment began then. The collection of essays called *Mince Pie* was published late in 1919 and there were still to appear, in 1920, certain overflowings of the Morley of the first period—the story of an Oxford undergraduate prank, called *Kathleen;* a book of verse, *Hide and Seek;* and more essays in *Pipefuls*. But that was to be about all. Something very definite had happened to the young man who was so friendly with everybody, who was forever talking about William McFee, who wrote forty-seven letters and notes a day, who had made a cult of quaintness and who liked to be called Kit and to have the resemblance of his name to that of Christopher Marlowe's stretched into a fanciful resemblance of personalities and writing. Some lone reviewer, speaking harshly; or some slight wound received in the house of one of his friends; or the shifts and vicissitudes of commercial enterprise—dissatisfaction with what he had already done, a thirtieth birthday, a wish to do something he had yet to do—together or singly may have been the agents of the change. Only the change itself matters. And what was that? It was not that Chris became less friendly, or autographed fewer dozens of copies of a new book of his, or loved the Elizabethans less or the work of Theodore Dreiser more. But a retractation took place, an alteration of ideas went on . . . aided, it may be, by the uniformity with which American magazine editors rejected a short story called **"Referred to the Author,"** one of the contents of Morley's book *Tales from a Rolltop Desk*—a story which Morley himself thinks marks the definite line between his old work and new.

V

Those who care for the poet of "households of two or more" will find him most readily now in the volume called *Chimneysmoke* (1921), which is a representative selection from the earlier books of verse, *Songs for a Little House, The Rocking Horse,* and *Hide and Seek.* Vincent O'Sullivan has said that the Morley here represented belongs with "the English intimists, Herrick, George Herbert, Cowper, Crabbe." Writing an introduction for the English edition of *Chimneysmoke,* E. V. Lucas remarked: "Domesticity has had many celebrants, but I cannot remember any one work in which such a number of the expressions of Everyman, in his capacity as householder, husband and father, have been touched upon, and touched upon so happily and with such deep and simple sincerity. The poet of 'The Angel in the House' was, I suppose, a predecessor; but Coventry Patmore was a mystic and a rhapsodist, whereas Mr. Morley keeps on a more normal plane and puts in verse, thoughts and feelings and excitements that most of us have known but have lacked the skill or will to epigrammatise. If we are to look in literature for a kindred spirit to Mr. Morley's we find it rather in the author of 'The Cotter's Saturday Night.'"

Morley's new book of essays, *The Powder of Sympathy,* shows the man changed and changing. It would be impossible to detect any loss of humour or cheerfulness in such papers as those on Sir Kenelm Digby or the Morley

automobile, Dame Quickly (to be succeeded some day by the more impressive Dean Swift). But the satire in **"The Story of Ginger Cubes"** is not less complete or sharp for being throughout good-natured; and in his piece on **"The Unknown Citizen"** Morley seems to me to strike a single magnificent chord in which satire and humour are simply notes underlain by the deep bass of pathos and truth. The new book of poems, *Parson's Pleasure,* shows that where there was so much *Chimneysmoke* a fire burns also. This book has an inspiring and inspiriting essay for preface—one far too quotable; I must resist it. Instead, let me give the first sonnet in the **"Memoranda for a Sonnet Sequence"**:

> The herb Lunaria, old books aver,
> If gathered thus and so, in moony patches,
> Has property of mystic opener
> When laid upon the fastest locks and latches.
> In this respect, the moonplant duly matches
> The magic of the poets, who bestir
> Their art to loosen spirit's careful catches
> And split our secret bolts like gossamer.
>
> To sprinkle moonseed on the tight-locked soul
> Bidding it open, or stand soft ajar—
> To sprinkle moonseed, gathered thus and so,
> This is the poet's honourable rôle.
> Like some old Tudor captain bound afar
> I hear him crying *Inward! Inward Ho!*

St. John Adcock (essay date 1928)

SOURCE: "Christopher Morley," in *The Glory That Was Grub Street: Impressions of Contemporary Authors,* The Musson Book Company, 1928, pp. 237-46.

[*In the following essay, Adcock praises Morley's versatility but cautions that such diversity can lead to a lack of focus.*]

It has been said often enough—I have said it often enough myself—and it must be true since it has been said so often, that it is as unfortunate for an author to be versatile as it is for a man to be born with three heads. With such a superfluity of natural gifts he may win notoriety and some money as a freak in a side-show, but he can hardly hope to succeed in getting himself taken so seriously that the management will put his variety entertainment in large type at the top of the bill as the great star turn in the exhibition. In spite of the proverb, it is found in practice that even two heads are not better than one, and there can be no doubt whatever that more than two amount to a catastrophe. A wise man, finding himself thus endowed and ambitious to rise and be received in the best and highest circles, will concentrate on one and, at all risks, amputate the others.

The versatile author is faced with the same problem. People in general may talk as if they admired an Admirable Crichton, but in their hearts they distrust him; he rather bewilders them, and they are much likelier to excuse themselves from following him by putting him aside as a jack-of-all-trades. For of course he is difficult to follow, and only the enterprising minority, whose tastes are sufficiently catholic, care to keep track of him. Instead of going steadily ahead, always along the same road, he is continually making excursions into byways, and if he cannot break himself of this habit, before it is too late, decide what goal he wants to reach and go straight for it, he usually ends by leaving most of his followers lost in those different byways and arriving nowhere in particular, at last, with nobody much at his heels.

I am not suggesting that this is going to be the awful fate of Christopher Morley; it might have been; but there are clear signs that he has so far only been feeling industriously around to find himself and the way he ought to travel; and that he has found them. As Hugh Walpole says in a preface to **Thunder on the Left**, Morley's gifts "were as many as they were dangerous, and that especial danger of finding life too enchanting to be true is difficult to escape because it becomes so easily a habit". He has been described to me—unhappily I have never met him—as a big, genial, friendly man, with an intense interest and joy in life; "a fellow of infinite jest" and fantasy, but one who is a tremendous worker and brings a fresh enthusiasm to every sort of work he is moved to do. You could not read much that he has written without guessing at something of this; you would guess from its glancing alertness and sense of spontaneity, that even if some of it had been done as part of a journalist's regular job, he had put his heart as well as his mind into it and found pleasure in the doing; you would guess he had been having a good time, letting his fancy and imagination range at large, catching at every kind of idea they brought home to him and carelessly embodying each in its different, appropriate medium, because he happens to have a breadth and brilliance of capacity which enabled him to do so. As a result, counting two written in collaboration, he has in the last sixteen years published five-and-twenty books of poems, serious and humorous, short stories, sketches, essays, novels, skits, and a few plays. His wildest burlesque and the most thoughtful and restrained of his poems, essays, stories have often been touched with a characteristic fantasy, whimsical, satirical or graciously tender, that has brought them into an elusive harmony; otherwise he has been a very Proteus in the various forms he has used. That is the real way how to be happy though literary, but, for the reasons suggested, it is not the way to a stable popularity, nor a sure way, as a substitute for concentration, in which an author can develop the greatest of his gifts. And you may depend that Morley knows this, for it looks as if he were beginning to act accordingly.

He was born in 1890, at Haverford, Pennsylvania, and, having graduated at Haverford College, went as a Rhodes Scholar to Oxford, from 1910 to 1913. While he was still at Oxford, in 1912, his first book, a book of poems, **The Eighth Sin**, was published by B. H. Blackwell, the well-known publisher of that city. He returned to America, and for five years was on the editorial staff of the great publishing house of Doubleday, Page & Co. Then he took to journalism, and was successively associated with the *Ladies' Home Journal, Philadelphia Public Ledger,* the New York *Evening Post* (to which he began to contribute his lively column, **The Bowling Green**, in 1920), and the *Saturday Review of Literature.*

Meanwhile, in 1917, appeared his first prose fiction, **Parnassus on Wheels** and a second volume of poems **Songs from a Little House**. In 1918 came a collection of his essays, **Shandygaff**; next year, more poems, **The Rocking Horse,** more fiction, **The Haunted Bookshop,** a skit on prohibition, **In the Sweet Dry and Dry**, and another book of essays, **Mince Pie**. That was a year of plenty, and 1920 rivalled it, with the sketches and essays, **Travels in Philadelphia**, a story, **"Kathleen"**, **Pipefuls**, another book of essays, and **Hide and Seek**, which contains some of the best poems of his that I have read. It contains, for instance, that sonnet, **"In an Auction Room"**, touching with a wry humour and poignance on the sale of Keats's love letters, and closing with the ironic comment:

> "Song that outgrew the singer! Bitter love
> That broke the proud hot heart it held in thrall.
> Poor script, where still those tragic passions
>   move—
> *Eight hundred bid: fair warning: the last call:*
> The soul of Adonais, like a star. . . .
> *Sold for eight hundred dollars—Doctor R.!"*

The next year (1921) brought a further three books, **Tales from a Rolltop Desk, Plum Pudding** (essays), and another collection of his poems, **Chimneysmoke**. If, as a poet, Morley's place is on the lower slopes of Parnassus, there is the individual note and the same charm of fancy and sentiment in a good deal of his verse that you find in his prose, breaking in there at times on his drollest and most irresponsible moods. Very characteristic of him are the lines **"To a Post-Office Inkwell"** (in **Chimneysmoke**), characteristic of his insight of the homely beauty and significance that is in common, everyday things:

> "How many humble hearts have dipped
> In you, and scrawled their manuscript!
> Have shared their secrets, told their cares,
> Their curious and quaint affairs!
>
> Your pool of ink, your scratchy pen,
> Have moved the lives of unborn men,
> And watched young people, breathing hard,
> Put Heaven on a postal card."

A later book of verse, **Translations from the Chinese** (1922) is in a very different vein, as you may gather from the fact that the verses are translations of such Celestial poets as No Sho and Mu Kow, and that Morley confesses his sole knowledge of Chinese was derived from laundry slips. To summarise the remainder of my catalogue, between 1922 and to-day we have had from him, in collaboration with Don Marquis, **Pandora Lifts** *the Lid;* we have had *The Arrow,* four volumes of essays, *The Powder of Sympathy, Inward Ho! Religio Journalistici,* and as delightful a miscellany of travel and general sketches as any he has done, *The Romany Stain,* a one-act play, *Rehearsal,* and his two latest collections of poems, *Parsons' Pleasure,* and *Toulemonde.* In addition, for like Browning's careful host I have left the finest wine till last, there are *Where the Blue Begins* (1922) and *Thunder on the Left* (1926).

With *Where the Blue Begins* Morley seemed, at one stride, to pass his Rubicon and stand among authors who are to be taken seriously. Until then, I suppose, he was looked upon by many of us rather as a clever trifler, a brilliant journalist and miscellaneous writer whose multifarious work suggested that he had greater gifts than he had yet realised or exerted himself to employ. That was, I am afraid, our notion of him over here, though they knew him better and he had a considerable vogue in his own country. But when we read *Where the Blue Begins* we woke up to a recognition of its strange power and originality, and to the fact that he had suddenly outrivalled himself. It is a novel, but not of the orthodox pattern; it would be more at home bracketed with "Gulliver's Travels"; for it is a blend of allegory, fantasy, satire, fable, poetry and philosophy. It is a story of Gissing, the dog, who lives in a world of dogs, where the animals think and talk and act much as if they were human beings. Gissing seeks for the meaning of life, as men do, broods on religion, is sceptical of its teachings and tries to find God in the world. After a splendidly successful interlude as a dog of business, he enters the Church as a lay reader, and moved one Sunday to exceed his authority mounts the pulpit and preaching of the mystery of Godhead tells his audience their idea of Him and of serving Him with trivial ceremony and ritual is all "on too petty a scale", and urges them to believe "it is even possible God may be a biped". Whereupon all the dogs in the congregation, led by a canine Bishop, rise in such a howling of indignant fury that he is compelled to flee for safety. He escapes to the sea and gets aboard a ship as a stowaway. Here, having won the confidence of the captain, he soon contrives, by means of a ruse, to scare the crew and passengers into going off in the boats, and he sails on alone, an erratic and uncharted course, which brings him finally to unknown land. He goes ashore, and after some wandering, comes upon a ragged tramp seated by a fire in a thicket, and at this unwonted sight of a man he quivers with emotion, goes forward with feelings of joy and worship, to nestle his head contentedly on the vagrant's knee, satisfied that he has at last found God. Presently, he runs off reluctantly to see that the ship is safely moored, and discovers it dwindled to a toy boat and the vast ocean to nothing but the lake near his own house.

Like all allegory it is not always easy of comprehension; it is full of spiritual suggestion, here and there it is susceptible of more than one interpretation, and will probably mean different things to different readers. You can enjoy the wit and satire and the oddly fantastic story

of it for their own sakes, but its covert parody of human life, thought and practice gives it a deeper interest and the inner significances you glimpse in mystical poems and parables.

Somewhat of this is true also of *Thunder on the Left,* which is too well known by now for it to be necessary for me to attempt anything much of a summary. Briefly, it is a tale of a party of children gathered to celebrate the tenth birthday of one of them, Martin. They talk of their elders, of whether grown-ups are really happy and how impossible it is to find out, because if you question them they will never tell you things. They decide that they will, as a new kind of game, get into the country of the grown-ups as spies on them, and then "bring in a report". In blowing out the birthday candles each child has one wish, and as a consequence of Martin's wish the second chapter opens with the story of George Granville and his wife, Phyllis. With the development of the story other children of the birthday party take part in it, but, like Phyllis, they have arrived at years of maturity. In due course comes Martin himself, grown to manhood but still a boy in mind, and it dawns upon you, after a while, that Martin is, in fact also George, and that in his own name he is only there as the boy-spy. The experiences of these people who have projected themselves into the future and are living the lives that may be theirs in twenty years' time are subtly and suggestively handled. They seem real, but have an occasional consciousness of their unreality; there is an elusive air of gramarye about it all, but the men and women are very human in their emotions and their relations with one another, and have gone through enough to know that everything is not easy for their elders, before it all fades like a dream and they are back at the party which is just breaking up, and Martin, at least, has some memory of what has passed. Here, again, you may not always be sure in every detail of exactly what Morley intends to convey, but the meaning of the fantasy as a whole is so clear that even he who runs can read it. There is wit and worldly wisdom and whimsical satire in this as in *Where the Blue Begins* and the humour is so rarely strained or thin that such passing flaws count for no more against the charm and skill of these two remarkable books than do spots on the sun. A dramatic version of *Thunder on the Left* has been as successful as the novel. Morley has been compared with Barrie; I think a comparison with Chesterton might be truer; but he is so little like and so much unlike both it is futile to compare him with either.

Richard D. Altick (essay date 1942)

SOURCE: "Average Citizen in Grub Street: Christopher Morley After Twenty-Five Years," in *The South Atlantic Quarterly,* Vol. XLI, No. 1, January, 1942, pp. 18-31.

[*In the following essay, Altick points to Morley's faded reputation as a writer.*]

There is, in each man's heart,
Chinese writing—
A secret script, a cryptic language;
The strange ideographs of the spirit,
Scribbled over or half erased
By the swift stenography of daily life.
   "The Palimpsest" from *Translations from the
Chinese*

Few people nowadays can be accused of taking Christopher Morley too seriously. But there is an equal error in taking him too much for granted. Thanks to the *succès de scandale* of **Kitty Foyle** his name is now more than ever a household word in America. For the past twenty-five years the presses have uttered his books with melancholy regularity. His burly figure, his beard, and his eternal pipe are familiar to lecture audiences from coast to coast. His easily kindled enthusiasm for each season's new books has won for him, among thousands of casual readers, the authority once enjoyed by Professor Phelps. In his extraprofessional moments he has appeared in such diverse roles as honorary night watchman at the Central Park Zoo and frequent guest on "Information Please." Perhaps it is his very ubiquitousness on the American scene which has denied him the close and dispassionate scrutiny accorded to other authors of his rank: like many another familiar institution, he has never been thought worthy of serious attention. It is a fault that should be remedied.

The chief task of Morley's critic is to find reasons for the decline of a reputation that many readers once felt sure was merely the prelude to literary fame. In his earlier years Morley was looked upon by his critics as a writer of great promise. After a decent period had elapsed and that promise showed no signs of substantial fulfillment, reviewers of each of his successive books exchanged their hopefulness for impatience, the occurrence of passages of true distinction even in his worst writing having made them reluctant to dismiss him finally as a flash in the pan. Of late years they have ceased even to be impatient, and their perfunctory notices now usually suggest that Morley's latest book will be sure to please Morley's fans, and no others need apply.

Yet even today it is impossible to forget that Morley once wrote **Thunder on the Left** (1925), a book whose delicate, haunting charm has not evaporated with the passage of the years. How did the man who was capable of producing a book of this stamp come to persuade himself that he was serving the same high ideals of art when he exposed the stream of a "white-collar girl's" consciousness in **Kitty Foyle** (1939)? It is a question not unworthy of our attention. It involves (if I may adopt for a moment the Morleyan manner) the spiritual odyssey of a descendant of Alexander Smith and Henry Ryecroft, set adrift in a world of shining skyscrapers—and hungry presses.

I

Morley's chief literary qualities are unbridled whimsicality, bookishness, a rich but disorderly prose style, an air of philosophical perplexity, and a passion for the appurtenances of ordinary life as lived by Americans in the twentieth century. Today most of us find those qualities intolerably cloying; Morley resolutely works the same old vein, but he long since stopped panning gold. Yet these were the very same elements which once were responsible for his being viewed as one of the most promising of our younger writers. If we forget our own satiation with them and regard them in historical perspective, we can understand why Morley was welcomed as a fresh and original spirit in American journalism.

The most discerning early estimate of Morley was written by Vincent O'Sullivan for the British *New Witness* in 1919. The critic made much of something which Morley's later career has caused us almost entirely to forget: namely, that he originally belonged far more to the English tradition than to the American. This young columnist on the Philadelphia *Evening Ledger* was, said O'Sullivan, "one of the very few American writers who continue the English literary tradition in a country where that tradition is dying fast, and where the spoken, and to a considerable extent the written, language is drawing farther and farther away from English as it is used in England." It was an acute comment; for Morley, though a Pennsylvanian by birth, was the son of English parents, had been a Rhodes scholar, and by sheer Anglicism of temperament had far deeper sympathies with the urbane tradition of Chesterton, Belloc, Beerbohm, and Lynd than with any of the American schools which were then fashionable.

An unusual combination of temperament, education, and wide reading allowed young Morley to give high promise as an American exponent of the classic informal essay. He had great personal charm, which made his Montaigne-like egotism not only acceptable but ingratiating; and the elderly tranquillity of his two colleges, Haverford and New College, Oxford, had joined with a certain habitual serenity of mind to give him an air of mellowness remarkable in so young a man. Every good essayist is a poet in his way, but Morley's poetic inclinations were notable. Not only was his facile light verse of enough merit to remind some extravagant people of Herrick, but his prose as well was characterized by a free play of romantic imagination and a true poet's choice of phrase. And, to top it off, he had a rich cultural background and a passion for reading which, by the time he published his first essays, had put him in possession of a vast stock of bookish knowledge, some of it unimportant but all of it entertaining.

These, then, were young Morley's indubitable assets, the things which caused reviewers to become thoughtful over him. His liabilities were those usually found in a new writer who has not had time to mature or to discipline himself. He was too discursive, his egotism often overstaying its welcome; he was over-allusive; he frequently allowed his poetic whimsicality to run away with him. But these were the excesses of a high-spirited youth, and they could be remedied in time. The most excellent of ales has too much froth when it is first poured.

When he began writing, Morley's interest was concentrated in the quaint and sentimental aspects of modern everyday life. His first essays, collected in such volumes as *Shandygaff* (1918), *Mince Pie* (1919), *Pipefuls* (1920), *Travels in Philadelphia* (1920), and *Plum Pudding* (1921), were, with the exception of notes on his innumerable literary hobbies, which are still characteristic of him, almost all light-hearted soliloquies on the humble joys of the suburbanite and the humors of a Grub Street runner. His philosophy was, as he said, a kind of dishpantheism (the pun being typical of the hundreds which bespeckle his earlier books): "I find the kitchen the shrine of our civilization, the focus of all that is comely in life. The ruddy shine of the stove is as beautiful as any sunset. A well-polished jug or spoon is as fair, as complete and beautiful, as any sonnet. The dish mop, properly rinsed and wrung and hung outside the back door to dry, is a whole sermon in itself." That his essays in this vein had a very genuine charm cannot be doubted; such papers as "On Filling an Inkwell," "The Urchin at the Zoo," "Thoughts on Cider," "An Early Train," and "On Being in a Hurry," with their comfortable English air of domesticity, remedied what had long been a blind spot in the American literary view of life. From the first, Morley revealed himself to be an enthusiast for the contemporary; but he preferred to view his times in their more picturesque, more intimate phases—in the microcosm of a modest bungalow on Long Island or an obscure chophouse in lower Manhattan.

It was not long, however, before critics, readers, and, apparently, author also tired of "his too prolonged genuflection at the shrine of the assiduously quaint," as one reviewer put it. All the time that he had been discoursing on the felicities of commuting and raising a family, there were suggestions in Morley's writing that his true concern lay deeper. In "Walt Whitman Miniatures" (1919), for instance, we read: "How much we need a Whitman today, a poet who can catch the heart and meaning of these grievous bitter years. . . . " This, in the light of what he was about to do, was not a mere routine expression of a hackneyed sentiment. And again in "Confessions of a 'Colyumist'" (1920) we find this straightforward declaration of his sense of the dignity of his literary mission: "To catch some hint of the meaning of all this, to present a few scrawled notes of the amazing interest and color of the city's life, this is the colyumist's task as I see it. It is a task not a whit less worthy, less painful, or less baffling than that of the most conscientious novelist."

It is not surprising, then, that in 1922, when the publishers' salesmen, seeing Morley's name on their new list, expected to receive "another book about an old bookstore" (they had previously done quite well with *The Haunted Bookshop,* a sequel to *Parnassus on Wheels*), they were given instead a strange little tale about a dog named Gissing, who deserted the cozy certainties of his suburban home and wandered out into the enormous world in quest of the meaning that underlay the mounting crescendo of noise and haste that was civilization. He went straight to New York.

> In the city which is maddest of all, Gissing had come to search for sanity. In the city so strangely beautiful that she has made even poets silent, he had come to find a voice. In the city of glorious ostent and vanity, he had come to look for humility and peace. . . . I know all that can be said against her; and yet, in her great library of streets, vast and various as Shakespeare, is beauty enough for a lifetime. O poets, why have you been so faint? Because she seems cynical and crass, she cries with trumpet-call to the mind of the dreamer; because she is riant and mad, she speaks to the grave sanity of the poet.

Gissing's own spiritual quest, in **Where the Blue Begins,** marking as it did the real beginning of Morley's own, stands as a prophecy of his entire subsequent career.

From that time on, without for a moment abandoning his literary enthusiasms or losing his keen zest for the small pleasures and whims of life, Morley became more and more engrossed in the philosophical problem of "this burning, maddening civilization." That is lofty language to use of a man who has been so playful and so trivial in all that he has written of his saunterings through the modern world. But as Dr. Canby, his former colleague on the *Saturday Review of Literature,* once said, "His humor is only the bubbling over of a rich nature which without his joy in living might have taken tragedy for its issue." Without in the least implying that a frustrated tragedian lurks beneath his motley, I believe we are justified in discounting to some extent his habitually humorous manner, his trick of smothering incisive thought under a cozy blanket of style. We may take his questionings seriously. He has always been bothered by the bigness, the variety, and what he calls "the St. Vitus" of our age. He has felt a desire to derive some mystic significance from it all—a desire as earnest as the religious fervor of the Quakers among whom he was raised. "In the vastness of the scene," he wrote in "Brooklyn Bridge" (ca. 1920), "one looks . . . for some guiding principle of arrangement by which vision can focus itself."

But that is all the further he has ever gotten; his essays and novels still abound with picturesque expressions of his sense of the need for formulation. Today, watching the glint of sunlight on the RCA tower, he seems to be thinking the same comfortably indecisive thoughts and having the same vague, delicious, romantic feelings that he had twenty years ago when he adored Diana atop the old Madison Square Garden. He would, of course, have it no other way. His most conspicuous trait is his tremendous contentment, which is never really disturbed by those gentle philosophical troublings about which he likes to write his most poetic paragraphs.

II

Thus Morley has always remained the journalist (using the word, in his own manner, as if it still meant what its Latin root suggests). He has never really looked beyond the day; he has never flirted with true philosophy, or even become moderately profound. And by inquiring for the causes of this blithe superficiality of outlook we may, I think, discover the essential nature of Morley's literary habit.

In the first place, he has an inexhaustible fund of animal spirits. He cannot be truly contemplative because he is too much alive, too much a part of all he surveys. The gusto which characterized his earliest papers has persisted undiminished through a quarter century of constant writing. His many gifts include the knack of writing engaging children's stories; and in his more serious work too he has remained the essential child, a wanderer among skyscrapers, fascinated beyond expression with the enormous variety of this world in which he dwells. To him, despite all his conscientious urge to probe deeper, the modern scene remains a gigantic hurly-burly of color and motion, an endlessly diverting pageant of appearances. Besides, he has not only the eyes of an artist but the informal essayist's faculty of noticing and enjoying small details. He is entranced alike by the "Euclidean paradise of solids, veined with parallels of silver" of the Empire State Building and by every small particular of the brisk, efficient routine of a transcontinental airplane trip. A man who takes such immense delight in a ride in the locomotive cab of a fast train cannot reasonably be expected, I suppose, to lose himself in deep thought.

Again, Morley has always had the idea that to "be human" is the highest use one can make of the gift of life. He admires, above everything else, the spectacle of a man or woman leading a "vulgar, jocund, carnal, beautiful, rueful" existence, thoroughly absorbed in everyday affairs, deriving the most pleasure from every tiny impression that strikes his senses, and humorously cultivating his small vices. His own lively humanity, whether spoken of in the first or the third person, has always been the staple of his most characteristic work. He loves to assume the incognito of the Average Citizen, whom he conceives as being so wrapped up in his small personal concerns that he is sensible of the existence of cosmic mysteries only in moments of vague uneasiness, from which he finds escape again in the trivialities of commonplace life. Since in the normal run-of-the-mill human being the twin native flames of poetry and philosophy are, according to the popular idea, turned down to the size of the pilot light on a gas stove, Morley, in order to conform to his own conception of strict "humanity," must moderate his own flames accordingly. If he must talk at all about the verities and such matters, it must be in the manner in which his Richard Roes do so: in the terms appropriate to flat-dwellers, and with an air of apology that suggests actual fright at coming, for an instant, full face with things from which they ordinarily are able to avert their gaze.

The long series of verse **"Translations from the Chinese"** offers us perhaps the best idea of the extent to which Morley, in his dual role of poet and Average Citizen, has succeeded in capturing and making articulate the underlying spirit of the age. The "Translations" purport to be the random comments of a Chinese mandarin who wanders through this country applying his mellow Confucian wisdom to such contemporary phenomena as neon lights and automats. The chief value of these and similar collections of *pensées,* which are heavily indebted to the *Trivia* of Morley's fellow-Haverfordian, Logan Pearsall Smith, is the chief value, indeed, of all of Morley's communion with the present: the mandarin's naïveté in the midst of the American Present directs our attention to the interest inherent in the *minutiae* of our everyday life, which have become so familiar to us that they are scarcely noticed. Their main weakness is also that of Morley's writings at large: the philosophical reflections which are hung on his little impressions of life in the city and along the main highways are almost invariably clever—but they are all distressingly inconsequential.

The most characteristic of Morley's extended prose studies of Today is **Human Being** (1932), an attempt, as the author remarks, "to catch a human being in the very act of being human—and to set it down without chemical preservatives." But it has far more value as a congeries of impressions of contemporary life than as a sympathetic record of the spiritual life of Richard Roe (the Average Citizen of the book) or as a faintly implied satire of the forces in our age which keep a man's spiritual fires safely but stodgily banked. It is in effect a receptacle for the thousands of tiny observations which Morley has made as he has moved wide-eyed through the world—reports on Sunday newspapers, bath towels, the intimate routine of office buildings, talkies, display windows, the subway. As the raw material of social history it is invaluable, but as a sensitive study of personal lives in modern urban civilization it is a bitter disappointment—mainly because Morley's mind, as he says of Richard Roe's, "was busy and happy as he admired this vivid show, yet he would have been rather speechless to any inquiry as to what he was thinking."

Intense joy in the outward aspects of life as it is lived in modern America, then, and sedulous worship of the "human" are two chief elements in the Morleyan temperament. Add a third, overdevelopment of the sentimental faculty, and there is little further need to ask the reasons for his failure to do anything important with the fine materials at his command. Though his sentimentality has produced some notable nostalgic passages in such books as the autobiographical "novel" **John Mistletoe** (1931), it has inhibited the exercise of the keen critical spirit which otherwise might manifest itself when Morley looks at his age. He is too passionately enamored of his mistress to be able to survey her very objectively. "Even Hell, you must admit, has always had its patriots," he once wrote, addressing **"A New Yorker a Hundred Years Hence"** (1921). "And how we loved this strange, mad city of ours, which we knew in our hearts was, to the clear eye of reason and the pure, sane vision of poetry, a bedlam of magical impertinence, a blind byway of monstrous wretchedness. And yet the blacker it seemed to the lamp of the spirit, the more we loved it with the troubled eye of flesh." All his talk about New York and the civilization of which it is the fountainhead and symbol has this same tone of blind, or if not blind at least obstinately optimistic, adoration. Morley has always been too pleased to feel a subtle emotional bond between himself and the subject of his meditations to be able to achieve a truly philosophical perspective. And he has always shown a reluctance to consider the seamier aspects of his shining city; even when he admits their existence, he perfumes them from the atomizer of his vocabulary until even degradation seems to have a jocund side. "It would be misleading to dwell too heavily on any elements of wisdom or anxiety in Richard Roe's thought," he wrote, in excellent self-criticism. "He was well aware of the world's enormous sinking-fund of misery. Yet even so it looked to him as though the *status quo* had high and humorous merits."

Morley worships at many shrines, but at none more fervently than Walt Whitman's; and recalling what that rugged one-time denizen of Broadway did with his To-day helps us to understand why Morley has never made equally permanent literature of the materials supplied by our own times. He is a humorist in the gentle English romantic tradition. He can never see a filling station as a blatant defacement of wayside beauty, for he possesses a remarkable faculty for filtering out the ugly from his impressions. Nor can he see that filling station as a symbol of modern commercial aggression, for he has little or no capacity for social indignation. Rather he must portray the cluster of pumps before which he draws one of "Dame Quickly's" successors as a monastic haven for modern highway pilgrims, the attendant as a genial abbot. Looking at one thing, Morley cannot help being reminded of something more romantic; or at least infusing that object, however utilitarian it may be, with a highly romantic coloring which sometimes borders on the ludicrous.

Thus Morley has been his own worst enemy. If he has never achieved anything greater than splendid fragmentary images of skyscrapers, if he has for the most part been content to be a connoisseur of (to use his own word) "hodiernal" humors—of ingenious gadgets and advertising signs and passing fads—it is the inevitable result of his failure to curb his own exuberance. Writing of Heywood Broun, Morley made what amounts to the most acute analysis to date of his own shortcomings: "His profession as daily columnist, . . . his diffusion among sociable and generous concerns, increased the temperamental discursiveness of his mind. He was too humane, too genuinely interested in people, for the savage concentration required by art. His mind, I used to think, was sometimes as disorderly as his person." When he seeks to delve beneath the appearances of things, he is as baffled as any of his Average Citizens.

He has the will to be a philosopher, but none of the patience. His life, which he lives seemingly for the sole purpose of writing about it, is portrayed as a perpetual bout between the "carnal" and the philosophical—a bout in which the outcome is never in question.

III

But undoubtedly Morley's failure to fulfill the promise of his early books can also be attributed to the circumstances under which he first achieved notice. He appeared on the scene at a time when the characteristic tone of his first writing, a high-spirited fusing of the bookish and the worldly, was most welcome. The years following the war saw a wide democratization of American literary interest. Morley, a journalist whose peculiar gift was the ability to look at books with the eye of a "human being" and at life with the eye of a bookman, was foreordained to be the most articulate leader of the popular literary movement. His gospel, as first announced in ***Parnassus on Wheels,*** was to be the liveliness, the humaneness, of literature; and as extended in ***The Haunted Bookshop,*** in Roger Mifflin's harangues on the part books should play in the mending of the human spirit, it was to include the timeliness of all good literature. Indeed, it may fairly be said that Morley's unashamed enthusiasm for the contemporary was the trait most responsible for his popularity. He made good reading because he loved life, the sort of life his readers knew, and he also made it easy for them to like it, because he was adept at giving them bookish authority for doing so.

Because popularity came so soon, Morley had no time to discipline himself, to learn economy and restraint and self-effacement. He found that he had defined his position very early in the game, and that henceforth he must maintain it: a practical journalist can do nothing else. He had a public which knew what it wanted and expected to have it. And so he was never to call himself to account for his disorderliness and his superficiality. The product he marketed had to adhere to certain specifications which he himself, alas, had formulated and popularized. The Morleyan brand of essay and novel has been quite consistent; it has also been indifferent to improvement. In the end, it has been the undoing of its manufacturer.

His style today is a curious and unhappy blend of classic English and modern newspaper and street usage. One would not be severe with Morley on this account had he not frequently been the eloquent champion of the older standards of literary craftsmanship, and supposedly a believer in the existence of certain objective canons of taste which a self-respecting writer will impose upon himself. Furthermore, he has himself been counted among the leading American stylists. Therefore the average literary quality of his recent work, entirely apart from its content, may well cause distress to those who saw in his initial essays a much needed reaffirmation of older English literary principles.

Even in his earlier prose Morley was a libertarian in the matter of grammar. His punctuation and what the schoolteachers call "sentence sense" were, like the rest of him, wayward. But such lapses were, on the whole, infrequent. Today, however, solecisms crowd one upon another, thicker than you will find them in the ordinary badly-edited newspaper. Such locutions as "somewhat embarrassment on both sides," "myself I'm pleased that," and "one of the most unique collections" are scarcely in the best tradition. Nor does the conscientious literary craftsman pass for the press such a phrase as this: "the disconcerting habit of some known beacons being thriftily turned off on moonlit nights."

Morley's present literary standards reach their lowest level, however, in connection with vocabulary. Throughout his career he has been, to use Dr. Canby's phrase, "a drunkard in vocabularies." He has accumulated and used a vast assortment of uncommon words, especially Latinisms, archaisms, and terms lifted from special vocabularies. He has used these words with charm, and although sometimes he has succumbed to an apparent compulsion to insert a showy, unfamiliar word where an ordinary one would do as well, their savor and their rich connotations have added to the lively scholarliness of his prose. But his unusual sensitivity to words leads him grievously astray as he indulges his passion for the contemporary; for his work has become a dumping ground, not only for those older Americanisms and colloquialisms which are now accorded a place in the reputable writer's vocabulary, but also for street talk and contemporary slang of extremely dubious appropriateness.

His language therefore is an incongruous hodgepodge in which the stately Latinism of *The Anatomy of Melancholy* rubs an uneasy elbow with the lingo of the subway rider. *Blattidae* [*sic*], *oecumenical, sphygmograph, tirpitzed*[*!*], *piaffing, inenarrably, caducity,* and *appetent* are found side by side with *hootch, holler,* and *fed up,* which are embodied in Morley's prose without even the implied apology of quotation marks. For abundant illustration of what I mean, open **Inward Ho!** (1923) at almost any page and read a few paragraphs of Morley's prose, which is at its best level in these half-humorous, half-brooding meditations. And then, taking one of the last installments of the Bowling Green, the department which Morley conducted for many years in the *Saturday Review,* you will come upon such a sentence as this, "We were wishing that all the deluxe book designers and collectors of goofiana would read the pages . . . devoted to pantywaist printing," or this, "Even so I can see that in this here now streamlining, as publicized, there's a trace of hooey." Further comment would be superfluous. It is not necessary to deny modern street talk the raciness which it unquestionably possesses to appreciate the dismal effect Morley produces when he mixes it indiscriminately with the language of the bookworm.

Morley has simply extended his preoccupation with the "human," the supposedly divine average, to language. If the Average Citizen cares nothing for the more moderate niceties of grammar and has an unconquerable addiction to the slang and clichés of the day, Morley too must take the easy position that anything that is current is coin. Hence Bowling Greens that are no more than ten years old, were they to be collected now, would require annotation. Morley not only writes *of* the present day; he seems content to address himself only to the reader who opens his pages while the ink is still damp.

IV

This view of Christopher Morley is admittedly not a happy one. It tempts us to recall the quarrel he had with O. O. McIntyre, shortly before the latter's death, over some alleged plagiarism. The irresistible suggestion of a resemblance between the erstwhile champion of the old English literary tradition and the popular Hearst columnist raises the question of whether Morley, despite his pretensions, is any more than a literary McIntyre: a gossipy chronicler of small occurrences in the world of books, a treasurer of personal trivia only slightly more profound than Pepys.

Certainly the average quality of his work now requires Morley to be ticketed as nothing more exalted than a journalist. But, as I remarked in the beginning, his temperament, his literary sympathies, and his background would have fitted him, had he been taken firmly in hand at a young age, for a career in serious writing: if not in poetry, certainly in essays, and even in novels. I do not mean to suggest that he would have made a Thomas Wolfe or even an American J. B. Priestley; but a candid examination of all his work will show that he has on numerous occasions demonstrated the actual fineness of his gifts. It is an enduring pity that there should be so much truth in Carl Van Doren's remark that Morley had been mellow before he had a chance to become ripe.

And yet there are certain indisputable achievements to enter upon Morley's record. His chit-chat upon books and their writers has had a great and on the whole very salutary influence on American reading tastes. His multifarious literary enthusiasms, exposed in many good essays, have led thousands of readers who might otherwise never have known them to turn to Whitman, to Walton, to Donne, and to such comparatively neglected writers as Alexander Smith and George Borrow. In an age preoccupied with proletarianism and "revolt" of every description, he insisted upon the abiding greatness of the older writers. If he has earned no other praise, he must receive his due reward as our most persuasive apostle of bibliophilism.

Some of his detractors have taken him to account for his placid acceptance of the world in which he finds himself. No doubt he would have a larger stature today had he tempered his adoration of the Present with a little social criticism, and discriminated between the "high and humorous merits" of our modern world and the vulgarity and injustices which accompany them. But even so, he has provided a sorely needed corrective for the pessimism and cynicism so rampant in the literature of the twenties and early thirties. Especially in an era of clamorous revolt do journalism and literature cry out for a healthy optimist with a spirit capable of detecting traces of beauty in frequencies to which we are ordinarily not tuned—an optimist whose lively imagination can endow even the ugly with a measure of romance.

And from the enormous bulk of his work a discerning editor could precipitate a residue of enduring literary value. A critical anthology of Morley's writing would devote its major space, I suppose, to his familiar essays, some of which have already won a permanent place in the annals of contemporary American prose. His best literary pieces have a value which is not merely enforced by the fact that American literature has been so bare of the true bookish essay. And a judicious selection of his light verse would prove still to possess sparkle and wit.

In the last decade, however, Morley seems to have fancied himself most as a novelist. As a writer in this form he will certainly be remembered for *Thunder on the Left,* one book in which he hovered very close to real art. *Thunder on the Left,* like the later novels, has for its theme the undefinable spiritual unrest which haunts men and women in the modern world: in this instance, the uneasiness that arises from recollections of childhood. In it, Morley revealed himself as still able to divert his eyes from the trivialities of contemporary existence sufficiently to portray emotional experiences in timeless terms. The novels from *John Mistletoe* on, however, are too flooded with concrete manifestations of the moment. The occasional emotional *malaise* of Mistletoe, of Richard Roe, even of Kitty Foyle, is either lost in a mass of circumstantial detail or irretrievably cheapened by the author's insistence upon "contemporary" means of expression.

Morley's career, one hopes, is by no means over. To those who have been disturbed by the frequent but never sustained gleams of excellence in his work, it has thus far been a disappointment. We may hope that sometime he will find resolution enough to turn his back upon his poetic incoherences and write the distinguished sort of prose we expected from him in the beginning. And we may hope even more, perhaps, that he will cease to smile tenderly upon his Average Citizens in their perpetual inability to collect their thoughts, and encourage them to pursue their ideas, no matter where they lead.

Milton M. Gordon (essay date 1947)

SOURCE: "'Kitty Foyle' and the Concept of Class as Culture," in *The American Journal of Sociology,* Vol. LIII, No. 3, November, 1947, pp. 210-17.

[*In the following essay, Gordon discusses* Kitty Foyle *and its view of upper-class American life as a cultural metaphor for the era.*]

The traditional approaches to the concept of social class[1] can, on the whole, be placed under one of two categories: (1) economic analysis of income stratification, or the relation of groups to the means of production and (2) class consciousness—that is, concern with the presence or lack of a feeling of class identification. Each has its shortcomings.

Discussion of social class in terms of economic factors alone begs the peculiar function of the social scientist, who should be able to include economic factors in his analysis but not be circumscribed by them, whereas the question of the existence of class consciousness is also a component part of the problem but not an inclusive frame of reference. As Simpson has pointed out:

> Class consciousness is a highly important element in class analysis, but it enters as an objective factor to be studied only after we are aware as to what we mean by class. The presence of classes in a society could not possibly be dependent upon class consciousness, because the degrees of consciousness of individuals vary even among those of identical relative modes of life and we would be forced to accept what men *think* they are as final indication of what they are. Propaganda concerning the equality of all individuals might lead individuals to accept themselves as equal to each other. . . . whereas their material equality is nowhere evident.[2]

The concept of social class can, however, be best approached through the anthropological concept of "culture." In other words, whatever the means by which they have evolved and whatever the degree of psychological awareness of the process on the part of those concerned, social classes in America constitute somewhat separate subgroups in American society, each with its own cultural attributes of behavior, ideas, and life-situations. From the point of view of "class as culture," then, analysis may subsequently be made of the status differentials involved, the historical reasons for the development of classes, the differential rewards obtained from society by the various classes, the avenues and methods of social mobility, and similar problems.

The cultural approach to class is based on two assumptions: (1) that classes are "little worlds" within which a particular individual carries on most of his important social relationships (the point must be made, of course, that there are innumerable spatially separated units of the same class) and (2) that the experience of growing up in a particular class is reflected in one layer, so to speak, of the individual's personality structure. Warner and Lunt have called this aspect of personality structure directly traceable to group experience the "social personality."[3] A review of the research literature on social class published since 1941 reveals that, although never explicitly stated, the concept of class as culture is implicit in the recent important group of studies carried out by Warner, Lunt, Srole, Davis, and the Gardners.[4] It is interesting to note, too, that the director and initiator of these studies, W. Lloyd Warner, was trained in the discipline of cultural anthropology.

The writer is at present making a study of the concept of social class as it has been handled in the American novel of the period between two World Wars, in which the hypothesis that the cultural implications of social class have been perceptively realized and presented by leading American novelists is being investigated. As an example, the novel *Kitty Foyle,*[5] by Christopher Morley, is analyzed from the point of view of its contribution to the "class-as-culture" concept. *Kitty Foyle* is especially interesting to the sociologist of class because it deals largely with the upper class in American life, a group which, for a number of reasons, has not often been the object of sociological investigation.

The locale of *Kitty Foyle* is Philadelphia; the author himself comes from the upper-class Philadelphia background of which he writes. The plot revolves around the love affair of Kitty, the daughter of a lower-class family of Irish descent living in an industrial section of the city, and Wynnewood Strafford, who lives with his family in Philadelphia's fashionable residential section, the "Main Line." The story takes place during the early 1930's and is told in the first person by Kitty, in retrospect. In a sense, Kitty, in her observations of the mores and behavior patterns of the upper class acts as the anthropological alter ego of Morley, viewing the upper class from the outside. How did Kitty and Wynnewood Strafford meet? As a result of the fact that Kitty's father, now a night watchman, had once been associated in a semiservant capacity with an upper-class institution. He had been groundkeeper at one of the suburban cricket clubs and coach at a private school:

> I suppose Philly is the last place in America where it still matters to be a gentleman. Of course, the old man wasn't, but he was on intimate terms with gentlemen on account of cricket. At the clubs, and at the big private school where he was coach, he knew all the Rittenhouse Square crowd when they were just boys. He was invited to cricket club dinners and used to sing Irish songs for them. There's nobody so snobby about keeping up social hedges as somebody who isn't himself quite the real McCoy. For Pop, men who didn't know about cricket hardly existed. . . .
>
> It was on account of cricket that Wyn first came to the house; he was getting some old scorebooks for that Hundred Years of Philadelphia Cricket they printed. . . . [pp. 14-15].

The association of class position and geographical locale—in other words, some primary group community interaction—is vital to the validity of the class-as-culture concept. This association is repeatedly made in *Kitty Foyle.* The term "Main Line," which refers to the suburban communities strung out along the main westerly tracks of the Pennsylvania Railroad, is used synonymously with "upper class." As a matter of fact, a subtle grading of the class position of various suburbs, including an internal grading of the Main Line itself, is indicated in one passage. Ruminates Kitty:

> People who wouldn't live on the Main Line for fear of being high-hatted go out to Oak Lane and Elkins Park. You wouldn't believe how complicated social life can be till you know about the Philadelphia suburbs. It's a riot. Wyn had a theory about how certain kind of people wouldn't dare live further out the Main Line than Merion [p. 131].

Wyn's family is pictured as living far enough out on the Main Line—at St. David's—and as having a town house on Rittenhouse Square, in central Philadelphia, the earlier residential locale of the Philadelphia upper class. Kitty's home, on the other hand, is in a distinctly unfashionable industrial section,

> just around the corner from Orthodox Street. That's in Frankford, and a long way from the Main Line, if you know what that means in Philly. It's freight trains and coal yards and factories and the smell of the tanneries down by Frankford Creek. . . . [p. 6].

Kitty's mother had come from a section of Philadelphia of higher social standing than her father: "Mother came from Germantown, which is pretty much top shelf compared to Frankford" (p. 2). But perhaps not from the most fashionable part of Germantown:

> And the old faded photograph of Mother when she was still a young lady in Germantown before she married into Frankford. That's quite a gulf, if you don't know it; though Pop when he got peeved, would say when you get that far down Wissahickon Avenue it's not Germantown but Tioga. Mother said Nonsense, we even had a station in Germantown named for us, Upsal. Who ever heard of a station called Foyle? Then Pop would call her his little chicken from Wissahickon which always tickled her. . . . [pp. 60-61].

Another geographical identification, the association of shopping areas and downtown streets with class, is interestingly made:

> Of course it's no use to think you won't meet people in Philly. All the shopping that amounts to anything socially is along those few blocks on Chestnut and Walnut, and sure enough one day when I went out for lunch I ran into Wyn. There had to be comedy about it, he was standing by the curb scraping one of those beautiful brown shoes on the edge. He said, "Kitty, this is very embarrassing, I walked on some chewing gum, I can't imagine where."
>
> "What were you doing on Market Street?"[6] I asked, and he said, "Kitty, you're adorable" [pp. 215-16].

And in another passage, Kitty, by this time living in New York, discusses class and geography in that city:

Then I walked up Fifth Avenue all the way to the Plaza and back again, looking in windows and trying to figure out whether women looked different from Philly. I was kind of disappointed. Of course I didn't know then what I do now, you don't see the really smart women on Fifth; they're mostly on Madison and Park Avenue. As a matter of fact Fifth Avenue isn't as smart as the right blocks on Chestnut St. [in Philadelphia]. There's too much of it, and a Public Library and Woolworth's, and clearances of Philippine lingerie certainly drag it down. . . . [p. 162].

If our hypothesis of "class as culture" is valid, class patterns of dress should be discernible. Kitty shows an acute awareness of upper-class patterns of attire: informality and simplicity, expensive material, and, among males, an emphasis on casual tweeds and flannels. In her first meeting with Wyn, when he drops in to talk with her father about cricket, she recalls that he was wearing "old gray pants and the soft shirt, and the cricket club blazer." At first, Kitty's reaction to this deviation from her lower-class stereotype of upper-class clothes was not favorable:

I only thought "My God, does he work at a bank in that outfit?" . . . Darby Mill, Old St. David's meant nothing to me. How could I guess how much swank there is in that intentional shabbiness [p. 107].

On another occasion she recalls Wyn's first formal call at the house: "All I can see is an attractive tweed suit in a kind of tobacco brown, and the loveliest deep maroon woolen socks" (p. 19).

As it becomes increasingly clear to her that her affair with Wyn is complicated by the separation of their two worlds, she makes an effort to escape by going to Chicago. Wyn follows her and turns up at her room: "Wyn, west of Paoli! Just the few days I'd been away I'd got used to the way men dress in Chicago,[7] pressed very sharp and neat, and provincial snap-brim hats, and Wyn looked almost foreign" (p. 145).

To celebrate the fact that Wyn came to Chicago to be with Kitty, at the cost of missing the Philadelphia Assembly, the annual upper-class ball, they decide to go dining and dancing in evening clothes:

When I was all equipped he sent me back to Molly's in a taxi and got himself a readymade evening suit. I bet it was the only time Wyn Strafford wore ready mades, and he looked almost too Ritzy. He said he did a few somersaults over the bed to take the shine off [p. 149].

In discussing her Uncle Elmer who lived in the mid-West, Kitty says: "He had genius for choosing the wrong kind of clothes, tweeds that were the color of straw and would have given Wyn apoplexy" (p. 55).

Later in the course of Kitty's life, while she is attempting to break off the affair with Wyn, she goes to New York,

and there eventually meets a Jewish doctor named Mark Eisen. Lonely and impressed with Mark's professional competence and intelligence, she begins to go out with him. But the cultural aspects of Jewish middle-class life to which she is introduced bother her. In a paragraph of reminiscing about Wyn, one evening she mentions clothes:

There's a roof of some hotel I can see right from my office desk. The women come out on the terrace and I can see them pause just an instant in the doorway to feel beautiful and sure and to know the dress will float just right as they step off the sill. Their escorts, just like it might be you behind me, following politely right after. You wouldn't be wearing a dentistry coat and a cummerbund, though, and looking like something in café society. Did you make a snob out of me, big boy! I could wring Mark Eisen's neck when I see his clothes, poor sweetheart; and how hard he tries. Always too nifty, always too shiny like cellophane, that's them [pp. 126-27].

Appraising Mark's appearance at a summer gathering, she writes:

Of course Wyn got me so conditioned about men's clothes that I hate to see them overdressed. Mark's striped pants, creased like a knife-edge, would blackball him at any cricket club, and those black and white yachting shoes with perforated breathing holes were definitely Hollywood. What put Big Casino on the outfit was a polo shirt wide open to the fur and a blue tweed coat with a handkerchief made of the same stuff as the shirt. That's pretty terrible, because a man ought to look like he's put together by accident, not added up on purpose. Poor old Mark, you could just see he'd been spending his Saturday afternoons figuring out this cruising kit [pp. 232-33].

He's got the same kind of sureness professionally that the Main Line has socially. He's got respect for intelligence like the Main Line has for flannel pants without any crease in them [pp. 203-4].

About class patterns of women's clothes, Kitty has less to say. On one occasion, however, while demonstrating perfume in a Philadelphia department store, she meets the woman Wyn has eventually married and commenting on her possibilities of attractiveness, says:

She might get that wholesome tweed-skirt, Wayne-Devon and Paoli[8] look. . . . Her manners were so pleasant it would be hard to know was she really dumb or not; of course all those vintage Main Liners pride themselves to be just lovely with the lower classes as long as they don't go beyond their proper station, which would probably be Overbrook [p. 214].

One of the characteristics of Wyn's class (in Warner's terms, it would be the upper-upper class of Philadelphia) is its careful lack of ostentation. Wyn's station wagon (in itself traditionally connected with upper-class status), as he calls at the Foyle house, is described as follows:

I looked out the window and saw a weather-stained old station wagon, and painted on the side of it in small green letters DARBY MILL, OLD ST. DAVID'S.

In line with her early lower-class stereotypes, Kitty evaluates this shabbiness in an amusing mistake:

In the car were some big piles of shingles baled up with wire. Pop had been saying for I don't know how long that we must get new shingles for the backhouse roof, it leaked on him when he was sitting in there. I supposed he ordered some without telling me, and ran downstairs just to see that he wasn't getting cheated.

"Is that the man for the backhouse?" I said as I went into the room. Pop cackled with laughter and the visitor rose politely. I could feel my pure and eloquent blood doing its stuff. It was Wyn [p. 106].

Years later, when Kitty has begun to see the status implications of a shabby station wagon, she writes as follows of an unexpected encounter with Wyn's wife:

I get off at 30th Street Station and walk out for a cab, and Jesusgod comes a station wagon pulling up under those pillars marked DARBY MILL. Not a nice old tumble-down station wagon neither but bran shiny new. I bet Ronnie wouldn't understand how much smarter the old one was [p. 208].

And in the scene describing Wyn's call at the Foyle home, when he leaves, Kitty apologizes to her father:

"I thought Mr. Strafford must be in the lumber business," I said.

"Jesusgod," exclaimed the old man. "Don't you ever read your *Ledger?* Strafford, Wynnewood and Company, the oldest private bank in Philly. Darby Mill, that's the name of their country place; there's an old sawmill on the crick out there, where they cut up the logs for Washington at Valley Forge. Honey, those folks are so pedigree they'd be ashamed to press their pants. They hire someone to drive the Rolls for a year before they use it, so it won't look too fresh."

"I think that's just as silly as the opposite." [Kitty notes that she replied.] I think so still [pp. 107-8].

This drive for unostentation goes as far as using circumlocutions to avoid public identification with names connoting prestige:

Wyn said he was getting a lot of work done because he'd taken leave of absence from the bank and his family were all away at their summer cottage in Rhode Island. He had a funny phobia about saying "Newport." I soon got to spot that habit of the Main Line crowd, kind of ashamed to let on how swell they are. Jesusgod they don't even brood on it in secret, they just know [p. 110].

An interesting sidelight on the use of the term "Esquire" among the upper classes is thrown in one paragraph; Wyn for a time engages in an eventually abortive attempt to produce a magazine in Philadelphia patterned after the *New Yorker,* and Kitty becomes his secretary:

I learned a lot about letters in the office of *Philly* because when I addressed one to Parry I remembered Pop's talk about the high-toned Esq and I wrote it Mr. Parrish Berwyn Esq which Wyn said was wrong. If you're Esq you can't be Mr. at the same time. I think I was rather cute, I said suppose I'd ever write you a letter would it be Wynnewood Strafford Esq VI or Wynnewood Strafford VI Esq? He said at Old St. David's or even at Rittenhouse Square it was his father was really the Esq and he himself was only Wynnewood Strafford VI, but if writing to an office it was better to put Mr. because there you were just the honest tradesman. It seems a man can't properly be Esq away from his inherited private property. To put Esq on a business letter is New York phony or the Nouveau Long Island touch, he said [pp. 138-39].

The reason for *Philly*'s failure comes from the mouth of Molly, Kitty's shrewd mid-western friend:

It sounds like fun. . . . But if I get the town from what you've told me I don't think it'll work. The *New Yorker*'s grand because it's edited by a lot of boys who are both smart and ambitious. You haven't got 'em like that here. If they're really peppy they clear out. And the *New Yorker*'s got a readymade public of all kinds of people who have an awful yen to be In the Know. It's a kind of inferiority. But I don't believe Philadelphia gives a damn about being In the Know. It prefers not to be or it thinks it's there already. The people on top are so damn sure they know it all they don't want to learn anything new; and the people underneath know they haven't got a Chinaman's chance. I think it's rather swell to have one town that simply doesn't give a damn except be comfortable. Why does your friend want to give it the needle? If I were you I'd let Philly be like old Pattyshells. Leave it wag its tail on the porch [pp. 117-18].

Class differences reveal themselves in speech. Morley uses the device of having his lower-class heroine tell the story in racy, slangy prose; but pronunciation and inflection are obviously difficult to present on a printed page without the use of phonetics, and he makes no attempt at it. In one place, however, he has Kitty comment on the speech of Rosey Rittenhouse, one of Wyn's upper-class friends:

I think of Rosey's voice sometimes, that easy well-bred Philadelphia accent that seems to fit them like a suit of good tweeds. The kind of voice people only get when they've had good meals and good sleep for several generations and horses in the stable [p. 159].

Religious affiliation and class are not dealt with extensively in **Kitty Foyle,** but the close historical association of Quakerism with the upper class in Philadelphia is indicated by the fact that several of Wyn's friends, including Rosey, are specifically mentioned as being members of this sect. A theological discussion is reported:

> We sat by a big fireplace and talked. . . about religion. Wyn said what he liked about Quakerism was the idea of salvation piped direct to the individual, what they called the Inner Light, everybody has it for himself. A kind of neon tubing I guess. Rosey said he wasn't so sure there wasn't something to be said for Indirect Lighting too, like the Catholics. "But don't quote me, I'll be thrown out of Swarthmore Meeting" [p. 159].

What happens when second-generation lower-class Irish tangles with the Main Line? It is to Morley's credit that when Wyn indicates a serious interest in Kitty Foyle to his family,[9] there are no "Go, and never darken my door again," or "You must choose between us" scenes. As a matter of fact, the Straffords' first response to the situation is to invite Kitty to a house party at their country home. Kitty goes reluctantly. As all concerned, with the possible exception of Wyn, had envisaged, Kitty's formal introduction to the Main Line is not a success:

> It was a mistake. Of course Wyn had done what any man would, told everybody to be lovely to me and they were so god damn lovely I could have torn their eyes out. I was the only one that wasn't in the union. That crowd, if they stopped to think about it, would reckon that Ben Franklin was still a boy from the wrong side of the tracks, so what could they think about me. Somebody wanted to know if I was one of the Iglehart Foyles from Baltimore or the Saltonstall Foyles from Pride's Crossing. I said no pride ever crossed our family except when the old man carried his bat against Merion C.C. That was Wyn's fault, he tried to ease the situation by making everybody drink too many old fashioneds. But it helped because good old Rosey Rittenhouse turned the talk on cricket and said he wished he could get more girls to show some intelligence about it. . . . I knew either I or the rest of them didn't belong, and the embarrassment went around the dinner table all wrapped up in a napkin like that wine bottle the butlers carried.

> Even in a Thanksgiving rainstorm, what a lovely lovely place. When I saw Wyn's old faded station wagon out in a hitching shed I asked him to drive me home. Of course he wouldn't and he couldn't. I was supposed to stay the night and I had to go through with it. "I hope you'll rest well," Mrs. Strafford said, "will you want the maid to undress you?" Jesusgod, I blushed like one of those Cornell chrysanthemums. I wanted to say there's only one person here who's good enough to undress me. Wyn saw me turn red, he kept his eyes on me all evening bless him and came across the room to see what was going wrong.

> "You mustn't try to get up in the morning, we'll all sleep late," Mrs. Strafford said.

> "I've got to get to the office," I said. "We're closing up and I want to leave everything clean."

> "Oh, I'm so glad Wyn is giving up that dreadful magazine," she said. "I don't think Philadelphia enjoys that sort of persiflage."

> Either she or I must have been pronouncing that word wrong up to then.

> "We know damn well they don't," was what I had a yen to say, but by God K. F. had herself under control.

> "I don't know what I would do without Kitty," said Wyn, trying to help. In fact I *won't* do without her. Maybe she'll come and help me at the bank" [pp. 134-35].

It is then that Kitty decides to leave Philadelphia:

> "I'm going to Chicago," I said, unexpectedly. I didn't know myself I was going to say it. I'd had a letter from Molly a day or two before. All of a sudden I saw what came next. Wyn was terribly startled, and what a flash of, well, thankfulness, I saw in Mrs. Strafford's eyes. Poor lady, she was only playing on the signals they'd taught her. I could see that down under she had a respect for me, she'd like to have me around if it could have been allowed.

> "Really, that's very interesting," she said. "Do you know people in Chicago? We have some very pleasant acquaintances in Lake Forest."

> "My best friend has a job at Palmer's, she's in the furnishing department."

> "The modern girls are so courageous, I think it's wonderful how enterprising they are."

> I looked around at the enterprising modern girls. They were showing a good deal of knee sprawled on the sofas with brandy and sodas and members of the Racquet Club, or they were screeching at ping pong in the game room, or playing some baby chess they called b'gammon. I felt homesick for a good filing case somewhere [pp. 135-36].

Kitty expresses her understanding of the endogamous nature of the Main Line:

> The Main Line girls Bill and Parry were accustomed to have to spend so much time on clothes and stuff they don't have a chance to figure out a good line of hidden-ball formations. The Assembly gazelles know they're practically doomed to the clutches of someone in their own set, why waste good energy in broken field running? [p. 133].

The reaction of Wyn's family is obviously not personal hostility toward Kitty. It seems simply to represent a realistic understanding of the separate and distinct nature of the different social worlds from which their son and Kitty come and a feeling of the hopelessness of bringing them together. In a later passage Kitty hints that Wyn's family "were working on him" to discourage the match, and she even indicates her belief that for a time when Wyn's visits are infrequent, he has resolved to "shake" her "out of his system" (p. 151). But this effort fails. Kitty is described as being a most attractive young lady, and their relationship has already reached the stage of sleeping together.

Kitty feels increasingly that the situation cannot be resolved in marriage and makes up her mind to accept an offer of a job in New York. The denouement, however, comes when Wyn's family, believing that Wyn is determined to marry Kitty, take the advice of Mr. Kennet, described as a Quaker banker, and an old friend of the family, and, in despair, propose a cultural renovation for Kitty:

> "Well then I've got to tell you," Wyn said. "Uncle Kennet has a big idea, he wanted to explain it to you himself. He says you're just exactly the girl for me, Kitty, and the girl the family needs, and he wants to send you. . . to college for a year and then maybe go abroad a year and meanwhile I'll try to get some education myself[10] and be ready for you."

> Oh Jesusgod I don't know exactly how you said it, Wyn. It was something like that. My poor baby, how could you know what that would do to me the way I was just then. Maybe that nice old man with his *thee* talk could have sold it to me; I don't know. I had a kind of picture of some damned family conference and the Straffords and their advisers trying to figure out how the curse was going to be taken off Kitty Foyle. So that was it, they were going to buy the girl with an education, and polish off her rough Frankford edges, were they, and make her good enough to live with stuffed animals' heads and get advertised in the *Ledger.* I can still see your face, my poor baby, when I turned on you. I felt hot inside my throat and on the rims of my ears.

> "You can tell Uncle Ken he's a white slaver. Listen, Wyn Strafford, I'll be your girl whenever I feel like it because I love you from hell to breakfast. But I wouldn't join the little tin family if every old Quaker with an adding machine begged me to. No, not if they all went back to college and got themselves an education. So they tried to sell you the idea they'd trim up Kitty so she could go to the Assembly and make Old Philadelphia Family out of her, hey? Cut her out of a copy of *Vogue* and give her a charge account and make a Main Line doll out of her. They can't do that to Kitty Foyle. Jesusgod, that's what they are themselves, a bunch of paper dolls."

> Remember you stopped the Buick just before we cut down a tree with it. Better maybe if we had. You just looked at me, and tried to light a cigarette and your hand shook pushing in the dashboard lighter. You were so rattled you threw the lighter away, you thought it was a match. I loved you specially because you hadn't shaved. I thought how the old man would rise green from his grave if he heard a proposition like that. I felt tears coming like those waves you swam through and I had to hurry to say it:—

> "By God, I'll improve *you* all I want but you can't improve me" [pp. 174-75].

And so Kitty leaves Philadelphia and becomes a "white-collar" girl in New York. Although the affair continues on occasional week ends, both Kitty and Wyn are resigned to the hopelessness of bringing their worlds together. The meetings become less frequent, and one day Kitty reads in the society columns of a New York newspaper of Wyn's engagement to "Miss Veronica Gladwyn of 'Welshwood' near King of Prussia." The tenuous threads of individual attraction that had connected the two cultural worlds have at last broken, and Kitty and Wyn proceed along their separate ways, nursing their wounds but gradually being reabsorbed into their respective social spheres. In a striking introspective dialogue with herself, sometime later, Kitty reflects on the affair and shows an amazingly keen and poignant understanding of the social issues:

> Q. Did you make Wyn happy?

> A. I think so. Yes, I know so.

> Q. Then why did you leave him?

> A. If I had done what he wanted, other people would have made him unhappier than I could have made him happy.

> Q. What do you mean?

> A. He was the product of a system. He was at the mercy of that system.

> Q. Is it not your conviction that there are now no systems? That the whole of society is in flux?

> A. Not in—I mean, not where Wyn lives.

> Q. Was not the way you left him rather cruel?

> A. Damn you, I was afraid you'd ask that. Yes, it was. But I *had* to be tough with him, otherwise he'd always have felt he had been unfair to *me,* and it would have made him wretched.

> Q. You think, then, he is not unhappy now?

> A. Yes. No. Ask that again, please.

> Q. You think Wyn is happy now?

> A. I think his life is full of delightful routine. He has what the government calls Social Security. Oh, and how. Read the *Public Ledger* on Sundays, or whatever papers they have now.

> Q. You think you could have made something more important of him?

A. I could have taught him to do the Wrong Thing sometimes.

Q. What, in Philadelphia?

A. We could have lived somewhere else.

Q. Are you quite fair to Philadelphia?

A. I am thinking of it only as a symbol. Actually I love it dearly.

Q. But are they not the most charming people in the world?

A. Of course. But the enemies of the Future are always the very nicest people.

Q. You think the Future should be encouraged?

A. That's a goofy question, my darling; it's on our necks already. And oh, God, Wyn was so much interested in it when he had a chance. What a man he might have been if everything hadn't been laid in his lap.

Q. Is your mind going to go round and round like this indefinitely?

A. How's about going to bed and try for some sleep [pp. 28-29].

Kitty Foyle, by means of her literary creator, has played the role of the sociologist of the culture of classes.

NOTES

[1] See, e.g., Page's summary of the work of the "Fathers" of American sociology in social class, Charles H. Page, *Class and American Sociology* (New York: Dial Press, 1940).

[2] George Simpson, "Class Analysis: What Class Is Not," *American Sociological Review,* IV, No. 6 (1939), 829.

[3] W. Lloyd Warner and Paul S. Lunt, *The Social Life of a Modern Community* ("Yankee City Series," Vol. I [New Haven: Yale University Press, 1941]), pp. 26-27.

[4] *Ibid.;* Warner and Lunt, *The Status System of a Modern Community* ("Yankee City Series," Vol. II [New Haven: Yale University Press, 1942]); W. Lloyd Warner and Leo Srole, *The Social Systems of American Ethnic Groups* ("Yankee City Series," Vol. III [New Haven: Yale University Press, 1945]); Allison Davis, Burleigh B. Gardner, and Mary R. Gardner, *Deep South* (Chicago: University of Chicago Press, 1941); see also W. Lloyd Warner, Robert J. Havighurst, and Martin B. Loeb, *Who Shall Be Educated* (New York and London: Harper & Bros., 1944), which contains an analysis of "Yankee City" materials not previously published.

[5] Christopher Morley, **Kitty Foyle** (Philadelphia: J. B. Lippincott Co., 1939); reprinted in an edition by "Penguin Books" (New York, 1944); all page numbers subsequently referred to are from the "Penguin Books" edition.

[6] Market Street in Philadelphia corresponds roughly to Forty-second Street in New York City: shooting galleries, hamburger stands, cheap movie houses, and inexpensive stores.

[7] In contrast to Wyn, "men in Chicago" obviously means "middle-class men."

[8] Stops on the Main Line.

[9] Kitty's own mother and father are dead before the affair reaches its climax.

[10] Just what Wyn means by this remark is not quite clear. He is already described as being a graduate of Princeton.

Guy R. Lyle (essay date 1963)

SOURCE: "Ethos of a Man of Letters," in *The Emory University Quarterly,* Vol. XIX, No. 3, Fall, 1963, pp. 137-43.

[*In the following essay, Lyle praises Morley as an outstanding poet, novelist, and man of letters. In addition, Lyle examines the various elements that constitute a typical Morley novel.*]

> Read, every day, something no one else is reading. Think, every day, something no one else is thinking. Do, every day, something no one else will be silly enough to do. It is bad for the mind to be always part of unanimity.

These words appear in **The Man Who Made Friends with Himself**, a novel by Christopher Morley, published some fourteen years ago. Morley died in 1957.

In his day, Christopher Morley achieved what must certainly be the ambition of most writers: his books sold well, and at the same time received high praise from the best contemporary critics—Henry S. Canby, J. Donald Adams, Vincent Starrett, and Harrison Smith, to name but a few. Not only did he write profusely, but he was considered a leading figure in the cultural life of his day. No one was asked more frequently to write introductions to launch a reprint of the classics; no one was more sought after for cocktails, autograph parties, or lecture programs. He paid posthumously for this fame by comparative neglect ever since. "Literary fashion is always a rotary club," he once wrote, "it goes through its own strange cycles."

Christopher Morley has been truly called a man of letters. He is first of all a poet. His early poems such as **Songs for a Little House** glorified the simple; his later poems, both light and serious, were sophisticated. **Spirit Level**, published one year after Hiroshima, contains that noble epigram:

> There is another atom to be split—
> The fatal rivalry of sovereign nations.

as well as the humorous satirical piece, entitled *Fin de Siecle:*

> Said Toulouse-Lautrec to Felicien Rops,
> "Old boy, I think your stuff is tops."
>
> Said Felicien Rops to Toulouse-Lautrec,
> "Yours is pretty good too, by heck."
>
> Said Daumier,
> "Their work's Grade A,
> But those boys ought to get out in the air
> And not read so much Baudelaire."

His essays are as tweedy, pipe-smoking, and homey as their titles: *Shandygaff, Streamlines, Plum Pudding,* and *The Ironing Board.* In them he writes about post office inkwells, subways, railway terminals, automats, food, drink, and other things which have no glamor of distance or time but to which he gives the glamor of his own creation. His easy platform manner, burly figure, magnificent beard, and eternal pipe made him a familiar figure to college audiences throughout the country. It was under these circumstances that I first met him. I was sitting in the second balcony of a college auditorium listening to a soliloquy at two dollars a minute. Morley was getting the two dollars. I call his talk a soliloquy, because he seemed more interested in listening to the pleasant sound of his own voice than in reaching any particular destination. He might have been chasing butterflies, for all of that, for whenever he caught sight of an especially bright-winged idea, he pursued it with much glee, quite careless of where it might lead him.

Christopher Morley was born on the campus of Haverford College. He once said he was born many times, "perhaps the first of which was on the rough coconut matting of a little iron gallery that runs around the old wing of the library at Haverford College. I was about eight years old, and was lying on my stomach reading." His parents came from Woodbridge, England, made famous by FitzGerald of Omar Khayyám fame. His father was a mathematician. Christopher and his two brothers, Frank and Felix, attended Haverford; all three were chosen Rhodes Scholars. In an early collection of poems, *Parsons' Pleasure*, he writes:

> Two breeding-places I have known
> Where germinal my heart was sown;
> Two places from which I inherit
> The present business of my spirit:
> Haverford, Oxford, quietly
> May make a poet out of me.

Christopher wrote fourteen novels. *Kitty Foyle* was his most popular success. In a partially facetious and decidedly premature obituary of himself, written for a biographical reference book, he said: "*Kitty Foyle*, which caused indignation in many readers, was an unexpected revelation, told in the person of an Irish-American 'white collar girl,' of the mind and heart and biology of a young woman of the 1930's." Morley knew women with a deeper intuition than most. Dead women—dead for him because the love of life had gone out of them or was inhibited—he neither liked nor understood; but if, as with Kitty Foyle, they were all too human in body and still vital in soul, then he had extraordinary powers for blending the intimacy of the diary with the detachment of the analyst.

Morley considered *The Man Who Made Friends with Himself*, his last novel, as his best. There is little in the way of plot. Richard Tolman, literary agent, commutes between Long Island and New York. Although he is the narrator, his story is presented as a memoir found after his death. At home in suburban Wending Ways, he leads a comfortable life, attended by Mealie, his colored housekeeper, who entertains her employer in language which *Time* considered extravagant even for Amos 'n' Andy. His New York office is presided over by shapely Miss Tally, who "drew an immaculate blank when brains were distributed" but makes herself invaluable to Tolman because of her "total immersion in the lifestream of her own time and class." Tolman's heart belongs to a young woman psychiatrist, Zoe, whose name means "life," and whose personableness is heightened by a familiarity with Bartlett which makes her almost Tolman's equal in identifying and capping quotations. Feeling out of sorts, Tolman takes a vacation at home, spends his evenings soliloquizing or in company with his neighbors Betty and Sharpy Cullen, keeps in touch with Zoe, and makes contacts with a shadow man who is real enough to precede him on his walks and phantasmal enough to light his cigarette with a firefly. As the plot unfolds, the reader begins to suspect a connection between the shadow man and a mysterious sealed manuscript in the safe at Tolman's office.

Tolman ends his vacation by returning to Zoe and to New York. On their way to meet the Cullens, who are to accompany them to dinner at the Grillparzer Club, Tolman and Zoe stop by his office to open the sealed manuscript, which turns out to be a stack of blank paper with a seven-word title. Tolman is not surprised, but Zoe is concerned when he mumbles "It's my unwritten sonnets. So all my life is blank pages." During the dinner at the Grillparzer, a fire breaks out in the kitchen. The novel's ending is dramatic, unexpected, and tragic.

In reading *The Man Who Made Friends with Himself* one must keep in mind the author's background. Morley was a published poet, and reviewer, journal editor, reader in a publishing house, newspaper reporter, columnist, and writer of everything from plays to travelogues before he emerged from his twenties. He was literally drenched in print. His forte was the personal essay, which accounts for his habit of constant digression—a habit which impaired his success as a novelist. "Me, I like books that encourage the mind to wander," Tolman says. "My thoughts are natural vagrants." In the light of this, it is not surprising to find Tolman quoting or paraphrasing Chaucer, Shakespeare, Herrick, Hazlitt,

Stevenson, Melville, Coleridge, Wordsworth, Kipling, Elizabeth Barrett Browning, Matthew Arnold, and dozens of others of subaltern rank. Tolman is no less a connoisseur of literature than Morley. Hundreds of beautiful verses and thoughts continue to haunt his memory. More intimately still, they are incorporated into the very substance of his thinking. He is loquacious, inconsequential, witty, and epigrammatic. There is nothing contrived; the quips, the quotes, the epigrams, flow from a well-stocked purse. Morley is sensitive to words. "My life is difficult," he writes, "because I love words." Here are a few sample Tolmanisms to reward those who like words, wit, and a subtle mind:

> My favorite prejudice is that I'm completely unprejudiced.

> Gluttons of morning air know there are only a few hours of God every day; say from 9 to 3. . . . About 3 (a.m. or p.m.) the angle turns from acute to obtuse; the Book of Lamentations begins. . . .

> The smartest women were wearing a sideswipe hairdo that dated from the Wife of Bath, but didn't know the jokes that went with it. Yet they loved to believe their minds were fashionably foul.

> Man is bored, disgusted, and eager to destroy himself. He is crippled by his vast burden of consciousness; the only animal in whom this horror has been laid. Man is too witty to survive.

> *Life* and *Time* were Sharpy's Yale and Harvard.

> April sharpens her colored pencils and writes fresh palimpsest on the wrinkled brown parchment of last winter.

> A man who has his initials on his pajamas must be uncertain of himself. Surely you should know who you are by bedtime.

> I had a notion to go to the Quaker meeting at Marathon next Sunday, but they might be folksy with me at the front door. When I am really worshipping, I like to be left alone.

> Historians needle people in the aftermath, where it hurts most, but has least effect.

> What sociologists see, after giving the data a brisk raking, is only the hair that got left in the comb.

A second ingredient of a Morley novel is symbolism, analogy, fantasy. It is Morley's strength, even though it weakens the structure of his novels, to see symbolism and analogy in the hazard of the everyday. There are two lobes to the suburb of Wending Ways where Tolman lives. The smart, the brokerage, the business-like, take the electric line at Marathon for the city; the simple folk, so Tolman says, take the slower, sooty, steamline at Salamis. "The electric line crosses an appalling high, dangerous trestle, only too plain an allegory of our civilization." Tolman broods over the various specters of mid-twentieth century:

> It wasn't just in myself, I saw signs of it everywhere. All decent people were weary; the world was in a bag's end, and not a sleeping bag either. Overtired men were flying around the earth, in overloaded planes, to try to patch the seams.

He is not cheerful about nuclear overkill:

> When stupid people murder stupid people I'm not interested. They're better dead anyway. When intelligent people murder themselves, or are nullified by inertia, or stereotyped by publicity, it's serious. When I see a whole civilization committing suicide. . . .

Little by little Tolman associates the unearthly sound of his anxiety with the mysterious stranger who precedes him on his walks and comes to haunt his dreams. He confesses that he is fascinated by the man, who more and more takes on the image of another and more real Richard Tolman. Tolman is not only cursed with sensitivity but with modern self-consciousness. His talks with his apparitional double are the manifestation of his deviation from the normal or conformity. It is not so much a matter of him starting all over again or of relearning the art of living as it is of Zoe inviting him to do so— to seek inner peace by getting better acquainted with his real self. Moreover, it appears absolutely necessary that Tolman must disappear in order to reveal his true identity. His real name is Toulemonde. Morley's approach to his age is too oblique for its values to be easily recorded. One cannot indicate more exactly the profound sense of his allegory, but Sharpy Cullen proves he has well understood the lesson when he says: "I loved the guy, but the one I need to make friends with is myself."

A third Morley requirement in a novel is the expression of his own engaging human qualities. His charm as a living person spills over into each of his novels. He frankly admires the man or woman who leads a "vulgar, jocund, carnal, beautiful, rueful" existence. By vulgar he means the taste and expression of the common people. Tolman has his comfortable, suburban home, a colored cook Mealie, a piebald cat named Chiropody, two kittens Shall and Will (few people know them apart), his neighbors Betty and Sharpy Cullen, his well-shevelled secretary, Miss Tally, and the lovely Zoe, who practices psychiatry. His relationship to these people, most especially to Zoe, forms the human story of this novel. Like all males of experience, Tolman is a little afraid of Zoe, which is perhaps the reason he understands her. There is as much casual sex and drinking in *The Man Who Made Friends with Himself* as in any modern novel but it is relative to the time and place, and most hearty readers will not disapprove. What they will complain about, however, and with reason, is the failure of the characters to come alive. Morley allows a promising plot to become so bedeviled by word-play, symbolism, analogy, and private enthusiasms for books and authors that he scarcely gives his characters a chance to breathe. This is not to overlook his descriptive power nor the manifestation of his own joy of living as revealed in his creations. There are those wonderful, high-summer days, blazing, somnolent, the morning glories ready to sprout blue, the melodrama of the tiger lilies at their most carnal. The recurring symbolism of the tiger lilies throughout the novel is powerful, tender, poignant. "The shadow stripes were gone from the sun, but poor Sharpy's lilies renewed the theme. She was never so beautiful; it was hard to tell in the summer afternoon, but at least part of her face was laughing at me. Love, and the absurdity love understands, lifts silliness to sacrament."

Jon Bracker (essay date 1965)

SOURCE: An Introduction to *Bright Cages: Selected Poems and Translations from the Chinese*, by Christopher Morley, edited by Jon Bracker, University of Pennsylvania Press, 1965, pp. 13-34.

[*In the following essay, Bracker examines Morley's poetic career and traces the influences that informed its development.*]

Although well known as the author of **Parnassus on Wheels, Where the Blue Begins, Thunder on the Left,** and **Kitty Foyle,** Christopher Morley thought of himself as essentially a poet and wanted to be remembered as such. Late in his career he confided, "I have never been completely happy except when writing verse. I've the horridest feeling that after it's too late for me, someone will say, 'He wrote poetry.'" When given the opportunity in 1942 of making a selection of his writing for Whit Burnett's anthology, *This Is My Best,* Morley contributed four poems, remarking, "I hope it will not startle you if I say I think I should prefer to enter your caravan as a poet rather than in other possible disguises. . . poetry was and remains my first love."

Morley's first book, **The Eighth Sin,** appeared in 1912 when he was twenty-two years old, and his last, **Gentlemen's Relish,** was published in 1955, two years before his death; both were volumes of verse. Enough poems for sixteen additional collections were written during a remarkably productive career. The selection of poems in **Bright Cages,** however, was made from twenty-two books, all but one of them out of print, because the best of Morley's verse spilled over into two novels, a collection of essays, and an early autobiography. Thus made available for the first time is the finest poetry of Christopher Morley; readers may now sympathize with the poet's own conviction that "some of his verse is more important than has been recognized."

. . . . .

The opening sentence of Morley's autobiographical **John Mistletoe** is: "To be deeply rooted in a place that has meaning is perhaps the best gift a child can have." The influence of Haverford, where "Kit" Morley enjoyed the first ten years of his life, was a strong one in the formation of the poet. Today a suburb of Philadelphia, Haverford in the '90's must have been a lovely place. In the spring one can still see "the dropping flit" of the maple seeds which Morley described as "coat-hangers for a fairy's closet." Born in a house on the lawn of Haverford College, where his father taught mathematics, the young boy grew up in an arcadian setting. "How like an English nobleman's park!" was the exclamation of one British visitor. There men in white trousers played cricket on green fields, ducks swam in the pond which local children would skate on in winter, and in another area of the extensive grounds, violets showed through a coverlet of pine needles on the floor of the woods. Haverford endowed Morley with a sense of place. The Quaker institution affected him with its quiet beauty and "feeling of permanence." In the production of a poet, Morley suggested, it is helpful if he know "one coign of ground pluperfectly"; under these ideal conditions

> Her bend of soil, her smell of air
> Bottom the clearness of his mind,
> Make a deep shining there, and pass
> To inmost in, as mercury behind
> A lucid pane, makes looking glass. . . .

Although he added that it makes little difference where this process takes place, one suspects that Morley had Haverford in mind when he wrote the lines.

At the age of nineteen, attending Haverford as a student, Morley fell in love and "reinvented the sonnet." Such attempts at verse as **"To Her"** and **"Omnia Vincit Amor"** appeared in the college magazine. "The nymphs of Bryn Mawr," Morley later stated, "are responsible for more juvenile verse in Eastern Pennsylvania than statisticians dream."

Also responsible for Morley's interest in writing poetry were two Haverford instructors. Professor of English and a specialist in the English ballad, Dr. Francis B. Gummere intoned "Lord Randall" in a voice of impressive timbre and resonance, the memory of which was to haunt Morley and would encourage him to write his "Ballad of New York, New York." With other students Morley visited in the teacher's home and sat before the fireplace over which Gummere had carved three lines by Walter Von Der Vogelweide: "Er minnet iemer deste baz / Swer von minnen etewaz / Hoeret singen oder lesen." Translating the lines as "Who hear something sung or read / Of sweet love and how it sped / Are the better lovers," Morley was to use them as his motto for **The Middle Kingdom,** a later collection of verse. Smoking a "Robin Hood" cigar—the picture of an outlaw on the band was a pleasant reminder of folk ballads—Gummere spoke to the boys about Chaucer, Milton, or perhaps of his favorites among the modern writers, Stevenson, Meredith, and Hardy. In gratitude to Gummere, who died in 1919, Morley dedicated **Gentlemen's Relish** (1955) to the teacher "born one hundred years ago and still, for his pupils, truly alive." Supplementing Gummere's influence, Dr. Albert E.

Hancock, an enthusiast of Keats' poetry, introduced Morley to the poets of the Romantic Period. When Morley in turn showed evidence in poetry of his own acquaintance with and interest in Shakespeare, Herrick, Pope, Wordsworth, Byron, Lamb, and their fellows, it was a way of passing on a lesson learned.

Although at Haverford Morley had been introduced to illustrious constellations of poets and had written verse of his own, he recorded in **John Mistletoe** the fact that, at the time, he and his classmates thought of literature "as something definitely Beyond the Horizon." It was not until Morley attended Oxford as a Rhodes Scholar that he came under the influence of literature as "a present living reality." There he saw Henry James and Robert Bridges receive honorary degrees, and met Sir William Osler, Sir Sidney Colvin, and Logan Pearsall Smith. "The great hall of the Examination schools was crowded to the windowsills," Morley recalled, when Belloc lectured on Rabelais; Chesterton was another favorite of the students. To read Beerbohm's Oxford farce, *Zuleika Dobson,* in its setting soon after the publication in 1911, to have John Masefield burst upon one from the pages of the *English Review,* was to learn that literature was not wholly contained within college texts.

The writers he saw and the poems he read made Morley himself eager to "lay the rhymester's switch across the rosy buttocks of the Muse," as he characteristically described the act in a poem written at the time. In years to come, critics would point to the year 1912 as the beginning of a renaissance of English poetry, but Morley maintained that at Oxford he "did not have to wait ten years to know that; I knew it then. I was sure of it: I was helping to write it."

The verses which Morley produced at Oxford were ballades in the hearty Belloc-Chesterton manner; rondeaus and rondels inspired by his reading, in a village on the outskirts of the forest of Fontainebleau during a spring vacation, of Charles d'Orléans, Villon, and Ronsard; and parodies of Raleigh and Herrick. The titles of the poems give glimpses of the charm of Oxford student life: **"Ballad of Shop-Windows in the High," "To Venus in the Ashmolean," "Mint Julep Night,"** and **"The Passionate Student to His Junior Bursar."** The poems, which show technical adroitness and felicity of phrase, as in the description of the river Isis, "through the cloth of green, stitching her silver way . . ." or the picture of a fish in a pool: "so tame he comes / To lip your fingers offering crumbs," were, in addition, many of them, love poems with the refreshing quality of sincerity. For it was during this period that Morley met and fell earnestly in love with Helen Booth Fairchild, an American he had met in London. She was the "Only Begetter" of the poems which in the fall of 1912 were published by B. H. Blackwell as **The Eighth Sin.** The title comes from a letter by John Keats: "There is no greater sin after the seven deadly than to flatter oneself into the idea of being a great poet." Another interpretation was that of a critic in New York during

the late '20's who said that the eighth sin was the price which the small bluish gray paper-covered book, of which only 250 or 300 copies had been printed, brought in the rare book market.

It would be unjust to condemn Morley's juvenilia for being no more than competent and engaging light verse not particularly different from that produced by fellow Oxford students, for the poet himself was aware of their slightness and later included only one poem from the volume in his first retrospective collection. He was to write of **The Eighth Sin,** "The perpetrator, if he thinks of it at all, thinks of it fondly as a boy's straggling nosegay, somewhat wilted in a hot eager hand, clumsily tied together with honest love."

The New York City which attracted Morley on his return from Oxford was an exciting place to seek a career. The second sight which impressed him on arrival (the first had been the starry ceiling of Grand Central Station) was the gold statue of Diana on the old Madison Square Garden, a shining silhouette against the sky; she became for Morley a symbol of this stimulating phase of his life, a symbol he used more than once in his poetry.

So recently smitten, he became enamored again, this time of a city. "A pricklejoy for poets," Morley called Manhattan, and also "the greatest unwrit poem in the world." Exploring her streets as he sought a niche in the literary world, Morley encountered for the first time the Flatiron Building, which seemed to him a ship whose prow pointed up Fifth Avenue; heard the chimes of the Metropolitan Life Insurance Building tower; and saw flocks of pigeons wheel over Madison Square. The city seemed to be growing up around him. Even at night work continued on the digging of the foundation for the Altman Building; the Empire State Building, the exposed framework on the pinnacle of which Morley was to climb as guest of the builder, was still going up.

Although his position with Doubleday, Page and Company—a "Grub Street Runner," the young factotum called himself—was at its Garden City press on Long Island, Morley lived for a number of months in the city. He was to become a suburbanite but kept in contact with city life when he returned to work at the Manhattan offices of the *New York Evening Post* and *The Saturday Review of Literature;* Morley also wrote for a while from a Nassau Street hideaway which he called "the kennel." During the '40's he went three times a week to an office on West 47th Street; this sanctum, four flights up in an elevatorless building, he called "Sciatica."

One of the areas of New York which Morley came to know well was the journalistic district of Park Row. Dropping in on Don Marquis at the *Sun* offices, watching the stenographers chatting over their lunches as they sat on benches in St. Paul's burial ground, or exploring every book and cranny of an alluring side street, Morley, in William Rose Benét's description, "roved the streets with a wild paronomastic enthusiasm nothing could quell." His forays were an expression of a devotion to Manhattan which Simeon Strunsky called "one of the great love stories of history."

The details of the lifelong affair are recorded in Morley's poetry: the panorama of faces in the subway, the sounds at night of traffic in the streets, the tiny fluffs of milkweed blown into the city on an October day; these are the pictures Morley drew, partly recreated from notes taken on the spot, partly the products of happy memories. One of his longer efforts, the excellent **"Ballad of New York, New York,"** captures much of the essence of "the Town so big men name her twice, / Like so: N'Yawk, N'Yawk"; Morley was proud of the poem, which he worked out over a period of ten months, and believed that in it were "a few of those lightning strokes of phrase and purview that lift feet over hedges." If he had written nothing else than this poem, which is already being quoted in print and is making its way into anthologies, Christopher Morley would have earned the right to be called a poet.

In 1914 Morley married Helen Fairchild, and the young couple set up housekeeping in a little cottage on Oak Avenue, Hempstead, Long Island. The domesticity which Morley enjoyed in the following years was celebrated in verses which made him a poet popular with the public. *Songs For a Little House,* the first of three collections of poetry of this period, is typical of Morley's early style. In traditional forms and with an acceptance of established poetic conventions ("For rhyme," he wrote, "is still the quiet pool / Where Beauty is reflected,") Morley sang of the joys of married life. Soon after, with the birth of the first of his four children, he began to write poems about children and for them. There are grandparents today who quote with pleasure the opening lines of Morley's **"To a Child":**

> The greatest poem ever known
> Is one all poets have outgrown:
> The poetry, innate, untold,
> Of being only four years old.

And there are young men and women who recall the refrain of another of Morley's widely reprinted verses for children: "Animal crackers and cocoa to drink, / That is the finest of suppers, I think."

It is not easy to write dispassionately of one's children, but Morley managed to do so fairly often. Even such a humble subject as a high chair, with one of his daughters in it, is transformed by Morley's skill:

> This is the battlefield that parents know
> Where one small splinter of old Adam's rib
> Withstands an entire household offering spoons.
> No use to gnash your teeth. For she will go
> Radiant to bed, glossy from crown to bib
> With milk and cereal and a surf of prunes.

The key to Morley's early popularity as a poet—and *The Rocking Horse* and *Hide and Seek,* which followed

Songs For a Little House in quick succession, met with a warm enough reception to warrant their collection, with several new poems, in *Chimneysmoke* (1921), an illustrated gift edition of the **"Lyrics for Households of Two or More"**—was his unabashed sentimentality. Morley felt few qualms over depicting the homelier aspects of human existence. After all, had not Herrick, Cowper, and Crabbe, all respected poets, dealt with similar subjects? "To the devil with those who pretend to ridicule sentiment," Morley declared. "There is room for enlightened sentiment, aerated by humor, stiffened with irony and self mockery, but not devoid of compassion."

Most of the early poems were written in the evenings after a day at the office. Writing with a fountain pen which he used as a staff pen, dipping it into the bottle of ink so as to have enough time to think but not so much time that he knew he was thinking, Morley might begin by putting down a phrase he had formulated on the walk home from the station or a rhyme he had found during the day. As time passed he would become too excited to sit at the desk any longer; "standing over the table leaning on elbows" was his self-description. Too absorbed to keep his pipe lit, Morley would continue to write until he became aware of the two dangers which lay in wait: the icebox and the sofa. Cursing himself for giving in to his appetite, Morley would drink milk from a bottle the top of which, he noted approvingly, read "Grand Gorge." Then the icebox pan was emptied into the insect-loud night. Sometimes the desk to which he returned seemed "built of slippery elm, full of knots, cut in the dark while a brindle cat was mewing. There was drowsy syrup in its veins." After a short nap on the couch, the tired young writer would go off to bed for the night, although there might yet be a vault from bed at four o'clock in the morning to record a thought he did not want to lose.

The poems of this second period, it must be admitted, were written not only from the love of writing but also for the extra cash they would bring in. The expenses of a young householder were barely met by Morley's salary. As his verses were accepted by the large family magazines, he discovered that an audience for his work was growing. He began to write for this audience and produced some ephemeral verse. But if there were critics who borrowed Morley's own term, "dishpantheism," to describe what they disliked in his early verse, there were others to give him reassurance and praise. "Elinor Wylie referred to several of his lyrics as matter of which Herrick himself might be proud," reported William Rose Benét, adding that he himself felt of Morley's **"In the Mermaid Cafeteria"** that "Herrick did things differently, but he did no one thing any better. The elucidating phrases of this poem are remarkable. It should become a classic." It was this poem in particular that Elinor Wylie regarded so highly; Morley, apparently quite seriously, told of her offering, when she saw the lines in manuscript, any of her unpublished verses in return for the privilege of being allowed to publish the poem as her own.

In 1917 Morley moved his family to Philadelphia, where he became briefly, as he put it, "one of the little group of wilful men who edit the *Ladies' Home Journal*." The next year he was conducting a daily column for the *Philadelphia Evening Public Ledger*; there in a rolltop desk was born the first of his "translations from the Chinese," which are not translations at all, but original poems, often with an Oriental flavor, which sometimes deal with Oriental subjects. First, as "Synthetic Poems," they were Morley's mild burlesque of the then new imagism. But Morley "also had a feeling that free verse, then mainly employed as the vehicle of a rather gaudy impressionism or of mere eccentricity, might prove a viable medium for humorous, ironic, and satiric brevities. . . . "

The Oriental aspect was added to the "translations" after Morley read in the fall of 1918 the just-published first of Arthur Waley's important translations, *170 Chinese Poems,* and learned "that the ancient Chinese poets themselves were both wise and humorous." Enjoying a vogue in America, Oriental verse influenced poets whose work was known to Morley: Witter Bynner (*The Beloved Stranger*, 1919) and Amy Lowell (*Fir-Flower Tablets*, 1921). *A History of Japanese Poetry* by Curtis Hidden Page—the recipient of Morley's poem entitled **"To C.H.P."**—was published in 1923. "To paraphrase the old English song," Morley wrote, "it was 'Loud sing Hokku' all across the map."

Returning to the New York scene in 1920, Morley found "a landscape bizarre enough to move him deeply" and the first of the poems actually printed as "translations from the Chinese" appeared. In the beginning the verses were attributed to such pseudo-poets as "No Sho," "O B'Oi," "Po Lil Chile," and "P'Ur Fish," but, as their creator later described the process, "little by little my Chinese sages began to coalesce and assume a voice of their own. I became not their creator but their stenographer. I began to feel a certain respect and affection for the 'Old Mandarin' who was dimly emerging as their Oriental spokesman. I began to realize that the mind speaks many languages, and some of its sudden intuitions and exclamations are truly as enigmatic to us as Chinese writing. . . . " As the "Old Mandarin" took shape, Morley's verses became more poetic. Their creator no longer felt a need to apologize humorously for his lack of knowledge of Chinese, based largely as it was on the reading of laundry slips, which caused him when in doubt as to the exact meaning of a phrase always to translate it as "a bowl of jade filled with the milk of moonlight."

Although Morley thought of the "translations" as a whole as essentially American in tone, it is interesting to consider the comments of Pearl Buck, whose qualifications as an American novelist of Chinese life make her a critic worth listening to. She wrote to Morley in 1932:

> Of course, as you know, I have considered your poems in the mandarin mood quite matchless, and I have never understood how it was an American or even an Occidental could write them. After I met you, however, I divined in you a certain quality of the mandarin, and then came to the conclusion that either you had once been a mandarin in some previous life, or that the mandarin quality, which I consider invaluable because it is both precious and rare, is more universal than I thought. The explanation depends on whether one is Oriental or Occidental at bottom; you may choose the one you like better.

There is a universal quality to the "translations," yet it is also true that, in the later poems, the "Old Mandarin" came to sound a great deal like Morley, or the "Old Man" as he was known to family and intimate friends. Indeed, Louis Greenfield, Morley's office manager for a number of years, writes that the poet was actually called the "Old Mandarin" by close associates; in any case, both the fictional character and his creator were occasionally referred to by the abbreviation "O.M."

Morley had hoped that someday the "translations," which appeared over a period of thirty-five years and were sometimes published along with his regular poems, might be separately collected; the best of them appear together in **Bright Cages** in a division of their own. Now one can see why as early as 1927 Leonard Bacon, the distinguished writer of light verse, claimed that "if Mr. Morley had never done anything other than **Translations From the Chinese** he would still be a notable figure. . . . Few poets restore more generously the mystery that our own clumsy hands have rubbed from the butterfly wings of the familiar."

In 1920 Morley moved his family to a large house in Roslyn, Long Island; he called the rambling structure "Green Escape" and lived there until his death thirty-seven years later. Soon after the move, a change could be perceived in Morley's writings. He became less the journalist—for he had produced many essays and much popular fiction since his return from Oxford—and more the creative writer, less the versifier and more the poet. It was the writing, in 1921, of an unmarketable short story, **"Referred to the Author,"** Morley maintained, that marked the dividing line if one were to be drawn. The next year saw the publication of his first important novel, the allegorical **Where the Blue Begins**, which was prefaced with a lyric in which Morley expressed his determination to break through the elements which held him pent and to "make his furious sonnet." More and more he wanted to be able to give up the hack work which had been necessary, and to get on to the projects which could engage his heart as well as his head. The little collection of fervently philosophical essays, **Inward Ho!**, which came out in 1923, further indicated Morley's new and serious concerns. In 1923 also he left the *New York Evening Post*, for which he had conducted a weekly column for three years. The poem **"Grub Street Recessional"** is Morley's verse farewell to the newspaper world, as **Religio Journalistici** (1924) is his prose goodbye. Although that year he became a contributing editor of *The Saturday Review of Literature* and wrote for the magazine once a week for fourteen years, Morley now only commuted to Manhattan for part of the week and was able to do a portion of his writing at home. As the sale of his prose works increased and his reputation grew, Morley became financially somewhat less dependent on pleasing an audience, particularly in poetry, which he wrote now more from private desire than public demand.

Suburban life agreed with him. The village where William Cullen Bryant had lived was a small community when Morley arrived; as a matter of fact, the first kerosene lamps were installed because he complained of bumping into a cow one night on the walk home from the station. Morley saw Roslyn grow and did not hold aloof from its life but weeded beets in the community garden during World War II and successfully campaigned against the renovation of the fascinatingly grotesque old Long Island Railroad station-house. A familiar figure in his worn blue sweater and comfortable trousers, he could be seen walking with his beloved spaniel, Corky, along the winding roads of Roslyn Estates; in his hip pocket a memorandum book "caressed the natural curvature."

In the summer Morley liked to clip the lawn with the office shears with which he had compiled several collections of essays. In the fall he raked and burned leaves and chopped wood for the furnace; when it became too cold to write in "the Knothole," the log cabin on an adjoining wood-lot, Morley retreated to the house where he had a study bursting with books and papers, on the shelves, tables, the floor, and even, for a while, on an ironing board. In the spring he observed how the white propellors of the backyard dogwood tree spun in the breeze; at night Orion stalked the sky while in the rose bushes fireflies "morsed about."

Life in Roslyn not only gave Morley material for a number of his finest poems, but also provided the setting for his last novel, the partially autobiographical *The Man Who Made Friends With Himself.* Richard Tolman, a literary agent who is the main character of the novel, expresses in verse his and Morley's enthusiasm for existence:

> The least last latest trivial thing
> Is what empowers me to sing:
> The labile sweetness of the rose,
> Or peonies, pepper to the nose;
> How, on your memory, imprint
> The sharpness of my backyard mint?

This was the problem that Morley set himself to solve: the communication of universal sensations. In *John Mistletoe* he had said:

> One of the things I shall miss most when I am dead
> Will be walking with naked feet on bare floors
> In summer nights, when the hardwood boards
> Are deliciously tepid to the palms of the feet.
> For if you love life you should love it all over
> And even feet have their privileges.

Knowing that after he was gone no one would notice things just as he had, Morley left us in poetry a legacy of his loves.

It is tempting to try to divide a man's career into neat compartments, each one exhibiting greater virtues until one can crown the person an indisputably major figure. "Juvenilia" is the easiest label to make stick, and "early work" is not hard to apply, but after that the going gets rougher and the man's writing will not always fall into three groups to be called "mature," "more mature," and "most mature." Having said this, one still feels that in the case of Morley the publication of the large retrospective collected *Poems* of 1929 marks a division worth noting. In the volume Morley collected all of the poetry he wished to preserve; he omitted all of *The Eighth Sin* and a number of poems from the other early volumes. A few new poems, among them two charming lyrics, were added.

Included in the *Poems* was the unusual long poem, *Toulemonde,* which had been published separately the previous year. In this work Morley took as his theme the meaning of a man's life; it was a theme he was to return to more than once, and particularly in the adventures of Richard Tolman, whose name is an adaptation of "Toulemonde," or "everybody." The form, however, of blank verse varied with interludes of song, was not entirely successful and although Morley felt a strong affection for the poem and returned to the theme in later shorter *Toulemonde* poems, most reviewers agreed that the volume was not one of his best.

If during the early '20's Morley showed an increased concentration on the problems of the art of writing, he was faced in the early '30's—his forties—with problems in the art of living. His recent two year fling at play producing in Hoboken had ended in financial difficulties and the shock of discovering the dishonesty of a trusted associate. Morley began to take stock of himself and the more bohemian aspects of his theatrical experience lost some of their allure. He had a "concern"—in the Quaker sense—to tell of an examined life and did so in *John Mistletoe,* his reflective, poetic autobiography, which was published in 1931. Succeeding years showed a somewhat mellowed man.

After the juvenilia of 1912 and the early celebrations of domesticity of 1914-29, a third period of Morley's verse is represented in *The Middle Kingdom, Spirit Level, Poetry Package,* and *The Ballad of New York, New York, and Other Poems;* the poems in these collections were written in the years 1929-50. In them Morley's individual voice is heard more clearly than in preceding collections. Here are the poetic milestones of the passage of time. One of the most successful is **"Ammonoosuc,"** a ballad which describes a deeply felt experience in Morley's life, a return to nature which rejuvenated the poet and committed him to rededication. Of the poem William Rose Benét wrote, "Emerson is one of my gods as a poet, and I get the same feeling when I read:

> Where her crystal overran it
> I lay down in channeled granite;
> Braced against the pushing planet
> I bathed in Ammonoosuc.

The last two lines Emerson would have wished to write." Another moving experience, the marriage of his daughter Louise, is the subject of **"For a Daughter's Wedding."** Also among the poems of this period is the tender description of Morley's fifteen-year-old spaniel, through which Corky may well join the company of Cowper's Beau and Elizabeth Barrett Browning's Flush. Realizing that he, too, was advancing in years, Morley wrote his fortunately premature **"Nightsong of Lord Culverin on the Drawbridge of Castle Querulous,"** the lovely last lines of which call for no editorial comment:

> Soft airs, wing-beetles, crowd about!
> Good night, my lovers. My lamp is out.

Some of the best poems of Morley's middle period appeared in *Poetry Package,* a book which has a curious publishing history. Thirty-six years earlier Morley had bought a magazine on the train which brought him to New York City; in it an advertisement for William Rose Benét's *Merchants From Cathay* caught his eye. "Would it ever be possible," he mused, "for me also to get some poems printed, and even maybe to meet, just once and a while, men of printed poems and musical names. . . ." Morley and Benét did meet and become close friends in the early '20's. Now, in 1949, another advertisement caught Morley's eye. A large New York department store was offering, among other books in a "Sale of the Unsalable," a book of poems by Benét and one by himself together as a "Poetry Package" for a dollar. At Morley's suggestion, then, the two poets selected the best poems from among their most recent and had them published by Louis Greenfield in an attractive paperbound volume. The co-authors of *Poetry Package* were only identified by their initials on the cover and title page; inside, the poems were attributed to "D. D." and "P. C.," which only initiates would recognize as "Dove Dulcet" and "Pigeon Cove," pseudonyms under which Morley and Benét, respectively, had published verse. The introduction, signed only "Cuckoo," was actually by the respected critic Chauncey Brewster Tinker; the motif was further carried out by a cover caricature of the poets as birds, Benét a pigeon operating a typewriter with one toe, and Morley a bearded and bespectacled dove writing with a quill pen. When the book came out, Morley told an interviewer that it had been published in memory of another collaboration, the *Lyrical Ballads* of Wordsworth and Coleridge.

Like Thomas Hardy, whose poetry he admired, Morley wrote some of his finest poems toward the end of a long writing career. Writing of Hardy, Morley could have been speaking of himself:

> Someone is sure to reiterate the old legend that it was pique or deep indignation at fool criticisms that turned Hardy from the novel to poetry. That

seems to me inconceivable. A man of his vitality and toughness writes as and how he pleases; and the sequence of a man's work obeys laws deeper than publicity. He turned to poetry, one may guess, because he could better express in that measure what he wanted to say.

After completing *The Man Who Made Friends With Himself,* Morley wrote to friends that "I have a sudden horrid feeling, probably glandular, that I am grown up; therefore I now devote myself to the only perfect excitement I have ever had, writing verse." He was not displeased with past performances and for Christmas, 1951, sent to friends a privately printed pamphlet, *A Pride of Sonnets,* which contained nineteen previously published poems. Among them was the charming **"Charles and Mary,"** which Walter De La Mare had chosen as one of twenty-four sonnets, some of them by such masters as Shelley, Keats, and Wordsworth, for "Sweet as Roses, A Little Treasury of Sonnets," which appeared in *The Saturday Book* for 1950. The sonnet form was a favorite of Morley's; his success with the conventional structure is shown in the sixteen examples in *Bright Cages.*

The fourth and final division in Morley's career as a poet is that of the poems produced after a stroke suffered in 1951 temporarily paralyzed his right arm and hand. Painfully he taught himself to type again (Morley had given up writing with a fountain pen in the late '30's, in an attempt to simplify his style). In his slow recovery from illness, Morley discovered that "when a word makes its way safely and scribably from skull to fingers . . . I probably really mean or want it." Enough poems were written for a final collection, *Gentlemen's Relish,* before a second stroke two years before his death in 1957 made both speech and writing impossible.

The approach of death can be seen in several poems in the volume, but the book itself is full of life. **"Elected Silence: Three Sonnets,"** for example, in which Morley pays tribute to the memory of William Rose Benét, who had died in 1950, is refreshingly free from elegiac formality. Another individual treatment of the theme of death is the witty **"Morning After,"** in which, asked by St. Peter what he would most enjoy in Heaven, the poet answers: "To learn again how words, well shuffled, / Can sort miraculously into rhyme; / Or better still, read as for the first time / One of the Adventures of Sherlock Holmes." Morley thought of himself, with some reason, as a forgotten man in his last years, but the once popular poet was not bitter towards a fickle public. He felt that he had written well and was content. As he expressed it in verse:

> All passion spent, and all publicity,
> My telephone not numbered in the book,
> Nowhere will you find a happier man.
> All birds are redbreast in the setting sun.

. . . . .

As to the technical aspects of the poetry, one wonders just what service would be performed for the reader were we to approach Morley's verse with the various tools of the critic—to count the number of syllables and ascertain the stresses, noting the sequence of feminine and masculine rhymes both internal and external, carefully paying attention to the distinctions between a rondeau and a rondel, a ballad and a ballade, and finally to correctly label the various specimens like so many butterflies preserved in an exhibit case. It is well, perhaps, to note that Morley successfully essayed a number of complicated French verse forms in addition to being adept at the more usual English ones, to remark that on occasion he wrote *vers libre* but that, except for the "translations from the Chinese," he was basically an old-fashioned poet for whom rhyme was important. If one were to read some of Morley's favorite poets—Austin Dobson, Sir William Watson, and Robert Louis Stevenson, as well as Keats, Shelley, and Wordsworth—one might better assess what he attempted, but it may well be better simply to read and enjoy each poem separately.

One thinks wryly of the teacher who told his students, "Go home and appreciate these poems by Monday." But even such a respected writer as T. S. Eliot has defined the critic he was most grateful to as "the one who can make me look at something I have never looked at before, or looked at only with eyes clouded by prejudice, set me face to face with it, and then leave me alone with it. From that point, I must rely upon my own sensibility, intelligence and capacity for wisdom."

Perhaps the editor might remark that the **"Wooing Song for Sir Toby"** was written to supplement the action of Shakespeare's *Twelfth Night,* in which Morley felt that Sir Toby and Maria marry too precipitately; it may be helpful for the reader to know, too, that the Sir Kenelm mentioned in the poems is Sir Kenelm Digby, the seventeenth century English naval commander, diplomat, and author. Further interest may be derived from the poems if one is reminded, when reading **"Oh to Be in 'Bartlett' Now That April's Here,"** that Morley edited two versions of *Familiar Quotations;* when reading **"Portrait of a Mathematician,"** that Morley's father was a noted geometer; and that the Chateau de Missery of the poem was an estate on the Cote d'Or at which Morley was once a guest. But basically such information is small beer; if the lines are good it cannot make them better and if they are bad, it cannot help at all. Morley's poetry, it need only be noted, exhibits symbolism without recourse to private mythology, knowledge without offensive pedantry, and complexity with neither wilful obscurity nor any of the seven types of ambiguity discovered by William Empson and embraced so ardently by the gradgrind mind. No, Christopher Morley's poetry is too honest and too human and communicates too directly with the reader for an explicator to feel very much at home. As Morley's **"Old Mandarin"** put it:

> I am weary
> Of critical theory.

> I'm empiric
> About a lyric.

> Either it sings
> Like a happy peasant,
> Or—one of those things—
> It just doesn't.

In the opinion of the editor, the poems which follow sing.

Gerald Weales (essay date 1978)

SOURCE: "The State of Letters: Did You Once See Morley Plain?," in *The Sewanee Review,* Vol. LXXXVI, No. 2, Spring, 1978, pp. 326-30.

[*In the following essay, Weales offers a posthumous retrospective of Morley's works.*]

> There is nothing more pathetic than the case of the author who is the victim of a supposedly critical essay.
> —Christopher Morley, *Shandygaff*

If I knew where to find a complete file of *The Double Six,* the 66th Infantry Regiment newspaper that a group of us put out in Garmisch after World War II, I could have another look at an essay called "Old Brandy, Old Briars, Old Books." It was written by a friend of mine who drank sparingly, smoked badly, and read fitfully. A lineal descendant of the English familiar essay, by way of the *litry* columns that used to decorate most American newspapers, it was a gem of sorts. It has been much on my mind lately because I have been reading Christopher Morley. Morley was a serious drinker, a heavy smoker, an inveterate reader—in every way a professional where Wig was clearly an amateur. I do not know whether Wig ever read Morley, but the effusion on the Old Bs could have been written only in an atmosphere created by writers who could say in all semiseriousness, as Morley did in *John Mistletoe,* "To discover the poets for one's self, and to learn to drink decently, with a sense of ritual, are part of a gentleman's education."

To be reading Christopher Morley in 1977 is admittedly a bit unusual. Except for *Parnassus on Wheels* and *The Haunted Bookshop, which* Lippincott has kept in print in its 1955 illustrated companion volumes, all of Morley's best-known works are out of print. There is a collection of verse and another of prefaces, both from university presses; and a scholarly reprint house has discovered that *Shandygaff* is in the public domain. There are a few other available Morley items, but only *Ex Libris Carissimis*, his 1931 Rosenbach lectures, is in paper covers. Morley, who always celebrated the publisher as businessman (vide *John Mistletoe, Human Being, Swiss Family Manhattan*), would see this last as a clear sign that there is no unfulfilled audience out there.

It was *Three Hours for Lunch* that brought me back to Morley. Not the book itself—for Helen McK. Oakley's biography has little to say about Morley as man or author, nothing to make me want to read him again. Oakley's work is amiable and anecdotal, full of obvious errors, touched occasionally with sound critical comments. She calls **Human Being** "thin and vitiated" and sees Morley as a flawed poet, but it is in those comments which seem to be intended affectionately—"the stream of sentimentality that ran through much of Morley's writings"; "lifelong passion for words, for involved locutions, and copious verbiage"—that she best catches the qualities that make Morley so hard to read today. As for Oakley's errors, a single example can stand for her pervasive carelessness. On Morley's discovery of Hazlitt at Oxford, she writes, "The volumes were ponderous Victorian tomes, but Kit sped through them from the first page of volume one to the last page of the final volume, as was his habit when adopting a new literary enthusiasm." In **John Mistletoe,** from which she gets the anecdote, Morley finds Hazlitt in "a modern edition," and, "smatterer then as now, he only dabbled in that great set of books." The publication of *Three Hours for Lunch,* made me wonder how a man who once cut so large a figure on the popular literary scene could have disappeared so completely, surfacing in an inadequate biography from an almost unknown press.

"Morley said of himself that he wished to be remembered as a poet," Oakley writes, "but I am sure he would settle for being remembered as a person." I doubt that any writer would make that settlement, but there is aptness in it because it was Morley himself who provided his chief subject. He began as a poet, which in Morley's case never meant anything other than a writer of light verse, a genre that feeds on personal incident and old-hat epiphany. When he moved from freelance journalism to a regular column—in the Philadelphia *Evening Public Ledger* and then the New York *Evening Post* (the celebrated Bowling Green, a name that followed him to the *Saturday Review of Literature,* which he helped to found)—he discovered the perfect rostrum from which to project Christopher Morley, the convivial companion, the good friend, the inventor of clubs ("Three Hours for Lunch" is an example), the lover of books and food and pipes and drink, the dropper of names, the reluctant family man and unwilling sinner, the embryonic encyclopedist. In his longer works he continued to be a columnist, working in fragments, parentheses, interruptions. Although he was attracted to popular literary forms—from the spy story of **The Haunted Bookshop** to the soap opera of **Kitty Foyle**—he never really mastered the genres, having little interest in plot or the conventional use of character. He had an exclamatory belief in human complexity ("to catch a human being in the very act of being human—and to set it down without chemical preservatives" is the task Hubbard sets himself in **Human Being**), but he never violated popular genres to put flesh on stereotype. More often he wrenched character from function, using the people in his books as lightly animated excuses for standard Morley turns—thumbnail travelogues, literary lectures, job descriptions, ruminations on life. Chapter 14

in **Human Being,** "The Railway Guide," is a prime example; virtually unreadable by anyone who does not share Morley's fondness for place names, it presumably tells us something about Richard Roe, the protagonist of the novel, but it is obviously Morley bemused. Richard Roe is a traveler for a publisher so that Morley can use, as he does in many ways, his young man's memories of life at Doubleday, Page, and his insider's sense of how the "Trade Winds" blow; and Roe is briefly a theater manager because Morley has just been in the theater business in Hoboken. Paul goes on a lecture tour in **Swiss Family Manhattan** because Morley has been that route, and he appears before a book-club committee so that Morley can comment, a bit wryly, on his judgeship for the Book-of-the-Month Club. Even Helen McGill in **Parnassus on Wheels** and Kitty Foyle, the narrator-heroines who are his most fully realized characters, are often forced to stand in for Morley (vide Helen on food, Kitty on Chicago). There are cross-references from book to book, from book to column, so pervasive that a Morleyana network is created. True believers who would recognize the signals—the familiar ideas (that discontent begins with thinking), names (Don Marquis, Vachel Lindsay), places (Leary's, the House of Dooner)—must have believed that, more than once, they saw Christopher Morley plain.

The interesting thing about Morley in retrospect is how much is left out. No one expects a popular columnist to be St. John of the Cross, and in one of the first of the Bowling Green columns (February 11, 1920) he answers a presumably fictional question from a reader, "Are you going to bare your soul in it?", with the comic assurance that "our soul has extremely low visibility." Yet Morley throws out hints of depths unplumbed. "My friend often gave a convincing exterior of hilarity, but there may have been many a darkness within," writes Morley in **John Mistletoe**—Morley on Mistletoe which means Morley on Morley—and it is characteristic that even when he suggests a darkness he has no intention of penetrating, he hedges its existence with the conditional "may have been." A few sentences later he quotes himself in another of his disguises, the Old Mandarin, and comments on the poet as one who means "much more than he says in his verses." Morley's art, then, is a means of not telling, even in those works—fiction, memoir—which might have let him escape the limits of the column. When his books appear to deal with potentially difficult subjects—marital discord (**Thunder on the Left, Human Being**), spiritual discontent (**Where the Blue Begins**), war and peace (**The Haunted Workshop, The Trojan Horse**)—they only approach the danger spots and retreat to familiar Morley ground. Paradoxically the rumination that runs rampant in his work, which might have led to more serious (or more comic) treatment of the human condition, becomes instead an excuse to avoid dramatic presentation. Having reread **Kitty Foyle** and been surprised that it had once been a best-seller, I passed it on to a friend with a greater capacity for what was once called woman's fiction; she handed it back after fifty pages with "It's all exposition."

It is in the matter of "indelicatessen"—to use one of Morley's terrible puns—that his habit of avoidance is most obvious. He has a reputation for being a hell of a fellow (or, at least, one of the boys), "somewhat profane in his private correspondence," as he says in *John Mistletoe;* but his work is almost dainty, even when Kitty Foyle falls off the roof. "Those sales boys are rough talkers, as rough as Shakespeare or James Joyce," says Hubbard in *Human Being.* "There's a lot of things I've got to try to convey without saying them." This is Christopher Morley protecting his audience perhaps, but the primness seems closer to home. At most he is naughty, as when he has clam broth in a "clam brothel" (*Mistletoe*). Only once, in an early poem, **"The New Altman Building,"** does he manage a funny dirty line, and that is the best example of accidental double entendre this side of James Whitcomb Riley's serious love poems. Contemplating the Altman girders, he thinks of his own unhappy attempt to build with words: "We . . . / Have wept to see our dear erections fall; / Have wept—then flung away our tools, and laughed."

Many of the Morley devices and much of his style contribute to the feeling in his work that there is no emotional, or even intellectual, reality beneath the busy surface. The pseudonymous selves that filled his columns—the Dulcet brothers, the Old Mandarin, Sir Kenelm Digby, P.E.G. Quercus—are journalistic conveniences that become the hesitant masks of *John Mistletoe,* in which Morley is sometimes "I" and sometimes Mistletoe, and of *Human Being,* in which the authorial "I" shares the narrator's voice with Hubbard, with Roe, with Hubbard's informants. This is not the ambiguity that enriches, but a reluctance to offer a self that can be blamed for anything—the bizarre underside of his failure to provide a character free of its creator's crotchets. The ornate language which is little more than a silly game in *Gentles, Attend!* (the broadside he wrote in 1920 to introduce a friend to the "jocund harbourage" of the Philadelphia he had just left) becomes an intrusion in the longer works, an imposition of artificiality on events, relationships, ideas which are reaching for a kind of truth. The elaborate puns, the bite-sized philosophic thoughts, the occasional lyric flights become screens between reader and subject. As Denis Dulcet in **"Frank Confessions of a Publisher's Reader"** he gives examples of bad writing, but the essay begins "In my youth I was wont" and the last paragraph finds him calling out "Perpend, brothers! Let us order a tierce of malmsey and talk it over!" As this early essay indicates, Morley practiced overwriting even though he recognized it. After a passage in *Where the Blue Begins* full of words like *ostent* and *riant* and phrases like *this terrene orb,* he adds, "So, in a mood perhaps too consciously lofty, Gissing was meditating."

The most attractive thing in Morley's work at this distance is the sense of missionary zeal that informs it. Morley is a reader who wants to share his passion with others. "Everywhere I go I will bring people a message about good books in the world," he wrote in *The Bookseller's Blue Book* (October-February 1914-1915), a passage that looks toward *Parnassus on Wheels.* His first and most appealing novel, *Parnassus* sends Roger Mifflin and his traveling book-wagon to carry the good word across the New England countryside. Morley carried the word himself, in the *Post* and the *Saturday Review* and through the Book-of-the-Month Club. Oakley quotes a letter Morley wrote to a BOMC subscriber who had complained about Ross Lockridge's *Raintree County* in which he disavows the "murderous purpose of improving anyone." This is of a piece with the distrust of critics and teachers which runs all through his work—even when he is acting as critic or teacher—but it does not belie the fact that he had an enthusiasm to sell. The difficulty is that Morley's literary tastes were fixed about the time of the first world war. The essays in *Shandygaff* (1918)—the affectionate pieces on R. L. Stevenson, Don Marquis, Rupert Brooke, William McFee, Hilaire Belloc, Walter de la Mare—somehow set his literary limits. Although some later writers do get into his **"Golden Florins,"** the book list at the end of *Ex Libris Carissimis,* sharing space with the classic authors he admired—Chaucer, Shakespeare, Swift, Keats, Blake, Fielding—he never gets much beyond the 1917 essay on Marquis in which he says that the three best critics in America are Marquis, Simeon Strunsky, and O. W. Firkins and the three leading poets, Marquis, William Rose Benét, "and (perhaps) Vachel Lindsay." It is not the specific writers (Strunsky and Firkins do not last in the Morley honor list) but the critical assumptions that are important in understanding Morley. He was always an idiosyncratic reader and a literary journalist who admired the great dead writers and the comfortable living ones, who introduced the metaphor of books as explosives into *The Haunted Bookshop* but never cared much for his contemporaries who might be lighting literary fuses.

Like an avuncular Colossus he did bestride his narrow world, but these days he seems more Ozymandias than Caesar.

FURTHER READING

Bibliography

Brown, H. Tatnall, Jr., and Lyle, Guy R. *A Bibliography of Christopher Morley.* Washington, DC: The Scarecrow Press, 1952, 198 p.
    An extensive and thorough bibliography of works by and about Morley.

Biography

Bracker, Jon, and Wallach, Mark I. *Christopher Morley.* Boston: Twayne Publishers, 1976, 145 p.
    A general and comprehensive biography.

Hughes, Babette. *Christopher Morley: Multi ex Uno.* Seattle: University of Washington Book Store, 1927, 28 p.

A biographical sketch set in verse.

Oakley, Helen McKelvey. *Christopher Morley on Long Island.* Roslyn, N.Y.: The Christopher Morley Knothole Association, 1967, 28 p.

A biographical sketch published by Morley's admiration society. This society is named after a literary monument built in Morley's honor.

———. *Three Hours for Lunch: The Life and Times of Christopher Morley.* New York: Watermill Publishers, 1976, 382 p.

Considered the definitive biography of Morley.

Criticism

Aiken, Conrad. "Poets as Reporters." *The Dial* 64 (11 April 1918): 351-53.

A review of *Songs for a Little House* that faults the sentimentality in Morley's verse.

Breit, Harvey. "Christopher Morley." In his *The Writer Observed,* pp. 67-71. Cleveland and New York: The World Publishing Company, 1956.

Examines Morley's passion for literature, particularly the works of Joseph Conrad.

Canby, Henry Seidel. "Persons and Personalities: Christopher Morley." In his *American Estimates,* pp. 61-70. New York: Harcourt Brace and Company, 1929.

Examines Morley's personality, especially his zest for life, and how this enthusiasm manifested itself in his writings.

Eales, John. "Reviews of Books: *The Man Who Made Friends with Himself.*" *Life and Letters* 64, No. 149 (1950): 77-80.

An assessment of Morley's novel as witty but ultimately tedious.

McCord, David. "Christopher Morley." *The English Journal* XIX, No. I (January 1930): 1-9.

A brief overview of Morley's extensive body of work. McCord praises Morley's essays and novels but contends that his poetry leaves much to be desired.

Teller, Walter. "The Way It Is: In the Transcendent Hour." *The American Scholar* 34, No. 3 (Summer 1965): 458-82.

Teller reflects on his experiences with Morley as a professor.

VanGelder, Robert. "An Interview with Christopher Morley." In his *Writers and Writing,* pp. 334-38. New York: Charles Scribner's Sons, 1946.

An interview with Morley in 1942. In the interview, Morley explains "Anglo-American osmosis," which is his description of the emerging relations between the United States and England.

The following sources published by Gale contain additional coverage of Morley's life and works: *Contemporary Authors,* Vol. 112; *Dictionary of Literary Biography,* Vol. 9.

Edwin Muir

1887-1959

(Also wrote under the pseudonym Edward Moore.) Scottish poet, critic, novelist, journalist, translator, and autobiographer.

This entry presents criticism on Muir that was published between 1925 and 1990. For further coverage of Muir's life and works, please see *TCLC* 2.

INTRODUCTION

A prominent Scottish poet and critic of the mid-twentieth century, Muir is also remembered as the translator who first brought the works of Franz Kafka to an English-speaking audience. After beginning his career as a critic and journalist, Muir started producing poetry in his mid-thirties and over the next three decades developed an individual, visionary style outside the main currents of Modernist poetry then prevalent. In his works he often drew on his early experiences on the Orkney islands off the northern coast of Scotland and on the disparity between his recollections of this pastoral idyll and the gritty, urban life he later experienced in Glasgow. In an appreciation of Muir's poetry the critic Kathleen Raine wrote in 1961: "Time does not fade [Muir's poems], and it becomes clear that their excellence owes nothing to the accidental circumstances of the moment at which the poet wrote, or we read, his poems; they survive, as it were, a change of background, and we begin to see that whereas the 'new' movements of this or that decade lose their significance when the scene changes and retain only a historical interest, Edwin Muir, a poet who never followed fashion, has in fact given more permanent expression to his world than other poets who deliberately set out to be the mouth-pieces of their generation."

Biographical Information

Muir was born the youngest of six children in a tenant farming family that worked a succession of farms in the Orkney Islands before high rents drove them to Glasgow in search of more secure financial prospects in 1901. The transition from an agricultural life that was closely tied to ancient traditions and the cycles of nature to an industrial and commercial life in Glasgow was devastating to the family, and Muir's father, mother, and two brothers died within five years of the move. Muir himself later compared the psychological fracture he experienced to an episode of time travel when he wrote, "I was born before the Industrial Revolution, and am now about two hundred years old. But I have skipped about a hundred and fifty of them. I was really born in 1737, and till I was fourteen no time-accidents happened to me. Then in 1751 I set out from Orkney for Glasgow. When I arrived I found that it was not 1751, but 1901, and that a hundred and fifty years had been burned up in my two days' journey. But I myself was still in 1751, and remained there for a long time. All my life since I have been trying to overhaul that invisible leeway." In Glasgow with little formal education, the fourteen-year-old Muir began work as an office clerk and subsequently held various positions, including a stint in a local bone factory. He began writing poetry in 1913, and quickly found publication in the *New Age*. However, he ceased writing poetry within a couple of years, turning instead to journalism. In 1919 he married Willa Anderson, a teacher and linguist. His marriage represented for Muir the most important event of his life, as his wife encouraged him to move to London, to pursue a career in journalism, and to undergo a course of psychoanalysis in order to grapple with fears and guilt related to his disrupted youth and the deaths in his immediate family. Muir was hired as an assistant editor for the *New Age,* and he later contributed reviews to such periodicals as the *Atheneum,* the *Scotsman,* and the *Freeman.* In 1921 the Muirs began an extended stay on the Continent, living first in Prague, and later in Dresden, Salzburg, and Vienna. Throughout the 1920s Muir gained a wide reputation as a critic with such works as *Latitudes* (1924) and *The Structure of the Novel* (1928) and began a series of collaborations with his wife on translations of the works of Gerhart Hauptmann, Franz Kafka, and Lion Feuchtwanger, among others. His works of poetry during this period included *First Poems* (1925) and *Chorus of the Newly Dead* (1926). The Muirs returned to England in 1927—the same year that Muir's first novel, *The Marionette,* was published—and took up residence in Surrey. Over the next two decades they lived variously in England and Scotland. With a well-established career as a critic and translator providing security, Muir undertook a series of projects during the 1930s, including a biography of the Calvinist leader John Knox, the autobiographical novels *The Three Brothers* (1931) and *Poor Tom* (1932), poetry in *Variations on a Time Theme* (1934), travel and history writing in *Scottish Journey* (1935), and political pamphleteering in *Social Credit and the Labour Party: An Appeal* (1935). In 1941 Muir accepted a position in Edinburgh with the British Council and was assigned to Prague in 1945 and Rome in 1949. The 1940s encompassed a period of heightened poetic output for Muir, with such works as *The Narrow Place* (1943), *The Voyage, and Other Poems* (1946), and *The Labyrinth* (1949). He returned to Scotland in 1950 when he was named warden of Newbattle Abbey College. He spent one year teaching at Harvard in the mid-1950s and returned to England, where he continued to write, completing his final poetry collection *One Foot in Eden* in 1956. Muir died at Swaffam, near Cambridge, in 1959.

Major Works

Muir's most important works may be divided into several genres, including poetry, criticism, translation, and autobiography. He began writing poetry at a relatively late age and over the course of several decades worked out an individual style for which he gained recognition late in his life. Such early works as *First Poems* and *Chorus of the Newly Dead* contain Muir's initial attempts to treat the central subjects and themes of his writing, including his idyllic childhood in Orkney and the loss of innocence brought on by his move to Glasgow. Works in his later collections, including *Variations on a Time Theme, The Narrow Place, The Voyage, and Other Poems, The Labyrinth,* and *One Foot in Eden,* further explore the theme of the journey, incorporate Muir's characteristic use of myth, folklore, visions, and dreams, and reveal his abiding concern with time and timelessness. Closely related to Muir's poetry is his autobiographical writing in *The Story and the Fable* (1940), which was later revised and issued as *An Autobiography* (1954). For Muir autobiography represented a voyage of self-discovery, and he blended both the outer ("story") and inner ("fable") aspects of his personal history, creating a work that reveals in prose the same visionary style, dominant themes, and central concerns already noted in his poetry.

As a critic, Muir was prolific, writing hundreds of reviews during his long career. Many of his essays and reviews have been collected in the volumes *Latitudes, Transition: Essays on Contemporary Literature* (1926), and *Essays on Literature and Society* (1949). In his one extended critical analysis, *The Structure of the Novel,* Muir identified and discussed such major forms as the novel of action, the character novel, the dramatic novel, and the chronicle novel. Throughout his career Muir advocated a close connection between literature and life, and thus rejected much of New Criticism with its close reading of poetry because in his view it tended to distance the poet from the audience. In one of his most controversial works, *Scott and Scotland: The Predicament of the Scottish Writer* (1936), Muir offended nationalists with his assertion that Scottish literature would be better served by the use of the English language, rather than Scots.

Muir's translations, which he produced in collaboration with his wife, are also counted among his significant works chiefly for their impact in bringing important German-language authors to the attention of English-speaking readers. Among the works that the Muirs translated are *Jud Süss,* by Lion Feuchtwanger, which became a best-selling novel in 1927, the *Poetic Dramas* of Gerhart Hauptmann (1925), *The Sleepwalkers,* by Hermann Broch (1932), and Kafka's *The Castle* (1942), *The Trial* (1945), and *In the Penal Colony: Tales and Short Pieces* (1948).

Critical Reception

Because he remained outside the main currents of modern poetry and criticism throughout his career, Muir did not create a sensation as a young man, nor did he enter the literary establishment easily through his association with other writers of the period. Instead, his critical reputation and popularity grew steadily as his poetic skills developed, culminating in numerous awards and honors that paid homage to his immense contributions to British literature. Early critics of his poetry praised his evocation of mood and noted his reliance on traditional poetic methods and structures. Late in his life, commentators recognized his singular achievement and drew attention to the close relation of Muir's autobiography to his poetry. Examining the body of his work, academic critics of the 1960s identified such key subjects and themes as time, the journey, innocence and experience, and the randomness of evil, and drew attention to Muir's use of myth and imagery from heraldic tradition. Admirers included T. S. Eliot, who edited a volume of Muir's poetry and ranked Muir "among the poets who have added glory to the English language." Interest in Muir has continued into the late decades of the twentieth century, particularly focusing on the connection between his poetry and his autobiography, Muir's interpretation of his own life in mythic terms, and his inquiry into human nature and the nature of memory and imagination as revealed in *The Story and the Fable.*

PRINCIPAL WORKS

We Moderns: Enigmas and Guesses [as Edward Moore] (criticism) 1918

Latitudes (criticism) 1924

First Poems (poetry) 1925

Poetic Dramas, by Gerhart Hauptmann [translator; with Willa Muir] (poetic dramas) 1925

Chorus of the Newly Dead (poetry) 1926

Transition: Essays on Contemporary Literature (criticism) 1926

Jud Süss, by Lion Feuchtwanger [translator; with Willa Muir] (novel) 1927; also published as *Power,* 1928

The Marionette (novel) 1927

The Ugly Duchess, by Lion Feuchtwanger [translator; with Willa Muir] (novel) 1927

The Structure of the Novel (criticism) 1928

John Knox: Portrait of a Calvinist (biography) 1929

The Three Brothers (novel) 1931

Poor Tom (novel) 1932

Six Poems (poetry) 1932

The Sleepwalkers, by Hermann Broch [translator; with Willa Muir] (novel) 1932

The Great Wall of China, by Franz Kafka [translator; with Willa Muir] (short stories) 1933

Variations on a Time Theme (poetry) 1934

Scottish Journey (nonfiction) 1935

Social Credit and the Labour Party: An Appeal (essay) 1935

Scott and Scotland: The Predicament of the Scottish Writer (criticism) 1936

Journeys and Places (poetry) 1937

America, by Franz Kafka [translator; with Willa Muir] (novel) 1938

The Present Age from 1914 (criticism) 1939

The Story and the Fable (autobiography) 1940; revised and enlarged as *An Autobiography*, 1954

The Castle, by Franz Kafka [translator; with Willa Muir] (novel) 1942

The Narrow Place (poetry) 1943

The Trial, by Franz Kafka [translator; with Willa Muir] (novel) 1945

The Scots and Their Country (nonfiction) 1946

The Voyage, and Other Poems (poetry) 1946

The Politics of "King Lear" (lecture) 1947

In the Penal Colony: Tales and Short Pieces, by Franz Kafka [translator; with Willa Muir] (short stories) 1948

Essays on Literature and Society (essays) 1949; revised and enlarged edition, 1965

The Labyrinth (poetry) 1949

Collected Poems, 1921-1952 (poetry) 1952

Prometheus (poetry) 1954

One Foot in Eden (poetry) 1956

Collected Poems, 1921-1958 (poetry) 1960; revised and enlarged edition, 1963

The Estate of Poetry (lectures) 1962

Selected Poems (poetry) 1965

Selected Letters of Edwin Muir (letters) 1974

Edwin Muir: Uncollected Scottish Criticism (criticism) 1981

CRITICISM

Marie Luhrs (essay date 1925)

SOURCE: "Piety and Peace," in *Poetry,* Vol. 27, No. 1, October, 1925, pp. 50-1.

[*In the following review, Luhrs focuses on structure and mood in* First Poems.]

American poetry in the past few years has been so obsessed by painted lips, anatomical love, bright colors, and solid images that a book like Edwin Muir's **First Poems** is stimulating and refreshing by reason of its drabness. A drabness, however, that does not arise from a sparse imagination or a watery technique, but from an observation that is accurate without being obtrusive. The tone of the book is quiet, and its path is peace. Horses and houses, reveries and remembrances are the subjects of Mr. Muir's inspiration. He writes nearly every poem in quatrains, and lets his idea ramble slowly down many stanzas instead of trying to pack every line with pictures and moods. He has an unusual preoccupation with the universal and the philosophical even when writing about such humble particulars as grass. **"Anatomy,"** which is the only poem short enough to quote, happily illustrates his reflective method:

> My feet walk to a hidden place
>   Whence no path issues; my eyes range
> Through immobility of space.
>   Towards changelessness my members change.
>
> My flesh a ripening fruit, my blood
>   A crimson brook which tends toward death;
> My reins a black and secret bud
>   Which breaks in everlasting breath.
>
> My lusts, a beauty-bearing tide,
>   Move stealthily as if bent on crime.
> My heart, self-moved, against my side
>   Beats like Eternity in Time.

Some of his separate lines and phrases are wonderfully expressive without being spectacular. He speaks of grass as

> Climbing, a tiny host, up mountain sides.

And in another place:

> Where each moist blade sweats one clear
>   glistening drop.

This stanza about horses is almost impressionistic, yet it is in no way gaudy or bizarre:

> And oh the rapture, when, one furrow done,
> They marched broad-breasted to the sinking sun!
> The light flowed off their bossy sides in flakes;
> The furrows rolled behind like struggling snakes.

The ballads which make up the last part of the little volume are curiously mystical and philosophical for that naive form. One of them, **"The Ballad of Eternal Life,"** has a distinct tang of the *Ancient Mariner.*

Mr. Muir's virtues are also his faults. The numerous quatrains and the placid moods grow monotonous when his phrases take a dull or prosy turn. But he is worth watching. Mysticism and simplicity and peace are rare qualities in this hour. And originality is more valuable than metric fluency or fashionable mannerism.

Humbert Wolfe (essay date 1926)

SOURCE: "Two Intellectuals," in *The New Criterion,* Vol. IV, No. I, January, 1926, pp. 205-8.

[*In the following review, Wolfe identifies the strengths of Muir's early poems.*]

The poetry of restraint, of emotional repression has in the last few years received notable adherents. The birth of this movement has been in the main Transatlantic, and may perhaps be attributed to a conscious reaction against the excessive sweetness in the American tradition. There have been two distinct attacks on literary easiness. With Ezra Pound, H.D., and the Imagists a resolute offensive was delivered on form. An attempt, not wholly unsuccessful, was made to prove that normal metrical tricks were unnecessary, and that poetry, when unadorned, was most adorned. Dullards, who did not recognise the exquisite balances in Pound's verse, reduced his discovery to babble, and we were presented by some of his followers with poetry not merely naked, but actually flayed.

That was the attack on form. The attack on substance was led by Mr. T. S. Eliot, and he numbered among his host Richard Aldington and Conrad Aiken, to name only two of many. Mr. Eliot himself has endeavoured to invest verse with a pregnancy and a hardness that is Eastern in its esoteric intensity, but Western in that it is the intensity of free, and not trammelled, thought. In *The Waste Land* he contrived in a few hundred lines to write at least the chapter-headings of a few hundred volumes. It was a great achievement, but a dangerous example not only for others, but for himself. A point may well be reached when so much is said in so little that the meaning disappears altogether, or is only to be apprehended with the emotion which rewards the solution of a cross-word puzzle.

I do not say that Mr. Aiken has reached that point in *Senlin*. It must be remembered that this is not his most recent work, and that therefore no final conclusions can be derived from it. But a work of art must be judged by itself, and by itself, for me, *Senlin* confuses mystery with profundity. Do not let me be misunderstood. Like *The Waste Land, Senlin* is a relentless intellectual attempt to present a system of philosophy in the enchanted shorthand of verse, and, as that, more than a little is accomplished, but not enough. One is entitled, in the face of the bid for intellectual supremacy made by Mr. Aiken, to ask what his metaphysical system is, and when that question is pressed home there seems to be no reply, or only the murmur 'mysticism', a philosophic creed which I have always regarded as an ignoratio elenchi. 'Senlin' is a city; 'Senlin' is an ancient wood; 'Senlin' is a desert; 'Senlin' is where

> 'Neighing far off in the haunted air
> The unicorns come down to the sea';

'Senlin' watches the burial of his city's dead; 'Senlin' is a tree

> 'And among the pleasant leaves hang sharp-eyed
>   birds
> While cruel roots dig downward secretly,'

'Senlin' is with the mummies of Cleopatra and Senebisto. 'Senlin' is all these things in his origins, but above all

> 'a helpless gesture of mist above the grasses.'

It is with that helpless gesture that I quarrel, it is of that mist that I am shy. The are of the mind is, or

should be, hard and clear, because all that is durable and lucid is there created. But if the mind gestures helplessly in the mist, then we have exchanged thought, which is our own, for emotion which is everybody's and nobody's.

Nor does 'Senlin' break into the light with his 'preoccupations', which are not less vulnerable because they are described in advance as futile.

'I am a room,' says 'Senlin', 'a house, a street, a town.' 'Senlin' ties his tie at the mirror but

> 'There are suns beneath the floor.'

'Senlin' sees a woman. Did she seek to attract him? He cannot guess, but, while he ponders, he smooths his hair and remembers the forbidden stairway up which he climbed with his sweetheart long ago. Then it is noon, and a street piano playing.

'Do not disturb my memories, heartless music!' 'Senlin' cries. It is evening.

> 'Death himself in the dusk gathering lilacs.'

Death approaches, says 'Senlin'. But 'Senlin' has yet time to climb 'the golden-laddered stair.'

> 'I ascend the golden-laddered hair
> of the harlot-queen of time.'

And now comes silence, 'Alone, in silence'.

Again beauty is spilt, almost indifferently as though Mr. Aiken were afraid of being caught with it about him. But it is a beauty in a mist, so we end with 'Senlin's' 'Cloudy Destiny':

> 'Yet we would say—this was no man at all;
> But a dream we dreamed, and vividly recall;
> And we are mad to walk in wind and rain,
> Hoping to find, somewhere, that dream again.'

That is exactly what you of all persons shouldn't say, Mr. Aiken. In the ultimate vision there are, or should be, no clouds, and since you are occupied with that go back and brush them away with the witches broom of your beauty.

Mr. Muir is also an intellectual, though in a different mode. While Mr. Aiken appears deliberately to choose his medium, and gives the impression of being able to write in any mode he may like, Mr. Muir makes it painstakingly, and sometimes almost painfully, clear that he is still the servant of his manner. The roughnesses are not wholly deliberate, the obscurities not always intentional, and his occasional failures to carry out his original scheme undesigned. But that is only to say, as he admits in his title, that these are **First Poems**. As such they are encouraging, even exciting. In **'Betrayal'**, for example, he is able to refashion one of the oldest tragedies in the world thus:

'And nothing now of Beauty stays,
Save her divine and witless smile.
For still she smiles, and does not know
Her feet are in the snaring lime.
He who entrapped her long ago,
And kills her, is unpitying Time.'

That is new, vigorous, breathing, and there is much more as good, and as fresh in Mr. Muir's work. His difficulty, as I see it, will be perfectly to relate his sensibility, which is profound, to his power of expression, which is as yet uncomplete. If he can achieve a perfect unity, the result will be distinguished poetry.

Hayden Carruth (essay date 1955)

SOURCE: "Edwin Muir's Autobiography," in *Poetry,* Vol. 87, No. 1, October, 1955, pp. 50-2.

[*In the following essay, Carruth reviews* An Autobiography *and discusses the relation of the work to Muir's achievement in poetry.*]

Several years ago, in a review of his **Collected Poems,** I said that Edwin Muir was one of the three or four greatest living writers of poetry in English—or words to that effect; I have lost the exact reference. It was a broad statement, embarrassingly broad, and of course I wish I hadn't made it. Not because I think the judgment itself is so very far from the truth of the matter, but rather because such exclusive remarks about living authors always imply a strict comparative view of literature, whereas in fact poems or groups of poems are only occasionally and partially comparable, and to say otherwise is to be both unrealistic and unfair. I knew these things when I made my statement, and I knew that I should probably regret my words later on; but I wrote them anyway, out of exasperation with what seemed to me the almost willful refusal of American readers to pay any attention to Muir's work. It wasn't as if Muir were a young poet just starting out; I was reviewing a collected edition of his poetry. But his poems, many of which struck me as superb, had received very little attention in this country, and I thought perhaps I could write something about them which would startle people so much that they would at least make the effort to look them up.

So far as I can see, my attempt was a teetotal failure. Muir's poems are no better known here now than they were before his **Collected Poems** was published. Either my judgment must be completely wrong, or American readers, having no longer an Ezra Pound to instruct them, must be singularly comatose when it comes to poetry from overseas.

Or is there perhaps a third alternative, less damaging to all concerned? Muir has not been completely unknown in this country. A few of his poems have been published from time to time in our magazines. In the Twenties, he contributed regularly to *The Freeman,* and other of his prose pieces have appeared occasionally over here.

Moreover, there was a period when Muir and his wife became what he has called "a sort of translation factory," and some of their translations, especially the beautiful ones from the novels and stories of Kafka, have been read by many Americans. In other words, Muir has done his full share of hack writing, though at a high level and always with skill and good taste; as a result, he has seemed for a long time to be one of those figures whose names are quite familiar to us as part of the structure of British literary society but whose precise places in it we are inclined to be rather hazy about. In such circumstances, it takes a special effort to discover what a man's merits really are.

A fourth alternative, of course, is that nobody read my review.

I hope that Muir's **Autobiography** will attract readers to his poetry, but there is a good chance that it won't. Like most autobiographical writings by poets, it is quite frankly a secondary work, a little fragmentary and inconclusive. The first two-thirds of it appeared in England in 1940 as **The Story and the Fable,** and the last third seems to have been tacked on hurriedly. I don't mean to say that it is a bad book; on the contrary, it is a good book and contains much that is informative and well written and even wise; and probably we should not expect a poet to put as much effort into meeting the formal demands of discursive prose as he does into the more resilient figures of poetry. What I do mean to say is that Muir's **Autobiography** is in a real sense supplementary to his poetry: it can be read with enjoyment for its own sake, but its full meaning will not be apparent to readers who are unacquainted with the poems.

Muir's story is one which we associate more typically with American experience than with British. It is the story of the boy who is born and bred in a rural, primitive, agricultural community, drifts into the shabby and brutal underground of industrial society, and emerges at last with a refined intellectual and emotional awareness which is rather unstable but which serves to reacquaint him in a dissociated way with some of the values of his childhood environment. In Muir's case, the early environment is Orkney (if the book had no other merit, it might at least establish in American minds once and for all the difference between the Orkneys and the Hebrides) and the story continues in such cities as Glasgow, London, Prague, Dresden, Rome, &c. Muir has seen a tremendous amount of ugliness and bad luck, and much of his **Autobiography** is imbued with sadness. But he writes with such a gentle, thoughtful manner that the whole book has an air of decrescendo about it, not at all painful. In fact, parts of it are not as painful as they probably ought to be.

Naturally there were times of good luck too, and one of them certainly was the successful though uncompleted course of psychoanalysis which Muir underwent at about the time he was beginning to write seriously. Perhaps if the analysis had been completed, Muir would not have been able to use it as fruitfully as he has. It is clear that his treatment went just far enough to relieve the most troublesome symptoms and to provide him with the means to conceptualize his experience of bad luck and alienation. This is where the autobiography comes closest to the poems. In his discussion of the analysis and of the dreams which became increasingly important to him, Muir writes without a trace of the clinical cant we usually expect from those who have experienced psychotherapy, and he shows how the material of dreams influenced and reinforced, but did not dominate, his poetic method. One feels that the Orkney farmer's uncommon sense came safely through it all. For Muir has found in dreams, not the echoes and grace notes of the surrealists, but the dominant voice of history; he is, in a sense, a subrealist; and his writing, both his poetry and his *Autobiography,* contains the durability which we in this country find in the works of such poets as Robert Frost.

From this side of the Atlantic one notices the similarities between Muir and Yeats much more, I am sure, than do those who are closer to them both. It is a matter of temperaments. For all his aestheticism, Yeats never lost his sense of history or his respect for the earth under his feet. If experience had dealt barbarously with him, if he had lived through the smashup of 1939-49, one feels that his essential toughness and his syncretistic way of looking at things might have produced a book like Muir's *Autobiography.* Perhaps the chief thing to be said about both men is that, though indisputably artists and hence unrelievedly aware of the multiplex catastrophe into which the race is debouching itself, they refused the separate, uncontaminated roles of lamentation and prophesy, and insisted on the duty of the individual organism to deal constructively with whatever materials are at hand.

John Holloway (essay date 1960)

SOURCE: "The Poetry of Edwin Muir," in *The Hudson Review,* Vol. XIII, No. 4, Winter, 1960-61, pp. 550-67.

[*In the following essay, Holloway assesses the relation of Muir's poetry to modern literary movements and cultural trends.*]

The recognition which any poet seeks from any reader is first and foremost a detailed attention to his poems; and a comprehension and appreciation of them, not in order to clarify a literary landscape or solve a critical problem, but for their own sake. Because of this, the most direct way in which one can offer recognition to Muir's achievement as a poet is to concentrate closely upon his individual poems. Yet in the present state of literary and critical opinion, one cannot, in Muir's case, make this one's first move. There is a general problem about the literary and critical horizon which must be dealt with as a preliminary. In turning to it, I should be sorry even to seem to use Muir's work for the mere purpose of clarifying it: I hope to clarify it in

order that his work many transpire more lucidly. There is the end, the generalities are the means.

There is at present, as there has been for generations, something of a current of discussion as to what poetry should be, and how far the poetry of the past, or new verse as it appears, lives up to what it should be. In cultivated conversation, in reviews and articles in literary or academic or critical journals, on the radio, or in public lectures—in all these, the poetry-reading public encounters a veritable bombardment of ideas about what poetry should be and what it should not be, a bombardment of categories, by the presence or absence of which poetry may be commented on, discussed, and assessed. Tentacular roots, richness and solidity of imagery, verbal inter-animation, chastity of diction, tone and tonelessness, concreteness and concrete meaning, syntax, a vernacular quality of language in diction and in rhythm—that probably does not exhaust the current tools of poetic criticism. There are the ideas that are there, ready to be reached for, whenever someone who is well up in current controversy wants to discuss a poem. They are our stock in trade.

There is no need to sweep these critical tools aside, or to argue that they cannot be applied to Muir's poetry; that it does not illustrate such ideas nor have such qualities. Certainly, there are other recent poets in whose verse such qualities as so-called inter-animation of words, or metaphorical life, or colloquial strength, are more conspicuous than they are in his. This is partly because the critic's admiration for some of these qualities is itself a historical phenomenon: to take an example, our admiration for complex verbal and metaphorical texture is not the result of a revelation from the Medes and the Persians, but of the influence of ideas about poetic texture which have largely come to us from a certain school of practising poets, to wit the French *Symbolistes* and in particular Mallarmé. Muir's work points back in other directions which will be discussed below. But there is perhaps a more important reason why the favourite poetic qualities of today show less conspicuously in Muir's work than in that of some other recent poets. It is that in the end all these qualities are not the decisive signs of poetic achievement, but the subordinate and derivative ones. They are means to the major poet's ends, not the ends themselves. Certainly, they have their interest; but it is best expressed by saying that these favoured qualities, these qualities that a poem is likely to have today if its writer is equipped and *avant-garde,* are of the kind which by themselves will enable a poem to interest for not just a day, but a year and a day. No longer. By themselves, they have no significance save to contribute another little swirl and eddy to the lively flux, the surface animation, of contemporary literary to-ing and fro-ing. On their own, they have their place somewhere in what one might almost call the journalism about current literature which is an increasing menace to the truly creative writer. Minor poets, intrigued with them, will concentrate on them, and make them conspicuous in their work. The more important writer will be more concerned with the more important things which lie behind. This was Muir's case; in his work what ought to appear only as means to something greater than itself, strictly does so.

Thus to look in Muir's poetry only for metaphorical complexity or for concreteness or for vernacular strength, will not be to come back empty-handed; but to miss the end, for the sake of the means to it, miss the big things for the sake of the small ones. As we read his poetry—this is a sign of its stature—we are likely to find ourselves being driven out of our conventionalities, into a first-hand contact with certain major realities of the poetic art. What is rich metaphor *for?* What is concreteness *for?* What is complexity *for?* What is vernacular strength *for?* Only while the answers to these questions are alive in our minds, shall we see what is remarkable not on the mere periphery, but at the centre, of his poems.

An outstanding poem is far from simply an interesting pattern of language. Every outstanding poem is a self-contained and completed *deed* of the imagination—and at one and the same time a record of that deed—which has penetrated into the realities, and the humanly important realities, of human life; and normally, the formal qualities, the "beauty" of the poem, are essentially a part of this, and are nothing but the issuing into words of the fullness and directness and at the same time economy—nothing superfluous, nothing digressive—with which that deed of the imagination has been performed. I say deed of the *imagination,* because the social scientist penetrates, and sometimes at least penetrates deeply, into humanly important realities. But the writer and the poet is concerned not only with the plain facts of what happens, of life; he is concerned also with the forces it holds in reserve, with its potentialities, its hidden strength for all that is remarkable, all that is good, all that is evil. This is why the poet—the poet particularly—may go in his work so far beyond anything that one could call a description of life in the realist's sense, that one begins almost to think that the interest of his poem can lie wholly in the intrinsic strangeness and newness of the imaginary world it describes; that its thrilling fantasy carries no reference back to our ordinary world at all. That is an error. Light cast from a great distance may carry its own decisive revelation. And when we see that this is so, and how it is so, in the poems which strike us as most "imaginative" and least "realistic," I believe that we are then equipped to recognize not only what Muir has achieved, but also the distinctive kind of that achievement, and the distinctive place and affiliations which it has in recent European art, a matter about which more must be said later on.

With these fundamental issues in mind we can turn, for example, to a late poem of Muir's like **"Milton,"** and at once recognize its primary merits, as opposed to its derivative and secondary ones.

> Milton, his face set fair for Paradise,
> And knowing that he and Paradise were lost

> In separate desolation, bravely crossed
> Into his second night and paid his price.
> There towards the end he to the dark tower came
> Set square in the gate, a mass of blackened stone
> Crowned with vermilion fiends like streamers
>   blown
> From a great funnel filled with roaring flame.

> Shut in his darkness, these he could not see,
> But heard the steely clamour known too well
> On Saturday nights in every street in Hell.
> Where, past the devilish din, could Paradise be?
> A footstep more, and his unblinded eyes
> Saw far and near the fields of Paradise.

I can see someone trying to praise this poem on account, perhaps, of the muscular quality of "blackened stone"—which, to be sure, conveys a quite different meaning from what "black stone" would convey; and the common-language quality of "on Saturday nights" or "devilish din" (indeed, his cup is full, he can claim ambiguity and wit here as well); and also the concreteness of "Fiends like streamers"; and a few more bits and pieces taken from here and there in the poem. But this response would be a pathetic one. It would be on a level with that of the man who cannot read classical Egyptian hieroglyph and yet prides himself on having given an adequate account of a passage of hieroglyph, when he has praised the sharp edges of the inscription (which he doesn't even *know* is an inscription) and the realism of the fish and the five different birds. An alternative response to the poem, less frivolously out of proportion but still inadequate, would be to praise it purely as creating a "poetic world," the "landscape of Muir's imagination," as if this were something we entered and enjoyed purely for its own newness or strangeness, and not, also, for its reference back to the world of our own realities. For the landscape of a poet's imagination (Muir's or indeed Dante's) is a semi-transparent one: through it, we glimpse our own. And this is the great fact, of which the little fact, the concrete common-language quality of some phrases in this poem, **"Milton,"** is the servant. If we are to imagine the noise in Muir's Hell as a "steely clamour known too well on Saturday nights in every street," we know where we are. To wander in this imaginary landscape, to experience its strangeness and terror, is to re-enter our own real landscape by an unexpected and revelatory gate. If Hell is like that, we are forced to say with Mephistopheles in Marlowe's *Doctor Faustus:* "why this is Hell, nor am I out of it." *There,* the poet's imaginary and created world, has illuminated *here,* our real one.

Similarly with the most striking part of the poem, the brilliant image of the gate of blackened stone

> Crowned with vermilion fiends like streamers
>   blown
> From a great funnel filled with roaring flame.

This is no mere science fiction vividness. Take away that they are fiends, that it is Hell of which this is the gate, and the bold colours are still there, but the inner strength, the deeper rightness and relevance—by a paradox, the *humanity* of the image—has gone. The great gate that leads in like a funnel but not out, the great destructive powers, bold and exultant, all-too-human and yet inhuman, which surround it, make no merely entertaining and merely horrific fairy-tale picture. They have their reference back to certain great lines of force, if you like, which run through reality; to the standing potentialities of human life. Nor is that the whole of the reference back of the poem; other major lines of force enter into it, because it is a reminder of how there is also in men a steadfastness and intrepidity and indeed pride which can break through those evil powers; and find, or make, a settled good beyond them. Nor is it a mere parable or allegory of these matters, to be interpreted point by point: what makes it a remarkable poem, what gives it its formal beauty, is the artistry—selection and economy and completeness—which has fined down and intensified a narrative into a single unshakeable unity, with the memorableness, the burning insistence, of an icon.

Muir was slow, I believe, to reach this level of achievement. The best illustration of that fact is perhaps the contrast between **"The Return,"** from his 1943 volume, and **"Telemachos Remembers,"** from that of 1956. Both of these centre upon the same topic Penelope waiting for Ulysses during the years of his absence, and how she spent the time at her loom, keeping the suitors at bay by weaving herself a bridal gown during the daytime and unstitching it in secret at night. The later poem is much richer and more detailed than the first, but that is no mere trick of concreteness. It is because by the time he came to write it, Muir saw more deeply into how men and women live; what shapes their life, what quality life can have. Muir could now imagine the whole mythical incident better. Everything in the second poem reads truer and goes deeper. The first Penelope's vague guiding idea of "order and right and hope and peace," becomes the second's more exact and relevant "pride and fidelity and love." The particularized reality of the scene matters to us because it truly embodies just these more general qualities of mind, and therefore contributes to a superbly integrated work of art. The second poem also spreads its vision much more widely than the first, for it sees how the plight of Penelope is only another version of that of Ulysses: her loom is his treadmill. This is why, in the second poem, it was worth Muir's while to render the loom and its web of warriors in terms of which a ready-made criticism could so easily praise the otherwise gratuitous concreteness. Finally, the beautiful orderliness and completeness of the second poem, as against the comparative repetitiveness and jerkiness in the first, are no abstract formal excellence; they are the embodiment of the writer's complete and ordered vision of what he has imagined, the mirror in words of the quality of his vision, his imagination of what life can be like, the dignity in tribulation which it can achieve.

Here is the crucial passage from **"The Return"**:

Sole at the house's heart Penelope
Sat at her chosen task, endless undoing
Of endless doing, endless weaving, unweaving,
In the clean chamber. Still her loom ran empty
Day after day. She thought: 'Here I do nothing
Or less than nothing, making an emptiness
Amid disorder, weaving, unweaving the lie
The day demands. Ulysses, this is duty,
To do and undo, to keep a vacant gate
Where order and right and hope and peace can
   enter.
Oh will you ever return? Or are you dead,
And this wrought emptiness my ultimate
   emptiness?'
She wove and unwove and wove and did not
   know
That even then Ulysses on the long
And winding road of the world was on his way.

And here, a little more condensed and oblique in approach, but in the end immensely superior, is **"Telemachos Remembers"**:

Twenty years, every day,
The figures in the web she wove
Came and stood and went away.
Her fingers in their pitiless play
Beat downward as the shuttle drove.

Slowly, slowly did they come,
With horse and chariot, spear and bow,
Half-finished heroes sad and mum,
Came slowly to the shuttle's hum.
Time itself was not so slow.

And what at last was there to see?
A horse's head, a trunkless man,
Mere odds and ends about to be,
And the thin line of augury
Where through the web the shuttle ran.

How could she bear the mounting load,
Dare once again her ghosts to rouse?
Far away Odysseus trod
The treadmill of the turning road
That did not bring him to his house.

The weary loom, the weary loom,
The task grown sick from morn to night,
From year to year. The treadle's boom
Made a low thunder in the room.
The woven phantoms mazed her sight.

If she had pushed it to the end,
Followed the shuttle's cunning song
So far she had no thought to rend
In time the web from end to end,
She would have worked a matchless wrong.

Instead, that jumble of heads and spears,
Forlorn scraps of her treasure trove.
I wet them with my childish tears
Not knowing she wove into her fears
Pride and fidelity and love.

The present line of thought—that the foundation of Muir's achievement as a poet is not a voguish manipulation of language, but the embodiment in verse of a deep and true apprehension of life—may be taken a step further by considering another poem written about 1950, **"Orpheus' Dream."** To turn to it serves as a reminder that Muir is, with Graves perhaps, the outstanding British love poet since Yeats; though it is the love not of passion, but of deep mutual intimacy and affection. **"Orpheus' Dream"**, like **"Telemachos Remembers"**, takes its start in a Greek myth; but to see the poem as a "recreation of myth" is almost not to see it at all. Again, there is much in the setting and the imagery of this poem which is reminiscent of neo-Platonic ideas about the existence of the soul before birth, or the heavenly world and the world of sense; and of the traditional imagery in which these ideas have many times been embodied. But nothing could be more to squander this fine poem, than to see it merely as expressing doctrines to which few of us will give credence. The poem speaks not *of* these, but *through* them, of the potentialities of our own experience—of what fulfilment in lasting love is like, of how it can come, of what it can yield. Nor of course is the poem a statement of these things; everything about it— and here is its integrity, its unity, its beauty—embodies them and helps to cast the reader's mind into a condition where these things, and the emotions which attend them, are felt with the force of an intuition. That is true of the two scenes or images, charged with calm and quiet and gentleness, with which the poem opens and closes: Eurydice appearing in the skiff of Orpheus, the ghost of Eurydice alone on her throne in the underworld. It is true of the shift, unobtrusive yet almost startling once noticed, from the third person to the second, and back again, in the course of the poem. It is true also of the very rhythms of the poem, so unassertive and yet so full of calm buoyant life; and of the beautiful opening out and closing in, as it were, of what it has to say; and of the almost naive lucidity of the diction. Wherever the reader turns, he finds some new detail contributing to the effect of the whole; and the work of the whole is to record, with a serene finality, something which matters in life itself, and to record it in the mirror, a diminishing and yet a magnifying glass, of a poem:

> And she was there. The little boat,
> Coasting the perilous isles of sleep,
> Zones of oblivion and despair,
> Stopped, for Eurydice was there.
> The foundering skiff could scarcely keep
> All that felicity afloat.
>
> As if we had left earth's frontier wood
> Long since and from this sea had won
> The lost original of the soul,
> The moment gave us pure and whole
> Each back to each, and swept us on
> Past every choice to boundless good.
>
> Forgiveness, truth, atonement, all
> Our love at once—till we could dare
> At last to turn our heads and see
> The poor ghost of Eurydice,
> Still sitting in her silver chair
> Alone in Hades' empty hall.

If we bring to this poem nothing but the current coin of critical analysis, we can even so find something there. We can single out, for example, the rhythmic control of emphasis:

> The little boat,
> Coasting the perilous isles of sleep,
> Zones of oblivion and despair,
> Stopped, . . .

and:

> Forgiveness, truth, atonement, all
> Our love at once, till we could dare
> At last to turn our heads . . .

Certainly, in passages like these, Muir shows himself for a deft and intelligent craftsman in verse. But comparatively speaking, how trivial, how futile praise in these terms would be, unless as the merest preliminary; unless we see craftsmanship as serving something greater than craftsmanship, serving in fact the new modes of vision of the poet which have led him to the new modes of being which he creates in his verse.

On the other hand, I can see a more futile criticism still, one which complained of a general lack of concreteness, lack of realization, in such phrases as "the moment gave us pure and whole/Back each to each"; and "boundless good"; and "all our love at once." "This is too vague!" I can hear the critic say. "What do these phrases mean? Why is the poem not specific, why does it not *say?*"— ignoring the fact, first, that largely it does say, in its whole largeness and gentleness, its simplicity and absence of local complication: qualities which are in part created by just the open, simple diction of which my imaginary critic complains. Ignoring also, one should add, the fact that we do not come to the reading of poetry with all the nakedness and ignorance of a babe unborn. We come to it with our experience of life and our care for it, our own emotions and insight. The poet, saying just so much, from us elicits more. He can enlarge the horizons of our imagination because it already *has* horizons, towards which his poem can turn our mind's eye. This is a large subject, and one cannot pursue it; one can only add that the opposite view, that which sees poetic merit only in poetry which pushes rich novelty of detail and what I believe is known as "specificity" to a maximum point, is simply a recent and, to judge by analogy, transient fashion which falls into a plain story of historical development: in particular of the historical accident whereby Mallarmé and Hopkins could be discovered at about the same time.

I suspect that there may be something notably of our own age in the particular way in which it interested Muir to write of love between men and women: not as what is called "romantic" love, nor as what we find celebrated in much of Donne's verse, but as the relaxed yet profound affection which supervenes upon sustained intimacy. However this may be, I leave it aside because there are other respects in which Muir was very conspicuously, as poet, a register of his own time and of some of its major forces. It is a strange thing—unless we remember Muir's years in Germany after the first war, or in Prague until after its fall, following the second—to notice how this quiet and elderly poet, living a comparatively retired life, was deeply concerned with the modern world (insofar as it is a world of war, totalitarianism, terrorism and the displaced person) at a time when his younger contemporaries, almost without exception, have either left these topics to others, or exploited them in a style which will bear no inspection. Indeed, although the 1930s were to some extent Muir's prentice years as a poet, he ranks high among the (in a broad sense) "political" poets of that decade; and if we enquire why it has been that he deepened and strengthened his awareness of political realities right up to the end of his life, whereas the other political poets of that time have on the whole, as poets, done the opposite, the reason is not far to seek. It is that, to the reader of today, much of the so-called political poetry of the 1930's was really a compromise between treating major political realities on the one hand, and being inclined to satisfy certain minor and transient poetic fashions on the other. Thus (though my purpose is not to disparage Auden's work as a whole) consider the first verse of *Danse Macabre:*

> It's farewell to the drawing-room's civilized cry,
> The professor's sensible whereto and why,
> The frock-coated diplomat's social aplomb,
> Now matters are settled with gas and with bomb.

or alternatively, this description, from *The Age of Anxiety,* of an air-raid on a town.

>   we laid our eggs
> Neatly in their nest, a nice deposit
> Which instantly hatched; houses flamed in
> Shuddering sheets as we shed our big
> Tears on their town . . .

These passages have their own qualities. As one reads them, ideas about how poetry ought to use plain language, ought to be astringent and witty, ought to draw readily on the tone of irony, ought to take subjects and metaphors from ordinary life, all flood into one's mind. And ought to cause it nothing but pain. For it is exactly this, which still comes in for praise in a stock way, that turns those passages into frivolous period pieces, devoid of serious contact with the realities they purport to describe. In Muir's verse this in the long run disabling voguishness never appears. That is why he does not lend himself to chaffering in the current coin of critical parlance, and why to study his work, is to be driven all the time to challenge that current parlance. In his verse, we hear the accents of one who is in another world from that of the poetically or the critically smart thing; we hear, at last, the voice of a poet speaking with complete directness and sincerity, with a total absence of literary flyness and manoeuvring, because he is wholly engrossed in what he writes of, and in making it into a poem wholly in his own way. It is this stellar remoteness from the vogue, and this only, which can make a

poem endure; everything conflicting with it, however subtle and sophisticated, will in the long run make verse at the best trivial, and at the worst—or perhaps this *is* the best—forgotten.

Most of Muir's more important political poems, or poems showing his concern with what one might call the basic rhythms of modernity—**"The Labyrinth"**, say, **"The Good Town"**, **"The Combat"**, **"Adam's Dream"**, or a still uncollected poem like **"The Last War"**—are comparatively long, and of a kind which makes short extracts unprofitable. A more convenient example, therefore, is the poem **"Troy,"** published as early as 1937. Though a pre-war poem, though one set (as so often with Muir) in the world of classical myth, though there are verbal echoes of Eliot, yet for all that, the poem strikes today's reader as a vision of post-war Europe, of the chaos of the late 1940s. Moreover (whatever may be said of verbal echoes) the attitude of the poem, and the awareness which lies behind it, are quite different from Eliot, and notably Muir's own. And equally distinctive of Muir is what might be termed the *mode* in which it makes its principal statements.

> He all that time among the sewers of Troy
> Scouring for scraps. A man so venerable
> He might have been Priam's self, but Priam was
>   dead,
> Troy taken. His arms grew meagre as a boy's,
> And all that flourished in that hollow famine
> Was his long, white, round beard. Oh, sturdily
> He swung his staff and sent the bold rats
>   skipping
> Across the scurfy hills and worm-wet valleys,
> Crying: 'Achilles, Ajax, turn and fight!
> Stop cowards!' Till his cries, dazed and
>   confounded,
> Flew back at him with: 'Coward, turn and fight!'
> And the wild Greeks yelled round him.
> Yet he withstood them, a brave, mad old man,
> And fought the rats for Troy. The light was rat-grey,
> The hills and dells, the common drain, his Simois,
> Rat-grey. Mysterious shadows fell
> Affrighting him whenever a cloud offended
> The sun up in the other world. The rat-hordes,
> Moving, were grey dust shifting in grey dust.
> Proud history has such sackends. He was taken
> At last by some chance robber seeking treasure
> Under Troy's riven roots. Dragged to the surface.
> And there he saw Troy like a burial ground
> With tumbled walls for tombs, the smooth sward
>   wrinkled
> As time's last wave had long since passed that way,
> The sky, the sea, Mount Ida and the islands,
> No sail from edge to edge, the Greeks clean gone.
> They stretched him on a rock and wrenched his
>   limbs,
> Asking: 'Where is the treasure?' till he died.

One thing is especially remarkable about this poem: its essential structure is to be a progress through a series of sharply created images; yet these are images which immediately establish themselves as having nothing to do with *Imagism*—with the pleasing pictures, faithfully observed, entirely for the sake of what they looked like, of Hilda Dolittle, T. E. Hulme or others. Muir's images—first the "brave, mad old man" fighting the rats, then the grey, rat-like landscape, then ruined Troy "like a burial ground," and finally the victim stretched out on the rock, are not offered us at all as models of close sensuous observation or intricate concrete realization in a subtly inter-playing verbal texture. Rather, it seems—and in Muir's later and sparer poems it seems much more—as if the poet has broken through all this, as if through a surface: and has confronted us, by what is a kind of skeletal presentation, with the essential quality of a deeply disturbing reality. Not, if you like, the suave intricacies of daytime observation, but the poignant or frightening diagrams of dream or nightmare: *icons*—this word seemed the obvious one to use earlier on—*icons* which rivet the attention and at their most powerful seem to stamp themselves indelibly upon the mind. In the poems already quoted, from **"Milton"** onwards, this is the most recurrent feature.

At this point I turn to Muir's place in the artistic achievement of the twentieth century. He was not only the contemporary of Beckett—**"Troy"** must have reminded the reader of Beckett's work—but also the translator of Kafka and student of Rilke. This means that he has his place in a movement in the arts of Europe as a whole, which comes a whole generation later than the French poets who, it seems, still dominate critical thought in England. This in part is why his work does not fit in; why some critically-minded readers hardly know what to make of him. Perhaps the point will come clearly out if recent poetry is considered in a context of painting. Mallarmé, in his *Crise de Vers* of 1894, said that in true poetry the poet should "cède l'initiative aux mots, par le heurt de leur inégalités mobilisés." The effect of this would be that words could kindle "reflets réciproques comme une virtuelle trainée de feu sur des pierreries." Where could we find the nearest analogue in painting to this beautiful surface intricacy? I suggest, the earlier work of the French Impressionists: Monet, Renoir, Pissarro: their inter-play of objects through colour, shadow and reflection, to create a dazzling, glittering, infinitely subtle orchestration of light. But Muir's work reminds one, precisely, of the painters who rejected Impressionism; less the French ones of the end of the nineteenth century (though they certainly belong to the story too) than the German ones of the early twentieth century, with their consciousness of the element of horror, chaos, and nightmare in life, and their seeking to represent, even with a certain radical indifference to surface appearance, the stark and abiding inner essence of reality. And the statements of these painters themselves, about what they tried to do, chime decisively with what is to be seen in Muir's poetry. Paul Klee took as his slogan, "from the model to the *archetype*"; Max Beckmann, a year after Muir published **"Troy,"** said "What I try to show in my work is the idea which lies behind ·so-called reality. I strive to find the bridge that leads from the visible to the invisible, like the famous cabalist . . . My figures come and

go as luck or misfortune bids them. I try to transfix them stripped of their accidental superficial characteristics." And in 1915 Franz Marc, writing his "Aphorisms from the Front"—the German Western Front—said this: "Everything has its shell and kernel, semblance and being, . . . the fact that we only grope at the shell . . . that we are so blinded by the mask of things that we cannot find the truth—how does that refute the inner definiteness of things?" These three Expressionist painters are all saying what could be taken as a statement of Muir's deepest concern; the plain fact is that Muir (like Beckett) is a reflection in literature not of Impressionism but of Expressionism. Here is the relevance of Kafka. The labyrinthine threadings to and fro in Kafka's *Castle* and *Trial* are in one sense, to be sure, complex enough. But they are not Mallarméan complexities at all: or better, a comparison with Mallarmé's contemporary Huysmanns' novel *A Rebours* brings out the point. Kafka is not, as Huysmanns was, asking his reader to sense subtle gradations, modifications, nuances, of his hero's experiences page by page. Rather, he presents in essence the same experience over and over, varying only on the surface, until we are left with a characteristically Expressionist achievement: an inescapable icon of the Castle or of the Court on the one hand, and one of the mere human individual as seeker on the other. And what is memorable about both books is that these polar extremities are impressed indelibly upon the reader's mind as the two basic realities which underlie every complexity of surface appearance. In Kafka's short stories, as might be expected, this icon quality is even clearer: the man with the hideous wound in "The Country Doctor," for example; the lighted door and door keeper of "Before the Law"; and everything, indeed, in that remarkable microcosm of Kafka's longer works, "The Burrow."

This whole trend is an important movement in the arts of Europe during the present century (the painter Rouault is also prominent in it); and a valid reflection of the element of horror and chaos in the contemporary world or the recent past. If it were more widely understood in England and America, we should also understand, for example, some of Eliot's verse better than we do; for he is not simply a Symbolist poet, but very much a Post-Symbolist. That these movements are comparatively unfamiliar here, save I assume among specialists in the visual arts, is perhaps a measure of what we have been spared in real life; and Edwin Muir—along with Willa Muir, who played a vital part in the enterprise of translating Kafka—will one day have a place in our cultural history simply as having been among the first to introduce them, in literature, to the English-speaking world.

Yet—the most important point of all—in Muir's own verse, so far as we find those trends at work, we find them having undergone a decisive transmutation. To the layman's eye at least, German Expressionist painting of the early years of this century is impressive for its courageous, unflinching confrontation of what is harsh and brutal in life, and for the power with which it concentrates this vision into the picture. But in its rigid insistence on this, it is with few exceptions a school of hardness and dread. A windowless room in which the only object was a painting by Max Beckmann would be long remembered; but not long endured. Turning to Kafka, we find that he can indeed write, in his Aphorisms, "we were fashioned to live in Paradise"; but the idea is one which enters his work very much tangentially. Nightmare and bewilderment and savage humour dominate it; the deliverance from these is something which the author could no more than reach for, and in the main we feel this reaching forward only as the novels peter out to their unfinished ends.

To turn back to Muir's poems is to encounter a diametrical opposite. **"Milton"** did not show Hell merely, but a triumph over it; **"Telemachos Remembers,"** not deprivation merely, but deprivation conquered by simple integrity; the old man in **"Troy"** was no symbol of the chaos and brutality within which he had to live and die, but rather, an embodiment of the human powers which these cannot touch. The great central fact about Muir's work is that although in his vision of life the powers of evil were great, ultimately the powers of good and goodness were greater; and they were greater because they were also humbler, more primaeval, nearer to life in its archaic simplicity, which Muir was able to see not far below life's surface distractions. This, in the end, is the inner vision of joy which the iconic quality of his verse predominantly serves; and it is this sense of the simple but spacious powers of goodness held by life in reserve, that is ultimately what demands, and what justifies, Muir's simple but often monumental imagery; and his grave and lucid rhythms; and the honesty and spareness of his diction. This positive quality, this sense of a trust finally reposed in man and what is in man, does not make Muir a greater artist than the others with whom I have associated him; and in fact, Kafka is clearly a greater writer than he. But it makes him significantly different, and to many readers will make his work an endearing source of strength. "Far inland shines the radiant hill," Muir wrote in **"Outside Eden,"** one of his last poems. We do not understand his work unless we see how central to its achievement is that radiance, and how it works down into the movement of the verse word by word. To emphasize how I am not now speaking merely of Muir's "philosophy", but of something which is to be felt through the whole tissue of many of his poems, I take **"The Annunciation,"** of about 1950. Again, we have a myth: this time not Greek but Christian. The iconic quality is unmistakable; but it is not in any mere comment, it is in the innermost feel of the poem, evoked as this is by the rhythms and the language, that the centre of Muir's vision of life must be traced:

> The angel and the girl are met.
> Earth was the only meeting place.
> For the embodied never yet
> Travelled beyond the shore of space.
> The eternal spirits in freedom go.

> See, they have come together, see,
> While the destroying minutes flow,
> Each reflects the other's face
> Till heaven in hers and earth in his
> Shine steady there. He's come to her
> From far beyond the farthest star,
> Feathered through time. Immediacy
> Of strangest strangeness is the bliss
> That from their limbs all movement takes.
> Yet the increasing rapture brings
> So great a wonder that it makes
> Each feather tremble on his wings.

> Outside the window footsteps fall
> Into the ordinary day
> And with the sun along the wall
> Pursue their unreturning way
> That was ordained in eternity.
> Sound's perpetual roundabout
> Rolls its numbered octaves out
> And hoarsely grinds its battered tune.

> But through the endless afternoon
> These neither speak nor movement make,
> But stare into their deepening trace
> As if their gaze would never break.

There is no more need to be a Christian in order to admire that, than there was to be a Greek to admire **"Telemachos Remembers."** What is required is only to be a man, to be able to recognize what is an illumination of a part of life, or of one great direction of life's potentiality. Muir's work as a whole reminds us that it is something like this, and no astuteness with words for anything *but* this, which is the primary concern of the poet and therefore of the critic. Our first debt of gratitude to Muir should be for what he has done; for the body of achievement in poetry which he has left for our admiration and delight, even our sustainment. But it is proper to add to that, a recognition of how his work reminds us, with his own characteristic unassumingness and limpidity, of these basic truths about poetry; and does so in a period when, for many, the reminder is a timely one.

Joseph H. Summers (essay date 1961)

SOURCE: "The Achievement of Edwin Muir," in *The Massachusetts Review*, Vol. II, No. 2, Winter, 1961, pp. 240-60.

[*In the following essay, Summers surveys Muir's most important works in such genres as autobiography, criticism, and poetry.*]

With the publication of Edwin Muir's *Collected Poems* (1952), his *Autobiography* (1954), and *One Foot in Eden* (1956), many readers made the disconcerting discovery that someone had been writing important poetry and prose for a number of years without their attention or help. Despite all the praise that those volumes have received, many of Muir's new admirers have still not fully recognized the range of his achievement. Born in 1887, Muir published his first volume of prose in 1918 and his last volume of poetry in 1956. At the time of his death in 1959, he was still writing new poems and working on a book on the Scottish ballads. He published seven volumes of literary and social criticism (including one volume disguised as a travel journal), three novels, two volumes of autobiography, a biography, ten volumes of poetry, and innumerable reviews and essays. There was also a period when Muir and his wife, Willa Muir, "turned [themselves] into a sort of translation factory" and produced among other works (by Hauptmann and Broch, for example) those translations of Kafka which are in themselves works of art.

The *Autobiography* provides the best introduction to Muir's work. When he published the first part of it in 1940, Muir explained the reason for its title, *The Story and the Fable:*

> It is clear that no autobiography can begin with a man's birth, that we extend far beyond any boundary line which we can set for ourselves in the past or the future, and that the life of every man is an endlessly repeated performance of the life of man. It is clear for the same reason that no autobiography can confine itself to conscious life, and that sleep, in which we pass a third of our existence, is a mode of experience, and our dreams a part of reality. In themselves our conscious lives may not be particularly interesting. But what we are not and can never be, our fable seems to me inconceivably interesting. I should like to write that fable, but I cannot even live it; and all I could do if I related the outward course of my life would be to show how I have deviated from it; though even that is impossible, since I do not know the fable or anybody who knows it. One or two stages in it I can recognize: the age of innocence and the Fall and all the dramatic consequences which issue from the Fall. But these lie behind experience, not on its surface; they are not historical events; they are stages in the fable.

Muir came as near to writing that "impossible" autobiography as anyone I know. It is a beautiful book. In its detailed accounts of the most important events of his life, both sleeping and waking, one can recognize the sources of some of the most moving passages in his poetry and fiction.

The *Autobiography* also dramatizes the relation of Muir's "story" to the smaller "fable" of the modern western artist. The "mythical" life of most of the significant twentieth-century artists seems to include alienation and despair—or nausea. They have been exiles from any homeland, wandering in a hostile realm, and they have often produced their most moving works from the very heart of that experience. They have been haunted by time. Muir, too, experienced alienation, despair and nausea. As an Orkneyman in Glasgow, London, Prague, Dresden and Rome, as a Scotsman writing in English, as an "English writer" translating continental

literature, he was always an exile or an alien. Time was one of his major themes. But Muir's time was not congruent with the time of upper middle-class civilization in England and America. His experience of the modern trauma was largely completed before 1921. Most of his writing came after; it reflects a life in the process of recreation rather than of disintegration. And Muir's life before the trauma was also not the characteristic modern one, for it began with fourteen years in a pre-industrial society and landscape, an Orkney in "pre-history" where a child could experience an "age of innocence," a natural vision of life and death. Muir seemed to have lived a longer span of the world's history than is generally given to any mortal.

When his father moved the family to hideously industrialized Glasgow, Muir descended into the modern hell:

> . . . like everybody else I stubbornly set myself not to see what was before my eyes every day. This in time produced a sense of inward squalor, the reflection of the outward misery that I pushed away from me; and finally I reached a stage where I almost ignored my surroundings, lost the natural delight in my eyes which I had once had, and shielded my senses by shutting them off from what perpetually violated them.

Within a few years his parents and two of his brothers were dead: "I was too young for so much death." With fantastic jobs in a beer-bottling factory and a "bone factory," meaningless love affairs, and his fierce attempts to educate himself (he attended concerts because Nietzsche approved of them), Muir experienced concomitantly his intellectual, social and psychological crises. He was led in dreams and visions to the brink of sanity.

We Moderns is our chief contemporary witness to the crises. A collection of short notes and a few satirical verses which had appeared in *The New Age,* it was published in 1918:

> In these notes I generalized in excited ignorance on creative love and the difference between it and pity, which I unhesitatingly condemned; I pointed out such facts as that humility is really inverted pride, and that the true antithesis of love is not hate but sympathy: whenever I hit upon a paradox which lay conveniently near the surface I took it for the final truth.

It is a painful book, and it is difficult to believe that the same man could have written it, with its rash of exclamation points and Germanicized abstract nouns, and some of the essays which appeared six years later. One can glimpse the idealism underneath the fury, and there are bits of interesting judgment; but the shrill affirmations betray the suffering and insecurity which produced this desperate act of will.

"I lived for most of these years in a sort of submarine world of glassy lights and distorted shapes, enclosed in a diver's bell which had grown to my shoulders." *The*

Marionette (1927), the novel about the "idiot" Hans, shows the mode of such perception and, partially, the process of a returning recognition of the external world. David's climactic meditation in *The Three Brothers* (a novel set in the period of the Scottish Reformation which Muir published in 1931) is one of the most moving realizations of despair which I know. But Muir could have written that passage, with all its personal echoes, only after the experience itself was past and could be seen. The story of Muir's rediscovery of the will to live is largely the story of his marriage to Willa Muir, his psychoanalysis in London in 1920 and 1921, and his discovery of beauty in Czechoslovakia and Germany in the 'twenties. Those events were associated with the rediscovery of his childhood world in the Orkneys, the events and images which, refined through dreams, represented his essential values.

Muir's later intellectual and literary development was remarkably independent. He rejected the program of the Scottish nationalists. He believed that the fragmentation of Scottish life had anticipated the fragmentation of modern life in general by a number of centuries ("the centre has not held in Scotland for four hundred years"); Scots had ceased to be the language of serious thought for so long that Muir believed any attempt to revive it as a literary language must fail. (He rejected from his *Collected Poems* all of his early poems in Scots, including the delightful **"Ballad of the Flood."**) After his early intoxication with Nietzsche, there was a time in the 'twenties when he thought Freud "seemed to provide an explanation for all experience"; and in the 'thirties he published an interesting pamphlet, *Social Credit and the Labour Party: An Appeal,* which indicated his individual allegiance to both those movements. But his theoretical enthusiasms did not have much effect on either his poetry or his criticism; and in his associations with fashionable intellectual movements, he was oddly unfashionable. He was never, for example, "properly" apologetic for the lack of "realism" in his early advocacy of Fabian socialism: he neither tried to make his position look realistic nor did he indicate that he had changed his mind particularly. What he learned from Freud did not resemble what most intellectuals learn from Freud. And in our days of dramatic conversions and dogmatic positions, it is almost shocking to read Muir's simple account of how, on the night of February 28, 1939, he discovered while taking off his waistcoat that he had been a Christian for some time without knowing it. Muir decided to join no church, and he confined the prose statement of his experience to one diary entry and a few paragraphs of the *Autobiography.*

Muir never truly belonged to a group or a "movement." For a critic and a poet in our age, such independence provided, in compensation for a certain loneliness, unexpected advantages.

As a critic, Muir combined the usually disparate functions of the reviewer for the press, the historical critic, and the critic concerned with fundamental principles. He was interested in fiction as well as poetry, and in works of all periods. He had a wider acquaintance with German and Slavic literatures (and probably less familiarity with Romance literature) than is customary today. He was not at all afraid that he might commit himself unquestionably in favor of a work which impressed no one else or might damn a work which others loved. He accepted naturally the critic's duty to define limitations as well as virtues, but he resisted the temptation to demand one kind of literary effect from all works. He was not pompous and he was not dull. His writing is always clear.

Muir's first significant volume of criticism was *Latitudes* (1924), which concerned Burns, Scottish ballads, Conrad, Dostoevsky, Ibsen, Nietzsche, and various general topics. *Transition: Essays on Contemporary Literature* (1926) contained individual essays on Joyce, Lawrence, Virginia Woolf, Stephen Hudson, Huxley, Strachey, Eliot, Edith Sitwell and Robert Graves. *The Structure of the Novel* (1928), his best known volume in America, was followed by *Scott and Scotland: The Predicament of the Scottish Writer* (1936). *The Present Age: From 1914* was designed as the fifth volume of Bonamy Dobrée's *Introductions to English Literature.* It had the immediate misfortune of publication in the year 1939, when the "present" suddenly became the past, and it was largely ignored. It is a substantial work, and today the period 1914-1939 seems to provide a fortuitous unit with more reality for literature than any other we have yet discovered in the twentieth century. The most important critical volume was *Essays on Literature and Society,* published in 1949.

Such a body of criticism over such a period of time inevitably recalls Eliot. But in his comments on Eliot in *Transition,* Muir made clear some of the essential differences. He began with a simple acknowledgment of Eliot's importance: "There is probably no writer of our time who has said more things about the art of literature which are at once new and incontrovertible than Mr. T. S. Eliot." He went on to describe Eliot's virtues, including by the way one of those simple, illuminating sentences which are a hallmark of Muir's criticism: "His critical method consists in pressing a small lever and in thereby releasing an unsuspectedly heavy weight." It was when he turned to Eliot's attitude toward "tradition" that Muir's independence emerged. He admired the central formulation in "Tradition and the Individual Talent":

> Admirable and profound words—yet why is it that in spite of them Mr. Eliot always appears to us to underestimate the free character of tradition, the fact that in its living perpetuation it gives the artist his proper liberty, and is not so much a thing to be submitted to or imposed as to be discovered and welcomed? The influence of tradition on Mr. Eliot's criticism is not to make it uniformly bold and comprehensive, but more generally to make it cautious. He often draws back where a genuinely classical writer, a writer in the

full stream of tradition, knowing the dangers, seeing the raised eyebrows of all the past and hearing the warnings of the present, would have gone on. Mr. Eliot feels answerable to tradition for every judgment he makes: but this accepted responsibility, while it gives his criticism weight, sometimes makes it curiously timid. Thus, if his enthusiasms are never wild, his understatements sometimes are. One is struck by the sheer oddity when he describes Goethe's *Faust* as "a very able and brilliant poem," and when, admitting that a few "many sided" men must "probably" be conceded to history, he adds: "Perhaps Leonardo da Vinci is such." It is as easy to lose one's sense of proportion through excessive caution as through excessive rashness.

In *The Present Age,* Muir made his major criticism explicit: "In Eliot we cannot but be conscious of a deep mistrust of liberty." After quoting the formulation in *After Strange Gods* about the "homogeneous" population desired in the Christian society, Muir remarked simply, "These are his requirements for a healthy traditional society; but the tradition is not the English one."

The differences between Muir's and Eliot's "traditions" are more than matters of literary taste: they imply a difference in attitude toward human experience and ultimate value. Muir was harshest and clearest when he described T. E. Hulme's use of the conception of Original Sin:

> Behind all Hulme's literary criticism was the dogma of Original Sin. Though it was not new, he succeeded in making a scoop of it and set it out in headlines. He was not quite disinterested, that is to say, in his employment of it; to him it was a convenient rejoinder to the romantics. All his public statements implied an invisible contemporary opponent; and he had in an exaggerated form the snobbery which consists in saying today what a good number of people will be saying tomorrow. He insisted therefore on the irreconcilable aspect of any truth; and to give Original Sin a sensational value, he calmly ignored the complementary hypothesis of redemption. He looked on attentively while man fell, and turned his eyes away while man picked himself up again, or was picked up. . . . he says: "As man is essentially bad, he can only accomplish anything of value by discipline—ethical and political." This is neither the religious nor the humanist point of view; in saying that man can accomplish anything of value *only* by discipline, Hulme would have had neither Aquinas nor Luther nor Calvin to support him, for he allowed nothing for Grace. The first part of his thesis, that man is essentially bad, is religious, though wrongly stated; the second part, that man can accomplish anything of value only by discipline is purely secular: it is the worldly philosophy of the dictator and of the realistic practical man in general.

"Eliot is a far more balanced and substantial critic than Hulme, and far less under the influence of mere reaction."

But that part of Eliot's "tradition" which derives from or resembles Hulme's, Muir opposed with "the English tradition, especially on its heretical libertarian side," which he then felt was exemplified in the criticism of Herbert Read:

> From Original Sin one may draw either the conclusion that man must be supervised into salvation, or the conclusion that man must be given the freedom to work out his salvation. The difference is roughly the difference between Catholicism and Protestantism; and on the plane of criticism it is roughly the difference between Eliot and Read.

I should tend to substitute the name of Muir himself for that of Read.

The figures whom Muir considered, each with some admiration, in *Literature and Society,* indicate how wide and how individual his own literary tradition was: Robert Henryson, Chapman, Shakespeare, Sterne, Burns, Scott, Browning, Hardy, Hölderlin and Kafka. The list is by no means exhaustive (surely Wordsworth and Hugo von Hofmannsthal must be included among those who seriously influenced Muir), but how oddly unfashionable it sounds! What possibly can such a random group of writers have in common? And how could one man "seriously" like them all?

The degrees of liking differed, and with some of these figures Muir had decided reservations (Chapman, Scott, Browning and Hardy, for example). Yet when one reads the essays carefully, particularly with some memory of Muir's poetry and of his other prose, one discovers that there is a thread of "tradition" which unites them. It is a very simple quality: each of these writers possessed an individual vision, in some sense unique, of the human condition; and each achieved a form either by inheritance or discovery or invention, which gives body to that vision and makes it communicable. Muir's tradition cannot be divorced from the individuals (or perhaps the visions) which compose it: it is always open to expansion. It includes, with almost equal facility, the comic and the humorous, as well as the tragic and the ironic, and it excludes no major writer. Most radically of all, it places technical dexterity firmly in a subordinate position to primary vision. It is the latter fact which makes possible such an unusual judgment today as Muir's remark, "Ingenuity was Rilke's besetting sin."

The test of a critic, of course, is how much illumination he furnishes us. Muir had a gift for "simple" and memorable formulations which, often in a sentence, cast new light on figures and issues—and often destroyed, almost casually, reams of obscurantist commentary. Our impression of Muir's essays is so predominantly one of "justness" that we may not remember how much wit is involved, yet it was Muir who remarked of the "morality" in Auden's early poems, "It suggests a crowd so eager to be a team that every member is busy pulling up his neighbour's socks and has no time to attend to his own." One could construct a small anthology of such remarks: "Mr. Empson's poetry is obscure, intelligent and intricate, and contains some beautiful lines and various kinds of ambiguity." "To Galsworthy the poor were a middle-class problem." "Hardy takes a short cut to tragedy by reducing life to a formula. He gets rid beforehand of the main obstacle to tragedy, which is man's natural inclination to avoid it." "The incompatibility between the natural man and his political aims makes Mr. Hemingway's later works sentimental in a curious way; it is as if we saw Caliban looking through the eyes of Prospero, and, without Prospero's rod, swearing to perform Prospero's miracle with his naked fist." Or on the early Aldous Huxley: "Because people are one thing and appear another, as they have always done and for their self-preservation must always do, he is enraged. . . . He has the moral rage, without the morality, of a satirist; and although the effect is unintentional, sometimes he gives the impression of sitting on the fence, of a little irresolutely trying to make the worst of both worlds."

Yet such a series of quotations may give the wrong impression, for Muir's criticism did not depend upon the wisecrack, and it was more often appreciative than destructive. The chief distinction of the individual essays derives from the fact that each presents a clear account of a writer's work, seen both in its historical situation and in an unhistorical, "absolute" context of human and aesthetic value. One may disagree with details or even with the entire judgment (I happen to believe that in his published writings Muir showed misunderstanding of Swift and a failure to respond to much of Yeats), yet one never doubts the value of the sane, double vision; it presents the issues clearly, the issues with which we ourselves must come to terms if we wish to make a different or a "better" judgment. In 1939, for example, Muir remarked that Pound's best poetry is the "comment of a craftsman," that his virtues were largely medieval virtues, similar to Dunbar's. But this, for Muir, did not automatically guarantee Pound's stature as a major literary figure: "Pound is the archetypal poet, or the mere poet, who rises to greatness in an age of faith when men's conception of life is given to them complete, objectively, and all that the poet has to do is to say it out. But in a sceptical age where the poet has both to shape his conception of life and say it out, these virtues cannot come to fulfilment; they fight against the times and the times against them."

Much of Muir's criticism might be dismissed in a technological age as "moral" rather than "literary," but I believe that one of his most exciting gifts was the ability to show precisely those situations in which the moral sphere impinges directly on the literary. In his essay on Spengler, for example, Muir remarked, "The essential thing here is Spengler's inflection, not what he says"; he then defined the "pseudo-man of action," a moral type which has become increasingly familiar since the nineteenth century:

Many people before him have held that man is a beast of prey; Hobbes did so. But he did not think it was a noble or edifying fact; he did not romantically exalt the lion, the tiger and the shark, and exhort men to become like them. . . . The pseudo-man of action alone romanticises brutality in this way, and by the pseudo-man of action I do not mean the man who, but for physical or other incidental defect, might have become a great figure in history, but the man who lives in a dream of action, imagining that by the ardour of his dreams he influences events. Carlyle behaves in this way when he exhorts Cromwell at the critical point of battles, forgetting that his exhortations come two centuries too late; Nietzsche, when he constitutes himself the official midwife of a Superman who is never born; and Spengler, when he implies that in writing about history he is in some way making it. A man who is not framed for action will commit the most shocking errors in writing about it and violate the moral sense of ordinary people without being in the least conscious that he is doing so.

The moral and aesthetic grounds for Muir's rejection of Communism were one:

Communism presented itself as a strange, solidly made object, very like a huge clock, with metal bowels, no feelings, and no explanation for itself but its own impenetrable mechanism; it was neither glad nor sad, and reverenced only its own guaranteed working. . . . To forgive an enemy was a sin against the system; to forgive an erring brother was reprehensible weakness. I tried to think of ordinary people, husbands and wives, fathers and mothers and children, lovers and friends and to imagine them all as unforgiving and unforgiven, on principle and not merely by inclination; and I realized that it was impossible to wish this and to understand mankind. To think in such ways either kills or falsifies the imagination.

What Muir opposed is clear: any system which stultifies the imagination, which does not leave a place for the recognition of individual experience and individual vision as the primary values. It is this principle which made coherent his attacks on Communism and fascism, on the "religion" of T. E. Hulme and the newer "naturalism" of a host of writers, on an "historical sense" which reduces literature and life itself to mere records of mechanized or casual "responses," and on a relativism by which "it is possible to prefer anything to anything else: a well-grown tiger to Socrates or Christ, brutality to kindness, cunning to honesty, treachery to good faith." This principle underlies his attacks on criticism which demands or values only one type of "psychology" or attitude, that which confuses ingenuity with profundity, and that which values works solely on the bases of historical or political considerations.

In literature, however, the force which Muir most consistently and valiantly attacked is the force of fashion. Fashion has the power to reduce, to falsify, to vulgarize almost any individual vision: Wordsworth probably furnished Muir's prime example. It was this perception which made Muir write, "In the modern world the power most solidly obnoxious to the artist is not the public but the intelligentsia."

In his early appreciations of Joyce, Lawrence and Kafka, Muir was presenting his individual discoveries, not following fashion. His admiration was based largely on the belief that these men had avoided "being assimilated by the age." They were opposed at every instance to the fashionable writers, the majority of writers:

> The majority of writers accept fashion blindly, never feel the abnormal need to question, are either satisfied with things as they seem, or else are content with a mood of wonder which cannot goad them beyond itself . . . they may have a regard for art; they are sometimes within their limitations sincere; but their decisive limitation is that they speak out of the Zeit Geist as if they were speaking in their sleep. . . . They are mere expressions of the thing of which as artists they should be the contemplators. If they have enthusiasm it is not their enthusiasm, if disillusion, not their disillusion, if thoughts, not their thoughts. They are manifestations of a literary fashion, and it is in the essential nature of fashion to blind us to its meaning and the causes from which it springs; to everything, in fact, except the inevitability of the conformity it demands.
>
> There are two ways in which the writer may avoid being assimilated by the age; one is by struggling with it, the other is by escape. Both imply an intense apprehension of the spirit of the age, and both are in greater or less measure salutary.

In 1926, Muir identified Aldous Huxley as "our best example of the fashionable writer," Joyce as that "of the artist expressing the age by an uncompromising opposition to it," Lawrence as "the grand example in our age of the poet of escape." To oppose fashion, the writer must have a vision of himself and his age and the "normal" life of man. Muir takes us back almost to Milton: the significant writer must be a man of significant vision; the great writer, the man of great vision.

In his thirty-fifth year when he was living in Germany, Muir began to write poetry. I doubt that any other living poet began in such a fashion:

> I had no training; I was too old to submit myself to contemporary influences; and I had acquired in Scotland a deference towards ideas which made my entrance into poetry difficult. Though my imagination had begun to work I had no technique by which I could give expression to it. There were the rhythms of English poetry on the one hand, the images in my mind on the other. All I could do at the start was to force the one, creaking and complaining, into the mould of the other. . . . I began to write poetry simply because what I wanted to say could not have gone properly into prose. I wanted so much

to say it that I had no thought left to study the form in which alone it could be said.

> I certainly knew far too little about myself; yet I feel now that, in spite of the troubles brought about by my ignorance, I was more fortunate than the young poet (I was not even young) who knows too much or thinks he knows too much about poetry, and solves with ease the technical problems which I could not solve at all. To think of poetry like this makes it a simple and businesslike, and may make it almost a clever thing. I wrote in baffling ignorance, blundering and perpetually making mistakes. I must have been influenced by something, since we all are, but when I try to find out what it was that influenced me, I can only think of the years of childhood which I spent on my father's farm in the little island of Wyre in Orkney, and the beauty I apprehended then, before I knew there was beauty.

Although the *Collected Poems: 1921-1951* is really a selection and contains few of the earliest poems, it shows Muir's development as a poet; it also shows that his unusual point of departure made for an unusual terminus.

One strain of modern poetry at its best has been called "dramatic," but it is often dramatic in a special sense. The poem is usually concerned not with a complete action but with a specific natural or psychological scene, the end of action or, more often, an explanation of why action is impossible; as Muir has remarked of Browning, the poet is "concerned with the *dramatis personae* rather than with the play, he set[s] himself to find out what the *dramatis personae* really thought of the play, privately." The language itself furnishes the central point of interest; the "action" of the poem is largely the action of the words upon each other. Complexity of language is essential to the life of the poem.

Muir always, however, strove for simplicity rather than complexity, for clarity rather than density of texture. He was primarily concerned with vision rather than with language. In his best poems the language comes close to that pure ideal of "translation" which Simone Weil once described in a letter to Gustave Thibon:

> The effort of expression has a bearing not only on the form but on the thought and on the whole inner being. So long as bare simplicity of expression is not attained, the thought has not touched or even come near to true greatness. . . . The real way of writing is to write as we translate. When we translate a text written in some foreign language, we do not seek to add anything to it; on the contrary, we are scrupulously careful not to add anything to it. This is how we have to translate a text which is not written down.

Muir could use such a diction and have his poems still remain poems because his subject was also not the usual one. The poems are rarely concerned with a particular personality in a particular time and place. They are concerned with man, and the time is either all time or one of the recurrent times of man, and the place is the world, the prehistoric and the historic, this world and the next. They are saved from formlessness by the fact that Muir saw life in terms of narrative. The modes of the narrative are largely the pilgrimage, the journey of discovery, and the battle; and the living fragments of the narrative are found in dreams, in visions, in the cycles of nature and man's life, in heraldry and myth. So we have **"Ballad of Hector in Hades," "Tristram's Journey," "The Enchanted Knight"**; the meditations of **"Oedipus,"** of **"Moses,"** and of Theseus escaped from **"The Labyrinth."** We have the heraldry of the dragon and the sphinx, the lion, the helmet, **"The Castle," "The Grove," "The Gate"**; and we have continually **"The Myth," "The Old Gods," "The Fall,"** and **"The Journey Back."** These themes do not, of course, guarantee the poetry. Other poets, long before Muir, have played with such material; but Muir was never trivial. He never treated the mythic as the simply historical or as the external: it reflected the poet's serious and often suffering perception of his own experience.

Muir usually chose traditional forms, each of which he used with increasing distinction: the ballad stanza, blank verse, *terza rima,* the sonnet, the simple three-stress or four-stress line in quatrains or short stanzas—with occasionally freer adaptations which indicated that his desire was not for an image of perfect symmetry. We are never at a loss to determine grammatical constructions, to identify recondite allusions, to work out the implications of verbal ambiguities, or to extricate various voices from an aural montage; and the imagery is almost never fully private: it is the stuff of the dreams and myths of everyman. Yet with all their simplicity and apparently "old-fashioned" conventions, the poems are anything but conventional or obvious. They are often deeply and rewardingly "obscure," with the obscurity of the dreams and myths themselves. They compel attentive meditation: with it, their relations to the timely as well as the timeless quietly expand.

The elements in the visions of Muir's poems were largely constant during the past thirty years, but their relationships changed. In the early poems time is characteristically the enemy, the destroyer rather than the partial creator of the myth. The fall of man seems in no sense happy: "Where I lie now I stood at first." Although there are earlier moments when the lost world is recaptured as a living thing, **"The Letter,"** from *The Narrow Place,* marks a new point of vision from which time may be glimpsed as blessing as well as curse:

> Tried friendship must go down perforce
> Before the outward eating rage
> And murderous heart of middle age,
> Killing kind memory at its source,
> If it were not for mortality,
> The thought of that which levels all
> And coldly pillows side by side
> The tried friend and the too much tried.

In **"The Human Fold,"** "There's no alternative here but love." There continue to be moments of the heraldic, timeless vision, but there is a new vision of man, often pathetic, but savoring more of nobility than of beastliness:

> but here our sight is bound
> By ten dull faces in a round,
> Each with a made-to-measure glance
> That is in misery till it's found.
> Yet looking at each countenance
> I read this burden in them all:
> 'I lean my cheek from eternity
> For time to slap, for time to slap.
> I gather my bones from the bottomless clay
> To lay my head in the light's lap.'

In the poems which follow, **"The Recurrence"** and **"The Good Man in Hell"** (the most Herbertian poem in modern poetry), time is again partial deliverer as well as destroyer; life is affirmed together with the dream. In **"The Ring,"** the beasts in human form become horrors in their timelessness, "new, all new." From this point until the beautiful final poem in *Collected Poems,* the true animals are seen as part of the timeless, unchanging order, but man becomes a monster if, losing memory, he attempts to live like them in an eternal present.

Despite the preponderance of mythical poems, it is not true that Muir avoided the contemporary subject. His **"Reading in Wartime"** is one of the best poems in English about the last war, and his **"To Ann Scott-Moncrieff"** is not only a fine poem but one of the few modern personal elegies which is not actually embarrassing. Often the mythical poems are contemporary to a degree that some readers have not recognized. Their resonance derives partially from the fact that in them the images from dreams, from past literature, and from contemporary political and social experience coincide.

To give only one example, one must begin with the nightmare hallucination which Muir experienced on a tram in Glasgow one evening in 1919, when he suddenly saw all the people there—and in the world—as monstrous animals, a menagerie "living an animal life and moving towards an animal death as towards a great slaughterhouse." That moment haunted his poetry and fiction for some years. Muir's continued reading of *King Lear,* among other experiences, helped to transform that image from a general vision of humanity to a particular vision of the dehumanized, of evil. *The Politics of "King Lear,"* Muir's lecture at Glasgow in 1946, provides implicitly an account of that transformation. The villains in Lear "are so close to the state of nature that they hardly need to reflect: what they have the power to do they claim the right to do. Or rather the power and its expression in action are almost simultaneous." These human "beasts" "are quite rational, but only on the lowest plane of reason, and they have contempt for other ways of thinking which comes from a knowledge of their own efficiency." They see other human beings and events merely as means to their own ends:

To regard things in this way is to see them in a continuous present divested of all associations, denuded of memory and the depth which memory gives to life. Goneril and Regan, even more than Edmund, exist in this shallow present, and it is to them a present in both senses of the word, a gift freely given into their hands to do with what they like. Having no memory, they have no responsibility, and no need, therefore, to treat their father differently from any other troublesome old man. This may be simply another way of saying that they are evil, for it may be that evil consists in a hiatus in the soul, a craving blank, a lack of one of the essential threads which bind experience into a coherent whole and give it a consistent meaning. The hiatus in Lear's daughters is specifically a hiatus of memory, a breach in continuity; they seem to come from nowhere and to be on the way to nowhere; they have words and acts only to meet the momentary emergency, the momentary appetite.

The innocent and the monstrous "animals" and *Lear* appear in many of the poems; by 1946, the holocaust of the political "new order" had cast upon them a general, hideous, and compelling light. All are present again in **"The Usurpers,"** reintensified by the "new order" which Muir had then seen in Czechoslovakia. The poem is "contemporary," but it is not propaganda. It extends to an exact and pitying vision of all men who have reached the lower limits of humanity in the heart of nihilism:

> There is no answer. We do here what we will
> And there is no answer. This our liberty
> No one has known before, nor could have borne,
> For it is rooted in this deepening silence
> That is our work and has become our kingdom.
> If there were an answer, how could we be free?
> It was not hard to still the ancestral voices:
> A careless thought, less than a thought could do it.
> And the old garrulous ghosts died easily,
> The friendly and unfriendly, and are not missed
> That once were such proud masters. In this air
> Our thoughts are deeds; we dare do all we think,
> Since there's no one to check us, here or
>   elsewhere.
> All round us stretches nothing; we move
>   through nothing,
> Nothing but nothing world without end. We are
> Self-guided, self-impelled and self-sustained,
> Archer and bow and burning arrow sped
> On its wild flight through nothing to tumble down
> At last on nothing, our home and cure for all.

One Foot in Eden, Muir's last volume of poetry, is also, I believe, his best. One feels a particular excitement and pleasure in this indication that Muir's poetic technique became consistently more flexible and skillful as his vision accreted and deepened, that he wrote his finest poetry after he was sixty years of age. In this volume he moved from the most relaxed and colloquial effects to the visionary and incantatory—often in one poem. The sonnet, **"Milton,"** on the opening page, gives promise of the range which follows:

> Milton, his face set fair for Paradise,
> And knowing that he and Paradise were lost
> In separate desolation, bravely crossed
> Into his second night and paid his price.
> There towards the end he to the dark tower came
> Set square in the gate, a mass of blackened stone
> Crowned with vermilion fiends like streamers
>   blown
> From a great funnel filled with roaring flame.
>
> Shut in his darkness, these he could not see,
> But heard the steely clamour known too well
> On Saturday nights in every street in Hell.
> Where, past the devilish din, could Paradise be?
> A footstep more, and his unblinded eyes
> Saw far and near the fields of Paradise.

"Milton" introduces the subjects as well as styles of the poems which make up the first half of *One Foot in Eden.* I should imagine that a large number of these poems will become well known to all readers of modern poetry: **"The Animals," "Adam's Dream," "The Annunciation," "The Christmas," "The Lord," "One Foot in Eden"** and **"The Emblem,"** at the minimum. They concern largely the mythic, and they include two or three of the best frankly Christian poems which we have in English. The colloquial strain reaches its fullest development in **"Antichrist":**

> When he forgives
> It is for love of sin and not of the sinner. . . .
>
> His vast indulgence is so free and ample,
> You well might think it universal love.

In the visionary poems, Muir did not abandon the colloquial for any sort of "poetic diction"; the language becomes simpler than ordinary speech as it renders the emblematic scene. The emblem itself is the central metaphor, and a more sensuous or metaphorical language would only distract. Muir shaped his "plain style" to create delicately dramatic and lyrical effects, as in **"Orpheus' Dream":**

> And she was there. The little boat,
> Coasting the perilous isles of sleep,
> Zones of oblivion and despair,
> Stopped, for Eurydice was there.
> The foundering skiff could scarcely keep
> All that felicity afloat.

The sonnet **"To Franz Kafka"** introduces, in the second half of the book, a group of poems more individual and local in their references than most of Muir's earlier poems. "Dear Franz, sad champion of the drab / And half," contrasts both with "the authentic ones, the worst and best" and with the collective first-person of the poem, "we, the proximate damned, presumptive blest." Kafka as the triumphant witness at the Judgment is an inspiration. He

> would watch the tell-tale shames drift in
> (As if they were troves of treasure) not aloof,
> But with a famishing passion quick to grab

Meaning, and read on all the leaves of sin
Eternity's secret script, the saving proof.

The **"Effigies"** which follow are five portraits of isolated souls, individuals among "the proximate damned."
The first, which begins, "His glances were directive,
seemed to move / Pawns on a secret chessboard," has
the physical precision of a night-mare:

> When he was dying
> The pieces sauntered about the board
> Like lawless vagrants, and would not be
>   controlled.
> He would whisper 'Stop,'
> Starting awake, and weep to think they were free.

"Double Absence," another poem from this section of
the book, is, I believe, the first of Muir's poems which
concerns primarily a "real" scene, a specific time in a
specific place: moonrise one evening at Newbattle Abbey (the worker's college near Edinburgh where Muir
was Warden from 1950 until his Norton Professorship at
Harvard, 1955-1956). It is a beautiful poem, and it may
shock us with its reminder of how infrequently Muir
used the scenic realism characteristic of so much of the
best modern poetry. It is not that Muir disliked such
poetry, with its fresh observation of physical particulari-
ties which makes us see the world as new; it is merely
that for his imagination the remembered or the dreamed
scene usually had a greater reality than the immediately
observed one.

Throughout most of its pages, *One Foot in Eden* shows
a continuation and a deepening of the former strains. In
his making of memorable poems, Muir never, for long
at least, was willing to settle for half a world. He was
not the apostle of asceticism but of fulfillment. He desired both the mythical and the physical, the angels and
the animals, "the story and the fable." **"Day and Night"**
represents his central position:

> I wrap the blanket of the night
> About me, fold on fold on fold—
> And remember how as a child
> Lost in the newness of the light
> I first discovered what is old
> From the night and the soft night wind.
> For in the daytime all was new,
> Moving in light and in the mind
> All at once, thought, shape and hue.
> Extravagant novelty too wild
> For the new eyes of a child.
> The night, the night alone is old
> And showed me only what I knew,
> Knew, yet never had been told;
> A speech that from the darkness grew
> Too deep for daily tongues to say,
> Archaic dialogue of a few
> Upon the sixth or the seventh day.
> And shapes too simple for a place
> In the day's shrill complexity
> Came and were more natural, more
> Expected than my father's face
> Smiling across the open door,

> More simple than the sanded floor
> In unexplained simplicity.

> A man now, gone with time so long—
> My youth to myself grown fabulous
> Like an old land's memories, a song
> To trouble or to pleasure us—
> I try to fit that world to this,
> The hidden to the visible play,
> Would have them both, would nothing miss,
> Learn from the shepherd of the dark,
> Here in the light, the paths to know
> That thread the labyrinthine park,
> And the great Roman roads that go
> Striding across the untrodden day.

Muir's achievement in poetry and prose is larger than
the merely literary. He did not share in the modern attempts to deify poetry, or language, or even the human
imagination. Implicit in all of his works is the recognition that there are things more important than literature—life and love, the physical world, the individual
spirit within its body: those things in which the religious man recognizes the immediate work of God.
Muir's triumph was less in the technological realm of
communication than in the vastly more difficult realm
of sensitivity, perception, wisdom, the things which he
communicated. It was a triumph made possible only, in
the familiar paradox, by humility.

Ralph J. Mills, Jr. (essay date 1963)

SOURCE: "Eden's Gate: The Later Poetry of Edwin
Muir," in *The Personalist*, Vol. XLIV, No. 1, January,
1963, pp. 58-78.

[*In the following essay, Mills examines key subjects and
themes in Muir's later poetry.*]

It is difficult to think of Edwin Muir without calling to
mind those simple, lonely, and nearly anonymous figures populating so many of his poems. However modestly he spoke of his life in *An Autobiography* and elsewhere, it was, as Stephen Spender once remarked of it,
a pilgrimage, an interior journey which gave a fundamental spiritual meaning to his actual travels. Though
Muir traveled a good deal in his lifetime, in a certain
profound sense he never left the environment into which
he was born—his father's small, productive farm in the
midst of the Orkney Islands. When he was still young,
his father sold the farm and the family departed for the
mainland. The sudden introduction to the modern urban
world of Glasgow only superficially covered Muir's at-
tachment to the place of his origins; for the entire movement of his inner and outer life was an odyssey homeward bound: a return to those beginnings and an attempt
to understand them in terms of the larger patterns of
human existence. The poetry of Edwin Muir is a record
of his journey, and I have discussed some of its main
lines of development elsewhere.[1] But there remain the
poems of his homecoming, that is, the work of his later

years which gives a final shape to his writings, his life, and the vision embracing both. This work includes *One Foot in Eden* (1956) and the miscellaneous poems gathered from magazines and unpublished manuscripts and appended to the new edition of his *Collected Poems* (London: Faber, 1960) by the poet's widow, Willa Muir, and J. C. Hall.

A passage from his "Extracts from a Diary, 1937-1939" in *The Story and the Fable,* the initial version of his autobiography, helps to explain, through a fantasy on the disruptive experiences of his youth, the consciousness of time that is peculiarly Muir's own:

> I was born before the Industrial Revolution, and am now about two hundred years old. But I have skipped a hundred and fifty of them. I was really born in 1737, and until I was fourteen no time-accident happened to me. Then in 1751 I set out from Orkney for Glasgow. When I arrived I found it was not 1751, but 1901, and that a hundred and fifty years had been burned up in my two days' journey. But I myself was still in 1751, and remained there for a long time. All my life since I have been trying to overhaul that invisible leeway. No wonder I am obsessed with Time.

The gap between the industrial city and the primitive agrarian community is one the poet was never really able to draw closed. And that was not due to any lack of realism on Muir's part, but rather to his innate comprehension of the permanent, though often obscured, destiny which it is man's task to fulfill. It is impossible for me to quote here all of the copious material from *An Autobiography* which would demonstrate the fact that Muir's notion of the good life sprang first from the experience of his childhood years in the Orkneys, but I believe it is undeniably the case. That way of farm life was an ancient way, its rhythms and practices long embedded in human consciousness. Hardly touched by the swelling tides of commerce and technology, the farm families lived out their existence, performed their labors, within the bounds of their own culture and tradition—derived from "legend, folk-song, and the poetry and prose of the Bible"—something they had preserved because of their remoteness which most of Europe was rapidly losing. Inside this community, the life of the family provided the circle within which young Muir moved. The figures of father and mother, protective, loving and strong, recur in his poetry as representative of man and woman, the inhabitants of earth from time immemorial, mythical in stature yet perfectly human. The naturalness and uncomplicated beauty of this manner of life he later recognized as closest to the actual purpose of existence.

Speed and change were foreign to the Orkney atmosphere; so it seemed, Muir tells us, that life underwent no real alteration from day to day but was "only one day endlessly rising and setting." This spell imparted to Muir his sense of timelessness and immortality, later confirmed by dreams and visionary experiences. With Vaughan, Traherne, and Wordsworth, he views childhood as a repetition in the individual of primordial human innocence before the Fall. Adolescence begins to shatter the unity of the child's world, and he succumbs to guilt. In Muir's case, the dissolution of childish perceptions was aggravated by the shift from the Orkney farm to Glasgow. But that rural life stayed in memory, so that Muir's psychoanalysis in London years later returned him in dreams and images to the island landscape. Those dreams—many of them re-told in *An Autobiography*—appear to be a generative force behind Muir's decision to write poetry. Indeed, a number of the pieces from *First Poems* (1925) have their sources in dreams or trance-like visions to be found in the autobiography. From the dreams grew the poet's awareness of the dual nature of human existence: the "story"—the history of our daily lives and our personalities—and the "fable"—the religious and mythological drama of man known only fragmentarily in dreams or moments of revelation but involving each person in the whole human legend of Innocence, the Fall, a subsequent life in time, the quest for its meaning and for the lost earthly paradise. In the future lies the final restoration of man to his original state, his inheritance before the Fall. The vision of this end and beginning of all things occupies a prominent place in Muir's final poems.

From the earliest of Muir's poems on, we are made aware of the presence of a lost condition of life that belongs to man by right. But it is not fixed in its identity as Eden until Muir becomes more conscious of what he is looking for. The dreams and visions which were his, the accumulated experience of life, convinced him of a lack in our condition. Through his inner life, Muir was granted images of a wholeness and harmony essential to existence, but missing from it except in dream, myth, and religion. His late poems attempt to organize that vision of the world as it was intended to be; and they reach backward in time to the Creation and look forward to a day when things will be much the same as they were at the end of the earth's first week. Hints of this lost estate are spread over Muir's writings after 1926 and finally become explicit in *The Labyrinth* (1949), most obviously in a poem called "**The Transfiguration**" near the close of the book. Based on the memory of a dream,[2] this poem makes one of the most complete statements of Muir's faith concerning the meaning and destination of all forms of earthly life, and so prepares for the religious tone of the poems in *One Foot in Eden*. The poem, which is about the Second Coming, opens with a sudden resurgence of new life that circulates through every creature, through inanimate things, and simultaneously purges the old life:

> So from the ground we felt that virtue branch
> Through all our veins till we were whole, our
>   wrists
> As fresh and pure as water from a well,
> Our hands made new to handle holy things,
> The source of all our seeing rinsed and cleansed
> Till earth and light and water entering there
> Gave back to us the clear unfallen world.

What occurs is not a substitution of one world for another, a change in the nature of *things,* but a change in the nature of man. His blindness to reality drops like scales from his eyes; his senses truly commune with their objects, and these are found to be sacred and good in themselves, worth more than our careless use of them.

The arrival of "that virtue" is unexpected, freely given and freely received; the moment of its happening could be any point in time. True to his reason, the poet questions the vision in the poem. Is it merely an instant's hallucination,

> Or did we see that day the unseeable
> One glory of the everlasting world
> Perpetually at work, though never seen
> Since Eden locked the gate that's everywhere
> And nowhere?

While the location of Eden, as Muir knows, cannot be placed geographically unless it is in the landscape of heart or imagination, that does not affect the truth of the "fable." Instead, we understand how an essential area of man's inner life was sealed off by the Fall and has remained a forgotten territory. The changes which bring about a release may be spiritual, yet they happen not only in man but—as a result of his cleansed perception—in the earth itself. The first sign of change comes through the earth, making explicit man's ties with his physical surroundings. The impression given is one of total reconciliation, which is also the completion of everything according to its own nature:

> Yet the world
> We saw that day made this unreal, for all
> Was in its place. The painted animals
> Assembled there in gentle congregations,
> Or sought apart their leafy oratories,
> Or walked in peace, the wild and tame together,
> As if, also for them, the day had come.
> The shepherds' hovels shone, for underneath
> The soot we saw the stone clean at the heart
> As on the starting-day. The refuse heaps
> Were grained with that fine dust that made the
>   world;
> For he had said, 'To the pure all things are pure.'

Following this, murderers and outcasts, self-seekers and liars emerge from the shadows to join with the figure of Jesus who, in Muir's original dream as in the poem, appears in their midst. This momentary vision—for that is all the longer it lasts before familiar reality returns—evokes the end of life in time as we know it. Jesus comes, we are told, because "all mankind from end to end of the earth" has called Him "with one voice." The request is answered by purification of the created world and of human actions. Everything is forgiven, no one judged. Evil, I think Muir would say, flourishes in man through his existence in time, through the distortions of personality that time and circumstance devise to imprison the true self. In the final day of Muir's vision, that self attains freedom from the bonds time has put upon it; history is likewise undone:

> In our own time,
> Some say, or at a time when time is ripe.
> Then he will come, Christ the uncrucified,
> Christ the discrucified, his death undone,
> His agony unmade, his cross dismantled—
> Glad to be so—and the tormented wood
> Will cure its hurt ane grow into a tree
> In a green springing corner of young Eden,
> And Judas damned take his long journey
>   backward
> From darkness into light and be a child
> Beside his mother's knee, and the betrayal
> Be quite undone and never more be done.

The poem concludes in the idea of redemption and the reversal of history. Two things are of importance here and for the next decade in Muir's thought and art. First, Muir's apocalyptic vision sees the world made over, not destroyed—though there are a few exceptions to this—and second, the substance of such poems is prophetic: they disclose a condition which does not yet exist, and can only be realized poetically.

The resolution of human destiny is the mystery Muir sought to uncover in all his poems; but he never forgot that the destiny was a common one, its secrets were universal. He never indulged himself, for that reason, in a system of private symbols and criticized Yeats and Rilke on that score. Muir was closer to his own description of Hölderlin, whose poetic "meanings . . . seem to arise as a direct response to a vision." Thus Muir is never at pains to expound the figures of his verse for the reader: they are constant and themselves. Life is not woven by this poet into a complex network of mythology and psychology; it is experienced as a mythology, but one which is universally recognizable when seen. Muir everywhere withdraws his personality from his poems and tries to let his vision stand alone, rendered as pure as possible. The images, meanings, and associations on which the poetry depends are part of a fund of inherited knowledge in the western world.

Love, faith, the sense of mystery, of the unfathomable heart of existence, and the persistent feeling that time and the world as we daily experience them reveal a fundamental absence in ourselves, a twist in our natures, constitute the central "discoveries" Muir makes—discoveries, he insists, that men in each generation need to make over again. From them his religious convictions emerge, his awareness that what man gathers in the way of understanding comes from "the Source of the mystery itself, by the means which religious people call Grace." And the later poems, in keeping with Muir's attitude, are religious and create images of the world in its beginning simplicity and harmony—of the flaw which initiated man's condition but made its fulfillment greater for all of that—and proffer the figures of myth and Bible, and the divine figure of Christ, as permanent depictions of the "fable" itself.

The assumed order of things on which Muir calls in his poems is a spiritual order that likewise invests the concrete world of people and things. Whatever or whoever appears in a poem, a swallow or wasp, Franz Kafka or Prometheus, each stands for itself or himself—with, of course, the values attached to such a one. The sonnet, **"Milton,"** which opens *One Foot in Eden,* displays this practice; for the physical and spiritual ordeals of the 17th century poet serve as a paradigm of the human situation as Muir sees it:

> Milton, his face set fair for Paradise,
> And knowing that he and Paradise were lost
> In separate desolation, bravely crossed
> Into his second night and paid his price,
> There towards the end he to the dark tower came
> Set square in the gate, a mass of blackened stone
> Crowned with vermillion fiends like streamers
>   blown
> From a great funnel filled with roaring flame.
>
> Shut in his darkness, these he could not see,
> But heard the steely clamour known too well
> On Saturday nights in every street in Hell.
> Where, past the devilish din, could Paradise be?
> A footstep more, and his unblinded eyes
> Saw far and near the fields of Paradise.

The action here is an abbreviated form of man's pilgrimage or of the later stages of the "fable": the passage through time; the trial and suffering by evil; and a revelation of a dimension past time which occurs with the same miraculous flash that begins **"The Transfiguration."** Muir's sonnet introduces a group of poems which seek to renew the eternal correspondence of the human, the mythical, and the divine stories within the compass of their figurative language.

In **"The Animals"** and **"The Days,"** poems following **"Milton,"** Muir explores poetically the themes of *The Book of Genesis*: Creation and the Fall and the present order of the universe. Man, the poet believes, is responsible for the fundamental breach dividing him from creation and Creator. Thus these poems maintain a double focus: the condition of the world before man flawed its unity and the human estate as it now is stand side by side. The animals, who populated earth previous to man, remain unsullied by the Fall; only we have changed our order of existence:

> They do not live in the world,
> Are not in time and space.
> From birth to death hurled
> No words do they have, not one
> To plant a foot upon,
> Were never in any place.

These creatures are granted a legendary or archetypal status; for them

> All is new and near
> In the unchanging Here
> Of the fifth great day of God,
> That shall remain the same,
> Never shall pass away.

This is one of Muir's finest revelations of the difference time makes in the universe. The Creation, which took place outside the temporal process introduced by the Fall, holds its objects in eternal poise, though man has been separated from those unchangeable origins by his defection. That timeless state which the animals still inhabit lies beyond us yet passes its imprint from generation to generation like a marvelous scripture upon brain and flesh, and is pictured in our dreams; that state is the Eden where Muir's poetic quest ends.

This theme enlarges in **"The Days"** to cover the whole week of Creation, and the poem notes in detail the present relation of man to that pristine condition. Starting with the "World" from whom "the seven days came," Muir elaborates in lyric fashion the activities of Creation, the "inhuman burgeoning," the gradual emergence of land, forest and meadow, the awesome birth of beasts, then man. A decisive break occurs with man's appearance, and the remainder of the poem turns on the situation of human life as it has been since the Fall. The images following this break intermingle the two conditions of being and so illustrate the discrepancy between a unified and a fallen order. The poem concludes in a desire to achieve once more the fullness of the seventh day of the first week:

> And now see in the sun
> The mountains standing clear in the third day
> (Where they shall always stay)
> And thence a river run,
> Threading, clear cord of water, all to all:
> The wooded hill and the cattle in the meadow,
> The tall wave breaking on the high sea-wall,
> The people at evening walking,
> The crescent shadow
> Of the light-built bridge, the hunter stalking
> The flying quarry, each in a different morning,
> The fish in the billow's heart, the man with the net,
> The hungry swords crossed in the cross of
>   warning,
> The lion set
> High on the banner, leaping into the sky,
> The seasons playing
> Their game of sun and moon and east and west,
> The animal watching man and bird go by,
> The women praying
> For the passing of this fragmentary day
> Into the day where all are gathered together,
> Things and their names, in the storm's and the
>   lightning's nest,
> The seventh great day and the clear eternal
>   weather.

Perfection and imperfection blended; these two overlapping orders emphasize the disunity of existence. A moment of wholeness at the end of the poem promises a final day of reconciliation when the "fable" will reach conclusion by a return to its beginning—the purity and completeness of the Creation week. Opposition and alteration would then be unknown; everything would stand forth, entirely itself, in the timeless present we call eternity.

Still, the stress falls, in Muir's poetry, on *human* experience. The earth does not vanish into an ethereal paradise, but assumes its true character, what it was intended to be. Muir's province is the human; he never denies it. How else should we explain the poems on *Genesis;* the story of Abraham's wanderings and those of his sons; the fully human emotions that run through the portrayals of Orpheus, Telemachus, and Prometheus; or the human mission Jesus accomplishes by His suffering and example—the donation of sacred meaning to flesh and life in the act of Incarnation? This abiding sense of the purification of man's existence so that it may be lived as it was conceived to be lived stayed with Muir to the last. One of his most beautiful poems, **"The Brothers,"** composed very late in life, embodies the theme of purification in a dream which is also a vision of the transfigured human self. Unlike Muir's more universal representations, this one has a poignant personal note: the brothers are the poet's own, and were lost to him at an early age and in great agony.

> Last night I watched my brothers play,
> The gentle and the reckless one,
> In a field two yards away.
> For half a century they were gone
> Beyond the other side of care
> To be among the peaceful dead.
> Even in a dream how could I dare
> Interrogate that happiness
> So wildly spent yet never less?
> For still they raced about the green
> And were like two revolving suns;
> A brightness poured from head to head,
> So strong I could not see their eyes
> Or look into their paradise.
> What were they doing, the happy ones?
> Yet where I was they once had been.

The barrier between the two worlds has real substance, yet we are painfully conscious, along with Muir, that the place his brothers inhabit in a state of endless joy does not differ much from our familiar world except by certain qualities present there. We cannot fully define these qualities, though we view their manifestation in the boys' elation, their play, and in the blinding light that wraps them round. When Muir compares the brothers' appearance now with their previous earthly appearance, the dream expires:

> I thought, How could I be so dull,
> Twenty thousand days ago,
> Not to see they were beautiful?
> I asked them, Were you really so
> As you are now, that other day?
> And the dream was soon away.
>
> For then we played for victory
> And not to make each other glad.
> A darkness covered every head,
> Frowns twisted the original face,
> And through that mask we could not see
> The beauty and the buried grace.
>
> I have observed in foolish awe
> The dateless mid-days of the law

> And seen indifferent justice done
> By everyone on everyone.
> And in a vision I have seen
> My brothers playing on the green.

The two spheres of being could not differ more. A world in which games are played for the winner's satisfaction is a world dominated by the egoism and selfish needs of the personality. The burning suns used to describe the boys suggest a self-possession and unity of being which the darkened, ravaged faces had formerly disguised. Like Blake in "The Echoing Green," Muir envisages the innocent in the midst of games that seem a ritual of the blessed, and so a celebration of earthly life as it was meant to be—a ceaseless interchange of love and joy. Death does not preclude this state, for the boys continue to live and remain, in some enigmatic but profound sense, participants in the world, though not the world as we fumblingly try to cope with it.

The same innocent joy to which the brothers gain access receives legendary form in **"The Other Oedipus,"** a remarkable poem depicting the fallen king in a state contrary to conventional notions of him. Torture and suffering, the burden of inexorable fate, have driven Oedipus and his companions through the haze of madness and death into another dimension where they attain a divine foolishness akin to the brothers' happy game:

> Remembered on the Peloponnesian roads,
> He and his serving-boy and his concubine,
> White-headed and light-hearted, their true wits
>   gone
> Past the last stroke of time into a day
> Without a yesterday or a to-morrow,
> A brightness laid like a blue lake around them,
> Or endless field to play or linger in.

This is another emblematic image of the paradisiacal condition; and the key word of the poem is "storyless"—the attribute of Oedipus and his friends according to Muir. "Story," we recall, is the history of the individual personality in the broken world of time. Oedipus has passed through his "story" and into the final phase of the "fable," where he presently exists.

The metamorphoses undergone by the persons in these and other poems of Muir must be seen as exemplary of the larger return of man to his original situation of innocence and freedom. Thus Eden is the culminating vision for Muir, but one which the poetry only approximates. Eden lies in the midst of every labyrinth and maze, favorite symbol in this poet's work, and at the end of each road or way. When Muir reaches the gate to this abandoned kingdom—that forbidden territory of the soul in which God can be met—and we with him, there we are halted and forced to spend our days. Such is the lesson taught us in **"Outside Eden,"** where the matter is directly put:

> A few lead in their harvest still
> By the ruined wall and broken gate.

Far inland shines the radiant hill.
Inviolable the empty gate,
Impassable the gaping wall;
And the mountain over all.

These relics and the landscape belong to the first days of the world, and to a different situation for man. In spite of their dilapidation, wall and gate serve as effective bulwarks to entry: the problems here are spiritual, not physical or geographical. The landscape beyond the wall was lost with Adam's sin. It is also the center of creation; the image of the mountain is that of "the Sacred Mountain—where heaven and earth meet . . . situated at the center of the world," as Mircea Eliade describes this universal religious symbol.[3] The story of the Creation and the Fall is a conscious memory of those who live near the "ruined gate" and await the conclusion of history, when the gate will swing open again and man will be released from his sentence. The inhabitants of this land (they are much like the Orkney Islanders Muir knew) are simple and devout people who accept their human status with a durable faith:

Guilt is next door to innocence.
So here this people choose to live
And never think to travel hence,
Nor learn to be inquisitive,
Nor browse in sin's great library,
The single never-ending book
That fills the shelves of all the earth.
There the learned enquirers look
And blind themselves to see their face.
But these live in the land of birth
And count all else an idle grace.

The concluding lines of the poem lead the reader as far as poetry can *within the limits of the human situation;* that is, Muir extends, through his imagery, man's possibilities in his circumstance as far as they will go. Any further extension would sever human relations with the world and make of the poetic act a sham gnostic venture, the presentation of a false reality. Muir refuses such deception, for man's destiny is intimately linked with the earth. Eden, with man in it, belongs to the divine foundation of things. Man and his natural habitation grow together: each shares the given burden of imperfection; each is veined with the ore of lost unity and perfection. So the poem must finish at the edge of time:

Their griefs are all in memory grown
As natural as a weathered stone.
Their troubles are a tribute given
Freely while gazing at the hill.
Such is their simplicity,
Standing on earth, looking at heaven.

That is Muir's complete statement of a common human heritage. His visionary poems, such as **"The Transfiguration," "The Brothers," "The Road," "Orpheus' Dream," "The Horses,"** and others, momentarily reach over the periphery of our condition to retrieve hints, glimpses, and images of its ultimate outcome. All reflect the "fable," but in various ways. Some provide the beginnings of the "fable" as it has come down to us in the Bible; these poems have a basis in tradition. But the visionary poems, though universal or archetypal in their symbolism, emerge from the poet's direct experience in dreams and trances of mythical proportion. In either case, the poem draws us back into the unseen movements of the "fable" as I have hastily outlined it. Since, as Muir says himself, the "fable" cannot be fully known because we are living it, its revelations must come to us clothed in various garb.

The "story," we know, consists of the life of the person in the world under the rule of time. Yet, undesirable as our sort of existence may seem at times, with its pain, cruelties, and losses, there is no doubt that the "fable" could not exist without it. If the original Fall had not occurred, Muir says in the title poem of *One Foot in Eden,* man would never have learned to value the spiritual possessions that are his. The agonies of existence provoke human attainments unthinkable in a universe lacking the imperfection stamped upon ours:

But famished field and blackened tree
Bear flowers in Eden never known.
Blossoms of grief and charity
Bloom in those darkened fields alone.
What had Eden ever to say
Of hope and faith and pity and love
Until was buried all its day
And memory found its treasure trove?
Strange blessings never in Paradise
Fall from these beclouded skies.

Thus Muir sees the meaning, which the experience of the "story" lends its hidden counterpart. Without the long journey through the wastes of time occupying the poet's attention from *Variations on a Time Theme* (1934) through the poems on the wanderings of Abraham in his later books, there would be nothing to gain, no kingdom to seek, no wrong to redeem and undo, no virtues to be achieved. The Fall and the exile resulting from it seem to Muir portions of the divine means of conferring a greatness on man not otherwise obtainable.

The threat to life as it might be, to the person and to society, in Muir's poetry consists of an illusory reversal of the good, or of the desired end. In another sense, we might say this illusion dominates wherever and whenever the "story" is taken for the whole of reality. Travelling along those roads as a pilgrim, which is what we find ourselves doing when we read Muir, we notice how false appearances many times put us off the track. A road seems to lead directly to the lost Eden, but then it carefully guides the traveler right past his goal. The world that Theseus discovers in **"The Labyrinth"** consists of an endless series of rooms opening into one another. He is rescued only by a vision of the gods who transcend this elaborate deception. Even the last lines of **"The Incarnate One"** insist upon the blind alleys, distorting mirrors, idols and unreal gods that blot out any accurate observation of reality:

The generations tell
  Their personal tale: the One has far to go
Past the mirages and the murdering snow.

Illusion and abstraction, rooted far down in man and
nature, prevent the return to Eden's gate, corrupt the
visions of transfiguration into ideals of power, isolation
and hate. If we examine Muir's later poems with any
care, we quickly realize that many of them are concerned solely with these illusions and their outcome: the
direct antithesis of the poet's belief in a lasting blessedness and in the completion of the "fable."

The problem of evil haunts much of the poetry Muir
wrote near the end of his life. His preoccupation with
the evil influence of perversity, illusion, and deceit is
evident in some of his best poems of these years:
**"Antichrist," "After a Hypothetical War," "After
1984," "The Last War," "The Ballad of Everyman,"
"Nightmare of Peace," "The Day before the Last
Day."** Muir must have been acutely conscious that the
way of the "fable"—its substance and reality—would
seem impotent and negligible if it were not set against
the other, more familiar reality of our present-day
existence: a perpetual nightmare of massive, inhuman
historical and political forces lumbering across the
face of the earth, decorated with the pennants of ideology and belief. Gentle, humble man that he was,
Muir struck out in old age with all his poetic strength
at these forces.

The lies and deceptive appearances created by the Antichrist in the poem of that title assume even more tangible form in **"The Ballad of Everyman,"** where peace
and the dove, as we employ them in our political strategies, are mendacities—an empty word, a stuffed image.
Everyman stands alone in the ballad as the repository of
those virtues of simplicity, honesty, justice, and love
which now have lost their currency:

Stout Everyman set out to meet
  His brothers gathered from every land,
And make a peace for all the earth
  And link the nations hand to hand.

He came into a splendid hall
  And there he saw a motionless dove
Swung from the roof, but for the rest
  Found little sign of peace or love.

Two days he listened patiently,
  But on the third got up and swore:
'Nothing but slaves and masters here:
  Your dove's a liar and a whore.

Disguised police on the high seats,
  In every corner pimps and spies.
Good-bye to you; I'd rather be
  With friends in Hell or Paradise.'

While this beginning section points the poem in the
direction of a contemporary parable on international
relations, the next part finds the poet speaking in the

first person and narrating a dream. The dream links this
portion of the poem to Muir's other visionary poems,
many of which take place in sleep or at its borders.
Mythological elements mingle with the curious but inexorable laws of the dream-work to provide a vision
horrifying in its outcome:

Night after night I dream a dream
  That I am flying through the air
On some contraption old and lame
  As Icarus' unlucky chair.

And first I see the empty fields—
  No sign of Everyman anywhere—
And then I see a playing field
  And two great sides in combat there.

And then they change into a beast
  With iron hoofs and scourging tail
That treads a bloody harvest down
  In readiness for the murdering flail.

And then a rash of staring eyes
  Covers the beast, back, sides and head,
And stare as if remembering
  Something that long ago was said.

And the beast is gone, and nothing's there
  But murderers standing in a ring,
And at the center Everyman.
  I never saw so poor a thing.

Curses upon the traitorous men
  Who brought our good friend Everyman down,
And murder peace to bring their peace,
  And flatter and rob the ignorant clown.

Muir envisages in these stanzas—and more specifically
in **"The Day before the Last Day"**—something like a
false apocalypse, for the beast is not sent to punish the
unregenerate world but to destroy the vestiges of truth
and honor left there. The death of Everyman at the
hands of this monster ushers in—we cannot avoid the
implication—an age dictated by lies and meaningless
abstractions. The lost Eden is buried beyond recovery;
the "story" triumphs and earth belongs to the "masters"
of the poem's opening section.

But this picture of human destiny is a false one, an
extension of human folly. Frequently, Muir's poems
about wars to come and the police state are poems of
purgation; that is, they conduct the reader through
periods of self-willed, lacerating experience to a closing outlook of calm and the restoration of perennial
virtues. **"After 1984," "The Last War,"** and **"The
Horses"** are examples of a revival of human responsibility and simplicity following conflict and catastrophe of grand proportions. Commitment to the "fable"
lies deep in man's nature and grows out of faith and
feeling; once made, it must be kept. Muir's later poems draw close to the boundary of that sacred space
where the "fable" will reach fulfillment, a space
locked within each person and at the center of every
created thing. How we shall step over that boundary

is not clear, but that we will finally do so is asserted in many poems. We can only live out the "fable"; accept the way which, in the poet's words, "leads on."

In what is apparently the last poem he worked upon, Muir contemplates briefly the meaning of his pilgrimage, the voices that spoke within him as he went, and, in a glance, the journey's finish—that moment when the barriers fall, when image and reflection, object and shadow, move together and are one:

> I have been taught by dreams and fantasies
> Learned from the friendly and the darker
>   phantoms
> And got great knowledge and courtesy from the
>   dead
> Kinsmen and kinswomen, ancestors and friends
> But from two mainly
> Who gave me birth.
>
> Have learned and drunk from that unspending
>   good
> These founts whose learned windings keep
> My feet from straying
> To the deadly path
>
> That leads into the sultry labyrinth
> Where all is bright and the flare
> Consumes and shrivels
> The moist fruit.
>
> And there dry at last time takes away
> And taking leaves all things in their right place
> An image of forever
> One and whole.
>
> And now that time grows shorter, I perceive.
> That Plato's is the truest poetry,
> And that these shadows
> Are cast by the true.

The Eden whose radiance and beauty everywhere touch the poems has a counterpart in Plato's realm of ideas. But both these worlds exist beyond the capacity of words to call them up except in metaphors and fragments, in momentary glimpses that are mere approximations. The eternal harmony of beings and things in that condition, as Muir was aware, constitutes its own language, not only the "truest" but the purest poetry.

NOTES

[1] In *Accent,* Winter 1959. The present essay extends some of the material taken up in that more general account of Muir.

[2] *An Autobiography* (London: Hogarth Press, 1954), pp. 54-57.

[3] *The Myth of the Eternal Return,* trans. W. R. Trask (New York: Pantheon, 1954), p. 12.

Sister M. Joselyn (essay date 1963)

SOURCE: "Herbert and Muir: Pilgrims of Their Age," in *Renascence: A Critical Journal of Letters,* Vol. XV, No. 3, Spring, 1963, pp. 127-32.

[*In the following essay, Joselyn identifies similarities in the poetry of George Herbert and Muir.*]

When R. P. Blackmur described Edwin Muir as a "Herbert without a parish or a doctrine or any one temple to construct," he characterized both the negative and positive qualities of Muir's religious verse. Although almost all of Muir's poetry may be characterized as religious in a broad sense, much of it is not religious in the same way that Herbert's work is, for it possesses characteristics which are distinctly modern. Eight poems in the Evergreen edition of the *Collected Poems* demonstrate the resemblances as well as the differences of the two poets and provide an accurate illustration of the peculiar amalgam of seventeenth century and contemporary religious sensibility which we see in Muir.

It is easy to list the surface resemblances between Muir and Herbert: tendency toward paradox, prevailing sweetness of tone, use of narrative situations to reveal moral or spiritual truths, self-conscious dialogue with the Deity, frequent use of the quatrain, simple diction, and so on. Perhaps the greatest difference between the poets lies in the degree of certainty with which each is able to close off the dialogue with conscience—or God. To put it another way, each poet catches a certain amount of recalcitrant experience in his religious net, but one net has much larger meshes than the other. The man who finds it harder to catch all that he sees in any net is of course Muir, the modern man.

Muir's **"The Prize"** and Herbert's "Peace" illustrate both the similarities and the differences in the poets' general religious feelings. Each poet is both probing the meaning of life and dramatizing the examination as a search. Muir queries, "Did we come here . . . / That we might win the prize that took us so?"; Herbert says, "I sought thee in a secret cave, / And ask'd, if Peace were there." But while Herbert unhesitatingly terms this goal of all life Peace, Muir's protagonist never succeeds in naming it. "Was it some ordinary sight, a flower. . . . Or was it one sole thing, a certain door / Set in a wall, a half-conjectured scene . . . ?" Muir's quester encounters many false answerers. Herbert's also progresses through several alternatives, but he finally receives a sure directive when "a reverend good old man" provides him with wheat and the counsel to make bread of it, for "that repose / And peace, which ev'ry where / With so much earnestness you do pursue / Is onely there." For Muir, however, though the existence of the "prize" is certain ("that far within the maze serenely lies"), we "Wander the countless roads" and we "forget, lost in the countless names." The modern man's search for ultimate meaning remains open-ended and tends only to affirm the search itself, but Herbert almost by formula locates value within the context of theological and revealed beliefs.

Muir's **"The Good Man in Hell"** presents a kind of religious fable for which one would instinctively (but mistakenly, as it turns out) expect to find a counterpart in Herbert, for the theme of the magnificence of love—its power in the form of hope to disrupt even hell—would appear to be as congenial to the older poet as to Muir. Moreover, the poem's limpid quatrains, its use of a curious narrative to illuminate a spiritual truth, its strategically ordered concrete detail ("Hell's little wicket gate," "the curse climb slowly to his throat," "Forcing his praying tongue to run by rote"), its paradoxes ("Or speak the truth only a stranger sees"; "Kindle a little hope in hopeless Hell") are much in Herbert's vein. But what is not like Herbert is that the poem's final insight places the source of love or hope within "the good man," rather than in God. Thus the poem's resolution comes about not in terms of Christ or of an eternal truth in the form of a dogma but in a vision which, if taken seriously, annihilates the Christian categories: "One doubt of evil would bring down such a grace, / Open such a gate, all Eden would enter in, / Hell be a place like any other place, / And love and hate and life and death begin." The last stanza of **"The Good Man in Hell"** may indeed be read simply as a hyperbolic description of love's power and thus a further classification of "watch beside Hell's little wicket gate / In patience for the first ten thousand years." It also strongly suggests that vis-à-vis Christian terms, heaven and hell are only extreme forms of man's ordinary existence. By locating both terms of extreme experience though retaining traditional names for them, Muir creates the curiously nightmarish quality so characteristic of contemporary vision. Both Muir's heaven and hell are more impressively terrifying than Herbert's could ever be because they explode the traditional extra-personal categories and place all sanctions within one unaided and undefended human being. While the tone of Muir's poem is quietly, even sweetly, reflective, as is often the case in Herbert, it is also halting, tentative, hypothetical: "Would he. . . . Would he at last . . . ?" Even the "revolution" rests on a statement of something less than fact—"*would* bring such a grace."

Two Muir poems which probe into the human situation in more particular terms, **"Sorrow"** and **"Comfort in Self-Despite,"** evoke strong remembrances of Herbert. Though there is no exact parallel in the older poet, the most cursory reading of **"Sorrow"** convinces that such a poem could not have been written had not Herbert written before him. The peculiarly modest sweetness of the self-debate, the lowering sense that terrible cosmic issues are being joined behind the poem's decorous façade; the insistence that both sides of the antinomy must be resolved accompanied by an understanding that the resolution will be accomplished at the cost of anguish; the characteristic disposition of the rhythm in small, falling cadences ("Until I have it so, or so, / And want it so")—all these are Herbert's. There are many poems in Herbert which deal with the feelings of a soul wrapped in grief, for whom indeed suffering has become a permanent condition, and many which measure accurately man's folly and sottishness, but very few of these, in contrast with Muir's "I cannot be resigned. . . ." present a final vision of life as dark or permanently out of joint. Even in what is perhaps Herbert's gloomiest poem, "The Pilgrimage," the soul does continue on its journey; though certain of death it is also certain of things beyond death that are at least no worse. For Herbert, sorrow is separation from God; for Muir, the modern man, it is the absence of joy that he *ought to have*.

Muir's **"Comfort in Self-Despite"** invites comparison with Herbert's "The Method" and has affinities with "Nature" and "Unkindness." In "The Method" and in **"Comfort in Self-Despite"** the protagonist conducts a self-examination; he analyzes a state of disequilibrium and distress and tries to ascertain its cause—Muir, in relation to a friend, Herbert, as might be expected, in relation to God. Both are concerned with moral implications as well as psychological analysis and both ask, can any good come from this state of revulsion? Both answer in terms of a paradox, Muir finding that remorse for carping at a friend leads him to remembrance of "The pure and touching good no taunt could kill," Herbert instructing himself, "Down with thy knees, up with thy voice. / Seek pardon first, and God will say, / *Glad heart rejoyce*."

In Muir's **"Sorrow"** and in four similar poems of Herbert ("The Crosse," "The Answer," "Employment (1)," "Affliction (IV)") the poets dramatize man's confrontation not with a particular suffering but with his essential human misery, a condition, or more likely the condition, of existence. Muir's confrontation is conducted in solely human terms, but Herbert's poems show several gradations of attitude from naturalism to a supernatural view of man's dilemma. Actually, **"Sorrow"** begins at a stage of experience after the confrontation; Muir knows he must come to terms with the pains of the human situation and is seeking a way to do so: "Sorrow, / Be you my second trade. / I'll learn the workman's skill / And mould the mass of ill. . . . " But Herbert customarily begins by representing his pain in concrete detail, calling himself "Broken in pieces, all asunder," "A thing forgot," "no link of thy great chain," "in all a weak disabled thing," and asserting that "These contrarieties crush me: these crosse actions / Dow winde a rope about, and cut my heart." Next, both poets attempt a stoic solution as a way of coming to terms with life's ills. Indeed, this is the only alternative Muir exploits, telling himself he must make a "pact with sorrow" and "wring from sorrow's pay / Wealth joy would soon toss away—/ Till both are balanced. . . . " Herbert's attempted stoicism takes two forms, a riddling one in which he declares that if his friends wish to characterize him as an "exhalation," he has "one reply, / Which they that know the rest, know more than I"; and a kind of Christian stoicism representing less than his usual joyous acceptance of God's doings: "since these thy contradictions / Are properly a cross felt by thy Sonne, / With but foure words, my words, *Thy will be done.*"

But in the conclusion of **"Sorrow,"** Muir abandons stoicism, showing by the qualifier "If it were only so . . ." that he never did believe in it. In the end, there is too much pain in the world, and Muir cannot resign himself, "Knowing that we were made / By joy to drive joy's trade. . . ." Herbert suffers no less, but in two of the four poems attains a full Christian affirmation and acceptance of the meaning of earthly woes. He always prays first for God's help ("dissolve the knot, / As the sunne scatters by his light / All the rebellions of the night"), certain that it will be forthcoming; then "these powers, which work for grief" shall "Labour thy praise, and my relief, / With care and courage building me, / Till I reach heav'n, and much more, thee."

In **"Twice-Done, Once-Done"** and in Herbert's "The Holdfast" the poets concern themselves with the individual man's predicament and with his past, trying to relate these two realities. Both study man in relation to Adam, with the crucial difference that for Herbert Christ intervenes between himself and the first parent.

Herbert's sonnet opens with one of his recurring topics, how to be virtuous, but Muir's eight quatrains plunge at once into a presentation of the circular or cyclic aspects of man's history, which turns out to be not so much a repetition or a recapitulation as a solidarity; ultimately there is one existence. Eliot-like, Muir sees that the past and the future exist only in the present (though Muir does not reverse the axiom), and that goal and process are one—"Yet we the latest born are still / The first ones and the last," for "first and last is every way, / And first and last each soul, / And first and last the passing day, / And first and last the goal." Since existence is solidarity, says Muir, let us "Abolish the ancient custom" and stop blaming Eve for the primordial wrong; is it not simply a fact that "Many a woman since Eve was made / Has seen the world is young, / Many and many a time obeyed / The legend-making tongue"? Also commenting on the moral plane is the curious, seemingly irrelevant central stanza of the poem in which Muir prays Father Adam and Mother Eve to "Make this pact with me: / Teach me, teach me to believe, / For to believe's to be." Here again, Muir is naturalizing or secularizing the myth. To be is to believe in the self, but we can only be what we remember and on account of our remembrance, which has already determined us; thus, literally, "Nothing yet was ever done / Till it was done again, / And no man was ever one / Except through dead men."

Herbert's speculations lead him to Adam in a less direct manner than Muir's, and are prefaced by two paradoxes—"to have nought is ours, not [only] to confesse / That we have nought," and all things are "more ours by being his [God's]." This is very close to Muir's human-solidarity insight, but is placed in an explicitly Christian

context by the qualifying and concluding statement which immediately follows in Herbert's sonnet: "What Adam had, and forfeited for all, / Christ keepeth now, who cannot fail or fall." Herbert's belief would paraphrase Muir into the Christian paradox that "Nothing yet was ever done until it was done by Christ, and no man was ever one except through Christ." When Christ became the new Adam, Adam—in himself and in all the redeemed—became Christ.

In the last three poems of Muir which we shall consider, **"The Intercepter," "The Way,"** and **"The Law,"** the poet introduces God more plainly, and it is God in some of the various Herbertian guises of hunter, haunter, preceptor, lover, and host. In Herbert, God can play these roles simultaneously (indeed the typical "plot" of a Herbert poem centers in the protagonist's attempt to determine which role God is playing at a given moment) or successively, as in peripety, but in Muir's poems, God tends to play only one role at a time. Perhaps this is a way of saying that the conceits of Muir's religious verse tend to operate on the verbal level alone, and not simultaneously on the verbal and ontological (or theological) levels, as do Herbert's. Thus **"The Intercepter,"** which presents the most shadowy and rudimentary version of a personal God, introduces the deity in the guise of a nay-sayer only, a kind of Puritan conscience writ large, which turns out in the rather inept closing quatrain to be only the protagonist's conscience after all. In tone, **"The Intercepter"** is cool, moderate, even detached, lacking the petulancy of Herbert when he confronts a God he does not care for, but also lacking Herbert's loving, paradoxical reconciliation with the haunter-hunter-lover. Muir never threatens to "change the service, and go seek / Some other master out," but neither is he capable of the triumphant Herbertian *cri de cœur,* "Ah my deare God! though I am clean forgot, / Let me not love thee, / If I love thee not."

"The Way," which has certain affinities with Auden's "O Where Are You Going," resembles much more Herbert's "The Pilgrimage." Using the traditional figure of a journey as an image of the spiritual life, both Herbert and Muir narrate in first person the encounters and uncertainties of the way. Neither poet can tell how the journey ends, for in terms of the allegory neither has completed the way. For once, however, it is Herbert who ends on the somberer note: having heard the cry *"None goes that way / and lives,"* the traveller adds, "If that be all . . . / After so foul a journey death is fair." Muir concludes simply, "The road leads on." The poems differ also in the fact that Muir directly addresses his account to a "Friend," while Herbert narrates to a general audience, although at one time he cries, "Alas my King! / Can both the way and end be tears?"

The Muir poem which in some respects most resembles Herbert and at the same time best speaks for the modern religious sensibility is **"The Law,"** written in four stanzas of looser idiom than Muir customarily uses and revolving around a series of paradoxes which both provide structural form and define the themes. Muir opens his poem with an apostrophe to God under three names, Law, Good, and Truth, at the same time defining both God and man by means of a negative relationship between them: "my Law / Which I serve not," "my Good / Which I prize not," "my Truth / Which I seek not." The next stanza, which reaches a level of exalted awe rare in Muir's religious verse, details the human-divine relationship in terms of man's inevitable failure to serve a God to whom he can never be adequate. In the third stanza, again speaking paradoxically, Muir considers man's positive failures, his "disservices," suggesting that good and evil can be identified only in terms of each other. The last stanza of the poem carries this paradox to its furthest extent in the assertion, "If I could hold complete / . . . The wrong side of Heaven, / O then I should know in not knowing / My truth is my error."

Characteristically, Muir makes a close approach to God, almost a capitulation, and then retreats, this time into a conceit expressing a profound respect for skepticism, rather than into naturalism. In Herbert's "The Reprisall," the soul is as awed as Muir's at the spectacle of how God outdoes man, and also questions what part sin can have in this relationship of overpowering love. But Herbert's typical gesture is one of repentant love, and his final conceit states a theological truth: "though I can do nought / Against thee, in thee I will overcome / The man, who once against thee fought." Several other Herbert poems closely resemble **"The Law,"** especially "The Call" ("Such a Way, as gives us breath: / Such a Truth, as ends all strife; / Such a Life, as killeth death"), the lovely lyric "Discipline," and "Love I," a sonnet ("Immortal love, . . . / Sprung from that beautie which can never fade; / How hath man parcel'd out thy glorious name. . . . ")

In a verse generally so impeccably one with its thought that it almost ceases to be art, Edwin Muir has well represented the modern man of religious sensibility, speaking in a new, existential voice which has also affinities with the great seventeenth-century metaphysicals. Muir's journey, as David Galler remarks, has taken him from the "equivocal ignominy of non-election" (sonnet to Kafka) towards the realization that non-election is neither equivocal nor ignominious. In the end, it is not a journey Herbert would—or could—have taken, though his voice echoes in Muir's.

Elgin W. Mellown (essay date 1964)

SOURCE: "The Development of A Criticism: Edwin Muir and Franz Kafka," in *Comparative Literature*, Vol. 16, No. 3, Fall, 1964, pp. 310-21.

[*In the following essay, Mellown traces Muir's influence as a translator and critic of the works of Franz Kafka.*]

The Growth of Franz Kafka's reputation in England and America has been studied by several writers,[1] yet only passing attention has been given to Edwin and Willa Muir, the translators who brought his works before the English-reading public. They not only translated Kafka's major writings, but also found publishers for them in England, while Muir's criticism helped to advance the reputation of the novelist. This essay is an examination of his criticism in order to show how its changes and developments afford an insight into Kafka criticism in general.

Edwin Muir, born in the Orkney Islands in 1887, left school at the age of fourteen and, until 1919, worked as a clerk in and around Glasgow, meanwhile educating himself as best he could.[2] In 1913 he began contributing poems, essays, and aphorisms to the London *New Age*. On the advice of A. R. Orage, editor of the newspaper, he studied Nietzsche, reading the philosopher in the translation edited by Dr. Oscar Levy; his early devotion to the German writer may have been partly responsible for his subsequent interest in the German language. In 1919 Muir married Willa Anderson, M.A. in classics from St. Andrews and a teacher in a London college. Encouraged by his success in writing for the *New Age* (a collection of his aphorisms from the weekly newspaper had been published in 1918),[3] Muir decided to make journalism his profession, and he and his wife moved to London. He soon became the assistant editor of the *New Age;* but within two years he found he could support himself by free-lance journalism, and he and his wife went to central Europe.

Unlike other "expatriates" of the period, they made their life on the continent an education, learning languages and entering into the literary life of the places they visited. They went first to Prague in September 1921; while they did not meet Kafka, they had letters of introduction to other writers and were frequently in the company of Karel Čapek. Encouraged perhaps by the example of their friend Paul Selver, who was becoming known as a translator from the Czech, they began to learn that language; but in March 1922, they moved to Hellerau, the suburb of Dresden where A. S. Neill had organized his first international school,[4] and took up German. Mrs. Muir taught in the school while her husband read and wrote poems and essays. They subsequently lived in other cities, but continued to study German; by the autumn of 1923 they were reading Hugo von Hofmannsthal and coming "under his enchantment."[5] The essays which Muir wrote at this time show his realization of the opportunities which lay in introducing contemporary German and Austrian literature to English-speaking audiences.

Between 1921 and 1924 Muir supported himself and his wife chiefly by writing essays and book reviews for the New York *Freeman*. When the periodical was discontinued in the early spring of 1924, he had to find some other means of making a living. Mrs. Muir resumed teaching in Neill's school, which had been removed to the Sonntagberg, near Rosenau, Austria. Providentially they were requested by B. W. Huebsch, the American publisher of Muir's *Latitudes* (New York, 1924), a collection of essays, to translate three of Gerhardt Hauptmann's plays.[6]

Their translating began thus as a stopgap, but was to become their principal source of income and to occupy most of their time until 1940. They began work light-heartedly. Mrs. Muir has told the present writer of their amusement as they translated Hauptmann's dramas, correcting one another's mistakes. The plays were followed by Hauptmann's novel, *The Island of the Great Mother* (London, 1925). It was, however, their third translation that made them known as translators—Lion Feuchtwanger's *Jew Süss* (London, 1926; American title, *Power*), published in England by Martin Secker. This best seller of 1927[7] was partly responsible for the publication of the translation of Kafka's *The Castle* in 1930; Secker had doubted the popularity of *Jew Süss* and had published it only after Muir persuaded him that the novel would be a success.[8] Its immense sales in England and America convinced Secker of the value of Muir's advice; hence he was willing to accept *The Castle* when the Muirs translated it.

Kafka's novel was the Muirs' tenth translation. It was preceded by Feuchtwanger's *The Ugly Duchess, Two Anglo-Saxon Plays,* and *Success,* Hauptmann's *Veland,* "Ludwig Renn's" *War,* Ernst Glaeser's *Class of 1902,* and the works already named. These books were all published in England by Secker, who had trade agreements for rights of translation with various German publishing houses. But *The Castle,* first published in 1926 in Munich by Kurt Wolff Verlag, was not covered by these agreements. According to Mrs. Muir, her husband read an article on Kafka in the late 1920s, became interested in him, and bought copies of his novels. The Muirs translated *The Castle* because they believed in the genius of its writer, and through their influence were able to get the translation published. They supported themselves by their translations; their work on such a doubtful risk as Kafka is proof of their faith in him.

Muir wrote an **"Introductory Note"** for *The Castle* which begins, "Franz Kafka's name, so far as I can discover, is almost unknown to English readers."[9] This **"Note"** has been referred to as a "historical curiosity";[10] but, as Wilhelm Emrich sensibly points out in his *Franz Kafka* (Bonn, 1958), it and Muir's introductions to *The Great Wall of China* (London, 1933) and *America* (London, 1938) have "naturgemäß das Kafka-Bild in England und Amerika wesentlich mitbestimmt."[11] In this introduction of Kafka to the English public, Muir gives some facts about his life and recounts how the novels came to be published in Germany. He then considers the meaning of the novel and, aware of Kafka's strangeness to an English audience, interprets the unfamiliar in terms of the familiar, advising that

> Perhaps the best way to approach *The Castle* is to regard it as a sort of modern *Pilgrim's Progress,* with the reservation, however, that the "progress" of the pilgrim here will remain in question all the time, and will be itself the chief, the essential problem. *The Castle* is, like *The Pilgrim's Progress,* a religious allegory; the desire of the hero in both cases is to work out his salvation.

But, since Kafka was "a religious genius" who wrote in "an age of scepticism," his hero knows only that "the goal and the road indubitably exist, and that the necessity to find them is urgent." The novelist

> begins with . . . the barest possible [postulates]; they are roughly these: that there is a right way of life, and that the discovery of it depends on one's attitude to powers which are almost unknown. What he sets out to do is to find out something about those powers, and the astonishing thing is that he appears to succeed.

The form of this **"Note"**—a definition of the tradition to which Kafka's work belongs and criticism in terms of such a tradition—is similar to that used by Muir in the essays collected in *Transition* (London, 1926), studies of nine contemporary English writers; and his analysis of *The Castle* is related to his own concepts of man's life. His finding one of Kafka's "axioms" to be "that at all times, whatever we may think, the demand of the divine law for unconditional reverence and unconditional obedience is beyond question," reflects, for example, the conclusion of his dramatic poem, **"The Field of the Potter,"** first published in *Six Poems* (Warlingham, 1932).[12] In it Judas is pictured as resigning himself to his fate: "He chose," the disciple says in reference to Christ, "and I was chosen. No one knew Him." Muir's Judas recognizes and bows before the same divine law which the poet finds presented by Kafka. In the earlier *First Poems* (London, 1925) and *Chorus of the Newly Dead* (London, 1926), written before he read Kafka, Muir frequently considers man's life in the image of the road; and the second work allows one to see why he considers that Kafka's knowledge about the "powers" is "astonishing." In this "sequence" of poems "the dead . . . look back at the life they . . . left and contemplate it from their new station";[13] and at one point the "Chorus" exclaims:

> It was decreed. We cannot tell
>   Why harlot, idiot or clown
> Lived, wept and died. We cannot spell
>   The hidden word which drove them down.
> But looking towards the earth we see
> The chart, deep-scored, stretched rigidly,
> And all they did beneath the sun
> Writ clear until the world is done.
>   (Chorus V, stanza 3)

Muir's observation here and in other early poems is limited to effects; and he marvels at Kafka's apprehension of causes.

This limited observation is largely due to Muir's immature thought, yet it is also related to the Calvinistic teaching which influenced his early life. Indeed, the pessimism produced by this upbringing became more pronounced in his work during the 1930s. Influenced by the growing political unrest on the continent and chafing under the drudgery of turning German novels into English, Muir began to doubt man's capacity to understand the "powers" which govern him and even his ability to find his "road." This attitude may be seen in the **"Introductory Note"** to *The Great Wall of China.* According to a "Publisher's Note" in *The Castle,*[14] *The Trial* was to be published next; but in *The Great Wall* Muir writes that he "thought it expedient to interpose between [the two novels] the present volume, which gives a more clear and general notion of Kafka's intentions as an artist and thinker than any of his earlier works."[15] The translator was aware that his job did not end with translation; he had also to help create a public for the novelist. Again Kafka is presented as pre-eminently a philosopher:

> The problem [Muir writes] with which all Kafka's work is concerned is a moral and spiritual one. It is a twofold problem: that of finding one's true vocation, one's true place, whatever it may be, in the community; and that of acting in accordance with the will of heavenly powers. But though it has those two aspects it was in his eyes a single problem; for a man's true place in the community is finally determined not by secular, but by divine, law, and only when, by apparent chance or deliberate effort, a man finds himself in his divinely appointed place, can he live as he should. Many people slip into their place without being aware of it; others are painfully conscious of the difficulty, the evident impossibility, of finding any place at all; and nobody has been more clearly and deeply conscious of it, I think, than Kafka.

Muir's own point of view is different; rather than looking at man and the "powers" above him, he sees man and the world about him. The difficulties of day-to-day life had become more apparent to Muir, and he passes by thoughts of "salvation" to emphasize the novelist's more temporal concerns.

This consideration of man's quest for his "true place" in Kafka's work is closely related to Muir's own ideas as they are expressed in the first version of his autobiography, *The Story and the Fable* (London, 1940), where he decides that the Orkney Islands at the time of his childhood possessed an "order" of society like that which existed before the Industrial Revolution; in this society men instinctively knew their place. Later, in the W. P. Ker Lecture, *The Politics of "King Lear"* (Glasgow, 1946), Muir forthrightly declared that between 1539 and 1649 "the medieval world with its communal tradition" gave way to "the modern individualist world."[16] But this concern with society had long figured in his thought, and was deep enough to influence even his more ephemeral work. In a 1934 review of *A Book of Scottish Verse,* edited by R. L. Mackie, he contrasts pre- and post-sixteenth-century Scots verse and decides that the earlier came from a society with a "centre" and the later from

a society which was not "a whole civilization."[17] From the early 1930s Muir became increasingly aware of the individual's difficulty in finding a place in the disintegrating society of modern civilization; and his awareness of the problem may have been responsible for his finding it in Kafka.

In 1933 the English public was not prepared to accept Kafka; four years passed before *The Trial* was published by Gollancz, followed in 1938 by *America,* published by Routledge. An "Epilogue" by Max Brod was included in *The Trial,* but no introduction. The English edition of *America,* however, includes an **"Introductory Note."** Muir's opinion of Kafka is not significantly different from his earlier views, although, having read Broad's *Franz Kafka, eine Biographie* (Prague, 1935), he is more aware of the relationship between Kafka's work and his life. The critic's use of such biographical material is justified, he writes, because

> No imaginative writer chooses his theme; it is chosen for him by the experience which has most deeply affected him. To trace back the inspiration of Kafka's stories to his relations with his father is not to belittle them or to give them a merely subjective validity. The extraordinary thing in Kafka was the profundity with which he grasped that experience and worked it out in universal terms, until it became a description of human destiny in general into which countless meanings at once ambiguous and clear, could be read.[18]

Kafka's works are considered to be allegorical. Even though *America,* "the happiest of Kafka's stories, is not allegorical; yet there is something semi-allegorical, or at least representative, about the hero, Karl Rossmann. All Kafka's main figures have this quality; they are not mere individuals; they are images of man in conflict with fate. There are various points, or stations in that conflict."

Muir's criticism of Kafka before 1938 takes for granted the novelist's intention of creating allegories based on man's spiritual life. Such an attitude is not unreasonable, yet one should remember that in the 1930s Muir was writing *Variations on a Time Theme* (London, 1934), a sequence of poems which "L. M." described as being similar to "a type of Royal Academy picture of a decade or so back—stilted allegorical nudes walking through a grey landscape,"[19] as well as the poems in *Journeys and Places* (London, 1937), the volume which prompted the *TLS* reviewer's statement that "Mr. Muir has always been a metaphysical poet."[20] While few of these poems are completely allegorical, Muir's use of extended metaphors gives them a "semi-allegorical" character, and their themes have generally to do with contrasts between man's ideal and the actual lives. The poet's criticism, whether true or not, is intimately connected with the philosophical problems explored and the techniques employed in his own poetry.

With the outbreak of war in 1939 the market for translations of German novels died away, and the Muirs, who felt they had become "a sort of translation factory,"[21] were forced to find other ways of making a living, although in 1940 they published excerpts "From Kafka's Diaries" in two periodicals.[22] In the same year Muir wrote a lengthy essay for *A Franz Kafka Miscellany* (New York, 1940); the essay shows how his understanding of Kafka had developed in the decade since he first studied *The Castle,* as well as how his criticism is related to his personal life. In February 1939, he had realized that he "was a Christian, no matter how bad a one."[23] This experience may account for his bluntly stating in 1940 that Kafka

> believed in the fundamental tenets of religion, divine justice, divine grace, damnation and salvation; they are the framework of his world. The problem which possesses him is how man, stationed in one dimension, can direct his life in accordance with a law belonging to another, a law whose workings he can never interpret truly, though they are always before his eyes.[24]

Muir also asserts that Kafka held "the dogma of the incommensurability of divine and human law which he adopted from Kierkegaard," and that this "dogma" is the "source of Kafka's humour . . . a comedy of cross-purposes on a grand scale." Ten years earlier Muir had seen in Kafka merely the presentation of man's religious problems, a description in far-reaching terms but without any commitment by the novelist to a religion. Now with the renewal of the critic's own religious faith, he finds in Kafka a positive belief which he describes in theological terms. He realizes that, because of this belief, Kafka's hero does not, and need not, understand the divine laws which govern him; that, indeed, the novelist's realization of this truth makes life bearable and brings "gleams of pure humour" into the "nightmare atmosphere" of *The Castle* and *The Trial.*

Muir continues to use the word allegory for "the form into which [Kafka] threw his two great religious narratives," but he stresses the imaginative invention in the novels rather than their symbolism. Studying their plots, a critical practice which he advocated in *The Structure of the Novel* (London, 1928), he emphasizes that Kafka's humor "can only be shown by showing how he manages the action of his stories." Since "every action is perfectly reasonable,"

> Kafka's most ordinary scenes have a fullness which gives them simultaneously several meanings, one beneath the other, until in a trivial situation we find an image of some universal or mythical event such as the Fall. That is the way in which his allegory works. He has been blamed for confusing two worlds, for introducing real people and then by a sudden twist making all their actions symbolical and bringing them into contact with mythical figures. But that was exactly what he set out to do. Pure allegory could not have expressed his conception of life or his idea of man's moral problem. His hero does not have to walk a beaten road like Christian in *The Pilgrim's Progress,*

overcoming set dangers, refusing set temptations, and after each victory drawing nearer to his destination. He did not deny that this road existed; but he found it very hard to distinguish.

Thus, while "Bunyan's allegory is a kind of demonstration," Kafka's "is rather an investigation which is both urgent and dramatic, for on its outcome depends the hero's salvation." Such "action . . . is a sort of dialectic, a progress from one position to the next. The final position, since it is not in this life, is unattainable, and so the allegory can never be finished." This "allegory" gives more "than the traditional symbols of religion, or than a new interpretation of them," and, indeed, "the imaginative logic of the narrative builds up a particularized system of relations which exist by their own right. Kafka's world did not take shape in obedience to these traditional symbols. He arrived at them by mere observation of life as he saw it." In 1930 Muir had emphasized the similarities between Bunyan and Kafka; now he sees the differences to be more important—that Bunyan's allegory is a strict framework imposed from without, while Kafka's is in a sense organic, developing with the action of the story. Not only is Muir's understanding of Kafka's particular type of symbolism deeper, but he is also more conscious of Kafka's artistry; the novelist's "temper," Muir writes, "is throughout that of an honest, unassuming workman; he measures and puts together his metaphysical world with the painstaking thoroughness of a mason building a house both to be worked and to be lived in."

Between 1930 and 1940 Muir's ideas about Kafka show a movement away from strict, limiting definitions of the subject and an increased awareness of the writer as an artist. This critical development is not unrelated to Muir's own artistic development. His poems in *The Narrow Place* (London, 1943) and later volumes are generally recognized to possess an artistic quality not present in his earlier work, and indeed he is almost the only English poet whose major poems were written in his old age; he was fifty-six years old when *The Narrow Place* was published. While certainly no single event was alone responsible for this late development, there is ample evidence that Muir's religious experience in 1939 was an important factor in releasing his creative power. The development of his verse is also paralleled by a change in his prose style; the involved, finely written sentences of 1930 give way to a plain, straightforward expression of thought.[25] His criticism of Kafka shows a similar change: one may judge the earlier criticism to be a reflection of Muir's own artistic aims (and a result of his own creative agonies), since the later criticism reveals such a wider range of knowledge concerning Kafka's significance.

Muir's last study of Kafka was published in 1947. In it his critical attitude is almost directly opposed to that which he held in 1930 and corresponds with the mature concept of life found in his later poetry. Some of his ideas in these later poems are typically expressed in "A

Birthday" (*The Voyage and Other Poems,* London, 1946). The only knowledge man must have is that a road leads through his life; an attitude of "acceptance and gratitude" will be enough to take him along this road:

> Before I saw the wood
> I loved each nook and bend,
> The track going right and wrong;
> Before I took the road
> Direction ravished my soul.
> Now that I can discern
> It whole or almost whole,
> Acceptance and gratitude
> Like travellers return
> And stand where first they stood.
>
> (Lines 21-30)

Muir's tranquil acceptance of life is the chief influence on the 1947 essay, entitled **"Poznámka k Franzi Kafkovi"** when it was first published in Czech in the commemorative volume *Franz Kafka a Praha* (Prague, 1947) and called **"Franz Kafka"** in Muir's *Essays on Literature and Society* (London, 1949).[26] In it he passes over his earlier estimation of the novelist as a "thinker" beset by religious problems to deal with him as "a great story teller." Kafka always "starts with a general or universal situation" which, being "story-less," forces him to make up the story he tells. "No foundation in fact, no narrative framework, no plot or scene for a plot is there to help him; he has to create the story, character, setting and action, and embody in it his meaning." Muir's attention in 1940 to Kafka's plots reaches its logical conclusion, for the critic considers the novels solely as narratives.

Again Muir brings in the metaphor which he uses so frequently in his poems:

> The image of a road comes into our minds when we think of [Kafka's] stories; for in spite of all the confusions and contradictions in which he was involved he held that life was a way, not a chaos, that the right way exists and can be found by a supreme and exhausting effort, and that whatever happens every human being in fact follows some way, right or wrong.

Muir pays little attention to the external forces which influenced Kafka, for by 1947 his critical practice was to treat each subject as an entity within itself. Thus, while Kafka's understanding of "the irreconcilability of the divine and the human law" was "confirmed" by Kierkegaard, yet "he must himself have made that reading independently"; and indeed "the supreme originality of Kafka's work does not lie in his reading of the universal position, which he shared with Kierkegaard at some points, but in his story-telling, by means of which he created a world." Being himself now more aware of the problems of creating an art form, Muir realizes that artistry is of the supreme importance; Kafka "is a great story-teller both by his art and by the interest and value of what he says. And the value of what he says does not depend on the truth of his metaphysical structure . . ."

He creates "endlessly surprising" inventions: "The scenes and figures and conversations seem to rise out of nothing, since nothing resembling them was there before. We contemplate things which we see for the first time." Indeed, Kafka "resurrected and made available for contemporary use the timeless story, the archetypal story, in which is the source of all stories."

The most noteworthy development of Muir's criticism is in his general attitude to Kafka's artistic purpose. In almost direct opposition to the ideas he had held for more than fifteen years, he writes:

> these stories are not allegories. The truths they bring out are surprising or startling, not conventional and expected, as the truths of allegory tend to be. They are more like serious fantasies; the spontaneous expression of Kafka's genius was fantasy, as his early short stories show . . . But no designation of his art is satisfying. We can see what it was not; to find a name for it is of little consequence.

Edwin Muir was obviously of first importance in bringing Franz Kafka to an English-speaking audience, and his influence upon this audience, while less calculable, was certainly very important. The translations of Kafka were the result of collaboration. Mrs. Muir, in a letter to the present writer, tells how they "tore a book in two, did half each, then I went over Edwin's translation and he went over mine, and the result was a seamless garment." (They were responsible for translating well over thirty novels, and, in addition, Muir translated Hauptmann's *Veland,* London, 1929, by himself; his wife was ill at the time. Mrs. Muir, using the name "Agnes Neill Scott," translated at least six novels by herself, including works by Hans Carossa and C. Winsloe.)[27]

Muir's criticism of Kafka was doubtlessly influenced by the personal preoccupations which also found expression in his poems; yet the reciprocal nature of this influence must not be overlooked. In *An Autobiography* Muir describes how "At one stage [in translating Kafka] the stories continued themselves in our dreams, unfolding into slow serpentine nightmares, immovably reasonable."[28] Many of Muir's poems, being based on "universal situations," inevitably remind one of Kafka's stories; and certainly Kafka, even if he did not directly influence Muir, strengthened the poet's faith in his own ideas.

Muir's criticism of Kafka helps the general reader to understand the novelist, but it is also important for the insight it affords into criticism in general and into criticism of Kafka in particular. The parallel which I have drawn between Muir's development as a poet and the development of his ideas about Kafka shows that even the "disinterested" critic with a complete knowledge of his subject can never be absolutely detached from his own personality. Muir's criticism of Kafka is a specific example of the general conclusions about the uneven development of criticism in the past three hundred years which George Watson makes in his study, *The Literary Critics* (London, 1962): "The great critics," he writes, "do not contribute: they interrupt."[29] Their interruption is not based on any change in the value of the work under discussion, but on their own personal development and understanding. Particularly for the artist who, like Kafka, has concerned himself with "universal situations," there can be no definitive criticism; and his work will always give rise to divergent opinions, the causes of which can be found in the critic himself, and the value of which is not unrelated to the critic's worth in other literary activities.

NOTES

[1] Including P. K. Ackermann, "A History of Critical Writing on Franz Kafka," *GQ,* XXIII (1950), 105-113. See also Klaus Jonas, "Franz Kafka: An American Bibliography," *Bull. of Bibliography,* XX (Sept.-Dec., 1952; Jan.-Apr., 1953), 212-216, 231-233; with supplement by Ann Benson, XXII (Jan.-Apr., 1958), 112-114.

[2] Biographical details are from Edwin Muir, *An Autobiography* (London, 1954) and from information given to the present writer by Mrs. Willa Muir.

[3] *We Moderns* (London, 1918), published under the pseudonym "Edward Moore," which Muir used until 1922. H. L. Mencken included the work in his "Free-Lance" series (New York, 1920) under Muir's own name.

[4] Neill and Mrs. Muir were friends at St. Andrews; the school is described in his *A Dominie Abroad* (London, 1923).

[5] *An Autobiography,* p. 219.

[6] *The Dramatic Works. Poetic Dramas [Indipohdi, The White Saviour, A Winter Ballad],* VIII (London, 1925).

[7] Mrs. Q. D. Leavis, in *Fiction and the Reading Public* (London, 1932, 1939), lists *Jew Süss* as a "best-seller" of 1927, including it among "translations that affected popular fiction and taste" (pp. 335, 330).

[8] *An Autobiography,* p. 228. According to Mrs. Muir, Secker was so doubtful of the novel's success that he required Feuchtwanger to pay for the translation; the Muirs had no share in the book's profits.

[9] The following passages by Muir are from his "Introductory Note," *The Castle* (London, 1930), pp. v-xii, where they are italicized. The ideas in this introduction are considerably expanded, but not modified, in Muir's "A Note on Franz Kafka," *Bookman* [New York], LXXII (1930), 235-241. In this "puff direct" for the American edition of *The Castle* he considers Kafka's debts to Kierkegaard and Pascal, discussing not only *The Castle* but *The Trial* and *America* as well. He quotes and summarizes Kafka's work with untempered enthusiasm. In this essay he also stresses the religious, allegorical nature of *The Castle* and *The Trial.* In his conclusion he writes: "For anyone who wants to

have a serious imaginative treatment of religion, Kafka is infinitely more satisfying than Dostoievski" (p. 241).

[10] Anon., "Note," *The Castle,* rev. ed. with additional material tr. Eithne Wilkins and Ernst Kaiser (London, 1957), p. 7.

[11] Page 436.

[12] Privately printed at the Samson Press. The poem is entitled "Judas" in Muir's *Journeys and Places* (London, 1937); it is not included in his *Collected Poems* (London, 1930, 1963).

[13] *An Autobiography,* p. 223.

[14] *The Castle,* p. xii.

[15] The following passages by Muir are from his "Introductory Note," *The Great Wall of China, And Other Pieces* (London, 1933), pp. vii-xvi.

[16] This lecture is most accessible in Muir's *Essays on Literature and Society* (London, 1949), pp. 31-48, especially pp. 32-33.

[17] *Spectator,* CLII (Apr. 20, 1934), 625. The problem is also a central one in Muir's *Scott and Scotland* (London, 1936).

[18] The following passages by Muir are from his "Introductory Note," *America* (London, 1938), pp. v-xii.

[19] [?Louis MacNeice], "Poems by Edwin Muir," *New Verse,* No. 9, June 1934, p. 20.

[20] "A Metaphysical Poet," Jan. 15, 1938, p. 41.

[21] *An Autobiography,* p. 222.

[22] *New Statesman,* XXI (Mar. 29, 1941), 321-322; *SRL,* July 26, 1941, pp. 3-4.

[23] *An Autobiography,* p. 247.

[24] The following passages by Muir are from "Franz Kafka," *A Franz Kafka Miscellany* (New York, 1940), pp. 55-66.

[25] This difference may easily be seen by comparing his essay "Laurence Sterne," *Bookman,* Mar., 1931, pp. 1-5, with the revision of it, *Essays on Literature and Society,* pp. 49-56.

[26] Muir had gone to Prague in Aug. 1945 as director of the British Institute, serving also as visiting professor of English at the Charles University. Mrs. Muir does not remember the name of the friend who translated the essay into Czech. It is printed in English in the *Essays on Literature and Society,* pp. 120-124, from which all quotations are taken. Michael Hamburger, in his

perceptive study, "Edwin Muir," *Encounter,* Dec. 1960, pp. 46-53, draws attention to the importance of this essay, although he fails to realize that it was also published in English:

"Not only Muir's admiration for Kafka, but his understanding of the works, deepened with time . . . In his Introductions to the translations, Muir had interpreted Kafka's fiction as allegory; it was not till 1947 that he corrected this view and stressed the purely imaginative character of Kafka's works.

"But this important disclaimer, contributed to a Czech publication, was never noticed in England. Muir's realisation that there is no key to Kafka's fiction has a direct bearing on his own later works."

[27] Information from Mrs. Muir; her pseudonym may have been derived from the names of their friends, A. S. Neill and Francis George Scott, the composer.

[28] *An Autobiography,* p. 240.

[29] Page 11.

J. R. Watson (essay date 1964)

SOURCE: "Edwin Muir and the Problem of Evil," in *The Critical Quarterly,* Vol. 6, No. 3, Autumn, 1964, pp. 231-49.

[*In the following essay, Watson identifies in Muir's poetry such central themes as the journey, the passage of time, and the randomness of evil.*]

In an essay on Henryson in *Essays on Literature and Society,* Edwin Muir quotes the epitaph from *The Testament of Cresseid:*

> Lo, fair Ladyis, Crisseid, of Troyis toun,
> Sumtyme countit the flour of Womanheid,
> Under this stane lait Lipper lyis deid.

'No other Scottish poet,' says Muir, 'has risen to this high and measured style, and Henryson himself does not attain it often, though he does as often as the subject requires it. Yet it is a style which one would have expected to suit the Scottish genius, with its seriousness and its love of compressed utterance.' These Scottish qualities may be detected in Muir's own poetry, particularly in his later poetry, where he attains a compression of utterance which had previously escaped him; and although he wrote in English, his poetry remains unmistakably un-English, as un-English as the poetry of Yeats in a different way. Yeats, said Muir, had 'expressed the central reality of Ireland', and he had done so 'not by clinging to Irish dialect, but by adopting English and making it into a language fit for all its purposes'. Muir also adopted English: but he differed from Yeats in having a greater interest in European problems and ideas. He lived in Europe for much of his writing life, shared the same cultural background with many German thinkers, and fostered it through his work on European writers. Through them, Muir escapes from what he calls the 'provincialism' of Scottish literature; he connects in his own work the seriousness of the Scottish tradition with the seriousness of a writer like Kafka, so that we find in Muir's work a preoccupation with the fundamental questions of the human condition which extends the Scottish tradition and links it with the European. He wrote of Kafka, whom he translated:

> The frustration of the hero is an intrinsic part of Kafka's theme; and it is caused by what in theological language is known as the irreconcilability of the divine and the human law; a subtle yet immeasurable disparity.

These ideas were confirmed by Kafka's reading of Kierkegaard, but they sprang originally from his personal experience; and in the same way, Muir's own version of the frustration of the hero is based upon his own experience. In Muir's case, there is a constant awareness of the need to find some meaning and purpose in life which can exist beside the realities of pain and disease and suffering, a continual attempt to grapple with what may be broadly called the problem of evil. It is this problem which informs a great deal of Muir's greatest poetry, the poetry of seriousness and compressed utterance, of the Scottish and also of the European tradition.

II

The story of Muir's early life is beautifully told in his *Autobiography* (1954). It begins with the childhood on the farms in Orkney, which ended when he was fourteen, when a bad landlord and then a poor farm forced his father to give up farming. The family moved to Glasgow in 1901. The terrible story of the years which followed shows quite clearly how the young Muir encountered the problem of evil in its most horrible form. 'The first few years after we came to Glasgow,' he wrote, 'were so stupidly wretched, such a meaningless waste of inherited virtue that I cannot write of them even now without grief and anger'. First of all his father, who had strained his heart working on the farm, died of heart failure; then his brother Willie died of consumption. This was followed by the worst experience of all, the death of his brother Johnnie by the slow agony of a tumour on the brain; and a few months after that, his mother died. 'I was too young,' wrote Muir, 'for so much death'. He described the walks which he took with Johnnie to Queen's Park, during the early course of the disease, 'as detached and cold as monks'; and the futility of his prayers outlined the problem of pain unmistakably:

> All autumn I had prayed, night after night, that Johnnie would get better. As the pain increased and he became a mere substance upon which it worked like a conscientious artisan, there seemed to be no sense in praying, and if there was a God I told myself that he was deaf or indifferent.

The experiences of these years underpin the essential seriousness of Muir's poetry with a personal urgency. They also appear in two of the three novels he wrote, *The Three Brothers* (1931) and *Poor Tom* (1932). In the first of these there is the death of a young man from consumption, and in the second a death that resembles Johnnie's. The brothers also appear in one or two of Muir's poems: there is a poem called **'The Brothers'**, in which he sees them playing happily in Paradise as he dreams; and in his poem **'Variations on a Time Theme'** he throws up an image of himself 'twice-armoured in the flesh of Cain'. This suggests a certain guilt about his brothers' deaths, which is easily explicable psychologically, particularly as the three brothers had strong personalities which did not always blend:—

> we played for victory
> And not to make each other glad.

By the time Muir was eighteen his family 'looked as if it had been swept by a gale'. Eventually, as he put it, 'I climbed out of these years, but for a long time I did not dare to look back into them'; even in 1954 they were 'still painful and still blurred in my mind'. The course of psychoanalysis which he underwent in London many years later threw up a great deal of the past which he had tried to keep buried; meanwhile the pointless brutality which he witnessed in the slums of Glasgow gave some indication of a pattern of life, a terrifying pattern of predestined dreariness and motiveless pain. Muir relates two vivid memories: one of a large muscular woman beating a small man whom she said had been her seducer, the other of an encounter between two men:

> . . . one of them, who looked serious and respectable and not particularly angry, raised his fist slowly every now and then, and, as if objectively, hit the other man, who stood in silence and never tried to defend himself. At last an older man said, "Why dinna you let the chap alane? He hasna hurt you." But the serious young man replied, "I ken he hasna hurt me, but I'm gaun tae hurt him!" And with a watchful look round him he raised his fist again.

Muir relates these two memories to the experiences of his own life:

> I did not want to see any more; but the scene and particularly the words of the serious young man— the other said nothing at all—took hold of my mind as if they were an answer to some question which, without my knowing it, had been troubling me: perhaps Johnnie's slow and painful death, during which, without being able to return a single blow, he had been battered so pitilessly. In both these memories there was the quality of Scottish Calvinism: the serious young man's reply had the unanswerable, arbitrary logic of predestination; and the encounter of the red-haired woman with her seducer, when both were so greatly changed that their original sin might have been committed in another world, and yet lived on, there in that slum, was a sordid image of fate as Calvin saw it. Somewhere in these two

incidents there was a virtue of a dreary kind, behind the flaunted depravity: a recognition of logic and reality.

At this stage of his life, these experiences 'took hold' of Muir's mind 'as if they were an answer to some question'; they helped to explain, in their own version of meaningless evil, the evil of Johnnie's death, and they gave something to which that death could be related, so that it no longer existed as a piece of solitary horror. This was not an answer, however, so much as a confirmation that such things happen, that naked and brutal evil does exist. The greatness of Muir's poetry lies in his struggle to find a deeper and more meaningful answer to this problem, an answer which admits the good which exists in the world but which nevertheless faces the reality of evil squarely and sensitively. Muir's complete integrity, in both his life and his poetry, was the quality remarked upon by T. S. Eliot in a recent broadcast: it springs, in his poetry, from the ground of personal experience recaptured in poetry, so that the optimism of the conclusion is hard-won, and never trite or superficial.

Up to and including his book *The Labyrinth* (1949), two themes appear again and again to embody the problem, and they are present, though less dominantly, in the poems written after 1949. The first of these is the theme of time, the second the theme or image of the journey. Both are obviously connected with Muir's early experience: it was through the inevitable process of time that he passed from the family life on the Orkney farm to the years of horror on the south side of Glasgow, while the journey which took the family there was not just a journey from one place to another, but a journey from happiness to misery, a plunge 'out of order into chaos.' These themes of time and of the journey dominate *Variations on a Time Theme* (1934). The poem is in ten sections: it describes man on his journey, losing his happiness:

> Where did the road branch?
> Where did the path turn like an enemy turning
> Stealthily, suddenly, showing his other face
> After the knife stroke?

The child is in Paradise, and not conscious of Time and all that it stands for:

> A child in Adam's field I dreamed away
> My one eternity and hourless day,
> Ere from my wrist Time's bird had learned to fly,
> Or I had robbed the Tree of which I die,
> Whose boughs rain still, whose fruit wave-green
>   shall fall
> Until the last great autumn reddens all.

Afterwards, like the children of Israel, man wanders through the wilderness of the world. Throughout his journey he is surrounded by Time, which is an evil power because it makes life meaningless and empty:

> If there's no crack or chink, no escape from Time,
> No spasm, no murderous knife to rape from Time

The pure and trackless day of liberty;
If there's no power can burst the rock of Time,
No Rescuer from the dungeon stock of Time,
Nothing in earth or heaven to set us free:
Imprisonment's for ever; we're the mock of Time,
While lost and empty lies Eternity.

Time is hostile to meaningful life because it passes over good and evil indifferently:

Time brings down the day
Like a great wrestler, fells it like a tree
With all its fruit, defeat or victory.

To this destroying power man is fastened, like a martyr to a fire-wheel:

Time's a fire-wheel whose spokes the seasons turn,
And fastened there we, Time's slow martyrs, burn.

There are some, like Heidegger's unauthentic man, who do not mind this, or do not notice it; others, like the martyrs looking up to heaven, gaze upward in search of a life of some purpose, beyond the cycle of birth, growth, decline and death:

And a few with eyes uplifted through the blaze
Let their flesh crumble till they're all a gaze
Glassing that fireless kingdom in the sky
Which is our dream as through Time's wood we fly
Burning in silence or crying the ancient rhyme:
'Who shall outsoar the mountainous flame of
    Time?'

Opposed to these visionaries, the restless, searching ones, are those to whom Time's fire-wheel is 'but a pleasant heat', who are indifferent to beauty, goodness and cruelty alike. This becomes explicit in the penultimate section of the poem, where Muir speaks of a figure 'Packed in my skin from head to toe':

His name's Indifference.
Nothing offending he is all offence;
Can stare at beauty's bosom coldly
And at Christ's crucifixion boldly;
Can note with a lack-lustre eye
Victim and murderer go by; . . .

This indifference is the result of the evil of Time's meaningless progression:

If I could drive this demon out
I'd put all Time's display to rout.
Its wounds would turn to flowers and nothing be
But the first Garden. The one Tree
Would stand for ever safe and fair
And Adam's hand stop in the air.

The driving out of the demon is a vision of something beyond Time, which accompanies the opposite factor to indifference, the Soul. The Soul's foundation is in pity, and this is why it fights indifference. Pity is essential for the conquering of indifference, and this is Muir's answer in this poem to the problem of evil: pity would gladly abolish evil from the earth, but if it did, indifference would reign supreme—

Pity would cancel what it feeds upon,
And gladly cease, its office done.
Yet could it end all passion, flaw, offence,
Would come my homespun fiend Indifference
And have me wholly.

The last section of the poem, 'Who curbed the lion long ago . . . ?', is the most difficult. I think its meaning is connected with Muir's idea about the fabulous in human life, and it is best understood by reference to Muir's distinction in the **Autobiography** between the 'Story' and the 'Fable' (in its original form as published in 1940, Muir's account of his life was entitled **The Story and the Fable**). The story part of a man's life is that 'outward life' which 'goes on in its ordinary routine of eating, drinking, sleeping, working, and making money in order to beget sons and daughters who will do the same.' The fable is 'what we are not and can never be', the significant and meaningful pattern from which we all deviate, the immortality which we can only glimpse: yet the very meaning of our lives is in this deviation and these glimpses—

Human beings are understandable only as immortal spirits; they become natural then, as natural as young horses; they are absolutely unnatural if we try to think of them as a mere part of the natural world. They are immortal spirits distorted and corrupted in countless ways by the world into which they are born; bearing countless shapes, beautiful, quaint, grotesque; living countless lives, trivial, sensational, dull; serving behind counters, going to greyhound races, playing billiards, preaching to savages in Africa, collecting stamps . . .

The opposite to this is the way of thinking of man as a kind of superior animal, and Muir relates an experience on a tramcar in Glasgow when he had just such a vision of humanity:

The tramcar stopped and went on again, carrying its menagerie; my mind saw countless other tramcars where animals sat or got on or off with mechanical dexterity, as if they had been trained in a circus; and I realized that in all Glasgow, in all Scotland, in all the world, there was nothing but millions of such creatures living an animal life and moving towards an animal death as towards a great slaughter-house.

Man is bound to this kind of life, Muir says, 'by necessity and guilt'; time is then the great inexorable power. Yet it is possible to see man's life in the light, not of highly-trained animal life, but of a deviation from immortality, in relation to the fable which gives it meaning and sense. 'I shall attend,' he says,

and listen to a class of experiences which the disbeliever in immortality ignores and dismisses as irrelevant to temporal life. . . . They come when I am least aware of myself as a personality

moulded by my will and time: in moments of
contemplation when I am unconscious of my body,
or indeed that I have a body with separate
members; in moments of grief or prostration; in
happy hours with friends; and, because self-
forgetfulness is most complete then, in dreams
and day-dreams and in that floating, half-discarnate
state which precedes and follows sleep. In these
hours there seems to me to be knowledge of my real
self and simultaneously knowledge of immortality.

This idea helps to explain the importance of dreams in
Muir's poetry and in the *Autobiography:* they are proofs
of the validity of the fable—

If I describe a great number of dreams in this
book I do so intentionally, for I should like to
save from the miscellaneous dross of experience
a few glints of immortality.

It is this contrast between 'the miscellaneous dross of
experience' and the 'glints of immortality' which is the
addition to *Variations on a Time Theme* made by the
last section. It represents the fable element in life by the
use of visionary animals, the lion and the dragon, once
alive, now 'empty as shape and cold as rhyme' on a
shield. Their heraldic posture serves two functions: to
remind us that they were once alive, fabulous, and to
indicate that, though they are dead, they still have a
meaning. Beyond the shield we can glimpse the 'fabulous wave far back in Time' when they existed and had
some kind of real meaning. Now they are present in
human life but cut off from their background, allowing
the temporal process of life, the story, to go on in its
non-meaning way, never casting a look backwards in
the direction of significant memory:

Here now heraldic watch them ride
This path far up the mountain-side
And backward never cast a look;
Ignorant that the dragon died
Long since and that the mountain shook
When the great lion was crucified.

It is impossible to decide with any exactitude what the
dragon is, or what the crucified lion represents. On the
banner, perhaps, it is the lion of Scotland; but why crucified? And why, on the banner, is it wingless—or
rather, why did it have wings in the first place? The best
way to resolve these difficulties, I think, is to treat this
imagery as vaguely representative of the fabulous: that
in some way the lion and the dragon and the crucifixion
are significant together because they stand for the wonderful fable-type occurrences which are so important for
Muir. Thus their exact identity is not important, because
they stand together for the glimpses of something meaningful—though one cannot help thinking that the poem
would have gained something if Muir had been more
precise at this point. But there is no doubt that for Muir,
to forget these fabulous things, the dragon, the crucified
lion, the shaking of the mountain, is to invite the figure
of Indifference, and to remember them is to call into
action the feelings of pity. Thus the fabulous and the

pitiful go together in their opposition to the meaningless
animal-like existence which is the 'story', with its complete subjection to the theme of time without any variation. When we do have variation in the Time theme,
through dreams and glimpses of the fabulous, we have
looks back on the journey which give us the perspective
on life to relate it to the immortal.

III

Armed with these connections and this complex of ideas
from *Variations on a Time Theme* we can approach
Muir's next book, *Journeys and Places* (1937). Poems
like **'The Mountains'** and **'The Road'** deal with the
inevitable journey and the inexorable passing of time. In
the poem **'Merlin',** the question he puts to the old wiz-
ard is this:

Will there ever be a singer
Whose music will smooth away
The furrow drawn by Adam's finger
Across the meadow and the wave?
Or a runner who'll outrun
Man's long shadow driving on,
Break through the gate of memory
And hang the apple on the tree?

The runner who will hang the apple on the tree again
will transform life by bringing back into it the fable, by
breaking through the gate of memory and thus upsetting
the course of time, for time and memory are interdependent. Similarly outside the progression of time, and thus
preserved from evil, is the figure of the old man chasing
the rats in the sewers of Troy in the poem **'Troy'.** He
remains under the ground during the sack of Troy, and
is therefore ignorant of it until he is brought to the
surface by robbers plundering the ruins. Then he is
suddenly brought face to face with an evil reality as he
becomes aware of the city's destruction and undergoes
the torture from which he dies:

And there he saw Troy like a burial ground
With tumbled walls for tombs, the smooth sward
wrinkled
As Time's last wave had long since passed that
way,
The sky, the sea, Mount Ida and the islands,
No sail from edge to edge, the Greeks clean gone.
They stretched him on a rock and wrenched his
limbs,
Asking: 'Where is the treasure?' till he died.

This portrait of the 'brave, mad old man' is a fine
imaginative capturing of the idea that time and evil go
together. In his sewer he lives out his own fable, pretending that the rats are Ajax or Achilles and shouting
after them as they run away. His fable is enacted in the
darkness, so that he becomes conscious of evil as soon
as he is brought out into the light of day. Evil, in fact,
is part of the inescapable reality of life above the surface
of the earth; it exists in the same way as the landscape
does. The figure of the old man has no alternative to
offer: he only escapes for a while by hiding, and sooner

or later he was bound to receive a rude awakening. Evil was there all the time, although he had never met it, just as Muir himself was relatively happy and unaware of pain and suffering until he came to Glasgow.

The next development in Muir's poetry is the provision of a more convincing and meaningful alternative to evil than this escape. In the next two books, *The Narrow Place* (1943) and *The Voyage* (1946), the peace and happiness of his married life take a place in his philosophy: love is the opposing force to evil as pity was to indifference in *Variations on a Time Theme*. In **'The Annunciation'**, for instance, love gives liberty from the 'iron reign' of time, material considerations (the Story):

> Now in this iron reign
> I sing the liberty
> Where each asks from each
> What each most wants to give
> And each awakes in each
> What else would never be,
> Summoning so the rare
> Spirit to breathe and live.

and **'The Commemoration'** ends:

> This strand we weave into
> Our monologue of two,
> And time cannot undo
> That strong and subtle chain.

Although these two books still contain poems which celebrate the dangers of evil, like **'The Castle'**, or the destruction of happiness, like **'The Little General'**, Muir is quietly and insistently optimistic about the power of good:

> One doubt of evil would bring down such a grace,
> Open such a gate, all Eden would enter in,
> Hell be a place like any other place,
> And love and hate and life and death begin.

This is the last verse of **'The Good Man in Hell'**, which not only suggests a kind of unreality of evil, so that it can be overthrown by doubting its existence, but also represents the struggle of life, the opposition of good and evil in the world, as a good thing in itself. Muir's own realization in his life of the lessening of evil after the act of faith in his marriage and leaving Glasgow in 1919, contains within it something of the doubt of a continuing evil. Now, in his poetry, love makes sense, even though it is surrounded by cruelty, as it is in **'In Love For Long'**, the concluding poem of *The Voyage:*

> This love a moment known
> For what I do not know
> And in a moment gone
> Is like the happy doe
> That keeps its perfect laws
> Between the tiger's paws
> And vindicates its cause.

Love here provides a purpose and significance in life; its opposite is a frame of mind in which everything seems pointless. This is a development of the indifference of *Variations on a Time Theme,* and it is found very clearly in the poem which gives its name to Muir's next collection, *The Labyrinth* (1949). The temptation for Theseus, even after he has killed the Minotaur and left the labyrinth, is to believe that the world itself is nothing but a great maze, that life is pointless and moral effort useless. A paragraph from Muir's essay on Kafka helps to illuminate this, and indeed the whole idea of the journey in his poetry:

> The image of a road comes into our minds when we think of his stories; for in spite of all the confusions and contradictions in which he was involved he held that life was a way, not a chaos, that the right way exists and can be found by a supreme and exhausting effort, and that whatever happens every human being in fact follows some way, right or wrong.

Theseus has a bad spirit which tells him the opposite of this:

> 'No need to hurry. Haste and delay are equal
> In this one world, for there's no exit, none,
> No place to come to, and you'll end where you are,
> Deep in the centre of the endless maze.'

Theseus-Muir replies emphatically:

> I could not live if this were not illusion.
> It is a world, perhaps; but there's another.

This other world is the world of the fable and the vision:

> For once in a dream or trance I saw the gods
> Each sitting on the top of his mountain-isle,
> While down below the little ships sailed by,
> Toy multitudes swarmed in the harbours,
>   shepherds drove
> Their tiny flocks to the pastures, marriage feasts
> Went on below, small birthdays and holidays,
> Ploughing and harvesting and life and death,
> And all permissible, all acceptable,
> Clear and secure as in a limpid dream.

Above this landscape the gods hold their conversation:

> And their eternal dialogue was peace
> Where all these things were woven, and this our life
> Was as a chord deep in that dialogue, . . .
> That was the real world; I have touched it once,
> And now shall know it always.

Muir saves this vision from becoming Olympian and complacent by the ending of the poem: however strong this vision of order and good, the evil fear keeps on asserting itself:

> Oh these deceits are strong almost as life
> Last night I dreamt I was in the labyrinth,
> And woke far on. I did not know the place.

So even in dreams the pointlessness can be felt. This pervasiveness of evil, and an intense realization (sometimes through symbol) of what it means in terms of everyday life, is the characteristic advance made by *The Labyrinth* in Muir's treatment of the problem. There is the other dream poem, 'The Combat', showing the conflict between some kind of good and some kind of evil in its fierce picture of the fighting animals; the helplessness of 'The Child Dying'; and above all, perhaps, a relating of the problem of evil to the political situation of the time—to the Second World War in 'The Journey Back', and to the Communist take-over in Prague in 1948 (which Muir witnessed) in 'The Good Town':

> No family now sits at the evening table;
> Father and son, mother and child are *out,*
> A quaint and obsolete fashion. In our houses
> Invaders speak their foreign tongues, informers
> Appear and disappear, . . .
> . . . If you see a man
> Who smiles good-day or waves a lordly greeting
> Be sure he's a policeman or a spy.
> We know them by their free and candid air.

Side by side with this political conception of evil is an equally strong affirmation of the power of love in *The Labyrinth.* Love conquers time in 'Love's Remorse' and 'Love in Time's Despite', and remains when everything else has passed away, the all-including power, as in the 'Song' near the end of the book:

> The quarrel from the start,
> Long past and never past,
> The war of mind and heart,
> The great war and the small
> That tumbles the hovel down
> And topples town on town
> Come to one place at last:
> Love gathers all.

From *Variations on a Time Theme,* through the three intermediate books to *The Labyrinth,* there is a consistent line of development. The attempt to capture the feelings and the meaning of love in poetry goes hand in hand with a similar effort to objectify the power of evil. Thus by the time of writing *The Labyrinth* Muir had succeeded in relating the thin abstractions of Pity and Indifference to the world of 1949. This development clears the way for his greatest treatment of the problem of evil, in his next book, *One Foot in Eden* (1956).

IV

In the *Autobiography* Muir relates the occurrence of a kind of religious experience which happened to him in February 1939. His wife was recovering from an illness in a nursing home, and as he was returning home from visiting her, he saw some children playing marbles on the pavement. In the way it had 'come round' again at its own time, the game 'seemed a simple little rehearsal for a resurrection, promising a timeless renewal of life'. That evening, he says,

> going to bed alone, I suddenly found myself (I was taking off my waistcoat) reciting the Lord's Prayer in a loud, emphatic voice—a thing I had not done for many years—with a deep urgency and profound disturbed emotion. . .˙. as I stood in the middle of the floor half-undressed, saying the prayer over and over, meaning after meaning sprang from it, overcoming me again with joyful surprise; and I realized that this simple petition was always universal and always inexhaustible, and day by day sanctified human life.

Muir goes on to state his religious beliefs. He had always, he says, believed in God and immortality; now 'I realized that, quite without knowing it, I was a Christian, no matter how bad a one; . . . I had a vague sense during these days that Christ was the turning-point of time and the meaning of life to everyone, . . . '

The themes of Muir's poetry at this time reflect this belief, and so does the imagery, to a smaller extent. He was not a member of any church, however, chiefly because he had an antipathy towards the Church of Scotland. He had written a biography of John Knox, discovering in the process that he 'came to dislike him more and more', and he felt that the Scottish Reformation had had a disastrous effect upon the intellectual and cultural life of the country. While England was developing the Elizabethan drama,

> Knox and Melville clapped their preaching palms
> And bundled all the harvesters away,
> Hoodicrow Peden in the blighted corn
> Hacked with his rusty beak the starving haulms.

and under their preaching, literature, and particularly dramatic poetry, withered and died. The result was disastrous:

> This matter of dramatic poetry, indeed, or rather the lack of it, was probably crucial for Scottish literature; and if that is so, then the Reformation truly signalized the beginning of Scotland's decline as a civilized nation.

Muir's dislike of the Church of Scotland springs from the fact that it was somehow on the side of the Story rather than the Fable, chained to time, reducing the vision and the mystery of the Incarnation to its own level of comprehension. As he was later to write in that powerful poem, **"The Incarnate One."**

> The Word made flesh here is made word again,
> A word made word in flourish and arrogant crook.
> See there King Calvin with his iron pen,
> And God three angry letters in a book,
> And there the logical hook
> On which the mystery is impaled and bent
> Into an ideological instrument.

This disengagement with the official church in Scotland suggests one reason why Biblical and Christian imagery do not play a very large part in Muir's poetry up to and including *The Labyrinth.* Believer though he was, the church stood between him and a full imaginative grasp of Christian faith and symbol. Between *The Labyrinth* and *One Foot in Eden,* however, came a period of a little over a year when Muir worked for the British Council in Rome. There, with the whole tradition of Italian visual images before him, he came to an over- whelming realization of what became for him the fact of the Incarnation. In the *Autobiography* he makes an explicit contrast between this revelation and the religion of the United Presbyterian Church of his youth in Orkney, where—

> I was aware of religion chiefly as the sacred Word, and the church itself, severe and decent, with its touching bareness and austerity, seemed to cut off religion from the rest of life and from all the weekday world, as if it were a quite specific thing shut within itself, almost jealously, by its whitewashed walls, furnished with its bare brown varnished benches unlike any others in the whole world, and filled with the odour of ancient Bibles. It did not tell me by any outward sign that the Word had been made flesh.

Instead, says Muir, 'there was the minister', and de- scribes Mr. Pirie and Mr. Webster, who were in charge of the churches of Rousay and Garth. 'In figures such as these,' he says,

> the Word became something more than a word in my childish mind; but nothing told me that Christ was born in the flesh and had lived on the earth.

Now comes the great experience of Rome:

> In Rome that image was to be seen everywhere, not only in churches, but on the walls of houses, at cross-roads in the suburbs, in wayside shrines in the parks, and in private rooms. . . . A religion that dared to show forth such a mystery for everyone to see would have shocked the congregations of the north, would have seemed a sort of blasphemy, perhaps even an indecency. But here it was publicly shown, as Christ showed himself on the earth.

One Foot in Eden shows the influence of this experi- ence in its confident use of traditional Christian imagery and symbol, and its assured rhythms. Italy seems to have released something, to have shown Muir that meaningful statements about life could be made in this way, using the elements of Christian belief. All the themes which attend the problem of evil, the time prob- lem, the Story and the Fable, the idea of life as a jour- ney, are woven into the fabric of the Christian story and interact with it. The result is a poetry so rich in mean- ing and so assured in form that it appears like a sudden late blossoming of Muir's art and makes much of the earlier poetry seem tentative and half-formed. Reading the early books again, after *One Foot in Eden,* one is aware of something repressed, perhaps of Muir's Scot- tish background quietly asserting itself, preventing such an open statement of belief: 'A religion that dared to show forth such a mystery for everyone to see would

have shocked the congregations of the north, would have seemed a sort of blasphemy, perhaps even an inde- cency'. Brought up among such congregations, Muir wrote for years with their repressive ideas behind him, and only in Italy did he shake them off. The result is found in *One Foot in Eden:* Muir stands on common ground with his readers, and this leads to an obvious increase in the compressed utterance of his great theme.

Not all the poems of *One Foot in Eden* are Christian, or use Christian imagery. I have singled out this quality as the characteristic advance of the book and the back- bone of its greatest poems. It might be thought that the Christian content would limit the appreciation of these, but I do not think that this is so. Consider '**The Annun- ciation**', a poem which springs directly from one of the Italian experiences, related in the *Autobiography*—

> I remember stopping for a long time one day to look at a little plaque on the wall of a house in the Via degli Artisti, representing the Annunciation. An angel and a young girl, their bodies inclined towards each other, their knees bent as if they were overcome by love, 'tutto tremante', gazed upon each other like Dante's pair; and that representation of a human love so intense that it could not reach farther seemed the perfect earthly symbol of the love that passes understanding.

The poem manages to convey a kind of breathtaking wonder at the happening, beneath which we can see the old theme of love and time, the problem solved by the visitor from another world:

> The angel and the girl are met.
> Earth was the only meeting place.
> For the embodied never yet
> Travelled round the shore of space.
> The eternal spirits in freedom go.
>
> See, they have come together, see,
> While the destroying minutes flow,
> Each reflects the other's face
> Till heaven in hers and earth in his
> Shine steady there. He's come to her
> From far beyond the farthest star,
> Feathered through time. Immediacy
> Of strangest strangeness is the bliss
> That from their limbs all movement takes.
> Yet the increasing rapture brings
> So great a wonder that it makes
> Each feather tremble on his wings.
>
> Outside the window footsteps fall
> Into the ordinary day
> And with the sun along the wall
> Pursue their unreturning way.
> Sound's perpetual roundabout
> Rolls its numbered octaves out
> And hoarsely grinds its battered tune.
>
> But through the endless afternoon
> These neither speak nor movement make,
> But stare into their deepening trance
> As if their gaze would never break.

As John Holloway has well said, 'There is no more need to be a Christian to admire that, than there was to be a Greek to admire **"Telemachos Remembers"**.'[1] The coming of the angel to Mary becomes a symbol of love coming to a person, making time meaningless, bringing heaven to earth, while outside, time and the footsteps 'Pursue their unreturning way'. Thus the poem says something similar to the sonnets in **The Labyrinth,** 'Love's Remorse' and **'Love in Time's Despite'**; the difference between it and them is that by joining the idea to the idea of the Annunciation, Muir obtains a great leap forward into universally significant meaning. The love which in the earlier poems was the love of one man for one woman, becomes part of the wider scheme of material and spiritual values which make up human life, representing the timeless spiritual qualities as opposed to the noisy Roman afternoon outside the window. In some of these poems, Time is still the great destroyer, as it is in the poem which gives its name to the collection, **'One Foot in Eden'.** Here everything begins in innocence, and is corrupted by Time: although the root is clean, the foliage and the fruit are burned and blackened.

> One foot in Eden still, I stand
> And look across the other land.
> The world's great day is growing late,
> Yet strange these fields that we have planted
> So long with crops of love and hate.
> Time's handiworks by time are haunted,
> And nothing now can separate
> The corn and tares compactly grown.
> The armorial weed in stillness bound
> About the stalk; these are our own.
> Evil and good stand thick around
> In the fields of charity and sin
> Where we shall lead our harvest in.
>
> Yet still from Eden springs the root
> As clean as on the starting day.
> Time takes the foliage and the fruit
> And burns the archetypal leaf
> To shapes of terror and of grief
> Scattered along the winter way.
> But famished field and blackened tree
> Bear flowers in Eden never known.
> Blossoms of grief and charity
> Bloom in these darkened fields alone.
> What had Eden ever to say
> Of hope and faith and pity and love
> Until was buried all its day
> And memory found its treasure trove?
> Strange blessings never in Paradise
> Fall from these beclouded skies.

In his book on Edwin Muir, Professor Butter notes the heraldic imagery running through this poem.[2] The stalk is bound, for instance, by an 'armorial' weed; and this image takes us back to the lion and the dragon at the end of *Variations on a Time Theme*. The answer to the problem of evil in **'One Foot in Eden'** is an extension of the idea of Pity in the earlier poem, but here it is extended into a superb rhetorical question:

> What had Eden ever to say
> Of hope and faith and pity and love
> Until was buried all its day
> And memory found its treasure trove?

Time brought with it the evil of the Fall, but also memory, and the qualities which make life human and worth living, 'strange blessings'. The optimism of this idea is reinforced by the assured and insistent rhythm of the octosyllabic couplets, skilfully and subtly varied to make a poem which is at once a tightly compressed utterance and a source of deep and rich meaning.

The first poem in the collection, **'Milton',** should be enough to draw our attention to the influence of Muir's great predecessor in the poetic treatment of the problem of evil. The man who wrote the beginning of the third book of *Paradise Lost* had his own personal experience of pain and suffering, and the need to explain the world, to justify the ways of God, without ignoring it. This personal background to their approach to the problem is one feature which Milton and Muir share; and I think that one or two specific instances of Miltonic influence can be detected in *One Foot in Eden.* The basic structural image of the title poem is that of the field filled with corn and tares, charity and sin, inextricably intertwined; and while this may have come direct from the Bible, it may also, considering the preoccupation with the Fall which Muir shows in these poems, have come from *Areopagitica*: 'Good and evil we know in the field of this world grow up together almost inseparably'. The germ of the poem is in this sentence, particularly if we consider the context of Adam's sin in which it is placed in *Areopagitica*. From Milton also may have come the suggestion for the great vision of pity and compassion after the Fall in **'Adam's Dream',** which ends:

> And he remembered all, Eden, the Fall,
> The Promise, and his place, and took their hands
> That were his hands, his and his children's hands,
> Cried out and was at peace, and turned again
> In love and grief in Eve's encircling arms.

The idea behind the poem is no different from that of *Variations on a Time Theme*—that pity is one of the results of the problem of evil, and that without suffering and evil pity would not exist; but now Muir has linked the idea with one of the great mythological concepts of mankind—the personal solution and the great story are joined into one.

Pity requires suffering and evil for its existence; pity is a divine attribute, so that through suffering one attains to Paradise. This is the subject of **'Milton',** in which Muir dives back into the past to recapture the feeling of a brawling Saturday night in the Glasgow slums:

> Milton, his face set fair for Paradise,
> And knowing that he and Paradise were lost
> In separate desolation, bravely crossed
> Into his second night and paid his price.
> There towards the end he to the dark tower came
> Set square in the gate, a mass of blackened stone

Crowned with vermilion fiends like streamers
   blown
From a great funnel filled with roaring flame.
Shut in his darkness, these he could not see,
But heard the steely clamour known too well
On Saturday nights in every street in Hell.
Where, past the devilish din, could Paradise be?
A footstep more, and his unblinded eyes
Saw far and near the fields of Paradise.

Milton's first approach to Paradise is too easy, too straightforward; the optimistic Milton of the *Areopagitica* has to be succeeded by the blind, disappointed Milton who out of his very suffering found the justification of the ways of God to men, in order to find the true Paradise, to attain to real sight. In the lines,

But heard the steely clamour known too well
On Saturday nights in every street in Hell,

Muir again shows his ability to generate a feeling that here is personal experience made myth, that the Glasgow street brawls are what Hell is really like. This is life seen against the background of the fable, everything becoming meaningful, seen for what it really is, placed in proportion. It is this which saves his religious poetry from a narrowness which a system of belief might otherwise produce: Muir is dealing with the meaning of his experience and never tries to impose a meaning from without. Moreover, the anti-clerical strain in his poetry continues to be represented in poems like **'The Incarnate One'**, and in poems written after the publication of *One Foot in Eden* like **'The Church'** and **"There's Nothing Here"** (a soliloquy spoken by Muir's cousin Sutherland, awaking after death to find himself in Heaven). In **'The Church'** Muir remembers those—

who house together in Hell,
Cooped by ingenious theological men
Expert to track the sour and musty smell
Of sins they know too well.

In the same way, the Heaven which Sutherland finds himself in is far too pious and good for his natural and unaffected personality, because it is a place without evil and hence without life, a creation of 'ingenious theological men'. Unlike the parsons, Kafka understood, as Milton had done: sin and evil are necessary for understanding, pity and redemption. Part II of *One Foot in Eden* begins with a sonnet to Kafka, which balances the **'Milton'** sonnet at the beginning of Part I. Kafka is the great champion of the inadequate, watching their encounter with 'the authentic ones', finding something in the very inadequacy:

But you, dear Franz, sad champion of the drab
And half, would watch the tell-tale shames drift in
(As if they were troves of treasure) not aloof,
But with a famishing passion quick to grab
Meaning, and read on all the leaves of sin
Eternity's secret script, the saving proof.

In these ways, Muir modifies the Christian ideas of Heaven and Hell, redemption and salvation, so that they

remain true to his personal memories and experience. In this way he is able to use the whole apparatus of Christian thinking to give his ideas a wider significance, without becoming tied to a code of belief and appearing to be a narrow dogmatist. Throughout the volume we are aware of the Scottish temperament in Muir reminding him that life is hard, that 'This is a difficult land', that Abraham did not live to see the Promise come, that there are times when God seems dead, 'a blindfold mask on a pillar of dust'. In *One Foot in Eden* Muir recognizes all this and approaches Christianity from these experiences; and the poems are the result of this combination of experience and belief.

V

Some of the developing ideas of Muir's poetry around this theme of the problem of evil can be seen on a parallel course in the *Essays on Literature and Society* (1949). In this collection of essays, the critical problems which interest him are closely related to his main poetic themes. We find fragmentary glimpses of what is to become complete in *One Foot in Eden*—the recognition of evil, and the reasons for its existence—in many of the essays. Muir writes with understanding of Hardy's conception that 'misfortune is a principle of the universe', for he had experienced such beliefs himself when he saw the brutality in Glasgow after Johnnie's death. Similarly, he knows that Browning was not just confidently optimistic, that he knew something about frustration, about 'the uniqueness and separation of the individual, the imperfection of human life'. From another point of view he is fascinated by the tragedies of Chapman: Bussy D'Ambois and Byron are 'unfallen men among the fallen', they are 'images of man in his original virtue; there is nothing else quite like them in English literature'. Time and its work is seen in the essay on Scott, who had once been violently in love, and who put the episode of Williamina Stuart-Belsches behind him to plunge into a life of compromise outside his Eden; and in the essay on Hölderlin who, like Muir, was preoccupied with 'the mystery of time and eternity'. As the Second World War gave Muir a more accurate insight into the nature of evil, we have the lecture on King Lear in which Goneril, Regan and Edmund represent a kind of Elizabethan *Realpolitik*, subscribing to 'interest and force, the gods of the new age'. In the essay on Spengler, which shows how far Muir had got Nietzsche out of his system, he writes of the fight between two views of life—

the religious view, which is also that of the artist, and the historical view. The virtue of the first— not its supreme virtue, which is its truth, but its relative pragmatic virtue—is that it gives meaning to the actual life we live, and accounts to us for ourselves. . . . The old view of life sees endless variety and complexity in human existence, and yet makes certain fundamental distinctions: good and evil, truth and falsehood, guilt and innocence. The new historical view as expressed by Spengler sees no essential variety in human existence at all, but only the category of power, or, in other words, of necessity; and yet, in spite of its simplicity, it leads to no conclusion: it remains on the plane of pure relativity. And on the plane of pure relativity it is possible to prefer anything to anything else: a well-grown tiger to Socrates or Christ, brutality to kindness, cunning to honesty, treachery to good faith.

It is the gradual development of Muir's thought in this fight which we have been observing—his insistence on the importance of the fabulous, that which gives meaning to life, while yet recognizing the inescapable necessity of evil. The development of his thought towards the completeness of *One Foot in Eden* is gradual, because while Muir is striving for something which will give a clue to the total meaning of life, he allows nothing which has not been proved upon the pulses. This is why the Christian imagery is so restrained until the visit to Italy, for before then it did not mean much to him.

The search for completeness, finally, is one reason why Muir did not write in Scots but in English. He used the word himself in an important paragraph in *Scott and Scotland* (1936)—'a Scottish writer who wishes to achieve some approximation to completeness has no choice except to absorb the English tradition'. Completeness for Muir meant an answer to the problem of evil, to the basic questions of our human conditions, which would be both philosophical and personal, combining thought, imagination and experience. He worked towards it slowly, with an integrity which appears in his faithfulness to experience, until in *One Foot in Eden* he attains to that religious view which is also that of the artist, which 'gives meaning to the actual life we live, and accounts to us for ourselves'.

NOTES

[1] "The Poetry of Edwin Muir", *Hudson Review,* 13, pp. 550-567.

[2] *Edwin Muir* (Writers and Critics Series), pp. 89-90.

Elgin W. Mellown (essay date 1965)

SOURCE: "Autobiographical Themes in the Novels of Edwin Muir," in *Wisconsin Studies in Contemporary Literature,* Vol. 6, No. 2, Summer, 1965, pp. 228-42.

[*In the following essay, Mellown traces Muir's artistic development through an examination of his use of autobiographical material in* The Marionette, The Brothers, *and* Poor Tom.]

During his lifetime Edwin Muir was probably best known as a professional journalist who specialized in reviewing novels and in translating, with his wife, various German books.[1] To a more select audience he was a valued poet, novelist, and literary critic, and to Scottish readers he was a sometimes tart commentator on the contemporary political scene. Indeed there were few literary forms which Muir did not use with skill, and while today his poetry is receiving ever more favorable attention, any estimate of his literary achievement must be based on the sum of his diverse accomplishments, for they all reflect, to a greater or lesser extent, his individuality. In *An Autobiography* (1954) and many of the later poems his personality is clearly evident, yet his three novels, written in his middle-age and ostensibly works of fiction, also show the development of his personality and even have their genesis in autobiographical sources. The novels were published within a five-year period, *The Marionette* appearing in 1927, *The Three Brothers* in 1931, and *Poor Tom* in 1932.[2]

Each novel centers upon one main character, a young man who in spite of apparent differences actually portrays the author. The differences between these three fictional characters reflect the maturing of Muir's personality and the development of his understanding of himself. *The Marionette* was published eight years after Muir, then thirty-one years old, married, gave up his job as a clerk in a Glasgow ship-building firm, and went to London to work as a journalist. Shortly afterward he and his wife moved to central Europe, where for several years they supported themselves by free-lance journalism. They studied the German language and its literature and immersed themselves in the cultural life of such cities as Vienna, Prague, Salzburg, and Dresden. In the spring of 1925 they went to St. Tropez, in the south of France, "where the living was cheap." There they began to translate Lion Feuchtwanger's *Jud Süss* for Mr. Martin Secker. "At the approach of winter," Muir writes in *An Autobiography,* "we went to Menton, where we lived, still translating, in a little house on the side of a hill above the town. I began to write my story about Salzburg, and my wife sat down to a novel she had been turning over in her mind for a long time."[3] His "story" was *The Marionette;* Mrs. Muir's novel was *Imagined Corners,* not published until 1931. Although Muir had published three books of essays and two of poems in addition to his journal-writing, *The Marionette* was his first prose fiction. It was not a conventional first novel. The *Times Literary Supplement* reviewer described it as "a curious book: indeed, one cannot call it a novel at all, but a *conte* the artistic purpose of which is obscure." The reviewer praised "the carefulness of the writing, the precision of the detail, the obvious rhythm, and the completeness of the construction," yet he found that "the studied objectivity of the presentation leaves a reader who does not instinctively respond to grope uncertainly for the reason why the emotions and reactions of a half-witted boy should have any but a pathological importance."[4] Hans, the "half-witted boy" who is the principal figure, is not (as I hope to show) actually a *character,* but rather one aspect of his creator, while his being placed in Salzburg is determined largely by Muir's wish to introduce the Austrian landscape, which also appears in some of the *First Poems* (1925) and in the *Chorus of the Newly Dead* (1926), and to utilize Salzburg's famous marionette theater. The latter supplies the 'heroine' of the novel, the Gretchen marionette (from the miniature production of *Faust*) with whom Hans falls in love.[5]

Between his first and second novels, Muir wrote *The Structure of the Novel* (1928), a critical study for the Hogarth Lecture Series, and *John Knox, Portrait of a Calvinist* (1929), a biography commissioned by Jonathan Cape; in addition he translated a number of German works with his wife. *The Structure of the Novel* would appear to be a helpful adjunct to a study of Muir's novels, but actually the title is misleading: the work is about the *philosophy* of the novel and is valuable as the critic's rather than the novelist's consideration of the form. The biography of Knox is actually more important to the student of Muir's thought, because the historical research for this work proved to Muir that the Reformation was the most important influence on contemporary Scottish life and also convinced him that the agrarian life he had known as a child in the Orkney Islands was typical of life from time immemorial, that he had indeed lived an 'archetypal' existence between his birth in 1887 and the removal of his family to Glasgow in 1901.

Muir's belief in his archetypal childhood colored much of his later work, including his second novel, *The Three Brothers,* in which he describes his childhood in terms of fictional, sixteenth-century characters. He had no difficulty in placing these autobiographical events in the time setting of the Reformation, for believing that there was no difference between his own time and that of the sixteenth century, he wrote of them without attempting to recreate a historical period in the style of such a novelist as Feuchtwanger. With the exception of the melodramatic events of the second part of the novel, *The Three Brothers* is much the same story as is found in An *Autobiography,* told there in the first person.[6]

The Three Brothers had brought Muir back to his native land, and in his last novel he considered not merely his own country but his own time as well: *Poor Tom* takes place in Glasgow during the first decade of the century and is a barely disguised account of the formation of Edwin Muir's own social attitudes. While it may well have been influenced by some of the works which the Muirs had translated—"Ludwig Renn's" *War* (1929) and *After War* (1931) and Feuchtwanger's *Two Anglo-Saxon Plays* (1928) deal, for instance, with the awakening of social consciousness—an awareness of politics and society is so much a part of the literature of the time that *Poor Tom* was probably not so much influenced by other works as it is a product of the same Zeitgeist. This contemporaneous quality of *Poor Tom* is true also of *The Three Brothers* and *The Marionette,* a historical novel and a surrealistic fantasy respectively, for each is typical in its kind of its year. Muir attempted in each novel to use a popular form, yet each is imprinted with his personality, which makes his novel stand out from others of the same type.

The three novels are all concerned with approximately the same period of adolescency in the main character's life. Although these three young men—Hans the Austrian idiot, David the sixteenth-century Scotsman, and Mansie the twentieth-century Glaswegian—appear to be dissimilar in character, their real difference comes from the distance at which their creator places them before the reader. Hans, the idiot, is the most removed, since his psychological condition alienates him from even the other characters in the novel. That it was not Muir's intention to portray another "idiot boy" (as Faulkner was to do with his Benjy) can be seen in his inconsistent handling of point of view in relation to Hans, for Hans' abilities vary widely. At times he possesses a poet's vision: "A lizard scuttling across the stones would make the place insecure [to Hans]. He saw nature as a terrifying heraldry. The cat, the lizard, and the wasp were embattled forces armed for war, carrying terror and death on their blazoned stripes, their stings, claws, and tongues. He could only run away from them to the vacancy of his room." (pp. 7-8) And again Hans is like a mystic or seer (pp. 8-9):

> Once when he was with his nursemaid on the crest of the Kapuziner Berg he saw a sight which he remembered always afterwards. The evening was still; the sun was setting behind the mountains; from the town, whose roofs were gilded by the light, came the sound of bells. Beneath him, overhanging a little precipice, lay a sloping bank, very green in the level light, and over it, in silence, three black dogs were coursing. Their snouts tied to the ground, their sides sharpened, their eyes desperate, they flew around in circles; sometimes their paws spurned clods and stones over the cliff, but they never stopped. Round them the turf glowed, every blade of grass glittered with a vivid, wakening green, but they seemed to have no kinship with it; they were as chill and dark as the mould beneath. Hans knew that the ground had once been a grave, and he had a vision of the spirit, a few feet underground, racing the dogs and maliciously leading them on. When the last rays left the mound all three stopped, tumbled over one another, and leapt round their master who was sitting near. But Hans was afraid.

Yet most often Hans is merely an idiot who may awaken pity, but whose insight is nil and whose apprehension is so worthless that the novelist completely passes it by: "It was too cold for [Hans] to sit in the shed. Accordingly the dolls and the dolls' house were installed in his bedroom, but although he spent all his time there he paid little attention to them. Sometimes he sat mute and vacant; sometimes he walked restlessly to and fro as if seeking release." (p. 52)

In contrast to Hans, David and Mansie are placed very close to the reader. Muir handles the sixteenth-century characters as if they were contemporaries; he mentions historical events and makes dramatic use of them, but *The Three Brothers* is not a period novel with a detailed reconstruction of a particular time and place. The historical setting is valuable to the novelist mainly because it gives him an objective point of view for handling incidents from his own life. Thus for example David hears his mother speak to the laborer Sutherland (pp. 25-26):

> One day Mrs. Blackadder burst out on Sutherland when they were all seated at their midday meal, accusing him of having been out again the night before. The twins stopped eating and gazed at him; his face was changing under their eyes and growing grave and important. Now they would know all about it at last, they thought, but Sutherland's words only cast them into deeper perplexity. "I swear on my oath, mistress, that I wasna away from this house all night. I'll no' deny though," he added, as if trying to remember, "that I mightna have been out in the yard in the dawing on a matter of needcessity." Mrs. Blackadder laughed scornfully, and their father said: "Needcessity! Ay, Sutherland, we ken your needcessity." And later, after Sutherland had left, he said, as if to himself: "Why, the man canna look at them, it seems, without them getting in the family way!" It was more than ever a mystery to the twins, and for days afterwards they gazed at Sutherland in respect and wonder, and were a little afraid of him when he joked with them.

The portrait of Sutherland is actually a direct copy of Muir's cousin Sutherland, who lived with the family in the Orkneys. The sketch of the cousin in *An Autobiography* is in the same vein as the account in the novel: "His language [Muir writes] was very free, and his advances shockingly direct, but always with a show of reason. He never tried to show 'the women why they should yield to him, but concentrated on the much more subtle question 'Why not?' a question very difficult to answer. He was the father of a number of illegitimate children, and I remember my father once saying in a vexed voice, 'Why, the man canna look at a woman, it seems, withoot putting her in the family way!' I was too young at the time to understand these words." (p. 17) Other incidents handled in *The Three Brothers* from a third-person point of view—those of a betrayed woman attacking her seducer, two men fighting in the street, the deaths of David's mother and his brother Sandy, and others—are given in *An Autobiography* as the first-person experiences of Edwin Muir. But were the incidents of the novel entirely fictitious, then the sensitive, personal outlook of David Blackadder, so exactly that of Edwin Muir as it is expressed in *An Autobiography* and other writings, would allow him to be treated as a projection of the novelist's own personality.

Having used autobiographical details in an historical setting, Muir evidently gained the confidence to treat them in their own setting and time in *Poor Tom,* juxtaposing for dramatic effect the actual events of almost a decade into a fictional two-year period. It is true that Muir disclaimed autobiographical sources for the novel,[7] but the evidence of the novel itself outweighs his protestations. Indeed the best chapters are those about events which he describes in *An Autobiography* as his own experiences during his youth and early manhood in Glasgow. Among these is the account of Mansie's becoming a Socialist, the highpoint being his participation in a May Day parade in Glasgow. He marches with the Clarion Scouts, "enclosed in peace" and "embedded in fold after fold of security." He looks about him and sees a man carrying a little girl on his shoulder (pp. 102-104):

> Mansie could not take his eyes from her, and when the procession began to move, when, in a long line like the powerful and easy rise and fall of a quiet surge, the ranked shoulders in front of him swung up and down, bearing forward on their surface that gay and fragile little bark, unexpected tears rose into Mansie's throat. But when presently from the front of the procession the strains of the "Marsellaise" rolled back towards him over the surface of that quietly rising and falling sea, gathering force as it came until at last it broke round him in a stationary storm of sound in which his own voice was released, he no longer felt that the little girl riding on the shoulder of the surge was more beautiful than anything else, for everything was transfigured. . . .   His arms and shoulders sprouted like a tree, scents of spring filled his nostrils, and when, still gazing in a trance at the bare-headed man with the little girl on his shoulder, he also took off his hat, his brows branched and blossomed. . . .

The procession passes through the slums and Mansie's euphoria influences even his attitude to the jeering crowds along the way. After the procession reaches Glasgow Green, "the spell did not lose its power, and Mansie wandered from platform to platform, where Socialist orators, still transfigured so that he scarcely recognized them, spoke of the consummated joys of the future society where all people would live together in love and joy." (pp. 105-106)

In *An Autobiography* Muir describes his political experiences more obliquely than in the novel, yet his attitude to them is the same. About 1906 he joined the Clarion Scouts, a "*do* something to make the world better" club fostered by Robert Blatchford's newspaper, the *Clarion.*[8] By the time he was twenty-one he had been converted to Socialism, which gave him "a future in which everything, including myself, was transfigured. . . . My sense of human potentiality was so strong that even the lorrymen and the slum boys were transformed by it; I no longer saw them as they were, but as they would be when the society of which I dreamed was realized. . . . For the first time in my life I began to like ordinary vulgar people, because in my eyes they were no longer ordinary or vulgar, since I saw in them shoots of the glory which they would possess when all men and women were free and equal. . . . It was a state which did not last for long; but having once known it I could sometimes summon it back again." (p. 113) The detachment of this later evaluation is in fact also present in *Poor Tom,* for the description of the May Day parade continues with Mansie wondering "whether he had talked a great deal of nonsense during the day," and deciding that "everything was allowed." He ends the day in his original "blissful security" (pp. 106-107), and the bubble of euphoria bursts only in the following chapter: "As his exaltation of the last few days gradually oozed out of him and he returned to a more comfortable size it was actually a relief—he couldn't but admit it to himself, it was an undeniable relief, though it left a sort of empty feeling somewhere. His feet were on the earth again. Strange how easily you slipped back into your old feelings! And when a man turned round to him and asked how he had liked his first procession, he said carelessly: 'Oh, it was quite all right in its way.'" (p. 109) Muir's change of style between the two chapters is intentional: the account of the parade is elated and high-flown and reinforces the quality of Mansie's experience, while the style of passages concerning Mansie's every-day life is pedestrian. The high-flown prose reveals Muir's most successful writing, for here, as in the early poems, he is closest to success when closest to bathos.

The Three Brothers and *Poor Tom* may profitably be studied as works embodying actual details taken from the novelist's personal experiences, but the relationship of *The Marionette* to Muir's life is found in the use of themes which appear both in the other novels and in the novelist's own life. The most important link between the three novels is found in the theme of the hero and his brothers. The theme is quite obvious in the two later novels, while in *The Marionette* it is treated in a stylized manner not dissimilar to that of the ballet *Petrouchka*, then all the rage with the avant-garde. The realization that the three male dolls are Hans' "brothers" helps one to understand that Hans is himself as limited as a wooden doll, powerless to act for himself and subject always to stronger wills. Muir's picture of him may be taken as a rendition in fiction of his own attitude to his life in earlier years. The sketch he gives of himself in the "Fairport" chapter of *An Autobiography* shows the same submissiveness that is exaggerated to a surrealistic level in the character of Hans, whose inarticulateness appears to correspond to Muir's own failure to make any satisfactory response to life for so many years before his marriage.

The reader must view Hans as being on the level of a wooden doll if he is to appreciate the role which the Gretchen marionette plays in the novel. She fills the same part that Ellen (in *The Three Brothers*) and Helen (in *Poor Tom*) play, that of the betraying heroine.[9] Possibly because his characters were so thoroughly disguised Muir employed more violent action in this story than in his other two works. The betrayal in *The Marionette* (which has many overtones depending on the Crucifixion) takes place in the garden of Hans' home when neighborhood boys throw stones across the fence at Hans and the Gretchen marionette, which is with him, does not 'protect' him but remains with the other wooden dolls. The climax of the novel occurs when Hans 'murders' Gretchen by repeatedly piercing her body with a nail: the symbolism is perhaps too apparent.

This theme of the betraying heroine is also present in the other two novels. The treatment of the theme in *The*

Three Brothers is almost as spectacular as that in *The Marionette:* David is actually betrayed by Ellen, who is seduced by his twin-brother Archie and later murdered by a former fiancé. In *Poor Tom* there is little melodrama in the betrayal, which is of Tom. It is symbolized in Chapter Four when Helen throws the locket which Tom gave her into the sea. Mansie feels that Helen's turning to him is in some way the cause of Tom's illness, and he finally gives up Helen to reconcile himself with his brother and to remain constantly by his deathbed. The themes of the hero and his brothers and the betraying heroine are thus related through fraternal rivalry and jealousy, exemplified in the love of the brothers for the same girl.

Other familial relationships in the novels provide themes which can be traced directly to Muir's own life. The death of the hero's mother is in each novel an important influence upon him: Hans' mother dies at his birth and David's mother, half-way through the novel, while the death of Mansie's mother is predicted through the closing chapters of the novel. The father-son relationship is more mechanically formed: either the son is extremely close to his father, as Hans and David are, each being indeed the sole object of his father's love, or the son has no contact at all with the father, as is the case with Mansie.

The connection of these and other themes with Muir's life is to be found in the first chapters of *An Autobiography,* and especially in the chapter entitled "Glasgow." Edwin, born in 1887, was the youngest child of four sons and two daughters and consequently knew his father only as an old man. He tells how the Muir family left their native Orkney Islands in 1901 to settle in the bustling city of Glasgow, a move from a pre-Industrial, agrarian society to the depths of an industrialized squalor. Mr. and Mrs. Muir brought their family to Glasgow because the older children had gone there to work; but Mr. Muir was unable to adjust to the ways of city life and soon died, and in steady succession came the deaths of the son Willie (from consumption), of another son, Johnnie (from a brain tumor), and of the mother, who, weakened from nursing her sons, died of an internal disease. These deaths, all within a period of four years, as well as the many difficulties of adjusting to the life of the city, were critical influences upon the adolescent Muir and helped to cause a neurotic condition which he only began to master after a course of psychoanalysis begun in 1920 in London. As a part of this treatment his analyst, Dr. Maurice Nicoll, asked him to write down his dreams and waking images.[10] Although the exercise was designed largely to make Muir objectify his fears and hidden thoughts, it also confronted him with the workings of his subconscious mind, and he quickly became aware of the latent poetry hidden there.

As early as December 23, 1920, he had written about the Super-Ego in a "prose-poem" entitled **"Man and His Brother,"**[11] and by the summer of 1922, he had turned a number of his dreams into poems with such titles as **"Rebirth"** and **"Ballad of Eternal Life."**[12] Prose versions of them, taken from the notebook in which he originally recorded his dreams, are given in *An Autobiography*. His purpose in writing these poems appears to have been analogous to that of Robert Graves in some of his post-war poetry. In *Mirror of Minds,* Professor Geoffrey Bullough, discussing the "new psychology" as it appears in modern poetry, writes that "Coming back from the First World War bitter and almost broken in mind, Mr. Graves used poetry as a means of recuperation and brought the repressed anguish of recent experience into the open by means of lyrics and anecdotes suffused with a quality of nightmare. The poetry of this phase . . . is distinguished . . . by a realization of the Freudian nature of the release afforded."[13] Professor Bullough points out that "In time Graves passed out of this phase," and suggests that "perhaps his cure came from realizing the causes of his trouble and from writing openly about it."[14] Although positive evidence is not available, it is quite probable that Dr. Nicoll encouraged Muir (who was supporting himself through his writing) to use his work as psychological therapy. Whether or not Muir was so advised, he found that poetry could objectify and purge his fears, as he states clearly in *An Autobiography* when he describes "the day when Freddie Sinclair chased me home. . . . he wanted to fight me again, but I was afraid. . . . afterwards I was so ashamed of that moment of panic that I did not dare to speak of it to anyone, and drove it out of my mind. I was seven at the time. . . . I got rid of that terror almost thirty years later in a poem describing Achilles chasing Hector round Troy, in which I pictured Hector returning after his death to run the deadly race over again. . . . The poem cleared my conscience." (pp. 42-43)

In the same way Muir's novels may be considered as attempts to objectify and rid himself of certain fears and emotions. They especially reveal his relationships with his immediate family. In *The Marionette* and *The Three Brothers* he creates a father-son relationship which is fairly obviously a wish-fulfillment based upon his own experiences as the youngest son of an old father. In *Poor Tom* he restricts himself to the actual situation, giving the father no part in the development of Mansie. Likewise, in the same novel his treatment of the mother is based upon the actual truth: Mrs. Manson is a background figure whose presence, if shadowy, influences the characters and events. In his first novel he attempts not to write about the mother-son relationship, because, we may speculate, the death of his mother, an event which haunted him for many years, was too close to him to be externalized, even in the surrealistic disguise which *The Marionette* afforded him. In his second novel he reverses his relationship with his own parents, making David (his proto-self) the favorite of the father and not of the mother, who indeed rejects him in favor of his twin-brother, Archie. One need not be a Freudian, or even a psychologist, to appreciate this mechanical reversal and use of opposites.

Muir's treatment of these autobiographical themes in his novels is related to his own personal development,

the record of which is found in *An Autobiography*. The story of the first novel is at the furthest possible remove from the author, who protects himself from discovery and personal criticism by making the principal figure a half-wit, a type of character through whom any emotion can be expressed. In his second novel, Muir, achieving an ever greater objectivity in his life, is able to treat his story in an almost direct fashion, interposing only a time difference between his novel and the autobiographical events therein chronicled. Finally in *Poor Tom* he handles his story in a perfectly direct manner, using both the scene and time of the actual events. Muir's increased objectivity about himself is also seen in his treatment of the heroes in *The Three Brothers* and *Poor Tom*. David Blackadder is an ideal character, a person enjoying relationships such as Muir may have desired for himself, while Mansie Manson is Muir himself, seen in the harshest light possible.

While these themes are more or less directly related to the novelist's own life, they also possess a mythical quality or pattern: the themes are archetypal, significant not merely for Muir alone, but for men in all ages. Of these archetypal themes, the most important is that of the hero's search for an understanding of his life, and indeed, all three novels might well be called *initiation* novels. In *The Marionette* and *The Three Brothers* the father is directly responsible for the son's abortive attempts at understanding himself: Hans, because of his withdrawn condition, can never come to grips with life, and David, because of his innocence, cannot understand the world until he moves farther away from his Eden. The first novel ends somewhat abruptly because the writer realized that Hans, as a fictional character, could never complete the search and hence was of no further value. *The Three Brothers,* however, ends with the search continuing: David wishes to leave his father, and "It was decided that he should try England first, and if he did not like it go over to Holland to his friend Cranstoun." (p. 343) Finally, in *Poor Tom* the hero's search is rewarded, for as Mansie stands by Tom's coffin he is rewarded by a vision of the world and his place in it (pp. 251-254):

> Mansie stood without moving, breathed in the scent of the lilies, and no longer felt any desire to go away; for though he knew that he was standing here in the parlour with his dead brother, something so strange had happened that it would have rooted him to a place where he desired far less to be: the walls had receded, the walls of the whole world had receded, and soundlessly a vast and perfect circle—not the provisional circle of life, which can never be fully described—had closed, and he stood within it. He did not know what it was that he divined and bowed down before: everlasting and perfect order, the eternal destiny of all men, the immortality of his own soul; he could not have given utterance to it, although it was so clear and certain; but he had a longing to fall on his knees. . . . Nothing less than death could erase all wrong and all memory of wrong, leaving the soul free for perfect friendship. . . . He wanted to experience

again, like someone learning a lesson, all that he had already experienced; for it seemed a debt due by him to life from which he had turned away, which he had walked round until his new road seemed the natural one, although it had led him to places where all life was frozen to rigidity. . . . He was in haste to begin, and with a last glance at Tom's face, which he could only dimly discern now, for darkness was falling, he left the room and closed the door after him.

Significantly, Edwin Muir wrote no more novels when he had finished **Poor Tom.**

. . . . .

Muir uses autobiographical themes extensively in his novels and poems, although his skill varies considerably between the two forms. Writing in prose, he learned by 1932 to handle such themes directly and without the intervention of any disguises. In poetry, however, he was longer in gaining the necessary skill to use them successfully, for only in **The Narrow Place** (1943) and subsequent volumes does one find the poetic equivalent of **Poor Tom**—a handling of autobiographical themes which is both detached and intimate. His succeeding volumes of verse show his ultimate achievement in relying upon personal experiences—both actual and psychic—and gloriously vindicate the fumbling technique found in the earlier volumes of poetry and prose. Muir's novels are to be valued for their own worth, as well as for having provided scope for a major poet to develop his use of autobiographical themes as basic literary sources.

Muir's three novels are certainly integral parts of his personal and æsthetic development, but how is Muir to be regarded as a novelist? Because of his limited output and its restricted range, he obviously stands apart from the development of the modern novel. Yet his use of events and themes which though personal have a general applicability, deserves more recognition than has been given to him as a novelist; and his practice relates his novels and poems to the work of the not inconsiderable number of autobiographical writers of the nineteen-twenties and 'thirties. The student of Muir's work may consider the novels as extensions to **An Autobiography,** while the psychologist may view them as psychological therapy in action, but the beginning novelist might well read them as models of how the novelist turns particular, personal facts into general, universally accepted statements of truth.

NOTES

[1] This essay has been drawn from my University of London Ph.D. dissertation, "The Literary Achievement of Edwin Muir" (1962). I am grateful to Mrs. Willa Muir for allowing me to visit her at her home in Cambridgeshire and for numerous letters about her husband's work. I am also indebted for information to Professor Peter Butter, Queen's University, Belfast, who is writing the official biography of Muir.

[2] Contemporary reviewers generally appreciated the novels, but they were never reprinted and since today copies of them are difficult to find, plot summaries may be helpful to the reader.

The setting of *The Marionette* (London and New York, 1927) is modern Salzburg and its two main characters are a middle-aged widower named Martin Scheffer and his feebleminded son Hans. The housekeeper Emma takes care of Hans, and Martin ignores him until she insists that his fourteenth birthday must be recognized. Martin then attempts to bring the boy out of his vacancy by gaining his confidence, walking with him and taking him to the marionette theater. Hans is fascinated by the miniature production of *Faust,* and his father secures the Gretchen marionette for him, which joins his collection of dolls in the doll-house built on Martin's orders for him. Martin appears to hope that Hans' interest in the little world of the marionettes will awaken in him an interest in or a grasp of the larger world of reality. But the dolls only increase Hans' confusion about himself and reality, and eventually the father realizes that he can do nothing for his son. In the abrupt conclusion the reader is told that Martin becomes reconciled to Hans' condition and that they live out their days happily enough.

The Three Brothers (London and New York, 1931), a *bildungsroman* of the Scottish Reformation, is the story of David Blackadder and his relationship with his father, a renaissance humanist; with his twin-brother, Archie, his 'evil genius'; and with his older brother Sandy, a fanatic Calvinist. David lives on the family farm and is educated by his father; he goes to St. Andrews to study and then to Edinburgh, where he is frustrated in his love-affair with Ellen, who is seduced by Archie. Ellen is subsequently murdered by her former fiancé, who also wounds Archie; and Sandy dies of consumption, having renounced Calvinism for the more liberal tenets of the Anabaptists. David frees himself from his twin-brother's influence and leaves Scotland for England and the Continent.

Poor Tom (London, 1932) takes place in Glasgow during 1911-1913; it is the story of the brothers Tom and Mansie, their mother Mrs. Manson, and their cousin Jean. The action is slight; indeed in Chapter Nineteen, an essay on Christianity and socialism, no mention is even made of the story. Mansie, the main character, is disliked by Tom because Mansie has achieved social and business successes beyond Tom's powers and has taken his sweetheart Helen from him. Tom begins to drink and injures his head in a fall while drunk. The injury causes a brain tumor, and the second half of the novel is a description of his prolonged illness and eventual death. During his illness Mansie breaks his engagement to Helen and makes a reconciliation with his brother. The last pages of the novel give Mansie's "vision" of the world and of his place therein.

Numbers in parentheses throughout my text will refer to the English editions.

[3] Edwin Muir, *An Autobiography* (London, 1954), pp. 228, 229-230. Numbers in parentheses throughout my text will refer to this edition.

[4] May 19, 1927, p. 352.

[5] Echoes of Goethe's *Faust* appear throughout *The Marionette;* and on the title page of the novel appears the second stanza of the lyric from *Wilhelm Meister's Lehrjahre* beginning "Wer nie sein Brot mit Tränen ass."

[6] In spite of Muir's interposing four centuries between his fictional autobiography and himself, he was probably following the lead provided him by Mrs. Muir in both her first and second novels, *Imagined Corners* (London, 1931) and *Mrs. Ritchie* (London, 1933). Both are set in contemporary Scotland and appear to have direct connections with Mrs. Muir's life, both before and after her marriage. They provide a contrast to Muir's works, being suffused with a sharp, satirical tone that never enters his novels. Mrs. Muir has told me that copies of *Mrs. Ritchie,* an exposé of Scottish motherhood and Calvinism, were burned in the streets of several Scottish towns shortly after the publication of the novel.

[7] Professor Peter Butter has described to me a letter which he read from the novelist to his sister Clara (who appears to have been the model for the character Jean in *Poor Tom*) in which Muir assures her that the work is not autobiographical.

[8] Laurence Thompson, *Robert Blatchford: Portrait of an Englishman* (London, 1951), p. 130.

[9] The main characters in the novels are all linked by similar vowel combinations in their names: *e/e* appears in the female names (Gretchen, Ellen, and Helen), while *a/i* (or *ie* or *y*) is employed in the male names (Hans, Martin, David, Archie, and Mansie).

[10] Dr. Nicoll was identified as Muir's analyst by Michael Hamburger in his essay "Edwin Muir," *Encounter,* XV (December, 1960), 47. Nicoll was an exponent of Jungian ideas; and his work with Muir was an important influence on the young writer (see *An Autobiography,* pp. 157-65).

[11] The *New Age,* XXVIII (December 23, 1920), 96. This poem has not been reprinted.

[12] These poems were also printed in the *New Age,* XXXI (June 8 and July 6, 1922), 72, 121-22. Revisions of them are included in Muir's *First Poems* (London, 1925).

[13] London, 1962, pp. 229-30.

[14] *Ibid.,* p. 231.

Daniel Hoffman (essay date 1966)

SOURCE: "Edwin Muir: The Story and the Fable," in *The Yale Review,* Vol. LV, No. 3, March, 1966, pp. 403-26.

[*In the following essay, Hoffman examines myth and tradition underlying Muir's poetry.*]

In the last poem before his death Edwin Muir wrote,

> I have been taught by dreams and fantasies
> Learned from the friendly and the darker
>   phantoms
> And got great knowledge and courtesy from the
>   dead. . . .

Now that his poems are completed, his debts to fantasies and dreams and to the past are clear. His own past had itself the pattern of a quest which disclosed its direction only as it went along, a pattern of continual revelation. And that direction seems a recapitulation in a single life of the fall of a society from pastoral innocence to the sufferings of modern man. Muir knew at first hand not only the dour poverty of the industrial slums but the sufferings of wartime Europe. He was a witness to the Communist seizure of power in Czechoslovakia and the resulting repression of his democratic friends. The latter half of his life, lived mainly on the Continent in Prague, Dresden, France, and Rome, contributed some materials to his poetry, but the main outline of Muir's imaginative experience was determined by his first thirty-five years. After his boyhood on his father's farm in the remote Orkney Islands, Muir's family was dispossessed by a harsh landlord. Luckless thereafter, they tried to start life anew among the still harsher exactions of the Glasgow slums. There followed in quick succession the heart-breaking deaths of both parents and two brothers. Edwin Muir subsequently found a job in a bone-factory where animal waste was converted into fertilizer, a nightmare parody of the inhuman industrialism which had crushed the ancient cohesiveness of Scotland as a people, as it had destroyed the Muir family. There, amid the fetid stink of rotting meat, Edwin lived in a state of shock, in a situation like that in a tale by Kafka, whose work Muir, with his wife Willa Anderson, would translate into English. Muir's intellectual awakening began with the influence of Heine, then of Nietzsche. Psychoanalysis in his middle thirties loosed the subconscious life of "dreams and fantasies" which he controlled in poems of remarkable poignance and power.

As a poet who seeks his truths in "dreams and fantasies" Edwin Muir summons the phantoms of his own unconscious life, with the certainty that these are not merely the tormented or triumphant imaginings of one particular man but take their forms and reveal their meanings as part of the inheritance of the race. In his ***Autobiography*** Muir has much to say about his dreams and their sources in childhood memories stirred up by later conflicts. It is quite clear that the images of animals, of struggles, of journeys, of recurrent visitations in certain landscapes attained by great effort and endured with a sense of inevitability—all these materials are akin to those patterns of memory which Jung has proposed as the Archetypes, residing not in exterior experience but inherent in the human mind. It is clear, too, that a workable correlation exists between such a theory of psychology and the Platonic conception of reality, a conception particularly attractive to a poet who inherits the intellectual attitudes of late Romanticism.

Platonism and Jungian archetype pass dramatically into one another in Muir's poem **"Hölderlin's Journey"** (1937). This is one of the many poems in which Muir sends his protagonist on a pilgrimage through life; in many of the others the destination is only partially revealed, but in this poem, based upon the life of a poet Muir much admired and translated, the journey ends in a perfect epiphany of despair:

> The evening brought a field, a wood.
>   I left behind the hills of lies,
> And watched beside a mouldering gate
>   A deer with its rock-crystal eyes.
>
> On either pillar of the gate
>   A deer's head watched within the stone.
> The living deer with quiet look
>   Seemed to be gazing on
>
> Its picture death—and suddenly
>   I knew, Diotima was dead,
> As if a single thought had sprung
>   From the cold and the living head.

Like Socrates, like Hölderlin, Muir has learned from Diotima that we attain to knowledge of the Forms by passing from love of the beautiful to love of the idea of beauty. Her death then means the extinction of the Platonic possibility, "a broken mind," the end of the imagination's power to unite created things with uncreated perfection. Muir does not usually use philosophical terms or tropes in his verse, and Plato occurs rarely again—as in the very last lines of his *Collected Poems:*

> And now that time grows shorter, I perceive
> That Plato's is the truest poetry,
> And that these shadows
> Are cast by the true.

If one conceives of life as the reiteration of archetypal patterns, it is necessary to devise a way of making the accidents of a particular existence conformable to the necessities of a preordinate pattern. The title of the first version of Muir's *Autobiography* indicates his terms for doing this. He called the account of his life until the age of thirty-five *The Story and the Fable.* What he means by "fable" and "story" is explained in this passage from the *Autobiography:* he is speaking of the correspondences between his dreams of animals and his childhood experience in a farming community:

> If I were recreating my life in an autobiographical novel I could bring out these correspondences freely and show how our first intuition of the world expands into vaster and vaster images, creating a myth which we act almost without knowing it, while our outward life goes on its ordinary routine of eating, drinking, sleeping, working, and making money in order to beget sons and daughters who will do the same. . . .

It is clear that no autobiography can begin with a man's birth, that we extend far beyond any boundary line which we can set for ourselves in the past or the future, and that the life of every man is an endlessly repeated performance of the life of man. It is clear for the same reason that no autobiography can confine itself to conscious life, and that sleep, in which we pass a third of our existence, is a mode of experience, and our dreams a part of reality. In themselves our conscious lives may not be particularly interesting. But what we are not and can never be, our fable, seems to me inconceivably interesting. I should like to write that fable, but I cannot even live it; and all I could do if I related the outward course of my life would be to show how I deviated from it, though even that is impossible, since I do not know the fable or anybody who knows it. One or two stages in it I can recognize: the age of innocence and the Fall and all the dramatic consequences which issued from the Fall. But these lie behind the experience, not on its surface; they are not historical events, they are stages in the fable.

What is this myth, this fable, which we try to live but cannot even fully know? Muir conceives of it in partly Christian, partly Platonic terms. He speaks of a Fall from the age of innocence, and we think at once of Adam's fall—Muir's last book of verse was titled *One Foot in Eden*—and of Wordsworth's "Intimations of Immortality" in childhood. If one is tempted to see Muir as a religious poet, and rightly so, one must be warned by his assertion, "I do not know the fable or anybody who knows it"; for Edwin Muir, though a deeply religious spirit, remained to the end a seeker of this fable, not a receptor of the revelations of others. He is as free, and in his patient and gentle way indeed as bold, with Christian theology as he is in adapting to his own needs the patterns of mythology received from the ancient world.

As he tells us, his dreams are rooted in childhood memories, and he has learned not only from "dreams and fantasies" but "got great knowledge and courtesy from the dead . . . from two mainly / Who gave me birth." We would therefore do well to look first at the life Edwin Muir knew as a child, to see "how our first intuition of the world expands into vaster and vaster images, creating a myth which we act almost without knowing it."

His childhood on farms in the Orkney Isles, to the north of Scotland, gave Muir a sense of fulfilment and perfection outside of time:

> Over the sound a ship so slow would pass
>   That in the black hill's gloom it seemed to lie.
> The evening sound was smooth like sunken glass,
>   And time seemed finished ere the ship passed
>   by.

Yet even in this idyllic tranquillity there were menacing natural shapes and forces, the exactions of the weather and the frightening energy of animals:

Those lumbering horses in the steady plough
On the bare field—I wonder why, just now,
They seemed terrible, so wild and strange,
Like magic power on the stony grange.

Perhaps some childish hour has come again,
When I watched fearful, through the blackening
    rain,
Their hooves like pistons in an ancient mill
Move up and down, yet seem as standing still. . . .

"Our first childhood is the only time in our lives when we exist within immortality," Muir has written, "and perhaps all our ideas of immortality are influenced by it." This orthodox Romantic sentiment runs strong in Muir, and strong is the memory of that time within time that was beyond time. In his poem about the horses, though, even that remembered Eden is menaced by "conquering hooves" that "Were ritual that turned the field to brown." Threatened though it was by those huge mechanistic beasts imposing change upon a changeless landscape, he still longs to recapture it—

Ah, now it fades! it fades! and I must pine
Again for that dread country crystalline,
Where the blank field and the still-standing tree
Were bright and fearful presences to me.

His childhood was clustered with "bright and fearful presences." His father was a good man, patient and loving but luckless; he would have made a fine informant had there been a Lady Gregory or a Campbell of Islay to take down his tales:

My father's stories were mostly drawn from an earlier age, and I think must have been handed on to him by his own father. They went back to the Napoleonic wars, the press gang, and keelhauling, which still left a memory of terror in Orkney. But in his own time he had known several witches, who had 'taken the profit of the corn,' turned the milk sour, and wrecked ships by raising storms. . . . The devil himself, as Auld Nick, sometimes came into these tales. . . . My father had also a great number of stories about the Book of Black Arts. This book could be bought only for a silver coin, and sold only for a smaller silver one. It ended in the possession of a foolish servant-girl who paid a threepenny-piece for it. It was very valuable, for it gave you all sorts of worldly power; but it had the drawback that if you could not sell it to some one before you died you would be damned. . . . My father also knew the horseman's word—that is, the word which makes a horse do anything you desire if you whisper it into its ear. . . . From what my father said I imagine that the word was a shocking one.

His mother's memory too was filled with old tales of shipwrecks, phantom vessels sailing past the cliffs, nocturnal appearances of spectral Danes. The Orkneys, like Ireland or Wales, have an ancient culture, partly Gaelic but more dominantly Viking in its heritage. Had Yeats been an Orkneyan, or had Muir pursued in the Orkneys such interests as Yeats followed in Ireland, there were

materials aplenty in the still available traditions of those northern islands for a recreated literature of ancient myth and epic action. As late as in his father's generation one could hear in the oral tradition versions of the ancient *Norse Tales* translated by Dasent, the folktale analogues of the Norse and Danish epics. The islands are honeycombed with burial mounds, Pictish barrows in which live a subterranean race of supernatural beings. There are circles of standing stones inscribed in ogham characters, and among the farmer folk, marriages and crops are controlled by the growing of the fruitful or waning of the fruitless moon, while fishermen are loath to start a voyage if their boat has been turned widdershins against the direction of the sun. And again, a poet with the haunted imagination of Robert Graves would have revelled in the fact that the largest island of the Orkneys is named Pomona, for the Roman goddess of fruit trees; or in memories of the witch at Stromness "who sold favorable winds to mariners at the low charge of sixpence"; or in the knowledge that the drowned dead are turned into seals, and that sea-fairies inhabit the waters, and that fishermen can show you near Stronsay the Mermaid's Chair in which she sings, enchanting the waters. And, at New Year's Eve, Orkneyans were used to troop from house to house, one dressed as the scapegoat Hobby Horse, and sing,

Here we hae brought our carrying-horse—
    We're a' Queen Mary's men;
A mony a curse licht on his corse;
    He'll eat mair meat than we can get;
He'll drink mair drink than we can swink,
    And that's before our Lady.

These details of Orkneyan folklore may well have been available to Muir; I take them from a local history published in 1869. The hobbyhorse victim of a Christianized White Goddess is in fact the subject of a fine contemporary poem, *The Mari Lwyd,* by the Welsh poet Vernon Watkins. But Muir makes none of these myths or folktales part of his own myth, as Graves or Yeats assuredly would have done. He could not assimilate naturally a heritage which he felt history had denied him; differing with C. M. Grieve ("Hugh MacDiarmid") on the possibility of Scotland's contemporary writers using dialect, Muir points out that the Scot habitually thinks in English but feels in Gaelic; Scottish life does not provide an organic community on which a national literature can be based. These conditions account for the strange fact that "Scotland is a country whose past has been moulded by poetry but which has produced very few poets." Unlike Yeats, who believed it his mission to create in the Irish a sense of nationality, or Graves, who had no need to concern himself with politics to discern an eternal truth, Muir feels debarred from much of his Celtic and Viking background, though his need for a unifying mythical interpretation of life is no less great than theirs.

In his poem **"Merlin,"** Muir tries to summon Druidic spells such as those that worked for Yeats and Graves—belief in the Celtic Otherworld, in the power of magic—as an alternative to Christian responsibility for sin in a world of change:

O Merlin in your crystal cave
Deep in the diamond of the day,
Will there ever be a singer
Whose music will smooth away
The furrow drawn by Adam's finger
Across the meadow and the wave?

. . . . .

Will your magic ever show
The sleeping bride shut in her bower,
The day wreathed in its mound of snow
And Time locked in his tower?

Although this poem has an incantatory rhythm, the questions it asks are asked because considered impossible of fulfilment. For Muir there is no escape from time through magic. He finds his freedom from time not in Merlin's outworn spells but through re-experiencing the Fable, as we shall see. Muir speaks of pagan antiquity in another poem, **"The Old Gods,"** which makes an interesting comparison to Yeats's long search for what the beggar found at Windy Gap, or to those old gods who swooped from Graves's Rocky Acres, "Terror for fat burghers on the plains below." (Auden, too, in "A New Age," conceived of the old gods as taking violent revenge upon the reasonable era that succeeded their reign.) But in his calm sonnet Muir sees neither the self-obliterating ecstasy of Yeats, nor the primordial avengers of Graves and Auden. Characteristically, his view is more humane than theirs. He sees the undying conflict between eternity and time, between perfection and change, as having been somehow reconciled in the reign of the old gods, and this reconciliation of the opposites that make our life difficult to bear compels his wonder. Muir does not call his "old gods and goddesses" by their names, and in the context of his other work it seems most probable that they answer not to the names of Celtic or Norse pagandom but to the same names Homer invoked. Despite his experience at first hand of Orkney folk life, when Muir thinks of antiquity it is to Troy and Greece that his mind turns.

We may identify his three most important themes as the Matter of Scotland, the Matter of Troy, and the Matter of the Fable. The first two are landscapes in which the protagonist's journey in the third takes place; in these real or imagined places are revealed the origin, destination, and meaning of his fabulous journey.

The Matter of Scotland is a double *donnée* for Muir. It comprises his remembered rural childhood, with its special qualities, and his adult consciousness of Scottish culture.

Muir's memories of his first ten years on the islands of Pomona and Wyre center on infantine intuitions of immortality, and on the ritualistic quality of the communal life there. His earliest memory is one of timeless tranquility and escape from change or pain:

I was lying in some room watching a beam of slanting light in which dusty, bright motes slowly danced and turned, while a low murmuring went on somewhere, possibly the humming of flies. My mother was in the room, but where I do not know; I was merely conscious of her as a vague, environing presence. . . . The quiet murmuring, the slow, unending dance of the motes, the sense of deep and solid peace, have come back to me since only in dreams. This memory has a different quality from any other memory in my life. It was as if, while I lay watching that beam of light, time had not yet begun.

This moment may seem, from the viewpoint of our day-life, to be a mere infantile regression, a flight from reality similar in feeling to Yeats's's poems of retreat into an island hermitage and a "bee-loud glade." From a position of greater sympathy to Muir's view of life we may recognize a more positive significance in his timeless moment, as he himself does in **"The Myth,"** a poem from his 1946 volume, *The Voyage:*

My childhood all a myth
Enacted in a distant isle;
Time with his hourglass and his scythe
Stood dreaming on the dial,
And did not move the whole day long
That immobility might save
Continually the dying song,
The flower, the falling wave.

Childhood meant not only the dreamlike trance when "time seemed finished ere the ship passed by," but also a cycle of violence as the environing world went through its seasonal changes of begetting and slaughter;

A child could not grow up in a better place than a farm; for at the heart of human civilization is the byre, the barn, and the midden. When my father led out the bull to serve a cow brought by one of our neighbours it was a ritual act of the tradition in which we have lived for thousands of years, possessing the obviousness of a long dream from which there is no awaking. When a neighbour came to stick a pig it was a ceremony as objective as the rising and setting of the sun; and though the thought never entered his mind that without that act civilization, with its fabric of customs and ideas and faiths, could not exist—the church, the school, the council chamber, the drawing-room, the library, the city—he did it as a thing that had always been done in a certain way. There was a necessity in the copulation and the killing which took away the sin, or at least, by the ritual act, transformed it into a sad, sanctioned duty.

It is thus the transformation through ritual of necessary action into sanctioned duty that redeems life from chaos. Such repetitions create the unchanging forms which extend through time and give us the grace of merging our individual existences with an eternal existence.

Nothing yet was ever done
Till it was done again,
And no man was ever one
Except through dead men,

for, as Muir adds in the same poem, "Even a story to be true/ Must repeat itself." The idea of discovering freedom through participation in our underlying fable is itself frequently repeated in Muir's poems.

> We meet ourselves at every turn
> In the long country of the past.
> There the fallen are up again
> In mortality's second day,
> There the indisputable dead
> Rise in flesh more fine than clay
> And the dead selves we cast away
> In imperfection are perfected. . . .

There is still another way in which "the long country of the past" endowed Edwin Muir with a special implication. As a Scot the past of his country meant not only his own memories but the time when Scotland was a nation; as a poet, the Scottish past suggested to him the era when the greatest Scottish poetry had flourished. And as the son of an Orkneyan farmer, Muir looked not to the courtly poetry of Dunbar and Allen Ramsay, nor to the sentimental songs of Burns, but to the Scottish ballads. In a **"Complaint of the Dying Peasantry"** he recalls the glory of those ballads, and now laments:

> The singing and the harping fled
> Into the silent library;
> But we are with Burd Helen dead
> And with Sir Patrick lost at sea.

Although Muir wrote but few ballads, the tragic view of fate found in the best Scottish balladry is central to his own understanding of life. His two essays on balladry in *Latitudes* (1924) and *The Estate of Poetry* (1955; published 1962) are among the best of his critical writings. His understanding of the intensity with which passion in the ballads appears simplified because pure, came from some analogy within himself to the character of the ballad-writers, and from his comprehension of the life that made the ballads possible. No one who has written about ballads has known their poetic qualities or the conditions of their origin with like authority.

By "the estate of poetry" Muir means "the actual response of a community to the poetry that is written for it: the effective range and influence of poetry." In his discussion of the relation of poetry to society in our own day he looks back to the ballad community, extending in time unchanged to the heroic age, as a condition when that relation was most intimate, far-reaching, and fruitful. Now, however, we no longer have, or are, a true community, an audience. Instead we have to deal with a new thing: a public. "It seems to be an impersonal thing, a collectivity which, if you break it up, does not reduce itself to a single human being, but at best into chunks of itself, sections, percentages." It speaks in clichés, slogans, "the language of the third party and the onlooker." But poetry is the instrument of the imagination, "that power by which we apprehend living beings in their individuality, as they live and move, not as ideas or categories. . . . The public seems designed for one purpose and the poet for another."

The ballad community on the other hand appears as analogous for society to the unfallen state of childhood for the man. Muir does not sentimentalize or falsify the primitive life of such a community. Yet here was an audience that participated in the dramatic action and cherished an art that was traditional, not "popular" or condescending. Here poetry presents a tragic acceptance of the life of reality and its surrounding mysteries, in which the natural and the supernatural (whether Heaven, Hell, or pagandom) were intermingled. Here great themes were handled, at their best, with brevity, strength, and passion. To such a community poetry is "a natural thing, an exercise of the heart and the imagination," expressing "an ancestral vision simplified to the last degree." Muir bids the contemporary poet ignore the modern public, that abstraction, and write for his true audience, which he creates by assuming that it exists. Somehow, among the statistical fractions of the public, live the individual readers whose humanity he can reach only by being true to his own. The growing reputation of Muir's poems is a validation of his hope, and a testament to his heroic conception of the poet's privileged obligation.

When Muir began to write poems—he was 38 years old when his *First Poems* appeared in 1925—he began by taking over to his own needs traditional usages: the lyric soliloquy, and the ballad. In fact the major attempts in *First Poems* were offered by three ballads, two of which he later omitted from his work; fortunately they have been restored in the posthumous *Collected Poems.* Although by no means among his faultless poems, they tell us much about the sensibility that was later refined in other poems (not ballads). One of these early efforts is Muir's only excursion into writing in Scots dialect. It is called **"Ballad of the Flood"**:

> Last night I dreamed a ghastly dream,
>   Before the dirl o' day.
> A twining worm cam out the wast,
>   Its back was like the slae.
>
> It ganted wide as deid man gant,
>   Turned three times on its tail,
> And wrapped itsel the warld around
>   Till ilka rock did wail.

This strong opening with the supernatural serpent's sudden appearance is clearly modelled on "The Laily Warm and the Mackrel of the Sea." But Muir's "twining worm" is no enchanted princess; it is an apocalyptic dragon, portending the destruction of the world. In 39 stanzas Muir tells the tale of the unrepenting folk sunk in sin, and Noah's building of the Ark. With the deluge and the sailing forth his ballad successively echoes "Sir Patrick Spens" and the "The Daemon Lover":

> The first day that auld Noah sailed
>   The green trees floated by.
> The second day that auld Noah sailed
>   He heard a woman's cry.
>
> And tables set wi' meats were there,
>   Gowd beakers set wi' wine,

And twa lovers in a silken barge
  A-sailing on the brine.

They soomed upon the lanely sea
  And sad, sad were their een.
'O tak me in thy ship, auld man,
  And I'll please thee, I ween.'

'Haul off, haul off,' auld Noah cried,
  'Ye comena in to me!
Drown deep, drown deep, ye harlot fause,
  Ye wadna list to me.

She wrang her hands, she kissed her make,
  She lap into the sea,
But Noah turned and laughed fu' loud:
  'To hell, I wat, gang ye!'

This vindictive condemnation of the sinner is the dominant tone of the ballad, not wholly ameliorated by the later echoes of "The Ancient Mariner" or the concluding promise of a rebirth of mankind.

"Ballad of the Flood" is what the Scotch call a *dour* poem. It is the first poem of Muir's to retell part of the Matter of the Bible as the Matter of the Fable; most of such poems are, like the "Ballad," drawn from the Old Testament. The stories of Adam and Abraham reveal stages in Muir's Fable. But more significantly, I think, "Ballad of the Flood" shows directly the repressive and vengeful Calvinism which repelled Muir in the Scottish character. In a poem called "Scotland 1941"—a polemical poem unusual for Muir—he writes,

We were a tribe, a family, a people.
Wallace and Bruce guard now a painted field,
And all may read the folio of our fable,
Peruse the sword, the sceptre and the shield.
A simple sky roofed in that rustic day,
The busy corn-fields and the haunted holms,
The green road winding up the ferny brae.
But Knox and Melville clapped their preaching
    palms
And bundled all the harvesters away,
Hoodicrow Peden in the blighted corn
Hacked with his rusty beak the starving haulms.
Out of that desolation we were born.

Thus we pass from the Matter of the Fable to the Matter of Scotland. If on the one hand the Matter of Scotland gave Muir images of the unfallen purity of childhood, menaced by terrible animal powers and the turning of time, on another his fate as a Scot made Muir poignantly aware of disinheritance, of the fall from glory, as a cultural, not only a personal, theme. With scathing irony in "Scotland 1941" he puts the Reformers Knox, Melville, and Peden at the head of his list of those who have robbed his land of the unity of culture enjoyed when "We were a tribe, a family, a people." Later in the poem he attacks the mean materialism by which the Scotch completed their own spiritual disfranchisement: We, he writes, who

crush the poet with an iron text,
How could we read our souls and learn to be? . . .

Now smoke and death and money everywhere,
Mean heirlooms of each fainter generation,
And mummied housegods in their musty niches,
Burns and Scott, sham bards of a sham nation,
And spiritual defeat wrapped warm in riches,
No pride but pride of pelf.

To the theme of the Fall (whether of Man or of a nation) we shall return, but first let us follow the consequences of the Calvinism which Muir exhibits in "Ballad of the Flood" but spurns in "Scotland 1941." This theme recurs in one of his most memorable poems. Characteristic of Muir, there the power of the statement derives from the transformation of the theme into a complex of images which came to him in dreams and seem to have nothing to do with the circumstances in his actual life that drove them into his unconscious. The poem is "The Combat," recounting a horrible nightmare of defenselessness in unmitigated battle with aggressive power, yet all but victorious in its capacity for eternal suffering. These abstract qualities are imagined as beasts, one an allegorical gryphon, the other a soft and furry slug. The stanza is a five-line, two-rhyme unit, in merry octasyllabics, jigging along as unadapted to its grim tale as is the ballad meter to its. There is something indefinably terrifying in this vision of struggle without end between the unappeasably destructive element and the undefeatable passivity of pure suffering:

It was not meant for human eyes,
That combat on the shabby patch
Of clods and trampled turf that lies
Somewhere beneath the sodden skies
For eye of toad or adder to catch.

And having seen it I accuse
The crested animal in his pride,
Arrayed in all the royal hues
Which hide the claws he well can use
To tear the heart out of the side.

"The Combat" seems in fact to be the crystallization in verse of several memories and dreams, the memories dreamlike, the dreams long remembered. One is of two animals in endlessly recurrent battle. This seems the direct source of the poem, but its real source lies behind the dream. Later in his *Autobiography* he recalls two sordid incidents in Glasgow. A large muscular woman is pummeling a "little, shrinking man," cursing him for having seduced her and started her ruin; "I do not know how it ended," he writes, "for the thud of the big, red-haired fist on the man's face sickened me. The crowd looked on without interfering." And in another crowd he came on a young man systematically punching another who made no effort to defend himself. When queried by a bystander, "Why dinna you let the chap alone? He hasna hurt you?" the assailant replied, "I ken he hasna hurt me, but I'm gaun tae hurt him!" and continued to slug his unresisting enemy.

These dismal scenes struck Muir "as if they were an answer to some question which, without my knowing it, had been troubling me." What is behind these dreams and memories is the merciless suffering which his brother Johnnie had endured in a protracted death from a brain tumor.

In both these memories there was the quality of Scottish Calvinism: the serious young man's reply had been the unanswerable, arbitrary logic of predestination; and the encounter of the red-haired woman with her seducer, when both were so greatly changed that their original sin might have been committed in another world, and yet lived on, there in that slum, was a sordid image of fate as Calvin saw it. Somewhere in these two incidents there was a virtue of a dreary kind, behind the flaunted depravity: a recognition of logic and reality.

In the poem the inexorable fight goes on, but the victor cannot win, the victim slips away, until once more they meet,

> And all began. The stealthy paw
> Slashed out and in. Could nothing save
> These rags and tatters from the claw?
> Nothing. And yet I never saw
> A beast so helpless and so brave.
>
> And now, while the trees stand watching, still
> The unequal battle rages there.
> The killing beast that cannot kill
> Swells and swells in his fury till
> You'd almost think it was despair.

It seems an impertinence to extract significances beyond those given by the poem itself, and they are the more compelling for growing not out of causes but out of being. There is no attributed motive for either beast, they simply act out their natures. While the context of Calvinist predestination is suggested by Muir's *Autobiography,* in his book *The Labyrinth* this poem is closely followed by one called **"The Interrogation."** There, at the border of a country (it is surely Czechoslovakia after the Communist *coup d'état*), when "We could have crossed the road but hesitated, / And then came the patrol". . . .

> We have stood and answered through the
>   standing day
> And watched across the road beyond the hedge
> The careless lovers in pairs go by,
> Hand linked in hand, wandering another star,
> So near we could shout to them. We cannot
>   choose
> Answer or action here,
> Though still the careless lovers saunter by
> And the thoughtless field is near.
> We are on the very edge,
> Endurance almost done,
> And still the interrogation is going on.

Between the "careless lovers" in "the thoughtless field" and the unwitting victims of suspicion and hatred there is no speech. Muir's compassion is moved by impersonal vengefulness menacing the dignity of the individual, whether its source be an authoritarian religion or a police state. Man's individuality is precious to Muir,

for it is as individuals, if only as victims, that we can retrace the outlines of the Fable, and so be delivered from chaos and suffering into the knowledge of grace.

A second early ballad is among his most successful poems. The origin of his **"Ballad of Hector in Hades"** was the memory of a childhood fight with another boy. In a momentary period of childish aggressiveness, Muir had had an earlier fight with Freddie Sinclair over possession of a knife, which he had won. But their second encounter was a debacle.

> What I was so afraid of I did not know; it was not Freddie, but something else; yet I could no more have turned and faced him than I could have stopped the sun revolving. As I ran I was conscious only of a few huge things, monstrously simplified and enlarged: Wyre, which I felt under my feet, the other islands lying round, the sun in the sky, and the sky itself, which was quite empty. For almost thirty years afterwards I was so ashamed of this moment of panic that I did not dare to speak of it to anyone, and drove it out of my mind. I was seven at the time and in the middle of my guilty fears. On that summer afternoon they took the shape of Freddie Sinclair, and turned him into a terrifying figure of vengeance.

Muir exorcised that fear thirty years later "in a poem describing Achilles chasing Hector round Troy," where Hector returns "after his death to run the deadly race over again." Their encounter is described with that scrupulous attention to the minutest tactile details ("The grasses puff a little dust / Where my footsteps fall") that obsess the combatants in the tales of Stephen Crane and Hemingway, or in Robert Graves's *Good-bye to All That.* At the re-enactment of the fatal blow,

> The sky with all its clustered eyes
>   Grows still with watching me,
> The flowers, the mounds, the flaunting weeds
>   Wheel slowly round to see.
>
> Two shadows racing on the grass,
>   Silent and so near,
> Until his shadow falls on mine.
>   And I am rid of fear.
>
> The race is ended. Far away
>   I hang and do not care,
> While round bright Troy Achilles whirls
>   A corpse with streaming hair.

"I could at last see the incident whole by seeing it as happening, on a great and tragic scale, to someone else." This is the transforming and therapeutic power of the imagination, dependent upon unconscious "solutions of the past projected into the present, deliberately announced as if they were a sibylline declaration that life has a meaning . . . depending on a different system of connected relations from that by which we live." Not that Muir accepts the proposition Mr. Graves was expounding at about the time this poem was written, that such therapeutic power is the purpose of poetry for both poet and reader. Yet this curative imaginative power to come to terms with fears and repossess the wholeness of life by a transcendent conception of destiny is, for Muir, the most precious material from which poetry may be made. When, as in this ballad, the material and the means of its expression coalesce, he writes his most valuable poems.

"Ballad of Hector in Hades" is the earliest use Muir makes of the Matter of Troy. His use of this Homeric material is markedly different from Yeats's. The conception of Helen by Jove upon Leda does not, in Muir's mind, mark the supersession of an epoch; nor is he drawn to Helen as an heraldic representation of mortal beauty in immortal dress. It is the destruction of Troy and the return of Odysseus to the faithful Penelope which fascinate Muir, the themes of mortal defeat and predestined journey. Neither does Muir think of himself as a modern Homer, as did Yeats. A modest poet, as he was a modest man, Muir aims only to capture or recapture intimations of life's meaning from what "sibylline declarations" come to him. Although his imagination is seemingly passive, awaiting the revelation of its materials, he is in fact boldly synoptic in the expression of his themes once they announce themselves.

In his scrupulous study of Muir, R. P. Blackmur has likened the poet to Virgil. The analogy, though at first surprising, bears out well our perception that Muir is among the last—indeed perhaps *the* last—of poets who can conceive of history as a continuous reiteration of human destiny. The Rome of which Muir is chronicler is not an empire but a faith. I do not mean the Roman Church, but faith in the continuity of Christendom as a mode of feeling, as a civilization. Blackmur takes courage for his thesis from Muir's assertion, at the end of the *Autobiography,* that he "discovered in Italy that Christ had walked on earth, and also that things truly made preserve themselves through time in the first freshness of their nature. So the northern child of Calvinism was in middle age awakened to a sensuous as well as a spiritual perception of what the Mediterranean world might take for granted."

But I would modify our view of Muir as Virgil's heir by acknowledging his sympathy, or his bias, in using the Tale of Troy. It is true that Aeneas was a Trojan, but the *Aeneid* is of course more concerned with the hero's triumphs in Latium than with the destruction of his first homeland. Blackmur, commenting on the "Ballad of Hector in Hades," observes that "within our psyches we all run in great heat around that wall, and it makes little difference whether the other fellow is Hector or Achilles." Yet Muir distinctly sees himself not as Achilles. As the now-vanquished former champion he is Hector, and in other poems he is a Trojan slave serving the victorious Greeks, or a mad old man left behind by the conquering Argives to live in the sewers of ruined Ilium until tortured to death by wandering brigands. I think that as a Scotsman Muir found his sympathy not with the triumphant imperialist Greeks who dominated the ancient world, but with the futile heroism of the defeated people. Allowing for stylistic alternation in these two passages between the Eliotic and rhetorical, a tone of lamentation such as informs the first appears again in the second:

> The rat-hordes,
> Moving, were grey dust shifting in grey dust.
> Proud history has such sackends.
>
> Such wasted bravery idle as a song,
> Such hard-won ill might prove Time's verdict
>   wrong,
> And melt to pity the annalist's iron tongue.

The first is from "Troy," the second from "Scotland 1941." As Muir interpreted her fate, Troy offered images of a fallen city, a society destroyed despite its valor as much by its own natural flaws as by the power of its enemies. His sense of Scotland's history as well as his own experiences made Muir acutely aware of social inequities and of individual responsibility for them. His *Scottish Journey,* a book describing Scotland in the depression, should rank with Orwell's chronicles of that decade. Like attitudes toward society and history inform Muir's poems on Troy. The soliloquist of "A Trojan Slave" tells us that history itself is a reduplication of fate, just as Hector relives his dying. The speaker, now enslaved to Greeks, was formerly enslaved by the Trojans who may well have fallen because "they would not arm us, and preferred / Troy's ruin lest a slave should snatch a sword." This poem (published in 1937) clearly speaks with the same sense of injustice that runs through *Scottish Journey* and the early chapters of Muir's *Autobiography.* In his imagination Scotland's fate has been endured before, on the Trojan plains.

In Muir's thought both the Matter of Scotland and the Matter of Troy are subordinated to his most insistent theme, the Matter of the Fable, which indeed the lesser themes exemplify. In poems in which he tried to discover the Fable independently of the concrete situations these lesser themes provided, however, Muir often wrote gropingly or abstractly. He felt early the compulsion toward an intuitive understanding of destiny, but what full course of action the Fable required was not revealed to him until the end of his life. Thus its first treatment, in the early "Ballad of the Soul," is, as Kathleen Raine observes,

> halting and obscure; the archetypal images come so thick and fast that they fail by reason of their too great purity, their insufficiently incarnated quality. Yet few poets can ever have started to write from an inspiration more authentically imaginative.

In this early ballad Muir imagines the world's destruction by fire and flood, then in journeys reminiscent of "The Ancient Mariner" he sees or takes part in apocalyptic struggles (similar to that later in "The Combat"). The phantasmagoria dissolves in a promised rebirth, but when the protagonist questions its meaning "then the fading dream/Had nothing more to say."

Life itself is the journey Muir's imagination records, and its destination is hidden in winding corridors and narrow places, though hinted at in recurrent glimpses of a perfection and a peace independent of the changes wrought by time. The pilgrimage is rendered larger than reality in **"The Mythical Journey"** (1937); now the episodes, though as "archetypal" as any in **"Ballad of the Soul,"** are more effective because drawn from recognizable mythologies rather than the private symbolism of dreams.

"The Mythical Journey" takes mankind from its origin **"First in the North,"** amidst malevolent nature and bitter spirits—"Tall women against the sky with heads covered,/The witch's house. . . . " Escaping from "The twice-dead castle on the swamp-green mound," we enter a natural world of plenitude and freedom.

> But the ship hastened on and brought him to
> The towering walls of life and the great kingdom
> Where he wandered seeking that which sought
>   him. . . .

Now we seem poised for the revelation of Who it is we seek. Once that were known, man's intellect could come into conscious activity and construct a philosophy of life and a theology of supernatural reality which could be transmitted from one to another generation. Without such certainty we are each individual seekers, retracing in our aloneness the archetypal processes that can only be intuitively apprehended but not consciously understood. The one who is both sought and seeker, this poem tells us, remains

> Beyond all knowledge. Only the little hills
> Head-high, and the winding valleys,
> Turning, returning, till there grew a pattern,
> And it was held. And there stood both their
>   stations
> With the hills between them. And that was the
>   meaning.

As a poetry of revelation these lines are sadly wanting in intensity; the abstractness of the situation makes nearly impossible the expression of the thought in images of tactile reality, and the verse rhythms are accordingly slack. Introduction of the traditional image of the Tree of Knowledge in an unexpected way makes for a livelier if inconclusive ending:

> That which he had sought, that which had sought
>   him,
> Glittered in death. And all the dead scattered
> Like fallen stars, clustered like leaves hanging
> From the sad boughs of the mountainous tree of
>   Adam
> Planted far down in Eden. And on the hills
> The gods reclined and conversed with each other
> From summit to summit.
>   Conclusion
> Without fulfilment. . . .
>   Beneath its branches
> He builds in faith and doubt his shaking house.

"The Mythical Journey" begins before legend and concludes "Without fulfilment" before history has begun. What made possible Muir's success in his later poems was the slowly-nurtured encompassing of actuality by his imagination so fully committed to the archetypal rather than to the accidental. The poems in ***One Foot in Eden*** accept reality—"This is a difficult country, and our home." The title poem of that book welcomes it, for "Strange blessings never in Paradise/Fall from these beclouded skies." The Fortunate Fall places man in the grip of time, of history, of change, but also makes possible "hope and faith and pity and love." Muir's gift is for seeing life as unified and history as continuous in the great clarification of the journey of the soul. We each fall anew from Eden and retrace the long voyage through the narrow place and the perilous place in search of the sufficient place. The journey may be through the life-long labyrinth, or through the adventurous seas which detained Odysseus on his homeward way; when all is done and sung we return to the sacred place from which our life began. These themes, frequently reiterated, are not however in themselves the guarantees of successful poems, whatever their validity psychologically. For the Fable needs at every point the Story, to dramatize its incarnation and make its action relevant to human life. The Story must redeem the Fable from abstraction. When there is no historical reality in which the Fable is both concealed and revealed, no tactile world, no solid landscape, no living characters nor believable chimaeras, in short no story, there is only the Fable. And as the fate of the word itself suggests, fables are illusory and not to be believed but for the sake of the moral—which is to say, we have an inferior imaginative action to the incarnation of truth in life. But when Muir fuses his Fable with his stories, whether of his own remembered childhood on the farm above the bay, or stories of Hector and Priam and the crazed survivor of the fallen city, or of Odysseus reentering the hall where time has been woven and unwound, or the stories of Old Testament patriarchs or the dreamed combat of beasts, the shape of life and the meaning become clear together.

Muir's Fable resembles the Christian story—without the Redeemer. Perhaps it is his unexorcised Calvinism (as well as Romantic longing) which makes the Fall, rather than Christ's rising, the moment of greatest psychological power in the pattern. But if Muir is a recusant Calvinist he is so in his own fashion; he cannot believe in a redemption through another's sacrifice—it must be won by his own sufferings, whose meaning he must seek himself. Each man is his own Adam, and Second Adam. In Muir we find religious feeling, religious conviction unsupported by religious dogma. Repelled by the inexorable and unforgiving logic of Calvinism, and distrusting equally the facile emotionalism of evangelical Christianity, Muir, with the aid of psychoanalysis, discovered a secular myth of divine things. This he held with piety and hope, evoked by painful processes of self-knowledge and patient receptivity to transcendent truths which come not from the exercise of will or reason but from the submerged treasuries of mankind's common dream.

Though indeed a gentle and forgiving man, Muir is neither a theological thinker nor a programmatic ethical poet. He tells us neither what we should believe nor how we should behave. His poetry has no intellectual platform, his myth requires no revision of history, as do those of Yeats and Graves. It is partly a matter of temperament; Muir is a patient extractor of meaning from event, not an imposer of willed unity upon experienced chaos. If his result is seemingly more tenuous than Yeats's intellectual suit of mail or than Graves's all-absorbing psychomachia, Muir does not require of us such self-surrender, such undeviating acquiescence to his own particular view of reality. He tells us his Fable and his Story, and when in his poems the two coalesce

> you shall know
> Before you Troy goes up in fire,
> And you shall walk the Trojan streets
> When home are sailed the murdering fleets,
> Priam shall be a little boy,
> Time shall cancel time's deceits,
> And you shall weep for grief and joy
> To see the whole world perishing
> Into everlasting spring.

He compels our assent not by the force of an argument but by the clarity with which he has illuminated a part of the deepest truth our culture can give us.

Fredrick Garber (essay date 1966)

SOURCE: "Edwin Muir's Heraldic Mode," in *Twentieth Century Literature,* Vol. 12, No. 2, July, 1966, pp. 96-103.

[*In the following essay, Garber focuses on Muir's use of symbols and images from heraldic tradition in his poetry.*]

Animals, in Edwin Muir's autobiography, occur and reoccur in contexts of guilt and necessity, visions of human bestiality, and dreams that take a variety of moods and shapes reaching back into the racial unconscious. In one passage, Muir recalls a long, fabulous age of pre-history, "populated by heraldic men and legendary beasts," in which our immediate connections with animals revealed themselves when we endowed our heroes with the metaphors of the fox's cunning and the lion's courage, and through this made heroes and totems that embodied the qualities we admired.[1] We worshipped some animals and killed others, and the killing left in us a haunting ambivalence, clothed in ritual, that shared equally in guilt and necessity. Now, however, our relations to animals are so much less immediate and personal that these old feelings seem somewhat absurd, and we dismiss them as unnecessarily sentimental. Yet, Muir says, "our dreams and ancestral memories speak a different language."[2]

Heraldry, for Muir, is still another version of the language that speaks, through dreams and archetypes, in the voice of the racial unconscious. Until the publication of *The Labyrinth* in 1949, images derived from armorial bearings bulk large in the totality of his poems. Muir probably knew little about the complex traditions and involuted nomenclature of this highly specialized art, but enough, certainly, had attracted him, and so strongly, that we can rightfully speak of his concern as an obsession. As early as 1934, in the last of his *Variations on a Time Theme,* Muir had shown how heraldry, and especially its animals, worked for him:

> Who curbed the lion long ago
> And penned him in this towering field
> And reared him wingless in the sky?
> And quenched the dragon's burning eye,
> Chaining him here to make a show,
> The faithful guardian of the shield?
>
> A fabulous wave far back in Time
> Flung these calm trophies to this shore
> That looks out on a different sea.
> These relics of a buried war,
> Empty as shape and cold as rhyme,
> Gaze now on fabulous wars to be.[3]

The lion and the dragon, fabulous beasts to begin with (the lion was winged), having survived as trophies of a past war, are now penned and chained, turned into heraldic animals. Some vital relationship between themselves and their world has been buried, although they are unaware of the change; the lion's wings are clipped, the dragon's fiery eye quenched. One gazes from the flag, the other guards the shield. Like the heraldic animals in **"The Human Fold,"** they are symbols from an old pagan religion. Perhaps a pallid, unimaginative rationalism puts fabulous beasts only on flags and shields. If so, too much that is vital in our lives has been buried, aspects of which we were more conscious when animals were totemic and men were likened to beasts. Yet these primitive strata of awareness appear again elsewhere, in our dreams and, sublimated and stylized, in the abstract heraldic designs we create as images of our pride.

In **"The Covenant,"** a poem written a decade later, Muir explicitly ties in these ideas to his preoccupations with a lost Eden and our journey from and to it. In dreams, "in sleep-walled night . . . the heraldic crest of nature / Shines out again," and we glimpse the original covenant, the primal unity of god, fabulous creature and man and woman. Here Muir does not use heraldry to indicate a decline in intensity, as he did in the tenth *Variation* (where it was "Empty as shape and cold as rhyme") but as an image of a past glory, pure though hidden, emergent in subliminal strata beyond the reach of the conscious mind that in Muir always symbolizes the daily round hiding our links with the past. The heraldic crest signifies the permanence of Eden, its stubborn continuation in our lives; though, in this poem at least, there is no guarantee that Eden will eventually re-emerge in a higher innocence. Both the tenth *Variation* (which was published separately under the title **"Heraldry"**) and **"The Covenant"** illustrate the function of the heraldic in establishing our relations to what has preceded us, whether those relations seem to be desiccated or, on a closer look, vital but by no means obvious.

Heraldry, then, for Muir, symbolizes order, tradition and history, a meaningful, recognizable continuity in time. In this, his treatment is perfectly consistent with the art itself. Heraldry, very much an art of time and history, is a microcosmic, abstract, stylized version of patterns of order and continuity, significant not only to the bearers but to one as obsessed with time and its passage as Muir. Heraldic devices need not symbolize anything in particular or do more than identify the bearer; they may be, simply, designs. But, expressly symbolic or not, their very existence suggests (or, one should say, insists) that stable patterns can be found, that time is not merely a flux of momentary events following each other in meaningless sequence, that figures, representative or abstract, can be both in the flux and part of a demonstrable order. For heraldry affirms continuity in time as well as the passage of it, and the simultaneous presence of both of these factors must have attracted Muir, since continuity is an order derived from the flux, while the passage is within it. Throughout his whole life he sought for images to substantiate his feeling that we have come from somewhere important, and that the journey itself is significant. In his earlier, Nietzschean phases (lasting into the thirties), this took the shape of the idea of eternal recurrence, which he ultimately refuted in **"The Recurrence"** and **"Robert the Bruce"** with images from Christianity. His later concept of the Fable stressed that "the life of every man is an endlessly repeated performance of the life of man."[4] And, of course, the archetypes that he mentions everywhere have the same function of asserting both the life of the transient individual, and his position in an enduring, sufficient, immortal order (e.g., **"The Sufficient Place"**).

This mode of seeing enabled Muir to transpose, in **"The Little General,"** the childhood memory of a stunted, dapper, bad landlord, who returned to his fields every year to shoot birds, into the image of an occurrence described ironically as "like the pious ritual of a faith." Spring becomes, for a moment, a season of carnage rather than burgeoning life, though the death itself recurs in an eternal relationship, another version of that same, strange war of man and animal that haunted Muir all his life:

> Up on the hill a remnant of a tower
>   Had watched that single scene for many a year,
>
> Weaving a wordless tale where all were gathered
>   (Hunter and quarry and watcher and fabulous
>   field),
> A sylvan war half human and half feathered,
>   Perennial emblem painted on th shield
>
> Held up to cow a never-conquered land
>   Fast in the little General's fragile hand.

But the grand totemic world of heraldic men and legendary beasts has thinned out into this, a meaningless ritual slaughter without the accompanying awareness of guilt and necessity that gave the earlier ritual much of the meaning it had, certainly most of its imaginative

import. At one level the poem defines a failure of tradition. The slaughterer himself is slight and over-delicate, the whole affair disgusting. Still, that should not obscure the fact that this is ritual. Whatever the character of the participants, it seems more to the point that the heraldic image painted on the shield signifies a permanent, ineluctable order in things, archetypal and therefore, somehow, right. Yet Muir (whose sardonic note has never received its due) designs for the shield an image which, as he phrases it, seems to be a fabulous heraldic beast, a man-bird rather than a man and a bird. Aggressor and victim blend in the slaughter and come together, ironically, into a unified ordered whole, the heraldic image that holds within itself the passage of time.

Thus, even the little general takes his place in a grand design, the "space and order magistral" that Muir, in a rare moment of public introspection on his art, speaks of in another poem, **"The Emblem"**:

> I who so carefully keep in such repair
> The six-inch king and the toy treasury,
> Prince, poet, realm shrivelled in time's black air,
> I am not, although I seem, an antiquary.
> For that scant-acre kingdom is not dead,
> Nor save in seeming shrunk. When at its gate,
> Which you pass daily, you incline your head,
> And enter (do not knock; it keeps no state)
>
> You will be with space and order magistral,
> And that contracted world so vast will grow
> That this will seem a little tangled field.
> For you will be in very truth with all
> In their due place and honour, row on row.
> For this I read the emblem on the shield.

By now the components are familiar: the realm, apparently dried up in the blasts of time, that runs parallel to our daily round; and the fact that, within the realm, once we enter and observe, all are found in their proper positions in a hierarchy that Muir never defines in more detail than this. Nor did he need to give it a more precise definition. Muir was most concerned with establishing what that realm was like in relation to the daily round that was hardly aware of it. More he did not know, nor claim to know. But he could demonstrate, through his poems and their inner life, much of the quality, the "feel" of what he spoke of as archetypal or fabulous, and he did so through a peculiar stylization that partakes heavily of the aesthetics of heraldry, with some side glances at Yeats winding up his golden nightingales.

Heraldic devices rarely communicate anything like a total realistic image, although exact delineations of one object or another may well appear in them. Heraldry is, above all, a highly stylized art, high artifice, and armorial bearings present abstract designs and / or images composed in patterns that may be symbolic or pure decoration or some variant combination of both. The images themselves are frequently distorted for effect or import, the familiar heraldic lion being stylized into a form no feline could own and survive. Particular qualities may be exaggerated for meaning or design, others simplified or played down. The heraldic device has to create a tightly organized order of meaningful inter-relationships, and the more complicated the device—that is, the more it shows about certain relationships in the real world—the more it becomes a self-contemplating, abstract thing of artifice. The designs of heraldry represent, as microcosms, some aspects of the world, but their components need not be entirely of it, although they may come from it. Certainly, their stylization puts them beyond any conventional definition of naturalism. For one of the most important aspects of the heraldic mode—the distortions, exaggerations, elongations of the figures—satisfies the basic premise of the heraldic that what it designates is an order perceptible within the natural scheme of things but not subject to its vicissitudes. (Even if the figures are more or less natural, the intricate, abstract ordering of the design creates the identical sort of autotelic, microcosmic world.) These are images "out of nature," supplied by artists like those Grecian goldsmiths Yeats admired and with whom Muir could, to some degree, sympathize, though Byzantium could hardly be the world of his dreams. As in Yeats, artifice is both a means of getting beyond the flux and a symbol of one's being there. To use Muir's terms, heraldic form asserts the triumph of the Fable over the Story. Or, in another way, it illustrates the Story become Fable.

And that, for Muir, was precisely the point. He wanted, as we have seen, an image, composed of elements of the flux, which was, at the same time, beyond the flux. The Story, each individual life, had to be seen as it related to the Fable, the archetypal, fabulous vision of which our lives are dim, imperfect, flickering reflections. Heraldry, obviously tailor-made as a source for Muir, could supply much of what he wanted: the timefulness and timelessness, the images organized into a coherent, orderly pattern. But there were some things it could not do, and here Muir's own terms are more helpful than others because they define more accurately what he wanted to achieve. Never did he reject the earthly, although he saw life as a mixture composed largely of pain, frustration, blindness and the death of hope. Here and nowhere else must we live out the Story and find a rudimentary happiness until we reach immortality. Therefore, although Muir wanted to create effects like those in heraldry, he could not accept completely, for his own work, the distortion usually associated with the heraldic device. Muir did not want the un-natural. He wanted his images to be of nature, not out of it. But he also refused the merely naturalistic, as any reader of his criticism of the twenties, especially on writers like Arnold Bennett, would know. Even earlier than that, in his days of writing epigrams for *New Age,* he could say (rather lamely) to Bennett:

> Why, pray, so garrulous of wood and leather,
> Eating, the clock, the bathroom, and the weather?
> Why on *existence* do you always dwell?
> Is it because you've naught of *Life* to tell?[5]

The elements of the world of his poems had to be recognizably those of our world, for it was our lives that his poems spoke of and reflected upon. Yet the poems also had to reveal, insofar as it could be done, the world of the Fable, and show its relationship to dream and archetype, all the ancestral memories. Muir did not depend entirely on heraldry to do this for him. More frequent than the crests, the shields and even the winged lions are other figures he designed, human and animal, with all of the atmosphere and much of the quality of the heraldic, although they themselves do not necessarily come out of that tradition. Like Hölderlin, who taught him so much, Muir created his world out of ours, but transformed it into the substance of prophetic vision.

A poem like **"The Road,"** from the volume ***Journeys and Places,*** involves a series of images designed to get at a central drama of timelessness where everything—birth and death, departure and shipwreck—exists simultaneously and permanently:

> The lion crouching in the centre
>   With mountain head and sunset brow
> Rolls down the everlasting slope
>   Bones picked an age ago,
> And the bones rise up and go.
>
> There the beginning finds the end
>   Before beginning ever can be,
> And the great runner never leaves
>   The starting and the finishing tree,
>   The budding and the fading tree.
>
> There the ship sailing safe in harbour
>   Long since in many a sea was drowned.
> The treasure burning in her hold
>   So near will never be found,
>   Sunk past all sound.

Clearly not our world, not a situation we could experience directly, this is equally as clearly about us. The microcosm Muir creates, with nothing in it of the special, the local or the idiosyncratic, is yet, at the same time, a detailed, vividly rendered, specific and concrete affair. (Both Blake and Hölderlin achieve similar effects, the manner being appropriate to apocalyptic poetry.) The lion, the runner and the ship are by no means abstractions, though neither are they this or that particular runner or ship. Nor would it, on the other hand, be accurate to call the poem allegorical, although it incorporates an extended description: we search in vain for one to one relations in it. These objective things, happening in that place, are what they say they are, are their meaning. The meaning lies in the things themselves and not in some commentary running along with them.

Muir achieves the effect of the heraldic through a type of simplification that leaves the object bare, pure and direct. He removes the idiosyncratic without a concomitant removal of detailed objectivity. These figures, more natural than Yeats's golden nightingale or the elongated heraldic lion, are still somewhat stylized. But Muir does not dislocate or fragment external reality as did Rimbaud or the German Expressionists in order to make a new one. His animals, roads and castles are recognizable as such, seen with all the sharpness and accuracy one could ask for. The beasts in his poems are neither real nor fake, stuffed nor savage, but fabulous in Muir's particular sense. And the purity of the language parallels the purity of the objects: the complexity of the poem is not verbal but in what the words point to, the nature of the inner world Muir creates. Almost none of the drama of his poetry in this vein comes out of the interplay among the words. For Muir, words are only secondarily counters existent in their own right, to be explored for ambiguity and allusion (though he was always prone to an imaginative pun). Mainly, they are vehicles stripped clear of everything but things and ideas—animals, Prague or Time. His language has to be both self-effacing and exceptionally precise. It is the things and ideas that fuse, dramatically, into intricate inner relationships. Impersonal and objective (heraldry is necessarily impersonal, for it celebrates the bearer and not the artist), his poems at their best are triumphant renderings of universal experience in a recognizable style, a personal idiom unmistakably his own.

Yet, with all of the advantage that Muir derived from heraldry, its glory and its tradition, he did, after all, eventually reject it as he moved where the heraldic could not follow him, into an order whose teleology he found more satisfactory. Two poems from *The Narrow Place* signal this change and one, in particular, establishes the causes of it. In **"The Recurrence"** Muir goes through the familiar Nietzschean idea with a distaste obvious in the images he chooses to exemplify it:

> All has been that ever can be,
> And this sole eternity
> Cannot cancel, cannot add
> One to your delights or tears,
> Or a million million years
> Tear the nightmare from the mad.
>
> Have no fear then. You will miss
> Achievement by the self-same inch,
> When the great occasion comes
> And they watch you, you will flinch,
> Lose the moment, be for bliss
> A footlength short.

Joy, after all, can recur as easily and logically as the pain Muir reveals, but the weight of most of his images (he speaks once or twice of "delights" or "the happy") tends toward a representation of earthly life as bitter, treacherous and hard, and thus of the recurrence as an endless prison sentence, punishing us for we know not what. "All done before," Muir says. But, as often in his poems, the last stanza changes the whole pattern by putting the previous assertions into a new moral· and temporal perspective:

> But the heart makes reply:
> This is only what the eye
> From its tower on the turning field
> Sees and sees and cannot tell why,
> Quarterings on the turning shield,
> The great non-stop heraldic show.

> And the heart and the mind know,
> What has been can never return,
> What is not will surely be
> In the changed unchanging reign,
> Else the Actor on the Tree
> Would loll at ease, miming pain,
> And counterfeit mortality.

The statement is clear but the images surprising. The heraldic is still in time, most emphatically so as indicated by the "quarterings on the turning shield," for the quarterings are divisions and subdivisions claiming temporal relationships and affirming continuity. Muir does not change his ideas about heraldry here; he changes only the perspective in which he sees it. For the heraldic can see only the recurrence; or, to phrase it in terms of Muir's images, the heraldic can only see. That is, it is bound to the corporeal, the empirical, where an imaginative faith would appear to be inconceivable. But Muir now envisions that which breaks the eternal recurrence and, necessarily, has to come in from beyond the cycle of time to do so. The limitations of heraldry were becoming clear to him.

Another and more curious version of this shift in thinking occurs in **"The Grove,"** with its full panoply of heraldic figures populating, like the images on a tapestry, the grove through which one must go in this world. The grove smothers, but beyond it is brightness, freedom, air:

> We trod the maze like horses in a mill,
> And then passed through it
> As in a dream of the will.
> How could it be? There was the stifling grove,
> Yet here was light; what wonder led us to it?
> How could the blind path go
> To climb the crag and top the towering hill,
> And all that splendour spread. We know
> There was no road except the smothering grove.

Beyond is immortality, while life, as elsewhere in Muir, is not entirely a pleasant experience, though it is indeed rich and fascinating. This odd, quasi-allegorical variation of the quest image basic to Muir's poems shows a pattern like that in "Ode to a Nightingale" or *Young Goodman Brown,* a movement into the inner darkness and out again to the light. Muir's image carries with it all the overtones of self-exploration implicit in other variations on the theme including his own (cf. **"The Labyrinth"**) but with his personal vision of another dimension in things.

Heraldry could not, finally, yield what Muir wanted because the heraldic is essentially secular. Its landscape is the setting of parable, and renders universal experience into palpable form, but heraldic imagery was, for Muir, something more and less than the Christian. It implies, for one thing, war, the human struggle to conquer and order, and thus a selfishness and destructiveness that Muir finally wanted to see as part of the Story and not the Fable. Much of his heraldic imagery is explicitly martial, even in his novels:

But a lizard scuttling across the stones would make the place insecure. He saw nature as a terrifying heraldry. The cat, the lizard and the wasp were embattled forces armed for war, carrying terror and death on their blazoned stripes, their stings, claws and tongues.[6]

For another thing, when the images of Christianity did take over in his work, it became clear that what Muir had wanted was what only Christianity could supply, a release from the cycle of time. Like heraldry, Christianity partakes of both Story and Fable, this life and the eternal pattern. What frightened Muir about Nietzsche's vision was the sense of being trapped, caught in an endless round (e.g., the ending of the seventh *Variation*). Christianity was able to free Muir from his horror and despair.

Finally, we know of his fascination in later years with the idea of Incarnation. His movement toward that fascination led him from heraldry to a religion that was the enemy of abstraction (see **"The Incarnate One"**). It would clearly falsify Muir's thinking and his life to say that he became anything like an orthodox Christian; but even in his Nietzschean days he had hated the abstract. The image of a personal god—warm, alive and on this earth—could do little less than fascinate him in a way that heraldry, with all its intriguing emphasis on order but its concomitant tendency toward abstraction, could not. Muir, no dogmatist, embraced those aspects of Christianity which satisfied his own needs and preoccupations. He shifted from one mode to another but never changed radically his way of looking at the world. For him it was always emblematic of another reality that manifests itself everywhere in our lives. In his last known poem he speaks of time

> which takes away
> And taking leaves all things in their right place
> An image of forever
> One and whole.
>
> And now that time grows shorter, I perceive
> That Plato's is the truest poetry
> And that these shadows are cast by the true.

NOTES

[1] Edwin Muir, *An Autobiography* (London, 1964), p. 47.

[2] *Ibid.,* p. 48.

[3] All quotations of the poems are taken from Edwin Muir, *Collected Poems,* 2nd ed. (London, 1964).

[4] *Autobiography,* p. 49, and cf. p. 114.

[5] *New Age,* XVIII (1916), 496.

[6] *The Marionette* (New York, 1927), p. 4.

Thomas Merton (essay date 1967)

SOURCE: "Arts and Letters: The True Legendary Sound," in *The Sewanee Review,* Vol. LXXV, No. 2, Spring, 1967, pp. 317-24.

[*In the following essay, Merton discusses Muir's poetry in relation to the views advanced in his critical writings and lectures.*]

A recent popular survey of English philosophy since 1900 gives us a useful appraisal of the respectable grammarians of our day. It also includes, as an afterthought, a chapter on metaphysics. The chief purpose of this chapter is, of course, to remind us that there are no metaphysicians in England. At the same time the author gives us to understand that there is no justification for metaphysics anyway. Of such an attitude Edwin Muir would have said that it was a "denial of the roots"—and he would have added that such a denial cannot be made without cost.

Muir is one of those who intuitively realize that the giving of names is a primordial metaphysical act of the human intelligence—the Edenic office of the poet who follows Adam and reverifies the names given to creatures by his first father. Sartre (who has not much else in common with Muir!) brings this out clearly in writing of Francis Ponge. "The thing awaits its name. The giving of a name is a metaphysical act of absolute value; it is the solid and definitive union of man and thing because the *raison d'être* of the thing is to require a name and the function of man is to speak and give it one." Beneath the surface of this statement one can guess an existentialist fluidity which has nothing to do with the Biblical and epic solidity of Muir's grasp of the act of being. Whether or not Muir ever read *La Nausée* he would surely have been repelled by the meditation of Roquentin on the root in the park!

The poetry of Edwin Muir gives evidence of profound metaphysical concern: concern for the roots of being, for being in act, manifested by numinous and symbolic qualities. He does not seek these roots out of curiosity, nor does he find them in speculative and dialectical discussion. As a poet, Muir felt himself compelled to "divine and persuade"—to divine in the sense of a water-diviner finding hidden springs; to persuade, not by demonstration but by sharing the water with others.

It would of course be misleading to call Muir a "metaphysical poet". Intellectual irony, wit, and "conceits" are absent from his verse. But we must not forget the metaphysical preoccupations of Wordsworth, Coleridge, and even more of Blake. Muir as critic more than once quotes the lines of "Tintern Abbey" about the "eye made quiet by the power of harmony" seeing into "the deep life of things". The business of the poet is to reach the intimate, that is ontological, sources of life which cannot be clearly apprehended in themselves by any concept, but which, once intuited, can be made accessible to all in symbolic and imaginative celebration. The poetic experience of Muir, rich and varied and reaching out on various levels of depth, sometimes seeks out the ground itself of being:

> It is not any thing
> And yet all being it is;
> Being, being, being
> Its burden and its bliss.
> How can I ever prove
> What it is I love?

At other times (and here he is more articulate) he shows that he could equal Rilke's power of "inseeing" (*Einsehen*) by which the poet "lets himself into the very center" of the particular existent that he sees. In Rilke's words, he becomes able to see the thing from the very point where it springs from the creative power of God, and is "approved" by God.

I think that we can find the best examples of Muir's "inseeing" in some of his poems about horses. Horses awed and fascinated him, and consequently some of his most inspired imaginative writing is about them: they were to him splendid and numinous archetypes, because of the extraordinary innocence of his vision of them as a child on a farm in the Orkney Islands.

We must remember that Muir's poetry rests on a substratum of authentically primitive experience. He was an Orkney islander, a peasant's child in one of the last primitive communities of Europe.

Muir speaks in his *Autobiography* of looking up at his father's huge plough-horses with "a combination of emotions which added up to worship in the Old Testament sense".

> Everything about them, the steam rising from their soft, leathery nostrils, the sweat staining their hides, their ponderous irresistible motion, the distant rolling of their eyes which was like the revolution of rock-crystal suns, the waterfall sweep of their manes . . . the plunge of their iron-shod hoofs striking fire from the flagstones filled me with a stationary terror and delight for which I could get no relief.

His reference to the Old Testament, and this quoted passage, suggest that he was thinking of the cosmic praise of the Creator in Job or the Psalms.

Muir, who had left the Orkneys in his teens to work under abominable conditions in Glasgow, always resented the industrial society in which he had to live. He never adjusted to it and retained a thoroughly romantic contempt for it. He could thus say, typically, that it is possible to write poems about horses and not about cars because horses have "a life of their own". The horse becomes for him a symbol of the primitive and natural world as opposed to the artificial and unnatural world of modern technology. This artificial world is one in which he thinks there is no real place for poetry at all: it is

essentially anti-poetic and Muir's estimate of the possibility of poetry's surviving in it is to say the least "depressed". His half-admitted hope for poetry lies rather in the guess that technology will prove self-destructive. In his private and sometimes curiously striking eschatology Muir has a poem about the sudden spontaneous return of "the horses" to the wreckage of a world that has finally smashed itself by its own machines. T. S. Eliot, a great admirer of Muir, singled this poem out for special mention in his preface to the *Collected Poems.* Actually, one of Muir's very first poems about horses is even more typical of his imaginative insight. It is the same vision of childhood referred to above, now embodied in a poem of Blakian power and intensity:

> Their conquering hooves which trod the stubble down
> Were ritual that turned the field to brown,
> And their great hulks were seraphim of gold,
> Or mute ecstatic monsters on the mould.
>
> And oh! the rapture, when, one furrow done,
> They marched broad breasted to the sinking sun!
> The light flowed off their bossy sides in flakes;
> The furrows rolled behind like struggling snakes.
>
> But when at dusk with steaming nostrils home
> They came, they seemed gigantic in the gloam,
> And warm and glowing with mysterious fire
> That lit their smouldering bodies in the mire.
>
> Their eyes as brilliant and as wide as night
> Gleamed with a cruel apocalyptic light,
> Their manes the leaping ire of the wind
> Lifted with rage invisible and blind.

Muir did not completely agree with Rilke's explanation of "inseeing". He thought it "Platonic". He was the enemy of all abstractions. His imagination, like his metaphysic, was Biblical and Homeric as well as Celtic. It was never Platonic (and the question arises: was the object of Rilke's inseeing merely the "Platonic idea"? Possibly this was a misjudgment on Muir's part). Still, Muir writes of animals as Rilke did, guessing at their vision of the world as uninfluenced by any self-consciousness, any introspection, any reflective memory, any language: purely looking outward and not knowing what their own names are.

> But these have never trod
> Twice the familiar track,
> Never never turned back
> Into the memoried day.
> All is new and near
> In the unchanging Here. . . .

Muir's metaphysical insight into the numinous and sacred which does not underlie but actually *is* the ordinary reality of our world, was not an other-worldly mysticism. On the contrary, it was the ground of a deep and humane sympathy which expressed itself, for instance, in praise of Rabelais (in a remarkable essay on Panurge and Falstaff). On this metaphysical insight rests the sound sense of his critical essays, particularly about the novel.

Some of his poems treat love in a way that shows deep insight into the metaphysic of the person. The sweep of his vision, which is constantly aware of the beginning and the end of all things, naturally demands of him poems of theological scope, in which he rejects the austere Calvinism to which he was temporarily converted in adolescence. Later he turns, as we see in his *Autobiography,* to a warmer and more "Mediterranean" theology of the Incarnation and the Cross. Still he responds to Milton in a magnificent visionary poem (the first of his most important book), **"One Foot in Eden".**

> Milton, his face set fair for Paradise,
> And knowing that he and Paradise were lost
> In separate desolation, bravely crossed
> Into his second night and paid his price.
> There towards the end he to the dark tower came
> Set square in the gate, a mass of blackened stone
> Crowned with vermilion fiends like streamers
>   blown
> From a great funnel filled with roaring flame.

The strong contrasting colors are those of the Italian primitives. Sometimes his eschatology almost suggests that of Hieronymus Bosch. Here he describes a city reflected in a river, seeming to fall apart in anticipation of Judgment Day.

> In its mirror
> Great oes and capitals and flourishes
> Pillars and towers and fans and gathered sheaves
> Hold harvest home and Judgment Day of fire.
> The houses stir and pluck their roofs and walls
> Apart as if in play and fling their stones
> Against the sky to make a common arc
> And fall again. The conflagrations raise
> Their mountainous precipices. Living eyes
> Glaze instantly in crystal change.

These few examples, sufficient to give at least a fair idea of Muir's poetic imagination, also show him to be a writer with little or no technical sophistication. Muir began writing poetry, almost under compulsion, in early middle-age. It was a psychological and spiritual necessity for him. He did not imitate Eliot or Pound or anyone else then in fashion: he wrote as he felt, in the ballad tradition that had still been alive in the community into which he was born, and in the tradition of Wordsworth and the romantics he had read in his youth. He was never able to become deeply concerned with technical problems in poetry, whether as a poet or as a critic. As a poet he struggled to get the archetypes under control by means of the most obvious and familiar forms. He wanted to get the big symbols out and make them clear.

"I began to write poetry," he tells us in the *Autobiography,* "simply because what I wanted to say could not have gone properly into prose. I wanted so much to say it that I had no thought left to study the form in which alone it could be said."

Muir's poetry seeks the reconciliation of the inner and outer man, of the world of the present with its roots in the past. It aims at unity, and the power which restores this living unity is imagination. In the poetic imagination the heroes of Homer and the Biblical patriarchs not only manifest themselves and make themselves comprehensible to the poet and reader, but they "coexist" with him. Their typological experience is seen as realized in the crises of the poet's own life. Psychoanalysis played a very important part in Muir's life of inner struggle and seems to have liberated in him an altogether unusual creative power. (Contrast Rilke who, probably with equally good reasons, refused to be analyzed fearing that analysis, in "healing" his wounds, might relax fruitful tensions on which his creative power depended.)

The two books of critical lectures and essays which concern us here show Muir to be a reader of sound and catholic judgment, profoundly humane and careful not to do violence to authors or characters in the interests of any pet theory of his own. *The Estate of Poetry,* containing his Norton Lectures, is preoccupied with the relation of the poet to his audience. His *Essays on Literature and Society* range widely over poetry, the novel, and drama, and even include an essay on Spengler. In both these books Muir, as critic, returns again and again to what, for him, is the most important question: imagination. Imagination is for him at once poetic and metaphysical: "By imagination I mean that power by which we apprehend living beings and living creatures in their individuality as they live and move and not in their ideas and categories." The power of the poet's imaginative vision (in which of course the reader can participate) is that it directs our eye to beings in such a way as to *"feel the full weight and uniqueness* of their lives". Here as a matter of fact the poet has a prerogative which the speculative and abstract metaphysician might be tempted to deny him out of envy: the power to see being *in the concrete* and not by pure abstraction; to see it in its *individual actualization*—and even to express it as its concreteness. Both the vision and the expression of the individual evade technical and discursive ontology. Hence Muir's sense of mission in constantly reaffirming the vital necessity of poetic imagination in our age. Without it, we can have no real participation in the rich experience of the past. But the hubris of the present consists precisely in dismissing the past as irrelevant except to the prying and classifying eye of the specialist who studies it without ever realizing its relationship, and consequently its relevance, to ourselves. "When outward change becomes too rapid and the world around us alters from year to year, the ancestral image grows indistinct and the imagination cannot pierce to it as easily as it once could. . . . " A tragic loss, for then we no longer realize what it means that "our life is a rehearsal of lives that have been lived over and over." Not that we are meant to repeat, for repetition's sake, a series of futile and obsolete patterns: but there are in us inherited meanings and symbols which never come to life, never "connect" in our own existence, if we cannot identify with others in the present and in the past. Muir is concerned with imagination not only in order that there may be good poetry, but in order that man himself may survive.

Muir was distrustful of strictly technical and professional critical disciplines. He thought our refined modern criticism too esoteric, and felt that it was only a symptom of a generally bad condition in literature. This is the main theme of **The Estate of Poetry.** The "natural estate" of poetry is that in which the poet is in direct contact with an audience to which he speaks or sings his own poems. He needs no interpreter and no mediator. Poetry is then a general possession—the author himself may be forgotten, or may be a collective person. For Muir, then, the natural estate of poetry was already deranged by printing, which put the book definitely between the poet and the reader. (Readers of manuscripts in Rome and the Middle Ages usually read *aloud.* Monastic texts are punctuated for *singing.*) With the printed book poetry is not "heard". It becomes visual, mental, abstract. In his deep gloom about the modern world, Muir saw only more and more hopelessness ahead as technology came more and more to intervene between man and nature, man and the reality and immediacy of his own being. Poetry is now, he thought, in a "depressed state". Muir was in fact in despair about the modern world and felt that the poet was in a hopeless predicament, completely cut off from a popular audience, with no one to talk to, still less to sing to. Muir apparently had no inkling of the possibilities that have since surprised us: the influence of young Soviet poets reading their works in the parks, or the power exercised by an admittedly unruly poet like Bob Dylan making use of modern media. Dylan may certainly have more in common with *Mad* comics than with Shakespeare but he is nevertheless definitely conscious of a poetic vocation and has communicated an authentic fervor to an audience that is deeply involved. For Muir, the poet has become the helpless and passive prey of the critic. Poetry having now become not an experience but a problem, it is necessary to write problematical poems that critics will be interested in discussing. If the critics ignore you, you are no poet.

Indeed, what really matters is not so much the poem as the crowning brilliancy of its critical analysis. The poem is only an occasion. Thus poetry is only a humble, ordinary, rather useless tree which justifies its existence by allowing criticisms to bloom all over its branches like orchids. So, Muir says, the poet having lost contact with a living and popular audience has turned in despair to the consolations of an imprisoned and "kept" existence. Poets have locked "themselves into a hygienic prison in which they speak only to one another and to the critic their stern warder". Such a situation gives Muir claustrophobia.

Doubtless Muir is too pessimistic. His romantic allergies incline him to some exaggeration and he is perhaps too negative in his estimate of critical methods. Yet it is true that they may become, as he says, machines into which the poem is put in order to achieve a result already in the teacher's mind. As a result poetry itself tends to become artificial, unnatural, unimaginative, a formalistic exercise without interest except for those who have a private code they like to play games with.

Muir's own poems are, then, deliberately left in a state which many readers might consider crude and naïve. He could easily be neglected, except for the fact that poets now seem to be reading him with considerable interest, not for the way he says things but for what he actually says; not for the sophistication of his technique but for his imaginative power and his concern for "the creation of a true image of life". Muir is no doubt a poet who wrote to be read aloud. He wrote with his ear attuned to his own inflections and some of his poems scan with difficulty when skimmed over with the eye. I do not know if he was a good reader himself, but perhaps these poems should be given the benefit that he demanded for all poetry: and then they would reveal to us their "true legendary sound". This is perhaps essential to poetry, which is "the communication of something for which no other kind of speech can serve". Muir himself was not a technical but a charismatic poet, and he was faithful to his special grace: his keen awareness that "The first allegiance of any poet is to imaginative truth."

Elizabeth Huberman (essay date 1972)

SOURCE: "Initiation and Tragedy: A New Look at Edwin Muir's 'The Gate'," in *PMLA,* Vol. 80, No. 1, January, 1972, pp. 75-9.

[*In the following essay, Huberman discusses innocence and experience in "The Gate."*]

Although since Edwin Muir's death ten years ago, his prestige as a poet has steadily increased, his poetry has been subjected to remarkably little critical examination. His **Collected Poems** (1952, 1960) and his final volume, **One Foot in Eden** (1956), were widely and for the most part favorably reviewed; many warm appreciations of his entire work appeared both in the United States and in England at the time of his death; and over the years a few general studies of his poetry, or of certain themes in his poetry, have been published in various journals and surveys of contemporary verse. Aside from Peter Butter, however, in his booklet, *Edwin Muir* (New York: Grove Press, 1962), and in his full-length biography and critique, *Edwin Muir: Man and Poet* (New York: Barnes and Noble, 1967), very few critics have scrutinized any of Muir's individual poems in close detail. Particularly, and rather surprisingly, no one has explored the complexities and ambiguities of one of the key poems to the understanding of Muir's work as a whole: the quiet yet disturbing poem called **"The Gate."**

Whether by accident or design, the physical location of this poem in Muir's final **Collected Poems** (p. 110) announces its strategic importance. For it not only occurs in the volume, **The Narrow Place** (1943), that marks a transformation in Muir's vision of life, from almost unrelieved darkness to the possibility, at least, of light, but it also stands precisely at the center of this volume, where it represents the nadir of horror and desolation, the extreme of Muir's commitment to despair.

Once this point is passed, once the threshold of this "gate" is crossed, a renewal of hope and joy takes place, as the remaining poems of *The Narrow Place* and succeeding volumes gradually reveal. But **"The Gate"** itself deals unsparingly with the loss of innocence, the initiation of the child into the mysteries and corruption of the adult world, and the ultimate cruelty and betrayal which lie at the center of that world. It is the direct confrontation with evil which must be endured, according to many of Muir's later poems, before there can be any true knowledge of good.

The whole structure of the poem, indeed, signals a terrifying downward plunge from light into dark, from safety into loss and fear. A strong caesura in the twelfth line ("And made them strange as gods. / We sat that day") divides the twenty-four freely handled blank verse lines of the poem almost exactly in half, and in each half there is a parallel descending movement. Beginning in both cases with the phrase "We sat" and the image of two children huddled securely against a protecting wall, both sections of the poem immediately qualify that security. It is a "stern" security in the first half; the walls "frown" upon the children; and in the second half the children are "outcast" as well as "safe." But whereas in the opening section the threat to the children is only implied in the care their guardians take to mask their "tell-tale faces," and in the "shame" they feel for the "rich food" that seems to make their bodies indecent, in the second section that threat is realized. The children's familiar world shrivels before their eyes, leaving them outside, outcast, as they have been by the adult world. And now, when they have no other refuge, the "huge gate" that they must turn and enter swings open behind them. Like a tolling bell, the four successive heavy stresses of the last line ("And then behind us the *huge gate swung* open") mark the inevitable end of innocence, the beginning of a strange, disturbing future.

To a certain extent this downward spiral of the poem might be characterized in the terms Muir himself used in *An Autobiography,* where he observed from his own experience that "in a child's mind there is at moments a divination of a hidden tragedy taking place around him, that tragedy being the life he will not live for some years still, though it is there, invisible to him, already."[1] The first half of "The Gate" records one of those moments of divination. The second half is the entry into tragedy. But although such a description indicates the prevailing set of the poem, it does not take into account a secondary movement which is also in operation. This is a movement of passage, an initiation rite, which is as firmly structured into the poem as the descent into tragedy, and is perhaps more important in determining the tone, the emotional coloring of the whole poem. For while there is fear in **"The Gate,"** there is neither pity nor any sense of tragic purgation. Once the two brief glimpses of safety and innocence are past, there is only a confluence of painful feelings: shame, revulsion, disillusion, loneliness, and dread of the unknown.

The initiation theme opens with the word "Outside," strategically placed at the beginning of the second line. The children in the poem are apparently "outsiders." For some reason they do not belong with their fathers inside the fortress, but must remain "outside" the walls. Their entrance into the fortress is, in fact, explicitly forbidden, tabooed. The fourth-line sentence, "We could not enter there"—again, positioned for emphasis—clearly implies prohibition as well as inability, and the idea of prohibition is reinforced by the "frowned" and "stern" of the preceding line. With the fifth and sixth lines, the basis of the interdiction develops: the children are still too immature, their "palates" too "unpracticed" for the "gross and strong" quality of life within the walls; and the note of coarseness, indecency, even corruption, sounded by "gross" strongly suggests that the secrets which the children are not permitted to penetrate are sexual. The fact that the fathers feel forced, in dealing with the children, to assume a lost innocence, to mask their "tell-tale faces" (blushing? leering?) still further confirms the presence of the sexual mystery, while their "shame / For the rich food that plumped their lusty bodies" establishes that presence beyond a doubt. For not only is the shame which adults feel before children most often a shame for their more fully developed sexual characteristics, but that full development is plainly indicated here, in "plumped" and "lusty bodies." To be sure, the motive for the "shame" is said to be the "rich food" which fed these bodies, rather than the bodies themselves; but eating and other forms of sensuality are often connected, as the phrase "unpracticed palates," a euphemism for physical immaturity, implies, and as William Empson notes in his essay on *Alice in Wonderland.* By coincidence, Empson even uses Muir's phrase, "rich food," which he says is "the child's symbol for all luxuries reserved for grownups."[2] And preeminent among those luxuries is, of course, the imperfectly understood but fearfully attractive sexual act. That this is Muir's symbolism too, his choice of the word "lusty" to modify "bodies" clearly proves. For "lusty" not only speaks its own meaning; it encloses "lust."

At this point, however, the first section of the poem comes to an end, and in the second section the mood and the focus of attention shift. The play on "outcast" and "castaway" emphasizes once more the children's exclusion from adult life, but the fleshly mysteries of that life are no longer suggested. Instead, the children's own world comes into view, a landscape recognizable as a version of Muir's own childhood landscape in the Orkneys. The smooth green hillock is the mound known as the Castle near his father's farm. The pond is perhaps the sound between the islands which he often watched from the Castle hill:

> Long time he lay upon the sunny hill,
> To his father's house below securely bound.
> Far off the silent, changing sound was still,
> With the black islands lying thick around.[3]

But a comparison between these two renderings of the same scene immediately shows a vast difference. While the four lines just quoted from Muir's early poem, **"Childhood,"** are touched with Wordsworth's "visionary gleam," the hill and pond of **"The Gate"** are sunless. The "scene" is "well-worn"—perhaps well-loved, but certainly not new or bright. Although the hillock is pleasantly "smooth and green," it is also "small," as if outgrown. And smallness, smoothness, and greenness all seem the qualities of toys, "intended" indeed for children, "for us alone and childhood," but intended also to narrow the view, not expand it to any glimpse of "that imperial palace" of our origins. The "still pond," which opens "upon no sight a quiet eye," lovely as it is, similarly closes the view, closes it to nothing at all, and the "little stream," with its music-box tinkle, has nowhere to go once it runs down the toy-like slope.

Even before the shrunken twenty-first line announces the fact, "But suddenly all seemed old," the fact is evident: the childhood world of the poem has already lost its largeness and splendor. It is "old" because the children are "old"; they have grown up. In a succession of sighing s's and sh's, which echo the "shore" of the sad fifteenth line, "As castaways thrown upon an empty shore," the twenty-first, -second, and -third lines simultaneously lament and describe the final withering of this already faded scene. The two who were once children are "outside" again, this time outside their lost youth. But whereas, as children, they were excluded from the stronghold of adult life, now, as adults themselves, they are ready for admission. The image of the fortress, with all its suggestions of the sexual mystery, returns; the gates swing open, and the *rite de passage,* the initiation, is on the point of accomplishment.

Thus, viewed as patterned on a ritual of initiation into maturity, **"The Gate"** takes a forward direction, steps over a threshold. As patterned on the theme of lost innocence, the tragic change from an early Eden to the fallen world we all live in, the poem moves downward. But to encompass this complete doubling of theme and movement in the short space of twenty-four lines; to achieve the peculiarly ambivalent quality, the special density of texture which characterizes the poem, both extreme compression and economy of means were requisite, and it is necessary to be aware of this compression and economy if the full extent of the technical dexterity of the poem is to be recognized.

Since, for example, both the forward and the downward curves of the poem take their start, whatever their conclusions, from the point of unspoiled childhood, that point must be definitely established. Without it, downward and forward lose their meaning. On the other hand, it must remain only a point. Expanded, it would interfere with the set of the poem, which is all toward darkness and disillusion. In a single line at the beginning of the poem, therefore, all that is needed is beautifully provided: "We sat, two children, warm against the wall." The alliterating w's, the comfortable assonance of "warm" and "wall," bind the line into a close unity; the image of the wall repeats the idea of encircling

protection; and the number of children, "two," is just right: a company, not a crowd; a diminutive Adam and Eve in a minimal Eden. With slightly less of an Edenic flavor, the same scene is recapitulated in the line and a half which introduce the second section of the poem: "We sat that day / With that great parapet behind us, safe." But after that, no more. A vision of security has been granted. The rest of **"The Gate"** is given over to erosion of that security, again by a complex of small, deft touches.

The second line, for instance, "Outside the towering stronghold of our fathers," does not directly undermine the snug circle of the first, but it firmly draws a line between that circle and the one that really matters. It also sets up less friendly walls, too high for children to climb. The *f* of "fathers" is disturbingly echoed by "frowned" in the third line, and once more by "fortress" in the fourth, where the danger that has been intimated suddenly comes into the open: the very walls that supposedly guard the children actually contaminate them. The "fortress," their "safe protection," is the center and source of a life too "gross and strong" for them to bear; and the word "gross," as we have seen, defines the nature of the contagion.

It is, of course, the now grown-up children, looking back, who relate these events, who tell of the futile deceptions practiced to protect them, while still innocent, from the corruption of their elders. But this distancing increases rather than diminishes the intensity of the experience. The "we" who were once the children see an irony the real children could not have recognized in the tender care of the guardians, "who had long since lost" their own innocence for the still undamaged "innocence" of the children; and they see the further irony of the fact that what the guardians sought to cherish they simultaneously destroyed, by the "tell-tale faces" they could not altogether hide, and by their disturbingly developed bodies. At the same time, they seem to react with all their original uneasy wonder at the mysterious "shame" of these guardians, at the inappropriate "childish mask" they felt impelled to put on, and at their perplexingly large and different bodies, "strange as gods." (Is there perhaps a hint here of some primitive initiation ceremony, with masked dancers representing fertility deities?) In any event, knowing and yet recalling the feel of not knowing, these former children, as narrators, give the poem the sense of a double point of view which, like a stereoscope, adds a third dimension of depth to the picture.

Double point of view, double movement, double theme, all work together to produce that ambivalence, that density we have already noted. But there are more doubles yet. Part of the word pattern of the poem is a play on doubles: on the surviving "innocence" of the children in the first half of line seven, for instance, and on the lost "innocence" of their fathers in the latter half of the next line. Or again, the "safe" of line five, where the security of "safe protection" is balanced against the threat of "too gross and strong," is repeated again, still in a context of security, in line thirteen, only to be coupled in the next line with an "outcast" that immediately cancels all safety. And "outcast" itself, repeated twice in the same line, becomes the pivotal word on which the movement of the second half of the poem turns, away from what seemed safety, "With that great parapet behind us," to a realization that such safety was only exclusion from two worlds. Then, in a recapitulation of that insight, "outcast" is transmuted into "castaway" in the desolation of the fifteenth line, "As castaways thrown upon an empty shore."

Patterns of assonance and alliteration, too, not only create an unusually rich, although subdued, music, as in the line: "That opened upon no sight a quiet eye," with its interweaving of *t, n, p, o,* and *i* sounds. They also point up the play on doubles and on opposites: the *ou* in the forbidding "Outside" in line two is immediately echoed in the equally forbidding "towering," and again in "frowned" and "down." The "*security*" of line three is ominously "*stern*"; the reiterated *p*'s of "unpracticed palates" call special attention to this significantly strange phrase; the *a*'s in "tell-tale faces" and "shame" mock the clumsy pretense of the preceding "grave play." If the *l*'s in the childhood scene have a soothing quality, as in "well-worn," "hillock," "small," "alone," "still," they nevertheless recall the suggestive "plumped" and "lusty," and they predict the weary, disillusioned "all," "old," "dull," and "sullen." From "plumped" and "lusty," too, come the first [Ë] sounds that recur again, in increasingly mournful tone, throughout the last lines: "dull," "shrunken," "shut," "sullen," and finally, emphatically, "swung." For on that word, as on the earlier "outcast," much of the impetus of the poem depends; this is the word that completes, sadly in either case, the motion down or in.

Yet finally, of course, it is on something more basic than any particular words or sound sequence, or even any patterns of initiation or loss, that the motion and the fundamental ambivalence of the poem depend. And that something is the underlying image, the picture of a fortress outside whose walls two children sit until at last the gates open to admit them. For the fact is that the movement of **"The Gate,"** from security outside the walls to some unimaginable, blank horror when the "huge gates" swing open, is contrary to all the usual expectations of such an image. The danger is customarily outside the fortress; refuge, within. Although this contrary current runs deep, almost unnoticed, under the more obvious details of the poem, nevertheless it qualifies these details, however imperceptibly, and it helps to account for the sense of oppression, of fear and betrayal, which the poem as a whole conveys.

What is more, this same contrary current reveals a relationship, otherwise easily overlooked, between this poem and a major strain in Muir's work apparently very different from either the initiation or the loss of Eden themes; and this, as Butter notes in his shorter study,

Edwin Muir, is the apprehension of treachery from within.[4] In its earliest forms this motif was most often involved with time. Time, for instance, was the traitor who caught poor Beauty in a snare in **"Betrayal"** in Muir's *First Poems,* and "inly" wasted her flesh away. Again, in his next major volume, *Variations on a Time Theme,* time was the traitor who trapped mankind in the wilderness and kept it from the promised land. Even in **"The Gate,"** although time is not specifically mentioned, it is still the passage of time which brings the children to maturity and opens for them the gate of a frightening future. But treachery for Muir can wear other and more intimate shapes than that of time. In Section Nine of *Variations,* treachery wears man's own skin. "Packed in my skin from head to toe,"[5] lives the root of all evil, indifference; and from within the stronghold of man's own heart, indifference betrays every virtue that heart inclines to. Similarly, in Muir's novel, *The Three Brothers,* this same callous indifference takes the form of one of the twins, Archie Blackadder, who lives side by side with his "good" twin, David, only to frustrate, and, of course, betray him. For Archie, "a pleasant enough wee beast himself,"[6] is that inseparable animal half of the human soul without which, according to Muir's reiterated thesis, man would not be man, yet with which there can be no permanent peace. Archie is the traitor who thrives in every man, who *is* one aspect of every man; he is the eternal evil at the core of life.

Significantly, to symbolize this existence of evil at the center, which is the basic theme of the novel, Muir uses precisely the same image he uses in **"The Gate,"**—the image of a fortress impregnable without, but open, through the gate, to treachery within. In **"The Castle,"** too, a poem in his next volume, *The Voyage,* he uses very briefly the same image and almost the very words of the novel, to express the same theme:

> There was a little private gate,
> A little wicked wicket gate,
> The wizened warder let them through.[7]

But in *The Three Brothers* he repeats and elaborates. When David, still a little boy, asks his father to explain how the Calvinists managed to get into the Castle at St. Andrews and kill the Cardinal, the elder Blackadder answers: "Ay, but just listen a wee. If you go round the corner of the castle what should you come to but another gate, a wee thing that ye would hardly notice, a wee, wicked-looking wee gate" (pp. 12-13). Then, David wonders, "A man can be killed in the middle of a castle?" And Blackadder admits, "Aye, it's so" (pp. 15-16).

As David grows up, he discovers there are many gates to the middle of the castle, many ways by which danger and destruction can enter the strongest and inmost keep. War, for example, breaks many castles down. His own brother Archie constantly betrays him and brings him trouble. Death insidiously attacks his mother, his other brother, and his sweetheart. Even the trusting animals of the farm are led to slaughter, until David finally sees in everything the sheer naked terror of existence. No-where is there any "security, nor any trust that was kept by the powers of the world." He thinks then of "Cardinal Beaton butchered in the inmost chamber of the Castle, and the pig, nourished and petted, and at last dragged out into the sunlit yard, and its throat cut by the hands which had fondled and fed it," and he asks himself, as he had asked his father, "What help was there in this world save in God alone?" (p. 272). But what help was there in God, who if the universe was cruel, "was its burning centre and axle?" (p. 273). And this, the awful cruelty at the heart of the universe, at the center where help and trust ought most to be looked for, *this* is the deep core of terror which in **"The Gate"** cancels our expectations of a stronghold and makes the move from outside into "the inmost chamber of the Castle" a descent into the heart of darkness.

NOTES

[1] New York: Seabury Press, 1968, p. 33.

[2] *"Alice in Wonderland:* The Child as Swain," *Some Versions of Pastoral* (Norfolk, Conn.: New Directions, 1950), p. 264.

[3] Edwin Muir, *Collected Poems* (New York: Oxford Univ. Press, 1965), p. 19. All quotations from *Collected Poems* by Edwin Muir. Copyright 1960 by Willa Muir. Reprinted by permission of Oxford Univ. Press, Inc.

[4] New York: Grove Press, 1962, pp. 85-87.

[5] *Collected Poems,* p. 50.

[6] *The Three Brothers* (New York: Doubleday, 1931), p. 240.

[7] *Collected Poems,* p. 129.

Christopher Wiseman (essay date 1972)

SOURCE: "Edwin Muir's 'The Labyrinth': A Study of Symbol and Structure," in *Studies in Scottish Literature,* Vol. X, No. 2, October, 1972, pp. 67-78.

[*In the following essay, Wiseman offers a close examination of "The Labyrinth," particularly focusing on Muir's symbolist techniques and the nonlogical structure of the poem.*]

The poems in *The Labyrinth* (1949) were written in Czechoslovakia between 1945 and 1948, when Edwin Muir was Director of the British Institute in Prague. These were dramatic and tragic years for Muir; so much so that on his return to England in 1948 he suffered a breakdown and withdrew into a state of despairing apathy, "a dead pocket of life",[1] for several months. On his arrival in Prague, after a journey through countries scarred and altered from the war, Muir had been horrified

by stories of Nazi atrocities during the recent occupation and the effect this had had on the Czech people, but even more disturbing was the ferment of political intrigue, culminating in the "Putsch" of 1948 when Russia effectively and brutally took over the country. This sudden *coup* was reinforced by a sinister and pervasive apparatus of secret police, informers, censorship, and personal and artistic repression and, in this climate of fear and suspicion, Muir found it almost impossible to function.

Willa Muir writes of these years that "the unrest, the flurries from pessimism to optimism which ravaged the country ravaged Edwin and me as well",[2] and many of the poems in *The Labyrinth* exhibit the poet's shocked awareness of how great political machines can dehumanise and brutalise individual lives. The problem of evil and suppression obsesses him, and in no other volume of his poetry do we sense so sharply what M. L. Rosenthal calls his "infinite sadness, and the repressed hysteria that underlies it."[3] Here the redemptive possibilities of Eden and eternity, towards which his symbology had been moving, become swamped and negated by an overwhelming sense of man caught in time, in social and political necessity. The shadow of the labyrinth broods over this collection, manifesting itself as an agent of blockage, interrupting and disorientating man on his journey back to Eden. Poems like **"The Combat," "The Interceptor," "The Interrogation," "The Helmet" "The Good Town," "The Usurpers"** are informed with a barely controlled violence of feeling and a political awareness new in Muir's work, even though the negative experience itself was by no means new to him, being a parallel in many ways to the violent sense of threat and disorientation he had experienced as a boy when he moved from Orkney to the industrial squalor of Glasgow. At that time he felt he had moved into time from eternity, into disintegration from wholeness and unity, and the "fearful shape of our modern inhumanity"[4] which impinged so sickeningly on him in Prague is an integral component of that symbolic Fall, the loss of Eden, he had experienced in the labyrinth of Glasgow's slums some forty years previously. The recurrence of this destructive ghost, released from a place in his mind he had thought sealed, must have been terrible.

The title poem of *The Labyrinth* dramatically embodies this sense of terror and loss of certainty. Not only is it interesting in terms of its desperate tone of nightmare, its sense of the lost self and its obsessive concern with psychological blockage, but it illustrates fully, for the first time, Muir's use of symbolist techniques. It is as if the new urgency of the content, the violence of the conflict of positive and negative potencies, has forced him into dramatic technical experiment, and, instinctively it seems, he uses classic symbolist devices. In this poem, and frequently in his poetry from this volume on, Muir employs a non-logical structure, dislocating tenses and confusing dream and reality in an attempt to free his symbols from the restrictions of time and space. And this deliberate movement in and out of time and reality is reinforced, as I hope to demonstrate, by a highly expressive use of syntax and metre.

In a broadcast, Muir described the genesis of **"The Labyrinth"**.

> Thinking there of the old story of the labyrinth of Knossos and the journey of Theseus through it and out of it, I felt that this was an image of human life with its errors and ignorance and endless intricacy. In the poem I made the labyrinth stand for all this. But I wanted also to give an image of the life of the gods, to whom all that is confusion down here is clear and harmonious as seen eternally.[5]

This account makes clear the central strategy of the poem—the juxtaposition of the images of confused man and harmonious gods, of the Fall and Eden—but the result is, in fact, far richer than Muir intimates here.

"The Labyrinth" is a highly complex poem. It draws together all Muir's great symbols—Eden, the Fall, time, the journey, the labyrinth—into a coherent and fully realised structure which resolves itself perfectly while remaining accessible to many levels of interpretation and response. The poem starts with the hero looking back at the labyrinth:

> Since I emerged that day from the labyrinth,
> Dazed with the tall and echoing passages,
> The swift recoils, so many I almost feared
> I'd meet myself returning at some smooth corner,
> Myself or my ghost, for all there was unreal
> After the straw ceased rustling and the bull
> Lay dead upon the straw and I remained,
> Blood-splashed, if dead or alive I could not tell
> In the twilight nothingness (I might have been
> A spirit seeking his body through the roads
> Of intricate Hades). . . .[6]

We are immediately presented with a vision of chaos; the protagonist (Theseus/Muir/Everyman) dazed and lost, splashed with blood, not knowing whether he is dead or alive. The labyrinth is deliberately likened to Hades, as a symbol of anti-Eden or anti-Heaven. It is the country of fallen man, removed from his beginnings and diverted from his true journey. But Muir immediately opposes this opening symbol with a compensatory vision of Eden:

> . . . ever since I came out
> To the world, the still fields swift with flowers,
>   the trees
> All bright with blossom, the little green hills, the
>   sea,
> The sky and all in movement under it,
> Shepherds and flocks and birds and the young
>   and old,
> (I stared in wonder at the young and old,
> For in the maze time had not been with me;

This vision of growth, of archetypal simplicity, with everything untroubled and in its place, heightens the effect of the labyrinth by contrasting emblematic pastoral colours with the "twilight nothingness", and the full potentiality of life and growth with the sterile half-life of the fallen condition. Through the device of the line

"For in the maze time had not been with me", Muir now switches tenses, taking us back into the labyrinth with an evocation of bewilderment and helplessness:

> I had strayed, it seemed, past sun and season and
>   change,
> Past rest and motion, for I could not tell
> At last if I moved or stayed; the maze itself
> Revolved around me on its hidden axis
> And swept me smoothly to its enemy,
> The lovely world). . . .

This is close to Kafka's nightmare world of disoriented man confronted with vast hostile organisations which lead him to doubt the authenticity and validity of his existence. The labyrinth undermines the self. Unlocated in time and space, the struggle for individual survival is made desperate by the absence of fixed points by which the self can find balance and perspective.

Up to this point, Muir has distanced this vision of chaos and insanity by placing it firmly in the past as a memory of the now safe traveller. Now he takes even that prop away by bringing the labyrinth into the present, continuing the Kafka-like images of helpless disorientation of perception:

> . . . since I came out that day,
> There have been times when I have heard my
>   footsteps
> Still echoing in the maze, and all the roads
> That run through the noisy world, deceiving
>   streets
> That meet and part and meet, and rooms that open
> Into each other—and never a final room—
> Stairways and corridors and antechambers
> That vacantly wait for some great audience,
> The smooth sea-tracks that open and close again,
> Tracks undiscoverable, indecipherable,
> Paths on the earth and tunnels underground,
> And bird-tracks in the air—all seemed a part
> Of the great labyrinth. And then I'd stumble
> In sudden blindness, hasten, almost run,
> As if the maze itself were after me
> And soon must catch me up.

The protagonist is not free from the experience of terror. The self remains threatened and paranoid as the past presses into the present. The Eden-vision is undermined and becomes fragile and semi-permanent in face of this reassertion of terror. The labyrinth is no longer a myth of time past but a massive reality reaching into the hoped-for stability of the present. The hero remains confused, uncertain of his actuality, split into the labyrinth-man and the religious visionary:

> But taking thought,
> I'd tell myself, 'You need not hurry. This
> Is the firm good earth. All roads lie free before you.'
> But my bad spirit would sneer, 'No, do not hurry.
> No need to hurry. Haste and delay are equal
> In this one world, for there's no exit, none,
> No place to come to, and you'll end where you are,
> Deep in the centre of the endless maze.'

Here the opposing symbols of the poem converge and move into direct confrontation. But just as the voice from the labyrinth, "my bad spirit", seems triumphant, Muir brings us back to the vision of Eden and the life of the gods, almost desperately invoking another world, which, by its transcendent properties, can perhaps defeat the chaos which threatens to overwhelm the protagonist:

> I could not live if this were not illusion.
> It is a world, perhaps; but there's another.
> For once in a dream or trance I saw the gods
> Each sitting on the top of his mountain-isle,
> While down below the little ships sailed by,
> Toy multitudes swarmed in the harbours,
>   shepherds drove
> Their tiny flocks to the pastures, marriage feasts
> Went on below, small birthdays and holidays,
> Ploughing and harvesting and life and death,
> And all permissible, all acceptable,
> Clear and secure as in a limpid dream.
> But they, the gods, as large and bright as clouds,
> Conversed across the sounds in Tranquil voices
> High in the sky above the untroubled sea,
> And their eternal dialogue was peace
> Where all these things were woven, and this our life
> Was as a chord deep in that dialogue,
> An easy utterance of harmonious words,
> Spontaneous syllables bodying forth a world.

This great vision of the gods is an expansion of the lines in the early poem **"The Mythical Journey"**:

>   And on the hills
> The gods reclined and conversed with each other
> From summit to summit.[7]

but in the symbolic structure of **"The Labyrinth"** the vision takes on a much wider significance. In this world everything is permissible and without tension. The gods preside over a place of harmony, "Where all these things were woven," and the labyrinth, in comparison, becomes small and inconsequential. The problem of time, however, is further confused here by the poet, for the vision of harmony occurred "once in a dream or trance." The world of the gods is a dream-reality, unconnected to the time-place of the labyrinth, and expressed with all the precise vagueness of a dream. The scene on which the gods look down is filled with "toy multitudes" and "tiny flocks"; the ships are "little", birthdays and holidays are "small", giving simultaneously an impression of unreality, of a toy landscape, and the sense of the striking new perspective from the high world of the gods. The gods themselves remain unconcrete, symbolised as insubstantial voices, creating only a vast music over the human landscape.

The next six lines defiantly celebrate the redemptive authenticity of this vision:

> That was the real world; I have touched it once,
> And now shall know it always. But the lie,
> The maze, the wild-wood waste of falsehood, roads
> That run and run and never reach an end,
> Embowered in error—I'd be prisoned there
> But that my soul has birdwings to fly free.

The conflicting symbols of the maze and Eden are temporarily reconciled here by the insistence upon a fortifying, Platonic reality, by which the pressures of actuality can be transcended. The tense is present once more, with the hero looking back on his vision while still conscious of the "wild-wood waste of falsehoods"—the labyrinth—pulling at his feet.

But the poem can not end here. Once again, Muir deliberately confuses the tenses, modifies the conclusion, and reaches for the ambiguity of the symbolic conflict:

> Oh these deceits are strong almost as life.
> Last night I dreamt I was in the labyrinth,
> And woke far on. I did not know the place.

We are left to decide whether last night's dream is the same as the early experience in the labyrinth, or whether it is a further vision of the former reality. Certainly we have been led back into the world of vision, having moved in and out of time and actuality throughout the poem, and the last line, because it leaves us stranded outside the safety of the concrete world of here and now, is charged with a vague menace. "I did not know the place" demonstrates once more the dislocation of time and space around which the structure of this poem is built. Ending in this way with a return to disorientation, Muir leaves us not with the vision of the gods but with the knowledge of nightmare, threat, bewilderment. The gestures towards a healing unity are proved to be no more than tentative, and the gap between human and divine reality, between time and eternity, falsehood and truth, remains strongly implicit.

This summary of the structure of **"The Labyrinth"** permits us to look more closely at the details of the symbolist method employed by Muir. We have seen how the poet works with two opposing symbols—the labyrinth and Eden—to create tension and meaning. I have deliberately avoided trying to interpret these symbols more widely, but it is clear that they are extremely rich and resonant, generating both personal and universal meaning. **"The Labyrinth"** is a completely symbolistic poem—non-rational, non-conceptual, non-allegorical—where the symbols, as we have seen, do not stay located in time or space, but are endlessly shifting between past and present actuality and vision. In this way they become centres of many overlapping circles of meaning, where oppositions are emphasized and resolved in a completely non-logical manner. There is no either/or in the symbolist imagination as there is in the logical process. In this poem, the labyrinth does not represent either the Fall of man or insanity, say; it encompasses the Fall and emotional blockage, loss of control, the political terror in Prague, the sour and squalid tenements of Glasgow, the labyrinth of the original Greek myth, the awareness of death, the soul's dark night, the sterile technological world of secondary objects and Muir's experience of Kafka's stories. And yet the symbol is more than all of these. Similarly, the world of the gods in the poem embraces Eden and Orkney, the harmonious relationship with the animals, pre-industrial life, positive religious experience, a celebration of poetic creation and a healing return from madness and confusion. In addition, we must remember that the poem tells us that both of these symbols derive from dreams or trances. This poem shows clearly the possibilities of the symbolist method, moving imperceptibly from level to level, place to place, tense to tense; from the world of myth to the real world of Prague; from Orkney to Glasgow; from sanity to madness. All this is achieved by the use of the two symbols, which Muir leaves next to each other to mean what they can. This is the essence of the symbolist method, and the essence of Muir's art. Time is not process; symbol is not tied to concept, as in allegory; inner and outer worlds become inseparable. The poet makes just one act of perception, through the symbols, which transcends analytic thought; the symbols are not reminders of meaning as much as sources of meaning, striving to define themselves. In this poem, the dark vision of the labyrinth is threaded by the bright symbol of rebirth and harmony; the conflicting symbols acting as generating elements in an undifferentiated stream of thoughts, feelings, perceptions and associations.

Writing about Whitman's great elegy for Lincoln, Charles Feidelson describes the symbolistic act of creation:

> The act of poetizing and the context in which it takes place have continuity in time and space but no particular existence. Both are 'ever-returning'; the tenses shift; the poet is in different places at once; and at the end this whole phase of creation is moving inexorably forward.
>
> Within this framework the symbols behave like characters in a drama, the plot of which is the achievement of a poetic utterance [8]

"The Labyrinth" is not *about* a labyrinth, nor *about* Muir's personal experience; rather it *enacts* the symbolic journey through the dark in terms of the vision of light. It is a perfect example of how the successful symbolist poem actually embodies what it is about by its use of symbol, syntax and prosody, and this poem clearly gives the lie to those who play down Muir's technical abilities.

For instance, J. C. Hall has claimed that "in this poem 'The Labyrinth' Muir sustains the first sentence for thirty-five lines without metrical support."[9] This is demonstrably untrue. **"The Labyrinth"** is written in regular metre, often loose, but with a five-stress line throughout. The syntax and metre are complex, and they are vital to the poem's effect and to the presentation of the symbolism.

The first sentence does, indeed, go on for thirty-five lines, enacting in its tenuous, uncertain, broken syntax the stumbling journey through the labyrinth. The pentameter lines use many foot-substitutions to enhance the syntactical re-enactment of the theme, letting the language speed up or fall away in flat despair. Let us consider lines 8 - 15:

```
           /    /      x   /   x x / x  /    x   /
 8  Blood-splashed, if dead or alive I could not tell
        x  x  /  x   /  x  /   x /    x   /
    In the twilight nothingness (I might have been
      x / x /   x    x /  x / x       x   /
10  A spirit seeking his body through the roads
       x  / x x   /   x   /  x  /  x x   /
    Of intricate Hades)—ever since I came out
       x  x  /    x   /   x    /      /   x
12  To the world, the still fields swift with
          /  x    x   /
       flowers, the trees
         /    /    x  /  x    x  / x x    /
    All bright with blossom, the little green hills,
         x   /
       the sea,
       x   /   x  / x /    x    x  / x /
    The sky and all in movement under it,
       /   x   x    /      x   /   x x    /
15  Shepherds and flocks and birds and the young
       x    /
       and old
```

Here we see only one line of regular iambic pentameter. Of the forty feet in the eight lines, there are no fewer than fourteen non-iambic substitutions, occurring not only in the usual first but in all of the five positions. This is a highly patterned poetry, but rhythmically extremely flexible. In these lines, too, we can see the labyrinthine effect of the syntax: the parenthesis introducing a new image and followed immediately by the change of tense and location; the run-on lines; the switch in tempo (and stress pattern) in line 12 to indicate the sudden emergence into the world of Eden; the many monosyllabic words, arranged in a simple catalogue form, in lines 12 - 15, which contrast formally with the much more tortured description of the labyrinth itself.

This order of technical complexity continues through the whole poem performing a vital expressive function. After the long first sentence, the syntax and the metrical pattern alter perceptibly. Short sentences, appropriate to the dialogue between the good and bad spirit, as well as imaging the desperate haste to leave the maze behind, are suddenly given a strikingly regular metrical base:

```
     x  /  x   /   x    /  x   /  x   /
    In sudden blindness, hasten, almost run,
     x /  x   /   x   /  x  /  x /
    As if the maze itself were after me
     x   /  x   /   x   /  x  /   x    /
    And soon must catch me up. But taking thought,
     x  /  x   /  x    /   x / x   /
    I'd tell myself, 'You need not hurry. This
```

These lines, dealing with actuality, are perfectly regular, but with the great vision of the gods we return to the earlier pattern of long sentences and many non-iambic feet, giving an immediate effect of non-reality, of dream. Of seventeen lines describing the vision of the gods, only three are regular iambic pentameter and there are only two sentences. But again, emerging from this dream of the gods, the syntax and metre bring us back to reality, moving forcefully and purposefully back into regularity to conclude the poem:

```
  /   x  x  /   /   / x   /    x  /
That was the real world; I have touched it once,
  x   /   x   /   x / x   /   x  /
And now shall know it always. But the lie
  x   /   x   /   x   /  x / x   /
The maze, the wild-wood waste of falsehood, roads
  x   /   x   /   x   / x  /   x   /
That run and run and never reach an end,
  x   /   x   x  / x   /   x   /  x   /
Embowered in error—I'd be prisoned there
  /   /   /   x  /   x   /   x   x  /  /
But that my soul has birdwings to fly free.
  x   /   x   /   x   /   x  /  x  /
Oh these deceits are strong almost as life.
  x   /   x   /  x  x  / x  / x  /
Last night I dreamt I was in the labyrinth,
  x   /   x  / x / x   /   x  /
And woke far on. I did not know the place.
```

Here the metrical resolution enforces the poem's conclusion. The iambic pulse now dominates so strongly that the earlier irregularities have been absorbed. The syntax, culminating in the last short sentence, is strong and tight, giving force to the poem's ending. Thus we can see that the prosody of the poem is highly expressive, itself symbolising dream and the time-space dislocation through irregularity, and actuality through insistent regularity. Throughout **"The Labyrinth,"** metre and syntax are, in this way, an organic part of the poem's movement in and out of actuality and dream. The shifting of tenses, the slackening and tightening of the metre, the negative and positive uses of syntax, all combine with the richness of the symbols to embody the poem's many levels of meaning. In this way, the experience of **"The Labyrinth"** is rendered not only by the symbols but by the movement of the lines, as the processes of frustration, stasis, growth and fruition are expressed and embodied in the poem's sound. In sound, as in the conflict of symbols, when one tension is resolved another begins, thus creating a formal complexity which perfectly embodies the psychological complexity which lies behind the maze/Eden conflict.

Before leaving this poem, it is worth turning briefly to Kafka in relation to the symbol of the labyrinth. In particular, Muir's critical writing on Kafka helps to clarify the relationship between the hero and the two opposing symbols, which lies at the heart of this poem. In an essay on Kafka, Muir writes:

> The image of a road comes into our minds when we think of his stories, for in spite of all the confusions and contradictions in which he was involved he held that life was a way, not a chaos, that the right way exists and can be found by a supreme and exhausting effort, and that whatever happens every human being in fact follows some way, right or wrong. . . . He looks ahead and sees, perhaps on a distant hill, a shape which he has often seen before in his journey, but always far away, and apparently inaccessible; that shape is justice, grace, truth, final reconciliation, father, God. As he gazes at it he wonders whether he is moving towards it while it is receding from him, or flying from it while it is pursuing him. He is tormented by this question, for it is insoluble by human reasoning . . . the right turn may easily chance to be the wrong, and the wrong the right.[10]

and later in the same essay, Muir refers to "the frustration of the hero . . . caused by what in theological language is known as the irreconcilability of the divine and the human law; a subtle yet immeasurable disparity."[11]

These remarks are remarkably relevant to Muir's own work and to **"The Labyrinth"** in particular. The central symbol of the journey; the "supreme and exhausting effort" to find the right way; the distant goal, apparently inaccessible, which is "final reconciliation"; the frustrated, tormented self; the "irreconcilability of the divine and the human law"—these are strongly present in **"The Labyrinth"**, embodied by the two symbols. Ultimately, the fallen hero—as much Everyman in Muir as in Kafka—struggling towards the grace and fulfilment of a transfigured reality is at the centre of Muir's imaginative vision. We know that translating Kafka had affected Edwin Muir and his wife deeply. He records that "At one stage the stories continued themselves in our dreams, unfolding into slow serpentine nightmares, immovably reasonable."[12]

The labyrinth of this poem reflects this serpentine nightmare perfectly and we must agree with Elgin Mellown that "many of Muir's poems . . . inevitably remind one of Kafka's stories; and certainly Kafka, even if he did not directly influence Muir, strengthened the poet's faith in his own ideas."[13]

"The Labyrinth", for all its vision of the gods, is one of Muir's most serious explorations of frustration, evil and terror. He is struggling to acquire a "negative capability"; to find a means of preserving the self and the vision of harmony and joy in a world seemingly bent on destroying them. He pits an imaginative reality against the forces of darkness, refusing to meet despair on its own terms, but translating the battle into a symbolic conflict which escapes from time and place, but which still can move towards integration and resolution. As a result, this is not a poem of defeat, but one more stage on the journey towards truth. At the age of sixty, Muir is only now able to treat, through symbol, his knowledge of the hideous gap between human reality and the world of the gods. In **"The Labyrinth"** he peers over the abyss of insanity and despair, but does not go over. There is a defiance embodied in the positive symbols which precludes their annihilation by the negative. Although balance has been lost, and the values of imagination, love, individuality, freedom are almost extinguished by the impersonal power of the will and political necessity, the possibilities of integration and rescue remain implicit, unkillable; the thread leading out of the maze is there in this poem, elusively and weightlessly beckoning as it floats in dream and hope. It is a thread which will eventually lead Muir out into the positive landscape of *One Foot in Eden* (1956), where the labyrinth shrinks under the confidently asserted pressure of symbols of growth and regeneration.

The Labyrinth shows Muir's slow struggle with the forces of evil, played out through the combat of symbols. Only by perfecting his technique so that his symbols could range freely and untethered over time and space could he cope with the intensity of concrete reality by assuming it into a larger pattern. The price he paid for overcoming the threat of annihilation was high. Back in England he had "the vacant stare of a shell-shock case after a modern war",[14] and the poems in this volume are the record of a war, symbolic and psychological, but as strenuously fought as any physical conflict. Muir's breakdown demonstrates that however remote his poetry sometimes seems, it is a deeply involved, though symbolic, treatment of highly personal experience. *"The Labyrinth"* is a record of a human being moving sluggishly but desperately in the dark underworld of his own spiritual crisis; that it is also a universal statement of man's relationship with evil and his instinctive and insistent craving for the numinous is a tribute not only to Muir's wisdom and knowledge, but to his suddenly matured poetic techniques, which enable him, through symbolist devices, to link the particular and personal with the universal in an urgent and distinctive way.

NOTES

[1] Edwin Muir, *An Autobiography* (London: The Hogarth Press, 1954), p. 274.

[2] Willa Muir, *Belonging* (London: The Hogarth Press, 1968), p. 234.

[3] M. L. Rosenthal, *The Modern Poets* (New York: Oxford University Press, 1965), p. 138.

[4] *An Autobiography*, p. 271.

[5] "Chapbook," B.B.C. Radio, 3 September 1952.

[6] Edwin Muir, *Collected Poems*, 2nd ed. (London: Faber and Faber, 1960), pp. 163-65.

[7] *Collected Poems*, p. 63.

[8] Charles Feidelson, *Symbolism and American Literature* (Chicago: University of Chicago Press, 1953), p. 22.

[9] J. C. Hall, ed., *Collected Poems of Edwin Muir* (New York: The Grove Press, 1957), p. 3.

[10] Edwin Muir, "Franz Kafka," *Essays on Literature and Society*, Revised ed. (London: The Hogarth Press, 1965), p. 121.

[11] *Ibid.*, p. 122.

[12] *An Autobiography*, p. 240.

[13] Elgin W. Mellown, "The Development of a Criticism: Edwin Muir and Franz Kafka," *Comparative Literature*, Vol. xvi, No. 4 (Fall, 1964), 321.

[14] *Belonging*, p. 244.

Brian Keeble (essay date 1973)

SOURCE: "In Time's Despite: On the Poetry of Edwin Muir," in The *Sewanee Review*, Vol. LXXXI, No. 3, July-September, 1973, pp. 633-58.

[*In the following essay, Keeble discusses the major symbols, themes, and philosophical views apparent in Muir's poetry.*]

As this, our most dreadful century yet, moves into its last quarter, it becomes even more difficult to deny that the total collapse of our civilization is imminent. The dream of an earthly paradise, bequeathed us by the nineteenth-century idea of "progress" and "evolution", seems as far off as ever before. The labyrinthine struggle in the maze of our own making is characterized by one thing above all else—our seeming refusal to allow any light from a source higher than that of our own "humanity" to throw an illuminating ray upon the nature of a chaos that is in reality the manifestation of our state of mind. As a consequence of our "humanism" the contingencies of time and space determine Truth, and individual experience becomes the measure of all things. Empirical and statistical laws, ever reformed and reforming, mirror the shifting values of that state of mind. But all men, whatever their lot, search for God, however they might disguise that search and however confused they may become as to the object of the search. The man has not yet lived who has not wanted peace and certainty within himself. But there is little hope of an Absolute in a world in which everything is made to seem relative. When the only criteria of Truth are the contingencies of the material world, man must abandon any hope of a God as the Supreme Principal of the Creation and assume that matter itself gives rise to mind.

Fortunately there are some few that, because of circumstance or disposition, do not give up the search and, urged by an inner compulsion, do feel the need to renew themselves, through their art, from the timeless Truth of the perennial Tradition. Edwin Muir stands apart as one of a small number of poets who, in feeling the need to put their art to the service of such a permanent Reality, have had the wisdom also to realize that this in no way entails the necessity of abstraction.

Muir's imaginative vision rests essentially upon a metaphysical view of the world of creation. For him that world was an Icon for contemplation, so that he belongs with those artists of the past who have understood that the natural object is always and alone the most apt symbol of the Reality that transcends nature. Abstraction involves a passive retreat into the indirect "fantasy" world of the psyche; whereas to see the natural world as a qualitative expression of immutable Truth involves the operation of a faculty of intellection that "knows" actively, intuitively, and directly. It knows itself to be the object of that Reality. In this way the natural world and its objects, conceived as the qualitative symbols of a spiritual Reality, become the criteria of Truth. Thus space symbolizes the Universal Intellect in which an upward movement implies spiritual elevation and a downward movement implies degradation. The world of time; the world beyond time; the horse; the road; the maze; the lost Eden: these and other symbols of Muir's vision characterize the inner principles of his own being. In this sense he was a "visionary" poet whose cosmology encompassed the domain of Universal possibility to an extent far greater than that of many who are thought of, misleadingly, as "major" poets.

"We live in a world created by applied science, and our present is unlike the present of any other age. The difference between our world and the world of imagination is growing greater, and may become so great that the one can hardly understand any longer the other." That was how Muir spoke of a world in which he found himself ill at ease, a world which he felt it his vocation to oppose with whatever gifts of the imagination were his to deploy. More and more that world has become all but exhausted by the effort to catalogue the logical relationships, and their implications, that exist between phenomena. From the standpoint of a mentality thus busy with horizontal relationships a poet who seeks to rediscover vertical correspondences must seem something of an anomaly. To ascribe Being to a world beyond appearances rather than to the accumulation of undeniable facts presented by the growth of the material sciences; to find "Reality" in the immutable, intangible world that appearances mask; to do this in the face of currents of thought that proclaim quite another view, takes a particular kind of courage and strength of vision. When the operations of the mind have come to have only a speculative significance, as must be the case when the methods of science hold sway in all departments of thought, then perhaps only the poet is left to restate the eternal truths.

> The norm of human existence remains. There are certain beliefs which are natural to man, for they satisfy his mind and heart better than any alternative ones. The mark of such beliefs is their completeness; they close the circle. In a state of irremediable imperfection such as man's, the circle can be closed only by calling on something beyond man; by postulating a transcendent reality. So the belief in eternity is natural to man; and all the arts, all the forms of imaginative literature, since they depend on that belief, are equally natural to him. When that belief partially fails, imagination suffers an eclipse, and art becomes a problem instead of a function.

In holding to such a position Muir and certain other poets have paid their price in terms of current esteem.

Except by a small but not inconsiderable body of admirers, their poetry has been thought of as largely irrelevant, not to say old-fashioned, to what is seen as a fruitful direction for poetic "development". But there has, since Muir's death, been a healthy and renewed interest in the work of this poet who has never been in the forefront of poetic innovation but whose verse nevertheless is found to touch consistently upon those perennial truths left untouched by more strident voices.

But for a very small part, all modern art is a systematized form of "self-expression". It has become necessary for "personality" to become the whole subject of art, since those doctrines that teach of art as the making accessible of that which transcends the human have long since been discarded in favor of more humanistic values. In his poetry, Muir sought to go beyond the mere elaboration of these moods of the psycho-physical "self". Although personal subjective experience serves as a first point of reference, there is, underlying his work, a consistent denial, by implication, that such experience can be an end in itself. Again and again the poems are concerned with that part of momentary experience that never dies. Such experience is always viewed from the standpoint of the larger backcloth that is all human existence. It is the constant succession of this existence that is the "fable" of his vision. Beneath it is the constant sense of the unity and interdependence of all life and particularly an interpenetration of the spiritual and the material qualities such as one finds in poems of Wordsworth and the Ballads which he admired so much. For Muir the unity of multiplicity that constitutes the natural world affirms the Reality of God. No further proof is needed. It falls peculiarly within the province of the poet to express that Reality that science can never prove. St. Thomas said proof of Being is impossible "not because of failure but because of superabundance of light".

Muir's poetic apprenticeship was in the best tradition: he was self-taught. Not that his learning lacked quantity or quality; but, unhampered by an academic training, he remained true throughout his life to an instinctive grasp of his own destiny as a poet. At a time when myth, symbol, the beautiful and the good (Plato's "remembering" of a latent knowledge) were being discredited as a significant dimension of the poet's craft, Muir slowly wrought his imaginative vision by discovering to what extent these were latent in his own existence. That vision has its roots in the traditions of his Orkney childhood.

> My childhood all a myth
> Enacted in a distant isle;
> Time with his hourglass and his scythe
> Stood dreaming on the dial,
> And did not move the whole day long
> That immobility might save
> Continually the dying song,
> The flower, the falling wave.
> And at each corner of the wood
> In which I played the ancient play,
> Guarding the traditional day
> The faithful watchers stood.

A child in Adam's field I dreamed away
My one eternity and hourless day,
Ere from my wrist Time's bird had learned to fly,
Or I had robbed the Tree of which I die,
Whose boughs rain still, whose fruit wave-green
   shall fall
Until the last great autumn reddens all.

Thus the experiences of childhood became the central "myth" (symbol in action) of his cosmology. The events of his later years fed and colored it.

A man now, gone with time so long—
My youth to myself grown fabulous
As an old land's memories, a song
To trouble or to pleasure us—
I try to fit that world to this,
The hidden to the visible play,
Would have them both, would nothing miss,
Learn from the shepherd of the dark,
Here in the light, the paths to know
That thread the labyrinthine park.

Like other "imaginative" poets before him Muir held constantly to the presence of that "hidden" world. Unlike those, however, he did not attempt to elaborate a complete system of cosmic correspondences, but won for himself a maturing vision by a continuing search for that which was constant within himself. Its essence was to be located in the memory of his childhood innocence, the simple and direct experiences of which are celebrated in **"Childhood"**, the first of his *Collected Poems,* and itself a symbol of the mature man's lost Eden. Of this Eden, maturity is the very destroyer; yet in turn it can also prepare us for the task of winning back a measure of its simplicity and dulled radiance. And so, in his poems, seen through the vicissitudes of adult experience childhood is always there, like a calm remembered landscape in summer at the end of the "journey" or "labyrinth" of daily life.

And that great movement like a quiet river,
Which always flowing yet is always the same,
Begets a stillness. So that when we look
Out at our life we see a changeless landscape,
And all disposed there in its due proportion,
The young and old, the good and bad, the wise
   and foolish,
All these are there as if they had been for ever,
And motionless as statues, prototypes
Set beyond time, for whom the sun stands still.

The purpose of the "journey back to see my kindred" is to

Seek the beginnings, learn from whence you came,
And know the various earth of which you are made

and at the end of this spiritual "voyage" is an inner summit,

Whose height
Will show me every hill,
A single mountain on whose side
Life blooms for ever and is still.

The journey, which must pass through

. . . the sultry labyrinth
Where all is bright and the flare
Consumes and shrivels
The moist fruit

is undertaken in "fallen" conditions dictated by time and is hazardous, encompassing

. . . what the eye
From its tower in the turning field
Sees and sees and cannot tell why,
Quarterings on the turning shield,
The great non-stop heraldic show.

Moreover there comes the realization that the beginning is also the end, for the one who journeys the journey and the goal are one and the same, being a transmutation of the knowing subject.

Yet in this journey back
If I should reach the end, if end there was
Before the ever-running road began
And race and track and runner all were there
Suddenly, always, the great revolving way
Deep in its trance;—if there was ever a place
Where one might say, 'Here is the starting-point,'

. . . . .

If I should reach that place, how could I come
To where I am but by that deafening road,
Life-wide, world-wide, by which all come to all,

. . . . .

Borne hither on all and carried hence with all,
We and the world and that unending thought
Which has elsewhere its end and is for us
Begotten in a dream deep in this dream
Beyond the place of getting and of spending.

As always it is the natural that must at once veil and reveal the ultimate Reality. There remain appearances which we must strive to go beyond, back to the source of our individual existence in eternal Being, along "ever-running roads" that themselves "seemed a part of the great labyrinth"; and the journey starting "where you are deep in the centre of the endless maze". The "maze" and "labyrinth" symbolize the inner tension that arises from the effort of vigilance to steer a path between the entangled demands of matter and Spirit. On the one hand there is the psycho-physical "ego" that must subdue the multifarious distractions of the relative domain, and on the other the inner Self that must hold on to the permanence and truth, amid change and illusion, of the Absolute.

For Muir, man is compelled to make sense of this his most frequent experience; truly death is "elsewhere its end". In striving to master its intricate pattern he is in fact discovering the true extent of his own being as a mystery.

I have fitted this or that into the pattern,
Caught sight sometimes of the original
That is myself—

but since

Time's handiworks by time are haunted

all that is under the sun comes under the governance of
death and our efforts are carried out under the constant
threat of being overtaken by time the destroyer; and the
Tree of Life and immortality on which are the "fruits"—
rewards of action along the "way" of the Spirit that is
beyond the temporal sense—is disfigured, and

Time takes the foliage and the fruit
And burns the archetypal leaf
To shapes of terror and of grief.

For the pattern can reveal itself only to the extent that
we are able to free ourselves from the temporal and
material standpoint of consciousness:

. . . there's no bargain you can drive with time
All this is insufficient.

But with spiritual vigilance some measure of freedom
ensues.

I have had such glimpses, made such tentative
Essays to shape my life, have had successes,
Whether real or apparent time will tell.

But such efforts to retrace the contours of the essential
Self have only an ultimate meaning when the world of
duration and events is brought into relation with the
eternal world where time, sequence, and change no
longer involve us in their flux of renewal and decay. They
are not separate but interdependent worlds only seemingly
divided by human consciousness, being manifestations, on
different levels, of the same one eternal Being.

The poet's initiation into the mystery came, as he tells us,
with the singing of traditional ballads in his childhood.
"They were born out of a tradition so ancient and so indisputable that it required no explanation, and passed beyond
opinion." And as to the eternal world through which to
view the temporal—"This supernatural world embodied for
the peasantry their sense of the mystery surrounding them,
in which they saw at one glance and with no incongruity, Christian revelation and natural magic." This childhood contact with the supernatural had far-reaching consequences when, later in life, Muir began to write poetry. It
was to undergo a gradual and natural metamorphosis into
a transcendent vision akin to Plato's Real World but
viewed from the context of the "fable". The whole of his
mature poetry is founded on the belief, common to traditional doctrines, that the individual mind embodies the
Universal Intellect, and is alone capable of "knowing" the
Real in an intuitive act of cognition. In the poems the
world of nature is always seen as the conjunction of the
actuality of this world and the immanence of the Spirit.

About the well of life where we are made
Spirits of earth and heaven together lie,

So deep their dream of pure commingled being.

A Christian poet "by convergence of symbol" rather
than by "subscription to doctrine", as Kathleen Raine
has pointed out, Muir saw that it was to vindicate the
transcendent Intellect that Christ died on the cross that
men might see the "way" to redeem their "fallen" condition. Were this not the case, then

What is not will surely be
In the changed unchanging reign,
Else the Actor on the Tree
Would loll at ease, miming pain,
And counterfeit mortality.

From this truth, as from the "maze" that obscures the
"way", there is no escape, since even

Love's agonies, victory's drums
Cannot huddle the Cross away.

The themes of Muir's poetry are few and relatively accessible, yet they share that complexity all art must have
that touches upon the roots of the human mystery. Time
and eternity; the lost Eden; the labyrinth or "road" of
daily life (the return to the primordial ground of our
being), with its endeavors, frustrations, joys, and sufferings (the losing and regaining the "way"): these themes
are constantly explored in the light of an ever deeper
and more enriched experience. But for all the metamorphoses they undergo, the themes revolve around one
central truth; the return to the archetypal "Self". The
journey from this world of time to the eternal world,
symbolized by Orpheus's journey, is seen in Platonic
terms in that beautiful poem **"Orpheus' Dream"**.

As if we had left earth's frontier wood
Long since and from this sea had won
The lost original of the soul,
The moment gave us pure and whole
Each back to each, and swept us on
Past every choice to boundless good.

In another poem, **"Adam's Dream"**, Muir explores the
united themes of the Fall and time. Adam's state of
innocence (archetypal man's) before the Fall was "his
age long daydream" which knowledge of his own innocence provided. After the Fall, no longer innocent, he
dreams at a more "self"-conscious level, a dream of life as
a sequence of meaningless events without form or proportion that take place in the desert wastes of a plain, filling

As by an alien arithmetical magic
Unknown in Eden, a mechanical
Addition without meaning, joining only
Number to number in no mode or order
Weaving no pattern.

This is the growth of the mind's rational faculty (dis-
criminative knowledge as opposed to unitive knowledge

of the divine), which the poet saw was in danger, left to its own devices, of subduing the mind's ability to unify the various and disparate experiences of the senses, and without which the mind has no intelligible grasp over life.

> 'This is time',
> Thought Adam in his dream,

and he becomes slowly aware of the true meaning of the Fall—an awareness of the burden of duration overriding the timeless moment of joy.

> Adam longed
> For more, not this mere moving pattern, not
> This illustrated storybook of mankind
> Always a-making, improvised on nothing.

He recognizes in the faces of the people who begin to inhabit the plain that they too share his "fallen" condition—are in fact himself.

> At that he was among them, and saw each face
> Was like his face, so that he would have hailed
>   them
> As sons of God but that something restrained him.
> And he remembered all, Eden, the Fall,
> The Promise, and his place, and took their hands
> That were his hands, his and his children's hands.

Conscious as he is of his now less than divine state, his "human" love for Eve is all that is left to remind him, like a dim reflection, of his former love in God—love that creates the world since these are principles of the eternal and timeless NOW.

> . . . the first great dream
> Which is the ground of every dream since then.

In the metaphysical terms of the perennial Tradition it remains man's vocation to "find" the point at which his individuality loses its identity in the original "ground" of Being. In Muir's poetic terms that is the point of the journey through the "maze" or along the "ever winding" road. The journey through life's perplexities "fallen" man is pledged to undertake, since from that which is redeemed all has come and all must return.

> There the beginning finds the end
>   Before beginning ever can be,
> And the great runner never leaves
>   The starting and the finishing tree,
>   The budding and the fading tree.

And each must undertake the journey for himself, so the task presents itself ever anew.

> We through the generations came
> Here by a way we do not know
> From the fields of Abraham,
> And still the road is scarce begun.

Like the wandering Odysseus, each must tread "the treadmill of the turning road", such a road as "cuts off the country of Again", where events in time never recur but leave only the movement forward, the inner journey, man's perennial spiritual adventure.

Man enters the labyrinth as a consequence of the Fall from Eden, his creation in time and matter entailing loss of the Spirit. By an understanding of the patterns of the maze man struggles back to the center—traditionally Paradise regained, the heavenly Jerusalem. Man's responsibility is to accept the burden placed upon him—all attempts to deny it arise from a less than responsible view of human destiny. Traditionally, as for Muir, the Fall represents the incarnation of the Spirit. Man as "purely divine essence" dies into time—a world of temporary existence. It is the nature of the Fall that, on the threshold of adulthood, is mirrored in the growth of "self"-consciousness. In this Miltonic-sounding passage from Section III of **"Variations on a Time Theme"**, the poet refers directly to that period of his own life when, as a young man, the vision of his childhood's innocence was lost to the inner eye:

> Alas! no heavenly voice the passing told
> Of that last Eden; my own bliss I sold.
> Weary of being one, myself conspired
> Against myself and into bondage hired
> My mortal birthright.

In our need to recover that innocence, given naturally to the child, we must seek its experience in full conscious awareness of our condition in the temporal, mutable world. And such a world is "strange to one lately in Eden".

But man is not entirely alone with his burden, for the natural world that surrounds him has its part to play in the necessity of cosmic harmony. Even the most superficial reading of Muir's poems will make it apparent that animals have a large and important part in the vision. According to Genesis they were created before man and exist in a purer state, and so do not partake of the Fall to the extent that man does. Because of their greater innocence in this respect they have a symbolic significance as embodiments of spiritual forces, so that man, who has banished the Angels from his imaginative world, has always before him some living evidence, through these its mediators, of the spiritual world,

> . . . as if they had been sent
> By an old command to find our whereabouts
> And that long-lost archaic companionship.

That is how he speaks of them ("their coming our beginning") in **"The Horses"**. In another poem, **"The Late Swallow"**, the swallow, a reincarnation of an Angel, is urged by the poet to return to the radiance at the source of spiritual light in the face of oncoming darkness; an age, like the day, is coming to an end for want of that all-informing light.

By now it should be apparent that in upholding the view that life begins in the quality of consciousness, not in material well-being, Muir's poetry is a plea for the supremacy of a transcendent metaphysic—that science of the Real—over all forms of knowledge. Plato has said of this world that it is the only one of which knowledge is possible, and his expression of it exercised a continuing influence over Muir's thinking throughout his life.

> I have thought of death,
> And followed Plato to eternity,
> Walked in his radiant world.

This "radiant world" is seen for the imaginative purposes of the vision as a blend of the Biblical and Platonic (Intelligible) worlds. The two worlds meet in the later poetry: the mythological world of the Greek heroes and the Christian world of the Bible. The influence of Genesis and parts of the New Testament in particular is very strong in the poems contained in *One Foot in Eden.* In **"Prometheus"**, for instance, the hero, chained and suffering on the rock, reflects on the fate of modern man the materialist caught in the vortex of his own blind and willful destruction. But he visualizes the last day as one in which Christ, should He be found, listens to the story of how man has turned his back upon his only salvation. It is this salvation, this knowledge of his own rightful origin and end, which forms the point around which the poetic allegiances of the later poetry gather and clarify.

For Muir, this radiance consistently suffuses the natural world as is evident throughout the poems. Its symbol, the supernal sun, is nothing less than the light of Truth, that "clear unfallen world" which must always serve as the measure of the creation. That is the theme of **"The Transfiguration"**.

> So from the ground we felt that virtue branch
> Through all our veins till we were whole, our wrists
> As fresh and pure as water from a well,
> Our hands made new to handle holy things,
> The source of all our seeing rinsed and cleansed
> Till earth and light and water entering there
> Gave back to us the clear unfallen world.
> We would have thrown our clothes away for
>   lightness,
> But that even they, though sour and travel stained,
> Seemed, like our flesh, made of immortal
>   substance.

Such a vision, subjective and subject to man's very imperfections, is always open to doubt;

> Was the change in us alone,
> And the enormous earth still left forlorn,
> An exile or a prisoner?

But the mind can hold on to this essential and qualitative world only when it is prepared for a meeting on equal terms.

> For he had said, 'To the pure all things are pure.'

We all too often forget that over and above its existential nature, the created world has only the qualities the mind ascribes to it.

> Was it a vision?
> Or did we see that day the unseeable
> One glory of the everlasting world
> Perpetually at work, though never seen
> Since Eden locked the gate that's everywhere
> And nowhere?

That world is the only world that the mind can grasp as an intelligible whole, since any rational explanation of the temporal world must fail to account for the mystery of the Being that makes such discursive operations of the mind possible;

> . . . the world
> We saw that day made this unreal, for all
> Was in its place.

Ultimately there is no turning back from the informing presence of the truths of the Spirit—Reality or vision, this we have seen. But for the poet no less than for us, such moments of illumination are all too brief and leave sorrow mingled with hope in their wake.

> If it had lasted but another moment
> It might have held for ever! But the world
> Rolled back into its place, and we are here,
> And all that radiant kingdom lies forlorn,
> As if it had never stirred; no human voice
> Is heard among its meadows, but it speaks
> To itself alone, alone it flowers and shines
> And blossoms for itself while time runs on.

This world of the Spirit, latent by necessity in the human intellect, carries with it a knowledge of man's ultimate origin and end;

> . . . pilgrim man
> Travels foreknowing to his stopping place,
> Awareness on his lips, which have tasted sorrow,
> Foretasted death.

For man's needs it is wholly sufficient; a knowledge of it makes it inconceivable that things should be otherwise, for none

> That comes complains, and all the world comes
>   here,
> Comes, and goes out again, and comes again.
> This is the Pattern, these the Archetypes
> Sufficient, strong, and peaceful. All outside
> From end to end of the world is tumult.

And since it is the measure of the natural world, a knowledge of this eternal world alters forever our existence in the temporal world.

> If a man
> Should chance to find this place three times in time
> His eyes are changed and make a summer silence
> Amid the tumult.

And its freedom is such as cannot be had from any other source.

That was the real world; I have touched it once,
And now shall know it always. But the lie,
The maze, the wild-wood waste of falsehood, roads
That run and run and never reach an end,
Embowered in error—I'd be prisoned there
But that my soul has bird wings to fly free.

As Kathleen Raine has said, "Nearly all he wrote has the luminosity of an inspired vision."

The influence of Plato can be traced in a number of the poems, explicit in some, implicit in others; so that in looking back over a lifetime's search for the True and the Good it was only natural that Muir should pay homage to the one who had been his unfailing guide throughout much of the search.

> And now that time grows shorter, I perceive
> That Plato's is the truest poetry,
> And that these shadows
> Are cast by the true.

Despite the lasting influence of Plato, however, Muir remained, as we have seen, a Christian poet. The diverse strands of his vision formed a synthesis whose framework was metaphysical but whose coloring was Christian and symbolic. Because of its essential unity there is in his work little of what, in the work of others, we call "development", for he was always able to find within himself the inspiration for his poetry. He had little need to search among remote cultures or periods of history as poets like Yeats and Pound have done. His use of Greek myths indicates that he looked upon their content as being perennially true and contemporaneous with the "fable" of his own life—indeed, as comprising a dimension of it.

To gain some idea of this unity, as well as the shift of emphasis that did take place, we have only to compare the imagery of the earlier poems with that of the later ones. We can see in this how far Muir was to go in giving his response to the external world a "luminous" expression. In the earlier poems the imagery of animals is used in a relatively natural way. No less important, the animals are nonetheless components of the landscape that contains them in a way that is reminiscent of Wordsworth's nature poetry. In the later poems, however, they have a much more transparent significance, being clearly symbolic of those instincts that link man to a basic pattern of existence in harmony with the natural world. The later poems reflect the greater depth and complexity Muir was to achieve in his mature verse. The world of nature has that element of numinous transparency, betokening a realization of the interdependence of the spiritual and material that always characterizes metaphysical thought.

Although the vision remained essentially the same throughout, the body of the poetry does fall fairly naturally into four groups. The earliest group, that of the work up to and including *Journeys and Places,* with its beginnings in dream and the Ballads, is characterized by a gradual discovery of the themes of the vision. The second group includes the three volumes published in the 'forties and most of the poems from *One Foot in Eden.* Here we find a deepening elaboration of the themes of the vision. The third group of poems is formed by some of the later poems from *One Foot in Eden,* such as **"If I could know"** and **"Into Thirty Centuries Born",** as well as the first section of the Uncollected Poems. Here the tone is one of profound doubt and questioning with a sense of crisis underlying the vision. With the fourth group, that of the remaining Uncollected Poems, the tone of doubt and crisis gives way suddenly to an expression of renewed and deepened faith.

With the later poetry we are in a territory rich with overlay in its depth of meaning. Here the substratum of our understanding must be a knowledge taken from the whole of Muir's work. The by now customary themes are reworked and woven into a new translucent texture, now somber with doubt (**"If I could know"**, **"Desolation"**, **"The Last War"**), now firm and bright as the vision again reveals itself (**"The Voices"**, **"The Poet"**). The central point of reference is that questioning dialogue between the world of the Real beyond time and the world of suffering in time; between the efficacy of the spiritual world and the demands of a practical existence and that which unites the two. Comparing these with the poems of the 'forties, we find a more frequent concern with contemporary events. There is a greater conscious awareness of the enigma of "that imperfect mystery". The themes themselves are "enlisted in the enigma's exploration" and

> Salute the outer and inner strife,
> The bickering between doubt and faith.

The serenity and wholeness of the inner vision are threatened by fears that are foreign to its calm illumination. It is as if the poet wished to prove his vision capable of maturity and responsibility by squaring it, through faith, against an increasing sense of his own involvement with a world where the desolation of spirit becomes daily more apparent.

> The desolations have no word nor music,
> Only an endless inarticulate cry
> Inaudible to the poetry-pampered ear.
> The desolations tell
> Nothing for ever, the interminable
> Civil war of earth and water and fire.
> These have to do with our making.

The vision is less secure, less insulated. There are moments of profound doubt.

> Make me to see and hear that I may know
> This journey and the place towards which I go.

Could it be that the intangible is, after all, without efficacy; that there comes a time when, with the vision lost,

> . . . we could not see
> The beauty and the buried grace.

The manifestations of the beautiful change grow old and hinder our efforts to divine their source which "we always seek and never find". But what of the nagging thought that

> Perhaps if found, the good and the beautiful end.

In that meeting-ground between the physical world and the spiritual world we recognize through it, there is perplexity with

> Word at odds with common word,
> A child's voice crying 'Let me be!'
> In a world he could not touch,
> And others saying, 'Be in time',
> With such a strange anxiety.

And the perplexity never diminishes while we fail to go beyond the rapid succession of events and stimuli that constitute the world of time and appearances.

> You who hear the avalanche
> Must fabricate a temporal tale
> To bring the timeless nightingale
> And swallow to your trysting place.

But at such moments, with brain baffled and with eyes unseeing, we have the soul as guide to "keep the bond when faith and beauty leave". For this faculty of intellection, traditionally symbolized by the "eye of the heart", is alone capable of perceiving "in an endless stasis . . . what was given before you opened your eyes upon the changing world". There, the continual flux that makes for uncertainty is halted; there is certainty.

Like some miraculous resurgence of faith, the crisis which underlies these late poems is triumphantly subdued in the last poems of all. Every line is here shot through with a marvellous autumnal radiance. The question mark, which appeared earlier with such regularity, now disappears like mist before the rising sun. This fact alone is sufficient to justify a distinction between the later and the very last poems. One of the first of this group, **"The Poet"**, bears the characteristic stamp of the group as a whole—a tone of confident assertion. The poet speaks of the inscrutable mystery that is love and faith.

> And in bewilderment
> My tongue shall tell
> What mind had never meant
> Nor memory stored.
> In such bewilderment
> Love's parable
> Into the world was sent
> To stammer its word.

Such love guides us to the timeless realities which we embody but which are not accessible to conceptual or rational thought.

> Heaven sent perplexity—
> If thought should thieve

> One word of the mystery
> All would be wrong.
> Most faithful fantasy
> That can believe
> Its immortality
> And make a song.

Of this resurgence these opening lines from **"Dialogue"** indicate the calm confidence and radiance which are the result of a fresh and stronger grasp on the inner vision, enabling the poet to see the vicissitudes of the world around him in a fresh light.

> I never saw the world until that day,
> The real fabulous world newly reborn,
> And celebrated and crowned on every side.

> Yet that first world was beautiful
> And true, stands still where first it stood.

The closing lines of the poem make use of a theme that recurs throughout the last poems.

> I have known men and horses many a day.
> Men come and go, the wise and the fanciful.
> I ride my horse and make it go my way.

The theme of horse and plough appears and reappears, and, through the perspective of the past that is in us, we come to a realization that the patient cultivation of those distant Elysian fields is the most profound and satisfying task that man can set himself. In that landscape and no other

> . . . each bush and tree
> Stands still within the fire,
> And the bird sits on the tree.
> Three horses in a field
> That yesterday ran wild
> Are bridled and reined by light
> As in a heavenly field.
> Man, beast and tree in fire,
> The bright cloud showering peace.

(These horses are distant cousins, as it were, of the two-winged steeds to which Plato likened the human soul: higher emotions and bodily cravings that must be brought into harmony.)

For Pound, emotion and rhythm were uncounterfeiting and uncounterfeitable, and strict attention to such things as the sequence of consonants, duration of vowels, agreement of emotion and rhythm are aspects of poetic craft for which Pound and Yeats are justly revered; but these were never the central concern for Muir. The thesis rather than the voice is all-important; only seldom is his verse "about to sing" [We can see from the two late poems **"Ballad of Everyman"** and **"Nightmare of Peace"** that Muir had the capacity to rethink and recast the same poem into completely different forms. Could it be that the late poem beginning "I have heard you cry" is an unfinished reworking of the earlier **"The Strange Return"**? Certainly at one point they contain similar and identical lines.]. Each word acts as support and pointer towards the essential truth of the poem, which in turn represents a dimension of the whole vision. For the most part everything in the poems strives to one end. Their strength lies in the undeviating resolve of their direction. As Kathleen Raine has said, his vision was "of an unswerving inner certainty, an integrity, an indifference to fashion, that made him never seek to please, but only to bear witness to the truth that was in him". No great "smith", but one whose work offers a vision unique as it is uniquely fulfilled. That vision he had whole when he began to write poetry at an age when most poets are either established or have grown sterile. He had something to say that no other poet of this century felt the need to say. Yet, for all that, we feel a sense of familiarity within his world. His reputation will strengthen as men come to understand that by his poetic vision he gave back to us a dimension we have all but ignored, one which the scientific viewpoint has done its best to discredit and one which the modern world stands most in need of—the dimension of the Spirit. The formal elegance of the sonnet **"The Emblem"** gives expression to this dimension in language that alone is worthy of it.

Muir had only the scraps of a living tradition in which to nourish his vision. It was for him as it must seem for any poet, the faculty of imagination.

> Imagination unites us with humanity in time and space; by means of it we understand Hector and Achilles in their distant world, and feel the remote emotion in a Chinese poem; in such things we are at one with universal mankind and ourselves. That is the work of the imagination, and our lives would not have any meaning without it.

Only by the intelligible principles that this dimension offers are we able to distinguish between the various modes of Being; otherwise confusion and lack of order must reign. Only by the light of its central transcendent Truth can we attempt to give each thing its proper place in the hierarchy of creation. That scheme Muir visualized in the context of man's ancestry. "We can feel but we cannot see life whole until it has been placed in some kind of past where it discovers its true shape." The symbolism with which he gave it shape—less "far-fetched" than that of Yeats—is no less profound for being "ready-to-hand".

In his *Autobiography* the poet spoke of how he came to realize that he shared with Traherne a common belief that childhood and immortality are bound together. Indeed, there are passages, particularly in the "Third Century" of Traherne, that would seem to refer directly to the core of the Scotsman's vision of that Eden towards which he was perforce, like us all, constantly to struggle.

> Those pure and Virgin Apprehensions I had from the Womb, and in that Divine Light wherein I was born, are the Best unto this day, wherein I can see the Universe. By the Gift of GOD they attended me into the World, and by His special favour I remember them till now. Verily they seem the Greatest Gifts His Wisdom could bestow, for without them all other Gifts had been Dead and Vain. They are unattainable by Book, and therefore I will teach them by Experience. Pray for them earnestly; for they will make you Angelical, and wholly Celestial. Certainly Adam in Paradise had not more sweet and Curious Apprehensions of the World, than I when I was a child. . . . I knew by Intuition those things which since my Apostasie, I Collected again. . . . I seemed as one Brought into the Estate of Innocence. . . . I saw all the Peace of Eden; Heaven and Earth did sing my Creator's Praises. . . . Is it not strange, that an infant should be heir of the whole World . . . but all things abide eternally as they were in their proper places . . . so that with much ado I was corrupted and made to learn the dirty devises of this world, which now I unlearn, and become, as it were, a little child again that I may enter into the Kingdom of God.

The fact that we refer to this as "poetic" prose is merely to beg the question. Suffice it to say that these lines stand as commentary on the whole life and work of Edwin Muir.

Janet Adam Smith (essay date 1974)

SOURCE: "Where We Should All Be," in *Encounter,* Vol. XLIII, No. 3, September, 1974, pp. 79-82.

[In the following review, Smith praises Muir's letters.]

> *Art is for me the only way of growing, of becoming myself more purely; and I value it for myself, I know it is my good, the only real good for me, and the personal feeling, the personal integration seems to me more and more the thing that really matters. Given that, other things will become right, for one will be alive and have therefore some criticism of life.*

One of the pleasures of reading these letters is to observe how steadfastly Edwin Muir held to this faith through a life whose outward circumstances were so often so unpropitious to art.

The earliest letter, tender and understanding, is to a girl Muir had been fond of in his Glasgow days; it is dated March 1919, when he was 32. Behind lay the uprooting from Orkney, the death of his parents and two brothers in Glasgow, the awful years working in the bone-factory in Greenock. Soon after came his marriage to Willa Anderson, whose devotion and energy freed him from the drudgery of his clerking and launched him on his life as a writer. Letters from their early wandering years describe their life in Prague, Dresden, Vienna, the Mediterranean, at a time when good wine could be had for 3d a bottle and St Tropez was "a little fishing village . . . a rather primitive, but pretty place." But this book is not an autobiography-through-letters: some stages of Muir's life are hardly represented (no letters from the bad days in Glasgow and Greenock, very few from Prague 1945-48 when he lived through the Communist *coup*), though the editor's chronology and notes make it easy to fill in gaps and grasp allusions. The book is about being, rather than doing; it is the record of a questing mind, and the revelation of a truly good man.

Muir knew he had to be a poet, but he never demanded that the world should therefore treat him more kindly or exempt him from the common lot. To live, he took on the bread-and-butter work of translation and regular novel-reviewing, and redeemed them from drudgery by the spirit in which he did them. His uncomplaining acceptance of such work, and his generosity shine from this letter of March 1933 to his Glasgow brother-in-law George Thorburn:

> At Christmas we were down to £1.10.0, with no job in prospect, the rent due, myself down with the 'flu. In the first week of the year I got a job from Gollancz, also a huge book to translate; and the same week *The Listener,* quite out of the blue, offered me the job of reviewing novels for them. So that out of hopelessness we were raised in a few days to comparative comfort. I've hardly ever felt more thankful in my life. I'm sending £4 for you and Lizzie as a thanks-offering, and hoping that it will be of some little use. We're all right for several months to come at least, and can quite well afford it.

In 1940, when they were living at St Andrews, and thin wartime periodicals had little space for reviews, Muir went back to a clerk's job at the Food Office in Dundee, wryly noting that he could get no teaching work in Scotland because

> I found that my lack of an academic degree is a most astonishing obstacle: in Scotland nothing but a certificate of some kind seems to be recognised as really meritorious.

This particular drudgery could not be redeemed, and after a few months his body rebelled. Illness and enforced rest

> made me realise that I had been rushing on like a madman, past my true self, living my own actual unique life as if it belonged to anyone at all, or to someone whom I had no concern with, someone who did not matter in the least to me. . . . The result of my tranquillity . . . has been a little freshet of poetry.

With such a firm sense of where *his* real life lay, Muir could be endlessly generous to others. He could be a sharp critic, saying of Wyndham Lewis—

> He is unhappy, and he uses his intellect to conceal this from himself; not only to make his unhappiness appear the norm, but to make it almost admirable. There is a devastating absence of joy in his work, something wall-eyed and self-willed. . . .

But there is no hint of any competitiveness in his attitude to fellow-writers, and he could do justice to talents quite unlike his own: he was one of the first critics to appreciate Ivy Compton-Burnett. Poetry, and the criticism of poetry, could never be for him an area of aggression, as it sometimes seems today; and for poets there was ready sympathy and encouragement, and hopes that *their* springs would flow even though his own might be dry. To Kathleen Raine he wrote:

> We all feel that we shall never write another poem, and feel it sometimes for long stretches: I think it is a common experience, and very painful, and very unpleasant, until the gates open again.

And to Norman MacCaig:

> I keep seeing poems by you everywhere, with friendly envy (if there is such a thing: I hope there is). How lovely to have the spring flowing freely (you are really to be envied) and not monotonously either, but with more variety than ever before.

He would have liked more readers, but was not bothered by reputation. In 1938 he wrote:

> As for my poetry, it has never "taken on", except for Willa, a few friends, a few poets like Walter de la Mare, and that is naturally discouraging, but would never make me give up the writing of it, when the impulse comes. But encouragement, on the other hand, strengthens the impulse. . . . I've acquired a certain reputation, not a big one, by going on writing poetry; but that is almost worthless, for it is not a matter of understanding, and understanding is the only thing of any use to a man who is saying what he thinks.

Nor was he bothered about trends, fashion, being in the swim. After praising Stephen Spender (in 1935) for the "freedom and naturalness and inventiveness of your use of language", he went on:

> I have naturalness in my own poetry, but I'm afraid I often lack freedom and inventiveness, which are qualities that can't be picked up and put in, and so I shall have to do without them. . . . I think we are all far too much moved by a spirit of emulation, and when something "new" appears feel almost in conscience bound to produce something new, whereas if we wrote from the solidest basis within ourselves we should produce something that is new.

To the literary world Muir sat lightly, though it gave him his living; his real interest was elsewhere. He was quite unperturbed when a row broke over his head on the publication of his **Scott and Scotland,** with Hugh MacDiarmid calling for his blood; and surprised when, late in life, the honours came—degrees from Edinburgh, Prague and Cambridge, the C.B.E., the Charles Eliot Norton lectures at Harvard.

Towards the end of his life, he welcomed the idea of writing a book on the Ballads, because it will give me time for something which I shall enjoy doing and take me back again into the roots of poetry, where we should all be, and away from fashion.

As Eliot observed after his death, Muir seemed not much concerned with technique, "but under the pressure of emotional intensity, and possessed by his vision, he found almost unconsciously the right, the inevitable way of saying what he wanted to say."

The vision to which he was so steadfast is in his wonderful *Autobiography,* and in his poems: in **"The Transfiguration"** where all creation shares with man the glory of the moment; in **"The Horses"** where nature comes back to a world struck by a nuclear holocaust; in **"The Road"** where time has stopped and history has rolled back:

> There the beginning finds the end
>   Before beginning ever can be,
> And the great runner never leaves
>   The starting and the finishing tree,
>   The budding and the fading tree.

It is a vision both other-worldly and deeply human, of an imaginative order existing beyond the confines of one person's life, yet able to enrich every human life.

> Seen deeply enough the life of the most ordinary human creature, who has to feel or bear all these final things, seems to me portentous, past all theorising, all relevance to optimism or pessimism. So that for myself the affirmation of life is not conditioned by my having to think life a happy business, and it has very little to do with love, except that love which is an attempt to comprehend, to imagine, everything, terrible as well as pleasant.

Muir—who had left the Kirk in youth and never felt he could join any other church—had in full measure the power that Keats called Negative Capability. Writing to Stephen Spender about "death and the fortuitous snuffing-out of life" he says—

> I can't accept any religious explanation that I know of, any more than you. I would rather have the problems themselves, for from an awareness of them and their vastness I get some sort of living experience, some sense even of communion, of being in the whole in some way, whereas from the explanations I should only get comfort and reassurance and a sense of safety which I know is not genuine.

In one of the last letters I had from him, from Harvard, he spoke of a girl who had left a lecture by I. A. Richards "in bewilderment." "That's splendid", Richards had said when Muir passed the comment on, "that's where one should start." And Muir called the poem he then wrote **"The Poet"**, for it was where he started too.

> And in bewilderment
> My tongue shall tell
> What mind had never meant
> Nor memory stored.
> In such bewilderment
> Love's parable
> Into the world was sent
> To stammer its word . . .
>
> Heaven-sent perplexity—
> If thought should thieve
> One word of the mystery
> All would be wrong.
> Most faithful fantasy
> That can believe
> Its immortality
> And make a song.

Letters can bring the dead to life. As I read these, I hear Edwin's soft Orkney voice, and count myself lucky to have had as friend a man who, in his gentle and humorous way, was as near a saint as ever I expect to meet.

Christopher Wiseman (essay date 1974)

SOURCE: "Edwin Muir's Last Poems," in *The University of Windsor Review,* Vol. X, No. 1, Fall-Winter, 1974, pp. 5-20.

[*In the following essay, Wiseman discusses Muir's poems of the late 1950s.*]

In the **Collected Poems**[1] are thirty-nine poems written by Edwin Muir between the time **One Foot in Eden** was accepted by Faber in 1955 and his death in 1959. Of these, twenty-two were published in periodicals or sent to Faber in manuscript form, six were found in typescript after his death, and the remainder were reconstructed from his papers. Had he lived to publish another collection, Muir would certainly have made revisions to some of these poems, but as they stand these last poems contain some of his finest work which has been curiously neglected by the critics.

Perhaps the most surprising thing about these poems, when one remembers that Muir was in his late sixties and seventies when they were written, is the amount of technical and thematic innovation. New extensions of the symbolist techniques he had developed in **The Labyrinth** (1949) and **One Foot in Eden** (1956) are clearly evident here, as well as experiments with new dialogue forms. In terms of his symbology, the great symbols he had explored in his earlier work—Eden, the Fall, the labyrinth, the journey—are here energised by a new rawness of surface texture and an insistent relating of these symbols to social and political actuality. There is still the same swaying conflict between loss and gain, destruction and creation, time and eternity, which was always the core of his apprehension of life, but whereas in **The Labyrinth** the positive symbols were almost swamped by a massive invasion of the negative, and in **One Foot in Eden** the positive symbols seemed at times too easily accepted, there is more of a balance in the late poems. Muir never forgot evil and suffering—he had twice broken down under the pressure of experiences which deprived him of his vision of Eden and which blocked him and held him in the labyrinth—but late in his life he learned how to absorb the Fall into a great vision of pattern and flux which is sustained by a higher reality. Late in his life Muir can accept that suffering is inevitable and is ultimately a means to knowledge which shapes life and gives it meaning. Indeed, the vision of Eden may emerge from the very heart of evil and break-down; the tragedies of the Story are assumed into the underpinning Fable, as the recourse to eternity, incarnated in the poetic symbol, is released into time.

Several of the late poems clearly demonstrate Muir's continuing concern with technique. In many of his finest poems he had previously used symbolist methods—spatio-temporal dislocation, an obsession with time, the deliberate releasing of symbol from referential points, a strong reliance on metre and syntax as expressive controlling agents—and even at the end of his life he was experimenting with these devices and refining them.

"The Song" is perhaps the most completely symbolist poem Muir wrote. Not only does the poem use dream material but it departs from Muir's own developed system of symbols. The poem moves disturbingly through various levels of dream-experience and reality, transcending time and space; it remains unlocated within myth, biography or any known symbology, which allows the symbolism to develop freely and attain an almost musical state of non-conceptuality. **"The Song"** comments on itself as it proceeds, creating its own meanings, disintegrating, resolving and confirming itself purely in its own terms, its own time and space. The poem is a self-enclosed, non-referential act feeding on itself, using the ambiguities of tense to drive the reader line by line through the time of the poem.

The core of this poem is a dream of a fabulous creature, a symbol from somewhere else invading reality and bearing witness to a vast anguish, a "wound in the world's side," before it leaves. But this vision of the creature is complicated by the observing "I" of the poem, whose responses are continuously recorded. The opening lines distort time and reality, as a necessary pre-requisite for the introduction of the beast:

> I was haunted *all that day by memories* knocking
> At a disused, deaf, dead door of my mind
> Sealed up *for forty years by myself and time.*
> They could not get to me nor I to them.
> And yet they knocked. And since I could not
>   answer,
> *Since time was past* for that sole assignation,
> I was oppressed by the unspoken thought
> That they and I were not contemporary,
> *For I had gone away. Yet still in dreams*
> *Where all is changed, time, place, identity,*
> Where fables turn to beasts and beasts to fables,
> And anything can be in a natural wonder,
> These meetings are renewed, dead dialogues
> Utter their antique speech.

> *That night I dreamed*
> That towards the end of *such another day*
> Spent in such thoughts, but *in some other place,*
> I was returning from a long day's work—
> *What work I have forgotten*—and had to cross
> A park *lost somewhere in the world,* yet now
> Present and whole to me as I to it:
>
>   (my italics)

The italicised phrases show the deliberate attempt to confuse the time and place of the experience and remove it from the exigencies of logic. The experience is elusive but seems suggestively close to Muir's own early years in Glasgow and London, when the harmony and order of his Orkney childhood were so brutally undermined and he was cut off from the "memories knocking." Also in those lines we see a celebration of dream and archetype which is ultimately a description of Muir's own art. When the unconscious is admitted "fables turn to beasts and beasts to fables/And anything can be in a natural wonder." This lies at the heart of the poem's symbolism, where everyday reality is penetrated by forces from outside our time and place.

The poem continues with the dream of the great creature, come into suburbia like some monster in a science-fiction film:

> . . . from the park poured out the resonant
>   moaning
> Of some great beast in anguish. Could it be
> For us, I wondered dreaming, the strange beast
>   mourned,
> Or for some dead once done and done for ever
> And done in vain?

Again the words "I wondered dreaming" allow the poem to move simultaneously on two levels, commenting on the dream as it is being recorded. The beast is massive, like a cliff, and strange beyond description:

> As heavy as earth it stood and mourned alone,
> Horse, or centaur, or wide-winger Pegasus,
> But far too strange for any fabulous name.

The creature's presence and its enormous private grief impinge upon the dreamer who runs away but remains close enough to listen to the "long breath drawn by pain, intolerable." The poem moves to a climax as the creature moves, in a strange combination of gentleness, holiness and brute strength:

> I thought, now it will move. And then it moved.
> The moaning ceased, the hoofs rose up and fell
> Gently, as treading out a meditation,
> Then broke in thunder; the wild thing charged the
>   gate,
> Yet could not pass—oh pity!—that simple barrier
> (Subservient to any common touch),
> Turned back again in absolute overthrow,
> And beat on the ground as if for entrance there.
> The dream worked on. The clamour died; the hoofs
> Beat on us common ground; silence; a drumming
> As of wild swans taking their highway south

From the murdering ice; hoofs, wings far
   overhead
Climbing the sky; pain raised that wonder there;
Nothing but pain. The drumming died away.

These remarkable lines combine dream narrative with comment on the narrative. The unreality of the scene is magnified and echoed by the distorted syntax of the penultimate sentence. The only remaining certainty for the observer is that "pain raised that wonder there; / Nothing but pain."

The poem concludes with twelve lines which question the significance of the beast and the vision of pain:

Was it these hoofs, I thought, that knocked all day
With no articulate message, but this vision
That had no tongue to speak its mystery?
What wound in the world's side and we unknowing
Lay open and bleeding now? What present anguish
Drew that long dirge from the earth-haunting
   marvel?
And why that earthly visit, unearthly pain?
I was not dreaming now, but thinking the dream.

There are no words to explain this experience; the words of **"The Song"** are events in themselves, not descriptive of events, and the vision creates and destroys its own existence without outside reference. The last four lines bring us one step closer to reality:

Then all was quiet, the park its own again,
And I on my road to my familiar lodgings
A world away; and all its poor own again.
Yet I woke up saying, 'The song—the song'.

The final note is one of celebration. The dream, so full of pain and fear, has been reduced, finally, to the only spoken words in the poem—"'The song—the song'." The vision is accepted with joy by the mind which had previously been "disused, deaf, dead" and "sealed up" and a process of transformation and liberation is complete. Through symbol Muir suggests a diagram of spiritual redemption. The narrator is altered in a significant way by the working on his mind of the great beast. The blocked mind can finally admit and transcend the knowledge of pain and suffering and the existence of a reality beyond the time and place of the park, the lodging house and the city suburb. On one level, the poem merely recounts a bizarre dream, but the symbolism insists upon wider meanings, however tentative.

Firstly, the poem is a discussion of the making of poetry. When open to the forces of dream and symbol, the imagination can "turn . . . beasts to fables"; the "I" of the poem, by "thinking the dream" can turn a one-dimensional, drab, blocked actuality into "the song." To achieve this, suffering and pain must be seen, felt, understood and accepted.

Secondly, it is difficult not to see references to Muir's own psychological journey here. This symbolic process from neurosis through vision and suffering to a final celebratory acceptance is the process of Muir's personal and poetic life. The stages correspond closely to his deep neurosis in Glasgow, the release of memory, vision and symbol through psycho-analysis, the slow but urgent coming to terms with evil and suffering in Prague and the final transcending vision which is incarnated in his poetry from *One Foot in Eden* onward.

It is possible, too, to feel a subdued Christian element in **"The Song."** The living presence from a higher world come to earth to bring understanding of a wider purpose and pattern is seen suffering intensely, as if bearing the whole world's pain. As with Christ, the great powers are not allowed to prevail in order to release it from necessary suffering. Here a simple park gate "defeats" the huge animal, just as a wooden cross "defeats" Christ. Here, too, following the agony, there is a mysterious upward rising from the world.

The symbolism cannot be made to bear, exclusively, on any one of these interpretations. It reverberates and moves too deeply and freely to be fixed in any way. The processes of liberation through poetry and the imagination and through mystical and religious sources all merge into one great utterance about the possibilities of man's defying the Fall into time and pain and achieving a vision which brings him closer to his true nature. This process dominates Muir's imagination, and in no other poem does he treat it with such a perfectly resolved tension between the experience he himself lived through and the universal experience be believed common to all men. It is only through a dramatic exploitation of symbolist technique that the poet is able to enact in such all-inclusive richness the vital human process of the integration of self.

Another example of technical virtuosity is **"Images."** On first appearance this seems to be three poems with no logical connection, but there exist clear relationships between the three—each comes at the same idea in a different way. The first section is deeply symbolistic in method, using symbol and syntax to describe symbol and syntax and their function in the creative act. The heart of the poem is a symbolic face, totally unidentified, which man must try to describe and recreate. The face seems to be a source of knowledge, like Keats' Moneta, and also the mystery of timelessness in art. The face, with its "lines of motionless desire," has to forego movement and exists in a timeless silence. Through a brilliant transition, Muir turns the lines on the face into the lines of poetry as he warns of the inability of mere syntax and language to recreate the felt knowledge of the face. Simultaneously he uses his own syntax to embody what he is saying about it:

Look once. But do not hope to find a sentence
To tell what you have seen. Stop at the colon:
And set a silence after to speak the word
That you will always seek and never find,
Perhaps, if found, the good and beautiful end.
You will not reach that place. So leave the hiatus
There in the broken sentence. What is missing
You will always think of.

This poetry is purely symbolist, describing itself and commenting on itself, using syntax as expressive agent, confusing present and future tenses, being concerned with the creation of art. What Muir suggests here is that the poetic symbol—the face—must be seen quickly and released without being contaminated by the individual observer. Although one glance at truth is never enough for man to know it, any further contact will interfere with its self-sufficiency. The poem asserts the existence of two planes of reality which must be joined, by art and symbol, before "the good and beautiful" vision can be experienced.

The second part of **"Images"** continues this idea. Its eighteen lines are contained in one sentence which unravels itself through stages of fear and confusion to a strong conclusion of permanent value, reminiscent of **"The Song."** Here, too, we have reference to Muir's familiar symbolism of the journey and the labyrinth as the poem describes the urgent necessity for the artist to forge serenity and song out of often desperate experience. The opening lines show the psychological labyrinth:

> You in imaginary fears
> Threading the terrors of a wood
> That has no place but in your mind . . .

The poem is deliberately freed from referential possibility by the insistence that the wood "has no place but in your mind" and the mind-breaking terrors are never specified.

From this point, the process of the artist is towards blindness from which comes vision and prophecy as he joins "blind Tiresias." Now he sees and feels clearly. The artistic symbol is here incarnated as a bird

> That sings at ease upon a branch,
> Time a long silence in its ear
> That never heard of time or space.

The "timeless nightingale"—the poetic symbol—is free of time and space. The poem celebrates Romantic and symbolist theories of poetry by its implied movement into the timeless world of the creative imagination to find inspiration, symbol and, ultimately, eternity. We are reminded strongly of Yeats' Byzantium poems but Muir is concerned with the identity of the symbol and its characteristics and not so much with the Yeatsian conflict in the mind of the artist/narrator.

The third poem again deals with the poetic symbol, itself symbolised here as a little god weaving, teasingly, through time and space, perfectly free in its magic powers. There is no human presence in this poem; no poet addressing or being addressed; no hint of autobiography. The god, or symbol, is allowed to dominate as Muir presents its possibilities and healing powers. The tone is lighter here, with a feyness and childish wryness as if the poet were telling a bedtime fairy-story:

> He is the little, sly, absconding god,
> Hides in the moment. Look and he is gone,

But turn away, and there he is back again.
He is more quick than movement,
Present and gone, absent and safe in hiding,
No spell can bind him.

Just as, in the first section of **"Images,"** the face could not be contained in language, so this god can not be found in time as he "Hides in the moment." He is not available to those who are over-seriously involved in time and time's things, or who have lost innocence of imagination:

> But idle fools and children
> Take him for granted, are at their ease with him,
> And he's the true friend of the absent-minded.

Those lines are followed by a strongly symbolist statement:

> He is too agile for time's dull iambics,
> Lightly drives in and out of stale duration,
> Poised on the endless present. There he is free,
> Having no past or future.

This is a justification of symbolist technique as a valid means of defeating time and space. The "endless present"—the condition of music—is achieved only by the free symbol. The poem ends with an assertion of value, modified by the sly tone:

> All things know him.
> And then are eased as by a heavenly chance.
> The greater gods sometimes in grave amusement
> Smile at his tricks, yet nod in approbation.

The symbol unites all things and brings healing and restoration to the fallen world of time and place.

Thus the three sections are really one. Each is directly concerned with the possibilities and limitations of art as a means of apprehending reality. The poetic symbol, seen as the face full of knowledge, the singing bird and the little god, can and does bridge the distance between this world and a higher one. However, visions of higher realities are temporary and fleeting because we have only "time's dull iambics" in which to embody our glimpses of eternity. **"Images"** is a justification and explanation of Muir's use of freely floating, non-anchored symbols as instruments which link time to eternity and, in so doing, bring balance and integration to the confused, disorientated psyche of man.

The technical control of the sustained images in each section and the remarkable integral expressiveness of the syntax are enhanced by the metrical virtuosity. The blank pentameter of the first and third sections are brilliantly handled, with suggestive foot substitutions, while the long sentence in the second section is controlled and modulated by rhymed, four-foot lines. One example of metrical virtuosity, almost humorous in its use, is the line "He is too agile for time's dull iambics." We would probably scan the line

x x / /   x x / /   x / x

which is about as far as a poet can get from "dull iambics" in a pentameter line. The double use of dipody and the extra syllable fracture the iambic line just as dramatically as the agile god escapes from the pattern of time. Many of Muir's late poems exhibit craftsmanship of a very high order which permits him to extend and modify his vision to the very end of his life.

We may usefully group **"An Island Tale," "The Brothers"** and **"The Two Sisters"** together. These poems, among the finest Muir ever wrote, are lyric elegies which treat death with a tone and a music which are wholly Muir's own; they are filled with a quiet acceptance of mortality and a poignant awareness of the workings of time.

In **"An Island Tale,"** an old lady dies on an island—perhaps Orkney; we do not need to know—and becomes the subject of a local ballad which celebrates the love and grief which "became her well." The poem, written from the viewpoint of the watchers at her death, rejects such an over-simplification by its insistence on the human reality of the event and the tragedy of time and death which work on beauty and life.

The first two stanzas achieve, through sound and tone, a great tenderness. The gravity and utter simplicity of language and feeling, the overwhelming sense of the dissolution of something valuable, ensure a powerful identification with the dying woman, which is essential for the ultimate success of the poem:

> She had endured so long a grief
> That from her breast we saw it grow
> Branch, leaf and flower with such a grace
> We wondered at the summer place
> Which set that harvest there. But oh
> The softly, softly yellowing leaf.

These lines have an immense compassion for humanity caught in time. They are seemingly effortless, but this is an earned ability, possible only when the personality of the poet himself has emerged from suffering and tragedy, and when this knowledge is allied to an unerring formal and technical instinct. This is one of Muir's most universal, timeless poems, in its embodiment of the potencies of growth and decay, and in its quiet humble reduction of emotional complexity into basic felt knowledge. The last question of the poem, which could so easily have been trite, attains, through the intense lyric build-up, a strong weight of significance:

> They sing her ballad yet,
> But all the simple verses tell
> Is, love and grief become her well.
> Too well; for how can we forget
> Her happy face when she was young?

The six-line tetrameter stanzas, rhymed a b c c b a, combine the rich close harmony of the central complex with the separated, more tentative rhymes of the first and last lines, giving each stanza a slow growth to a

point followed by a diminuendo, as sound and sense fall away and, faintly echoing, dissolve.

"The Brothers," an elegy for his brothers Willy and Johnnie, is the only direct poetic treatment of his family in all of Muir's poetry. When the family moved from Orkney to Glasgow, Muir, as a boy, saw his brothers and both parents die in a short space of time—events which contributed greatly to his unhappy years in Glasgow and his subsequent breakdown. Now, fifty years after the events, he is able to treat his brothers' deaths only because he dreamed of them.

The poem turns on the well-know human characteristic, inevitable after the death of a loved person, of guilt; of an overwhelming sense of not having valued, or shown an appreciation of value, until it is too late. **"The Brothers"** is an elegy, but also a plea for expiation, as the poet explains that he has only reached an understanding of the relationship with the passing of time. This realisation that only slow years have been able to bring vision serves to emphasise the poignancy of the poem, as Muir deals with time at its most cruel when it cuts down youth and innocence and thereby chokes the growth and potentialities of love. It is this awareness of loss, more terrible because of its quiet presentation, which informs the emotional centre of the poem.

A quiet progression of tonal and emotional logic develops in the poem's three sections. The first section describes in visual terms the dream-vision of the two brothers transfigured and mystically beautiful:

> Last night I watched my brothers play,
> The gentle and the reckless one,
> In a field two yards away . . .
> For still they raced about the green
> And were like two revolving suns;
> A brightness poured from head to head,
> So strong I could not see their eyes
> Or look into their paradise.

The hyperbole of "two yards away" and the pouring brightness are acceptable in the low-toned dream context and the unwavering certainty of the poet's statement. It is a vision of ecstacy, modified throughout by the implicit dimension of death and loss. The second section is concerned with the observer's own guilt and blindness:

> I thought, How could I be so dull,
> Twenty thousand days ago,
> Not to see they were beautiful?

And the final section resolves the poem by moving into wider, more public areas in order to examine, and implicitly condemn, the idea of justice in a world of inhumanity and tragedy. The lines have tremendous authority:

> I have observed in foolish awe
> The dateless mid-days of the law
> And seen indifferent justice done

By everyone on everyone.
And in a vision I have seen
My brothers playing on the green.

The protest against necessity and injustice could not be stronger and yet the lines have a meditative, resigned, falling cadence. The seemingly inconsequential last couplet, following the general statement on human conduct, provides the perfect conclusion. Totally simple, apparently unprotesting, it somehow welds together Muir's vision of his own private grief and guilt, the lack of humanity in the world at large, and a powerful acknowledgment of, and response to, the savage workings of time among the ruins of human hopes. That Muir's feelings strike so powerfully is largely due to his use of words suggesting youth, innocence and growth, against which the deaths of the brothers become increasingly obscene and unnatural; the language gently builds up a powerful emotional resistance to the fact of the deaths, to the realisation that contact is possible now only in dream and not reality.

"The Brothers" is a superb lyric, technically and tonally impressive, and containing deep, complex and universal feelings about the nature of death, bereavement, time and justice. Much less formally ambitious than his big symbolist poems, it is nevertheless, through the creative mingling of sound, tone, image and vision, one of his purest, most unflawed and most deeply felt poems.

In **"The Two Sisters"** Muir uses a perfectly regular song-like form. I print the poem in full:

> Her beauty was so rare,
> It wore her body down
> With leading through the air
> That marvel not her own.
> At last to set it free
> From enmity of change
> And time's incontinence
> To drink from beauty's bone,
> Snatching her last defence,
> She locked it in the sea.
>
> The other, not content
> That fault of hers should bring
> Grief and mismanagement
> To make an end of grace
> And snap the slender ring,
> Pulled death down on her head,
> Completed destiny.
> So each from her own place,
> Those ladies put to sea
> To join the intrepid dead.

The words of this poem are astonishingly simple and largely monosyllabic, the rhyme is full and straightforward, and, apart from the last line with seven syllables, the poem is completely accentual-syllabic throughout, having three feet and six syllables in each line. Yet, for all this, the poem exerts a tonal and emotional complexity which is strange and effective.

Firstly, we must realise that this is not—or not merely—a narrative. The images of the two dead sisters—one full of beauty; one full of grace and manners—lie side by side in time and place, completely unspecific, ultimately, in spite of the local concrete details. The two sisters may or may not have existed. They may be from life, from art or from the poet's imagination; contemporary or medieval. The only certain reality is "the sea" of "the intrepid dead," which exists as a free-moving symbol. The poem deals with human death and the effect of "time's incontinence" on the most delicate and rare human things. The two sisters engage in a contest with time before they consent to its demands, and it is this final consenting, or acceptance, which makes the poem so moving. Death comes finally without any protest. The human-beings are absorbed into a great natural process which means the end of struggle and some sort of fulfilment.

This technique of placing imprecisely located images side by side may lack precision, but in this poem it articulates to the sense something which could never be directly described. There is absolutely no comment from the poet here. Two deaths, two attitudes, two tones, are placed together to generate what meaning they can. As well as the overwhelming sense of dissolution into death, or mortality celebrated and elegised, there appears an attitude of chiding, of gentle mockery towards the two highly motivated ladies, who to preserve decently their attributes of good looks and good manners consciously choose death rather than a loss of appearance. This is done so mildly and affectionately by Muir that it remains merely an impression. Certainly there is no overt judgement, but rather a whimsical recognition of human concern with behaviour which lies tantalisingly next to the serious emotional knowledge of death.

What then is the emotion of the poem? It is not simply grief, nor gentle amusement. The emotion lies between the two, where the two things penetrate each other and reveal each other on a nonlogical level. It becomes a completely "felt" meaning, elusive but humanly recognisable and important, in which the fact of death, far from being reduced in potency by the mockery is heightened. In this context human fallibility and individual eccentricity become valuable beyond measure.

"The Two Sisters" celebrates life by celebrating death. It praises human strength and dignity by recognising human weakness, and this is done by the perfect blend of form and meaning. Suffering, to Muir at the end of his life, is a deep known mirror; his techniques now allow him to embody his knowledge in clear and luminous poetry, gracefully pointed and seemingly simple, but full of converged feeling.

"The Two Sisters" demonstrates Muir's ability to hold together in a single form the contradictions of a familiar world and the larger sanctions of a creative pattern which works through and beyond it. There are several late poems, however, which, by their insistence upon temporal pain and chaos, fail to penetrate to any redemptive higher reality. These are, after all, poems of the 1950's—the age of cold war, of "ban-the-bomb" marches, of political and military fears—and in poems like **"After a Hypothetical War," "After 1984," "The Last War," "The Tower," "Ballad of Everyman"** and **"The Day Before the Last Day,"** Muir demonstrates and embodies terror and disintegration. In a letter to Kathleen Raine, he wrote: "I know I have been writing some very queer poetry . . . with a good deal of new horror in it . . ."[2] and it is clear that in some of these last poems he is once again overwhelmed temporarily by terrible negative visions.

In **"The Horses"** (1956) Muir was able to modify the shock of nuclear destruction by allowing the survivors to establish relationship with "the strange horses" as a prerequisite of a new order, but in **"After a Hypothetical War"** there are no horses, no symbolic messengers of hope. Post-atomic existence here is a mixture of selfishness, greed, sterility of nature, overthrow of law, unnatural mutations, infection—in short, a total collapse of order and those values which make human life bearable. Never has Muir evoked such a terrible picture of distorted life and hell on earth without a balancing positive impulse. There is a weary sense of desperation in this poem, combined with an intensely realised depiction of twisted humanity and infected nature:

> Chaotic breed of misbegotten things,
> Embryos of what could never wish to be.
> Soil and air breed crookedly here, and men
> Are dumb and twisted as the envious scrub
> That spreads in silent malice on the fields.
> Lost lands infected by an enmity
> Deeper than lust or greed, that works by stealth
> Yet in the sun is helpless as a blindworm,
> Making bad worse. The mud has sucked half in
> People and cattle until they eat and breathe
> Nothing but mud.

This is the essence of chaos, with infection having undermined the very springs of life and the process of breeding. This desperate vision of a ruined world is softened only by its being projected as a hypothesis and by the fact that Muir uses no rant or bitterness and assumes no angry rhetorical stance.

In **"After 1984,"** the poet again evokes the sterile horrors of hell on earth:

> Start from ourselves even in our mind;
> Only a twisting chaos within
> Turned on itself, not knowing where
> The exit was, salvation gate.

But this poem ends in a regenerative transformation as the old men narrating the events describe the revolution which released them. Evil is defeated, but, as in many of those poems, the Fall is prominent as an agent of blockage and sterility. **"The Day Before the Last Day"** images an apocalyptic end of the world; **"The Refugees Born for a Land Unknown"** describes displaced lives and lost identity; **"Ballad of Everyman"** and **"Nightmare of Peace"** show the fragile self confronted by police states and "false-faced" assemblies of politicians; **"Petrol Shortage"** is set in a shattered post-war Europe; **"The Last War"** again postulates chaos—all these poems keep Muir's symbolism and his attitudes to experience firmly rooted in the actual. But overall the tone is one of acceptance. Only in **"After a Hypothetical War"** does the negative swamp the positive in a hopeless way and the authority Muir gains from reporting the negative strengthens his vision of the positive and gives it authenticity because it is so hard earned.

Probably the last poem Muir wrote, **"I have been Taught,"** is a credo, a summing up. For once Muir seems to be speaking directly through a first-person "I," without a mask. The poem discusses his beliefs about art and reality. His knowledge, he claims, comes from "dreams and fantasies," with its symbols both "friendly" and "darker"; from those who preceded him into death; from his parents; from the "founts" of ritual, art, and traditional sustaining patterns; from a knowledge of the dark places to the psyche, "the sultry labyrinth"; from time, which allows us glimpses of eternity. And now, finally, he sees that "Plato's is the truest poetry"; that the belief in perfect forms, of which our world is an imperfect reflection, does in fact sustain life. This last statement asserts pattern, eternity, love and art. The labyrinth and its power can never be forgotten but can be seen as part of something larger, more generous and life-enhancing which supports and illuminates existence.

In these late poems, Muir creates a world which is both remote and yet instantly recognisable. The instinctive search for the lost Eden is still modified by the labyrinth, but through the immense authority of his poetic techniques and a new calm wisdom, the poet succeeds in earthing man's everyday experience of mortality and pain into a rich inclusive pattern which harmoniously absorbs time into eternity, and good and evil into wide rhythms of potentiality. Edwin Muir's life and art come finally to a place of integration and perfected forms.

NOTES

[1] Edwin Muir, *Collected Poems* (London: Faber and Faber, 1960. Second edn. 1963).

[2] Quoted in Peter Butter, *Edwin Muir: Man and Poet* (Edinburgh: Oliver and Boyd, 1966), p. 272.

Roger J. Porter (essay date 1978)

SOURCE: "Edwin Muir and Autobiography: Archetype of a Redemptive Memory," in *South Atlantic Quarterly*, Vol. 77, No. 4, Autumn, 1978, pp. 504-23.

[In the following essay, Porter discusses memory and imagination in The Story and the Fable *and* An Autobiography.*]*

I

Among the appeals of reading an autobiography is its evocation of the writer's past, especially when the writer perceives that time as englobed and inviolable, existing beyond his reach. Like a Joseph Cornell box, constructed of old objects taken from studio cartons labeled "flotsam and jetsam" and "watch parts," an autobiography may charm us through the collecting and assembling instinct of the artist, who reclaims the fragments of his memory and composes them into an image, a unified assemblage speaking a certain remoteness. The fascination for us is exactly the enclosed pastness of the past, and its quality of continually receding behind the one who lived and, in a sense, has created it. If we indeed dwell in an age of nostalgia, autobiography would seem to be our primary vehicle for a journey into a lost time; unlike historical novels, which express a past as if it were present, autobiographies declare the past to be past. The autobiographer stands at the threshold of his past, and from the position of the narrative present takes us with him into his past; we always recognize that the earlier time exists only in the autobiographer's conscious act of memory, and therefore in a certain tension with his present. As the autobiographer edges us away from his past, we may feel the sense of loss with him, for childhood innocence and historical simplicities combine in our reading to suggest an unrecoverable world perhaps more attractive than our own.

But on another inspection we know this to be scarcely the case. We immediately suspect any reduction of childhood to unalloyed bliss; furthermore, we believe that the roots of our anxieties lie back there, the very origins of which may cause the autobiographer to dream somewhat sentimentally on that past in the first place, as if either in forgetfulness or desperation he seeks to forge an Edenic conception of the past. It is not only that memory may trick him, but he may also manipulate memory to serve his deepest wishes. I use the Cornell box as an image of the autobiographer's past because it too is a kind of sanctified space, transparent but sealed off, deeply recessed and visible yet wholly untouchable. Like an Eden it cannot be reentered except through the imagination. In effect the box asks to be taken as a kind of theater of the mind with items gathered and staged from the scenes of our own past, a memory box that is as much a skull as an environment. It both magnetizes us and holds us at bay, as any vision of Eden must. Its analogue in autobiographical theory is the separation between the narrated past and the present narrative situation.

Edwin Muir presents the example of an autobiographer who begins by evoking the past as a time apart—a special moment, preserved in the mind, that nurtured the most harmonious aspects of his being. Muir seeks to return to the past, for he views his childhood as shot through with Adamic significance, his later life as a kind of tragic fall away from the earlier timelessness. But he cannot collapse the present into the past, and the poignance of his autobiography is the futility of attempting to recapture what is gone. In the process, Muir begins to write autobiography as wish fulfillment, freighting the past with the burden of transcendent meaning. In his two autobiographies—*The Story and the Fable* (1940) and *An Autobiography* (1954)—Muir reveals how he struggled to hold to an ongoing and redemptive sense of his past, to preserve and virtually encapsulate it against the rush of history. Again and again he felt his life slip away from him, as the course of time counteracted his dream of recovery. What he could and did accomplish, however, was to make some peace with his predicament through the art of autobiography, not to freeze the past but to turn it into a kind of mythic narrative to keep the past from dissolving. And in so doing he complicates the past, seeing it as the source of his joy and his sorrow, both of which he must understand, especially in their relation to one another, in order to be free from a sentimentalized view of the past. Autobiography for Muir was a genre which would not so much recapture the past—an illusion he came to acknowledge—as give the past a special "plot," so that his "return" would function largely in a compensatory realm of art and might confer a unity to the life he had feared was no longer apparent even to himself. As a result Muir implicitly urges upon us a theory and strategy for the writing of autobiography.

The Story and the Fable takes Muir up to age 35, in 1922; *An Autobiography,* written five years before his death in 1959 at the age of 72, is essentially the earlier book with new chapters added, bringing the account of his life up to date. We may begin by examining the significance of the title of the original volume. Muir makes the distinction between "Story" and "Fable."

> It is clear that no autobiography can begin with a man's birth, that we extend far beyond any boundary line which we can set for ourselves in the past or the future, and that the life of every man is an endlessly repeated performance of the life of man. It is clear for the same reason that no autobiography can confine itself to conscious life, and that sleep, in which we pass a third of our existence, is a mode of experience, and our dreams a part of reality. In themselves our conscious lives may not be particularly interesting. But what we are not and can never be, our fable, seems to be inconceivably interesting. I should like to write that fable, but I cannot even live it; and all I could do if I related the outward course of my life would be to show how I have deviated from it; though even that is impossible, since I do not know the fable or anybody who knows it. One or two stages in it I can recognize: the age of innocence and the Fall and all the dramatic consequences which issue from the Fall. But these lie behind experience, not on its surface; they are not historical events; they are stages in the fable.

The problem that confronts an autobiographer even more urgently than other men is, How can he know himself? I am writing about myself in this book, yet I do not know what I am. I know my name, the date and place of my birth, the appearance of the places I have lived in, the people I have met, the things I have done. I know something of the society which dictates many of my actions, thoughts, and feelings. I know a little about history, and can explain to myself in a rough-and-ready fashion how that society came into being. But I know all this in an external and deceptive way, as if it were a dry legend which I had made up in collusion with mankind. This legend is founded on a sort of agreement such as children presuppose in their games of make-believe: an agreement by which years and days are given certain numbers to distinguish them, and peoples and countries and other things certain names: all this is necessary, of course, for the business of living. But it is a deception as well: if I knew all these figures and names I should still not know myself, far less the other people in the world, or the small number whom I call friends. This external approach, no matter how perfect, will never teach me about them or about myself. (pp. 48-49)[1]

The Fable is an archetype of the paradisal myth, a semblance of which one hopes to recapture by living as if the fundamental aspects of life were recurrent. But Muir seems to disavow the possibility of writing the Fable; he can only report the Story—his external life, the facts, phenomena, and contingencies of ordinary existence—or the appearances presented by others in the world. He begins a search for the meaning of his own past with an explicit acknowledgment of the writer's limitations. This misgiving is not merely the usual one of autobiographers—of imposing false images on the self to satisfy one's idealized conceptions; it is, rather, that his life can never be discerned so long as he treats only its "Story" and not the underlying myth. As autobiographer Muir will strive to convey more than "dry legend," or even commentary upon it; a deeper vision of the life is needed. This will involve a scheme that Muir fears may falsify unduly the truth of his life, and he wrestles with the problem of making a literary construct.

Hesitant to admit that autobiography can reveal the unconscious claims of a mind, Muir assumes that while the novelist can concentrate on the Fable side of a life, subordinating ordinary experience to the dream world of his characters, the autobiographer is bound by sheer facts—the Story.

> If I were recreating my life in an autobiographical novel I could . . . show how our first intuition of the world expands into vaster and vaster images, creating a myth which we act almost without knowing it, while our outward life goes on in its ordinary routine of eating, drinking, sleeping, working, and making money in order to beget sons and daughters who will do the same. I could follow these images freely if I were writing an autobiographical novel. As it is, I have to stick to the facts and try to fit them in where they will fit in. (p. 48)

Nevertheless, that Muir is writing an autobiography and not a novel is less of an inhibition than he imagines: the "intuition of the world" emerges from the facts, the Fable arises naturally from the Story, and he depicts "a myth which we act without knowing it." For Muir every event fits into a structure the significance of which is the burden of the autobiography to explore. Whenever Muir stands at a crisis in his life, a discussion of "the Fable" takes place. When he is about to leave the peace of his childhood farm in the Orkney Islands for the squalor of Glasgow, the move becomes analogous to the expulsion of Adam. When, after a period of deep depression he turns to Socialism, his vision of humanity transfigured is also described in Adamic terms:

> There are times in every man's life when he seems to become for a little while a part of the fable, and to be recapitulating some legendary drama which, as it has recurred a countless number of times in time, is ageless. The realization of the Fall is one of these events, and the purifications which happen in one's life belong to them too. (p. 114)

Muir constantly moves from the Story to the Fable, from the life to the mythic meaning of that life. Kathleen Raine notes that Muir once had a dream consisting entirely of the punctuation mark the colon. Muir's own interpretation was that the poet never knows all that he writes; he writes, in fact, only as far as the colon, but the mythic meaning or Fable of the writing and the life lies to the right of and beyond the colon.[2] Harold Bloom's description of myth is appropriate for Muir: "To make a myth is to tell a story of your own invention, to speak a word that is your word alone, and yet the story is so told, the word so spoken, that they mean also the supernal things and transcend the glory of the ego able to explain itself to others."[3] It is this urge that controls the design of Muir's work, as he subordinates the personalism of his story to a more transcendent, mythic way of seeing, in which a man is more than just a product of his special circumstances.

Muir's assertion of a self that is beyond mere appearance or role-playing suggests that the autobiography is dedicated to recovering whatever characteristics time and history have effaced. Muir views his "true" self as outside the boundary lines of conscious life, and his autobiography is largely an investigation of that self which seems hidden from and alien to the very man who is writing. Behind the threat of failure stands the inescapable epistemological problem for autobiographers: "How can I know myself?" Muir admits the impossibility: "I do not know who I am," but this assertion is not in itself the ultimate position of the book, for the entire autobiography is an attempt to probe the way he makes meanings: it is autobiography about the *process* of self-discovery in time.

The Story and the Fable especially has a Miltonic theme, as it moves from an original Eden of childhood to chaos, disillusionment, loss of selfhood, and finally approaches the recovery of a paradise within the autobiographer's mind. Muir poses a dualistic conception of self—someone living in a timeless, unchanging world, and mortal man aware of his limitations, compelled to acknowledge his ordinariness. We can trace Muir's attempt to regain the past as the writer turns deeper into himself to find the sources of a sustaining vision. The significance of childhood for Muir depends on his notions of innocence, myth, natural harmony, and timelessness; but he complicates his vision of childhood by stressing both its creative and destructive aspects. In childhood begins the motif of the double self: one who alternately sees his life shaped by myth and desire, and one who recognizes the impossibility of that idyllic vision. As Muir attempts to resolve this duality, we can judge his conception of autobiography as a mode to explore the continuities and discontinuities of selfhood.

II

Muir was born in 1887 on a small farm in the Orkney Islands and enjoyed a serene boyhood in the isolation of what he considered a rural paradise. Though Muir's long and beautiful first chapter takes him only to his eighth year, the analysis is patiently sustained, for he will ground every subsequent feeling and thought in those early reveries. *The Story and the Fable* is the quest for a renewal of an Edenic view of the world, circular, not linear, in form. There is, to be sure, a narrative progression from childhood to middle age; but the child is conditioned by what he imagines his life will be, and Muir's sense of himself *as he writes* determines the expressed view of childhood. "Turning backward" is both the method and the subject of the book; it shows Muir conscious of carrying a sense of time within him, and of time itself as a condition of his existence. The need to write autobiography follows the desire to recapture the early harmonious vision and to unify the life by measuring all later attitudes in terms of the earlier ones.

Muir begins the account with his closeness to the natural world.

> I can see the rough grey stones spotted with lichen on top of the Castle . . . but I cannot bring back the feelings which I had for them, the sense of being magically close to them, as if they were magnets drawing me with a palpable power. Reasonable explanations can be found for these feelings: the fact that every object is new to a child; that he sees it without understanding it, or understands it with a different understanding from that of experience—different, for there may be fear in it, but there cannot be calculation or worry; or even the fact that he is closer to things, since his eyes are only two or three feet from the ground, not five or six. Grass, stones, and insects are twice as near to him as they will be after he has grown up, and when I try to re-create my early childhood it seems to me that it was focused on such things as these, and that I lived my life in a small, separate underworld, while the grown-ups walked on their long legs several feet above my head on a stage where every relation was different. I was

dizzily lifted into that world, as into another dimension, when my father took me on his shoulders, so that I could see the roof of the byre from above or touch the lintel of the house door with my hand. But for most of the time I lived with whatever I found on the surface of the earth. . . . (pp. 20-21)

The perspective Muir gains when his father lifts him on his shoulders and thrusts him out of his element breaks the delicate interplay between child and natural world. Later Muir speaks of a child's wisdom of human existence as "a state in which the earth, the houses on the earth, and the life of every human being are related to the sky overarching them; as if the sky fitted the earth and the earth the sky" (p. 33). This "fit" depends upon a silent covenant which the child makes with nature exactly because he lacks experience and has no reason to question the goodness and "palpable power" of natural phenomena. Muir is passive, feeling joy in merely being surrounded by a familiar scene. A "completer harmony of all things with each other than he will ever know again" (p. 33) results from what the child possesses only for a few brief years, especially his diminished height and the geographical insularity of his home. All things are "compressed within" the island world, and there is no escaping any phenomenon. Later he comments: "We need a symbolical stage on which the drama of human life can play itself out for us, and I doubt whether we have the liberty to choose it. The little island was not too big for a child to see in it an image of life; land and sea and sky, good and evil, happiness and grief, life and death discovered themselves to me there . . ." (p. 206). In Muir's theater of perception all actors take on enormous significance; life beyond the self-contained island is irrelevant. The spatial constriction is important, for the confinement of the child's stage provides a source of easy familiarity and comfort. The island is like his own childhood mind—the repository of dreams and a place where all things are relevant to all others. Muir's autobiography builds on bedrock—the archetypal moments of a life—and he celebrates Orkney as the emotional and rhythmic center of his existence.

His first memory is from an indistinct time when he lay in his cradle:

> I was lying in some room watching a beam of slanting light in which dusty, bright motes slowly danced and turned, while a low murmuring went on somewhere, possibly the humming of flies. My mother was in the room, but where I do not know; I was merely conscious of her as a vague environing presence. . . . The quiet murmuring, the slow, unending dance of the motes, the sense of deep and solid peace, have come back to me since only in dreams. This memory has a different quality from any other memory in my life. It was as if, while I lay watching that beam of light, time had not yet begun. (p. 18)

The crucial phrase here is "environing presence"; his mother acts like the island itself, protecting the child by granting him a timeless serenity. All of Muir's remembering is based on this first sensuous moment. Throughout the autobiography Muir demonstrates his faith in the restorative power of images, and he will write autobiography out of the impulse to explain his memory, the way in which early experiences become part of the Fable; memories themselves are less important than the act of remembering.

A principal feature of the island is that it represents a world beyond time. "Time sat still on the wrist of each day with its wings folded." His parents are "fixed allegorical figures in a timeless landscape," and he sees them "as a stationary pattern, changing, yet always the same"; each day is a mirror image of the previous one, as if there were only "one day endlessly rising and setting." Muir's father rises "out of changelessness like a rock out of the sea" (pp. 24-25), and his image, which makes a kind of island of the father, connects security and insularity. Orkney creates a circle of contentment through geography and weathers: "The winter gathered us into one room as it gathered cattle into the stable . . . the sky came closer; the lamps were lit at three or four in the afternoon, and then the great evening lay before us like a world . . ." (pp. 30-31). Light and warmth provide a center of vitality, a place where the few elements in Orkney life come together in celebration of the ongoing power of that life, a place from which Muir can observe the changing of seasons in their unalterable cycles.

These aspects of Muir's childhood, as well as the legends that envelop his archaic community, define existence as a Fable. "The Orkney I was born into was a place where there was no great distinction between the ordinary and the fabulous; the lives of great men turned into legend" (p. 14). Muir's Orkney life stands on the brink of a primitive era, when there was little distinction between man and animal, and what is now legend and myth was reality. He sees some of this attitude in the Orkney of his youth: "When a neighbor came to stick the pig it was a ceremony as objective as the rising and setting of the sun" (p. 36), and this ceremonial orientation to experience assures the boy that all his actions have a transcendent, cosmic significance. The ritual surrounding the pig-killing validates its character as a sacrifice or mystery expressing the sacramental nature of life and helps create an intelligible order for the child, a way of coping with unknown and disturbing aspects of experience and of accepting even the violence he sees about him.

Muir suggests that our unconscious life goes back to such an archaic age, that any present event can be understood only when we realize the significance of its first enactment in mythical time—Eliade's "eternal return." Muir strives to banish concrete time or duration, and his existence as a child has meaning largely in relation to what transcends it. Much of the first chapter shows the autobiographer deliberately forcing his mind back into the past, uncovering successive layers of memory, as if the desire to assure himself that nothing new happens in the world can be realized by seeking the prototypical events in his own life, just as his earliest experiences seem to conform to more general prototypes in the life of man and nature. The perception that life re-creates primordial experience is mirrored in the act of writing an autobiography which partly demonstrates that re-creating the life is its own kind of renewal. Muir's assertion that much of his later life was spent in attempting to recapture an Edenic perspective suggests he is a kind of "natural autobiographer": he lives his life as if he were engaged in the act of writing about its recovery. The paradise literally may not be had again, but Muir will strive to uncover layers of "falsifying" experience that have intervened since Orkney and to find a new Edenic center within. Muir as a child may have known an unfallen world by intuition, but Muir the autobiographer attempts to recover it through the imagination.

But Muir gives us a more complex view of his childhood. Like the Eden of *Paradise Lost,* Orkney is not without elements that counter its harmony. The island possesses many attributes of the outside world Muir will confront later, and his need to internalize a paradisal vision results from knowledge that place alone can never suffice. Parallel to a hopeful myth of the childhood idyl runs a negative myth of fear, guilt, and joylessness, of potential fall in the child and the land. Muir is vulnerable even as a child, and the honesty of this recognition will determine the nature of his achieved consolations in the autobiography.

The first evidence of complexity stems from Muir's fears of the natural world. He is shocked by unexpected terrors and the realization that nature can distress as well as soothe. Certain insects represent the night that darkens childhood splendor:

> I could never bear to touch any of these creatures, though I watched them so closely that I seemed to be taking part in their life, which was like little fragments of night darting about in the sun; they often came into my dreams later, wakening me in terror. . . . The gravelocks and forkytails were my first intimation of evil, and associations of evil still cling 'round them for me, as, I fancy, for most people: popular imagery shows it. We cannot tell how much our minds are influenced for life by the fact that we see the world first at a range of two or three feet. (p. 21)

The natural world contains moral qualities, especially those of reliability or deception; certain flowers can be trusted, others "took on a faithless look." Muir speaks of a broken image contradictory to the harmony of all things; it brings "the sense of an unseen tragedy being played out around me" (p. 33). He is deliberately vague about this "unseen tragedy"; it takes no definite shape and is thus more terrifying.

This tension between "an unknown glory" and "an unseen tragedy" provides the drama of the early chapters. His confidence in the Edenic myth is shattered by the intrusion of a literally poisonous substance into the garden. Muir's father one day places a sack of toxic sheep-dip in a field and gives his son strict orders not to touch or go near it.

> I took care to keep away from it; yet after the sheep had been dipped and the sack destroyed I could not feel certain that I had not touched it, and as I took my father's words literally, and thought that even to touch the sack might bring death, I went about in terror. For my hands might have touched the sack. How could I know, now that the sack was gone and I had no control over the boy who might have touched it or might not have touched it, being quite unable to stay his hand in that other time and that other place? (p. 34)

Ironic Biblical overtones are present: his father is like Jehovah warning man from a forbidden temptation; abruptly the child creates a tension both within the self and between self and other.

> My fear went about with me, never leaving me: I would turn corners to get away from it, or shut myself in a little closet with one window, where there seemed to be no room except for myself; but the closet was big enough to hold my fear too. . . . I had actually gone away into a world where every object was touched with fear, yet a world of the same size as the ordinary world and corresponding to it in every detail: a sort of parallel world divided by an endless, unbreakable sheet of glass from the actual world. For though my world was exactly the same in appearance as that world, I knew that I could not break through my fear to it, that I was invisibly cut off, and this terrified and bewildered me. The sense that I was in a blind place was always with me, yet that place was only a clear cloud or bubble surrounding me, from which I could escape at any moment by doing something; but what that was I did not know. My sister, playing in the sun a few feet away, was in that other world; . . . I could not reach it by getting close to it, though I often tried; for when my mother took me in her arms and laid my head on her shoulder she, so close to me, was in that world, and yet I was outside. (pp. 34-35)

This is a remarkable passage, for Muir's sense of himself as a special being is now a nightmare vision of exclusion, the child's entrapping imagination itself the cause of his terror. No longer at the center of the idyllic island, he is imprisoned in his closet and cannot shut out fear any more than the fallen Adam can shut God or his own shame out of mind. The double world—one on each side of the glass or bubble—will haunt Muir for many years, and is a crucial motif in the autobiography. At this point he is cut off not only from the world outside himself but also from the familiar recesses of the self, for when nature no longer sustains him he creates a fantasy world that testifies to his alien state.

Orkney then is not mere paradise, for reality intervenes in the form of death, disillusionment and fear; the autobiography asserts the presence of pastoral's inevitable "counterforce," a feature of Muir's childhood which

"brings a world which is more 'real' into juxtaposition with an idyllic vision."[4] His pastoral vision is complex in that nature can arouse within the child himself disturbances and doubts of which he had not been aware, thus provoking self-consciousness. As the island phase draws to a close he depicts the separation of his family in terms that signal the end of a unified and confident self:

> . . . my family had been a stationary, indivisible pattern; now my brothers and sisters hardened into separate shapes, and without my knowing it division entered the world. . . . At its heart the family held together; there was no inward break, no enmity; it was as if something quite impersonal were scattering us to all quarters of the compass. . . . We were a family, but we were individuals too, moving each in a different direction, and straining the fabric of the family. (pp. 79-81)

Each of Muir's chapters has a geographical title, with change of place indicating his changing fortunes and new crises. The book takes the form of a quest, as Muir moves outward from the shelter of childhood to the "chaos" of Glasgow and as far as Prague, where he reaches his deepest conviction of man's degradation. The physical horror of Glasgow is "a quagmire," "a great, spreading swamp into which I might sink for good" (p. 104). With monotonous regularity the family falls to the grinding city: Muir's father's heart gives out climbing tenement steps; one brother dies of consumption, another of brain injury from a streetcar fall. Muir feels cut off from the outside, and returns to the image of glass enclosures: a bone factory where he is employed oppresses him with its stench of rotting flesh, and is separated from the freer, purer world beyond. But even that world appears fragile and evanescent, filling him "with apprehension, of which I did not know" (p. 140).

His inability to locate a definite object of fear corresponds to a more general failure to attain a stable self as he strains to find a meaningful relation with the world beyond himself: "I could grasp what was before my eyes only by an enormous effort, and even then an invisible barrier, a wall of distance, separated me from it. I moved in a crystalline globe or bubble, insulated from the life around me, yet filled with desire to reach it, to be at the very heart of it and lose myself there" (pp. 149-150). Muir splits himself into a gazer and an object gazed upon, searching for something buried within and simultaneously desiring to escape from himself. The glass bubble separating him from the world is symptomatic of the loss of his childhood myth, and all his efforts are to close the gap between present and past by regaining the origins of his preserving memory.

III

The question for Muir is how to conceive of past and present in some sustaining relationship. He joins with such modernists as Jung in celebrating myth as a way of retracing the roots of and reestablishing bonds with the primal sources of his own early experience. Like Jung, he stands on the brink between an older, romantic notion that locates significance in a transcendent order of the universe with which they long to merge, and a newer, modern notion that separates the self from any overarching scheme and throws man back on his own imagination, both freed from and anxious over the loss of such cosmic values. Muir seeks a return to a natural harmony, but finding that past irrecoverable, he must come to grips with his own character as he confronts the great enemies of modern man—mechanized power, impersonal forces, and spiritual doubt. Muir's autobiography demonstrates the conflict of a self revolted by alien experience but committed to penetrating the meaning of its existence. As he wrestles with this duality in his autobiography, Muir discovers that Fable and Story—myth and mundanity—work together in his complex fate.

Daniel Hoffman, in an article on Muir's poetry, has this to say in defense of the Story side of things:

> . . . the Fable needs at every point the Story, to dramatize its incarnation and make its action relevant to human life. The Story must redeem the Fable from Abstraction. When there is no historical reality in which the Fable is both concealed and revealed, no tactile world, no solid landscape, no living creatures nor believable chimeras, in short no story, there is only the Fable. . . . But when Muir fuses his Fable with his stories . . . the shape of life and the meaning become clear together.[5]

To dwell merely on the present story, however, would not only distort significance but would trap Muir in surface consciousness. The power of autobiography for Muir is that it allows him to connect experience across time, so that even if he cannot recover the past he can at least understand and feel a sense of continuity. As such, the Fable must predominate. Several passages from Jung's autobiography *Memories, Dreams, Reflections* state succinctly what Muir himself was searching for in his depiction of a life:

> My life is a story of the self-realization of the unconscious. Everything in the unconscious seeks outward manifestation, and the personality too desires to evolve out of its unconscious conditions and to experience itself as a whole. . . .
>
> What we are to our inward vision, and what man appears to be *sub species aeternitatis,* can only be expressed by way of myth. . . .
>
> I have now undertaken . . . to tell my personal myth. I can only make direct statements, only "tell stories." Whether or not the stories are "true" is not the problem. The only question is whether what I tell is my fable, my truth. . . .
>
> In the end the only events in my life worth telling are those when the imperishable world irrupted into this transitory one. That is why I speak chiefly of my inner experiences, amongst which I include my dreams and visions. . . .[6]

Muir, who had read Jung avidly as his theories were being published in the *New Age,* emphasizes the universal, archetypal elements in his life. He traces his plot to a collective unconscious beneath the individual one, subduing his personality and connecting himself with other men; for Muir autobiography must avoid too much concentration on the individual self (the self mired in personal history and contingencies). A series of conversions to Socialism, Jungian anthropology, and finally Christianity all signal Muir's submersion of personality into one form or another of collectivism. On the other hand this process involves a profoundly unsettling loss of selfhood, a fear of emptiness or of having only a series of multiple, even contradictory and perhaps inauthentic selves. Perhaps worse is the fear that if there *is* a central self it may remain unknown even to its possessor.

Muir seems to echo Arnold's "The Buried Life" in his efforts to discover and give voice to his feelings of anonymity: "Something in myself was buried. . . . I felt that I had gone too far away from myself" (p. 145); "at the center of myself I tried to assemble my powers and assert something there, though what I did not know" (p. 156). Muir's several "conversions" appear inadequate exactly by offering him facile alternatives to self-discovery. The central section of the autobiography focuses on the frightening self-confrontation in his psychoanalysis, which demolishes all the previous "purifications"; Muir's task in this part of the book is not merely to re-create his past but to cancel those falsifications which have deprived him of a reliable identity.

The very act of autobiography represents a way for Muir to rethink the relation between his paradisal and tormented selves. The autobiography is also the instrument for him to discern the connection between any given experience and the past which will explain its meaning. Autobiography delineates the relation between Story which threatens and the Fable which sustains. The only way to get beyond the crippling facts of experience, time, and change is to mediate between Story and Fable, to look through and beyond mere facts. At the conclusion of **The Story and the Fable** he reports how he realized he must compose autobiography in order to come to know himself, to gain "a first acquaintance with myself" (p. 193). The autobiography, which partly lifts Muir out of time, is his voluntary effort to refine his views of the unconscious life, a gesture toward identity. As we shall see, there are less voluntary means available to him—dreams and the results of psychoanalysis: autobiographical imagination, dreams, and visions culled from the subconscious all help to link present and past, Story and Fable, or at least to bring past and Fable to the surface.

Muir enters psychoanalysis, committed to an examination of the interior life and its relation to the Fable, but is reluctant to face up to his new discoveries. He labels his unconscious "a treacherous spy," and what follows is the indecision of a man torn between evasion and disclosure. A new wave of dread and disgust comes over him, as an older, idealized version of himself falls away revealing a core of "sensual desires and thoughts . . . unacknowledged failures and frustrations . . . self-hatred . . . shame and grief" (p. 158).

The inclusion of Muir's dreams and his own interpretations of them testify to his attempt to discover an order in the life, as he tries to fit the puzzles together and accept the complexities of his own nature. Dreams which acknowledge the primacy of the Fall or a timeless state of existence are honored for the qualities which ally them to Muir's art in the autobiography—the ability to see life as a coherent patterning of time. The dreams and interpretations correspond to the imaginative way of regarding himself that Muir calls for at the conclusion to *The Story and the Fable:* "In living that life over again I struck up a first acquaintance with myself. Till now, I realized that I had been stubbornly staring away from myself. As if I had no more choice than time, I had walked with my face immovably set forward, as incapable as time of turning my head and seeing what was behind me. I looked, and what I saw was myself as I had lived up to that moment when I could turn my head" (p. 193). When Muir turns back and looks *against* the flow of time, he draws attention to what he calls the timeless nature of life. Inquiring into the meaning of change produces a recognition that single events are less important than the traditional and mythic patterns which lie behind them and all individual destinies. The examined past becomes itself the present to be lived: ". . . when my past life came alive in me after lying for so long, a dead weight, my actual life came alive too as that new life passed into it; for it was new, though old; indeed, I felt that only now was I truly living it, since only now did I see it as it was, so that at last it could become experience. Without . . . looking and looking back, I might never have lived my life."[7] The key words are "at last it could become experience"; only when his vision of his early life can "go into" the everyday Story, when the past no longer seems remote and inaccessible, can he live it in such a way as to give it a continuing significance. This is a Bergsonian insistence on the continuity of the psychological life: no act is a totally isolated one, but all "go into" the Fable; our character is "the condensation of the history we have lived from our birth."[8] Autobiography is Muir's way to assert his selfhood even while he subordinates it to a more transcendent vision that locates the individual in history and in time.

IV

Muir's career after the psychoanalysis in London (1922) involves a continuous journeying throughout Europe. The pervasive sense of these elegiac chapters is of a world out of joint, political and social upheavals intensifying the tone of fear which runs through so much of the narrative. Even free colonies of artists and intellectuals distress him by their lack of direction: "They lived in an open landscape, without roads, or a stopping place, or any point of the compass" (p. 229). Spatial metaphors are important here because Muir thinks of these years as a pilgrimage: he remembers looking down from a mountaintop on tiny figures on distant roads and realizes that even casual journeys take on the appearance of a quest. This emblematic scene suggests his purposive vision: "I can only explain it by some deep archetypal image in our minds of which we become conscious only at the rare moments when we realize that our own life is a journey" (p. 217). Stephen Spender, in his autobiography *World Within World,* says about his meetings with Muir: "On each occasion I was struck by the integrity of purpose in his work and life, which make him seem a pilgrim from place to place rather than a wanderer like myself. Indeed he had the purpose which converted a line of shifting jobs into a spiritual pilgrimage" (p. 290). But Muir seems constantly adrift and fears he will fall short of his own expectations; the only hope comes with two incidents that leap over the accumulated futilities of his wandering years. The first is in 1939, when the sight of two children playing marbles recalls his own childhood and seems to promise "a timeless renewal of life" (p. 246). The other is in Rome, after the war, when he discovers what he takes to be a spontaneous sense of piety, a religion not cut off from human concern but made a part of people's ordinary lives. For Muir religion in Italy preserves a natural innocence he has always sought to recapture.

On the last page of the autobiography Muir declares that his development has been brought about by spiritual forces rather than by any conscious intent. "As I look back on the part of the mystery which is my own life, my own fable, what I am most aware of is that we receive more than we can ever give; we receive it from the past, on which we draw with every breath, but also—and this is a point of faith—from the Source of the mystery itself, by the means which religious people call Grace" (p. 281). But Muir's tone in the added sections is impersonal, even though impersonality is the condition he is protesting against. He quotes from his diary: "I can see men and women as really human only when I see them as immortal souls. Otherwise they are unnatural, self-evidently not what they are by their nature" (p. 246). The discussion of religion towards the conclusion of *An Autobiography* raises a question of autobiographical strategy. Is the ascent into faith sufficient to the complexity of the rest of the book? All along Muir struggles between Eden and the fallen world, joy and guilt, hope and fear. Even with the putative cure in London, the darker elements remain in some form, arising when the outside world collapses around him. At the end Muir tries to obliterate the previous doubts and uncertainties in a moment of revelation; yet in so doing he simplifies the character he has built. This leap of faith makes the rest of *An Autobiography* different from *The Story and the Fable,* both in tone and theme. The earlier book (which represents about two-thirds of the entire work) centers on the mind of the writer and the conflict between that side of him which would suppress awareness and that which would confront and deal with all that threatens the security of the self. The new section centers on society more than on self, and Muir is less concerned with his own psychological complexity.

One critic of autobiography has commented on some distinguishing features of the genre in a way as to suggest why we might feel diminished power in the section written since 1939:

> The "creative stamp," the distinguishing imaginative organization of experience, is in autobiography not supplied by intention, but by the felt relation to the life data themselves. The esthetic effect that gifted autobiographers instinctively if not always consciously seek would seem to be the poetry of remembered happenings, the intensity of the individual's strivings, the feel of life in its materiality.[9]

In the later part of the book Muir seems unable to dramatize the self as a figure of vital and central concern. The "life data" in **The Story and the Fable** are in the best sense "self-conscious"; the "felt relation" to them is expressed as a kind of dialogue—of Muir with himself, of Story with Fable. What we miss in the new part is the autobiographical self engaged with its own potentialities. When Muir moves out of isolation into the world, his voice too often becomes that of the historian, analyzing the external world but not the depths of the self. Muir is, as it were, "Story-ridden" at the end.

The book surrenders that persuasive structure which earlier saw *all* Muir's experience unified in the dialectic of innocence and Fall, and it covers over the darker elements to resolve everything too neatly. In **The Story and the Fable** Muir acknowledges his complications, and the autobiographical voice is never fixed—now pleading for understanding, now confessing his terrors, now poised in a mythic realm of his own creation, now sensing the fragility of such a conception. Life is viewed as essentially tragic, not because early happiness is blighted, but because the mind itself is unsettled and dislocated, made to confront itself and brought to desires which are often self-defeating. Muir is at his best when dealing with false starts, "conversions" that are evasions, "purifications" that cleanse nothing. But in the remainder of **An Autobiography** struggle and process are gone, autobiography no longer a mode of analysis but a record of achieved conviction. This is not to question the *authenticity* of the religious experience, only to say that what Irving Howe has called "the turnings and distensions of sensibility"[10] are ceased, as Muir's triumph forecloses further introspection. Even so reverent an autobiographer as St. Augustine cannot abandon his doubts and fears of backsliding, for in *The Confessions* he postulates a divided will that must always be reckoned with. Though he subordinates the frail human self to divine Providence, Augustine is always curious about the unpredictability of his own mind. As he says, "I have become a problem [or question] to myself."[11]

Muir momentarily recognizes there is loss in his gain:

> One of the disconcerting accidents of a writer's life is that if he reads again what he wrote, say thirty years before . . . he may appear quite strange to himself. . . . I fancy we all have sometimes this sense of strangeness, or of estrangement, when we look back, perhaps at some moment in our childhood, or at a boy waiting for a girl he loved or thought he loved—both gone and almost forgotten, never in any case to be recovered—or at a young man loitering in a summer dream beside a river which flows now into a different sea. (p. 224)

Perhaps the estrangement is that between the hero of the first book and the hero of the second, a moving one because it points to Muir's own fear that the Fable cannot be sustained, that the "dry legend which I had made up in collusion with mankind" will predominate in any life, and that the past is finally irrecoverable. Nevertheless, Muir's book does demonstrate how necessary it is for him both to reconstitute the past and to see his entire life as an extension and product of the contradictory nature of that past. And it movingly reveals that between this necessity and the burden of self-understanding lies the elemental task of all powerful autobiographical writing.

Finally, what can Muir's achievement tell us about autobiography as a reflective literary art? All autobiography is necessarily concerned with memory, and inevitably any autobiographer expresses some awareness of how his mind plays upon materials from the past. But Muir is more self-conscious of the workings and meaning of memory than perhaps any autobiographer since Augustine. In Book X of *The Confessions* Augustine's long meditation on memory stands as the head of autobiographical tradition by asserting that only through memory—our consciousness of consciousness across time—can we come to know ourselves; autobiography is the embodiment of memory, a re-collecting of what has been scattered: "Once [memories] have been dispersed, I have to collect them again, and this is the derivation of the word *cogitare,* which means *to think* or *to collect one's thoughts.* For in Latin the word *cogo,* meaning *I assemble* or *I collect,* is related to *cogito,* which means *I think. . . .* " What autobiographers think about is the process of becoming, and in the re-collection, re-creation and re-enactment of the past the writer discovers how he has evolved in time. As Augustine says, "In the vast cloisters of my memory . . . I meet myself." Turning to memory is the autobiographical act which argues against a fixed self or Aristotelian *telos;* it announces that our image of ourselves across time is problematic, a function of how we remember, for the object of our past selfhood lodges in the presence of ourselves, now. Muir's work is a radical statement that the past is a function of our present, that memory is a design and not merely a fact. Like Augustine's book, **The Story and the Fable** can almost be regarded as meta-autobiography, a study of the redemptive autobiographical imagination and not merely of the perceived past.

NOTES

[1] References in the text are to Muir's *An Autobiography* (London, 1954). I wish to thank Howard Wolf for his sensitive criticisms of an earlier version of this essay.

[2] "Edwin Muir: An Appreciation," *Texas Quarterly,* 4 (1960), 234.

[3] *The Visionary Company* (New York, 1961), p. 3.

[4] The term and the definition are Leo Marx's, from his *The Machine in the Garden: Technology and the Pastoral Ideal in America* (New York, 1964).

[5] Hoffman, "Edwin Muir: The Story and the Fable," *Yale Review,* 55 (1966), 425.

[6] *Memories, Dreams, Reflections,* trans. Richard and Clara Winston (New York, 1963), pp. 3-4. For a detailed account of the autobiographical aspects of Jung's writings, see James Olney: *Metaphors of Self: The Meaning of Autobiography* (Princeton, 1972), pp. 89-150.

[7] *The Story and the Fable* (London, 1940), p. 235.

[8] Henri Bergson: *Creative Evolution,* trans. Arthur Mitchell (New York, 1939), pp. 6-7.

[9] Alfred Kazin: "Autobiography as Narrative," *Michigan Quarterly Review,* 3 (1964), 212.

[10] *Literary Modernism* (Greenwich, Conn., 1967), p. 32.

[11] Saint Augustine: *Confessions,* trans. R. S. Pine-Coffin (London, 1961), p. 223. The following passages are from pp. 218-19 and 215.

Michael J. Phillips (essay date 1978)

SOURCE: "Muir and the Critics," in *Edwin Muir: A Master of Modern Poetry,* Hackett Publishing Company, Inc., 1978, pp. 137-59.

[*In the following essay, Phillips surveys critical assessments of Muir's work.*]

The nature and appeal of Muir's work have been the most important factor in the rise of his reputation; but the warm reception offered by discerning critics in the late fifties and the sixties has been a factor as well. The fact that Muir's poetry was published in his later years by Faber (a firm with which one associates T. S. Eliot) must have helped his cause considerably. The first *Collected Poems: 1921-1952*[1] appeared in 1952 in Great Britain with the Faber imprint, and the confidence of critics and readers must have been enhanced by Eliot's preface to the 1965 *Collected Poems:*

> And as I have grown older, I have come to realise how rare this quality is. That utter honesty with oneself and with the world is no more common among men of letters than among men of other occupations. I stress this unmistakable integrity, because I came to recognise it in Edwin Muir's work as well as in the man himself.[2]

In further tribute:

> Edwin Muir will remain among the poets who have added glory to the English language.[3]

The publication in Great Britain in 1965 of the *Selected Poems,*[4] edited by T. S. Eliot, added further prestige to Muir's name. The paperback edition of the *Collected Poems,*[5] published in the early years of the quality-paperback boom, had helped Muir in America, and his appearance at Harvard in the 1955-1956 academic year, to deliver the Charles Eliot Norton Lectures, commanded further respect. In Britain, J. C. Hall's pioneering pamphlet in the Writers and Their Work series in 1956,[6] gave Muir an early push and enhanced the poet's reputation, as did full-scale articles in the United States by Fred Grice in 1955[7] and Charles Glicksburg in 1956.[8] His later reviews in *The Listener*[9] from 1932 to 1958, in *The Observer*[10] from 1924 to 1958, and in *The New Statesman*[11] from 1919 to 1959 kept him in the public eye in one sphere more than is the case with many poets. According to J. C. Hall, it was only after the publication of *The Labyrinth*[12] in 1952 that Muir was recognized as an important voice by more than a minority of critics in England.[13] The reappearance in 1954 of the respected and popular *The Story and the Fable*[14] (1940) in a new form, as *An Autobiography,*[15] must have helped a great deal to familiarize readers with the poet. And with the 1962 publication in the Evergreen Profile Series of P. H. Butter's well-written study,[16] analyzing Muir's work from the viewpoint of the New Criticism, Muir received the book-length consideration he deserved. In the sixties, in full-scale articles by the poets Kathleen Raine,[17] Elizabeth Jennings,[18] and Thomas Merton,[19] three of the most important poets younger than Muir wrote about him in a single decade.

It is appropriate to speak of Thomas Merton, a poet associated with the monastic habit; before his death in 1968, he provided us with several acute insights into Muir's modes of thought and their manifestations in poetry. Merton's "The True Legendary Sound: The Poetry and Criticism of Edwin Muir" was published in the *Sewanee Review* in 1967. The monk established his continuity with what is becoming the principal thread in Muir scholarship: the fact that Muir looked at both intellectual and empirical reality in such a fresh and poetically compatible way that he cannot be ignored by anyone taking modern poetry, or life itself, seriously. As Merton sees it,

> Muir is, one of those who intuitively realize that the giving of names is a primordial metaphysical act of the human intelligence—the Edenic office of the poet who follows Adam and reverifies the names given to creatures by his first father.[20]

Merton hints at a postexistential opening for a poet like Muir who looks at things so freshly and uniquely—the poet steps into some of the "philosophical gaps" created by the great doctrines of Sartre.

The poetry of Edwin Muir gives evidence of profound metaphysical concern: concern for the roots of being, for being in act, manifested by numinous and symbolic qualities. He does not seek these roots out of curiosity, nor does he find them in speculative and dialectical discussion.[21]

He is, rather, one who reaches toward

> the intimate, that is ontological, sources of life which cannot be clearly apprehended in themselves by any concept, but which, once intuited, can be made accessible to all in symbolic and imaginative celebration.[22]

And

> Muir's metaphysical insight into the numinous and sacred which does not underlie but actually *is* the ordinary reality of our world, was not an other-worldly mysticism.[23]

Not only has the poet named some important things and provided glimpses of the sacred, but the very nature of what he has named is central.

> As a poet he struggled to get the archetypes under control by means of the most obvious and familiar forms. He wanted to get the big symbols out and make them clear.[24]

Thus Merton sees the poet's imagination as acting to produce a sense of unity between what is outside one's self and what is within, and at the same time coming to terms with the present and the past.

> In the poetic imagination the heroes of Homer and the Biblical patriarchs not only manifest themselves and make themselves comprehensible to the poet and reader, but they "coexist" with him.[25]

And a higher moral purpose is involved:

> Muir is concerned with imagination not only in order that there may be good poetry, but in order that man himself may survive.[26]

Also, according to Merton, Muir's poetry expressed something that could not have been said any other way—and it is precisely this uniqueness that explains the relevance of the Scotsman.

Elizabeth Jennings is close to Thomas Merton in her Christian interpretation of Muir, and her intelligent examination of the poetry is particularly welcome since she has emerged as one of the leading female poets of her own generation. She is comparable to Merton in her concern and appreciation of Muir's metaphysics, but her tone is that of a Christian layman, as distinct from a monastic.

> Muir was a visionary poet whose poems were both the source and the fulfilment of his vision; they did not crystallize a past experience but embodied it even while it was being experienced. There

was no question of feverishly seeking for appropriate imagery. The poetic, but also the visionary, experience came to him *in terms of* imagery. This is true of every poet but it needs to be remembered in any examination of the work of a visionary or mystical poet; for we tend to think that mystical poetry differs from other poetry in that the poet first experiences and afterwards searches for suitable imagery. This is not so at all. The vision *is* the words and images and only through them can it transcend them.[27]

We can see here that "imagism" (if there was ever such a thing) is extended to a definition of a type of "religious poetry"—the concretion of the mystical experience at the very moment of its occurrence in poetry. The last sentence is perhaps the most significant, when it is read along with the first sentence; although what we have here may be too narrow a definition of what might be called "visionary poetry," Jennings's description provides a successful and skillful working tool and is a real insight into the essential "isness" of the poems.

Jennings goes on to see Muir as close to the life of nature:

> The simple, primitive life of the soil, the immediacy of the changing seasons, the closeness of animal life, made a profound impression on him.[28]

One feels that she is struck by the quality of the abstraction (the "vision") in Muir's imagery, as well as by the concreteness; it is not merely nature's presence in the subject matter, but also the fact that the theme is involved with qualitative generalization as well as qualitative specificity, that is important. We can see that our "visionary poet," in his choice of subjects and in the outlining of the metaphysical wheels and the earth itself, is thereby touching the perennial universals—such as time—that nature offers. But more than this (more than just time),

> Muir saw the life of mankind as an endless journey through time, a journey continually repeating itself, continually reaching again the same stages.[29]

Thus the poetry of Muir is seen as close to the recurring facts of each man's or woman's life span in history—and in this journey through history in time the ontological coldness and loneliness can be conquered:

> Time is cold, pitiless—but it can be defeated; it can be defeated by being confronted with events outside time—by the Incarnation, the Passion and the Crucifixion of Christ.[30]

One can escape from the hard logic of time (as Jennings sees it) through the choice of Christian themes. By dealing with the language of Christ, by providing the necessary data, by defeating time throughout the body of the works, Muir thus "took the dogmas of Christianity and gave them a new and dramatic life."[31]

Change, rebirth, decay, changelessness, place, original sin in connection with the myth of Christ, childhood, the abuse of power, the duality of flesh and spirit, love, and death all take their place in Muir's tapestry of poetic language, according to Jennings. She almost says that our ability to accept the archetypes may not necessarily work through the myth of Christ, but rather may occur in a process where the individual becomes conscious of the stillness and flux of poetic forms and archetypes—the sacred language of poets like Muir. And to go beyond conceptions of Christ and universals, she sees in the poetry a condition where

> all is a movement yet all is also a stillness since repetition, renewal and regeneration are signs of permanence.[32]

In connection with these ideas, Jennings sees Muir's contribution to the English language as less spectacular, but perhaps as significant, as that of Pound or Eliot—and she may feel that the nature of Muir's expression is more important than any other.

> Muir's achievement is to have examined and appropriated that drama in intensely meditative but never merely abstract terms. The body of his work shows how a vision can often be most powerful when simplicity is at the centre of it—that simplicity which, as Eliot has said, costs 'not less than everything.'[33]

It is not really too far from here to regarding Muir as a mythmaker.

Kathleen Raine, in an attentive and inspired "Appreciation" of Edwin Muir, seems less concerned with establishing the monastic or mystical significance of Muir, as Merton did, or Muir's relation to the fundamentals of lay Christianity, as Jennings was to do; rather, she saw Muir as being more oriented toward expressing the harder-to-see side of a dual reality. She sees the body of his poetry as being important because it expresses a possible world behind the world we live in, a world of permanence as distinct from a changing world, a world of immortality as distinct from one of temporal existence. Her interpretation is not really very distant from that of Thomas Merton or of Elizabeth Jennings. Discussing Muir's essay **"Against Being Convinced"**[34] Raine takes up Muir's contention that philosophers cannot answer the question "What is life?"

> Though he [Muir] does not say so, he implies, I think, that to answer this question belongs to the poet; the poem communicates life, essence, which is indefinable; for the opposite of the philosopher, he says, would be "a thinker of an incredible simplicity, a spontaneity which would appear to be a piece of nature's carelessness."[35]

Speaking of the ways that poems either are faded by time or glow with time, she sees Muir's poems in the latter category:

> Edwin Muir's poems belong, as it seems, to the second kind: time does not fade them, and it

becomes clear that their excellence owes nothing to the accidental circumstances of the moment at which the poet wrote, or we read, his poems; they survive, as it were, a change of background, and we begin to see that whereas the "new" movements of this or that decade lose their significance when the scene changes and retain only a historical interest, Edwin Muir, a poet who never followed fashion, has in fact given more permanent expression to his world than other poets who deliberately set out to be the mouthpieces of their generation.[36]

The poet is seen as related to great modern mythological ideas such as those contained in Jung's writings. According to Raine, Muir conceives the "story" as the life of the individual, whereas the "fable" is the pattern built up by the common, shared universal experience of the human race. It is Muir's brilliant expression of the phenomena of this experience that explains his importance in connection with some of his younger contemporaries.

> Certainly Spender and Day Lewis felt strongly about world events; and Auden equals, indeed surpasses, Muir in descriptive vividness; but in Muir alone do we find "those hard symbolic bones" that Yeats found in Dante and Blake—political poets also—that give form to events.[37]

Later, in the same vein, she sees Muir as discovering late

> what was known early to Dante and Milton, and discovered in the course of their poetic thought by Coleridge, Shelley, Blake, and Yeats, the great symbolic language of tradition."[38]

This juxtaposition of Muir with both modern poets and great poets of the past is convincing and helpful, and Raine closes her article by showing that

> at his best, Muir achieved a poetic language at once powerfully mythological, yet concrete; symbolic, yet poignant with a particular joy or anguish.[39]

John Holloway, in a finely reasoned essay,[40] has insisted that Muir should not be judged by superficial or fashionable standards. For Holloway, facile reference to irony, concreteness, metaphorical life, vernacular strength, or the "wit" of the thirties does not prepare the way for adequate recognition of a poet of Muir's status and uniqueness; indeed, such concepts may be terribly misleading.

> It is that in the end all these qualities are not the decisive signs of poetic achievement, but the subordinate and derivative ones. They are means to the major poet's ends, not the ends themselves.[41]

With this comment in mind, however, a reader of poetry might be led astray. Holloway says one might take "realism" too seriously, or, in contrast, one might go to the opposite extreme: to a sentimental, nonreferential excess of imagination. In both cases the result may be a fundamental hollowness and emptiness.

> But the writer and the poet is concerned not only
> with the plain facts of what happens, of life; he
> is concerned also with the forces it holds in
> reserve, with its potentialities, its hidden strength
> for all that is remarkable, all that is good, all
> that is evil. This is why the poet—the poet
> particularly—may go in his work so far beyond
> anything that one could call a description of life
> in the realist's sense, that one begins almost to
> think that the interest of his poem can lie wholly
> in the intrinsic strangeness and newness of the
> imaginary world it describes; that its thrilling
> fantasy carries no reference back to our ordinary
> world at all. That is an error.[42]

Discussing the poems **"Milton,"**[43] **"The Return,"**[44] and **"Telemachus Remembers"**[45] in terms of the quality, importance, relevance, and centrality of their themes (death, the nature of a possible life after death, love, fidelity, and allegiance), Holloway comes to the conclusion that

> the foundation of Muir's achievement as a poet
> is not a voguish manipulation of language, but
> the embodiment in verse of a deep and true
> apprehension of life.[46]

Thus Holloway establishes "a deep and true apprehension of life" as the principal criterion for judging the poems. It is the high seriousness of Muir's poetry that Holloway appears to admire particularly.

> We see craftsmanship as serving something greater
> than craftsmanship, serving in fact the new modes
> of vision of the poet which have led him to the
> new modes of being which he creates in his verse.[47]

Thus, central to Holloway's interpretation is the fact that the poet has created poetic landscapes of emotion and intellect that are the manifestation in verse of a serious and probing appreciation of human experience, as well as the fact that the poetry leads us to a fresh vision and therefore fresh experiences of reality.

Holloway goes on to assert Muir's high place among the political poets of the thirties—a role not heretofore emphasized. Poems like **"The Labyrinth,"**[48] **"The Good Town,"**[49] **"The Combat,"**[50] **"Adam's Dream,"**[51] **"The Last War,"**[52] and **"Troy"**[53] are seen to give Muir an elevated position, for in these poems it is not a matter of "models" (speaking of **"Troy"**)

> of close sensuous observation or intricate concrete
> realization in a subtly interplaying verbal texture.[54]

It is rather the case that Muir, in the social poems, has

> broken through all this, as if through a surface:
> and has confronted us, by what is a kind of skeletal
> presentation, with the essential quality of a deeply
> disturbing reality.[55]

Going somewhat further than this, Holloway sees Muir as not being in direct relationship with the French Impressionists and Symbolists. Instead, as a poet, he emerged from the horror, harshness, brutality, frankness and despair of German Expressionism—most significantly out of the labyrinthine nightmare world of Franz Kafka in *The Castle*[56] and *The Trial,*[57] which Muir translated (one might also mention Muir's translations of Lion Feuchtwanger, Shalom Asch, and Hermann Broch). According to Holloway, Muir observed, confronted, and reacted to the twentieth-century history and art of central Europe. As Arnold Toynbee might say, there were the real facts and those depicted—the preludes and the aftermaths: then there was an inevitable reaction, which is involved in Muir's poems. Or as Holloway puts it (in probably the best sentences ever written on Muir):

> The great central fact about Muir's work is that
> although in his vision of life the powers of evil were
> great, ultimately the powers of good and goodness
> were greater; and they were greater because they
> were also humbler, more primaeval, nearer to life
> in its archaic simplicity, which Muir was able to
> see not far below life's surface distractions. This,
> in the end, is the inner vision of joy which the
> iconic quality of his verse predominantly serves;
> and it is this sense of the simple but spacious
> powers of goodness held by life in reserve, that is
> ultimately what demands, and what justifies,
> Muir's simple but often monumental imagery; and
> his grave and lucid rhythms; and the honesty and
> spareness of his diction.[58]

Helen Gardner, seeing Muir as having evolved out of touch with the usual, ordinary educational experience (and thereby raising some questions about modern education), is struck by Muir's sweet temper and profound contact with the "nature of things and the destiny of mankind"[59] and by the high quality of his education of himself. We discover that he is one of the poets that she has "read and reread." For Gardner

> Muir's strength and distinction as a poet lie in his
> fidelity to his experience and in his conviction that
> that experience has a more than personal meaning.
> His poetry has an extreme purity of intention. It has
> no "palpable design on us." It states, or implies
> through images and symbols, convictions about the
> nature of things and the destiny of mankind. It is
> often content to state them simply, by rendering the
> image in its fullness. It gives us what he calls the
> "fable or myth of man" as glimpsed in the life-
> history of an individual of great intellectual integrity
> and rare spiritual sweetness and strength.[60]

To pick a particular example, Gardner sees an analogy between Muir's sensitivity to animals as documented in *An Autobiography* (and poems like **"The Combat"** and **"Horses"**[61]) and Wordsworth's own reaction to mountains. But in Muir's case one has

> an extraordinary power of rendering, without the
> intrusion of adult feeling and adult reflection, the
> clear, bright, unmoral world of childish vision.[62]

She sees him as being concerned in the poetry with two great legends or myths in combination: the myth of the fall of man or expulsion from paradise, and the myth of universal purification. For Gardner, the early traumas in Muir's life through death in the family, general deprivation, and his own hard experiences from the time at the farm through his teens and twenties made him conscious of the story of the Fall of Man. Then a kind of reaction to a vision of original evil set in in later life:

> Both visions—of a fall from innocence to experience, an expulsion from Paradise, and of a redemption into a world that was not the world of childhood, but the world of man remade and glorified—were insistent visions.[63]

The visions were rather spontaneous, too, as Muir did move in the course of his life from the farm to the city, and then to some of the particular centers of European civilization. In the later years the immediate environment around him was more sedate and more civilized. In a way, he enacted the movement and development of civilization from the rural to the urban.

Gardner sees Muir as maintaining a lifelong poetic relation to the concept of eternal recurrence—the idea, in the most particular sense, that life can be thought of as meaningless in that each "lifetime" involves the repetition of the same problems of life—and that one always recurs, always comes back to earth, back to time, and back to life without an escape from the process. Muir's poetry does not merely establish a context of meaning in relation to these ideas; it also deals with the problem unsentimentally. For instance, in **"The Stationary Journey,"** imagination, although it possesses redeeming grace, is only

> A dream! the astronomic years
>   Patrolled by stars and planets bring
> Time led in chains from post to post
>   Of the all-conquering Zodiac ring.[64]

Central to Muir's deliberations on human process is a consideration of both play and serious action in man's life (as in place poems like **"The Hill"**),[65] as well as a consideration of manifestations of wisdom, knowledge of both good and evil, innocence, and "profound knowledge" in relation to the time process (as is carried out in poems such as **"The Hill," "The Road"** ("The great road stretched"),[66] or **"The Mountains"**).[67] Gardner speaks then of Muir going beyond the mere naming, combining, and revivifying of some of our metaphysical categories and concerns. She sees him as dealing squarely with the realities of the dream process and then bringing these dreams to poetic life. In every case, this metaphysical and imaginative exploration is done with appropriate emotion and completeness:

> Wisdom, as distinct from knowledge, intellectual brilliance, or technical competence, is something we look for to poets, or should look for. He has great power to communicate, through the verbal recreation of visible and tangible experiences,

invisible truths. Of all the poets of our century, none has, with less pretention or with more gentleness, made us more truly aware of the pathos, the grandeur and the mystery of our common humanity.[68]

Gardner's essay, in short, is primarily valuable for its knowledgable generalizations and the clusters of small insights it provides. It is metaphysical and humanistic in its exploration of Muir's imagination, but its basic orientation is not particularly religious.

R. P. Blackmur's essay "Edwin Muir: Between the Tiger's Paws,"[69] published in 1959, remains the most individualistic, as well as the most striking and penetrating, critical work in the Muir canon. It is unique and highly imaginative, containing a proliferation of insights into the poetry; it serves as a reminder of how the best of the New Criticism helped the cause of serious poetry in this century. Striking out at what he feels is the growing professionalism of poetry, Blackmur sees in Muir simpler processes at work:

> The professional poet and his poetry should be seen as the collapsing chimaeras they mainly, and of necessity, are; then we could scratch where we itch. Then, too, we could enjoy for the hard and interesting things *they* are, the verses made by quite unprofessional poets like Edwin Muir out of honest and endless effort and the general materials of their language.[70]

To develop his growing vision of Muir, he suggests interesting comparisons and contrasts between Virgil and the man from Orkney. Both men existed at times of great empires, and in both men there was the existence of piety, or *pietas;* Blackmur sees this latter quality as springing out of the resolution of conflicts involved in the mutual cooperation that the existence of empire itself involved. But Muir achieves a kind of "harmony" in his habit of thought:

> This difficulty in achieving harmony indeed seems the characteristic difficulty of the human condition in our times, and it sometimes seems possible only to think it in verse.

> To say that this is what Muir has done, is another way of saying something about the attractive force of Muir's verse: he has made his harmony in the thought—not the numbers, the *thought*—of his verse: verse for him is the mode of his thoughtful piety, the mode of the mind's action where his piety is not only enacted for him but takes independent action on its own account and for us: when it does, it becomes poetry.[71]

Deliberating on Muir's comments in *An Autobiography* about his life in Rome, Blackmur sees that the poet is particularly struck by the rage, terror, and human conflicts that have vanished while the still worthy products of that civilization (the architectural structures, for example) linger on. Blackmur speaks of the ruins and artifacts as a kind of allegory—suggesting that Muir's own verse is the modern equivalent of Roman ruins:

The allegory which Rome provided for Muir out of the monuments and fountains of human ruins and aspirations, and which he records in his prose, is a kind of prefiguration of the allegory—the effort to make things speak further for themselves than our mere words can signify alone—which he completes in his verse. I should like to point out that these allegories are not—as so many of our allegories are nowadays—puzzles or evasions or deliberate ambiguities or veilings of purpose, and they do nor require interpretation according to anything but the sense of intimacy in experience approached or observed with piety in order to accept what is there.[72]

Muir's language is the common educated language:

I mean the allusions which are very nearly a part of the substance of our mind, so early were they bred in us by education and conversation: the allusions we can make without consciousness of their meanings, but which, when we do become conscious of their meanings, are like thunder and lightning and the letting go of breath.[73]

To illustrate the harmony and *pietas* as effects of Muir's poetry, Blackmur quotes from **"The Good Man in Hell"**:

One doubt of evil would bring down such a grace,
   Open such a gate, all Eden would enter in,
Hell be a place like any other place,
   And love and hate and life and death begin.[74]

For Blackmur

this looks backwards, through a little theology, into our most backward selves where we abort, but need not, human action in the hell of the wilfully wrong affirmation: it is that lethargy of sensation, or boredom of perception, which feels only the wrong good.[75]

In characters like Penelope, in **"The Return,"** we find evidence of "great tenderness" and "annunciation bringing incarnation." Such poems show us the writer, Muir, as "like all of us in those moments when we put meaning into our words."[76] The poems are, to Blackmur, "gestures of recognition" and examples of "thinking in verse." They make

an old script, an older and different alphabet, out of the general mystery and the common intuition, inescapably present, when looked at, in our regular vocabulary of word and myth and attitude.[77]

For further example, Blackmur reminds us that in **"The Ballad of Hector in Hades"**[78] Muir attacks the racial nightmares through giving us their therapeutic and reminding forms; in **"The Enchanted Knight"**[79] Muir recognizes and identifies a type of love in its perverse, narcissistic aspects; and in a more general sense, a poem like **"The Island"**[80] extends justified sympathy to a point:

And simple spells make unafraid
The haunted labyrinths of the heart,

And with our wild succession braid
The resurrection of the rose.

"The Annunciation ('Now in this iron reign')"[81] is seen to give an alternative to dramatic evil in love. Everywhere in the poem is "pietas," a power of generalization reminiscent of Emily Dickinson, and gesture that is morally and aesthetically appropriate to the specific occasion. Muir emerges from this essay as a poetic thinker on a par with Ezra Pound or T. S. Eliot, one who is engaged with the particulars of tradition in the most vital way. He has always an adequate vision, Blackmur points out, with respect to "pietas" and "harmony," qualities through which the moral, aesthetic, and religious foundations of his metaphor acquire an adequate stature.

A discussion in terms of the comprehensive and useful short critical study of Edwin Muir by P. H. Butter is most helpful at this point. Butter fills in facts about the poet's life, insofar as the life influenced the poetry. Born on a small farm in the Orkneys, the poet came to reflect in his poems "a sense of unity, of timelessness and of splendour."[82] These characteristics came from both the quality of the earlier family life, the natural identification of the child-poet with the country around him, and the freshness with which the child viewed reality.

The journey out of Eden began at the age of six with the onset of a consciousness of change, of death, and of guilt.[83]

The family proved to be unable to cope with the problems of farming, and, by the onset of his teen years, Muir was living in Glasgow, an experience that hastened the progression from innocence to experience; the harshness of the urban environment and the conclusive breakup of the family heightened the stresses of the period for the young man. An interest in socialism and a respect for the ideas of Nietzsche—as well as an urge to self-education—characterized Muir in his twenties.[84] Shortly after meeting his wife and marrying, he moved to London and became an assistant on the *New Age;* by this means of employment he launched his career as a journalist. These events, his marriage, and his undergoing of complete psychoanalysis were the key happenings in his early thirties. After the summer of 1921 Muir and his wife were in Central Europe (Prague, Dresden, and Hellerau), and by 1924 they had started their translating activities. Most of the next 35 years were spent in England and Scotland, with prolonged periods in the south of France, Czechoslovakia, Rome, and America. According to Butter, Muir's full childhood, his experience of industrial life, his contact with culture in the great cities, his cosmopolitanism, the years of teaching, and his marriage combined to give him a good, full, and adequate life for a poet.

Butter goes on to deal with Muir's prose and poetry—assuming, perhaps correctly, that the criticism and translation are subordinate.[85] However, Butter reminds us that

He was concerned with the imaginative truth of what a writer conveys, and with details of style only in so far as these are a writer's means of embodying his vision. As we have seen, he thought that criticism could be the starting point for "an inquiry into the human spirit."[86]

In the early poems, Butter comments,

> one feels the presence of strong and genuine emotions struggling for expression, but the words fail in precision.[87]

From the typically descriptive sketches in *First Poems,*[88] Muir moved to the complex *Chorus of the Newly Dead,*[89] and then to the more adequate and realized *Variations on a Time Theme.*[90] Butter sees the themes of the last work centered upon the ideas that, paradoxically, there exist in our sensibilities both a consciousness of mortality and a consciousness of immortality, that we are imprisoned in a for ordained length of time while alive, and that we still experience moments of freedom and timelessness. Adding *Journeys and Places*[91] to his list of Muir's less successful works, Butter concludes that it was really in and after *The Narrow Place*[92] in 1943 that Muir extended the range of the poet's powers by looking more to the outward, external world rather than to the imaginative, inner world. He concludes that

> If he had been able to do nothing but look back and till over and over again the small field of his childhood memories, his inspiration would surely, like Wordsworth's, have dried up. He was to show himself able to assimilate new experiences as well as to achieve clearer understanding of past ones, to look out at the world around him and to apprehend the patterns, revealed in myth, which underlie history.[93]

Keeping in mind what amounts to a kind of metaphysical set of assumptions, we can find in the 1943 book of poems

> an advance on what had gone before both in skill and in range. There is a greater mastery of a variety of metrical forms and of rhythmical effects.[94]

The result in future works (from 1943 on) is an illumination of the contemporary experience—an advance on those who know nothing but the fragmentary experience of the present. The earlier poems hinted at invisible, suggestive qualities; but in *The Narrow Place,* the poet has instead embodied the larger significance in appropriate language in the text of the poem itself.

For Butter *The Voyage and other Poems*[95] shows significant accomplishments. First and foremost, one finds a highly accomplished and skillful mastery of the poetic medium. As important as this is Muir's voice, which gives the impression that he is engaging in personal conversation with the reader. There is also an absence of sentimentality, as well as a kind of mature serenity. At this point Butter finds less resistance to reality, and

discovers the dominance of a concomitant growth in the attributes of acceptance and gratitude. We find in Muir the attestation of a new kind of knowledge growing to wisdom as a result of the poet's victories over experience. Examining **"The Transmutation,"**[96] **"Time Held in Time's Despite,"**[97] **"For Ann Scott-Moncrieff (1914-1943),"**[98] **"A Birthday,"**[99] **"All We,"**[100] and **"In Love for Long,"**[101] Butter finds evidence of a philosophic transformation that is not so much the finding of an escape from time, but rather "an escape from the conception of time as a closed circle."[102] The poet does not achieve salvation by dreaming and delineating another world in light of time being a kind of prison; rather he concentrates on developing a profounder vision of that world—as in the case of this group of poems, an exploration is achieved of how "transmutation" works itself out. The "transmutation" occurs in the case of the particular discussed—whether love, friendship, nature, marriage, artistic creation, or a possible deity. With this proliferation of effects, Butter tells us, Muir achieves a kind of wholeness or adequate comprehensibility that is unique and satisfying.

To move on to the poems of *The Labyrinth* is to find some of Muir's greatest achievements, and, according to Butter, his most consistently high level of accomplishment in the earlier collections. With the newly acquired wisdom that comes with the aging process, the poet was able to look backward most skillfully. Edwin Muir was always searching inward in the imagination and outward in the external environment for patterns; what he found he chose to illustrate by means of myth, dreams, history, and imaginative metaphor. Contrasting the poem **"The Labyrinth"** with **"The Transfiguration,"**[103] Butter finds the difference between the nightmare world of the former poem and the "transmutations" and "resurrections" of the latter significant for gaining a comprehension of the duality of Muir's vision—and therefore his continual lack of sentimentality. We sense in the former poem a profound awareness of evil; in the latter "verse artifact," the poet could make a very sharp poetic contrast between a vision of the gods and the threads of history. In another sense, this second poem speaks of these moments when life is entirely holy and significant to humans; this is in sharp contrast to the schizophrenia depicted in **"The Labyrinth."** For Butter, **"The Transfiguration"** is equivalent to the idea or ideal of a millennium. Yet Muir never erected a system of belief on the basis of his positive experiences; presumably, he was never that confident about reality. And finally, another poem, **"The Combat,"** reminds us of the sharp contrast between good and evil in the book if the work is taken as a whole. Butter finds that *The Labyrinth* is imbued with a "luminous simplicity," that "image and theme are more perfectly united," and that the "range and complexity of reference of the symbols is greater" than before.[104]

One Foot in Eden goes beyond particular themes into a scheme for history itself in the opening section. It is a matter of a more comprehensive vision of the whole of human history than he had attempted before.[105]

The idea of the "resurrection of Christ in the flesh" is seen as a key to the approaches to history in these poems exploring the history of the race, or the "fable." The Christ myth—particularly the motifs of incarnation and transmutation—serve as helpful assumptions for all the poems, in that they add the fabulous element and are seen to serve as a bridge between the real world (or, to put it another way, the eternal world) and the world of history. This is true also with respect to the references to Eden, which are likewise serving something different from ordinary reality, and are thereby relating to something closer to the moments of birth and of death than to real life, as we live it daily. Not only do we find this dualism with respect to the "real world" and the "world beyond worlds"; even within the "world," Muir gives us evidence both in history and in the present moment, according to Butter:

> The perpetually renewed beauty of nature is not presented simply as a symbol pointing to something beyond itself; in a sense it is Eden, existing now and always,[106]

For Butter, in some of the poems, we come to contemplate the image as eternally present (the *idea* "root," as distinct from just a particular root) and therefore absolute in its implications.

To put it another way, Butter says:

> In Christ the antinomy of flesh and spirit, time and eternity is resolved. The Word became flesh, Christ walked the earth as a person. The infinite value of each person and the rightness of expressing divine mysteries through images are among the implications of this.[107]

It should be remembered that Butter stresses the fact that in this book, as in the earlier ones, one finds in Muir a variety of types of poems as well as differentiated subject matter.

Turning to the conclusions derived from this semi-definitive examination of the poems, and speaking very generally, Butter finds joy—"the expression of a deep, abiding joy in things that endure"[108] as distinct from a superficial gaiety. He finds significance in the quality of the love poems, and worth in the poems that express his gratitude toward the past. For Butter, Eden is the time of childhood and old age—living in the world (or simply what is called "experience," comes in between these two periods. In Muir's poetry, according to Butter, there is "a greater sense of wholeness, of tensions having been resolved"[109] than in Yeats. He finds a "pondering on experiences which have been mastered,"[110] and, in light of this, the appropriate "slow and grave and unobtrusive rhythms."[111] As he sees it, the poems

> frequently develop a closely-knit argument; and the bringing-together of a number of thoughts and images into a single sentence helps to show their connexion.[112]

Means are subordinated to ends, and

> the lines glow when charged with strong thought and feeling, as they usually are.[113]

The writing is almost always "austere, competent and uninflated."[114] And finally, it is perhaps most relevant that Muir is able

> to make real some imagined landscape or incident from mythology or dream.[115]

Muir speaks

> with complete honesty out of his bewilderment as out of his faith, and though making something whole and well made in his song did not do violence to the mystery of life by claiming to be able to contain it in any neat formula.[116]

For Butter, in closing, "the nightmares characteristic of our century are all present in his poems."[117]

NOTES

[1] *Collected Poems: 1921-1952* (London: Faber, 1952).

[2] T. S. Eliot in Muir's *Collected Poems* (New York: Oxford University Press, 1965), p. 3.

[3] Ibid., p. 4.

[4] *Selected Poems* (London: Faber, 1965).

[5] *Collected Poems* (New York: Grove, 1957).

[6] J. C. Hall *Edwin Muir; Writers and Their Work* no. 71 (London: Longmans, 1956).

[7] Fred Grice, "The Poetry of Edwin Muir," *Essays in Criticism* 5 (1955), pp. 243-252.

[8] Charles Glicksburg, "Edwin Muir: Zarathustra in Scotch Dress," *Arizona Quarterly* 12 (1956), pp. 225-239.

[9] Listed in Mellown, *Bibliography of the Writings of Edwin Muir*, pp. 79-115.

[10] Ibid., pp. 69-116.

[11] Ibid., pp. 59-116.

[12] *The Labyrinth* (London: Faber, 1949).

[13] Hall, *Edwin Muir*, p. 7.

[14] *The Story and the Fable* (London: Harrap, 1940).

[15] *An Autobiography* (London: Methuen, 1968).

[16] Peter Butter, *Edwin Muir* (New York: Grove, 1962).

[17] Kathleen Raine, "Edwin Muir: An Appreciation," *Texas Quarterly* 4 (1961), pp, 233-245.

[18] Elizabeth Jennings, "Edwin Muir as Poet and Allegorist," *London Magazine* 17 (1960), pp. 43-56.

[19] Thomas Merton, "The True Legendary Sound: The Poetry and Criticism of Edwin Muir," *Sewanee Review,* 75 (1967), pp. 317-324.

[20] Ibid., p. 317.

[21] Ibid., pp. 317-318.

[22] Ibid., p. 318.

[23] Ibid., p. 320.

[24] Ibid., p. 321.

[25] Ibid., p. 322.

[26] Ibid., p. 323

[27] Jennings, "Edwin Muir as Poet and Allegorist," p. 43.

[28] Ibid.

[29] Ibid.

[30] Ibid., p. 44.

[31] Ibid.

[32] Ibid., p. 45.

[33] Ibid., p. 56.

[34] *Latitudes* (London: Melrose, 1924), pp. 230-239.

[35] Raine, "Edwin Muir: An Appreciation," p. 234.

[36] Ibid., p. 233.

[37] Ibid., p. 236.

[38] Ibid., p. 243.

[39] Ibid., p. 239.

[40] John Holloway, "The Poetry of Edwin Muir," *Hudson Review* 13(1960-1961), pp. 550-567.

[41] Ibid., p. 551.

[42] Ibid., p. 552.

[43] "Milton," p. 207.

[44] "The Return," pp. 166-167.

[45] "Telemachus Remembers," pp. 219-220.

[46] Holloway, "The Poetry of Edwin Muir," p. 557.

[47] Ibid., p. 559.

[48] "The Labyrinth," pp. 163-165.

[49] "The Good Town," pp. 183-186.

[50] "The Combat," pp. 179-180.

[51] "Adam's Dream," pp. 210-212.

[52] "The Last War," pp. 282-285.

[53] "Troy," p. 71.

[54] Holloway, "The Poetry of Edwin Muir," p. 562.

[55] Ibid.

[56] Franz Kafka, *The Castle* (London: Secker, 1965).

[57] Franz Kafka, *The Trial* (London: Secker, 1968).

[58] Holloway, "The Poetry of Edwin Muir," pp. 565-566.

[59] Helen Gardner, *Edwin Muir: The W. D. Thomas Memorial Lecture* (Cardiff: University of Wales, 1961), p. 11.

[60] Ibid., pp. 10-11.

[61] "Horses," pp. 19-20.

[62] Gardner, *Edwin Muir,* p. 14.

[63] Ibid., p. 10.

[64] "The Stationary Journey," pp. 57-59.

[65] "The Hill," pp. 60-61.

[66] "The Road" ("The great road stretched"), p. 223.

[67] "The Mountains," pp. 59-60.

[68] Gardner, *Edwin Muir,* p. 26.

[69] R. P. Blackmur, "Edwin Muir: Between the Tiger's Paws," *Kenyon Review* 21 (1959), pp. 419-436.

[70] Ibid., p. 419.

[71] Ibid., p. 421.

[72] Ibid., p. 423.

[73] Ibid.

[74] "The Good Man in Hell," p. 104.

[75] Blackmur, "Edwin Muir: Between the Tiger's Paws," p. 424.

[76] Ibid., p. 426.

[77] Ibid., p. 428.

[78] "Ballad of Hector in Hades," pp. 24-26.

[79] "The Enchanted Knight," p. 74.

[80] "The Island," pp. 248-249.

[81] "The Annunciation ('Now in this iron reign')," p. 117.

[82] Butter, *Edwin Muir,* p. 1.

[83] Ibid., p. 5.

[84] Early poems in the *New Age,* under Muir's pseudonym, Edward Moore, as early as 1913, suggest that Muir had begun writing publishable poetry in his late twenties.

[85] What should be kept in mind by the reader is that the exercise of criticism for Muir was the best means of keeping track of what was happening in literature. At the same time his views have often proved to be highly influential, as well as in most cases essentially correct. I believe there is no well-known modern poet who has left a more adequate record of a concern for the stream of modern imaginative literature, and Muir is unique in terms of the sheer quantity of his critical work centering upon modern developments in English literature.

[86] Butter, *Edwin Muir,* p. 36.

[87] Ibid., p. 51.

[88] *First Poems* (London: Hogarth, 1925).

[89] Muir, E., *Chorus of the Newly Dead* (London: Hogarth, 1926).

[90] *Variations on a Time Theme* (London: Dent, 1934).

[91] *Journeys and Places* (London: Dent, 1937)

[92] *The Narrow Place* (London: Faber, 1943).

[93] Butter, *Edwin Muir,* p. 65.

[94] Ibid., p. 67.

[95] *The Voyage and Other Poems* (London: Faber, 1946).

[96] "The Transmutation," pp. 154-155.

[97] "Time Held in Time's Despite," p. 155.

[98] "For Ann Scott-Moncrieff (1914-1943)," pp. 156-157.

[99] "A Birthday," pp. 157-158.

[100] "All We," p. 158.

[101] "In Love for Long," pp. 159-160.

[102] Butter, *Edwin Muir,* pp. 75-76.

[103] "The Transfiguration," pp. 198-200.

[104] Butter, *Edwin Muir,* p. 87.

[105] Ibid.

[106] Ibid., p. 89.

[107] Ibid., p. 91.

[108] Ibid., p. 102.

[109] Ibid., p. 105.

[110] Ibid., p. 106.

[111] Ibid.

[112] Ibid., p. 107.

[113] Ibid.

[114] Ibid., p. 108.

[115] Ibid., p. 110.

[116] Ibid., p. 116.

[117] Ibid.

P. H. Gaskill (essay date 1980)

SOURCE: "Hölderlin and the Poetry of Edwin Muir," in *Forum for Modern Language Studies,* Vol. XVI, No. 1, January, 1980, pp. 12-32.

[*In the following essay, Gaskill examines "the various ways in which Muir's knowledge of Friedrich Hölderlin's life and work manifests itself in his own poetry."*]

From the time of his first acquaintance with the work of the German poet, in Hellerau in 1922/3, until his death in 1959, Edwin Muir remained a great admirer of the poetry of Hölderlin. There were naturally other poets for whom he had a very high regard, including not a few who wrote in German. One is nevertheless justified in claiming that Hölderlin meant something special for Muir. His discovery of Hölderlin coincided with his first serious attempts to write poetry. Over the years that followed he devoted four substantial essays to Hölderlin, reviewed books on him, featured him as the protagonist in a major poem, and had him very much in mind in one of his last literary statements about the nature of poetry and the poet.[1] In so far as Muir was indebted to any individual poet, one would expect the influence of Hölderlin to be significant. Attempting to assess, with any degree of precision, the influence of one major poet upon another, is of course an extremely problematic undertaking, particularly so when they work in different languages, with all that implies here by way of cultural, geographical, and historical distance. It is not the primary concern of the essay to "prove" a dependent relationship between Muir and Hölderlin. Muir is a fine poet in his own right, and could and would have become one without knowing anything of Hölderlin. It would probably be foolhardy to look for immediate and decisive formative influences on the work of a man who begins to write poetry at the mature age of thirty-five, the time for naïve assimilation being long past, nor would one expect him to be consciously derivative. Accordingly, this is less an attempt to determine the role of Hölderlin in Muir's poetic development than an examination of the various ways in which Muir's knowledge of Hölderlin's life and work manifests itself in his own poetry.

The most obvious indication in Muir's verse of his interest in Hölderlin is the occurrence of the German poet's name in two poems written in the mid-1930s. In order of publication (and probably writing) the first of these is a little known poem, **"No more of this trapped gazing . . ."**, which appeared as one of **"Four Poems"** in March 1936 in the *London Mercury*. It was never subsequently republished.[2] One reason for Muir's apparently not wishing to include it in either edition of his collected poems, apart from general dissatisfaction with it, may well have been the numerous echoes of other of Muir's poems which the reader is likely to detect.[3] One of these is of particular interest in the context of this study. The poem as a whole reflects Muir's dominant concern with time and eternity, mortality and immortality. Together with another of the **"Four Poems"**, later entitled **"The Law"**, it presents a vision of the temporal world as a twisted, reverse image of eternity. In **"The Law"** we read:

> If I could know ingratitude's
> Bounds I should know gratitude;
> And disservice done
> Would show me the law of service;
> And the wanderer at last
> Learns his long error.
>
> If I could hold complete
> The reverse side of the pattern,
> The wrong side of Heaven,
> O then I should know in not knowing
> My truth in my error.
>
> (C.P., 107)[4]

The same paradox is expressed in **"No more of this trapped gazing . . ."**;

> If you could hold
> Complete in one great glance this reverse pattern
> (That's all you see) you'd be a god, although

> On the wrong side of Heaven.
>   Mad Hölderlin
> Praised God and Man, cut off from God and Man
> In a bright twisted world.

The mention of Hölderlin immediately calls to mind the final stanza of **"Hölderlin's Journey"**:

> So Hölderlin mused for thirty years
>   On a green hill by Tübingen,
> Dragging in pain a broken mind
>   And giving thanks to God and men.
>
> (C.P., 68)

Whether the similarity has any bearing on the interpretation of either poem is another matter, but in view of the argument between critics concerning the ending of **"Hölderlin's Journey"**, it should at least be noted. Common to both poems is Muir's preoccupation with Hölderlin's madness, something which is also evident in the two essays he devoted to Hölderlin during this period.[5] What it means here is by no means immediately clear. Twenty years later Muir called Hölderlin the "great modern representative figure" of poetic "divine madness", in the context of a discussion of his own **"The Poet"**.[6] It is possible that the madness of Hölderlin in these two poems might be in some sense related to Platonic "Heaven-sent perplexity". Yet at the same time the "bright twisted world" and the "dragging in pain" of a "broken mind" seem to point rather to Hölderlin's actual clinical insanity, with its degradation and anguish. It is true that the "praising" and "giving thanks", together perhaps with the punning "muse(d)", might suggest Hölderlin's poetry as the likely medium, but doubtful whether this could be seen here as a representative manifestation of the creative spirit. In **"No more of this trapped gazing . . ."** (which continues: "These sights are not for your deciphering"), it is the reader, and perhaps the poet himself, who throughout the poem is addressed as "you". Accordingly, when the mention of Hölderlin is immediately followed by a reference to another great German (and then to Caesar)—

> Beethoven lived
> In such a world as your one—

the implication would seem to be that this is a world from which Hölderlin has been permanently detached, "cut off". The context might suggest that his alienation comes about as a result of the attempt to grasp the reverse pattern in its entirety, the detachment being a necessary precondition of the "great glance", a kind of Archimedean point outside reality. If this were intended to suggest one means of escape from the "trapped gazing" of the first line—it is rather the most extreme form of indulging in it—it would be a drastic remedy, and not conducive to insight into ultimate mysteries. For bright and twisted as is Hölderlin's world, so too must be his vision. It is, after all, the knowledge of the "wrong side of Heaven"; and the usefulness of such knowledge (which is envisaged in **"The Law"**) is lost on Hölderlin, since, in gaining it, he has forfeited the foothold on reality which would enable him to relate the "reverse pattern" to a putative right side. He is cut off, both from God and Man. His praising is that of an idiot.[7]

In **"No more of this trapped gazing . . ."** Hölderlin's name occurs alongside those of Agamemnon, Odysseus, Nausicaa, Beethoven and Caesar. In **"Hölderlin's Journey"** he is the central figure, and in thirteen of the fifteen stanzas, all but the first and last, his is the first-person voice we hear. The poem itself appeared in the collection *Journeys and Places* (1937), and comes immediately after **"Tristram's Journey"**. Willa Muir has written of the general darkening background against which most of these poems came into being:

> None of the Journeys or the Places was a direct representation of raw personal experience. Feelings of bewilderment, of baffled loss, of mental trouble, of "conclusion without fulfilment", are transmuted by his imagination into other strange, remote forms. Tristram goes mad and recovers, Hölderlin goes mad and does not recover . . .[8]

This bewilderment, it should be noted, is of a different order from that later experienced by Muir's **"Poet"**. It is not the "bewilderment" in which the "tongue shall tell / What mind had never meant / Nor memory stored", the bewilderment in which "Love's parable / Into the world was sent / To stammer its word" (C.P., 286). It has in fact much more in common with the bewilderment which Muir earlier detected in much contemporary poetry:

> The response of the poet to this world is not pessimism, for pessimism is a reasonable and traditional thing; it is rather a bewilderment and distress of mind. The poet is not concerned because ideals do not correspond to realities (a great source of pessimistic poetry); he is hardly concerned with ideals at all. His bewilderment springs from something far more complex: the feeling that reality itself has broken down, that even the simple emotions, the instinctive reactions, are disorientated and lead us astray. This bewilderment has not the absoluteness of pessimism, but it is nevertheless more completely without consolations.[9]

It is as well, perhaps, to bear this passage in mind when we consider **"Hölderlin's Journey"**, particularly its enigmatic ending which has been taken by one critic as signifying a celebration of Hölderlin's final achievement, a serene acceptance and reconciliation of opposites.[10]

Any consideration of Muir's Hölderlin in this poem ought really to confront the question of how legitimate it is to refer outside the poem to the historical Hölderlin, at least as Muir saw him, in order to resolve difficulties of interpretation. In her sensitive examination of **"Hölderlin's Journey"** Elizabeth Huberman supports her "optimistic" interpretation of the poem's conclusion by pointing out that it was in his madness that Hölderlin produced some of his "greatest and most radiant poetry", this being his way of "giving thanks to God and men".[11] It is clear that the critic knows something, if not

very much, about Hölderlin's life and work, her main source being Muir himself. One critic who appears to know nothing at all about Hölderlin is Daniel Hoffman. Significantly, he sees the journey as ending in a "perfect epiphany for despair".[12] He also takes the Diotima of the poem to be the Diotima of Socrates, rather than Susette Gontard, Hölderlin's beloved. It obviously makes a difference to our understanding of the poem whether we assume the journey itself to be motivated by a frantic desire for reunion with the loved one, or rather a search for the mediator of Platonic possibilities. Hoffman's ignorance is presumably real, rather than assumed for the purposes of interpretation, but such an approach could be defended. In 1936 Muir wrote to Stephen Spender about **"Hölderlin's Journey"**:

> The poem is by no means perfect, and it is a purely imaginary and I am afraid personal description of Hölderlin's real journey, which has haunted me ever since I first read about it, why, I don't know enough about myself to say.

In a later letter he writes:

> I am glad you liked the Hölderlin, which was not, of course, in the least like Hölderlin: but that journey has always appealed to my imagination.[13]

"Purely imaginary", "not in the least like Hölderlin" (the person or the poetry?)—such expressions must make us cautious about bringing external knowledge to bear on an interpretation of the poem. Nevertheless, if we are to make sense of it, it is perhaps difficult to avoid doing this.

Muir's Hölderlin may be no more like the real Hölderlin than his Odysseus, Penelope, Tristram, Theseus, etc., are "like" the legendary figures on whom they are based. On the other hand, Hölderlin is no legend—he lived and wrote poetry, he loved a woman he called Diotima, and he did make a journey from Bordeaux which he apparently completed in a state of mental disturbance. Frantic and hazardous journeys, motivated by news or an intuition of the plight of the beloved, from whom the hero has been separated, are not uncommon in the Ballads which Muir so greatly admired. This might partly explain his attraction to the Hölderlin story, also his treatment of it here. But it is necessary to know who is meant by Diotima, as Hoffman's misunderstanding clearly shows. An acknowledgment of the relevance of some background knowledge to an understanding of the poem is provided by Muir himself in the form of an explanatory note with which he prefaces *Journeys and Places*:

> The references in one of the new poems may need some explanation, for Hölderlin is little known in this country except as the name of a German poet. The journey of which I try to give an imaginary account is one which he made in the summer of 1805. Hardly anything is known about it. He was at that time in Bordeaux as a tutor, having been driven from the house of the woman he loved in Germany by an angry husband. The woman was

Susette Gontard, the wife of a Frankfort business man: she is the Diotima of the poems. In the midsummer heat of 1805 Hölderlin set out on foot from Bordeaux. He arrived in Germany several weeks later, ragged, emaciated, and out of his mind. It is recorded that he passed through Arles. Susette was dead when he arrived. He partly recovered, and during that short period wrote some of his finest poetry; but he presently relapsed again, and for the last forty years of his life suffered from a form of insanity.[14]

Quite apart from its possible application to an interpretation of the poem, the note itself is of interest. One factual inaccuracy, Muir's mistake about the year (the journey was made in 1802), is of no significance, since Muir gets it right in an essay written not long before.[15] Other misrepresentations appear at first sight to be attributable to excessive reliance on antiquated sources. Hölderlin's actual journey has appealed to the imaginations of others besides Muir, and numerous stories of varying degrees of literary merit have been written about it.[16] The inspiration for most of these comes from Moritz Hartmann's *Eine Vermuthung* (1852) which purports, or pretends to purport, that the deranged poet wandered into the grounds of a château in Blois on the Loire on his way back from Bordeaux. The story, which is certainly fictional, was taken at face value by Hellingrath, who quotes most of it in his edition (which Muir knew), and is also made much of by E. M. Butler in her *Tyranny of Greece over Germany*.[17] Muir is likely to have known about this speculation, and since one might reasonably find stone deers' heads on pillars at the entrance to a château drive, it is tempting to suppose that Muir might be alluding to this story in his poem (stanzas 7-8). On the other hand, Hölderlin had told Schwab that he had visited Paris—this could only have been on the return journey, since it is known that he went to Bordeaux via Lyon—and Hartmann knew this, hence the location for his story mid-way between Bordeaux and the capital. Unless Muir, whose memory could play strange tricks with names, has somehow managed to turn Blois into Arles, the mention of Arles must remain a mystery. It is too persistent to be based on anything but what could be regarded by Muir as solid evidence. He keeps repeating that "it is recorded that" Hölderlin passed through there on his return, the earliest such reference being in 1923.[18] I have been unable to trace any possible source.

Disregarding details about the route taken, Muir's account of the journey here essentially agrees with that which was current in the second half of the nineteenth century: Hölderlin, possibly having heard of Susette's illness, suddenly leaves Bordeaux, wanders across France, and arrives in Germany with his mind shattered by the news of her death. The account is based on the assumption that Hölderlin left Bordeaux at the beginning of June, and arrived home about a month later, Susette having died on 22 June. However, some fifty years before Muir wrote **"Hölderlin's Journey"** documentary evidence had been produced which established that Hölderlin left Bordeaux shortly after 10 May (having planned the journey beforehand), and that he passed the frontier at Strasbourg-Kehl on 7 June, two weeks before Susette's death (which followed an illness of only ten days).[19] It is virtually certain that he did not hear of her death until the beginning of July, when the news served to exacerbate an already agitated mental state. All the relevant evidence is fully incorporated into the notes to the Hellingrath edition. It was even known to David Gascoyne, whose knowledge and understanding of Hölderlin were much more superficial than Muir's.[20]

Let it be stressed that the above in no way constitutes a comment on the legitimacy of Muir's treatment of the journey in the poem, in which it seems to be suggested (stanza 13) that Diotima may even have been dead before Hölderlin left Bordeaux (although there are also nineteenth-century precedents for that assumption). The poem, after all, presents a purely imaginary description of the journey, by Muir's own admission. It does, however, seem probable that Muir himself accepts the account he gives in the explanatory note, and that he is not deliberately tampering with history in order to make for a more interesting subject for his poem. It is also reasonable to suppose that he intended the note to be helpful for the reader. He is, of course, selective in his choice of detail, notably by ignoring the time-span between Hölderlin's ejection from the Gontard household and his move to Bordeaux—in reality over three years, as Muir knew. Whereas in earlier accounts Muir has Hölderlin's insanity occurring in Bordeaux, and in a revised version not long preceding the poem can also give space to the conjecture that his madness was caused by sunstroke,[21] here he is at pains to establish in the reader's mind an association between the violent severing of the relationship, the exile in Bordeaux, the sudden flight back towards Germany, Diotima's death, and the onset of Hölderlin's madness. Telescoped in this way, the actual events, as Muir saw them, certainly have the makings of a fine tragic ballad. And it is tragic.

Wherever Hölderlin wrote his "most radiant poetry", it was not "on a green hill by Tübingen", as Muir knew very well. In his essays he is always careful to differentiate between the great poetry he took Hölderlin to have written after the death of Diotima and his first breakdown in 1802, and what he wrote after his final collapse in 1806, in which, as Muir writes, the "real demoralisation of Hölderlin's mind" becomes evident.[22] The note itself carefully points out that some of Hölderlin's finest poetry was written during a "short period" (not thirty or forty years) when he had partially recovered, and it can therefore in no sense be associated with the Tübingen "musing" of his insanity. If we are to invoke our knowledge of Hölderlin's poetry, it has to be said that the poems of his madness proper consist of simple, often touching little rhymed stanzas on nature and the seasons, with the odd moral platitude or personal reflection, and bearing no observable relation to the ambitious, highly complex hymns in free rhythms, such as "Patmos", the product of a mind stretched to breaking-point, but still intact. The last two lines of Muir's poem—

> Dragging in pain a broken mind
> And giving thanks to God and man

—can far better be applied to the poetry of Hölderlin's actual insanity, effectively evoking the strange contradiction between the idyllic nature of much of the verse and the distressed condition of the unfortunate poet who produced it. Moreover, nothing in the poem prepares the reader even remotely for any note of harmony or reconciliation at the end, and it is doubtful whether it would be found by anyone who knew nothing of Hölderlin apart from Muir's note. And even if one shares Muir's interest in the German poet, the final lines of **"Hölderlin's Journey"** are surely more likely to suggest tragedy and pathos: a man who had stood at the intellectual summit of his age, conversing with Schelling and Hegel as equals, producing monumental hymns which evoke for Muir himself "a sense of a vast whole, a universal dispensation which is the life of mankind from beginning to end",[23] is reduced to a pathetic shadow of himself, writing harmless incoherent little ditties in provincial, not to say clinical and mental isolation—the ironic association of the "green hill" here being surely that it is "far away".[24] These lines seem to echo the accounts of the insane Hölderlin, profuse in his utterances of gratitude to his mother, to Zimmer and his family, who looked after him, conferring on all and sundry the most elevated titles, protesting his orthodoxy at the sight of the pantheistic slogan above Waiblinger's desk, soothed by the natural world around him, but driven to frenetic jabbering by his own inability to follow through a line of thought:

> Das Angenehme dieser Welt hab ich genossen.
> Der Jugend Freuden sind wie lang! wie lang!
>   verflossen.
> April und Mai und Junius sind ferne.
> Ich bin nichts mehr, ich lebe nicht mehr gerne.

"We feel that when Hölderlin wrote these lines the world in which his imagination had lived was not only in ruins but vanished without a trace, leaving merely the carpenter's house in Tübingen and his daily round."[25]

The omission from the poem of any reference to the productive twilight period between 1802 and 1806 is not the least significant of the biographical liberties taken by Muir, but is certainly justified in terms of the inner logic of **"Hölderlin's Journey"** itself. When he begins his journey, Hölderlin is not mad, "but lost in mind". His search for Diotima takes him through an increasingly treacherous and menacing external world in which he vainly tries to solve "the mean riddle" of tallying appearance with reality (stanza 5). The revelation of Diotima's death is followed by the experience that reality itself has broken down:

> The hills and towers
> Stood otherwise than they should stand,
> And without fear the lawless roads
> Ran wrong through all the land.
>
> Upon the swarming towns of iron
> The bells hailed down their iron peals,

> Above the iron bells the swallows
> Glided on iron wheels.

> (stanzas 11-12)

He is left with a realization of the meaninglessness and futility of the journey itself:

> For now I know
> Diotima was dead

> 'Before I left the starting place;
>   Empty the course, the garland gone,
> And all that race as motionless
>   As these two heads of stone.'

> (stanzas 13-14)

If, at the beginning of the poem, Hölderlin is "lost in mind" because "time and space had fled away / With her he had to find", her death betokens its final collapse. Time and space, having fled with Diotima, have now died with her. They are frozen in the mad poet's final lines. Hölderlin's tenuous link with reality, sustained by the hope of reunion with Diotima, is severed beyond repair. He is left in a timeless limbo of chaos and separation, cut off from God and the world and himself. This is a conclusion without fulfilment, and without consolation.

This is not to deny that the poem does appear to contain paradoxes and fundamental ambiguities. The fourteenth stanza, quoted above, which for Hoffman suggests the "extinction of the Platonic possibility", is taken by Huberman to represent victory through enlightenment: "In recognizing the truth of Diotima's death, Hölderlin simultaneously recognizes the fixed pattern, the appropriately Platonic form, as it were, of his search for her."[26] The contradiction, or confusion, seems to be related to Muir's fascination with time, and the way this is interpreted by critics. Muir's thinking was certainly deeply influenced by Plato, and indeed St Augustine, so that it is tempting to look at the poetry in terms of neat dualisms and antinomies which may or may not be capable of resolution. The treatment of time in Muir's poems is often ambivalent, in the sense that the temporal world can be seen either positively or negatively in relation to the non-temporal, and that the non-temporal is by no means always to be equated with the eternal. As P. H. Butter has pointed out with regard to **"The Labyrinth"**, the maze from which the protagonist of that poem manages to escape is not simply representative of life trapped in time, since on the contrary it is in the labyrinth that a kind of timeless hell is experienced—

> For in the maze time had not been with me
> (C.P., 164)

—whereas in the vision of the "real world" towards the end of the poem all the changing events of life are contained, and time and eternity, men and gods, are seen to be in ultimate harmony.[27] It is when the possibility of such a unitive vision is absent, or appears to be denied, that reality assumes a menacing aspect. Life becomes entangled in the "maze, the wild-wood waste of falsehood, roads / That run and run and never reach an end" (C.P. 165). It is only in relation to eternity that time has meaning, and change and progression become possible. Seen immanently, as a closed world, the temporal is paradoxically transformed into something static, a nightmarish frozen waste of eternal recurrence and sad stationary journeys.[28] Hölderlin's final lines represent, not enlightenment, but regression, ultimate entrapment in the maze. This would be the fate of the protagonist of **"The Labyrinth"**, "But that my soul has birdwings to fly free" (C.P. 165). The wings of Hölderlin's soul have been broken and he is left dragging them in pain.[29]

There naturally remain many unanswered questions about **"Hölderlin's Journey"**. Most perplexing, perhaps, is the temporal progression within the poem itself. It appears at first to be linear and straightforward: Hölderlin leaves Bordeaux; there follows an account of the journey as seen by Hölderlin himself; by the end of the journey he has been overtaken by madness, and then come the thirty years of insanity in Tübingen. But by contriving to see the journey through Hölderlin's own eyes, Muir has turned the account into a recollection of the already mad poet. "*So* Hölderlin mused for thirty years . . .", which seems initially to mean "then", "after this experience", ought perhaps to suggest "thus", "in this way". The account of the journey would then actually constitute Hölderlin's Tübingen "musing". It would cease to be a real journey at all, but rather represent the illusory wandering of an autistic mind through a world of its own creation. The time sequence within the recollection itself also seems complex. It begins in what appears to be an ordered manner; in fact, for one from whom time and space have fled, Hölderlin provides a surprising degree of temporal and topographical detail—

> The morning bells rang over France
>   From tower to tower. At noon I came
> Into a maze of little hills . . .
>
>   (stanza 2)
>
> The evening brought a field, a wood . . .
>
>   (stanza 7)

The month-long journey is compressed into a single day. This has the effect both of conveying the urgency of the search which motivates the journey (for which there is no parallel in **"Tristram's Journey"**), and emphasizing the collapse of time which follows the "evening" revelation of Diotima's death. This revelation comes initially in the ninth stanza as a result of the encounter with the stone and living deer, the former seen as the latter's "pictured death". Hölderlin is held by this image and sees "All moving things so still and sad", adding:

> But till I came into the mountains
> I know I was not mad
>
>   (stanza 10)

The next two stanzas bring the chilling account of the "change", already quoted, with the hills and towers standing otherwise than they should stand, the lawless

roads, the swarming towns of iron . . . It seems at first that the experiences related in these stanzas refer to a continuation of the journey, following the realization of Diotima's death. However, the journey itself has lost its purpose, and in the thirteenth stanza we find that Hölderlin has not moved, but is still watching the deer. The terrifying transformation of reality is in fact projected backwards onto the things already seen and experienced during the preceding "day", the hills, the bells and the towers. That little "head-high" hills should now be seen as mountains is the first example of the dislocation of Hölderlin's perception. In this re-enactment of the onset of insanity the threefold repetition of "iron" in the twelfth stanza evokes both the extinction of life and soul, and the grating of Hölderlin's mental processes. His account ends in an image of absolute petrefaction. Whether the poem's final stanza, which has been called one of the most serious and moving in English poetry,[30] ought, poetically, to be able to redeem Hölderlin, is surely very much open to doubt.

. . . . .

When Muir told Spender that his Hölderlin was "not in the least like Hölderlin", he might have been referring, not simply to the fictive nature of his account of the journey, but also to the poetry itself which in no sense represents an approximation to Hölderlin's manner, either in sanity or madness. In an earlier letter to Spender, written in October 1935, Muir claimed to have read the prophetic poems of Hölderlin again and again for the last twelve years.[31] If any trace of that reading were to be shown in Muir's own verse, one would expect to find it above all in **"Hölderlin's Journey"**. In fact, both in form and imagery, this poem is as typical of Muir as any other written during this period. The maze of little head-high hills, with its associations of entrapment (stanzas 2 ff.),[32] the near-numinosity of the encountered beast (stanzas 7 ff.)[33], roads running wrong (stanza 11),[34] the stationary journey (stanza 14),[35] all are unmistakably characteristic of Muir, as indeed is the mainly octosyllabic four-line stanza, with its rhyme on the second and fourth lines. Some attempt has ben made by two critics to detect echoes from Hölderlin in the poem. J. C. Hammer, despite pointing to some striking similarities between the imagery of Hölderlin and Muir in other poems, is somewhat unconvincing here, concentrating on the poetry of Hölderlin's insanity with its occasional allusions to pain and mental suffering.[36] Elizabeth Huberman finds affinities with "Patmos", which is indeed the poem which seems to have made the deepest imprint on Muir's imagination. There may be a case for arguing a similarity between the little hills of **"Hölderlin's Journey"** and the "Gipfel der Zeit" of the opening stanza of "Patmos",[37] but this should not be pressed too far: in Muir's poem it is the sinister hills which obscure and conceal, whereas in Hölderlin's it is the abysses between the peaks which separate the "loved ones". If any one poem of Hölderlin's might have inspired **"Hölderlin's Journey"** to a significant degree, one would expect it to be "Menons Klagen um Diotima". There are indeed motifs common to both poems, though these must be to some extent naturally conditioned by the similarity of theme. One thinks particularly of the fruitless searching of the protagonist, lost in a maze of deceptive paths, and the effect which the loss of the beloved has on his perception of the external world.[38] A significant difference, however, is that Menon is able rationally to come to terms with the suffering occasioned by the loss of Diotima (the poem was written before Susette's death and Hölderlin's first breakdown). In the end Menon finds himself able to offer thanks—"So will ich, ihr Himmlischen! denn auch danken"—and confidently proclaims that his damaged wings are mended—"Die blutenden Fittige sind ja / Schon genesen".[39] The last lines of Muir's poem read like an ironic comment on the illusory nature of this recovery.

A passage which seems to have struck Muir is the extraordinary opening stanza of what is now known as the third version of "Mnemosyne":

> Reif sind, in Feuer getaucht, gekochet
> Die Frücht und auf der Erde geprüfet und ein
>   Gesez ist
> Daß alles hineingeht, Schlangen gleich,
> Prophetisch, träumend auf
> Den Hügeln des Himmels. Und vieles
> Wie auf den Schultern eine
> Last von Scheitern ist
> Zu behalten. Aber bös sind
> Die Pfade. Nemlich unrecht,
> Wie Rosse, gehn die gefangenen
> Element' und alten
> Geseze der Erd. Und immer
> Ins Ungebundene gehet eine Sehnsucht . . .
> (StA. II, 197, 1-13)

Possibly the fourth and fifth lines of this are echoed at the end of the fourth of the *Variations on a Time Theme:*

> The prophet dreams on the peak
> (C.P., 44)

One is more strongly reminded of a stanza in the last of Muir's *Collected Poems,* "I have been taught . . .". The poet is grateful that his feet are kept from straying to the deadly path—

> That leads into the sultry labyrinth
> Where all is bright and the flare
> Consumes and shrivels
> The moist fruit
> (C.P., 302)

Of even greater interest, however, is the question of a possible influence on the formulation "ran wrong" in **"Hölderlin's Journey"** (stanza 11), and also **"The Three Mirrors"** (C.P., 140). In his perceptive and stimulating essay on Muir's poetry W. N. Dodd observes how in lines such as—

> And without fear the lawless roads
>   Ran wrong through all the land

—Muir develops "tutta una sua dimensione espressiva, creando una specie di limbo esistenziale sospeso fra spazialità e moralità." One evident example is the expression "lawless roads". Words such as "narrow", "crooked", "straight", are traditionally ambivalent, capable of application either in a physical or a moral sense. "Lawless" belongs unambiguously to the moral sphere, and would not normally be applied to a road. Another example is the predicate, "ran wrong", which at the same time suggests a breakdown in the physical world—things *go* wrong, cease to function properly—and also, by means of "estrangement" of the common expression, emphasizes or recaptures the moral connotation of the adverb.[40] There is a strikingly similar strangeness about the expression "unrecht gehen" in Hölderlin's poem, which is also the effect of an unusual conjunction of verb and adverb. The sense seems to be that the imprisoned elements and old laws of the earth run away, break loose, bolt like horses (a variant has "durchgehen"), but the unfamiliar use of the adverb "unrecht" manages to convey the impression of disorderly, irregular, and misdirected movement, and also, by its negation of "Recht" (= law), an appropriate awareness of the anarchistic implications. Admittedly, here it is not explicitly the roads which run wrong, though they are lawless enough, as is evidenced by the epithet "bös" (= evil, malicious). That Hölderlin shares with Muir a predilection for odd, but precise combinations of moral and spatial associations (probably partly deriving in both poets from early immersion in biblical language), can be seen elsewhere in his work. A good example is to be found in "Lebenslauf":

> Herrscht im schiefesten Orkus
>   Nicht ein Grades, ein Recht noch auch?
> (StA. II, 22, 7 f.)

The relevance of Hölderlin to the geometry of Muir's imaginative world is apparent in his fascination with the image in "Patmos" of "God's quiet sign in the thundering sky and Christ standing beneath it His life long", which for Muir expresses the union of the two truths, a truth transcending time, and a truth immanent in time, permanence and alternation.[41] He associates it with his own image of timeless human life as the intersection and interpenetration of a stationary beam falling from heaven and the craving, aspiring dust rising for ever to meet it, in denial or submission, in ignorance or comprehension.[42] Muir has a natural, and perhaps traditional tendency to think of the eternal and the temporal, the ideal and the phenomenal, the Fable and the Story, in terms of the vertical and the horizontal. The intersection of the two is the point at which the connection between the Story and the Fable is realized. W. N. Dodd is able to show the subtle and consistent use to which a conventional religious perspective is put in Muir's poetic imagery. Even such innocuous and commonplace verbs as "stand" and "lie" acquire significance by reference to their respective planes, and all that these connote in Muir's poetry.[43] Given this system of spatial-moral correspondences, it is not surprising that a central myth of the Fable which is behind the Story of everyone's life can be depicted in a literal and physical manner (painfully so). In **"For Ann Scott-Moncrieff"** Muir writes of sinner and saint, and all who strive to make themselves whole, being—

> Smashed to bits by the Fall
>
> (C.P., 157)

Nothing in Hölderlin's work corresponds to Muir's fascination with the Fall, although of course a philosophically secularized version of the events of Genesis iii. permeates his thinking and that of many other German writers of the period. Nevertheless, it is not difficult to see why, of all Hölderlin's poems with the exception of "Patmos", it is "Hyperions Schiksaalslied" which made the deepest impression on Muir's own verse, its imagery passing most naturally and seamlessly into his. Dealing, as it does, with change and changelessness, the dual existence of gods and men, the irremediable division of life, the poem was bound to attract Muir's attention:

> "You wander up there in the light," he says in one of the most beautiful of his earlier lyrics, the "Schicksalslied," "on soft lawns, spiritual beings ["seelige Genien"] . . . Fateless, like the sleeping child, breathe the heavenly ones. Chastely nourished in separate ["bescheiden"!] buds, the spirit blooms in them for ever, and spiritual eyes gaze in still, eternal clarity." "But to us," he cries:

> But to us is given
> In no state to rest;   ["auf keiner Stätte"]
>   They vanish ["schwinden"], they fall,
>   The suffering mortals,
>   Blindlings from one
>   Hour to another,
>   Like water from cliff
>   To cliff flung downward,
>   Yearlong into the unknown below.[44]

The first part of this contrasting vision is responsible for one of the most obvious echoes from Hölderlin in all of Muir's poetry. In the sixth section of **"The Journey Back"** Muir writes:

> They walk high in their mountainland in light
> On winding roads by many a grassy mound
> And paths that wander for their own delight.
>
> There they like planets pace their tranquil round
> That has no end, whose end is everywhere,
> And tread as to a music underground,
>
> An ever-winding and unwinding air
> That moves their feet though they in silence go,
> For music's self itself has buried there,
>
> And all its tongues in silence overflow
> That movement only should be melody.
>
> (C.P., 174)

The lines left untranslated by Muir have not been forgotten:

> Glänzende Götterlüfte
>   Rühren euch leicht,
>   Wie die Finger der Künstlerin
>   Heilige Saiten[45]

It seems clear that Muir has made good and deliberate, and unquestionably legitimate use of Hölderlin's poem to express his own vision of "pure commingled being" (C.P., 285). For traces of the reverse side, as presented in the harrowing last stanza of the "Schiksaalslied", we have to turn to other poems, despite the deceptive first line of the seventh section—

> Yet in this journey back

—which, as Hammer notes, seems to recall "Doch uns ist gegeben . . .". The third of the *Variations on a Time Theme* (1934) begins—

> A child in Adam's field I dreamed away
> My one eternity and hourless day,
> Ere from my wrist Time's bird had learned to
>   fly . . .
>
> (C.P., 42)

—and ends—

> As he who snatches all at last will crave
> To be of all there is the quivering slave,
> *So I from base to base slipped headlong down*
> Till all that glory was my mountainous crown.
> Set free, or outlawed, now I walk the sand
> And search this rubble for the promised land.
>
> (C.P., 43)[46]

Other examples might include **"The Transmutation"**, which speaks of "we who fall / Through time's long ruin" (C.P., 154), and even **"Reading in War-time"** where armies fall like forests, "The iniquitous and the good / Head over heels hurled" (C.P., 148).[47] A delightful poem in Muir's last collection, devoid of at least mythological gravity, contemplates with compassion the ending of a late wasp which has fed on the poet's marmalade through the dying summer:

> And down you dive through nothing and through
>   despair
>
> (C.P., 253)

When Willa Muir writes of Muir's first acquaintance with Hölderlin, through the mediation of Iwar von Lücken, she observes: "To Edwin Hölderlin's gods sitting on their mountain tops became very dear."[48] This seems to allude to a possible influence on Muir's own **"The Mythical Journey"** and **"The Labyrinth"**, both of which have gods conversing with each other from summits or mountain-isles. The vision in **"The Labyrinth"** is particularly impressive in its attempt to "give an image of the life of the gods, to whom all that is confusion down here is clear and harmonious as seen eternally."[49] It is difficult not to think of Hölderlin when we read:

> But they, the gods, as large and bright as clouds,
> Conversed across the sounds in tranquil voices

High in the sky above the untroubled sea,
And their eternal dialogue was peace
Where all these things were woven, and this our life
Was as a chord deep in that dialogue,
An easy utterance of harmonious words,
Spontaneous syllables bodying forth a world.

(C.P., 165)

It is even more difficult to say exactly what one is reminded of. The imagery is closer to passages in *Hyperion* than to any of the poems, though Muir cannot be said with any certainty to have even read Hölderlin's novel.[50] As Muir clearly saw, Hölderlin went to great lengths to overcome the fundamental dualism posited in the "Schiksaalslied" (probably too far for Muir's liking), and the pursuit of a unitive vision such as the above is common to both poets. Its achievement can even be expressed in identical images—both write of the "marriage-feast", the "Brautfest", of heaven and earth, men and gods.[51] The main difference lies in Muir's abiding Platonism—the above is a momentary glimpse, not a permanent possession, and a transcendent perspective is maintained—and, related to this, in the approach to the gods themselves. It is perhaps also a matter of temperament. Pantheist though he may have been, Hölderlin retained to an unusual degree for his period a sense of religious awe. His gods, even if ultimately benevolent, threaten by their very presence. Their approach is often associated with danger, and the fear of the poet is that we shall be found wanting, meaning by that our incapacity to sustain exposure to the unmediated deity. The tranquillity of Muir's vision here has no parallel in the work of Hölderlin's maturity. Given the intensity and dynamism of his gods, one cannot imagine them even "sitting" (**"The Labyrinth"**) on their summits, let alone "reclining" (**"The Mythical Journey"**).

Despite these obvious differences it is understandable that, given Muir's major concerns, it should be Hölderlin's prophetic poetry, the so-called "vaterländische Gesänge" (rather than the longer odes and elegies), which most impressed him. He immediately recognized "Patmos" as the greatest of these, and few would argue with his taste. Its influence on his own poetry is, however, diffuse and difficult to isolate. Most of the echoes seem to come from the first stanza of the poem. For instance, the "light-built bridge", which casts a crescent shadow in **"The Days"** (C.P., 209), surely echoes lines 6 ff. of "Patmos" with the "leichtgebaute Brüken". More interesting, perhaps, is Muir's assimilation of lines 9-10:

Drum, da gehäuft sind rings
Die Gipfel der Zeit

If one disregards the implications of "Zeit", there is a striking reminiscence in **"A Trojan Slave"**:

. . . the *mountain-rings*
On every side. They are like toppling snow-
wreaths
Heaped on Troy's hearth

(C.P., 72; my italics)

Similarly in **"The Mountains"**, with something of the millennial "vastness" of "Patmos":

See on the harvest fields of time
The mountains *heaped* like sheaves

(C.P., 60; my italics)

The use of "heaped" in these examples has the same quality of strangeness in English as does Hölderlin's "gehäuft" in German, and this is no doubt intentional. In those poems in which it occurs, for instance in **"The Refugees"**—

A few years did not waste
The heaped up world

(C.P., 96)

—it invariably reflects the perspective of a fallen or alienated state of being. Disregarding Hölderlin's equivalent strangeness, one wonders whether Muir's particular kind of "Verfremdungseffekt" might not be commonly achieved by the literal translation of more conventional German imagery. Certainly, no study of Muir's poetic language could afford to leave his knowledge of German out of account.[52]

It seems likely that a later stanza of "Patmos" exercised some influence on **"Sappho"**. In the eighth Hölderlin refers to the voluntary self-eclipse of Christ, the abnegation of divine power:

Denn izt erlosch der Sonne Tag,
Der Königliche, und zerbrach
Den geradestralenden,
Den Zepter, göttlichleidend, von selbst,
Denn wiederkommen sollt' es
Zu rechter Zeit. Nicht wär es gut
Gewesen, später, und schroffabbrechend, untreu,
Der Menschen Werk . . .

(108-15)

Elements of this complex passage seem to go into the lines where Muir has Sappho driving her victim (herself) to the "penal rock"—

Angry, abrupt, broken-off edge of time

(C.P., 131)

"Schroff" in German has the sense of both "harsh" and "abrupt", and "schroffabbrechend" in Hölderlin's poem continues the image which begins with the "breaking" of the divine sceptre. Muir's image is considerably more emphatic and immediately meaningful, conveying, as it does, both the sudden ending of life through murderous intent and the actual manner of execution. Nevertheless, a similar procedure seems to be at work in both poems: virtually the same expression—"schroffabbrechend", "abrupt, broken-off"—is used figuratively in a conventional temporal sense, and at the same time the literal force of the verb is recovered by its association with something physical—a sceptre, or a jagged rock. This results in a by now familiar strangeness, for though one may easily break off a piece of rock, it is seldom done abruptly; and the abrupt breaking-off of an object which is itself the symbol for something else seems even more complicated.

Muir devoted much attention to one of the later, fragmentary versions of "Patmos", and a passage which held particular fascination for him was the following:

> Johannes. Christus. Diesen möcht'
> Ich singen, gleich dem Herkules, oder
> Der Insel, welche vestgehalten und gerettet,
>   erfrischend
> Die benachbarte mit kühlen Meereswassern aus
>   der Wüste
> Der Fluth, der weiten, Peleus. Das geht aber
> Nicht. Anders ists ein Schiksaal. Wundervoller.
> Reicher, zu singen. Unabsehlich
> Seit jenem die Fabel. Und jezt
> Möcht' ich die Fahrt der Edelleute nach
> Jerusalem, und das Leiden irrend in Canossa,
> Und den Heinrich singen. Dass aber
> Der Muth nicht selber mich aussezze. Begreiffen
>   müssen
> Diss wir zuvor. Wie Morgenluft sind nemlich die
>   Nahmen
> Seit Christus. Werden Träume. Fallen, wie
>   Irrtum
> Auf das Herz und tödtend, wenn nicht einer
>   Erwäget, was sie sind und begreift.
>
>   (StA. II, 181 f., 151-66)

In his essay on "Patmos" Muir writes that it is impossible in a translation to give any idea of the expressiveness of this passage, in which the images of time seem to crowd in so thickly on the poet that he can only mention them in passing.[53] He does, however, pay tribute to it in his own poem, **"Moses"**:

> We did not see and Moses did not see,
> The great disaster, exile, diaspora,
> The holy bread of the land crumbled and broken
> In Babylon, Caesarea, Alexandria
> As on a splendid dish, or gnawed as offal.
> Nor did we see, beyond, the ghetto rising,
> Toledo, Cracow, Vienna, Budapesth
>
>   (C.P., 130)

The similarity lies both in the vastness of the historical sweep and the paratactic listing of names. In **"Scotland 1941"** it is people, not places:

> Montrose, Mackail, Argyle, perverse and brave
>   (C.P., 98)

The paratactic breathlessness of Hölderlin's late style (immediately preceding his madness) can also be found in Muir. A good example, one of many possible, is given by Anne Marie Le Bon who quotes from **"Oedipus"**:

> Their will in them was anger, in me was terror
> Long since, but now is peace. For I am led
> By them in darkness; light is all about me;
> My way lies in the light; they know it; I
> Am theirs to guide and hold . . .
>
>   (C.P., 190)[54]

And yet it seems unwise to attempt to ascribe Muir's style in this and other poems to specific influences. K. L. Goodwin tells us that the staccato movement of such poems as **"Troy"** (C.P., 71), and the loose syntactical linkages, especially with the "Ands", derive from Ezra Pound.[55] This may well be true. Equally it emphasizes Hölderlin's modernity.

There is perhaps one stylistic consideration which is not out of place here. W. N. Dodd, without, as he admits, having read Muir's essays on Hölderlin, turns his attention to such lines as—

> Evil and good stand thick around
> In the fields of charity and sin
>
> . . . fells it like a tree
> With all its fruit, defeat or victory
>
> A beast so helpless and so brave
>
> Until the stony barrier break
> Grief and joy no more shall wake

—and comments on Muir's obvious predilection for the yoking together of opposites. He also notes the sometimes unusual use of conjunctions: "A prima vista l'abitudine quasi inveterata del poeta di legare le coppie antitetiche con 'and' o 'or', e solo eccezionalmente con 'but', 'though', 'yet', farebbe pensare che la sua intenzione fosse quella di creare paradossi." He concludes, however, that the manner in which the elements of these contradictory pairs are linked argues a fundamental equivalence, conferring on the pairs themselves a curious semantic neutrality. It emphasizes the essential polarity which is a permanent condition of this world, the world of the Story.[56] The observation is certainly relevant, and all the more striking for coming remarkably close to what Muir himself observed in Hölderlin:

> There are other statements which become strange because 'and' is used where one would expect 'but'; it is as if Hölderlin's imagination were so full that he had to use the uniting conjunction instead of the qualifying one:
>
> Near is the god
> And hard to grasp
>
>   ("Patmos", 1 f.)
>
> . . . what would appear a qualification or a contradiction in an ordinary statement is in Hölderlin's world the self-evident continuation of a simple assertion.[57]

There are differences, of course. Oxymoronic expressions, with or without a grammatical conjunction, in Hölderlin's poetry invariably betoken a condition of fulfilment (almost to excess), as Muir seems to recognize.[58] This is not always true of Muir, and it seems to depend very much on the perspective adopted in the individual poem whether the "and" suggests irresolvable contradiction, or reconciliation, meaningful conjunction *sub specie aeternitatis.*[59] Be that as it may, it is curious that Muir should make an observation about Hölderlin, which others can make about Muir himself. It is also unlikely that he was unaware of his own poetic practice. One of the best examples of Muir's using an "and" where the sense would apparently demand a "but" is provided by the following lines:

> Dragging in pain a broken mind
> *And* giving thanks to God and men.

(my italics)

Clearly, much more could be said on the subject of Muir and Hölderlin. One could, for instance, examine their respective attitudes to the classical world, their treatment of traditional myths in their poetry—both seem to turn more naturally to Greece and the Middle East of the Bible than to the mythologies of their homelands, despite the example of respected contemporaries (Klopstock, Yeats), and both are highly individualistic in their departures from the données of the myths they choose. These are, however, matters which ought properly to find their place in a more strictly comparative study. Even on the more disreputable level of "echo-hunting", more examples could have been offered. I have tried to restrict myself to those which might be seen as having some relevance to Muir's poetic practice. It is interesting that, as far as I am aware, there are none to be found in poems written before 1933. This seems to suggest that Muir's rapid critical assimilation of Hölderlin preceded poetic assimilation of him by some ten years. For evidence of immediate German influence on Muir's early poetry one would have to look to others, probably Hofmannsthal. Hölderlin's influence, when it comes, is significant and lasting. It is by no means restricted to the mid-1930s which is the time when Hölderlin actually becomes a subject of poems. The disquieting fact that, if the interpretation given here is correct, Hölderlin emerges from these poems as a lunatic, may well be attributable to the generally oppressive circumstances in which they were conceived. It does not vitiate the assertion that Hölderlin's significance for Muir's poetry was probably as great as that of any other single poet, foreign or British.

NOTES

[1] See P. H. Gaskill, "Edwin Muir as a critic of Hölderlin", *FMLS*, XIV (1978), 345-364; also Muir's letter to Janet Adam Smith, 26 September, 1956, in *Selected Letters of Edwin Muir* (edited by P. H. Butter, London, 1974), pp. 187 f., on the subject of "The Poet".

[2] The full text may be found in Robert B. Hollander, *A Textual and Bibliographical Study of the Poems of Edwin Muir* (dissertation, Columbia University, 1962), p. 119.

[3] For example, 'The Town Betrayed', 'The Law', 'Hölderlin's Journey', also the first version of 'The Place of Light and Darkness'.

[4] C.P. = *Edwin Muir: Collected Poems* (London, 1960).

[5] For the dating of these essays, which are essentially identical with those which subsequently appeared in *Essays on Literature and Society,* see 'Muir as a critic of Hölderlin', pp. 354 f.

[6] See note 1 for reference. It seems that, had Muir remodelled the poem as he intended, it might well have become another Hölderlin poem.

[7] Cf. The Idiot in *Chorus of the Newly Dead* (London, 1926), p. 5: "I laughed, I wept, / Felt stinging pain, / Over and over / But all was vain, / For bright and vacant / Was my brain." A similarly curious use of "bright" may be found in 'The Escape' (C.P. 128): "A land of bright delusion".

[8] *Belonging* (London, 1968), p. 198.

[9] *Transition* (New York, 1926), p. 186.

[10] Elizabeth Huberman, *The Poetry of Edwin Muir: The Field of Good and Ill* (New York, 1971), pp. 93 f.

[11] Huberman, p. 94.

[12] Daniel Hoffman, *Barbarous Knowledge: Myth in the Poetry of Yeats, Graves, and Muir* (London, 1967), p. 228.

[13] *Selected Letters,* pp. 92 f.

[14] *Journeys and Places* (London, 1937), p. vii.

[15] "Hölderlin's 'Patmos'", in *The European Quarterly,* I (4), (February, 1935), 241-255.

[16] See Adolf Beck, *Hölderlin: Sämtliche Werke,* Grosse Stuttgarter Ausgabe (= StA.), (Stuttgart, 1946-78), VII (2), pp. 202 ff.

[17] Butler (London, 1933), p. 203. Any claims raised on behalf of the authenticity of the Hartmann story are effectively demolished by Beck in "Moritz Hartmanns 'Vermuthung'", *Hölderlin-Jahrbuch* (1952), pp. 50-67.

[18] "A Note on Friedrich Hölderlin", in *Scottish Nation,* I (11 September 1923), 15.

[19] See C. C. T. Litzmann, *Archiv für Litteraturgeschichte,* 15 (1887), p. 67; also Beck, "Zu Hölderlins Rückkehr von Bordeaux", *Hölderlin-Jahrbuch* (1950), 72-97.

[20] Gascoyne, *Hölderlin's Madness* (London, 1938), p. 6.

[21] See "Friedrich Hölderlin", in *Adelphi* (May 1926), p. 800; "Hölderlin's 'Patmos'" (1935), p. 242. The sunstroke hypothesis was first propounded in earnest by the elder Litzmann, but seems to go back as far as Schelling—see StA. VII (3), 453.

[22] "Friedrich Hölderlin" (1938), *Essays on Literature and Society* (London, 1965), p. 90.

[23] "Hölderlin's 'Patmos'", *Essays on Literature and Society,* p. 94.

[24] Elizabeth Huberman makes much of the "green hill", perhaps overlooking the full cruelty of what happened on it. Interestingly, her "traditional hill of peace and holiness" (p. 93) becomes for Muir "a squat hill-top by Jerusalem" ("The Killing", C.P. 224).

[25] "Friedrich Hölderlin", p. 91.

[26] Hoffman, p. 228; Huberman, p. 93.

[27] P. H. Butter, *Edwin Muir: Man and Poet* (London, 1966), p. 217.

[28] Cf. "The Recurrence" (C.P. 102 ff.), "Variation II" (C.P. 40); also "The Road" (C.P. 61 f.).

[29] Both Huberman and J. C. Hammer, "Friedrich Hölderlin in England" (dissertation, Hamburg, 1966), p. 26, find in the penultimate line of the poem a suggestion of broken wings, and as Hammer remarks the image is actually applied to Hölderlin by Butler, p. 206. It is also conceivable that Muir had in mind Hölderlin's request for wings in the first stanza of "Patmos", a request which is answered in that poem, as the ensuing magnificent aerial journey clearly implies (something which is unlikely to be repeated by the mad poet at the end of "Hölderlin's Journey").

[30] Michael J. Phillips, "Edwin Muir: poet, critic, and translator" (dissertation, Indiana, 1972), p. 80.

[31] See Butter's note, *Selected Letters,* p. 85.

[32] Cf. C.P. 43 f., 63, 125, 140.

[33] The most striking parallels are to be found in Muir's prose—see *The Story and the Fable* (London, 1940), p. 22, for horses with eyes like "rock-crystal suns"; see also *Poor Tom* (London, 1932), p. 172, for Mansie's encounter with the horse and the simultaneous conviction that his brother will die (I am grateful to Mr Ritchie Robertson for drawing my attention to this passage).

[34] Cf. C.P. 140, 185, 213, also 165.

[35] Cf. C.P. 40, 57 ff.

[36] Hammer, p. 59.

[37] Huberman, p. 92.

[38] Cf. StA. II, 75 ff., lines 1-14, 57-70.

[39] Lines 109, 115 f. See also first version, StA II, 72, line 55.

[40] W. N. Dodd, "La grammatica della visione: Uno studio della poesia di Edwin Muir", in *Paragone Letteratura,* 280 (1973), 42 f.

[41] "Hölderlin's 'Patmos'", *Essays,* p. 102.

[42] See *The Story and the Fable,* p. 198.

[43] Dodd, p. 45; the clearly horizontal "dragging" of Hölderlin's mind ought to be relevant here.

[44] "A Note on Friedrich Hölderlin", in *The Freeman,* 7 (1 August 1923), 489. Together with two stanzas from "Patmos" in the same article, this represents Muir's earliest translation from Hölderlin, and the only one he published of the "Schiksaalslied'.

[45] These "echoes" in the "Variation" are also noted by Hammer, p. 48.

[46] "Blindlings", in line 20 of the "Schiksaalslied", which is perhaps quite deliberately given as "blindlings" (= blind persons) in Muir's translation, actually means "head-long". The italics are mine.

[47] Cf. Hammer, p. 50.

[48] *Belonging,* p. 75.

[49] Muir's comment in "Chapbook", BBC Radio, 3 September 1952, as quoted by Christopher Wiseman, "Edwin Muir's 'The Labyrinth'", *Studies in Scottish Literature* 10 (1972/3), p. 68.

[50] He mentions it twice in all his writings, saying no more than that it is a prose romance which tells the story of Hölderlin's love affair with Susette Gontard. If Muir read it, he would have been impressed by a passage in Diotima's "swansong": "Beständigkeit haben die Sterne gewählt, in stiller Lebensfülle wallen sie stets und kennen das Alter nicht. Wir stellen im Wechsel das Vollendete dar; in wandelnde Melodien theilen wir die grossen Akkorde der Freude. Wie Harfenspieler um die Thronen der Ältesten, leben wir, selbst göttlich, um die stillen Götter der Welt, mit dem flüchtigen Lebensliede mildern wir den seeligen Ernst des Sonnengotts und der andern" (StA. III, 148).

[51] "Der Rhein", StA. II, 147, line 180; "The Christmas" in *One Foot in Eden* (London, 1956), p. 38—admittedly, here it is Christ who accomplishes the miracle, and the poem's relative orthodoxy may be responsible for its being left out of the *Collected Poems.*

[52] Cf. for example the syntactic peculiarity of this line from "The Day" (C.P. 122): "The in eternity written and hidden way".

[53] "Hölderlin's 'Patmos'", *Essays,* pp. 98 f.

[54] Le Bon, "Edwin Muir" (dissertation, Paris, 1975), p. 254.

[55] Goodwin, *The Influence of Ezra Pound* (London, 1966), p. 211.

[56] Dodd, pp. 37 f.

[57] "Friedrich Hölderlin", *Essays,* pp. 88 f.

[58] Cf. the polar unities of the first stanza of "Hälfte des Lebens"; in the second stanza of the same poem absence of fulfilment is expressed through absence of contrast.

[59] Cf. the second and third stanzas of "The Three Mirrors" (C.P. 140 f.); also "One Foot in Eden" (C.P. 227).

Philip Dodd and M. Lapsley (essay date 1982)

SOURCE: "Is Man No More Than This? A Consideration of Edwin Muir's 'The Story and the Fable'," in *Studies in Scottish Literature,* Vol. XVII, 1982, pp. 13-22.

[*In the following essay, Dodd and Lapsley argue that the central concern of Muir's autobiography is neither self-reflection nor self-definition, but an inquiry into the definition of humanness.*]

In *The Story and the Fable* and in a letter written at the time of its composition, Edwin Muir poses a question which reveals the nature of his concern in the autobiography. His repeated question is neither the orthodox autobiographical 'Who am I?' nor the question John Ruskin asks himself in *Praeterita* when speaking of his desire for a vocation—"What should I be, or do?"[1] If the former indicates an anxiety about personal identity, and Ruskin's question involves a concern with self-definition in a social sense, Muir's question is of the very nature of man:

> . . . I am taking notes for something like a description of myself, done in general outline, not in detail, not as a story, but as an attempt to find out what a human being is in this extraordinary age which depersonalizes everything.
>
> (*Letters* 100)

> The problem that confronts an autobiographer even more urgently than other men is, How can he know himself? I am writing about myself in this book, yet I do not know what I am.
>
> (*SF* 55)

> But they [a man's actions] are not of much help to us when we set out to discover what we are, and there is a necessity in us, however blind and ineffectual, to discover what we are.
>
> (*SF* 57)

We propose to argue that in *The Story and the Fable* Muir apprehends and judges the available definitions of "what a human being is" through his evaluation of the social orders and the religious and secular faiths which enshrine those definitions.

In Muir's discussion of *King Lear* in the autobiography, and in its progeny, "**The Politics of *King Lear,*"** he discerns in Shakespeare's play two conceptions of society, conceptions which, his autobiography reveals, are of crucial importance to his understanding of contemporary life. Indeed such are the parallels which Muir sees between the world of *King Lear* and his own world that the very personal vocabulary of moral discrimination and evaluation which he employs in his judgement of the conceptions of society in Shakespeare's play also enables him to comprehend and place the social orders of his own experience. Muir argues that the "conflict in Lear is a conflict between the sacred tradition of human society, which is old, and nature [animal nature], which is always new, for it has no background" (*SF* 60). For him, the "communal tradition, filled with memory" of Lear is opposed to the "new conception of society" of Goneril, Regan and Cornwall who are "merely animals furnished with human faculties" (**PKL** 47, 40, *SF* 59): their "life in the moment . . . their want of continuity, their permanent empty newness, are sufficient in themselves to involve them with nature, for nature is always new and has no background" (**PKL** 43). Representatives of a "brand-new order," and here Muir is explicit about their contemporary relevance for him, they point to "*laissez-faire* and the struggle for existence and the survival of the fittest so dear to the Victorian economists" (**PKL** 36, 43). What "they have the power to do they claim the right to do"; for "having no memory, they have no responsibility" (**PKL** 38, 41). Both in *King Lear* and in his own life Muir perceives an opposition between an old communal order which recognises custom and memory, and an individualistic "brand-new order" which denies all relationships other than those of power.

In *The Story and the Fable* Muir records two antithetical social orders of his own experience: the "good order" of Wyre and the "chaos" of Glasgow (*SF* 72). Of Wyre he writes:

> The farmers did not know ambition and the petty torments of ambition; they did not realize what competition was . . . they helped one another with their work when help was required, following the old usage; they had a culture made up of legend, folk-song, and the poetry and prose of the Bible; they had customs which sanctioned their instinctive feelings for the earth; their life was an order, and a good order.
>
> (*SF* 71-2)

Muir stresses that the inhabitants of Wyre acknowledge their dependence not only on each other but on the animal world: as the life of animals "had to be taken and the guilt for it accepted, the way of taking it was important, and the ritual arose, in which were united the ideas of necessity and guilt, turning the killing into a mystery" (*SF* 53). Yet though the Wyre social order is a good one, a co-operative one, it is threatened by a new kind of society represented by the figure of the Muir's landlord. Our awareness of Muir's belief that the traditional is the "distinctively human" (***Trans*** 208), and that only nature is "new," would be sufficient to dictate our hostile judgment of the landlord with his castle, a "brand-new one like a polished black-and-white dice" (***SF*** 13); but his association with such newness is only one of several suggestions that he is, in terms of the assumptions of the Wyre community, a new kind of man. The animal world, whose relation with the human world is, for the Wyre community, a "sacred" one (***SF*** 53), is for the landlord merely the object of his sport (***SF*** 13-4), as are, in a different way, his fellow men. The master of his tenants' fortunes, as his identification with the "black-and-white dice" would suggest, he drives the Muir family "out of the farm by his exactions" (***SF*** 14). The landlord with his "dapper walk" foreshadows the "dapper," "new owner" of the firm in the "chaos" of Glasgow whose arbitrary sacking of his employees gives Muir his first concrete realisation of the "power of an employer" (***SF*** 13, 153): "I was beginning to see that my job was at the mercy of any chance" (***SF*** 151). Absolved from the "plague of custom" (***PKL*** 37), such figures as the landlord and the factory owner are of the "new" competitive order: what they "have the power to do they claim the right to do" (***PKL*** 38).

At the age of eight Muir moves from Wyre to Garth on the mainland of Orkney. With its "rich shopkeepers" and "clean, businesslike school" whose headmaster pulls Muir towards him "as he might have pulled a lever," Garth can be seen, within the moral scheme of the autobiography, as a "stepping-stone" on the way to commercial and industrial Glasgow (***SF*** 79, 80, 93). After five years on Pomona the Muir family finally leave Orkney and journey to Glasgow—a journey which Muir understands not merely as a geographical shift but also as an irrevocable temporal shift, into the twentieth century: from 1751 to 1901 (***SF*** 263). The principle of the "new society" (***SF*** 108, 109) of Glasgow and Fairport in which Muir and his family are plunged is competition not co-operation, and the dominant relationship is a financial one. Even salvation is seen in the light of a "good business proposition" (***SF*** 103). If on Wyre the relation of the human and animal worlds is a "personal relation" (***SF*** 53), at Fairport it shrinks to an economic one at the bone factory whose "repellently clean" head-office in Glasgow (***SF*** 153) remains a polite distance from the source of its profits: "the last relics of well-tended herds which had browsed and copulated in the rich fields of Scotland" (***SF*** 164). The ruling principle of this *laissez-faire* society, "looking after yourself" (***SF*** 109), is quickly grasped by Muir's older brothers as they are (and the language of social Darwinism is here explicit) at an age "when adaptation becomes conscious and deliberate" (***SF*** 109). But Muir's parents are too old to understand or adapt to this "new" order and are destroyed. ("**The Politics of *King Lear***" makes plain Muir's understanding of the relationship of the "new" order and the doctrine of the survival of the fittest.)

If Wyre is a "protective" and "fostering" order (***SF*** 263)—Muir is born, and note the curious preposition,

"into" Orkney (***SF*** 12)—all that the "chaos" of Glasgow and Fairport ensures is utter deprivation; Muir suffers homelessness, the deaths in his family, his own continual illnesses, his incessant wanderings from job to job, and his succession of lodgings. In the chapter on Wyre the word "gathered" can be used of both the human and natural worlds, thus suggesting their communion: on Sunday evenings Muir's father "gathered us together to read a chapter of the Bible," and at the onset of the long nights the "winter gathered us into one room as it gathered the cattle into the stable and the byre" (***SF*** 27, 32). All that can subsequently be "gathered" is associated with poison and dissolution: "the poisonous stuff" of Muir's adolescent state, as of his Glasgow years, "gathered" in him (***SF*** 102, 133); and decaying animal bones are "gathered by diligent hands" for the Fairport bone factory (***SF*** 164). Certainly then, the ways of life of Orkney and Glasgow seem to be antithetical. On Wyre beggars are known only in traditional songs (***SF*** 30), and if, in Garth, they are encountered, they are "always taken in and given food" (***SF*** 95). Only in Glasgow do the Muirs learn that "you must not take a beggar in and give him something to eat, but must slam the door at once in his face" (***SF*** 106). But if, on Wyre, a "new" conception of man as a competing animal appeared, in Glasgow an old conception of man as a co-operating being does linger on, in the figure of the slum doctor who successfully treats Muir for an ailment which other doctors, with whom Muir had spent "many a useless half-crown" (***SF*** 122), had failed to do. With the successful doctor who found "some excuse whenever I asked him how much I owed him" (***SF*** 122-3), Muir felt he was "intelligently collaborating" (***SF*** 123).

It is evident, then, that Wyre and Glasgow nourish two radically different conceptions of man: man as a co-operating being, and man as a competing animal preying on his fellows. But nevertheless Muir does not pretend that pre-industrial Wyre is available as a model for the men and women of industrial towns. At best the memory of Wyre serves for Muir in ***The Story and the Fable*** as a chief inspiration towards a humanly satisfactory society of the modern world. For the way of life of his first home possesses, in its rooted patterns of work with their corresponding ceremonies, "custom, tradition, and memory" (***SF*** 260), the necessary conditions of a co-operative life. It is within such an order—one never to return—that Muir spends, at the Bu, the first stage of his childhood, a period of his life when, to use his own terms, he lived "within immortality" (***SF*** 26). (Compare Wordsworth, "But trailing clouds of glory do we come / From God, who is our home.") The description of those early days is replete with acknowledgments that "human life is not fulfilled in our world, but reaches through all eternity" (***SF*** 203): Muir's first definite memory is of baptism (***SF*** 18); biblical exegesis is a common subject of argument in the Wyre home (***SF*** 64); and Sunday night signals the family prayers in which Edwin waits for the words: "'an house not made with hands, eternal in the heavens'" (***SF*** 27). The immemorial customs of Wyre and the adherence of its community to the rhythms of the seasons ensure that Wyre is a community "in which everybody possessed without thinking about it much the feeling for a permanence above the permanence of one human existence, and believed that the ceaseless flux of life passed against an unchangeable background. . . . They felt also that there was a relation between the brief story of man and that unchangeable order" (**DeN** 148-9). Muir's first home and the first stage of his childhood are both lost at the same time; and with the loss of these two inheritances, which had sanctioned his belief that life "reaches through all eternity," Muir has to evolve his subsequent faiths purely out of his own experience.

It is at Garth, a "stepping-stone" on the way to Glasgow, that Muir first locates his heaven not in an eternal future but in a temporal one, in an adulthood which as an adolescent he imitates and of which he speaks in religious terms: a "state which I longed to reach, in which I divined an unknown glory" (**SF** 83). He lives as an adolescent at Garth, as he will live in later life in Glasgow, not in the present but in a desired future: "I could not see things with my own eyes; instead I tried to see them as I thought my father and my mother and Sutherland saw them" (**SF** 77): to cite Wordsworth's "Ode" again, "As if his whole vocation / Were endless imitation." Nothing is done for its present sake, all for the adult life which is to come. But, if it is at Garth that we have our first indication that Muir's heaven might be precipitated "from the transcendental to the historical plane," to use the words of **Poor Tom** (Muir's earlier attempt to face some of the issues of the autobiography: **PT** 231), it is in Glasgow, after the deaths of so many of his family, that Muir's heaven is firmly located through his socialism in a temporal future. The journey of a "hundred and fifty years" from Orkney to Glasgow (**SF** 263) which Muir undertakes is, as he makes clear in **Poor Tom,** analogous to that temporal journey which takes place when a "man of our time . . . is converted from a Christian creed to one of the modern faiths" (**PT** 185), which for Muir are purely secular faiths. What meaning such modern faiths can give to the life of a man is, from one standpoint, the subject of the Glasgow and Fairport chapters.

In Glasgow Muir is very soon deprived both of his family and of his religious belief, and suffers, as we have already mentioned, continual bouts of illness, the loss of several jobs, and the lack of a stable home. He gradually comes to accept the creed of socialism which offers him the hope of re-release from his present painful experience, allowing him to "escape from the world I had known with such painful precision" into a "future in which everything, including myself, was transfigured" (**SF** 133). Muir's socialism is a deterministic creed which holds that "when the evolution reached a certain point a revolution would painlessly follow . . . as the logical consummation of the evolutionary process preceding it" (**SF** 132). His faith in the future, which his socialism nourishes, slowly hardens and shows itself to be inhuman as he comes to believe with Nietzsche that life is "guiltless and beyond good and evil," and that

"the future did not lie with mankind at all, but with the Superman": "I was not interested any longer in descriptions of suffering, for suffering had no place in the vision of mankind I still clung to, where all vice and weakness and deformity were transcended" (**SF** 58, 143). Both Muir's socialism and the curious mixture of socialism and Nietzscheanism (**SF** 150) which he later adopts set the moving principle of good outside man in the inevitable evolution of the universe towards a "heaven on earth" (**Letters** 112) and, in so doing, make of man a compliant passenger on that journey. The character of the journey is given concrete expression in the tramway of Glasgow with its inexorable, mechanical, simple forward movement, with its propulsion of its passenger, who is released from the burden of choice, in a determined direction and to a set destination.[2] The image of the tramway is crucial to the Glasgow and Fairport chapters: it is on a tram that Muir has his Nietzschean vision of animal man "moving towards an animal death as towards a great slaughter-house" (**SF** 59); on another tram, a glimpse of his future as a clerk (**SF** 151); and on another, his conversion to socialism (**SF** 131, see also **SF** 119, 120, 176).[3]

Muir does not deny his socialism a certain kind of redemptive power, and he describes it as a "pure, earthly vision" (**SF** 134): "My sense of human potentiality was so strong that even the lorry-men and the slum boys were transformed by it; I no longer saw them as they were, but as they would be when the society of which I dreamed was realized" (**SF** 133). It is a faith which engenders in him a "hygienic love" by which "the future had already purified in anticipation what it would some time purify in truth" (**SF** 134). His conversion to socialism is itself a cleansing of the "poisonous stuff" that had "gathered" in him during his early Glasgow years (**SF** 133). The exact nature of the purification that the vision of socialism can effect is described by Muir in **Poor Tom** (1932), in a vocabulary close to that of the autobiography, as a chemical purification:

> Like the visions of the saints, the Socialist vision is one of purification, and arises from man's need to rid himself of his uncleanness, the effluvia of his body and the dark thoughts of his mind. Yet the Socialist does not get rid of them in the fires of death, from which the soul issues cleansed and transfigured, but rather by a painless vaporisation of all that is urgent and painful in a future which is just as earthly as the present. . . . it is a chemical or bio-chemical purity, not a spiritual. It is what is left when man eliminates from himself all that is displeasing, unclean and painful.

> (**PT** 190-1)

What Muir achieves in exposition in **Poor Tom** finds realisation in **The Story and the Fable** in the Fairport bone factory which, in conjunction with the image of the tramway, allows Muir to gather up fully the implications inherent in his conception of the man of "modern faiths." The bone factory, whose "*clean* and indifferent chemistry" reduces to "*pure* dry dust," to "dry, *sterilized* residue," the unclean decaying bones (*SF* 164, 165), operates as an image of the way in which a "hygienic" socialism evades what in man is irremediably "displeasing, unclean and painful." One remembers that Muir describes his socialism as a "*pure,* earthly vision" engendering a "*hygienic* love," and speaks of the revolution being "painlessly achieved" (our emphases). He also notes that his reading of Nietzsche confirmed him in a "vision of mankind . . . where all vice and weakness and deformity were transcended." Muir is able to evade, with his gaze set firmly on a purified future ("I flung myself into it, lived in it" [*SF* 133]), what is "unclean" and sinful in himself and others until his "very painful" psychoanalysis in London (*SF* 187).

The psychoanalysis, which shakes him with "disgust and dread" of himself (*SF* 188), forces him to recognise that he shares with all men the same *impure* thoughts: "every one, like myself, was troubled by sensual desires and thoughts, by unacknowledged failures and frustrations causing self-hatred and hatred of others, by dead memories of shame and grief which had been *shovelled* underground long since because they could not be borne" (*SF* 188). (Compare the bones of Fairport which "were *shovelled* along with the maggots into the furnaces" [*SF* 155, our emphases].) The religious man confronts "these things" and, in so doing, wins "a certain liberation from them" (*SF* 188); the man of secular faiths merely attempts to avoid them. The importance of the psychoanalysis for Muir is twofold. First, he realizes that man is a creature of sin in need of expiation and not beyond good and evil; and second, he begins to apprehend, although in a simplified way, that human beings are understandable only as "immortal spirits" (*SF* 203):

> I realized that immortality is not an idea or a belief, but a state of being in which man keeps alive in himself his perception of that boundless union and freedom, which he can faintly apprehend in Time, though its consummation lies beyond Time. This realization that human life is not fulfilled in our world, but reaches through all eternity, would have been rejected by me some years before as an act of treachery to man's earthly hopes; but now, in a different way, it was a confirmation of them, for only a race of immortal spirits could create a world for immortal spirits to inhabit.

> (*SF* 202-3)

The experience of self-reflection in London is resumed and intensified a short time afterwards in Dresden, in a period of idleness and contemplation which Muir had not known since the age of fourteen:

> . . . when at last I looked back at that life . . . it seemed to me that I was not seeing my own life merely, but all human life. . . . In turning my head and looking *against* the direction in which Time was hurrying me I won a liberation and a new kind of experience.

> (*SF* 234-5)

Muir's italicisation of "against" explicitly announces the nature of his victory over the "ceaseless flux" of time, and his final liberation from those secular beliefs which imaged in the inexorable forward movement of the tram insist that man's life is determined.

With Dresden Muir effectively closes his account of his life, an account whose purpose, according to the author himself, was an attempt to find out "what a human being is in this extraordinary age." Certainly in *The Story and the Fable* Muir, as we have seen, has grasped and judged the conceptions of man enshrined in religious and secular faiths and in co-operative and competitive social orders. But, notwithstanding such an achievement, he ends his autobiography on a provisional note: "So here for the present I leave it" (*SF* 236). This should not surprise us when we remember that Muir, firm in his belief that man is an "immortal spirit" (*SF* 249) and a co-operating being, sees himself in 1940 adrift in a world which increasingly recognises no social relationships other than those of power. The diary chronicles the Spanish civil war, the Munich agreement, the persecution of the Jews, and the invasion of Czechoslovakia by Hitler's armies which Muir appropriately expresses through an animal metaphor: "We had no premonition then that history, in Oswald Spengler's words, 'would take them by the throat and do with them what must be done'" (*SF* 229). The problem of envisaging a modern social order capable of nourishing and sustaining, as did Wyre, man's co-operative nature evades resolution in *The Story and the Fable* and continues to obsess Muir in the revised *An Autobiography* (1954). But in *The Story and the Fable* Muir has at least laid bare the available past and present definitions of man and, in so doing, has clarified for himself his position and his choices in "this extraordinary age."

NOTES

[1] *The Works of John Ruskin,* ed. E. T. Cook and A. Wedderburn (London, 1903-12), XXXV, 312. Page references to the following editions of Edwin Muir's works will be inserted parenthetically in the text using the abbreviated titles indicated below: (*Trans*) *Transition* (London, 1926); (*PT*) *Poor Tom* (London, 1932); (*SF*) *The Story and the Fable* (London, 1940); (*Letters*) *Selected Letters of Edwin Muir,* ed. P. H. Butter (London, 1974). The following abbreviations are used for the essays collected in *Essays on Literature and Society* (London, 1949): (PKL) "The Politics of *King Lear*"; (DeN) "The Decline of the Novel."

[2] It is interesting to note that Muir translated Kafka's "On the Tram" which associates the surrender of the will with movement on a tram: "I have not even any defence to offer for standing on this platform, holding on to this strap, letting myself be carried along by this tram . . ." (Franz Kafka, *Wedding Preparations in the Country and Other Stories* [Harmondsworth, 1978], p. 98).

[3] In his description of creeds of temporal life which deny immortality Muir, in letters written around the time of

the composition of *The Story and the Fable,* uses phrases that suggest that the tramway does gather up concretely his sense of a purely temporal existence. He says of history that we "are moved about, caught, wedged, clamped in this machinery," and that if this was all he could believe in "he would hand back his ticket" (*Letters* 108, 112).

J. Brooks Bouson (essay date 1982)

SOURCE: "Poetry and the Unsayable: Edwin Muir's Conception of the Powers and Limitations of Poetic Speech," in *Studies in Scottish Literature,* Vol. XVII, 1982, pp. 23-38.

[*In the following essay, Bouson discusses Muir's attempts to elucidate through poetry such fundamental human experiences as the passage of time and the loss of innocence.*]

Often described as a visionary,[1] Edwin Muir wrote under necessity as he attempted to convey his inner world of memories, dreams, and visions. Having apprehended in isolated, timeless moments a transcendental framework underlying the structure of human experience, Muir was obsessed not only with time but with the felt tension between time and the timeless; and hence, he became a poet not only of the journey through time and place but also a poet who tried to convey the timeless vision apprehended at the core of human experience. Like all those who attempt to communicate the visionary experience, Muir was deeply aware of both the powers and limitations of language.

Aware of the "story that never can be told," the irreducibly simple and utterly unsayable story of silent immortality, Muir realized that the ultimate mysteries of life elude poetic speech. But he also realized that poetry, the speech grown from the darkness of the unconscious, offered him a way of knowing and a way of penetrating what he called the "fable" of life, the archetypal myth of Innocence and the Fall.[2] Although his visionary experiences occurred only in brief flares of illumination, poetic art, as a nexus of verbal energy and imaginative insight, empowered him to commemorate his momentary glimpses of that elusive world. In the timeless, ordered world of art, he momentarily was redeemed from time's disorder; in the self-enclosed, gemlike world of poetic contemplation, he uncovered a world that was boundless and unfathomably precious.

Art, Muir realized, has a deep power to give shape and intensity to experience. As the artist creates order out of chaos, so he creates a new structure of existence—a new time and place—in the midst of our everyday world. When we cross the threshold and enter the concentrated, magical realm of art, as Muir indicates in the sonnet **"The Emblem"** (230-1),[3] we pass beyond the horizons of our daily world:

> I who so carefully keep in such repair
> The six-inch king and the toy treasury,
> Prince, poet, realm shrivelled in time's black air,
> I am not, although I seem, an antiquary.
> For that scant-acre kingdom is not dead,
> Nor save in seeming shrunk. When at its gate,
> Which you pass daily, you incline your head,
> And enter (do not knock; it keeps no state)
>
> You will be with space and order magistral,
> And that contracted world so vast will grow
> That this will seem a little tangled field.
> For you will be in very truth with all
> In their due place and honour, row on row.
> For this I read the emblem on the shield.

Likening the toy to the emblem and drawing a further analogy between these and the poem—for "toys," as Muir states in an article, "are the first works of art in our experience" and help us to "recapture the feelings of the first artist and the first spectator"[4]—the speaker-poet discloses the child-like wonder he feels both as a creator and spectator of the artistic object. Although the artist may appear to be nothing more than an "antiquary" and his fashioned world of myths and symbols nothing more than a shrunken, insignificant toy kingdom, the world of the artistic imagination is a world of "space and order magistral." Although the world of the imagination may appear to be inaccessible and elusive, it is both approachable and penetrable for we pass the "gate" to its realm "daily." It is a world open to all men—all men may achieve that same vision. When we imaginatively perceive the "contracted world" of the artistic object or poem and succumb to its formalized magic, we enter a place so vast and ordered that our daily world of time appears, by comparison, both chaotic and trivial: it seems but a "little tangled field." Through art we triumph over time and chaos. And through art we uncover the dynamic coherence of life as we find ourselves "in very truth with all / In their due place and honour, row on row." The formal, ordered world of art opens wide the gate of vision and gives us a perspective of the wholeness and totality and unexpected magic of human life.

And art also, as Muir indicates in **"The Myth"** (144-5), can reveal the pattern and meaning of existence by linking the individual to the timeless world of innocence, a world known in childhood and subsequently lost. As Muir contemplates the span of his life in the quiet music of this poem, he uncovers what endures from his first world through the artistic imagination. Looking back, in the first stanza of the poem, to his childhood on the small island of Wyre, located in the Orkney Islands, he sees it as something fabulous, a "myth / Enacted in a distant isle" (1-2). Childhood, from the perspective of the sojourner in time, the wayfarer now "past the prime" (25) of his life, remains a potent icon before the eye of the imagination. For during that brief, unconscious moment of childhood, the poet exists in a sacred, self-enclosed world of primal blessedness, a world filled with the interpenetrating spiritual presence of the "faithful watchers" (12), the unearthly guardians of innocence. And in that brief but eternal moment, he exists in eternity: he exists in a world in which time remains suspended so that "immobility might save / Continually the dying song, / The flower, the falling wave" (6-8).

Although, as Muir indicates in the second stanza, that first world is lost during the "tragi-comedy" of youth (13), a vital link to that eternal world is retained. For the war fought during adolescence, a war of "dreams and shames" (14), is "Waged for a Pyrrhic victory / Of reveries and names" (15-6)—it is waged, at great cost, for the poetic imagination. For through the "name," i.e., poetic language, he can recover and hold intact his world of "reverie," those elusive memories, momentary visions, and fleeting dream images which link him to his timeless childhood world. While the reverie and the name are hurled against the ever-encroaching reality of "flesh and blood" (18), the poet, in his manhood, shapes an art that retains something of the radiance of his lost world:

> And there in practical clay compressed,
> The reverie played its useful part,
> Fashioning a diurnal mart
> Of radiant east and west.
>
> (21-4)

And it is the poetic imagination and that mysteriously present but elusive world of the spirit which survives "past the prime" (25) of manhood, Muir indicates in the final stanza. For when the designs of "flesh and bone" grow "halt and lame" (29-30)

> Unshakeable arise alone
> The reverie and the name.
> And at each border of the land,
> Like monuments a deluge leaves,
> Guarding the invisible sheaves
> The risen watchers stand.
>
> (31-6)

The poet, faithful to the world of the poetic imagination—the world of the reverie and the name—, remains in touch with the timeless world of childhood, the world of the unearthly "watchers." When the "deluge" of time's wave passes over him, he reaps a rich spiritual harvest as he apprehends the mysterious core of life, the self-enclosed world of sacredness and integral reality.

Not only committed to the intangible world of the reverie and the name, Muir is also committed to the deep and potent magic of the racial unconscious. He is a poet who has been "taught," he tells us in the last poem he wrote, "by dreams and fantasies" and by the "friendly and the darker phantoms" (302, 1-2) of the imagination. In **"The Song"** (257-9), Muir describes how a vivid dream vision, an unearthly visitation by one of the "darker phantoms" of the racial memory, kindles the poetic imagination, man's song-creating faculty. In the opening lines of the poem, the speaker describes the inception of the poetic process in the elusive world of

unconscious memories. Haunted by memories that knock at "a disused, deaf, dead door" (2) of the mind and yet remain unformed and remote—"They could not get to me nor I to them. / And yet they knocked" (4-5)—the speaker initially feels "oppressed" (7) because he is cut off from his unconscious world. Yet in dreams, he realizes, where one's consciousness of self as a being in time and place is suspended as one enters the world of the fable, "These meetings are renewed, dead dialogues / Utter their antique speech" (13-4). For in the world of dreams where "fables turn to beasts and beasts to fables," anything "can be in a natural wonder" (11-2).

And so it is in a dream that the speaker passes beyond the borders of his daily world as he opens himself up to the creative—and song-making—faculties of the unconscious and confronts the irreducible otherness of this hidden, magical realm. For when the speaker, in his dream, returns home from a "long day's work" (18) and crosses a park, a "Utilitarian strip of grass and trees— / A short-cut for poor clerks to unhallowed rooms" (22-3), he encounters an inexpressibly strange beast: "As heavy as earth it stood and mourned alone, / Horse, or centaur, or wide-winged Pegasus, / But far too strange for any fabulous name" (39-41). When the dreamer is brought within sight of the "great beast in anguish" (26)—a beast that mourns for the Fall of man, a "deed once done and done for ever / And done in vain" (28-9)—he is brought in sight of an inarticulate mystery. At once gentle and fearsome, submissive and forceful, the creature moves, its hoofs "treading out a meditation" (52) and then, breaking out in thunderous sound, the "wild thing" charges at the park gate but is unable to pass that "simple barrier" (53-4). When the creature with "hoofs, wings far overhead" (61), climbs the sky, the vision passes: "pain raised that wonder there; / Nothing but pain. The drumming died away" (62-3). As the world of the fable crystallizes only to dissolve again into the familiar world of everyday reality, the dreamer questions the source of his mysterious vision:

> Was it these hoofs, I thought, that knocked all
>   day
> With no articulate message, but this vision
> That had no tongue to speak its mystery?
> What wound in the world's side and we
>   unknowing
> Lay open and bleeding now? What present
>   anguish
> Drew that long dirge from the earth-haunting
>   marvel?
>
> (64-9)

Although the moment of vision passes with the ascension of the Pegasus-like creature—a creature symbolic both of the world of the fable and the magical realm of poetic insight[5]—the experience holds the speaker in its peculiar power. The speaker retains, upon awakening, a memory of the beast's "dirge":

> Yet I woke up saying, 'The song—the song'.
>
> (75)

The miracle of the "song"—something given to the speaker-poet—redeems him from the pain and suffering of his vision of the Fall. Now that the "disused, deaf, dead" door of the unconscious has been opened and the poetic imagination has been stimulated, the speaker-poet is ready to translate the inarticulate dream "song" into a poetic "song." Through the formalized cadence of poetic speech, he will attempt to convey his visionary experience.[6]

A poet inspired by dreams in which "fables turn to beasts and beasts to fables" and in which "dead dialogues / Utter their antique speech," Muir is also a poet who knows the "delicacy / Of bringing shape to birth" (**"All We,"** 158, 7-8), and the difficulty of sustaining the moment of poetic inspiration. He is a poet who must find the "right moment"[7] if he is to create verse that is "both simple and unexpected"[8] for the "poetic state, the state in which poetry is produced, is a state balanced more or less exactly between the conscious and the unconscious, between inspiration and formulation. . . . "[9] There is "no knowing," Muir explains as he describes how lines sometimes occurred spontaneously in his mind, "when such things will come, or where."[10] And when the "right moment"—a moment such as that described in **The Song**"—did come and Muir felt the premonitions of a poem, he needed solitude and silence to sustain the poetic state, as he indicates in the conversational tones of **"The Visitor"** (198), a rare public statement by Muir on the creation of verse. In the abrupt opening lines of the poem, the speaker-poet asks to be left in privacy so he can receive his "delicate," ghostlike muse who stands waiting at the threshold—the "door"—of consciousness:

> No, no, do not beguile me, do not come
> Between me and my ghost, that cannot move
> Till you are gone,
> And while you gossip must be dumb.
>
> (1-4)

Through the natural speech cadences of these lines, Muir creates an intensely personal poetry, poetry that has the ring of authenticity. The tone of this "half-uttered scarcely whispered plea" (11) is at once hushed (an effect created through the combined use of prolonged vowel and muted consonant sounds) and urgent (an effect produced through the use of repetitions, especially of negative assertions, such as *no . . . no/do not . . . do not*). We are made privy to the speaker-poet's increasing distress as the subdued tension of the first few lines of the poem gives way before the speaker's frustration, a frustration verbally betrayed through the use of hyperbole (to describe the "din" of a whispered plea) and irony (to describe the intruder's gossip as "great tidings"):

> But I would be alone
> Now, now and let him in,
> Lest while I speak he is already flown,
> Offended by the din
> Of this half-uttered scarcely whispered plea
> (So delicate is he).

> No more, no more.
> Let the great tidings stay unsaid.
>
> (7-14)

In the final lines of the poem, we find an open avowal of the speaker-poet's anxiety:

> For I must to the door,
> And oh I dread
> He may even now be gone
> Or, when I open, will not enter in.
>
> (15-8)

Distressed by the thought that his delicate, elusive muse has fled, he fears that he has squandered that precious moment given to him, the moment of poetic inspiration when the intangible worlds of the reverie and the name fuse together in the poet's consciousness.

A poet inspired by a ghostly muse and by those visionary glimpses into the world of the fable, Muir is also inspired by those moments in which he comes to a deep awareness of the absolute value of life. In the celebratory poem **"In Love for Long"** (159-60) Muir captures and makes formal the magic of an experience he had during the war years while sitting in the countryside and gazing at the scene around him. "Suddenly and without reason," he recalls, he felt a deep and abiding fondness for the hills, the cottages, the clouds, the soft, subdued light, and for the very ground he sat upon, and he realized that he loved these things "for themselves."[11] Seeking to give concrete form to his experience of an irreducible and irresistible love, a love grounded in the soil of this world, Muir attempts to grasp, in the verbal space of the poem, that mysterious force which grasped him, that force from which "there's no escape," and that force which challenges his powers of poetic expression:

> I've been in love for long
> With what I cannot tell
> And will contrive a song
> For the intangible
> That has no mould or shape,
> From which there's no escape.
>
> (1-6)

As he tries to penetrate the enigma of "what" it is he loves in these simple, trimeter lines with their mixture of simple and Latinate diction, the speaker-poet poses a riddle. Giving a series of clues to the identity of the mysterious thing he loves, he invites the reader to become involved in the process of discovery. Though what he loves is "not even a name," yet it is "all constancy" (7-8). It is simultaneously as fleeting and airy as a "breath" and as "still" and stable as "the established hill" (11-12). Whether "Tried or untried," it is "the same," and it is an essential part of his being for it "cannot part" from him (9-10). What he loves resides in paradox and contradiction for he loves the very stuff of "being" itself:

> It is not any thing,
> And yet all being is;

Being, being, being,
Its burden and its bliss.
How can I ever prove
What it is I love?

(13-8)

What he loves cannot be grasped through the reason nor can it be localized or confined by the intellect, and therefore, he cannot "prove" it. What he loves can only be grasped in a poetic song of simplicity and child-like intensity.

Though the "happy moment" of love passes—for time crushes it "beneath and above / Between to-days and morrows" (21-2)—the speaker-poet recovers, in its integral time-space unit, a world of innocence, joy, and fulfillment. His love is "A little paradise / Held in the world's vice" (23-4):

This love a moment known
For what I do not know
And in a moment gone
Is like the happy doe
That keeps its perfect laws
Between the tiger's paws
And vindicates its cause.

(31-7)

Though vulnerable and doomed by time, his "moment" of profound love, like the "happy doe" found in the tiger's grasp, "vindicates its cause" by the very fact of its existence. In the moment of love he discovers a dynamic world of perfected order and value. As the poet "contrives a song" to celebrate the freedom and joy which emerge within the boundless moment of love, he seeks to create verse of a higher order, verse which tells what he "cannot tell" and gives shape to the "intangible / That has no mould or shape."

Driven to create poetry by the ecstatic moment of love, Muir is also driven by the quieter moments of poetic contemplation and reflection, by those "transformations of reality which the imagination itself creates"[12] those transformations of reality which bring one towards the limits of language. "I have always had a particular feeling," Muir states in a letter, "for that transmutation of life" found "occasionally in poetry" and "sometimes in one's own thoughts when they are still."[13] In the sonnet **"The Transmutation"** (154-5), a poem which Muir liked "best" of all his sonnets,[14] he gives formal expression to his enigmatic experience of the imaginative transmutation of life. Employing an unresolved syntax in the first three and one-half lines to convey a feeling of wonder, the speaker-poet describes, in the lingering music of this poem, a moment of value redeemed from time:

That all should change to ghost and glance and
    gleam,
And so transmuted stand beyond all change,
And we be poised between the unmoving dream
And the sole moving moment—this is strange

Past all contrivance, word, or image, or sound,
Or silence, to express, that we who fall
Through time's long ruin should weave this
    phantom ground
And in its ghostly borders gather all.

(1-8)

As the speaker-poet celebrates the unutterably "strange" transforming vision which so "changes" things to reveal their unchanging core, so he celebrates that which cannot be grasped: the elusive "ghost," the fleeting "glance," and the intangible "gleam." It is this unlocalized world—a world hovering between dream and reality and time and the timeless—which is the poet's domain. Although life in time is a protracted fall through the flawed (i.e., ruined) world of time and place and towards the final "ruin" of decay and dissolution, and although time's process is irrevocable and irreversible, the poet can recover essence from time's substance. In the "ghostly borders" of an isolated and framed moment of contemplation, the poet can encompass the "all"—the essence—of reality and "weave" from these ethereal strands an enduring design.

The speaker-poet discovers, interwoven in this contemplative vision, a world of utter simplicity and human significance. For here he envisions not only the innocent realm of first childhood where "incorruptible the child plays still" and the world in which the lover "waits beside the trysting tree," but also the self-contained world in which "The good hour spans its heaven, and the ill" (9-11). He has been granted what Muir believes to be the "supreme vision of human life," the reconciling vision in which both the good and ill "have their place legitimately."[15] In this iconic realm of contemplation, the worlds of innocence, love, and good and ill remain "Rapt in their silent immortality" (12): they are held in dynamic suspension by the mysterious power of the transforming vision.

Although, as the concluding couplet suggests, the transmuted world of vision does not have a permanent, tangible existence in our world—it exists "*As in commemoration of a day / That having been can never pass away*" (13-4, my italics)—and although, when the vision passes the speaker-poet must return to the world of "time's long ruin," yet he has transcended, during the moment of contemplation, the dissolving and ruinous flux of time. And he has fashioned, out of his experience, a formal poetic utterance. He has poetically commemorated a moment of vision, a moment "poised between the unmoving dream / And the sole moving moment"; he has reverentially held in memory and celebrated the magic of an experience strange "Past all contrivance, word, or image, or sound, / Or silence, to express." Brought to the threshold of "silent immortality," he has been within sight of what Muir, in another poem, describes as the "story that never can be told" (**"The Bargain,"** 189, 11).

Paradoxically, at the point Muir has everything to say he discovers his inability to say anything. For as he approaches, in moments of contemplation, the world of "silent immortality," so he approaches the borderline of the unsayable. Though he can, through poetic speech, give form and intensity to the visionary, and though he can commemorate and make formal his experience of the transmutation of life by telling it and shaping it into a poem, there is something which the poet apprehends but must leave unsaid. There is that final mystery which defies poetic formulation, as Muir indicates in a late poem, **"Images I"** (260), in which he gives poetic utterance to a dream he had and subsequently related to Kathleen Raine, a dream he felt conveyed the "deepest truth" about the act of writing:

> The dream was a very simple one: it consisted of a semicolon. The meaning of this semicolon, as it revealed itself to the dreamer, was that the poet never knows all that he writes: he writes only, as it were, as far as the semicolon; beyond the statement is something more, that completes his meaning. We can never define it, for it is not finite in its very nature; yet it is part of the poem, and part of what the poet communicates to the reader.[16]

In the poem—which can be conceived either as a self-dialogue or as an address by the speaker-poet to another writer or to the reader—this "truth" about writing is conveyed as the speaker directs the "you" of the poem to behold the inexpressible mystery of that which is at once intimate and immediate and yet elusive and symbolic: the human face. Combining, in the abrupt opening statement of the poem, a familiar tone with a cryptic command to "look" at a face—a face which is never identified or described—, Muir conveys to the reader something of the suddenness and mysteriousness of the moment of revelation described in the poem:

> Take one look at that face and go your way.
>
> (1)

"One look" at this face is sufficient. Seen in a moment of illumination, this face provides a direct awareness of a mystery deeper than life, a mystery that resides in paradox. Although the cares and burdens of time have left their mark in the "lines" of this face, the "yearning" evident in these features, with their "lines of motionless desire / Perpetually assuaged yet unappeased" (2-4), discloses a deep-seated hunger for something outside of time, something glimpsed in a moment of self-forgetfulness when the temporal, private identity has been shed and the alien distance intervening between the self and the real overcome. For

> These are your lineaments, the face of life
> When it is quite alone, and you forgotten.
>
> (6-7)

A manifestation of the individual and universal man, this face conveys to the observer a deep truth about life, a truth which can never be defined or stated as the speaker explains in the self-referential lines that follow, lines that, as critic Christopher Wiseman puts it, use syntax as an "expressive agent" to create a poetry which describes and comments on itself:[17]

> Look once. But do not hope to find a sentence
> To tell what you have seen. Stop at the colon:
> And set a silence after to speak the word
> That you will always seek and never find,
> Perhaps, if found, the good and beautiful end.
> You will not reach that place. So leave the hiatus
> There in the broken sentence. What is missing
> You will always think of.
>
> (8-15)

Paradoxically, only silence can speak; only the "hiatus," the missing word in the sentence, can convey the mystery perceived by the observer. For the direct awareness of mystery cannot be captured by language or shaped and structured through words and syntax: the totality of the observer's experience defies formulation. If his experience could, somehow, be articulated, the "good and beautiful" vision might be lost through the transformation of his immediate, intuitive knowledge into conscious, verbal knowledge. And if he were to "scan" (16) that face once again, he might read himself into his experience: he might leave, on that face, his own "personal load of trouble and desire" (17) and so lose the moment of disinterested contemplation. Though his revelatory insight is fleeting, it is also whole, a totality: "You cannot add to it nor take away" (18). Having witnessed the mystery of that face, the observer must rely on the "imperfect mystery" of the "limping sentence" for there is nothing more he can "think or say" (19-20). And he must rely on memory: "And do not forget. But look once at that face" (21).

Aware of the inexhaustible mystery of human life, Muir speaks, as he indicates in **"The Poet"** (286), written several years before his death, "in bewilderment":

> And in bewilderment
> My tongue shall tell
> What mind had never meant
> Nor memory stored.
> In such bewilderment
> Love's parable
> Into the world was sent
> To stammer its word.
>
> (1-8)

Possessed by the overwhelming presence of love, the poet becomes a vessel through which love's word is conveyed. But he relays his knowledge only imperfectly when he embodies it in language: he must "stammer" the deep truth he has apprehended. He does not force his visionary experience into the predetermined structures of rational thought, for he realizes that "If thought should thieve / One word of the mystery / All would be wrong" (18-20). In moments of poetic inspiration, when the rational processes of the mind are submerged and the poet enters the world of "ghost and glance and gleam," he travels beyond time's framework and stands in the presence of ultimate reality:

Where traveller never went
Is my domain
Dear disembodiment
Through which is shown
The shapes that come and go
And turn again.

(11-6)

In touch with the imponderable mysteries of life, Muir is in touch with the profound sources of poetry. As he states in the last poem he wrote:

And now that time grows shorter, I perceive
That Plato's is the truest poetry,
And that these shadows
Are cast by the true.

(302, 19-22)

Telling the untellable tale through the "limping sentence" with its missing word, the poet says more than he can ever know through the conscious mind. "What I shall never know," Muir states in **"The Poet,"** "I must make known" (286, 9-10). Although he must "Stop at the colon: / And set a silence after to speak the word" which he seeks and cannot find, he communicates a profound truth which exists beyond systems and beyond the words of poetry. As he creates his song out of his deep spiritual awareness, commemorating his momentary glimpses of a transmuted, perfected world, he communicates, however imperfectly, a knowledge that transcends and fulfills us. Through his song, and its deep inwardness, Muir reveals to us the boundless mystery and hidden significance of the human experience.

NOTES

1 Muir is frequently placed in the company of the great visionary poets of the English tradition, poets such as Herbert, Vaughan, Blake, Wordsworth, and Coleridge. See, for example, J. C. Hall, *Edwin Muir,* British Council Writers and Their Work Series, No. 71 (London, 1956), p. 31; Elizabeth Huberman, *The Poetry of Edwin Muir: The Field of Good and Ill* (New York, 1971), pp. 7-9; Thomas Merton, "The True Legendary Sound: The Poetry and Criticism of Edwin Muir," *Sewanee Review,* 75 (Spring 1967), 318; and Ralph Mills, Jr., "Edwin Muir's Poetry: An Introductory Note," *The Newberry Library Bulletin,* 6 (Nov. 1963), 78.

2 The "fable" of Innocence and the Fall is one of the central themes in Muir's poetry. Muir became obsessed with the "fable" of life because of his own life experiences. As he states in *An Autobiography* (London, 1954; rpt. New York, 1968), p. 114: "There are times in every man's life when he seems to become for a little while a part of the fable, and to be recapitulating some legendary drama which, as it has recurred a countless number of times in time, is ageless. The realization of the Fall is one of those events, and the purifications which happen in one's life belong to them too."

3 Page and line references to the *Collected Poems* (New York, 1965) will be indicated parenthetically within the text.

4 "Toys and Abstractions," *Saltire Review,* 9 (Winter 1957), 36.

5 It is also possible to find, as Christopher Wiseman points out (in "Edwin Muir's Last Poems," *University of Windsor Review,* 10 [Fall-Winter 1974], 9), a "subdued Christian element" in this poem: "The living presence from a higher world come to earth to bring understanding of a wider purpose and pattern is seen as suffering intensely, as if bearing the whole world's pain. As with Christ, the great powers are not allowed to prevail in order to release it from necessary suffering. Here a simple park gate 'defeats' the huge animal, just as a wooden cross 'defeats' Christ. Here, too, following the agony, there is a mysterious upward rising from the world." And one might add, the image of the "wound in the world's side" also reflects the "subdued Christian element" found in "The Song."

6 We can carry this process one step further. The poem "The Song" *is* Muir's translation of his dream experience into a poetic "song."

7 *Selected Letters of Edwin Muir,* ed. P. H. Butter (London, 1974), p. 146.

8 Ibid., p. 143.

9 Ibid., p. 89.

10 Ibid., p. 179. In his biography of Muir, P. H. Butter discusses this in more detail. As Butter states (in *Edwin Muir: Man and Poet* [Edinburgh, 1966], pp. 190-191): "Muir always waited for a poem to knock on the door, for inspiration. He could not—or at least did not—stimulate inspiration in himself by deliberately setting himself tasks. He waited—sometimes for a long time. Then perhaps sitting on the top floor of an Edinburgh tram, 'looking at the windows flying past, feeling as if I were in no fixed place, as if I were nowhere,' he would find odd lines coming into his mind which he recognised as the beginning of a poem. Or this might happen in company, and he would withdraw right out of the conversation, and Mrs Muir would nudge her neighbour and say 'birth is coming.' Then he would need perhaps quite a long period of gestation, walking by himself preferably in the country, before he would write down the poem and work at it with the top of his mind."

11 Cited by Butter in *Edwin Muir: Man and Poet,* p. 206, from the B.B.C. "Chapbook," 3 Sept. 1952. As Muir recalls in a B.B.C. broadcast: "'I was up at Swanston in the Pentlands one Saturday morning during the War. It was in late summer; a dull, cloudy, windless day, quite warm. I was sitting in the grass, looking at the thatched cottages and the hills, when I realised that I was fond of them, suddenly and without reason, and for themselves,

not because the cottages were quaint or the hills romantic. I had an unmistakable warm feeling for the ground I was sitting on, as if I were in love with the earth itself, and the clouds, and the soft subdued light. I had felt these things before, but that afternoon they seemed to crystallise, and the poem came out of them.'"

[12] From the B.B.C. "Chapbook," 3 Sept. 1952. Cited by Butter, p. 222.

[13] *Selected Letters,* p. 148.

[14] Ibid., p. 157.

[15] "Yesterday's Mirror: Afterthoughts to an Autobiography," *Scots Magazine,* NS 33 (Sept. 1940), 406.

[16] Kathleen Raine, "Edwin Muir: An Appreciation," *Texas Quarterly,* 4 (Autumn 1961), 234. Although the poem is about a colon and not a semicolon, this dream is undoubtedly a source of "Images I."

[17] Wiseman, p. 10.

Avrom Fleishman (essay date 1983)

SOURCE: "Muir's Autobiography: Twice More in Eden," in *Figures of Autobiography: The Language of Self-Writing in Victorian and Modern England,* University of California Press, 1983, pp. 369-87.

[*In the following essay, Fleishman compares Muir's autobiographical writing in* The Story and the Fable *and* An Autobiography *focusing on his mythic interpretation of his experiences in the latter.*]

With Edwin Muir's *An Autobiography* (1954), the self-awareness of the self-writer in foregrounding the traditional autobiographical figures reaches a moment of fulfillment. It is only one such moment, to be sure, for in the years between Muir's first and his expanded versions of the text, other autobiographers were conducting formal experiments in full awareness of living in an age after the fall into generic self-consciousness. Muir's work is the distillation of a tradition rather than the founding of a new one—for all its copious use of dream materials from the age of Freud to enlarge upon conscious experience. Its exercises in Freudian interpretation now have an air of early modernist mustiness about them, but its array of biblical figures, archetypal patterns and prophetic—though winningly modest—rhetoric continues to give *An Autobiography* the kind of luminous power we associate with *The Prelude* as a definitive autobiography.

That this power exerts itself on most of Muir's critics is, however, something of an irony, for their rendition of the work—a *de rigueur* synopsis opens most studies of his poetry[1]—captures only its sequence as a story without straining to discover the pattern or fable to which

Muir himself aspired. The terms of this distinction are those of the first version, *The Story and the Fable* (1940), and are set out at several places in *An Autobiography:*

> It is clear that no autobiography can begin with a man's birth, that we extend far beyond any boundary line which we can set for ourselves in the past or the future, and that the life of every man is an endlessly repeated performance of the life of man. It is clear for the same reason that no autobiography can confine itself to conscious life, and that sleep, in which we pass a third of our existence, is a mode of experience, and our dreams a part of reality. In themselves our conscious lives may not be particularly interesting. But what we are not and can never be, our fable, seems to me inconceivably interesting. I should like to write that fable, but I cannot even live it; and all I could do if I related the outward course of my life would be to show how I have deviated from it; though even that is impossible, since I do not know the fable or anybody who knows it. One or two stages in it I can recognize: the age of innocence and the Fall and all the dramatic consequences which issue from the Fall. But these lie behind experience, not on its surface; they are not historical events; they are stages in the fable.[2]

This approach to the autobiographical project carries echoes of Jungian archetypalism and has been so interpreted, but Muir's psychological thinking reveals no theoretical ties to Jung's and is rather of the classical, literary variety—more germane to Muir's highly productive career as a literary critic. There is, nonetheless, an aporia of intellectual fuzziness or genuine mystery—it is hard to tell which it is—in Muir's theory of the fable, one which may be filled by Jungian interpretation as well as by others. In speaking of the shape of his life, the above passage distinguishes between the universal fable and the individual's deviations from it, suggesting that the underlying pattern of one's personal experience constitutes *another* fable, departing significantly and apparently balefully from the universal one. I shall call this personal arrangement Muir's myth and distinguish it from the fable—a religious truth about human destiny, which neither Muir nor the present writer has been able to discover—as well as from the story, the specific enactments of the myth that make up the narrative of the autobiography. For in expanding his work from its first version, Muir not only filled in the events of his biography from 1922 to the time of writing but also ran through the myth or pattern of his early years at least twice over. *An Autobiography* is not merely an extension of *The Story and the Fable* but a codification of it as the perennial myth of Muir's life, and it deserves to be treated in some detail as a formal construct in order to grasp the full measure of his achievement.

. . . . .

Muir's story of his early childhood in the unspoiled landscape and folk community of the Orkney Islands has been so often recounted that I shall content myself with only a brief excerpt to stress its figural mode of presentation. Speaking of his parents, he declares:

> I never thought that they were like other men and women; to me they were fixed allegorical figures in a timeless landscape. Their allegorical changelessness made them more, not less, solid, as if they were condensed into something more real than humanity; as if the image "mother" meant more than "woman," and the image "father" more than "man." . . . That world was a perfectly solid world, for the days did not undermine it but merely rounded it, or rather repeated it, as if there were only one day endlessly rising and setting. Our first childhood is the only time in our lives when we exist within immortality, and perhaps all our ideas of immortality are influenced by it. (ch. 1, pp. 24-25)

Although these ideas have been expressed in many languages and explained by many theories, the terms employed here insist on the child's repetition of the conditions of Eden—with father and mother as generic Adam and Eve—even in these rocky and sea-swept northern isles.

So, too, with the events of later childhood:

> I have often fancied, too, that in a child's mind there is at moments a divination of a hidden tragedy taking place around him, that tragedy being the life which he will not live for some years still, though it is there, invisible to him, already. And a child has also a picture of human existence peculiar to himself, which he probably never remembers after he has lost it: the original vision of the world. I think of this picture or vision as that of a state in which the earth, the houses on the earth, and the life of every human being are related to the sky overarching them; as if the sky fitted the earth and the earth the sky. Certain dreams convince me that a child has this vision, in which there is a completer harmony of all things with each other than he will ever know again. There comes a moment (the moment at which childhood passes into boyhood or girlhood) when this image is broken and contradiction enters life. (ch. 1, p. 33)

The fall into division and self-consciousness, after an "original vision of the world" in which "the sky fitted the earth and the earth the sky," is here psychogenetically reported and plausibly explained, yet it is clearly a latter-day version of the philosophical and religious fables on which autobiographers have long modeled their personal sense of loss. Without bombast and, at this stage, without elaborate use of biblical terminology, Muir writes the story of his early years in terms of the Platonic-Christian fable of human life, before going on in his further pages to personalize it as myth.

The more palpable forms in which the fall occurs are registered as "childish guilt" (at touching a prohibited sack of dangerous sheep dip), unwilling submission to the regimentation of school ("I disliked school from the start"), and the threat of violence—told in the account of "the day when Freddie Sinclair chased me home" and immortalized in the poem **"Ballad of Hector in Hades."**[3] But the full scope of the fall is felt only when the family is driven from its farm by a "bad landlord" and sinks steadily to the Glasgow slums:

> My first years in Glasgow were wretched. The feeling of degradation continued, but it became more and more blind; I did not know what made me unhappy, nor that I had come into chaos. We had lived comfortably enough in Orkney, mainly on what we grew; but here everything had to be bought and paid for. . . . My elder brothers had already grasped the principle of this new society, which was competition, not co-operation, as it had been in Orkney. . . . Though we imagined that we had risen in some way, without knowing it we had sunk into another class. . . . We were members of the proletariat, though at that time we had never heard the name. Happily my brothers kept their jobs, and we did not have to become acquainted with the abyss over which we lived. (ch. 3, pp. 92-93)

But the abyss is there, if not that of unemployment and destitution, that of illness and death. Mother, father, and two brothers are dead within two years.

Although Muir survives his illnesses, he reaches another depth of his exile when he takes a clerk's job in a plant processing charcoal from waste bones:

> When I left the office in Glasgow I had no picture of the job I was going to. . . . As I stood there [at "Fairport" station] I became aware of a faint insinuating smell. I paid no attention to it. I should have done so. . . . It was a gentle, clinging, sweet stench, suggesting dissolution and hospitals and slaughter-houses, the odour of drains, and the rancid stink of bad, roasting meat. On hot summer days it stood round the factory like a wall of glass. (ch. 4, pp. 130-31)

Though rendered with naturalistic detail and disarming simplicity, the account moves through scenes resembling a medieval dance of death: "There were old, faithful hands in the place who had spent their lives among the bones. . . . They made free with the bones, humorously flinging them at one another as they sat at their midday meal in the bone-yard; the older ones cynically stirred their tea with a pointed dry bone" (ch. 4, p. 131). From this hellish scene it is a short step to a sense of general depravity and of one's own implication in it: "I had nothing to do with the stuff out of which the firm ground its profits. Yet I could not stave off a feeling of degradation" (ch. 4, p. 132). Trying to do his work with strict accuracy and "cleanliness," he is put constantly in the wrong by the incompetence of others: "I ended by acquiring a habitual bad conscience, a constant expectation of being accused" (ch. 4, p. 133). Thus was formed the English translator of Kafka—of novels about the unreasonable workings of a castle and a trial dooming man to alienation and condemnation, about a system of life in which some universal fault puts every man in the "constant expectation of being accused."[4]

After these elementary structures of the child in an uncorrupted nature, his fall into personal guilt and insecurity, and exile to infernal realms of social life, the succeeding phases of Muir's early career become considerably more complex. As a prototypic modern intellectual, his philosophical and political questing takes in a fair number of the ideologies prevailing early in this century: Nietzscheanism, socialism, Freudianism, etc. Though he receives intellectual and emotional support from his wife—"My marriage was the most fortunate event in my life" (ch. 4, p. 154)—and from his editor, A. R. Orage, his mental state can readily be compared with the long-gathering crises that spiritual autobiographers have recounted. Even some of the terms are the same, as Muir experiences the "Methodist" conversion stage, which Mill also named "conviction of sin" (ch. 5, p. 158).

At this critical point Muir undergoes psychoanalysis, a phase of his development that has been badly overestimated by his critics. Far from providing him with clarification and serenity, the analysis is shown in *An Autobiography* to fall far short of his native insight. In a typical situation, Muir's analyst "indicated the sexual symbolism of the dream, which by this time I could read for myself. . . . Yet these things, though obvious enough, did not seem applicable to the dream, which was unearthly, or rather unhuman, and so in a sense unsexual" (ch. 5, p. 163). In a similar case, the disparity between the figures of psychological health and the biblical fable is even more heavily stressed: "The longing to fling myself down from a height (which comes into both dreams) is immediately associated with the analyst's exhortations to come down to earth, to accept reality; but it also brings to my mind images of the Fall and of the first incarnation, that of Adam, and another image as well, which is my image of timeless human life as the intersection and interpenetration of a stationary beam falling from heaven and the craving, aspiring dust rising for ever to meet it . . ." (ch. 5, p. 166).

It is not through Freud that Muir comes into self-possession but through the traditional language of the seventeenth-century poets, recounting their spiritual travail and triumph. In this process of conversion—Muir uses the term in its verb form—the mediator is no psychoanalyst but a rather strange and otherwise little known friend, John Holms, "the most remarkable man I ever met" (ch. 5, p. 180). Although he is always quoting Wordsworth at Muir, sometimes to apply to his own mental distress and sometimes to Muir's, Holms's affinities lie in an earlier century; the plebeian Muir is careful to point out that "he was descended from John Ferrar, the brother of Nicholas Ferrar, who founded the religious community of Little Gidding" (ch. 5, p. 177). In Holms's company, Muir has what can surely be classed as an epiphanic experience, though it comes in the medium of poetry:

> The very first day that I met him he started to quote Donne (whom I did not know at that time) as we returned from our long summer day in the country. . . . he went on to the opening verse of *The Relic,* stopping in delight over "the last busy day" and the picture of the resurrected soul waiting by the lover's grave to "make a little stay." For the last half-hour we had been meeting a long line of courting couples moving in the opposite direction: as we leaned on the gate they went on passing us, a millennial procession in the calm evening light. Perhaps it was this that recalled to Holms Traherne's "orient and immortal wheat, which never should be reaped, nor was ever sown," for he began to recite the passage, which moved me more deeply than Donne. He held Traherne's and Vaughan's and Wordsworth's theory of childhood, which was bound up with his belief in immortality; in time he converted me to it, or rather made me realize that my own belief was the same as his. (ch. 5, p. 179)

Following on this epiphany, a sense of renewal and return to origins is not long in coming: "These good hours [with Holms] always brought a sense of abundance, or numerous herds, rich fields, full streams, endless food and drink—all things gladly fulfilling the law of their nature—and was like a return to Adam's world" (ch. 5, p. 180). It is only in the following years, when the Muirs begin to make the most of their first Continental adventures, that the renewal is portrayed as a psychological recovery as well as a return to the bounties of childhood:

> We left for Dresden about the end of March [1922], and from the start loved the fine, spacious city. There during the hot, idle summer I seemed at last to recover from the long illness that had seized me when, at fourteen, I came to Glasgow. I realized that I must live over again the years which I had lived wrongly, and that every one should live his life twice, for the first attempt is always blind. . . . In turning my head and looking *against* the direction in which time was hurrying me I won a new kind of experience; for now that I no longer marched in step with time I could see life timelessly, and with that in terms of the imagination. . . . I did not feel so much that I was rediscovering the world of life as that I was discovering it for the first time. (ch. 6, pp. 192-93)

But as his citation of Proust suggests (in a number of sentences I have omitted), this "first time" feeling is connected with the sense of liberation "from the order of time." The past is not retrieved for its own sake but is seen as the focus of a new vision—"*against* the direction" of time. The transformation of the familiar but forgotten into the uncanny and newly discovered is an act of the imagination, and Muir here joins not only Proust but also Wordsworth among the high exemplars of a special form of transformative power, the imagination of the past.

What the traditional language of Muir's recuperation does not reveal is the extent to which he was experiencing the entire process over again at the time he wrote of it. Completed in 1939, *The Story and the Fable* follows in the wake of an intense religious experience that Muir had in February of that year and that he reports in its place in the final text (ch. 11, pp. 246-47). The special feature of this event is its Christian burden, and although Muir's conversion was never of an orthodox kind, his later writings are as much imbued with New Testament figures as with those of the Old. Perhaps even more decisive for the form that the completed autobiography eventually took, in 1946 he read Augustine's *Confessions* "with intense attraction and repulsion: it seems to me one of the greatest of books; the description of the ecstasy [the leave-taking at Ostia] unsurpassed by anything else I know."[5] By the following year, he had made the *Confessions* into an encompassing norm for autobiography. Comparing his own subjective and particularist method with Herbert Read's objective and generalizing one, he concludes: "Both methods are equally good, I think; when they are combined, as in Augustine's *Confessions,* they produce something terrifically impressive."

The model autobiography is made to stand for yet another norm in an article Muir published in 1940, **"Yesterday's Mirror: Afterthoughts to an Autobiography."** Here three ways of looking into one's memory are described. They are the three modes of vision set out in the poem **"The Three Mirrors."** Beyond the realist's way—he sees only the world's wrongs because he has forgotten childhood—and the way of the man who remembers childhood and sees "an indefeasible rightness beneath the wrongness of things," there is another vision:

> The world which the mystical poet sees is a world in which both good and evil have their place legitimately; in which the king on his throne and the rebel raising his standard in the market place, the tyrant and the slave, the assassin and the victim, each plays a part in a supertemporal drama which at every moment, in its totality, issues in glory and meaning and fulfillment. . . . St. Augustine saw it and so did Blake; it is the supreme vision of human life, because it reconciles all opposites; but it transcends our moral struggle, for in life we are ourselves the opposites and must act as best we can.[6]

This mode of vision is presumably the one Muir found himself winning through to; it is an advance on the despair and the naïve optimism of his earlier mirrors. It is an Augustinian-Blakean-mystical viewpoint, according to his essay, but the special qualities Muir attaches to it seem more distinctly those of a personal myth that he was evolving for himself. Without reference to a Christian dispensation, the myth reconciles all the conflicting and random experiences of a life in a "supertemporal drama"—neither a theodicy nor a rationale but a formal narrative that hangs together as all one story, one's own.

The apparent "bottom line" of *The Story and the Fable* is its concluding sentence; although complaining about

his late start as a poet, Muir announces that in the year of his recovery (1922) he began to write poetry. But the continuation of the autobiography as he composed it in the 1950s does not hew to this line of professional or visionary vocation. Having been stirred by his religious experience in 1939—and by later experiences which *An Autobiography* will recount—he described the further stages of life in the twenties and after in terms similar to those with which he began: lost and recovered Edenic scenes.

The new milieu is vastly different, to be sure: Central Europe during a period of violent social change rather than the remote and timeless Orkneys. But here, too, his imagination of the past is fully in control:

> We lived there [Dresden] in ignorance, not looking ahead. In spring we watched the sweet-smelling lime blossom coming out on the trees bordering the streets, and in summer spent a great deal of time on the banks of the river, sun-bathing among the seal-like Saxons whose skin was tanned to a Red Indian brown: a pleasant, vacant life without a trace of boredom, for everything round us was strange. . . . All this was thirty years ago, and with one half of my mind I can look at it historically, while the other half still sees it as I saw it then, wrapped in its own illusions. We lived, it seems to me now, in a climate of "new ideas," and looked forward to a "new life" which would be brought about by the simple exercise of freedom, a freedom such as had never been formulated before in any terms, since it too was new. (ch. 8, pp. 198-99)

With hindsight, Muir can see that the Weimar period's enthusiasms—like the Dalcroze eurhythmics in which he joined at Hellerau—were not so novel as claimed and that the appeal to primal innocence in bodily movement and personal relations was a latter-day variant of a perennial human urging. The "new life" to be fostered by "new ideas" of self-congratulation and heavy sunbathing was ignorant and illusory but nonetheless effective:

> The German landscape, as I have said, helped to foster it. There was something in the appearance of the woods which seemed to invite nature-worship, and from nature-worship to worship of our own nature, which we were modestly practising, was an easy step. The trees solicited us to be natural, since they were natural, to be young, since they renewed their youth every year, to be child-like, since we could easily feel as we wandered among them that we were children of nature. (ch. 8, p. 202)

In this unlikely setting, Muir renews not merely his childhood insouciance but his fable of it, and we are told on successive pages about Vaughan and Traherne and the *Wandervögel* balladeers.

After a stay in Italy with Holms—an unsatisfactory one, as the English mystic is off his form as a *cicerone* of Latin culture—Muir returns to *Mitteleuropa* and receives his first foretaste of the coming fall. At Salzburg, he is impressed enough by the beauty and strangeness of the scene to store up impressions for a novel, *The Marionette,* a surrealistic fantasy about an idiot boy who falls in love with such an object.[7] But the more surrealistic fantasies in this city are those which are published in the local newspapers: "We read with astonishment of ritual murders still happening, and of curious Jewish perversions, described in detail, of which we had never heard. A little time afterwards we met some intelligent Austrians who maintained against all we could say that Ramsay Macdonald and Bernard Shaw were Jews: they must be, for they were subverters of society" (ch. 8, p. 214). Returning to Vienna, they find the first signs of the coming debacle: "The misery in Vienna created its own nightmare. We did not know that the nightmare would end in the slaughter of a people" (ch. 8, p. 218). But there are already strong indications that this is a society in disintegration.

Returning to England after four years of innocence and experience, the Muirs gradually achieve a measure of literary success, though without financial security, and in the thirties they come to lead the literary life of Hampstead. These pages are condensed and only half-attentive to the inner life, but when the family suffers a near-disaster the original urgency and weight return to Muir's prose. After their son, an only child, is hit by a car, he suffers longer from his psychological than from his physical trauma, and the parents decide to remove to a quieter place. Without explaining his thought process, the autobiographer makes clear the significance of his decision:

> A friend got a furnished house for us in St. Andrews. But first we went to Orkney, so that our son should have a complete rest. . . . I had not been back to Orkney for many years; few of the people I had known were there still; but the beauty of the light showered from the wide sky and reflected from the spreading waters, and diffused, a double radiance, over the bright fields, was the same beauty I had known as a child; and the loneliness of every shape rising from the treeless land, the farm houses and the moving outlines of men and women against the sky, had, as then, the simplicity of an early world. The peace helped to still Gavin's fears. (ch. 10, pp. 241-42)

Whatever fears are being stilled here are not the son's alone as Muir clearly creates or seizes the opportunity to relive and rewrite his childhood once again. It is not only a pattern of psychic repetition that is being formed here but a pattern of narrative and lyrical writing. This practice becomes the myth of which Muir makes his poetry over the last decades of his life, reaching a grand finale in his last volume, *One Foot in Eden* (1956).

. . . . .

Despite Muir's satisfaction in finding himself once more in Eden, his myth became so compelling that he had to make the cycle of exile and return all over again after the war.[8] If his version of the Christian fable was fueling his poetry during these years, his created myth of childhood, fall, and return was dominant over his personal fortunes—or at least over his conception of them. In adding these later episodes to the final pages of his autobiography, Muir followed the myth pattern that he had used twice over in telling of his earlier losses and recoveries.

After spending the war years with the British Council in Edinburgh, Muir was appointed director of the British Institute in Prague in 1945. As the chapter title "Prague Again" suggests, his sense of the voyage is one of uncanny repetition. But the conditions of an occupied city in a war-torn continent make difficult a recovery of earlier days of liberated innocence: "The new impression was more vivid and less agreeable than I had expected; it was as if whole series of familiar objects were presenting themselves a second time and asking to be digested again. During my first few weeks in Prague I felt I was in a strange place, and was teased by the fancy of another city, the same and yet not the same, whose streets I or someone very like me had walked many years before" (ch. 12, p. 255). It soon emerges that the city has not merely been changed by time but has suffered a range of experiences known only to sermons on hell and records of the holocaust. Looking at pictures of the former German overlords with friends, the widow of a resistance leader "pointed at one young man and said without expression: 'That is the one who strangled my husband.' But it might have been any of the others. They stared out from the photographs with the confidence of the worthless who find power left in their hands like a tip hastily dropped by a frightened world. Though they had done so many things to satisfy their revenge on mankind there was no satisfaction in their faces, and no hope" (ch. 12, p. 261).

Yet worse is to come, for the brief hopes raised by the withdrawal of the Russian troops come to an end when the Communist party enacts a classic coup d'état. Muir finds that the narratives of Kafka, which he had been translating as existential allegories, were close to becoming literal histories: "We heard of the attempt of the students to reach the President. The police had blocked the main street to the Castle, and the students took another route. When they reached the Castle they found it shut and soldiers on guard. An officer raised his sword as a warning to them to keep back" (ch. 12, p. 266; cf. p. 270). Powerless to do more than look on at the extinction of liberty, Muir deepens his identification with individuals suffering the moral equivalent of the national crisis. A Czech acquaintance is given the choice of keeping her job by becoming a Communist or asserting her Catholic faith and losing her means of supporting her invalid father and mother. He is never to learn the outcome of this paradigmatic situation, for conditions at Charles University become so repressive as to force his departure. As soon as he arrives back in England, he suffers a breakdown "and fell plumb into a dead pocket of life which I had never guessed at before" (ch. 13, p. 274). His depression may be reduced to a psychiatric regression, but given its moral and political inducements, it seems better to view it as Muir's renewed apprehension of the fallen human estate.

Fortunately, there is Edenesque relief at hand, if not return to Scotland (until a later time), at least a sojourn in a cultural paradise. Muir is assigned to direct the British Institute in Rome and finds both the city and the workplace immensely congenial:

> it was a new experience to know people who spoke from the heart, simply and naturally, without awkwardness, and put all of themselves, heart and soul, into what they said. I had known fresh and natural speech among Orkney farmers living close to the cattle and the soil, but not till now among men and women moulded by city life. . . . The humanity was perfectly natural, but I knew that naturalness does not come easily to the awkward human race, and that this was an achievement of life.

> . . . I felt, the first morning I called at the Institute that I was breaking into an Eden. . . . The Institute remained a sort of talkative Eden and was the most friendly, kind, busy place imaginable. (ch. 13, pp. 275-76)

It is not only his Italian co-workers and the office camaraderie that give the exhausted Muir the impulse to resort again to his archetypes but the larger culture in which they are placed. Even Roman history becomes adaptable to the Edenic vision: "The history of Rome is drenched in blood and blackened with crime; yet all that seemed to be left now was the peace of memory. . . . The grass in the courtyard of the Temple of the Vestals seemed to be drenched in peace down to the very root, and it was easy to imagine gods and men still in friendly talk together there" (ch. 13, p. 277). It is evidently easy for Muir, in his relieved state of mind and with its controlling structures, to imagine this Hölderlinian conclave (Muir's poem on the Romantic-classicist poet comes readily to mind). More difficult to assimilate—because more sketchily articulated—is the sudden reverence Muir feels for the images of Catholicism that mark the city. The pull toward Christian spirituality continues to draw Muir steadily, but he never commits himself to a religious conversion, preferring the articles of his private faith, though they draw on the tradition for their images.

Returning to Scotland at last, as warden of an experimental workingmen's college, Muir has leisure to write the continuation of his autobiography, but his embarrassment or diffidence in promulgating his myth shows up at the close:

> Some kind of development, I suppose, should be expected to emerge, but I am very doubtful of such things, for I cannot bring life into a neat pattern. If there is a development in my life—and

it seems an idle supposition—then it has been brought about more by things outside than by any conscious intention of my own. I was lucky to spend my first fourteen years in Orkney; I was unlucky to live afterwards in Glasgow as a Displaced Person. . . . In my middle thirties I became aware of immortality, and realized that it gave me a truer knowledge of myself and my neighbors. Years later in St. Andrews I discovered that I had been a Christian without knowing it. I saw in Czechoslovakia a whole people lost by one of the cruel turns of history, and exiled from themselves in the heart of their own country. I discovered in Italy that Christ had walked on the earth, and also that things truly made preserve themselves through time in the first freshness of their nature. . . . As I look back on the part of the mystery which is my own life, my own fable, what I am most aware of is that we receive more than we can ever give; we receive it from the past, on which we draw with every breath, but also—and this is a point of faith—from the Source of the mystery itself, by the means which religious people call Grace. (ch. 13, pp. 280-81)

Although Muir's religious meditations and personal version of Christianity have come up in the autobiography, they have not been allowed to shape his "development"—certainly no decisive conversion pattern or pilgrimage has been suggested, even in displaced form. At the final sentence, an enormous weight is placed on the unanticipated and unearned, on the fable of Christian redemption, and the term *Grace* is appropriated for it.

Yet *An Autobiography* has seen the formal reenactment of a pattern—twice over again, after the first and most telling sequence—in a personal life interpretation, which I have called Muir's myth. For this pattern, Muir has employed a Judeo-Christian mythos of a more elementary kind: the fable of Eden and the Fall, of lost innocence and diminished powers. He fills this abstract space with various sources of creative energy: the love and care of wife and child, the imagination of the past, the islands of human civility and rich culture, which occasionally survive the horrors of modern politics. In returning to primary values, deeply imagined and at least temporarily realized, Muir has renewed a universal fable that comes earlier than Christianity, lies deeper perhaps than religion, and comprehends the endemic autobiographical drift to recapitulate one's origins and end—to make oneself whole again and at last.[9]

NOTES

[1] E.g., Elizabeth Huberman, *The Poetry of Edwin Muir: The Field of Good and Ill* (New York, 1971), ch. 1; or Christopher Wiseman, *Beyond the Labyrinth: A Study of Edwin Muir's Poetry* (Victoria, Can., 1978), ch. 1.

[2] Edwin Muir, *An Autobiography* (New York, 1968 [1954]), ch. 1, pp. 48-49; I quote the American paperback edition in the text. Cf. another summative passage on the fable and the Fall at ch. 3, p. 114.

[3] Edwin Muir, *Collected Poems: 1921-1958* (London, 1960); the poem appeared originally in *First Poems* (1925).

[4] Muir's long bout of translating and writing about Kafka has been well summarized in Elgin W. Mellown, *Edwin Muir* (Boston, 1979), pp. 39-44; it is tempting to find parallels between Muir's changing views of Kafka's narrative and allegory and his performance in narrating and allegorizing his own life.

[5] *Selected Letters of Edwin Muir*, ed. P. H. Butter (London, 1974), p. 127 (Nov. 15, 1940); the quotation that follows is from p. 128 (April 16, 1940).

[6] Quoted in P. H. Butter, *Edwin Muir: Man and Poet* (New York, 1967), pp. 186-87.

[7] In addition to this fiction, Muir wrote an autobiographical novel, *Poor Tom* (1932), with a Glasgow setting of illness and death; Mellown, *Edwin Muir*, pp. 70-80, treats these and the novel *The Three Brothers* (1931) as autobiographical in varying ways.

[8] For a contrary view of the later chapters, see Roger J. Porter, "Edwin Muir and Autobiography: Arch of a Redemptive Memory," *South Atlantic Quarterly*, 87 (1978): 521-22; *An Autobiography* "surrenders that pervasive structure which earlier saw *all* Muir's experience unified in the dialectic of innocence and Fall, and it covers over the darker elements to resolve everything too neatly."

[9] "The expulsion from Paradise is in its main significance eternal: Consequently the expulsion from Paradise is final, and life in this world irrevocable, but the eternal nature of the occurrence (or, temporally expressed, the eternal recapitulation of the occurrence) makes it nevertheless possible that not only could we live continuously in Paradise, but that we are continuously there in actual fact, no matter whether we know it here or not." The words are not Muir's but Kafka's, in the translation by Muir and his wife, Willa Muir, *Parables* (New York, 1947), p. 25.

Sheila Lodge (essay date 1985)

SOURCE: "The Politics of Edwin Muir's Autobiographies," in *Prose Studies*, Vol. 8, No. 2, September, 1985, pp. 97-117.

[*In the following essay, Lodge reconsiders prevailing views of Muir's political development as suggested by his autobiographical writings through an examination of his contributions to the* New Age *during the 1920s.*]

On publication, Edwin Muir's *The Story and the Fable*[1] was hailed as "a book of outstanding delicacy and integrity."[2] Michael Hamburger described *An Autobiography* as a "singularly honest and lucid account,"[3] while Rex Warner almost ran out of adjectives in gushing that these writings should be labelled "gentle and wise, modest, vivid and illuminating."[4] Alfred Kazin referred to Muir as "a giver of testimony"; and Stephen Spender, with a note of meekly resigned puzzlement, commented that "it is difficult to criticise a work which gives a single-minded impression of integrity."[5] No less an authority than T. S. Eliot sought to stress Muir's "unmistakable integrity";[6] but even this tribute is less revealing than that paid by Richard Hoggart.

Hoggart's 1965 lecture on autobiography to the Royal Society of Literature draws upon his established sensitivity to ideological bias in writings from and about the working classes; yet, having neatly dispatched the sentimentalities of a clutch of unmemorable memoirs, he too falls back on the matter of Muir's "integrity." Autobiography depends, he argues, on "questions of tone or voice," and he continues:

> For myself, I would like to find a voice which would carry a wide and deep range of attributes and emotions without being socially self-conscious or derivatively literary. Among modern autobiographers I know hardly anyone who has found this tone, this clarity which seems almost like talking to oneself, since no one is being wooed. Edwin Muir's autobiography has this quality, and about it one can properly use terms like 'sensitive integrity'. He was a poet, and he used his poetic skills here in a disciplined way.[7]

Hoggart's use of quotation marks here seems to suggest a certain disquiet underlying the apparent approbation; but he remains incapable of breaking through the confusion of the earlier reviewers. He knows that the tone which convinces him of Muir's "sensitive integrity" can only be a product of the "poetic skills" to which he makes obeisance; he knows that he is dealing not with a natural object found by chance but with a literary text deliberately fashioned for publication and carefully constructed to make a certain impression on the reader: and yet part of that impression is the conviction that no impression whatever had been intended at all. At the end of a most intricately and cleverly patterned work, Muir's autobiographical persona writes, "I cannot bring life into a neat pattern"—and the critics believe him! If we were to continue Hoggart's metaphor, we might say that he has not been wooed by Muir's text so much as raped. This essay outlines some of the arguments which support a less ingenuous reading of Muir's prose, and which help reveal the complex of ideological pressures which determined its character.

If Muir is transported from England to Scotland, his autobiographies cease to be seen as the stronghold of purity and integrity which the persona was designed to make them seem. In Scotland, Muir is not simply the latest in a long line of English mystical writers that stretches from Traherne and Vaughan to Eliot;[8] he is primarily seen as a political writer, author of *Scott and Scotland* (1936), the major attack on the Scottish Literary

Renaissance and the most cogent defence of the Unionist ideology to be written this century. In this context, *The Story and the Fable* is the representation of what Chris Grieve/Hugh MacDiarmid described as Muir's "own little personal Whipsnade,"[9] a self-indulgent self-examination by which he attempted to exclude from history the political and cultural debate which the initial reaction to *Scott and Scotland* suggested that he had lost. And exclude it Muir most certainly did. If the autobiographies are Muir's rewriting of his personal history, created to compensate for the apparent failure of his attempted rewriting of Scotland's history, then they work simply by denying space—by denying time—to those elements of his earlier commitments which were no longer compatible with his new devotion to the role of religious and "apolitical" mystic. This is the great success of the writer Edwin Muir: that he has triumphed in determining which aspects of the totality of his work are to be seen as constituting his oeuvre and as bearing the development of his ideology. The extent of Muir's victory is seen, for example, in Peter Butter's biographical study where he writes of the *New Age* material that "Muir would not wish much attention to be paid to this early work," and then himself dispenses with it in a superficial account which condemns the writing of four or five years in a page and a half.[10] Such naivety not only accepts Muir's self-image unquestioningly: it also underestimates the degree of literary ability which Muir employed in constructing that image.

I

In an important article on "History and the Scottish Novel," Cairns Craig began with W. B. Gallie's argument in *Philosophy and the Historical Understanding* that "all history [is] founded upon the processes of narrative: history is the construction of story out of the amorphous, fragmented, hypothetical totality of what has happened to occur." Narrative, however, is essentially teleological:

> "it is chiefly in terms of conclusion—eagerly awaited as we read forward and accepted at the story's end—that we feel and appreciate the unity of a story"; and the ultimate teleology of the historical story is the present.[11]

If the skills Muir uses in producing his autobiographies are seen not as "poetic" (in Hoggart's phrase) but as those of a novelist (and Muir had already made "stories" out of his life in writing two—arguably, three—autobiographical novels in *The Marionette* [1927], *The Three Brothers* [1931] and *Poor Tom* [1932]), then an analysis of them reveals a literary methodology of selection and presentation which remains notable for its skill and cleverness, but which can no longer be shielded from investigation by the claim that the autobiographies simply represent intuitions of essential mystery.

Gallie claims that it is the ending of the story, the present, which makes sense of the past by explaining the final position of the writer. The clue to Muir's ideological terminus in his autobiographies is first apparent in the conclusion to *The Story and the Fable.* The narrative which he constructs in 1940 out of the events of his life goes only so far as the removal to Dresden in 1922: but there is a concluding section headed "Extracts from a Diary, 1937-39." The passages themselves are a miscellaneous collection. Although they do admit of political reflection in a more direct manner than *An Autobiography* was to do, these reactions are placed within a discourse primarily preoccupied with varieties of religious and transcendental experience (dreams, visions, aphorisms).

An Autobiography, distanced by eighteen years from the storm surrounding *Scott and Scotland,* and produced by a Muir who had given up almost entirely his engagement with Scottish and socialist concerns, shows a much greater confidence in the explanatory role of transcendental mysticism. It is significant that here again he returns to the form of the diary, from which he now takes just one extract:

> It was the last day of February 1939—when I saw some schoolboys playing at marbles on the pavement; the old game had 'come round' again in its own time, known only to children, and it seemed a simple little rehearsal for a resurrection, promising a timeless renewal of life. I wrote in my diary next day:

> Last night, going to bed alone, I suddenly found myself (I was taking off my waistcoat) reciting the Lord's Prayer in a loud, emphatic voice—a thing I had not done for many years—with deep urgency and profound disturbed emotion. While I went on I grew more composed; as if I had been empty and craving and were being replenished, my soul stood still; every word had a strange fullness of meaning which astonished and delighted me. It was late; I had sat up reading; I was sleepy; but as I stood in the middle of the floor half-undressed, saying the prayer over and over, meaning after meaning sprang from it, overcoming me with joyful surprise; and I realized that this simple petition was always universal and always inexhaustible, and day by day sanctified human life.

> I had believed for many years in God and the immortality of the soul. (*A,* 246).

As soon as Muir has given the diary account of his conversion, his first impulse is, as always, to redefine the past in its light, again replacing change with discovery: he had "believed *for many years* in God." And this is the process that is repeated throughout the autobiographies, so that all his life is shown only in its relation to this transcendentalist faith of the late thirties. Consequently, he announces quite early in the work,

> I shall attend and listen to a class of experiences which the disbeliever in immortality ignores, or dismisses as irrelevant to temporal life. The experiences I mean are of little practical use and have no particular economic or political interest. (*A,* 54).

As we have seen from Butter, this claim to have selected material for these books according to its relevance to other-worldly concerns has been widely welcomed by Muir's critics. Only Q. D. Leavis dared publicly to suggest that something had been lost in his decision not to write "that invaluable account of the central literary world in the formative post-war years, the era of *The Calendar of Modern Letters* and *The Athenaeum,* Eliot's poetry and the early Virginia Woolf and all the rest"; but she too put this heretical thought aside in admitting that Muir remained "notable for his integrity" and conceding that he could "hardly be blamed for writing his own book and not the one we wanted."[12] "Blamed," no: but this compliance in reading Muir only in the context in which he chose to direct us to read it leads directly to the kind of intellectual bullying of which Roger Knight is guilty when he attempts to warn off the sceptic:

> The directive to the reader of Muir's own work is clear: if it does not exercise his 'capacity for admiration', he had better leave it alone.[13]

The irony is that in seeking for literary gossip (albeit of the higher order) Mrs Leavis had identified one of the prime absences in Muir's work, one of the silences in the text: his life as a literary critic.

But as already mentioned, Scottish critics and historians make much of the events of the twenties and thirties, of the literary and critical battles which Muir omits. To Grieve, Muir was less the man of integrity and the private individual than the collaborator who had sold out his country's culture to become the "leader of the white-mouse faction of the Anglo-Scottish literati."[14] Yet such attacks came from the same Grieve who in 1925 had hailed Muir as "incontestably in the first flight of contemporary critics of *weltliteratur*" [*sic*].[15] The source of the rupture was, of course, *Scott and Scotland.* In that work the argument depends on the premise that Scotland has somehow dropped out of History, and that Scott consequently lived in "a temporal Nothing . . . dotted with a few disconnected figures arranged at abrupt intervals" (2). Since Scotland is not part of the historical process, it follows that there can be no change which will bring her out of the cultural malaise which Muir defines: and so this narrative leads inexorably to the conclusion that "Scotland can only create a national literature by writing in English" (111). Such a version of the past, justifying such prognosis, gives the lie to the autobiographies' contention that spiritual issues had always taken precedence in Muir's life, and opens the way to other moments being seen as the determining crisis—or crises—in his story. And the paradox remains that, whereas the autobiographies claim overtly to be rebuttals of the kind of political interest displayed in *Scott and Scotland,* both the two studies of self and the examination of Scott share the denial of historical progress ("some kind of development, I suppose, should be expected to emerge, but I am very doubtful of such things" [*A,* 280]) which makes them, at a deeper level, part of the project of rewriting Scottish history that lay at the heart of the Renaissance Movement. Muir's versions may come to conclusions quite different from those of the *Scottish Chapbook, Albyn* or the *Drunk Man:* but the burden of his works is identical.

By analysing the ways in which the autobiographies deny significance to the history of Muir's political development, selecting and shaping his story to highlight and propagandise the religiose conservatism which the failure of those politics had brought about, it is possible to give an alternative reading of *The Story and the Fable* and *An Autobiography* as narrative constructions, in such a way as to open up access to a wider and deeper understanding of the historical constraints within which Muir wrote.

II

In an article published shortly after *The Story and the Fable* appeared, Muir wrote:

> I tried to make clear the pattern of my life as a human being existing in space and moving through time, environed by mystery. After I had finished, I went over the manuscript many times, seeking to make the pattern clearer, and felt like a man with an inefficient torch stumbling through a labyrinth, having forgotten where he entered and not knowing where he would come out.[16]

Here, the concession that the autobiography is a deliberate literary creation, a manuscript actively worked over many times to stress *the* pattern, is defused by the persona's only being allowed to work "to make the pattern *clearer*"; and the image of the professional writer is quite overshadowed by that of the clumsy, forgetful persona's inefficiency. The reader's attention is directed away from the process of writing which is the ostensible subject of this text, and towards the progress of the narrator, that innocent "environed by mystery" but bravely coping with the maze. Such language is typical of the later Muir's strategy: "environed," for instance, implies that being surrounded by "mystery" is man's natural habitat, and it encourages the acceptance of Muir's anti-intellectual philosophy.

The pattern to which Muir refers is, naturally, defined as being inaccessible to intellectual investigation:

> It is clear that no autobiography can begin with a man's birth, that we extend far beyond any boundary line which we can set for ourselves in the past or the future, and that the life of every man is an endlessly repeated performance of the life of man. . . . In themselves our conscious lives may not be particularly interesting. But what we are not and never can be, our fable, seems to me inconceivably interesting. I should like to write that fable, but I cannot even live it; and all I could do if I related the outward course of my life would be to show how I have deviated from it; though even that is impossible, since I do not know the fable or anybody who knows it. One or

two stages in it I can recognize: the age of innocence and the Fall and all the dramatic consequences which issue from the Fall. But these lie behind experience, not on its surface; they are not historical events; they are stages in the fable. (*S & F*, 55)

But Muir's art is that of the bluff. He tells us that he cannot make the pattern clear so that we do not investigate too closely its inconsistencies, do not suspect him of propagandising: yet the work in which he tells us this is itself structured in such a way as to present an image of the Fable which takes a religious form as reflected here in the references to the Fall. And this form is in turn validated by Muir's offering of his own conversion to Christianity as the climax of the familiar structure of the *Bildungsroman*.

The autobiographies logically cannot be the investigative exercise which the imagery of the man with the dim torch would seek to suggest. After 1939, Muir could not step outside of his religious commitment in order to examine it "objectively"; he necessarily and consistently wrote from within it. Consequently, the notion that there is an independent, objective pattern to which Muir fits his own poor experience as best he can must be seen not as an account of his progress towards the theory of the story and the fable, but as an instance of that theory's operation.

The values which structure this pattern are slowly brought together in the opening chapters of the book, long before their theoretical significance—for Muir or for the reader—is expounded. The most consistent element—not surprisingly—is religion itself. Often, the touch is very light indeed: St Magnus's cathedral, for instance, is said to be "the most beautiful thing within sight" of the Bu farm (*A*, 16); but this apparently descriptive fact is turned into a point of a very different order when the narrator adds that "it rose every day against the sky until it seemed to become a sign of the fable in our lives," anachronistically attributing to his childhood (and to all his family—and all the residents of Orkney?) the belief held by the man of 1940. Again, although he claims to remember nothing of the routine of his first seven years (*A*, 19), he nonetheless displays almost total recall of his baptism. Family prayers are singled out as being among his "happiest memories," creating "a feeling of complete security and union among us as we sat reading about David or Elijah" (*A*, 26): as in **Scott and Scotland,** where the ideal unified sensibility is located only in pre-Reformation Scotland, religious harmony here creates a community which Muir depicts—through the use of the first person plural—as unified. Organised religion, however, is tainted with Calvinism even so late as the 1890s, and it meets little approval: Muir's participation in revivalist meetings is attributed to a child's fear of exclusion—but this too takes on a more narrowly political force when the feelings of distaste established here are invoked to disparage his later

Socialist convictions: "my conversion to Socialism," he needs only say, "was a recapitulation of my first conversion at fourteen" (*A*, 113).

The Orcadian routine of the late nineteenth century is quickly established as the good life, and one prefiguring that of his later beliefs. This life becomes the touchstone against which all later experience is measured. For example, the speakers at the Clarion Scout meetings which Muir attended in Glasgow are presented as self-seeking charlatans (*A*, 112), but their political engagement is also denigrated by being contrasted with the quietism on Orkney. The landlord whose exactions drove the family from farm to farm and finally into Glasgow is discussed only in the context of a single shooting trip to the islands, and the terms of that description—"a mere picture" (*A*, 115)—suggests that this role in the capitalist system is parallel with his activity as a hunter of game birds: that it may not be a particularly pleasant role is conceded, but on the grounds that it belongs to a larger pattern which transcends its apparent evil it is allowed to pass unquestioned.

There is another emblematic distinction in the contrast of prevalent attitudes to beggars in Orkney and on the mainland. In the islands, men such as John Simpson—regarded almost as blessed fools, being "not right in the mind"—are "always taken in and given food" (*A*, 82); one of the first things the reader is told about the adjustment to city life is that

> beggars were perpetually ringing the bell, and we did not learn for weeks that you must not take a beggar in and give him something to eat, but must slam the door at once in his face. (*A*, 91)

Glasgow is cast throughout as the antithesis of Orkney, presaged by such bad omens as his father's cold, the dark and windy day of travel and the dirty train awaiting the family when they had docked (*A*, 90). Leading into the chaos of family deaths, personal illness and the degradation of the bone factory, Glasgow is opposed to the rural idyll which it replaces.

In reading the presentation of Muir's pre-literary life, then, it is possible to discern the elements of the structures which underpin the autobiographies' ideological purpose as a whole. The country is seen as being intrinsically better than the city because it is depicted as having "natural" links with a religious (Christian) faith that is expressed in the terms of the "organic" peasant community. It is a fairly conventional mixture of Rousseau, Wordsworth and T. S. Eliot, though none the less potent for that.

But the project of deconstructing these images of his life can only be properly tackled when the independent evidence about Muir's life becomes available with which to challenge his own version of his past. Such evidence becomes available when we turn to the time Mrs Leavis longed to know about, his years in London in the early 1920s, and to the writing that he did for *The New Age* in that period.

III

Most of those who have researched the intellectual history of Britain in the first decades of this century will agree on at least one thing: that the full significance of *The New Age* has yet to be realised by the majority of readers. Edited by A. R. Orage, it was undoubtedly the most wide-ranging of contemporary magazines in that heyday of periodical journalism, seeking to keep its readers abreast of the latest developments in every field of thought, from psychoanalysis and philosophy to physics, as well as fulfilling the functions of a more conventional literary and cultural review. Above all, much work remains to be done on the journal's politics, and on the role of the journal from 1919 (starting a few months before Muir joined the staff as assistant editor) as propagator of Major Douglas' Social Credit economics. Certainly, by early in 1920, even a cursory reading of the paper would show that those writing for the periodical regarded working for the success of what had become "the Douglas–*New Age* Scheme" as their *raison d'être*.

Shortage of space prevents a full analysis here: but it is important to note that the columns which Muir regularly contributed to *The New Age* during these years show little sign of the Guild Socialist or Nietzschean ideas which had originally attracted his attention, and are entirely in keeping with the new ethos. And it is particularly important, in relation to the strategy of the autobiographies, that at this early date the use of a literary persona is signalled by the use of a precisely anglicised pseudonym, "Edward Moore."

The major part of Muir's contributions in this period involved the production of "Our Generation," ninety-six articles which were published almost weekly from November 1920 to September 1922, and which consist of comments on three or four topical issues or events of the week. The point of view is that of someone overtly committed to social credit and completely lacking in any doubts or fears about tackling the most sensitive political or cultural problems, from the miners' strike and unemployment to the role of the Anglican bishops.

These columns, however, were not just simple occasional pieces: they sought to fulfil a mission. It was not until 1934 that Lewis Grassic Gibbon wrote off the Scheme as a "bourgeois funk-fantasy;"[17] in the 1920s and early '30s, many (including Eliot, Grieve, Lewis, Pound and Gunn) saw it as the only salvation from the alternatives of Communist or Fascist totalitarianism. Muir's problem was to devise a literary strategy by which he, as a writer whose ideology had been most strongly determined by being a working-class Scot, could persuade his largely English, middle-class audience of the virtues of Douglasism. Consequently, "Moore"s' chief

characteristics are his blunt common sense, his lack of arrogance, and his persistent belief that the truth is perfectly clear and easy for men of goodwill to discern if only they will disabuse themselves of the conventions of capitalist ideology, the "superstitions" against which his co-propagandist Pound would rail in adjacent columns. And just to be on the safe side, "Moore" shows a marked predilection to talk in the first person plural, and to make explicit contrasts between the habits of "we English" as opposed to the mores of the Scots! Yet the reader of the autobiographical accounts of these years would get a completely different impression from that derived from the primary sources.

After their London wedding in June 1919, Muir returned to Glasgow and Willa Anderson set about finding a place where they might live. Having rented and furnished rooms in Guilford Street, she was astonished to find on her arrival in Scotland that her husband had yet to resign his job in a Renfrew office. "But you said you didn't want to be a clerk all your life, and that you wanted to get out of Glasgow," she protested. "But I'm earning three pounds seventeen and six *a week*," he replied.[18] In Willa's memoir, this anecdote performs several roles. Showing how little she knew of her husband and emphasising her greater adventurousness, it also supports the image of his unworldliness: by 1968, the date of the publication of *Belonging,* with knowledge of his success and with inflation having made the security of his wage seem negligible, his appeal to an economic argument seems slightly ridiculous, an excuse for his timidity and a result of his inability to discuss his neuroses. But the fact that Muir was concerned about his earnings is at least discernible in his wife's autobiography: his own autobiography suggests that at the time the matter was of no interest whatsoever. Implying that they were infected by their surroundings with a Peter Pan-like insouciance, he claims that he and his wife existed

> in a suspended state, waiting for work, not really apprehensive, for we could not imagine the possibility of not finding it: the work was there, invisible for the present, and one day it would appear. When we were tired of looking for it we went to Kensington Gardens, and in complete idleness dreamt through the afternoon. (*A,* 155)

Once again, like all good things, work is depicted as simply waiting to be discovered. But since Muir's psychological difficulties continued in London and beyond, despite several months of psychoanalysis, the discrepancy between the anguished protestations recalled by Willa and the confident ease of Edwin's account cannot be explained simply by the fact of their having left Glasgow. The *Autobiography*'s description reinforces the impression that Muir—seen here as too interested in "dreams" to be "really apprehensive" about diurnal economic realities—had *always* acknowledged the dominance of the transcendental.

In fact, Willa had lost her job in a ladies' college on her marriage, and was able to find only less well-paid work at a crammer's, so when Muir accepted Orage's offer of £3 for three days work each week, the loss of nearly a quarter of his income must have imposed the kind of difficulties he had anticipated from Scotland. The autobiography discounts this entirely, slanting the image of the past to help create the feeling that the supremacy of transcendentalism in the autobiographical persona is the inevitable realisation of his "true" self. And this strategy of selecting the aspects of the period which can be turned to congruence with his later concerns is followed throughout the description of his time in London and his continuing association with *The New Age.*

The account of his career during these years, for example, is very thin. Having mentioned that reviewing for *The Athenaeum* and providing drama criticism for *The Scotsman* boosted his income to an acceptable level (*A,* 157), he makes no comment on the manner in which this new work was approached nor on its relationship with his contemporary editorial training. Instead, emphasis is placed on his personal life. Having arranged for Muir to join the paper, Orage's first role in the "London" chapter is not as editor of *The New Age* but, surprisingly, as the provider of Muir's introduction to psychoanalysis through his friendship with Maurice Nicoll and his colleagues (*A,* 157). Moreover, having chosen to ignore the interest possibly inherent in a description of the Jungian analytic method he underwent in the early 1920s, Muir concentrates exclusively on his subjective experiences. The five-page account of a particularly vivid "waking dream" details such religious images as Muir and his wife rising on angels' wings to sit on the shoulders of "a gigantic figure clad in antique armour, sitting on a throne with a naked sword at his side" (*A,* 162); and although other dreams are left in comparative obscurity, the cumulative effect of their description is to suggest that the spiritual—and, tangentially, the poetic—development they signify is what is most important about the period. Further, the similarly protracted account of his friendship with John Holms (*A,* 177-81) also stresses the personal side of this stage of his life at the expense of his public and literary development.

The autobiography does give some space to his association with *The New Age,* but this is largely taken up by a discussion not of the paper itself but of the personalities surrounding it. Orage's influence is not discussed in terms of his writings, but in the impressionistic terms of Muir's interpretation of his character, and this derives from the autobiographical persona's transcendental Christianity. Consequently, passages apparently praising Orage resolve themselves into indictment, on the grounds of his failing to achieve the kind of spirituality held to be the standard within the autobiography. For example, his skill as an editor is seen as a gift for clarifying thought, but only at the expense of altering its essential character: "his mind," says Muir,

> was peculiarly lucid and sinuous, and could flow round any object, touching it, defining it, laving

it, and leaving it with a new clarity in the mind. From a few stammering words he could divine a thought you were struggling to express, and, as if his mind were an objective clarifying element, in a few minutes he could return it to you cleansed of its impurities and expressed in better words than you could have found yourself. This power was so uncanny that at first it disconcerted me, as if it were a new kind of thought-reading. Sometimes the thought was not quite the thought that I had had in mind, and then I was reassured; perhaps, indeed, it was never quite the same thought, though it came surprisingly close to it. He was a born collaborator, a born midwife of ideas, and consequently a born editor. His mind went out with an active sympathy to meet everything that was presented to it, whether trifling or serious; and his mere consideration of it, the fact that his intelligence had worked on it, robbed it of its triviality and raised it to the level of rational discourse. (*A,* 172)

Consistent with the anti-intellectual bias of the autobiography, Orage's intuitive qualities are praised—his ability to "divine" a thought, his attitude of "active sympathy"—while his skill in objective expression is referred to as "uncanny," as if it were the cheap trickery of "a new kind of thought-reading." His seriousness of approach and generalist orientation are turned into a lack of discrimination as he deals equally with the (undefinedly) "significant" and "trivial," and his major success is described as an ambiguous talent for elevating unimportant matters to the level of rational discourse.

Having undermined his intellectual career, the autobiography goes on to attack Orage's spiritual interests by implying an ineradicable dilettantism. "Ever since his youth," it is claimed, Orage

> had taken up and followed creeds which seemed to provide a shortcut to intellectual and spiritual power. He had been a theosophist, a member of a magic circle which included Yeats, a Nietzschean, and a student of Hindu religion and philosophy. He was convinced that there was a secret knowledge behind the knowledge given to the famous prophets and philosophers. . . . It was this that made him throw up *The New Age* a few months after I had left it, and put himself under Gurdjieff's directions at Fontainebleau. (*A,* 173)

The derogatory suggestion that for all his self-discipline Orage was seeking only a shortcut cancels out the tribute paid in acknowledging that he was prepared to "sacrifice everything and take upon him any labour, no matter how humble or wearisome or abstruse" (*A,* 173-4), in the interests of his quest. Enthusiasm untempered by discrimination is shown to lead to an unreliable lack of constancy. (Muir's own enthusiasms could form a list at least as long and perhaps less adventurous: but, of course, by this stage the reader is aware that Muir's true religious core was always safely hovering in the background, waiting its cue in St Andrews.) There is real cruelty in giving the pretentious yoga mantra which

Orage recommended to the Muirs ("Brighter than the sun, purer than the snow, subtler than the air is the self, the spirit within my heart. I am that self, that self am I", *A,* 173); and an account of a book he gave them cataloguing "all the spiritual dominations, principalities and powers giving the exact numbers and functions of each" (*A,* 173) emphasises further the tendency to crankiness in such matters. This eccentricity is not even seen as being original: rather, it is a given characteristic of the *New Age* circle as a whole, as represented by Mitrinović.

The decision to introduce Mitrinović at this point was not arbitrary. That he and Orage are analogous figures is suggested by using an account of a book which he lent to Muir, to imply the absurdity of his ideas. Noting that it was a French volume and that it described "the history of man since his birth in Atlantis, when he was a headless emanation with flames shooting from his open neck" (*A,* 175) is sufficient to complete the impression of his oddity derived from the account of his thought:

> He was a man for whom only the vast processes of time existed. He did not look a few centuries ahead like Shaw and Wells, but to distant milleniums, which to his apocalyptic mind were as near and vivid as to-morrow. He flung out the wildest and deepest thoughts pell-mell, seeing whole tracts of history in a flash, the flash of an axe with which he hewed a way for himself through them, sending dynasties and civilizations flying. . . . He would arrive with a large bottle of beer under each arm and talk endlessly about the universe, the creation of the animals, the destiny of man, the nature of Adam Kadmon, the influence of the stars, the objective science of criticism (for he held that it was possible to determine the exact greatness of every poet, painter and musician and set it down in mathematical terms), and a host of things which I have since forgotten. (*A,* 174-5)

The hint of violent apocalypse in the image of Mitrinović wielding a flashing axe against the centuries seems out of joint with the list of his rather abstract interests and mildly silly convictions such as the project of a mathematically formulaic aesthetic; but this is because what Muir claims to have "forgotten" is that the column Mitrinović largely wrote for *The New Age* under the joint name "M. M. Cosmoi," "in an English of his own, filled with energy but difficult to understand" (*A,* 174), was savagely anti-semitic, and that, whatever its unspecified influence on Orage, Muir himself had found it deeply attractive. "Our Generation" would appeal to its precepts as authority in discussion of contemporary events, as for example when it was suggested that an English Jew should be appointed Indian Viceroy:

> There is no question of impugning the qualities of the Jewish people. Their tact, ability and character it is impossible not to admire; but as the writers of World Affairs have insisted, they are not members of the Aryan race, and cannot undiluted be made the instruments for the Aryanisation of the world. Yet the Press talks of sending Lord

Reading to India as the representative of Aryandom, and only a few have made any protest against it. Nevertheless, everyone would feel it was wrong if Lord Reading were called Sir Rufus Isaacs. (*The New Age,* 13 Jan. 1921, 124-5)

There are several reasons why Muir might wish to hide this allegiance, including the disgust at anti-semitism aroused by his experiences in Europe between the wars and the possibility that the views expressed by "Moore" were not necessarily held with absolute conviction by Muir even in 1921. Whichever took precedence in 1940, the autobiography's intention is clearly to suggest that Muir in the early 1920s observed the follies of his fellow contributors and even of his editor from a secure position within his own ideology.

That the ideology involved an apolitical stance is made clear when Muir refers to Orage's attempts to persuade him to write the weekly editorial of the paper. His efforts are said to have met with an uncompromising integrity:

> I was capable of doing only one thing, which was to write what I thought in my own way. I did not have Orage's intense interest in politics. I did not possess real political intelligence, and although in Orage himself this would merely have inspired him to acquire an interest in politics and create in himself a political intelligence, in me it had the opposite effect; I thought that if I yielded I should be unfaithful to what talent I had. Orage at last gave up his attempt to get me to write the 'Notes of the Week' and uncomplainingly continued them himself. (*A,* p. 171)

Orage is here made to serve as the political figure against which Muir's apolitical stance may claim to be defined. There is a curious movement, if the passage is read in context, whereby apparent self-depreciation resolves itself as self-congratulation. Muir describes himself negatively in relation to Orage—he was "capable of doing only one thing" in contrast to the polymathic editor; he could only "write what I thought in my own way" whereas Orage could articulate, albeit with alterations, another's ideas for him; he "did not possess real political intelligence" and was not inspired by this absence as he says Orage would have been—but within the autobiography's rhetoric, the episode takes the cast of the denial of a temptation to which Muir refuses to "yield" for fear of being "unfaithful" to his true, transcendentalist self. By this choice of vocabulary and use of negative syntactic structures, that which appears in terms of the ideology of the *New Age* as churlish inadequacy is read in terms of transcendental Christianity as heroic steadfastness; and one more indictment, that of attempting to entice Muir into the foreign world of politics against his natural inclination, is added to the charges of intellectual confusion and spiritual dilettantism against the *New Age* circle and its political ethos.

Conspicuous by its absence from the autobiographies is any discussion of the nature of that political ethos: the attempt is rather to condemn by association, using the crankiness of its adherents to blacken the ideology they espoused. The critics have drawn from this the conclusion Muir had designed concerning his own articles: Butter's dismissal of the *New Age* material is not based on any inherent quality of the articles themselves, but justified because in them

> he [Muir] was sometimes uncharacteristically ill-tempered and carping, sometimes too confident on matters of which he was ignorant. He adopted the stance, distasteful to him later, of a prophet denouncing his contemporaries for spiritual impotence while himself having nothing very precise or securely-held to offer.[19]

The complaint is not that the writings are "uncharacteristic," but that Muir was behaving "uncharacteristically" in producing them, and this again reveals the depth of the conviction that criticism of his works should be determined solely by the degree to which they conform to the image created in the autobiography—the picture of a man whose spirituality lifted him above or beyond such evidence of temporal fallibility as being impatient or poorly informed. Butter can see that in "Our Generation" Muir was "adopting a stance": but he is blind to the idea that some or all of his later writings may have used the same strategy. Assuming that the autobiography is true to the *real* Muir and that everything else must thereby be false, he moves on, unconcerned with the reasons for this uncharacteristic mendacity. For Butter, Muir becomes interesting only after he has achieved spiritual calm and has something "precise or securely held to offer"; the processes which determined the nature of that special knowledge are regarded as irrelevant.

In his account of his interest in Nietzsche's writings, Muir says that the "infatuation" was unnaturally prolonged "since they gave me exactly what I wanted: a last desperate foothold on my dying dream of the future" (*A*, 126). Apart from fostering the political pessimism of the 1940s, this suggests that his Nietzscheanism, passing by 1919, was the final manifestation of his political concerns and commitments. Yet "Our Generation" begins in 1920 as the most politically optimistic gesture of his literary career, reflecting his confidence in his ability to infiltrate a foreign cultural formation (the operation of the English literary periodical) and to choose a sector of that formation, *The New Age,* which would offer the opportunity to direct his writings towards changing the entire economic, political and cultural workings of capitalism.

It was, of course a misplaced faith. He may have left the paper in 1922, but he did not leave social credit ideology behind, as his pamphlet *Social Credit and the Labour Party: An Appeal* (1935) shows. In itself, this argument only proves that Muir was not very clever at politics: Pound's reading of Douglas led him to Mussolini's fascism, after all. But the irony is that the price Muir paid for admission to Orage's circle was an anglicisation which denied exactly those Scottish and working-class elements of his experience which had first brought him to engage with the political system. It

was this idea of an English "core" culture which he then used to deny Scottishness, before he retreated into a religious denial of all temporal reality.

IV

Considerations of space prevent my detailing all the ramifications of such a reading for studies of Muir's works, and from even beginning an examination of his writings which would seek to integrate the other biographical and non-biographical determinants of his ideology, such as the movement towards high Anglicanism and Anglo-Catholicism among the English literati of the 1930s and '40s, the effects of the market for autobiography on the style, form and techniques used, even the influence of the publisher of the two autobiographies: the Hogarth Press. Nonetheless, I would hope that the outline of such a reading at least points out that there is an interpretation of Muir's life that reveals a pattern of recurrent crises and revaluations, and that this thoroughly denies the structure whereby a single, significant moment of revelation dominates all. That instant may have been chosen to determine the representation of the life in the writing: but that is a subject of quite a different order.

APPENDIX

The significance of Muir's revisions to *The Story and the Fable* (1940) for republication as *An Autobiography* (1954):

Although Muir's ideology underwent no major revision after 1939, it did continue to develop, and the differences between the two published versions of his life— *The Story and the Fable* and *An Autobiography*—show a distinct movement over the intervening fourteen years towards a deeper distrust of the remnant of his early political idealism, and a greater confidence in his handling of tone and persona as propagandist devices against that ideology. I can find no evidence of editorial influence on either version of the autobiography, and indeed Muir's comments in contemporary letters on struggling with revisions support the supposition that the texts were fashioned by him alone.

Some of the alterations are, of course, merely a matter of bringing facts up to date. For example, the death of his sister Elizabeth leads him to change the single paragraph which refers to his relationships with her and his other sister, Clara. After his assertion that she had "an eager mind and a spirit equal to anything" he omits the phrase "and still has," and he amends "she died some years ago" (of Clara) to "both are now dead" (94/80). More interesting are those changes which relate to the dominant areas of conflict within his ideology (notably, as so often with Muir, concerning his socialism and his Scottishness) and those which embody his response to that conflict in the creation of a literary persona. In each of these cases Muir can be seen to be reinforcing his transcendentalism.

Muir wrote *The Story and the Fable* around the time of his religious conversion in 1939, so it is not surprising that it should carry vestigial traces of the socialist interpretation of society which he had been expounding—albeit in the version diluted for middle-class taste implicit in Social Credit philosophy—as recently as 1935, in *Social Credit and the Labour Party.* But for the persona of *An Autobiography,* even these remnants are unacceptable: the changes he makes here suggest that he finds such references too overtly concerned with temporal and political reality. For example, in discussing the Scottish Enlightenment philosophers' thesis that the human personality is distorted by modern society's demand for specialisation, he had originally written:

> These things are of enormous importance, and we shall never settle them until the miner can live a civilized life and the stockbroker has disappeared. (57)

Echoes of the concept of class struggle, with the ultimate victory of the proletarian over the bourgeois, are resolutely stripped from this sentence in the 1954 version:

> These things are of enormous importance, and we shall never settle them until the miner and the stockbroker live a civilized life. (*A,* 51)

Similarly, in condemning the conditions in which he had lived in the slums of Glasgow, Muir first makes specific attacks on those who have become complacent about their social origins since they managed to escape from them: "successful business men and Labour leaders who wear their youth as if they were flaunting a dingy decoration" clearly worry the old member of the I.L.P., as is emphasised by his naming them again ("Members of Parliament or business magnates or trade-union leaders") within the same paragraph (*S & F,* 12). In *An Autobiography,* this attack is turned into a more general observation when he complains of any "successful men" (*A,* 110), thus reducing the sense of the precise phenomenon of upward social mobility eroding class consciousness and political radicalism. He actually goes further, inserting at the end of this section a new sentence which convicts him of a complacency perhaps different in kind but nonetheless arising from the same causes and equivalent in significance to that which he has just condemned:

> There has been a great improvement in the lot of the poor since the time I am speaking of, and that is one of the entirely good achievements of our century. (*A,* 110)

This implies that all social problems existed only in the past, and thus political activity in the present could carry no humanistic justification.

In the account Muir gives of his stay in Prague in the early 1920s, he devotes a paragraph in *The Story and the Fable* to the destruction by the Nazi invaders of the communal, organic life he claims to have sensed in Czechoslovakia:

> Karel Čapek died shortly after the seizure of his country by Germany, whether of his illness or of a broken heart I do not know. After the Prague in which he was 'Karlicku' to everyone and where he could walk about as he liked, the new Prague must have seemed like a prison-yard. We met many other Czech writers. I dread to think what may have happened to them now; even if no physical harm has come to them their life has been snatched away, and their Prague no longer exists. We spent many evenings in their houses; we were taken into their lives. We had no premonition then that history, to use Oswald Spengler's words, 'would take them by the throat and do with them what must be done'. The idea of history taking people by the throat pleased Spengler. (*S & F,* 229)

By omitting this section from *An Autobiography* (189), Muir implies that the only danger to social life in Prague comes from the later repression of the Communist regime. To have actively decided to cut from the text his earlier condemnation of Fascism implies at least that by 1954 he regarded repression inspired by right-wing convictions as being less contemptible than that resulting from left-wing dogmas. While the Communist takeover which he witnessed when working for the British Council must understandably have been most vivid in his mind in 1954, this excision reveals, if nothing else, a propagandist thrust out of keeping with the notion of the apolitical but generally compassionate persona.

There is a further set of such political examples to be noted in the final section of *The Story and the Fable,* "Extracts from a Diary, 1937-39." The omission of these pieces from the revised version of the book was obviously caused by the general restructuring of the work; yet it is pertinent to note that cutting these passages altogether rather than working them into the new pattern changes the overall effect of the writing and helps create the different tones of the two autobiographies. Significantly, among the most interesting passages from the "Extracts" are the one that asks: since "the rich live on the poor: why should they sneer at them as well?" (242), and that which defines Nazism as the inevitable extension of nineteenth-century materialism, industrialism and ideals of "progress" (257). Again, the loss of these passages greatly reduces the impression of any political interest on the part of "Moore"'s persona.

In *The Story and the Fable,* references to the problematic status of Scotland and to his own Scottishness are less numerous than political observations, perhaps because the quarrel over *Scott and Scotland* was barely three years old in 1939. However, there are two significant alterations to passages dealing with Scottish Nationalism. The first comes in relation, again, to his affection for pre-war Prague. In 1939 he had written admiringly of Čapek's popularity with all sections of the population:

> This warm, easy-going contact could only have been possible in a small town, and it was the first thing that made me wish that Edinburgh might

become a similar place and that Scotland might be a nation again. (*S & F*, 228)

The 1954 version ends simply with the pious hope "that Edinburgh might become a similar place" (*A*, 189), and the question of how that happy result is to be achieved is completely ignored, thereby rendering the matter of political nationalism irrelevant.

The second consideration of nationalism is another of the "Diary" extracts omitted from the 1954 version. Arguing against imperialism on the grounds that "mankind has never managed to do anything as it should be done" due to the impossibility of achieving full knowledge of all circumstances from within the temporal world, he continues:

> Because of this I believe that men are capable of organising themselves only in relatively small communities, and that even then they need custom, tradition and memory to guide them. For this reason I believe in Scottish Nationalism, and should like to see Scotland a self-governing nation. In great empires the quality of individual life declines: it becomes plain and commonplace. The little tribal community of Israel, the little city state of Athens, the relatively small England of Elizabeth's time, mean far more in the history of civilization than the British Empire. I am for small nations as against large ones, because I am for a kind of society where men have some real practical control of their lives. I am for a Scottish nation, because I am a Scotsman. (*S & F*, 260)

It seems incontrovertible that this passage was originally a reply to MacDiarmid's contemporary attacks on *Scott and Scotland;* albeit implicitly, it certainly puts paid to the insistence of many Muir critics that he never deigned to respond to Grieve's invective, even if only by showing his continuing confusion on the subject! While the Eliotesque cast of thought here is perfectly in keeping with the notion of the small, organic community which *An Autobiography* resolutely propagandises, Muir chooses to exorcise its specific application to his own background from the later publication.

Other changes are further instances of the increased conservatism of the older Muir. For example, in writing of the rise from the slums of successful business men and Labour leaders, he had earlier felt it necessary that he should deny that he had himself shared any such ambition:

> I have never had any social ambition, nor do I have any literary ambition beyond the wish to write well; I am not much concerned whether I have or lack a reputation. To be a Member of Parliament would not excite me, and if I were one I should not look back on my youth in self-approval and think that I have done a great thing by rising from fourteen shillings a week to six hundred pounds a year. (*S & F*, 129-30)

Contemporary letters which show Muir's keenness to make his mark in the literary world of the twenties ("even a column . . . done regularly and conscientiously, should waken a little respect. And it is only a beginning."; "I want primarily to get some kind of hearing in England.") reveal that this vaunted humility is part of his creation of the other-worldly persona. The omission of the passage from *An Autobiography* (110) shows Muir exercising a greater degree of subtlety than fourteen years previously.

Again, he cuts almost a full page from his description of his friendship with John Holms (*S & F*, 213/ *A*, 178), referring specifically to their shared love of argumentative debate. This may be because he no longer wishes it to be recorded that he once contended that, had he been Christ, he would not have consented to be crucified: such opinions don't quite fit with the non-contentious orthodoxy of the *Autobiography*'s persona. Alternatively, the cut may have been made because the passage acknowledges the fact that Willa seems deeply to have disliked Holms, and to have had grave misgivings about the nature of the friendship. The notion of Muir experiencing domestic disharmony is as inappropriate to the persona as the experience of political activism. The general effect of this deletion is to intensify the sense that Muir sits in judgement on his friend, and finds him (like Mitrinović and Orage and the political discussion group in St Andrews) to have fallen short of the transcendentalism he had later espoused himself.

If most of the changes charted here show the greater confidence and subtlety of *An Autobiography* over *The Story and the Fable,* there is also one example which reveals a greater degree of caution to have been characteristic of the writing of the older Muir. Having quoted in the first version of his life an excerpt from his article **"Impressions of Prague,"** he comments: "These reflections were set down when my impressions of Prague were fresh; they were sincere, on the whole, though romantically touched up" (*S & F*, 226). All that follows the semi-colon here is omitted from *An Autobiography* (187): to admit that he was a professional writer, that he did not always remain more than "on the whole" sincere, and that he was capable of literary manipulation by having "touched up" what purported to be direct recording of autobiographical fact, was too near to admitting the nature of his current practice to be allowed to stand.

However, for all the significance of these instances, the greatest difference of *An Autobiography* from *The Story and the Fable* is, of course, in the structural development of the work. Like Muir's two Scottish novels, *The Three Brothers* (1931) and *Poor Tom* (1932), *The Story and the Fable* ends with a series of extracts from a diary. The sense of open-endedness in *The Story and the Fable* is an illusion worked by the form, since the final section is an unflinching exposition of Muir's faith in the order of the "mediaeval communal feeling," and, following from the impossibility of its realisation in the modern world ("I do not think there is anything admirable in being up to date, apart from the fact that it is necessary" [263]), his implicit transcendentalism. *An*

Autobiography, on the other hand, is more conventionally shaped, with no pretence at openness of ending: here Muir, having asserted that "I cannot bring life into a neat pattern" (280), has the nerve to bring his book—which in terms of the literary artefact precisely constitutes his "life"—to a perfectly neat ending, with all the satisfaction of the happy ending of a novel, and of a completed and successful pattern of development. And here the Christianity is explicitly avowed:

> As I look back on the part of the mystery which is my own life, my own fable, what I am most aware of is that we receive more than we can ever give; we receive it from the past, on which we draw with every breath, but also—and this is a point of faith—from the Source of the mystery itself, by the means which religious people call Grace. (*A,* 282)

Emphasising the personal again and again ("I look back," "my own life," "I am most aware"), yet talking in the plural voice ("we receive," "we can ever give," "we draw"), he creates a balance that suggests the image of the impartial writer unwilling to foist his own opinions upon the reader while constantly impressing on him or her the need to do so. And by suggesting that "Grace" is a term he cannot bring himself to use he implies an entirely undogmatic faith that is nonetheless held with the absoluteness of any theologian. Such techniques show Muir to have developed between 1940 and 1954 a surer conviction in his own ideas, a stronger confidence in his ability to propagandise them through the medium of his autobiography, and a greater willingness to define and control the ideological context in which all his writing, poetry and prose, was to be read.

NOTES

All works published in London unless otherwise stated.

[1] Muir's autobiography appeared in two forms, *The Story and the Fable* (1940) being revised for republication as *An Autobiography* in 1955. For a detailed account of the differences between the two, see the appendix to this article. Where the distinctions are not of consequence, references are to *An Autobiography,* since this was reprinted in 1980 and is much more widely available.

[2] Unsigned review, *TLS* (1 June 1940), 268.

[3] "Connections Everywhere," *The Spectator,* CCXIV (18 June 1965), 791.

[4] *London Magazine,* I (Dec. 1954), 80.

[5] "A Dream-Haunted Giver of Testimony," *New York Times Book Review* (13 March 1955), 4; "Being Alive," *New Statesman and Nation* (22 June 1940), 778.

[6] Introduction to *Selected Poems of Edwin Muir,* (London: Faber, 1965), p. 4.

[7] *Essays in Diverse Hands, Being the Transactions of the Royal Society of Literature,* XXXIII (1965), pp. 28-9.

[8] There are many English and American critics who see Muir in this way; the most recent advocate of this approach is Roger Knight, *Edwin Muir: An Introduction to his Work* (London: Longman, 1980).

[9] "On Making Beasts of Ourselves" (1949): reprinted in *The Uncanny Scot,* ed. Kenneth Buthlay (London: MacGibbon and Grey, 1968), p. 149.

[10] Peter Butter, *Edwin Muir: Man and Poet* (London & Edinburgh: Oliver & Boyd, 1966), pp. 73-4.

[11] Cairns Craig, "The Body in the Kitbag: History and the Scottish Novel," *Cencrastus* 1 (1979), 18.

[12] "The Literary Life Respectable," *Scrutiny,* IX (1940-1), 170-1.

[13] Knight, p. 5.

[14] *Lucky Poet* (London: Methuen, 1943), p. 21.

[15] "Edwin Muir," *The Scottish Educational Journal* (4 Sept. 1925).

[16] "Yesterday's Mirror: Afterthoughts to an Autobiography," *The Scots Magazine,* n.s. XXXIII, 5 (Aug. 1940), 404.

[17] *A Scots Quair: Grey Granite* (London: Jarrolds, 1934), p. 101.

[18] Willa Muir, *Belonging: A Memoir* (London: Hogarth Press, 1968), pp. 30-1.

[19] Butter, p. 73.

Elizabeth Huberman (essay date 1987)

SOURCE: "The Growth of a Poem: Edwin Muir's 'Day and Night'," in *Studies in Scottish Literature,* Vol. XXII, 1987, pp. 106-14.

[*In the following examination of "Day and Night," Huberman traces "a pattern of development from manuscript to poem."*]

Because it is not often that the original seed from which a poem grew can be identified, and that growth traced, a single manuscript sentence in an undated notebook among Edwin Muir's papers in the National Library of Scotland is of particular importance. For that sentence, "Now I lie down and wrap the night about me,"[1] is manifestly the seed out of which developed the entire poem, **"Day and Night,"** printed in Muir's last collection, *One Foot in Eden.* But merely to say this, of course, is not enough. The case requires proof. Just how did the poem emerge from this beginning? How did its three stanzas unfold, image by image and syllable by syllable, from this one sentence? Naturally, there is now no way to reconstruct the process of composition in Muir's mind; yet from careful study of both poem and sentence, as well as of Muir's other writings—particularly his **Collected Poems** and the two versions of his autobiography—it is possible to show a pattern of development from manuscript to poem, from seed to final flower.

Obviously, no proof is needed to show the likeness between the original sentence and the first two lines of the poem: "I wrap the blanket of the night / About me, fold on fold."[2] The two are almost identical. But once the poem continues, different ideas and images inevitably appear. Take the four lines:

> And remember how as a child
> Lost in the newness of the light
> I first discovered what is old
> From the night and the soft night wind.

Now there is a child, there is daylight and a contrast of day with night and new with old, none of which were apparently present in that first sentence. Yet when carefully considered, that sentence does contain all these elements in latent form. For although it mentions no child, it definitely suggests a child's action in wrapping the night, like a security blanket, about him. More, the first lines of the poem confirm this suggestion. Both sentence and poem evoke a childhood scene, with the child lying bundled in bed, secure and warm. Again, the first clause of the manuscript sentence—"Now I lie down"—points plainly to a child's world and a child's trust in the protection of sleep, since these are words that echo the traditional children's bedtime prayer: "Now I lay me down to sleep, / I pray the Lord my soul to keep." When the child himself materializes in the third line of the poem, therefore, his appearance simply makes explicit what was implicit in the original note.

So, too, are the other major themes and structural patterns which determine the course of the poem implicit in that note. For instance, the image of night as the child's blanket, a source of warmth and comfort, readily leads to the contrasting idea that the day is somehow less trustworthy, while this in turn leads both to the child's daytime confusion in the poem's fourth line and to the continuing opposition, throughout the poem, of day and night, light and dark. What is more, diction and structure of the manuscript sentence indicate that the speaker, the "I," is not a child. Rather, it is an adult—indeed, according to the third stanza, an old man—who by repeating a childhood gesture recaptures the child he used to be. As the poem's third line states, he "remembers" that child's feelings, and by this remembering, which is rooted in the manuscript note, he sets up the contrast between man and child, present and past, which becomes another ongoing pattern in the poem, reflected not only in the imagery but even in the syntax, in the alternation of present and past tenses.

Still another pair of opposites—new and old—likewise develops logically from that original sentence, since where present and past are implied, as we have just seen, there must necessarily be new and old. According to ancient tradition, too, there must also be new and old where there are day and night. For in all creation myths the day is secondary. Night is primary, pre-existent; the day is made new. Yet here a paradox develops. Although day and the present suggest the new, and night and the past the old, it is the old man in the poem who is nevertheless associated with the new, and the child with the old. Is the thread of argument tangled? No; what seems a tangle is actually a prefiguring of the poem's eventual reconciliation of the opposite poles on which it is structured. As in so many of his poems, here too in **"Day and Night"** Muir has used paradox to arrive at the final harmony his vision perceived; and the discernible presence of paradox in the very germ of the poem is simply one more proof that the shape of the whole is indeed there, in that germ.

Yet the seed is not the whole, only the beginning. The next step, therefore, is to follow the poem as it grows by attracting related images from Muir's entire range of experience, memory, and dream into the pattern preordained in the seed. The child, for example, who already in the manuscript sentence was safely folded in the night and by implication lost in the day, is very much an embodiment of Muir's own childhood experience, as he recorded it in **An Autobiography.** Seeking the cause of his early sense of closeness to little things, such as certain flowers and leaves, lichen on rocks, even a yellow toy whistle, he suggests that a "reasonable" explanation might be the "fact that every object is new to a child, that he sees it without understanding it, or understands it with a different understanding from that of experience . . ."[3] What, indeed, then, could be more bewildering than the multitude of strange objects from an adult world that the child sees all around him, and sees moreover, as Muir points out (p. 20), from a level of only two or three feet from the ground? No wonder he is in the poem's fourth line, "Lost in the newness of the light," not at home in a country where he lacks experience to judge things, and where the only relationship to be found is with things as small as himself.

On the other hand—and until the end there is always an "other hand" in this poem, since it grows by swinging from one pole to its contrary—the night is a refuge from this newness; and in the sixth and seventh lines: "I first discovered what is old / From the night and the soft night wind," the poem shifts back from the day to the protecting dark. But more than a shift to an opposite pole takes place here. Because the night has now become teacher as well as protector, there is a crucial change in the character of the poem. Mystery enters, suspense develops, the pace quickens, all as a result of the question suggested in these two lines: What is it that is "old," that the night teaches? To increase the suspense and the pace and compound the mystery, the poem provides no immediate answer. Instead, it veers back once more to the day and for the remaining five lines of the stanza elaborates on a child's experience of the day, as Muir remembered it:

> For in the daytime all was new,
> Moving in the light and in the mind
> All at once, thought, shape and hue.
> Extravagant novelty too wild
> For the new eyes of a child.

But underneath these lines, the question of the preceding lines goes on working, accelerating the drive to the second stanza, with its powerful, provocative opening line: "The night, the night alone is old," and intensifying the force of the answer that stanza gives.

All the while, too, the sound pattern of the poem accentuates and channels this drive towards the second stanza. The "fold/child" rhyme of the first quatrain of course refers back to the manuscript association of the child with the protective character of the night, but it also leads forward to the crucial "old" of the fifth line, where the question of what the night teaches is first posed. Then the "wild/child" rhyme of the first stanza's final couplet joins in, to make a persistent chiming that points directly to the first line of the second stanza, where "old" is the rhyme word once more. Clearly, this line is charged with a special significance, which its own distinctive arrangement of sounds makes even clearer. There are the emphatically repeated "night", the alliteration of "night" with the *"n"* of "alo*n*e," and the echoing vowels in "alone" and "old." With all this, there can be no doubt but that something important is to be said.

What is said, however, depends on two very special areas of Muir's life—his childhood in the Orkney Islands and his dreams. We have seen that he retained from his early years the feeling of what is was like to be little and lost in adult surroundings. But he retained as well a rather contrary memory, which he believed is every child's heritage: an original vision of existence, a sense of being in a place where he is at home and where, according to *An Autobiography,* "the earth, the houses on the earth, and the life of every human being are related to the sky overarching them, as if the sky fitted the earth and the earth the sky" (p. 33). This is of course an image of the Orkney Muir knew, but it was also, for him, the world as it was first created; it was Eden. Since Eden is already lost, however, although as Muir observed, the child does not realize this until he grows into adolescence, it is really a world that lies far back in time, both in the child's past and in the history of the race. It is "old" connotes in the very special sense of the word peculiar to Muir. For what "old" connotes in this sense and in the poem is neither "ancient" nor "outworn," but something altogether different, derived from Muir's feelings about a child's first perceptions of the life around him. This "old" evokes the world as it was in the beginning, before the Fall.

Along with this childhood sense of an unfallen world, Muir's dream experiences enter the poem. Most adults, he recognized, no longer remember their early intuition of the world, nor would Muir perhaps have remembered, despite his recollection of so many childhood impressions, were it not for his dreams. Throughout his life, they kept that first vision alive for him, as repeated passages in *An Autobiography* tell us. "Certain dreams," he wrote, convinced him that every "child has this vision, in which there is a completer harmony of all things with each other than he will ever know again" (p. 33). Or later, "Sleep tells us things both about ourselves and the world which we could not discover otherwise" (p. 54). Dreams, sleep, the night, in other words, played a part in Muir's life that most of us never imagine. They taught him about that part of reality that the waking day keeps hidden; and when we see this, we see what lies behind the mysterious transition in the poem, from night as protector to night as teacher and guide. For Muir, night and dreams were the source of buried knowledge, a connection with the "old" first world; and it is this world, that still remains beneath the conscious business of daily living, that is invoked in Muir's repeated use of the word "old" and in the content of the entire second stanza:

> The night, the night alone is old
> And showed me only what I knew
> Knew, yet never had been told:
> A speech that from the darkness grew
> Too deep for daily tongues to say,
> Archaic dialogue of a few
> Upon the sixth of the seventh day.
> And shapes too simple for a place
> In the day's shrill complexity
> Came, and were more natural, more
> Expected than my father's face
> Smiling across the open door,
> More simple than the sanded floor
> In unexplained simplicity.

Because it is this "old" world that a child naturally inhabits until he enters the world of experience, of the "day's shrill complexity," he is completely at home in this first, simple place. It is a place of which he already "Knew, yet never had been told." Further, the language spoken there, the "Speech that from the darkness grew / Too deep for daily tongues to say," is already familiar to him, too. For although in one sense this language of the dark is the language of dreams, the speech Muir referred to when he wrote that "our dreams and ancestral memories speak a different language" (p. 48) from that of the waking world, and tell us different things, in another sense it is far more. It is also the language spoken on the "sixth or the seventh day" of Creation, since from **"Ballad of the Soul"** in his *First Poems* to an entire sequence in his last volume, the question of what the world was like in the beginning continued to fascinate Muir. He experimented with it in poem after poem. No wonder, then, that when the child's perception of the "old," the early world, took shape in **"Day and Night,"** Muir's own preoccupation with the Genesis theme should be drawn into the poem too, and with marvelous effect. When the two trisyllabic Greek derivatives, "archaic dialogue," of the fifth line in this second stanza suddenly break into the slow march of Anglo-Saxon monosyllables in the preceding lines, it is as if the tongues of those few creatures inhabiting Eden then had miraculously for the first time broken into speech.

In the remaining lines of this stanza there is yet another instance of the accretion of dream and memory around the poem's central seed, since what these lines present is a clearer picture of the "old" world, the child's country where everything is accepted because everything is familiar and expected. The miracle of speech astonishes the reader, but not, apparently, the child. In his mind, the way things are is the way they should be, because that is how they have always been. Whatever the "shapes" about him, they are naturally a part of this original society. They are more simple and reassuring than his own father's smiling face, because it was actually as such images of immemorial changelessness and simplicity, Muir remembered in *An Autobiography,* that he first saw his father and mother. Looking back over the years when he knew them "as a man and a woman, like, or almost like, other men and women," Muir recalled that as a child he did not see them this way. To him then "they were fixed allegorical figures in a timeless landscape." Further, "their allegorical changelessness made them more, not less solid, as if they were condensed into something more real than humanity. . . . " (p. 24). As if, indeed, they were the primeval "shapes" of Eden, so that in the poem's movement back in time, back beyond father or mother, both parents are naturally displaced by their own images, and the undefined "shapes" assume their simplicity, solidity, and timelessness.

From that farthest point in the past and the dark, however, the poem now swings back once more to the light and returns to the present where it began. In the last stanza, it is again the adult speaker of the first few lines who is speaking, again looking back on his childhood:

> A man now, gone with time so long—
> My youth to myself grown fabulous
> As an old land's memories, a song
> To trouble or to pleasure us—
> I try to fit that world to this,
> The hidden to the visible play,
> Would have them both, would nothing miss,
> Learn from the shepherd of the dark,
> Here in the light, the paths to know
> That thread the labyrinthine park,
> And the great Roman roads that go
> Striding across the untrodden day

But now there is a difference. Now instead of trying to recover his childhood in his imagination, he steps back to view his youth from the distance of age, and with this shift in perspective attracts to the poem still another cluster of perceptions that are peculiarly Muir's, and that need to be recognized as such to be fully understood. When the speaker calls his youth "fabulous," for example, in the line: "My youth to myself grown fabulous," he uses a word that not only bears Muir's signature

but carries his particular slant of meaning. "Fabulous" to him was not "fantastic," as it is often understood, but more real than everyday reality. The title of the first version of *An Autobiography,* for instance, was *The Story and the Fable,* with the story referring to the narrative of surface events and the fable to the underlying universal reality revealed, as we have seen in discussing this poem, in childhood, in dreams, and in moments of vision. In a famous passage in *An Autobiography,* where he describes the Orkneys where he was born, he says they were "a place where there was no great distinction between the ordinary and the fabulous" (p. 14); and again the "fabulous" is not unreal, but an extension of reality—an extension now being lost, Muir grieved, "under the pressure of compulsory [and therefore standardized] education" (p. 14). To give just one more example: in his 1946 collection, *The Voyage* a poem called **"The Myth"** applies this approximate synonym of "fable" to his childhood: "My childhood all a myth / Enacted in a distant isle."[4] But there too the myth is the true reality; it is what endures. After the passage of a lifetime, "Unshakeable arise alone / The reverie and the name." Thus although the "fabulous" in **"Day and Night,"** so smoothly equated to a "song" or an "old land's memories," may seem at first glance to dissolve the speaker's youth into mere shadow, in terms of Muir's usage it does quite the opposite. Both "song" and "memories," indeed, like "fable," are the stuff of the timeless reality that underlies time.

Once this is understood, the rest of the stanza follows logically, as otherwise it does not. It is because the "fabulous," the "hidden" world is so real, as the entire poem up to this point has demonstrated, that the speaker wants to fit it together with the world whose reality we all take for granted: the "visible," the ordinary. A life in which the two worlds are at variance is inevitably fragmented. A life where they are integrated can recover, on a new level which incorporates the shock of experience, the wholeness and harmony of the child's first vision. And it is the purpose of this final stanza, as was prefigured in the original manuscript sentence, to achieve this reconciliation and recover this vision. In a strong rhythmic pulse, like a wave gathering weaker currents into its rush, the stanza brings all the opposites on which the poem has been built—man and child, present and past, day and dark, new and old—into a final harmony as the speaker seeks "to fit that world to this, / The hidden to the visible play."

Yet seeking through personal effort alone is not enough. With a sudden lift of tone and an opening of meaning to still wider reaches than have so far been touched, the poem turns from the simple volition implied in "I try to fit" and "Would have them both, would nothing miss," to a kind of prayer, which recalls the prayer embedded in the manuscript note from which the whole poem has grown. There, in that sentence, was the hint of the child's "Now I lay me down to sleep." Here, in the phrase, "shepherd of the dark," is a hint of the Twenty-third Psalm: "The Lord is my shepherd." Certainly both are related, so that the poem comes full circle on this level too, as in the return to the present tense. Almost as certainly the second prayer springs from the first. But in any case both acknowledge that the deliberate will is not sufficient to achieve the unity of conscious and unconscious life—of day and night—that the speaker here desires. Only through the power of the hidden reality made known to us in dream and vision can that unity be won; and it is therefore to the "shepherd of the dark," the night as yet more than teacher—as priest, and even perhaps as Christ, since Muir decided near the end of his life that he was a Christian—that the speaker turns for guidance through both day and night.

Just as the meaning of night is once more enlarged here, so the paths through which the night must guide us are further complicated, since even as the poem draws to its close—curving back to the manuscript prayer and asserting on a deeper level the original need for night—it still continues to exert a magnetic pull on related images in Muir's mind. With "the paths . . . / That thread the labyrinthine park" the whole constellation of labyrinths and mazes, roads running crooked and leading nowhere, that recur over and over in Muir's poems, particularly in his long poem called **"The Labyrinth,"** now all enter into this poem too. Yet the case is not the same. Where earlier the labyrinth had no exit, or only a dubious one—even the relatively affirmative **"The Labyrinth"** concludes with a return of the image in dreams—here there is no question but that a way out does exist. The key to that way can be learned from the shepherd of the dark. What was an image of frustration and despair in other poems now becomes a measure of this poem's triumph over frustration and despair. Inevitably, that earlier desperation continues to sound here, like background noise, but it serves to emphasize by contrast the speaker's new mood of affirmation, possibly even of faith.

Similarly, the prayer here recalls a much earlier poem, **"The Day,"** from Muir's 1943 volume, *The Narrow Place.* That too was a prayer for the speaker to be shown the right road, or rather to be given the "clarity and love" to know and choose the already "in eternity written and hidden way"[5] that was his own. And that sense, that the road is there waiting, if one has the "clarity and love," the insight, to recognize it, of course underlies and reinforces the plea in **"Day and Night."** It is such insight that the speaker would learn from the "shepherd of the dark." At the same time, the concept of an eternally established road on which **"The Day"** was based, not only foreshadows the tremendous image of the concluding lines in **"Day and Night"**: ". . . the great Roman roads that go / striding across the untrodden day." but also illustrates a shade of meaning in that image which might not otherwise be apparent: the direction to be followed, the direction that leads out of the endless maze and into a life where day and night fit together in harmony, is a direction imprinted from the beginning on the soul. "Before I took the road, / Direction ravished my soul,"[6] Muir wrote in **"A Birthday"** in *The Voyage,* and that intimation of a road that is right because it is

one's own, of a way clear and straight as any of the Roman roads that can still be seen, cutting across the landscape of contemporary Britain, if one only listens to the true sources of wisdom, brings the whole structure of **"Day and Night"** to a fitting close.

For the poem too has followed a predestined course, from the original picture of the child lying down at night and praying the Lord his soul to keep from the day's confusion, to the final image of the grown man praying likewise, to the "shepherd of the dark" for the knowledge to keep his soul on the right road through both day and night. All along the way, as Muir's deepest intuitions, memories and dreams have clustered around the original seed noted in his manuscript book, that seed, that sentence: "Now I lie down and wrap the night about me," has determined the pattern in which all the poem's images have been arranged, the meanings they have accumulated, and the direction in which they have led.

NOTES

[1] Undated manuscript note, Muir Collection, Department of Manuscripts, National Library of Scotland, Edinburgh.

[2] Edwin Muir, "Day and Night," *Collected Poems* (New York: Oxford University Press, 1965), pp. 239-40.

[3] (New York: Seabury Press, 1968), p. 20. Succeeding references to this volume are included in my text.

[4] *Collected Poems,* p. 144.

[5] *Ibid.,* p. 122.

[6] *Ibid.,* p. 158.

Nancy Dew Taylor (essay date 1989)

SOURCE: "Edwin Muir's Penelope Poems," in *Studies in Scottish Literature,* Vol. XXIV, 1989, pp. 212-20.

[*In the following essay, Taylor discusses Muir's repeated use of the story of Penelope in his poems.*]

> "Nothing yet was ever done
> Till it was done again"

In our day poetry is more often read with the eyes than the voice, and its spoken quality—that power of language to move—is often lost. When it is heard, as all poetry ought to be, the mind creates pictures from the sounds. Read aloud, for instance, these lines from **"Telemachos Remembers"** by Edwin Muir:

> Twenty years, every day,
> The figures in the web she wove
> Came and stood and went away.
> Her fingers in their pitiless play
> Beat downward as the shuttle drove.

Slowly, slowly did they come,
With horse and chariot, spear and bow,
Half-finished heroes sad and mum,
Came slowly to the shuttle's hum.
Time itself was not so slow.
And what at least was there to see?
A horse's head, a trunkless man,
Mere odds and ends about to be,
And the thin line of augury
Where through the web the shuttle ran.[1]

Heard, that one line—"the thin line of augury"—in a single flash throws in front of the mind a maelstrom of images: massed heads, wild, wide-eyed horses; helmeted men; a jumble of spears and arrows, all glinting with movement. Seeing that thin line on the loom—the line between created and yet-to-be-created, between past and future—seeing the line brings into focus the whole of the loom, with its chaotic groups of threads in parallel lines running at odd angles to each other: the confusion of creation. It is an unbelievably *visual* line of poetry.

Such a line impels the hearer to Muir's *Collected Poems;* once there, one discovers five poems concerning Penelope. To write five poems about the same person is odd enough; add to that fact that in three of them Muir emphasizes the same aspect of Penelope's story, her weaving, and the fascination of the poet for this character and her story becomes even more apparent. An attempt to fathom this fascination is the purpose of this article.

In his poetry Muir is much preoccupied with Eden and the figure of Christ and with the subjects of time and war. He is interested in how to make the most of our timed lives, in discovering why we are in time, in the cyclical nature of time—particularly its wheel-like ability to crucify if we do not learn to control and make good use of it. Above all else, Muir's poetry implies that in order for the race to endure, humanity must discover its convictions, that it must have the strength of those convictions.

Once these themes and preoccupations are recognized, connections between the Penelope poems and the others begin to suggest themselves. In this study, **"The Return of the Greeks"** needs to be considered along with **"Penelope in Doubt,"** so the discussion of the poems will not be chronological. And although it may be difficult to go from Odysseus' homecoming "back" to three poems that deal with Penelope's years of waiting, the three poems which emphasize her weaving will be examined last. They contain the heart of Muir's fascination with Penelope.

"The Return of the Greeks" is a good example of a Muir poem that presents the differences between war and real life. For ten years the Greeks have lived with deep knowledge of the literal walls of Troy and with the possibility of imminent death. On their return home the warriors are stunned to find that life goes on and that home seems somehow smaller—what they have missed has been enlarged by memory until the real things appear unreal.

The Greeks come home "sleepwandering" (2), a lovely, concocted word which implies both sleepwalking and the absent, still "wandering" Odysseus (as does the word *scar* in 5). Their ships blunder over the bar; they have been soldiers so long they have almost forgotten how to sail. The "boundless" sea-vistas (20), the "squat and low" hills (24) don't look right; the up-close, "towering" (18) walls of Troy have knocked out their sense of perspective, both literal and figurative. The "vinerows" (33) probably remind them of "an alley steep and small" (17),[2] but "the parcelled ground" (32) is totally different from the battlefield which knew no neat lines of demarcation. They are shocked by empty space (23) because for years they have been "reading" (7) "the huge heartbreaking wall" (14).

The Greeks cannot get used to being at home, where there is ". . . never a change" (33).[3] They find "a childish scene / Embosomed in the past" (26-7), a world so seemingly trite and strange that were it not for their grey-haired wives and their sons grown shy and tall, they would go back, raise the defeated walls, and begin the battles again. Just how much they are tempted to do so is evidenced by the change in wording from "But for" (37) to "In spite of" (42).

But they stay. And Penelope, alone in her tower, watches the men as, hesitantly, then more surely, but always slowly, they enter their homes with their wives. ". . . within an hour" (45) she knows she will still be alone, that Odysseus is not among them. "In her tower" (43, 38) she watches: not *from* her tower. The tower remains her prison, and she remains in it, imprisoned alone, looking down "upon the show" (44). Muir's word choice here is a further attempt to alienate Penelope from the action around her, an attempt to portray her as observer or audience separate from the action of the drama. This separation is, of course, what Penelope does not want, so the irony of *show* is a good choice.

A kind of irony exists as well in the way Muir sets up this poem. The first and last lines of each stanza end with the same word. The recurring words give a sense of the sleepwandering Greeks' reactions and their dazed condition. They are an evidence of "The past and the present bound / In one oblivious round / Past thinking trite and strange" (34-6). The repetition also suggests the triteness of this life versus the life of war ("trite and strange" are one of the two examples of *two* words—a phrase—being repeated in the first and last lines). The strongest case might be made for the repetitious words representing a prison. Each stanza is confined within the two words just as Penelope is confined within her tower. Her solitariness in the tower in the last stanza effectively contrasts with the second example of more than one word being repeated: "came home" (1, 6): these words emphasize her separation from the rest of the Greeks.

In **"Penelope in Doubt"** Penelope experiences the same kind of dazed reaction to Odysseus' return as the Greek soldiers displayed in their return ten years earlier.

White-haired, her eyes bleached pale by time's passage, Penelope surveys her white-haired husband with the shrivelled scar. She stands there listening to Odysseus as he describes a brooch.[4] She remembers it as he talks, marvels that the hound and doe remain unchanged by time. As she listens, she wonders: despite the proofs of brooch and scar, is this really Odysseus?

Her hesitancy in answering this question grows out of more than just their changed physical appearances. Faced with him, she suddenly realizes they are both totally different people, people changed by experience. "How many things in her had died" (14)? Who was he now, this stranger, "who had seen too much, / Been where she could not follow" (19-20)? "How could she know / What a brown scar said or concealed?" (22-3). If she thinks his tale of hound and doe both "strange" (17) and "idle" (13), what will he think when she tells him what *she*'s been doing, day in and day out, for twenty years? In her confusion Penelope perhaps even equates the two of them with the doe and the hound; are they not irrevocably bound one to the other? Such a possibility is suggested by the rhyme scheme, abccba, of each stanza, a metrical device which also implies the going away of Odysseus followed by his return and might also imply the weaving and unweaving of Penelope's years.

"Penelope in Doubt" concerns the return of Odysseus, but **"The Return of Odysseus"** does not deal with what its title suggests. Odysseus is still "on the long and winding road of the world" (27-8). The poem is about Penelope, about her long wait for Odysseus' return. And Muir's picture of her is certainly imaginative: in stanza one we find that Penelope has let the outer part of the house go to the dogs and cattle and all strangers. The onomatopoeic "flapped," "lolling," and "babbler" help create the noise and sense of disorder which pervade the outer house. All manner of men come there as to a public market; they lean on the walls, spit on the floor, eye without interest newcomers. We remember here Homer's description of Odysseus' actual homecoming; the "guests" at first regarded a newcomer without interest, then with jeers, then—as they realized who he was—with fear and trembling. But in this disordered house—dusty, crumbling, weedy—no one expects Odysseus. The last line of the first stanza, however, reminds the reader of him: "All round the island stretched the clean blue sea"—and the word *clean* both contrasts with the description of the outer rooms and leads perfectly into the second stanza.

Here, at the heart of the house, sits Penelope, weaving. "Sole" (14) implies both *lonely* and *soul* and *only*—in the sense that only where Penelope is do we find cleanliness and order. This stanza reveals as well the reason Penelope has allowed the outer house to lie open, to decay: if the door is open, so to speak, then "order and right and hope and peace can enter" (23) in the form of Odysseus, who, on his return, will bring these things back into the house with him.

Odysseus can tend to these outer attributes because Penelope has maintained "at the house's heart" (14) the soul of both herself and their home. Penelope *is* the heart of the house. Here she sits at her "chosen" task: "endless undoing / Of endless doing, endless weaving, unweaving" (15-6). Here, paradoxically, we again encounter disorder: the unweaving of the day's work. Penelope describes it as "an emptiness / Amid disorder, weaving, unweaving the lie / The day demands" (19-21). But then she puts a name to it: duty. Her duty is "To do and undo, to keep a vacant gate" (22), both of which are necessary to assure the return of Odysseus which the title speaks of. Only by holding her suitors at bay (to do and undo) and only by expecting Odysseus (the vacant gate) to make things right upon his return can she get through her long days and years of waiting. The poem, then, is about duty and about warding off the despair which breaks out of her soul in the lines "'Oh will you ever return? Or are you dead, / And this wrought emptiness my ultimate emptiness?'" (24-5).

Telemachos, as a child, might have asked these same questions. His poem about his mother begins, however, with an adult observation full of awe: "Twenty years, every day." (This same feeling recurs in stanzas four and five: "How could she bear the mounting load?"—16.) His descriptions of the figures Penelope weaves are a combination of both childish memories and adult perspective; her "Half-finished heroes," he says, were "sad and mum" (8), much like Penelope herself. It is his description of the heads, of both horses and men, in the work, along with the insinuation of movement in "odds and ends about to be" (13) that creates the maelstrom image, as though "that jumble of heads and spears" (31) were being carried along on a wave denoting both the passion of Penelope and the passions of war. Penelope has, in effect, woven her fear into this tapestry.[5]

Here we come to a central question: why does Penelope weave this particular scene over and over? Would she not grow tired of the monotony of it? Why would she not weave the picture of Odysseus' voyage over the waves on his way home to her or why not weave their actual reunion? But after knowing her definition of duty, this scene seems the only possible one Muir could have given her to weave. In this battle scene are all her deepest fears: Odysseus being killed in battle, Odysseus being swept away by a maelstrom at sea. If she did not keep herself in such fear, perhaps she would give in and finish the tapestry, give up on Odysseus' return, let herself be claimed by a suitor. Thus she weaves not possibly happy scenes but ones that remind her of her fear and her duty.

Everything—all these thoughts of Penelope's; the whole of her future, of "the task grown sick from morn to night, / From year to year" (22-3); her memories of her life with Odysseus, the "forlorn scraps of her treasure trove" (32)—all these are foretold in "the thin line of augury" (14). Telemachos wonders if even the *loom* did not grow "weary" (21). Yet if she had finished it, he says, she would have "worked a matchless wrong" (30), for it represents and portrays "her ghosts" (17), her *fears*—"Pride and fidelity and love" (35). If she does not hold pride and fidelity and love in jeopardy, she may begin to take them for granted and thereby lose them.[6]

If we wonder why Telemachos thinks her finishing the piece would have worked a matchless wrong, we can find the answer, or part of it, in **"Song for a Hypothetical Age."** Here Penelope's weaving is used as a parable, so before we can examine it, we must try to see why Muir chooses her story as a parable for this particular poem.

The hypothetical age Muir describes is one in which there is no personal grief. We of the hypothetical age are "exempt from grief and rage"; we "Rule here our new impersonal age" (3-4). History's and time's cycles turn to an age in which there is much to mourn for, yet none to do the mourning (8), for we have forgotten how to grieve "In a world to order grown" (10), a world so orderly that even justice is idle (9). Like the new age, justice is impersonal (4) and does not weep. We have taught ourselves not to grieve: have found "a smoother tale to tell / Where everything is in its place/And happiness inevitable" (14-6).

But happiness is never inevitable, Muir believes, and he proves it by telling a parable of Penelope. Once upon a time, he says, there was a woman named Penelope who for twenty years wove and unwove a web all day. This web might have been her masterpiece—if she had let it have its way (i.e., get finished)—a masterpiece that would have driven "all artistry to despair" (23). Such a masterpiece, in bringing despair to artists, would have "set the sober world at play / Beyond the other side of care, / And lead a fabulous era in" (24-6). In other words, if artists refused to write or weave because Penelope had made the great masterpiece no one could ever hope to equal, the world would be set at play, would be ushered into a new, fabulous (in the sense of *feigned* or *astonishing*) age—a hypothetical age, in fact. The reason such a new age of play would be created is that artists are those who remind us of "despair," of the "sober world"; without them, we would think the world was merely play, that happiness was inevitable.

But, Muir continues in the fable, Penelope did not finish this possible masterpiece.

> "Where I begin
> Musty I return, else all is lost,
> And great Odysseus tempest-tossed
> Will perish, shipwrecked on my art.
> But so, I guide him to the shore"
>
> (27-31).

"But so"—by not finishing—Penelope remains true to her duty, faces her despair, will begin again. Her weaving and unweaving, which she has sometimes described as "an emptiness / Amid disorder," is exactly what will keep the world human and humane.[7]

Thus the poet can say to the hypothetical age: unpetrify your heart; do not let "Heart and earth [be] a single stone" (37). Break the stony barrier—weep, grieve—for unless we do this, "Grief and joy no more shall wake" (39). Although this mention of "joy" in the last line shocks (it seems totally opposite to "inevitable happiness," and the poem has been about the necessity to grieve), the word *joy* is not just thrown in. Muir implies that if we have not grief, neither can we have that which is its opposite, joy: this is the message he sings for the hypothetical age.

Muir's fascination with Penelope, then, lies in her artistry and its relationship with duty. He is obsessed with her as a representative not only of duty but of constancy, even constancy under pressure from time and social forces (in allegories, constancy was the old Latin *fortitudo,* the strength of conviction under duress). Yet I believe the last three poems give us a clue to a deeper fascination Penelope holds for him: she represents the duty and/ or role of the artist, both as an individual and as a member of society. The weaving and tearing up thus become a metaphor for the artist's work, the continuing attempt to create a great work, the constant frustration of having missed the mark, followed by a need to start again.

Seen in this light, Penelope's "making an emptiness/ Amid disorder" in **"The Return of Odysseus"** represents work worth doing in the highest sense; the fear that her "wrought emptiness" might become her "ultimate emptiness" is a fear not contemptible of but full of praise for things "wrought." The weary loom and "the task grown sick from morn to night, / From year to year" in **"Telemachos Remembers"** are evidences of the difficulty of creation; "the shuttle's cunning song" is a warning against the creator's becoming so involved with his work that he forgets both the "real world" and his true purpose, the purpose outlined in the parable **"Song for a Hypothetical Age."**

In **"Twice-Done, Once-Done,"** the poem from which the title of the paper is taken, Muir is concerned with our connectedness to the past which allows us to find life in the present. This is precisely what Penelope was doing in her weaving; it is certainly one of the themes of Muir's work. Daniel Hoffman states it as follows:

> It is thus the transformation through ritual of necessary action into sanctioned duty that redeems life from chaos. Such repetitions create the unchanging forms which extend through time and give us the grace of merging our individual existence with an eternal existence.[8]

Two other lines in **"Twice-Done, Once-Done"**—"Even a story to be true / Must repeat itself" (23-4)—give us another clue into Muir's fascination with Penelope: in her story he found one worth repeating. Penelope, too, had found a story worth repeating. Perhaps, like Muir, whose approach to her story was different each time, Penelope herself—artist that she obviously was—did not weave the same scene all the time. Perhaps she, too, had her favorite themes and wove them using her favorite images, but never wove them in the same way twice.

NOTES

[1] References to line numbers in individual poems, all found in *Collected Poems* (New York, 1965), will be placed in the body of the paper.

[2] The vinerows and alley both remind the reader of "The Narrow Place," title poem of Muir's third volume of poems. And "The Narrow Place" reminds one of the first poem in "Variations on a Time Theme."

[3] Elizabeth Huberman's extended explication of this poem, in *The Poetry of Edwin Muir: The Field of Good and Evil* (New York, 1971), is excellent; her emphasis on the tone and theme of boredom is particularly enlightening.

[4] Both Christopher Wiseman in *Beyond the Labyrinth: A Study of Edwin Muir's Poetry* (Victoria, BC, 1978, pp. 206-7) and P. H. Butter in *Edwin Muir: Man and Poet* (London, 1966, p. 288) quote a passage from Muir's 1957 notebook on the genesis of this poem. Muir states that he had an actual brooch in mind. In the poem itself, we cannot know the brooch was one Odysseus was describing rather than one he had taken with him to Troy, perhaps, and brought back. Nor does Muir, in the poem, describe "the dog fastened to the fawn's throat, the fawn striking at him with its slender hoofs." Since that information does not appear in the finished poem, the image can be read also as one of the endless chase, one applicable to Penelope's doubts.

[5] John Holloway ("The Poetry of Edwin Muir," *The Hudson Review*, 13 (Winter 1960-1), p. 555) suggests it is a bridal gown.

[6] Roger Knight, in *Edwin Muir: An Introduction to His Work* (New York, 1980), p. 193, states "pride and fidelity and love are not given; they must be endlessly created and recreated."

[7] P. H. Butter quotes a BBC address by Muir, "Scottish Life and Letters," on this subject. If Penelope, "the great image of love and constancy," had finished the web, she "would have achieved the supreme work of art, but in doing so would have renounced her humanity" (p. 253).

[8] *Barbarous Knowledge: Myth in the Poetry of Yeats, Graves, and Muir* (New York, 1967), p. 238. Holloway would agree; in his fine article he claims that one of Muir's primary themes is that of "the dignity in tribulation" (p. 555).

W. S. Di Piero (essay date 1990)

SOURCE: "On Edwin Muir," in *Shooting the Works: On Poetry and Pictures*, Triquarterly Books, 1990, pp. 59-69.

[*In the following essay, Di Piero considers sources, themes, and philosophical viewpoint in Muir's poetry.*]

Reviewing the *Collected Poems* in 1955, Edwin Muir criticized Wallace Stevens for following too obediently the aesthetic patterns contrived by his own mind, and for allowing his speculative nature to turn him away from life "to an imaginary world of beautiful objects, of peaches and pears." Stevens's desired world, even if occupied with things that satisfy the senses, remains a place which Muir calls "a legendary world without a legend." What he means, I think, is that Stevens's imagination, though much at ease among the fabulous, lacked the grounding and precedence of fable, that he could speculate on techniques of the mythy mind but did not possess such a mind. Frost was the more appealing poet, because he wrote about human action and choice as if they were already legend; Muir even singled out, in a 1943 review of Frost's work, the buck that crashes into view at the end of "The Most of It" as "a fine legendary image." Muir's critical judgments, like most of his poems, were rooted in his early experience. He was born and raised in the islands of Orkney, and in his *Autobiography* he writes about the ordinary blend of the fabulous and the normal in his native place: islanders sometimes encountered "fairicks" dancing on the shore in moonlight; a man who sailed out to find a mermaid returned to tell of his conversation with her; feats of great strength were reported and remembered as among the Achaeans; Muir's own father told him of witches that he knew. These were a few of the facts absorbed by the young boy who would later speak of childhood as the only period in life when we live in immortality because we are without a sense of the policing exactions of time. He describes childhood as a perfect unselfconscious repetition, "one day endlessly rising and falling." The ordinary activities of farm life fused in his young imagination to the heroic stories he heard from islanders and those he read in the few books available to him. When cows were brought to the bull he and the other children were shut inside the house, but to him the voices he heard in the yard were the cries of warriors fighting or playing heroic games. His poetry was a remaking or recapitulation of essential fables. His early life gave him not only subject matter but also legendary patterns on which he modeled narrative forms. In one of his late essays he remarked that "we become human by repetition." And poetry becomes more humane and more responsive to the whole of our existence by virtue of its recapitulations: "In the imagination that repetition becomes an object of delighted contemplation, with all that is good and evil in it, so that we can almost understand the saying that Hector died and Troy fell that they might turn into song."

Muir's people were tenant farmers subject to their landlords' needs. When Muir was fourteen his family had already worked three farms; the last of them was the worst, with dreary damp quarters and miserable land. That was when they decided to emigrate to Glasgow. Later he would recall life in Orkney as "a good order." That order, already destabilized by the tough existence on their last farm, was shattered when they moved to the city. Within two years his parents and two brothers were dead. The city did not destroy the family, though the circumstances of urban life did wear away the health of Muir's father. But the removal, the dislocation, took the family out of the familiar religious and social formations which sustained and to some degree protected them physically and spiritually. Muir soon commenced a succession of menial office jobs that allowed him to make his way in the world. One was in a bone factory in Fairport where for two years he breathed the stench of furnaces that reduced to charcoal carloads of maggot-covered bones. Orkney may have been a hardscrabble place, but there at least the elements of life, fabulous and actual, were fused into sensible rhythms, and the ancient order of guilt and sacrifice attached to the slaughtering of animals was still intact. Working in a bone factory, Muir was living through one kind of fall from a known, felt unity.

The story of the fall is often retold in his poetry, along with the dream of ritual purification and the restoration of a whole order. His adult intellectual life, in fact, can be mapped as a series of attempted restorations or, as I think of them, conversions, where the soul seeks to heal lesions, to mend its divisiveness. The *Autobiography* concludes with this:

> I was lucky to spend my first fourteen years in Orkney; I was unlucky to live afterwards in Glasgow as a Displaced Person. . . . Because a perambulating revivalist preacher came to Kirkwall when I was a boy, I underwent an equivocal religious conversion there; because I read Blatchford in Glasgow, I repeated the experience in another form, and found myself a Socialist. In my late twenties I came, by chance, under the influence of Nietzsche. . . . In my middle thirties I became aware of immortality, and realized that it gave me a truer knowledge of myself and my neighbors. Years later . . . I discovered that I had been a Christian without knowing it.

The becalmed, processional summation of his experience has the measured quality of much of his poetry—it's the plainness and orderly simplicity of fable.

By the time he began to write poetry at the age of thirty-five, after having launched himself as a critic and essayist, Muir was by his own report too old to be vulnerable to contemporary influences. He came to poetry an already formed intellectual, and he admitted that his deference toward ideas made his beginnings as a poet quite difficult. That deference never left him, and a distinguishing feature of his poems is that they are concept heavy. He could never quite express in poetry what it *feels* like to work a thought, and the mixed feeling-tones we often experience in moments of consciousness are so muted or thinned out in his poetry that they hardly seem to exist. His image world is more a bearer of ideas than of feelings. He felt that the task of the poet is "to make his imaginative world clear to himself . . . [but that] world in becoming clear may grow hard and shallow and obscure the mystery which it once embodied." Muir wanted to write a poetry that embodied the essential

mysteries of existence and civilization. The danger of shallowness becomes all the greater when a poet's imaginative world exists, like Muir's, as a succession of emblematic settings, events, and personages stilled and heraldic like a frieze. He kept his world clear not by enlarging or diversifying his image hoard but by refining its essential concepts and by varying the fabulous contexts poem to poem. He is like the bard who tells the same story three ways, each time with a different shape and import but always recognizably the same.

In the *Autobiography* he writes that "there are times in every man's life when he seems to become for a little while a part of the fable, and to be recapitulating some legendary drama which, as it has recurred a countless number of times, is ageless." His poems are ritual enactments of this kind, and they do not concern themselves only with recapitulated human actions. Seasons exist for him as legends. In an early poem, **"When the Trees Grow Bare on the High Hills,"** feeling the surprising buoyancy and weightlessness of things in autumn the poet becomes "Mere memory, mere fume / Of my own strife, my loud wave-crested clamor, / An echo caught / From the mid-sea / On a still mountain-side." The transformation of self into memory is some kind of purification ritual wherein finally "Attainment breathes itself out, / Perfect and cold." Muir seems to have believed the poet to be a permeable consciousness suffused at once by the instant and by the completed past—any poem then becomes a ritual offering of that consciousness, purified of personality. The haunted tone so peculiar to Muir's work comes from the way any moment in a poem can swim away in the echo chamber of the past's endless repetitions. His poems do not show the stress of deliberations, the kind of aggrieved scruples we hear in so much of Eliot's poetry; they present recapitulated suffering as if it were an unchanged moral sentence. In one of his finest poems, **"Ballad of Hector in Hades,"** the Trojan hero is doomed to recall Achilles' pursuit and the chase around the walls of the city. (The poem recapitulates a childhood experience when Muir was chased home from school by a local bully.) Hector remembers, for himself and us, the bright beauty of the physical world, "The little flowers, the tiny mounds, / The grasses frail and fine." He remembers, too, how the bright world converges on his shame and all of nature bears witness to his flight: "The sky with all its clustered eyes / Grows still with watching me, / The flowers, the mounds, the flaunting weeds / Wheel slowly round to see." His own death is now legend in his consciousness, and the singular feeling tone is relief that his humiliation is over, though the image that concludes the poem is the one we know must repeat in Hector's mind: "While round bright Troy Achilles whirls / A corpse with streaming hair."

The fall of Troy is one of the recurrent legends in Muir's poetry. Its destruction and the dispersal of its inhabitants represented for him the wartime devastations and displaced populations of the 1930s and 1940s. Legends survive in large part because they are essentially static, unchanging, always somewhat aloof from the rattlings and travails of daily life. They lie beyond fact. Muir's enterprise was to disclose the legendary within familiar facts. In **"Troy"** an old man "so venerable / He might have been Priam's self, but Priam was dead," lives among Troy's sewers, fighting off the rats that have overtaken the city. Looters capture, torture, and interrogate him, "Asking: 'Where is the treasure?' till he died." In another poem, **"A Trojan Slave,"** we see the idea-trace even more darkly drawn. Thirty years after the fall of his city, the old slave regards his master as "a Grecian dolt, / Pragmatic, race-proud as a pampered colt." For all his hatred of the Greeks, a "cold aspiring race," his deeper spite is reserved for the Trojans who, even as their city fell, refused to arm their servants: "And while they feared the Greeks they feared us most." The war, as the slave reviews it, was a system of fatal vanities built up on class and racial arrogance. The disintegration of class distinctions and racial divisiveness was one of the aspirations of the Socialism that Muir embraced in his early twenties (though he detested the Marxist view of necessary class war), and we hear it in the slave's view of what could have saved Troy. But there is also in the slave's monologue the sourness and anger of Nietzschean *ressentiment,* that source of power and righteousness for the disenfranchised which, Nietzsche argued, was at the center of the rise of Judeo-Christian morality. For the slave, the fall of the great city remains, "as if in spite, a happy memory."

Muir's 1924 collection of essays *Latitudes* contains a piece titled **"A Note on the Scottish Ballads"** in which he says that Scottish writers usually come from humble ranks whereas English writers most often come from the cultivated classes. Though he had no university education, Muir became an extremely cultivated man, a much sought after translator and reviewer, but these structures were built on the bedrock of Orkney culture. The plainness of his poems—I mean not just the unadorned diction but also the preservation of event and figure as primeval foreground—speaks for an ambition he saw realized in the ballads: "The ballads go immediately to that point beyond which it is impossible to go, and touch the very bounds of passion and of life." But Muir was too much a pious ironist, and became too much a European intellectual, to touch those extremities in his work. His poems are filled with elemental settings and actions which do not of their own possess elemental feelings. Poems like **"The Town Betrayed," "The Return of Odysseus," "The Interrogation," "Outside Eden,"** the beautiful **"The Transfiguration"** and many others are pageant presentations of life; they *present* the "passion, terror, instinct, action" that he found and cherished in ballad literature, but they don't seethe with the experience of those intensities. The textures of actuality have not been brought over into the language textures. This has something to do with the meditative quality of Muir's work. He praises ballads for their energy, their refusal of meditative delay, their "ecstatic living in passion at the moment of its expression and not on reflection, and the experiencing of it therefore

purely, as unmixed joy, as complete terror." We sometimes most admire that which lies beyond our own temperamental capacities or which we feel is irrecoverable. Muir admired in the ballads that complete, oblivious inhabiting of momentary feeling, of elemental joy, fear, or sorrow, which his own poetry does not enact, cannot enact because it is so mediated by reflection. His poems powerfully illustrate, exemplify, and report sudden passion, they do not embody it. Scenic clarity and the high relief of anecdote matter more to him than emotional intensity, and his favorite imaginative arrangement is of figures in a landscape.

The series of poems he wrote in the early 1940s with titles like **"The Threefold Place," "The Original Place," "The Unattained Place,"** and so forth, are mostly about imaginary homecomings and original places. Home, stranger, man and woman, "leaf and bird and leaf," threshold, city walls, messengers, "silver roads"—these are the figures and landmarks in the poems. They have the simplicity Muir valued in the ballads, but they are presented with a self-awareness not found there. **"The Sufficient Place"** is a legend about what suffices, the moment in consciousness when balance and peace obtain in a household while "All outside / From end to end of the world is tumult." The household, the man and woman standing at the threshold "simple and clear / As a child's first images," are set forth as mythic categories: "This is the Pattern, these the Archetypes." That intellectual theatricalization, the self-conscious designation of the vision, marks a reflective estrangement that the poems themselves time and again seek to overcome. In the most unsettling of this group, **"The Dreamt-of Place,"** Muir dreams he sees two birds cutting across the air like Dante's two mating doves, Paolo and Francesca, leading the souls lost to love. But this is a place untroubled by orthodox judgment, free from damnation. The old god does not rule here: "The nightmare god was gone / Who roofed their pain." Hell greens out and becomes a natural continuation of *il dolce mondo* above-ground. The dead and the living reconcile into one continuity:

> This is the day after the Last Day,
> The lost world lies dreaming within its coils,
> Grass grows upon the surly sides of Hell,
> Time has caught time and holds it fast for ever.

First world, last world, dream world are all one in the poem, and they compose the kind of visionary tableau Muir was finest at creating. His clearest signature, however, comes with the turn in the last few lines. Within his dream-vision of the place of redemption, of unity and harmony, comes a thought: "Where is the knife, the butcher, / The victim? Are they all here in their places? / Hid in this harmony? But there was no answer." The mind and heart can put the question to the dream, but the dream—legendary, heraldic, typical—is unresponsive, sealed off, keeping its own mysterious wisdom. Muir's imagination never strayed far from Eden's gate, from the sedate perfections of the Golden Age, but this inclination was jolted and countered by the experience of his own disordered nightmarish time. What dream of a golden place can keep down bloodguilt, paranoia, and the knowledge of genocide? This poem is one of his finest because it tells with massiveness and credibility and completeness the simple story of a dream-persuasion overturned by waking doubt, waking knowledge. But that suspicion comes to us at such a vulnerable moment, when we have already been converted by the authority of the imagination of the dream, that we are then drawn even closer to some final derangement.

When he writes of refugee populations, outcasts of Paradise, homeland, town, or family (the images in Ingmar Bergman's *Shame* could have been modeled on Muir's poetry) he often inducts himself among "the always homeless, / Nationless and nameless." His "we" is an autobiographical fact; after leaving Orkney he spoke of himself as a Displaced Person. It is also a moral and political commitment to suffer history among others, to negotiate moral qualities in a world where Nietzsche's project of the transvaluation of all values seemed to have gotten stuck terrifyingly halfway, half-realized, a monstrous intellectual creature whose handsome but unfinished leonine and raptor features were blended into beautiful but not fully articulated human ones. In **"The Good Town,"** once all the normal balances of moral relation are disrupted by two wars and their ensuing occupations, all those clarities are made opaque by the new mediators—policemen, informants, collaborators. The change causes the teller of the tale, a townsman, to question what they all (perhaps too complacently) regarded as the essential goodness of their place and which now seems to have been "conquered" by evil. He realized, though, that moral balance is not governed like fluid levels: you cannot readjust it by increasing or decreasing quantities, or by controlling local pressures and gravities. The bad, in order to succeed, may take on the color of the prevailing good. The good, intact but enslaved, may take on the hue of the wicked in order to pass unnoticed, unpunished: "We have seen / Good men made evil wrangling with the evil, / Straight minds grown crooked fighting crooked minds." The poem, for all its cool archetypal presentation, describes actual historical patterns lived out by populations in occupied territories (and even more exactly by the experiences of partisan cadres throughout Europe in the 1940s). It all tells us how the failure of the will to question and refine the moral-political values we hold most dear, and most (pridefully) representative, will weaken those same values and induce a complacency that breeds corruption and equivocation. The populace described in **"The Good Town"** have become moral refugees; they live in their native place as displaced souls.

Muir somewhere says that Eden's gate is everywhere and nowhere. That also describes the center of a labyrinth, as well as the disorientation induced by night crossings, border flights, interrogations, displacements without destinations. In **"The Labyrinth"** Theseus, or Thesean consciousness, has finally escaped the maze, which was a condition of pure alienation, perfect of its kind with a center everywhere and all else undifferentiated "place." Once restored to "its enemy / The lovely world," Theseus suffers the maze in memory, in his ordinary experiences of "all the roads / That run through the noisy world, deceiving streets / That meet and part and meet, and rooms that open / Into each other." He has a dream vision that momentarily dissolves the labyrinth's after-image which so confuses his life, a vision of a world overseen by gods, "each sitting on top of his mountain-isle." The round of human events, the repetitions of birthdays, marriages, holidays, of "Ploughing and harvesting and life and death," exist within the harmonies made by the gods' conversation. Everything is woven into harmonious celestial dialogue. It's a vision of the Peaceable Kingdom as a perfect sentence. And that, now, is the real world to Theseus, though it exists only as one vision in the image-hoard that also includes the recurrent dream of the maze that concludes the poem. That repeated dream knocks the dreamer back into his alienated life; whenever it recurs he wakes to feel momentarily lost: "Oh these deceits are strong almost as life. / Last night I dreamt I was in the labyrinth, / And woke far on. I did not know the place."

Muir's entire career can be viewed as a struggle against what he described in a 1949 essay on Spengler as the cry of historical necessity over the life of the individual. He was converted to Socialism in his twenties, but he could not accept Marxism, which he felt makes the historical process "the sole significant embodiment of life." He believed that while humankind works out its destiny in time, in history, its meaning in the world and to itself derives from the soul's immortality. Muir knew that the artistic mind shares this view with the religious mind. The view has a pragmatic virtue in that "it gives meaning to the actual life we live, and accounts to us for ourselves." Out of this comes his concept of the imagination, stated late in life in *The Estate of Poetry,* as "that power by which we apprehend living beings and living creatures in their individuality, as they live and move, and not as ideas or categories." As a definition grounded in elemental sympathy, it is winning but too nice. Muir's poetics finally are circumscribed by a sense of decency, of human goodness and sympathy, which verges sometimes on advocacy and which in the rhythms and language of his verse is transmuted into sober, diligent, modest normalcy. While he removes the human from the mechanical press of history, he refits the individual into a legendary narrative which itself tends to be overdetermining. Muir is certainly a religious poet by his own definition, but he is one who in the language of his poems abjures sacred decoration; and although we hear tell of aspiration and grief and joy in his poetry, we are seldom brought close to the incoherent cravings and indecencies of appetite and need, or the shriek of want and sorrow. His ambition to pursue our originating fables in the ordinary experience of the modern individual, and to conduct the pursuit in an almost puritanically plain style, equipped him to retell what he called "the great and the little glooms."

FURTHER READING

Bibliography

Hoy, Peter C., and Mellown, Elgin W. *A Checklist of Writings about Edwin Muir.* Troy, N.Y.: The Whitson Publishing Company, 1971, 80 p.
>   Secondary bibliography including book reviews, periodical essays, and sections in books.

Mellown, Elgin W. *Bibliography of the Writings of Edwin Muir,* 2nd ed. London: Nicholas Vane, 1966, 137 p.
>   Includes books and pamphlets; contributions to books, periodicals, and newspapers; translations; an index of poems and essays; and a list of selected critical studies.

Biography

Butter, P. H. *Edwin Muir: Man and Poet.* Edinburgh: Oliver & Boyd, 1966, 314 p.
>   Authorized biography which includes extensive criticism of Muir's writings as well as excerpts from his diaries and letters.

Criticism

Aitchison, James. *The Golden Harvester: The Vision of Edwin Muir.* Aberdeen: Aberdeen University Press, 1988, 215 p.
>   Considers such central themes of Muir's work as the Fall, Conflict, the Journey, and Reconciliation.

Bouson, J. Brooks. "A Poet 'Taught by Dreams and Fantasies': Muir's Dual Vision of Human Nature." In *The Scope of the Fantastic—Culture, Biography, Themes, Children's Literature: Selected Essays from the First International Conference on the Fantastic in Literature and Film,* edited by Robert A. Collins and Howard D. Pearce, pp. 115-25. Westport, Conn.: Greenwood Press, 1985.
>   Concludes that "Muir's poetry derives from a series of waking visions that revealed, in unearthly, fantastic scenes replete with fabulous monsters, the myths of humankind's creation and spiritual destiny."

Butter, P. H. *Edwin Muir.* Edinburgh: Oliver & Boyd, 1962, 120 p.
>   Examines Muir's works in criticism, fiction, autobiography, and poetry.

Crick, Joyce. "Kafka and the Muirs." In *The World of Franz Kafka,* edited by J. P. Stern, pp. 159-74. New York: Holt, Rinehart and Winston, 1980.
>   Considers "what part [Edwin and Willa Muir] played in the making of Franz Kafka's world . . . what they did for his English reputation, and what picture of Kafka English-speaking readers carry away from their translations."

Eliot, T. S. "Preface." In *Selected Poems,* by Edwin Muir, edited by T. S. Eliot, pp. 9-11. London: Faber and Faber, 1965.
>   Praises the integrity of Muir's poetic vision and asserts "Muir will remain among the poets who have added glory to the English language."

Finney, Brian. "Myths and Dreams in Autobiography." In his *The Inner I: British Literary Autobiography of the Twentieth Century,* pp. 186-206. London: Faber and Faber, 1985.
>   Discusses *An Autobiography* as an example of autobiographical writing that subordinates personal history to myth, particularly noting Muir's concepts of "story" (the external facts of a life) and the "fable" (one's inner life).

Gregory, Horace. "The Timeless Moment in Modern Verse: Edwin Muir." In his *Spirit of Time and Place,* pp. 201-05. New York: W. W. Norton, 1957.
>   Offers an overview of Muir's poetry, concluding that Muir "in casting off mere provincial mannerisms and dialects has made his own language that restores the strength of a Scottish tradition . . . and given it universal character and meaning."

Hall, J. C. *Edwin Muir.* London: Longmans, Green, 1956, 36 p.
>   Introductory study of Muir's work offering discussion of his life, critical reputation, prose, and poetry.

Hamburger, Michael. "Edwin Muir (1960)." In his *Art as Second Nature: Occasional Pieces, 1950-74,* pp. 86-102. Cheadle Hulme, Cheshire, England: Carcanet New Press, 1975.
>   Offers a personal portrait of Muir in a review of *Collected Poems.*

Handel, Amos. "The Sense of Estrangement from One's Previous Self in the Autobiographies of Arthur Koestler and Edwin Muir." *Biography* 9, No. 4 (Fall 1986): 306-23.
>   Explores "the meaning and connotation of one's sense of estrangement from his past self as it is especially expressed in the autobiographical narratives of Koestler (1952, 1954) and Muir (1940, 1954).

Hoffman, Daniel. "The Story and the Fable." *Barbarous Knowledge: Myth in the Poetry of Yeats, Graves, and Muir,* pp. 225-56. New York: Oxford University Press, 1967.
>   Examines myth, folklore, fantasy, and dreams in Muir's works.

Huberman, Elizabeth. *The Poetry of Edwin Muir: The Field of Good and Ill.* New York: Oxford University Press, 1971, 251 p.
>   Explores "through analysis of the most important poems in each of Muir's volumes, the major themes of his poetry, the directions in which these themes have developed, and the technical resources through which they have been patterned and expressed."

————. "The Broch/Muir Correspondence: Teaching Each Other." *Modern Austrian Literature* 22, No. 2 (1989): 45-57.
Traces correspondence between Hermann Broch and the Muirs relating to their translation of *The Sleepwalkers*.

Keeble, Brian. "Edwin Muir: Our Contemporary and Mentor." *Agenda* 12-13, No. 4-1 (Winter-Spring 1975): 79-87.
Reconsiders Muir's achievement in terms of fashion and tradition in modern poetry.

Knight, Roger. *Edwin Muir: An Introduction to His Work.* London: Longman, 1980, 210 p.
Traces Muir's literary development through close analysis of selected prose and poetry.

MacLachlan, C. J. M., and Robb, D. S., eds. *Edwin Muir Centenary Assessments.* Aberdeen: Association for Scottish Literary Studies, 1990, 146 p.
Collects papers delivered at the Edwin Muir Centenary Conference held in June 1987 at St. Andrews, Scotland.

McCulloch, Margery. *Edwin Muir: Poet, Critic and Novelist.* Edinburgh: Edinburgh University Press, 1993, 128 p.
Presents a chronological consideration of Muir's major works focusing on his "search for meaning and values in the unstable, mundane world."

Mellown, Elgin W. *Edwin Muir.* Boston: Twayne Publishers, 1979, 181 p.
Study of Muir's life and works, including chronological consideration of his poetry.

Merwin, W. S. "Four British Poets." *Kenyon Review* XV, No. 3 (Summer 1953): 461-76.
Reviews *Collected Poems* concluding that "The best of [Muir's] poems—and they are not few—are of a scope, power and stature which rank him among the genuinely important poets of our time."

Morgan, Edwin. "Edwin Muir." In his *Essays,* pp. 186-93. Cheadle, Cheshire, England: Carcanet New Press, 1974.
Broadly discusses subjects, themes, and techniques of Muir's poetry.

Pittock, Murray G. H. "'This Is the Place': Edwin Muir and Scotland." *Scottish Literary Journal* 14, No. 1 (May 1987): 53-72.
Discusses symbols of Scottish heraldry, history, landscapes, and battles in Muir's poetry.

Read, Herbert. "Edwin Muir." In his *The Cult of Sincerity,* pp. 178-84. London: Faber and Faber, 1968.
Brief memoir discussing Muir's background, personal manner, and poetry.

Rosenthal, M. L. "MacDiarmid and Muir." In his *The Modern Poets: A Critical Introduction,* pp. 131-40. New York: Oxford University Press, 1960.
Identifies Muir as a "dynamic type" of British writer who "embodied in his career much of the development, and motivation, of advanced thought of his time."

Stegmaier, Edmund. "Edwin Muir's *Scottish Journey* and the Question of Violence." *Scottish Literary Journal* 19, No. 2 (November 1992): 50-60.
Examines the theme of violence in *Scottish Journey*.

Wiseman, Christopher. *Beyond the Labyrinth: A Study of Edwin Muir's Poetry.* Victoria, B.C.: Sono Nis Press, 1978, 252 p.
Studies Muir's techniques for using symbols in an "attempt to place him squarely in the tradition of post-symbolist poetry," and offers close examination of Muir's later poetry.

The following sources published by Gale contain further information on Muir's life and works: *Contemporary Authors,* Vol. 104; *Dictionary of Literary Biography,* Vols. 20, 100; *Twentieth-Century Literary Criticism,* Vol. 2.

Heiti Talvik

1904-1947

(Full name Heiti Talviken) Estonian poet.

INTRODUCTION

Talvik is recognized as a pivotal member of the "Logomancers," a group of Estonian poets between the world wars who prescribed cultural and spiritual solutions to social and political problems. Talvik integrates disparate European philosophical and literary schools of thought and the Judaic writings of Lev Issakovich Schwartzmann (Lev Shestov) to construct a small but consistent body of work that strongly emphasizes ethical themes and individual self-control. His poems show an adept handling of short poetic forms and an austere and precise treatment of Romantic and spiritual themes. While his literary output is small, amounting to slightly more than one hundred published poems, Talvik is admired as one of Estonia's great poets of the twentieth century.

Biographical Information

Talvik was born in the seaside resort Parnu on Estonia's West coast. His father was a physician and professor of forensic medicine who was widely read in philosophy, and his mother was a musician and appreciator of classic literature. His parents' scientific and cultural background strongly influenced Talvik's later poetry. He attended Tartu University, where one of his instructors was Estonian poet Gustav Suits, and he roomed with Friedebert Tuglas, a founder of the Young Estonia group in the 1920s, member of Siuru, an Estonian poetry movement of the 1930s, and a renowned critic of Estonian literature. For a time, Talvik and Tuglas were the central focus of Tartu's literary community, entertaining other writers for discussions in their home. These poets are often grouped together as the Estonian Logomancers. Individually the Logomancers adhered to no specific literary influence or style but shared a concern with social and ethical issues that is often characterized as similar to themes addressed by nineteenth-century Romantic writers. Talvik familiarized himself with the works of Dante Alighieri, French Symbolists Paul Claudel and Charles Baudelaire, philosophers Søren Kierkegaard and Henri Bergson, mystic Jacob Bohme, critic Julien Benda, Nikolai Gogol, and Lev Shestov. Talvik left Tartu before graduating, published his first poem in 1925, and married the poet Betti Alver in 1937. Following that year, Talvik published only five more poems. He was unable to publish during the German and Russian occupations of Estonia, and was arrested during the Russian occupation. According to most biographical sources, Talvik was released prior to his death, which is usually believed to have occurred in 1947.

Major Works

Talvik placed very high demands on his poetry, and allowed publication of only two collections in his lifetime, *Palavik* and *Kohtupaev*. Publication of *Palavik* was arranged by Talvik's friends who printed only six hundred copies, all of which sold almost immediately. He destroyed much of his early work and later drafts of unpublished poems, while his later manuscripts disappeared after they were confiscated by Soviet soldiers. Many of these poems contain stark images of contemporary life, which in Talvik's experience confronted equal threats from Nazi Germany, European Fascism during the 1930s, and the Stalinist Soviet Union. In addition to documenting the political turmoil prevalent in Europe, Talvik's poems are concerned with the spiritual malaise of both himself and the European community. Like the works of T. S. Eliot, Talvik's poetry reveals his belief that Western civilization is in decline due to the abandonment of moral and ethical behavior. The work of the two poets also shares the common influence of French Symbolist poet Jules LaForgue. Talvik's poetry implies that the dire circumstances facing Estonia and all of Europe in his time could be mitigated by a return to traditional values. He underscores this theme by constructing poems that reveal a formal and disciplined style, which many critics believe reflects Talvik's desire to create order in a world collapsing into chaos. In *Palavik*, Talvik employs images culled from his father's vocation as a mortician, including death, disease, and putrefaction, to depict a world that is on the verge of self-destruction. Throughout these poems, however, critics have detected a note of subdued optimism, suggesting that Talvik considered the solutions suggested in his poetry an amelioration for Europe's troubles. The poetry collected in *Kohtupaev* is perceived by critics to exhort Estonian politicians and cultural figures to practice and encourage responsible behavior.

PRINCIPAL WORKS

Palavik (poetry) 1934
Kohtupaev (poetry) 1937

CRITICISM

W. K. Matthews (essay date 1953)

SOURCE: "Phases of Estonian Poetry," in *Anthology of Modern Estonian Poetry,* translated by W. K. Matthews, University of Florida Press, 1953, pp. xv-xxix.

[*In the following essay, Matthews presents a historical context in which to understand Estonian poetry of the twentieth century.*]

I

Estonian folksong possesses a tradition which appears to go back considerably beyond the thirteenth century, when the Estonian people lost their freedom and were converted by the sword to German Catholicism. The heroic ballads alluded to in medieval Scandinavian sources incline us to conjecture that originally Estonian folksong was sung by minstrels and had a masculine intonation. This would seem to have been lost with loss of independence. The numerous songs which have survived to this day are sung by women and reflect mainly feminine modes of thought and feeling.

Estonian poetry in the narrower sense of this word has not been deeply influenced by folksong, because until recently the nature and significance of the latter were not adequately understood. Even during the period of national awakening (1860-1880), when it was widely imitated, the prevailing romanticism was apt to dilute its racy vitality.

Verse composition in Estonian began without the intervention of folk poetry in the first half of the seventeenth century, when a group of German clergy and teachers in Tallinn, familiar with the discipline of the *leges opitianae,* made flippant and patronising use of the language for occasional verse of no literary merit, and Heinrich Stahl inserted wooden renderings of Lutheran hymns in his *Hand- und Hausbuch für das Fürstentumb Ehsten in Liffland I-II* (1632-1638). The first writer of purely Estonian origin was Käsu Hans, whose arid, but not altogether unpoetical, lament on the destruction of Tartu by the armies of Peter the Great in 1708 (*Oh, ma waene Tardo liin!*) follows the uninspired baroque tradition established by the German versifiers. Even at the beginning of the nineteenth century Estonian poetry was still under German tutelage. The Estophils Heinrich Rosenplänter and J. W. L. von Luce had encouraged their German fellow-countrymen to study Estonian folksongs, old and new, and Count Peter von Manteuffel, Heinrich Wahl, R. J. Winkler, and P. H. von Frey imitated them more or less successfully. Incomparably superior to these well-intentioned poetasters was the promising philologist and poet, Kristjan Jaak Peterson (1801-1822), whose premature death was a grave loss to Estonian poetry. He was of Estonian extraction and one of the first of his nationality to enter Tartu University after the emancipation of

the Estonian peasantry from serfdom. This is the earliest significant name in the history of Estonian literature. But Peterson remained entirely unknown until his poetry was disinterred by Gustav Suits at the beginning of this century.

Some decades after Peterson's death Estonian poetry reached sudden romantic pinnacles in the patriotic ardour of Lydia Jannsen (Koidula) and the meditative humanity of F. R. Fählmann and F. R. Kreutzwald. The last is best known as the author of that noble mosaic "The Kalevid" (*Kalevipoeg,* 1857-1861), which, like the Finnish epic *Kalevala,* became a symbol and buttress of national pride.

Koidula's lyrics and Kreutzwald's epic were the verbal and emotional reflections of a movement which resisted oppression from above not with physical force, but with organised knowledge. In the eighteen-sixties begins a brief and hopeful period of national awakening marked by the foundation of Estonian schools, theatres, and literary societies, and by the confident and courageous use of the Estonian vernacular. The national movement, directed against German hegemony, had been supported by the Russian Government. But towards the beginning of the eighteen-eighties this support was withdrawn in the interests of "panslavism." German hegemony was replaced by Russian, and a period of intensive russification set in. The poetry of the period of national awakening (*ärkamisaeg*) survived in epigonic form as variations on receding literary themes: Koidula's fire had sunk to the embers of Jaan Bergmann and M. J. Eisen. The period of russification continued till the revolution of 1905, but more than a decade before this date Estonians had begun to take active measures to protect themselves. The focus of the national movement had now shifted from the south to the north, where it assumed an urban and socialist complexion. But Tartu and the south still remained nationally significant. The oldest surviving Estonian newspaper, "Postman" (*Postimees*), founded by Koidula's father, the author J. W. Jannsen, in 1857, had been taken over by Jaan Tônisson in 1896, and he and his more enlightened colleagues now exercised a steadying influence on the trend of national sentiment.

With the growth of urban nationalism the romantic moods of the period of national awakening gave place to realism, which in literature was reinforced by the spirit of the age and its West European manifestations. The realistic approach is found chiefly in contemporary Estonian prose—in the plays of August Kitzberg and the fiction of Eduard Wilde—but it was not overlooked by the poets of the eighteen-nineties. Even such distinctly romantic temperaments as K. E. Sööt (b. 1862) and Anna Haava (b. 1864) illustrate the formative impingement of realism. The latter, for instance, sets out in the stereotyped Heinesque manner to develop a narrow range of lyrical themes and ends up with free verse and with bolder and richer chords. But it is Juhan Liiv (1864-1913) who shows the impress of the new attitude most clearly. The romantic veneer of his early verse wears off in trenchant satire and tragic introspection.

His own mental ailment as much as the spirit of the age determines his inclinations now. Liiv, however, goes beyond realism. His agonies lead him on to neoromanticism and symbolism. Lucid moments during his later years record as in a mirror not only his sufferings, but often enough a synthesis of these with the moral humiliations of his oppressed country. And the longing for physical regeneration echoes in the larger hope of national liberty, which finally speaks with the lips of messianic prophecy.

Juhan Liiv was loved and admired by the writers of the Young Estonia (*Noor-Eesti*) group, the creators of modern Estonian literature. But their youthful enthusiasm seems to have caused him more distress than pleasure. In a poem addressed to his admirers (*Noor-Eestile* "To Young Estonia") Liiv urges them not to honour *him,* but to choose as leader a man "grown up in light" and conscious of his aims, and as such better able to show them the way. This poem belongs to the year of the first Russian revolution; 1905 also dates a revolution in Estonian poetry.

II

Though the revolution of 1905 was suppressed in blood, its effect soon afterwards was to check the progress of russification and to bring economic and cultural relief to the Estonian people. The growth of material prosperity was accompanied by a considerable growth in the numbers of the Estonian educated class, and freedom of expression revived the party spirit and political journalism. The new tolerance towards ideas and ideologies favoured the development of a national culture. Schools and universities filled with Estonians, the publishing house "Estonian Literature" (*Eesti Kirjanduse Selts*) and the Estonian National Museum (*Eesti Rahva Muuseum*) were founded, the Tartu and Tallinn theatres ("Vanemuine" and "Estonia") opened larger premises, and translations of good books multiplied.

Even before the revolution of 1905 Estonian national consciousness had found expression in secret political and literary societies at the gymnasia (grammar schools), especially in Tartu, Pärnu, and Kuressaare. In Tartu, Gustav Suits, then a pupil of the local gymnasium, founded a society called Friends of Literature (*Kirjanduse sôbrad*), which between 1901 and 1902 published three numbers of the album "Irradiations" (*Kiired*), containing contributions by writers of the older generation as well as by adolescent authors. The object of "Irradiations" was to promote original literature and criticism and the translation of important books from foreign languages. After the appearance of the third number the publication was officially prohibited, but the activity of the youths continued in secret. In 1902 the nationalist literary society, The Estonian Sower (*Eesti Külvaja*), was inaugurated and before long had amassed a library containing the works of Nietzsche, Tolstoy, Ibsen, Darwin, Brandes, Marx, and Kautsky. This society was unearthed and disbanded by the police, but, like its predecessor, soon transformed itself into another. The new society came

into existence in 1903 under the name Union (*Ühisus*) and had manifestly literary leanings, its members being interested chiefly in French literature. During 1903 Suits was in Finland, where he made the acquaintance of Finnish writers and conceived the idea of issuing a literary publication modelled on the "Young Finland" (*Nuori Suomi*) album, to celebrate the centenary of Kreutzwald's birth. The idea materialised only in the spring of 1905, when the first "Young Estonia" (*Noor-Eesti*) album appeared. In the meantime Suits had revived the Friends of Literature society with the help of Friedebert Tuglas (Mihkelson), Johannes Aavik, and Bernhard Linde, and with Villem Ridala (Grünthal), then living in Kuressaare, as a sort of corresponding member. These afterwards adopted the name Young Estonia, and the most important movement in Estonian literature was inaugurated.

In the first Young Estonia album Suits wrote: "More culture! More European culture! Let us be Estonians and at the same time let us become Europeans." These exhortations came ultimately to represent the aims of the Estonian intelligentsia not merely in literature, but in politics, for Young Estonia was much more than a literary movement. Its literary bias, however, was strong. The study of European, especially French, literature concentrated attention on problems of expression and led to a determined effort to reform and enrich the Estonian language, to cultivate style, and to foster and develop literary criticism. The philological side of the effort was ably carried out by Aavik; the critical, by Suits. In his essays "Aims and Views" (*Sihid ja vaated,* 1906) the latter emphasises the significance of the individual as against the national and, following Nietzsche, demands a maximum of moral liberty. But not until the appearance of the second Young Estonia album in 1907 are these views illustrated in full. The second album resurrects the poetry of the individualist K. J. Peterson and offers significant contributions by such leaders of the movement as Tuglas and Suits. The third album (1909) widens the breach with the past by offering three naturalistic poems by Jaan Oks and translations of the French decadents from Baudelaire to Verlaine. The individualism and aestheticism of the movement is symbolised in the heroine of Aavik's story "Ruth." From now on the cult of form predominates, and the remaining Young Estonia albums (the fourth appeared in 1912, the fifth in 1915) are consecrated to it. The individualist bent of the Young Estonia group brought it into conflict with conservatives who viewed its criticism and practice as revolutionary. But its influence on the young was complete. To these it brought contacts with new worlds and new modes of thinking. Thanks to Young Estonia, West European literature became familiar to the responsive and appreciative among the Estonian intelligentsia.

The Young Estonia movement was eclectic, favouring no particular literary inspiration, but drawing sustenance from several. Yet its general tenor was neoromantic and symbolistic. These adjectives fully qualify the poetry of Suits, and the first may be confidently applied to the tranquil nature poems of Ridala. Symbolism blended with impressionism also characterises the contemporary lyrics of Ernst Enno, but this poet held aloof from clique and movement and cultivated an hermetic individualism.

The external influences which affected the work of the Young Estonia poets were mainly French and Italian. Baudelaire, Verlaine, and Verhaeren appealed to Suits; Carducci and d'Annunzio to Ridala. Such influences favoured the cult of form and style. And the exquisite technique of the Romance poets inspired Aavik's and Ridala's attempt to "renovate" the mother tongue. These, with Suits and the representative of imaginative prose, Friedebert Tuglas, raised Estonian literature to a level of distinction. Their work was concentrated into a period covering just over a decade, between two revolutions.

III

At the peak of its development the Young Estonia movement was interrupted by the outbreak of the First World War, which put a temporary end to literary activity in Estonia. When the war and the Russian revolution of 1917 had prepared the way for the Estonian war of independence, interest in literature immediately revived. The signal for renewed literary activity coincided with the return of Tuglas and Wilde from exile in the spring of 1917. Soon afterwards Tuglas, with the poets Artur Adson, Marie Under, and Henrik Visnapuu, and the novelist August Gailit, formed the literary society "Siuru" (so named after a legendary bird in "The Kalevid"). Most of these authors had already contributed to the Young Estonia albums, so that their debut in the Siuru albums had all the characteristic marks of maturity. Three such albums appeared between 1917 and 1919, and the items included in them illustrate the salient features of the Young Estonia movement, namely, aestheticism, individualism, fantasy, and the cult of form. The repressions of the war and revolution years were now followed by the inevitable moral reaction. Visnapuu in "Amores" (1917) and Marie Under in her "Sonnets" (*Sonetid*, 1917) gave candid expression to erotic sentiment in their pursuit of egocentric pleasures. The Siuru albums too emphasised the individual and his instincts in transparent terms, though these often enough were borrowed from other languages. A peculiar fondness for exotic words led to the overloading of Estonian with grotesque alien doublets. Another feature of Siuru poetry was a tendency to enlarge the individual into the social. This tendency became general after the liquidation of the Siuru group in 1919. Two years later most of the members of Young Estonia and Siuru combined to form the cultural and political association Tarapita, to wage war against the stubborn anticultural elements in Estonian society.

Ultraindividualism in politics, morals, and literature exerted an influence on language. Aavik's inventiveness went beyond the innovations that are now usually accepted. Some of his suggestions read like the fantastic and grotesque stories he was in the habit of translating to illustrate his lexical principles. But fundamentally his reforms were sane and sound, and because of them the Estonian language has become a vigorous and adaptable medium of expression.

IV

A tendency to substitute realistic for romantic moods is evident in the later practice of members of the Siuru group and in the social interests of its metamorphosis Tarapita. It is even more apparent in the work of certain hangers-on of the movement, though these remain romanticists at heart.

A thoroughgoing reaction to romanticism could obviously come only from a younger generation, to whom war and revolution and their emotional reflexes were mainly hearsay. Such a reaction is illustrated by a short-lived periodical called "Literary Orbit" (*Kirjanduslik Orbiit*, 1929-1930), which received contributions mainly from prose authors. The poets of the Orbit movement, including Juhan Sütiste, were more robust than their predecessors and took little or no interest in refinements of language and in the individualist pose. They were drawn to slum life and to the cause of the inarticulate and levelling masses. Like the English left-wing poets of the nineteen-thirties, they had a profound social consciousness. But unlike these, they largely succeeded in suppressing their egoisms and in harnessing their talents to the service of their country.

The depersonalisation of poetry was apparently carried too far because of the fluency and lack of self-criticism characteristic of the Literary Orbit poets. A still younger body of authors had meanwhile appeared. These, like the Young Estonia and Siuru poets, had been brought up on European literature, but they did not constitute a group and were free from the Bohemian snobbery of the aesthetes. For international culture, whether aesthetic, like that of the Young Estonia and Siuru, or sociological, like that of the Literary Orbit, they substituted a national culture, and for the impersonal art of the last-mentioned, a personal art chastened by study and comparison. Native as well as foreign influences were not lacking in their work. The subtleties of Suits and the alien irradiation of the French and Russian Symbolists had left felicitous traces. There was a general refinement in the use of language and more often than not the presence of a prosodic conscience. Yet the technical acquisitions had been critically sifted and applied to the sober reproduction of the prevailing emotional atmosphere. This reflected the pessimism of the times—as apparent in Estonia as elsewhere—and a new romantic radiance. Professor Ants Oras, the poet-translator, collected and commended the work of the younger generation in his anthology "Logomancers" (*Arbujad*, 1938). The title suggests a common purpose, perhaps till then subconscious, and certainly unformulated in a manifesto or embodied in a coterie. But the illustrative material shows how strikingly diverse and individually aloof were the new talents. Uku Masing's Scriptural and Protestant mysticism is unique, and the Blok-like pessimism of Heiti Talvik has nothing in common with the subdued nature-love of Bernard Kangro, or the witty reserve of Betti Alver with the vernal spontaneity of Kersti Merilaas. The work of all these and of several others found Estonian poetry emerged from the pains of rebirth and advancing towards the promise of a strenuous maturity.

V

This was the Estonian literary scene and these were most of its principal actors up to the middle of that fateful June of 1940, when the sudden and bewildering irruption of Soviet forces and the Communist *coup d'état,* which quickly followed, put an end to Estonian political and literary independence, and the activities of Estonian writers were curtailed and restricted by the imposition of Leninist standards from above. The years 1940 and 1941 were relatively uncreative. Literature had been diverted into the official channel of socialist realism, and such writers as had previously shown interest in proletarian themes either continued to give expression to this interest or, where it had become dormant, revived it.

The Soviet occupation led ultimately to the liquidation of the Estonian publishing enterprises Estonian Literature (*Eesti Kirjanduse Selts*) and Young Estonia (*Noor-Eesti*), which were replaced by the State Literary Centre (*Riiklik Kirjanduskeskus*) with its various departments. The magazines "Creative Art" (*Looming*) and *Varamu,* the latter as "Pentagon" (*Viisnurk*), were converted into instruments of Soviet propaganda, and both ceased publication with the German invasion of 1941.

On the outbreak of hostilities between the U.S.S.R. and Germany, Estonia, like the other two Baltic States, at first became a battlefield, then came under German occupation, and was finally incorporated in the newly constituted province of Ostland. Under the Germans, whose arrival had raised hopes of a freer creative activity, national expression was for the most part muzzled, as it had been under the Communists, and the Soviet-sponsored literary movement remained in abeyance. The years 1941-1944 proved to be as disappointing as the first experience of foreign occupation. Like most of their compatriots, those Estonian authors who had not fled with the Russians lived on in a state of passive resistance. Their difficulty may be seen, for instance, in the experience of Betti Alver, whose newest book was vetoed by the German censor. Visnapuu, however, was allowed to edit the purely literary magazine "Rainbow" (*Ammukaar*), of which three numbers were printed at irregular intervals between 1942 and 1944, and the publishing house "Young Estonia" was given the opportunity of renewing its activities, but these resulted in the publication of nothing significant and came to an end with the second coming of the Communists in 1944.

The Soviet regime and its author-representatives were restored to power in the latter half of 1944, and the conditions prevailing in 1940-1941 reappeared. When the second Soviet occupation seemed inevitable, Estonian writers at home were faced with the choice of Soviet ideology or exile, and this led ultimately to the schism which now divides Estonia into two literary camps.

Contemporary Estonian literature has two foci—one at home and the other abroad, the latter partly in Sweden, partly in Germany. The German centre, which was intellectually less important than the Swedish from the outset, has been gradually disintegrating with the emigration of Estonian "displaced persons" to other countries. Its characteristic representative Henrik Visnapuu, champion of East Baltic and "Balto-Scandian" unity, died recently in the United States, and others, including a small group of young poets headed by Arved Viirlaid, are in England. Even the Swedish centre has latterly lost some of its younger members; nevertheless it still remains, as it was in 1944, the nucleus of independent Estonian culture. Stockholm is now the home of nearly all the major Estonian poets, including Suits and Marie Under, and publishes nearly all the principal Estonian periodicals. Here, after a short spell in Helsinki (1944), the literary periodical "Estonian Creative Art" (*Eesti Looming*) appeared in 1945-1946 as a worthy successor to the great Tartu monthly. The editorial board included Suits, Ants Oras, and Karl Ristikivi, and the expressed aim of the periodical was contained in a modification of the Young Estonia slogan "Let us be Estonians and become Europeans" (*olgem eestlased ja saagem eurooplasteks*) to "Let us be Estonians and Europeans" (*olgem eestlased ja eurooplased*), in order to meet the inevitable demand of a resuscitated independent Estonia for national and international culture. "Estonian Creative Art" ceased publication in 1946, and for almost two years after that no periodical of quite the same order and purpose was published to serve the intellectual needs of the Estonian community in Stockholm. At last, in 1948, the urgent demand for a literary and learned periodical was met by the issue of the rather bulky stencilled publication "Word" (*Sôna*). It was the organ of a group of writers and artists known as *Tuulisui,* and two of its three editors were the poets Raimond Kolk and Kalju Lepik. It was avowedly an attempt to fill the gap left by the disappearance of "Estonian Creative Art" and was intended to provide "a free forum" for Estonian authors, critics, and scholars, its limits being determined not by point of view, but by literary and intellectual quality. True to its programme, "Word" did not confine itself exclusively to Estonian interests, but introduced its readers to contemporary West European ideas and letters. "Word" appeared in Stockholm and gave ample scope for self-expression to young poets as well as to those with an established reputation. An even more important literary periodical began to appear in May, 1950, under the title of "Scorched Earth" (*Tulimuld*) and the editorship of Bernard Kangro, who in his preface to the first number declared that the periodical was intended to "preserve and develop Estonian culture, to unite all those Estonians who desire culture, and to rouse Estonian youth and bind it to its ancient and vigorous national culture." Like "Word," this periodical prints not only original imaginative literature, but critical articles and documented scholarly essays. It represents the latest development in the extraordinary and almost incredible literary activity, which only about seven per cent of the total population of Estonia has made possible.

This activity was stimulated to some extent by the Estonian publishing house Orto, which began work at Vadstena (Sweden) in 1944 and has since then regularly issued reprints of Estonian classics, as well as new writing. Nevertheless it would be a mistake to imagine that most of the Estonian verse published in Sweden bears the Orto imprint. A great deal of it has appeared in periodicals, and several books of verse, for instance Bernard Kangro's, have been printed privately. As striking as the number and artistic appearance of the many verse-collections are their high average level of achievement and the variety of talent displayed in them. Older authors, like Suits, Marie Under, and Artur Adson, continue to publish characteristic work in periodicals and, apart from Suits, whose "Fire and Wind" (*Tuli ja tuul*) came out in 1950, have not had a book printed for several years. In contrast to them, Bernard Kangro published six collections between 1945 and 1952, and the much younger Kalju Lepik four between 1946 and 1951. The latter has already established himself as an original poet, and there are several other contemporaries, for instance Raimond Kolk, the dialect poet, Ivar Grünthal, and Reet Veer (Vellner), in whose work there are definite signs of personal and poetical integrity.

In Kangro's periodical "Scorched Earth" Henrik Visnapuu is mentioned as its American editor. Till quite recently this versatile and productive poet was one of the forces of Estonian literary activity in Germany. Visnapuu was important also as an organiser, for it was he who founded the German branch of the World Society of Estonian Literature (*Ülemaailmaline Eesti Kirjanduse Selts*) at the IRO camp at Geislingen (Württemberg) in 1949, with the object of "organising nationally-minded Estonian culture-workers all over the world" in an effort to preserve and develop the national tradition. The literary reflection of this undertaking was the quarterly symposium "The Gatherer" (*Koguja*), one of whose editors was Pedro Krusten, who is now in the U.S. This publication reflects the term rather than the peak of an intense literary activity, which, astonishingly enough, was not brought to a standstill even by the increased cost of book production resulting from the currency reform in Germany. Karl Kesa's substantial and well-printed anthology "Blue Weave" (*Sinikangas*, 1948), covering Estonian poetry from K. J. Peterson to Raimond Kolk, may be taken as a salient illustration of the spirit of perseverance which has stimulated this activity and successfully overcome all obstacles and difficulties. This anthology also represents a persistent and salutary demand for poetry among Estonians in exile.

Such a demand is the best augury for the development of expatriate Estonian poetry, though the exodus of Estonians from Germany overseas may exercise an injurious effect in the long run, unless the Estonian groups in the Americas and the Antipodes can survive as cultural units. Indeed, the very existence of an Estonian literature in exile very largely depends on the existence of a relatively numerous and educated reading public. The numbers of the Estonian community in Europe were highest in 1945-1946 and since then have gradually declined. The decline has led to depletion and diminution of the main centres and to the establishment of new ones elsewhere. But even this inevitable process of decentralisation can be counterbalanced to some extent by active collaboration among the various scattered centres, and realisation of such a possibility has led to the multiplication of branches of national organisations like the Estonian National Fund and the World Society of Estonian Literature, to the revival of the Young Estonia (*Noor-Eesti*) Press in Stockholm, and to the foundation of the very enterprising Estonian Authors' Cooperative Society (*Eesti Kirjanike Kooperativ*), which has already published an outstanding series of original prose works and some books of verse in Lund.

The strength of Estonian poetry in exile at the present time resides in its possession of a notable body of authors, including several of those who were actively associated with its most significant modern movements. Its weakness is mostly a function of time, for without a new generation to cultivate it, this poetry and, in fact, expatriate Estonian literature in general can hardly be expected to survive. Naturally enough its attitude has been conservative rather than progressive, for it has tended on the whole to reproduce the models and manners of a decade ago. This has been acutely felt by the editors of "Word," and one of them, Ilmar Talve, has expressly urged the desirability of adapting the pre-war literary tradition to changing needs. Here we have a sane approach to national literature in exile which refuses to neglect the tendency to change characteristic of all living literatures.

Ivar Ivask (essay date 1960)

SOURCE: "'The Logomancers': 1934," in *Estonian Poetry and Language: Studies in Honor of Ants Oras*, edited by Viktor Koressaar and Aleksis Rannit, VC Kirjastus Vaba Eesti Estonian Learned Society in America, 1965, pp. 280-7.

[*In the following essay, originally published in 1960, Ivask compares Talvik with other members of the Logomancers Group of Estonian poets, admiring the idealistic qualities of his poetry.*]

THE "LOGOMANCERS": 1934

> Our task is to enclose in slim stanzas
> the blind rage of the elements.[1]
>
> Heiti Talvik

A reaction was bound to come against both the stylistic refinement of "Young Estonia" and the experimental subjectivism of "Siuru". It came in the twenties, when some groups of writers began to demand greater "closeness to life", even "proletarian" realism instead of Symbolism and Expressionism. They found their mouthpiece in the periodical *Literary Orbit*. Poetry in particular suffered by this change in the general literary climate. Soon the social was exulted above the individual. Events of the day were described in free verse, which in turn encouraged laxity of form and journalistic fluency. Estonian verse became impersonal, verbose, and provincially limited in its outlook and sympathies. For a while it almost seemed as if "Young Estonia" had hardly existed as a major cultural influence. Suits himself had ceased writing verse. Under alone in these years achieved full mastery, coming to occupy the elevated but solitary position of an acknowledged living classic.[2]

The young democratic state itself underwent a number of far-reaching political changes during these crucial years—partly on account of the world economic crisis, partly because of the increasing trend towards totalitarianism abroad. The year 1934 saw several political developments come to a sudden head. The president dissolved the parliament, the political activity of all parties was forbidden, and an authoritarian regime (although mild in its effects) was set up. It is against this literary and political ferment that we have to view the emergence of a new generation of poets in the thirties.

The poets and writers of "Young Estonia" had moved between Tartu and Helsinki, those of "Siuru" between Tartu and Tallinn, but the young generation of poets was firmly centered in Tartu. They were all connected with the academic life of the university and—with few exceptions—even shared membership in the same student organization ("Veljesto"). Having grown up during their country's years of independence, they had naturally attended schools in their own native language, not Russian or German. Being Estonians as well as Europeans seemed to them in no need of special stressing. No literary côterie was formed, nor were any violent manifestoes issued. There was no urgent need anymore to publish separate albums in the tradition established by "Young Estonia" and "Siuru". Since 1923 there existed the excellent literary magazine *Looming* (Creation) in which they could publish their verse. Yet these young poets were recognizable for their common insistence on the primacy of cultural and spiritual values rather than on any programmatically distorted, foggy concept of "closeness to life". They shared an intense awareness of world literature in obvious distinction from the writers represented by the *Literary Orbit*. From the latter they also differed in their careful craftsmanship that sometimes resulted in a formal discipline akin to classicism. Still their poetry was by no means an aesthetic abstraction of pure poetry divorced from concrete life; their ethical bias was strong.

These poets began to publish in periodicals around 1930 and their first books came out between 1934-38. Of the outstanding poets of this generation, Heiti Talvik made his début somewhat ahead of the others in 1934, when his collection *Fever* appeared. The title captures well the restless state of the country caught between two mighty totalitarian camps in the West and the East, harbouring deep-set political problems of its own. It was around the idealistic Talvik that the other young poets gathered, among them Betti Alver, Bernard Kangro, Kersti Merilaas (b. 1913), and August Sang (b. 1914), without forming any strictly defined literary school. When Talvik and Alver later married, they constituted as famous a nucleus for a literary movement as had Under and Adson in the days of "Siuru". It seems that only the theologian Uku Masing had no contacts with this circle of friends, though he definitely belongs to the same generation.

Friedebert Tuglas was the leading literary critic to emerge from "Young Estonia". "Siuru", too, could boast of an interesting critic in the person of the minor poet Johannes Semper, author of books on *The French Mind* and Whitman. In the thirties, the growing influence of a third important critic, Ants Oras, was rapidly telling. Educated at Oxford, he was teaching English literature at Tartu University. His great impact upon the poets of this decade came from his stimulating essays on Estonian and European writers as well as from his many fine translations from the major literatures of Europe. It was he who selected and prefaced an anthology from the poetry of the new literary generation. Published in 1938, the title finally gave a name to these poets—*Logomancers*, magicians of the word or, in Estonian, "Arbujad".

In attempting to characterize the "Logomancers" as a group, critics have come up with several suggestions. A. Oras himself speaks of a new poetic Romanticism[3] and calls all the poets Neo-Symbolists.[4] W. K. Matthews talks likewise of a new romantic radiance[5] while K. Ristikivi terms the trend neo-classical.[6] We are reminded more of the Neoparnassian movements of "Clarism" and "Acmeism" in modern Russian letters. "Acmeism" crystallized around the poet Nikolay Gumilev in 1913. Gumilev liked Shakespeare, Rabelais, Villon, Théophile Gautier, and the French Parnassians—a literary taste shared by Talvik. Both professed an admiration for Pushkin. Gumilev's definition of "Acmeism" or "Adamism" (a firm and manly vision of life) must have pleased the Estonian poet, since it demanded among other things, "A greater balance of powers and a more precise notion of the tie between subject and object than was the case with Symbolism."[7] Gumilev died before a Communist firing squad, while Talvik's fate was quite similar—he died after incarceration in a Red prison. However, the possible influence of "Acmeism" should not be overemphasized, since there were several other influences upon Talvik's verse that have to be regarded as at least as significant. And if we consider such "Logomancers" as Kangro and Masing, whose verse evinces little affinity with the ideals of "Acmeism", then it becomes clear that the critic has to be wary in claiming any major influences upon them *as a group*. The "Logomancers" were perhaps the least homogeneous major literary movement in Estonian poetry.

The debt of these extremely form-conscious poets of the thirties to "Young Estonia", that is Suits and Ridala, will be readily granted. But Liiv's haunting cadences also return sometimes in Kangro and Alver. Even deeper than these influences may have been that of the many-sided poetry of Under. The dramatic restlessness and self-analysis in Talvik more than once recalls the same qualities in Under. Certain traces of her irony are to be found in Alver's early, very different kind of poetry, while Alver's later turning towards greater simplicity and warmth of expression owes possibly much to the example of Under. Masing's attempt to fuse Expressionist imagery with the solemnity of the Psalms was clearly foreshadowed in the poems Under wrote between 1919 and 1922. Kangro and Merilaas, too, drew some inspiration from their great predecessor.[8] In short, the "Logomancers" owe as much to the main tradition of Estonian poetry as to European literature.

HEITI TALVIK: DAY OF JUDGMENT

Ants Oras has called Heiti Talvik "the poet with the greatest sense of ethical responsibility in his generation".[9] Talvik was born in 1904 in Pärnu, a seaport and well-known resort on the West coast of Estonia. His father was a physician with strong philosophical interests who became professor of Forensic Medicine at Tartu after World War I. His mother was a fine pianist. In due course the future poet enrolled at the university in order to study literature and languages. One of his teachers was Gustav Suits. During his student days he lived in a small attic-room in the house of Friedebert Tuglas, one-time founder of "Young Estonia" and later member of "Siuru". As a student, Heiti Talvik read widely and voraciously—far beyond the requirements for passing the necessary examinations. He made a try at one of these examinations and even chose a topic for a thesis to be written under Professor Suits (about Gogol's humour), but then decided not to graduate after all and to devote himself entirely to poetry. Talvik's first poem was published in 1925.

Fellow students with similar literary interests began to cluster around the young poet whose definite convictions lent him an air of natural authority. What attracted them to Talvik were personal as well as intellectual qualities. Personally he charmed all those who came in contact with him by his courteous kindliness and great consideration toward others. Behind his brilliant conversation could be felt an uncompromising attitude in matters of the spirit, reflecting inner integrity and true nobility. With his Dantesque profile he had in no time earned the nickname of "Habsburg". There was about him the aura of a dedicated monk or priest, although he certainly did not shun the bohemian symposia of his friends and other poets.

The frequent gatherings in Talvik's tiny room actually became—in the amusing words of an eyewitness—a third, private academy in addition to the popular coffee-house "Werner" and, of course, the university itself. From these meetings radiated a new awareness of literary standards. The discussion was usually preceded by Talvik's readings from his celebrated notebook (called the "brown bacillus" on account of its brown leather binding). It contained his favourite poems and passages culled from his extensive reading, which included such diverse authors as Villon, Rabelais, Bellman, Gogol, Heine, Leopardi, Poe, Baudelaire, Rimbaud, Dostoyevsky, in addition to Homer, Dante, Shakespeare, Cervantes. Of contemporary poets he liked to quote Blok, Heym, and Tuwim (the Polish poet of "Skamander" fame). Sometimes the conversation strayed into the more abstract field of philosophy and then ideas of Kierkegaard, Soloviev, even the thought of the mystic Jacob Böhme would capture the imagination of those present. But the talk would sooner or later revert to Dante, probably Talvik's favourite poet.[10] The selection of names is indicative of Talvik's own tastes and inclinations as a poet. Oras reports that Talvik expected from literature "structure, bone, a definite outline, energy" which stood for "spiritual greatness, personality, fire—not narcosis".[11] No wonder, that this particular generation in Estonian poetry is decisively marked by formal discipline, which does not degenerate into an aesthetic end in itself. It is coupled more often than not with alert intellectual inquiry, a realization of the larger philosophic issues peculiar to our age. Although these young poets differed greatly among themselves with regard to background and temperament, still all of them shared a dislike for mere literary improvisation and irresponsible trifling in matters of art. It is precisely this correlation of formal rigour with ethical responsibility that made Talvik so effective an influence on his circle—"not as teacher, adviser, but simply as a human magnet",[12] explains A. Aspel, one of his friends and best critics.

In the early thirties Talvik married a young poetess from his circle, Betti Alver. Both were equally devoted to the pursuit of their art and inspired one another to ever greater achievements (though their disdain for practical matters did not improve their material situation). Talvik's uncompromising attitude, his immense self-criticism did not permit him to turn out in rapid succession translations or essays for periodicals; Alver published more, prose as well as translations. The traditional gatherings of the student-poets were continued in the couple's slightly larger lodgings. The atmosphere, even though marked by more maturity, must have been somewhat like that at discussions held by English undergraduate poets at Oxford and Cambridge in the early thirties. When the second Russian occupation was imminent in 1944, Talvik stayed with his wife in their native country. He was imprisoned in 1945 and died after his release from prison in 1947.

It is against this background that we have to view the poems of Heiti Talvik. It is the poetry of a passionately searching and fighting idealist. This quality makes him very much a part of the main tradition of Estonian poetry, which has been characterized by Ants Oras in the following manner: "Estonian literature has so far been of necessity the literature of a fighting people and its greatest names are—on various levels—names of spiritual fighters. . . . Quiet contemplation has had little room in it, since history has not left much time to Estonians for silent meditation."[13] In order to print Talvik's first book of poems, his friends got up an ad hoc "publishing house" and risked an edition of 600 copies. To everybody's surprise, all of them were sold (partly, perhaps, because of the zeal with which friends acted as salesmen). *Fever* came out in 1934 and contained Talvik's poems from 1924—1934, forty-five in all. The reader today, aware of the poet's subsequent development, no longer mistakes its occasionally "decadent" images of death and decay for the incurable disease of a corrupt organism, but takes them for a passing fever. *Fever* actually represents an act of purification, a kind of purgatory, clearly shown to be a temporary state in both the opening and the concluding poem of the volume. The first poem is entitled **"Legendary"** and evokes the trusting wonder of childhood, when the poet with his small brother wandered along the native coast: "Across the white promontory, Through the radiant day there glistens our shore. There we shall disappear—a golden seed in our breast. The growing gift of the eternal sun." This piece is intentionally placed in strong contrast to the feverish search of the rest of the book, which leads through malice, death, and dissolution, yet ends with a real "Liberation"—a discovery of the world of the spirit that is not subject to transitoriness. I quote: "God's whip hit the water And my wreck was thrown against a reef. From my heart the seal was broken, From my lips—the red wax. So my senses were freed from the flesh And the Tempter quit my hearth. My ribs turned into harpstrings That await the Musician." The poet's spirit emerges as clean from all kinds of temptations and doubts as a skeleton from the putrefied flesh.

The cause of Talvik's fever is a profound preoccupation with death. Whatever the biographical explanation for it, this fear is clearly present in cynical confessions and descriptions such as **"After the Revolution"**, **"Blasphemous Ballad / Pastiche à la Villon"**, **"Across Graves"**, **"Despair"**, or **"Corpse on the Shore"**. Another poem does not promise more than **"Hangover Reflections"**, yet its motto from Dostoyevsky's *The Possessed*, "My whole life God has tormented me", alerts the reader. We find these lines: "Ah, but around man's throat there hangs a noose The end of which is in Your hands—and that's the soul." It is interesting to note that in spite of the obvious metaphysical bent of many of these poems, they also often evince a fine sensitivity towards nature. Besides the already quoted poem **"Legendary"**, we recall here, as examples, **"Winter Night"**, the balladic **"On the Reefs"**, and **"In the Swamp"**.

Fever has to be seen as Talvik's *Waste Land*, an act of catharsis that is accomplished by looking unflinchingly at all that is vile in one's self and in life at large. This constitutes the first phase of Talvik's spiritual quest as a poet. *Day of Judgment* (1937) represents its second phase. The title, inspired by the Old Testament, fits the basically prophetic character of the book. A section of early poems (1925—1931) and the translations of some poems by Blok are followed by two sequences, **"Dies irae"** and **"In the Twilight of the Gods"** (1934—1937). They constitute the most memorable achievement of this collection. In these cycles the prophet and judge of his time is fully revealed, but—characteristically for Talvik's honesty—a judge who sits in severe judgment on himself as well. A. Oras sees the essential quality of these poems in their ethical sensibility: "More intensely than most he sensed the approaching 'twilight of the gods', the weakening of the moral fibre of the western world whose bulwarks seemed to crumble so easily under the impact of totalitarian dogma and practice . . . The poet's greatest task for him was to impose spiritual order on the threatening chaos." He sees further a relationship with Julien Benda's philosophy, the Estonian poet being "one of the few 'clerks' absolutely refusing to have any truck with the Great Betrayal."[14]

Talvik in his new rôle as poet-prophet has matured sufficiently to perceive besides his own condition the human condition as such. He castigates his country's often smug self satisfaction, its political short-sightedness and the drowsiness of his fellow poets who are caught sleeping "around the extinguished lamp" in a truly apocalyptic time. Many such poems are what the Germans call *Zeitdichtung,* but on so high a level that in epigrammatic sharpness and metaphysical depth they may surpass even the remarkable achievement of Suits in this genre.[15] Talvik's style has become more dense, more economic; the few ornamental details derived from the decadent poets have disappeared entirely. The prophetic criticism expressed in this style may seem at times almost Marxist or nihilistic in its sweeping radicalism. He attacks the church for its weakness and envisions the revolution dawning like a bloody sun above the jungle of the cities. Yet such quotes can easily be countered by others that lash out sarcastically against the mere numbers of the mob, its messianic delusions. The truth is that the poet is attacking all hard and fast dogmas, their badly compromised pseudo-solutions: "Dogmas are the stronghold of cowards Which is attacked by Chance". Talvik's answer to this predicament is an extreme measure: "Our God remains unshaped by human hands And our way, regardless of the mind's fetters, Leads back to life". Spiritual rebirth is characterized in these terms: "What does it help that Mammon has come into our yard? In his plenty rotted the ground of our being. It is time to renounce fame, wealth, and one's brother, In order to find one's self again—Pristine purity in the pangs of birth and transformation". The superhuman purity of God appears to have only a very indirect effect upon this process of renewal. But this impression is quickly corrected in the **"Songs of Lucifer"**, in which God breaks into the Luciferian or human sphere: "I shouted as much as my blood had strength,

And awoke—between Your bridegroom's hands". This God, however, is still essentially the Jehovah of the Old Testament as described in the **"Chorus of Slaves"**: "Stern is our Lord of Peril, Yet He is what we want. / In streams of fire descending, He rules whom Moses saw. Stay free in His unbending, Inexorable law!"[16] A. O.). Indeed, the poet has come a long way from the **"Blasphemous Ballad"**. The Day of Judgment is past, and after the agonizing night there dawns a new morning. Thus, appropriately, the second collection of Talvik ends with the symbolic poem **"Morning"** that celebrates a new-found sense of mission and of personal ethical-religious responsibility towards life and mankind: "It is time to spur the stallion Up the range of cliffs, In order to fling from there An iron gauntlet into the face of night".

The final position that Heiti Talvik arrived at as poet is embodied in four poems which were published in literary journals from 1939 to 1942. In the year of the outbreak of World War II, the Estonian poet printed what is perhaps his most moving poem, entitled simply **"Sunset"**—the sunset of old Europe, of the independence of his native country, of humane values in general. He begins with the lament that "Soon no hand grows tender roses, Mutely crumble croft and palace", which is followed by apocalyptic visions of destruction and death. But death is seen in an altogether new, consoling light, since "Corpses lie with bloated bellies, But like silver gleam their features". In this rapid disintegration of a humane way of life, the poet has the courage to advocate the paradoxical attitude of Christian love and forgiveness: "Now that friend stalks friend, that kindling Thunderclouds of wrath await us, Let us deal our only dwindling Loaf to those who jeer and hate us" (A. O.). Talvik's spiritual evolution has come full circle. On a higher plane he has arrived at the purity of heart which he so movingly described in the opening poem of his first book. It had been a metaphysical search all along. Once the existential anxiety of death was conquered, Talvik proceeded from the I to the We. After having discovered the inexorable Jehovah of the Old Testament, he finally achieved a union of Man and Man, Man and God in the love of Christ. Talvik's small body of poetry constitutes the most essential and lucid expression of man's ancient quest for spiritual truth and integrity in Estonian poetry.[17]

NOTES

[1] Heiti Talvik, *Kogutud luuletused* (Stockholm, 1957), p. 109.

[2] Karl Ristikivi, *Eesti kirjanduse lugu* (Stockholm, 1954), p. 120.

[3] "Estonian Poetry", p. 9.

[4] *Storia*, p. 65.

[5] Matthews, *Anthology*, p. XXII.

[6] *Eesti kirjanduse lugu*, p. 120.

[7] Renato Poggioli, *The Poets of Russia, 1890-1930* (Cambridge, 1960), p. 214.

[8] Ivar Ivask, "Eesti lüürika bilanss sajandi keskel", *Tulimuld*, No. 3 (1959), p. 193.

[9] Oras, *Storia*, p. 60.

[10] Harald Parrest, "Heiti Talvik", *Tulimuld*, No. 6 (1954), pp. 324-329.

[11] "Heiti Talvik" in H. Talvik, *Kogutud luuletused*, p. 5.

[12] Aleksander Aspel, "Heiti Talviku isiksus ja luule", *Mana*, No. 4 (1958), p. 9.

[13] "Heiti Talvik" in H. Talvik, *Kogutud luuletused*, p. 5.

[14] Oras, *Storia*, p. 60-61.

[15] Aspel, op. cit., p. 23.

[16] *Mana*, No. 4 (1958), p. 6.

[17] Aspel, op. cit., p. 24.

Aleksis Rannit (essay date 1976)

SOURCE: "Heiti Talvik, From Decadent Dream to Martyrdom," in *Journal of Baltic Studies*, Vol. VIII, No. 2, Summer, 1977, pp. 142-9.

[*In the following essay, which was originally presented to the 39th P.E.N. International Congress, Rannit isolates such philosophical influences on Talvik's poetry as Henri Bergson, Lev Shestov, and Judaism.*]

Estonia, my native country, and her literature are little known to the world at large; thus I think it would be helpful to recall a few facts from her historical and literary life. Proto-Estonians and Estonians, as shown by archaeological discoveries, have inhabited the shores of the Baltic Sea for at least five to six millennia. Yet Estonia is seldom mentioned or described in the writings of classical antiquity. Although Tacitus wrote of a people called "Aestii," it is not clear whether he meant the Estonians themselves or their neighbours. Much later, Alfred the Great and the medieval chroniclers gave the first descriptions of the country, some of them full of enthusiasm. And it was also in the medieval period that the Estonian folk epic *Kalevipoeg* (*The Son of Kalev*) was conceived. The late Norman Holmes Pearson of Yale University has praised this epic highly; and in view of the power and unity of the whole composition, as well as its metaphorical richness and musicality, Professor Pearson's praise is not undeserved. *Kalevipoeg* has been translated into German, Russian, Finnish, Swedish, Czech, Hebrew and other tongues; but unfortunately it has not yet been rendered into such major languages as English, French, Spanish, Arabic or Chinese.

Estonia lost her independence as early as the thirteenth century, in the course of Christendom's expansion toward the East. At the beginning of that century Germany and Denmark—two equally powerful countries—attacked Estonia simultaneously from the South and North. After a war of nearly three decades, the much smaller Estonian army was forced to surrender, and the country was divided between her conquerors.

Yet the creative spirit of the Estonians remained unbroken, and, during the next seven centuries, under the rule of various larger powers, one million people in Estonia produced a treasury of 400,000 folk songs, giving her the richest folklore of any European country. Strangely enough, a small population is often a positive factor in a nation's creativity. Smaller countries often possess and enjoy a greater cultural intensity and productivity than larger ones. And that is not only a contemporary phenomenon. We can recall how early medieval Iceland, whose population at the time was only 10,000, gave birth to the immortal poems of the *Edda*. For more recent examples, we need only look to Danish, Norwegian, and Finnish literature, the Celtic revival, or the neo-Greek tradition.

Estonian literary poetry, in the sense of *Kunstdichtung,* started to develop in the seventeenth century; but it was only at the beginning of the nineteenth that there appeared a truly significant poet, Kristjan Jaak Peterson (1802-1822). Since then, and especially in the first decade of this century, Estonia has been engaged in the intensification and refinement of her poetic language. He modern verse reached its maturity after her victory over Soviet Russia in the War of Liberation of 1918-1920. It was only then - for those two brief decades between the two world wars - that Estonia enjoyed national independence in the contemporary sense. That was a time of sudden brilliant flowering in my country, a veritable renaissance in literature and in all the arts, as well as in the structure of our government and society. There was also during this period a sense of precariousness in the newly won achievements, a kind of tension, resulting in a calling-up of inner resources to sustain something so precious and unique as freedom. But in 1939 a secret Soviet-Nazi agreement decided the fate of the Baltic nations, and, as a result, Estonia was occupied and annexed by the Soviet Union. Needless to say, this put an end to the growth and expansion of a free Estonian culture. The intensiveness of the inner life of Estonian intellectuals continued, nonetheless, relying on inner energies for survival. What was and is left, is only a sort of secret existential freedom—one that has to be won every minute in concealment, and is so much the more perilous for that.

It was around 1940, the time of the Soviet annexation of Estonia, that Heiti Talvik reached the summit of his poetic faculties; tragically enough, it was thereafter that the Soviet government arrested him and took his life. Talvik was born in 1904. His father was a professor of medical jurisprudence, his mother a pianist. His father's constant discussion of crime, suicide and sickness, combined with his mother's passionate interest in music and literature, helped produce the striking dark-and-light background of Talvik's poetry. Talvik studied for several years at the Estonian University of Tartu. Despite the small number of Estonian Jews, this was the only university in all of Europe to have a chair in Hebrew Language and Literature - a fact that is significant for an understanding of Talvik's development. While his main interests were poetry and philosophy, and, later, comparative religion, Talvik was particularly influenced by Judaism, as seen through the eyes of Lev Isaakovich Shvarchman, better known as Lev Shestov (1866-1938), a Russian philosopher in exile. The poets who inspired Talvik's restless thought were many, beginning with Propertius, Dante, Villon, Rabelais, Pushkin, Goethe and Baudelaire, and ending with Blok, Rilke, Léon-Paul Fargue, Claudel and the Russian emigre lyricist, Georgij Ivanov.

Talvik's known works consist of only 104 pieces, predominantly shorter poems. They are divided between two books, *Palavik* (*Fever*), 1934, and *Kohtupäev* (*Doomsday*), 1937. These collections form, in the one hand, an allegory, or extended symbolization, of Talvik's youth; on the other hand, they also form the autobiography of a soul in its journey through the chaos of our century. There is a definite contrast in the poems between the all too frequent disasters of war, the horrors of Nazism, the "bloody sun" of the October counter-revolution, on the one hand—and, on the other, the private spiritual torments of Talvik's own disasters, the corrosive effects of the dreariness which saps the will. Talvik's agitated desires revolve in circles, rising and falling, shifting and changing, until at last his very feelings appear to destroy themselves by their own internal power. The poem **"Ristimine"** (**"Baptism"**) is in this sense a summing-up of Talvik's rather adolescent, neo-Dantesque and symbolist vision:

> Flame streaked along the lightning's crackling train;
> A reek of burning stuck into my senses;
> The tempest's stony shrilling won terrain;
> And granite hail crashed through the loose
>   defences.
>
> A thunder-cloud, swelling like quarry smoke,
> Poured out its lap in an unending torrent,
> And, where the lightning-gutted heavens broke,
> A shadow fell on me, winged and abhorrent.
>
> An eagle fiercer than Medusa's dyes
> Sank its twin claws into my brain's tough leather;
> Green malice stared out of its frozen eyes;
> And hail beat down on each triumphant feather.
>
> It has stayed with me since—an evil shade
> That urges my sick senses towards their pyre.
> Already, where my dream-leaves lie decayed,
> Spring the black tongues of life's deciduous fire.

This careful translation by the late Professor William K. Matthews of London University conveys little of the specific musicality and rhythmical energy of the original; and thus it is necessary to recite the poem in Estonian:

Tuld haaras välgu praksuv süütenöör,
ozooni lõhn mu verre lõikas vahe.
Lõi pragisema tormi kivilõõr
ja maha prahvatas graniitne rahe.

Ränk äiksepilv kui suitsev kivimurd
mu põue põrmuks kallas oma süle.
Ja säält, kus valgust lõhkes taevakurd,
üks pime vari langes minu üle.

Üks kotkas hirmsam kui Meduusa pää
l i küüned põlevad mu kurnat ajju.
Ta silmist roheline välkus jää
ja rahe peksis tema tiibu laiu.

Ta jäi mu kannule kui paha vaim,
ta marru kihutas mu haiged meeled.
Ja sääl, kus närbus luule habras taim,
nüüd loitvad elutule mustjad keeled.

This poem is not very original in its conception; apart from the influence of symbolist dramatism, it is chiefly based on the world-view and aesthetics of the French Decadents. The search for the unnatural, the excessive self-analysis, the morbidity as well as the feverish hedonism, are all-too-recognizable. But the poem is not without positive qualities, especially as revealed in its complex metaphorical structure and in the progressive intensification of its quantitative rhythms.

Talvik's mind is occassionally haunted by the great Baudelaire—despite the latter's malicious dandyism. In his **"Lutsiferi laulud"** (**"Songs of Lucifer"**) Talvik echoes Baudelaire's famous "Les Litanies de Satan" ("Litanies of Satan")—but how differently! The Estonian poet transforms himself into a bride, who wants to be raped by Satan, but who decides to perish first, in a dream of erotic religiosity, sustained by negative mysticism. The rendering of this poem, done by Matthews, reads as follows:

I heard your hand upon my spirit's portal
And rushed to open this in bridal pallor.
But I have not slaved for you with each mortal
Pulse.

There has been enough in me of valour
To lacerate your pride and flout your vision,
To hurl myself down from the temple wall,
And yearning for your love in mock derision,
To perish in my fall.

And in Estonian it sounds like this:

Su koputusi kuulsin hingeuksel
ja sööstsin avama. Oo mõrsjanõrkust!
Kuid orjata Sind i g a l veretuksel—
ei iialgi!

Mul küllalt jätkus kõrkust
Su pilgu särapaistel sigatseda,
Su templiharjalt puruks kukkuda,
Su järel hullupööra igatseda
ja siiski hukkuda . . .

From these narrowly egocentric limits full of Bergsonian flux—which can too easily justify a psychic, as well as physical, drunkenness—Talvik moved toward more universal experience and more objective perceptions, both in his poetry and in his social criticism. In the latter he devoted his talent and energy to exposing the growing influence of Fascism, in all its manifestations; and in the cycle of poems "Dies Irae" written as early as 1934, he pronounced the death sentence of Nazism itself. I wish that some of the fine poets of our time would render this cycle into their own languages. The poems included there are among the best written on this subject in *any language*. Only the most perfect single lines of Majakovskij or Neruda can compete with their carefully crafted magnetism, and spiritually Talvik stands much higher.

After unmasking the growing nightmare of modern Europe, Talvik engaged in the battle against the disintegration of artistic unity. He even thought that a superb purism in prosody—mathematical principles of control in language—could save us from becoming utterly inhumane. With the prophetic validity of a true formalist, he wrote:

It is our duty to force the blind rage of nature
into a slender line of verse.

And in Estonian:

Meie kohus on sundida saledasse stroofi
elementide pime raev.

But the purity of form, and the authority of reason alone, did not satisfy Talvik for very long. In 1932, he came under the influence of the philosopher Lev Shestov, mentioned earlier. Shestov's book, *Afiny i Ierusalim* (*Athens and Jerusalem*) wrought a profound change in Talvik's life and work. The home in philosophical rationalism, according to Shestov, was Athens—while Jerusalem is the home of faith, of an existential feeling which opens the way to mystery and pure possibility. Through Shestov's eyes, Talvik—the Lutheran, the Protestant—saw the necessity of complete obedience to the laws of Jehovah, in order to achieve salvation. In **"Orjade Koor"** (**"The Chorus of Slaves"**), one of the central poems of his last years, Talvik expresses his final vision most cogently:

When wilt thou free us, Prophet,
God's breath on burning lips,
From knavery's barren profit,
From slavery's scarring whips?

Our masters' scourge is stinging,
Our masters' praise is worse.
Our fevered eyes see, clinging
To tainted homes, our curse.

The timid turned and fled us—
We choose the desert track.
The meats of Egypt fed us—
You give us what we lack!

Through regions gaunt and sterile
We venture, starved and gaunt.
Stern is our Lord of Peril,
Yet He is what we want.

In streams of fire descending,
He rules whom Moses saw.
Stay free in his unbending,
Inexorable law!

The German rendering is even closer to the original. Both translations were made by Ants Oras, himself a permanent poet of the Estonian tongue and a teacher of Talvik:

Prophet, o komm und rette,
vom Hauch des Herrn durchloht,
uns von der Knechtschaft Kette,
der Knechtschaft eklem Brot!

Der Vögte Hieb verwundet,
das Lob der Vögte brennt,
der Striemen Blut bekundet
die Schmach, die keiner nennt.

Die Zagen lass zaudern und klagen,
doch uns in Wüstenein
lass Not und Tod ertragen,
um sterbend frei zu sein.

Ägyptens Fleisch verschmähn wir,
verschmähn Ägyptens Spott.
Zum strengsten Gotte gehn wir,
zum wahren, einzigen Gott.

Zum Gott, der Judahs Stamme
auf Sinais Grat erschien
in harter Satzung Flamme:
sie macht uns frei und kühn.

Sublimity, says Coleridge, is Hebrew by birth. Very different from the organ music of the Hebrew language and yet equally space-creating is the Estonian original of this *Hymnus:*

Suur prohvet, kunas küll viid sa,
Jehoova hinguset kant,
meid eemale orjapiitsa
ja orjaroogade mant.

On kibedad kupjahoobid,
veel kibedam kupjakiit
ja paksu poriga loobit
on iga me uksepiit.

Las halin jääb argade hooleks,
meid aga kõrbe vii.
Ja kui me ka nälga kooleks—
pääsi on olla prii.

Egiptuse leib ja humal—
end puhtaks rookigem neist.
On range juutide jumal,
kuid meie ei taha teist.

Ta Siinai harjale laskus.
mis tuliallikais keeb,
ja tema seaduste raskus
meid vabaks ja võimsaks teeb.

Here form becomes content; spiritual obedience and asceticism-in-faith become liberty. But for his love of individual existentialist freedom Talvik paid dearly. After 1940, when Estonia came under Soviet rule, he was not permitted to publish a single poem in the Soviet press. His actual date of death is not known. He was arrested by the Soviet police and spent some time in several prisons, and then he was sent to a concentration camp on the river Ob' in Siberia. In the government-controlled publications of Soviet-occupied Estonia, the year of his death has been given variously as 1945, 1946, and 1947. Talvik's fate reminds us of another significant poet, Osip Mandelstam, who perished in another Soviet concentration camp, near Vladivostok. Officially, the Soviets have given Mandelstam's date of death as 1938, 1940, and 1941. It is also true that we do not know, for example, the actual death date of Francois Villon; but then of course, besides being a very important poet, Villon was also a wanted criminal. Yet the fact that, today, some five centuries after Villon's death, in a so-called civilized world, two great poets, two national figures, can disappear without a trace is something which should make us uneasy. Nevertheless, as in Mandelstam's case, our astonishment is aroused not by the tragic fate which the Estonian poet shared with the millions of people under Soviet "law," but by his permanent greatness. We are struck most of all by his achievement of the dynamic harmony of conviction, concentration and objectification under which the highest kinds of poetry are produced.

I am thankful to the Muse of History, because I (the only one in a family of six) personally survived the first Soviet occupation as well as the Nazi occupation of Estonia. But I am also grateful to destiny—and perhaps faith—which has enabled me to come to Israel, Heiti Talvik's imagined land, and speak here about him, who never saw this country, but to whose religious and intellectual heritage he was attached, and whose people, spread throughout the world, he loved.

Edward Westermarck

1862-1939

(Full name Edward Alexander Westermarck) Finnish philosopher, sociologist, and anthropologist.

INTRODUCTION

Westermarck is best known for combining his sociological and anthropological research to create philosophical works pertaining to human marriage customs, Moroccan anthropology, and the foundations and evolution of human morality. In perhaps his most important work, *The Origin and Development of the Moral Ideas* (1906-08), Westermarck postulated that societal values are conditioned responses to human sentiment and not objectively established truths. Westermarck further supported his thesis in *Ethical Relativity* (1932), in which he elaborated on his previous claims that morality derives more from human emotions and sentimentality than from objective sources. In these works, Westermarck relied extensively on his sociological and anthropological research into social standards regarding suicide, slavery, infanticide, euthanasia, and human sacrifice performed as professor at the University of London and several Finnish colleges to verify his assertion that subjective standards determine morality. Westermarck eschewed German metaphysical philosophy, being influenced instead by such British empiricist philosophers John Stuart Mill, Adam Smith, Edmund Spenser, and David Hume, as well as anthropologists Charles Darwin and Sir James Frazer.

Biographical Information

Westermarck was born in Helsinki, Finland. His father was a university professor of Latin, and his mother was daughter of the university's librarian. An asthmatic child who spoke both Swiss and English, Westermarck attended Book's Lyceum and the Swedish Normal Lyceum, and earned degrees in philosophy from the University of Finland. In 1887, he traveled to England's British Museum to further research his doctoral thesis on human marital customs, resulting in his first major work, *The History of Human Marriage* (1896). In 1894, Westermarck became docent at the University of Helsingfors, as well as teaching at the Academy of Abo. From 1898 to 1902, he lived in Morocco while researching the country's social customs and supernatural beliefs. This field research resulted in several works, including *Ritual and Belief in Morocco* (1926) and *The Wit and Wisdom of Morocco: A Study of Native Proverbs* (1930). Westermarck pursued concurrent tenures at the University of London's School of Economics and Finland universities. An agnostic for the majority of his adult life, Westermarck brought his opinions and research into human morality to bear in his last major work, *Christianity and Morals* (1939), a work that historically documents breaches of social morality by Christian practitioners in the name of Jesus Christ.

Major Works

In *The History of Human Marriage*, Westermarck countered prevailing notions that primitive cultures engaged in promiscuous sexual practices, and argued that marital customs are universal throughout human anthropological history. In this work, Westermarck relied heavily on Charles Darwin's theory of natural selection. Westermarck later revised the work and published it as three volumes in 1926. His next major work, *The Origin and Development of the Moral Ideas*, took Westermarck nearly twenty years to finish. Introducing his belief that moral judgements are emotional rather than intellectual responses, the work traces the evolution of morality throughout human history. The reliance of *The Origin and Development of the Moral Ideas* on Westermarck's knowledge in the fields of sociology and anthropology caused the work to be classified more as a study in those fields rather than a distinct philosophical work, a judgement Westermarck endeavored to alter with what is considered to be the more solidly philosophical *Ethical Relativity*. Responding to critical charges that a relative consideration of moral issues could result in dangerous and unchecked behavior, Westermarck wrote: "Ethical subjectivism instead of being a danger is more likely to be an advantage to morality. Could it be brought home to people that there is no absolute standard in morality, they would perhaps be on the one hand more tolerant, and on the other hand more critical in their judgements." In these works, Westermarck acknowledges the writings of Adam Smith, whose *Theory of Moral Sentiments* Westermarck greatly admired. Westermarck's contribution to the field is generally acknowledged as challenging preconceived notions that ethical principles exist apart from human psychology and biology, as well as reason and knowledge. As humankind evolves and their environmental stimuli changes, wrote Westermarck, so too does their societal code. These moral beliefs become so inculcated into a society's behavior pattern that they are no longer aware that their reactions are emotion-based. In his last work, *Christianity and Morals*, Westermarck attempted to show Christianity as historically having a negative impact on Western morality.

PRINCIPAL WORKS

The History of Human Marriage (sociology) 1891; re-
vised 1921
The Origin and Development of the Moral Ideas (phi-
losophy) 1906-08
Ritual and Belief in Morocco (sociology) 1926
Memories of My Life (memoirs) 1929
Wit and Wisdom in Morocco (nonfiction) 1930
Ethical Relativity (philosophy) 1932
Three Essays on Sex and Marriage (essays) 1934
Christianity and Morals (philosophy) 1939

CRITICISM

Evander Bradley McGilvary (essay date 1907)

SOURCE: A review of *The Origin and Development of
the Moral Ideas,* in *The Philosophical Review,* Vol.
XVI, No. 1, January, 1907, pp. 70-8.

[*In the following review of* The Origin and Development
of the Moral Ideas, *McGilvary favorably examines
Westermarck's theory that moral emotions are negative
results of societal disapproval.*]

The author of *The History of Human Marriage* has in
[*The Origin and Development of the Moral Ideas*]
taken up the larger problem of the history of human
morality. He brings to his task, of course, the same
wonderful erudition and the same rare critical acumen
that characterized his former book. The result is what
we should expect of Westermarck.

The introductory words remind one of Locke's account
of the way in which he was led to write his *Essay.* "The
main object of this book will perhaps be best explained
by a few words concerning its origin.

"Its author was once discussing with some friends the
point how far a bad man ought to be treated with kindness. The opinions were divided, and, in spite of much
deliberation, unanimity could not be attained. It seemed
strange that the disagreement should be so radical, and the
question arose, Whence this diversity of opinion? Is it due
to defective knowledge, or has it a merely sentimental
origin? And the problem gradually expanded. Why do the
moral ideas in general differ so greatly? And, on the other
hand, why is there in many cases such a wide agreement?
Nay, why are there any moral ideas at all?

"Since then many years have passed, spent by the author
in trying to find an answer to these questions. The present
work is the result of his researches and thoughts.

"The first part of it will comprise a study of the moral
concepts: right, wrong, duty, justice, virtue, merit, &c.

Such a study will be found to require an examination
into the moral emotions, their nature and origin, as also
into the relations between these emotions and the various moral concepts. There will then be a discussion of
the phenomena to which such concepts are applied—the
subjects of moral judgments. The general character of
these phenomena will be scrutinised, and an answer
sought to the question why facts of a certain type are
matters of moral concern, while other facts are not.
Finally, the most important of these phenomena will be
classified, and the moral ideas relating to each class will
be stated, and, so far as possible, explained" (pp. 1, 2).

In Chapter I the author lays down his fundamental thesis of "the emotional origin of moral judgments." "That
the moral concepts are ultimately based on emotions
either of indignation or approval, is a fact which a certain school of thinkers have in vain attempted to deny.
The terms which embody these concepts must originally
have been used—indeed they are still constantly so
used—as direct expressions of such emotions with reference to the phenomena which evoked them. Men pronounced certain acts to be good or bad on account of the
emotions those acts aroused in their minds, just as they
called sunshine warm and ice cold on account of certain
sensations which they experienced, and as they named a
thing pleasant or painful because they felt pleasure or
pain. But to attribute a quality to a thing is never the
same as merely to state the existence of a particular
sensation or feeling in the mind which perceives it.
Such an attribution must mean that the thing, under
certain circumstances, makes a certain impression on
the mind. By calling an object warm or pleasant, a person asserts that it is apt to produce in him a sensation
of heat or a feeling of pleasure. Similarly, to name an
act good or bad, ultimately implies that it is apt to give
rise to an emotion of approval or disapproval in him
who pronounces the judgment. Whilst not affirming the
actual existence of any specific emotion in the mind of
the person judging or of anybody else, the predicate of
a moral judgment attributes to the subject a tendency to
arouse an emotion. The moral concepts, then, are essentially generalisations of tendencies in certain phenomena to call forth moral emotions" (pp. 4, 5).

There seems to be a confusion here which is worth
noticing. The ordinary man, in saying that sunshine is
warm, does not necessarily mean that it produces in him
a warm sensation. He may mean actually to attribute to
the sunshine an objective quality of warmth. What he
means to assert, *i. e.,* the content of his assertion, may
or may not be in accordance with the facts; but whether
his assertion, in the meaning it has for him, is confirmed or refuted by the facts has nothing to do with the
question what his meaning is. If the truth of a statement
were the criterion of its meaning, no statement could
ever be false. Now, it may be that moral predicates, as
a matter of fact, do not belong to acts *per se,* and that
our emotions are the causes of our moral predications;
but this, even if true, does not tell us the meaning of the
moral predicates. An example will illustrate the point. *A*

is not guilty of theft (matter of fact), and yet my dislike for him (cause of my judgment) leads me, wholly against the facts, to interpret the chain of evidence as pointing to his guilt. Now when I say that he stole, my meaning is not to be interpreted from my motive, which is personal dislike: I do not mean to say that I hate the man. Nor is the meaning to be interpreted from the actual facts: else I could be made to mean that he did *not* steal. But Westermarck, in interpreting the meaning of moral predications, uses a principle that would justify these absurd constructions. He confuses the question of the *causes* prompting to moral judgments, with the very different question as to the *meaning* of moral predication. Both questions are treated indiscriminately in the chapter on the emotional *origin* of moral judgments.

But if moral judgments always mean to express only our emotional attitudes, how comes it that they have objectivity ascribed to them? This "illusive" objectivity is ascribed to them "partly on account of the comparatively uniform nature of the moral consciousness" (p. 9), and partly on account of custom (*ibid.*). "Society is the school in which men learn to distinguish between right and wrong. The headmaster is Custom, and the lessons are the same for all. The first moral judgments were pronounced by public opinion; public indignation and public approval are the prototypes of the moral emotions. As regards questions of morality, there was, in early society, practically no difference of opinion; hence a character of universality, or objectivity, was from the very beginning attached to all moral judgments" (p. 9). But, "besides the relative uniformity of moral opinions," due to custom and to the similarity of emotional constitution in men, "there is another circumstance which tempts us to objectivise moral judgments, namely, the authority which, rightly or wrongly, is ascribed to moral rules. From our earliest childhood we are taught that certain acts *are* right and that others *are* wrong. Owing to their exceptional importance for human welfare, the facts of the moral consciousness are emphasised in a much higher degree than any other subjective facts. . . . Thus the belief in a moral order of the world has taken hardly less firm hold of the human mind, than the belief in a natural order of things" (p. 14). "Authority is an ambiguous word. It may indicate knowledge of truth, and it may indicate a rightful power to command obedience. The authoritativeness attributed to the moral law has often reference to both kinds of authority. The moral lawgiver lays down his rules in order that they should be obeyed, and they are authoritative in so far as they have to be obeyed. But he is also believed to know what is right or wrong, and his commands are regarded as expressions of moral truths" (p. 15).

"The presumed objectivity of moral judgments thus being a chimera, there can be no moral truth in the sense in which this term is generally understood" (p. 17), and "if there are no general moral truths, the object of scientific ethics cannot be to fix rules for human conduct," but "to study the moral consciousness as a fact" (p. 18).

Dr. Westermarck frankly characterizes his general theory of the emotional origin of the moral concepts as "ethical subjectivism" (pp. 18, 19). He denies its dangerous consequences, although, of course, even if there were such, they would not disprove the truth of the theory. Ethical subjectivism, as propounded by the author, "certainly does not allow everybody to follow his own inclinations; nor does it lend sanction to arbitrariness and caprice. Our moral consciousness belongs to our mental constitution, which we cannot change as we please. We approve and we disapprove because we cannot do otherwise. Can we help feeling pain when the fire burns us? Can we help sympathising with our friends? Are these phenomena less necessary, less powerful in their consequences, because they fall within the subjective sphere of experience? So, too, why should the moral law command less obedience because it forms part of our own nature?" (p. 19). In fact, instead of being a dangerous doctrine, the adoption of it would bring about beneficial results. Men would become "more tolerant in their moral judgments," and there would be more progressiveness in the moral life (p. 20).

If, now, moral judgments are those that are called forth by moral emotions, the question next arises as to what are the moral emotions. This question is answered at length in Chapters II, III, IV. "These emotions are of two kinds: disapproval, or indignation, and approval. They have in common characteristics which make them moral emotions, in distinction from others of a non-moral character, but at the same time both of them belong to a wider class of emotions, which I call retributive emotions. Again, they differ from each other in points which make each of them allied to certain non-moral retributive emotions, disapproval to anger and revenge, and approval to that kind of retributive kindly emotion which in its most developed form is gratitude" (p. 21). "Moral disapproval is a kind of resentment and akin to anger and revenge," and "moral approval is a kind of retributive kindly emotion and akin to gratitude" (p. 22). There is a long discussion of the nature of resentment and revenge, but into this we cannot go here. The position upheld by Westermarck, against Steinmetz, is that revenge is not indiscriminate in its application, but is directed normally towards the aggressor. Even the fact of collective responsibility among primitive peoples does not interfere with this theory. "The fact that punishments for offences are frequently inflicted, or are supposed to be inflicted, by men or gods upon individuals who have not committed those offences, is explicable from circumstances which in no way clash with our thesis that moral indignation is, in its essence, directed towards the assumed cause of inflicted pain. In many cases the victim, in accordance with the doctrine of collective responsibility, is punished because he is considered to be involved in the guilt—even when he is really innocent—or because he is regarded as a fair representative of an offending community. In other cases, he is supposed to be polluted by a sin or a curse, owing to the contagious nature of sins and curses. The principle of social solidarity also accounts for the efficacy ascribed to vicarious expiatory sacrifices; but in may instances expiatory sacrifices only have the character of a ransom or bribe" (pp. 69, 70).

But though moral disapproval is a species of resentment, "its aggressive character has become more disguised" in the course of evolution (p. 73). Forgiveness has taken the place of retaliation, in some of the more advanced civilizations. "The rule of retaliation and the rule of forgiveness, however, are not so radically opposed to each other as they appear to be. What the latter condemns is, in reality, not every kind of resentment, but non-moral resentment; not impartial indignation, but personal hatred. It prohibits revenge, but not punishment" (p. 77). Now in punishment the ground motive is retributive. The author undertakes to show that neither the deterrent nor the reformatory theory of punishment does justice to the facts, and he subjects both theories to a critical examination. His conclusion can be expressed in two sentences. "Punishment can hardly be guided exclusively by utilitarian considerations, but requires the sanction of the retributive emotion of moral disapproval" (p. 82), and "the principle of reformation has thus itself a retributive origin" (p. 88).

In Chapter IV the author discriminates moral disapproval from anger and revenge, and moral approval from gratitude. One of the *differentiæ* is the disinterestedness of the moral emotions. "The predicate of a moral judgment always involves a notion of disinterestedness. . . . A moral judgment may certainly have a selfish motive; but then it, nevertheless, pretends to be disinterested, which shows that disinterestedness is a characteristic of moral concepts as such" (p. 101). "Disinterestedness, however, is not the only characteristic by which moral indignation and approval are distinguished from other, non-moral, kinds of resentment or retributive kindly emotion. It is, indeed, itself a form of a more comprehensive quality which characterises moral emotions—apparent impartiality" (p. 103). "A moral emotion, then, is tested by an imaginary change of the relationship between him who approves or disapproves of the mode of conduct by which the emotion was evoked and the parties immediately concerned, whilst the relationship between the parties themselves is left unaltered. At the same time it is not necessary that the moral emotion should be really impartial. It is sufficient that it is tacitly assumed to be so, nay, even that it is not knowingly partial" (p. 104). "Finally, a moral emotion has a certain flavour of generality" (p. 104). The generality is illusory, but still when one judges morally, one feels that his judgment *would be* shared if other people knew the act and all its attendant circumstances as well as he does himself, and if, at the same time, their emotions were as refined as are his own. This feeling gives to his approval or indignation a touch of generality, which belongs to public approval and public indignation, but which is never found in any merely individual emotion of gratitude or revenge" (pp. 104-5).

Now another problem arises. How comes it that the emotions of resentment and non-moral gratitude acquire these touches and flavors of disinterestedness, impartiality, and generality? Chapter V, "The Origin of the Moral Emotions," answers this question.

As to disinterestedness, the answer is easy. "It is obvious, then, that sympathy aided by the altruistic sentiment—sympathy in the common sense—tends to produce disinterested retributive emotions" (p. 111). This reminds one of Adam Smith's *Theory of the Moral Sentiments,* to which the author refers in this connection. But when Westermarck comes to account for generality and impartiality as *differentiæ* of moral emotions, he emphasizes the social environment, which Adam Smith did not make very much of. The problem here seems also to change on our hands. "However, the real problem which we have now to solve is not how retributive emotions may become apparently impartial and be coloured by a feeling of generality, but why disinterestedness, apparent impartiality, and the flavour of generality have become characteristics by which so-called moral emotions are distinguished from other retributive emotions. The solution of this problem lies in the fact that society is the birthplace of the moral consciousness; that the first moral judgments expressed, not the private emotions of isolated individuals, but emotions which were felt by the society at large; that tribal custom was the earliest rule of duty" (pp. 117, 118). "The most salient feature of custom is its generality. Its transgression calls forth public indignation; hence the flavour of generality which characterises moral disapproval. Custom is fixed once for all, and takes no notice of the preferences of individuals. By recognizing the validity of a custom, I implicitly admit that the custom is equally binding for me and for you and for all the other members of the society. This involves disinterestedness; I admit that a breach of the custom is equally wrong whether I myself am immediately concerned in the act or not. It also involves apparent impartiality; I assume that my condemnation of the act is independent of the relationship in which the parties concerned in it stand to me personally, or, at least, I am not aware that my condemnation is influenced by any such relationship. And this holds good whatever be the origin of the custom" (pp. 120, 121).

But while custom explains the disinterestedness, impartiality, and generality of moral emotions, "custom is a moral rule only on account of the indignation called forth by its transgression. In its ethical aspect it is nothing but a generalisation of emotional tendencies, applied to certain modes of conduct, and transmitted from generation to generation. Public indignation lies at the bottom of it" (p. 121).

Having thus examined in detail the nature and the origin of the moral emotions, the author proceeds in Chapter VI to analyze the moral concepts, which are "generalisations of tendencies in certain phenomena to call forth" these "moral emotions" (p. 5). This analysis is in order to show the connection between the moral concepts and the moral emotions.

One of the most striking features of the analysis is that many of the concepts usually considered to be positive in character are, according to the author's analysis, negative, and are directly connected with the emotion of disapproval, not with that of approval. "Ought" is analyzed into a conation *plus* a potential indignation at the thought that what ought to be done may be omitted. "The conation expressed in 'ought' is determined by the idea that the mode of conduct which ought to be performed is not, or will possibly not be, performed. It is also this idea of its not being performed that determines the emotion which gives to 'ought' the character of a moral predicate. The doing of what ought not to be done, or the omission of what ought not to be omitted, is apt to call forth moral indignation—this is the most essential fact involved in the notion of 'ought.' Every 'ought'-judgment contains implicitly a negation" (p. 135). Duty is treated as synonymous with obligation. Even "right," whether used as an adjective or as a noun, expresses a moral conception that is essentially negative. Wrong (adjective) is not defined as not-right, but on the contrary, right (adjective) is defined as not-wrong. "The concept of 'right,' then, as implying that the opposite mode of conduct would have been wrong, ultimately derives its moral significance from moral disapproval. This may seem strange considering that 'right' is commonly looked upon as positive and 'wrong' as its negation. But we must remember that language and popular conceptions in these matters start from the notion of a moral rule or command. . . . But the fact which gives birth to the command itself is the indignation called forth by the act which the command forbids, or by the omission of that which it enjoins" (pp. 138-9). "Right" as a substantive is also treated negatively. "To have a moral right to do a thing means that it is not wrong to do it," and also "that it would be wrong of other people to prevent" the doing of it (p. 139). Still again, "an act is 'just,' in the strict sense of the word, if its omission is unjust" (p. 142).

Of course there are moral conceptions that are rooted in the emotion of approval. They are goodness, virtue, merit, etc.; but the moral attitude is predominantly negative, one of disapproval, rather than of approval, hence the generalizations of tendencies which put us into the moral attitude must result in negative conceptions rather than in positive.

These six chapters just reviewed in some detail, present the most important features of Westermarck's ethical theory. There are six other chapters devoted to theory, and the remaining portion of the volume, pp. 327-716, is not so much theory as statement of fact. The subjects treated, ethnographically and historically, are homicide in general; the killing of parents, sick persons, children; feticide; the killing of women, and of slaves; the criminality of homicide influenced by distinctions of class; human sacrifice; blood revenge and compensation; the punishment of death; the duel; bodily injuries; charity and generosity; hospitality; the subjection of children; the subjection of wives; and slavery.

Every one who is acquainted with *The History of Human Marriage* is prepared to find a most painstaking and comprehensive, one is tempted to say exhaustive, presentation of accessible facts bearing on the general subject of the book. The interpretation of these facts may here and there be questioned, but the important thing is to have the facts collected so as to be within easy reach. Ethical theorists should find the work invaluable, as thus furnishing them with concrete facts to rest their theories on or to test their theories by. The sociologist will find illuminating discussion of many customs, while the general reader, if interested in matters of universal human concern, cannot fail to get much pleasure and instruction from the reading of the book.

Altogether it is perhaps safe to say that the work is the most important contribution to ethical literature within recent years.

Ruth Benedict (essay date 1932)

SOURCE: "Absolute Virtue a Delusion," in *New York Herald Tribune Books,* Vol. 8, No. 42, June 26, 1932, p. 3.

[*In the following review of* Ethical Relativity, *Benedict agrees with Westermarck's thesis that no universals for morality exist, and asserts that tolerance and discrimination are worthy substitutes.*]

No one in our generation has done more to take ethics out of the realm of fantasy than the venerable Professor Westermarck. With the publication, years ago, of his *History of the Moral Ideas* he put forward with full documentation his essential conclusion. It is a criticism of the theory of the still, small voice of conscience and its validity, the voice Kant said was the human claim on divinity, and which school after school of ethics has made the arbiter of absolute and cosmic Right. Westermarck, approaching the problem from the angle of his vast collections of anthropological contradictions, was not so sanguine. As he showed, there has never been a virtue so clean-cut that all peoples agreed upon it. He might have shown, likewise, that all peoples have favorite and darling virtues for which they show the most fantastic readiness to scrap all human values, and with which they allow no tampering. But as for Absolute Virtue, it is a contradiction in terms.

Normative ethics has upheld the opposite contention. Normative ethics is the philosophic counterpart of our private assurance that our moral convictions are no mere matter of opinion; there is a right, there is a wrong, that eternally corresponds in the cosmos to the course of action to which we commit ourselves. With this Professor Westermarck does not wholly disagree. There *is* something wrong that corresponds everywhere in every society to the code of the good life. It is the life that that society enjoins. The virtues and the vices of any culture are not the consequence of its success in following its ethical precepts; the ethical precepts are the reflections, somewhat straightened and doctored always, of the life custom lays down. Ethics has always been an apologia for customary behavior, and to derive Absolute Right from our local schemes is to measure the cosmos by a provincial footrule.

Professor Westermarck's argument carries still farther. If, as he shows, the moral consciousness was in its early forms anything but the individual conscience reproducing an eternal verity, what has given morality everywhere its characteristic claims to impartiality and universal validity? We do not generalise anger and being in love—the non-ethical emotions—and demand that all persons feel them alike at the same situations. We should be surprised if when our car is bumped by another every one should jump out of their passing cars as angry as we are. But when it is a matter of righteous indignation and the other moral emotions, the matter is different. The teaching of evolution was fought in Dayton not on the ground of personal offense but on that of an impartial wrong, and those who fought appealed with assurance to a moral sentiment they could rely upon in others. Why is it that the moral emotions are at least not knowingly partial, and stand in this respect over against all other emotions? Because, says Westermarck, of the very fact that morals reflect customary behavior of the group. Customs are public habits, and, more than that, rules of conduct, and when they are not complied with man feels a malaise, a disapproval, which he reads off as a law of absolute right and wrong. It is because the source of this feeling, which is everywhere morality, is in the group and its rules of behavior, and because it thus transcends the individual and his immediate preferences that the moral emotions are characterized by this claim to universal validity and impartiality. The authority assigned to conscience is the echo of the unanimous agreement of the culture upon the particular behavior in question. Early morality mistook its tribal customs for Plato's prototypes, and normative ethics carries on the delusion.

Ethical Relativity is a systematic presentation of Professor Westermarck's position and a rebuttal of the arguments of the exponents of other schools. In his earlier, volumes he has been content to present collections of data and to draw conclusions from them. In this book he examines in some detail the theories of his opponents. Quite rightly, he is not disturbed by their protest that to take away absolute validity from our particular code of behavior is to destroy the good life. As he says, the knowledge that our local and temporary rules are not universal fiat makes for tolerance in our judgments of others' conduct, and for discrimination in our consideration of our own. He denies that his position is subversive. It merely falls into the category of those things that challenge customary opinion and cause those who hold them acute malaise. As soon as the new opinion is embraced as customary belief, it will be another trusted bulwark of the good life. There is nothing in the thesis that he puts forward that is intrinsically difficult for morality to incorporate.

The positive gains are many. As he abundantly shows, normative ethics has always been under the necessity of establishing on one or another absolute basis the fleeting codes of a generation. We have only to pass in review the systems of ethics that have held that their pet virtues were enunciated by self-evident intuitions that are unchangeable. In an excellent chapter Westermarck examines Kant from this point of view. This great philosopher sought to deduce ethics, not from a mere intuition or from the tendency of the organism to seek satisfactions, as most theorists have been content to do, but from pure reason, and what he drew up amounts to a speculative background for the most extreme puritanic distrust of human impulses. Desire for pleasure, he pointed out as the great obstacle to morality, and he made it a first principle that no acts have moral worth except those that are done for duty's sake. All his arguments center upon conscious resistance to temptation, and he throws out all exceptions to the moral rules because, as Westermarck says, "of his peculiar idea that they could have no other ground but the individual's desire to modify the rule in his own favor." In Spartan fashion, too, he threw out consequences in so far as they related to the situation in hand. The world's greatest effort to derive an absolute basis for ethics resulted in a scheme that has only casual validity for a generation that has ever so slightly shifted its cultural position. We are not likely to fare better with the schemes with which we justify our virtues of the present moment. The absolute is a fire that has always burned men's fingers, and the possibility of an ethic that shall find place for tolerance and discrimination seems to lie in the direction Professor Westermarck has pointed out.

William Curtis Swabey (essay date 1942)

SOURCE: "Westermarckian Relativity," in *Ethics*, Vol. LII, No. 2, January, 1942, pp. 222-30.

[*In the following excerpt, Swabey assesses Westermarck's ethical relativism.*]

In his *Concept of Morals*[1] Professor Stace conducts a vigorous attack on ethical relativism, in the course of which he mentions, without discussing in any detailed way, Edward Westermarck's *Ethical Relativity.* Whatever difficulties there may be in Westermarck's denial of objective moral truth, it seems clear to the present writer that there is a considerable element of validity in what we may call "the emotional theory of moral judgment." This is, in general, the theory that the use of all such "ethical predicates" as right, wrong, noble, base, wicked, honorable, etc., is connected with the expression of certain specific "moral emotions," namely, approval and disapproval. These are the feelings of a real or imaginary spectator viewing actions in their respective contexts; it may be that the spectator is the agent himself. Morally good actions awaken in the mind of a disinterested spectator a certain glow of approval; morally bad actions are those which awaken indignation. In one sense right actions are those merely not disapproved; men, again, have rights in the sense that there are certain things which it would be wrong to prevent them from doing, etc. It is not necessary to reproduce here Westermarck's admirable system of definitions; we may sum it up in the simple equations:

The morally good = the approved;
The morally bad = the disapproved.

These definitions leave the question as to who the judge is wholly unanswered. The judge or spectator is indeterminate, a mere *x*. What is right for one spectator is wrong for another. Who is *the* judge? No matter, since every man must in the end judge for himself. Each necessarily identifies the expressions of his own feelings with parts of a code of absolute truth; each regards the pronouncements of his own heart, saying, "This is right," "This is wrong," as the decrees of God.

Now to Professor Stace this seems a very shocking situation and one which, if generally acknowledged, can bring about only the downfall of society. In substance the charges which Stace brings against relativism run as follows:

1. "Ethical relativity can only end in destroying the conception of morality altogether, in undermining its practical efficacy, in rendering meaningless many almost universally accepted truths about human affairs, in robbing human beings of any incentive to strive for a better world, in taking the life-blood out of every ideal and every aspiration which has ever ennobled the life of man."[2] The objection, then, is that ethical relativism simply cancels the idea of morality altogether.

2. Ethical relativity renders meaningless all attempts to compare the standards of various communities with one another in respect of their moral worth.[3]

3. The whole notion of moral progress becomes a delusion under this assumption. *Better* can only mean "more like us."[4]

4. We find that the larger groups have smaller groups within them, each of which has its own standards. How can it be just to judge, let us say, a gangster by the standards accepted by the community as a whole and not merely those of his own gang? In the end, "all moral valuation thus vanishes. There is nothing to prevent each man from being a rule unto himself. The result will be moral chaos and the collapse of all effective standards."[5] We should have to prove that two individuals have the same standards before we could compare them. In the end we can only judge each individual by his own moral standards.

Westermarck had said that ethical subjectivism "instead of being a danger is more likely to be an advantage to morality. Could it be brought home to people that there is no absolute standard in morality, they would perhaps be on the one hand more tolerant and on the other hand more critical in their judgments."[6] To this, Professor Stace replies as follows:

Certainly, if we believe that any one moral standard is as good as any other, we are likely to be more tolerant. We shall tolerate widow-burning, human sacrifice, cannibalism, slavery, the infliction of physical torture or any other of the thousand and one abominations which are, or have been, from time to time, approved by one moral code or another.[7]

Now there should be no doubt that ethical judgment, in some sense, claims universal validity. This results from the fact that moral judgments, being in the form of logical assertions, are subject to the laws of logic. If I believe that widow-burning is an abomination, I can by no means tolerate the contradictory opinion. The contrary attitude must appear as blindness or perversity. Even if it is true that moral judgments are expressions of emotions, yet these emotions are real and intense and essentially intolerant on important matters. We can by no means adopt an attitude of indifference toward what appear to us to be atrocities and brutalities. And if we postulate—as, in fact, we must, for practical purposes—an objective moral truth, we can speak meaningfully of differences of worth between diverse cultures as well as of moral progress. In all this there is no more egotism or vanity than there is in any case in which we dare to judge for ourselves about a matter of fact or of logic.

Furthermore, it is not likely that any civilized person, on adopting the emotional theory, will throw away his old feelings and become tolerant toward widow-burning, cannibalism, slavery, the infliction of physical torture, or any other phase of savagery. Or, if men are so unfixed in their emotions, the remedy cannot be in the adoption of the philosophical theory of objective moral truth but must be practical, such as the setting-up of a strong government or of an authoritative religion. As if in anticipation of Professor Stace's attack, Westermarck, on the page preceding that which Stace quotes, questions whether his theory is really a danger to morality. His theory, he says,

cannot be depreciated by the same inference as was drawn from the teachings of the ancient Sophists, namely, that if that which appears to each man as right or good stands for that which is right or good, then everybody has the natural right to follow his caprice and inclinations and to hinder him doing so is an infringement on his rights. My moral judgments spring from my own moral consciousness; they judge of the conduct of other men, not from their point of view but from mine, not in accordance with their feelings and opinions about right and wrong, but according to my own. And these are not arbitrary. We approve and disapprove because we cannot do otherwise; our moral consciousness belongs to our mental constitution, which we cannot change as we please.[8]

We may perhaps interpret this as meaning that we judge of the actions of others by asking whether it would be right for us to do certain things if we were in their place; the answer to this question gives us what each of us regards as absolute right and wrong. At the same time we cannot help acknowledging a certain moral goodness in those who follow their moral judgments even when their judgments contradict our own.

It is to be noted that the difficulty of having to judge each man by his own standards arises on the theory of "absolute" moral truth very much in the same way that it does in the system of ethical relativism. If there is a set of absolute moral truths or code of "eternal and immutable morality," a problem arises with regard to those individuals who are ignorant of these moral truths. It would seem quite unfair to blame an individual for doing "what he thinks right" even though he may thereby be committing a crime. Even though we are absolutists of the deepest die, we must distinguish between subjective and objective right, unavoidably using our own judgment as revealing objective right. One may cite in this connection a statement from Richard Price's *Review of the Principal Questions in Morals* (1758), which shows the way in which the most decisive ethical objectivism recognizes that there is a sense in which a man must be judged by his own standards.

> Abstract virtue is, most properly, a quality of the external action or event. It denotes what an action is, considered independently of the sense of the agent; or what, in itself and absolutely, it is right such an agent, in such circumstances, should do; and what, if he judged truly, he would judge that he ought to do. Practical virtue, on the contrary, has a necessary relation to and dependence upon the opinion of the agent, concerning his actions. . . . . Moral agents are liable to mistake the circumstances they are in, and consequently to form erroneous judgments concerning their own obligations. . . . . But when they are, in any manner mistaken, it is not to be imagined, that there is nothing remains obligatory; for there is a sense in which it may be said that what any being, in the sincerity of his heart, thinks he ought to do, he indeed ought to do and would be justly blamable if he omitted to do, though contradictory to what, in the former sense, is his duty.[9]

The point to be noted is that the problem as to whether a man is to be judged by his own standards is quite distinct from the problems either of absolutism versus relativism or of rationalism versus emotionalism. Moralists of every school must face the distinction between objective and subjective right. An anarchist assassinating a president is undoubtedly doing a wrongful action, as most of us see it—an action which it is our duty to prevent him from doing if we possibly can. Such actions are wrong, and yet they do not involve the moral badness of the man who does them, however difficult it may be to realize this truth. The anarchist's action regarded as sacrificing his own life for the sake of an ideal is of a sort to awaken our emotional applause and to appear noble or heroic when we view it in its isolated character. There is a sense, then, on any theory, in which a man can be judged only by his own standards, since for him it would be wrong to obey any others. This sort of judgment is not that given by the magistrate, whose duty it

is to enforce socially accepted standards and to bring heterodox consciences into line, if necessary, by force.

Westermarck is quoted by Stace as saying that ethical subjectivism would make men more tolerant, a statement which Stace interprets in a bad sense. But Westermarck goes on to explain his assertion in a way which makes it clear that he, at least, thought that in certain ways ethical subjectivism would make us more strict:

> In every society the traditional notions as to what is good or bad, obligatory or indifferent, are commonly accepted by the majority of people without further reflection. By tracing them to their source it will be found that not a few of these notions have their origin in ignorance and superstition or in sentimental likes or dislikes, to which a scrutinizing judge can attach little importance; and, on the other hand, he must condemn many an act or omission which public opinion, out of thoughtlessness, treats with indifference.[10]

According to Westermarck himself, therefore, the effect to be anticipated from tracing our moral opinions back to the emotional experiences which they express is by no means an indiscriminate toleration of all sorts of abominations but rather a critical sifting of our moral judgments, which leaves standing only those judgments which are sincere, only those which express our real feelings of approval and disapproval. Such a sifting, Westermarck believed, would be favorable to morality, that is to say, favorable to those evaluations which Westermarck himself, as a civilized human being, would have made. It would result in increased tolerance in certain directions but in increased severity in others.

The ethical predicates are, in form, names of properties of actions and characters; ethical judgments have the form of propositions assigning these predicates to actions, classes of actions, and characters. It is, of course, true that in literal meaning such predicates and judgments do not refer to the feelings of the person who makes the judgment but to the action or character which is the subject of the assertion. To those who accept a literal-minded philosophy of naïve realism with regard to the sensuous qualities of things, the thought that beauty and nobility and vileness, etc., should not be literally intrinsic qualities of actions and men no doubt seems highly sophistical. However, modern critical philosophy regards both common sense and science as containing a goodly amount of construction. Words and sentences cannot be interpreted literally. Thus science speaks of mass, energy, space-time, events, electrons, etc., without meaning to be taken quite literally; common sense speaks of things, causes, and selves without being able to give an exact account of its meaning. It is intellectually crude and unmannerly to insist that sentences must mean exactly what they mean literally, or else nothing at all. Taken literally, a judgment that an action possesses rightness or wrongness would always be false, just as a judgment predicating a secondary quality is always literally false. An action may be said to be objectively right or wrong in the sense that it possesses the *power* of evoking the emotions of approval and disapproval, just as a physical thing may be described as hot or cold because of its ability to produce certain sensations. But whose approval? Modern intuitionists, such as G. E. Moore and Sir W. David Ross, press this question and demand a definite answer. Is it the emotions of the agent, of *any* judge, of all men or a majority of men, past, present, and future, or a majority of Englishmen, etc.? The answer can only be that ethical terms, as used by the plain man, have no precise or unambiguous meaning. When we praise or blame, we are not ordinarily conscious of any "standing alone"; we feel that the great majority of respectable men are with us or would be if they saw the facts of the case as we do. In the last analysis, if we cannot obtain a social backing for our approval or disapproval, we are willing to explain our judgments as simply the expression of our own feelings.

It is easy to overemphasize the variability of moral judgments. Human nature is fundamentally the same in all men, as Professor Stace points out, but men living under different conditions and in groups of different degrees of advancement have various social habits which express themselves in diverse moral judgments. If we could subtract all that is due to training and to peculiar conditions, including beliefs regarding causal influences and supernatural agencies, we should probably find that men and women, in all times and places, are much the same. Westermarck, while emphasizing the variability of moral judgments, nevertheless points out that this variability is largely with regard to the intellectual conditions of moral judgment.

> The variability of moral valuation depends in very large measure upon intellectual factors of another kind, namely, different beliefs relating to the objective nature of similar modes of conduct and their consequences. Such difference of ideas may arise from different situations and external conditions of life, which consequently influence moral opinion.[11]

This is the explanation, according to Westermarck, of parent-killing, infanticide, and other similar practices. Religious belief, again, is a powerful factor, since it includes beliefs on the consequences of conduct. "When we study the moral rules laid down by the customs of savage peoples we find that they in a very large measure resemble the rules of civilized nations."[12] The chief differences refer to the rights granted to nonmembers of the tribe and in consideration of animals; these are due to variations in the range of altruistic sentiment.

There are, then, differences of moral judgment connected with different customs and institutions; those customs may be called universal, if there are such, without which no society could exist. It would be rash to attempt to specify just what such universally necessary social habits must be; every society, it would seem, would place some value on truthtelling, promise-keeping, loyalty to the group and to leaders, and probably on respect for property in one form or another. Social groups adopt laws and customs which they believe to be to their advantage; the individual is trained in these conventions from infancy and acquires habits of praise and blame which he rarely revises in any fundamental way.

At first glance, the emotional theory seems to place a restriction on our attitude toward life. If it is true that moral evaluations are emotional expressions, it would seem that we should abstain from praise and blame and merely record the facts of people's desire and choice. This conclusion, however, is unwarranted. The emotional theory is merely a matter of philosophy from which nothing follows of a normative or imperative nature. In saying that the predicate *wrong* belongs to an action only as an expression of the feelings of some person acting as an impartial spectator, we do not deny that the action is wrong in the only sense in which an action can be wrong. Assuredly the emotional view cannot be taken to imply the theory that all actions are indifferent; for ethical indifference means that the action has been considered with reference to our positive and negative feelings and evokes neither. It does not follow, then, that because moral judgments are expressions of emotion that they should not, or ought not, be passed, since the emotional theory is offered as a statement of fact, and no statement of fact has any direct implication as to what ought to be done. The emotional theory, as a psychological fact, might causally engender a cessation of praise and blame, but there is no evidence to show that so abstract a theory can actually have any such effect on our practical and emotional lives.

The fact which gives life to the general aversion to the emotional theory among ethicists and practical moralists of all types is that it seems, on the face of it, to deny the phenomenal reality of right and wrong, morally good and morally bad. Now this phenomenal reality of moral distinctions is an indubitable and unchanging fact of human experience and corresponds to the intensity of our feelings of approval and disapproval. The practical moralist responds to relativism as the plain man does when he first learns of the Lockean theory of secondary qualities or of Berkeley's doctrine that "sensible things" exist only in the mind. But the fact is that the phenomenal reality of moral values remains after the acceptance of the emotional theory just as it was before. Furthermore, the very meaning of the ethical terms presupposes a certain detachment or impartiality. The use of such words as "wrong," "unjust," etc., is not to express our sorrow at pain or loss but to express the fact that we feel (or believe that we *would* feel were we detached spectators) an emotion of disapproval with regard to the character of such actions; our feelings are "supposed" to be against these actions *as such*, whoever was agent or patient in them. In practice it is true that moral judgment is often an expression of self-interest. Thus two individuals or nations who have conflicting interests are almost sure to express disapproval of each other. This is the common hypocrisy of life; men rarely deal with each other as honest egoists, free from moralizing cant; they become liars and self-deceivers when they use the language of right and wrong, a language which implies a godlike aloofness. The ethical predicates, in the struggle of life, become weapons; the perception, however, that these words are not used in true detachment and impartiality awakens disgust and even an aversion to any use of a language so commonly abused.

The moral emotions are by definition emotions of approval or disapproval felt by persons as disinterested spectators. They are directed on the *what* of actions in various patterns of circumstance, that is, on the universal form of classes of actions. This is at least part of what is generally meant by the "universal validity" of moral standards; it is the fact that each of us, in every feeling of praise of blame, is passing judgment on all actions, whether done by others or by ourselves, which are similar in character and circumstance to the one we have in mind. Now this claim to apply to all acts of the same kind is what is expressed in the time-honored golden rule of Confucius and Jesus and by the categorical imperative of Kant. "Do not that to another, which thou thinkest unreasonable to be done to thyself," said Hobbes, to quote only one of the many statements which have been given of this thought. This involves the notion that an action which would be "unreasonable" if done by A to B is "unreasonable" if done by B to A. This doctrine is accepted by Stace and is explained by him as the theory of the intrinsic equality of all men. The proposition is indeed a formal logical law, going back to the truism that A is A. It is a consequence of the fact that the moral emotions are directed on universals, i.e., on the recurrent patterns of actions in their contexts; if we disapprove of a given act, we admit that we would disapprove of that act if we were the doers of it. A man who does that which he condemns in another necessarily disapproves of his own action and to that extent of himself. The follower of the golden rule, on the other hand, is at peace with himself if he merely avoids doing what he condemns in others; if he does positively what he applauds others for doing, he can enjoy the applause of his own mind. On the other hand, such a man may not gain the approval of others as far as his actions are concerned, since there may be a difference of opinion as to what is right. But these others, even though condemning his actions, would feel a certain sympathetic approval if, for a moment, they could see his life from *his* point of view and share sympathetically his self-approval. In the case of the bad man, even one who has externally done right actions (i.e., actions of which we approve) when we place ourselves in his position, we feel disapproval, since we know how much this man disapproves of himself.

The golden rule, according to Westermarck, is an expression of the disinterestedness and impartiality of the moral emotions. "All this means is that resentment and retributive kindly emotion are moral emotions if they are assumed by those who feel them to be uninfluenced by the particular relationship in which they stand both to those who are immediately affected by the acts in question and to those who perform the acts."[13] We may elaborate this proposition as follows. If I approve my friend's action, or my own action, the supposition is that I would approve a similar action done by *anyone* in the same circumstances. Or, if there is some action done to me of which I disapprove, then since my disapproval is supposed to have been felt as a disinterested spectator, it follows that I must disapprove of that same action if done by myself. We test the genuineness of our impartiality in approving of some action of our own by asking whether we would approve of this action if done by another to us; or again we test the genuineness of our impartiality in disapproving the action of another to us by asking whether we would blame ourselves if we did this thing to another. Westermarck says of Sidgwick's law of equity that the proposition is true but tautological.

> When I pronounce an act to be right or wrong, good or bad, I mean that it is so quite independently of any reference it may have to me personally or to the particular relationship in which I stand to him who is immediately affected by the act and to him who performs it. This is implied in the very meaning of those and all other moral predicates on account of the disinterestedness and impartiality that characterizes the moral emotions, from which all moral concepts are derived.[14]

But how does Westermarck know that the moral emotions *ought* to be disinterested, when as a matter of fact they are commonly the reverse? It is evident that he performed an analysis of the *meaning* of the moral concepts and gained a certain insight which less thoughtful persons never succeed in gaining. According to Westermarck, such principles as Sidgwick's law of equity or the golden rule or the categorical imperative are merely tautologies. Whether we call these propositions tautologies or insights of reason is a question of verbal usage; at any rate, the meaning of these "tautologies" is not easily grasped or easily applied in life. The conclusion we reach seems to be a formal absolutism combined with a material relativity; the supreme principle is the postulate of impartiality, but this is empty unless combined with particular approvals and disapprovals.

NOTES

[1] W. T. Stace, *The Concept of Morals* (New York: Macmillan Co., 1937).

[2] *Ibid.,* p. 45.

[3] *Ibid.,* p. 46.

[4] *Ibid.,* p. 48.

[5] *Ibid.,* p. 53.

[6] *Ethical Relativity,* p. 59.

[7] *Op. cit.,* p. 58.

[8] *Op. cit.,* pp. 58-59.

[9] Selby-Bigge, *British Moralists*, II, 175. Sir W. David Ross comes to a similar conclusion in his closely reasoned *Foundations of Ethics* (London: Oxford University Press, 1939), p. 163.

[10] *Op. cit.*, p. 59.

[11] *Op. cit.*, p. 184.

[12] *Ibid*, p. 197.

[13] *Ibid.*, p. 93.

[14] *Op. cit.*, p. 12.

Claude Levi-Strauss (essay date 1945)

SOURCE: "The Work of Edward Westermarck," in *Acta Philosophica Fennica*, Vol. 34, 1982, pp. 654-67.

[*In the following excerpt, originally published in 1945, Levi-Strauss memorializes the recently deceased Westermarck as the spokesman for an era of sociological thought.*]

I

The death of Edward Westermarck was felt by all sociologists with a special sadness. It awakened memories, it provoked reflections, which infinitely expanded the bounds of the very real sorrow caused by the passing of a master who was among the greatest of his time.

In the case of Westermarck, indeed, it was not simply a renowned scholar who passed away; an entire era of sociological thought came to an end. And that on two accounts. Westermarck was the last and most famous representative of the English Anthropological School; he embodied, with an exceptional, militant power, a current of thought which renewed our social and moral understanding, and out of which grew the first efforts to develop a comprehensive description of mankind. But Westermarck revealed this affiliation not only in his theory; he affirmed it as well, in a more intimate and touching manner, in his person. The very advanced age at which he died made him less a continuator than a survivor. This old man of seventy-four years who would still dispute in 1936 with those he considered daring innovators—Lowie, Radcliffe-Brown, and others—had known Tylor; he had for many years carried on discussions with Frazer and, among us, with Durkheim. He was the last of this group of men of truly exceptional temperament, industry, erudition, and fecundity, who performed at the end of the nineteenth century the same role for the social sciences that the Renaissance masters did for modern thought.

Westermarck was born in Helsinki in 1862. His university studies ended in 1889 with a doctoral thesis on **"The Origin of Marriage"**; it was the embryo of his first large-scale work, **The History of Human Marriage**,[1] which immediately compelled recognition, first, by the ease and charm with which considerable erudition served the discussion of often austere themes and, second, by virtue of two important innovations: one, in method, placed sociological discussion within the framework of biological evolution; the other consisted in the striking repudiation of the theory of primitive promiscuity which dominated the period.

From 1906 to 1908 Westermarck published **The Origin and Development of the Moral Ideas**.[2] One finds there an attempt to interpret systematically the nature and origin of the moral judgments, conjoined with an inquiry of great scope intended to verify the theory by concrete proof. The eclecticism which governed this dual conception assured the work a lasting success, shown clearly by the publication date of the first French translation,[3] twenty years after the original. His last work, **Ethical Relativity**,[4] brings out his conclusions within the realm of moral theory.

In 1906 Westermarck was named Professor of Practical Philosophy at the University of Helsinki. The University of London assigned him a course in sociology in 1904, and in 1907 it conferred on him its chair in sociology. He had to teach alternately in London and in Helsinki, keeping a term in each city, until the establishment of the Swedish university known as the Åbo Akademi. He left Helsinki in 1918 to assume the rectorship of the new university until 1921, and he taught there until his final years.

These heavy teaching duties did not rule out fieldwork. He sojourned often in Morocco, and an important part of his work is devoted to monographs on folklore, dealing mainly with the relationship between moral ideas and magical beliefs. Especially worthy of mention are **"The Magic Origin of Moorish Designs,"**[5] **"Midsummer Customs in Morocco,"**[6] *Marriage Ceremonies in Morocco*,[7] and, finally, a comprehensive work in two volumes, **Ritual and Belief in Morocco**.[8]

These works not only are of keen interest to the student of Africa; they also shed special light on Westermarck's conceptions of the connections between ethnology and folklore, on the one hand, and between theoretical reflection and practical research, on the other. It is, moreover, the fieldworker whom the Royal Anthropological Institute had wanted to reward when it bestowed on Westermarck the Rivers Memorial Medal in 1928. Several years previously, Rivers had paid homage to him in his celebrated article on "The Disappearance of Useful Arts."[9]

II

In reviewing **The History of Human Marriage**, Tylor wrote in 1891: "The distinguishing character of Dr. Westermarck's whole treatise is his vigorous effort to work the biology-side and the culture-side of anthropology into one connected system."[10] Westermarck himself saw in his criticism of the theory of promiscuity not only the historical origin of his work, but also the basis of his subsequent methodological thinking. In 1890 it was generally believed that "primitive man lived in a state of promiscuity, where individual marriage did not exist, where all the men in a horde or tribe had indiscriminately access to all the women, and where the children born of these unions belonged to the community at large." And in the article **"Methods in Social Anthropology,"** from which those lines are taken and which constitutes his philosophical testament, Westermarck immediately adds: "I commenced my work as a faithful adherent of that hypothesis."[11]

What dissuaded him—and this is quite significant for understanding the development of his thought—was not social facts considered in themselves, but the problems that result from the theory of promiscuity when one claims to integrate the phenomena of social evolution with the more general process of biological evolution. In becoming "acquainted with the doctrine of organic evolution" he reached "the conclusion that the social habits of the anthropoids must throw some light on those of primitive man."[12] Thus, at the very dawn of his scientific career, that fundamental tendency emerged which immediately brought him into conflict with Durkheim and his school and at the same time with Frazer and, later, with both the "cultural anthropologists" of the United States and the "pure sociologists" of the school of Radcliffe-Brown: namely that, for Westermarck, sociological explanation is never satisfactory in itself, and that, to grasp a phenomenon in an intelligible form, it is necessary to transcend the social and to attain the underlying psychological level always, and the biological level whenever possible.

The criticism of promiscuity is revealing in this respect. According to Westermarck, the facts prove that the family is the social unit among gorillas and chimpanzees; the orangutan and gibbon also live in a monogamous family. Moreover, ethnographic investigations show that the family is a universal institution among mankind. From this double observation, "an evolutionist . . . is therefore naturally inclined to believe that it [marriage] existed among primitive man as well."[13]

This conclusion is reinforced by some arguments inspired by Darwinism: where family life was spontaneously established, natural selection must have favored couples; among the great apes, in fact, the small number of young, combined with the long duration of infancy, required that the male, by an acquired instinct, take care of the female and the young. All these considerations are valid for the human species.

In being the first to reject the theory of promiscuity, Westermarck anticipated by a good twenty years the general agreement of specialists; but there are objections to his argument and the postulates which it implies. If promiscuity had existed in certain human societies, it would have been as a cultural innovation and not as a natural survival. Thus, the example of the anthropoids

would be of no value. But above all, it was very risky to attempt to resolve the relative uncertainties about the first stages of human life by appealing to still more fragile hypotheses about the way wild primates live. On this subject, one is always reduced to conjectures; this was even truer fifty years ago.[14]

But, for Westermarck, the theory of marriage conceals a deeper aim. The tie it establishes between sociology and biology is valuable not only in itself; if it is justified, it confers on sociology a scientific value as great as that of biology, and perhaps even greater. If social institutions are, as Westermarck thinks, based on instincts, they become explicable to the extent that we succeed in reducing the one to the other. However, the sociologist is better placed than the biologist, since the latter is entirely ignorant of the causes of the organic variations presupposed by natural selection. On the contrary, the causes of social phenomena are accessible. Sociological method is the method suitable for discovering the causes of social phenomena.

III

By his insistence on a wholly explanatory sociology, by his conviction that only the fundamental characteristics of human nature can furnish such an explanation, Westermarck allies himself with the defenders of the comparative method. Discovery of similarities among beliefs and institutions, classification of these resemblances, explanation according to a psychological or biological law—such, according to him, is the proper direction of the social sciences. He did not rule out *a priori* the interpretation of phenomena by cultural borrowings or contacts, but he systematically restricted the field of their application. Indeed, how should we understand identical behavior in animals of the same species, if not by identity of nature? "From seeds of the same kind very similar plants spring up."[15] And reversing the diffusionist thesis, Westermarck thought that not only did geographical proximity and historical intimacy among various peoples fail to support explanation of the similarity of their institutions in terms of reciprocal borrowings; on the contrary, they reinforced the probability that each of the peoples evolved independently. The more similar they are, the more likely it is that they will generate the same social or moral traits. This distrust of historical or local explanation appears also in his African monographs. The ocellate decoration found on Moroccan ceramics, and the Ionian capital of the Greeks, do not necessarily have the same geographical origin; but they both should be interpreted with reference to the magical belief that the eye protects against the evil eye.[16] For Westermarck, the diffusionist method is based exclusively on external analogies; it is the method of a museum researcher, not of the sociologist.

One can indeed refuse *a priori* to explain the most universal characteristics in terms of cultural contacts: right to property, punishment, blood ties, marriage, prohibition of incest, exogamy, slavery, etc. But even when the historical connection has been established, nothing further has been accomplished with respect to explanation. How did the phenomenon appear in the first place? For there must have been a beginning. Now it is by means of comparison that the ultimate origin is discovered in the residue common to all similar institutions. But psychological explanation can succeed, if need be, even without points of comparison: "Very frequently the knowledge of the cause of a certain custom found among one people is suggestive of the meaning of the same or similar customs among other peoples."[17] This extrapolation is justified, for Westermarck, solely by the recognition of the existence, among all peoples, of a bond of "common humanity."

His evolutionist intransigence tolerated, even at the end of his life, only two reservations. He confessed that the English School compromised itself by two sorts of carelessness, the first being an abuse of the interpretation of obscure phenomena as "survivals" of other better known phenomena. But a custom cannot be the survival of another custom from which one could not recognize it as logically descended. Thus, Briffault interprets the loan of a wife as a survival of promiscuity, by likening the guest to the clan-brother. But why did the survival persist in the exceptional case of the guest and not in the normal and regular case of the clan-brother? Besides the "extravagant and uncritical" use of the principle of survival, the evolutionists were guilty of another excess, namely their tendency "to infer . . . from the prevalence of a custom or institution among some savage peoples . . . that this custom or institution was a relic from a stage of development which the whole human race once went through."[18] Westermarck thus attacked Lewis Morgan and the fifteen celebrated stages which universally would have preceded monogamous marriage. But in the process of banishing unilinear sequences, he condemned himself to tracing very perfunctory evolutionary systems, since institutions, according to him, always had the same origin and tended always toward the same end.

IV

For Westermarck, indeed, evolutionary explanation is always limited, and often contradicted, by the search for ultimate causes in the realm of psychology. This second tendency of his thought exhibits itself especially in his great work *The Origin and Development of the Moral Ideas.* In the first part, the author attempted to link various moral rules to some constitutional disposition of human nature in general, already existing in the most primitive societies known. He thought, indeed, that there are no qualitatively different kinds of morality, but a single Morality, of which the different moralities are only progressive approximations—in short, the point of view of ancient natural philosophy. But to this is added, as in eighteenth-century authors, the feeling—contradictory to the thesis stated above—that morality is a complex matter, and that it is indispensable to study it in its historical manifestations, which can, moreover, always be reduced to a few basic feelings.

By an obvious paradox, a work which presents itself above all as a study of facts thus begins with the declaration of a moral system which is completely finished before any reference to the social has been proposed or suggested. All moral judgment, according to Westermarck, has its origins in a special category of emotions which he calls retributive emotions; confronted with the actions of others, we sometimes display anger or indignation, sometimes benevolence and sympathy. This very simple emotional process can be discovered through introspection. Is this enough to establish the sphere of morality? Doubtless no, because it is found in animals as well as in men. But to the extent that it offers a start toward systemization, that it exhibits "a certain flavour of generality," that it ultimately furnishes the basis for an *a priori* deduction of the fundamental categories of duty, right, justice, injustice, good, merit, and virtue— to this extent, the general foundations of morality are provided, with their character of permanence and universality. It is still Kantianism, but of a diluted variety.

Thus, social observation could not claim to explain morality; it could not even discover the general orientation of morality, because when the framework is established the content has also been established, to a large degree. Social observation can, at most, supply a proof or, more accurately, an illustration of the psychological thesis and permit the precise definition of deviations, interruptions, aberrations, and progress with respect to a predetermined goal. The defects of the method are readily apparent. As Rivers expressed it, "it leaves us at the end just where we were at the beginning. . . ."[19] But, what is worse, the fault affects the method itself by which social facts are treated and the rigor with which they are introduced, criticized, and compared. Durkheim, after the publication of the work, had reproached Westermarck for this quite vigorously. He had shown, at the same time, how the initial psychological postulate (which is that of the entire English Anthropological School) had encouraged Westermarck to be content with what Durkheim called "a hasty and disorganized review": if one thinks that the origins of morality should be sought among the most permanent dispositions of human nature, then "instead of limiting and circumscribing the field to grasp the specifics, it will be necessary to extend it as far as possible [by studying heterogenous peoples] in order to demonstrate the very general processes which are sought."[20] Facts are merely accumulated, rather than chosen for clarity and illustration. The rigor of philosophical thought is diminished when attention is deflected toward empirical investigation, while the integrity of empirical investigation is weakened by its subordination to the justification of predetermined philosophical theories.

As a result, each chapter of *The Origin and Development of the Moral Ideas,* despite its lively style, the lightness of its discussion, and the interest aroused by the wealth of information, leaves a general feeling of dissatisfaction and the vague suspicion that the effort displayed is not proportional to the result obtained. The celebrated discussion between Frazer and Westermarck with respect to *The History of Human Marriage* provides a good example.[21]

When Frazer concluded his analysis of the prohibition of incest by proposing, as the ultimate explanation, certain magical beliefs related to the infertility of women, he himself was conscious of the weakness of this appeal. On the one hand, the beliefs in question presupposed the existence of the prohibition he wanted to infer from them; on the other hand, they have too specialized and limited a character to give a satisfactory account of an almost universal custom. But Frazer at least tried in this way to explain one cultural fact by another. Westermarck, on the contrary, after stating the criticisms just mentioned, declares that "the home is kept pure from incestuous intercourse neither by laws, nor by customs, nor by education, but by an instinct which . . . makes sexual love between the nearest kin a psychical impossibility."[22] This impossibility is the product of habit, which itself results from the close living conditions of the kin. Now here the psychological method backfires, not only for the reason that this "impossibility" admits of exceptions, but also that society does not forbid individuals (including brothers and sisters) from having sexual intercourse simply because of their living in close proximity, but rather because of their family relationship. This interdiction extends to all the individuals who can be regarded as kin, even if no actual proximity exists among them. In other words, the origin of the prohibition is found neither in the physiological tie of kinship nor in the psychological tie of proximity, but in the exclusively institutional tie of fraternity or paternity.

But Westermarck could not admit that the origin of a moral rule is found anywhere but in the deepest recesses of human nature. "All [theories of the prohibition of incest] presuppose that men avoid incestuous marriages only because they are taught to do so."[23] Can a social rule have any other source? But a theory which makes morality an autonomous reality could recognize neither learning nor forgetting: "Even when the meaning of a custom is obscure or lost, the field-worker's knowledge of the native mind and its modes of thinking and feeling may enable him to make valuable conjectures."[24] But if one thus makes the native mind the microcosm of the culture of the group, one runs the risk of replacing the concrete history of the society being studied not—as might be thought—with its underlying, universal, psychological bases, but with the by-products deposited by folklore in gullible minds. Westermarck considered fieldwork as the indispensable basis of all legitimate sociological speculation, and, against Radcliffe-Brown and Rivers, he cited his nine years of Moroccan investigations. It does not at all diminish the great value of his monographic work to recall that it has more to do with folklore than with ethnography. But at the theoretical level also, he explicitly confused the two disciplines.[25] Westermarck was willing, as seen above, to reconstruct the psychological history of customs by forcing individual minds beyond the limits of forgetfulness, but "the immediate data" of the native mind seemed to

him just as capable of accounting for the entirety of institutions. In his **"Midsummer Customs in Morocco,"**[26] he does not hesitate to reject the interpretation proposed by Frazer of the Midsummer Day fires as survivals of solar or rain rites, for the sole reason that the Berbers who were questioned had no recollection of any meaning of that sort. Individual forgetfulness of this meaning does not prove, however, that the practice never had such a meaning.

v

These psychological abuses have led some theorists of polemical bent to express very severe judgments. Thus, Radcliffe-Brown declared that "in England we have very little of anything that is called sociology" and that "any explanation of a particular social phenomenon in terms of psychology, i.e., of processes of individual mental activity, is invalid. . . . "[27] Westermarck replied to these attacks with great bitterness, and they were, so far as they concerned him, quite unjust. In the course of a discussion of the relationship between psychology and sociology, he one day interrupted Rivers by asking him how he claimed to explain blood feuds, if not by the desire for revenge; and Rivers replied to him that, on the contrary, it is the psychology of revenge which is unintelligible without the knowledge of blood feuds. In choosing to see customs and social rules only as the historical expression of internal, psychical, or organic tendencies, one reduces culture to a mundane and illusory manipulation of an autonomous psychological phenomenon, independent of all objective experience. Real events, migrations, wars, contacts, borrowings, inventions, and destructions are (in principle, if not in fact) eliminated as causes of the appearance or disappearance of such and such an institution among a given people at a specific time and place. The history and geography of human groups are abolished.

However, as far removed as Westermarck was from the direction taken by the social sciences during the last years of his life, in his work one encounters a very great number of foreshadowings, often prophetic suggestions, of ideas that are now generally accepted. And, by a curious paradox, if his psychological method constantly restricted the scientific scope of his work, nevertheless because of his lively appreciation of psychology his thought was, in many respects, in advance of the theories of his time. The psychological aspect of his thought gives it a freshness and vigor that make Westermarck the most contemporary of the great masters of the English School.

Undoubtedly its monumental character remains the most striking feature of his work. Not only has there never been a more immense effort at synthesis in the realm of the social sciences, but this effort is always sustained by a truly prodigious erudition. The compilation of authors is done with constant care to cite only reliable evidence. Nowhere, save with Frazer, can one find so considerable a compendium of information about human opinions.

But above all, one can never insist enough on the importance of the step which Westermarck took to free sociology by eliminating the theory of promiscuity, which had been interposed like a distorting filter between primitive psychology and our own. It tainted the former with what could seem to observers a scandal, an absurdity, or an enigma. It obliged theorists to multiply, endlessly and hopelessly, intermediary institutions, since it was necessary to account for the hypothetical transition between two forms of marriage as opposite as could be imagined: promiscuity and monogamous marriage. Thus, an ever deeper ditch was dug between the primitives and ourselves. To be sure, Westermarck's critique is not satisfactory. The best proof of this is that the refutation of the theory of promiscuity, which struck a decisive blow against sociological evolutionism, is based by him, essentially, on an evolutionary argument. Yet not exclusively. Behind the apparatus of proofs and discussions, one perceives the solid and enduring basis of his work: a human sympathy and a good psychological sense which, without fail, preserved him from the excesses of the theorists. Morocco apart, he never had direct contact with true primitives; but a sort of secret intuition prevented him from attributing to their institutions motives or explanations which were completely irreducible to this norm of "common humanity" to which he so often referred.

Thus, his "psychologism" has had two consequences, the one negative and the other positive, but both fertile. In the first place, the contradiction his work exhibits between the diversity of collected facts and the simplicity of proposed explanations has helped his successors to understand that psychological factors, precisely because they are universal and permanent, cannot explain social phenomena which are diverse, particular, and contingent. Through an almost automatic reaction to the theories of the English School, there emerged the distinction between *nature* and *culture,* which has made possible the cultural and historic interpretation of social phenomena.

But if cultures should be treated as specific and often heterogenous phenomena, it will not be forgotten in the future that the individuals who participate in these cultures are united by a bond of psychological brotherhood, and that, despite the diversity of their technologies, their beliefs, or their customs, the primitive African or American and the civilized European are, as individuals, similar and receptive to each other, and they react through the same mechanisms, although within different frameworks.

This concept of "permanent humanity" and this belief in a psychological constant constitute both the basis and the great originality of Westermarck's work. They go hand in hand. In particular, they are at the bottom of his criticism of the unilinear evolutionism of Spencer and Lewis Morgan. Human evolution did not consist, for him, in a passage through more and more heterogeneous stages, but in a perilous and progressive confirmation of fundamental concepts and tendencies. The evolutionary system which furnishes the general framework of *The History of Human Marriage,* as well as the specific frameworks of each chapter of *The Origin and Development of the Moral Ideas,* is basically the following: first, primitive mankind, where confused and varied approximations of the main psychological and moral needs of man are detected; then, with the intermediate civilizations of antiquity and the Middle Ages (Egypt, Greece, Rome, Christian Europe, India, China, Mexico), a series of deformations and specializations in comparison to these primitive tendencies; and, finally, from the time of the Renaissance and with the development of critical thought, a progressive rationalization which tends to lead mankind toward a refined consciousness and implementation of fundamental needs. He had thus foreshadowed one of the most original conceptions of contemporary sociological thought. His interpretation of the intermediate civilizations as being outside the general process of evolution heralds the diffusionist theory of Rivers and Elliot Smith, who see in Mediterranean civilization not a necessary transition, but an historical event at once exceptional, sensational, and formidable.

Moreover, Westermarck took constant care to underline the similarities between the moral customs of cultures which seemed very disparate and to restore to the great civilizations, whose heirs we consider ourselves to be, the responsibility for rules or customs which we habitually label "savage": this confers on his work a critical value and militancy of which he was fully aware. Moral evolution had for him one meaning: it should bring mankind nearer to an ideal of liberalism and rationalism, it should emancipate it from errors and prejudices. He was thus the first to be aware of the sterile conservatism of unilinear evolutionism, which justified all institutions by depicting them as inescapable forms of a necessary development. But, for Westermarck, the role of sociology was not to justify what was, nor what is, but to construct what ought to be. He considered the relativist critique as an instrument of spiritual emancipation.

To be convinced of this, it is enough to recall one of the last disputes he carried on, at the end of his life, against a disciple of Briffault who took up against him the defense of promiscuity. The injustice toward his work seemed to him to reside less in the false interpretation of his arguments or in the misunderstanding of the proofs which for fifty years had accumulated in his favor, than in the accusation, which seemed to him intolerable, that he wanted to establish the morality of monogamous marriage on a transcendent basis by criticizing promiscuity. And, wishing to summarize the significance of half a century of scientific activity, he concluded with this sentence: "Both in my book *The Origin and Development of the Moral Ideas,* which appeared before the war, and in my recent book *Ethical Relativity,* I have emphatically refuted the objectivity and absoluteness of all moral values."[28]

NOTES

[1] Edward Westermarck, *The History of Human Marriage, Part I: The Origin of Human Marriage* (Helsinki:

Frenckell & Son, 1889); and *The History of Human Marriage,* with an Introductory Note by Alfred R. Wallace (London: Macmillan and Co., 1891).

[2] Westermarck, *The Origin and Development of the Moral Ideas,* 2 vols. (London: Macmillan and Co., 1906-8).

[3] Westermarck, *L'Origine et le développement des idées morales,* trans. Robert Godet, 2 vols. (Paris: Payot, 1928-29).

[4] Westermarck, *Ethical Relativity,* International Library of Psychology, Philosophy, and Scientific Method (London: Kegan Paul, Trench, Trubner & Co., 1932).

[5] Westermarck, "The Magic Origin of Moorish Designs," *The Journal of the Anthropological Institute of Great Britain and Ireland* 34 (1904): 211-22.

[6] Westermarck, "Midsummer Customs in Morocco," *Folk-Lore* 16, no. 1 (March 1905): 27-47.

[7] Westermarck, *Marriage Ceremonies in Morocco* (London: Macmillan and Co., 1914).

[8] Westermarck, *Ritual and Belief in Morocco,* 2 vols. (London: Macmillan and Co., 1926).

[9] W. H. R. Rivers, "The Disappearance of Useful Arts," in *Festskrift tillegnad Edvard Westermarck i anledning av hans femtioårsdag den 20 November 1912* (Helsinki: J. Simelii arvingars boktryckeri, 1912), pp. 109-30.

[10] Edward B. Tylor, review of *The History of Human Marriage, The Academy* 40, no. 1013 (3 October 1891): 289.

[11] Westermarck, "Methods in Social Anthropology," *Journal of the Royal Anthropological Institute* 66 (July-December 1936): 223.

[12] Ibid.

[13] Ibid., p. 224.

[14] Westermarck, moreover, insisted upon the fact that progress in zoological observation has confirmed his thesis. See Westermarck, "On Primitive Marriage: A Rejoinder to Mr. V. F. Calverton," *The American Journal of Sociology* 41, no. 5 (March 1936): 565-84.

[15] Westermarck, "Methods," p. 228.

[16] Westermarck, "Magic Origin," pp. 217, 222.

[17] Westermarck, "Methods," p. 232.

[18] Ibid., p. 236.

[19] Rivers, "Sociology and Psychology," in *Psychology and Ethnology* (London: Kegan Paul, Trench, Trubner & Co., 1926), p. 10.

[20] Émile Durkheim, "Sur l'évolution générale des idées morales," *L'Année sociologique* 10 (1905-6): 385.

[21] See J. G. Frazer, *Totemism and Exogamy: A Treatise on Certain Early Forms of Superstition and Society,* 4 vols. (London: Macmillan and Co., 1910), 4: 92-99, and Westermarck's "Additional Note" in the second edition of *The Origin and Development of the Moral Ideas,* vol. 2 (London: Macmillan and Co., 1917), pp. 747-50.

[22] Westermarck, *History* (1891), p. 544.

[23] Ibid.

[24] Westermarck, "Methods," p. 241.

[25] Ibid.

[26] Westermarck, "Midsummer Customs," pp. 44-47.

[27] A. R. Radcliffe-Brown, "The Present Position of Anthropological Studies," in *The Advancement of Science: 1931,* Addresses Delivered at the Centenary Meeting of the British Association for the Advancement of Science (London: British Association, 1931), pp. 27, 14.

[28] Westermarck, "On Primitive Marriage," p. 584.

C. Wright Mills (essay date 1948)

SOURCE: "Edward Alexander Westermarck and the Application of Ethnographic Methods to Marriage and Morals," in *An Introduction to the History of Sociology,* edited by Harry Elmer Barnes, The University of Chicago Press, 1948, pp. 654-67.

[*In the following excerpt, Mills draws comparisons between Westermarck's work and the writings of Sir Henry Maine and Charles Darwin.*]

I. THE LIFE AND WORKS OF WESTERMARCK

It depends on the definition into which the tally is made, but, not counting hillbillies, peasants, and folk-societies, there are something under one hundred major cultural types of nonliterate people on the globe today. Since the eighteenth century they have been "data" for social thinkers. Exhausting work, good minds, and a lot of money have been spent in exploiting them. Many of their languages have been learned. Detailed graphs have been constructed of their family and social organization. They have been lived among. Thin, mensurative instruments have been pushed around their heads. Their very existence, as well as the details of their lives and minds, have been the object of many theories. They have been much explained, and they have been used in various and imaginative explanations of the development of mankind.

If we conceive of the history of intellectual doctrine as a series of learned conversations, we may designate

Westermarck as one given to monologues. Twice he monopolized the round table—on two topics: (1) the origin and history of kinship structures and rules and (2) the character and history of moral ideas.[1] He also spoke on ethics,[2] but the philosophers could not believe it, and the ethnologists, although respectful, were not interested in "philosophy."

Most of his traveling was to the British Museum and in shuttling between London and Finland, but he left the round table occasionally and went to Morocco and came back with three collections which had only a small audience.[3] A triangle with points in London, Finland, and Morocco encompasses the major movements of Westermarck's life. He was close to academic contexts by antecedents and location. Born in Helsingfors, in 1862, he breathed out a sickly childhood, being barred from the romp and game of associates of his own age. As an undergraduate he took a strong dislike to German metaphysics, was attracted greatly to English empiricism, and became an agnostic. He remained an agnostic, being quietly but firmly hostile to religion all his life.

He must have conceived of the marriage study around 1887; in that year he came to the British Museum for library materials. Fourteen years later the book appeared. In the meantime, as a professor of moral philosophy he taught at Helsingfors, escaping these duties in 1893 and 1897 for periods of work in London. He met and was associated with such men as Shand, Tylor, Marett, Branford, and the Maecenas, J. Martin White, who was instrumental in securing for him a university lectureship in sociology at the University of London in 1907. At the same time he held the chair of moral philosophy at Helsingfors and spent his summers in field work in Morocco. Intermittently, he was active in Finnish politics. But his life was filled mostly with scholarship up to the last days. He died on September 3, 1939.[4]

II. THE ORIGINS, EVOLUTIONS, AND FORMS OF MARRIAGE

The "conversation" into which Westermarck plumped his monumentally sized tomes on marriage and the family had been going on for some time. Since many of the logically possible positions concerning the origin and early forms of marriage had already been taken, it is to be expected that Westermarck had antecedents. There were those who were upholding and those who were contraverting theories similar to those with which Westermarck's name was to be connected. Sir Henry Maine (*Ancient Law* [1861]) had held the primordial cell of social development to be the patriarchal family and had voiced other views similar to those that Westermarck was to enunciate. However, Maine had not supported his notion with primitive materials; his sources were largely Roman. Bachofen (*Das Mutterrecht* [1861]), using Greek data primarily, had challenged the notion of the patriarchate as the first form of the family. Tylor, in his review *of The History of Human Marriage,* made it clear that Westermarck was not the first to reject primitive promiscuity; Tylor himself had never sponsored it.[5]

The primary objective of those who have studied family organizations and marriage rules among primitive peoples has been the reconstruction of the sequence of forms which are antecedent to those now existent. Taking existent types as the end-product, other forms have been scaled according to their degrees of difference and similarity to them; various features of contemporary culture have been treated as survivals from, putatively, earlier stages that no longer exist; also the mating behavior of anthropoids have been used analogously.

Perhaps the prevailing views on the topic were those of the classical evolutionists, represented by such men as Post, McLennan, Lubbock, and Morgan. Using the comparative method and positing certain stages to have been universally followed, the evolutionists set forth the following scheme:

In the beginning was promiscuity. "Society" was without form; chaos prevailed and unregulated sex intercourse. Then groups of women, related or not, were looked upon as wives of groups of men, related or not. But the clans came forth: tribes were divided into these hereditary social units, and these were composed of blood relatives and also of some who were not so related. Thus social organization became more clearly formed. At first, and dominantly, this form was maternal in principle: the children belonged to the clan of their mothers. Later the gens developed: the children belonged to the gentes of their fathers. Finally, after all this had passed, the monogamous family (and the village) became the basic units of organization.

It was against this view that Westermarck formulated what impressed many as a definitive and adequate counterstatement. He did not think mankind had to go through so much to reach monogamy. Man was originally monogamous. Rejecting primitive promiscuity in the first well-rounded attack on that notion, Westermarck asserted that a paternalistic family was the earliest, and universal, social unit. It was present in the most primitive tribes, in those having no clan structure; and it persisted among all those which had acquired such structures of kinship. Westermarck attempted to refute the precedence of matrilineal over patrilineal descent. He set forth alternative explanations for observed social forms which had been explained by the evolutionists as survivals of group marriages and promiscuity.

His evidence was gathered, as seems to have been a custom of the day, illustratively; it was of two kinds—ethnographic and from the anthropoids, which he indicated as being given to pair arrangements of some permanence. In both cases his evidence has been strongly imputed to have been selected for the theory. He profusely illustrated the alleged fact that hunters and fishers, whom the classical evolutionists considered "most primitive" economically, were, in the main, monogamous. He set forth many detailed cases around which argument over the question could swirl.

Besides these two modes of proof there was another: Westermarck grounded the idea of a universal and original monogamous patriarchate in the realm of Darwinian biology and in what passed (and "still passes") for a psychology. He supported the Darwinian view of the family, bottomed on male possessiveness and jealousy, with monopoly by force later becoming enshrined in custom. He argued from supposedly universal "psychological causes" to social forms. He accepted "mere instincts" as playing a "very important part in the origin of social institutions."[6] This mode of proof supported and was supported by the evidence from the anthropoids. I shall comment later upon the psychological inadequacy of Westermarck's thinking.

How do present-day American ethnologists stand on the question of the origin and sequence of marriage forms? In so far as they permit themselves an opinion on such a large question, they are, as a group, closer to Westermarck than to the Morgan type of evolutionist. But their reasons are not his. Such men as Boas, Kroeber, Lowie, and Malinowski hold that the biosocial unit of the monogamous family seems to be a very fundamental and prevailing one in existent preliterate societies. However, properly speaking, we know of no such institution as "*the* primitive family"; there are many and diverse types of organization among primitive peoples, some quite similar to "modern" forms, some not. At the "lowest levels" of society, family life is quite varied. There seems to be no thoroughly acceptable evidence that a "stage" of promiscuity ever existed. The father, the mother, the child, and their net of relationships are primary. By various types of extension their interrelationships have grown into such (often complex) groupings as the clan and into such arrangements as group marriage. The latter occurs but rarely and then as an outgrowth of previous conditions of individual marriage. The family and village groupings are near-universal units of social organization; they extend "from the beginning"; they persist through all the other forms.

But, in the main, modern ethnologists have not answered the sort of questions and topics which formed the theme of the evolutionists' and Westermarck's work on marriage and family structures. They have dropped the questions. They have given up the search for origins. They no longer seek all over the world, albeit via libraries, for "the fundamentally primitive" condition. It is a methodological refusal to ask a question whose answer presumably would rest upon evidence that is not available. And, more important, the quest for origins is a significant and compulsive problem only within a framework which assumes the fundamental conception of evolutionism: a universal uniformity of development through stages. The legitimacy and the significance of the origin hunt died with the evolutionists.

From present elements found in nonliterate cultures, modern ethnologists do not *readily* infer into a constructed past, certainly not into a "stage" arbitrarily postulated as previously existent. Such an element is studied functionally in a context that is seen; it is not interpreted as evidence for an affiliated context supposed to have been there but which is now forever vanished.

III. ON METHOD AND COMPILATION

In a growing science it is often over questions of method that arguments hover; and it is through this sphere that individuals really shape deeply and lastingly the contour of their science. If you spread out the histories of various sciences, you see that compilations of fact are not important unless they are logically connected with sharp theory and incisive method. Theory, fact, and method are the inseparable rungs of the ladder to scientific fame. Methodology is what others can take away from an individual's work and use themselves. You will learn very little, save industry, from Westermarck as methodologist.

The model of thought which informed the classical evolutionists was not the paradigm drawn from physics of Descartes; nor was it the scheme of Hegel. It was Spencer's, and back of Spencer lay the geology and biology of the early nineteenth century, and alongside of him sat Darwin. Among others, Comte had used a comparative method. Spencer used it more generously, and it was from Spencer that the classical evolutionists derived their way of thinking. Like them, Westermarck used the comparative method, but with this scheme and method he dug out of the British Museum, and presented to the round table, an alternative sequence of the forms of marriages and families and of kinship structures in general.

Unlike the classical evolutionists, Westermarck rejected *in toto* the small interpretative trick with which any kind of rabbit can be made to appear from anybody's sleeve of abstractions: the theory of survivals. He thought it was based on speculation, that it took unfair advantage of empirical materials. And in this he has been vindicated.

But the concrete way of work utilized by Westermarck was the famous little-slips-of-paper-piled-topically-and-write-it-up-method.[7] It was the encyclopedic and comparative method. The data so collected suffer in general in that they are not oriented so as to be crucial empirical evidence in the solution of carefully defined problems. In ethnological work this method has been rejected for a more specialized reason: it dislocates particular phases and bits of a "total culture" and tears societal features from their contexts.[8] Given the present ethnographic norms for the determination of whole facts, the result is plain and simple inaccuracy.[9] Also, since the cultural world is a big place with a lot in it, such grab-bag methods are bound to result in ethnographic inadequacy, for even encyclopedias are selective. A severe appraisal of Westermarck's method, sources, and work has been written by R. Lowie. After commenting on the profusion of documents used in an amazingly uncritical way, he states: "Not only are there inconsistencies . . . but bad, good, and indifferent sources are cited indiscriminately . . . even good sources are abused. . . . Westermarck neither appraises his evidence discriminatively nor becomes absorbed in his cultural phenomena; and while his views on early family life largely coincide with current doctrines, we are not able to discover any signal advancement of ethnology due to his writings."[10] Yet, in so far as ethnography in its quest for facts and more facts around the turn of this century implemented a concretizing of social science, Westermarck's Darwinian ethnography helped. He did live with the Moors for nine years.

For many ethnologists, however, Lowie has carved an epitaph that cannot easily be rubbed off the tomes of Westermarck with their six to twelve footnotes per page.[11]

IV. THE NATURAL HISTORY OF SOCIAL INSTITUTIONS

But other thinkers with other interests sat at the round table of intellectual history. Some of them listened to Westermarck's monologue and took away certain influences and certain models of thought. By some sociologists, Westermarck is remembered as among the first to shift the focus from old-fashioned history to the "natural history of social institutions." If a sociological standpoint occurs when historical studies become studies of the regular growth of institutions, then Westermarck's *History of Human Marriage* is one of the earliest wholesale sociological studies. The book may be viewed as a large-scale natural history of a social institution. In this connection Westermarck writes:

> Like the phenomena of physical and psychical life those of social life should be classified into certain groups and each group investigated with regard to its origin and development. Only when treated in this way can history lay claim to the rank of a science in the highest sense of the term, as forming an important part of Sociology, the youngest of the principal branches of learning. Descriptive historiography has no higher object than that of offering materials to this science.[12]

The sociological interest in historical and ethnological materials was greatly augmented by Darwinian doctrine, and Westermarck's work is dominated by the Darwinism of *The Descent of Man*. The direct translation of Darwinian principles into social interpretation imaginatively ran itself to a brief end in such men as Gumplowicz. The other line of development was the classical evolutionist and, following in partial reaction to it, the historical and institutional evolutionism of such men as Westermarck.

England was one of the several places where idiographic facts got caught up in a level of abstraction. In England, history and ethnography were used as stuffing for natural histories. In so far as English thinkers have imprinted patterns upon American sociology, it is by means of this notion of the natural history of social institutions. And Westermarck was a big man among them.

His view of sociology is indicated clearly in the above quotation. He had no systematic view of the scope of the discipline; it was synthetic, a collection of studies dealing with all aspects of social life. His own interest was in the comparative study of social institutions, which he thought of as sets of social relations regulated and sanctioned by "society." In American publications he is also classed as a forerunner of folk, or, more usually, of "cultural," sociology. In this connection, W. I. Thomas, in his influential course on social origins, told his classes that *The Origin and Development of Moral Ideas* was an important book to purchase, but, he added, "because of the wealth of material rather than for theory."[13]

Ward and Giddings and their generation knew Westermarck at firsthand, and he seems to have influenced Cooley in his formulation of the importance of primary groups, although how much or in what way, we do not know. Cooley writes: "The best comparative studies of the family, such as those of Westermarck or Howard, show us. . . . a universal institution . . . . as more alike the world over than. . . . an earlier school had led us to suppose."[14] Cooley also cites him as rendering evidence for Cooley's cherished primary ideal of "the universality of kindness and the kindly ideal."[15] Yet it cannot be denied that Westermarck has not been, and is not now, of any focal importance in the actual work of American sociologists.

V. THE PSYCHOLOGICAL MODE OF EXPLANATION AND BIOLOGICAL METAPHYSICS

Closely tied in with the comparative method but also standing weakly by itself, there is in the recorded thinking of Westermarck an instinctivist psychology. This psychology is linked to a model of causal explanation, and both are determined by the Darwinian notion of survival value. Westermarck used "cause" interchangeably with "origin." By these terms he meant the *biological* condition which determined a phenomenon or which lent to it a biological survival value. Thus the cause and origin of marriage lie in the need of prolonged parental care and protection. Mammals, including human beings, with such instinctive proclivities are favored by processes of natural selection. Upon such instincts (in 1936 Westermarck called them "primeval habits," and "feelings"[16]) rests the origin and persistence through various kinship vicissitudes of the family grouping. The basic explanatory apparatus upon which rests the application of causal analysis is, for Westermarck, the Darwinian theory of natural selection. This theory is used in accounting for the "psychological" tendencies and structures of men. Such tendencies and structures are the causes and lead to the motives underlying social groups and relationships. Hence, "in the last analysis," the *real* hub of the wheel of social life is found to be biological conditions. This was the metaphysical bent which underlay the psychology of the day.

It is because the "instincts and sentiments" underneath it are deep in the universal organic makeup of man as animal[17] that the family existed "from the beginning" and will probably continue to exist in times not yet here.

Any reconstruction or explanation of social institutions must be based on "the fundamental causes" which Westermarck took to be biological and psychological in nature. "I put particular stress," he says, "upon the psychological causes. . . . and more especially I believe that the mere instincts have played a very important part in the origin of social institutions and rules."[18]

Thus, although Westermarck treated his ethnographic data in terms of the concept of social institution, he relied for their ultimate explanation upon psychobiological theory. Robertson Smith[19] criticized his **History of Human Marriage** on two related grounds: It is not "natural" history, for an institution is "controlled by public opinion and regulated by law." Second, to treat the study as a *natural* history of pairing involves the assumption that "the laws of society are at bottom mere formulated instincts, and this assumption really underlies all our author's theories. His fundamental position compels him. . . . to hold that every institution connection with marriage that has universal validity, or forms an integral part of the main line of development is rooted in instinct, and that institutions which are not based on instinct are necessarily exceptional and unimportant for scientific history."

Such a writer as Sir Edward B. Tylor considered that Westermarck had executed a valuable attempt to work out the biological and cultural sides of anthropology into a connected scheme.[20] But today, when one of the major emphases in ethnology is sociological psychology, it is not necessary to detail the reasons why Westermarck's formulation and assumptions are outmoded and otiose. The Durkheim school and also Rivers[21] criticized him for "explaining" social phenomena on a "psychological" basis, told him to watch it, but he shook them off.

VI. THE SOCIOLOGY OF MORALS AND THE THEORY OF ETHICS

Perhaps the ground tone of all Westermarck's writing is a persistent interest in moral codes and in ethical theories. The initial problem which led to the three volumes on marriage was that of sexual modesty. Later this concern expanded to include all relations between the sexes.

This drive toward a sociology of morals is one component of Westermarck's work which I believe could, but probably will not, influence the direction of American sociological interests. A sociology of morals, worthy of the name, cannot be said to exist among American social thinkers. Their intellectual tradition harbors certain hard phrases, distinctions, and many logical knots, which hang by the neck any attempt really to analyze moral phenomena. The theoretically inadequate work of Sumner is still for most the last word. An adequate social psychology of moral rules and judgments has not yet been written.

But if a sociology of morals were to be developed, Westermarck[22] would be written of as *one type* of its "forerunners." His voluminous synthesis of ethnographic material[23] was one of the pioneering books that placed the *historical* and *grossly empirical* aspect of ethics on a much more secure foundation. He documents moral variability; he presents data on the evolution of ethical behavior; his collection of facts shows a "connection" of custom with morals.[24] He shows morals as an early religious function.[25] One comes from his books with an absorbed realization of the *factual*[26] relativity of moral ideas. In his books the divine-origin view of morals is bathed in a lethal bath of facts. His name must be placed on the list of those who helped hammer out a naturalistic view of morals, even though *its* theoretical basis was mistaken. There is in Westermarck much timber that was growing in his time and that must be cleared from his work by a sociology of morals. Perhaps the utilization of his large body of anthropological materials in reconstructing the evolution of morals is vitiated by an uncontrolled comparative method. But the generic weakness in his thought on morals, as in his thought on kinship, lies in its psychological foundations.

His data show custom to be related to morals. It may be said that Westermarck misstates the point of these data: although he recognizes a certain objectivity and disinterestedness[27] as a characteristic of custom, he is so dominated by a subjective psychology that he is able to write: "Custom is a moral rule only on account of the indignation called forth by its transgression. . . . it is nothing but a generalization of emotional tendencies."[28]

The ultimate basis of moral judgments is individual and emotional. Moral concepts are generalizations of emotions that are within us. In certain cases specific emotions underpin certain moral concepts. Moral disapproval is a form of resentment, and moral approval is a form of retributive kindly emotion.[29] These two are distinctly *moral emotions*. Psychologically, Westermarck is not a bad bedfellow for McDougall, and certainly he would not fail to welcome Adam Smith if he had brought his "sentiments" with him.[30] Moral judgments spring from the individual's "own moral consciousness; they are judgments of other's conduct from one's own point of view and in accordance with one's own feelings and opinions about right and wrong." Although relative, they are not arbitrary, for we approve and disapprove "because we cannot do otherwise; our moral consciousness belongs to our mental constitution which we cannot change as we please."[31]

Yet, factually, "there is no absolute standard in morality."[32] Hence Westermarck must posit innate emotional differences to account for the ethnographic fact of a variety of moral judgments. He falls back upon the notion of an innate "emotional constitution."[33] The basic moral factor in evolution springs not from social relations but from individual sentiments of praise and blame. Westermarck evolutionized the Adam Smith of the "Moral Sentiments."

He speaks of "the evolution of the moral consciousness" which to "a large extent consists in its development from the unreflecting to the reflecting, from the unenlightened to the enlightened."[34]

Although, as I have indicated, the excessively psychological and subjective interpretation given by Westermarck to his data makes it necessary to give us the explanatory structure of his thought, the gross data are still valuable for certain purposes and there are also scattered inklings which a sociology of morals would wish to consider carefully and possibly to develop.

VII. THE MORAL

The younger generation of American ethnologists and sociologists do not know Westermarck at firsthand. It is possible to receive gracefully the Ph.D. degree in ethnology, and certainly in sociology, without ever opening any one of his books. In diluted fashion his effort lives in passages in histories of social thought and in the chapters of symposiums.[35] But he is not a direct determinant of the working day of American social scientists.

Searching the pages of contemporary texts, monographs, and symposiums you will find few references to Westermarck. You do find scattered bits of information ("In Java, among the. . . . "), with his name footnoted, or references to, or paragraph summaries of, his theories of incest and ornament and the monogamic family.

Why is this? Why did this man have his best time in other times and then drop from the running in the operative, the pivotal, footnotes of fresh writing? Many general and perhaps some social reasons could be given, but I think there are two more or less specific ones.[36]

One reason is that between Westermarck and us there stands a modern sociological psychology which comprises a new view of the role of biological elements in social systems and which excludes the psychological as explanatory, making physiological science a strict counterpart and a parallel endeavor to work within a sociological perspective. With varying degrees of adequacy, ethnologists are grasping and using this view; it forms one of the more fruitful trends of interest in modern American ethnology. The past is written and used in terms of the present, and Westermarck does not contribute to this trend.

The other reason is the changed status of "fact" within the accepted models of inquiry. Westermarck got hold of a lot of "facts," but he used them either in a kind of planless empiricism or like a philosopher illustrating his feelings in the grand manner. His facts do not now appear to be crucial. They are not caught up in a firm mesh of theory, which they prove or disprove. The comparative method and the evolutionist theory, within which his facts make sense, have been overthrown for new models of inquiry and new and perhaps more modest theory. That is the history of the changing content of science. And so his books bore us a little because their masses of fact seem irrelevant to our theoretic directions.

Encyclopedic compilation prevails over analytic theory, and he is heavy with obsolete problems. The undisturbed dust on his volumes is an object lesson in method and in the ways of setting up problems.

These things might have been forgiven if he had possessed the synoptic mind that can squeeze from masses of data the analytically characterizing sentence. But Westermarck did not write such sentences. Maybe he made some of the men at the intellectual round table get up and thenceforth look to their facts. But he does not give us anything to look to them through; he sat at some other round table with other chairmen.

NOTES

[1] *The History of Human Marriage* (London, 1901). The major propositions of these three volumes are to be found in a one-volume edition, *A Short History of Marriage* (New York, 1926); and in *The Origin and Development of Moral Ideas* (2 vols.; London, 1906). He also considered *The Future of Marriage in Western Civilization* (New York, 1936).

[2] *Ethical Relativity* (New York, 1932).

[3] *Marriage Ceremonies in Morocco* (London, 1914); *Ritual and Belief in Morocco* (2 vols.; London, 1926); *Wit and Wisdom in Morocco: A Study of Native Proverbs* (London, 1930); see also "The Belief in Spirits in Morocco," *Acta academiae Aboensis, Humaniora,* I (Helsingfors, 1920), 1-167.

[4] The best life-history in brief compass is to be found in M. Ginsberg's "The Life and Work of Edward Westermarck," *Sociological Review* (Eng.), January-April, 1940; see also, for self-told account, Westermarck's *Memories of My Life* (New York, 1929), trans. A. Barnewl.

[5] *Academy,* XL (October 3, 1891), 288 ff.

[6] *History of Human Marriage,* p. 5.

[7] See Westermarck, *Memories of My Life.*

[8] It is interesting to note the way in which museum arrangements reflect ethnological theory and vice versa. Westermarck's books are arranged like the museums set up by Pitt-Rivers. Both reflect evolutionist theory. The present method of arrangement is "regional," and the corresponding theory incorporates such notions as "cultural area" and the necessity for contextual work.

[9] There is a remarkable criticism of Westermarck written in 1900 by Karl Pearson (*Grammar of Science*). After criticizing the "obscurity attaching to the use of the words force and cause" (p. 132), he adds that "to find sequences of facts. . . . we must follow the changes of one tribe or people at a time. We cannot trace the successive stages of social life except by minute investigation of facts relating to one social unit" (p. 359).

[10] *The History of Ethnological Theory* (New York, 1937), p. 98-99.

[11] Before leaving Westermarck as ethnologist, however, it must be recorded that the common idea of him as merely an armchair librarian is mistaken. Those who hold such a view are sentenced to thirty days with the very flat idiographic descriptions in *Ritual and Belief in Morocco* and the ethnographic pages of "The Belief in Spirits in Morocco." These works show that Westermarck knew what a campstool felt like; they do not harbour any conclusions, and they have not entered into the stream of American social science. Although the bulk of *Wit and Wisdom in Morocco* consists of a mere compilation of proverbs (with full Arabic texts), there is a 63-page Introductory Essay (embodying the Frazer lecture of 1928), which contains a neat set of characterizing criteria for *proverbs,* an empiric taxonomic scheme, and notes on their societal function. It should also be mentioned that two of Westermarck's more specific theories still run through writers on these topics (see the *Encyclopaedia of the Social Sciences,* articles by Reo Fortune on "Incest" [VII, 621] and by Ruth Bunzel on "Ornament" [XI, 496]).

[12] *The History of Human Marriage,* p. 1.

[13] *Source Book for Social Origins* (Boston, 1909), p. 911 and 869.

[14] *Social Organization* (New York, 1909), p. 24.

[15] *Ibid.,* p. 40.

[16] *The Future of Marriage in Western Civilization,* pp. 5, 264.

[17] Hence, given the biologistic premises, the relevance of the mating habits of the cognate species of anthropoid.

[18] *The History of Human Marriage,* p. 5.

[19] *Nature,* XLIV, 270 (cited by Park and Burgess, *An Introduction to the Science of Sociology,* pp. 16-17).

[20] Tylor, *op. cit.,* pp. 288 f.

[21] See the critical reviews in *Revue philosophique,* 1907, pp. 409 ff.; *L'Année sociologique,* X, 283 ff., XI, 274 ff.; W. H. R. Rivers, "Survival in Sociology," *Sociological Review;* VI, 304 ff., and "Sociology and Psychology," *ibid.,* IX, 3 ff.

[22] Along with Hobhouse, *Morals in Evolution* (London, 1906); Sumner, *Folkways* (Boston, 1906); and Spencer, *The Data of Ethics* (New York, 1879).

[23] *The Origin and Development of Moral Ideas* (2 vols.; London, 1906).

[24] But see below.

[25] *Op. cit.,* II, 745.

[26] But, as we shall see, in his interpretation of moral phenomena and in his ethics it is clear that moral ideas are relative to "the emotions they express" and not to social factors, e.g., custom (see *Ethical Relativity,* p. 289).

[27] See, e.g., *Origin and Development of Moral Ideas,* I, 120-21; cf. also A. Smith's notion of the "impartial spectator" and "sympathetic resentment."

[28] *Ibid.,* I, 121.

[29] *Ethical Relativity,* p. 89.

[30] *Ibid.,* see p. 71 for laudatory references to *The Theory of Moral Sentiments.*

[31] *Ethical Relativity,* pp. 58-59.

[32] *Ibid.,* p. 59.

[33] *Moral Ideas,* I, 11: "The emotional constitution of man [which underlies moral phenomena] does not present the uniformity uniformity as the human intellect." The very engaging manner in which Westermarck uses his very pliable psychology to account for what he considers to be another fact should be noted: "The general uniformity of human nature accounts for the great similarities which characterize the moral ideas of mankind. . . . . But at the same time these ideas also represent racial differences" (*ibid.,* II, 742). Although "different external conditions" and "different measures of knowledge" [*Ethical Relativity,* p. 187] may also be reasons for these variations, "the most common differences of moral estimates have undoubtedly a psychical origin [ultimately 'emotional']" (*Moral Ideas,* II, 742).

[34] *Moral Ideas,* I, 10.

[35] See H. E. Barnes and Howard Becker, *Social Thought from Lore to Science* (Boston, 1938), and *Contemporary Social Theory* (New York, 1940).

[36] I am here concerned *only* with immanent reasons, not those, if any, to be found by a sociological analysis of his work in its various societal contexts. See V. F. Calverton's ideological imputations, "The Compulsive Basis of Social Thought," *American Journal of Sociology,* March, 1931; also Westermarck's reply (*ibid.,* March, 1936).

G. E. Moore (essay date 1965)

SOURCE: "The Nature of Moral Philosophy," in *Philosophical Studies,* Routledge & Kegan Paul Ltd., 1965, pp. 310-39.

[*In the following excerpt, Moore disagrees with Westermarck's notion that moral indignation can be consistent from one individual to the next.*]

I should like, if I can, to interest you to-night in one particular question about Moral Philosophy. It is a question which resembles most philosophical questions, in respect of the fact that philosophers are by no means agreed as to what is the right answer to it: some seem to be very strongly convinced that one answer is correct, while others are equally strongly convinced of the opposite. For my own part I do feel some doubt as to which answer is the right one, although, as you will see, I incline rather strongly to one of the two alternatives. I should like very much, if I could, to find some considerations which seemed to me absolutely convincing on the one side or the other; for the question seems to me in itself to be an exceedingly interesting one.

I have said that the question is a question *about* Moral Philosophy; and it seems to me in fact to be a very large and general question which affects the whole of Moral Philosophy. In asking it, we are doing no less than asking what it is that people are doing when they study Moral Philosophy at all: we are asking what sort of questions it is which it is the business of Moral Philosophy to discuss and try to find the right answer to. But I intend, for the sake of simplicity, to confine myself to asking it in two particular instances. Moral Philosophy has, in fact, to discuss a good many different ideas; and though I think this same question may be raised with regard to them all, I intend to pick out two, which seem to me particularly fundamental, and to ask it with regard to them only.

My first business must be to explain what these two ideas are.

The name Moral Philosophy naturally suggests that what is meant is a department of philosophy which has something to do with morality. And we all understand roughly what is meant by morality. We are accustomed to the distinction between moral good and evil, on the one hand, and what is sometimes called physical good and evil on the other. We all make the distinction between a man's moral character, on the one hand, and his agreeableness or intellectual endowments, on the other. We feel that to accuse a man of immoral conduct is quite a different thing from accusing him merely of bad taste or bad manners, or from accusing him merely of stupidity or ignorance. And no less clearly we distinguish between the idea of being under a moral obligation to do a thing, and the idea of being merely under a legal obligation to do it. It is a common-place that the sphere of morality is much wider than the sphere of law: that we are morally bound to do and avoid many things, which are not enjoined or forbidden by the laws of our country; and it is also sometimes held that, if a particular law is unjust or immoral, it may even be a moral duty to disobey it—that is to say that there may be a positive conflict between moral and legal obligation; and the mere fact that this is held, whether truly or falsely, shows, at all events, that the one idea is quite distinct from the other.

The name Moral Philosophy, then, naturally suggests that it is a department of philosophy concerned with morality in this common sense. And it is, in fact, true that one large department of Moral Philosophy is so concerned. But it would be a mistake to think that the whole subject is *only* concerned with morality. Another important department of it is, as I shall try to show, concerned with ideas which are *not* moral ideas, in this ordinary sense, though, no doubt, they may have something to do with them. And of the two ideas which I propose to pick out for discussion, while one of them is a moral idea, the other belongs to that department of Moral Philosophy, which is not concerned solely with morality, and is not, I think, properly speaking, a moral idea at all.

Let us begin with the one of the two, which is a moral idea.

The particular moral idea which I propose to pick out for discussion is the one which I have called above the idea of moral obligation—the idea of being morally bound to act in a particular way on a particular occasion. But what is, so far as I can see, precisely the same idea is also called by several other names. To say that I am under a moral obligation to do a certain thing is, I think, clearly to say the same thing as what we commonly express by saying that I ought to do it, or that it is my duty to do it. That is to say, the idea of moral obligation is identical with the idea of the moral "ought" and with the idea of duty. And it also seems at first sight as if we might make yet another identification.

The assertion that I ought to do a certain thing seems as if it meant much the same as the assertion that it would be wrong of me *not* to do the thing in question: at all events it is quite clear that, whenever it is my duty to do anything, it would be wrong of me not to do it, and that whenever it would be wrong of me to do anything, then it is my duty to refrain from doing it. In the case of these two ideas, the idea of what is wrong, and the idea of what is my duty or what I ought to do, different views may be taken as to whether the one is more fundamental than the other, or whether both are equally so; and on the question: *If* one of the two is more fundamental than the other, which of the two is so? Thus some people would say, that the idea of "wrong" is the more fundamental, and that the idea of "duty" is to be defined in terms of it: that, in fact, the statement "It is my duty to keep that promise" merely means "It would be wrong of me not to keep it"; and the statement "It is my duty not to tell a lie" merely means "It would be wrong of me to tell one." Others again would apparently say just the opposite: that duty is the more fundamental notion, and "wrong" is to be defined in terms of it. While others perhaps would hold that neither is more fundamental than the other; that both are equally fundamental, and that the statement "it would be wrong to do so and so" is only equivalent to, not identical in meaning with, "I ought not to do it." But whichever of these three views be the true one, there is, I think, no doubt whatever about the equivalence notion of the two ideas; and no doubt, therefore, that whatever answer be given to the question I am going to raise about the one, the same answer must be given to the corresponding question about the other.

The moral idea, then, which I propose to discuss, is the idea of duty or moral obligation, or, what comes to the same thing, the idea of what is wrong—morally wrong. Everybody would agree that this idea—or, to speak more accurately, one or both of these two ideas—is among the most fundamental of our moral ideas, whether or not they would admit that all others, for example the ideas of moral goodness, involve a reference to this one in their definition, or would hold that we have some others which are independent of it, and equally fundamental with it.

But there is a good deal of difficulty in getting clear as to what this idea of moral obligation itself is. Is there in fact only one idea which we call by this name? Or is it possible that on some occasions when we say that so and so is a duty, we mean something different by this expression from what we do on others? And that similarly when we say that so and so is morally wrong, we sometimes use this name "morally wrong" for one idea and sometimes for another; so that one and the same thing may be "morally wrong" in one sense of the word, and yet *not* morally wrong in another? I think, in fact, there are two different senses in which we use these terms; and to point out the difference between them, will help to bring out clearly more the nature of each. And I think perhaps the difference can be brought out most clearly by considering the sort of moral rules with which we are all of us familiar.

Everybody knows that moral teachers are largely concerned in laying down moral rules, and in disputing the truth of rules which have been previously accepted. And moral rules seem to consist, to a very large extent, in assertions to the effect that it is always wrong to do certain actions or to refrain from doing certain others; or (what comes to the same thing) that it is always your duty to refrain from certain actions, and positively to do certain others. The Ten Commandments for example, are instances of moral rules; and most of them are examples of what are called negative rules—that is to say rules which assert merely that it is wrong to do certain positive actions, and therefore our duty to refrain from these actions; instead of rules which assert of certain positive actions, that it is our duty to do them and therefore wrong to refrain from doing them. The fifth commandment, which tells us to honour our father and mother, is apparently an exception; it seems to be a positive rule. It is not, like the others, expressed in the negative form "Thou shalt *not* do so and so," and it is apparently really meant to assert that we ought to do certain positive actions, not merely that there are some positive action from which we ought to refrain. The difference between this one and the rest will thus serve as an example of the difference between positive and negative moral rules, a difference which is sometimes treated as if it were of great importance. And I do not

wish to deny that there may be some important difference between seeing only that certain positive actions are wrong, and seeing also that, in certain cases, to refrain from doing certain actions is just as wrong as positively to do certain others. But this distinction between positive and negative rules is certainly of much less importance than another which is, I think, liable to be confused with it. So far as this distinction goes it is only a distinction between an assertion that it is wrong to do a positive action and an assertion that it is wrong to refrain from doing one: and each of these assertions is equivalent to one which asserts a duty—the first with an assertion that it is a duty to refrain, the second with an assertion that a positive action is a duty. But there is another distinction between some moral rules and others, which is of much greater importance than this one, and which does, I think, give a reason for thinking that the term "moral obligation" is actually used in different senses on different occasions.

I have said that moral rules seem to consist, *to a large extent,* in assertions to the effect that it is always wrong to do certain *actions* or to refrain from doing certain others, or the equivalent assertions in terms of duty. But there is a large class of moral rules, with which we are all of us very familiar, which do not come under this definition. They are rules which are concerned not with our *actions,* in the natural sense of the word, but with our feelings, thoughts and desires. An illustration of this kind of rule can again be given from the Ten Commandments. Most of the ten, as we all know, are concerned merely with actions; but the tenth at least is clearly an exception. The tenth says "Thou shalt not covet thy neighbour's house, nor his wife, nor his servant, nor his ox, nor his ass, nor anything that is his," and, unless "covet" is merely a mistranslation of a word which stands for some kind of action, we plainly have here a rule which is concerned with our *feelings* and not with our actions. And one reason which makes the distinction between rules of this kind and rules concerned with actions important, is that our feelings are not, as a rule, directly within the control of our will in the sense in which many of our actions are. I cannot, for instance, by any single act of will directly prevent from arising in my mind a desire for something that belongs to some one else, even if, when once the desire has arrived, I can by my will prevent its continuance; and even this last I can hardly do *directly* but only by forcing myself to attend to other considerations which may extinguish the desire. But though I thus cannot prevent myself altogether from coveting my neighbour's possessions, I can altogether prevent myself from stealing them. The action of stealing, and the feeling of covetousness, are clearly on a very different level in this respect. The action is *directly* within the control of my will, whereas the feeling is not. *If* I will not to take the thing (though of course some people may find a great difficulty in willing this) it does in general follow directly that I do not take it; whereas, if I will not to desire it, it emphatically does not, even in general, follow directly that no desire for it will be there. This distinction between the way in which our feelings and our actions are under the control of our wills is, I think, a very real one indeed; we cannot help constantly recognising that it exists. And it has an important bearing on the distinction between those moral rules which deal with actions and those which deal with feelings, for the following reason. The philosopher Kant laid down a well-known proposition to the effect that "ought" implies "can": that is to say, that it cannot be true that you "ought" to do a thing, unless it is true that you *could* do it, *if* you chose. And as regards one of the senses in which we commonly use the words "ought" and "duty," I think this rule is plainly true. When we say absolutely of ourselves or others, "I ought to do so and so" or "you ought to," we imply, I think, very often that the thing in question is a thing which we *could* do, *if* we chose; though of course it may often be a thing which it is very difficult to choose to do. Thus it is clear that I cannot truly say of anyone that he ought to do a certain thing, if it is a thing which it is physically impossible for him to do, however desirable it may be that the thing should be done. And in this sense it is clear that it cannot be truly said of me that I ought not to have a certain feeling, or that I ought not to have had it, if it is a feeling which I could not, by any effort of my will, prevent myself from having. The having or the prevention of a certain feeling is not, of course, strictly ever a *physical* impossibility, but it is very often impossible, in exactly the same sense, in which actions are physically impossible—that is to say that I could not possibly get it or prevent it, even if I would. But this being so, it is plain that such a moral rule as that I ought not to covet my neighbour's possessions is, if it means to assert that I ought not, in that sense in which "ought" implies "can," a rule which cannot possibly be true. What it appears to assert is, absolutely universally, of *every* feeling of covetousness, that the feeling in question is one which the person who felt it *ought* not to have felt. But in fact a very large proportion of such feelings (I am inclined to say the vast majority) are feelings which the person who felt them could not have prevented feeling, if he would: they were beyond the control of his will. And hence it is quite emphatically *not* true that none of these feelings *ought* to have been felt, if we are using "ought" in the sense which implies that the person who felt them *could* have avoided them. So far from its being true that absolutely *none* of them ought to have been felt, this is only true of those among them, probably a small minority, which the person who felt them *could* have avoided feeling. If, therefore, moral rules with regard to feelings are to have a chance of being *nearly* true, we must understand the "ought" which occurs in them in some other sense. But with moral rules that refer to actions the case is very different. Take stealing for example. Here again what the Eighth Commandment appears to imply is that absolutely every theft which has ever occurred was an act which the agent ought not to have done; and, if the "ought" is the one which implies "can," it implies, therefore, that every theft was an act which the agent, if he had chosen, could have avoided. And this statement that every theft which has

been committed was an act which the thief, *if* he had so willed, could have avoided, though it may be doubted if it is absolutely universally true, is not a statement which is clearly absurd, like the statement that every covetous desire could have been avoided by the will of the person who felt it. It is probable that the vast majority of acts of theft have been acts which it was in the power of the thief to avoid, if he had willed to do so; whereas this is clearly not true of the vast majority of covetous desires. It is, therefore, quite possible that those who believe we ought never to steal are using "ought" in a sense which implies that stealing always *could* have been avoided; whereas it is I think quite certain that many of those who believe that we ought to avoid all covetous desires, do not believe for a moment that every covetous desire that has ever been felt was a desire which the person who felt it could have avoided feeling, if he had chosen. And yet they certainly do believe, in some sense or other, that no covetous desire *ought* ever to have been felt. The conclusion is, therefore, it seems to me, unavoidable that we do use "ought," the moral "ought," in two different senses; the one a sense in which to say that I ought to have done so and so does really imply that I could have done it, if I had chosen, and the other a sense in which it carries with it no such implication. I think perhaps the difference between the two can be expressed in this way. If we express the meaning of the first "ought," the one which does imply "can," by saying that "I ought to have done so and so" means "It actually *was* my duty to do it"; we can express the meaning of the second by saying that *e.g.* "I ought not to have felt so and so" means *not* "it *was* my duty to avoid that feeling," but "it *would* have been my duty to avoid it, *if* I had been able." And corresponding to these two meanings of "ought" we should, I think, probably distinguish two different sorts of moral rules, which though expressed in the same language, do in fact mean very different things. The one is a set of rules which assert (whether truly or falsely) that it always actually *is* a duty to do or to refrain from certain actions, and assert therefore that it always is in the power of the agent's will to do or to refrain from them; whereas the other sort only assert that so and so *would* be a duty, if it *were* within our power, without at all asserting that it always is within our power.

We may, perhaps, give a name to the distinction I mean, by calling the first kind of rules—those which do assert that something actually is a duty—"rules of duty," and by calling the second kind—those which recommend or condemn something not in the control of our wills—"ideal rules": choosing this latter name because they can be said to inculcate a moral "ideal"—something the attainment of which is not directly within the power of our wills. As a further example of the difference between ideal rules and rules of duty we may take the famous passage from the New Testament (Luke 6, 27) "Love your enemies, do good to them that hate you, bless them that curse you, pray for them that despitefully use you." Of these four rules, the three last may be rules of duty, because they refer to things which are plainly, as a rule, at least, in the power of your will; but the first, if "love" be understood in its natural sense as referring to your feelings, is plainly only an "ideal" rule, since such feelings are obviously not directly under our own control, in the same way in which such actions as doing good to, blessing or praying for a person are so. To love certain people, or to feel no anger against them, is a thing which it is quite impossible to attain directly by will, or perhaps ever to attain completely at all. Whereas your behaviour towards them is a matter within your own control: even if you hate a person, or feel angry with him, you can so control yourself as not to do him harm, and even to confer benefits upon him. To do good to your enemies may, then, really be your duty; but it cannot, in the strict sense, be your duty not to have evil feelings towards them: all that can possibly be true is that it would be your duty if you were able. Yet I think there can be no doubt that what Christ meant to condemn was the occurrence of such feelings altogether; and since, if what he meant to assert about them in condemning them, would have been certainly false, if he had meant to say that you *could* avoid ever feeling them, I think it is clear that what he meant to assert was *not* this, or not this only, but something else, which may quite possibly be true. That is to say, he was asserting an ideal rule, not merely a rule of duty.

It will be seen that this distinction which I am making coincides, roughly at all events, with the distinction which is often expressed as the distinction between rules which tell you what you ought to *be* and rules which tell you merely what you ought to *do;* or as the distinction between rules which are concerned with your inner life—with your thoughts and feelings—and those which are concerned only with your external actions. The rules which are concerned with what you ought to *be* or with your inner life are, for the most part at all events, "ideal" rules; while those which are concerned with what you ought to do or your external actions are very often, at least, rules of duty. And it is often said that one great difference between the New Testament and the Old is its comparatively greater insistence on "ideal" rules—upon a change of heart—as opposed to mere rules of duty. And that there is a comparatively greater insistence on ideal rules I do not wish to deny. But that there are plenty of ideal rules in the Old Testament too must not be forgotten. I have already given an example from the Ten Commandments: namely the rule which says you ought not to covet anything which belongs to your neighbour. And another is supplied by the Old Testament commandment, "Love thy neighbour as thyself," if by "love" is here meant a feeling which is not within our own control, and not merely that the Jew is to *help* other Jews by his external actions. Indeed, however great may be the difference between the Old Testament and the New in respect of comparative insistence on ideal rules rather than rules of duty, I am inclined to think that there is at least as great a difference, illustrated by this very rule, in another, quite different, respect—namely in the kind of rules, *both ideal and of duty,* which are insisted on. For whereas by "thy

neighbour" in the Old Testament there is plainly meant only other Jews, and it is not conceived either that it is the duty of a Jew to help foreigners in general, or an ideal for him to love them; in the New Testament, where the same words are used, "my neighbour" plainly is meant to include all mankind. And this distinction between the view that beneficent action and benevolent feelings should be confined to those of our own nation, and the view that both should be extended equally to all mankind,—a distinction which has nothing to do with the distinction between being and doing, between inner and outer, but affects both equally—is, I am inclined to think, at least as important a difference between New Testament and Old, as the comparatively greater insistence on "ideal" rules. However, the point upon which I want at present to insist is the distinction between ideal rules and rules of duty. Both kinds are commonly included among moral rules, and, as my examples have shown, are often mentioned together as if no great difference were seen between them. What I want to insist on is that there is a great difference between them: that whereas rules of duty do directly assert of the idea of duty, in the sense in which to say that something is your duty implies that you *can* do it, that certain things are duties, the "ideal" rules do *not* assert this, but something different. Yet the "ideal" rules certainly do, in a sense, assert a "moral obligation." And hence we have to recognise that the phrase "moral obligation" is not merely a name for one idea only, but for two very different ideas; and the same will, of course, be true of the corresponding phrase "morally wrong."

When, therefore, I say that the idea of "moral obligation" is one of the fundamental ideas with which Moral Philosophy is concerned, I think we must admit that this one name really stands for two different ideas. But it does not matter for my purpose which of the two you take. Each of them is undoubtedly a moral idea, and whatever answer be given to the question we are going to raise about the one, will also certainly apply to the other.

But it is now time to turn to the other idea, with which I said that Moral Philosophy has been largely concerned, though it is not, strictly speaking, a moral idea, at all.

And I think, perhaps, a good way of bringing out what this idea is, is to refer to the Ethics of Aristotle. Everybody would admit that the fundamental idea, with which Aristotle's Ethics is concerned, is an idea which it is the business of Moral Philosophy to discuss; and yet I think it is quite plain that this idea is not a moral idea at all. Aristotle does not set out from the idea of moral obligation or duty (indeed throughout his treatise he only mentions this idea quite incidentally); nor even from the idea of moral goodness or moral excellence, though he has a good deal more to say about that; but from the idea of what he calls "the human good," or "good for man." He starts by raising the question what the good for man *is,* and his whole book is arranged in the form of giving a detailed answer to that question. And I think we can gather pretty well what the idea is, which he calls by this name, by considering what he says about it. There are two points, in particular, which he insists upon from the outset: first, that nothing can be good, in the sense he means, unless it is something which is worth having for its own sake, and not merely for the sake of something else; it must be good *in itself;* it must not, like wealth (to use one example which he gives) be worth having merely for the sake of what you can do with it; it must be a thing which is worth having even if nothing further comes of it. And secondly (what partly covers the former, but also, I think, says something more) it must, he says, be something that is "self-sufficient": something which, even if you had nothing else would make your life worth having. And further light is thrown upon his meaning when he comes to tell you what he thinks the good for man is: the good, he says, is "mental, activity—where such activity is of an excellent kind, or, if there are several different kinds of excellent mental activity, that which has the best and most perfect kind of excellence; and also" (he significantly adds) "mental activity which lasts through a sufficiently long life." The word which I have here translated "excellence" is what is commonly translated "virtue"; but it does not mean quite the same as we mean by "virtue," and that in a very important respect. "Virtue" has come to mean exclusively *moral* excellence; and if that were all Aristotle meant, you might think that what he means by "good" came very near being a moral idea. But it turns out that he includes among "excellences," intellectual excellence, and even that he thinks that the best and most perfect excellence of which he speaks is a particular kind of intellectual excellence, which no one would think of calling a moral quality, namely, the sort of excellence which makes a man a good philosopher. And as for the word which I have translated "activity," the meaning of this can be best brought out by mentioning the reason which Aristotle himself gives for saying that mere excellence itself is not (as some of the Greeks had said) the good for man. He says, truly enough, that a man may possess the greatest excellence—he may be a very excellent man—even when he is asleep, or is doing nothing; and he points out that the possession of excellence when you are asleep is not a thing that is desirable *for its own sake*—obviously only for the sake of the effects it may produce when you wake up. It is not therefore, he thinks, mere mental excellence, but the *active exercise* of mental excellence—the state of a man's mind, when he not only possesses excellent faculties, moral or intellectual, but is actively engaged in using them, which really constitutes the human good.

Now, when Aristotle talks of "the good for man," there is, I think, as my quotation is sufficient to show, a certain confusion in his mind between what is *good* for man and what is *best* for man. What he really holds is that *any* mental activity which exhibits excellence and is pleasurable is *a* good; and when he adds that, if there are many excellences, *the* good must be mental activity which exhibits the *best* of them, and that it must last through a sufficiently long life, he only means that this is necessary if a man is to get the *best* he can get, not

that this is the *only* good he can get. And the idea which I wish to insist on is not, therefore, the idea of "*the* human good," but the more fundamental idea of "good"; the idea, with regard to which he holds that the working of our minds in some excellent fashion is the only good thing that any of us can possess; and the idea of which "better" is the comparative, when he says that mental activity which exhibits some sorts of excellence is *better* than mental activity which exhibits others, though both are good, and that excellent mental activity continued over a longer time is *better* than the same continued for a shorter. This idea of what is "good," in the sense in which Aristotle uses it in these cases, is an idea which we all of us constantly use, and which is certainly an idea which it is the business of Moral Philosophy to discuss, though it is not a moral idea. The main difficulty with regard to it is to distinguish it clearly from other senses in which we use the same word. For, when we say that a thing is "good," or one thing "better" than another, we by no means always mean that it is better in this sense. Often, when we call a thing good we are not attributing to it any characteristic which it would possess *if it existed quite alone,* and if nothing further were to come of it; but are merely saying of it that it is a sort of thing from which other good things do in fact come, or which is such that, when accompanied by other things, the whole thus formed is "good" in Aristotle's sense, although, by itself, it is not. Thus a man may be "good," and his character may be "good," and yet neither are "good" in this fundamental sense, in which goodness is a characteristic which a thing would possess, if it existed quite alone. For, as Aristotle says, a good man may exist, and may have a good character, even when he is fast asleep; and yet if there were nothing in the Universe but good men, with good characters, all fast asleep, there would be nothing in it which was "good" in the fundamental sense with which we are concerned. Thus "moral goodness," in the sense of good character, as distinguished from the actual working of a good character in various forms of mental activity, is certainly not "good" in the sense in which good means "good for its own sake." And even with regard to the actual exercise of certain forms of moral excellence, it seems to me that in estimating the value of such exercise relatively to other things, we are apt to take into account, not merely its intrinsic value—the sort of value which it would possess, if it existed quite alone—but also its effects: we rate it higher than we should do if we were considering only its intrinsic value, because we take into account the other good things which we know are apt to flow from it. Certain things which have intrinsic value are distinguished from others, by the fact that more good consequences are apt to flow from them; and where this is the case, we are apt, I think, quite unjustly, to think that their intrinsic value must be higher too. One thing, I think, is clear about intrinsic value—goodness in Aristotle's sense—namely that it is only actual occurrences, actual states of things over a certain period of time—not such things as men, or characters, or material things, that can have any intrinsic value at all. But even this is not sufficient to distinguish intrinsic value clearly from other sorts of goodness: since even in the case of actual occurrences, we often call them good or bad for the sake of their effects or their promise of effects. Thus we all hope that the state of things in England, as a whole, will really be better some day than it has been in the past—that there will be progress and improvement: we hope, for instance, that, if we consider the whole of the lives lived in England during some year in the next century, it may turn out that the state of things, as a whole, during that year will be really better than it ever has been in any past year. And when we use "better" in this way—in the sense in which progress or improvement means a change to a *better* state of things—we are certainly thinking partly of a state of things which has a greater intrinsic value. And we certainly do not mean by improvement merely *moral* improvement. An improvement in moral conditions, other things being equal, may no doubt be a gain in intrinsic value; but we should certainly hold that, moral conditions being equal, there is yet room for improvement in other ways—in the diminution of misery and purely physical evils, for example. But in considering the degree of a real change for the better in intrinsic value, there is certainly danger of confusion between the degree in which the actual lives lived are really intrinsically better, and the degree in which there is improvement merely in the *means* for living a good life. If we want to estimate rightly what would constitute an intrinsic improvement in the state of things in our imagined year next century, and whether it would on the whole be really "good" at all, we have to consider what value it would have if it were to be the last year of life upon this planet; if the world were going to come to an end, as soon as it was over; and therefore to discount entirely all the promises it might contain of future goods. This criterion for distinguishing whether the kind of goodness which we are attributing to anything is really intrinsic value or not, the criterion which consists in considering whether it is a characteristic which the thing would possess, if it were to have absolutely no further consequences or accompaniments, seems to me to be one which it is very necessary to apply if we wish to distinguish clearly between different meanings of the word "good." And it is only the idea of what is good, where by "good" is meant a characteristic which has this mark, that I want now to consider.

The two ideas, then, with regard to which I want to raise a question, are first the moral idea of "moral obligation" or "duty," and secondly the non-moral idea of "good" in this special sense.

And the question with regard to them, which I want to raise, is this. With regard to both ideas many philosophers have thought and still think—not only *think,* but seem to be absolutely convinced, that when we apply them to anything—when we assert of any action that it ought not to have been done, or of any state of things that it was or would be good or better than another, then it *must* be the case that *all* that we are asserting of the thing or things in question is simply and solely that

some person or set of persons actually does have, or has a tendency to have a certain sort of feeling towards the thing or things in question: that there is absolutely no more in it than this. While others seem to be convinced, no less strongly, that there *is* more in it than this: that when we judge that an action is a duty or is really wrong, we are *not* merely making a judgment to the effect that some person or set of persons, have, or tend to have a certain sort of feeling, when they witness or think of such actions, and that similarly when we judge that a certain state of things was or would be better than another, we are *not* merely making a judgment about the feelings which some person or set of persons would have, in witnessing or thinking of the two states of things, or in comparing them together. The question at issue between these two views is often expressed in other less clear forms. It is often expressed as the question whether the ideas of duty and of good or value, are or are not, "objective" ideas: as the problem as to the "objectivity" of duty and intrinsic value. The first set of philosophers would maintain that the notion of the "objectivity" of duty and of value is a mere chimera; while the second would maintain that these ideas really are "objective." And others express it as the question whether the ideas of duty and of good are "absolute" or purely "relative:", whether there is any such thing as an absolute duty or an absolute good, or whether good and duty are purely relative to human feelings and desires. But both these ways of expressing it are, I think, apt to lead to confusion. And another even less clear way in which it is put is by asking the question: Is the assertion that such and such a thing is a duty, or has intrinsic value, ever *a dictate of reason?* But so far as I can gather, the question really at issue, and expressed in these obscure ways, is the one which I have tried to state. It is the question whether when we judge (whether truly or falsely) that an action is a duty or a state of things good, *all* that we are thinking about the action or the state of things in question, is simply and solely that we ourselves or others have or tend to have a certain feeling towards it when we contemplate or think of it. And the question seems to me to be of great interest, because, if this is all, then it is evident that all the ideas with which Moral Philosophy is concerned are merely psychological ideas; and all moral rules, and statements as to what is intrinsically valuable, merely true or false psychological statements; so that the whole of Moral Philosophy and Ethics will be merely departments of Psychology. Whereas, if the contrary is the case, then these two ideas of moral obligation and intrinsic value, will be no more purely psychological ideas than are the ideas of shape or size or number; and Moral Philosophy will be concerned with characteristics of actions and feelings and states of affairs, which these actions and feelings and states of affairs would or might have possessed, even if human psychology had been quite different from what it is.

Which, then, of these two views is the true one? Are these two ideas merely psychological ideas in the sense which I have tried to explain, or are they not?

As I have said, I feel some doubts myself whether they are or not: it does not seem to me to be a matter to dogmatize upon. But I am strongly inclined to think that they are not merely psychological; that Moral Philosophy and Ethics are not mere departments of Psychology. In favour of the view that the two ideas in question are merely psychological, there is, so far as I am aware, nothing whatever to be said, except that so many philosophers have been absolutely convinced that they are. None of them seem to me to have succeeded in bringing forward a single argument in favour of their view. And against the view that they are, there seem to me to be some quite definite arguments, though I am not satisfied that any of these arguments are absolutely conclusive. I will try to state briefly and clearly what seem to me the main arguments against the view that these are merely psychological ideas; although, in doing so, I am faced with a certain difficulty. For though, as I have said, many philosophers are absolutely convinced, that "duty" and "good" do merely stand for psychological ideas, they are by no means agreed *what* the psychological ideas are for which they stand. Different philosophers have hit on very different ideas as being the ideas for which they stand; and this very fact that, if they *are* psychological ideas at all, it is so difficult to agree as to *what* ideas they are, seems to me in itself to be an argument against the view that they are so.

Let me take each of the two ideas separately, and try to exhibit the sort of objection there seems to be to the view that it is merely a psychological idea:

Take first the idea of moral obligation. What purely psychological assertion can I be making about an action, when I assert that it was "wrong," that it ought not to have been done?

In this case, one view, which is in some ways the most plausible that can be taken, is that in every case I am merely making an assertion about my own psychology. But what assertion about my own psychology can I be making? Let us take as an example, the view of Prof. Westermarck, which is as plausible a view of this type as any that I know of. He holds that what I am judging when I judge an action to be wrong, is merely that it is of a sort which *tends* to excite in me a peculiar kind of feeling—the feeling of moral indignation or disapproval. He does not say that what I am judging is that the action in question *is actually* exciting this feeling in me. For it is obviously not true that, when I judge an action to be much more wrong than another, I am always actually feeling much indignation at the thought of either, or much more indignation at the thought of the one than at that of the other; and it is inconceivable that I should constantly be making so great a mistake as to my own psychology, as to think that I am actually feeling great indignation when I am not. But he thinks it is plausible to say that I am making a judgment as to the *tendency* of such actions to excite indignation in me; that, for instance, when I judge that one is much more wrong than the other, I am merely asserting the fact,

taught me by my past experience, that, if I were to witness the two actions, under similar circumstances, I should feel a much more intense indignation at the one than at the other.[1]

But there is one very serious objection to such a view, which I think that those who take it are apt not fully to realise. If this view be true, then when I judge an action to be wrong, I am merely making a judgment about my own feelings towards it; and when you judge it to be wrong, you are merely making a judgment about yours. And hence the word "wrong" in my mouth, means something entirely different from what it does in yours; just as the word "I" in my mouth stands for an entirely different person from what it does in yours—in mine it stands for me, in yours it stands for you. That is to say when I judge of a given action that it was wrong, and you perhaps of the very same action that it was not, we are not in fact differing in opinion about it at all; any more than we are differing in opinion if I make the judgment "I came from Cambridge to-day" and you make the judgment "*I* did not come from Cambridge to-day." When *I* say "That was wrong" I am merely saying "That sort of action excites indignation in me, when I see it "; and when you say "No; it was not wrong" you are merely saying "It does not excite indignation in *me,* when I see it." And obviously both judgments may perfectly well be true together; just as my judgment that I did come from Cambridge to-day and yours that you did not, may perfectly well be true together. In other words, and this is what I want to insist on, if this view be true, then there is absolutely no such thing as a difference of opinion upon moral questions. If two persons think they differ in opinion on a moral question (and it certainly seems as if they sometimes *think* so), they are always, on this view, making a mistake, and a mistake so gross that it seems hardly possible that they should make it: a mistake as gross as that which would be involved in thinking that when you say "I did not come from Cambridge to-day" you are denying what I say when I say "I did." And this seems to me to be a very serious objection to the view. Don't people, in fact, sometimes really differ in opinion on a moral question? Certainly all appearances are in favour of the view that they do: and yet, if they do, that can only be if when I think a thing to be wrong, and you think it not to be wrong, I mean by "wrong" the very *same* characteristic which you mean, and am thinking that the action possesses this characteristic while you are thinking it does not. It must be the very *same* characteristic which we both mean; it cannot be, as this view says it is, merely that I am thinking that it has to my feelings the very same relation, which you are thinking that it has not got to yours; since, if this were all, then there would be no difference of opinion between us.

And this view that when we talk of wrong or duty, we are not merely, each of us, making a statement about the relation of the thing in question to our own feelings, may be reinforced by another consideration. It is commonly believed that some moral rules exhibit a *higher* morality than others: that, for instance a person who believes that it is our duty to do good to our enemies, has a higher moral belief, than one who believes that he has no such duty, but only a duty to do good to his friends or fellow-countrymen. And Westermarck himself believes that, some moral beliefs, "mark a stage of higher refinement in the evolution of the moral consciousness."[2] But what, on his view can be meant by saying that one moral belief is higher than another? If A believes that it is his duty to do good to his enemies and B believes that it is not, in what sense can A's belief be higher than B's? Not, on this view, in the sense that what A believes is true, and what B believes is not; for what A is believing is merely that the idea of not doing good to your enemies tends to excite in him a feeling of moral indignation, and what B believes is merely that it does not tend to excite this feeling in *him:* and both beliefs may perfectly well be true; it may really be true that the same actions do excite the feeling in A, and that they don't in B. What then, could Westermarck mean by saying that A's morality is higher than B's? So far as I can see, what, on his own views, he would have to mean is merely that he himself, Westermarck, shares A's morality and does not share B's: that it is true of him, as of A, that neglecting to do good to enemies excites his feelings of moral indignation and not true of him as it is of B, that it does *not* excite such feelings in him. In short he would have to say that what he means by calling A's morality the higher is merely "A's morality is *my* morality, and B's is not." But it seems to me quite clear that when we say one morality is higher than another, we do not merely mean that it is our own. We are not merely asserting that it has a certain relation to our own feelings, but are asserting, if I may say so, that the person who has it has a better moral taste than the person who has not. And whether or not this means merely, as I think, that what the one believes is true, and what the other believes is false, it is at all events inconsistent with the view that in all cases we are merely making a statement about our own feelings.

For these reasons it seems to me extremely difficult to believe that when we judge things to be wrong, each of us is merely making a judgment about *his own* psychology. But if not about our own, then about whose? I have already said that the view that, if the judgment is merely a psychological one at all, it is a judgment about our own psychology, is in some ways more plausible than any other view. And I think we can now see that any other view is *not* plausible. The alternatives are that I should be making a judgment about the psychology of all mankind, or about that of some particular section of it. And that the first alternative is not true, is, I think, evident from the fact that, when I judge an action to be wrong, I may emphatically *not* believe that it is true of all mankind that they would regard it with feelings of moral disapproval. I may know perfectly well that some would not. Most philosophers, therefore, have not ventured to say that this is the judgment I am making; they say, for instance, that I am making a judgment about the feelings of the particular society to which I belong—

about, for instance, the feelings of an impartial spectator in that society. But, if this view be taken, it is open to the same objections as the view that I am merely making a judgment about my own feelings. If we could say that every man, when he judges a thing to be wrong, was making a statement about the feelings of all mankind, then when A says "This is wrong" and B says "No, it isn't," they would really be differing in opinion, since A would be saying that all mankind feel in a certain way towards the action, and B would be saying that they don't. But if A is referring merely to his society and B to his, and their societies are different, then obviously they are not differing in opinion at all: it may perfectly well be true both that an impartial spectator in A's society does have a certain sort of feeling towards actions of the sort in question, and that an impartial spectator in B's does not. This view, therefore, implies that it is impossible for two men belonging to different societies ever to differ in opinion on a moral question. And this is a view which I find it almost as hard to accept as the view that *no* two men ever differ in opinion on one.

For these reasons I think there are serious objections to the view that the idea of moral obligation is merely a psychological idea.

But now let us briefly consider the idea of "good," in Aristotle's sense, or intrinsic value.

As regards this idea, there is again a difference of opinion among those who hold that it is a psychological idea, as to *what* idea it is. The majority seem to hold that it is to be defined, somehow, in terms of desire; while others have held that what we are judging when we judge that one state of things is or would be intrinsically better than another, is rather that the belief that the one was going to be realized would, under certain circumstances, give more pleasure to some man or set of men, than the belief that the other was. But the same objections seem to me to apply whichever of these two views be taken.

Let us take desire. About whose desires am I making a judgment, when I judge that one state of things would be better than another?

Here again, it may be said, first of all, that I am merely making a judgment about my own. But in this case the view that my judgment is merely about my own psychology is, I think, exposed to an obvious objection to which Westermarck's view that my judgments of moral obligation are about my own psychology was not exposed. The obvious objection is that it is evidently not true that I do in fact always desire more, what I judge to be better: I may judge one state of things to be better than another, even when I know perfectly well not only that I don't desire it more, but that I have no tendency to do so. It is a notorious fact that men's strongest desires are, as a rule, for things in which they themselves have some personal concern; and yet the fact that this is so, and that they know it to be so, does not prevent them from judging that changes, which would not affect them personally, would constitute a very much greater improvement in the world's condition, than changes which would. For this reason alone the view that when I judge one state of things to be better than another I am merely making a judgment about my own psychology, must, I think, be given up: it is incredible that we should all be making such mistakes about our feelings, as, on this view, we should constantly be doing. And there is, of course, besides, the same objection, as applied in the case of moral obligation: namely that, if this view were true, no two men could ever differ in opinion as to which of two states was the better, whereas it appears ·that they certainly sometimes do differ in opinion on such an issue.

My judgment, then, is not merely a judgment about my own psychology: but, if so, about whose psychology is it a judgment? It cannot be a judgment that all men desire the one state more than the other; because that would include the judgment that I myself do so, which, as we have seen, I often know to be false, even while I judge that the one state really is better. And it cannot, I think, be a judgment merely about the feelings or desires of an impartial spectator in my own society; since that would involve the paradox that men belonging to different societies could never differ in opinion as to what was better. But we have here to consider an alternative, which did not arise in the case of moral obligation. It is a notorious fact that the satisfaction of some of our desires is incompatible with the satisfaction of others, and the satisfaction of those of some men with the satisfaction of those of others. And this fact has suggested to some philosophers that what we mean by saying that one state of things would be better than another, is merely that it is a state in which more of the desires, of those who were in it, would be satisfied at once, than would be the case with the other. But to this view the fundamental objection seems to me to be that whether the one state was better than the other would depend not merely upon the number of desires that were simultaneously satisfied in it, but upon what the desires were desires for. I can imagine a state of things in which all desires were satisfied, and yet can judge of it that it would not be so good as another in which some were left unsatisfied. And for this reason I cannot assent to the view that my judgment, that one state of things is better than another is merely a judgment about the psychology of the people concerned in it.

This is why I find it hard to believe that either the idea of moral obligation or the idea of intrinsic value is merely a psychological idea. It seems to me that Moral Philosophy cannot be merely a department of Psychology. But no doubt there may be arguments on the other side to which I have not done justice.

NOTES

[1] E Westermarck, *The Origin and Development of Moral Ideas,* Vol. I, pp. 4, 13, 17-18, 100-101. On p. 105,

however, Westermarck suggests a view inconsistent with this one: namely that, when I judge an action to be wrong, I am not *merely* asserting that it has a tendency to excite moral indignation in me, but am also asserting that other people *would be* convinced that it has a tendency to excite moral indignation in them, if they "knew the act and all its attendant circumstances as well as [I do], and if, at the same time their emotions were as refined as [mine]."

[2] Ibid. p. 89.

Georg Henrik Von Wright (essay date 1965)

SOURCE: "The Origin and Development of Westermarck's Moral Philosophy," in *Acta Philosophica Fennica,* Vol. 34, 1982, pp. 25-60.

[*In the following excerpt, originally published in 1965, Wright relies on unpublished proceedings of the Philosophical Society of Finland to illustrate Westermarck's intellectual development.*]

I

The main purpose of this essay is to clarify a bit of intellectual history having to do with Edward Westermarçk's scholarly activities. Very little has been written about Westermarck's moral philosophy and the development of his thinking within the context of the history of ideas generally. We know that he labored for nearly twenty years on his great work *The Origin and Development of the Moral Ideas*[1] and it would be natural to suppose that his ideas went through many phases, with earlier thoughts being abandoned in favor of later ones. But not much is known about Westermarck's early development as a philosopher. On the contrary, doubt has even been expressed as to whether anything can be said on the subject.

Thus the late Professor K. Rob. V. Wikman, addressing the Finnish Society of Sciences in 1942 on the subject of Westermarck's theory of ethical relativity, said that he did not know when and where Westermarck originally got his ideas about an emotivist ethics, although he ventured the opinion that "the theoretical foundations of his moral philosophy had already been formed by the time Westermarck set off one spring day in 1898 to explore foreign climes [i.e., Morocco]."[2]

Twenty years later, in a paper read to the Westermarck Society in connection with the centenary celebrations of the philosopher's birth, Wikman spoke as follows: "Unfortunately we know too little about the progress of the work to be able to form any clear opinion of the development of Westermarck's philosophical ideas during the period 1893-98."[3] Wikman then conjectured that Westermarck's ideas probably began to take their final form when he was living in London.[4]

As a matter of fact, these claims about the difficulty of explaining Westermarck's development are too pessimistic. There exists a hitherto unused source which provides a surprising amount of information about these matters, namely the (unpublished) proceedings of the Philosophical Society of Finland for the years 1887-1913.[5] By reference to this material I hope to show that Westermarck's chief contributions to moral philosophy were the outcome of an interesting and complex development, which had already in large measure been completed before he set out on his grand tour in 1898. It goes without saying that his philosophical development continued further in the decade preceding the appearance in 1906 and 1908 of the two volumes of *The Origin and Development of the Moral Ideas,* as well as during the quarter century that separates that work from his *Ethical Relativity.*[6] Even later, when he was translating *Ethical Relativity* into Swedish, one can observe slight shifts of emphasis in his thinking. However, I shall confine my discussion here to the earliest, yet most significant, phase of Westermarck's philosophical development, an understanding of which serves to illuminate his principal achievement, *The Origin and Development of the Moral Ideas*—probably the most important philosophical work ever written by a Finn.

II

Westermarck became an undergraduate in 1881 and took his first degree five years later. He explains in his memoirs that his final examination was delayed by nearly a year on account of his struggle with Greek, a subject in which he nevertheless gained no qualification.[7] His main subject was aesthetics and modern literature, with general history and philosophy as subsidiaries. At first, Westermarck seemed most interested in aesthetics: he went to C. G. Estlander's lectures and participated with enthusiasm in meetings of the Aesthetical Society, of which he was secretary for a time. He also enjoyed success in his historical studies, under the tutelage of J. R. Danielson-Kalmari, and at one point he seems to have had the idea of expanding his honors thesis in history into a dissertation. The last of Westermarck's degree subjects was philosophy. For this, he attended no lecture courses, and his first contact with the professor, Thiodolf Rein, was when he submitted his honors thesis for examination. The title of the thesis was **"Does Civilization Increase the Happiness of Mankind?"**[8]

One can hardly say that this thesis gives any hint of the nature and independent thinking Westermarck was later to show in philosophical matters. It deals for the most part with the pessimistic philosophies of life and culture fashionable at that time, which had been expressed most thoroughly by Edward Hartmann in his *Philosophie des Unbewussten.* In his thesis, Westermarck used various arguments to discredit this "cultural pessimism." His thinking is lucid throughout and at times he makes acute observations. It is evident that he was familiar with the classical utilitarian theories about pleasure and pain and also with the notion of a "hedonic calculus."

Westermarck concludes that "civilization does not decrease the feeling of pleasure while correspondingly increasing the feeling of pain; on the contrary, it modifies the relationship between the two types of feeling, to the advantage of feelings of pleasure. . . . "[9] The optimism implied here probably remained characteristic of Westermarck to the end to his life.

III

I think it is correct to say that Westermarck was not particularly knowledgeable philosophically, and although he was one of Finland's greatest scholars his philosophical reading remained slight and one-sided throughout his life.

The first philosopher Westermarck studied seriously was probably Immanuel Kant. Emma Irene Åström, the first woman in Finland to be awarded a master's degree in philosophy, tells us in her memoirs that for her final examination for Professor Rein she had to read Kant's *Kritik der reinen Vernunft,* the *Kritik der praktischen Vernunft,* and the *Kritik der Urteilskraft.*[10] Westermarck most likely read the same books for his own examination five years later, and if so these three critiques would have constituted his basic education in philosophy.

However, in his memoirs Westermarck says explicitly that he was not greatly inspired by his study of Kant's philosophy,[11] and in his works on moral philosophy Westermarck criticizes no other philosopher so often and so tenaciously as he does Kant. At first glance, the contrast between the moral philosophy of Kant and Westermarck seems extreme. Westermarck is a subjectivist and a relativist who bases morals on feelings. Kant tries to derive an objective and absolute system of morals from a priori principles of practical reason. Closer study, however, reveals remarkable similarities. For example, Westermarck, like Kant, stresses the fact that the primary subject of a moral judgment is the internal motive of an act (the intention, mental state, or will "behind" the act) and not the external result.[12] Another similarity is to be found in Westermarck's idea that moral feelings are disinterested and impartial—one thinks immediately of Kant's idea about generalizability as a criterion of the moral maxim.

Westermarck says that he became distrustful of German metaphysics at an early stage, but was attracted by English empirical philosophy.[13] He appears to have had no close contacts with French philosophy, unlike his Finnish colleagues Hjalmar Neiglick, who was one year his senior, and the slightly younger Rolf Lagerborg, both of whom were deeply influenced by French philosophy, psychology, and sociology.[14]

It was not easy for Westermarck to familiarize himself with the English philosophers, because he was still unable to read English at the time he took his degree. He thus had to rely on translations and on commentaries in other languages.

Westermarck's interest in things English was probably stimulated by a German work he read while preparing for his degree, Hettner's *Literaturgeschichte des 18ten Jahrhunderts.* In his study of Westermarck and his English friends, Yrjö Hirn explains that it was from Hettner's work that Westermarck learned to appreciate the eighteenth-century English empirical philosophers.[15] Before taking his degree, Westermarck also read Buckle and Macaulay in Swedish. We know, moreover, that as an undergraduate he read John Stuart Mill and Herbert Spencer's evolutionary philosophy. Mill's *Three Essays on Religion* and Spencer's *First Principles* had been published in Swedish translations, and the other parts of Spencer's great *System of Synthetic Philosophy* were available to Westermarck in German. All these writers and works are mentioned by Westermarck in his memoirs.[16]

It is clear from the bibliography of his honors thesis that by 1886 Westermarck was familiar with the German translations of Adam Smith's *The Theory of Moral Sentiments,* Mill's study of utilitarianism, Hartley's *Observations on Man,* and Hutcheson's principal work on moral philosophy. He also refers to the original versions of Bain's *The Emotions and the Will* and Sully's book, *Pessimism.* Westermarck's actual knowledge of Sully's ideas probably derived at least in part from conversations with the English philosopher and psychologist, whom he met by chance when walking in the Norwegian mountains in the summer of 1885. "This was the beginning of an acquaintance to which I have owed much in my life," wrote Westermarck."[17] Sully was indispensable later as Westermarck's guide to English society, especially during his first visit to England in 1887, and they were lifelong friends. Another contemporary, whose works Westermarck got to know while still an undergraduate and who presumably had some importance for him, was the Danish philosopher Harald Høffding. Westermarck mentions in his memoirs that he had Høffding's *Psykologi* with him for occasional reading when he was in the fells in Norway in the summer of 1885.[18] To celebrate Høffding's eightieth birthday in 1923, Westermarck published an article about him in the newspaper *Åbo Underrättelser.* "For those of us who were students in the 1880s," he wrote, "Høffding's psychology was a revelation."[19] Westermarck was particularly impressed by Høffding's defense of the so-called identity thesis (the parallel theory, monism, neo-Spinozism) concerning the relationship between body and mind.[20] Yet there is little of Høffding's influence in Westermarck's ethics: their points of view are related, but only remotely. At a meeting of the Sociological Society in London in 1904, the two men even appear to have been at odds with each other.[21]

IV

The thinker who made the deepest and most lasting impression on Westermarck was not, however, a philosopher. In Westermarck's life and work as a whole—in his philosophy, sociology, and writings on religion—it was Charles Darwin whose influence was paramount,

and it is necessary to study Westermarck against the background of Darwin's doctrines, which were so all-pervasive in European intellectual circles in the late nineteenth century.

As far as I can tell Westermarck did not become acquainted with Darwin's ideas until after he had graduated, and then his first direct contact was with *The Descent of Man* in Swedish translation. We have Westermarck's own word for it that this book was of the greatest possible significance for his later work.[22] The experience of reading Darwin convinced Westermarck of the necessity of learning English in order to have access to the anthropological sources quoted.

Westermarck says that it was during his twenty-fifth year that he finally learned enough English to be able to read a book in that language.[23] Probably this was during the spring of 1887, for he made his first visit to England in the autumn of that year and there read Darwin's *Life and Letters,* which had just been published. In his reminiscences he says of the book that it was "a lesson both in humility and in strict scientific method."[24]

More explicitly, he affirms that it was the reading of Darwin which put him on the track that led to the writing of his great work on marriage.[25] The first stage was his doctoral dissertation, *The Origin of Human Marriage,*[26] which he defended in Helsinki in 1889. The dissertation was subsequently republished as the first part of a larger work, *The History of Human Marriage,*[27] which also included an introductory note by Alfred Russel Wallace, a friend and supporter of the great Darwin and himself one of the pioneers of the theory of evolution.

In the very first sentence of the doctoral dissertation a Darwinian note can be heard unmistakably. "It is in the firm conviction," says the author, "that the history of human civilization should be made an object of as scientific a treatment as the history of organic nature that I write this book."[28] The idea of the origin and development of human civilization—its institutions, customs, and practices—is basic to all of Westermarck's scholarly work. He shared this idea implicitly with other leading anthropologists, sociologists, and historians of morals and religion of his time; and above the classic studies of man and his achievements looms the mighty figure of Charles Darwin.

I shall not, however, discuss here Westermarck's work in relation to the theory of evolution, nor shall I consider the impressions and influences Westermarck received—from Darwin and others—during his first journey to England in 1887-88 or thereafter.[29]

V

Westermarck had no contact with the professor of philosophy before submitting his honors thesis for examination, because there were no compulsory seminars in those days.[30] There was, however, another forum for the exchange of philosophical thought which could in some respects be compared to a seminar. This was the Philosophical Society, founded in 1873 by Thiodolf Rein. Rein was thirty-five at the time and had succeeded Johan Vilhelm Snellman as professor of philosophy at the University of Helsinki.

In his memoirs, Rein himself does not have much to say about the meetings of the Philosophical Society.[31] But important insights are provided by the reminiscences of Emma Irene Åström and Westermarck, as well as by Arvi Grotenfelt in an article which appeared in a Festschrift to commemorate Rein's eightieth birthday.[32] We have access, finally, to the proceedings of the Philosophical Society itself, which often include copious notes about the lectures and discussions which took place.

The picture of Rein that emerges from these works is impressive. He was clearly a humble seeker after truth with a genuine taste for philosophical debate. It may be asked whether there have ever been such fervent and serious philosophical discussions in Finland as those which took place in the Philosophical Society in the last two decades of the nineteenth century, with Rein, Neiglick, and Westermarck as the main participants.

Westermarck provides this reminiscence of Rein and the debates in the Society:

> To value Rein's power as a teacher at its true worth it was essential to have heard him at the Philosophical Society. This was the darling of his heart. He had founded the Society a few years after his appointment as professor, remained faithful to it both as Rector and Vice-Chancellor, and still read papers there nearly fifty years after its foundation. The discussion often assumed the form of a duel, in which the contending parties were the chairman on the one hand and perhaps some young graduate on the other. Rank and age were forgotten; it was not the learned professor speaking, but an older comrade—so it seemed—who was trying to tempt others out to a tussle. It was evident that Rein enjoyed the dispute; *in verba magistri jurare* was a demand that he never dreamed of making. He did not spare facetious remarks at his opponent's expense, but he was never either bitter or crushing in his jokes. When it was all over the disciple might perhaps feel some self-reproach lest he should have treated his honoured master with less than due respect, but there was never any indication that the professor felt his dignity had been wounded in any way. . . . In the Philosophical Society, Rein's open-minded and humble search for truth was seen in its brightest light.[33]

It is possible that Rein's own creative gifts as a philosopher were swamped by the powerful influence of Snellman, but little by little he shook himself free of Snellman's Hegelianism. Although Rein never really made any important contribution to philosophy,[34] he had the dialectical gifts of a true philosopher and these were seen at their best in the discussions of the Philosophical Society. He was also open to new ideas. He was attracted, in the first place, by Lotze's attempt to combine the basic ideas of speculative idealism with the newer empirical, scientific way of thinking.[35] He was also influenced by John Stuart Mill, Darwin, and evolutionist philosophy generally.[36]

VI

In the proceedings of the Philosophical Society, Westermarck's name is mentioned for the first time in connection with a meeting held on 16 November 1888. Westermarck, incidentally, recorded the minutes of that meeting himself. He had just returned from his first stay in England, during the academic year 1887-88, and was principally preoccupied with putting the finishing touches to his doctoral dissertation. In the spring term of 1889, on 15 February, Westermarck read his first paper to the Philosophical Society. The subject was similar to that of his doctoral dissertation and had a somewhat tortuous title, typical of those times: "On the Method for an Ethnographically-based Sociology, Illustrated by an Investigation of the Earliest History of Marriage and the Family." I shall not discuss its contents here. It may be said, however, that when the first edition of *The History of Human Marriage* appeared in 1891, it became almost immediately the subject of a paper delivered to the Philosophical Society. The paper was read by Arvi Grotenfelt and it provoked an animated discussion.

A subject which often came up for discussion at meetings of the Society in the late eighties and throughout the following decade was the fashionable "parallel theory" of the relationship between body and mind, the physical and mental aspects of existence. Frequently this theory became the main issue for discussion as the evening progressed, even when it was not directly related to the stated topic of the meeting. Closely connected with the question of the relationship between body and mind was another popular topic of discussion, namely the problem of free will.

Rein was an opponent of the parallel theory. One of his objections to the theory was that it led to metaphysical materialism. He thought, moreover, that the parallel theory implied a strict determinism that denied free will. Rein was a defender of the mind as an independent substance and of free will—the latter because he believed that moral responsibility was impossible without it.

It seems that Rein never really formulated any clear idea about the relationship between the physical and the mental. In a sense he was a dualist; he thought there was causal interaction between body and mind—a view that was called into question by supporters of the parallel theory. At the same time he inclined to the view that matter was essentially spiritual in nature. He thus showed a predilection for the kind of metaphysical idealism which had its roots in Leibniz and which Lotze had at that time developed by relating it to the new scientific way of thinking.[37]

Opposing Rein were Neiglick and later Westermarck, who defended the parallel theory. A climax was reached in the dispute when Westermarck, leading off the debate on 20 November 1891, replied to the criticism of the parallel theory that Rein had offered in the second volume of his recently published book *Försök till en framställning af psykologien.* The discussion continued at the next meeting of the Society, this time with Rein speaking first. I surmise that Westermarck's article **"On Rein's Critique of the Monist Theory of the Mind,"** which appeared in 1892 in *Finsk Tidskrift,* and Rein's rejoinder in the same journal represent by and large the substance of these discussions.[38]

One of Westermarck's main arguments is that the causal effect of the mind on the body is incompatible with the law of the conservation of energy. Rein, for his part, tried to show, among other things, that the parallel theory was incompatible with Darwinism. His line of thought seems to have been this: If one is to use Darwinism to explain the evolution of awareness and of mental functions, it must also be admitted that the mind is distinct from material things and can intervene causally in the chain of physical events; otherwise, it is impossible to explain why mental phenomena are useful in the struggle for existence.[39]

Following his general line of thought on the relationship between body and mind, Westermarck also approved of determinism in the free will controversy. At a meeting of the Society on 8 April 1892, Westermarck introduced a debate on **"Free Will and Its Moral Significance."** In this polemic against Rein, Westermarck claimed that the supposition that the will is subject to the laws of causality is entirely compatible with man's responsibility for his own actions and does not undermine the basis of moral approval and disapproval.[40]

Westermarck's position on free will, as it was expressed in the Philosophical Society, can also be found in the thirteenth chapter of *The Origin and Development of the Moral Ideas.* In the book, however, his thoughts are much more subtly expressed and the material is better organized. In the proceedings of the Society one searches in vain for a proper explanation as to why determinism must not be confused with fatalism.

The contribution Westermarck made to the debates in the Philosophical Society on the parallel theory and his article on the same subject in *Finsk Tidskrift* were apparently his only excursions into the realm of theoretical philosophy. It is not unfair to say that, in the discussions of the Society, neither the opinions of Westermarck nor those of the other participants made any important contribution to philosophy. The whole dispute is nevertheless interesting historically. The opposing views about the parallel theory are a reflection of a crisis between two generations. The parallel theory, the identity hypothesis, neo-Spinozism, monism—so many different labels for what was really the same thing—are the various philosophical guises in which the intellectual

movement known as naturalism expressed itself. This movement, which was at its zenith in the 1880s, may also be seen as a philosophical reflection of the great changes in the scientific world view. It was an expression of the dominance of scientific methods of investigating both nature and human nature, of the belief that all events are subject to strict laws. Determinism was at the very heart of the movement, and many of its critics and adherents viewed metaphysical materialism as an inevitable corollary. Neither Neiglick nor Westermarck, however, accepted this consequence. Of all the supporters of the parallel theory in European philosophy at that time, it was Høffding, I think, who had the greatest influence on the Finnish advocates of the doctrine.

It was above all the law of the conservation of energy that was seen as the scientific prop for the parallel theory. But Darwinism also entered the picture.[41] Spencer, the "armchair philosopher" of the theory of evolution, supported one form of the parallel theory; so did Haeckel, the most eloquent of the doctrine's philosophical propagandists and popularizers in Western Europe. It is well known that Haeckel was one of those monists who came extremely close to accepting metaphysical materialism, and Westermarck had read the Swedish translation of his *Natürliche Schöpfungsgeschichte* shortly after graduation.[42]

VII

There was a somewhat surprising sequel to the deliberations of the Philosophical Society on the parallel theory.

In November 1895, some years after the discussions referred to, Westermarck addressed the society on the subject **"The Emotive States and Their Physical Expression."** He began by outlining the views of Darwin and Spencer on this topic and then proceeded to discuss the new theory of James and Lange, which had attracted much attention. Westermarck was clearly unwilling to accept the idea that the expression of emotion was the proximate cause of emotion—to paraphrase James, we do not cry because we are sorry or tremble because we are afraid, but on the contrary, we feel sorry because we cry, afraid because we tremble.[43] Discussion was continued at the first meeting of the Society in the spring term of 1896, when Yrjö Hirn spoke on "The Physiological Correlative of Emotion." Westermarck joined in the debate and again objected to the view that the expression of emotion was the cause of emotion.

The conversations in the Philosophical Society about the James-Lange theory stirred up the old dispute about the parallel theory. On 6 March 1896, Rein addressed the Society on "A Comparison between the Philosophy of Spinoza and the So-called Parallel Theory of Our Time." In this talk Rein repeated his earlier objections and was now more assured in his support of a monism in the style of Leibniz or Lotze. He asked specifically whether Westermarck could accept his present position, and Westermarck replied that he could not. At the same time, however, Westermarck wished to dissociate himself from the parallel theory, which he had earlier supported. I must confess that the reasons for Westermarck's change of position are not entirely clear to me. They are, however, connected with the problems involved in the notion of causality, and they have something to do with the contributions made by Westermarck to the earlier discussions about the James-Lange theory.[44]

The story, however, does not end here. One year later Westermarck unambiguously explained his new position with regard to the body-mind relationship in terms of idealism. It was not, however, the metaphysical idealism of Leibniz and Lotze (Rein's position), but rather that kind of epistemological idealism represented by the philosophy of the classic British empiricists, Berkeley and Hume.

Westermarck's acceptance of idealism was publicly formulated at a meeting of the Society on 19 February 1897. The debate was launched by Rein, on the theme "God as a Person." The exchange of opinions soon led to the old dispute about the two aspects of reality. Westermarck now claimed that only the mental is real, that the physical is only a species of the mental. It is reported in the minutes that the speaker, i.e., Westermarck, "was unable to accept the identity hypothesis, because it is unable to derive the physical from the mental. . . . The speaker's position was thus very near to radical idealism."

I do not wish to impute any special or deep meaning to Westermarck's idealistic position when considering his thought as a whole. I have no idea how profoundly he held this conviction or how long it persisted.[45] Westermarck's "idealistic" phase seems to me to be interesting primarily because it shows that between 1895 and 1897 he was strongly influenced by the great British empiricists. I do not know whether Berkeley enters the picture, but there is no doubt about the influence of Hume. Evidence for this can be found especially in the great interest Westermarck displayed in the problem of causality, both in his lecture on the emotive states in 1895 and in his contribution to many other debates.

I hope later to show that the years 1895-97 were decisive for the development of Westermarck's moral philosophy. The fact that he came down on the side of epistemological idealism confirms that Westermarck was deeply affected by Hume while his ideas about moral philosophy were assuming their final form.

VIII

I mentioned earlier that in his memoirs Rein makes only passing reference to the Philosophical Society, notwithstanding the fact that he both founded it and ran it for a number of years. Rein reports the founding of the Society on 18 October 1873 and adds: "I venture to believe that the interchange of thought over many important questions that has taken place at these meetings . . . has not been entirely unsuccessful in arousing reflection and clearing up ideas in those who have taken part in them, especially in the younger members of the University."[46]

Westermarck quotes the above passage in his memoirs, and comments: "Arousing reflection indeed! The writer of these lines, during one of the discussions, was aroused to a work on the origin and development of the moral ideas which was to occupy his thoughts for well-nigh twenty years."[47] Later in his memoirs he repeats the assertion that he received the original impulse to write *The Origin and Development of the Moral Ideas* at one of the meetings of the Philosophical Society. He even goes into some detail: "The discussion chanced to deal with the question as to how far a bad man should be treated with kindness. Opinions differed, and in spite of much deliberation they could not be reconciled. Whence this want of agreement? Was it due to defective knowledge or had it a merely sentimental origin?"[48]

In view of this interesting information about the origins of Westermarck's principal work, it is natural to ask whether the occasion referred to can be identified by consulting the proceedings of the Society. Unfortunately this is not possible. The only occasion that seems at all promising in this regard is the meeting held on 17 March 1893, when Arvid Järnefelt, who held a degree in law and was also a well-known writer and devotee of Tolstoy, led a debate on "The Punishment of Crime." In the manner of his mentor, Järnefelt condemned punishment as being a form of violence. Järnefelt was vigorously opposed in the ensuing discussion. It may be of interest to mention in passing that among those present at the meeting were two future Finnish presidents, K. J. Ståhlberg and J. K. Paasikivi. But Westermarck's name it not mentioned, and for a good reason: he was in Oxford. So much for the idea that Westermarck got the stimulus for his great work on morals at this meeting in March 1893.

The proceedings of the Society, then, give no hint as to which meeting Westermarck alluded to. Indeed, there are even grounds for doubting whether it was at a meeting of the Philosophical Society that Westermarck received his inspiration. Westermarck wrote his memoirs in 1926 and 1927. In the introduction to *The Origin and Development of the Moral Ideas,* written twenty years earlier, there is no special mention of a meeting of the Society, but we do find the following comment: "The main object of this book will perhaps be best explained by a few words concerning its origin. Its author was once discussing with some friends the point how far a bad man ought to be treated with kindness. The opinions were divided, and in spite of much deliberation, unanimity could not be attained."[49] It is therefore possible, though by no means certain, that the occasion Westermarck had in mind was not a meeting of the Philosophical Society but a private conversation with friends.

More important, however, than the kind of occasion that gave him the impulse is the date. In the introduction to

The Origin and Development of the Moral Ideas he simply says "Since then many years have passed. . . . "[50] In the passage from the memoirs quoted above, Westermarck speaks of a labor that occupied him for nearly twenty years. If this is correct, we are led back to the late 1880s. It is, furthermore, important to note that Westermarck says specifically in his memoirs that he had started to plan a work on the origin and development of moral awareness even before he had completed his book on marriage.[51] It is not clear, however, whether this is a reference to his dissertation (1889) or to the first edition of *The History of Human Marriage* (1891), although he probably was referring to the latter.

Westermarck's memoirs contain other references to dates which may be significant when considering the origins of his book on the moral ideas. In a passage where he speaks of the slow progress he is making with that work he observes:

> But I soon saw that the work which I had now undertaken was incomparably more difficult than its predecessor. Human marriage was a well-defined subject, whereas morality extends into infinity. . . . It took a full five years before my ideas of the nature of the moral emotions had become more or less settled, and in some other important questions my views did not clear up until much later. The disposition of the great subject took ten years before it was finally complete. . . . In the book on marriage the architecture was simple and developed almost of itself, but in the book on morals it was complicated and gave me much trouble. . . . I certainly could never dream that nearly eighteen years must pass before I should be able to hoist my flag on the roof.[52]

As I stated earlier, the first part of *The Origin and Development of the Moral Ideas* appeared in 1906 and the second part in 1908. If by hoisting his flag Westermarck meant, as is possible, that both volumes were finished and printed, then according to his own statement it was begun in 1890. In that very year, on 7 March, Westermarck talked to the Philosophical Society on the origins of the moral emotions. Almost exactly five years later, on 19 April 1895, he again addressed the Society on this subject. Whereas the 1890 lecture was principally a summing up of Darwin's ideas in *The Descent of Man,* the lecture of 1895 presented a detailed account of Westermarck's own theory of morals. The time gap between the two lectures and the difference in content accord well with Westermarck's statement that it took five years before his understanding of the nature of the moral emotions "became more or less settled."

We can thus propose the following timetable for the writing of *The Origin and Development of the Moral Ideas:* in 1890 Westermarck began to be seriously interested in problems about moral emotions; by 1895 he had developed his own theory on the subject; and thereafter eleven years were to pass before the printing of the first volume of his great work and thirteen years before the second.

When we consider the long time that elapsed between the lecture in 1895 to the Philosophical Society and the appearance in 1906 and 1908 of *The Origin and Development of the Moral Ideas*, it would be quite surprising to find that the main features of Westermarck's moral philosophy underwent no change. In fact there is a great difference between the ideas he expressed in the lecture and in the book. It is therefore interesting to see in what way his opinions changed, and we can reconstruct the development of his thinking fairly precisely with the aid of the minutes of the Philosophical Society.

IX

Westermarck's earliest known statement on questions of moral philosophy is contained in the lecture he delivered to the Society on 7 March 1890. It is worth noting that Westermarck probably first became interested in writing about morality as a result of Darwin's influence—just as, on his own admission, he was indebted to Darwin some years earlier for his interest in the study of marriage.

According to Darwin, moral emotions are based on social instincts.[53] We disapprove, for example, of parents who do not look after their children. Why? Because looking after children is necessary to the continuation of the group (society). The forms of behavior which are subject to moral approval or disapproval are, respectively, those which are useful for or detrimental to the preservation of the species. The origin of the moral emotions is thus explained by the principle of natural selection, and the same is true of conscience. If someone feels the pangs of conscience, it is because he disapproves of his own selfish behavior in the same way as he would disapprove of similar behavior by others. He judges himself by the standard of the general good.

In the debate that followed Westermarck's lecture, Rein made an interesting contribution. He stressed that it was not enough to consider an act moral because it derived from a social instinct to preserve the species. According to Rein it is also necessary that an act be done with the awareness of a general rule or norm, which must be obeyed in the individual case. Such awareness would hardly be possible for animals. He therefore concluded that moral emotions and moral deliberation are specifically human attributes. There is some truth in Rein's observations, as Westermarck was later to admit.

At the next meeting of the Philosophical Society, on 21 March 1890, questions of moral philosophy were again discussed. Hugo Pipping, later professor of Nordic languages, read a paper on Wundt's criticism of the ethics of Spencer.[54] In the debate Westermarck asserted that an action is ethical if it does not offend our moral feelings. The remark foreshadows one of the main theses of Westermarck's moral philosophy, namely the idea that moral concepts are ultimately based on emotions of (moral) approval or disapproval.[55]

Westermarck's opposition to utilitarianism should be seen in the light of his conviction that morality is based on emotions.[56] According to the classical utilitarian view, we approve or disapprove of something morally according to whether it increases or decreases human happiness; thus moral emotions are derivative from the purportedly highest value, happiness. But even in Darwinian moral theory, which Westermarck himself accepted, moral emotions are secondary—in this case to the power of the thing approved or disapproved to promote or retard the survival of the species. In this respect the Darwinian moral doctrine resembles utilitarianism, and the connection can be seen quite clearly in Spencer.

A number of years were still to elapse before Westermarck's thinking about the moral emotions took final shape, and even so the relationship between his ideas and utilitarianism never became completely clear. In the development of his views on moral philosophy the period 1890-94 can perhaps be called the Darwinian phase. In the minutes of the Philosophical Society during those years we often find Westermarck referring to the Darwinian idea that morality has a "survival value" in the struggle for existence.[57] He adds, in this connection, that morality is independent of religion.

X

It may be appropriate to say a few words here about Westermarck's view of religion, at least as it appears in the proceedings of the Society.

In the first meeting where Westermack's name is mentioned in the minutes, 16 November 1888, the subject was "How Scientific is Theology?" Rein led off the discussion, with Westermarck and others joining in. "Mr. Westermarck," we read, "saw Christian theology as merely part of the psychology of religious feeling, but he nevertheless was of the opinion that a separate chair of comparative religion could easily hold its own in the university." Both Rein and Neiglick argued, against Westermarck, that even when theology is understood as an empirical study of the phenomena of religious life, it covers a much wider area than simply the psychology of religious feeling. This is no doubt correct, but it may be observed in passing that, despite many efforts, the University of Helsinki had to wait until 1970 for the founding of a chair in comparative religion. When finally it was founded, it was placed in the theological faculty, which Westermarck would probably have considered inappropriate.

We find Westermarck expressing some interesting thoughts at a meeting held on 12 February 1892. The theme was "The Origins of Ethics" and it was again introduced by Rein. In both the lecture and the debate, the relationship between religion and morality was much to the fore. The report of the meeting gives rather a good picture of the near-utilitarian ethical viewpoint that Rein himself seems to have supported. According to Rein, the ultimate measure of good and evil is happiness—not, however, the happiness of the individual, but of all mankind. In principle, morality and religion are independent. Moral rules are valid, says Rein "not because they have a religious foundation, but by their very nature. Morality does not collapse if you remove religion. Religions have of course promoted morality, but this is because they contain, particularly within Christianity, moral elements." Westermarck spoke for an even more radical view. He claimed that ethical concepts have deeper roots than religious concepts, which accords well with his idea that ethical and legal concepts derive from instincts which have a "survival value" in the struggle for existence.

The idea that morality is independent of religion is, of course, completely consonant with the historical fact that religions have affected the moral life in different ways. There can also be different opinions about the nature and significance of such influences. Rein thought they had had a beneficial effect, that religions have made a positive contribution to moral behavior. Westermarck had another perspective. For him it was natural to stress those features in religions, and especially in the Christian religion, that are at odds with the demands of morality, which work against the improvement of the moral emotions. Westermarck saw a historical conflict rather than an alliance between religion and morality. He presented a detailed and well-documented statement of this point of view in his last work, *Christianity and Morals*,[58] which appeared in 1939, the year of his death. He had, however, already expressed his opinions clearly and pointedly at a meeting of the Philosophical Society on 2 March 1894. The title of his lecture was **"The Moral Content of the Christian Doctrine of Life after Death."** Westermarck condemned this doctrine as being immoral because of its egoism. (The same argument has a central place in Westermarck's moral criticism of Christianity forty-five years later.) The lively discussion that followed, reported in detail in the minutes, concentrated on the question "How essential to Christianity is the doctrine of reward or punishment after death?" Westermarck was at pains to stress—rightly, I think—that attempts to play down the distasteful elements in the Christian doctrine about life after death required a new interpretation of Christianity according to the tenets of a more enlightened age and not, as was often claimed, a return to an orthodox, original doctrine.

XI

In November 1894, Rein gave a lecture to the Society on one of his favorite subjects, natural law. Westermarck took part in the discussion and made use of the occasion to outline his thoughts, as he then formulated them, about the nature of the moral emotions and prescriptions. The report states that he also expressed the hope that "at some future time he might have the opportunity to present his ideas on this matter more fully."

His wish was fulfilled some six months later, on 19 April 1895, when he addressed the Society on the subject of **"Moral Emotion."** It seems therefore that his new theory about morals, which was explained in this lecture, had already been formulated earlier. In fact, Westermarck had already presented it in a series of university lectures on sociology. We have what is probably an accurate summary of these lectures, based on the notes of Leo Ehrnrooth. Ehrnrooth, who was later awarded a doctorate in law and became a senator, took these notes when he was an undergraduate, and they were distributed by the Academic Bookstore in Helsinki.[59] A comparison of these notes and the minutes of the Philosophical Society meeting reveals no significant differences.

In Westermarck's new theory, moral feeling is defined as "the feeling of pleasure or displeasure which arises when the idea of the specific intention of a given person's act is viewed in relation to the idea of the intention I myself would have had in his place."[60] It seems to me that this theory may be understood in the following manner. Let us suppose that a particular person has acted in a certain way. I picture to myself the intention he had, and, trying to put myself in his place, I ask myself whether I should have had the same intention. If I decide that my intention in so acting would have been the same as his, I get a feeling of pleasure, which could perhaps be described as "pleasure of agreement." If, on the other hand, I decide that my intention would have been different, perhaps even the opposite, I get a feeling of displeasure, which we can call the "displeasure of disagreement." These feelings of pleasure and displeasure are not in themselves identical with emotions of moral approval and disapproval. Moral emotions are a special case of the feelings just described; they are what Westermarck calls "relational emotions."[61] In order to be *moral* an emotion must fulfill another condition, which Westermarck calls "formal": the intentions—my own and the other person's—which are compared with respect to their conformity or disparity, must "come within the field of recognized general rules, or so-called moral commandments."

Moral commandments are expressions of what Westermarck calls the collective or general will of the group. They are prescriptions which indicate what the members of a group must do and what they may not do. Among other things, they enjoin respect for life and property, truthfulness in speech, the honoring of promises and agreements. If the will of one member of the group "differs from the collective will, he is disapproved of because of the displeasure that arises from the lack of agreement with the collectivity." As I understand it, Westermarck's theory implies that my approval or disapproval of another's act on the basis of the conformity or disparity of our intentions constitutes *moral* approval or disapproval if and only if my own intention accords with the collective will. If I reflect upon an earlier act of mine and conclude that my intention in doing it does not accord with the intention I would have if I were in the same situation today, I become distressed. In so far as the present direction of my will agrees with the collective will, this distress is called the pangs of conscience.

Undoubtedly Westermarck's theory can be questioned at many points. One may, for instance, ask whether the pleasure or displeasure that is supposed to result from the conformity or disparity of intentions really exists. It is not my aim, however, to evaluate the theory. Not long afterwards, Westermarck himself was to reject it in favor of a theory that was assuredly much more firmly based. On the other hand, it is interesting to look at one or two of the special features of Westermarck's moral theory of 1895.

Within the framework of the theory, Westermarck made his first attempt to identify the distinguishing characteristics of the moral emotions. At that time, he thought there were two such characteristics: first, moral emotions are by their very nature relational emotions, and second, they involve conformity with the collective will. He was later to change his opinion radically, substituting the concept of retributive emotions for that of relational emotions and replacing conformity with the general will by the characteristics of disinterestedness and impartiality.

Westermarck's view of the fundamental importance for the moral life of the collective will echoes the theory advanced at that time by the great French sociologist, Émile Durkheim. Durkheim's book, *De la division du travail social,* in which his views on moral philosophy are expressed, had appeared in 1893. There is no direct evidence that in 1894-95 Westermarck knew anything about Durkheim's work or ideas,[62] but the similarity of their thought is very striking.

In Finland the great champion of Durkheim's philosophical views was Rolf Lagerborg.[63] Westermarck's thinking was, in contrast, beginning to take a rather different turn. Nevertheless, I think that the great emphasis Westermarck placed on the importance of custom in his principal work on moral philosophy represents a continuation of his thinking from the time of the mid-1890s.[64]

XII

Westermarck's moral theory of 1895 seems to differ greatly from the theory he finally proposed in *The Origin and Development of the Moral Ideas* and *Ethical Relativity.* It may be supposed that his views developed gradually during his sojourns in England and Morocco at the turn of the century; indeed this is what has sometimes been claimed. But although there may be some truth in this description, I believe it is essentially erroneous. It is my contention—and I think the evidence supports it—that Westermarck's views developed very rapidly and underwent great changes in the two years following his lecture on "Moral Emotion"; that, broadly speaking, he had already arrived at his final conclusions when, as the first recipient of a Rosenberg travel grant, he went abroad in the autumn of 1897.

During the years I am now discussing, Westermarck spent the academic terms in Finland. He was acting professor of philosophy at the time, because Rein as

Vice-Chancellor was on leave of absence. In the year 1895 he made no journey abroad—"a unique time in my life," as he calls it in his memoirs.[65] The summer of 1897 saw him in Munich at an international psychology congress. Then, in the autumn of the same year he went abroad, and apart from an occasional short visit, remained outside Finland for eight whole years.

At the last spring meeting of the Philosophical Society in 1897, on 22 April, Westermarck gave a lecture entitled **"The Predicate in Moral Judgments."** The full report of this lecture in the proceedings of the Society shows that it was an earlier version of a talk he gave to the Aristotelian Society in London, which was published in 1900 in *Mind* under the title **"Remarks on the Predicates of Moral Judgments."**[66] The contents of his lecture to the Society are roughly as follows: he divides moral predicates into two basic types, which he calls "obligatory" and "meritorious." He says that the concept "contrary to duty" can be defined with the help of the concept "obligatory" and vice versa: acting contrary to duty is leaving undone that which is obligatory. The concept of the "permissible" can similarly be defined: that which is permissible is not contrary do duty. The word "ought" may be used instead of the term "obligatory," and instead of "contrary to duty" one may say "ought not," "wrong," or "immoral." (It is presupposed that one is talking of what is "obligatory" or what is "meritorious" in a moral sense.) Westermarck points out that in the view of some philosophers "meritoriousness has no independent existence in the field of morals."[67] According to these thinkers meritoriousness is merely one form of obligatoriness, or, putting it another way, the concept of "goodness" is a special case of the concept of "duty." Westermarck vigorously opposes this view.[68] He observes that acts which we call meritorious are not necessarily acts which we consider blameful or contrary to duty if left undone. Hence if duty is that which it is wrong to leave undone, it follows that meritorious acts are not identical with "obligatory" acts. The morally meritorious or good is something which, we may say, goes beyond duty. In more modern terms, it could be said that the concepts of duty and meritoriousness (or duty and goodness) cannot be defined in terms of each other, but are logically independent. Westermarck's point of view is by no means unique in the realm of moral philosophy. It is, however, independently elaborated and expressed with great clarity, particularly in his published works, and he makes a skillful defense of his ideas, especially against those who would reduce the concept of "goodness" to that of "duty." Perhaps I may be permitted to add that I believe Westermarck's viewpoint in this important question is, broadly speaking, correct.

Westermarck goes on to relate the two types of moral predicates to moral emotions of approval and disapproval. Meritoriousness, and kindred concepts like goodness and virtue, he associates with moral approval; obligatoriness and other similar concepts he connects with moral disapproval—we disapprove of what is contrary to duty (wrong, immoral). An act which is "obligatory," says Westermarck, "does not as such arouse a feeling of approval, but only to the extent to which it includes an element of meritoriousness. To say of a person that he did what he ought to do, is not to praise him." I believe that there is reason to concur with this view as well.

It is important to remember in this context that Westermarck thought that moral emotions had a primary position in relation to moral predicates. Acts are morally meritorious (good) *because* they are subject to moral approval, and conversely "contrary to duty" (wrong, immoral) *because* they are subject to moral disapproval. This naturally raises a question, which Westermarck formulates and answers in the following manner:

> What kind of emotions are moral approval and disapproval? We do not approve and disapprove merely in a moral sense. Moral disapproval is always a feeling of anger, in other words a feeling which is followed by a strong desire to punish; moral approval is always followed by the desire to reward. But not all desire to punish or reward is moral. The judgment 'X is wrong' does not simply mean that the person making the judgment desires to reproach or punish X,[69] but that X *deserves* reproach or punishment. The difference is that in the latter case all self-interest is excluded. The idea that disinterestedness is a characteristic of moral judgments is the basis of Kant's principle 'Act according to that maxim which you can will to be a universal law' and also of the Christian prescription 'Do unto others as you would have them do unto you.'[70]

In the lecture of 1897 Westermarck had thus abandoned his earlier idea that the defining characteristic of morality is its conformity with the collective will. He now proposed a new characteristic, which he calls "disinterestedness." In *The Origin and Development of the Moral Ideas* the characteristic in question is called "disinterestedness and impartiality." We find both terms used in the article in *Mind,* but only the former occurs in the report of the lecture given to the Philosophical Society.

Like the idea that goodness cannot be reduced to duty, so too the view that disinterestedness and impartiality are intrinsic features of moral judgments is not unique in the history of ethics. Westermarck himself alluded in his lecture both to Kant's demand for "generalizability" and to the "Golden Rule" of Christian ethics. Yet this view as it is expressed by Westermarck is one of the most valuable aspects of his moral philosophy, and his manner of treating it is both new and original.

It is especially suggestive to find Westermarck referring to Kant in his lecture of 1897. This shows that he was aware that something resembling one of the chief points of his ethical theory could be found in Kant.

However, Westermarck makes no mention of Kant either in the article in *Mind* or in those passages in *The Origin and Development of the Moral Ideas* where he considers disinterestedness and impartiality as special features of the moral emotions. This omission may obscure the relationship between his own thinking and other traditions of moral philosophy.

XIII

The question of the relationship between Westermarck's ethical theory and the ideas of his predecessors forms an interesting chapter in the development of philosophical thought, but I shall do no more here than offer a few random comments.

The prevailing view is that Hume and Smith áre the most important of the earlier thinkers who influenced Westermarck's theory. One could almost say, with respect to the history of ethics in England, that Westermarck rediscovered Hume and Smith after a century dominated first by utilitarian and then by evolutionary ethics. It is customary to stress especially the similarity between Westermarck and Smith. There are many references to Smith in Westermarck's published works and in both his philosophical writings and his memoirs he expresses admiration for Smith. The references to Hume are considerably less frequent, but Kant is often mentioned, although almost always disparagingly.

I do not wish to deny that Smith is Westermarck's close philosophical kin. Smith influenced Westermarck in three ways: first, in the view that "resentment and gratitude belong to the root-principles of the moral consciousness";[71] second, in Westermarck's selection of disinterestedness and impartiality as criteria of moral behavior—although here Kant was also important; and third, in the role allotted to sympathy in arousing feelings of approval or disapproval towards other people.

However, comparison between Westermarck and Hume, and particularly between *The Origin and Development of the Moral Ideas* and *A Treatise of Human Nature*, reveals far-reaching and often striking similarities, especially concerning the question of moral objectivity and truth. Westermarck's subjectivism and ethical relativism are in my opinion nearer to Hume than to Smith.[72]

It is not possible to say at what stage Westermarck came decisively under the influence of Smith. He was already familiar with the German translation of *The Theory of Moral Sentiments* at the time he was writing his honors thesis (1886). The thesis, however, contains but a single reference—and that hardly important—to the works of Smith. Westermarck's own copy of the original English text of *The Theory of Moral Sentiments* was printed in 1887.[73] The book shows signs of having been carefully read; words and phrases are underlined and there are occasional notes in the margin. So far as I can tell, however, there is nothing about the markings that would indicate when they were made. Moreover, there are no references to Smith either in the records of the proceedings of the Philosophical Society or in the notes taken by Ehrnrooth of Westermarck's sociology lectures. In an

interview he gave in 1898, however, Westermarck spoke enthusiastically and admiringly of *The Theory of Moral Sentiments* and its author.[74] If I may hazard a guess, I think Westermarck's real "experience" of Smith may not have taken place until the time of his stay in England at the turn of the century. If this is correct, then the main points of Westermarck's moral philosophy were arrived at without any direct influence from Smith. Conversely, there seem to be good grounds for saying that the influence of Hume was greatest precisely during the vital years 1895-97, when Westermarck was in Finland—the period which saw the final development of the main features of his moral philosophy.

XIV

A separate chapter is formed by Westermarck's lectures and discussions in the Philosophical Society on methodological questions. His very first lecture, on 15 February 1889, was called **"On the Method for an Ethnographically-based Sociology. . . . "** I shall not discuss it here; as a matter of fact, the lecture deals as much with Westermarck's theory of marriage and his refutation of the claim that primitive societies were promiscuous and matriarchal as with the question of sociological method.

Westermarck gave two lectures in 1896, **"The Task of Ethics"** (8 May) and **"On Philosophy and its Study"** (21 November). In the latter, he dealt in particular with the relationship between philosophy and certain of the sciences. He drew attention to the fact that in the university, empirical psychology and sociology were still "under the tutelage of philosophy," and he expressed the opinion that it could surely not be long before these disciplines were granted their autonomy. In reality half a century would elapse before permanent chairs·in these subjects were established in Finland.[75]

At an international psychology congress in Munich in 1896, Westermarck spoke on **"Normative und psychologische Ethik."** The report of the congress included a summary of his lecture,[76] and in 1976 the complete Swedish and German texts were discovered among Westermarck's papers in the Åbo Akademi. As the title makes plain, Westermarck distinguished two main types of ethics. The one attempts to provide standards for good and evil and to give prescriptive rules for human behavior; the other simply endeavors to describe exactly the standards actually used and to give an account of the rules actually obtaining in different societies. Westermarck uses the accepted term, "normative," to describe the first type of ethics; for the latter he uses the adjective "psychological." It might perhaps be better to use the word "sociological," but he never calls it that. More important than the question of terminology, however, is the fact that this second kind of ethics must, according to Westermarck, be an *empirical* study of morals—that is, of moral concepts and behavior—an adjunct to the natural history of man and his civilization. Only empirical ethics can be called a science; normative ethics cannot be scientific because it is impossible to find any general validity in norms and evaluations. Westermarck's belief that normative ethics is not scientific stems from his ethical subjectivism and his relativism. Normative ethics he sees as a kind of propaganda, but he does not deny that as such it may have great practical significance.

I wish to make two observations here about Westermarck's ethical ideas. The first concerns the division of ethics into normative and empirical psychological, sociological, historical). Such a division is not exhaustive. There is also a third basic type of ethical inquiry, which can be called the conceptual or logical analysis of value judgments, norms, and moral concepts (such as goodness, evil, duty, virtue, justice, etc.). This kind of study is nowadays often called meta-ethics, but most of what has traditionally been called ethics or moral philosophy is in fact of this type; examples can be found in Aristotle, Hume, Kant, and Mill. The same type of inquiry is manifested in Westermarck's theory about the relationship between moral judgments and truth; his idea that moral judgments derive from feelings of approval or disapproval; his view that moral emotions are disinterested and impartial; and his conception of the relationship between duty and merit. These theories are neither empirical descriptions of fact nor generalizations based on fact; on the contrary, they are (logical) investigations of concepts and judgments. It is true that Westermarck also made empirical studies of morality—perhaps on a greater scale than anyone before or since. Of the fifty-three chapters of *The Origin and Development of the Moral Ideas,* the last forty comprise a vast collection of material concerning the history of customs. Even the first thirteen chapters, the so-called "theoretical"—or as we may say, philosophical—part of that work, contain empirical material of such wealth that it sometimes seems to me to obscure rather than to illuminate the main argument.

There is no doubt that Westermarck had an erroneous idea about the *nature* of his moral theories. He regarded as an empirical study something which was, in fact, moral philosophy, and the misconception has regrettably led to some confusion. It does not, however, detract from the essential value and interest of his theories.

In the second place I wish to make a historical comment about Westermarck's distinction between normative and empirical ethics. The distinction was "in the air" at the time he was formulating his theories. This we see quite clearly in the works of the French writers Durkheim and Lévy-Bruhl. (In English and German moral philosophy the distinction had less importance.) Was it not Lévy-Bruhl who conferred upon ethics the name *science des moeurs?*

It seems worth asking whether Westermarck's views about the status of ethics were influenced by French thinkers of the time—particularly by Durkheim. We have already touched on this matter in connection with Westermarck's lecture of 1895 on the subject of the moral emotions. Although we have no direct evidence that Westermarck was influenced by the French school, the conceptual similarities concerning the nature and tasks of ethics may be indirect evidence of such influence.

A Finnish scholar before Westermarck had also made an eloquent plea in favor of the distinction between normative and empirical ethics. This was Hjalmar Neiglick. He never actually published anything on the subject of ethics, and the proceedings of the Philosophical Society reveal nothing about his interesting views on moral philosophy.[77] We get an insight into his ethical ideas, however, from a letter he wrote in 1886 to Waldemar Ruin.[78] In that letter he talked about his plans for writing a study on the feeling of sympathy, which he appears to have considered to be at the bottom of morality.

It is well known that Neiglick was sympathetic to French ideas and had good relations with French philosophers and psychologists. He had become acquainted with Durkheim during his prolonged sojourn in Leipzig (1885-86), where he wrote his doctoral dissertation under the guidance of Wundt. It is thought that he later corresponded with Durkheim, but in any case the letters have never come to light. We are thus not in a position to say whether Neiglick got his own ideas about the task of ethics as a result of French influence. Personally, I do not think it likely that Neiglick was indebted to such foreign influence, and his view that sympathy is the basis of morality is quite different from anything in Durkheim.

We cannot say with any certainty whether Westermarck's views about the nature of ethics and the importance of sympathy to the moral emotions owe anything to Neiglick. Westermarck states in his memoirs that Neiglick spoke to him about his plan for a study of sympathy, "but I cannot recall whether he mentioned anything about the ethical direction which, according to the letter to Ruin, he intended to give his work."[79] Westermarck goes on: "I scarcely think he gave me any thoughts which had not already occurred to me."[80]

The similarity between the thinking of Neiglick and Westermarck thus seems to have been quite fortuitous. It is of interest nevertheless to note that Westermarck's ethical views had been anticipated by another Finnish philosopher, who was at the same time Westermarck's close friend. Had Neiglick lived longer, it is quite possible that their work in the field of ethics would have been complementary and that they would have stimulated each other.

XV

Westermarck's active participation in the Philosophical Society came to an end in the spring term of 1897. In the autumn of the same year, he went on a long journey abroad, but in the spring of 1903 he was again in Finland, where he was acting professor of philosophy. In the minutes of the Philosophical Society, Westermarck is mentioned as being present at only one meeting during that spring term.

About the turn of the century, the Philosophical Society experienced a period of decline, and for two years there are not even any records of what transpired. In a letter he wrote to Westermarck in February 1901, Yrjö Hirn said that the activities of the society had come to an end.[81] No doubt it was significant that Westermarck was abroad and that Rein, as Vice-Chancellor, had relinquished his professorship as well as the chairmanship of the Society. Rein's successor in the chair of philosophy, and later also as chairman of the Society, was his nephew Arvi Grotenfelt.[82] In 1906, when the chair of philosophy was divided between theoretical and practical philosophy, Westermarck accepted an invitation to the chair of practical philosophy. At the same time he maintained his connections with the University of London (at the London School of Economics and Political Science), where he had been lecturer in sociology since 1904 and was to become professor of sociology in 1907.

There is little to say about Westermarck and the Philosophical Society after he became a professor. His name is hardly ever mentioned in the minutes of the Society. New figures begin to appear on the philosophical scene and new subjects are discussed. When, on 23 March 1908, Westermarck addressed the Society on the subject **"The Development of Morality,"** it was to be his last lecture.

On that occasion Westermarck explained how impartial approval and disapproval, which are the essence of moral judgments, embrace ever larger human communities as history advances. Primitive man reacted "morally" only towards the members of his own group (family, tribe, or nation); he did not, as a rule, feel retributive resentment over those misfortunes which affected members of other groups. For Westermarck complete disinterestedness of the retributive emotions is an ideal seldom reached in actual moral judgments. It seems, however, that retributive emotions are steadily developing in the direction of this moral ideal. In this matter, Westermarck was an "evolutionary optimist" and a child of his age. But he was not for all that artlessly naive—not even in the light of the moral setbacks experienced by mankind in the present century.

The second volume of *The Origin and Development of the Moral Ideas* appeared in 1908 and the great work was thus completed. Rolf Lagerborg commented on the contents of this volume in a lecture to the Philosophical Society, the minutes of which were kept by the eighteen-year-old Eino Kaila. The account is brief and it is not clear whether the debate was of any interest philosophically. We do not even know whether Westermarck himself was present.

In the proceedings of the Society, Westermarck's presence is mentioned for the last time in the minutes for 4 April 1913, which may be described as a historic occasion. It was at that meeting that Rein gave his last lecture to the Society. It was on a subject that had always been dear to him—natural law—and was entitled **"Must One Recognize the Existence of Natural Law, and If So in What Sense?"** In this lecture, Rein supported the kind of utilitarianism he had advocated consistently throughout his philosophical career: the ultimate basis for moral judgments is the idea of the "common" or "public" good (*bonum commune*). The report of the meeting states that "Professor Westermarck expressed a dissenting view of the origins of the principles of both natural law and ethics."

Thus these two friendly antagonists joined swords once again, on a stage which had many times witnessed their lively disputations. Rein was now seventy-five years old, Westermarck fifty, and it was a quarter of a century since they had first met in the Society. This meeting was probably the last one Westermarck attended—at least there is no evidence to the contrary.

A Festschrift in honor of Rein was published for his eightieth birthday on 28 February 1918.[83] Westermarck was at that time in England and was unable to send the article he had promised. A note in the Festschrift says that the article was to have dealt with utilitarianism, but it was never published and, as far as I know, there is no evidence of any manuscript. Possibly Westermarck did not even finish it. It could have shed further light on Westermarck's moral philosophy and could also have been a concluding contribution to the debate on utilitarianism which was carried on in the Philosophical Society throughout the Rein era.

NOTES

The present article is a revised version of a paper read to the Philosophical Society of Finland on 20 February 1963, entitled "Edvard Westermarck och Filosofiska föreningen." The paper dealt with the development of Westermarck's philosophy insofar as it could be traced in the proceedings of the Society. In the article I have also made use of some early source material which is not connected with Westermarck's role in the Society, but the actual framework has not been enlarged. It is therefore necessary to stress that I deal with only a limited aspect of Westermarck's overall philosophical development—approximately that period which came to an end with his long sojourn abroad, starting with his journey to England in the early autumn of 1897.

A number of hitherto unknown manuscripts by Westermarck were discovered by Timothy Stroup at the Åbo Akademi in 1976. These comprise several hundred pages, some handwritten, some typewritten. They contain, among other things, a preparatory study for *The Origin and Development of the Moral Ideas,* as well as the German and Swedish manuscripts of Westermarck's talk in 1896 to an international psychology congress in Munich. This "new" material provides a "missing link" between Westermarck's earlier and later ideas. For a discussion of Westermarck's philosophical development in the light of these manuscripts, see Stroup, *Westermarck's Ethics* (Turku/Åbo: Akademi, 1982).

NOTES

[1] Edward Westermarck, *The Origin and Development of the Moral Ideas,* 2 vols. (London: Macmillan and Co., 1906-8). Hereafter cited as *"ODMI."*

[2] K. Rob. V. Wikman, "Edvard Westermarcks etiska relativitetsteori," *Societas Scientiarum Fennica Årsbok-Vuosikirja* 21 B:1 (1942-43): 4-5.

[3] Wikman, "Edward Westermarck as Anthropologist and Sociologist," *Transactions of the Westermarck Society* 9, no. 1 (1962): 13.

[4] Ibid., p. 12.

[5] The manuscript of the Philosophical Society minutes, *Filosofisen Yhdistyksen Pöytäkirjat 1873-1915,* is preserved in the Department of Philosophy of the University of Helsinki. A chronological list of Westermarck's lectures to the Society is given at the end of the notes to this article. Since the minutes are not continuously paginated, reference is possible only to the date of the meeting.

[6] Westermarck, *Ethical Relativity,* International Library of Psychology, Philosophy, and Scientific Method (London: Kegan Paul, Trench, Trubner & Co., 1932). I have dealt with some of the detailed differences between the trains of thought in the two principal works in my article "Om moraliska föreställningars sanning," in the collection *Vetenskapens funktion i samhället,* Nordisk Sommar-universitet 1953 (Copenhagen: Munksgaard, 1954); see especially pp. 49-52.

[7] Westermarck, *Minnen ur mitt liv* (Helsinki: Holger Schildts Förlag, 1927). Quotations from this work are reproduced from the authorized English translation of Anna Barwell, published as *Memories of My Life* (London: George Allen & Unwin Ltd., 1929). Hereafter cited as *Minnen* and *Memories.* Westermarck describes his degree studies in *Minnen,* pp. 25-29, and *Memories,* pp. 27-31.

[8] Westermarck, "Gör kulturen människoslägtet lyckligare?," Box 77, Edward Westermarck Papers, Åbo Akademi Library, Turku/Åbo.

[9] Ibid., p. 134.

[10] Emma Irene Åström, *Mitt liv och mina vänner* (Helsinki: Söderström & Co., 1934), p. 143.

[11] "Not even the study of Kant's philosophy aroused any deeper feeling of admiration in my mind. In his *Kritik der reinen Vernunft* I thought even then that I could detect attempts to solve impossible problems, inconsistencies, arguments in a circle, formalistic constructions, an astonishing disposition to employ the same terms in different senses and other obscurities. His moral philosophy gave the impression of an exalted character, but contained strange and even incomprehensible propositions, unfounded postulates, and a moral law which was almost empty. His manner of presentment was often repulsive; I was glad to hear our Professor of Philosophy say once that Kant in his books had shown how *not* to write." *Memories,* p. 30; *Minnen,* p. 28.

[12] Westermarck seems to have thought this idea more or less self-evident. In *ODMI,* 1:205, he writes with reference to Sidgwick: "In this point moralists of all schools seem to agree." That is nevertheless an exaggeration.

[13] *Memories,* pp. 29-30; *Minnen,* p. 28. In his article "Studieresor i ungdomen," *K. D. F. Festskrift utgiven av Nylänningar* (Helsinki, 1925), Westermarck says (p. 26) that Locke, Hume, Spencer, and Mill had made a deep impression on him even before his first visit to England.

[14] See Rolf Lagerborg, "The Essence of Morals: Fifty Years (1895-1945) of Rivalry between French and English Sociology," *Transactions of the Westermarck Society* 2, no. 2 (1953): 15.

[15] Yrjö Hirn, "Edward Westermarck and his English Friends," *Transactions of the Westermarck Society* 1, no. 2 (1947): 42.

[16] *Memories,* pp. 29, 35, and 67; *Minnen,* pp. 27, 33, and 69.

[17] *Memories,* p. 49; *Minnen,* p. 47.

[18] *Memories,* p. 48; *Minnen,* p. 47.

[19] Westermarck, "Harald Høffding åttio år," *Åbo Underrättelser,* 11 March 1923, p. 3.

[20] See Harald Høffding, *Psykologi i Omrids paa Grundlag af Erfaring,* 3rd. ed. (Copenhagen: P. G. Philipsens Forlag, 1892), pp. 71-79.

[21] See *Memories,* p. 207; *Minnen,* p. 261. Rolf Lagerborg specifically calls Westermarck a "disciple of Høffding" in his *Edvard Westermarck och verken från hans verkstad under hans tolv sista år 1927-1939* (Helsinki: Svenska Litteratursällskapets i Finland Förlag, 1951), p. 165. I think this is an exaggeration.

[22] *Memories,* pp. 67-68; *Minnen,* p. 69.

[23] *Memories,* p. 68; *Minnen,* p. 69.

[24] *Memories,* p. 77; *Minnen,* p. 81.

[25] *Memories,* pp. 67-68; *Minnen,* p. 69.

[26] The full title was *The History of Human Marriage, Part I: The Origin of Marriage* (Helsinki: Frenckell & Son, 1889), but to avoid confusion with his later work, the dissertation will be referred to by the shorter title.

[27] Westermarck, *The History of Human Marriage* (London: Macmillan and Co., 1891).

[28] Westermarck, *Origin*, p. 1.

[29] Information about this can be found in Hirn, "Edward Westermarck."

[30] *Memories*, pp. 31-32; *Minnen*, pp. 29-30.

[31] Thiodolf Rein, *Lefnadsminnen* (Helsinki: Söderström & Co., 1918), p. 260.

[32] Arvi Grotenfelt, "Thiodolf Rein Filosofisessa Yhdistyksessä," *Juhlajulkaisu omistettu Th. Reinille hänen täyttäessään 80 vuotta, 28.II.1918* (Helsinki: Kustannusosakeyhtiö Otava, 1918), pp. 240-53. Among other things, Grotenfelt gives a lively description of the exchange of views between Rein and Neiglick at the meetings of the Philosophical Society.

[33] *Memories*, pp. 32-33; *Minnen*, pp. 30-31.

[34] See his somewhat plaintive but no doubt truthful words about himself in *Lefnadsminnen*, p. 264.

[35] Ibid., pp. 263-64.

[36] Ibid., pp. 215, 261-62.

[37] In *Memoirs*, p. 34 (*Minnen*, p. 32), Westermarck says that Rein was at one time a dualist, but that he later tended towards monism. Kalle Sorainen describes Rein as a consistent monist—that is, a metaphysical idealist—in his "Filosofinen yhdistys 75 vuotta," *Ajatus* 15 (1948): 191. Neither description is entirely accurate. Rein's ideas may be studied in the two published parts of his *Försök till en framställning af psykologin eller vetenskapen om själen*, 2 vols. (Helsinki: Finska Litteratur-Sällskapets tryckeri, 1876, 1891) and in the article "Nyare åsikter om förhållandet mellan själ och kropp," in *Öfversikt af Finska Vetenskaps-Societetens Förhandlingar* 48, no. 21 (1905-6): 22-38.

[38] Westermarck, "Professor Reins kritik af den monistiska själsteorin." *Finsk Tidskrift* 32, no. 1 (January 1892): 33-41, and Rein, "Om parallelteorin i psykologin: Genmäle till Herr E. Westermarck," *Finsk Tidskrift* 32, no. 4 (April 1892): 327-36.

[39] Rein's attempt to steer a course between Darwinism and the parallel theory can be seen more clearly in the lectures he gave to the Philosophical Society on 11 October 1889 and 14 February 1890. In the former, Rein proposed the following thesis for discussion: "If we accept the basic tenets of Darwinism, it is illogical to be a materialist, even in the sense of Spencer, for example." In the second lecture Rein spoke about "Some of the latest works in which the application of Darwinism to psychology is considered." At the meeting of 20 November 1891, when Westermarck replied to Rein's criticism of the parallel theory in *Försök till en framställning af psykologin*, Rein himself stressed once again that the parallel theory was incompatible with Darwinism. Yet it looks as though Westermarck's rejoinder obliged Rein to soften his position, because in his reply to Westermarck at the next meeting, on 4 December 1891, Rein simply says that Darwinism does not *support* the parallel theory. He expressed the same opinion in an article in *Finsk Tidskrift*.

[40] The typical Westermarckian concepts "approval" and "disapproval" are not mentioned in the minutes of this meeting. They are mentioned, however, in the minutes of the meeting held in February 1895, when free will was discussed again.

[41] Rein's use of Darwinism in attacking the supporters of the parallel theory was to some extent an attempt to pay them back in their own coin.

[42] *Memories*, p. 67; *Minnen*, p. 69.

[43] William James, "What is an Emotion?," *Mind* 9, no. 34 (April 1884): 190.

[44] In *Memories*, p. 34 (*Minnen*, p. 32), Westermarck says that during the years which followed his earlier (1891) exchange of ideas with Rein, he had modified his opinion because he found monism "untenable on account of the arbitrary way in which it handled the concept of causality. . . . " He adds that he had come to accept "empirical dualism." The minutes of the Society contradict this and we may suppose that Westermack's memory was faulty; his memoirs were written thirty years later.

[45] The somewhat inaccurate account of the discussions with Rein in the Philosophical Society which Westermarck gives in his memoirs suggests that his "idealistic" phase was superficial and short-lived. (See the previous note.)

[46] Rein, *Lefnadsminnen*, p. 260.

[47] *Memories*, pp. 32-33; *Minnen*, p. 31.

[48] *Memories*, p. 100; *Minnen*, p. 112.

[49] *ODMI*, 1: 1.

[50] Ibid.

[51] *Memories*, p. 100; *Minnen*, p. 112.

[52] *Memories*, p. 102; *Minnen*, p. 114.

[53] Darwin's theory of moral emotion is discussed more fully in *The Descent of Man and Selection in Relation to Sex*, 2 vols. (London: John Murray, 1871). See 1: 70-106, 158-84; 2: 391-94.

[54] Hugo Pipping, who was Westermarck's brother-in-law, was for some years an enthusiastic contributor to the

debates of the Philosophical Society. Unlike Neiglick and Westermarck, Pipping was a supporter of utilitarianism.

[55] Apparently Westermarck had not yet made use of the terms "approval" and "disapproval." (See note 40.)

[56] The report of the Society's meeting of 3 May 1895 also throws light on Westermarck's attitude to subjectivism and utilitarianism. The discussion was about the morality of suicide.

[57] For instance, at the meetings of 11 April 1890 and 12 February 1892.

[58] Westermarck, *Christianity and Morals* (London: Kegan Paul, Trench, Trubner & Co., 1939).

[59] (Westermarck), *Anteckningar i samhällslära enligt Dr. Edv. Westermarcks föreläsningar,* ed. Leo Ehrnrooth (Helsinki: Akademiska Bokhandeln, 1894).

[60] Quoted from minutes kept by Johannes Hedengren.

[61] In the minutes and also in *Anteckningar,* Westermarck makes a distinction between "self-contained" and "relational" emotions and considers the moral emotions to be in the latter category. I do not know whether this is Westermarck's own idea or whether he got it from some other writer. He does not advert to this distinction in *ODMI* or in his other printed works. In the 1895 lecture he refers to the discussion by Bain of the subject of "relational" feelings. So far as I know, Bain did not make this distinction between "self-contained" and "relational" feelings and he does not use these terms.

[62] According to Rolf Lagerborg, even as late as 1900 Westermarck had not studied Durkheim's ideas about morality; see his *Edvard Westermarck,* pp. 185-86, and "The Essence of Morals," p. 15. (The explanation given by Lagerborg is, however, hardly conclusive.) Perhaps it was Lagerborg himself who drew Westermarck's attention to Durkheim. Lagerborg's doctoral dissertation, *Moralens väsen* (Helsinki: Helsingfors Centraltryckeri, 1900), had appeared in 1900. In a note in *ODMI*, 1: 145, Westermarck mentions Durkheim's *De la division du travail social* and also Lagerborg's article "La nature de la morale," *Revue internationale de Sociologie* 11, nos. 5-6 (May-June 1903): 370-97, 441-72. In this note, Westermarck criticizes the idea expressed by Bain, Durkheim, and Lagerborg that morality is based on norms.

[63] See Jussi Tenkku, "Westermarck's Definition of the Concept of the Moral," *Transactions of the Westermarck Society* 9, no. 2 (1962): 25-28, 31.

[64] It does not become clear from the report whether Westermarck actually dealt with customs in the lecture of 19 April 1895. In *Anteckningar* the concept is dealt with thoroughly. He says among other things (p. 29): "Customs are those norms for conduct laid down by the organized social power, the collective will." And again (p. 41): "I define the commands of custom as the rules for conduct laid down by the collective will. I define ethical commands as the verbal expression of the collective will. Ethics, or morality, is the collective will itself."

[65] *Memories,* p. 123; *Minnen,* p. 146.

[66] Westermarck, "Remarks on the Predicates of Moral Judgments," *Mind* N.S. 9, no. 34 (April 1900): 184-204.

[67] Quoted from minutes kept by K. A. Moring.

[68] See also the analysis of the concepts "good," "virtue," "merit," "super-obligatory," and "indifferent" in *ODMI*, 1: 145-57.

[69] Perhaps this ought to read "punish the person who has done X."

[70] The wording here is taken from the Society's minutes, but it may be Westermarck's own. In any case it probably represents his thought accurately.

[71] Westermarck, "Remarks on the Predicates," p. 185. Westermarck refers here specifically to Smith.

[72] See Stroup, "Westermarck's Debt to Hume," in *Wright and Wrong: Mini-Essays in Honor of Georg Henrik von Wright,* ed. Krister Segerberg (Turku/Åbo: Åbo Akademi Forskningsinstitut, 1976), p. 79: "it is fair to remark that Westermarck's debt to Hume is greater than he admitted in his published writings. . . . "

[73] The book is the property of Professor Knut Pipping, who kindly lent it to me while I was preparing the present article.

[74] See F. J. Gould, "With Dr. Westermarck," printed in *The Literary Guide and Rationalist Review* N.S. 30 (1 December 1898): 185-87.

[75] At the University of Helsinki the chair of psychology was separated from the chair of theoretical philosophy in 1948. A permanent chair of sociology was established in 1945.

[76] (Westermarck), "Normative und Psychologische Ethik," *Dritter Internationaler Kongress für Psychologie* (Munich: Verlag von J. F. Lehmann, 1897), pp. 428-31.

[77] It should be pointed out that no records survive of the Society's proceedings for the academic years 1885-86 and 1886-87, nor for the autumn term of 1887. Neiglick was, however, abroad during the academic year 1885-86 and also during the greater part of the academic year 1886-87. This gap in the minutes is thus hardly important with regard to our knowledge of Neiglick's views, nor does it affect our knowledge of Westermarck. According to the records of membership, Westermarck joined the Society on 16 November 1888, although he could have attended meetings before that date.

[78] Extracts from the letter are quoted in Waldemar Ruin's article, "Två tänkare från vår brytningstid," in the collection *Från brytningstider: Minnen och erfarenheter II* (Helsinki: Söderström & Co., 1917), pp. 171-96.

[79] *Minnen,* p. 90. The passage does not appear in the English version.

[80] Ibid.

[81] The Student Aesthetic Society (Studenternas förening för konst och litteratur), which was founded at about that time, seems to some extent to have replaced it. That society was active up to the end of the year 1903. See Irma Rantavaara, *Yrjö Hirn I, 1870-1910* (Helsinki: Kustannusosakeyhtiö Otava, 1977), pp. 151, 166-79.

[82] It seems to be impossible to discover exactly when Rein resigned from the chairmanship of the Philosophical Society and when Grotenfelt took over. The last report in which Rein is mentioned as chairman is that of the meeting on 11 November 1898. In the report of the next meeting, on 3 March 1899, Grotenfelt is said to have been in the chair, but he does not appear to have been the official chairman. Reports of the proceedings during the year 1903 make it plain that Waldemar Ruin was then chairman. It is not until 1908 that we find Grotenfelt referred to specifically as the chairman.

[83] *Juhlajulkaisu omistettu Th. Reinille hänen täyttäessään 80 vuotta,* 28. II. 1918 (Helsinki: Kustannusosakeyhtiö Otava, 1918).

Timothy Stroup (essay date 1981)

SOURCE: "In Defense of Westermarck," in *Journal of the History of Philosophy,* Vol. XIX, No. 2, April, 1981, pp. 213-34.

[*In the following excerpt, Stroup urges modern readers to read Westermarck's work without prejudice from his critical detractors.*]

I

The history of ideas can be approached in two ways. The first treats its materials like fossils, to be unearthed as clues to the past. Occasionally these exciting discoveries shed light on current concerns, but that is by no means a necessary reward. There is instead the thrill of the search, of tracking down a neglected work, of finding an outlook that is intrinsically interesting, if not always fresh or vital. The other approach seeks out pioneers who have contributed to a continuum of intellectual progress. The aim is to establish theoretical pedigrees, to show the sources from which later refinements derive their inspiration. In some instances the stature of the innovator overshadows that of the followers, and a renascence or redirection of energies is required.

The ethical theory of the Finnish philosopher Edward Westermarck (1862-1939) repays study from either standpoint: his writings are of interest in their historical context and of value to contemporary philosophy. Yet subsequent commentators have seldom recognized either of these merits in Westermarck's work. This is not entirely true of Nordic writers, who have contributed scattered articles on his life and thought,[1] but otherwise Westermarck has suffered a shabby treatment in the four decades since his death. When he is remembered at all, it is usually by critics who attribute to him an untenable subjectivism, a paradigm of what must be avoided in analyzing ethical discourse. Most of Westermarck's interpreters have been guilty of judging him through eyeglasses—or blinders—of contemporary philosophical method or of letting their description be colored by its role in philosophical disputation. The result is distortion of the aims and orientation, as well as the substance, of Westermarck's moral philosophy, and misunderstanding can lead to easy dismissal.

Readers who come across Westermarck's work only through the filter of recent criticism may form the impression that his ethical theory consists of nothing more than a naive analysis of the meaning of moral judgments, that his massive study of moral beliefs was entitled not *The Origin and Development of the Moral Ideas* but *The Meaning of Moral Utterance.* Here are some samples of how Westermarck's theory has been described by others:

> He holds that what I am judging when I judge an action to be wrong, is merely that it is of a sort which *tends* to excite in me a peculiar kind of feeling—the feeling of moral indignation or disapproval.[2]

> [Westermarck defines] 'X is good' as 'I feel moral retributive kindly emotion towards X.'[3]

> To say that an action is reprehensible, according to Westermarck, is essentially to say: 'I have a tendency to feel moral disapproval toward the agents of all acts like this one.'[4]

> Westermarck held that when I call it [an action] right, I mean that *I* have a certain feeling about it.[5]

> According to Westermarck, every moral statement can be translated into an equivalent statement concerning the speaker's tendency to feel moral approval or disapproval. If I, for example, say 'This is bad,' and have, let us say, cruelty to animals in mind, then the statement has, according to Westermarck, the same meaning as the statement 'I have a tendency to feel moral disapproval with respect to cruelty to animals.'[6]

These authors were not the first to characterize Westermarck's view in this manner. Priority goes to Axel Hägerström, who as early as 1907 asserted that, on Westermarck's analysis, to say "that an action is good or bad means merely that it is calculated to arouse approval or disapproval."[7] Nor is Westermarck the only writer to be so described. In *Five Types of Ethical Theory* C. D. Broad claims, "Now for Hume the statement 'x is good' *means* the same as the statement 'x is such that the contemplation of it would call forth an emotion of approval towards it in all or most men.'"[8] However, there are passages in Hume which appear to support such an interpretation, for example, "So that when you pronounce any action or character to be vicious, you mean nothing, but that from the constitution of your nature you have a feeling or sentiment of blame from the contemplation of it."[9]

II

It may be instructive to reverse the usual procedure and to assess the philosophical persuasiveness of Westermarck's critics before considering their textual accuracy. Rather than first determining the extent to which their characterizations capture Westermarck's theory, it will be helpful to see what is so objectionable about the view they depict. To be sure, the critics display no consensus about the precise features of Westermarck's account, and it will make a difference in detail which picture is chosen; but for practical purposes a fairly general, inclusive formulation can be adopted, and the theory attributed to Westermarck will initially be viewed as a "plain subjectivism" which equates moral judgments with statements about the psychological tendencies of the individual who makes them.[10] This subjectivism is not so plain as it could be: talk of "tendencies" is already more sophisticated than simply identifying moral properties with existent psychological states. But a still cruder subjectivism is open to at least the same objections as this plain subjectivism, and there is little point in starting the analysis with the least tenable view, simply for the sake of completeness or to provide greater philosophical exercise along the road to plausibility.

There are many objections to plain subjectivism, some of them fatal. The classic criticism is the argument from ethical disagreement. This attack has passed through many hands: it was hinted at by Henry Sidgwick,[11] developed by G. E. Moore,[12] and today appears in a variety of contexts in the writings of many philosophers, including some of those already cited.[13] Moore's statement of the objection is as clear as any, and he specifically offers it as a criticism of Westermarck. Moore thinks that the wrongness of plain subjectivism is evident from a consideration of the nature of ordinary moral controversy. When two persons are engaged in a moral dispute, they think they are disagreeing about something. But Moore declares that the dispute would not be genuine if plain subjectivism were correct: one person would simply be describing his tendency to approve of something, another her tendency to disapprove of it. What purport to be competing ethical judgments are only lines from different autobiographies, and no contradiction occurs in their joint utterance; the "dispute" is illusory. As Moore puts it, "If two persons think they differ in opinion on a moral question . . . they are always, on this view, making a mistake, and a mistake so gross that it seems hardly possible that they should make it. . . . "[14]

Moore states the matter only in terms of ethical disagreement, but it is even more startling to criticize plain subjectivism on the grounds that it makes ethical agreement impossible. After all, sometimes the goal of engaging in an ethical dispute is to establish that the dispute is only apparent; fortunately, people are less likely to take pains to show that agreement is only apparent. Yet Moore's criticism applies equally to ethical agreement: if those who purport to agree are merely making pronouncements about their own psychological states or tendencies, how then can their statements be identical?

What can be made of Moore's point? Assume, for the time being, that he is correct in his descriptions of both ethical disagreement and the plain subjectivist analysis of moral judgments: moral argument is neither farce nor bagatelle, and for the plain subjectivist morality is reduced to psychology. Is Moore then victorious? What follows, rather, is that either the plain man or the plain subjectivist is making a "gross mistake," in Moore's words. (The "or" is, of course, non-exclusive.) Moore shows his customary preference for the plain man, but need he be so adverse to the philosopher? Admittedly, if plain subjectivism is offered as a theory of the ordinary or standard meaning of moral terms and judgments, then something is seriously wrong with it. In order to determine what, if anything, ethical judgments mean, some account has to be taken of how ethical judgments are actually used, which involves questions of what they are intended to do; and any analysis which greatly distorts the underlying psychology of moral utterance can be empirically refuted by what the plain man thinks.

But does the plain subjectivist merely report on usage? Consider the parallel case of a utilitarian who wants to equate goodness and happiness. To blunt Moore's open-question argument, the utilitarian might reply, "'Goodness' does not simply mean 'happiness.' My 'equation' is not merely tautological and trivial. It is a proposal as to how 'goodness' should be used, but it recognizes that the term has a certain allowable or fixed content. 'Goodness' does not mean just anything, but it should mean nothing more than 'happiness.'"

This may also be a tactic of the plain subjectivist, for the plain subjectivist is a moral skeptic who thinks there is nothing except psychological states to which moral judgments could refer. But it is another matter whether moral judgments therefore *do* refer to psychological states. The reduction of morality to psychology may be a challenge to revise our moral language, or at least our thinking about moral language. The trouble with such proposals, however, is that they themselves stand in need of the same justification they set out to provide. By recommending that we alter the linguistic terrain, they simply shift the justificational ground. Furthermore, viewed as an unabashedly stipulative theory of this sort, plain subjectivism grants, rather than meets, Moore's criticism, and the price may seem too high.

III

The plain subjectivist view thus has little to recommend it, either as an account of how we actually do use moral language or as a proposal about how we should use it. But was Westermarck a plain subjectivist to begin with? The answer is emphatically not, and to think otherwise mistakes the nature, extent, and direction of his account of moral judgments.

To view Westermarck as preeminently offering an account of the meaning of moral judgments is to distort the nature of his inquiry, a distortion all too understandable given subsequent meta-ethical concerns. But while Westermarck was a careful analyzer, sensitive to verbal nuance, he was no linguistic analyst in the contemporary sense. Rather, he approached ethics from the standpoint of a sociologist observing an empirical phenomenon. He wanted to determine the origins and development of moral beliefs, to investigate within a scientific, in particular an evolutionary, framework the factors which cause us to have the moral ideas we do. His overriding interest was psychological, and this is apparent from his earliest writings. In an unpublished honors thesis which he submitted in 1886 at the University of Helsinki,[15] there is a significant foreshadowing of the later features of Westermarck's thought: an effort to counter theorists of an objective ethics; an empiricist appeal to the data of moral behavior; an emphasis on the emotions, particularly the sympathetic emotions, in explaining moral ideas; and the view that civilization develops through social life, with a corresponding focus on society rather than the individual. Westermarck's formative years occurred during the end of the nineteenth century, and the predominant influences on his thought were Adam Smith, Charles Darwin, and James Frazer.[16] For more than fifteen years he was occupied with the detailed comparative research that culminated in *The Origin and Development of the Moral Ideas* (1906, 1908);[17] only a portion of the first volume is devoted to meta-ethical theorizing, the vast bulk of the work being a descriptive catalogue of moral beliefs from diverse times and places. Even Westermarck's most purely philosophical book, *Ethical Relativity* (1932),[18] is largely a restatement of views that had been settled a third of a century earlier. Consequently it is a chronological and interpretive howler to depict Westermarck's moral theory as the product of early logical positivism, as was the plain subjectivist view; instead, it is the product of an early British evolutionary sociology which stressed the empirical examination of human interaction and the influence of society and environment on behavior.

Even the language in which Westermarck's view is stated by his critics is alien to Westermarck himself. Krister Segerberg, for example, remarks that for Westermarck all moral statements can be "translated" into equivalent statements about the tendencies of the speaker.[19] Westermarck, however, seldom uses the word "translated," and he only briefly talks of "reducing" moral values to human thoughts; but clearly he does not use either word in its modern logical sense. "Translation" appears in the chapter on "The Moral Concepts" in *Ethical Relativity,* but comparison with Westermarck's later Swedish version of the passage reveals that what is meant is closer to "interpretation" or "rendering";[20] and the Swedish text eliminates, from the corresponding passage in the English original, any equivalent of the word "reduced."[21]

And where exactly can Westermarck's treatment of the meaning of moral judgments be found? The very question reveals the false emphasis given to Westermarck's account by recent critics, for, to take *Ethical Relativity* as an example, there are chapters on "The Supposed Objectivity of Moral Judgments" (which is a discussion of objectivist theories), "The Moral Emotions," "The Moral Concepts," "The Subjects of Moral Judgments" (by which Westermarck refers to those classes of things—conduct, acts, intentions, etc.—to which moral judgments are said to apply), "The Variability of Moral Judgments," and "The Emotional Background of Normative Theories." There is, however, no chapter devoted to the meaning of moral judgments, and Westermarck's discussion of this subject is relegated to two parts of the chapter on "The Moral Concepts," pages 114-17 and 141-47. Thus, the location and extent of Westermarck's treatment of ethical meaning should give some perspective to its place in his moral philosophy.

The direction of Westermarck's inquiry is also important: it proceeds from the moral emotions to the moral concepts to the moral judgments. His modern critics, however, tend to start at the end of this series and to assume that everything can be collapsed backwards. But as the progression occurs its nature changes as individual emotions become socialized and concepts take on a life of their own, and at the level of moral judgments the whole affair is a complex mixture of many components, including beliefs about ordinary matters of fact (e.g., who did what) as well as about supposed moral facts. Hence, it is highly misleading to say that Westermarck held that moral judgments only describe or express the moral emotions, or the tendencies to have moral emotions, of individuals.

IV

On the other hand, it could hardly be expected that so many eminent and intelligent critics would misinterpret Westermarck's view if the view itself were absolutely clear. It can be granted that the context and development of Westermarck's thought have seldom been known, and thus some distortion is inherent in any secondary account which considers only part of the data; and there is the obvious, if *ad hominem,* point that most of the critics do not primarily seek to understand Westermarck on his own terms, but rather use him for other expository purposes. Still, it must be conceded that what can be pieced together of Westermarck's account of the meaning of moral judgments makes a confused and confusing assemblage. There are three possible positions on the question of the truth-value of moral judgments, which correspond to differing views about their meaning and nature, and Westermarck seems at times to have held all three, despite the fact that they are mutually contradictory.

First, it can be held that moral judgments are neither true nor false. Westermarck begins *Ethical Relativity* by listing the various tenets of objectivism which he intends to dispute in the book. One of the implications of an objectivist view is that "it makes morality a matter of truth and falsity. . . . "[22] Later, after discussing the shortcomings of particular objectivist theories, Westermarck concludes that

> in my opinion the predicates of all moral judgments, all moral concepts, are ultimately based on emotions, and that, as is very commonly admitted, no objectivity can come from an emotion.[23]

Again, he states:

> But to speak, as Brentano does, of 'right' and 'wrong' emotions, springing from self-evident intuitions and having the same validity as truth and error, is only another futile attempt to objectivize our moral judgments.[24]

In *The Origin and Development of the Moral Ideas* Westermarck puts the point a little differently, but no less emphatically:

> The presumed objectivity of moral judgments thus being a chimera, there can be no moral truth in the sense in which this term is generally understood. The ultimate reason for this is, that the moral concepts are based upon emotions, and that the contents of an emotion fall entirely outside the category of truth.[25]

Second, it can be held, as the objectivist does, that moral judgments are either true or false, depending upon the particular judgment. Westermarck at times adopts such a view, but for seemingly naturalistic reasons. He observes in *The Origin and Development of the Moral Ideas* that

> it may be true or not that we have a certain emotion, it may be true or not that a given mode of conduct has a tendency to evoke in us moral indignation or moral approval. Hence a moral judgment is true or false according as its subject has or has not that tendency which the predicate attributes to it. If I say that it is wrong to resist evil, and yet resistance to evil has no tendency whatever to call forth in me an emotion of moral disapproval, then my judgment is false.[26]

And in *Ethical Relativity* he asserts:

> I thought it was generally recognized that every proposition is either true or false, and that this must consequently be the case also with the proposition 'this is good,' whatever be the meaning of its predicate. . . . If 'good' expresses a tendency to feel moral approval, then the proposition in question is, as already said, true if there really is such a tendency with regard to that of which goodness is predicated, and false if there is no such tendency—people are often hypocrites in their moral judgments.[27]

These remarks are the closest Westermarck ever comes to equating emotions and valuations, to adopting a plain subjectivist viewpoint. Even so, he thinks that it is not a proposition which expresses the emotional tendency, but rather a word or concept;[28] and his use of "expresses" is quite loose. Sometimes Westermarck does speak of moral concepts as "direct expressions"[29] of emotions, but more often he puts the relationship between a moral concept and an emotion back a stage: such concepts can be "traced back to,"[30] are "ultimately based on,"[31] emotions; emotions are "at the bottom of"[32] the moral concepts. Also, Westermarck has here confused the notions of truth and sincerity: If I say "X is good" and I approve of X, then my statement may be sincere, but it does not follow that it is true, although the statement that it is sincere may be true. The meaning of a moral judgment is not identical with the conditions under which it can be uttered sincerely.

Third, it can be held that all moral judgments are false. As W. C. Swabey has described a Westermarckian view, "Taken literally, a judgment that an action possesses rightness or wrongness would always be false."[33] Westermarck is, at one point in *Ethical Relativity,* forced into accepting this conclusion because he wants to hold three propositions which imply it: that all propositions are either true or false; that moral judgments are propositions; and that there is no moral truth. From these three assumptions it follows that moral judgments are all false, and Westermarck recognizes this:

> If, as I maintain, the objective validity of all moral valuation is an illusion, and the proposition 'this is good' is meant to imply such validity, it must always be false.[34]

There is no corresponding passage in *The Origin and Development of the Moral Ideas,* and this is an important instance in which *Ethical Relativity* goes beyond the earlier work.[35] It must be noted, however, that the passage which contains this error theory of moral judgments is not included in either of the two subsequent books which discuss moral judgments, *Christianity and Morals* and the Swedish translation of *Ethical Relativity.* But this is probably due to the nature of these last two works, rather than to a change in philosophical outlook: the former book includes only a précis of Westermarck's moral theory and the latter is in some respects an abridgement of the original.[36]

There is, thus, considerable doubt about the way in which Westermarck's theory of moral judgments should be interpreted. It may be that in reconstructing his view one "is not directly interpreting his words, but rather considering what position would be most in conformity with other aspects of his philosophy,"[37] as Páll Árdal has remarked of Hume. In what follows, therefore, two principles will be relied upon in trying to reorganize Westermarck's theory: generosity and development. According to the first principle, the least tenable view will not be attributed to Westermarck if there is another which accords as well with the textual evidence. The second principle prescribes that, within the chronological spectrum of an author's views, preference should be given to later formulations, on the obvious grounds that revisions usually indicate that prior analyses have been discarded as unsatisfactory. Both principles can, in fact, be satisfied by an examination of the record of Westermarck's writings, which shows a continuous move away from a plain subjectivist account.

V

One of Westermarck's first philosophical expositions contained an analysis of moral judgments that had elements of plain subjectivism. In his *Anteckningari samhällslära,* which were notes taken of his sociology lectures in the early 1890s, he advanced the view that "When I say that an intention is moral, this implies that I approve of the intention, and when I say that an [intention] is immoral, this implies that I disapprove of it."[38] It can be granted that there is no equivalence between moral judgments and moral emotions, but only an implication, yet neither is there any talk of tendencies. In **"The Origin and Growth of the Moral Ideas,"** an early draft of some chapters of *The Origin and Development of the Moral Ideas*, there is already some dissociation from the view that moral judgments must be accompanied by moral emotions, but there is also a good deal of confusion as to what really is going on when moral judgments are uttered. Westermarck tries, much like his critics after him, to discover a formula which is equivalent in meaning to the moral judgment, but he does so without success or consistency.[39] In *The Origin and Development of the Moral Ideas* itself the separation of existent moral emotions from moral judgments becomes complete, but tendencies are conjured up as links:

> But to attribute a quality to a thing is never the same as merely to state the existence of a particular sensation or feeling in the mind which perceives it. . . . Whilst not affirming the actual existence of any specific emotion in the mind of the person judging or of anybody else, the predicate of a moral judgment attributes to the subject a tendency to arouse an emotion.[40]

Ethical Relativity, however, marks a radical departure from the earlier accounts, because no longer are even tendencies expressed by the moral judgments. Instead, these tendencies are put back a stage and are viewed as being causally involved in the origin of the moral concepts. What happens, rather, when moral judgments are

made is that moral concepts, which ultimately have a subjective origin, are attributed as qualities to something. Westermarck's analysis here is so important that it is worth quoting at some length:

> The theory of the emotional origin of moral judgments I am here advocating does not imply that such a judgment affirms the existence of a moral emotion in the mind of the person who utters it: he may do so without feeling any emotion at all. No doubt, to say that a certain act is good or bad may be the mere expression of an emotion felt with regard to it, just as to say that the sun is hot or the weather cold may be a mere expression of a sensation of heat or cold produced by the sun or the weather. But such judgments express subjective facts in terms which strictly speaking have a different meaning. To attribute a quality to something is not the same as to state the existence of a particular emotion or sensation in the mind that perceives it. This, however, does not imply that the term used to denote the quality may not have a subjective origin. I maintain, on the contrary, that the qualities assigned to the subjects of moral judgments really are generalizations derived from approval or disapproval felt with regard to certain modes of conduct, that they are tendencies to feel one or the other of these emotions interpreted as qualities, as dynamic tendencies, in the phenomena which gave rise to the emotion. A similar translation of emotional states into terms of qualities assigned to external phenomena is found in many other cases: something is 'fearful' because people fear it, 'admirable' because people admire it. When we call an act good or bad, we do not *state* the existence of any emotional tendencies, any more than, when we call a landscape beautiful, we state any characteristics of beauty: we refer the subject of the judgment to a class of phenomena which we are used to call good or bad. But we are used to call them so because they have evoked moral approval or disapproval in ourselves or in other persons from whom we have learned the use of those words.[41]

This passage, with virtually no change in wording, reappears in the first chapter of *Christianity and Morals.*[42] It also provides the basis for the corresponding discussion in the Swedish translation of *Ethical Relativity,* but there are some variations which only serve to emphasize Westermarck's distance from plain subjectivism:

> The theory that all moral judgments are ultimately grounded on emotions does not imply that the person who utters such a judgment thereby expresses a moral emotion which he experiences on that occasion; he can do so without having any emotion at all. If I call an act good or bad, I attribute to the act a certain moral property, and this is, of course, not the same thing as saying that I experience a certain emotion on this occasion. But this by no means precludes that the property in question has a wholly subjective origin. On the contrary, I consider it to be obvious that the properties which are attributed to the subjects

of moral judgments are derived from tendencies to experience moral approval or disapproval, which formally are expressed as properties in the phenomena which call forth one or the other of these emotions.[43]

The Swedish version goes beyond the English in further dissociating the moral concepts from the moral emotions: in *Ethical Relativity* the qualities assigned by the moral predicates are "tendencies to feel one or the other of these emotions interpreted as qualities"; in the Swedish version these properties are "*derived* from tendencies."[44] At any rate, there can be little question that Westermarck, in these passages, sought to deny a plain subjectivist interpretation of his view of moral judgments.

Yet all doubt whatsoever is removed by three explicit statements in *Ethical Relativity.* In criticizing Bentham's analysis of moral concepts in terms of utility, Westermarck protests against any equation between naturalistic tendencies and moral judgments:

> Now the statement that a certain act has a tendency to promote happiness, or to cause unhappiness, is either true or false; and if rightness and wrongness are only other words for these tendencies, it is therefore obvious that the moral judgments also have objective validity. But it is impossible to doubt that anybody who sees sufficiently carefully into the matter must admit that the identification in question is due to a confusion between the meaning of terms and the use made of them when applied to acts on account of their tendencies to produce certain effects.[45]

Later, in commenting on aesthetic judgments, which, if anything, would be more prone to a plain subjectivist account because they are less objectivized, Westermarck observes:

> The aesthetic judgment makes claim to objectivity: when people say that something is beautiful, they generally mean something more than that it gives, or has a tendency to give, them aesthetic enjoyment. . . . [46]

Again in connection with aesthetic judgment, Westermarck remarks:

> He [W. D. Ross] admits that 'we do not *mean* by "beautiful" an attribute having even this sort of reference to a mind, but something entirely resident in the object, apart from relation to a mind'; but suggests that 'we are deceived in thinking that beautiful things have any such common attribute over and above the power of producing aesthetic enjoyment.' This view of beauty is precisely similar to my view of moral values. . . . [47]

Moreover, a marginal notation in Westermarck's copy of Moore's *Ethics* constitutes conclusive proof that Westermarck was not a plain subjectivist. At the passage where Moore states, "Each of us, according to this view, is merely making an assertion about *his own* feelings: when *I* assert that an action is right, the *whole* of what I mean is merely that *I* have some particular feeling towards the action . . . ,"[48] Westermarck has pencilled in an emphatic "No!"

VI

Westermarck's description of a moral judgment is this: We observe a certain action, say the taking by one person of another's money without permission. This action is of a kind which is traditionally called "theft." Theft is wrong; therefore this action is wrong:

> Particular modes of conduct have their traditional labels, many of which are learnt with language itself; and the moral judgment commonly consists simply in labelling the act according to certain obvious characteristics which it presents in common with others belonging to the same group.[49]

What is the justification for saying that theft is wrong? According to Westermarck, there is no objective justification. Why, then, do we call it wrong? To begin with, we could hardly do otherwise. As Westermarck says, "our moral consciousness belongs to our mental constitution, which we cannot change as we please."[50] We usually call theft wrong because it tends to give rise to emotions of disapproval within us and others, and because "wrong" is the term used to express disapproval; but the disapproval need not be specifically personal because we can uncritically accept value judgments from others who tend to feel disapproval or who themselves accept the judgment from still others.[51]

This is not intended as an analysis of meaning, but as a genetic account of the way in which moral words come to be used. No doubt when moral concepts first came into existence there was a fairly direct connection between them and the moral emotions. Westermarck calls such uses of moral concepts "the intrinsic meaning of the terms," and he stresses that he does not maintain that "those who use them are aware of this meaning. We are often unable to tell what is really implied in a concept we predicate to a certain phenomenon."[52] Such concepts take on a life of their own and their connection with feelings is often taken for granted or ignored; they are "mentioned without any distinct idea of their contents. The relation in which many of them stand to the moral emotions is complicated. . . . "[53] Although ultimately there is the implication, behind the use of these words, that actions of this sort tend to produce certain emotions—if there were not, sincere people would not bother to use them—there is no mere equation between their use and the emotions or emotional tendencies. On the contrary, the person who makes a moral judgment usually intends more by it than an expression of an emotion: "The enthusiast is more likely than anybody else to regard his judgments as true, and so is the moral enthusiast with reference to his moral judgments. The intensity of his emotions makes him the victim of an illusion."[54]

The relationship between moral emotions and moral judgments is far more complex, according to Westermarck, than is suggested by the plain subjectivist. More than the mere expression of emotions occurs when moral judgments are made: moral judgments contain an element of objectivizing. To the person who makes them, they are not merely subjective; rather they have objective, universal validity—they are true. Unfortunately, although Westermarck is otherwise very interested in moral psychology, he does not provide a detailed discussion of how this objectivizing occurs and what it consists of; he does not directly say much more than that objectivizing occurs when a subjective feeling is attributed as a quality to an object.[55]

But, as we might expect, he does comment on its origins.[56] A character of universality and apparent objectivity is lent to moral judgments by the comparatively uniform nature of moral beliefs, particularly within early societies, in which Westermarck thinks there was "no difference of opinion" regarding questions of morality.[57] This initial agreement is subsequently enhanced by its impression on consciousness through the medium of authority: "From our earliest childhood we are taught that certain acts *are* right and that others *are* wrong."[58] The authorities can be temporal or spiritual, personal or codified into custom, law, or public opinion. Furthermore, the tendency to assign objectivity to our subjective experience is a general, and not only a moral, propensity in mankind. Hume is the chief ancestor of Westermarck's view about objectivizing,[59] and both for him and for Westermarck objectivizing is not confined to the moral domain. If everyone observes a constant conjunction between events, the tendency is to think that the events *necessarily are* connected; if everyone experiences a sour taste from sucking a lemon, the tendency is to think that the lemon *really is* sour; if everyone, to use Westermarck's example,[60] says that a landscape is beautiful, the tendency is to think that the landscape *really is* beautiful. Whether in causal, sensory, aesthetic, or moral contexts, there is a propensity to assign the qualities we perceive to the objects to which they are related.

VII

While we could reasonably insist on a greater elaboration in *Ethical Relativity* of the concept of objectivizing, the immediate benefits of employing it in the analysis of moral judgments should be obvious. Any plain subjectivist account will fail to capture the actual meaning of moral judgments, and will have to rely on stipulative appeal. As J. D. Mabbott remarks,

> It is very easy (all too easy) to turn a beginner from being an objectivist to being a subjectivist. . . . But even the most stupid beginner is usually quite clear that he was not a subjectivist when he sat down in your armchair for treatment.[61]

This criticism does not apply to a theory which allows for objectivizing. It can be admitted that the plain man

is objectivist rather than subjectivist;[62] all that need be denied is that he is correct in so being. This, of course, requires the general refutation of objectivism, which is not the point here. There may not be any iron-clad argument to show the plain man's mistake, but only a fabric of persuasive arguments of the sort that Westermarck adduces in the first two chapters of *Ethical Relativity.* The present point is only that, by adopting the notion of objectivizing, Westermarck is able to counter Moore's attack and at the same time to give at least a partial account of the way in which moral judgments are used.

For Westermarck does defend himself, and rather well at that. In presenting an example in which one person says that some food is disagreeable and another person says that the same food is not disagreeable, he writes:

> We should undoubtedly assert that they have different opinions about it. On Professor Moore's view this shows that the two persons do not merely judge about their feelings but state that the food really is, or is not, disagreeable, and if they admitted that they only expressed their own feelings—as they most probably would if their statements were challenged—and yet thought that they differed in opinion, they would make a mistake almost too great to be possible. For my own part I venture to believe that most people would find it absurd if they *denied* that they had different opinions about the food. This follows from the fact that the subjective experience has been objectivized in the speech as a quality attributed to the object, and seems the more natural on account of the ambiguous meaning which the word 'opinion' has in common parlance, where it is used both for a judgment and for the expression of a feeling.[63]

The key word here is "objectivized." One person says the food is disagreeable, another that it is not disagreeable. Assume in this case that the relationship between the feelings and the moral judgments of the disputants is fairly straightforward, and that they make their judgments not automatically, insincerely, or because of tendencies, but with real fondness for and aversion to the food. And assume also, for the sake of simplicity, that agreeableness is broad enough to encompass indifference, so that agreeableness and disagreeableness would be logically incompatible and exhaustive if their attribution succeeded at all.

Of what, then, do the opinions in question consist? If we distinguish between the feeling and its objectification, do we reserve the term "opinion" only for the objectification, or does it apply to the whole bundle of feeling-plus-objectification, or can it stand for the feeling alone? Westermarck complains that the term is ambiguous; but Moore, in distinguishing between feeling and opinion, uses the latter term to refer to what Westermarck calls the objectification only. The disputants' difference of opinion is then more psychological than logical, because neither opinion is in fact true. Our conviction that the opinions differ results from the act of objectivizing. To say that the food is disagreeable is not to contradict a person who claims that it is agreeable. Both statements, indeed, embody the same false assumption: namely, that there is some property of disagreeableness or agreeableness inherent in the food. If the assumption were correct, the two statements would be contradictories; and it is the ignoring of the falsity of the assumption which makes the apparent contradictoriness of the statements seem actual.

Rather than "opinion," perhaps it is "differ" which is the troublesome word. Do the opinions of the disputants differ? If "differ" implies logical contradiction, then they do not differ, although they do something rather like differing: they make the same mistake of objectivizing which, it if were not a mistake, would have the consequence that they would differ in the strict sense. The disputants have the same false presuppositions in common: they assume that their moral claims describe actual properties of things and that the only point of disagreement is whether the thing has one property or another. There is an error in moral discourse, but it is subtler than Moore's "gross mistake": moral antagonists do not confuse attribution with expression, objectification with feeling; by tacitly "agreeing to disagree" they incorporate an objectivist ontology into their ethical language.

These considerations are sufficient to thwart Moore's criticism. He says, "Don't people, in fact, sometimes really differ in opinion on a moral question? Certainly all appearances are in favour of the view that they do. . . . "[64] But Moore cannot legitimately—that is, without begging the question—conclude that the facts of ethical dispute entail that the disputants really differ and not that they only do something like differing. His moral controversy argument succeeds only when objectivism is presupposed. The point here is not original; it was made more than two hundred years ago by Richard Price:

> It would, I doubt, be to little purpose to plead further here, the natural and universal apprehensions of mankind, that our ideas of right and wrong belong to the understanding, and denote real characters of actions; because it will be easy to reply, that they have a like opinion of the *sensible qualities* of bodies; and that nothing is more common than for men to mistake their own sensations for the properties of the objects producing them, or to apply to the object itself, what they find always accompanying it, whenever observed.[65]

Price's comment is interesting because it suggests that an appeal to our tendency to objectivize may have been a fairly standard ploy of his times, an "easy" and obvious reply to those who tried to base objective theories on common sense. Price had long before dismissed as useless the very argument that Moore and others later made so much of, even though Price and Moore were roughly on the same side of the ethical fence.

Viewed in this perspective, it is difficult to see how Moore's argument ever gets off the ground, because in order for two propositions to be contradictories one must be true and the other false, and that is precisely what is at issue over ethical objectivism. Consequently, Moore does not even claim quite this; rather, his argument is one of belief: we *think* that contradiction goes on in moral dispute. But what we believe is no conclusive proof of what actually occurs. If it were, the appeal to apparent contradiction would itself be unnecessary, because there is a general belief, at least implicitly, in the existence of objective ethical principles. Westermarck himself entered just this defense: nothing in the mere dictates of common sense in favor of moral objectivity can guarantee such objectivity. He makes this point in discussing criticisms by W. R. Sorley and Hastings Rashdall, but it holds equally for Moore:

> The whole argument is really reduced to the assumption that an idea—in this case the idea of the validity of moral judgments—which is generally held, or held by more or less advanced minds, must be true: people claim objective validity for the moral judgment, therefore it must possess such validity. The only thing that may be said in favour of such an argument is, that if the definition of a moral proposition implies the claim to objectivity, a judgment that does not express this quality cannot be a moral judgment; but this by no means proves that moral propositions so defined are true—the predicated objectivity may be a sheer illusion.[66]

Indeed, on Westermarck's account that is exactly what happens: our moral claims fail to state genuine, objective moral properties, but rather disclose the objectivizing tendencies of the persons who utter them. The common sense belief in moral objectivity does show, however, that any theory of moral discourse which attempts to capture the facts of moral psychology must allow for objectivizing, and hence that plain subjectivism is an inadequate analysis of moral meaning.

VIII

By adopting a notion of objectivizing and by putting some distance between moral judgments and moral emotions, it is possible to arrive at an account of moral judgments that avoids the obvious pitfalls of plain subjectivism. But such an account is not thereby a complete analysis of moral judgments. Westermarck was hardly in a position to offer such an analysis. In part he was a captive of his times, although this excuse is somewhat less applicable to his account in *Ethical Relativity*. He says there, "I thought it was generally recognized that every proposition is either true or false, and that this must consequently be the case also with the proposition 'this is good,' whatever be the meaning of its predicate."[67] There is no indication in any of his writings, despite the passages referred to earlier, that Westermarck ever *seriously* considered the possibility of a non-propositional theory of moral judgments.[68] To admit non-propositional elements into his account would have in no way jeopardized Westermarck's skepticism. Hägerström, also a non-objectivist, held such a view, although admittedly his approach was more radical and less sociological and empirical.[69] Nor would it have diminished the value of Westermarck's detection of the process of objectivizing, for there is no need to think that there is only one thing that goes on in moral discourse. Ethical judgments have a wide variety of uses: the imperative, the interjective or expressive, the prescriptive, the reportive, the persuasive, and the purportedly objective. Any account which tries to reduce moral language to only one of these functions will distort its subject, and will be prone to a number of legitimate attacks from opposing ethical camps. There is no single use, and efforts to find a simple formula which is equivalent in meaning to all moral judgments are misguided.

But this should not obscure the significant contribution of Westermarck, who was one of the few non-objectivist moral philosophers to call attention to what is one of the most common uses of moral judgments: to make purportedly objective claims.[70] In a time in which non-propositional accounts have had wide influence, it is a helpful corrective to recall this important function of moral language. Westermarck's account of moral judgments was confused because he never understood all of the functions of ethical discourse, but he did understand some of the functions, and in particular some which have eluded both the plain subjectivist and Westermarck's critics.

The main point which emerges above all others from this discussion is that it is necessary to guard against simplifying and distorting Westermarck's view by assimilating it to plain subjectivism: it is essential to overcome the temptation to say that Westermarck simply equated moral judgments with descriptions of the emotions or emotional tendencies. Here a principle of G. H. von Wright's can be invoked: "When one criticizes Westermarck's theory of the moral judgment, one should remember that Westermarck nowhere explicitly says that a sentence about moral value *means the same as* a sentence about a moral valuation."[71] Of course, the principle is somewhat too strong, because it applies, strictly speaking, only to Westermarck's later writings (although these are the very writings to which all the critics refer); but it does state an ideal for interpreting his mature moral philosophy: any mere equation between moral judgments and sentences about moral emotions should be abjured, whether the *definiens* is conceived of as an expression or as an assertion, as an outburst of feeling or as a report of feeling. It is important to recognize that Westermarck was not overly preoccupied with translations, reductions, and definitions of moral judgments;[72] he was more interested in origins, in causation.

IX

From this observation it does not follow that Westermarck committed the genetic fallacy. Indeed, what the genetic fallacy itself consists of is none too clear, because the term is often brandished merely to intimidate, without any precise indication of the nature of the charge being made.[73] Insofar as it calls attention to a crudely *ad hominem* attack against the personal characteristics of an opponent,[74] the genetic fallacy is wisely avoided, as Westermarck, of course, did. More plausibly, however, the imputation of geneticism may be an objection to confusing the present condition of a phenomenon with its original condition; causal explanation with the analysis of meaning; genetic context with truth and falsity; or fact with justification. In each of these cases, no valid complaint can be brought against Westermarck.

Westermarck was not concerned with origins alone, but with origins and development, and the very inquiry into the origins and development of a phenomenon cannot get started unless some distinction is made between the phenomenon and its history.[75] He held that the development of moral ideas entails that their present nature is in many respects different from their origin. On the other hand, moral beliefs do not spring up startlingly *ex nihilo,* but rather arise within a context which must be understood if the observer is to grasp their full import.

Nor did Westermarck confuse meaning with causation, if only because he was not primarily concerned with the meaning of moral judgments. As Kai Nielsen correctly asserts, Westermarck "had no very clear theory about the logical status of moral utterances. His value as a moral philosopher lay elsewhere."[76] Westermarck did have some insight into the function of moral judgments: he held that, in typical instances such as "Lying is wrong," they *attribute* a predicate to a subject. To this logical observation he appended a psychological explanation of the significance of the predicate or moral concept. For Westermarck there was more to moral philosophy than the treatment of moral utterances; in his work there is evident the difference "between those who want to make the analysis of the meaning of terms central to the philosophic enterprise, and those who prefer a broader view."[77] Westermarck was a consistent empiricist who approached moral phenomena as data which required a scientific explanation; he was not an analyst of the logic of moral discourse. By thinking that he collapsed value judgments directly into moral emotions, Westermarck's critics have made it easy to accuse him of a fallaciously genetic approach. By distinguishing between the two, it is possible to see how a framework which explains the phenomena of moral behavior in general will thereby provide some hints about the phenomena of moral language in particular.

Furthermore, it can be admitted that one cannot determine whether moral judgments are true simply by determining how they originate, but this does not imply that the two inquiries are unrelated. For a Westermarckian empiricist a judgment will be true if it corresponds to the facts; but moral facts have a peculiar elusiveness, and the skeptic can account for moral behavior without them by pointing to facts about human psychology. This sort of evidence is a supplement to, not a substitute for, the independent attack that Westermarck offered to show the failure of objective theorists to establish their claims.

Finally, having an understanding of the genesis of a person's moral beliefs is different from having a justification for those beliefs, but it is unlikely that a moral skeptic would commit this sort of genetic fallacy, since skepticism itself typically relies on the "is"-"ought" distinction in separating scientific and norm-active ethics. However, the distinction between fact and value can be recognized without disparaging the importance of facts to meta-ethics. Just as any non-stipulative definition must have some basis in the facts of linguistic usage, so also must any meta-ethical system have some basis in the facts of moral behavior. Even an ideal, imperative, normative morality, in telling us how we *should* act, must have some limit put on its content by the consideration of how we *can* act, which is a factual matter. At the meta-ethical level the role of fact is even more apparent. Non-vacuous theories will have some observable consequences and particular ethical epistemologies will have implications for actual moral disagreement. Ethical theories can ignore the facts of moral behavior only at the risk of encountering problematic anomalies; as Richard Brandt has observed:

> . . . it is awkward to say that ethical insight into what is fitting in particular situations is somehow an 'intuitive apprehension of an objective fact,' and at the same time to admit that some psychologists are right in supposing that one's particular 'insights' derive from the values of one's father and are a result of 'identification' with him (and would have been quite different if one's father's values had happened to be different).[78]

Meta-ethics cannot afford to isolate itself from all descriptive concerns.

X

The connection between empirical phenomena and ethical analysis is not merely negative. Westermarck's approach is skeptical in that he denies a normative moral reality; but in another sense Westermarck is a lot less skeptical about morality than are many of his opponents. Too often the claim that intuition provides genuine insight into morality serves only to limit the inquiry. Like the uncritical application of a notion of instinct in biology, intuition may lead to sterility in analysis; for if some moral concepts are indeed indefinable and known only through intuitive reflection, then there may not be too much more to say about them. On the other hand, an empiricist account like Westermarck's is able to comment with richness of detail about the actual facts of moral behavior. By foregoing Moral Facts the analysis can center on facts about morality; and Moorean opponents are not much more forthcoming about Moral Facts anyway, except to assert that they exist. This point was well made by Samuel Alexander in a review of **Ethical Relativity:**

> In these days when ethical works pour out from Oxford and Cambridge and elsewhere in a brilliant reactionary flood to prove that no account can be given of good or right it is a refreshment to have a writer who attempts to throw light on right and wrong and good by tracing them back to their origin. True enough, we cannot explain the flavour of good any more than we can explain why red is red. Yet just as we learn something vital about red by discovering its wave-length, so psychology and anthropology may give us vital and also hopeful knowledge about the nature of morals.[79]

Westermarck's account, therefore, is an attempt to view moral language as part of moral behavior generally and to trace behavior back to its ultimate psychological and biological roots. In doing this it succeeds in offering "a theory that, without any need for objective moral truths, covers the facts completely."[80]

But Westermarck's view has too frequently been distorted by mistaking the character of his inquiry. He did not approach moral philosophy as a latter-day linguistic analyst, but as an empirical social theorist who wrote his chief works in the first third of the twentieth century. In some respects there have been great advances in method since Westermarck's time, and these have encouraged neglect and misunderstanding of his position. From the standpoint of the history of ideas this is unfortunate, because knowledge of Westermarck's role in the early development of the sociology of morals enriches our perception of an intellectual epoch. But also from the standpoint of substantive contributions it is regrettable that Westermarck's work has been given an unfair hearing, for he had much to say about moral philosophy which could improve those dominant theories of the subject which have overlooked him.

It has, however, been all too tempting to resurrect Westermarck, if at all, in order to use him as a whipping-boy in the furtherance of some alternative position. Consequently, the main conclusions of his ethics are perverted and the details never get considered at all. In order to secure an audience for the many insights which Westermarck offered into human moral experience, it will be necessary to overcome the influence of "that class of controversialists who hold that we should reply not to what our adversary actually said, but to what he ought to have said if we are to triumph over him."[81]

NOTES

This is a revised version of a talk given at the University of Helsinki and the Åbo Akademi in April 1976.

[1] George Henrik von Wright, "Edvard Westermarck och Filosofiska föreningen," *Ajatus* 27 (1965): 123-61, and "Om moraliska föreställningars sanning," in *Vetenskapens funktion i samhället* (Copenhagen: Munksgaard, 1954), pp. 48-74; K. Rob. V. Wikman, "Edward Westermarck as Anthropologist and Sociologist," *Transactions of the Westermarck Society* 9, no. 1 (1962):

7-17, and "Edvard Westermarcks etiska relativitetsteori," *Societas Scientiarum Fennica Årsbok* 21B, no. 1 (1942-43) 1-20; Yrjö Hirn, "Edward Westermarck and His English Friends," *Transactions of the Westermarck Society* 1 ((1947): 39-51; Rolf Lagerborg, *Om Edvard Westermarck och verkan från hans verkstad under hans tolv sista år 1927-1939* (Helsinki: Svenska Litteratursällskapets i Finland Förlag, 1951); Krister Segerberg, "Moores kritik av Westermarck," *Årsskrift utgiven av Åbo Akademi* 56 (1971-72): 74-80; Jussi Tenkku, "Westermarck's Definition of the Concept of the Moral," *Transactions of the Westermarck Society* 9, no. 2 (1962): 21-35.

2 G. E. Moore, *Philosophical Studies* (London: Kegan Paul, Trench, Trubner & Co., 1922), p. 332.

3 Erik Stenius, "Definitions of the Concept 'Value-Judgment,'" *Theoria* 21, no. 2-3 (1955): 136.

4 Richard B. Brandt, *Ethical Theory: The Problems of Normative and Critical Ethics* (Englewood Cliffs, N.J.: Prentice-Hall, 1959), p. 166. An expanded formulation is given later in the same paragraph; see also p. 278.

5 Brand Blanshard, *Reason and Goodness* (London: George Allen & Unwin, 1961), p. 104. Blanshard does, however, recognize that Westermarck "never accepted the view held by the more extreme positivists that such judgment expresses *nothing but* emotion. It is not an exclamation merely; it is a genuine judgment, with its own truth or falsity. Still, as made by the plain man, he holds that its concepts are bogus concepts . . ." (p. 128).

6 Segerberg, p. 74. Similar characterizations are found in Morris Ginsberg, "The Life and Work of Edward Westermarck," *The Sociological Review* 32, no. 1-2 (January-April, 1940): 12; Roderick Firth, "Ethical Absolutism and the Ideal Observer," *Philosophy and Phenomenological Research* 12, no. 3 (March, 1952): 320; Paul Edwards, *The Logic of Moral Discourse* (New York: The Free Press, 1955), p. 55; Sven Krohn, *Die normative Wertethik in ihre Beziehung zur Erkenntnis und zur Idee der Menschheit.* Annales Universitatis Turkuensis B:69 (Turku: Turun Yliopisto, 1958), p. 119; von Wright, *Logik, filosofi och språk: Strömingar och gestalter i modern filosofi* (Stockholm: Bonniers, 1957), pp. 162, 208-9, and *The Varieties of Goodness,* International Library of Philosophy and Scientific Method (London: Routledge & Kegan Paul, 1963), p. 72; Konrad Marc-Wogau, *Studier till Axel Hägerströms filosofi,* Föreningen Verdandi (Falköping: Gummessons Boktryckeri, 1968), p. 23; and David A. J. Richards, *A Theory of Reasons for Action* (Oxford: Clarendon Press, 1971), p. 63.

7 Axel Hägerström, "I moralpsykologiska frågor," *Psyke* 2, no. 5 (1907): 274.

8 C. D. Broad, *Five Types of Ethical Theory,* International Library of Psychology, Philosophy and Scientific Method (London: Kegan Paul, Trench, Trubner & Co., 1930), pp. 84-85.

9 David Hume, *A Treatise of Human Nature,* ed. L. A. Selby-Bigge (Oxford: Clarendon Press, 1967), p. 469 (3.1.1). A quite different picture of Hume emerges when objectivizing elements in his account are emphasized; see note 59 below and especially J. L. Mackie, *Hume's Moral Theory.* International Library of Philosophy (London: Routledge & Kegan Paul, 1980).

10 More commonly Westermarck is described as a naturalist. For example, Carl Wellman, *The Language of Ethics* (Cambridge: Harvard University Press, 1961), p. 23: "Ethical naturalism has been ably represented by such men as Schlick and Perry. Westermarck, if one could pin down his careless writing, would probably belong in this category as well"; Charles L. Stevenson, *Facts and Values: Studies in Ethical Analysis* (New Haven: Yale University Press, 1963), p. 3: "The usual naturalistic theories of ethics that stress attitudes—such as those of Hume, Westermarck, Perry, Richards, and so many others—stress disagreement in belief no less than the rest"; and Brandt, p. 278: "He [Westermarck] is a naturalist and therefore thinks that the rational method for answering the questions of ethics is the method of science." If "naturalism" involves merely a scientific approach to ethics, then the term is appropriate for Westermarck; but if it entails an attitudinal objectivism, then it is similar to what is here referred to as "plain subjectivism." Perry himself saw that Westermarck was not this sort of naturalist; see his *General Theory of Value: Its Meaning and Basic Principles Construed in Terms of Interest* (New York: Longmans, Green and Company, 1926), p. 521.

11 Henry Sidgwick, *The Methods of Ethics,* 7th ed. (London: Macmillan and Co., 1907), p. 27.

12 Moore, pp. 333-35.

13 See A. C. Ewing, *The Definition of Good* (New York: The Macmillan Company, 1947), p. 5; Geoffrey Hunter, "Hume on 'Is' and 'Ought,'" *Philosophy* 37, no. 140 (April, 1962): 151-52; Jonathan Harrison, "Ethical Subjectivism," *The Encyclopedia of Philosophy,* ed. Paul Edwards, 8 vols. (New York: The Macmillan Company and the Free Press, 1967), 3:78-79; Richard Norman, *Reasons for Actions: A Critique of Utilitarian Rationality* (Oxford: Basil Blackwell, 1971), pp. 127-33; Bernard Williams, *Morality: An Introduction to Ethics* (New York: Harper & Row, 1972), p. 15. Moore's argument is accepted as convincing by Konrad Marc-Wogau, *Kritiska studier i socialfilosofi och etik* (Uppsala: Appelbergs Boktryckeriaktiebolag, 1939), pp. 106-7; von Wright, *Logik, filosofi och språk,* p. 209; and Blanshard, pp. 137-38.

14 Moore, p. 333. Moore also resorts to the moral controversy argument in *Ethics,* Home University Library of Modern Knowledge (London: Williams and Norgate,

1912), p. 101, where he says of two moral disputants, "They are no more contradicting one another than if, when onè had said, 'I like sugar,' the other had answered, '*I don't* like sugar.'" Von Wright has remarked (in conversation) that Moore told him that the chapter on "The Objectivity of Moral Judgments" in *Ethics* was in large measure written in response to Westermarck.

[15] Edward Westermarck, "Gör kulturen människoslägtet lyckligare?" Box 77, Edward Westermarck Papers, Åbo Akademi Library, Åbo (Turku), Finland. Hereafter cited as "EWP."

[16] See "The Influences on Westermarck's Thought," in Timothy Stroup, "Westermarck's Ethics" (D. Phil. thesis, Oxford University, 1977), pp. 153-87.

[17] Westermarck, *The Origin and Development of the Moral Ideas,* 2 vols. (London: Macmillan and Co., 1906-8). Hereafter cited as *"ODMI."*

[18] Westermarck, *Ethical Relativity,* International Library of Psychology, Philosophy and Scientific Method (London: Kegan Paul, Trench, Trubner & Co., 1932). Hereafter cited as *"ER."*

[19] Segerberg, p. 74.

[20] *ER,* p. 114; Westermarck, *Etisk relativism* (Helsinki: Söderström & Co., 1949), p. 69. Westermarck was a Swedish-speaking Finn who wrote most of his major works in English.

[21] *ER,* p. 3; Westermarck, *Etisk relativism,* p. 5.

[22] *ER,* p. 3.

[23] Ibid., p. 60.

[24] Ibid., p. 61.

[25] *ODMI,* 1:17. The same point is made in Westermarck, *Memories of My Life,* trans. Anna Barwell (London: George Allen & Unwin, 1929), p. 101.

[26] *ODMI,* 1:17-18.

[27] *ER,* p. 142.

[28] Segerberg, p. 77, n. 3, rightly notes that "it actually is the moral concepts and the moral emotions which are central to Westermarck's analysis, not moral statements."

[29] *ODMI,* 1:4.

[30] Ibid., p. 6.

[31] Ibid., p. 4; *ER,* pp. xvii, 60, 62.

[32] *ODMI,* 1:131.

[33] William Curtis Swabey, "Westermarckian Relativity," *Ethics* 52, no. 2 (January, 1942):226.

[34] *ER,* p. 142.

[35] On the contrary, there is a curious paragraph in *ODMI,* 1:105, in which Westermarck states that the assumption that moral judgments are shared by all who have a "sufficiently developed" moral consciousness "cannot, consequently, be regarded as a *conditio sine quá non* for a moral judgment, unless, indeed, it be maintained that such a judgment, owing to its very nature, is necessarily a chimera—an opinion which, to my mind, would be simply absurd."

[36] Westermarck, *Christianity and Morals* (London: Kegan Paul, Trench, Trubner & Co., 1939), and *Etisk relativism.* Hence, more than this one passage is missing from the chapter of the Swedish version. Westermarck ends the discussion at the equivalent of p. 141 of the English text, omitting in its entirety his reply to critics, pp. 141-47.

[37] Páll S. Árdal, *Passion and Value in Hume's Treatise,* (Edinburgh: Edinburgh University Press, 1966), p. 212.

[38] Leo Ehrnrooth, ed., *Anteckningar i samhällslära enligt Dr. Edv. Westermarcks föreläsningar* (Helsinki: Akademiska Bokhandeln, 1894), p. 38.

[39] Westermarck, "The Origin and Growth of the Moral Ideas," Addenda, EWP.

[40] *ODMI,* 1:4.

[41] *ER,* pp. 114-15. On p. 231 Westermarck appears to lapse momentarily into a view that ties tendencies to judgments rather than to concepts, but this is probably no more than a careless way of distinguishing between tendencies and existing emotions.

[42] Westermarck, *Christianity and Morals,* p. 15.

[43] Westermarck, *Etisk relativism,* p. 69.

[44] Emphasis added.

[45] *ER,* p. 5.

[46] Ibid., p. 48.

[47] Ibid., p. 145, n. 54.

[48] Moore, *Ethics,* p. 89. The italics are Moore's own. Westermarck's copy of the book is in the Åbo Akademi Library.

[49] *ODMI,* 1:9.

[50] *ER,* pp. 58-59. Adam Smith comments that "the sentiments of moral approbation and disapprobation, are

founded on the strongest and most vigorous passions of human nature. . . . " Smith, *The Theory of Moral Sentiments,* ed. D. D. Raphael and A. L. Macfie (Oxford: Clarendon Press, 1976), p. 200 (V.2.1.).

[51] *ODMI,* 1:3.

[52] *ER,* p. 116.

[53] *ODMI,* 1:5.

[54] Ibid., p. 17.

[55] *ER,* p. 117. There is a good account in Blanshard, pp. 108-9.

[56] *ER,* pp. 49-57; *ODMI,* 1:8-17.

[57] *ER,* p. 50; *ODMI,* 1:9.

[58] *ER,* pp. 50-51; *ODMI,* 1:14.

[59] Hume stated that taste "has a productive faculty, and gilding or staining all natural objects with the colours, borrowed from internal sentiment, raises in a manner a new creation." Hume, *An Enquiry concerning the Principles of Morals,* in *Enquiries concerning the Human Understanding and concerning the Principles of Morals,* ed. L. A. Selby-Bigge, 2nd ed. (Oxford: Clarendon Press, 1962), p. 294 (Appendix 1.5). See also Hume, *Treatise,* p. 470 (3.1.2): "Morality, therefore, is more properly felt than judg'd of; tho' this feeling or sentiment is commonly so soft and gentle, that we are apt to confound it with an idea, according to our common custom of taking all things for the same, which have any near resemblance to each other." An awareness of Hume's recognition of objectivizing may go some way towards solving problems of interpretation of the sort raised by Harrison in *Hume's Moral Epistemology* (Oxford: Clarendon Press, 1976), pp. 110-25, under the heading "Five views that might have been Hume's."

[60] *ER,* p. 115.

[61] J. D. Mabbott, *An Introduction to Ethics* (London: Hutchinson University Library, 1966), p. 99. The pre-philosophical moralist is not aware of this tendency to objectivize and does not think of moral judgments as mere descriptions or expressions of emotions. As Hume notes, "We do not infer a character to be virtuous, because it pleases: But in feeling that it pleases after such a particular manner, we in effect feel that it is virtuous." Hume, *Treatise,* p. 471 (3.1.2). The relation between emotion and judgment is more direct at the level of causation than of meaning.

[62] Westermarck talks of "the objective validity ascribed to them [moral judgments] by both common sense and by normative theories of ethics." *ER,* p. xvii. Moore—strangely—says that the plain subjectivist view is "very commonly held. . . . " Moore, *Ethics,* p. 87. In the margin of his copy Westermarck has noted "not the ordinary or common view!" This is not to deny that ordinary speakers often, and perhaps increasingly, pay lip-service to a surface relativism, rooted in naive tolerance, which is inconsistent with their deeper objectivism.

[63] *ER,* pp. 143-44. The example is obviously a poor one for the discussion of *moral* disagreement, but that does not affect the point at hand.

[64] Moore, *Philosophical Studies,* p. 334.

[65] Richard Price, *A Review of the Principle Questions in Morals,* ed. D. D. Raphael (Oxford: Clarendon Press, 1974), pp. 45-46. Mackie points out this passage in *Hume's Moral Theory,* p. 136.

[66] *ER,* p. 47. Westermarck cites (p. 42) Moore's own statement: "That a proposition appears to be true can never be a valid argument that true it really is." Moore, *Principia Ethica* (Cambridge: Cambridge University Press, 1903), p. 143.

[67] *ER,* p. 142.

[68] Segerberg, p. 77, thinks that there may be traces of value-nihilism, i.e., non-cognitivism, in Westermarck's writings, although he opts for a plain subjectivist characterization. A weaker claim has been made by Richard T. Garner and Bernard Rosen, *Moral Philosophy: A Systematic Introduction to Normative Ethics and Meta-Ethics* (New York: The Macmillan Company, 1967), p. 246, that "the correct conclusion is probably that he would have been a non-cognitivist had he seen that consistency required it. . . . "

[69] Hägerström, "I moralpsykologiska frågor"; *Om moraliska föreställningars sanning* (Stockholm: Albert Bonniers Förlag, 1911); and *Moralpsykologi* (Stockholm: Natur och Kultur, 1952).

[70] Notions of objectivizing can be found in Alexander Sutherland, *The Origin and Growth of the Moral Instinct,* 2 vols. (London: Longmans, Green, and Co., 1898), 2:316, 319; Hägerström, "Kritiska punkter i värdepsykologien," in *Festskrift tillägnad E. O. Burman på hans 65-års dag* (Uppsala: K. W. Appelbergs Boktryckeri, 1910), pp. 16-75; J. L. Mackie, "A Refutation of Morals," *Australasian Journal of Psychology and Philosophy* 24, no. 1-2 (September, 1946):77-90, and *Ethics: Inventing Right and Wrong* (Harmondsworth: Penguin Books, 1977); Richard Robinson, "The Emotive Theory of Ethics," in *Logical Positivism and Ethics,* Aristoleian Society Supplementary Volume 22 (London: Harrison and Sons, 1948), pp. 79-106; Leon Petrażycki, *Law and Morality,* trans. Hugh W. Babb, Twentieth Century Legal Philosophy Series 7 (Cambridge: Harvard University Press, 1955); and Harrison, "Moral Scepticism," Aristotelian Society Supplementary Volume 41 (London: Harrison and Sons, 1967), pp. 199-214.

[71] Von Wright, "Om moraliska föreställningars sanning," p. 54.

[72] Thus Perry, p. 130, wrongly asserts that Westermarck "attempted to *define* moral values in *terms* of moral opinion."

[73] The discussion of Rollo Handy, "The Genetic Fallacy and Naturalistic Ethics," *Inquiry* 2, no. 1 (Spring, 1959):25-33, and Norwood Russell Hanson, "The Genetic Fallacy Revisited," *American Philosophical Quarterly* 4, no. 2 (April, 1967):101-13, attempt to bring needed exactness to this field. Some of the comments which follow draw upon Handy.

[74] For examples, see Hanson, p. 101.

[75] Westermarck's recognition of this distinction is shown by his talk of the "intrinsic meaning" of terms (*ER,* p. 116) and by his comment (*ODMI,* 1:3) that "a moral estimate often survives the cause from which it sprang."

[76] Kai Nielsen, "Varieties of Ethical Subjectivism," *Danish Yearbook of Philosophy* 7 (1970): 85.

[77] Handy, p. 27. Handy does not apply this characterization specifically to Westermarck.

[78] Brandt, p. 115.

[79] Samuel Alexander, "Disinterested Resentment," *Manchester Guardian* 26, no. 759 (June 13, 1932):5. Westermarck himself put the point this way: "For while a moral intuition can be no more explained than a mathematical axiom, a moral emotion *can* be explained, as a particular emotional attitude arising under definite conditions. We can say *why* it arises, our mental constitution being such as it is, and the moral judgment may thereby be traced to its ultimate source." *ER,* p. 263.

[80] Blanshard, p. 120. Blanshard, of course, thinks that Westermarck's efforts are unsuccessful.

[81] Havelock Ellis, *Views and Reviews: A Selection of Uncollected Articles, 1884-1932,* vol. 2 (London: Desmond Harmsworth, 1932), p. 168; cited in Westermarck, *Three Essays on Sex and Marriage* (London: Macmillan and Co., 1934), p. 163.

Morris Ginsberg (essay date 1982)

SOURCE: "The Life and Work of Edward Westermarck," in *Acta Philosophica Fennica,* Vol. 34, 1982, pp. 1-22.

[*In the following excerpt, originally published in 1940, Ginsberg presents an overview of Westermarck's life and work.*]

Edward Westermarck was born in Helsinki on 20 November 1862. His father was the University Bursar, Nils Christian Westermarck, whose family moved to Finland from Sweden during the first half of the eighteenth century. By temperament reserved and outwardly cold, he yet evidently took a warm interest in his son's scientific aspirations and gave him complete freedom in the choice of his career. His mother was the daughter of Alexander Blomqvist, professor of the History of Learning and University Librarian. In contrast to his father, she had a sunny disposition which Westermarck in a great measure inherited. His memory of her was clearly dominated by a feeling of infinite devotion and affection. As a child Westermarck suffered from chronic catarrh complicated by asthma, and this prevented him from sharing in the normal active life of children of his own age and later from taking part in games and sports at school.

As an undergraduate Westermarck early developed an antipathy to German metaphysics, which, he concluded, "gave the impression of depth because it was so muddy." He was, on the other hand, greatly attracted by the English empiricists, where he found clearness and a sense of reality, and above all a readiness to test all hypotheses in the light of experience. In close connection with his philosophical studies Westermarck was deeply interested in religious questions, and here he was greatly influenced by Spencer's *First Principles* and Mill's essays on religion which he read in a Swedish translation. He rapidly became an agnostic and remained so for the rest of his life. In his later elaborate studies of religion there is to be detected, beneath the outwardly calm and detached exposition, a persistent mood of irritation and hostility. Yet in a deeper sense he was not without religious feeling. He retained throughout life a sense of the unfathomable mystery of the world and of the inherent limitations of human knowledge, but the only expression he found for this feeling was in music. Any attempt to embody it in a formulated creed was bound in his view to be tainted with anthropomorphism, and he even regarded all such efforts as blasphemous. His attitude to death and immortality was one of humble submission to the unknowable and acceptance of the inevitable, an attitude which again can hardly be described as irreligious.

The plan of writing a work on the origin and development of moral ideas came to Westermarck during the discussions at a philosophical society led by his teacher, Professor Thiodolf Rein, by whose candid and humble search for truth he was evidently deeply moved. The problem, however, on which he began to work was the limited one of the nature and origin of sexual modesty. He approached this along evolutionary lines. He made himself thoroughly familiar with the main principles of Darwinism and early saw that the theory of natural selection, especially in its application to instinct, was to prove of great importance in the study of social phenomena. He soon found that his problem raised the much wider question of the relation between the sexes and their historical development. He became interested in the hypothesis of primitive promiscuity, which Darwin took for granted, on the ground of the investigations made by Morgan, Lubbock, and McLennan, and at the age of twenty-five found it necessary to learn English in order to go back to the original authorities. He was soon convinced that the attempt to reconstruct the primitive forms of social institutions must lead to arbitrary conclusions unless their fundamental causes, i.e., their biological and psychological conditions, were first ascertained. In particular, we had, he thought, no right to assume the universal prevalence of any social phenomenon unless it could be shown that its causes were universally present and were not counteracted. He was thus led to the hypothesis that the family, consisting of father, mother, and children being rooted in essential, biological conditions already existed in primitive times, while the alleged causes, say, of group-marriage, or marriage by capture, were not such as to justify the belief in their universal prevalence at any stage of human civilization.

These general ideas gradually took shape in a plan to write a book on the history of marriage, and in 1887 he came to England in order to collect his material in the library of the British Museum, to him an island of bliss and a "very temple as well." Through Sully, with whom he formed an intimate friendship, he was introduced to intellectual circles in England. The book appeared with a preface by Wallace and had an immediate scientific success. The massive learning of the work so impressed reviewers that it was declared to be the "earnest labour of the chief part of a life-time." Later, Westermarck tells us, he came upon the belief that its author was a kind of patriarch, and twice he was taken for his own son. The publication of the book was in his own view the most momentous happening in his life. "It has been said," he adds, "that marriage has many thorns, but celibacy no roses. For my own part I would say that marriage has brought me many roses—and bachelorhood no thorns."

The success of the book on marriage encouraged Westermarck to proceed with his plans of a much larger inquiry into the origin and development of moral ideas. It is clear that the main concepts took definite shape in his mind quite early in his career, but it took nearly eighteen years to carry out the task he had set himself. His work was interrupted by teaching duties at his university, where he was appointed Docent in 1890; but in 1893 he was awarded a scholarship which enabled him to go back to the British Museum and to Oxford, where he met Tylor and Marett. A further scholarship in 1897 gave him three years' quiet work, which he again spent in England. At the meetings of the Aristotelian Society he renewed his acquaintance with English scholars, and it was here that he met Shand and became his warm friend. "I have in great measure," he tells us, "to thank my friend Shand for my conception of an English gentleman as seen at his best."

In planning his work on the comparative study of morals, Westermarck saw that it would be most useful to

him to acquire first-hand knowledge of other cultures than our own. He intended to go to the East to study both civilized and savage races. He sailed, however, first to Morocco and, realizing the difficulties involved in getting to know even a single country, he never went farther. In the course of three decades he spent altogether nine years in Morocco, and the results of his labors were embodied in his trilogy on the customs and ideas of the Moors.[1]

In 1903 Westermarck again visited England to arrange for the publication of the first volume of his *Moral Ideas*. It was then that he first met Victor Brandford, who invited his cooperation in a scheme for starting an English sociological society. Through Branford he made the acquaintance of J. Martin White, through whose generous benefaction the University of London was enabled to inaugurate the teaching of sociology, and later to establish professorships of sociology. As a Member of Parliament Martin White, it appears, came to the conclusion that it would be good for M.P.s to have a training in sociology, and his endowment was intended to provide facilities for such training. Under his benefaction Westermarck was appointed University Lecturer in Sociology for a period of three years, and during that period courses were also given by L. T. Hobhouse on comparative ethics and comparative psychology and by A. C. Haddon on ethnology. In 1907 a permanent chair in sociology was endowed, and Hobhouse was appointed to it. At the same time Westermarck's lectureship was converted into a chair with a five years' tenure. In 1912 the appointment was renewed for eighteen years more. Meanwhile Westermarck had been appointed to the chair of moral philosophy at Helsinki and the two posts were held by him concurrently. For a number of years he devoted the first two terms to his work at Helsinki, the summer term to the School of Economics, and the remaining summer months to his investigations in Morocco. In his scientific activities Westermarck adhered rigidly to the plans which he had formed when a young man. He lived long enough to realize these in his comprehensive works on the history of marriage, the origin and development of moral ideas, and on the ideas and customs of the Moors. On three occasions he took an active part in politics, namely, in organizing the International Address to the Tsar on behalf of Finland, in the movement for its independence during the war of 1914-18 and in the Åland campaign, and it is generally recognized that the services he thus rendered to his country were of the highest value. It is clear that the chief passion of his life was the pursuit of truth, and that he found his greatest happiness in those hours when he could work in peaceful solitude. Two other sources of happiness were given him—the love of nature and the experience of deep and enduring friendships. It is a great pleasure to those who knew and worked with Westermarck to have his own assurance that in the main he had achieved the goals which he had set to himself and that the sources of his happiness were not such as to run dry with advancing age. His capacity for the appreciation of beauty and for friendship grew no less with increasing years, and he continued with his scientific work right up to a few days before his death on 3 September 1939. There can be few people so justified as he was in declaring that if he had to live his life over again, he would on the whole follow the same path as he had in fact chosen.

In coming now to deal with Westermarck's work, I may best begin perhaps with his conception of the scope and methods of sociology. Sociology he defined as the science of social phenomena, and in this sense it was a collection of studies, including such disciplines as economics, politics, and the history of law. He himself was, however, most interested in developing that branch of sociology which he called the comparative study of social institutions, and the bulk of his work was devoted to this task. Social institution he defined as a social relationship regulated by society and sanctioned by it. The study of social institutions thus involves an account of the general nature of society and of the different forms in which it appears and of the sanctions and regulations employed by it. This is given in *The Origin and Development of the Moral Ideas,* in which the forms of social regulations are studied in detail and analyzed psychologically by reference to the fundamental emotions of approval and disapproval. The institution of marriage was dealt with in much greater detail in a number of works, in which it is examined both comparatively and in reference to the particular area of Morocco.

The method which he employed was in the main the comparative one. This aimed in the first place at a classification of the products of culture found among different peoples in different parts of the world; for example, the classification of religious beliefs and practices under the headings of animism, totemism, ancestor worship, polytheism, monotheism, or of marriage under the headings of marriage by capture, marriage by consideration, or monogamy, polygamy, polyandry, and group-marriage. From classification, he thought, we could move to causal explanation by a comparison of the circumstances common to a cultural phenomenon and those which could be shown to vary without corresponding variation in the phenomenon. Westermarck frequently uses the terms cause and origin interchangeably. By the cause of a social phenomenon he means in the first place the biological conditions determining it or at least giving it survival value. Thus the cause of marriage as an institution he finds in the need of prolonged marital and paternal protection. Such protection, he thought, was an indispensable condition of survival in the case of a species in which the number of the young is small, the period of infancy prolonged, and the supply of food such as to hinder a permanently gregarious mode of life. Through natural selection instincts would be developed impelling the male to stay with the female and the young and to care for them. These instincts, together with the sex instinct, are at the root of the family as an institution. Under their impulsion it became the habit in primitive times for a man and a woman or several women to live together and to rear their offspring in

common. The habit was sanctioned by custom and law, upheld by the tendency of members of the group to feel resentment against a man who forsook his mate and children. Of this set of relationships marriage is an integral part. As Westermarck puts it: marriage is rooted in the family rather than the family in marriage. Further, the instincts and sentiments which gave rise to the family are so deep-rooted that they are likely to preserve it, even though they may no longer be necessary for the survival of the race. In this example, which, I think, is typical of a good deal of Westermarck's work, causal explanation is in terms of the Darwinian theory of natural selection. In other cases the causes of social phenomena are sought in the motives which may be supposed to underlie them. Thus, in his study of human sacrifice, he argues that comparative investigation shows that human victims are offered in war, to avert or stop a famine or drought, to ward off perils from the sea, or to prevent the death of some particular person. This, he thinks, justifies the conclusion that human sacrifice is largely a method of life insurance, based on the idea of substitution.[2]

Two further points require elucidation. In the first place, Westermarck was not at all impressed by the objections raised against his views by the followers of Durkheim and others on the ground that social phenomena cannot be explained in terms of individual psychology. Who could deny, he argued, that even collective behavior involves the actions of individuals? When we speak of the customs or religion of a people, we refer to something that the individual members of it have in common, and, in the last resort, they are the outcome of mental activity. Further, the force by which customs are maintained can only in the long run be understood in terms of an analysis of the moral consciousness, and he thinks himself justified in concluding that this is ultimately based on the retributive emotions collectively felt and given a measure of generality and impartiality within a given community. In the study of particular social phenomena such as rites and ceremonies, Westermarck did not share the view held by Rivers that the task of disentangling the motives underlying them was hopeless. He thought that valuable information could be obtained, not so much from what natives say *about* their rites, as from what they say at the moment when they perform them, and he gives many examples of such interpretations from his own studies in Morocco.[3] Westermarck here perhaps oversimplifies the issue. He does not inquire into the various ways in which social forces react upon human motives by encouraging some and inhibiting others and by determining the manner in which they find expression. Unless this is done, it is difficult to account for the variations which Westermarck himself studies in the institutions and beliefs of mankind.

The second point that requires here to be mentioned relates to the use made by Westermarck of the theory of evolution. We have seen that in explaining social phenomena he was inclined to look for the biological conditions underlying them and to appeal to the theory of natural selection in accounting for the psychological make-up of man. He was not, however, interested in tracing stages of development, and in particular he repudiated in even his earliest writings the belief in a unilinear sequence of institutional stages. From the point of view of method, the reconstruction of the past, in the absence of direct historical evidence, stands on the same footing as the prediction of the future. In both cases it is necessary to know the causes of the phenomena and to ascertain whether they are likely to be operative in the period in question without being counteracted. Thus in dealing with the family Westermarck thinks we are justified in concluding that it existed already in primitive times, because the conditions necessitating it are then likely to have prevailed, and, further, that it is likely to persist in modern society, because the instincts and sentiments underlying it have become so deeply rooted that they will continue to demand satisfaction. The tracing of trends of change is likely to be misleading unless we are able at the same time to ascertain the causes of the changes. In the controversy between the diffusionists and the upholders of independent origination, Westermarck followed the lead of Tylor. Similarity in the cultural phenomena found among different peoples is to be ascribed "sometimes to the like working of men's minds under like conditions, and sometimes it is a proof of blood relationship or of intercourse, direct or indirect, between the races among whom it is found."[4]

In dealing with widespread or universal elements of culture, such as as the right of property, punishment, the various forms of marriage, the rules of exogamy, and so forth, the diffusionist hypothesis seemed to him in the highest degree improbable. But he was quite prepared to resort to diffusion in dealing with particular problems, such as those which are connected with decorative art or with proverbs, and he gives examples from his own studies in Morocco.[5]

The greatest difficulty of the comparative method is due to the necessity under which it labors of detaching or isolating cultural phenomena from their context and the risk it thus runs of distorting their real character. Of this risk Westermarck was well aware, but he thought that analysis and comparison were essential to sociology as to other sciences, and that if due caution was observed, the difficulties inherent in the method could in a large measure be overcome.

Passing now to the substance of Westermarck's work, I propose to confine attention to his theory of morals and to certain aspects of his study of marriage. In his moral theory Westermarck was profoundly influenced by Adam Smith, whose *Theory of Moral Sentiments* he considered as the most important contribution to moral psychology made by any British thinker,[6] and by the theory of natural selection. Adam Smith had given an analysis of approval and disapproval in terms of sympathy. We approve of the feelings of another when we recognize that, if we or rather an impartial spectator

were in the same situation, we should experience the same feeling, and we disapprove of them when on entering into the situation we cannot share those feelings. In his account of merit and demerit, Adam Smith had moreover laid special stress on the feelings of resentment and gratitude. According to him an action has merit if it is the approved object of gratitude and that has demerit which is the approved object of resentment. In other words, an act is meritorious if an impartial spectator can be expected to sympathize with the gratitude which it evokes, and, similarly, an act is to be condemned if the resentment aroused by it is likely to be shared by an impartial spectator. Westermarck's analysis starts with the emotions of gratitude and resentment, which he designates the retributive emotions and of which he gives a biological account in accordance with the theory of natural selection. He shows that gratitude or retributive kindly emotions has the tendency to retain a cause of pleasure, while resentment has the tendency to remove a cause of pain, and that these emotions are therefore both useful to the species. The difference in their prevalence is, he thinks, easily explained by the fact that living in groups is of advantage only to certain species and that even gregarious animals have many enemies but few friends. The retributive emotions are not however as such moral. They only become so if they acquire the three qualities of generality, disinterestedness, and impartiality. The disinterestedness is rendered possible by the presence in us of the power to sympathize with the feelings of others, and above all, by the altruistic sentiment which is an active disposition to promote the welfare of its object. The generality and impartiality of moral rules are due, he thinks, to the fact that they express not the emotions felt by isolated individuals, but those felt generally in a society in accordance with custom. Custom is general in its nature, i.e., it formulates what is expected from everyone in the same circumstances. Custom is also impersonal and impartial, i.e., is equally binding on all coming under the rule and under its influence there arises the feeling not so much that "I must do this" as that "this must be done." Westermarck has been accused of arguing in a circle in maintaining that custom is the factor responsible for making the retributive emotions disinterested and impartial, while holding at the same time that custom is a moral rule only on account of the disapproval called forth by its breach.[7] But I am not sure that the charge can be sustained. A moral emotion is, I take it, in Westermarck's view, a public emotion, that is, one likely to be felt generally in a given community. Customary rules are in their origin generalization of emotional tendencies, but having come to be established in a given community they are upheld by the tendency of their violation to arouse disapproval whether or not the act in itself, i.e., apart from its being condemned by custom, would arouse emotions in particular individuals. The circle is thus not vicious.

Westermarck describes his theory as a form of ethical relativity, and it is important to inquire what precisely he understands by relativity and how far his view can be consistently maintained. The most general form in which he states his theory is that the predicates of all moral judgments are ultimately based on emotions. To say that an act is good or bad is to say that it is apt to give rise to the emotions of approval or disapproval, or perhaps a little more accurately, to refer the act to a class of acts which have come to be called good or bad because of their tendency to arouse these emotions. The concepts of good and of ought are in his view distinct and not deducible from one another. But he repudiates the claim that either is ultimate and unanalyzable. The notion of goodness springs from the emotion of moral approval: that of duty from moral disapproval. Thus, to say that an act ought to be done implies that its omission has the tendency to arouse disapproval, and to say that it ought not to be done implies that its performance has the tendency to call forth disapproval. It is because the ought-judgment has implicit in it the notion of a prohibition that the idea of duty has come to carry with it a suggestion of antagonism to natural inclination, and that philosophers have even tended to restrict the notion of duty to acts that result from a successful struggle against opposite inclination. In a similar way Westermarck gives an analysis of other terms used in morals, such as right, wrong, just and unjust, merit, virtue, and vice. In all cases he thinks the qualities assigned to the subjects of moral judgments are generalizations derived from approval or disapproval and they indicate tendencies to arouse one or other of these emotions. The assertions made in ethical propositions are in this respect similar to the propositions asserting that something is fearful, lovable, wonderful, and the like. In short, what we are asserting is the presence of dynamic tendencies or the power of arousing certain emotions in the acts of which they are predicated. In this sense they may be true or false, since these tendencies are either present or absent in a given community. The approval or disapproval on the other hand being, in Westermarck's view, emotions, are not capable of being either true or false and to claim objective validity for them is therefore meaningless.

How far was Westermarck able to maintain this position consistently? To answer this question we must consider his views of the part played by reflection in the growth of the moral consciousness and his account of the variations of the moral judgments found in different societies. Since the higher emotions are stimulated by awareness of objects, they are bound to be affected by changes in knowledge. Thus our anger with a person who has told a lie may disappear or even change to approval when we discover that he acted from a desire to save life. In this way reflection has affected the emotions of approval and disapproval by revealing more fully the character of the objects which evoke them or by freeing them from associations which have gathered round them. A few illustrations may serve to make this clear. In the first place, we find gradually that indignation is properly directed only against acts deliberately intended to cause pain, and our anger dies when we realize that pain has been caused to us by an inanimate object or by

a person acting unwillingly or in ignorance of the consequence of his acts. Historically this has been of the greatest importance in the changes that have come about in the infliction of punishment. Primitive codes, for example, fail to distinguish clearly between intentional and unintentional acts, and animals, children, and lunatics are treated as punishable even in modern times. Important changes are now occurring in the treatment of crime, partly as a result of growing insight into the psychology of the immature or the mentally unsound. In these cases the growth of thought has affected the moral emotions by deepening our knowledge of the nature of the subject of moral judgments, that is to say, the character of the agent. In the second place, there are aversions and sympathies which Westermarck, following Bain, calls "disinterested" or "sentimental," that is, likes and dislikes which are not based upon direct experience of pleasure or pain; as when we dislike persons who differ from us in taste, habit, or opinion. These antipathies have affected the moral consciousness by leading people to regard as wrong many acts which are merely unusual, new, or foreign. The morality of sexual relations in particular has, in Westermarck's view, been profoundly influenced by these "sentimental" aversions. Examples are to be found in the condemnation, varying in intensity among different peoples, of auto-erotism and bestiality. They are regarded as immoral, not because they are known to cause harm, but because they inspire disgust. In the third place, religious or superstitious beliefs may affect our views of the nature of certain acts which then evoke our disapproval. In Westermarck's view the horror of homosexuality among the Hebrews, the Christians, and Zoroastrians is largely due to the fact that they associated it with the practices of infidels and therefore regarded it as a form of sacrilege. He argues that where no such religious influence has been operative, the moral attitude towards homosexual practices has been different and that in Christian Europe the growth of rationalism is bringing about important changes in the attitude of the law and of public opinion. Finally, many of our moral judgments are based, not on direct approval or disapproval of acts which are perceived to be the cause of pleasure or pain to others, but on sympathetic approval or resentment. In other words, we are inclined to get our resentments and approvals secondhand from those for whom we have a regard or who are in a position of authority. In this way, for example, punishment inflicted by society being regarded as an expression of the moral indignation of the community, may lead us to condemn an act which we should not otherwise regard as blameworthy. Acts which are in themselves harmless may thus, through ignorance, superstition, or prejudice, come to have opprobrium attached to them, and their condemnation becomes so deeply rooted in the moral tradition that no one ever thinks of inquiring into the original causes which led to their being regarded as immoral. In short, growing reflection may alter the direction of our emotions of approval and disapproval by revealing more fully the character of the agent, by dissipating superstitious beliefs which tend to endow acts with qualities which do not really belong to them, by revealing the existence of merely "sentimental" sympathies and antipathies, and by challenging traditional morality to disclose the original causes which brought given rules of morality into being. Westermarck thinks that comparative study shows that in a measure moral ideas have in the course of social evolution become more "enlightened" in all these respects, and that there is reason to believe that the influence of reflection upon moral judgments will steadily increase.

This account, Westermarck claims, is borne out by a study both of the differences and similarities that are found to exist in the moral judgments of different societies. With regard to the subjects of moral judgments, Westermarck concludes after a careful survey that in reflective morality moral approval and disapproval are felt with reference to persons on account of their conduct or to character conceived as the cause of their conduct. This is true in the main also of earlier and cruder phases of morality, though there is then no serious attempt to separate the external event from the will and there is an inclination to assume that the two always coincide. Hence, in part, the failure to distinguish clearly between intentional and unintentional acts and the ascription of blame or praise to agents whom the reflective mind cannot regard as strictly responsible. The fact that moral judgments are passed always on conduct and character is in harmony, Westermarck argues, with their origin in the retributive emotions. The latter are reactions towards a living being regarded as the cause of pleasure or pain, and they are not so regarded by the reflective mind unless they are taken to issue from the character or will of the agent considered as a continuous entity. Allowing then for differences in psychological knowledge, there is, according to Westermarck, no difference in principle between the moralities of different peoples regarding the subjects of moral judgments.

With regard to the content of moral rules, the result of Westermarck's elaborate study is to show that despite certain important differences there is a noteworthy similarity in the moral ideas of mankind. This similarity extends to the so-called uncivilized peoples:

> When we study the moral rules laid down by the customs of savage peoples we find that they in a very large measure resemble the rules of civilized nations. In every savage community homicide is prohibited by custom, and so is theft. Savages also regard charity as a duty and praise generosity as a virtue, indeed their customs relating to mutual aid are often much more exacting than our own; and many of them are conspicuous for their avoidance of telling lies.[8]

This similarity Westermarck explains as due ultimately to the fact that the emotions which the moral rules express are presumably similar in all groups of mankind. The differences which are found he attributes broadly to three causes, namely, differences in external circumstances

which affect the consequences of otherwise similar acts and thereby their moral import, differences in knowledge of the nature and consequences of acts due very often to the influence of religious and magical beliefs, and finally differences in the strength and range of the altruistic sentiment which affect the range of persons to whom moral rules are held to apply. Examples of the operation of the first set of causes are to be found in the practice of infanticide, which is in the main due to the hardships of savage life; and the practice of killing aged parents, which is connected with deficiencies in the food supply and is inspired by the necessity of saving the young and vigorous and the humane intention of putting an end to prolonged and hopeless misery. Examples of the second set of causes are to be found in the different attitudes adopted by different peoples to suicide, which, according to Westermarck, have been greatly influenced by religious beliefs, such as the duty of absolute submission to the will of God or, as in the case of Christianity, the importance ascribed to the moment of death. Numerous other instances can readily be given from the varied taboos found among different peoples. The most important divergence in moral attitudes concerns the range of persons to whom moral rules are held to apply. Though the rules inculcating regard for life, property, truth, and the general well-being of a neighbor are found in all societies, they are held to be binding only in reference to members of the same group. The range is widened with the expansion of the social unit, but the distinction between the tribesman and the stranger survives even today, and the fact that morality is still largely group morality is seen in the survival of war and the precariousness of the rules supposed to control behavior during war. Nevertheless, there has been a great advance in humanity with regard to the treatment of foreigners. Westermarck notes further that, so far as the teaching of the great moralists is concerned, the change from the savage attitude has been enormous. There is remarkable unanimity in this respect, in the teaching of all the higher religions. The doctrine of universal love is taught not only by Christianity but by Chinese thinkers, by the Buddhists and other Indian teachers, by the Greek philosophers, and the doctrine of a world citizenship was given definite content and historical importance by the Stoics. The most important cause of the extension of the range of moral rules has been the widening of the altruistic sentiment which has accompanied the increase in the size of social unit and the growth of intercourse between different societies. The change has been in the main due, according to Westermarck, to emotional rather than to cognitive factors. He argues further that variations in the range and intensity of the altruistic sentiment account also for the differences of moral opinion regarding the limits of the duty of self-sacrifice and the treatment of the lower animals.

We must now consider the bearing which this account of the part played by reflection in the growth of the moral judgment and of the variations of moral views among different peoples has upon the theory of ethical relativity. Westermarck himself notes that in so far as differences of moral opinion depend on differences of circumstances, or on knowledge or ignorance of facts, or on the influence of specific religious and magical beliefs, or on different degrees of reflection, they are perfectly compatible with the universal validity which is claimed for moral judgments.[9] Analogous differences of opinion may easily be shown to exist in other spheres of knowledge where no one would on their account call in question the possibility of establishing universally valid propositions. It may be added that moralists concerned to defend the claim to objective validity of moral truths have themselves explained the variety of opinion actually found, in terms which closely resemble the explanation given by Westermarck.[10] Westermarck, however, claims that there is an important class of differences in moral opinion illustrated by the differences in the range of persons to which moral rules are held to apply in different communities, which depend not on differences in knowledge but on differences of emotional dispositions, and he argues that variations of this sort are fatal to the supposed universality of moral judgments. I cannot find his argument at all convincing. It rests on an unreal separation of feeling and thought. It is possible that without the power of sympathy the truths of universalist ethics could neither be discovered nor become effective in practice, but this throws no light at all on the nature of the truths once they are discovered. Just as certain feelings are only possible at a given level of rational development, so it may well be that certain thoughts or beliefs only emerge under certain emotional conditions. Certainly in grasping the essential relations between men, the power of imaginative identification, of entering fully into the situation of others, must be of the highest value, and perhaps this power only reaches its greatest intensity under the influence of the social feelings.

The difficulty here raised besets, I think, the whole of Westermarck's discussion of the part played by reason in morals. He assigns to intellectual factors very important functions, but he does not realize that he is giving them a claim to authority which is not compatible with his relativistic outlook. The statement, for example, that in the course of social evolution morality has become more "enlightened" implies a value judgment which goes beyond his own emotional approval of certain of the changes that have occurred. It is indeed clear from Westermarck's account that the feelings of approval and disapproval are in themselves an insufficient guide to conduct. Apart from the "sentimental" antipathies and sympathies whose origin is obscure, many other feelings have been implanted in man under conditions which no longer prevail and can therefore be no longer relied upon as a criterion of well-being. This appears to be the case in much of the morality of sexual relations, and Westermarck even feels justified in concluding that "enlightened" people will probably come to look upon sexual acts as morally indifferent and as no "proper object for punishment or moral censure" save in so far as they may involve injury to others. To be called wrong he says "an act must be productive of other harm than the mere aversion it causes, provided that the agent has

not in an indecent manner shocked anyone's feelings."[11] But what is the meaning of the term "proper" in this context? As a mere matter of biological or sociological fact the aversions which are indirectly attached to acts as a result of social suggestion or of magical and religious beliefs are as proper as the primary resentments, that is, those directed against the infliction of pain, since presumably they are also rooted in the tendencies of human nature. It would seem then that discriminating or enlightened reflection does not remain satisfied with merely ascertaining the actual or probable tendencies to approval or disapproval in given societies, but also seeks to criticize them in the light of a conception of what is deserving of approval or disapproval.

There is another difficulty in connection with Westermarck's discussion of the relations between individual and social approval and disapproval. Sometimes he appears to suggest that for the emotion to be moral it is necessary that it should be "public" or general in a given community. Yet he recognizes the importance of moral innovators and he even thinks that such moral progress as has occurred has been largely due to the example of such innovators and their efforts to raise public opinion to their own standard of right.[12] I do not think that Westermarck succeeds in overcoming this difficulty, which in one form or another besets all sociological theories of ethics. In one place he suggests that all that is required to give to the retributive emotions of the exceptional individuals moral character is that these emotions should possess the characteristics of disinterestedness and impartiality originally due to the social influence of custom, and that in that case they may differ from public approval and disapproval either in intensity or with regard to the facts by which they are evoked. But surely this reference to the origin of impartiality is not very helpful. The value of the contributions of the moral innovators has often consisted, as Westermarck himself says, in showing that "the apparent impartiality of public feelings is an illusion," and, what is equally important, in showing that rules which are impartially applied may themselves be unjust. Why should such contributions be regarded as "progressive" or enlightened if the only criterion is public approval? In the end Westermarck has to appeal to an ideal society:

> Even when standing alone, he (the moral dissenter) feels that his conviction is shared at least by an ideal society, by all those who see the matter as clearly as he does himself, and who are animated by equally wide sympathies, and equally broad sense of justice. Thus the moral emotions remain to the last public emotions—if not in reality, then as an ideal.[13]

There is, however, in Westermarck's work no analysis of the concept of an ideal, and its use appears to introduce a value category for which it is difficult to find a place in his system.

Westermarck has defended his views with great vigor and lucidity, and has refuted many of the objections made to them convincingly. I have tried to look at his work, so to say, from within, and I do not find it quite self-consistent. Yet whatever criticisms may be made against his work regarded as a contribution to ethical philosophy, there can be no doubt of its value as a systematic and comprehensive sociological study of the moral ideas and customs of mankind. In this study he was a pioneer and he carried it out with an erudition, lucidity, and balance still unsurpassed.

Westermarck was led to his studies into the history of human marriage by his interest in the question of the origins of sexual modesty. The studies, however, came to cover the whole range of sexual relations and even in the later enlarged editions of the **History of Human Marriage,** only a single chapter is devoted to the question which initiated the whole inquiry, while in the first edition only a few lines are given to it. When it first appeared it was hailed everywhere as a scientific work of the highest importance. Of the later expanded edition I will quote the opinion of Havelock Ellis, with which I think most competent students would agree: "In its extended and mature shape it stands out as a monumental achievement in the field of scientific sociology, recalling the other great achievement of the same generation in an analogous field by Sir James Frazer, and with no other edifice of comparable magnitude in sight."[14] Out of the vast range of topics dealt with by Westermarck the two that have attracted most attention are perhaps his explanation of the origin and significance of the rules of exogamy and his theory of the universality and primitive character of the family. As to the first, his view, which he defends with great learning and skill, is that the cause of all incest prohibitions is to be found in the want of inclination for and consequent aversion to sexual intercourse between persons who have lived together in close intimacy from childhood. He thinks that there may be a biological explanation of this disinclination. There is, he urges, strong evidence showing that exclusive and prolonged inbreeding tends to be injurious to the stock, and in accordance with the theory of natural selection it is probable that the sexual instinct has been moulded to meet the requirements of the species. The biological explanation is, however, only offered as a hypothesis, while the psychological facts which it is intended to elucidate are taken by him to be proved by common experience. Westermarck's theory has been accepted by many authorities, including Havelock Ellis. On reviewing the discussion of this whole question in recent literature I am not, however, convinced by his argument. The biological explanation certainly cannot be regarded as safely established, but without it I cannot see how Westermarck can explain the transformation from mere indifference to aversion which according to him has occurred. No doubt we have parallel cases of indifference turning into dislike but hardly into a deep-seated aversion comparable to that with which incest is regarded. The aversion may, indeed, be caused by the prohibition, but then the prohibition has to be accounted for.

With regard to his views on the family it will be recalled that when he began his work he was inclined to accept the hypothesis then widely held that primitive man lived in a state of promiscuity. He soon discovered, however, that there was no real evidence for this hypothesis. He showed (i) that no known savage people either is or recently was living in such a state; (ii) that statements to the contrary from ancient writers are vague and untrustworthy; (iii) that in the case of peoples who have a form of group-marriage, the evidence suggests that it has arisen as a combination of polygyny with polyandry; (iv) that in the case of peoples alleged to have some kind of sex communism, in which several men have the right of access to several women, none of the women is properly married to more than one of the men and individual marriage subsists. Finally, he produces positive evidence that even among the food-gatherers and hunters, who might be supposed to live in conditions nearest to those in which primitive man lived, the family, consisting of parents and children, is a well-marked social unit. With regard to primitive man, he further argues, his general conclusion is strengthened by what is known of the social habits of the anthropoids, where the family unit, consisting of male, female or females, and young, has been shown to exist.

Westermarck's arguments both as regards the universality and the probably primitive character of the family have been widely accepted by anthropologists. Recently, however, his entire position has been fiercely attacked by Dr. Briffault in a huge work of three volumes entitled *The Mothers.* Much to the amusement of those who knew Westermarck, he is depicted as a defender and upholder of moral theology, and, what is more serious, he is accused of distorting the evidence and of ignoring facts which do not fit in with his theories. Westermarck has written a lengthy rejoinder[15] to Dr. Briffault, as he felt it "a matter of honour with me to defend myself against false indictments that cast a stain on my character as a scientist and an honest seeker after truth." He performs this task with a thoroughness which was to be expected, and no unbiased reader will have any doubt of his success. Dr. Briffault's general position can only be stated here very briefly. He tries to show that the primitive human group was not the family nor an aggregation of families but the "motherhood," i.e., the biological group formed by the mother and her offspring, "a group economically self-contained through the co-operation of brothers and sisters and one of which the sexual mate forms no partner." The sexual instincts are, in his view, subordinate in primitive humanity to the deeper ties due to the maternal instincts and the bonds of sentiment connected with kinship. Nor is there a gregarious instinct as such. Gregariousness is derivative, being the effect of the offspring's dependence upon maternal protection. The group of mothers with their offspring form the clan, and the clan relationship is therefore more primitive than the family system of relationship. Individual marriage has an economic origin. Economic association between sexual partners has tended to establish individual sexual claims, and in the latter stages of social development the betrothal of females has led to a retrospective restriction of sexual freedom and to the demand that the bride shall be a virgin. The paternal family begins to be important with the growth of private property, and the individual economic power of males and marriage acquires a social significance only when the paternal family has become a medium for the consolidation and transmission of private property. To establish his position Dr. Briffault traverses the entire range of social anthropology, and at every point heatedly disputes Westermarck's interpretation of the evidence. He seeks to show that matrilocal marriage is a custom of "almost universal distribution" in uncultured societies and that everywhere the paternal family has been preceded by the matrilocal family. He argues further that there is no known case of a primitive people insisting on prenuptial chastity except in societies which practice infant betrothal and marriage by purchase involving a high bride price; that there is no convincing evidence of the existence of monogamous institutions in any uncivilized peoples; that the existing cases of group-marriage and sex communism suggest that in their origin marriage regulations had no reference to individuals but to groups.

Anyone who takes the trouble of comparing Dr. Briffault's study and Westermarck's rejoinder will I think come to the conclusion that though the material used by both is often vague and ambiguous, Westermarck cannot rightly be charged with distorting the evidence in the interests of a preconceived theory, and those who knew him personally will only be strengthened in their admiration for his conspicuous candor and disinterestedness. It is obviously impossible here to examine the complicated problems raised in any detail. I have, however, in connection with the work in which I collaborated with the late Professor Hobhouse, had occasion to survey much of the evidence and will try to indicate my attitude to some of the points in this controversy.[16] I can see no ground for believing that matrilineal descent everywhere preceded patrilineal descent. The evidence does not prove the maternal principle to be decidedly characteristic of the lowest culture, though it does suggest that the paternal principle becomes more prominent in the pastoral stage, while among agricultural principles the two are nearly balanced. As to the precedence of the clan over the family, it appears that while the family is always found wherever the clan exists, there are cases of clanless tribes who nevertheless live in groups of families. Briffault's statements as to monogamy among primitive peoples are very sweeping. So far as the hunters and gatherers are concerned, it would seem on the evidence that monogamy is the prevailing practice, though not in most cases the strict rule. The evidence regarding prenuptial chastity is conflicting and extremely difficult to evaluate. But it does not seem to support the association alleged between marriage by purchase and prenuptial chastity; the most that can be said is that purchase tightens up a pre-existing prohibition. The cases of alleged group-marriage and sexual communism are difficult to analyze, but on Dr. Briffault's own showing there is in nearly every case some form of individual economic marriage alongside the relations which are permitted outside the narrow family. He has not, so far as I can see, produced any evidence of group-marriage in any strict sense, that is, of a number of males married collectively and on equal terms to a group of females. In any event, I see no ground for believing that group-marriage was at any stage universal.

The last work in English to come from the pen of Westermarck is an impressive volume dealing with the influence of Christianity upon moral ideas and practices.[17] Here he restates the conclusions he had reached on the nature both of religion and morality, and considers in detail the effect that Christian teaching and practice has had on the institutions of the family, property, and economic organization, war and slavery, and the duties of regard for life and truth. In each of these spheres he produces an array of carefully sifted facts, and impressively challenges the claim so often made for Christianity that it has proved itself the highest ethical force in the history of man. Certain difficulties inherent, I think, in his outlook and method become here apparent. In accordance with his own relativistic ethics Westermarck should have confined his study of Christian morality to a record of the emotional responses of Christian societies to different classes of acts and of the feelings aroused in other societies by the behavior of Christians. In fact, however, Westermarck does not impose this limitation upon himself, and his book abounds in value judgments for which general validity is claimed. A second difficulty arises from the fact that Westermarck's method does not enable us to disentangle and give due weight to the numerous factors involved in the history of civilization. If the advances in the direction of a more humane ethic cannot be attributed to Christianity alone, neither ought Christianity to be blamed for the backslidings, and there is much to be said for the view that often the most serious criticisms of Christianity have come from the Christians themselves. A parallel difficulty would, I think, be experienced by anyone who attempted to estimate the influence of rational thought on morals. Here too, alike in its failures and successes it would be difficult to disentangle what is due to thought as such, and what to the economic, political and religious factors with which it is interwoven. Despite these doubts, however, no one who reads the work can fail to be impressed by its massive erudition and the detachment with which a subject of profound emotional significance is here handled.

Westermarck has given a lively account of his work at the School of Economics and of his contacts with the students from all parts of the world who came to seek his guidance. Those who attended his seminars will always think of him with respect and affection and will recall his kindliness, his candor and tolerance, his singlemindedness in the pursuit of truth. In his own university in Finland he quite evidently exercised a profound influence. I should like to quote here a few words of appreciation from Eino Kaila, Professor in Theoretical Philosophy at Helsinki University:

His greatest importance for many of his pupils lay, in my opinion, in the fact that he opened for us the world of English thought. For three centuries our scientific life had been completely under German dominance. Westermarck was the first, at least among the representatives of the philosophical faculties, to make himself thoroughly at home in the English language. This attitude of his became even more stimulating to us because he so splendidly developed the English tradition within the sphere of social philosophy. We admire in him equally the great scientist and the noble personality who devoted his whole life to those studies which are most essential to the advance of culture.[18]

Westermarck has on several occasions expressed his high appreciation of the contribution made by English thinkers to the study of society, but most emphatically perhaps on what must have been one of his last visits to this country. "I am convinced," he said, in concluding his Huxley Memorial Lecture given at the Royal Anthropological Institute in 1936, "that there is no country in the world that can rival it in its achievements in social anthropology, whether pursued in the study or in the field, largely owing to its sterling qualities of lucidity and good sense." English scholars will assuredly feel that of these qualities Westermarck's own work was a magnificent example.

NOTES

[1] Edward Westermarck, *Marriage Ceremonies in Morocco* (London: Macmillan and Co., 1914); *Ritual and Belief in Morocco,* 2 vols. (London: Macmillan and Co., 1926); *Wit and Wisdom in Morocco: A Study of Native Proverbs,* with the assistance of Shereef 'Abd-es-salam el-Baqqali (London: George Routledge & Sons, 1930).

[2] Westermarck, *The Origin and Development of the Moral Ideas,* vol. 1 (London: Macmillan and Co., 1906), pp. 440-76. Hereafter cited as *"ODMI."*

[3] See Westermarck, "Methods in Social Anthropology," *Journal of the Royal Anthropological Institute* 66 (July-December 1936): 223-48.

[4] Edward B. Tylor, *Researches into the Early History of Mankind and the Development of Civilization,* 3d ed. (London: John Murray, 1878), p. 5.

[5] Westermarck, "Methods," pp. 226-33.

[6] Westermarck, *Ethical Relativity,* International Library of Psychology, Philosophy, and Scientific Method (London: Kegan Paul, Trench, Trubner & Co., 1932), p. 71. Hereafter cited as *"ER."*

[7] See John Dewey, "Anthropology and Ethics," in *The Social Sciences and Their Interrelations,* ed. William Fielding Ogburn and Alexander Goldenweiser (Boston: Houghton Mifflin Company, 1927), p. 28.

[8] *ER,* p. 197.

[9] *ER,* p. 196.

[10] See Dugald Stewart, *The Collected Works of Dugald Stewart,* ed. Sir William Hamilton, vol. 6 (Edinburgh: Thomas Constable and Co., 1855), p. 237; and Henry Sidgwick, *Lectures on the Ethics of T. H. Green, Mr. Herbert Spencer, and J. Martineau* (London: Macmillan and Co., 1902), p. 227.

[11] Westermarck, *The Future of Marriage in Western Civilisation* (London: Macmillan and Co., 1936), p. 255.

[12] Westermarck, *Christianity and Morals* (London: Kegan Paul, Trench, Trubner & Co., 1939), p. 15.

[13] *ODMI,* 1: 123.

[14] Havelock Ellis, Review of Westermarck, *Three Essays on Sex and Marriage,* in *The Sociological Review* 27, no. 1 (January 1935): 94.

[15] Westermarck, *Three Essays on Sex and Marriage* (London: Macmillan and Co., 1934).

[16] L. T. Hobhouse, G. C. Wheeler, and M. Ginsberg, *The Material Culture and Social Institutions of the Simpler Peoples; an Essay in Correlation* (London: Chapman & Hall, 1930).

[17] Westermarck, *Christianity.*

[18] This comment was kindly sent to me by Westermarck's friend and pupil, Miss Agnes Dawson.

Timothy Stroup (essay date 1982)

SOURCE: "Soft Subjectivism," in *Acta Philosophica Fennica,* Vol. 34, 1982, pp. 99-119.

[*In the following excerpt, Stroup classifies Westermarck's system of beliefs as "soft subjectivism."*]

I

The central question of moral philosophy, to which Edward Westermarck continually addressed himself, is whether moral judgments have objective validity. Can the statements which express our moral beliefs somehow be proved or conclusively established? Is there an objective moral order—a "realm" of moral facts—which justifies the claims we make about the conduct and character of ourselves and others?

Westermarck's answer is clearly negative. Against those who hold that fundamental moral principles are apprehended through acts of intuition or are necessary presuppositions which cannot be further derived, Westermarck maintained that "there can be no moral truth in the sense in which this term is generally understood," because "moral judgments are ultimately based, not on the intellect, but on emotions" and "no objectivity can come from an emotion."[1] Yet Westermarck's answer is not devastatingly negative; it is not destructive of all moral thought, as would be a crude nihilistic subjectivism, but rather can serve as the basis for an ethics which avoids the pitfalls of both objectivism and subjectivism.[2] By analogy with "soft determinism," I call such a view "soft subjectivism," and in what follows I shall explain what that view consists of, how it survives attacks which are fatal to less subtle variants, and how it provides a hopeful way of looking at human moral behavior.

II

The case against ethical objectivism is persuasive rather than conclusive. Westermarck nowhere attempts a single knock-down disproof of objectivism, but he clearly thinks that his analysis taken as a whole makes a very strong case.[3] His strategy is complex and runs along two distinct lines. On the one hand, he assesses and finds wanting the arguments that have been advanced by moral philosophers in support of an objective ethics. In the first two chapters of *Ethical Relativity* he offers a critique of several objectivist doctrines, including those of Mill, Sidgwick, Spencer, Bradley, and Hobhouse.[4] He cites inconsistencies, anomalies, oversights; he appeals to common usage against the overly confident objectivists; he deflates the notions of self-evidence and universality in morals. All this is useful as a preamble to the development of a substantive theory of ethics. Moral philosophy is a market-place of ideas in which new goods are necessary only when the existing supply is in some respects inadequate. In the case of ethical objectivism, continuing competition may itself be indicative of malaise. If moral judgments state moral facts, these facts must be of a peculiar sort: they fail to secure agreement and are ontologically odd and non-empirical.

Westermarck concludes that the arguments advanced by leading moral philosophers are in every case inadequate to the purpose of establishing an objectivist ethics. This does not in itself show that objectivism is false, but only that such a view is held for no good reason. But can we be sanguine about finding better support, given the strong inductive evidence of the failures of other philosophers and the difficulties of conceiving of what forms new arguments might take?

The second half of Westermarck's strategy begins with an examination of the facts of moral behavior in order to see what range of data a moral theory must explain and whether these facts are themselves suggestive of a theory. To this task Westermarck brought exceptional qualities of intellect and temperament. Particularly in *The Origin and Development of the Moral Ideas* he amassed a vast compendium of moral practices and beliefs, which enabled him to draw general conclusions about behavior based on the most systematic empirical study that was possible at the time he wrote. The result was, as Brand Blanshard has observed, "a theory that, without any need for objective moral truths, covers the facts completely."[5] And as Westermarck himself claimed, no other theory, "whatever arguments have been adduced in support of it, has been subjected to an equally comprehensive test."[6]

Thus, the real strength of Westermarck's ethical system comes from a combination of the philosophical refutation of specific objectivist theories and the ability to account for the evidence of morality in other terms. Neither half of the strategy is decisive on its own, in the sense of providing an inescapable proof of ethical subjectivism, but together they are persuasive and mutually supporting. Here I shall focus attention exclusively on Westermarck's positive conclusions about the nature of morality.

III

Westermarck's view can appropriately be called "soft subjectivism" because it takes a stance on the question of ethical objectivity similar in several ways to that taken by soft determinism on the question of the freedom of the will. Both views attempt to mediate between extremes, between rigid objectivism and nihilistic subjectivism on the one hand, and mechanistic determinism and wishful indeterminism on the other. Both views display a respect for scientific evidence in solving philosophical problems; while recognizing that philosophical analysis has its proper role in formulating questions and mapping the terrain, they hold that there is a fundamental issue of fact—of what there is—at the root of each problem. Both views attempt to counter certain intuitively convincing arguments from personal belief in favor of competing conclusions: the soft determinist maintains that a "feeling of freedom" is incapable of demonstrating contra-causal action, the soft subjectivist that our ordinary beliefs in moral objectivity do not establish that there are real values. Thinking things are so does not guarantee that they are so. Finally, both views attempt to account for moral concepts in ways that require revision, but not wholesale rejection, of our ordinary ways of assessing behavior. Both permit moral thinking to perform some of the functions that we believe are necessarily part of the moral life.

Since Westermarck's soft subjectivism is empirically based, it is helpful in approaching it to ask how the facts of moral behavior bear upon his moral theory. There are two such facts which are immediately striking: people speak, think, and act like ethical objectivists (although hardly with much philosophical awareness or articulation of this position); and the moral practices and beliefs of societies, and even of individuals within societies, show marked dissimilarities over many issues of importance. Taken together, these facts tell much about what Westermarck's view is and what it is not.

IV

People generally believe in objective moral values. Were this not so we would be at a loss to explain the vehemence with which arguments about right and wrong sometimes develop or the inhumane and brutal extremes towards which the banner of conscience can be carried, for we seldom get so exercised about matters of mere taste. Nor could we explain the objectivist bias of our language, in which "right" (to use only one example) means considerably more than "right in my opinion" or "right in the opinion of my society." This is not to deny that people often, and perhaps increasingly, pay lip-service to a surface relativism, rooted in naive tolerance, which is inconsistent with their deeper objectivism. But scratch a naive relativist and you get an ethical objectivist.

Any theory of moral discourse which attempts to capture the facts of moral psychology must allow for this commonsense belief in objective values. The less sophisticated emotive and attitudinal subjectivisms which were popular earlier in this century, and which I have elsewhere called "plain subjectivism,"[7] were deficient in just this respect if understood as analyses of first-order, unreconstructed, moral judgments. According to these views moral judgments merely express or report the feelings of the speaker; and, as G. E Moore has argued, if this were the case we could scarcely begin to account for the phenomenon of moral disagreement, for no contradiction could literally be occurring.[8]

But Westermarck was certainly no plain subjectivist. He stood quite outside the logical positivist, reductionist tradition of analyzing the logic of moral utterance. He was far more concerned with assessing the biological, sociological, and psychological influences on moral behavior in general, of which moral language is only one part. Yet he did have some insight into the functions of moral judgments. He held that, in typical instances, moral judgments *attribute* a predicate to a subject, and to this logical observation he appended a psychological explanation of the emotional derivation of the predicate. Moral judgments do not directly describe, report, or even express moral emotions, but rather ascribe to conduct and character properties which, given our objectivist outlook, are thought to be objective.

Hence, the relationship between moral emotions and moral judgments is far more complex, according to Westermarck, than is suggested by the plain subjectivist. More than the mere expression or description of emotions occurs when moral judgments are made: moral judgments contain an element of objectivizing. To the person who makes them, they are not merely subjective; rather, they have objective, universal validity—they are true.

Unfortunately, although Westermarck is otherwise very interested in moral psychology, he does not provide a detailed discussion of how this objectivizing occurs and what it consists of; he does not directly say much more than that we objectivize when we attribute a subjective feeling as a quality to an object.[9] But he does comment on its origins.[10] A character of universality and apparent objectivity is lent to moral judgments by the comparatively uniform nature of moral beliefs, particularly within early societies, in which Westermarck thinks there was "no difference of opinion" regarding questions of morality.[11] This initial agreement is subsequently enhanced by its impression on consciousness through the medium of authority: "From our earliest childhood we are taught that certain acts *are* right and that others *are* wrong."[12] The authorities can be temporal or spiritual, personal or codified into law, custom, or public opinion.

This tendency to assign objectivity to our subjective experience is a general, and not only a moral, propensity. Hume is the chief ancestor of Westermarck's view about objectivizing, and he has well described this projective tendency of the mind: taste, he claims, "has a productive faculty, and gilding or staining all natural objects with the colours, borrowed from internal sentiment, raises in a manner a new creation."[13] Both for Hume and for Westermarck, objectivizing is not confined to the moral domain. If everyone observes a constant conjunction between events, the tendency is to think that the events *necessarily are* connected; if everyone experiences a sour taste from sucking a lemon, the tendency is to think that the lemon *really is* sour; if everyone, to use Westermarck's example,[14] says that a landscape is beautiful, the tendency is to think that the landscape *really is* beautiful. Whether in causal, sensory, aesthetic, or moral contexts, there is a propensity to assign the qualities we perceive to the objects to which they are related.

Westermarck's identification of objectivizing must be understood against the background of his psychological account of the disinterested, impartial, and general emotions. In *The Origin and Development of the Moral Ideas* he views disinterestedness and impartiality as two distinct characteristics of moral emotions, although they are related because disinterestedness is a form of impartiality, and he introduces a third characteristic, "a certain flavour of generality."[15] In *Ethical Relativity* and *Christianity and Morals* disinterestedness is still a form of impartiality, but the notion of generality has disappeared.[16] At any rate, these three features of moral emotions which Westermarck proposed at one time or another are somewhat different from each other, but also have an element in common: they all represent a move towards universalization that distinguishes the moral emotions from other emotions.

All emotions are subjective, in the sense that they are felt by the person who has them and by no other person. But Westermarck thinks that some emotions, through social conditioning, come to have reference beyond the mere individual: "Society is the school in which we learn to distinguish between right and wrong."[17] These emotions are such that the person who has them thinks they would be shared by others if they "knew the act and all its attendant circumstances as well as he does himself, and if, at the same time, their emotions were as refined as are his own."[18] These public emotions of approval and disapproval differ from purely individual emotions like gratitude and revenge. As the usage of moral concepts becomes established through custom, the links to individual wants become more attenuated and the objectivity-claiming component becomes more pronounced.[19] It is then possible for people to learn particular moral concepts by recognizing, say, their commending function, and then to apply the concepts to those wants which they wish to commend. Therefore, the whole process of externalizing wants tends to be self-supportive: by wanting things we objectivize them and by objectivizing them we want them. And, at the final stage of the process, a moral judgment has been so conditioned that it is seen not as prompted by our wants at all, but rather as dictated by fairness or some other impartial or disinterested objectivity-claiming principle.

Westermarck's psychological investigation of the moral emotions, even if it isolates impartiality, disinterestedness, and generality as empirical characteristics of the phenomena, is quite a different matter from the *a priori* deduction of maxims for conduct based on these characteristics. Westermarck's task is one of definition, not of recommendation. If people who use the word "moral" to describe something generally imply that the thing has certain characteristics, this lexicographic observation does not imply the moral claim that it *really* is good to have those characteristics. Dictionaries are not bibles. But Westermarck's analysis does succeed, to an extent that plain subjectivism cannot, in capturing some important facts about how people think and talk morally.

Thus, in one crucial respect Westermarck and the objectivist are in agreement: both hold that moral judgments commonly are used to make objective claims. But for the objectivist these claims succeed or fail insofar as they correctly report an objective moral order, while for Westermarck the claims must always fail in that sense because there are no moral facts: "If, as I maintain, the objective validity of all moral valuation is an illusion, and the proposition 'this is good' is meant to imply such validity, it must always be false."[20]

To be sure, there is nothing in the logic of moral discourse that will settle the question of whether moral claims *do* state moral facts or are simply *thought to* state moral facts; that is a question about the world, not only about our description of it. This is why Westermarck's defense of soft subjectivism goes beyond mere attention to language and rightly focuses on the philosophical refutation of objectivist arguments and the alternative explanation of the empirical evidence of human behavior. This is where the heart of the problem lies.

V

Old-fashioned relativist theories of ethics normally proceeded from cultural relativism to ethical relativism. That is, they argued that there is diversity in the fundamental beliefs actually held from society to society, that there are no moral principles that *are* held in all societies, and from this they concluded that actions can be morally evaluated only within a particular society, that there are no moral principles which *should* be held in all societies.

But Westermarck's relativism is much more subtle than this. Indeed, even his acceptance of cultural relativism is noticeably guarded. One critic has attributed to him the view that "chaotic diversity of opinion is the rule in the moral realm;"[21] but this could not possibly square with Westermarck's own conception of the process of objectivizing, which owes its origins to the "comparatively uniform nature" of moral beliefs. Westermarck declares, "This objectivity ascribed to judgments which have a merely subjective origin springs in the first place from the similarity of the mental constitution of men. . . ."[22] Nor is there any reason to suppose that an ethics which bases itself on emotions cannot admit that human emotions show great similarities from person to person and society to society. What, then, does Westermarck see as the true scope of ethical diversity?

Consider first the cognitive causes of moral diversity, which can be attributed to different ideas about the objective nature of similar modes of conduct and the consequences of such conduct. On Westermarck's account, these differences arise in three specific ways. First, human moral behavior encompasses varying degrees of knowledge and reflection. Societies which manifest a high level of scientific sophistication will have different moral codes from those which rely on animistic explanations of natural events. In *Christianity and Morals* Westermarck cites an example: "at the lower stages of civilisation there is a considerable lack of discrimination between intentional injuries and accidental ones,"[23] and this imprecision is reflected in moral beliefs. Second, much moral diversity results from different ideas which arise from the different external circumstances in which people find themselves. Westermarck offers the practice of infanticide as an example.[24] Societies vary greatly in the extent to which they are favored by conditions propitious to life. Subsistence societies cannot tolerate large populations, and unlimited childbirth may be viewed as disadvantageous on economic grounds, although these considerations are seldom drawn so explicitly. The ultimate consequence is that two societies may agree to the general moral principle of placing a premium on human life, yet disagree about whether infanticide is necessary to avoid degrading the lives of those who cannot be cared for, or is abhorrent because it involves superfluous killing. Third, Westermarck cites differences in moral beliefs which result from superstition or religion, and this category is really a subcategory of the first: "In almost every branch of conduct we notice the influence which the belief in supernatural forces or beings or in a future state has exercised upon the moral ideas of mankind, and the great diversity of this influence."[25] In fact, Westermarck's last work, *Christianity and Morals,* is entirely devoted to tracing the extent to which a particular set of religious beliefs has resulted in elaborate codes of moral behavior.

The conclusion of Westermarck's inquiry into the rational bases of moral belief is that a great amount of diversity can be explained as resulting from intellectual factors and consequently provides no ammunition for the relativist:

> In so far as differences of moral opinion depend on knowledge or ignorance of facts, on specific religious or superstitious beliefs, on different degrees of reflection, or on different conditions of life or other external circumstances, they do not clash with that universality which is implied in the notion of the objective validity of moral judgments.[26]

But what about emotional differences? It can be conceded that the emotional characteristics of different peoples exhibit general similarities, and this is indeed what makes possible Westermarck's classification of the retributive emotions. Basic regularities in human temperaments set broad limits to emotional dissimilarities: "Certain cognitions inspire fear into nearly every breast. . . . "[27] But there is variation as well. To take one central example, the range of persons to whom the moral rules are held to apply varies from place to place and time to time. Variations of this sort are, for Westermarck, mainly due to variation in the sentiment of altruism, which has an emotional origin. The extent of altruism in a society is a function of many factors, the chief among them being the size of the social unit and the amount of intercourse with other societies: social isolation and differences of race, language, and customs work to inhibit the feeling, and peaceful intersocietal encounters foster it because prudence encourages friendliness in such relationships.[28]

Altruism is manifested in many ways. In "primitive" morality exclusive reference is made to members of the same community, and an act which is condemned when perpetrated against a member of the same tribe may be praised when an outsider bears its brunt; "civilized" society has not managed to obliterate this unequal treatment, but "both law and public opinion certainly show a very great advance in humanity with regard to the treatment of foreigners,"[29] and the improvement is even more noticeable in the injunctions of the normative systems of Western society than in the informal behavior of their adherents.

Nor need altruism have a merely human reference: it is evident in the attitude we take towards animals, although in this respect the so-called "civilized" societies have not always been very advanced. Yet Westermarck notes an improvement in nineteenth-century Europe in the kindness accorded to animals, and he believes that this can be accounted for partly by intellectual factors—for example, by more vivid reflection about what happens when animals suffer—but that emotional factors also enter in, with the result that diversity in moral judgments about animals prevails because there is a diversity of altruistic sentiment towards them:

> though greater intellectual discrimination may lessen the divergencies of moral opinion on the subject, nothing like unanimity may be expected, for the simple reason that humanity to animals is ultimately based on the altruistic sentiment, and sympathy with the animal world is a feeling which varies greatly in different individuals.[30]

Thus the specific manner in which moral rules have been extended so that they prohibit actions against strangers and animals reflects the nature and extent of the altruism that prevails in a society. Westermarck concludes, "Whatever part reflection may have played in the expansion of the moral rules—prudence has also, no doubt, had something to do with the matter—it seems to me obvious that the dominant cause has been the widening of the altruistic sentiment."[31]

Westermarck therefore maintains that there is some irreconcilable moral diversity which results from basic differences of emotional temperament, evident most clearly in differing displays of the sentiment of altruism. Unlike the cognitive causes of diversity, such emotional causes cannot readily be eliminated.

It would be rash to conclude from the simple fact of moral diversity that objectivism is false; dispute in itself does not show that neither disputant is right. But Westermarck does not make such a simple progression. Rather he examines, with analytical lucidity and meticulous detail, "the origin and development of the moral ideas" in order to demonstrate that many of the moral problems we pose for ourselves cannot be solved by sufficient observation and reflection, because they exhibit a tenacity which discloses the varying emotional reactions behind them. We therefore lead ourselves into perplexity when we try to determine which ethical theory possesses "the unique jewel of moral truth" and which are "only false stones."[32] But diversity does render extremely implausible any meta-ethical theory which claims that moral truth is readily grasped through simple acts of intuition:

> is it really possible to assume that defective 'moral illumination' could sufficiently explain the existence of so many different ethical theories, each of which is based on one or more principles regarded as self-evident intuitions, and as to some of which there is the same disagreement now as there was two thousand years ago?[33]

The existence of moral diversity thus tells strongly against simpler intuitionist objectivisms; and even though diversity *in itself* is not decisive against more sophisticated objectivisms, by providing the most persuasive causal explanation of the various ways—rational and emotional—in which differences in morals actually arise, Westermarck has driven one more nail into the objectivist's coffin.

VI

We can get closer to Westermarck's soft subjectivism by considering four objections that might be brought against it, two of them meta-ethical in character and two normative.

Among Westermarck's near contemporaries, his most influential opponent was G. E. Moore, who wrote the chapter on "The Objectivity of Moral Judgments" in his popular *Ethics* as an implicit response to Westermarck's views, and who explicitly criticized Westermarck in an essay on "The Nature of Moral Philosophy."[34] Moore argued that Westermarck tried to reduce moral judgments directly to moral emotions and thereby failed to account for moral controversy, which could never get a foothold if people were disputing merely idiosyncratic preferences. But such a characterization is a serious distortion of Westermarck's account of moral judgments, and the ensuing argument from disagreement—however fatal it may be to a plain subjectivist view—has no force against any analysis based on objectivizing.

From a psychological standpoint, both objectivism and soft subjectivism can account for the persistence of moral disagreement in a way that plain subjectivism cannot: ordinary moral antagonists incorporate an objectivist ontology into their ethical language, and on the basis of these common presuppositions particular disputes assume an appearance of substance transcending personal taste. It is not difficult at all to explain the *conviction* with which such disputes are thought to be genuine.

From a logical perspective, however, the soft subjectivist account differs from the objectivist. While the objectivist thinks that real disagreement, in the sense of logical contradiction, occurs in fundamental ethical disputes, the soft subjectivist claims that only something resembling contradiction occurs. Moral disputants make an error—however implicit, unconscious, and understandable that error may be—in thinking that the properties predicated by their moral judgments inhere in the subjects to which they are ascribed. They assume that their claims describe actual features of things and that the only point of disagreement is whether the thing has one feature or another—whether, say, it is *really* fair or *really* unfair. If there were no errors of presupposition, competing moral claims would be true contradictories; as it is, the soft subjectivist maintains, the claims only *appear* to be contradictories.

We can fully account for the psychological force of this appearance by appreciating the objectivist leanings that are part of the mental constitution of ordinary speakers,

and the deeper question of whether moral judgments state moral facts or embody false presuppositions cannot simply be settled by appeal to belief, to objectivist bias. As Westermarck declared of any such appeal:

> The whole argument is really reduced to the assumption that an idea—in this case the idea of the validity of moral judgments—which is generally held, or held by more or less advanced minds, must be true: people claim objective validity for the moral judgment, therefore it must possess such validity. The only thing that may be said in favour of such an argument is, that if the definition of a moral proposition implies the claim to objectivity, a judgment that does not express this quality cannot be a moral judgment; but this by no means proves that the moral propositions so defined are true—the predicated objectivity may be a sheer illusion.[35]

Nothing in the mere dictates of common sense in favor of moral objectivity can guarantee such objectivity. Even the soft subjectivist can account for the psychological lure of moral disagreement, and the objectivist cannot build real values only on figures of speech.

A second meta-ethical objection to an account like Westermarck's is that it commits the genetic fallacy. Although Westermarck himself has not often been singled out as exemplifying this failing, many people presume that any anthropologically or sociologically sensitive treatment of morality runs the risk of illicitly jumping from matters of fact to matters of justification.

Westermarck, however, was cautious in the way he used facts. Indeed, he even asserted that "facts in themselves leave me as a rule rather cold"; the challenge was to "extract from them something which they do not directly express," that is, hypotheses about the underlying forms of human behavior.[36] He held that to be acceptable an ethical theory must be set upon a solid evidentiary base and that this requires a description of the particular workings out in society of human psychological and biological endowments. Thus, *The Origin and Development of the Moral Ideas* was "so constructed that the comparative and historical treatment of the moral ideas in the last three-quarters of the book was necessary to confirm the general theory of the nature of the moral consciousness set forth in the earlier chapters."[37]

If we keep in mind the two strategies that Westermarck used against the objectivist—philosophical refutation and alternative explanation—it is unlikely that we will accuse him of a fallacious geneticism. The soft subjectivist who points to facts about biology and psychology in denying the existence of objective moral principles need not intend such an appeal as a substitute for, but only as a supplement to, an independent attack on the failures of the objectivists to prove their case. Yet it is a powerful appeal nonetheless. We cannot consistently tell whether individual utterances are true or false, justified or unjustified, simply by examining the psychology of their utterers, but we can conclude that certain categories of utterance, insofar as they have an ultimate, irreducible, and dominant emotional component, are not of the sort that lend themselves to rational settlement in the way that typically factual utterances do. If we can establish that moral judgments—whatever their form in ordinary language—have no more inherent claim to be stating moral facts than do mere expressions of feelings, and that moral judgments have purposes and functions that belie the rationalistic, intuitionistic pictures often drawn of them, then our logico-empirical study pays justificatory benefits. We shall have established that "the moral concepts are based upon emotions and that the contents of an emotion fall entirely outside the category of truth."[38]

VII

The two most popular normative objections to a Westermarckian soft subjectivism, and to relativism and subjectivism generally, are even more illuminative of their target than are the meta-ethical objections. With an undoubtedly unintended hint of paradox, critics of subjectivism have argued that it countenances nihilism on the one hand—the view that no moral principles are worthy of respect—and excessive tolerance on the other hand—the view that all moral principles should be generously respected as products of particular societies.

As a reading of his autobiography amply indicates, Westermarck was neither nihilistic nor tolerant of everything. But what theoretical basis can soft subjectivists have for holding some moral principles and rejecting others?

Moore asked just this question in his essay "The Nature of Moral Philosophy." Speaking again directly of Westermarck, he wondered how it could be said on such an account that one morality is higher than another—in other words, how the soft subjectivist can consistently claim there are no objective moral principles yet assert that one moral principle is a *better* guide to conduct than another.[39]

But Moore's perplexity can readily be dissolved by distinguishing between ordinary and reconstructed moral judgments. Ordinary moral judgments as made by ordinary moral speakers do make a claim to objectivity, according to Westermarck, and hence we can understand the sense in which they postulate "better" and "worse," even though they do not succeed in attributing objective properties. Soft subjectivists, on the other hand, recognize the error of objectivizing and should avoid it in their own pronouncements about morality; they should, as ordinary speakers do not, forgo professing the objective and universal validity of the moral emotions which they merely happen to feel.

From this, however, it scarcely follows that they must dispense with the language of morality entirely, for soft subjectivists still continue to feel moral emotions and

moral language can be used to express those emotions. All that is required of them, on grounds of consistency, is that the illusory belief that moral judgments state moral facts should no longer play a role in their moral psychology. They therefore are entitled to call one thing right and another wrong, but "right" and "wrong" will now have different meanings for them from those which they once had:

> every one of us makes use of the words sunrise and sunset, which are expressions from a time when people thought that the sun rose and set, though nobody now holds this view. Why, then, should not the ethical subjectivist be allowed to use the old terms for moral qualities, although he maintains that the objective validity generally implied in them is a mere illusion?[40]

Moral terms now relate not to facts at all, but to the soft subjectivists' endorsements of modes of conduct. Hence at the level of reconstructed moral judgments the soft subjectivist view begins to resemble prescriptivist and emotivist views.

Like those views, however, it has to overcome the worry that morality will seem arbitrary and insecure if robbed of the objective content normally ascribed to it. Westermarck thought his meta-ethical system provided well-tested empirical hypotheses about what there is—or, in the case of moral facts, about what there is not—and that it could not be disproven simply because it led to regrettable practical consequences:

> It is needless to say that a scientific theory is not invalidated by the mere fact that it is likely to cause mischief. The unfortunate circumstance that there do exist dangerous things in the world, proves that something may be dangerous and yet true.[41]

But he vehemently denied that the consequences of soft subjectivism would be regrettable. For one thing, the effect on moral argument would be fairly modest. So much of ordinary moral controversy is centered not around ultimate moral facts but around ordinary, everyday facts: it is based on incomplete information, careless assumptions, false applications, unconscious biases. At the level of fundamental moral principles, the soft subjectivist view does have distinct practical and theoretical consequences; but, given the tenacity with which moral emotions can resist unwelcome facts, we need scarcely fear that our present approbations and disapprobations would change drastically were soft subjectivism more widely accepted. There would still be plenty left for us to bicker about, and even if we recognized that there was no further rational way to settle some ethical questions, we could still resort to other means of persuasion.

Nor would soft subjectivism lead to an unacceptable arbitrariness at the fundamental level. If every vestige of the external validity of moral truths were removed, if ultimate moral judgments were seen as merely expressive and prescriptive, our moral judgments would not cease to have a basis: "why should the moral law command less obedience because it forms a part of ourselves?"[42] Morality is not some fragile, artificial device elaborately constructed to achieve an arbitrary goal, but rather a development through evolution of patterns of reacting to the natural settings in which people find themselves: "We approve and disapprove because we cannot do otherwise; our moral consciousness belongs to our mental constitution, which we cannot change as we please."[43] Moral emotions are well-settled responses to important concerns, and there are psychological, biological, and sociological methods for understanding how moral beliefs come to be what they are. At the level of fundamental belief, then, we can no longer *justify,* but we are still able to *explain* and we will still want to *recommend.*

Will we want to tolerate? This objection to soft subjectivism has generally taken two forms. It has been argued, most notably by Bernard Williams, that it is inconsistent to deny the objectivity of moral values yet to wax eloquent over the real virtues of tolerance.[44] But it should be clear from what has been said that Westermarck was guilty of no such contradiction because he made no claim that his moral judgments were absolute, objective moral prerogatives. Quite the contrary: he was fully aware of the commending function of moral judgments, and there is no reason why he should be forbidden to commend tolerance.

Alternatively, the objection from tolerance may be that the soft subjectivist is too tolerant and that some things should not be tolerated.[45] But why must a soft subjectivist believe in extreme tolerance? As Westermarck says:

> I do not even subscribe to that beautiful modern sophism which admits every man's conscience to be an infallible guide. If we had to recognise, or rather if we did recognise, as right everything which is held to be right by anybody, savage or Christian, criminal or saint, morality would really suffer a serious loss.[46]

Sometimes subjectivists and ethical relativists are pictured by their critics as holding that an action can be right in one society—not simply *thought* right, for that is only a descriptive, cultural relativism—and its opposite right in another society. Universal tolerance is then a small step, for why should we be intolerant of what is *right?* But Westermarck is more nearly claiming that each society is *wrong* in its objectivized claims about what is right, and once this is recognized there is no need to put up with whatever *feelings* others may happen to have. Hence, extreme tolerance, for Westermarck, is neither a universally binding moral fact nor a personal preference.

Yet it does seem both undeniable and welcome that a consequence of adopting soft subjectivism would be, within limits, a greater tolerance of other views—not the sort of tolerance that would embrace any atrocity condoned by some society, but one which showed greater respect for other persons and their circumstances. Our moral judgments, instead of being complacent towards ourselves and critical of others, would through greater understanding become more self-critical and more generous towards others: "Could it be brought home to people that there is no absolute standard in morality, they would perhaps be somewhat more tolerant in their judgments, and more apt to listen to the voice of reason."[47] Feelings can still be held intolerantly, but one of the props for intolerance—the self-satisfied, unreflective conviction of one's own absolute rightness—has been removed.

Far from leading to nihilism or excessive tolerance, soft subjectivism has consequences which its exponents can consistently and conscientiously recommend. Thus, Huntington Cairns has taken an aggressive stance in defending the normative implications of soft subjectivism:

> It seems to me that Professor Westermarck's general position from the point of view of the good life is immeasurably superior to that of his opponents. In judging moral precepts, if his view is adopted, the force of tradition is minimized and the role of reason is increased. This is a merit which few objective moralists can claim for the systems proposed by them.[48]

Fears about the practical effects of a soft subjectivist meta-ethics are misplaced. The moral horrors that have been and are being committed cannot be laid at the door of the soft subjectivist, but rather are fanatical extensions of dogmatic and cruel ethical objectivisms, for which a greater measure of ethical skepticism may be a helpful corrective.

VIII

From these various bits and pieces of Westermarck's view we can draw together the outlines of a soft subjectivist approach to ethics.

The chief contention of the soft subjectivist is that there can be no correspondence theory of moral truth, because there are no moral facts to which our moral judgments could coincide. As Hume has stated the matter:

> Take any action allow'd to be vicious: Wilful murder, for instance. Examine it in all lights, and see if you can find that matter of fact, or real existence, which you call *vice.* In which-ever way you take it, you find only certain passions, motives, volitions and thoughts. There is no other matter of fact in the case.[49]

Nor do efforts to provide a coherence theory of moral truth help much, because even the most attractive coherence theories are separated only by accuracy in describing ideas, appeal to personal taste, and complexity from consistent but close-minded dogmatism; all are shut off, in principle, from objective facts. Yet we have much to learn from a coherence approach insofar as it attempts simply to relate the common features of a human moral sense—not the inflated perceptual organ that earlier philosophers thought could grasp objective prescriptions, but only that part of our mental constitution which prompts us to feel moral approbation and disapprobation towards the actions we observe. After all, we make this moral sense our ultimate arbiter of the acceptability of moral principles so we should know more about it. With this as our task we could start with the armchair approach of John Rawls, interpreted merely as an inquiry into patterns of belief; move to the richer empirical studies of human moral behavior offered by Westermarck; and freshen the account with the latest findings of the human sciences, in particular of sociobiology.

To reach conclusions at the general level it is necessary to begin with the specifics of the social behavior of actual people. And because human beings are biological phenomena it is possible to place their conduct on a hard basis of fact by examining their intercourse with each other and with their environment, rather than by meditating on the metaphysical authenticity of their moral nature. In understanding why we behave the way we do morally, we uncover the fundamental emotional urges to which we are subjected. Through the continuous operation of the natural lottery, coupled with the harsh realities of struggle in an often uncongenial physical environment, we have been endowed after a long period of selection with fairly fixed ways of reacting to events—our behavior and even our corresponding perceptions of reality have been determined by our genetic and environmental conditionings. There is variation in detail, but also considerable uniformity on the large scale, in the way people act and react. Behavior has readily observable and distinguishable features, and in the case of moral behavior the specific emotions which give rise to moral beliefs can be isolated. These are retributive emotions, either of gratitude or resentment, which arise on an impartial and disinterested basis. And although we cannot draw any *normative* conclusions from the fact that natural selection influences the moral feelings—the crude evolutionisms of the nineteenth century made just this illicit jump from "is" to "ought"—we can incorporate the realities of evolutionary development into an *explanatory* account that provides further support for soft subjectivism:

> The origin of the retributive emotions may be explained by their usefulness to the species. Resentment, like protective reflex action, from which it has gradually developed, is a means of protection for the animal owing to its tendency to remove a cause of danger. The disposition to experience it may consequently be regarded as an element in the animal's mental constitution that has been acquired through the influence of natural selection in the struggle for existence.[50]

Some moral codes—those which exhibit certain ranges in the balance between selfishness and altruism, between aggression and cooperation—will equip people better than others in their struggle for survival and hence will tend to predominate over time. Like opposable thumbs, moral beliefs have survival value. But while this process appears to bestow a biological seal of approval on the normative, it can generate only the conviction of moral objectivity, not moral objectivity itself. Moral beliefs activated by retributive emotions—especially emotions of resentment, which dominate our moral thinking—can be *understood,* at least in part, in terms of their biological function, even though they cannot (as the earlier evolutionists thought) be *justified* by that function.

The soft subjectivist picture of the moral emotions is compatible with a world in which some moral practices resemble each other fairly widely—for example, the giving of preference to relatives over strangers—while others vary dramatically—for example, the kindness accorded to animals. It draws no hasty conclusion that diversity reveals the error of objectivism, but rather examines the reasons why diverse moral practices really are diverse in order to show that not all moral disputes can be assimilated to the model of theoretical disagreement.

By recognizing the social interplay of these moral emotions we can also understand the way in which the terms used to describe and name them originate. In turn, we can then have a secure foundation for appraising the role of language in expressing moral sentiments. The connection between language and emotions, however, is not necessarily direct. We cannot simply pick any moral judgment and expect to trace it immediately to an emotion in the person who utters it. Of course, if the judgment is uttered sincerely there usually is the implication that the utterer in fact has some attitude towards what he or she is talking about; otherwise there would be no point in using *moral* language. But this attitude may be one's own, that of some authority one respects, or even of society itself; and it may vary in intensity from deep conviction to near unconcern. Morality as a whole reflects our overriding concerns, but individual moral judgments may be only pale instances of them. All this, however, is implied by sincere moral utterance, and not part of the meaning of the utterance itself. Typically, to make an ordinary moral judgment is not consciously to describe, report, or even express a moral emotion, although it may have those effects, but rather to ascribe a property to something; and because most people are objectivists, even though not on explicit or philosophical grounds, the properties ascribed are thought to be objective. Westermarck's task was to show that this sort of moral attribution involves an error, which he did by tracing the properties attributed by moral concepts to their ultimate emotional foundation. Once this is done, it is not difficult to account for the phenomena of moral disagreement and moral dogmatism.

Furthermore, the soft subjectivist analysis of moral judgments resolves Hume's paradox that, although it may seem otherwise, reason itself has no motivating force.[51] On Westermarck's view, the inward link to emotions can account for the prescriptiveness of moral judgments, while the outward projection of emotions can explain the apparent objectivity of those judgments. Intuited "moral facts" cannot by themselves influence conduct, as Hume realized; but objectivized moral emotions not only, by projection, can masquerade as universal requirements, but also, through their emotional pedigree, can move us to action.

Soft subjectivism is skeptical in that it denies that there is an objective normative morality. But in another sense, soft subjectivists are much less skeptical about morality than are many of their opponents. Too often, the claim that intuition provides genuine insight into morality serves only to limit inquiry. Like the uncritical application of a notion of instinct in biology, reliance on intuition as an explanatory or justificatory device may lead to sterility in analysis; for if some moral concepts are known only through intuitive reflection, as Moore maintained, then there may not be much more to say about them. On the other hand, an empiricist account like Westermarck's is able to comment with richness of detail about the actual facts of moral behavior.[52] By forgoing "moral facts" the analysis can center on facts about morality; and Moorean opponents are not much more forthcoming about "moral facts" anyway, except to assert that they exist.

And soft subjectivism may produce benefits as well at the level of normative morality. Unlike crude objectivism it encourages us to take a critical attitude towards our own views and an understanding one towards the views of others. Unlike crude nihilism it recognizes the continuing existence of moral emotions that will need reconstructed moral principles for their expression. The soft subjectivist can echo Leslie Stephen's telling phrase, "I now believe in nothing to put it shortly; but I do not the less believe in morality. . . . "[53] And unlike crude relativism, which makes the individual the moral slave of society by basing all values on those which societies actually hold, soft subjectivism puts the individual at the center of the moral stage.

Hence, the soft subjectivist argues that values are neither discovered, non-existent, nor received. They are created—created by acts of individual choice. In Westermarck's words:

> Far above the vulgar idea that the right is a settled something to which everybody has to adjust his opinions, rises the conviction that it has its existence in each individual mind, capable of any expansion, proclaiming its own right to exist, and, if need be, venturing to make a stand against the whole world. Such a conviction makes for progress.[54]

NOTES

[1] Edward Westermarck, *The Origin and Development of the Moral Ideas*, 2 vols. (London: Macmillan and Co., 1906-8), 1:17; *Memories of My Life*, trans. Anna Barwell (London: George Allen & Unwin Ltd., 1929 [1927]),

p. 101; and *Ethical Relativity,* International Library of Psychology, Philosophy, and Scientific Method (London: Kegan Paul, Trench, Trubner & Co., 1932), p. 60. The first and third of these works are hereafter cited as *"ODMI"* and *"ER"* respectively.

[2] The terms "objectivism" and "subjectivism" are, of course, bundles of confusion. Thus, some attitudinal subjectivisms are objectivist in the sense that they ascribe *truth or falsity* to moral judgments that have been reduced to reports of feeling, and utilitarian objectivisms are subjectivist in the sense that they rest morality on calculi of *personal* pleasure. In what follows I understand objectivists, roughly and minimally, to be claiming that moral concepts can be used without qualifying expressions ("in my opinion," "according to society S," etc.) and that there is some method (the categorical imperative, the principle of utility, the original position under a veil of ignorance, etc.) for determining the *correct* application of these concepts.

[3] Responding with uncharacteristic belligerence to a personal attack, Westermarck even claimed that "in my recent book *Ethical Relativity* I have emphatically refuted the objectivity of all moral values." Westermarck, *Three Essays on Sex and Marriage* (London: Macmillan and Co., 1934), p. 335.

[4] *ER,* pp. 3-61.

[5] Brand Blanshard, *Reason and Goodness* (London: George Allen & Unwin Ltd., 1961), p. 120. Blanshard, nevertheless, takes exception to Westermarck's view.

[6] *ER,* p. 177. See also *ODMI,* 2:742.

[7] Stroup, "In Defense of Westermarck," *Journal of the History of Philosophy* 19, no. 2 (April 1981): 215. In the present article I have drawn on some sections from this previous paper, as well as from my "Westermarck's Ethical Relativism," *Ajatus* 38 (1980): 31-71.

[8] G. E. Moore, *Philosophical Studies,* International Library of Psychology, Philosophy, and Scientific Method (London: Kegan Paul, Trench, Trubner & Co., 1922), p. 333-34.

[9] *ER,* p. 117. There is a good account in Blanshard, *Reason,* pp. 108-9.

[10] *ER,* pp. 49-52; *ODMI,* 1:8-17.

[11] *ER,* p. 50; *ODMI,* 1:9.

[12] *ER,* pp. 50-51; *ODMI,* 1:14.

[13] David Hume, *An Enquiry concerning the Principles of Morals,* in *Enquiries concerning the Human Understanding and concerning the Principles of Morals,* ed. L. A. Selby-Bigge, 2nd ed. (Oxford: The Clarendon Press, 1962 [1748]), p. 294 (App. I.v.).

[14] *ER,* p. 115.

[15] *ODMI,* 1:104.

[16] *ER,* pp. 92-93; Westermarck, *Christianity and Morals* (London: Kegan Paul, Trench, Trubner & Co., 1939), p. 12.

[17] *ER,* p. 50. See also *ODMI,* 1:9.

[18] *ODMI,* 1:105. See also *ER,* p. 46.

[19] Westermarck observes, "It seems very probable that originally moral concepts were not clearly differentiated from other more comprehensive generalizations, and that they assumed a more definite shape only by slow degrees." *ER,* p. 118.

[20] *ER,* p. 142.

[21] Stuart L. Penn, "The Ethical Relativism of Edward Westermarck" (Ph. D. diss., Yale University, 1957), p. 2.

[22] *ODMI,* 1:8. On the next page Westermarck talks of the "comparatively uniform nature of the moral consciousness."

[23] Westermarck, *Christianity,* p. 34.

[24] *ER,* pp. 185-87.

[25] *ER,* p. 187.

[26] *ER,* p. 196.

[27] *ER,* p. 216.

[28] *ER,* p. 200.

[29] *ER,* p. 199.

[30] *ER,* p. 213.

[31] *ER,* p. 207. Or, to put it another way, "no intellectual enlightenment, no scrutiny of facts, can decide how far the interests of the lower animals should be regarded when conflicting with those of men, or how far a person is bound, or allowed, to promote the welfare of his nation, or his own welfare, at the cost of that of other nations or other individuals." *ODMI,* 1:11-12.

[32] *ER,* p. 4.

[33] *ER,* p. 43.

[34] Moore, *Philosophical Studies,* pp. 310-39.

[35] *ER,* p. 47. On p. 42 Westermarck cites Moore's own statement, in *Principia Ethica* (Cambridge: Cambridge University Press, 1903), p. 143: "That a proposition appears to be true can never be a valid argument that true it really is."

[36] Westermarck, *Memories,* p. 28.

[37] Ibid., p. 232.

[38] *ODMI,* 1:17. See also *ER,* p. 60.

[39] Moore, *Philosophical Studies,* pp. 334-35.

[40] *ER,* p. 49.

[41] *ER,* p. 58.

[42] *ER,* p. 59.

[43] *ER,* pp. 58-59.

[44] Bernard Williams, *Morality: An Introduction to Ethics* (New York: Harper & Row, 1972), pp. 20-21.

[45] W. T. Stace levelled such a charge against Westermarck in his *The Concept of Morals* (New York: The Macmillan Company, 1937), p. 58.

[46] *ODMI,* 1:19.

[47] *ODMI,* 1:20. See also *ER,* p. 59.

[48] Huntington Cairns, review of *ER,* in *The Baltimore Evening Sun,* 6 August 1932, p. 4.

[49] Hume, *A Treatise of Human Nature,* ed. L. A. Selby-Bigge (Oxford: The Clarendon Press, 1967 [1739]), p. 468. (III.i.).

[50] Westermarck *Christianity,* p. 7.

[51] Hume, *Treatise,* pp. 413-18. (II. iii. 3).

[52] Westermarck claimed (*ER,* p. 59) that "a theory which leads to an examination of the psychological and historical origin of people's moral opinions should be more useful than a theory which postulates moral truths enunciated by self-evident intuitions that are unchangeable." Samuel Alexander, in his review of *Ethical Relativity (Manchester Guardian,* 13 June 1932, p. 5) concurred: "it is a refreshment to have a writer who attempts to throw light on right and wrong and good by tracing them back to their origin. True enough, we cannot explain the flavour of good any more than we can explain why red is red. Yet just as we learn something vital about red by discovering its wave-length, so psychology and anthropology may give us vital and also hopeful knowledge about the nature of morals."

[53] Quoted in Quentin Bell, *Bloomsbury* (London: Weidenfeld and Nicolson, 1968), p. 24.

[54] *ODMI,* 1:20.

FURTHER READING

Bibliography

Stroup, Timothy. *Westermarck's Ethics*. Helsinki: Publications of the Research Institute of the Abo Akademi Foundation, 1982, 332 p.

> Presents a detailed listing of books and articles by and about Westermarck.

Criticism

Fletcher, Ronald. *The Making of Sociology: A Study of Sociological Theory, Volume Two: Developments*. New York: Charles Scribner's Sons, 1971, 855 p.

> Asserts that Westermarck attempted to use Darwinism to find biological causes for the necessary emergence of social institutions.

Hill, Thomas English. *Contemporary Ethical Theories*. New York: The Macmillan Company, 1950, 368 p.

> Declares *The Origin and Development of the Moral Ideas* a classic work of moral sentiment theories and admires the consistency of Westermarck's theories throughout his writing to differentiate him from the Logical Positivists.

Twentieth-Century
Literary Criticism

Cumulative Indexes
Volumes 1-87

How to Use This Index

The main references

> Calvino, Italo
> 1923–1985 .... CLC 5, 8, 11, 22, 33, 39,
> 73; SSC 3

list all author entries in the following Gale Literary Criticism series:

BLC = *Black Literature Criticism*
CLC = *Contemporary Literary Criticism*
CLR = *Children's Literature Review*
CMLC = *Classical and Medieval Literature Criticism*
DA = *DISCovering Authors*
DAB = *DISCovering Authors: British*
DAC = *DISCovering Authors: Canadian*
DAM = *DISCovering Authors: Modules*
   DRAM: *Dramatists Module*; *MST*: *Most-Studied Authors Module*;
   MULT: *Multicultural Authors Module*; *NOV*: *Novelists Module*;
   POET: *Poets Module*; *POP*: *Popular Fiction and Genre Authors Module*
DC = *Drama Criticism*
HLC = *Hispanic Literature Criticism*
LC = *Literature Criticism from 1400 to 1800*
NCLC = *Nineteenth-Century Literature Criticism*
PC = *Poetry Criticism*
SSC = *Short Story Criticism*
TCLC = *Twentieth-Century Literary Criticism*
WLC = *World Literature Criticism, 1500 to the Present*

The cross-references

> See also CANR 23; CA 85-88;
>   obituary CA116

list all author entries in the following Gale biographical and literary sources:

AAYA = *Authors & Artists for Young Adults*
AITN = *Authors in the News*
BEST = *Bestsellers*
BW = *Black Writers*
CA = *Contemporary Authors*
CAAS = *Contemporary Authors Autobiography Series*
CABS = *Contemporary Authors Bibliographical Series*
CANR = *Contemporary Authors New Revision Series*
CAP = *Contemporary Authors Permanent Series*
CDALB = *Concise Dictionary of American Literary Biography*
CDBLB = *Concise Dictionary of British Literary Biography*
DLB = *Dictionary of Literary Biography*
DLBD = *Dictionary of Literary Biography Documentary Series*
DLBY = *Dictionary of Literary Biography Yearbook*
HW = *Hispanic Writers*
JRDA = *Junior DISCovering Authors*
MAICYA = *Major Authors and Illustrators for Children and Young Adults*
MTCW = *Major 20th-Century Writers*
NNAL = *Native North American Literature*
SAAS = *Something about the Author Autobiography Series*
SATA = *Something about the Author*
YABC = *Yesterday's Authors of Books for Children*

20/1631
See Upward, Allen

A/C Cross
See Lawrence, T(homas) E(dward)

Abasiyanik, Sait Faik 1906-1954
See Sait Faik
See also CA 123

Abbey, Edward 1927-1989 .... **CLC 36, 59**
See also CA 45-48; 128; CANR 2, 41

Abbott, Lee K(ittredge) 1947- .... **CLC 48**
See also CA 124; CANR 51; DLB 130

Abe, Kobo 1924-1993 **CLC 8, 22, 53, 81; DAM NOV**
See also CA 65-68; 140; CANR 24, 60; DLB 182; MTCW 1

Abelard, Peter c. 1079-c. 1142 ...... **CMLC 11**
See also DLB 115, 208

Abell, Kjeld 1901-1961 .... **CLC 15**
See also CA 111

Abish, Walter 1931- .... **CLC 22**
See also CA 101; CANR 37; DLB 130

Abrahams, Peter (Henry) 1919- .... **CLC 4**
See also BW 1; CA 57-60; CANR 26; DLB 117; MTCW 1

Abrams, M(eyer) H(oward) 1912- .... **CLC 24**
See also CA 57-60; CANR 13, 33; DLB 67

Abse, Dannie 1923- . **CLC 7, 29; DAB; DAM POET**
See also CA 53-56; CAAS 1; CANR 4, 46, 74; DLB 27

Achebe, (Albert) Chinua(lumogu) 1930- **C L C 1, 3, 5, 7, 11, 26, 51, 75; BLC 1; DA; DAB; DAC; DAM MST, MULT, NOV; WLC**
See also AAYA 15; BW 2; CA 1-4R; CANR 6, 26, 47, 73; CLR 20; DLB 117; MAICYA; MTCW 1; SATA 40; SATA-Brief 38

Acker, Kathy 1948-1997 .... **CLC 45, 111**
See also CA 117; 122; 162; CANR 55

Ackroyd, Peter 1949- .... **CLC 34, 52**
See also CA 123; 127; CANR 51, 74; DLB 155; INT 127

Acorn, Milton 1923- .... **CLC 15; DAC**
See also CA 103; DLB 53; INT 103

Adamov, Arthur 1908-1970 **CLC 4, 25; DAM DRAM**
See also CA 17-18; 25-28R; CAP 2; MTCW 1

Adams, Alice (Boyd) 1926- **CLC 6, 13, 46; SSC 24**
See also CA 81-84; CANR 26, 53, 75; DLBY 86; INT CANR-26; MTCW 1

Adams, Andy 1859-1935 .... **TCLC 56**
See also YABC 1

Adams, Brooks 1848-1927 .... **TCLC 80**
See also CA 123; DLB 47

Adams, Douglas (Noel) 1952- .... **CLC 27, 60; DAM POP**
See also AAYA 4; BEST 89:3; CA 106; CANR 34, 64; DLBY 83; JRDA

Adams, Francis 1862-1893 .... **NCLC 33**

Adams, Henry (Brooks) 1838-1918 **TCLC 4, 52; DA; DAB; DAC; DAM MST**
See also CA 104; 133; DLB 12, 47, 189

Adams, Richard (George) 1920- **CLC 4, 5, 18; DAM NOV**
See also AAYA 16; AITN 1, 2; CA 49-52; CANR 3, 35; CLR 20; JRDA; MAICYA; MTCW 1; SATA 7, 69

Adamson, Joy(-Friederike Victoria) 1910-1980 **CLC 17**
See also CA 69-72; 93-96; CANR 22; MTCW 1; SATA 11; SATA-Obit 22

Adcock, Fleur 1934- .... **CLC 41**
See also CA 25-28R; CAAS 23; CANR 11, 34, 69; DLB 40

Addams, Charles (Samuel) 1912-1988 **CLC 30**
See also CA 61-64; 126; CANR 12

Addams, Jane 1860-1945 .... **TCLC 76**

Addison, Joseph 1672-1719 .... **LC 18**
See also CDBLB 1660-1789; DLB 101

Adler, Alfred (F.) 1870-1937 .... **TCLC 61**
See also CA 119; 159

Adler, C(arole) S(chwerdtfeger) 1932- . **C L C 35**
See also AAYA 4; CA 89-92; CANR 19, 40; JRDA; MAICYA; SAAS 15; SATA 26, 63, 102

Adler, Renata 1938- .... **CLC 8, 31**
See also CA 49-52; CANR 5, 22, 52; MTCW 1

Ady, Endre 1877-1919 .... **TCLC 11**
See also CA 107

A.E. 1867-1935 .... **TCLC 3, 10**
See also Russell, George William

Aeschylus 525B.C.-456B.C. .. **CMLC 11; DA; DAB; DAC; DAM DRAM, MST; DC 8; WLCS**
See also DLB 176

Aesop 620(?)B.C.-564(?)B.C. .... **CMLC 24**
See also CLR 14; MAICYA; SATA 64

Affable Hawk
See MacCarthy, Sir(Charles Otto) Desmond

Africa, Ben
See Bosman, Herman Charles

Afton, Effie
See Harper, Frances Ellen Watkins

Agapida, Fray Antonio
See Irving, Washington

Agee, James (Rufus) 1909-1955 **TCLC 1, 19; DAM NOV**
See also AITN 1; CA 108; 148; CDALB 1941-1968; DLB 2, 26, 152

Aghill, Gordon
See Silverberg, Robert

Agnon, S(hmuel) Y(osef Halevi) 1888-1970 **CLC 4, 8, 14; SSC 30**
See also CA 17-18; 25-28R; CANR 60; CAP 2; MTCW 1

Agrippa von Nettesheim, Henry Cornelius 1486-1535 .... **LC 27**

Aherne, Owen
See Cassill, R(onald) V(erlin)

Ai 1947- .... **CLC 4, 14, 69**
See also CA 85-88; CAAS 13; CANR 70; DLB 120

Aickman, Robert (Fordyce) 1914-1981 **C L C 57**
See also CA 5-8R; CANR 3, 72

Aiken, Conrad (Potter) 1889-1973 **CLC 1, 3, 5, 10, 52; DAM NOV, POET; SSC 9**
See also CA 5-8R; 45-48; CANR 4, 60; CDALB 1929-1941; DLB 9, 45, 102; MTCW 1; SATA 3, 30

Aiken, Joan (Delano) 1924- .... **CLC 35**
See also AAYA 1, 25; CA 9-12R; CANR 4, 23, 34, 64; CLR 1, 19; DLB 161; JRDA; MAICYA; MTCW 1; SAAS 1; SATA 2, 30, 73

Ainsworth, William Harrison 1805-1882 **NCLC 13**
See also DLB 21; SATA 24

Aitmatov, Chingiz (Torekulovich) 1928- **C L C 71**
See also CA 103; CANR 38; MTCW 1; SATA 56

Akers, Floyd
See Baum, L(yman) Frank

Akhmadulina, Bella Akhatovna 1937- **CLC 53; DAM POET**
See also CA 65-68

Akhmatova, Anna 1888-1966 **CLC 11, 25, 64; DAM POET; PC 2**.
See also CA 19-20; 25-28R; CANR 35; CAP 1; MTCW 1

Aksakov, Sergei Timofeyvich 1791-1859 **NCLC 2**
See also DLB 198

Aksenov, Vassily
See Aksyonov, Vassily (Pavlovich)

Akst, Daniel 1956- .... **CLC 109**
See also CA 161

Aksyonov, Vassily (Pavlovich) 1932- **CLC 22, 37, 101**
See also CA 53-56; CANR 12, 48

Akutagawa, Ryunosuke 1892-1927 **TCLC 16**
See also CA 117; 154

Alain 1868-1951 .... **TCLC 41**
See also CA 163

Alain-Fournier .... **TCLC 6**
See also Fournier, Henri Alban
See also DLB 65

Alarcon, Pedro Antonio de 1833-1891 **NCLC 1**

Alas (y Urena), Leopoldo (Enrique Garcia) 1852-1901 ....
TCLC 29
See also CA 113; 131; HW

Albee, Edward (Franklin III) 1928- **CLC 1, 2, 3, 5, 9, 11, 13, 25, 53, 86, 113; DA; DAB; DAC; DAM DRAM, MST; WLC**
See also AITN 1; CA 5-8R; CABS 3; CANR 8, 54, 74; CDALB 1941-1968; DLB 7; INT CANR-8; MTCW 1

Alberti, Rafael 1902- .... **CLC 7**
See also CA 85-88; DLB 108

Albert the Great 1200(?)-1280 ...... **CMLC 16**
See also DLB 115

Alcala-Galiano, Juan Valera y
See Valera y Alcala-Galiano, Juan

Andric, Ivo 1892-1975 .... **CLC 8**
See also CA 81-84; 57-60; CANR 43, 60; DLB 147; MTCW 1
Androvar
See Prado (Calvo), Pedro
Angelique, Pierre
See Bataille, Georges
Angell, Roger 1920- .... **CLC 26**
See also CA 57-60; CANR 13, 44, 70; DLB 171, 185
Angelou, Maya 1928-**CLC 12, 35, 64, 77; BLC 1; DA; DAB; DAC; DAM MST, MULT, POET, POP; WLCS**
See also AAYA 7, 20; BW 2; CA 65-68; CANR 19, 42, 65; CLR 53; DLB 38; MTCW 1; SATA 49
Anna Comnena 1083-1153 .... **CMLC 25**
Annensky, Innokenty (Fyodorovich) 1856-1909
TCLC 14
See also CA 110; 155
Annunzio, Gabriele d'
See D'Annunzio, Gabriele
Anodos
See Coleridge, Mary E(lizabeth)
Anon, Charles Robert
See Pessoa, Fernando (Antonio Nogueira)
Anouilh, Jean (Marie Lucien Pierre) 1910-1987
CLC 1, 3, 8, 13, 40, 50; DAM DRAM; DC 8
See also CA 17-20R; 123; CANR 32; MTCW 1
Anthony, Florence
See Ai
Anthony, John
See Ciardi, John (Anthony)
Anthony, Peter
See Shaffer, Anthony (Joshua); Shaffer, Peter (Levin)
Anthony, Piers 1934- .... **CLC 35; DAM POP**
See also AAYA 11; CA 21-24R; CANR 28, 56, 73; DLB 8; MTCW 1; SAAS 22; SATA 84
Anthony, Susan B(rownell) 1916-1991 **T C L C 84**
See also CA 89-92; 134
Antoine, Marc
See Proust, (Valentin-Louis-George-Eugene-) Marcel
Antoninus, Brother
See Everson, William (Oliver)
Antonioni, Michelangelo 1912- .... **CLC 20**
See also CA 73-76; CANR 45
Antschel, Paul 1920-1970
See Celan, Paul
See also CA 85-88; CANR 33, 61; MTCW 1
Anwar, Chairil 1922-1949 .... **TCLC 22**
See also CA 121
Apess, William 1798-1839(?)**NCLC 73; DAM MULT**
See also DLB 175; NNAL
Apollinaire, Guillaume 1880-1918**TCLC 3, 8, 51; DAM POET; PC 7**
See also Kostrowitzki, Wilhelm Apollinaris de
See also DLB 152
Appelfeld, Aharon 1932- .... **CLC 23, 47**
See also CA 112; 133
Apple, Max (Isaac) 1941-............... **CLC 9, 33**
See also CA 81-84; CANR 19, 54; DLB 130
Appleman, Philip (Dean) 1926- .... **CLC 51**
See also CA 13-16R; CAAS 18; CANR 6, 29, 56
Appleton, Lawrence
See Lovecraft, H(oward) P(hillips)
Apteryx
See Eliot, T(homas) S(tearns)
Apuleius, (Lucius Madaurensis) 125(?)-175(?)
CMLC 1
Aquin, Hubert 1929-1977 .... **CLC 15**
See also CA 105; DLB 53

Aquinas, Thomas 1224(?)-1274..... **CMLC 33**
See also DLB 115
Aragon, Louis 1897-1982.. **CLC 3, 22; DAM NOV, POET**
See also CA 69-72; 108; CANR 28, 71; DLB 72; MTCW 1
Arany, Janos 1817-1882 .... **NCLC 34**
Aranyos, Kakay
See Mikszath, Kalman
Arbuthnot, John 1667-1735 .... **LC 1**
See also DLB 101
Archer, Herbert Winslow
See Mencken, H(enry) L(ouis)
Archer, Jeffrey (Howard) 1940- ..... **CLC 28; DAM POP**
See also AAYA 16; BEST 89:3; CA 77-80; CANR 22, 52; INT CANR-22
Archer, Jules 1915- .... **CLC 12**
See also CA 9-12R; CANR 6, 69; SAAS 5; SATA 4, 85
Archer, Lee
See Ellison, Harlan (Jay)
Arden, John 1930-**CLC 6, 13, 15; DAM DRAM**
See also CA 13-16R; CAAS 4; CANR 31, 65, 67; DLB 13; MTCW 1
Arenas, Reinaldo 1943-1990 . **CLC 41; DAM MULT; HLC**
See also CA 124; 128; 133; CANR 73; DLB 145; HW
Arendt, Hannah 1906-1975 .... **CLC 66, 98**
See also CA 17-20R; 61-64; CANR 26, 60; MTCW 1
Aretino, Pietro 1492-1556 .... **LC 12**
Arghezi, Tudor 1880-1967 .... **CLC 80**
See also Theodorescu, Ion N.
See also CA 167
Arguedas, Jose Maria 1911-1969 **CLC 10, 18**
See also CA 89-92; CANR 73; DLB 113; HW
Argueta, Manlio 1936- .... **CLC 31**
See also CA 131; CANR 73; DLB 145; HW
Ariosto, Ludovico 1474-1533 .... **LC 6**
Aristides
See Epstein, Joseph
Aristophanes 450B.C.-385B.C.**CMLC 4; DA; DAB; DAC; DAM DRAM, MST; DC 2; WLCS**
See also DLB 176
Aristotle 384B.C.-322B.C. ... **CMLC 31; DA; DAB; DAC; DAM MST; WLCS**
See also DLB 176
Arlt, Roberto (Godofredo Christophersen) 1900-1942 ....
TCLC 29; DAM MULT; HLC
See also CA 123; 131; CANR 67; HW
Armah, Ayi Kwei 1939- . **CLC 5, 33; BLC 1; DAM MULT, POET**
See also BW 1; CA 61-64; CANR 21, 64; DLB 117; MTCW 1
Armatrading, Joan 1950- .... **CLC 17**
See also CA 114
Arnette, Robert
See Silverberg, Robert
Arnim, Achim von (Ludwig Joachim von Arnim) 1781-1831 ...... **NCLC 5; SSC 29**
See also DLB 90
Arnim, Bettina von 1785-1859 .... **NCLC 38**
See also DLB 90
Arnold, Matthew 1822-1888**NCLC 6, 29; DA; DAB; DAC; DAM MST, POET; PC 5; WLC**
See also CDBLB 1832-1890; DLB 32, 57
Arnold, Thomas 1795-1842 .... **NCLC 18**
See also DLB 55
Arnow, Harriette (Louisa) Simpson 1908-1986
CLC 2, 7, 18
See also CA 9-12R; 118; CANR 14; DLB 6; MTCW 1; SATA 42; SATA-Obit 47

Arouet, Francois-Marie
See Voltaire
Arp, Hans
See Arp, Jean
Arp, Jean 1887-1966 .... **CLC 5**
See also CA 81-84; 25-28R; CANR 42
Arrabal
See Arrabal, Fernando
Arrabal, Fernando 1932-.... **CLC 2, 9, 18, 58**
See also CA 9-12R; CANR 15
Arrick, Fran .... **CLC 30**
See also Gaberman, Judie Angell
Artaud, Antonin (Marie Joseph) 1896-1948
TCLC 3, 36; DAM DRAM
See also CA 104; 149
Arthur, Ruth M(abel) 1905-1979 ...... **CLC 12**
See also CA 9-12R; 85-88; CANR 4; SATA 7, 26
Artsybashev, Mikhail (Petrovich) 1878-1927
TCLC 31
See also CA 170
Arundel, Honor (Morfydd) 1919-1973**CLC 17**
See also CA 21-22; 41-44R; CAP 2; CLR 35; SATA 4; SATA-Obit 24
Arzner, Dorothy 1897-1979 .... **CLC 98**
Asch, Sholem 1880-1957 .... **TCLC 3**
See also CA 105
Ash, Shalom
See Asch, Sholem
Ashbery, John (Lawrence) 1927-**CLC 2, 3, 4, 6, 9, 13, 15, 25, 41, 77; DAM POET**
See also CA 5-8R; CANR 9, 37, 66; DLB 5, 165; DLBY 81; INT CANR-9; MTCW 1
Ashdown, Clifford
See Freeman, R(ichard) Austin
Ashe, Gordon
See Creasey, John
Ashton-Warner, Sylvia (Constance) 1908-1984
CLC 19
See also CA 69-72; 112; CANR 29; MTCW 1
Asimov, Isaac 1920-1992 **CLC 1, 3, 9, 19, 26, 76, 92; DAM POP**
See also AAYA 13; BEST 90:2; CA 1-4R; 137; CANR 2, 19, 36, 60; CLR 12; DLB 8; DLBY 92; INT CANR-19; JRDA; MAICYA; MTCW 1; SATA 1, 26, 74
Assis, Joaquim Maria Machado de
See Machado de Assis, Joaquim Maria
Astley, Thea (Beatrice May) 1925- ... **CLC 41**
See also CA 65-68; CANR 11, 43
Aston, James
See White, T(erence) H(anbury)
Asturias, Miguel Angel 1899-1974 **CLC 3, 8, 13; DAM MULT, NOV; HLC**
See also CA 25-28; 49-52; CANR 32; CAP 2; DLB 113; HW; MTCW 1
Atares, Carlos Saura
See Saura (Atares), Carlos
Atheling, William
See Pound, Ezra (Weston Loomis)
Atheling, William, Jr.
See Blish, James (Benjamin)
Atherton, Gertrude (Franklin Horn) 1857-1948
TCLC 2
See also CA 104; 155; DLB 9, 78, 186
Atherton, Lucius
See Masters, Edgar Lee
Atkins, Jack
See Harris, Mark
Atkinson, Kate .... **CLC 99**
See also CA 166
Attaway, William (Alexander) 1911-1986
CLC 92; BLC 1; DAM MULT
See also BW 2; CA 143; DLB 76
Atticus
See Fleming, Ian (Lancaster); Wilson, (Thomas) Woodrow

Bessie, Alvah 1904-1985 .... **CLC 23**
See also CA 5-8R; 116; CANR 2; DLB 26
Bethlen, T. D.
See Silverberg, Robert
Beti, Mongo ... CLC 27; BLC 1; DAM MULT
See also Biyidi, Alexandre
Betjeman, John 1906-1984 **CLC 2, 6, 10, 34, 43; DAB; DAM MST, POET**
See also CA 9-12R; 112; CANR 33, 56; CDBLB 1945-1960; DLB 20; DLBY 84; MTCW 1
Bettelheim, Bruno 1903-1990 .... **CLC 79**
See also CA 81-84; 131; CANR 23, 61; MTCW 1
Betti, Ugo 1892-1953 .... **TCLC 5**
See also CA 104; 155
Betts, Doris (Waugh) 1932- ...... **CLC 3, 6, 28**
See also CA 13-16R; CANR 9, 66; DLBY 82; INT CANR-9
Bevan, Alistair
See Roberts, Keith (John Kingston)
Bey, Pilaff
See Douglas, (George) Norman
Bialik, Chaim Nachman 1873-1934 **TCLC 25**
See also CA 170
Bickerstaff, Isaac
See Swift, Jonathan
Bidart, Frank 1939- .... **CLC 33**
See also CA 140
Bienek, Horst 1930- .... **CLC 7, 11**
See also CA 73-76; DLB 75
Bierce, Ambrose (Gwinett) 1842-1914(?)
TCLC 1, 7, 44; DA; DAC; DAM MST; SSC 9; WLC
See also CA 104; 139; CDALB 1865-1917; DLB 11, 12, 23, 71, 74, 186
Biggers, Earl Derr 1884-1933 .... **TCLC 65**
See also CA 108; 153
Billings, Josh
See Shaw, Henry Wheeler
Billington, (Lady) Rachel (Mary) 1942- **C L C 43**
See also AITN 2; CA 33-36R; CANR 44
Binyon, T(imothy) J(ohn) 1936- .... **CLC 34**
See also CA 111; CANR 28
Bioy Casares, Adolfo 1914-1984 **CLC 4, 8, 13, 88; DAM MULT; HLC; SSC 17**
See also CA 29-32R; CANR 19, 43, 66; DLB 113; HW; MTCW 1
Bird, Cordwainer
See Ellison, Harlan (Jay)
Bird, Robert Montgomery 1806-1854 **NCLC 1**
See also DLB 202
Birkerts, Sven 1951- .... **CLC 116**
See also CA 128; 133; CAAS 29; INT 133
Birney, (Alfred) Earle 1904-1995 **CLC 1, 4, 6, 11; DAC; DAM MST, POET**
See also CA 1-4R; CANR 5, 20; DLB 88; MTCW 1
Biruni, al 973-1048(?) .... **CMLC 28**
Bishop, Elizabeth 1911-1979 **CLC 1, 4, 9, 13, 15, 32; DA; DAC; DAM MST, POET; PC 3**
See also CA 5-8R; 89-92; CABS 2; CANR 26, 61; CDALB 1968-1988; DLB 5, 169; MTCW 1; SATA-Obit 24
Bishop, John 1935- .... **CLC 10**
See also CA 105
Bissett, Bill 1939- .... **CLC 18; PC 14**
See also CA 69-72; CAAS 19; CANR 15; DLB 53; MTCW 1
Bitov, Andrei (Georgievich) 1937- ... **CLC 57**
See also CA 142
Biyidi, Alexandre 1932-
See Beti, Mongo
See also BW 1; CA 114; 124; MTCW 1
Bjarme, Brynjolf
See Ibsen, Henrik (Johan)

Bjoernson, Bjoernstjerne (Martinius) 1832-1910 .... **TCLC 7, 37**
See also CA 104
Black, Robert
See Holdstock, Robert P.
Blackburn, Paul 1926-1971 .... **CLC 9, 43**
See also CA 81-84; 33-36R; CANR 34; DLB 16; DLBY 81
Black Elk 1863-1950 **TCLC 33; DAM MULT**
See also CA 144; NNAL
Black Hobart
See Sanders, (James) Ed(ward)
Blacklin, Malcolm
See Chambers, Aidan
Blackmore, R(ichard) D(oddridge) 1825-1900 **TCLC 27**
See also CA 120; DLB 18
Blackmur, R(ichard) P(almer) 1904-1965 **CLC 2, 24**
See also CA 11-12; 25-28R; CANR 71; CAP 1; DLB 63
Black Tarantula
See Acker, Kathy
Blackwood, Algernon (Henry) 1869-1951 **TCLC 5**
See also CA 105; 150; DLB 153, 156, 178
Blackwood, Caroline 1931-1996 **CLC 6, 9, 100**
See also CA 85-88; 151; CANR 32, 61, 65; DLB 14, 207; MTCW 1
Blade, Alexander
See Hamilton, Edmond; Silverberg, Robert
Blaga, Lucian 1895-1961 .... **CLC 75**
See also CA 157
Blair, Eric (Arthur) 1903-1950
See Orwell, George
See also CA 104; 132; DA; DAB; DAC; DAM MST, NOV; MTCW 1; SATA 29
Blair, Hugh 1718-1800 .... **NCLC 75**
Blais, Marie-Claire 1939- **CLC 2, 4, 6, 13, 22; DAC; DAM MST**
See also CA 21-24R; CAAS 4; CANR 38, 75; DLB 53; MTCW 1
Blaise, Clark 1940- .... **CLC 29**
See also AITN 2; CA 53-56; CAAS 3; CANR 5, 66; DLB 53
Blake, Fairley
See De Voto, Bernard (Augustine)
Blake, Nicholas
See Day Lewis, C(ecil)
See also DLB 77
Blake, William 1757-1827 . **NCLC 13, 37, 57; DA; DAB; DAC; DAM MST, POET; PC 12; WLC**
See also CDBLB 1789-1832; CLR 52; DLB 93, 163; MAICYA; SATA 30
Blasco Ibanez, Vicente 1867-1928 **TCLC 12; DAM NOV**
See also CA 110; 131; HW; MTCW 1
Blatty, William Peter 1928- **CLC 2; DAM POP**
See also CA 5-8R; CANR 9
Bleeck, Oliver
See Thomas, Ross (Elmore)
Blessing, Lee 1949- .... **CLC 54**
Blish, James (Benjamin) 1921-1975 . **CLC 14**
See also CA 1-4R; 57-60; CANR 3; DLB 8; MTCW 1; SATA 66
Bliss, Reginald
See Wells, H(erbert) G(eorge)
Blixen, Karen (Christentze Dinesen) 1885-1962
See Dinesen, Isak
See also CA 25-28; CANR 22, 50; CAP 2; MTCW 1; SATA 44
Bloch, Robert (Albert) 1917-1994 .... **CLC 33**
See also CA 5-8R; 146; CAAS 20; CANR 5; DLB 44; INT CANR-5; SATA 12; SATA-Obit 82
Blok, Alexander (Alexandrovich) 1880-1921

TCLC 5; PC 21
See also CA 104
Blom, Jan
See Breytenbach, Breyten
Bloom, Harold 1930- .... **CLC 24, 103**
See also CA 13-16R; CANR 39, 75; DLB 67
Bloomfield, Aurelius
See Bourne, Randolph S(illiman)
Blount, Roy (Alton), Jr. 1941- .... **CLC 38**
See also CA 53-56; CANR 10, 28, 61; INT CANR-28; MTCW 1
Bloy, Leon 1846-1917 .... **TCLC 22**
See also CA 121; DLB 123
Blume, Judy (Sussman) 1938- ... **CLC 12, 30; DAM NOV, POP**
See also AAYA 3, 26; CA 29-32R; CANR 13, 37, 66; CLR 2, 15; DLB 52; JRDA; MAICYA; MTCW 1; SATA 2, 31, 79
Blunden, Edmund (Charles) 1896-1974 **C L C 2, 56**
See also CA 17-18; 45-48; CANR 54; CAP 2; DLB 20, 100, 155; MTCW 1
Bly, Robert (Elwood) 1926- **CLC 1, 2, 5, 10, 15, 38; DAM POET**
See also CA 5-8R; CANR 41, 73; DLB 5; MTCW 1
Boas, Franz 1858-1942 .... **TCLC 56**
See also CA 115
Bobette
See Simenon, Georges (Jacques Christian)
Boccaccio, Giovanni 1313-1375 ... **CMLC 13; SSC 10**
Bochco, Steven 1943- .... **CLC 35**
See also AAYA 11; CA 124; 138
Bodel, Jean 1167(?)-1210 .... **CMLC 28**
Bodenheim, Maxwell 1892-1954 .... **TCLC 44**
See also CA 110; DLB 9, 45
Bodker, Cecil 1927- .... **CLC 21**
See also CA 73-76; CANR 13, 44; CLR 23; MAICYA; SATA 14
Boell, Heinrich (Theodor) 1917-1985 **CLC 2, 3, 6, 9, 11, 15, 27, 32, 72; DA; DAB; DAC; DAM MST, NOV; SSC 23; WLC**
See also CA 21-24R; 116; CANR 24; DLB 69; DLBY 85; MTCW 1
Boerne, Alfred
See Doeblin, Alfred
Boethius 480(?)-524(?) .... **CMLC 15**
See also DLB 115
Bogan, Louise 1897-1970 . **CLC 4, 39, 46, 93; DAM POET; PC 12**
See also CA 73-76; 25-28R; CANR 33; DLB 45, 169; MTCW 1
Bogarde, Dirk .... **CLC 19**
See also Van Den Bogarde, Derek Jules Gaspard Ulric Niven
See also DLB 14
Bogosian, Eric 1953- .... **CLC 45**
See also CA 138
Bograd, Larry 1953- .... **CLC 35**
See also CA 93-96; CANR 57; SAAS 21; SATA 33, 89
Boiardo, Matteo Maria 1441-1494 .... **LC 6**
Boileau-Despreaux, Nicolas 1636-1711 . **LC 3**
Bojer, Johan 1872-1959 .... **TCLC 64**
Boland, Eavan (Aisling) 1944- .. **CLC 40, 67, 113; DAM POET**
See also CA 143; CANR 61; DLB 40
Boll, Heinrich
See Boell, Heinrich (Theodor)
Bolt, Lee
See Faust, Frederick (Schiller)
Bolt, Robert (Oxton) 1924-1995 ..... **CLC 14; DAM DRAM**
See also CA 17-20R; 147; CANR 35, 67; DLB 13; MTCW 1
Bombet, Louis-Alexandre-Cesar

See Stendhal

Bomkauf
See Kaufman, Bob (Garnell)

Bonaventura .... **NCLC 35**
See also DLB 90

Bond, Edward 1934- **CLC 4, 6, 13, 23; DAM DRAM**
See also CA 25-28R; CANR 38, 67; DLB 13; MTCW 1

Bonham, Frank 1914-1989 .... **CLC 12**
See also AAYA 1; CA 9-12R; CANR 4, 36; JRDA; MAICYA; SAAS 3; SATA 1, 49; SATA-Obit 62

Bonnefoy, Yves 1923- ... **CLC 9, 15, 58; DAM MST, POET**
See also CA 85-88; CANR 33, 75; MTCW 1

Bontemps, Arna(ud Wendell) 1902-1973 **CLC 1, 18; BLC 1; DAM MULT, NOV, POET**
See also BW 1; CA 1-4R; 41-44R; CANR 4, 35; CLR 6; DLB 48, 51; JRDA; MAICYA; MTCW 1; SATA 2, 44; SATA-Obit 24

Booth, Martin 1944- .... **CLC 13**
See also CA 93-96; CAAS 2

Booth, Philip 1925- .... **CLC 23**
See also CA 5-8R; CANR 5; DLBY 82

Booth, Wayne C(layson) 1921- .... **CLC 24**
See also CA 1-4R; CAAS 5; CANR 3, 43; DLB 67

Borchert, Wolfgang 1921-1947 .... **TCLC 5**
See also CA 104; DLB 69, 124

Borel, Petrus 1809-1859 .... **NCLC 41**

Borges, Jorge Luis 1899-1986 **CLC 1, 2, 3, 4, 6, 8, 9, 10, 13, 19, 44, 48, 83; DA; DAB; DAC; DAM MST, MULT; HLC; PC 22; SSC 4; WLC**
See also AAYA 26; CA 21-24R; CANR 19, 33, 75; DLB 113; HW; MTCW 1

Borowski, Tadeusz 1922-1951 .... **TCLC 9**
See also CA 106; 154

Borrow, George (Henry) 1803-1881 **NCLC 9**
See also DLB 21, 55, 166

Bosman, Herman Charles 1905-1951 **TCLC 49**
See also Malan, Herman
See also CA 160

Bosschere, Jean de 1878(?)-1953 ... **TCLC 19**
See also CA 115

Boswell, James 1740-1795 . **LC 4; DA; DAB; DAC; DAM MST; WLC**
See also CDBLB 1660-1789; DLB 104, 142

Bottoms, David 1949- .... **CLC 53**
See also CA 105; CANR 22; DLB 120; DLBY 83

Boucicault, Dion 1820-1890 .... **NCLC 41**

Boucolon, Maryse 1937(?)-
See Conde, Maryse
See also CA 110; CANR 30, 53, 76

Bourget, Paul (Charles Joseph) 1852-1935 **TCLC 12**
See also CA 107; DLB 123

Bourjaily, Vance (Nye) 1922- .... **CLC 8, 62**
See also CA 1-4R; CAAS 1; CANR 2, 72; DLB 2, 143

Bourne, Randolph S(illiman) 1886-1918 **TCLC 16**
See also CA 117; 155; DLB 63

Bova, Ben(jamin William) 1932- ...... **CLC 45**
See also AAYA 16; CA 5-8R; CAAS 18; CANR 11, 56; CLR 3; DLBY 81; INT CANR-11; MAICYA; MTCW 1; SATA 6, 68

Bowen, Elizabeth (Dorothea Cole) 1899-1973 **CLC 1, 3, 6, 11, 15, 22, 118; DAM NOV; SSC 3, 28**
See also CA 17-18; 41-44R; CANR 35; CAP 2; CDBLB 1945-1960; DLB 15, 162; MTCW 1

Bowering, George 1935- .... **CLC 15, 47**

See also CA 21-24R; CAAS 16; CANR 10; DLB 53

Bowering, Marilyn R(uthe) 1949- .... **CLC 32**
See also CA 101; CANR 49

Bowers, Edgar 1924- .... **CLC 9**
See also CA 5-8R; CANR 24; DLB 5

Bowie, David .... **CLC 17**
See also Jones, David Robert

Bowles, Jane (Sydney) 1917-1973 **CLC 3, 68**
See also CA 19-20; 41-44R; CAP 2

Bowles, Paul (Frederick) 1910- **CLC 1, 2, 19, 53; SSC 3**
See also CA 1-4R; CAAS 1; CANR 1, 19, 50, 75; DLB 5, 6; MTCW 1

Box, Edgar
See Vidal, Gore

Boyd, Nancy
See Millay, Edna St. Vincent

Boyd, William 1952- .... **CLC 28, 53, 70**
See also CA 114; 120; CANR 51, 71

Boyle, Kay 1902-1992 **CLC 1, 5, 19, 58; SSC 5**
See also CA 13-16R; 140; CAAS 1; CANR 29, 61; DLB 4, 9, 48, 86; DLBY 93; MTCW 1

Boyle, Mark
See Kienzle, William X(avier)

Boyle, Patrick 1905-1982 .... **CLC 19**
See also CA 127

Boyle, T. C. 1948-
See Boyle, T(homas) Coraghessan

Boyle, T(homas) Coraghessan 1948- **CLC 36, 55, 90; DAM POP; SSC 16**
See also BEST 90:4; CA 120; CANR 44, 76; DLBY 86

Boz
See Dickens, Charles (John Huffam)

Brackenridge, Hugh Henry 1748-1816 **NCLC 7**
See also DLB 11, 37

Bradbury, Edward P.
See Moorcock, Michael (John)

Bradbury, Malcolm (Stanley) 1932- **CLC 32, 61; DAM NOV**
See also CA 1-4R; CANR 1, 33; DLB 14, 207; MTCW 1

Bradbury, Ray (Douglas) 1920- **CLC 1, 3, 10, 15, 42, 98; DA; DAB; DAC; DAM MST, NOV, POP; SSC 29; WLC**
See also AAYA 15; AITN 1, 2; CA 1-4R; CANR 2, 30, 75; CDALB 1968-1988; DLB 2, 8; MTCW 1; SATA 11, 64

Bradford, Gamaliel 1863-1932 ...... **TCLC 36**
See also CA 160; DLB 17

Bradley, David (Henry), Jr. 1950- ... **CLC 23, 118; BLC 1; DAM MULT**
See also BW 1; CA 104; CANR 26; DLB 33

Bradley, John Ed(mund, Jr.) 1958- .. **CLC 55**
See also CA 139

Bradley, Marion Zimmer 1930- **CLC 30; DAM POP**
See also AAYA 9; CA 57-60; CAAS 10; CANR 7, 31, 51, 75; DLB 8; MTCW 1; SATA 90

Bradstreet, Anne 1612(?)-1672 **LC 4, 30; DA; DAC; DAM MST, POET; PC 10**
See also CDALB 1640-1865; DLB 24

Brady, Joan 1939- .... **CLC 86**
See also CA 141

Bragg, Melvyn 1939- .... **CLC 10**
See also BEST 89:3; CA 57-60; CANR 10, 48; DLB 14

Brahe, Tycho 1546-1601 .... **LC 45**

Braine, John (Gerard) 1922-1986 **CLC 1, 3, 41**
See also CA 1-4R; 120; CANR 1, 33; CDBLB 1945-1960; DLB 15; DLBY 86; MTCW 1

Bramah, Ernest 1868-1942 .... **TCLC 72**
See also CA 156; DLB 70

Brammer, William 1930(?)-1978 .... **CLC 31**
See also CA 77-80

Brancati, Vitaliano 1907-1954 .... **TCLC 12**
See also CA 109

Brancato, Robin F(idler) 1936- .... **CLC 35**
See also AAYA 9; CA 69-72; CANR 11, 45; CLR 32; JRDA; SAAS 9; SATA 97

Brand, Max
See Faust, Frederick (Schiller)

Brand, Millen 1906-1980 .... **CLC 7**
See also CA 21-24R; 97-100; CANR 72

Branden, Barbara .... **CLC 44**
See also CA 148

Brandes, Georg (Morris Cohen) 1842-1927 **TCLC 10**
See also CA 105

Brandys, Kazimierz 1916- .... **CLC 62**

Branley, Franklyn M(ansfield) 1915- **CLC 21**
See also CA 33-36R; CANR 14, 39; CLR 13; MAICYA; SAAS 16; SATA 4, 68

Brathwaite, Edward Kamau 1930- . **CLC 11; BLCS; DAM POET**
See also BW 2; CA 25-28R; CANR 11, 26, 47; DLB 125

Brautigan, Richard (Gary) 1935-1984 **CLC 1, 3, 5, 9, 12, 34, 42; DAM NOV**
See also CA 53-56; 113; CANR 34; DLB 2, 5, 206; DLBY 80, 84; MTCW 1; SATA 56

Brave Bird, Mary 1953-
See Crow Dog, Mary (Ellen)
See also NNAL

Braverman, Kate 1950- .... **CLC 67**
See also CA 89-92

Brecht, (Eugen) Bertolt (Friedrich) 1898-1956 **TCLC 1, 6, 13, 35; DA; DAB; DAC; DAM DRAM, MST; DC 3; WLC**
See also CA 104; 133; CANR 62; DLB 56, 124; MTCW 1

Brecht, Eugen Berthold Friedrich
See Brecht, (Eugen) Bertolt (Friedrich)

Bremer, Fredrika 1801-1865 .... **NCLC 11**

Brennan, Christopher John 1870-1932 **TCLC 17**
See also CA 117

Brennan, Maeve 1917-1993 .... **CLC 5**
See also CA 81-84; CANR 72

Brent, Linda
See Jacobs, Harriet A(nn)

Brentano, Clemens (Maria) 1778-1842 **NCLC 1**
See also DLB 90

Brent of Bin Bin
See Franklin, (Stella Maria Sarah) Miles (Lampe)

Brenton, Howard 1942- .... **CLC 31**
See also CA 69-72; CANR 33, 67; DLB 13; MTCW 1

Breslin, James 1930-1996
See Breslin, Jimmy
See also CA 73-76; CANR 31, 75; DAM NOV; MTCW 1

Breslin, Jimmy .... **CLC 4, 43**
See also Breslin, James
See also AITN 1; DLB 185

Bresson, Robert 1901- .... **CLC 16**
See also CA 110; CANR 49

Breton, Andre 1896-1966 **CLC 2, 9, 15, 54; PC 15**
See also CA 19-20; 25-28R; CANR 40, 60; CAP 2; DLB 65; MTCW 1

Breytenbach, Breyten 1939(?)- . **CLC 23, 37; DAM POET**
See also CA 113; 129; CANR 61

Bridgers, Sue Ellen 1942- .... **CLC 26**
See also AAYA 8; CA 65-68; CANR 11, 36; CLR 18; DLB 52; JRDA; MAICYA; SAAS 1; SATA 22, 90

Bridges, Robert (Seymour) 1844-1930 **TCLC 1; DAM POET**

9; DAM NOV
See also CA 13-16R; CANR 11, 39, 64; DLBY
80; INT CANR-11; MTCW 1
Buell, John (Edward) 1927- .... CLC 10
See also CA 1-4R; CANR 71; DLB 53
Buero Vallejo, Antonio 1916- ..... CLC 15, 46
See also CA 106; CANR 24, 49, 75; HW;
MTCW 1
Bufalino, Gesualdo 1920(?)- .... CLC 74
See also DLB 196
Bugayev, Boris Nikolayevich 1880-1934
TCLC 7; PC 11
See also Bely, Andrey
See also CA 104; 165
Bukowski, Charles 1920-1994CLC 2, 5, 9, 41,
82, 108; DAM NOV, POET; PC 18
See also CA 17-20R; 144; CANR 40, 62; DLB
5, 130, 169; MTCW 1
Bulgakov, Mikhail (Afanas'evich) 1891-1940
TCLC 2, 16; DAM DRAM, NOV; SSC 18
See also CA 105; 152
Bulgya, Alexander Alexandrovich 1901-1956
TCLC 53
See also Fadeyev, Alexander
See also CA 117
Bullins, Ed 1935- CLC 1, 5, 7; BLC 1; DAM
DRAM, MULT; DC 6
See also BW 2; CA 49-52; CAAS 16; CANR
24, 46, 73; DLB 7, 38; MTCW 1
Bulwer-Lytton, Edward (George Earle Lytton)
1803-1873 .... NCLC 1, 45
See also DLB 21
Bunin, Ivan Alexeyevich 1870-1953TCLC 6;
SSC 5
See also CA 104
Bunting, Basil 1900-1985 ..... CLC 10, 39, 47;
DAM POET
See also CA 53-56; 115; CANR 7; DLB 20
Bunuel, Luis 1900-1983 .. CLC 16, 80; DAM
MULT; HLC
See also CA 101; 110; CANR 32; HW
Bunyan, John 1628-1688 ... LC 4; DA; DAB;
DAC; DAM MST; WLC
See also CDBLB 1660-1789; DLB 39
Burckhardt, Jacob (Christoph) 1818-1897
NCLC 49
Burford, Eleanor
See Hibbert, Eleanor Alice Burford
Burgess, AnthonyCLC 1, 2, 4, 5, 8, 10, 13, 15,
22, 40, 62, 81, 94; DAB
See also Wilson, John (Anthony) Burgess
See also AAYA 25; AITN 1; CDBLB 1960 to
Present; DLB 14, 194
Burke, Edmund 1729(?)-1797 LC 7, 36; DA;
DAB; DAC; DAM MST; WLC
See also DLB 104
Burke, Kenneth (Duva) 1897-1993CLC 2, 24
See also CA 5-8R; 143; CANR 39, 74; DLB
45, 63; MTCW 1
Burke, Leda
See Garnett, David
Burke, Ralph
See Silverberg, Robert
Burke, Thomas 1886-1945 .... TCLC 63
See also CA 113; 155; DLB 197
Burney, Fanny 1752-1840 .... NCLC 12, 54
See also DLB 39
Burns, Robert 1759-1796 . LC 3, 29, 40; DA;
DAB; DAC; DAM MST, POET; PC 6;
WLC
See also CDBLB 1789-1832; DLB 109
Burns, Tex
See L'Amour, Louis (Dearborn)
Burnshaw, Stanley 1906- .... CLC 3, 13, 44
See also CA 9-12R; DLB 48; DLBY 97
Burr, Anne 1937- .... CLC 6
See also CA 25-28R

Burroughs, Edgar Rice 1875-1950 . TCLC 2,
32; DAM NOV
See also AAYA 11; CA 104; 132; DLB 8;
MTCW 1; SATA 41
Burroughs, William S(eward) 1914-1997CLC
1, 2, 5, 15, 22, 42, 75, 109; DA; DAB; DAC;
DAM MST, NOV, POP; WLC
See also AITN 2; CA 9-12R; 160; CANR 20,
52; DLB 2, 8, 16, 152; DLBY 81, 97; MTCW
1
Burton, Richard F. 1821-1890 .... NCLC 42
See also DLB 55, 184
Busch, Frederick 1941- ..... CLC 7, 10, 18, 47
See also CA 33-36R; CAAS 1; CANR 45, 73;
DLB 6
Bush, Ronald 1946- .... CLC 34
See also CA 136
Bustos, F(rancisco)
See Borges, Jorge Luis
Bustos Domecq, H(onorio)
See Bioy Casares, Adolfo; Borges, Jorge Luis
Butler, Octavia E(stelle) 1947-CLC 38; BLCS;
DAM MULT, POP
See also AAYA 18; BW 2; CA 73-76; CANR
12, 24, 38, 73; DLB 33; MTCW 1; SATA 84
Butler, Robert Olen (Jr.) 1945-CLC 81; DAM
POP
See also CA 112; CANR 66; DLB 173; INT 112
Butler, Samuel 1612-1680 .... LC 16, 43
See also DLB 101, 126
Butler, Samuel 1835-1902 . TCLC 1, 33; DA;
DAB; DAC; DAM MST, NOV; WLC
See also CA 143; CDBLB 1890-1914; DLB 18,
57, 174
Butler, Walter C.
See Faust, Frederick (Schiller)
Butor, Michel (Marie Francois) 1926-CLC 1,
3, 8, 11, 15
See also CA 9-12R; CANR 33, 66; DLB 83;
MTCW 1
Butts, Mary 1892(?)-1937 .... TCLC 77
See also CA 148
Buzo, Alexander (John) 1944- .... CLC 61
See also CA 97-100; CANR 17, 39, 69
Buzzati, Dino 1906-1972 .... CLC 36
See also CA 160; 33-36R; DLB 177
Byars, Betsy (Cromer) 1928- .... CLC 35
See also AAYA 19; CA 33-36R; CANR 18, 36,
57; CLR 1, 16; DLB 52; INT CANR-18;
JRDA; MAICYA; MTCW 1; SAAS 1; SATA
4, 46, 80
Byatt, A(ntonia) S(usan Drabble) 1936- C L C
19, 65; DAM NOV, POP
See also CA 13-16R; CANR 13, 33, 50, 75;
DLB 14, 194; MTCW 1
Byrne, David 1952- .... CLC 26
See also CA 127
Byrne, John Keyes 1926-
See Leonard, Hugh
See also CA 102; INT 102
Byron, George Gordon (Noel) 1788-1824
NCLC 2, 12; DA; DAB; DAC; DAM MST,
POET; PC 16; WLC
See also CDBLB 1789-1832; DLB 96, 110
Byron, Robert 1905-1941 .... TCLC 67
See also CA 160; DLB 195
C. 3. 3.
See Wilde, Oscar
Caballero, Fernan 1796-1877 .... NCLC 10
Cabell, Branch
See Cabell, James Branch
Cabell, James Branch 1879-1958 .... TCLC 6
See also CA 105; 152; DLB 9, 78
Cable, George Washington 1844-1925 T C L C
4; SSC 4
See also CA 104; 155; DLB 12, 74; DLBD 13
Cabral de Melo Neto, Joao 1920- ... CLC 76;

DAM MULT
See also CA 151
Cabrera Infante, G(uillermo) 1929- .. CLC 5,
25, 45; DAM MULT; HLC
See also CA 85-88; CANR 29, 65; DLB 113;
HW; MTCW 1
Cade, Toni
See Bambara, Toni Cade
Cadmus and Harmonia
See Buchan, John
Caedmon fl. 658-680 .... CMLC 7
See also DLB 146
Caeiro, Alberto
See Pessoa, Fernando (Antonio Nogueira)
Cage, John (Milton, Jr.) 1912-1992 .. CLC 41
See also CA 13-16R; 169; CANR 9; DLB 193;
INT CANR-9
Cahan, Abraham 1860-1951 .... TCLC 71
See also CA 108; 154; DLB 9, 25, 28
Cain, G.
See Cabrera Infante, G(uillermo)
Cain, Guillermo
See Cabrera Infante, G(uillermo)
Cain, James M(allahan) 1892-1977CLC 3, 11,
28
See also AITN 1; CA 17-20R; 73-76; CANR 8,
34, 61; MTCW 1
Caine, Mark
See Raphael, Frederic (Michael)
Calasso, Roberto 1941- .... CLC 81
See also CA 143
Calderon de la Barca, Pedro 1600-1681 .. L C
23; DC 3
Caldwell, Erskine (Preston) 1903-1987CLC 1,
8, 14, 50, 60; DAM NOV; SSC 19
See also AITN 1; CA 1-4R; 121; CAAS 1;
CANR 2, 33; DLB 9, 86; MTCW 1
Caldwell, (Janet Miriam) Taylor (Holland)
1900-1985 ....
CLC 2, 28, 39; DAM NOV, POP
See also CA 5-8R; 116; CANR 5; DLBD 17
Calhoun, John Caldwell 1782-1850NCLC 15
See also DLB 3
Calisher, Hortense 1911-CLC 2, 4, 8, 38; DAM
NOV; SSC 15
See also CA 1-4R; CANR 1, 22, 67; DLB 2;
INT CANR-22; MTCW 1
Callaghan, Morley Edward 1903-1990CLC 3,
14, 41, 65; DAC; DAM MST
See also CA 9-12R; 132; CANR 33, 73; DLB
68; MTCW 1
Callimachus c. 305B.C.-c. 240B.C. CMLC 18
See also DLB 176
Calvin, John 1509-1564 .... LC 37
Calvino, Italo 1923-1985CLC 5, 8, 11, 22, 33,
39, 73; DAM NOV; SSC 3
See also CA 85-88; 116; CANR 23, 61; DLB
196; MTCW 1
Cameron, Carey 1952- .... CLC 59
See also CA 135
Cameron, Peter 1959- .... CLC 44
See also CA 125; CANR 50
Campana, Dino 1885-1932 .... TCLC 20
See also CA 117; DLB 114
Campanella, Tommaso 1568-1639 .... LC 32
Campbell, John W(ood, Jr.) 1910-1971 C L C
32
See also CA 21-22; 29-32R; CANR 34; CAP 2;
DLB 8; MTCW 1
Campbell, Joseph 1904-1987 .... CLC 69
See also AAYA 3; BEST 89:2; CA 1-4R; 124;
CANR 3, 28, 61; MTCW 1
Campbell, Maria 1940- .... CLC 85; DAC
See also CA 102; CANR 54; NNAL
Campbell, (John) Ramsey 1946-CLC 42; SSC
19
See also CA 57-60; CANR 7; INT CANR-7

Campbell, (Ignatius) Roy (Dunnachie) 1901-
1957 .... **TCLC 5**
See also CA 104; 155; DLB 20
Campbell, Thomas 1777-1844 .... **NCLC 19**
See also DLB 93; 144
Campbell, Wilfred .... **TCLC 9**
See also Campbell, William
Campbell, William 1858(?)-1918
See Campbell, Wilfred
See also CA 106; DLB 92
Campion, Jane .... **CLC 95**
See also CA 138
Campos, Alvaro de
See Pessoa, Fernando (Antonio Nogueira)
Camus, Albert 1913-1960 **CLC 1, 2, 4, 9, 11, 14,
32, 63, 69; DA; DAB; DAC; DAM DRAM,
MST, NOV; DC 2; SSC 9; WLC**
See also CA 89-92; DLB 72; MTCW 1
Canby, Vincent 1924- .... **CLC 13**
See also CA 81-84
Cancale
See Desnos, Robert
Canetti, Elias 1905-1994 **CLC 3, 14, 25, 75, 86**
See also CA 21-24R; 146; CANR 23, 61; DLB
85, 124; MTCW 1
Canfield, Dorothea F.
See Fisher, Dorothy (Frances) Canfield
Canfield, Dorothea Frances
See Fisher, Dorothy (Frances) Canfield
Canfield, Dorothy
See Fisher, Dorothy (Frances) Canfield
Canin, Ethan 1960- .... **CLC 55**
See also CA 131; 135
Cannon, Curt
See Hunter, Evan
Cao, Lan 1961- .... **CLC 109**
See also CA 165
Cape, Judith
See Page, P(atricia) K(athleen)
Capek, Karel 1890-1938 ... **TCLC 6, 37; DA;
DAB; DAC; DAM DRAM, MST, NOV; DC
1; WLC**
See also CA 104; 140
Capote, Truman 1924-1984 **CLC 1, 3, 8, 13, 19,
34, 38, 58; DA; DAB; DAC; DAM MST,
NOV, POP; SSC 2; WLC**
See also CA 5-8R; 113; CANR 18, 62; CDALB
1941-1968; DLB 2, 185; DLBY 80, 84;
MTCW 1; SATA 91
Capra, Frank 1897-1991 .... **CLC 16**
See also CA 61-64; 135
Caputo, Philip 1941- .... **CLC 32**
See also CA 73-76; CANR 40
Caragiale, Ion Luca 1852-1912 ..... **TCLC 76**
See also CA 157
Card, Orson Scott 1951- **CLC 44, 47, 50; DAM
POP**
See also AAYA 11; CA 102; CANR 27, 47, 73;
INT CANR-27; MTCW 1; SATA 83
Cardenal, Ernesto 1925- .... **CLC 31; DAM
MULT, POET; HLC; PC 22**
See also CA 49-52; CANR 2, 32, 66; HW;
MTCW 1
Cardozo, Benjamin N(athan) 1870-1938
TCLC 65
See also CA 117; 164
Carducci, Giosue (Alessandro Giuseppe) 1835-
1907
TCLC 32
See also CA 163
Carew, Thomas 1595(?)-1640 .... **LC 13**
See also DLB 126
Carey, Ernestine Gilbreth 1908- .... **CLC 17**
See also CA 5-8R; CANR 71; SATA 2
Carey, Peter 1943- .... **CLC 40, 55, 96**
See also CA 123; 127; CANR 53, 76; INT 127;
MTCW 1; SATA 94

Carleton, William 1794-1869 .... **NCLC 3**
See also DLB 159
Carlisle, Henry (Coffin) 1926- .... **CLC 33**
See also CA 13-16R; CANR 15
Carlsen, Chris
See Holdstock, Robert P.
Carlson, Ron(ald F.) 1947- .... **CLC 54**
See also CA 105; CANR 27
Carlyle, Thomas 1795-1881 . **NCLC 70; DA;
DAB; DAC; DAM MST**
See also CDBLB 1789-1832; DLB 55; 144
Carman, (William) Bliss 1861-1929 **TCLC 7;
DAC**
See also CA 104; 152; DLB 92
Carnegie, Dale 1888-1955 .... **TCLC 53**
Carossa, Hans 1878-1956 .... **TCLC 48**
See also CA 170; DLB 66
Carpenter, Don(ald Richard) 1931-1995 **C L C
41**
See also CA 45-48; 149; CANR 1, 71
Carpenter, Edward 1844-1929 .... **TCLC 88**
See also CA 163
Carpentier (y Valmont), Alejo 1904-1980 **CLC
8, 11, 38, 110; DAM MULT; HLC**
See also CA 65-68; 97-100; CANR 11, 70; DLB
113; HW
Carr, Caleb 1955(?)- .... **CLC 86**
See also CA 147; CANR 73
Carr, Emily 1871-1945 .... **TCLC 32**
See also CA 159; DLB 68
Carr, John Dickson 1906-1977 .... **CLC 3**
See also Fairbairn, Roger
See also CA 49-52; 69-72; CANR 3, 33, 60;
MTCW 1
Carr, Philippa
See Hibbert, Eleanor Alice Burford
Carr, Virginia Spencer 1929- .... **CLC 34**
See also CA 61-64; DLB 111
Carrere, Emmanuel 1957- .... **CLC 89**
Carrier, Roch 1937- **CLC 13, 78; DAC; DAM
MST**
See also CA 130; CANR 61; DLB 53; SATA
105
Carroll, James P. 1943(?)- .... **CLC 38**
See also CA 81-84; CANR 73
Carroll, Jim 1951- .... **CLC 35**
See also AAYA 17; CA 45-48; CANR 42
Carroll, Lewis ..... **NCLC 2, 53; PC 18; WLC**
See also Dodgson, Charles Lutwidge
See also CDBLB 1832-1890; CLR 2, 18; DLB
18, 163, 178; JRDA
Carroll, Paul Vincent 1900-1968 ...... **CLC 10**
See also CA 9-12R; 25-28R; DLB 10
Carruth, Hayden 1921- **CLC 4, 7, 10, 18, 84;
PC 10**
See also CA 9-12R; CANR 4, 38, 59; DLB 5,
165; INT CANR-4; MTCW 1; SATA 47
Carson, Rachel Louise 1907-1964 .. **CLC 71;
DAM POP**
See also CA 77-80; CANR 35; MTCW 1; SATA
23
Carter, Angela (Olive) 1940-1992 **CLC 5, 41,
76; SSC 13**
See also CA 53-56; 136; CANR 12, 36, 61; DLB
14, 207; MTCW 1; SATA 66; SATA-Obit 70
Carter, Nick
See Smith, Martin Cruz
Carver, Raymond 1938-1988 **CLC 22, 36, 53,
55; DAM NOV; SSC 8**
See also CA 33-36R; 126; CANR 17, 34, 61;
DLB 130; DLBY 84, 88; MTCW 1
Cary, Elizabeth, Lady Falkland 1585-1639
LC 30
Cary, (Arthur) Joyce (Lunel) 1888-1957
TCLC 1, 29
See also CA 104; 164; CDBLB 1914-1945;
DLB 15, 100

Casanova de Seingalt, Giovanni Jacopo 1725-
1798 .... **LC 13**
Casares, Adolfo Bioy
See Bioy Casares, Adolfo
Casely-Hayford, J(oseph) E(phraim) 1866-1930
TCLC 24; BLC 1; DAM MULT
See also BW 2; CA 123; 152
Casey, John (Dudley) 1939- .... **CLC 59**
See also BEST 90:2; CA 69-72; CANR 23
Casey, Michael 1947- .... **CLC 2**
See also CA 65-68; DLB 5
Casey, Patrick
See Thurman, Wallace (Henry)
Casey, Warren (Peter) 1935-1988 ..... **CLC 12**
See also CA 101; 127; INT 101
Casona, Alejandro .... **CLC 49**
See also Alvarez, Alejandro Rodriguez
Cassavetes, John 1929-1989 .... **CLC 20**
See also CA 85-88; 127
Cassian, Nina 1924- .... **PC 17**
Cassill, R(onald) V(erlin) 1919- .... **CLC 4, 23**
See also CA 9-12R; CAAS 1; CANR 7, 45; DLB
6
Cassirer, Ernst 1874-1945 .... **TCLC 61**
See also CA 157
Cassity, (Allen) Turner 1929- .... **CLC 6, 42**
See also CA 17-20R; CAAS 8; CANR 11; DLB
105
Castaneda, Carlos 1931(?)- .... **CLC 12**
See also CA 25-28R; CANR 32, 66; HW;
MTCW 1
Castedo, Elena 1937- .... **CLC 65**
See also CA 132
Castedo-Ellerman, Elena
See Castedo, Elena
Castellanos, Rosario 1925-1974 **CLC 66; DAM
MULT; HLC**
See also CA 131; 53-56; CANR 58; DLB 113;
HW
Castelvetro, Lodovico 1505-1571 .... **LC 12**
Castiglione, Baldassare 1478-1529 ...... **LC 12**
Castle, Robert
See Hamilton, Edmond
Castro, Guillen de 1569-1631 .... **LC 19**
Castro, Rosalia de 1837-1885 **NCLC 3; DAM
MULT**
Cather, Willa
See Cather, Willa Sibert
Cather, Willa Sibert 1873-1947 **TCLC 1, 11,
31; DA; DAB; DAC; DAM MST, NOV;
SSC 2; WLC**
See also AAYA 24; CA 104; 128; CDALB 1865-
1917; DLB 9, 54, 78; DLBD 1; MTCW 1;
SATA 30
Catherine, Saint 1347-1380 .... **CMLC 27**
Cato, Marcus Porcius 234B.C.-149B.C.
CMLC 21
Catton, (Charles) Bruce 1899-1978 .. **CLC 35**
See also AITN 1; CA 5-8R; 81-84; CANR 7,
74; DLB 17; SATA 2; SATA-Obit 24
Catullus c. 84B.C.-c. 54B.C. .... **CMLC 18**
Cauldwell, Frank
See King, Francis (Henry)
Caunitz, William J. 1933-1996 .... **CLC 34**
See also BEST 89:3; CA 125; 130; 152; CANR
73; INT 130
Causley, Charles (Stanley) 1917- .... **CLC 7**
See also CA 9-12R; CANR 5, 35; CLR 30; DLB
27; MTCW 1; SATA 3, 66
Caute, (John) David 1936- ..... **CLC 29; DAM
NOV**
See also CA 1-4R; CAAS 4; CANR 1, 33, 64;
DLB 14
Cavafy, C(onstantine) P(eter) 1863-1933
TCLC 2, 7; DAM POET
See also Kavafis, Konstantinos Petrou
See also CA 148

Cavallo, Evelyn
See Spark, Muriel (Sarah)
Cavanna, Betty .... CLC 12
See also Harrison, Elizabeth Cavanna
See also JRDA; MAICYA; SAAS 4; SATA 1,
30
Cavendish, Margaret Lucas 1623-1673LC 30
See also DLB 131
Caxton, William 1421(?)-1491(?) .... LC 17
See also DLB 170
Cayer, D. M.
See Duffy, Maureen
Cayrol, Jean 1911- .... CLC 11
See also CA 89-92; DLB 83
Cela, Camilo Jose 1916-CLC 4, 13, 59; DAM
MULT; HLC
See also BEST 90:2; CA 21-24R; CAAS 10;
CANR 21, 32, 76; DLBY 89; HW; MTCW 1
Celan, Paul .... CLC 10, 19, 53, 82; PC 10
See also Antschel, Paul
See also DLB 69
Celine, Louis-FerdinandCLC 1, 3, 4, 7, 9, 15,
47
See also Destouches, Louis-Ferdinand
See also DLB 72
Cellini, Benvenuto 1500-1571 .... LC 7
Cendrars, Blaise 1887-1961 ..... CLC 18, 106
See also Sauser-Hall, Frederic
Cernuda (y Bidon), Luis 1902-1963 CLC 54;
DAM POET
See also CA 131; 89-92; DLB 134; HW
Cervantes (Saavedra), Miguel de 1547-1616
LC 6, 23; DA; DAB; DAC; DAM MST,
NOV; SSC 12; WLC
Cesaire, Aime (Fernand) 1913-. CLC 19, 32,
112; BLC 1; DAM MULT, POET; PC 25
See also BW 2; CA 65-68; CANR 24, 43;
MTCW 1
Chabon, Michael 1963- .... CLC 55
See also CA 139; CANR 57
Chabrol, Claude 1930- .... CLC 16
See also CA 110
Challans, Mary 1905-1983
See Renault, Mary
See also CA 81-84; 111; CANR 74; SATA 23;
SATA-Obit 36
Challis, George
See Faust, Frederick (Schiller)
Chambers, Aidan 1934- .... CLC 35
See also AAYA 27; CA 25-28R; CANR 12, 31,
58; JRDA; MAICYA; SAAS 12; SATA 1, 69
Chambers, James 1948-
See Cliff, Jimmy
See also CA 124
Chambers, Jessie
See Lawrence, D(avid) H(erbert Richards)
Chambers, Robert W(illiam) 1865-1933
TCLC 41
See also CA 165; DLB 202
Chandler, Raymond (Thornton) 1888-1959
TCLC 1, 7; SSC 23
See also AAYA 25; CA 104; 129; CANR 60;
CDALB 1929-1941; DLBD 6; MTCW 1
Chang, Eileen 1920-1995 .... SSC 28
See also CA 166
Chang, Jung 1952- .... CLC 71
See also CA 142
Chang Ai-Ling
See Chang, Eileen
Channing, William Ellery 1780-1842 N C L C
17
See also DLB 1, 59
Chaplin, Charles Spencer 1889-1977CLC 16
See also Chaplin, Charlie
See also CA 81-84; 73-76
Chaplin, Charlie
See Chaplin, Charles Spencer

See also DLB 44
Chapman, George 1559(?)-1634LC 22; DAM
DRAM
See also DLB 62, 121
Chapman, Graham 1941-1989 .... CLC 21
See also Monty Python
See also CA 116; 129; CANR 35
Chapman, John Jay 1862-1933 .... TCLC 7
See also CA 104
Chapman, Lee
See Bradley, Marion Zimmer
Chapman, Walker
See Silverberg, Robert
Chappell, Fred (Davis) 1936- ..... CLC 40, 78
See also CA 5-8R; CAAS 4; CANR 8, 33, 67;
DLB 6, 105
Char, Rene(-Emile) 1907-1988CLC 9, 11, 14,
55; DAM POET
See also CA 13-16R; 124; CANR 32; MTCW 1
Charby, Jay
See Ellison, Harlan (Jay)
Chardin, Pierre Teilhard de
See Teilhard de Chardin, (Marie Joseph) Pierre
Charles I 1600-1649 .... LC 13
Charriere, Isabelle de 1740-1805 ..NCLC 66
Charyn, Jerome 1937- .... CLC 5, 8, 18
See also CA 5-8R; CAAS 1; CANR 7, 61;
DLBY 83; MTCW 1
Chase, Mary (Coyle) 1907-1981 ....DC 1
See also CA 77-80; 105; SATA 17; SATA-Obit
29
Chase, Mary Ellen 1887-1973 .... CLC 2
See also CA 13-16; 41-44R; CAP 1; SATA 10
Chase, Nicholas
See Hyde, Anthony
Chateaubriand, Francois Rene de 1768-1848
NCLC 3
See also DLB 119
Chatterje, Sarat Chandra 1876-1936(?)
See Chatterji, Saratchandra
See also CA 109
Chatterji, Bankim Chandra 1838-1894NCLC
19
Chatterji, Saratchandra .... TCLC 13
See also Chatterje, Sarat Chandra
Chatterton, Thomas 1752-1770 . LC 3; DAM
POET
See also DLB 109
Chatwin, (Charles) Bruce 1940-1989CLC 28,
57, 59; DAM POP
See also AAYA 4; BEST 90:1; CA 85-88; 127;
DLB 194, 204
Chaucer, Daniel
See Ford, Ford Madox
Chaucer, Geoffrey 1340(?)-1400 LC 17; DA;
DAB; DAC; DAM MST, POET; PC 19;
WLCS
See also CDBLB Before 1660; DLB 146
Chaviaras, Strates 1935-
See Haviaras, Stratis
See also CA 105
Chayefsky, Paddy .... CLC 23
See also Chayefsky, Sidney
See also DLB 7, 44; DLBY 81
Chayefsky, Sidney 1923-1981
See Chayefsky, Paddy
See also CA 9-12R; 104; CANR 18; DAM
DRAM
Chedid, Andree 1920- .... CLC 47
See also CA 145
Cheever, John 1912-1982 CLC 3, 7, 8, 11, 15,
25, 64; DA; DAB; DAC; DAM MST, NOV,
POP; SSC 1; WLC
See also CA 5-8R; 106; CABS 1; CANR 5, 27,
76; CDALB 1941-1968; DLB 2, 102; DLBY
80, 82; INT CANR-5; MTCW 1
Cheever, Susan 1943- .... CLC 18, 48

See also CA 103; CANR 27, 51; DLBY 82; INT
CANR-27
Chekhonte, Antosha
See Chekhov, Anton (Pavlovich)
Chekhov, Anton (Pavlovich) 1860-1904TCLC
3, 10, 31, 55; DA; DAB; DAC; DAM
DRAM, MST; DC 9; SSC 2, 28; WLC
See also CA 104; 124; SATA 90
Chernyshevsky, Nikolay Gavrilovich 1828-1889
NCLC 1
Cherry, Carolyn Janice 1942-
See Cherryh, C. J.
See also CA 65-68; CANR 10
Cherryh, C. J. .... CLC 35
See also Cherry, Carolyn Janice
See also AAYA 24; DLBY 80; SATA 93
Chesnutt, Charles W(addell) 1858-1932
TCLC 5, 39; BLC 1; DAM MULT; SSC 7
See also BW 1; CA 106; 125; CANR 76; DLB
12, 50, 78; MTCW 1
Chester, Alfred 1929(?)-1971 .... CLC 49
See also CA 33-36R; DLB 130
Chesterton, G(ilbert) K(eith) 1874-1936
TCLC 1, 6, 64; DAM NOV, POET; SSC 1
See also CA 104; 132; CANR 73; CDBLB
1914-1945; DLB 10, 19, 34, 70, 98, 149,
178; MTCW 1; SATA 27
Chiang, Pin-chin 1904-1986
See Ding Ling
See also CA 118
Ch'ien Chung-shu 1910- .... CLC 22
See also CA 130; CANR 73; MTCW 1
Child, L. Maria
See Child, Lydia Maria
Child, Lydia Maria 1802-1880 ...NCLC 6, 73
See also DLB 1, 74; SATA 67
Child, Mrs.
See Child, Lydia Maria
Child, Philip 1898-1978 .... CLC 19, 68
See also CA 13-14; CAP 1; SATA 47
Childers, (Robert) Erskine 1870-1922 T C L C
65
See also CA 113; 153; DLB 70
Childress, Alice 1920-1994CLC 12, 15, 86, 96;
BLC 1; DAM DRAM, MULT, NOV; DC 4
See also AAYA 8; BW 2; CA 45-48; 146; CANR
3, 27, 50, 74; CLR 14; DLB 7, 38; JRDA;
MAICYA; MTCW 1; SATA 7, 48, 81
Chin, Frank (Chew, Jr.) 1940- .... DC 7
See also CA 33-36R; CANR 71; DAM MULT;
DLB 206
Chislett, (Margaret) Anne 1943- ...... CLC 34
See also CA 151
Chitty, Thomas Willes 1926- .... CLC 11
See also Hinde, Thomas
See also CA 5-8R
Chivers, Thomas Holley 1809-1858NCLC 49
See also DLB 3
Chomette, Rene Lucien 1898-1981
See Clair, Rene
See also CA 103
Chopin, Kate TCLC 5, 14; DA; DAB; SSC 8;
WLCS
See also Chopin, Katherine
See also CDALB 1865-1917; DLB 12, 78
Chopin, Katherine 1851-1904
See Chopin, Kate
See also CA 104; 122; DAC; DAM MST, NOV
Chretien de Troyes c. 12th cent. - . CMLC 10
See also DLB 208
Christie
See Ichikawa, Kon
Christie, Agatha (Mary Clarissa) 1890-1976
CLC 1, 6, 8, 12, 39, 48, 110; DAB; DAC;
DAM NOV
See also AAYA 9; AITN 1, 2; CA 17-20R; 61-
64; CANR 10, 37; CDBLB 1914-1945; DLB

13, 77; MTCW 1; SATA 36

Christie, (Ann) Philippa
   See Pearce, Philippa
   See also CA 5-8R; CANR 4

Christine de Pizan 1365(?)-1431(?) .... **LC 9**
   See also DLB 208

Chubb, Elmer
   See Masters, Edgar Lee

Chulkov, Mikhail Dmitrievich 1743-1792**LC 2**
   See also DLB 150

Churchill, Caryl 1938- ..... **CLC 31, 55; DC 5**
   See also CA 102; CANR 22, 46; DLB 13;
   MTCW 1

Churchill, Charles 1731-1764 .... **LC 3**
   See also DLB 109

Chute, Carolyn 1947- .... **CLC 39**
   See also CA 123

Ciardi, John (Anthony) 1916-1986 . **CLC 10, 40, 44; DAM POET**
   See also CA 5-8R; 118; CAAS 2; CANR 5, 33;
   CLR 19; DLB 5; DLBY 86; INT CANR-5;
   MAICYA; MTCW 1; SAAS 26; SATA 1, 65;
   SATA-Obit 46

Cicero, Marcus Tullius 106B.C.-43B.C.
   CMLC 3

Cimino, Michael 1943- .... **CLC 16**
   See also CA 105

Cioran, E(mil) M. 1911-1995 .... **CLC 64**
   See also CA 25-28R; 149

Cisneros, Sandra 1954- . **CLC 69, 118; DAM MULT; HLC; SSC 32**
   See also AAYA 9; CA 131; CANR 64; DLB 122,
   152; HW

Cixous, Helene 1937- .... **CLC 92**
   See also CA 126; CANR 55; DLB 83; MTCW
   1

Clair, Rene .... **CLC 20**
   See also Chomette, Rene Lucien

Clampitt, Amy 1920-1994 ..... **CLC 32; PC 19**
   See also CA 110; 146; CANR 29; DLB 105

Clancy, Thomas L., Jr. 1947-
   See Clancy, Tom
   See also CA 125; 131; CANR 62; INT 131;
   MTCW 1

Clancy, Tom .. **CLC 45, 112; DAM NOV, POP**
   See also Clancy, Thomas L., Jr.
   See also AAYA 9; BEST 89:1, 90:1

Clare, John 1793-1864 **NCLC 9; DAB; DAM POET; PC 23**
   See also DLB 55, 96

Clarin
   See Alas (y Urena), Leopoldo (Enrique Garcia)

Clark, Al C.
   See Goines, Donald

Clark, (Robert) Brian 1932- .... **CLC 29**
   See also CA 41-44R; CANR 67

Clark, Curt
   See Westlake, Donald E(dwin)

Clark, Eleanor 1913-1996 .... **CLC 5, 19**
   See also CA 9-12R; 151; CANR 41; DLB 6

Clark, J. P.
   See Clark, John Pepper
   See also DLB 117

Clark, John Pepper 1935- .. **CLC 38; BLC 1; DAM DRAM, MULT; DC 5**
   See also Clark, J. P.
   See also BW 1; CA 65-68; CANR 16, 72

Clark, M. R.
   See Clark, Mavis Thorpe

Clark, Mavis Thorpe 1909- .... **CLC 12**
   See also CA 57-60; CANR 8, 37; CLR 30;
   MAICYA; SAAS 5; SATA 8, 74

Clark, Walter Van Tilburg 1909-1971**CLC 28**
   See also CA 9-12R; 33-36R; CANR 63; DLB
   9, 206; SATA 8

Clark Bekederemo, J(ohnson) P(epper)
   See Clark, John Pepper

Clarke, Arthur C(harles) 1917-**CLC 1, 4, 13, 18, 35; DAM POP; SSC 3**
   See also AAYA 4; CA 1-4R; CANR 2, 28, 55,
   74; JRDA; MAICYA; MTCW 1; SATA 13,
   70

Clarke, Austin 1896-1974 .... **CLC 6, 9; DAM POET**
   See also CA 29-32; 49-52; CAP 2; DLB 10, 20

Clarke, Austin C(hesterfield) 1934-**CLC 8, 53; BLC 1; DAC; DAM MULT**
   See also BW 1; CA 25-28R; CAAS 16; CANR
   14, 32, 68; DLB 53, 125

Clarke, Gillian 1937- .... **CLC 61**
   See also CA 106; DLB 40

Clarke, Marcus (Andrew Hislop) 1846-1881
   NCLC 19

Clarke, Shirley 1925- .... **CLC 16**

Clash, The
   See Headon, (Nicky) Topper; Jones, Mick;
   Simonon, Paul; Strummer, Joe

Claudel, Paul (Louis Charles Marie) 1868-1955
   TCLC 2, 10
   See also CA 104; 165; DLB 192

Claudius, Matthias 1740-1815 .... **NCLC 75**
   See also DLB 97

Clavell, James (duMaresq) 1925-1994**CLC 6, 25, 87; DAM NOV, POP**
   See also CA 25-28R; 146; CANR 26, 48;
   MTCW 1

Cleaver, (Leroy) Eldridge 1935-1998**CLC 30; BLC 1; DAM MULT**
   See also BW 1; CA 21-24R; 167; CANR 16, 75

Cleese, John (Marwood) 1939- .... **CLC 21**
   See also Monty Python
   See also CA 112; 116; CANR 35; MTCW 1

Cleishbotham, Jebediah
   See Scott, Walter

Cleland, John 1710-1789 .... **LC 2, 48**
   See also DLB 39

Clemens, Samuel Langhorne 1835-1910
   See Twain, Mark
   See also CA 104; 135; CDALB 1865-1917; DA;
   DAB; DAC; DAM MST, NOV; DLB 11, 12,
   23, 64, 74, 186, 189; JRDA; MAICYA; SATA
   100; YABC 2

Cleophil
   See Congreve, William

Clerihew, E.
   See Bentley, E(dmund) C(lerihew)

Clerk, N. W.
   See Lewis, C(live) S(taples)

Cliff, Jimmy .... **CLC 21**
   See also Chambers, James

Clifton, (Thelma) Lucille 1936- **CLC 19, 66; BLC 1; DAM MULT, POET; PC 17**
   See also BW 2; CA 49-52; CANR 2, 24, 42,
   76; CLR 5; DLB 5, 41; MAICYA; MTCW 1;
   SATA 20, 69

Clinton, Dirk
   See Silverberg, Robert

Clough, Arthur Hugh 1819-1861 ... **NCLC 27**
   See also DLB 32

Clutha, Janet Paterson Frame 1924-
   See Frame, Janet
   See also CA 1-4R; CANR 2, 36, 76; MTCW 1

Clyne, Terence
   See Blatty, William Peter

Cobalt, Martin
   See Mayne, William (James Carter)

Cobb, Irvin S. 1876-1944 .... **TCLC 77**
   See also DLB 11, 25, 86

Cobbett, William 1763-1835 .... **NCLC 49**
   See also DLB 43, 107, 158

Coburn, D(onald) L(ee) 1938- .... **CLC 10**
   See also CA 89-92

Cocteau, Jean (Maurice Eugene Clement) 1889-
   1963 ....

CLC 1, 8, 15, 16, 43; DA; DAB; DAC; DAM DRAM, MST, NOV; WLC
   See also CA 25-28; CANR 40; CAP 2; DLB
   65; MTCW 1

Codrescu, Andrei 1946-**CLC 46; DAM POET**
   See also CA 33-36R; CAAS 19; CANR 13, 34,
   53, 76

Coe, Max
   See Bourne, Randolph S(illiman)

Coe, Tucker
   See Westlake, Donald E(dwin)

Coen, Ethan 1958- .... **CLC 108**
   See also CA 126

Coen, Joel 1955- .... **CLC 108**
   See also CA 126

The Coen Brothers
   See Coen, Ethan; Coen, Joel

Coetzee, J(ohn) M(ichael) 1940- **CLC 23, 33, 66, 117; DAM NOV**
   See also CA 77-80; CANR 41, 54, 74; MTCW
   1

Coffey, Brian
   See Koontz, Dean R(ay)

Cohan, George M(ichael) 1878-1942**TCLC 60**
   See also CA 157

Cohen, Arthur A(llen) 1928-1986 . **CLC 7, 31**
   See also CA 1-4R; 120; CANR 1, 17, 42; DLB
   28

Cohen, Leonard (Norman) 1934- **CLC 3, 38; DAC; DAM MST**
   See also CA 21-24R; CANR 14, 69; DLB 53;
   MTCW 1

Cohen, Matt 1942- .... **CLC 19; DAC**
   See also CA 61-64; CAAS 18; CANR 40; DLB
   53

Cohen-Solal, Annie 19(?)- .... **CLC 50**

Colegate, Isabel 1931- .... **CLC 36**
   See also CA 17-20R; CANR 8, 22, 74; DLB
   14; INT CANR-22; MTCW 1

Coleman, Emmett
   See Reed, Ishmael

Coleridge, M. E.
   See Coleridge, Mary E(lizabeth)

Coleridge, Mary E(lizabeth) 1861-1907**TCLC
   73**
   See also CA 116; 166; DLB 19, 98

Coleridge, Samuel Taylor 1772-1834**NCLC 9, 54; DA; DAB; DAC; DAM MST, POET; PC 11; WLC**
   See also CDBLB 1789-1832; DLB 93, 107

Coleridge, Sara 1802-1852 .... **NCLC 31**
   See also DLB 199

Coles, Don 1928- .... **CLC 46**
   See also CA 115; CANR 38

Coles, Robert (Martin) 1929- .... **CLC 108**
   See also CA 45-48; CANR 3, 32, 66, 70; INT
   CANR-32; SATA 23

Colette, (Sidonie-Gabrielle) 1873-1954**T C L C
   1, 5, 16; DAM NOV; SSC 10**
   See also CA 104; 131; DLB 65; MTCW 1

Collett, (Jacobine) Camilla (Wergeland) 1813-
   1895 ....

NCLC 22

Collier, Christopher 1930- .... **CLC 30**
   See also AAYA 13; CA 33-36R; CANR 13, 33;
   JRDA; MAICYA; SATA 16, 70

Collier, James L(incoln) 1928-**CLC 30; DAM POP**
   See also AAYA 13; CA 9-12R; CANR 4, 33,
   60; CLR 3; JRDA; MAICYA; SAAS 21;
   SATA 8, 70

Collier, Jeremy 1650-1726 .... **LC 6**

Collier, John 1901-1980 .... **SSC 19**
   See also CA 65-68; 97-100; CANR 10; DLB
   77

Collingwood, R(obin) G(eorge) 1889(?)-1943
   TCLC 67

See also CA 117; 155
Collins, Hunt
See Hunter, Evan
Collins, Linda 1931- .... **CLC 44**
See also CA 125
Collins, (William) Wilkie 1824-1889**NCLC 1,
18**
See also CDBLB 1832-1890; DLB 18, 70, 159
Collins, William 1721-1759 . **LC 4, 40; DAM
POET**
See also DLB 109
Collodi, Carlo 1826-1890 .... **NCLC 54**
See also Lorenzini, Carlo
See also CLR 5
Colman, George 1732-1794
See Glassco, John
Colt, Winchester Remington
See Hubbard, L(afayette) Ron(ald)
Colter, Cyrus 1910- .... **CLC 58**
See also BW 1; CA 65-68; CANR 10, 66; DLB
33
Colton, James
See Hansen, Joseph
Colum, Padraic 1881-1972 .... **CLC 28**
See also CA 73-76; 33-36R; CANR 35; CLR
36; MAICYA; MTCW 1; SATA 15
Colvin, James
See Moorcock, Michael (John)
Colwin, Laurie (E.) 1944-1992**CLC 5, 13, 23,
84**
See also CA 89-92; 139; CANR 20, 46; DLBY
80; MTCW 1
Comfort, Alex(ander) 1920-**CLC 7; DAM POP**
See also CA 1-4R; CANR 1, 45
Comfort, Montgomery
See Campbell, (John) Ramsey
Compton-Burnett, I(vy) 1884(?)-1969**CLC 1,
3, 10, 15, 34; DAM NOV**
See also CA 1-4R; 25-28R; CANR 4; DLB 36;
MTCW 1
Comstock, Anthony 1844-1915 ...... **TCLC 13**
See also CA 110; 169
Comte, Auguste 1798-1857 .... **NCLC 54**
Conan Doyle, Arthur
See Doyle, Arthur Conan
Conde, Maryse 1937- .... **CLC 52, 92; BLCS;
DAM MULT**
See also Boucolon, Maryse
See also BW 2
Condillac, Etienne Bonnot de 1714-1780 **L C
26**
Condon, Richard (Thomas) 1915-1996**CLC 4,
6, 8, 10, 45, 100; DAM NOV**
See also BEST 90:3; CA 1-4R; 151; CAAS 1;
CANR 2, 23; INT CANR-23; MTCW 1
Confucius 551B.C.-479B.C. .. **CMLC 19; DA;
DAB; DAC; DAM MST; WLCS**
Congreve, William 1670-1729 **LC 5, 21; DA;
DAB; DAC; DAM DRAM, MST, POET;
DC 2; WLC**
See also CDBLB 1660-1789; DLB 39, 84
Connell, Evan S(helby), Jr. 1924-**CLC 4, 6, 45;
DAM NOV**
See also AAYA 7; CA 1-4R; CAAS 2; CANR
2, 39, 76; DLB 2; DLBY 81; MTCW 1
Connelly, Marc(us Cook) 1890-1980 .. **CLC 7**
See also CA 85-88; 102; CANR 30; DLB 7;
DLBY 80; SATA-Obit 25
Connor, Ralph .... **TCLC 31**
See also Gordon, Charles William
See also DLB 92
Conrad, Joseph 1857-1924**TCLC 1, 6, 13, 25,
43, 57; DA; DAB; DAC; DAM MST, NOV;
SSC 9; WLC**
See also AAYA 26; CA 104; 131; CANR 60;
CDBLB 1890-1914; DLB 10, 34, 98, 156;
MTCW 1; SATA 27

Conrad, Robert Arnold
See Hart, Moss
Conroy, Pat
See Conroy, (Donald) Pat(rick)
Conroy, (Donald) Pat(rick) 1945-**CLC 30, 74;
DAM NOV, POP**
See also AAYA 8; AITN 1; CA 85-88; CANR
24, 53; DLB 6; MTCW 1
Constant (de Rebecque), (Henri) Benjamin
1767-1830 ....
NCLC 6
See also DLB 119
Conybeare, Charles Augustus
See Eliot, T(homas) S(tearns)
Cook, Michael 1933- .... **CLC 58**
See also CA 93-96; CANR 68; DLB 53
Cook, Robin 1940- .... **CLC 14; DAM POP**
See also BEST 90:2; CA 108; 111; CANR 41;
INT 111
Cook, Roy
See Silverberg, Robert
Cooke, Elizabeth 1948- .... **CLC 55**
See also CA 129
Cooke, John Esten 1830-1886 .... **NCLC 5**
See also DLB 3
Cooke, John Estes
See Baum, L(yman) Frank
Cooke, M. E.
See Creasey, John
Cooke, Margaret
See Creasey, John
Cook-Lynn, Elizabeth 1930-.. **CLC 93; DAM
MULT**
See also CA 133; DLB 175; NNAL
Cooney, Ray .... **CLC 62**
Cooper, Douglas 1960- .... **CLC 86**
Cooper, Henry St. John
See Creasey, John
Cooper, J(oan) California .... **CLC 56; DAM
MULT**
See also AAYA 12; BW 1; CA 125; CANR 55
Cooper, James Fenimore 1789-1851**NCLC 1,
27, 54**
See also AAYA 22; CDALB 1640-1865; DLB
3; SATA 19
Coover, Robert (Lowell) 1932- **CLC 3, 7, 15,
32, 46, 87; DAM NOV; SSC 15**
See also CA 45-48; CANR 3, 37, 58; DLB 2;
DLBY 81; MTCW 1
Copeland, Stewart (Armstrong) 1952-**CLC 26**
Copernicus, Nicolaus 1473-1543 .... **LC 45**
Coppard, A(lfred) E(dgar) 1878-1957 **T C L C
5; SSC 21**
See also CA 114; 167; DLB 162; YABC 1
Coppee, Francois 1842-1908 .... **TCLC 25**
See also CA 170
Coppola, Francis Ford 1939- .... **CLC 16**
See also CA 77-80; CANR 40; DLB 44
Corbiere, Tristan 1845-1875 .... **NCLC 43**
Corcoran, Barbara 1911- .... **CLC 17**
See also AAYA 14; CA 21-24R; CAAS 2;
CANR 11, 28, 48; CLR 50; DLB 52; JRDA;
SAAS 20; SATA 3, 77
Cordelier, Maurice
See Giraudoux, (Hippolyte) Jean
Corelli, Marie 1855-1924 .... **TCLC 51**
See also Mackay, Mary
See also DLB 34, 156
Corman, Cid 1924- .... **CLC 9**
See also Corman, Sidney
See also CAAS 2; DLB 5, 193
Corman, Sidney 1924-
See Corman, Cid
See also CA 85-88; CANR 44; DAM POET
Cormier, Robert (Edmund) 1925-**CLC 12, 30;
DA; DAB; DAC; DAM MST, NOV**
See also AAYA 3, 19; CA 1-4R; CANR 5, 23,

76; CDALB 1968-1988; CLR 12, 55; DLB
52; INT CANR-23; JRDA; MAICYA;
MTCW 1; SATA 10, 45, 83
Corn, Alfred (DeWitt III) 1943- .... **CLC 33**
See also CA 104; CAAS 25; CANR 44; DLB
120; DLBY 80
Corneille, Pierre 1606-1684 .... **LC 28; DAB;
DAM MST**
Cornwell, David (John Moore) 1931-**CLC 9,
15; DAM POP**
See also le Carre, John
See also CA 5-8R; CANR 13, 33, 59; MTCW 1
Corso, (Nunzio) Gregory 1930- .... **CLC 1, 11**
See also CA 5-8R; CANR 41, 76; DLB 5, 16;
MTCW 1
Cortazar, Julio 1914-1984**CLC 2, 3, 5, 10, 13,
15, 33, 34, 92; DAM MULT, NOV; HLC;
SSC 7**
See also CA 21-24R; CANR 12, 32; DLB 113;
HW; MTCW 1
CORTES, HERNAN 1484-1547 .... **LC 31**
Corvinus, Jakob
See Raabe, Wilhelm (Karl)
Corwin, Cecil
See Kornbluth, C(yril) M.
Cosic, Dobrica 1921- .... **CLC 14**
See also CA 122; 138; DLB 181
Costain, Thomas B(ertram) 1885-1965 **C L C
30**
See also CA 5-8R; 25-28R; DLB 9
Costantini, Humberto 1924(?)-1987 . **CLC 49**
See also CA 131; 122; HW
Costello, Elvis 1955- .... **CLC 21**
Cotes, Cecil V.
See Duncan, Sara Jeannette
Cotter, Joseph Seamon Sr. 1861-1949 **T C L C
28; BLC 1; DAM MULT**
See also BW 1; CA 124; DLB 50
Couch, Arthur Thomas Quiller
See Quiller-Couch, SirArthur (Thomas)
Coulton, James
See Hansen, Joseph
Couperus, Louis (Marie Anne) 1863-1923
TCLC 15
See also CA 115
Coupland, Douglas 1961-**CLC 85; DAC; DAM
POP**
See also CA 142; CANR 57
Court, Wesli
See Turco, Lewis (Putnam)
Courtenay, Bryce 1933- .... **CLC 59**
See also CA 138
Courtney, Robert
See Ellison, Harlan (Jay)
Cousteau, Jacques-Yves 1910-1997 .. **CLC 30**
See also CA 65-68; 159; CANR 15, 67; MTCW
1; SATA 38, 98
Coventry, Francis 1725-1754 .... **LC 46**
Cowan, Peter (Walkinshaw) 1914- .... **SSC 28**
See also CA 21-24R; CANR 9, 25, 50
Coward, Noel (Peirce) 1899-1973**CLC 1, 9, 29,
51; DAM DRAM**
See also AITN 1; CA 17-18; 41-44R; CANR
35; CAP 2; CDBLB 1914-1945; DLB 10;
MTCW 1
Cowley, Abraham 1618-1667 .... **LC 43**
See also DLB 131, 151
Cowley, Malcolm 1898-1989 .... **CLC 39**
See also CA 5-8R; 128; CANR 3, 55; DLB 4,
48; DLBY 81, 89; MTCW 1
Cowper, William 1731-1800 . **NCLC 8; DAM
POET**
See also DLB 104, 109
Cox, William Trevor 1928- .... **CLC 9, 14, 71;
DAM NOV**
See also Trevor, William
See also CA 9-12R; CANR 4, 37, 55, 76; DLB

See also AAYA 4; CA 112; 115; CANR 37; CLR
  20; JRDA; MAICYA; SATA 36, 63, 102;
  SATA-Brief 30
Da Ponte, Lorenzo 1749-1838 .... **NCLC 50**
Dario, Ruben 1867-1916 .... **TCLC 4; DAM
  MULT; HLC; PC 15**
  See also CA 131; HW; MTCW 1
Darley, George 1795-1846 .... **NCLC 2**
  See also DLB 96
Darrow, Clarence (Seward) 1857-1938 **T C L C
  81**
  See also CA 164
Darwin, Charles 1809-1882 .... **NCLC 57**
  See also DLB 57, 166
Daryush, Elizabeth 1887-1977 ...... **CLC 6, 19**
  See also CA 49-52; CANR 3; DLB 20
Dasgupta, Surendranath 1887-1952 **TCLC 81**
  See also CA 157
**Dashwood, Edmee Elizabeth Monica de la Pas-
  ture** 1890-1943
  See Delafield, E. M.
  See also CA 119; 154
Daudet, (Louis Marie) Alphonse 1840-1897
  NCLC 1
  See also DLB 123
Daumal, Rene 1908-1944 .... **TCLC 14**
  See also CA 114
Davenant, William 1606-1668 .... **LC 13**
  See also DLB 58, 126
Davenport, Guy (Mattison, Jr.) 1927-**CLC 6,
  14, 38; SSC 16**
  See also CA 33-36R; CANR 23, 73; DLB 130
Davidson, Avram 1923-1993
  See Queen, Ellery
  See also CA 101; 171; CANR 26; DLB 8
Davidson, Donald (Grady) 1893-1968**CLC 2,
  13, 19**
  See also CA 5-8R; 25-28R; CANR 4; DLB 45
Davidson, Hugh
  See Hamilton, Edmond
Davidson, John 1857-1909 .... **TCLC 24**
  See also CA 118; DLB 19
Davidson, Sara 1943- .... **CLC 9**
  See also CA 81-84; CANR 44, 68; DLB 185
Davie, Donald (Alfred) 1922-1995 .**CLC 5, 8,
  10, 31**
  See also CA 1-4R; 149; CAAS 3; CANR 1, 44;
  DLB 27; MTCW 1
Davies, Ray(mond Douglas) 1944- ... **CLC 21**
  See also CA 116; 146
Davies, Rhys 1901-1978 .... **CLC 23**
  See also CA 9-12R; 81-84; CANR 4; DLB 139,
  191
Davies, (William) Robertson 1913-1995 **C L C
  2, 7, 13, 25, 42, 75, 91; DA; DAB; DAC;
  DAM MST, NOV, POP; WLC**
  See also BEST 89:2; CA 33-36R; 150; CANR
  17, 42; DLB 68; INT CANR-17; MTCW 1
Davies, W(illiam) H(enry) 1871-1940**TCLC 5**
  See also CA 104; DLB 19, 174
Davies, Walter C.
  See Kornbluth, C(yril) M.
Davis, Angela (Yvonne) 1944- **CLC 77; DAM
  MULT**
  See also BW 2; CA 57-60; CANR 10
Davis, B. Lynch
  See Bioy Casares, Adolfo; Borges, Jorge Luis
Davis, Harold Lenoir 1894-1960 ...... **CLC 49**
  See also CA 89-92; DLB 9, 206
Davis, Rebecca (Blaine) Harding 1831-1910
  TCLC 6
  See also CA 104; DLB 74
Davis, Richard Harding 1864-1916**TCLC 24**
  See also CA 114; DLB 12, 23, 78, 79, 189;
  DLBD 13
Davison, Frank Dalby 1893-1970 ..... **CLC 15**
  See also CA 116

Davison, Lawrence H.
  See Lawrence, D(avid) H(erbert Richards)
Davison, Peter (Hubert) 1928- .... **CLC 28**
  See also CA 9-12R; CAAS 4; CANR 3, 43; DLB
  5
Davys, Mary 1674-1732 .... **LC 1, 46**
  See also DLB 39
Dawson, Fielding 1930- .... **CLC 6**
  See also CA 85-88; DLB 130
Dawson, Peter
  See Faust, Frederick (Schiller)
Day, Clarence (Shepard, Jr.) 1874-1935
  TCLC 25
  See also CA 108; DLB 11
Day, Thomas 1748-1789 .... **LC 1**
  See also DLB 39; YABC 1
Day Lewis, C(ecil) 1904-1972 . **CLC 1, 6, 10;
  DAM POET; PC 11**
  See also Blake, Nicholas
  See also CA 13-16; 33-36R; CANR 34; CAP 1;
  DLB 15, 20; MTCW 1
Dazai Osamu 1909-1948 .... **TCLC 11**
  See also Tsushima, Shuji
  See also CA 164; DLB 182
de Andrade, Carlos Drummond
  See Drummond de Andrade, Carlos
Deane, Norman
  See Creasey, John
**de Beauvoir, Simone (Lucie Ernestine Marie
  Bertrand)**
  See Beauvoir, Simone (Lucie Ernestine Marie
  Bertrand) de
de Beer, P.
  See Bosman, Herman Charles
de Brissac, Malcolm
  See Dickinson, Peter (Malcolm)
de Chardin, Pierre Teilhard
  See Teilhard de Chardin, (Marie Joseph) Pierre
Dee, John 1527-1608 .... **LC 20**
Deer, Sandra 1940- .... **CLC 45**
De Ferrari, Gabriella 1941- .... **CLC 65**
  See also CA 146
Defoe, Daniel 1660(?)-1731 ..... **LC 1, 42; DA;
  DAB; DAC; DAM MST, NOV; WLC**
  See also AAYA 27; CDBLB 1660-1789; DLB
  39, 95, 101; JRDA; MAICYA; SATA 22
de Gourmont, Remy(-Marie-Charles)
  See Gourmont, Remy (-Marie-Charles) de
de Hartog, Jan 1914- .... **CLC 19**
  See also CA 1-4R; CANR 1
de Hostos, E. M.
  See Hostos (y Bonilla), Eugenio Maria de
de Hostos, Eugenio M.
  See Hostos (y Bonilla), Eugenio Maria de
Deighton, Len .... **CLC 4, 7, 22, 46**
  See also Deighton, Leonard Cyril
  See also AAYA 6; BEST 89:2; CDBLB 1960 to
  Present; DLB 87
Deighton, Leonard Cyril 1929-
  See Deighton, Len
  See also CA 9-12R; CANR 19, 33, 68; DAM
  NOV, POP; MTCW 1
Dekker, Thomas 1572(?)-1632 .. **LC 22; DAM
  DRAM**
  See also CDBLB Before 1660; DLB 62, 172
Delafield, E. M. 1890-1943 .... **TCLC 61**
  See also Dashwood, Edmee Elizabeth Monica
  de la Pasture
  See also DLB 34
de la Mare, Walter (John) 1873-1956**TCLC 4,
  53; DAB; DAC; DAM MST, POET; SSC
  14; WLC**
  See also CA 163; CDBLB 1914-1945; CLR 23;
  DLB 162; SATA 16
Delaney, Franey
  See O'Hara, John (Henry)
Delaney, Shelagh 1939-**CLC 29; DAM DRAM**

See also CA 17-20R; CANR 30, 67; CDBLB
  1960 to Present; DLB 13; MTCW 1
Delany, Mary (Granville Pendarves) 1700-1788
  LC 12
Delany, Samuel R(ay, Jr.) 1942-**CLC 8, 14, 38;
  BLC 1; DAM MULT**
  See also AAYA 24; BW 2; CA 81-84; CANR
  27, 43; DLB 8, 33; MTCW 1
De La Ramee, (Marie) Louise 1839-1908
  See Ouida
  See also SATA 20
de la Roche, Mazo 1879-1961 .... **CLC 14**
  See also CA 85-88; CANR 30; DLB 68; SATA
  64
De La Salle, Innocent
  See Hartmann, Sadakichi
Delbanco, Nicholas (Franklin) 1942- **CLC 6,
  13**
  See also CA 17-20R; CAAS 2; CANR 29, 55;
  DLB 6
del Castillo, Michel 1933- .... **CLC 38**
  See also CA 109
Deledda, Grazia (Cosima) 1875(?)-1936
  TCLC 23
  See also CA 123
Delibes, Miguel .... **CLC 8, 18**
  See also Delibes Setien, Miguel
Delibes Setien, Miguel 1920-
  See Delibes, Miguel
  See also CA 45-48; CANR 1, 32; HW; MTCW
  1
DeLillo, Don 1936- **CLC 8, 10, 13, 27, 39, 54,
  76; DAM NOV, POP**
  See also BEST 89:1; CA 81-84; CANR 21, 76;
  DLB 6, 173; MTCW 1
de Lisser, H. G.
  See De Lisser, H(erbert) G(eorge)
  See also DLB 117
De Lisser, H(erbert) G(eorge) 1878-1944
  TCLC 12
  See also de Lisser, H. G.
  See also BW 2; CA 109; 152
Deloney, Thomas 1560(?)-1600 .... **LC 41**
  See also DLB 167
Deloria, Vine (Victor), Jr. 1933- ..... **CLC 21;
  DAM MULT**
  See also CA 53-56; CANR 5, 20, 48; DLB 175;
  MTCW 1; NNAL; SATA 21
Del Vecchio, John M(ichael) 1947- ... **CLC 29**
  See also CA 110; DLBD 9
de Man, Paul (Adolph Michel) 1919-1983
  CLC 55
  See also CA 128; 111; CANR 61; DLB 67;
  MTCW 1
De Marinis, Rick 1934- .... **CLC 54**
  See also CA 57-60; CAAS 24; CANR 9, 25, 50
Dembry, R. Emmet
  See Murfree, Mary Noailles
Demby, William 1922-**CLC 53; BLC 1; DAM
  MULT**
  See also BW 1; CA 81-84; DLB 33
de Menton, Francisco
  See Chin, Frank (Chew, Jr.)
Demijohn, Thom
  See Disch, Thomas M(ichael)
de Montherlant, Henry (Milon)
  See Montherlant, Henry (Milon) de
Demosthenes 384B.C.-322B.C. ...... **CMLC 13**
  See also DLB 176
de Natale, Francine
  See Malzberg, Barry N(athaniel)
Denby, Edwin (Orr) 1903-1983 .... **CLC 48**
  See also CA 138; 110
Denis, Julio
  See Cortazar, Julio
Denmark, Harrison
  See Zelazny, Roger (Joseph)

1878-1957
See Dunsany, Lord
See also CA 104; 148; DLB 10

Dunsany, Lord .... **TCLC 2, 59**
See also Dunsany, Edward John Moreton Drax
Plunkett
See also DLB 77, 153, 156

du Perry, Jean
See Simenon, Georges (Jacques Christian)

Durang, Christopher (Ferdinand) 1949-**C L C
27, 38**
See also CA 105; CANR 50, 76

Duras, Marguerite 1914-1996**CLC 3, 6, 11, 20,
34, 40, 68, 100**
See also CA 25-28R; 151; CANR 50; DLB 83;
MTCW 1

Durban, (Rosa) Pam 1947- .... **CLC 39**
See also CA 123

Durcan, Paul 1944-**CLC 43, 70; DAM POET**
See also CA 134

Durkheim, Emile 1858-1917 .... **TCLC 55**

Durrell, Lawrence (George) 1912-1990 **C L C
1, 4, 6, 8, 13, 27, 41; DAM NOV**
See also CA 9-12R; 132; CANR 40; CDBLB
1945-1960; DLB 15, 27, 204; DLBY 90;
MTCW 1

Durrenmatt, Friedrich
See Duerrenmatt, Friedrich

Dutt, Toru 1856-1877 .... **NCLC 29**

Dwight, Timothy 1752-1817 .... **NCLC 13**
See also DLB 37

Dworkin, Andrea 1946- .... **CLC 43**
See also CA 77-80; CAAS 21; CANR 16, 39,
76; INT CANR-16; MTCW 1

Dwyer, Deanna
See Koontz, Dean R(ay)

Dwyer, K. R.
See Koontz, Dean R(ay)

Dwyer, Thomas A. 1923- .... **CLC 114**
See also CA 115

Dye, Richard
See De Voto, Bernard (Augustine)

Dylan, Bob 1941- .... **CLC 3, 4, 6, 12, 77**
See also CA 41-44R; DLB 16

Eagleton, Terence (Francis) 1943-
See Eagleton, Terry
See also CA 57-60; CANR 7, 23, 68; MTCW 1

Eagleton, Terry .... **CLC 63**
See also Eagleton, Terence (Francis)

Early, Jack
See Scoppettone, Sandra

East, Michael
See West, Morris L(anglo)

Eastaway, Edward
See Thomas, (Philip) Edward

Eastlake, William (Derry) 1917-1997 **CLC 8**
See also CA 5-8R; 158; CAAS 1; CANR 5, 63;
DLB 6, 206; INT CANR-5

Eastman, Charles A(lexander) 1858-1939
TCLC 55; DAM MULT
See also DLB 175; NNAL; YABC 1

Eberhart, Richard (Ghormley) 1904- **CLC 3,
11, 19, 56; DAM POET**
See also CA 1-4R; CANR 2; CDALB 1941-
1968; DLB 48; MTCW 1

Eberstadt, Fernanda 1960- .... **CLC 39**
See also CA 136; CANR 69

Echegaray (y Eizaguirre), Jose (Maria Waldo)
1832-1916 .... **TCLC 4**
See also CA 104; CANR 32; HW; MTCW 1

Echeverria, (Jose) Esteban (Antonino) 1805-
1851 .... **NCLC 18**

Echo
See Proust, (Valentin-Louis-George-Eugene-)
Marcel

Eckert, Allan W. 1931- .... **CLC 17**
See also AAYA 18; CA 13-16R; CANR 14, 45;

INT CANR-14; SAAS 21; SATA 29, 91;
SATA-Brief 27

Eckhart, Meister 1260(?)-1328(?) ... **CMLC 9**
See also DLB 115

Eckmar, F. R.
See de Hartog, Jan

Eco, Umberto 1932- **CLC 28, 60; DAM NOV,
POP**
See also BEST 90:1; CA 77-80; CANR 12, 33,
55; DLB 196; MTCW 1

Eddison, E(ric) R(ucker) 1882-1945**TCLC 15**
See also CA 109; 156

Eddy, Mary (Morse) Baker 1821-1910**T C L C
71**
See also CA 113

Edel, (Joseph) Leon 1907-1997 .. **CLC 29, 34**
See also CA 1-4R; 161; CANR 1, 22; DLB 103;
INT CANR-22

Eden, Emily 1797-1869 .... **NCLC 10**

Edgar, David 1948- ... **CLC 42; DAM DRAM**
See also CA 57-60; CANR 12, 61; DLB 13;
MTCW 1

Edgerton, Clyde (Carlyle) 1944- ...... **CLC 39**
See also AAYA 17; CA 118; 134; CANR 64;
INT 134

Edgeworth, Maria 1768-1849 .... **NCLC 1, 51**
See also DLB 116, 159, 163; SATA 21

Edmonds, Paul
See Kuttner, Henry

Edmonds, Walter D(umaux) 1903-1998 **C L C
35**
See also CA 5-8R; CANR 2; DLB 9; MAICYA;
SAAS 4; SATA 1, 27; SATA-Obit 99

Edmondson, Wallace
See Ellison, Harlan (Jay)

Edson, Russell .... **CLC 13**
See also CA 33-36R

Edwards, Bronwen Elizabeth
See Rose, Wendy

Edwards, G(erald) B(asil) 1899-1976**CLC 25**
See also CA 110

Edwards, Gus 1939- .... **CLC 43**
See also CA 108; INT 108

Edwards, Jonathan 1703-1758 .... **LC 7; DA;
DAC; DAM MST**
See also DLB 24

Efron, Marina Ivanovna Tsvetaeva
See Tsvetaeva (Efron), Marina (Ivanovna)

Ehle, John (Marsden, Jr.) 1925- .... **CLC 27**
See also CA 9-12R

Ehrenbourg, Ilya (Grigoryevich)
See Ehrenburg, Ilya (Grigoryevich)

Ehrenburg, Ilya (Grigoryevich) 1891-1967
CLC 18, 34, 62
See also CA 102; 25-28R

Ehrenburg, Ilyo (Grigoryevich)
See Ehrenburg, Ilya (Grigoryevich)

Ehrenreich, Barbara 1941- .... **CLC 110**
See also BEST 90:4; CA 73-76; CANR 16, 37,
62; MTCW 1

Eich, Guenter 1907-1972 .... **CLC 15**
See also CA 111; 93-96; DLB 69, 124

Eichendorff, Joseph Freiherr von 1788-1857
NCLC 8
See also DLB 90

Eigner, Larry .... **CLC 9**
See also Eigner, Laurence (Joel)
See also CAAS 23; DLB 5

Eigner, Laurence (Joel) 1927-1996
See Eigner, Larry
See also CA 9-12R; 151; CANR 6; DLB 193

Einstein, Albert 1879-1955 .... **TCLC 65**
See also CA 121; 133; MTCW 1

Eiseley, Loren Corey 1907-1977 .... **CLC 7**
See also AAYA 5; CA 1-4R; 73-76; CANR 6;
DLBD 17

Eisenstadt, Jill 1963- .... **CLC 50**

See also CA 140

Eisenstein, Sergei (Mikhailovich) 1898-1948
TCLC 57
See also CA 114; 149

Eisner, Simon
See Kornbluth, C(yril) M.

Ekeloef, (Bengt) Gunnar 1907-1968 **CLC 27;
DAM POET; PC 23**
See also CA 123; 25-28R

Ekelof, (Bengt) Gunnar
See Ekeloef, (Bengt) Gunnar

Ekelund, Vilhelm 1880-1949 .... **TCLC 75**

Ekwensi, C. O. D.
See Ekwensi, Cyprian (Odiatu Duaka)

Ekwensi, Cyprian (Odiatu Duaka) 1921-**CLC
4; BLC 1; DAM MULT**
See also BW 2; CA 29-32R; CANR 18, 42, 74;
DLB 117; MTCW 1; SATA 66

Elaine .... **TCLC 18**
See also Leverson, Ada

El Crummo
See Crumb, R(obert)

Elder, Lonne III 1931-1996 ....**DC 8**
See also BLC 1; BW 1; CA 81-84; 152; CANR
25; DAM MULT; DLB 7, 38, 44

Elia
See Lamb, Charles

Eliade, Mircea 1907-1986 .... **CLC 19**
See also CA 65-68; 119; CANR 30, 62; MTCW
1

Eliot, A. D.
See Jewett, (Theodora) Sarah Orne

Eliot, Alice
See Jewett, (Theodora) Sarah Orne

Eliot, Dan
See Silverberg, Robert

Eliot, George 1819-1880 **NCLC 4, 13, 23, 41,
49; DA; DAB; DAC; DAM MST, NOV; PC
20; WLC**
See also CDBLB 1832-1890; DLB 21, 35, 55

Eliot, John 1604-1690 ....**LC 5**
See also DLB 24

Eliot, T(homas) S(tearns) 1888-1965**CLC 1, 2,
3, 6, 9, 10, 13, 15, 24, 34, 41, 55, 57, 113;
DA; DAB; DAC; DAM DRAM, MST,
POET; PC 5; WLC**
See also CA 5-8R; 25-28R; CANR 41; CDALB
1929-1941; DLB 7, 10, 45, 63; DLBY 88;
MTCW 1

Elizabeth 1866-1941 .... **TCLC 41**

Elkin, Stanley L(awrence) 1930-1995 **CLC 4,
6, 9, 14, 27, 51, 91; DAM NOV, POP; SSC
12**
See also CA 9-12R; 148; CANR 8, 46; DLB 2,
28; DLBY 80; INT CANR-8; MTCW 1

Elledge, Scott .... **CLC 34**

Elliot, Don
See Silverberg, Robert

Elliott, Don
See Silverberg, Robert

Elliott, George P(aul) 1918-1980 .... **CLC 2**
See also CA 1-4R; 97-100; CANR 2

Elliott, Janice 1931- .... **CLC 47**
See also CA 13-16R; CANR 8, 29; DLB 14

Elliott, Sumner Locke 1917-1991 ..... **CLC 38**
See also CA 5-8R; 134; CANR 2, 21

Elliott, William
See Bradbury, Ray (Douglas)

Ellis, A. E. .... **CLC 7**

Ellis, Alice Thomas .... **CLC 40**
See also Haycraft, Anna
See also DLB 194

Ellis, Bret Easton 1964-**CLC 39, 71, 117; DAM
POP**
See also AAYA 2; CA 118; 123; CANR 51, 74;
INT 123

Ellis, (Henry) Havelock 1859-1939 **TCLC 14**

74; DLB 13; MTCW 1; SATA 66
Frye, (Herman) Northrop 1912-1991**CLC 24,
70**
See also CA 5-8R; 133; CANR 8, 37; DLB 67,
68; MTCW 1
Fuchs, Daniel 1909-1993 .... **CLC 8, 22**
See also CA 81-84; 142; CAAS 5; CANR 40;
DLB 9, 26, 28; DLBY 93
Fuchs, Daniel 1934- .... **CLC 34**
See also CA 37-40R; CANR 14, 48
Fuentes, Carlos 1928-**CLC 3, 8, 10, 13, 22, 41,
60, 113; DA; DAB; DAC; DAM MST,
MULT, NOV; HLC; SSC 24; WLC**
See also AAYA 4; AITN 2; CA 69-72; CANR
10, 32, 68; DLB 113; HW; MTCW 1
Fuentes, Gregorio Lopez y
See Lopez y Fuentes, Gregorio
Fugard, (Harold) Athol 1932-**CLC 5, 9, 14, 25,
40, 80; DAM DRAM; DC 3**
See also AAYA 17; CA 85-88; CANR 32, 54;
MTCW 1
Fugard, Sheila 1932- .... **CLC 48**
See also CA 125
Fuller, Charles (H., Jr.) 1939-**CLC 25; BLC 2;
DAM DRAM, MULT; DC 1**
See also BW 2; CA 108; 112; DLB 38; INT 112;
MTCW 1
Fuller, John (Leopold) 1937- .... **CLC 62**
See also CA 21-24R; CANR 9, 44; DLB 40
Fuller, Margaret .... **NCLC 5, 50**
See also Ossoli, Sarah Margaret (Fuller
marchesa d')
Fuller, Roy (Broadbent) 1912-1991**CLC 4, 28**
See also CA 5-8R; 135; CAAS 10; CANR 53;
DLB 15, 20; SATA 87
Fulton, Alice 1952- .... **CLC 52**
See also CA 116; CANR 57; DLB 193
Furphy, Joseph 1843-1912 .... **TCLC 25**
See also CA 163
Fussell, Paul 1924- .... **CLC 74**
See also BEST 90:1; CA 17-20R; CANR 8, 21,
35, 69; INT CANR-21; MTCW 1
Futabatei, Shimei 1864-1909 .... **TCLC 44**
See also CA 162; DLB 180
Futrelle, Jacques 1875-1912 .... **TCLC 19**
See also CA 113; 155
Gaboriau, Emile 1835-1873 .... **NCLC 14**
Gadda, Carlo Emilio 1893-1973 .... **CLC 11**
See also CA 89-92; DLB 177
Gaddis, William 1922-1998**CLC 1, 3, 6, 8, 10,
19, 43, 86**
See also CA 17-20R; 172; CANR 21, 48; DLB
2; MTCW 1
Gage, Walter
See Inge, William (Motter)
Gaines, Ernest J(ames) 1933- **CLC 3, 11, 18,
86; BLC 2; DAM MULT**
See also AAYA 18; AITN 1; BW 2; CA 9-12R;
CANR 6, 24, 42, 75; CDALB 1968-1988;
DLB 2, 33, 152; DLBY 80; MTCW 1; SATA
86
Gaitskill, Mary 1954- .... **CLC 69**
See also CA 128; CANR 61
Galdos, Benito Perez
See Perez Galdos, Benito
Gale, Zona 1874-1938**TCLC 7; DAM DRAM**
See also CA 105; 153; DLB 9, 78
Galeano, Eduardo (Hughes) 1940- ... **CLC 72**
See also CA 29-32R; CANR 13, 32; HW
Galiano, Juan Valera y Alcala
See Valera y Alcala-Galiano, Juan
Galilei, Galileo 1546-1642 .... **LC 45**
Gallagher, Tess 1943- ...... **CLC 18, 63; DAM
POET; PC 9**
See also CA 106; DLB 120
Gallant, Mavis 1922- ... **CLC 7, 18, 38; DAC;
DAM MST; SSC 5**

See also CA 69-72; CANR 29, 69; DLB 53;
MTCW 1
Gallant, Roy A(rthur) 1924- .... **CLC 17**
See also CA 5-8R; CANR 4, 29, 54; CLR 30;
MAICYA; SATA 4, 68
Gallico, Paul (William) 1897-1976 ..... **CLC 2**
See also AITN 1; CA 5-8R; 69-72; CANR 23;
DLB 9, 171; MAICYA; SATA 13
Gallo, Max Louis 1932- .... **CLC 95**
See also CA 85-88
Gallois, Lucien
See Desnos, Robert
Gallup, Ralph
See Whitemore, Hugh (John)
Galsworthy, John 1867-1933**TCLC 1, 45; DA;
DAB; DAC; DAM DRAM, MST, NOV;
SSC 22; WLC**
See also CA 104; 141; CANR 75; CDBLB
1890-1914; DLB 10, 34, 98, 162; DLBD 16
Galt, John 1779-1839 .... **NCLC 1**
See also DLB 99, 116, 159
Galvin, James 1951- .... **CLC 38**
See also CA 108; CANR 26
Gamboa, Federico 1864-1939 .... **TCLC 36**
See also CA 167
Gandhi, M. K.
See Gandhi, Mohandas Karamchand
Gandhi, Mahatma
See Gandhi, Mohandas Karamchand
Gandhi, Mohandas Karamchand 1869-1948
TCLC 59; DAM MULT
See also CA 121; 132; MTCW 1
Gann, Ernest Kellogg 1910-1991 ...... **CLC 23**
See also AITN 1; CA 1-4R; 136; CANR 1
Garcia, Cristina 1958- .... **CLC 76**
See also CA 141; CANR 73
Garcia Lorca, Federico 1898-1936**TCLC 1, 7,
49; DA; DAB; DAC; DAM DRAM, MST,
MULT, POET; DC 2; HLC; PC 3; WLC**
See also CA 104; 131; DLB 108; HW; MTCW
1
Garcia Marquez, Gabriel (Jose) 1928-**CLC 2,
3, 8, 10, 15, 27, 47, 55, 68; DA; DAB; DAC;
DAM MST, MULT, NOV, POP; HLC; SSC
8; WLC**
See also AAYA 3; BEST 89:1, 90:4; CA 33-
36R; CANR 10, 28, 50, 75; DLB 113; HW;
MTCW 1
Gard, Janice
See Latham, Jean Lee
Gard, Roger Martin du
See Martin du Gard, Roger
Gardam, Jane 1928- .... **CLC 43**
See also CA 49-52; CANR 2, 18, 33, 54; CLR
12; DLB 14, 161; MAICYA; MTCW 1;
SAAS 9; SATA 39, 76; SATA-Brief 28
Gardner, Herb(ert) 1934- .... **CLC 44**
See also CA 149
Gardner, John (Champlin), Jr. 1933-1982
**CLC 2, 3, 5, 7, 8, 10, 18, 28, 34; DAM NOV,
POP; SSC 7**
See also AITN 1; CA 65-68; 107; CANR 33,
73; DLB 2; DLBY 82; MTCW 1; SATA 40;
SATA-Obit 31
Gardner, John (Edmund) 1926-**CLC 30; DAM
POP**
See also CA 103; CANR 15, 69; MTCW 1
Gardner, Miriam
See Bradley, Marion Zimmer
Gardner, Noel
See Kuttner, Henry
Gardons, S. S.
See Snodgrass, W(illiam) D(e Witt)
Garfield, Leon 1921-1996 .... **CLC 12**
See also AAYA 8; CA 17-20R; 152; CANR 38,
41; CLR 21; DLB 161; JRDA; MAICYA;
SATA 1, 32, 76; SATA-Obit 90

Garland, (Hannibal) Hamlin 1860-1940
TCLC 3; SSC 18
See also CA 104; DLB 12, 71, 78, 186
Garneau, (Hector de) Saint-Denys 1912-1943
TCLC 13
See also CA 111; DLB 88
Garner, Alan 1934-**CLC 17; DAB; DAM POP**
See also AAYA 18; CA 73-76; CANR 15, 64;
CLR 20; DLB 161; MAICYA; MTCW 1;
SATA 18, 69
Garner, Hugh 1913-1979 .... **CLC 13**
See also CA 69-72; CANR 31; DLB 68
Garnett, David 1892-1981 .... **CLC 3**
See also CA 5-8R; 103; CANR 17; DLB 34
Garos, Stephanie
See Katz, Steve
Garrett, George (Palmer) 1929-**CLC 3, 11, 51;
SSC 30**
See also CA 1-4R; CAAS 5; CANR 1, 42, 67;
DLB 2, 5, 130, 152; DLBY 83
Garrick, David 1717-1779 ....**LC 15; DAM
DRAM**
See also DLB 84
Garrigue, Jean 1914-1972 .... **CLC 2, 8**
See also CA 5-8R; 37-40R; CANR 20
Garrison, Frederick
See Sinclair, Upton (Beall)
Garth, Will
See Hamilton, Edmond; Kuttner, Henry
Garvey, Marcus (Moziah, Jr.) 1887-1940
TCLC 41; BLC 2; DAM MULT
See also BW 1; CA 120; 124
Gary, Romain .... **CLC 25**
See also Kacew, Romain
See also DLB 83
Gascar, Pierre .... **CLC 11**
See also Fournier, Pierre
Gascoyne, David (Emery) 1916- .... **CLC 45**
See also CA 65-68; CANR 10, 28, 54; DLB 20;
MTCW 1
Gaskell, Elizabeth Cleghorn 1810-1865**NCLC
70; DAB; DAM MST; SSC 25**
See also CDBLB 1832-1890; DLB 21, 144, 159
Gass, William H(oward) 1924-**CLC 1, 2, 8, 11,
15, 39; SSC 12**
See also CA 17-20R; CANR 30, 71; DLB 2;
MTCW 1
Gasset, Jose Ortega y
See Ortega y Gasset, Jose
Gates, Henry Louis, Jr. 1950-**CLC 65; BLCS;
DAM MULT**
See also BW 2; CA 109; CANR 25, 53, 75; DLB
67
Gautier, Theophile 1811-1872 .. **NCLC 1, 59;
DAM POET; PC 18; SSC 20**
See also DLB 119
Gawsworth, John
See Bates, H(erbert) E(rnest)
Gay, John 1685-1732 .... **LC 49**
Gay, Oliver
See Gogarty, Oliver St. John
Gaye, Marvin (Penze) 1939-1984 ..... **CLC 26**
See also CA 112
Gebler, Carlo (Ernest) 1954- .... **CLC 39**
See also CA 119; 133
Gee, Maggie (Mary) 1948- .... **CLC 57**
See also CA 130; DLB 207
Gee, Maurice (Gough) 1931- .... **CLC 29**
See also CA 97-100; CANR 67; SATA 46, 101
Gelbart, Larry (Simon) 1923- .... **CLC 21, 61**
See also CA 73-76; CANR 45
Gelber, Jack 1932- .... **CLC 1, 6, 14, 79**
See also CA 1-4R; CANR 2; DLB 7
Gellhorn, Martha (Ellis) 1908-1998 **CLC 14,
60**
See also CA 77-80; 164; CANR 44; DLBY 82
Genet, Jean 1910-1986**CLC 1, 2, 5, 10, 14, 44,**

46; DAM DRAM
See also CA 13-16R; CANR 18; DLB 72;
DLBY 86; MTCW 1

Gent, Peter 1942- .... CLC 29
See also AITN 1; CA 89-92; DLBY 82

Gentlewoman in New England, A
See Bradstreet, Anne

Gentlewoman in Those Parts, A
See Bradstreet, Anne

George, Jean Craighead 1919- .... CLC 35
See also AAYA 8; CA 5-8R; CANR 25; CLR 1;
DLB 52; JRDA; MAICYA; SATA 2, 68

George, Stefan (Anton) 1868-1933TCLC 2, 14
See also CA 104

Georges, Georges Martin
See Simenon, Georges (Jacques Christian)

Gerhardi, William Alexander
See Gerhardie, William Alexander

Gerhardie, William Alexander 1895-1977
CLC 5
See also CA 25-28R; 73-76; CANR 18; DLB
36

Gerstler, Amy 1956- .... CLC 70
See also CA 146

Gertler, T. .... CLC 34
See also CA 116; 121; INT 121

Ghalib .... NCLC 39
See also Ghalib, Hsadullah Khan

Ghalib, Hsadullah Khan 1797-1869
See Ghalib
See also DAM POET

Ghelderode, Michel de 1898-1962CLC 6, 11;
DAM DRAM
See also CA 85-88; CANR 40

Ghiselin, Brewster 1903- .... CLC 23
See also CA 13-16R; CAAS 10; CANR 13

Ghose, Aurabinda 1872-1950......... TCLC 63
See also CA 163

Ghose, Zulfikar 1935- .... CLC 42
See also CA 65-68; CANR 67

Ghosh, Amitav 1956- .... CLC 44
See also CA 147

Giacosa, Giuseppe 1847-1906 .... TCLC 7
See also CA 104

Gibb, Lee
See Waterhouse, Keith (Spencer)

Gibbon, Lewis Grassic .... TCLC 4
See also Mitchell, James Leslie

Gibbons, Kaye 1960-CLC 50, 88; DAM POP
See also CA 151; CANR 75

Gibran, Kahlil 1883-1931 . TCLC 1, 9; DAM
POET, POP; PC 9
See also CA 104; 150

Gibran, Khalil
See Gibran, Kahlil

Gibson, William 1914- .. CLC 23; DA; DAB;
DAC; DAM DRAM, MST
See also CA 9-12R; CANR 9, 42, 75; DLB 7;
SATA 66

Gibson, William (Ford) 1948- ... CLC 39, 63;
DAM POP
See also AAYA 12; CA 126; 133; CANR 52

Gide, Andre (Paul Guillaume) 1869-1951
TCLC 5, 12, 36; DA; DAB; DAC; DAM
MST, NOV; SSC 13; WLC
See also CA 104; 124; DLB 65; MTCW 1

Gifford, Barry (Colby) 1946- .... CLC 34
See also CA 65-68; CANR 9, 30, 40

Gilbert, Frank
See De Voto, Bernard (Augustine)

Gilbert, W(illiam) S(chwenck) 1836-1911
TCLC 3; DAM DRAM, POET
See also CA 104; SATA 36

Gilbreth, Frank B., Jr. 1911- .... CLC 17
See also CA 9-12R; SATA 2

Gilchrist, Ellen 1935-CLC 34, 48; DAM POP;
SSC 14

See also CA 113; 116; CANR 41, 61; DLB 130;
MTCW 1

Giles, Molly 1942- .... CLC 39
See also CA 126

Gill, Eric 1882-1940 .... TCLC 85

Gill, Patrick
See Creasey, John

Gilliam, Terry (Vance) 1940- .... CLC 21
See also Monty Python
See also AAYA 19; CA 108; 113; CANR 35;
INT 113

Gillian, Jerry
See Gilliam, Terry (Vance)

Gilliatt, Penelope (Ann Douglass) 1932-1993
CLC 2, 10, 13, 53
See also AITN 2; CA 13-16R; 141; CANR 49;
DLB 14

Gilman, Charlotte (Anna) Perkins (Stetson)
1860-1935 ....

TCLC 9, 37; SSC 13
See also CA 106; 150

Gilmour, David 1949- .... CLC 35
See also CA 138, 147

Gilpin, William 1724-1804 .... NCLC 30

Gilray, J. D.
See Mencken, H(enry) L(ouis)

Gilroy, Frank D(aniel) 1925- .... CLC 2
See also CA 81-84; CANR 32, 64; DLB 7

Gilstrap, John 1957(?)- .... CLC 99
See also CA 160

Ginsberg, Allen 1926-1997CLC 1, 2, 3, 4, 6, 13,
36, 69, 109; DA; DAB; DAC; DAM MST,
POET; PC 4; WLC
See also AITN 1; CA 1-4R; 157; CANR 2, 41,
63; CDALB 1941-1968; DLB 5, 16, 169;
MTCW 1

Ginzburg, Natalia 1916-1991CLC 5, 11, 54, 70
See also CA 85-88; 135; CANR 33; DLB 177;
MTCW 1

Giono, Jean 1895-1970 .... CLC 4, 11
See also CA 45-48; 29-32R; CANR 2, 35; DLB
72; MTCW 1

Giovanni, Nikki 1943- CLC 2, 4, 19, 64, 117;
BLC 2; DA; DAB; DAC; DAM MST,
MULT, POET; PC 19; WLCS
See also AAYA 22; AITN 1; BW 2; CA 29-32R;
CAAS 6; CANR 18, 41, 60; CLR 6; DLB 5,
41; INT CANR-18; MAICYA; MTCW 1;
SATA 24

Giovene, Andrea 1904- .... CLC 7
See also CA 85-88

Gippius, Zinaida (Nikolayevna) 1869-1945
See Hippius, Zinaida
See also CA 106

Giraudoux, (Hippolyte) Jean 1882-1944
TCLC 2, 7; DAM DRAM
See also CA 104; DLB 65

Gironella, Jose Maria 1917- .... CLC 11
See also CA 101

Gissing, George (Robert) 1857-1903TCLC 3,
24, 47
See also CA 105; 167; DLB 18, 135, 184

Giurlani, Aldo
See Palazzeschi, Aldo

Gladkov, Fyodor (Vasilyevich) 1883-1958
TCLC 27
See also CA 170

Glanville, Brian (Lester) 1931- .... CLC 6
See also CA 5-8R; CAAS 9; CANR 3, 70; DLB
15, 139; SATA 42

Glasgow, Ellen (Anderson Gholson) 1873-1945
TCLC 2, 7
See also CA 104; 164; DLB 9, 12

Glaspell, Susan 1882(?)-1948TCLC 55; DC 10
See also CA 110; 154; DLB 7, 9, 78; YABC 2

Glassco, John 1909-1981 .... CLC 9
See also CA 13-16R; 102; CANR 15; DLB 68

Glasscock, Amnesia
See Steinbeck, John (Ernst)

Glasser, Ronald J. 1940(?)- .... CLC 37

Glassman, Joyce
See Johnson, Joyce

Glendinning, Victoria 1937- .... CLC 50
See also CA 120; 127; CANR 59; DLB 155

Glissant, Edouard 1928- . CLC 10, 68; DAM
MULT
See also CA 153

Gloag, Julian 1930- .... CLC 40
See also AITN 1; CA 65-68; CANR 10, 70

Glowacki, Aleksander
See Prus, Boleslaw

Gluck, Louise (Elisabeth) 1943-CLC 7, 22, 44,
81; DAM POET; PC 16
See also CA 33-36R; CANR 40, 69; DLB 5

Glyn, Elinor 1864-1943 .... TCLC 72
See also DLB 153

Gobineau, Joseph Arthur (Comte) de 1816-
1882 .... NCLC 17
See also DLB 123

Godard, Jean-Luc 1930- .... CLC 20
See also CA 93-96

Godden, (Margaret) Rumer 1907-1998 C L C
53
See also AAYA 6; CA 5-8R; 172; CANR 4, 27,
36, 55; CLR 20; DLB 161; MAICYA; SAAS
12; SATA 3, 36

Godoy Alcayaga, Lucila 1889-1957
See Mistral, Gabriela
See also BW 2; CA 104; 131; DAM MULT;
HW; MTCW 1

Godwin, Gail (Kathleen) 1937-CLC 5, 8, 22,
31, 69; DAM POP
See also CA 29-32R; CANR 15, 43, 69; DLB
6; INT CANR-15; MTCW 1

Godwin, William 1756-1836 .... NCLC 14
See also CDBLB 1789-1832; DLB 39, 104, 142,
158, 163

Goebbels, Josef
See Goebbels, (Paul) Joseph

Goebbels, (Paul) Joseph 1897-1945TCLC 68
See also CA 115; 148

Goebbels, Joseph Paul
See Goebbels, (Paul) Joseph

Goethe, Johann Wolfgang von 1749-1832
NCLC 4, 22, 34; DA; DAB; DAC; DAM
DRAM, MST, POET; PC 5; WLC
See also DLB 94

Gogarty, Oliver St. John 1878-1957TCLC 15
See also CA 109; 150; DLB 15, 19

Gogol, Nikolai (Vasilyevich) 1809-1852NCLC
5, 15, 31; DA; DAB; DAC; DAM DRAM,
MST; DC 1; SSC 4, 29; WLC
See also DLB 198

Goines, Donald 1937(?)-1974CLC 80; BLC 2;
DAM MULT, POP
See also AITN 1; BW 1; CA 124; 114; DLB 33

Gold, Herbert 1924- .... CLC 4, 7, 14, 42
See also CA 9-12R; CANR 17, 45; DLB 2;
DLBY 81

Goldbarth, Albert 1948- .... CLC 5, 38
See also CA 53-56; CANR 6, 40; DLB 120

Goldberg, Anatol 1910-1982 .... CLC 34
See also CA 131; 117

Goldemberg, Isaac 1945- .... CLC 52
See also CA 69-72; CAAS 12; CANR 11, 32;
HW

Golding, William (Gerald) 1911-1993CLC 1,
2, 3, 8, 10, 17, 27, 58, 81; DA; DAB; DAC;
DAM MST, NOV; WLC
See also AAYA 5; CA 5-8R; 141; CANR 13,
33, 54; CDBLB 1945-1960; DLB 15, 100;
MTCW 1

Goldman, Emma 1869-1940 .... TCLC 13
See also CA 110; 150

Goldman, Francisco 1954- .... **CLC 76**
See also CA 162

Goldman, William (W.) 1931- .... **CLC 1, 48**
See also CA 9-12R; CANR 29, 69; DLB 44

Goldmann, Lucien 1913-1970 .... **CLC 24**
See also CA 25-28; CAP 2

Goldoni, Carlo 1707-1793 **LC 4; DAM DRAM**

Goldsberry, Steven 1949- .... **CLC 34**
See also CA 131

Goldsmith, Oliver 1728-1774 . **LC 2, 48; DA; DAB; DAC; DAM DRAM, MST, NOV, POET; DC 8; WLC**
See also CDBLB 1660-1789; DLB 39, 89, 104, 109, 142; SATA 26

Goldsmith, Peter
See Priestley, J(ohn) B(oynton)

Gombrowicz, Witold 1904-1969 **CLC 4, 7, 11, 49; DAM DRAM**
See also CA 19-20; 25-28R; CAP 2

Gomez de la Serna, Ramon 1888-1963 **CLC 9**
See also CA 153; 116; HW

Goncharov, Ivan Alexandrovich 1812-1891 **NCLC 1, 63**

Goncourt, Edmond (Louis Antoine Huot) de 1822-1896 .... **NCLC 7**
See also DLB 123

Goncourt, Jules (Alfred Huot) de 1830-1870 **NCLC 7**
See also DLB 123

Gontier, Fernande 19(?)- .... **CLC 50**

Gonzalez Martinez, Enrique 1871-1952 **TCLC 72**
See also CA 166; HW

Goodman, Paul 1911-1972 ...... **CLC 1, 2, 4, 7**
See also CA 19-20; 37-40R; CANR 34; CAP 2; DLB 130; MTCW 1

Gordimer, Nadine 1923- **CLC 3, 5, 7, 10, 18, 33, 51, 70; DA; DAB; DAC; DAM MST, NOV; SSC 17; WLCS**
See also CA 5-8R; CANR 3, 28, 56; INT CANR-28; MTCW 1

Gordon, Adam Lindsay 1833-1870 **NCLC 21**

Gordon, Caroline 1895-1981 **CLC 6, 13, 29, 83; SSC 15**
See also CA 11-12; 103; CANR 36; CAP 1; DLB 4, 9, 102; DLBD 17; DLBY 81; MTCW 1

Gordon, Charles William 1860-1937
See Connor, Ralph
See also CA 109

Gordon, Mary (Catherine) 1949- **CLC 13, 22**
See also CA 102; CANR 44; DLB 6; DLBY 81; INT 102; MTCW 1

Gordon, N. J.
See Bosman, Herman Charles

Gordon, Sol 1923- .... **CLC 26**
See also CA 53-56; CANR 4; SATA 11

Gordone, Charles 1925-1995 **CLC 1, 4; DAM DRAM; DC 8**
See also BW 1; CA 93-96; 150; CANR 55; DLB 7; INT 93-96; MTCW 1

Gore, Catherine 1800-1861 .... **NCLC 65**
See also DLB 116

Gorenko, Anna Andreevna
See Akhmatova, Anna

Gorky, Maxim 1868-1936 **TCLC 8; DAB; SSC 28; WLC**
See also Peshkov, Alexei Maximovich

Goryan, Sirak
See Saroyan, William

Gosse, Edmund (William) 1849-1928 **TCLC 28**
See also CA 117; DLB 57, 144, 184

Gotlieb, Phyllis Fay (Bloom) 1926- .. **CLC 18**
See also CA 13-16R; CANR 7; DLB 88

Gottesman, S. D.
See Kornbluth, C(yril) M.; Pohl, Frederik

Gottfried von Strassburg fl. c. 1210- **CMLC 10**
See also DLB 138

Gould, Lois .... **CLC 4, 10**
See also CA 77-80; CANR 29; MTCW 1

Gourmont, Remy (-Marie-Charles) de 1858-1915 .... **TCLC 17**
See also CA 109; 150

Govier, Katherine 1948- .... **CLC 51**
See also CA 101; CANR 18, 40

Goyen, (Charles) William 1915-1983 **CLC 5, 8, 14, 40**
See also AITN 2; CA 5-8R; 110; CANR 6, 71; DLB 2; DLBY 83; INT CANR-6

Goytisolo, Juan 1931- . **CLC 5, 10, 23; DAM MULT; HLC**
See also CA 85-88; CANR 32, 61; HW; MTCW 1

Gozzano, Guido 1883-1916 .... **PC 10**
See also CA 154; DLB 114

Gozzi, (Conte) Carlo 1720-1806 .... **NCLC 23**

Grabbe, Christian Dietrich 1801-1836 **NCLC 2**
See also DLB 133

Grace, Patricia 1937- .... **CLC 56**

Gracian y Morales, Baltasar 1601-1658 **LC 15**

Gracq, Julien .... **CLC 11, 48**
See also Poirier, Louis
See also DLB 83

Grade, Chaim 1910-1982 .... **CLC 10**
See also CA 93-96; 107

Graduate of Oxford, A
See Ruskin, John

Grafton, Garth
See Duncan, Sara Jeannette

Graham, John
See Phillips, David Graham

Graham, Jorie 1951- .... **CLC 48, 118**
See also CA 111; CANR 63; DLB 120

Graham, R(obert) B(ontine) Cunninghame
See Cunninghame Graham, R(obert) B(ontine)
See also DLB 98, 135, 174

Graham, Robert
See Haldeman, Joe (William)

Graham, Tom
See Lewis, (Harry) Sinclair

Graham, W(illiam) S(ydney) 1918-1986 **CLC 29**
See also CA 73-76; 118; DLB 20

Graham, Winston (Mawdsley) 1910- **CLC 23**
See also CA 49-52; CANR 2, 22, 45, 66; DLB 77

Grahame, Kenneth 1859-1932 **TCLC 64; DAB**
See also CA 108; 136; CLR 5; DLB 34, 141, 178; MAICYA; SATA 100; YABC 1

Granovsky, Timofei Nikolaevich 1813-1855 **NCLC 75**
See also DLB 198

Grant, Skeeter
See Spiegelman, Art

Granville-Barker, Harley 1877-1946 **TCLC 2; DAM DRAM**
See also Barker, Harley Granville
See also CA 104

Grass, Guenter (Wilhelm) 1927- **CLC 1, 2, 4, 6, 11, 15, 22, 32, 49, 88; DA; DAB; DAC; DAM MST, NOV; WLC**
See also CA 13-16R; CANR 20, 75; DLB 75, 124; MTCW 1

Gratton, Thomas
See Hulme, T(homas) E(rnest)

Grau, Shirley Ann 1929- . **CLC 4, 9; SSC 15**
See also CA 89-92; CANR 22, 69; DLB 2; INT CANR-22; MTCW 1

Gravel, Fern
See Hall, James Norman

Graver, Elizabeth 1964- .... **CLC 70**

See also CA 135; CANR 71

Graves, Richard Perceval 1945- .... **CLC 44**
See also CA 65-68; CANR 9, 26, 51

Graves, Robert (von Ranke) 1895-1985 **CLC 1, 2, 6, 11, 39, 44, 45; DAB; DAC; DAM MST, POET; PC 6**
See also CA 5-8R; 117; CANR 5, 36; CDBLB 1914-1945; DLB 20, 100, 191; DLBD 18; DLBY 85; MTCW 1; SATA 45

Graves, Valerie
See Bradley, Marion Zimmer

Gray, Alasdair (James) 1934- .... **CLC 41**
See also CA 126; CANR 47, 69; DLB 194; INT 126; MTCW 1

Gray, Amlin 1946- .... **CLC 29**
See also CA 138

Gray, Francine du Plessix 1930- ..... **CLC 22; DAM NOV**
See also BEST 90:3; CA 61-64; CAAS 2; CANR 11, 33, 75; INT CANR-11; MTCW 1

Gray, John (Henry) 1866-1934 ...... **TCLC 19**
See also CA 119; 162

Gray, Simon (James Holliday) 1936- **CLC 9, 14, 36**
See also AITN 1; CA 21-24R; CAAS 3; CANR 32, 69; DLB 13; MTCW 1

Gray, Spalding 1941- **CLC 49, 112; DAM POP; DC 7**
See also CA 128; CANR 74

Gray, Thomas 1716-1771 **LC 4, 40; DA; DAB; DAC; DAM MST; PC 2; WLC**
See also CDBLB 1660-1789; DLB 109

Grayson, David
See Baker, Ray Stannard

Grayson, Richard (A.) 1951- .... **CLC 38**
See also CA 85-88; CANR 14, 31, 57

Greeley, Andrew M(oran) 1928- ..... **CLC 28; DAM POP**
See also CA 5-8R; CAAS 7; CANR 7, 43, 69; MTCW 1

Green, Anna Katharine 1846-1935 **TCLC 63**
See also CA 112; 159; DLB 202

Green, Brian
See Card, Orson Scott

Green, Hannah
See Greenberg, Joanne (Goldenberg)

Green, Hannah 1927(?)-1996 .... **CLC 3**
See also CA 73-76; CANR 59

Green, Henry 1905-1973 .... **CLC 2, 13, 97**
See also Yorke, Henry Vincent
See also DLB 15

Green, Julian (Hartridge) 1900-1998
See Green, Julien
See also CA 21-24R; 169; CANR 33; DLB 4, 72; MTCW 1

Green, Julien .... **CLC 3, 11, 77**
See also Green, Julian (Hartridge)

Green, Paul (Eliot) 1894-1981 **CLC 25; DAM DRAM**
See also AITN 1; CA 5-8R; 103; CANR 3; DLB 7, 9; DLBY 81

Greenberg, Ivan 1908-1973
See Rahv, Philip
See also CA 85-88

Greenberg, Joanne (Goldenberg) 1932- **CLC 7, 30**
See also AAYA 12; CA 5-8R; CANR 14, 32, 69; SATA 25

Greenberg, Richard 1959(?)- .... **CLC 57**
See also CA 138

Greene, Bette 1934- .... **CLC 30**
See also AAYA 7; CA 53-56; CANR 4; CLR 2; JRDA; MAICYA; SAAS 16; SATA 8, 102

Greene, Gael .... **CLC 8**
See also CA 13-16R; CANR 10

Greene, Graham (Henry) 1904-1991 **CLC 1, 3, 6, 9, 14, 18, 27, 37, 70, 72; DA; DAB; DAC;**

DAM MST, NOV; SSC 29; WLC
See also AITN 2; CA 13-16R; 133; CANR 35,
61; CDBLB 1945-1960; DLB 13, 15, 77,
100, 162, 201, 204; DLBY 91; MTCW 1;
SATA 20

Greene, Robert 1558-1592 .... **LC 41**
See also DLB 62, 167

Greer, Richard
See Silverberg, Robert

Gregor, Arthur 1923- .... **CLC 9**
See also CA 25-28R; CAAS 10; CANR 11;
SATA 36

Gregor, Lee
See Pohl, Frederik

Gregory, Isabella Augusta (Persse) 1852-1932
TCLC 1
See also CA 104; DLB 10

Gregory, J. Dennis
See Williams, John A(lfred)

Grendon, Stephen
See Derleth, August (William)

Grenville, Kate 1950- .... **CLC 61**
See also CA 118; CANR 53

Grenville, Pelham
See Wodehouse, P(elham) G(renville)

Greve, Felix Paul (Berthold Friedrich) 1879-
1948
See Grove, Frederick Philip
See also CA 104; 141; DAC; DAM MST

Grey, Zane 1872-1939 .. **TCLC 6; DAM POP**
See also CA 104; 132; DLB 9; MTCW 1

Grieg, (Johan) Nordahl (Brun) 1902-1943
TCLC 10
See also CA 107

Grieve, C(hristopher) M(urray) 1892-1978
CLC 11, 19; DAM POET
See also MacDiarmid, Hugh; Pteleon
See also CA 5-8R; 85-88; CANR 33; MTCW 1

Griffin, Gerald 1803-1840 .... **NCLC 7**
See also DLB 159

Griffin, John Howard 1920-1980 ..... **CLC 68**
See also AITN 1; CA 1-4R; 101; CANR 2

Griffin, Peter 1942- .... **CLC 39**
See also CA 136

Griffith, D(avid Lewelyn) W(ark) 1875(?)-1948
TCLC 68
See also CA 119; 150

Griffith, Lawrence
See Griffith, D(avid Lewelyn) W(ark)

Griffiths, Trevor 1935- .... **CLC 13, 52**
See also CA 97-100; CANR 45; DLB 13

Griggs, Sutton Elbert 1872-1930(?)**TCLC 77**
See also CA 123; DLB 50

Grigson, Geoffrey (Edward Harvey) 1905-1985
CLC 7, 39
See also CA 25-28R; 118; CANR 20, 33; DLB
27; MTCW 1

Grillparzer, Franz 1791-1872 .... **NCLC 1**
See also DLB 133

Grimble, Reverend Charles James
See Eliot, T(homas) S(tearns)

Grimke, Charlotte L(ottie) Forten 1837(?)-1914
See Forten, Charlotte L.
See also BW 1; CA 117; 124; DAM MULT,
POET

Grimm, Jacob Ludwig Karl 1785-1863**NCLC
3**
See also DLB 90; MAICYA; SATA 22

Grimm, Wilhelm Karl 1786-1859 .... **NCLC 3**
See also DLB 90; MAICYA; SATA 22

Grimmelshausen, Johann Jakob Christoffel von
1621-1676 .... **LC 6**
See also DLB 168

Grindel, Eugene 1895-1952
See Eluard, Paul
See also CA 104

Grisham, John 1955- .... **CLC 84; DAM POP**

See also AAYA 14; CA 138; CANR 47, 69

Grossman, David 1954- .... **CLC 67**
See also CA 138

Grossman, Vasily (Semenovich) 1905-1964
CLC 41
See also CA 124; 130; MTCW 1

Grove, Frederick Philip .... **TCLC 4**
See also Greve, Felix Paul (Berthold Friedrich)
See also DLB 92

Grubb
See Crumb, R(obert)

Grumbach, Doris (Isaac) 1918-**CLC 13, 22, 64**
See also CA 5-8R; CAAS 2; CANR 9, 42, 70;
INT CANR-9

Grundtvig, Nicolai Frederik Severin 1783-1872
NCLC 1

Grunge
See Crumb, R(obert)

Grunwald, Lisa 1959- .... **CLC 44**
See also CA 120

Guare, John 1938- . **CLC 8, 14, 29, 67; DAM
DRAM**
See also CA 73-76; CANR 21, 69; DLB 7;
MTCW 1

Gudjonsson, Halldor Kiljan 1902-1998
See Laxness, Halldor
See also CA 103; 164

Guenter, Erich
See Eich, Guenter

Guest, Barbara 1920- .... **CLC 34**
See also CA 25-28R; CANR 11, 44; DLB 5,
193

Guest, Judith (Ann) 1936- **CLC 8, 30; DAM
NOV, POP**
See also AAYA 7; CA 77-80; CANR 15, 75;
INT CANR-15; MTCW 1

Guevara, Che .... **CLC 87; HLC**
See also Guevara (Serna), Ernesto

Guevara (Serna), Ernesto 1928-1967
See Guevara, Che
See also CA 127; 111; CANR 56; DAM MULT;
HW

Guicciardini, Francesco 1483-1540 .... **LC 49**

Guild, Nicholas M. 1944- .... **CLC 33**
See also CA 93-96

Guillemin, Jacques
See Sartre, Jean-Paul

Guillen, Jorge 1893-1984 .... **CLC 11; DAM
MULT, POET**
See also CA 89-92; 112; DLB 108; HW

Guillen, Nicolas (Cristobal) 1902-1989 **C L C
48, 79; BLC 2; DAM MST, MULT, POET;
HLC; PC 23**
See also BW 2; CA 116; 125; 129; HW

Guillevic, (Eugene) 1907- .... **CLC 33**
See also CA 93-96

Guillois
See Desnos, Robert

Guillois, Valentin
See Desnos, Robert

Guiney, Louise Imogen 1861-1920 **TCLC 41**
See also CA 160; DLB 54

Guiraldes, Ricardo (Guillermo) 1886-1927
TCLC 39
See also CA 131; HW; MTCW 1

Gumilev, Nikolai (Stepanovich) 1886-1921
TCLC 60
See also CA 165

Gunesekera, Romesh 1954- .... **CLC 91**
See also CA 159

Gunn, Bill .... **CLC 5**
See also Gunn, William Harrison
See also DLB 38

Gunn, Thom(son William) 1929-**CLC 3, 6, 18,
32, 81; DAM POET**
See also CA 17-20R; CANR 9, 33; CDBLB
1960 to Present; DLB 27; INT CANR-33;

MTCW 1

Gunn, William Harrison 1934(?)-1989
See Gunn, Bill
See also AITN 1; BW 1; CA 13-16R; 128;
CANR 12, 25, 76

Gunnars, Kristjana 1948- .... **CLC 69**
See also CA 113; DLB 60

Gurdjieff, G(eorgei) I(vanovich) 1877(?)-1949
TCLC 71
See also CA 157

Gurganus, Allan 1947- . **CLC 70; DAM POP**
See also BEST 90:1; CA 135

Gurney, A(lbert) R(amsdell), Jr. 1930- . **C L C
32, 50, 54; DAM DRAM**
See also CA 77-80; CANR 32, 64

Gurney, Ivor (Bertie) 1890-1937 ... **TCLC 33**
See also CA 167

Gurney, Peter
See Gurney, A(lbert) R(amsdell), Jr.

Guro, Elena 1877-1913 .... **TCLC 56**

Gustafson, James M(oody) 1925- ... **CLC 100**
See also CA 25-28R; CANR 37

Gustafson, Ralph (Barker) 1909- ..... **CLC 36**
See also CA 21-24R; CANR 8, 45; DLB 88

Gut, Gom
See Simenon, Georges (Jacques Christian)

Guterson, David 1956- .... **CLC 91**
See also CA 132; CANR 73

Guthrie, A(lfred) B(ertram), Jr. 1901-1991
CLC 23
See also CA 57-60; 134; CANR 24; DLB 6;
SATA 62; SATA-Obit 67

Guthrie, Isobel
See Grieve, C(hristopher) M(urray)

Guthrie, Woodrow Wilson 1912-1967
See Guthrie, Woody
See also CA 113; 93-96

Guthrie, Woody .... **CLC 35**
See also Guthrie, Woodrow Wilson

Guy, Rosa (Cuthbert) 1928- .... **CLC 26**
See also AAYA 4; BW 2; CA 17-20R; CANR
14, 34; CLR 13; DLB 33; JRDA; MAICYA;
SATA 14, 62

Gwendolyn
See Bennett, (Enoch) Arnold

H. D. .... **CLC 3, 8, 14, 31, 34, 73; PC 5**
See also Doolittle, Hilda

H. de V.
See Buchan, John

Haavikko, Paavo Juhani 1931- .. **CLC 18, 34**
See also CA 106

Habbema, Koos
See Heijermans, Herman

Habermas, Juergen 1929- .... **CLC 104**
See also CA 109

Habermas, Jurgen
See Habermas, Juergen

Hacker, Marilyn 1942- **CLC 5, 9, 23, 72, 91;
DAM POET**
See also CA 77-80; CANR 68; DLB 120

Haeckel, Ernst Heinrich (Philipp August) 1834-
1919 ....

TCLC 83
See also CA 157

Haggard, H(enry) Rider 1856-1925**TCLC 11**
See also CA 108; 148; DLB 70, 156, 174, 178;
SATA 16

Hagiosy, L.
See Larbaud, Valery (Nicolas)

Hagiwara Sakutaro 1886-1942**TCLC 60; PC
18**

Haig, Fenil
See Ford, Ford Madox

Haig-Brown, Roderick (Langmere) 1908-1976
CLC 21
See also CA 5-8R; 69-72; CANR 4, 38; CLR
31; DLB 88; MAICYA; SATA 12

See Futabatei, Shimei

Hasek, Jaroslav (Matej Frantisek) 1883-1923
TCLC 4
See also CA 104; 129; MTCW 1

Hass, Robert 1941- ... **CLC 18, 39, 99; PC 16**
See also CA 111; CANR 30, 50, 71; DLB 105, 206; SATA 94

Hastings, Hudson
See Kuttner, Henry

Hastings, Selina .... **CLC 44**

Hathorne, John 1641-1717 .... **LC 38**

Hatteras, Amelia
See Mencken, H(enry) L(ouis)

Hatteras, Owen .... **TCLC 18**
See also Mencken, H(enry) L(ouis); Nathan, George Jean

Hauptmann, Gerhart (Johann Robert) 1862-1946 .... **TCLC 4; DAM DRAM**
See also CA 104; 153; DLB 66, 118

Havel, Vaclav 1936- ... **CLC 25, 58, 65; DAM DRAM; DC 6**
See also CA 104; CANR 36, 63; MTCW 1

Haviaras, Stratis .... **CLC 33**
See also Chaviaras, Strates

Hawes, Stephen 1475(?)-1523(?) .... **LC 17**
See also DLB 132

Hawkes, John (Clendennin Burne, Jr.) 1925-1998 .. **CLC 1, 2, 3, 4, 7, 9, 14, 15, 27, 49**
See also CA 1-4R; 167; CANR 2, 47, 64; DLB 2, 7; DLBY 80; MTCW 1

Hawking, S. W.
See Hawking, Stephen W(illiam)

Hawking, Stephen W(illiam) 1942- . **CLC 63, 105**
See also AAYA 13; BEST 89:1; CA 126; 129; CANR 48

Hawkins, Anthony Hope
See Hope, Anthony

Hawthorne, Julian 1846-1934 .... **TCLC 25**
See also CA 165

Hawthorne, Nathaniel 1804-1864 **NCLC 39; DA; DAB; DAC; DAM MST, NOV; SSC 3, 29; WLC**
See also AAYA 18; CDALB 1640-1865; DLB 1, 74; YABC 2

Haxton, Josephine Ayres 1921-
See Douglas, Ellen
See also CA 115; CANR 41

Hayaseca y Eizaguirre, Jorge
See Echegaray (y Eizaguirre), Jose (Maria Waldo)

Hayashi, Fumiko 1904-1951 .... **TCLC 27**
See also CA 161; DLB 180

Haycraft, Anna
See Ellis, Alice Thomas
See also CA 122

Hayden, Robert E(arl) 1913-1980 . **CLC 5, 9, 14, 37; BLC 2; DA; DAC; DAM MST, MULT, POET; PC 6**
See also BW 1; CA 69-72; 97-100; CABS 2; CANR 24, 75; CDALB 1941-1968; DLB 5, 76; MTCW 1; SATA 19; SATA-Obit 26

Hayford, J(oseph) E(phraim) Casely
See Casely-Hayford, J(oseph) E(phraim)

Hayman, Ronald 1932- .... **CLC 44**
See also CA 25-28R; CANR 18, 50; DLB 155

Haywood, Eliza (Fowler) 1693(?)-1756 **LC 1, 44**
See also DLB 39

Hazlitt, William 1778-1830 .... **NCLC 29**
See also DLB 110, 158

Hazzard, Shirley 1931- .... **CLC 18**
See also CA 9-12R; CANR 4, 70; DLBY 82; MTCW 1

Head, Bessie 1937-1986 **CLC 25, 67; BLC 2; DAM MULT**
See also BW 2; CA 29-32R; 119; CANR 25;

DLB 117; MTCW 1

Headon, (Nicky) Topper 1956(?)- ..... **CLC 30**

Heaney, Seamus (Justin) 1939- **CLC 5, 7, 14, 25, 37, 74, 91; DAB; DAM POET; PC 18; WLCS**
See also CA 85-88; CANR 25, 48, 75; CDBLB 1960 to Present; DLB 40; DLBY 95; MTCW 1

Hearn, (Patricio) Lafcadio (Tessima Carlos) 1850-1904 .... **TCLC 9**
See also CA 105; 166; DLB 12, 78, 189

Hearne, Vicki 1946- .... **CLC 56**
See also CA 139

Hearon, Shelby 1931- .... **CLC 63**
See also AITN 2; CA 25-28R; CANR 18, 48

Heat-Moon, William Least .... **CLC 29**
See also Trogdon, William (Lewis)
See also AAYA 9

Hebbel, Friedrich 1813-1863 **NCLC 43; DAM DRAM**
See also DLB 129

Hebert, Anne 1916- **CLC 4, 13, 29; DAC; DAM MST, POET**
See also CA 85-88; CANR 69; DLB 68; MTCW 1

Hecht, Anthony (Evan) 1923- **CLC 8, 13, 19; DAM POET**
See also CA 9-12R; CANR 6; DLB 5, 169

Hecht, Ben 1894-1964 .... **CLC 8**
See also CA 85-88; DLB 7, 9, 25, 26, 28, 86

Hedayat, Sadeq 1903-1951 .... **TCLC 21**
See also CA 120

Hegel, Georg Wilhelm Friedrich 1770-1831 **NCLC 46**
See also DLB 90

Heidegger, Martin 1889-1976 .... **CLC 24**
See also CA 81-84; 65-68; CANR 34; MTCW 1

Heidenstam, (Carl Gustaf) Verner von 1859-1940 .... **TCLC 5**
See also CA 104

Heifner, Jack 1946- .... **CLC 11**
See also CA 105; CANR 47

Heijermans, Herman 1864-1924 .... **TCLC 24**
See also CA 123

Heilbrun, Carolyn G(old) 1926- .... **CLC 25**
See also CA 45-48; CANR 1, 28, 58

Heine, Heinrich 1797-1856 **NCLC 4, 54; PC 25**
See also DLB 90

Heinemann, Larry (Curtiss) 1944- ... **CLC 50**
See also CA 110; CAAS 21; CANR 31; DLBD 9; INT CANR-31

Heiney, Donald (William) 1921-1993
See Harris, MacDonald
See also CA 1-4R; 142; CANR 3, 58

Heinlein, Robert A(nson) 1907-1988 **CLC 1, 3, 8, 14, 26, 55; DAM POP**
See also AAYA 17; CA 1-4R; 125; CANR 1, 20, 53; DLB 8; JRDA; MAICYA; MTCW 1; SATA 9, 69; SATA-Obit 56

Helforth, John
See Doolittle, Hilda

Hellenhofferu, Vojtech Kapristian z
See Hasek, Jaroslav (Matej Frantisek)

Heller, Joseph 1923- **CLC 1, 3, 5, 8, 11, 36, 63; DA; DAB; DAC; DAM MST, NOV, POP; WLC**
See also AAYA 24; AITN 1; CA 5-8R; CABS 1; CANR 8, 42, 66; DLB 2, 28; DLBY 80; INT CANR-8; MTCW 1

Hellman, Lillian (Florence) 1906-1984 **CLC 2, 4, 8, 14, 18, 34, 44, 52; DAM DRAM; DC 1**
See also AITN 1, 2; CA 13-16R; 112; CANR 33; DLB 7; DLBY 84; MTCW 1

Helprin, Mark 1947- **CLC 7, 10, 22, 32; DAM NOV, POP**
See also CA 81-84; CANR 47, 64; DLBY 85;

MTCW 1

Helvetius, Claude-Adrien 1715-1771 .. **LC 26**

Helyar, Jane Penelope Josephine 1933-
See Poole, Josephine
See also CA 21-24R; CANR 10, 26; SATA 82

Hemans, Felicia 1793-1835 .... **NCLC 71**
See also DLB 96

Hemingway, Ernest (Miller) 1899-1961 **C L C 1, 3, 6, 8, 10, 13, 19, 30, 34, 39, 41, 44, 50, 61, 80; DA; DAB; DAC; DAM MST, NOV; SSC 1, 25; WLC**
See also AAYA 19; CA 77-80; CANR 34; CDALB 1917-1929; DLB 4, 9, 102; DLBD 1, 15, 16; DLBY 81, 87, 96; MTCW 1

Hempel, Amy 1951- .... **CLC 39**
See also CA 118; 137; CANR 70

Henderson, F. C.
See Mencken, H(enry) L(ouis)

Henderson, Sylvia
See Ashton-Warner, Sylvia (Constance)

Henderson, Zenna (Chlarson) 1917-1983 **SSC 29**
See also CA 1-4R; 133; CANR 1; DLB 8; SATA 5

Henley, Beth .... **CLC 23; DC 6**
See also Henley, Elizabeth Becker
See also CABS 3; DLBY 86

Henley, Elizabeth Becker 1952-
See Henley, Beth
See also CA 107; CANR 32, 73; DAM DRAM, MST; MTCW 1

Henley, William Ernest 1849-1903 .. **TCLC 8**
See also CA 105; DLB 19

Hennissart, Martha
See Lathen, Emma
See also CA 85-88; CANR 64

Henry, O. .... **TCLC 1, 19; SSC 5; WLC**
See also Porter, William Sydney

Henry, Patrick 1736-1799 .... **LC 25**

Henryson, Robert 1430(?)-1506(?) ...... **LC 20**
See also DLB 146

Henry VIII 1491-1547 .... **LC 10**
See also DLB 132

Henschke, Alfred
See Klabund

Hentoff, Nat(han Irving) 1925- .... **CLC 26**
See also AAYA 4; CA 1-4R; CAAS 6; CANR 5, 25; CLR 1, 52; INT CANR-25; JRDA; MAICYA; SATA 42, 69; SATA-Brief 27

Heppenstall, (John) Rayner 1911-1981 **C L C 10**
See also CA 1-4R; 103; CANR 29

Heraclitus c. 540B.C.-c. 450B.C. .. **CMLC 22**
See also DLB 176

Herbert, Frank (Patrick) 1920-1986 **CLC 12, 23, 35, 44, 85; DAM POP**
See also AAYA 21; CA 53-56; 118; CANR 5, 43; DLB 8; INT CANR-5; MTCW 1; SATA 9, 37; SATA-Obit 47

Herbert, George 1593-1633 ..... **LC 24; DAB; DAM POET; PC 4**
See also CDBLB Before 1660; DLB 126

Herbert, Zbigniew 1924-1998 ..... **CLC 9, 43; DAM POET**
See also CA 89-92; 169; CANR 36, 74; MTCW 1

Herbst, Josephine (Frey) 1897-1969 **CLC 34**
See also CA 5-8R; 25-28R; DLB 9

Hergesheimer, Joseph 1880-1954 .. **TCLC 11**
See also CA 109; DLB 102, 9

Herlihy, James Leo 1927-1993 .... **CLC 6**
See also CA 1-4R; 143; CANR 2

Hermogenes fl. c. 175- .... **CMLC 6**

Hernandez, Jose 1834-1886 .... **NCLC 17**

Herodotus c. 484B.C.-429B.C. ...... **CMLC 17**
See also DLB 176

Herrick, Robert 1591-1674 **LC 13; DA; DAB;**

DAC; DAM MST, POP; PC 9
See also DLB 126
Herring, Guilles
See Somerville, Edith
Herriot, James 1916-1995**CLC 12; DAM POP**
See also Wight, James Alfred
See also AAYA 1; CA 148; CANR 40; SATA
86
Herrmann, Dorothy 1941- .... **CLC 44**
See also CA 107
Herrmann, Taffy
See Herrmann, Dorothy
Hersey, John (Richard) 1914-1993**CLC 1, 2, 7,**
9, 40, 81, 97; DAM POP
See also CA 17-20R; 140; CANR 33; DLB 6,
185; MTCW 1; SATA 25; SATA-Obit 76
Herzen, Aleksandr Ivanovich 1812-1870
NCLC 10, 61
Herzl, Theodor 1860-1904 .... **TCLC 36**
See also CA 168
Herzog, Werner 1942- .... **CLC 16**
See also CA 89-92
Hesiod c. 8th cent. B.C.- .... **CMLC 5**
See also DLB 176
Hesse, Hermann 1877-1962**CLC 1, 2, 3, 6, 11,**
17, 25, 69; DA; DAB; DAC; DAM MST,
NOV; SSC 9; WLC
See also CA 17-18; CAP 2; DLB 66; MTCW 1;
SATA 50
Hewes, Cady
See De Voto, Bernard (Augustine)
Heyen, William 1940- .... **CLC 13, 18**
See also CA 33-36R; CAAS 9; DLB 5
Heyerdahl, Thor 1914-....................... **CLC 26**
See also CA 5-8R; CANR 5, 22, 66, 73; MTCW
1; SATA 2, 52
Heym, Georg (Theodor Franz Arthur) 1887-
1912 .... **TCLC 9**
See also CA 106
Heym, Stefan 1913- .... **CLC 41**
See also CA 9-12R; CANR 4; DLB 69
Heyse, Paul (Johann Ludwig von) 1830-1914
TCLC 8
See also CA 104; DLB 129
Heyward, (Edwin) DuBose 1885-1940 **T C L C**
59
See also CA 108; 157; DLB 7, 9, 45; SATA 21
Hibbert, Eleanor Alice Burford 1906-1993
CLC 7; DAM POP
See also BEST 90:4; CA 17-20R; 140; CANR
9, 28, 59; SATA 2; SATA-Obit 74
Hichens, Robert (Smythe) 1864-1950 **T C L C**
64
See also CA 162; DLB 153
Higgins, George V(incent) 1939-**CLC 4, 7, 10,**
18
See also CA 77-80; CAAS 5; CANR 17, 51;
DLB 2; DLBY 81; INT CANR-17; MTCW
1
Higginson, Thomas Wentworth 1823-1911
TCLC 36
See also CA 162; DLB 1, 64
Highet, Helen
See MacInnes, Helen (Clark)
Highsmith, (Mary) Patricia 1921-1995**CLC 2,**
4, 14, 42, 102; DAM NOV, POP
See also CA 1-4R; 147; CANR 1, 20, 48, 62;
MTCW 1
Highwater, Jamake (Mamake) 1942(?)- **C L C**
12
See also AAYA 7; CA 65-68; CAAS 7; CANR
10, 34; CLR 17; DLB 52; DLBY 85; JRDA;
MAICYA; SATA 32, 69; SATA-Brief 30
Highway, Tomson 1951-**CLC 92; DAC; DAM**
MULT
See also CA 151; CANR 75; NNAL
Higuchi, Ichiyo 1872-1896 .... **NCLC 49**

Hijuelos, Oscar 1951- **CLC 65; DAM MULT,**
POP; HLC
See also AAYA 25; BEST 90:1; CA 123; CANR
50, 75; DLB 145; HW
Hikmet, Nazim 1902(?)-1963 .... **CLC 40**
See also CA 141; 93-96
Hildegard von Bingen 1098-1179 . **CMLC 20**
See also DLB 148
Hildesheimer, Wolfgang 1916-1991 ..**CLC 49**
See also CA 101; 135; DLB 69, 124
Hill, Geoffrey (William) 1932- **CLC 5, 8, 18,**
45; DAM POET
See also CA 81-84; CANR 21; CDBLB 1960
to Present; DLB 40; MTCW 1
Hill, George Roy 1921- .... **CLC 26**
See also CA 110; 122
Hill, John
See Koontz, Dean R(ay)
Hill, Susan (Elizabeth) 1942- .... **CLC 4, 113;**
DAB; DAM MST, NOV
See also CA 33-36R; CANR 29, 69; DLB 14,
139; MTCW 1
Hillerman, Tony 1925- . **CLC 62; DAM POP**
See also AAYA 6; BEST 89:1; CA 29-32R;
CANR 21, 42, 65; DLB 206; SATA 6
Hillesum, Etty 1914-1943 .... **TCLC 49**
See also CA 137
Hilliard, Noel (Harvey) 1929- .... **CLC 15**
See also CA 9-12R; CANR 7, 69
Hillis, Rick 1956- .... **CLC 66**
See also CA 134
Hilton, James 1900-1954 .... **TCLC 21**
See also CA 108; 169; DLB 34, 77; SATA 34
Himes, Chester (Bomar) 1909-1984**CLC 2, 4,**
7, 18, 58, 108; BLC 2; DAM MULT
See also BW 2; CA 25-28R; 114; CANR 22;
DLB 2, 76, 143; MTCW 1
Hinde, Thomas .... **CLC 6, 11**
See also Chitty, Thomas Willes
Hindin, Nathan
See Bloch, Robert (Albert)
Hine, (William) Daryl 1936- .... **CLC 15**
See also CA 1-4R; CAAS 15; CANR 1, 20; DLB
60
Hinkson, Katharine Tynan
See Tynan, Katharine
Hinton, S(usan) E(loise) 1950- **CLC 30, 111;**
DA; DAB; DAC; DAM MST, NOV
See also AAYA 2; CA 81-84; CANR 32, 62;
CLR 3, 23; JRDA; MAICYA; MTCW 1;
SATA 19, 58
Hippius, Zinaida .... **TCLC 9**
See also Gippius, Zinaida (Nikolayevna)
Hiraoka, Kimitake 1925-1970
See Mishima, Yukio
See also CA 97-100; 29-32R; DAM DRAM;
MTCW 1
Hirsch, E(ric) D(onald), Jr. 1928- .... **CLC 79**
See also CA 25-28R; CANR 27, 51; DLB 67;
INT CANR-27; MTCW 1
Hirsch, Edward 1950- .... **CLC 31, 50**
See also CA 104; CANR 20, 42; DLB 120
Hitchcock, Alfred (Joseph) 1899-1980**CLC 16**
See also AAYA 22; CA 159; 97-100; SATA 27;
SATA-Obit 24
Hitler, Adolf 1889-1945 .... **TCLC 53**
See also CA 117; 147
Hoagland, Edward 1932-................... **CLC 28**
See also CA 1-4R; CANR 2, 31, 57; DLB 6;
SATA 51
Hoban, Russell (Conwell) 1925- . **CLC 7, 25;**
DAM NOV
See also CA 5-8R; CANR 23, 37, 66; CLR 3;
DLB 52; MAICYA; MTCW 1; SATA 1, 40,
78
Hobbes, Thomas 1588-1679 .... **LC 36**
See also DLB 151

Hobbs, Perry
See Blackmur, R(ichard) P(almer)
Hobson, Laura Z(ametkin) 1900-1986**CLC 7,**
25
See also CA 17-20R; 118; CANR 55; DLB 28;
SATA 52
Hochhuth, Rolf 1931-.. **CLC 4, 11, 18; DAM**
DRAM
See also CA 5-8R; CANR 33, 75; DLB 124;
MTCW 1
Hochman, Sandra 1936- .... **CLC 3, 8**
See also CA 5-8R; DLB 5
Hochwaelder, Fritz 1911-1986**CLC 36; DAM**
DRAM
See also CA 29-32R; 120; CANR 42; MTCW 1
Hochwalder, Fritz
See Hochwaelder, Fritz
Hocking, Mary (Eunice) 1921- .... **CLC 13**
See also CA 101; CANR 18, 40
Hodgins, Jack 1938- .... **CLC 23**
See also CA 93-96; DLB 60
Hodgson, William Hope 1877(?)-1918 **T C L C**
13
See also CA 111; 164; DLB 70, 153, 156, 178
Hoeg, Peter 1957- .... **CLC 95**
See also CA 151; CANR 75
Hoffman, Alice 1952- .... **CLC 51; DAM NOV**
See also CA 77-80; CANR 34, 66; MTCW 1
Hoffman, Daniel (Gerard) 1923-**CLC 6, 13, 23**
See also CA 1-4R; CANR 4; DLB 5
Hoffman, Stanley 1944- .... **CLC 5**
See also CA 77-80
Hoffman, William M(oses) 1939- ...... **CLC 40**
See also CA 57-60; CANR 11, 71
Hoffmann, E(rnst) T(heodor) A(madeus) 1776-
1822 .... **NCLC 2; SSC 13**
See also DLB 90; SATA 27
Hofmann, Gert 1931- .... **CLC 54**
See also CA 128
Hofmannsthal, Hugo von 1874-1929**TCLC 11;**
DAM DRAM; DC 4
See also CA 106; 153; DLB 81, 118
Hogan, Linda 1947-.... **CLC 73; DAM MULT**
See also CA 120; CANR 45, 73; DLB 175;
NNAL
Hogarth, Charles
See Creasey, John
Hogarth, Emmett
See Polonsky, Abraham (Lincoln)
Hogg, James 1770-1835 .... **NCLC 4**
See also DLB 93, 116, 159
Holbach, Paul Henri Thiry Baron 1723-1789
LC 14
Holberg, Ludvig 1684-1754 .... **LC 6**
Holden, Ursula 1921- .... **CLC 18**
See also CA 101; CAAS 8; CANR 22
Holderlin, (Johann Christian) Friedrich 1770-
1843 ....
NCLC 16; PC 4
Holdstock, Robert
See Holdstock, Robert P.
Holdstock, Robert P. 1948-................ **CLC 39**
See also CA 131
Holland, Isabelle 1920- .... **CLC 21**
See also AAYA 11; CA 21-24R; CANR 10, 25,
47; JRDA; MAICYA; SATA 8, 70; SATA-
Essay 103
Holland, Marcus
See Caldwell, (Janet Miriam) Taylor (Holland)
Hollander, John 1929- .... **CLC 2, 5, 8, 14**
See also CA 1-4R; CANR 1, 52; DLB 5; SATA
13
Hollander, Paul
See Silverberg, Robert
Holleran, Andrew 1943(?)- .... **CLC 38**
See also CA 144
Hollinghurst, Alan 1954- .... **CLC 55, 91**

See also CA 104; DLB 201

James, P. D. 1920- .... CLC 18, 46
See also White, Phyllis Dorothy James
See also BEST 90:2; CDBLB 1960 to Present;
DLB 87; DLBD 17

James, Philip
See Moorcock, Michael (John)

James, William 1842-1910 .... TCLC 15, 32
See also CA 109

James I 1394-1437 .... LC 20

Jameson, Anna 1794-1860 .... NCLC 43
See also DLB 99, 166

Jami, Nur al-Din 'Abd al-Rahman 1414-1492
LC 9

Jammes, Francis 1868-1938 .... TCLC 75

Jandl, Ernst 1925- .... CLC 34

Janowitz, Tama 1957- .. CLC 43; DAM POP
See also CA 106; CANR 52

Japrisot, Sebastien 1931- .... CLC 90

Jarrell, Randall 1914-1965CLC 1, 2, 6, 9, 13,
49; DAM POET
See also CA 5-8R; 25-28R; CABS 2; CANR 6,
34; CDALB 1941-1968; CLR 6; DLB 48, 52;
MAICYA; MTCW 1; SATA 7

Jarry, Alfred 1873-1907 .. TCLC 2, 14; DAM
DRAM; SSC 20
See also CA 104; 153; DLB 192

Jarvis, E. K.
See Bloch, Robert (Albert); Ellison, Harlan
(Jay); Silverberg, Robert

Jeake, Samuel, Jr.
See Aiken, Conrad (Potter)

Jean Paul 1763-1825 .... NCLC 7

Jefferies, (John) Richard 1848-1887NCLC 47
See also DLB 98, 141; SATA 16

Jeffers, (John) Robinson 1887-1962CLC 2, 3,
11, 15, 54; DA; DAC; DAM MST, POET;
PC 17; WLC
See also CA 85-88; CANR 35; CDALB 1917-
1929; DLB 45; MTCW 1

Jefferson, Janet
See Mencken, H(enry) L(ouis)

Jefferson, Thomas 1743-1826 .... NCLC 11
See also CDALB 1640-1865; DLB 31

Jeffrey, Francis 1773-1850 .... NCLC 33
See also DLB 107

Jelakowitch, Ivan
See Heijermans, Herman

Jellicoe, (Patricia) Ann 1927- .... CLC 27
See also CA 85-88; DLB 13

Jen, Gish .... CLC 70
See also Jen, Lillian

Jen, Lillian 1956(?)-
See Jen, Gish
See also CA 135

Jenkins, (John) Robin 1912- .... CLC 52
See also CA 1-4R; CANR 1; DLB 14

Jennings, Elizabeth (Joan) 1926- . CLC 5, 14
See also CA 61-64; CAAS 5; CANR 8, 39, 66;
DLB 27; MTCW 1; SATA 66

Jennings, Waylon 1937- .... CLC 21

Jensen, Johannes V. 1873-1950 ...... TCLC 41
See also CA 170

Jensen, Laura (Linnea) 1948- .... CLC 37
See also CA 103

Jerome, Jerome K(lapka) 1859-1927TCLC 23
See also CA 119; DLB 10, 34, 135

Jerrold, Douglas William 1803-1857NCLC 2
See also DLB 158, 159

Jewett, (Theodora) Sarah Orne 1849-1909
TCLC 1, 22; SSC 6
See also CA 108; 127; CANR 71; DLB 12, 74;
SATA 15

Jewsbury, Geraldine (Endsor) 1812-1880
NCLC 22
See also DLB 21

Jhabvala, Ruth Prawer 1927-CLC 4, 8, 29, 94;

DAB; DAM NOV
See also CA 1-4R; CANR 2, 29, 51, 74; DLB
139, 194; INT CANR-29; MTCW 1

Jibran, Kahlil
See Gibran, Kahlil

Jibran, Khalil
See Gibran, Kahlil

Jiles, Paulette 1943- .... CLC 13, 58
See also CA 101; CANR 70

Jimenez (Mantecon), Juan Ramon 1881-1958
TCLC 4; DAM MULT, POET; HLC; PC
7
See also CA 104; 131; CANR 74; DLB 134;
HW; MTCW 1

Jimenez, Ramon
See Jimenez (Mantecon), Juan Ramon

Jimenez Mantecon, Juan
See Jimenez (Mantecon), Juan Ramon

Jin, Ha 1956- .... CLC 109
See also CA 152

Joel, Billy .... CLC 26
See also Joel, William Martin

Joel, William Martin 1949-
See Joel, Billy
See also CA 108

John, Saint 7th cent. - .... CMLC 27

John of the Cross, St. 1542-1591 .... LC 18

Johnson, B(ryan) S(tanley William) 1933-1973
CLC 6, 9
See also CA 9-12R; 53-56; CANR 9; DLB 14,
40

Johnson, Benj. F. of Boo
See Riley, James Whitcomb

Johnson, Benjamin F. of Boo
See Riley, James Whitcomb

Johnson, Charles (Richard) 1948-CLC 7, 51,
65; BLC 2; DAM MULT
See also BW 2; CA 116; CAAS 18; CANR 42,
66; DLB 33

Johnson, Denis 1949- .... CLC 52
See also CA 117; 121; CANR 71; DLB 120

Johnson, Diane 1934- .... CLC 5, 13, 48
See also CA 41-44R; CANR 17, 40, 62; DLBY
80; INT CANR-17; MTCW 1

Johnson, Eyvind (Olof Verner) 1900-1976
CLC 14
See also CA 73-76; 69-72; CANR 34

Johnson, J. R.
See James, C(yril) L(ionel) R(obert)

Johnson, James Weldon 1871-1938 TCLC 3,
19; BLC 2; DAM MULT, POET; PC 24
See also BW 1; CA 104; 125; CDALB 1917-
1929; CLR 32; DLB 51; MTCW 1; SATA 31

Johnson, Joyce 1935- .... CLC 58
See also CA 125; 129

Johnson, Judith (Emlyn) 1936- ..... CLC 7, 15
See also CA 25-28R; 153; CANR 34

Johnson, Lionel (Pigot) 1867-1902 TCLC 19
See also CA 117; DLB 19

Johnson, Marguerite (Annie)
See Angelou, Maya

Johnson, Mel
See Malzberg, Barry N(athaniel)

Johnson, Pamela Hansford 1912-1981CLC 1,
7, 27
See also CA 1-4R; 104; CANR 2, 28; DLB 15;
MTCW 1

Johnson, Robert 1911(?)-1938 .... TCLC 69

Johnson, Samuel 1709-1784LC 15; DA; DAB;
DAC; DAM MST; WLC
See also CDBLB 1660-1789; DLB 39, 95, 104,
142

Johnson, Uwe 1934-1984 .. CLC 5, 10, 15, 40
See also CA 1-4R; 112; CANR 1, 39; DLB 75;
MTCW 1

Johnston, George (Benson) 1913- ..... CLC 51
See also CA 1-4R; CANR 5, 20; DLB 88

Johnston, Jennifer 1930- .... CLC 7
See also CA 85-88; DLB 14

Jolley, (Monica) Elizabeth 1923-CLC 46; SSC
19
See also CA 127; CAAS 13; CANR 59

Jones, Arthur Llewellyn 1863-1947
See Machen, Arthur
See also CA 104

Jones, D(ouglas) G(ordon) 1929- ...... CLC 10
See also CA 29-32R; CANR 13; DLB 53

Jones, David (Michael) 1895-1974CLC 2, 4, 7,
13, 42
See also CA 9-12R; 53-56; CANR 28; CDBLB
1945-1960; DLB 20, 100; MTCW 1

Jones, David Robert 1947-
See Bowie, David
See also CA 103

Jones, Diana Wynne 1934- .... CLC 26
See also AAYA 12; CA 49-52; CANR 4, 26,
56; CLR 23; DLB 161; JRDA; MAICYA;
SAAS 7; SATA 9, 70

Jones, Edward P. 1950- .... CLC 76
See also BW 2; CA 142

Jones, Gayl 1949- .... CLC 6, 9; BLC 2; DAM
MULT
See also BW 2; CA 77-80; CANR 27, 66; DLB
33; MTCW 1

Jones, James 1921-1977 ...... CLC 1, 3, 10, 39
See also AITN 1, 2; CA 1-4R; 69-72; CANR 6;
DLB 2, 143; DLBD 17; MTCW 1

Jones, John J.
See Lovecraft, H(oward) P(hillips)

Jones, LeRoi .... CLC 1, 2, 3, 5, 10, 14
See also Baraka, Amiri

Jones, Louis B. 1953- .... CLC 65
See also CA 141; CANR 73

Jones, Madison (Percy, Jr.) 1925- .... CLC 4
See also CA 13-16R; CAAS 11; CANR 7, 54;
DLB 152

Jones, Mervyn 1922- .... CLC 10, 52
See also CA 45-48; CAAS 5; CANR 1; MTCW
1

Jones, Mick 1956(?)- .... CLC 30

Jones, Nettie (Pearl) 1941- .... CLC 34
See also BW 2; CA 137; CAAS 20

Jones, Preston 1936-1979 .... CLC 10
See also CA 73-76; 89-92; DLB 7

Jones, Robert F(rancis) 1934- .... CLC 7
See also CA 49-52; CANR 2, 61

Jones, Rod 1953- .... CLC 50
See also CA 128

Jones, Terence Graham Parry 1942- CLC 21
See also Jones, Terry; Monty Python
See also CA 112; 116; CANR 35; INT 116

Jones, Terry
See Jones, Terence Graham Parry
See also SATA 67; SATA-Brief 51

Jones, Thom 1945(?)- .... CLC 81
See also CA 157

Jong, Erica 1942- . CLC 4, 6, 8, 18, 83; DAM
NOV, POP
See also AITN 1; BEST 90:2; CA 73-76; CANR
26, 52, 75; DLB 2, 5, 28, 152; INT CANR-
26; MTCW 1

Jonson, Ben(jamin) 1572(?)-1637 .. LC 6, 33;
DA; DAB; DAC; DAM DRAM, MST,
POET; DC 4; PC 17; WLC
See also CDBLB Before 1660; DLB 62, 121

Jordan, June 1936-CLC 5, 11, 23, 114; BLCS;
DAM MULT, POET
See also AAYA 2; BW 2; CA 33-36R; CANR
25, 70; CLR 10; DLB 38; MAICYA; MTCW
1; SATA 4

Jordan, Neil (Patrick) 1950- .... CLC 110
See also CA 124; 130; CANR 54; INT 130

Jordan, Pat(rick M.) 1941- .... CLC 37
See also CA 33-36R

Kogawa, Joy Nozomi 1935- .. **CLC 78; DAC; DAM MST, MULT**
See also CA 101; CANR 19, 62; SATA 99

Kohout, Pavel 1928- .... **CLC 13**
See also CA 45-48; CANR 3

Koizumi, Yakumo
See Hearn, (Patricio) Lafcadio (Tessima Carlos)

Kolmar, Gertrud 1894-1943 .... **TCLC 40**
See also CA 167

Komunyakaa, Yusef 1947- **CLC 86, 94; BLCS**
See also CA 147; DLB 120

Konrad, George
See Konrad, Gyoergy

Konrad, Gyoergy 1933- .... **CLC 4, 10, 73**
See also CA 85-88

Konwicki, Tadeusz 1926- **CLC 8, 28, 54, 117**
See also CA 101; CAAS 9; CANR 39, 59; MTCW 1

Koontz, Dean R(ay) 1945- ..... **CLC 78; DAM NOV, POP**
See also AAYA 9; BEST 89:3, 90:2; CA 108; CANR 19, 36, 52; MTCW 1; SATA 92

Kopernik, Mikolaj
See Copernicus, Nicolaus

Kopit, Arthur (Lee) 1937- **CLC 1, 18, 33; DAM DRAM**
See also AITN 1; CA 81-84; CABS 3; DLB 7; MTCW 1

Kops, Bernard 1926- .... **CLC 4**
See also CA 5-8R; DLB 13

Kornbluth, C(yril) M. 1923-1958 .... **TCLC 8**
See also CA 105; 160; DLB 8

Korolenko, V. G.
See Korolenko, Vladimir Galaktionovich

Korolenko, Vladimir
See Korolenko, Vladimir Galaktionovich

Korolenko, Vladimir G.
See Korolenko, Vladimir Galaktionovich

Korolenko, Vladimir Galaktionovich 1853-1921 .... **TCLC 22**
See also CA 121

Korzybski, Alfred (Habdank Skarbek) 1879-1950 .... **TCLC 61**
See also CA 123; 160

Kosinski, Jerzy (Nikodem) 1933-1991 **CLC 1, 2, 3, 6, 10, 15, 53, 70; DAM NOV**
See also CA 17-20R; 134; CANR 9, 46; DLB 2; DLBY 82; MTCW 1

Kostelanetz, Richard (Cory) 1940- .. **CLC 28**
See also CA 13-16R; CAAS 8; CANR 38

Kostrowitzki, Wilhelm Apollinaris de 1880-1918
See Apollinaire, Guillaume
See also CA 104

Kotlowitz, Robert 1924- .... **CLC 4**
See also CA 33-36R; CANR 36

Kotzebue, August (Friedrich Ferdinand) von 1761-1819 ....
NCLC 25
See also DLB 94

Kotzwinkle, William 1938- ..... **CLC 5, 14, 35**
See also CA 45-48; CANR 3, 44; CLR 6; DLB 173; MAICYA; SATA 24, 70

Kowna, Stancy
See Szymborska, Wislawa

Kozol, Jonathan 1936- .... **CLC 17**
See also CA 61-64; CANR 16, 45

Kozoll, Michael 1940(?)- .... **CLC 35**

Kramer, Kathryn 19(?)- .... **CLC 34**

Kramer, Larry 1935- **CLC 42; DAM POP; DC 8**
See also CA 124; 126; CANR 60

Krasicki, Ignacy 1735-1801 .... **NCLC 8**

Krasinski, Zygmunt 1812-1859 .... **NCLC 4**

Kraus, Karl 1874-1936 .... **TCLC 5**
See also CA 104; DLB 118

Kreve (Mickevicius), Vincas 1882-1954 **TCLC 27**
See also CA 170

Kristeva, Julia 1941- .... **CLC 77**
See also CA 154

Kristofferson, Kris 1936- .... **CLC 26**
See also CA 104

Krizanc, John 1956- .... **CLC 57**

Krleza, Miroslav 1893-1981 .... **CLC 8, 114**
See also CA 97-100; 105; CANR 50; DLB 147

Kroetsch, Robert 1927- **CLC 5, 23, 57; DAC; DAM POET**
See also CA 17-20R; CANR 8, 38; DLB 53; MTCW 1

Kroetz, Franz
See Kroetz, Franz Xaver

Kroetz, Franz Xaver 1946- .... **CLC 41**
See also CA 130

Kroker, Arthur (W.) 1945- .... **CLC 77**
See also CA 161

Kropotkin, Peter (Alekseievich) 1842-1921 **TCLC 36**
See also CA 119

Krotkov, Yuri 1917- .... **CLC 19**
See also CA 102

Krumb
See Crumb, R(obert)

Krumgold, Joseph (Quincy) 1908-1980 **C L C 12**
See also CA 9-12R; 101; CANR 7; MAICYA; SATA 1, 48; SATA-Obit 23

Krumwitz
See Crumb, R(obert)

Krutch, Joseph Wood 1893-1970 ...... **CLC 24**
See also CA 1-4R; 25-28R; CANR 4; DLB 63, 206

Krutzch, Gus
See Eliot, T(homas) S(tearns)

Krylov, Ivan Andreevich 1768(?)-1844 **N C L C 1**
See also DLB 150

Kubin, Alfred (Leopold Isidor) 1877-1959 **TCLC 23**
See also CA 112; 149; DLB 81

Kubrick, Stanley 1928- .... **CLC 16**
See also CA 81-84; CANR 33; DLB 26

Kumin, Maxine (Winokur) 1925- **CLC 5, 13, 28; DAM POET; PC 15**
See also AITN 2; CA 1-4R; CAAS 8; CANR 1, 21, 69; DLB 5; MTCW 1; SATA 12

Kundera, Milan 1929- .. **CLC 4, 9, 19, 32, 68, 115; DAM NOV; SSC 24**
See also AAYA 2; CA 85-88; CANR 19, 52, 74; MTCW 1

Kunene, Mazisi (Raymond) 1930- .... **CLC 85**
See also BW 1; CA 125; DLB 117

Kunitz, Stanley (Jasspon) 1905- **CLC 6, 11, 14; PC 19**
See also CA 41-44R; CANR 26, 57; DLB 48; INT CANR-26; MTCW 1

Kunze, Reiner 1933- .... **CLC 10**
See also CA 93-96; DLB 75

Kuprin, Aleksandr Ivanovich 1870-1938 **TCLC 5**
See also CA 104

Kureishi, Hanif 1954(?)- .... **CLC 64**
See also CA 139; DLB 194

Kurosawa, Akira 1910-1998 . **CLC 16; DAM MULT**
See also AAYA 11; CA 101; 170; CANR 46

Kushner, Tony 1957(?)- **CLC 81; DAM DRAM; DC 10**
See also CA 144; CANR 74

Kuttner, Henry 1915-1958 .... **TCLC 10**
See Vance, Jack
See also CA 107; 157; DLB 8

Kuzma, Greg 1944- .... **CLC 7**
See also CA 33-36R; CANR 70

Kuzmin, Mikhail 1872(?)-1936 ...... **TCLC 40**
See also CA 170

Kyd, Thomas 1558-1594 **LC 22; DAM DRAM; DC 3**
See also DLB 62

Kyprianos, Iossif
See Samarakis, Antonis

La Bruyere, Jean de 1645-1696 .... **LC 17**

Lacan, Jacques (Marie Emile) 1901-1981 **CLC 75**
See also CA 121; 104

Laclos, Pierre Ambroise Francois Choderlos de 1741-1803 .... **NCLC 4**

Lacolere, Francois
See Aragon, Louis

La Colere, Francois
See Aragon, Louis

La Deshabilleuse
See Simenon, Georges (Jacques Christian)

Lady Gregory
See Gregory, Isabella Augusta (Persse)

Lady of Quality, A
See Bagnold, Enid

La Fayette, Marie (Madelaine Pioche de la Vergne Comtes 1634-1693 .... **LC 2**

Lafayette, Rene
See Hubbard, L(afayette) Ron(ald)

Laforgue, Jules 1860-1887 **NCLC 5, 53; PC 14; SSC 20**

Lagerkvist, Paer (Fabian) 1891-1974 **CLC 7, 10, 13, 54; DAM DRAM, NOV**
See also Lagerkvist, Par
See also CA 85-88; 49-52; MTCW 1

Lagerkvist, Par .... **SSC 12**
See also Lagerkvist, Paer (Fabian)

Lagerloef, Selma (Ottiliana Lovisa) 1858-1940 **TCLC 4, 36**
See also Lagerlof, Selma (Ottiliana Lovisa)
See also CA 108; SATA 15

Lagerlof, Selma (Ottiliana Lovisa)
See Lagerloef, Selma (Ottiliana Lovisa)
See also CLR 7; SATA 15

La Guma, (Justin) Alex(ander) 1925-1985 **CLC 19; BLCS; DAM NOV**
See also BW 1; CA 49-52; 118; CANR 25; DLB 117; MTCW 1

Laidlaw, A. K.
See Grieve, C(hristopher) M(urray)

Lainez, Manuel Mujica
See Mujica Lainez, Manuel
See also HW

Laing, R(onald) D(avid) 1927-1989 . **CLC 95**
See also CA 107; 129; CANR 34; MTCW 1

Lamartine, Alphonse (Marie Louis Prat) de 1790-1869 ....
NCLC 11; DAM POET; PC 16

Lamb, Charles 1775-1834 ..... **NCLC 10; DA; DAB; DAC; DAM MST; WLC**
See also CDBLB 1789-1832; DLB 93, 107, 163; SATA 17

Lamb, Lady Caroline 1785-1828 ... **NCLC 38**
See also DLB 116

Lamming, George (William) 1927- **CLC 2, 4, 66; BLC 2; DAM MULT**
See also BW 2; CA 85-88; CANR 26, 76; DLB 125; MTCW 1

L'Amour, Louis (Dearborn) 1908-1988 **C L C 25, 55; DAM NOV, POP**
See also AAYA 16; AITN 2; BEST 89:2; CA 1-4R; 125; CANR 3, 25, 40; DLB 207; DLBY 80; MTCW 1

Lampedusa, Giuseppe (Tomasi) di 1896-1957 **TCLC 13**
See also Tomasi di Lampedusa, Giuseppe
See also CA 164; DLB 177

Lampman, Archibald 1861-1899 ... **NCLC 25**
See also DLB 92

Lucas, Craig 1951- .... CLC 64
See also CA 137; CANR 71
Lucas, E(dward) V(errall) 1868-1938 T C L C
73
See also DLB 98, 149, 153; SATA 20
Lucas, George 1944- .... CLC 16
See also AAYA 1, 23; CA 77-80; CANR 30;
SATA 56
Lucas, Hans
See Godard, Jean-Luc
Lucas, Victoria
See Plath, Sylvia
Lucian c. 120-c. 180 .... CMLC 32
See also DLB 176
Ludlam, Charles 1943-1987 .... CLC 46, 50
See also CA 85-88; 122; CANR 72
Ludlum, Robert 1927-CLC 22, 43; DAM NOV,
POP
See also AAYA 10; BEST 89:1, 90:3; CA 33-
36R; CANR 25, 41, 68; DLBY 82; MTCW
1
Ludwig, Ken .... CLC 60
Ludwig, Otto 1813-1865 .... NCLC 4
See also DLB 129
Lugones, Leopoldo 1874-1938 .... TCLC 15
See also CA 116; 131; HW
Lu Hsun 1881-1936 .... TCLC 3; SSC 20
See also Shu-Jen, Chou
Lukacs, George .... CLC 24
See also Lukacs, Gyorgy (Szegeny von)
Lukacs, Gyorgy (Szegeny von) 1885-1971
See Lukacs, George
See also CA 101; 29-32R; CANR 62
Luke, Peter (Ambrose Cyprian) 1919-1995
CLC 38
See also CA 81-84; 147; CANR 72; DLB 13
Lunar, Dennis
See Mungo, Raymond
Lurie, Alison 1926- .... CLC 4, 5, 18, 39
See also CA 1-4R; CANR 2, 17, 50; DLB 2;
MTCW 1; SATA 46
Lustig, Arnost 1926- .... CLC 56
See also AAYA 3; CA 69-72; CANR 47; SATA
56
Luther, Martin 1483-1546 .... LC 9, 37
See also DLB 179
Luxemburg, Rosa 1870(?)-1919 ..... TCLC 63
See also CA 118
Luzi, Mario 1914- .... CLC 13
See also CA 61-64; CANR 9, 70; DLB 128
Lyly, John 1554(?)-1606LC 41; DAM DRAM;
DC 7
See also DLB 62, 167
L'Ymagier
See Gourmont, Remy (-Marie-Charles) de
Lynch, B. Suarez
See Bioy Casares, Adolfo; Borges, Jorge Luis
Lynch, David (K.) 1946- .... CLC 66
See also CA 124; 129
Lynch, James
See Andreyev, Leonid (Nikolaevich)
Lynch Davis, B.
See Bioy Casares, Adolfo; Borges, Jorge Luis
Lyndsay, Sir David 1490-1555 .... LC 20
Lynn, Kenneth S(chuyler) 1923- .... CLC 50
See also CA 1-4R; CANR 3, 27, 65
Lynx
See West, Rebecca
Lyons, Marcus
See Blish, James (Benjamin)
Lyre, Pinchbeck
See Sassoon, Siegfried (Lorraine)
Lytle, Andrew (Nelson) 1902-1995 ... CLC 22
See also CA 9-12R; 150; CANR 70; DLB 6;
DLBY 95
Lyttelton, George 1709-1773 .... LC 10
Maas, Peter 1929- .... CLC 29

See also CA 93-96; INT 93-96
Macaulay, Rose 1881-1958 .... TCLC 7, 44
See also CA 104; DLB 36
Macaulay, Thomas Babington 1800-1859
NCLC 42
See also CDBLB 1832-1890; DLB 32, 55
MacBeth, George (Mann) 1932-1992CLC 2, 5,
9
See also CA 25-28R; 136; CANR 61, 66; DLB
40; MTCW 1; SATA 4; SATA-Obit 70
MacCaig, Norman (Alexander) 1910-CLC 36;
DAB; DAM POET
See also CA 9-12R; CANR 3, 34; DLB 27
MacCarthy, Sir(Charles Otto) Desmond 1877-
1952 .... TCLC 36
See also CA 167
MacDiarmid, HughCLC 2, 4, 11, 19, 63; PC 9
See also Grieve, C(hristopher) M(urray)
See also CDBLB 1945-1960; DLB 20
MacDonald, Anson
See Heinlein, Robert A(nson)
Macdonald, Cynthia 1928- .... CLC 13, 19
See also CA 49-52; CANR 4, 44; DLB 105
MacDonald, George 1824-1905 .... TCLC 9
See also CA 106; 137; DLB 18, 163, 178;
MAICYA; SATA 33, 100
Macdonald, John
See Millar, Kenneth
MacDonald, John D(ann) 1916-1986 CLC 3,
27, 44; DAM NOV, POP
See also CA 1-4R; 121; CANR 1, 19, 60; DLB
8; DLBY 86; MTCW 1
Macdonald, John Ross
See Millar, Kenneth
Macdonald, Ross .... CLC 1, 2, 3, 14, 34, 41
See also Millar, Kenneth
See also DLBD 6
MacDougal, John
See Blish, James (Benjamin)
MacEwen, Gwendolyn (Margaret) 1941-1987
CLC 13, 55
See also CA 9-12R; 124; CANR 7, 22; DLB
53; SATA 50; SATA-Obit 55
Macha, Karel Hynek 1810-1846 .... NCLC 46
Machado (y Ruiz), Antonio 1875-1939T C L C
3
See also CA 104; DLB 108
Machado de Assis, Joaquim Maria 1839-1908
TCLC 10; BLC 2; SSC 24
See also CA 107; 153
Machen, Arthur .... TCLC 4; SSC 20
See also Jones, Arthur Llewellyn
See also DLB 36, 156, 178
Machiavelli, Niccolo 1469-1527LC 8, 36; DA;
DAB; DAC; DAM MST; WLCS
MacInnes, Colin 1914-1976 .... CLC 4, 23
See also CA 69-72; 65-68; CANR 21; DLB 14;
MTCW 1
MacInnes, Helen (Clark) 1907-1985 CLC 27,
39; DAM POP
See also CA 1-4R; 117; CANR 1, 28, 58; DLB
87; MTCW 1; SATA 22; SATA-Obit 44
Mackay, Mary 1855-1924
See Corelli, Marie
See also CA 118
Mackenzie, Compton (Edward Montague)
1883-1972 .... CLC 18
See also CA 21-22; 37-40R; CAP 2; DLB 34,
100
Mackenzie, Henry 1745-1831 .... NCLC 41
See also DLB 39
Mackintosh, Elizabeth 1896(?)-1952
See Tey, Josephine
See also CA 110
MacLaren, James
See Grieve, C(hristopher) M(urray)
Mac Laverty, Bernard 1942- .... CLC 31

See also CA 116; 118; CANR 43; INT 118
MacLean, Alistair (Stuart) 1922(?)-1987C L C
3, 13, 50, 63; DAM POP
See also CA 57-60; 121; CANR 28, 61; MTCW
1; SATA 23; SATA-Obit 50
Maclean, Norman (Fitzroy) 1902-1990 C L C
78; DAM POP; SSC 13
See also CA 102; 132; CANR 49; DLB 206
MacLeish, Archibald 1892-1982CLC 3, 8, 14,
68; DAM POET
See also CA 9-12R; 106; CANR 33, 63; DLB
4, 7, 45; DLBY 82; MTCW 1
MacLennan, (John) Hugh 1907-1990 CLC 2,
14, 92; DAC; DAM MST
See also CA 5-8R; 142; CANR 33; DLB 68;
MTCW 1
MacLeod, Alistair 1936-CLC 56; DAC; DAM
MST
See also CA 123; DLB 60
Macleod, Fiona
See Sharp, William
MacNeice, (Frederick) Louis 1907-1963C L C
1, 4, 10, 53; DAB; DAM POET
See also CA 85-88; CANR 61; DLB 10, 20;
MTCW 1
MacNeill, Dand
See Fraser, George MacDonald
Macpherson, James 1736-1796 .... LC 29
See also Ossian
See also DLB 109
Macpherson, (Jean) Jay 1931- .... CLC 14
See also CA 5-8R; DLB 53
MacShane, Frank 1927- .... CLC 39
See also CA 9-12R; CANR 3, 33; DLB 111
Macumber, Mari
See Sandoz, Mari(e Susette)
Madach, Imre 1823-1864 .... NCLC 19
Madden, (Jerry) David 1933- .... CLC 5, 15
See also CA 1-4R; CAAS 3; CANR 4, 45; DLB
6; MTCW 1
Maddern, Al(an)
See Ellison, Harlan (Jay)
Madhubuti, Haki R. 1942-CLC 6, 73; BLC 2;
DAM MULT, POET; PC 5
See also Lee, Don L.
See also BW 2; CA 73-76; CANR 24, 51, 73;
DLB 5, 41; DLBD 8
Maepenn, Hugh
See Kuttner, Henry
Maepenn, K. H.
See Kuttner, Henry
Maeterlinck, Maurice 1862-1949 ... TCLC 3;
DAM DRAM
See also CA 104; 136; DLB 192; SATA 66
Maginn, William 1794-1842 .... NCLC 8
See also DLB 110, 159
Mahapatra, Jayanta 1928- .... CLC 33; DAM
MULT
See also CA 73-76; CAAS 9; CANR 15, 33, 66
Mahfouz, Naguib (Abdel Aziz Al-Sabilgi)
1911(?)-
See Mahfuz, Najib
See also BEST 89:2; CA 128; CANR 55; DAM
NOV; MTCW 1
Mahfuz, Najib .... CLC 52, 55
See also Mahfouz, Naguib (Abdel Aziz Al-
Sabilgi)
See also DLBY 88
Mahon, Derek 1941- .... CLC 27
See also CA 113; 128; DLB 40
Mailer, Norman 1923-CLC 1, 2, 3, 4, 5, 8, 11,
14, 28, 39, 74, 111; DA; DAB; DAC; DAM
MST, NOV, POP
See also AITN 2; CA 9-12R; CABS 1; CANR
28, 74; CDALB 1968-1988; DLB 2, 16, 28,
185; DLBD 3; DLBY 80, 83; MTCW 1
Maillet, Antonine 1929- . CLC 54, 118; DAC

See also CA 115; 120; CANR 46, 74; DLB 60;
    INT 120
Mais, Roger 1905-1955 .... **TCLC 8**
    See also BW 1; CA 105; 124; DLB 125; MTCW
    1
Maistre, Joseph de 1753-1821 .... **NCLC 37**
Maitland, Frederic 1850-1906 .... **TCLC 65**
Maitland, Sara (Louise) 1950- .... **CLC 49**
    See also CA 69-72; CANR 13, 59
Major, Clarence 1936-**CLC 3, 19, 48; BLC 2;**
    DAM MULT
    See also BW 2; CA 21-24R; CAAS 6; CANR
    13, 25, 53; DLB 33
Major, Kevin (Gerald) 1949-.. **CLC 26; DAC**
    See also AAYA 16; CA 97-100; CANR 21, 38;
    CLR 11; DLB 60; INT CANR-21; JRDA;
    MAICYA; SATA 32, 82
Maki, James
    See Ozu, Yasujiro
Malabaila, Damiano
    See Levi, Primo
Malamud, Bernard 1914-1986**CLC 1, 2, 3, 5,**
    8, 9, 11, 18, 27, 44, 78, 85; DA; DAB; DAC;
    DAM MST, NOV, POP; SSC 15; WLC
    See also AAYA 16; CA 5-8R; 118; CABS 1;
    CANR 28, 62; CDALB 1941-1968; DLB 2,
    28, 152; DLBY 80, 86; MTCW 1
Malan, Herman
    See Bosman, Herman Charles; Bosman, Herman
    Charles
Malaparte, Curzio 1898-1957 .... **TCLC 52**
Malcolm, Dan
    See Silverberg, Robert
Malcolm X .... **CLC 82, 117; BLC 2; WLCS**
    See also Little, Malcolm
Malherbe, Francois de 1555-1628 .... **LC 5**
Mallarme, Stephane 1842-1898 **NCLC 4, 41;**
    DAM POET; PC 4
Mallet-Joris, Francoise 1930- .... **CLC 11**
    See also CA 65-68; CANR 17; DLB 83
Malley, Ern
    See McAuley, James Phillip
Mallowan, Agatha Christie
    See Christie, Agatha (Mary Clarissa)
Maloff, Saul 1922- .... **CLC 5**
    See also CA 33-36R
Malone, Louis
    See MacNeice, (Frederick) Louis
Malone, Michael (Christopher) 1942-**CLC 43**
    See also CA 77-80; CANR 14, 32, 57
Malory, (Sir) Thomas 1410(?)-1471(?)**LC 11;**
    DA; DAB; DAC; DAM MST; WLCS
    See also CDBLB Before 1660; DLB 146; SATA
    59; SATA-Brief 33
Malouf, (George Joseph) David 1934-**CLC 28,**
    86
    See also CA 124; CANR 50, 76
Malraux, (Georges-)Andre 1901-1976**CLC 1,**
    4, 9, 13, 15, 57; DAM NOV
    See also CA 21-22; 69-72; CANR 34, 58; CAP
    2; DLB 72; MTCW 1
Malzberg, Barry N(athaniel) 1939- ... **CLC 7**
    See also CA 61-64; CAAS 4; CANR 16; DLB
    8
Mamet, David (Alan) 1947-**CLC 9, 15, 34, 46,**
    91; DAM DRAM; DC 4
    See also AAYA 3; CA 81-84; CABS 3; CANR
    15, 41, 67, 72; DLB 7; MTCW 1
Mamoulian, Rouben (Zachary) 1897-1987
    CLC 16
    See also CA 25-28R; 124
Mandelstam, Osip (Emilievich) 1891(?)-1938(?)
    TCLC 2, 6; PC 14
    See also CA 104; 150
Mander, (Mary) Jane 1877-1949 ... **TCLC 31**
    See also CA 162
Mandeville, John fl. 1350- .... **CMLC 19**

See also DLB 146
Mandiargues, Andre Pieyre de .... **CLC 41**
    See also Pieyre de Mandiargues, Andre
    See also DLB 83
Mandrake, Ethel Belle
    See Thurman, Wallace (Henry)
Mangan, James Clarence 1803-1849**NCLC 27**
Maniere, J.-E.
    See Giraudoux, (Hippolyte) Jean
Mankiewicz, Herman (Jacob) 1897-1953
    TCLC 85
    See also CA 120; 169; DLB 26
Manley, (Mary) Delariviere 1672(?)-1724**L C
    1, 42**
    See also DLB 39, 80
Mann, Abel
    See Creasey, John
Mann, Emily 1952- .... **DC 7**
    See also CA 130; CANR 55
Mann, (Luiz) Heinrich 1871-1950 ... **TCLC 9**
    See also CA 106; 164; DLB 66, 118
Mann, (Paul) Thomas 1875-1955 **TCLC 2, 8,**
    14, 21, 35, 44, 60; DA; DAB; DAC; DAM
    MST, NOV; SSC 5; WLC
    See also CA 104; 128; DLB 66; MTCW 1
Mannheim, Karl 1893-1947 .... **TCLC 65**
Manning, David
    See Faust, Frederick (Schiller)
Manning, Frederic 1887(?)-1935 ... **TCLC 25**
    See also CA 124
Manning, Olivia 1915-1980 .... **CLC 5, 19**
    See also CA 5-8R; 101; CANR 29; MTCW 1
Mano, D. Keith 1942- .... **CLC 2, 10**
    See also CA 25-28R; CAAS 6; CANR 26, 57;
    DLB 6
Mansfield, Katherine**TCLC 2, 8, 39; DAB; SSC
    9, 23; WLC**
    See also Beauchamp, Kathleen Mansfield
    See also DLB 162
Manso, Peter 1940- .... **CLC 39**
    See also CA 29-32R; CANR 44
Mantecon, Juan Jimenez
    See Jimenez (Mantecon), Juan Ramon
Manton, Peter
    See Creasey, John
Man Without a Spleen, A
    See Chekhov, Anton (Pavlovich)
Manzoni, Alessandro 1785-1873 .... **NCLC 29**
Map, Walter 1140-1209 .... **CMLC 32**
Mapu, Abraham (ben Jekutiel) 1808-1867
    NCLC 18
Mara, Sally
    See Queneau, Raymond
Marat, Jean Paul 1743-1793 .... **LC 10**
Marcel, Gabriel Honore 1889-1973 . **CLC 15**
    See also CA 102; 45-48; MTCW 1
Marchbanks, Samuel
    See Davies, (William) Robertson
Marchi, Giacomo
    See Bassani, Giorgio
Margulies, Donald .... **CLC 76**
Marie de France c. 12th cent. - **CMLC 8; PC
    22**
    See also DLB 208
Marie de l'Incarnation 1599-1672 ...... **LC 10**
Marier, Captain Victor
    See Griffith, D(avid Lewelyn) W(ark)
Mariner, Scott
    See Pohl, Frederik
Marinetti, Filippo Tommaso 1876-1944**TCLC
    10**
    See also CA 107; DLB 114
Marivaux, Pierre Carlet de Chamblain de 1688-
    1763 .... **LC 4; DC 7**
Markandaya, Kamala .... **CLC 8, 38**
    See also Taylor, Kamala (Purnaiya)
Markfield, Wallace 1926- .... **CLC 8**

See also CA 69-72; CAAS 3; DLB 2, 28
Markham, Edwin 1852-1940 .... **TCLC 47**
    See also CA 160; DLB 54, 186
Markham, Robert
    See Amis, Kingsley (William)
Marks, J
    See Highwater, Jamake (Mamake)
Marks-Highwater, J
    See Highwater, Jamake (Mamake)
Markson, David M(errill) 1927- .... **CLC 67**
    See also CA 49-52; CANR 1
Marley, Bob .... **CLC 17**
    See also Marley, Robert Nesta
Marley, Robert Nesta 1945-1981
    See Marley, Bob
    See also CA 107; 103
Marlowe, Christopher 1564-1593 **LC 22, 47;**
    **DA; DAB; DAC; DAM DRAM, MST; DC
    1; WLC**
    See also CDBLB Before 1660; DLB 62
Marlowe, Stephen 1928-
    See Queen, Ellery
    See also CA 13-16R; CANR 6, 55
Marmontel, Jean-Francois 1723-1799 .. **LC 2**
Marquand, John P(hillips) 1893-1960**CLC 2,
    10**
    See also CA 85-88; CANR 73; DLB 9, 102
Marques, Rene 1919-1979 ..... **CLC 96; DAM
    MULT; HLC**
    See also CA 97-100; 85-88; DLB 113; HW
Marquez, Gabriel (Jose) Garcia
    See Garcia Marquez, Gabriel (Jose)
Marquis, Don(ald Robert Perry) 1878-1937
    TCLC 7
    See also CA 104; 166; DLB 11, 25
Marric, J. J.
    See Creasey, John
Marryat, Frederick 1792-1848 .... **NCLC 3**
    See also DLB 21, 163
Marsden, James
    See Creasey, John
Marsh, (Edith) Ngaio 1899-1982 **CLC 7, 53;
    DAM POP**
    See also CA 9-12R; CANR 6, 58; DLB 77;
    MTCW 1
Marshall, Garry 1934- .... **CLC 17**
    See also AAYA 3; CA 111; SATA 60
Marshall, Paule 1929- .. **CLC 27, 72; BLC 3;
    DAM MULT; SSC 3**
    See also BW 2; CA 77-80; CANR 25, 73; DLB
    157; MTCW 1
Marshallik
    See Zangwill, Israel
Marsten, Richard
    See Hunter, Evan
Marston, John 1576-1634**LC 33; DAM DRAM**
    See also DLB 58, 172
Martha, Henry
    See Harris, Mark
Marti, Jose 1853-1895**NCLC 63; DAM MULT;
    HLC**
Martial c. 40-c. 104 .... **PC 10**
Martin, Ken
    See Hubbard, L(afayette) Ron(ald)
Martin, Richard
    See Creasey, John
Martin, Steve 1945- .... **CLC 30**
    See also CA 97-100; CANR 30; MTCW 1
Martin, Valerie 1948- .... **CLC 89**
    See also BEST 90:2; CA 85-88; CANR 49
Martin, Violet Florence 1862-1915 **TCLC 51**
Martin, Webber
    See Silverberg, Robert
Martindale, Patrick Victor
    See White, Patrick (Victor Martindale)
Martin du Gard, Roger 1881-1958 **TCLC 24**
    See also CA 118; DLB 65

Martineau, Harriet 1802-1876 .... **NCLC 26**
See also DLB 21, 55, 159, 163, 166, 190; YABC 2

Martines, Julia
See O'Faolain, Julia

Martinez, Enrique Gonzalez
See Gonzalez Martinez, Enrique

Martinez, Jacinto Benavente y
See Benavente (y Martinez), Jacinto

Martinez Ruiz, Jose 1873-1967
See Azorin; Ruiz, Jose Martinez
See also CA 93-96; HW

Martinez Sierra, Gregorio 1881-1947**TCLC 6**
See also CA 115

Martinez Sierra, Maria (de la O'LeJarraga) 1874-1974 ....
TCLC 6
See also CA 115

Martinsen, Martin
See Follett, Ken(neth Martin)

Martinson, Harry (Edmund) 1904-1978**C L C 14**
See also CA 77-80; CANR 34

Marut, Ret
See Traven, B.

Marut, Robert
See Traven, B.

Marvell, Andrew 1621-1678 ... **LC 4, 43; DA; DAB; DAC; DAM MST, POET; PC 10; WLC**
See also CDBLB 1660-1789; DLB 131

Marx, Karl (Heinrich) 1818-1883 . **NCLC 17**
See also DLB 129

Masaoka Shiki .... **TCLC 18**
See also Masaoka Tsunenori

Masaoka Tsunenori 1867-1902
See Masaoka Shiki
See also CA 117

Masefield, John (Edward) 1878-1967**CLC 11, 47; DAM POET**
See also CA 19-20; 25-28R; CANR 33; CAP 2; CDBLB 1890-1914; DLB 10, 19, 153, 160; MTCW 1; SATA 19

Maso, Carole 19(?)- .... **CLC 44**
See also CA 170

Mason, Bobbie Ann 1940-**CLC 28, 43, 82; SSC 4**
See also AAYA 5; CA 53-56; CANR 11, 31, 58; DLB 173; DLBY 87; INT CANR-31; MTCW 1

Mason, Ernst
See Pohl, Frederik

Mason, Lee W.
See Malzberg, Barry N(athaniel)

Mason, Nick 1945- .... **CLC 35**

Mason, Tally
See.Derleth, August (William)

Mass, William
See Gibson, William

Master Lao
See Lao Tzu

Masters, Edgar Lee 1868-1950 **TCLC 2, 25; DA; DAC; DAM MST, POET; PC 1; WLCS**
See also CA 104; 133; CDALB 1865-1917; DLB 54; MTCW 1

Masters, Hilary 1928- .... **CLC 48**
See also CA 25-28R; CANR 13, 47

Mastrosimone, William 19(?)- .... **CLC 36**

Mathe, Albert
See Camus, Albert

Mather, Cotton 1663-1728 .... **LC 38**
See also CDALB 1640-1865; DLB 24, 30, 140

Mather, Increase 1639-1723 .... **LC 38**
See also DLB 24

Matheson, Richard Burton 1926- ..... **CLC 37**
See also CA 97-100; DLB 8, 44; INT 97-100

Mathews, Harry 1930- .... **CLC 6, 52**
See also CA 21-24R; CAAS 6; CANR 18, 40

Mathews, John Joseph 1894-1979 .. **CLC 84; DAM MULT**
See also CA 19-20; 142; CANR 45; CAP 2; DLB 175; NNAL

Mathias, Roland (Glyn) 1915- .... **CLC 45**
See also CA 97-100; CANR 19, 41; DLB 27

Matsuo Basho 1644-1694 .... **PC 3**
See also DAM POET

Mattheson, Rodney
See Creasey, John

Matthews, Greg 1949- .... **CLC 45**
See also CA 135

Matthews, William (Procter, III) 1942-1997 **CLC 40**
See also CA 29-32R; 162; CAAS 18; CANR 12, 57; DLB 5

Matthias, John (Edward) 1941- .... **CLC 9**
See also CA 33-36R; CANR 56

Matthiessen, Peter 1927-**CLC 5, 7, 11, 32, 64; DAM NOV**
See also AAYA 6; BEST 90:4; CA 9-12R; CANR 21, 50, 73; DLB 6, 173; MTCW 1; SATA 27

Maturin, Charles Robert 1780(?)-1824**NCLC 6**
See also DLB 178

Matute (Ausejo), Ana Maria 1925- .. **CLC 11**
See also CA 89-92; MTCW 1

Maugham, W. S.
See Maugham, W(illiam) Somerset

Maugham, W(illiam) Somerset 1874-1965 **CLC 1, 11, 15, 67, 93; DA; DAB; DAC; DAM DRAM, MST, NOV; SSC 8; WLC**
See also CA 5-8R; 25-28R; CANR 40; CDBLB 1914-1945; DLB 10, 36, 77, 100, 162, 195; MTCW 1; SATA 54

Maugham, William Somerset
See Maugham, W(illiam) Somerset

Maupassant, (Henri Rene Albert) Guy de 1850-1893
NCLC 1, 42; DA; DAB; DAC; DAM MST; SSC 1; WLC
See also DLB 123

Maupin, Armistead 1944-**CLC 95; DAM POP**
See also CA 125; 130; CANR 58; INT 130

Maurhut, Richard
See Traven, B.

Mauriac, Claude 1914-1996 .... **CLC 9**
See also CA 89-92; 152; DLB 83

Mauriac, Francois (Charles) 1885-1970 **C L C 4, 9, 56; SSC 24**
See also CA 25-28; CAP 2; DLB 65; MTCW 1

Mavor, Osborne Henry 1888-1951
See Bridie, James
See also CA 104

Maxwell, William (Keepers, Jr.) 1908-**CLC 19**
See also CA 93-96; CANR 54; DLBY 80; INT 93-96

May, Elaine 1932- .... **CLC 16**
See also CA 124; 142; DLB 44

Mayakovski, Vladimir (Vladimirovich) 1893-1930 .... **TCLC 4, 18**
See also CA 104; 158

Mayhew, Henry 1812-1887 .... **NCLC 31**
See also DLB 18, 55, 190

Mayle, Peter 1939(?)- .... **CLC 89**
See also CA 139; CANR 64

Maynard, Joyce 1953- .... **CLC 23**
See also CA 111; 129; CANR 64

Mayne, William (James Carter) 1928-**CLC 12**
See also AAYA 20; CA 9-12R; CANR 37; CLR 25; JRDA; MAICYA; SAAS 11; SATA 6, 68

Mayo, Jim
See L'Amour, Louis (Dearborn)

Maysles, Albert 1926- .... **CLC 16**

Maysles, David 1932- .... **CLC 16**
See also CA 29-32R

Mazer, Norma Fox 1931- .... **CLC 26**
See also AAYA 5; CA 69-72; CANR 12, 32, 66; CLR 23; JRDA; MAICYA; SAAS 1; SATA 24, 67, 105

Mazzini, Guiseppe 1805-1872 .... **NCLC 34**

McAuley, James Phillip 1917-1976 .. **CLC 45**
See also CA 97-100

McBain, Ed
See Hunter, Evan

McBrien, William Augustine 1930- .. **CLC 44**
See also CA 107

McCaffrey, Anne (Inez) 1926-**CLC 17; DAM NOV, POP**
See also AAYA 6; AITN 2; BEST 89:2; CA 25-28R; CANR 15, 35, 55; CLR 49; DLB 8; JRDA; MAICYA; MTCW 1; SAAS 11; SATA 8, 70

McCall, Nathan 1955(?)- .... **CLC 86**
See also CA 146

McCann, Arthur
See Campbell, John W(ood, Jr.)

McCann, Edson
See Pohl, Frederik

McCarthy, Charles, Jr. 1933-
See McCarthy, Cormac
See also CANR 42, 69; DAM POP

McCarthy, Cormac 1933- **CLC 4, 57, 59, 101**
See also McCarthy, Charles, Jr.
See also DLB 6, 143

McCarthy, Mary (Therese) 1912-1989**CLC 1, 3, 5, 14, 24, 39, 59; SSC 24**
See also CA 5-8R; 129; CANR 16, 50, 64; DLB 2; DLBY 81; INT CANR-16; MTCW 1

McCartney, (James) Paul 1942- **CLC 12, 35**
See also CA 146

McCauley, Stephen (D.) 1955- .... **CLC 50**
See also CA 141

McClure, Michael (Thomas) 1932-**CLC 6, 10**
See also CA 21-24R; CANR 17, 46; DLB 16

McCorkle, Jill (Collins) 1958- .... **CLC 51**
See also CA 121; DLBY 87

McCourt, Frank 1930- .... **CLC 109**
See also CA 157

McCourt, James 1941- .... **CLC 5**
See also CA 57-60

McCoy, Horace (Stanley) 1897-1955**TCLC 28**
See also CA 108; 155; DLB 9

McCrae, John 1872-1918 .... **TCLC 12**
See also CA 109; DLB 92

McCreigh, James
See Pohl, Frederik

McCullers, (Lula) Carson (Smith) 1917-1967 **CLC 1, 4, 10, 12, 48, 100; DA; DAB; DAC; DAM MST, NOV; SSC 9, 24; WLC**
See also AAYA 21; CA 5-8R; 25-28R; CABS 1, 3; CANR 18; CDALB 1941-1968; DLB 2, 7, 173; MTCW 1; SATA 27

McCulloch, John Tyler
See Burroughs, Edgar Rice

McCullough, Colleen 1938(?)- **CLC 27, 107; DAM NOV, POP**
See also CA 81-84; CANR 17, 46, 67; MTCW 1

McDermott, Alice 1953- .... **CLC 90**
See also CA 109; CANR 40

McElroy, Joseph 1930-................... **CLC 5, 47**
See also CA 17-20R

McEwan, Ian (Russell) 1948- .... **CLC 13, 66; DAM NOV**
See also BEST 90:4; CA 61-64; CANR 14, 41, 69; DLB 14, 194; MTCW 1

McFadden, David 1940- .... **CLC 48**
See also CA 104; DLB 60; INT 104

McFarland, Dennis 1950- .... **CLC 65**
See also CA 165

McGahern, John 1934-**CLC 5, 9, 48; SSC 17**
See also CA 17-20R; CANR 29, 68; DLB 14;
MTCW 1
McGinley, Patrick (Anthony) 1937- . **CLC 41**
See also CA 120; 127; CANR 56; INT 127
McGinley, Phyllis 1905-1978 .... **CLC 14**
See also CA 9-12R; 77-80; CANR 19; DLB 11,
48; SATA 2, 44; SATA-Obit 24
McGinniss, Joe 1942- .... **CLC 32**
See also AITN 2; BEST 89:2; CA 25-28R;
CANR 26, 70; DLB 185; INT CANR-26
McGivern, Maureen Daly
See Daly, Maureen
McGrath, Patrick 1950- .... **CLC 55**
See also CA 136; CANR 65
McGrath, Thomas (Matthew) 1916-1990**CLC
28, 59; DAM POET**
See also CA 9-12R; 132; CANR 6, 33; MTCW
1; SATA 41; SATA-Obit 66
McGuane, Thomas (Francis III) 1939-**CLC 3,
7, 18, 45**
See also AITN 2; CA 49-52; CANR 5, 24, 49;
DLB 2; DLBY 80; INT CANR-24; MTCW
1
McGuckian, Medbh 1950- ..... **CLC 48; DAM
POET**
See also CA 143; DLB 40
McHale, Tom 1942(?)-1982 .... **CLC 3, 5**
See also AITN 1; CA 77-80; 106
McIlvanney, William 1936- .... **CLC 42**
See also CA 25-28R; CANR 61; DLB 14, 207
McIlwraith, Maureen Mollie Hunter
See Hunter, Mollie
See also SATA 2
McInerney, Jay 1955-**CLC 34, 112; DAM POP**
See also AAYA 18; CA 116; 123; CANR 45,
68; INT 123
McIntyre, Vonda N(eel) 1948- .... **CLC 18**
See also CA 81-84; CANR 17, 34, 69; MTCW
1
McKay, Claude**TCLC 7, 41; BLC 3; DAB; PC
2**
See also McKay, Festus Claudius
See also DLB 4, 45, 51, 117
McKay, Festus Claudius 1889-1948
See McKay, Claude
See also BW 1; CA 104; 124; CANR 73; DA;
DAC; DAM MST, MULT, NOV, POET;
MTCW 1; WLC
McKuen, Rod 1933-........................... **CLC 1, 3**
See also AITN 1; CA 41-44R; CANR 40
McLoughlin, R. B.
See Mencken, H(enry) L(ouis)
McLuhan, (Herbert) Marshall 1911-1980
CLC 37, 83
See also CA 9-12R; 102; CANR 12, 34, 61;
DLB 88; INT CANR-12; MTCW 1
McMillan, Terry (L.) 1951- **CLC 50, 61, 112;
BLCS; DAM MULT, NOV, POP**
See also AAYA 21; BW 2; CA 140; CANR 60
McMurtry, Larry (Jeff) 1936-**CLC 2, 3, 7, 11,
27, 44; DAM NOV, POP**
See also AAYA 15; AITN 2; BEST 89:2; CA 5-
8R; CANR 19, 43, 64; CDALB 1968-1988;
DLB 2, 143; DLBY 80, 87; MTCW 1
McNally, T. M. 1961- .... **CLC 82**
McNally, Terrence 1939- .... **CLC 4, 7, 41, 91;
DAM DRAM**
See also CA 45-48; CANR 2, 56; DLB 7
McNamer, Deirdre 1950- .... **CLC 70**
McNeile, Herman Cyril 1888-1937
See Sapper
See also DLB 77
McNickle, (William) D'Arcy 1904-1977 C L C
89; DAM MULT
See also CA 9-12R; 85-88; CANR 5, 45; DLB
175; NNAL; SATA-Obit 22

McPhee, John (Angus) 1931- .... **CLC 36**
See also BEST 90:1; CA 65-68; CANR 20, 46,
64, 69; DLB 185; MTCW 1
McPherson, James Alan 1943-.. **CLC 19, 77;
BLCS**
See also BW 1; CA 25-28R; CAAS 17; CANR
24, 74; DLB 38; MTCW 1
McPherson, William (Alexander) 1933- **C L C
34**
See also CA 69-72; CANR 28; INT CANR-28
Mead, George Herbert 1873-1958 . **TCLC 89**
Mead, Margaret 1901-1978 .... **CLC 37**
See also AITN 1; CA 1-4R; 81-84; CANR 4;
MTCW 1; SATA-Obit 20
Meaker, Marijane (Agnes) 1927-
See Kerr, M. E.
See also CA 107; CANR 37, 63; INT 107;
JRDA; MAICYA; MTCW 1; SATA 20, 61,
99
Medoff, Mark (Howard) 1940- ... **CLC 6, 23;
DAM DRAM**
See also AITN 1; CA 53-56; CANR 5; DLB 7;
INT CANR-5
Medvedev, P. N.
See Bakhtin, Mikhail Mikhailovich
Meged, Aharon
See Megged, Aharon
Meged, Aron
See Megged, Aharon
Megged, Aharon 1920-........................ **CLC 9**
See also CA 49-52; CAAS 13; CANR 1
Mehta, Ved (Parkash) 1934- .... **CLC 37**
See also CA 1-4R; CANR 2, 23, 69; MTCW 1
Melanter
See Blackmore, R(ichard) D(oddridge)
Melies, Georges 1861-1938 .... **TCLC 81**
Melikow, Loris
See Hofmannsthal, Hugo von
Melmoth, Sebastian
See Wilde, Oscar
Meltzer, Milton 1915- .... **CLC 26**
See also AAYA 8; CA 13-16R; CANR 38; CLR
13; DLB 61; JRDA; MAICYA; SAAS 1;
SATA 1, 50, 80
Melville, Herman 1819-1891**NCLC 3, 12, 29,
45, 49; DA; DAB; DAC; DAM MST, NOV;
SSC 1, 17; WLC**
See also AAYA 25; CDALB 1640-1865; DLB
3, 74; SATA 59
Menander c. 342B.C.-c. 292B.C. ..... **CMLC 9;
DAM DRAM; DC 3**
See also DLB 176
Mencken, H(enry) L(ouis) 1880-1956 **T C L C
13**
See also CA 105; 125; CDALB 1917-1929;
DLB 11, 29, 63, 137; MTCW 1
Mendelsohn, Jane 1965(?)- .... **CLC 99**
See also CA 154
Mercer, David 1928-1980**CLC 5; DAM DRAM**
See also CA 9-12R; 102; CANR 23; DLB 13;
MTCW 1
Merchant, Paul
See Ellison, Harlan (Jay)
Meredith, George 1828-1909 . **TCLC 17, 43;
DAM POET**
See also CA 117; 153; CDBLB 1832-1890;
DLB 18, 35, 57, 159
Meredith, William (Morris) 1919-**CLC 4, 13,
22, 55; DAM POET**
See also CA 9-12R; CAAS 14; CANR 6, 40;
DLB 5
Merezhkovsky, Dmitry Sergeyevich 1865-1941
TCLC 29
See also CA 169
Merimee, Prosper 1803-1870**NCLC 6, 65; SSC
7**
See also DLB 119, 192

Merkin, Daphne 1954- .... **CLC 44**
See also CA 123
Merlin, Arthur
See Blish, James (Benjamin)
Merrill, James (Ingram) 1926-1995**CLC 2, 3,
6, 8, 13, 18, 34, 91; DAM POET**
See also CA 13-16R; 147; CANR 10, 49, 63;
DLB 5, 165; DLBY 85; INT CANR-10;
MTCW 1
Merriman, Alex
See Silverberg, Robert
Merriman, Brian 1747-1805 .... **NCLC 70**
Merritt, E. B.
See Waddington, Miriam
Merton, Thomas 1915-1968**CLC 1, 3, 11, 34,
83; PC 10**
See also CA 5-8R; 25-28R; CANR 22, 53; DLB
48; DLBY 81; MTCW 1
Merwin, W(illiam) S(tanley) 1927- **CLC 1, 2,
3, 5, 8, 13, 18, 45, 88; DAM POET**
See also CA 13-16R; CANR 15, 51; DLB 5,
169; INT CANR-15; MTCW 1
Metcalf, John 1938-........................... **CLC 37**
See also CA 113; DLB 60
Metcalf, Suzanne
See Baum, L(yman) Frank
Mew, Charlotte (Mary) 1870-1928 .. **TCLC 8**
See also CA 105; DLB 19, 135
Mewshaw, Michael 1943- .... **CLC 9**
See also CA 53-56; CANR 7, 47; DLBY 80
Meyer, June
See Jordan, June
Meyer, Lynn
See Slavitt, David R(ytman)
Meyer-Meyrink, Gustav 1868-1932
See Meyrink, Gustav
See also CA 117
Meyers, Jeffrey 1939-......................... **CLC 39**
See also CA 73-76; CANR 54; DLB 111
Meynell, Alice (Christina Gertrude Thompson)
1847-1922 .... **TCLC 6**
See also CA 104; DLB 19, 98
Meyrink, Gustav .... **TCLC 21**
See also Meyer-Meyrink, Gustav
See also DLB 81
Michaels, Leonard 1933- **CLC 6, 25; SSC 16**
See also CA 61-64; CANR 21, 62; DLB 130;
MTCW 1
Michaux, Henri 1899-1984 .... **CLC 8, 19**
See also CA 85-88; 114
Micheaux, Oscar 1884-1951 .... **TCLC 76**
See also DLB 50
Michelangelo 1475-1564 .... **LC 12**
Michelet, Jules 1798-1874 .... **NCLC 31**
Michels, Robert 1876-1936............. **TCLC 88**
Michener, James A(lbert) 1907(?)-1997 **C L C
1, 5, 11, 29, 60, 109; DAM NOV, POP**
See also AAYA 27; AITN 1; BEST 90:1; CA 5-
8R; 161; CANR 21, 45, 68; DLB 6; MTCW
1
Mickiewicz, Adam 1798-1855 .... **NCLC 3**
Middleton, Christopher 1926- .... **CLC 13**
See also CA 13-16R; CANR 29, 54; DLB 40
Middleton, Richard (Barham) 1882-1911
TCLC 56
See also DLB 156
Middleton, Stanley 1919-............... **CLC 7, 38**
See also CA 25-28R; CAAS 23; CANR 21, 46;
DLB 14
Middleton, Thomas 1580-1627 **LC 33; DAM
DRAM, MST; DC 5**
See also DLB 58
Migueis, José Rodrigues 1901- .... **CLC 10**
Mikszath, Kalman 1847-1910 .... **TCLC 31**
See also CA 170
Miles, Jack .... **CLC 100**
Miles, Josephine (Louise) 1911-1985**CLC 1, 2,**

14, 34, 39; DAM POET
See also CA 1-4R; 116; CANR 2, 55; DLB 48
Militant
See Sandburg, Carl (August)
Mill, John Stuart 1806-1873 .... **NCLC 11, 58**
See also CDBLB 1832-1890; DLB 55, 190
Millar, Kenneth 1915-1983 .... **CLC 14; DAM POP**
See Macdonald, Ross
See also CA 9-12R; 110; CANR 16, 63; DLB 2; DLBD 6; DLBY 83; MTCW 1
Millay, E. Vincent
See Millay, Edna St. Vincent
Millay, Edna St. Vincent 1892-1950 **TCLC 4, 49; DA; DAB; DAC; DAM MST, POET; PC 6; WLCS**
See also CA 104; 130; CDALB 1917-1929; DLB 45; MTCW 1
Miller, Arthur 1915-**CLC 1, 2, 6, 10, 15, 26, 47, 78; DA; DAB; DAC; DAM DRAM, MST; DC 1; WLC**
See also AAYA 15; AITN 1; CA 1-4R; CABS 3; CANR 2, 30, 54, 76; CDALB 1941-1968; DLB 7; MTCW 1
Miller, Henry (Valentine) 1891-1980**CLC 1, 2, 4, 9, 14, 43, 84; DA; DAB; DAC; DAM MST, NOV; WLC**
See also CA 9-12R; 97-100; CANR 33, 64; CDALB 1929-1941; DLB 4, 9; DLBY 80; MTCW 1
Miller, Jason 1939(?)- .... **CLC 2**
See also AITN 1; CA 73-76; DLB 7
Miller, Sue 1943- .... **CLC 44; DAM POP**
See also BEST 90:3; CA 139; CANR 59; DLB 143
Miller, Walter M(ichael, Jr.) 1923-**CLC 4, 30**
See also CA 85-88; DLB 8
Millett, Kate 1934-.............................. **CLC 67**
See also AITN 1; CA 73-76; CANR 32, 53, 76; MTCW 1
Millhauser, Steven (Lewis) 1943-**CLC 21, 54, 109**
See also CA 110; 111; CANR 63; DLB 2; INT 111
Millin, Sarah Gertrude 1889-1968 ... **CLC 49**
See also CA 102; 93-96
Milne, A(lan) A(lexander) 1882-1956**TCLC 6, 88; DAB; DAC; DAM MST**
See also CA 104; 133; CLR 1, 26; DLB 10, 77, 100, 160; MAICYA; MTCW 1; SATA 100; YABC 1
Milner, Ron(ald) 1938-**CLC 56; BLC 3; DAM MULT**
See also AITN 1; BW 1; CA 73-76; CANR 24; DLB 38; MTCW 1
Milnes, Richard Monckton 1809-1885 **N C L C 61**
See also DLB 32, 184
Milosz, Czeslaw 1911- **CLC 5, 11, 22, 31, 56, 82; DAM MST, POET; PC 8; WLCS**
See also CA 81-84; CANR 23, 51; MTCW 1
Milton, John 1608-1674**LC 9, 43; DA; DAB; DAC; DAM MST, POET; PC 19; WLC**
See also CDBLB 1660-1789; DLB 131, 151
Min, Anchee 1957- .... **CLC 86**
See also CA 146
Minehaha, Cornelius
See Wedekind, (Benjamin) Frank(lin)
Miner, Valerie 1947- .... **CLC 40**
See also CA 97-100; CANR 59
Minimo, Duca
See D'Annunzio, Gabriele
Minot, Susan 1956- .... **CLC 44**
See also CA 134
Minus, Ed 1938- .... **CLC 39**
Miranda, Javier
See Bioy Casares, Adolfo

Mirbeau, Octave 1848-1917 .... **TCLC 55**
See also DLB 123, 192
Miro (Ferrer), Gabriel (Francisco Victor) 1879-1930 .... **TCLC 5**
See also CA 104
Mishima, Yukio 1925-1970**CLC 2, 4, 6, 9, 27; DC 1; SSC 4**
See Hiraoka, Kimitake
See also DLB 182
Mistral, Frederic 1830-1914 .... **TCLC 51**
See also CA 122
Mistral, Gabriela .... **TCLC 2; HLC**
See Godoy Alcayaga, Lucila
Mistry, Rohinton 1952- .... **CLC 71; DAC**
See also CA 141
Mitchell, Clyde
See Ellison, Harlan (Jay); Silverberg, Robert
Mitchell, James Leslie 1901-1935
See Gibbon, Lewis Grassic
See also CA 104; DLB 15
Mitchell, Joni 1943- .... **CLC 12**
See also CA 112
Mitchell, Joseph (Quincy) 1908-1996**CLC 98**
See also CA 77-80; 152; CANR 69; DLB 185; DLBY 96
Mitchell, Margaret (Munnerlyn) 1900-1949 **TCLC 11; DAM NOV, POP**
See also AAYA 23; CA 109; 125; CANR 55; DLB 9; MTCW 1
Mitchell, Peggy
See Mitchell, Margaret (Munnerlyn)
Mitchell, S(ilas) Weir 1829-1914 ... **TCLC 36**
See also CA 165; DLB 202
Mitchell, W(illiam) O(rmond) 1914-1998**CLC 25; DAC; DAM MST**
See also CA 77-80; 165; CANR 15, 43; DLB 88
Mitchell, William 1879-1936 .... **TCLC 81**
Mitford, Mary Russell 1787-1855 ... **NCLC 4**
See also DLB 110, 116
Mitford, Nancy 1904-1973 .... **CLC 44**
See also CA 9-12R; DLB 191
Miyamoto, Yuriko 1899-1951 .... **TCLC 37**
See also CA 170; DLB 180
Miyazawa, Kenji 1896-1933 .... **TCLC 76**
See also CA 157
Mizoguchi, Kenji 1898-1956 .... **TCLC 72**
See also CA 167
Mo, Timothy (Peter) 1950(?)- .... **CLC 46**
See also CA 117; DLB 194; MTCW 1
Modarressi, Taghi (M.) 1931- .... **CLC 44**
See also CA 121; 134; INT 134
Modiano, Patrick (Jean) 1945- .... **CLC 18**
See also CA 85-88; CANR 17, 40; DLB 83
Moerck, Paal
See Roelvaag, O(le) E(dvart)
Mofolo, Thomas (Mokopu) 1875(?)-1948 **TCLC 22; BLC 3; DAM MULT**
See also CA 121; 153
Mohr, Nicholasa 1938-**CLC 12; DAM MULT; HLC**
See also AAYA 8; CA 49-52; CANR 1, 32, 64; CLR 22; DLB 145; HW; JRDA; SAAS 8; SATA 8, 97
Mojtabai, A(nn) G(race) 1938- **CLC 5, 9, 15, 29**
See also CA 85-88
Moliere 1622-1673**LC 10, 28; DA; DAB; DAC; DAM DRAM, MST; WLC**
Molin, Charles
See Mayne, William (James Carter)
Molnar, Ferenc 1878-1952 .. **TCLC 20; DAM DRAM**
See also CA 109; 153
Momaday, N(avarre) Scott 1934- **CLC 2, 19, 85, 95; DA; DAB; DAC; DAM MST,**

MULT, NOV, POP; PC 25; WLCS
See also AAYA 11; CA 25-28R; CANR 14, 34, 68; DLB 143, 175; INT CANR-14; MTCW 1; NNAL; SATA 48; SATA-Brief 30
Monette, Paul 1945-1995 .... **CLC 82**
See also CA 139; 147
Monroe, Harriet 1860-1936 .... **TCLC 12**
See also CA 109; DLB 54, 91
Monroe, Lyle
See Heinlein, Robert A(nson)
Montagu, Elizabeth 1720-1800 .... **NCLC 7**
Montagu, Mary (Pierrepont) Wortley 1689-1762 ....**LC 9; PC 16**
See also DLB 95, 101
Montagu, W. H.
See Coleridge, Samuel Taylor
Montague, John (Patrick) 1929- **CLC 13, 46**
See also CA 9-12R; CANR 9, 69; DLB 40; MTCW 1
Montaigne, Michel (Eyquem) de 1533-1592 **LC 8; DA; DAB; DAC; DAM MST; WLC**
Montale, Eugenio 1896-1981**CLC 7, 9, 18; PC 13**
See also CA 17-20R; 104; CANR 30; DLB 114; MTCW 1
Montesquieu, Charles-Louis de Secondat 1689-1755 .... **LC 7**
Montgomery, (Robert) Bruce 1921-1978
See Crispin, Edmund
See also CA 104
Montgomery, L(ucy) M(aud) 1874-1942 **TCLC 51; DAC; DAM MST**
See also AAYA 12; CA 108; 137; CLR 8; DLB 92; DLBD 14; JRDA; MAICYA; SATA 100; YABC 1
Montgomery, Marion H., Jr. 1925- .... **CLC 7**
See also AITN 1; CA 1-4R; CANR 3, 48; DLB 6
Montgomery, Max
See Davenport, Guy (Mattison, Jr.)
Montherlant, Henry (Milon) de 1896-1972 **CLC 8, 19; DAM DRAM**
See also CA 85-88; 37-40R; DLB 72; MTCW 1
Monty Python
See Chapman, Graham; Cleese, John (Marwood); Gilliam, Terry (Vance); Idle, Eric; Jones, Terence Graham Parry; Palin, Michael (Edward)
See also AAYA 7
Moodie, Susanna (Strickland) 1803-1885 **NCLC 14**
See also DLB 99
Mooney, Edward 1951-
See Mooney, Ted
See also CA 130
Mooney, Ted .... **CLC 25**
See also Mooney, Edward
Moorcock, Michael (John) 1939-**CLC 5, 27, 58**
See also AAYA 26; CA 45-48; CAAS 5; CANR 2, 17, 38, 64; DLB 14; MTCW 1; SATA 93
Moore, Brian 1921- **CLC 1, 3, 5, 7, 8, 19, 32, 90; DAB; DAC; DAM MST**
See also CA 1-4R; CANR 1, 25, 42, 63; MTCW 1
Moore, Edward
See Muir, Edwin
Moore, G. E. 1873-1958 .... **TCLC 89**
Moore, George Augustus 1852-1933**TCLC 7; SSC 19**
See also CA 104; DLB 10, 18, 57, 135
Moore, Lorrie .... **CLC 39, 45, 68**
See also Moore, Marie Lorena
Moore, Marianne (Craig) 1887-1972**CLC 1, 2, 4, 8, 10, 13, 19, 47; DA; DAB; DAC; DAM MST, POET; PC 4; WLCS**
See also CA 1-4R; 33-36R; CANR 3, 61;

CDALB 1929-1941; DLB 45; DLBD 7;
MTCW 1; SATA 20
Moore, Marie Lorena 1957-
See Moore, Lorrie
See also CA 116; CANR 39
Moore, Thomas 1779-1852 .... NCLC 6
See also DLB 96, 144
Morand, Paul 1888-1976 .... CLC 41; SSC 22
See also CA 69-72; DLB 65
Morante, Elsa 1918-1985 .... CLC 8, 47
See also CA 85-88; 117; CANR 35; DLB 177;
MTCW 1
Moravia, Alberto 1907-1990 CLC 2, 7, 11, 27,
46; SSC 26
See Pincherle, Alberto
See also DLB 177
More, Hannah 1745-1833 .... NCLC 27
See also DLB 107, 109, 116, 158
More, Henry 1614-1687 .... LC 9
See also DLB 126
More, Sir Thomas 1478-1535 .... LC 10, 32
Moreas, Jean .... TCLC 18
See also Papadiamantopoulos, Johannes
Morgan, Berry 1919- .... CLC 6
See also CA 49-52; DLB 6
Morgan, Claire
See Highsmith, (Mary) Patricia
Morgan, Edwin (George) 1920- .... CLC 31
See also CA 5-8R; CANR 3, 43; DLB 27
Morgan, (George) Frederick 1922- .. CLC 23
See also CA 17-20R; CANR 21
Morgan, Harriet
See Mencken, H(enry) L(ouis)
Morgan, Jane
See Cooper, James Fenimore
Morgan, Janet 1945- .... CLC 39
See also CA 65-68
Morgan, Lady 1776(?)-1859 .... NCLC 29
See also DLB 116, 158
Morgan, Robin (Evonne) 1941- .... CLC 2
See also CA 69-72; CANR 29, 68; MTCW 1;
SATA 80
Morgan, Scott
See Kuttner, Henry
Morgan, Seth 1949(?)-1990 .... CLC 65
See also CA 132
Morgenstern, Christian 1871-1914 . TCLC 8
See also CA 105
Morgenstern, S.
See Goldman, William (W.)
Moricz, Zsigmond 1879-1942 .... TCLC 33
See also CA 165
Morike, Eduard (Friedrich) 1804-1875 NCLC
10
See also DLB 133
Moritz, Karl Philipp 1756-1793 .... LC 2
See also DLB 94
Morland, Peter Henry
See Faust, Frederick (Schiller)
Morley, Christopher (Darlington) 1890-1957
TCLC 87
See also CA 112; DLB 9
Morren, Theophil
See Hofmannsthal, Hugo von
Morris, Bill 1952- .... CLC 76
Morris, Julian
See West, Morris L(anglo)
Morris, Steveland Judkins 1950(?)-
See Wonder, Stevie
See also CA 111
Morris, William 1834-1896 .... NCLC 4
See also CDBLB 1832-1890; DLB 18, 35, 57,
156, 178, 184
Morris, Wright 1910-1998 CLC 1, 3, 7, 18, 37
See also CA 9-12R; 167; CANR 21; DLB 2,
206; DLBY 81; MTCW 1
Morrison, Arthur 1863-1945 .... TCLC 72

See also CA 120; 157; DLB 70, 135, 197
Morrison, Chloe Anthony Wofford
See Morrison, Toni
Morrison, James Douglas 1943-1971
See Morrison, Jim
See also CA 73-76; CANR 40
Morrison, Jim .... CLC 17
See also Morrison, James Douglas
Morrison, Toni 1931-CLC 4, 10, 22, 55, 81, 87;
BLC 3; DA; DAB; DAC; DAM MST,
MULT, NOV, POP
See also AAYA 1, 22; BW 2; CA 29-32R;
CANR 27, 42, 67; CDALB 1968-1988; DLB
6, 33, 143; DLBY 81; MTCW 1; SATA 57
Morrison, Van 1945- .... CLC 21
See also CA 116; 168
Morrissy, Mary 1958- .... CLC 99
Mortimer, John (Clifford) 1923-CLC 28, 43;
DAM DRAM, POP
See also CA 13-16R; CANR 21, 69; CDBLB
1960 to Present; DLB 13; INT CANR-21;
MTCW 1
Mortimer, Penelope (Ruth) 1918- .... CLC 5
See also CA 57-60; CANR 45
Morton, Anthony
See Creasey, John
Mosca, Gaetano 1858-1941 .... TCLC 75
Mosher, Howard Frank 1943- .... CLC 62
See also CA 139; CANR 65
Mosley, Nicholas 1923- .... CLC 43, 70
See also CA 69-72; CANR 41, 60; DLB 14, 207
Mosley, Walter 1952- . CLC 97; BLCS; DAM
MULT, POP
See also AAYA 17; BW 2; CA 142; CANR 57
Moss, Howard 1922-1987 CLC 7, 14, 45, 50;
DAM POET
See also CA 1-4R; 123; CANR 1, 44; DLB 5
Mossgiel, Rab
See Burns, Robert
Motion, Andrew (Peter) 1952- .... CLC 47
See also CA 146; DLB 40
Motley, Willard (Francis) 1909-1965 CLC 18
See also BW 1; CA 117; 106; DLB 76, 143
Motoori, Norinaga 1730-1801 .... NCLC 45
Mott, Michael (Charles Alston) 1930-CLC 15,
34
See also CA 5-8R; CAAS 7; CANR 7, 29
Mountain Wolf Woman 1884-1960 .. CLC 92
See also CA 144; NNAL
Moure, Erin 1955- .... CLC 88
See also CA 113; DLB 60
Mowat, Farley (McGill) 1921-CLC 26; DAC;
DAM MST
See also AAYA 1; CA 1-4R; CANR 4, 24, 42,
68; CLR 20; DLB 68; INT CANR-24; JRDA;
MAICYA; MTCW 1; SATA 3, 55
Mowatt, Anna Cora 1819-1870 ..... NCLC 74
Moyers, Bill 1934- .... CLC 74
See also AITN 2; CA 61-64; CANR 31, 52
Mphahlele, Es'kia
See Mphahlele, Ezekiel
See also DLB 125
Mphahlele, Ezekiel 1919-1983 CLC 25; BLC
3; DAM MULT
See also Mphahlele, Es'kia
See also BW 2; CA 81-84; CANR 26, 76
Mqhayi, S(amuel) E(dward) K(rune Loliwe)
1875-1945 ....
TCLC 25; BLC 3; DAM MULT
See also CA 153
Mrozek, Slawomir 1930- .... CLC 3, 13
See also CA 13-16R; CAAS 10; CANR 29;
MTCW 1
Mrs. Belloc-Lowndes
See Lowndes, Marie Adelaide (Belloc)
Mtwa, Percy (?)- .... CLC 47
Mueller, Lisel 1924- .... CLC 13, 51

See also CA 93-96; DLB 105
Muir, Edwin 1887-1959 .... TCLC 2, 87
See also CA 104; DLB 20, 100, 191
Muir, John 1838-1914 .... TCLC 28
See also CA 165; DLB 186
Mujica Lainez, Manuel 1910-1984 ... CLC 31
See also Lainez, Manuel Mujica
See also CA 81-84; 112; CANR 32; HW
Mukherjee, Bharati 1940-CLC 53, 115; DAM
NOV
See also BEST 89:2; CA 107; CANR 45, 72;
DLB 60; MTCW 1
Muldoon, Paul 1951-CLC 32, 72; DAM POET
See also CA 113; 129; CANR 52; DLB 40; INT
129
Mulisch, Harry 1927- .... CLC 42
See also CA 9-12R; CANR 6, 26, 56
Mull, Martin 1943- .... CLC 17
See also CA 105
Muller, Wilhelm .... NCLC 73
Mulock, Dinah Maria
See Craik, Dinah Maria (Mulock)
Munford, Robert 1737(?)-1783 .... LC 5
See also DLB 31
Mungo, Raymond 1946- .... CLC 72
See also CA 49-52; CANR 2
Munro, Alice 1931- .... CLC 6, 10, 19, 50, 95;
DAC; DAM MST, NOV; SSC 3; WLCS
See also AITN 2; CA 33-36R; CANR 33, 53,
75; DLB 53; MTCW 1; SATA 29
Munro, H(ector) H(ugh) 1870-1916
See Saki
See also CA 104; 130; CDBLB 1890-1914; DA;
DAB; DAC; DAM MST, NOV; DLB 34, 162;
MTCW 1; WLC
Murdoch, (Jean) Iris 1919-CLC 1, 2, 3, 4, 6, 8,
11, 15, 22, 31, 51; DAB; DAC; DAM MST,
NOV
See also CA 13-16R; CANR 8, 43, 68; CDBLB
1960 to Present; DLB 14, 194; INT CANR-
8; MTCW 1
Murfree, Mary Noailles 1850-1922 ... SSC 22
See also CA 122; DLB 12, 74
Murnau, Friedrich Wilhelm
See Plumpe, Friedrich Wilhelm
Murphy, Richard 1927- .... CLC 41
See also CA 29-32R; DLB 40
Murphy, Sylvia 1937- .... CLC 34
See also CA 121
Murphy, Thomas (Bernard) 1935- ... CLC 51
See also CA 101
Murray, Albert L. 1916- .... CLC 73
See also BW 2; CA 49-52; CANR 26, 52; DLB
38
Murray, Judith Sargent 1751-1820 NCLC 63
See also DLB 37, 200
Murray, Les(lie) A(llan) 1938-CLC 40; DAM
POET
See also CA 21-24R; CANR 11, 27, 56
Murry, J. Middleton
See Murry, John Middleton
Murry, John Middleton 1889-1957 TCLC 16
See also CA 118; DLB 149
Musgrave, Susan 1951- .... CLC 13, 54
See also CA 69-72; CANR 45
Musil, Robert (Edler von) 1880-1942 T C L C
12, 68; SSC 18
See also CA 109; CANR 55; DLB 81, 124
Muske, Carol 1945- .... CLC 90
See also Muske-Dukes, Carol (Anne)
Muske-Dukes, Carol (Anne) 1945-
See Muske, Carol
See also CA 65-68; CANR 32, 70
Musset, (Louis Charles) Alfred de 1810-1857
NCLC 7
See also DLB 192
My Brother's Brother

See Chekhov, Anton (Pavlovich)
Myers, L(eopold) H(amilton) 1881-1944
TCLC 59
See also CA 157; DLB 15
Myers, Walter Dean 1937-. **CLC 35; BLC 3;**
DAM MULT, NOV
See also AAYA 4, 23; BW 2; CA 33-36R;
CANR 20, 42, 67; CLR 4, 16, 35; DLB 33;
INT CANR-20; JRDA; MAICYA; SAAS 2;
SATA 41, 71; SATA-Brief 27
Myers, Walter M.
See Myers, Walter Dean
Myles, Symon
See Follett, Ken(neth Martin)
Nabokov, Vladimir (Vladimirovich) 1899-1977
CLC 1, 2, 3, 6, 8, 11, 15, 23, 44, 46, 64;
DA; DAB; DAC; DAM MST, NOV; SSC
11; WLC
See also CA 5-8R; 69-72; CANR 20; CDALB
1941-1968; DLB 2; DLBD 3; DLBY 80, 91;
MTCW 1
Nagai Kafu 1879-1959 .... **TCLC 51**
See also Nagai Sokichi
See also DLB 180
Nagai Sokichi 1879-1959
See Nagai Kafu
See also CA 117
Nagy, Laszlo 1925-1978 .... **CLC 7**
See also CA 129; 112
Naidu, Sarojini 1879-1943 .... **TCLC 80**
Naipaul, Shiva(dhar Srinivasa) 1945-1985
CLC 32, 39; DAM NOV
See also CA 110; 112; 116; CANR 33; DLB
157; DLBY 85; MTCW 1
Naipaul, V(idiadhar) S(urajprasad) 1932-
CLC 4, 7, 9, 13, 18, 37, 105; DAB; DAC;
DAM MST, NOV
See also CA 1-4R; CANR 1, 33, 51; CDBLB
1960 to Present; DLB 125, 204, 206; DLBY
85; MTCW 1
Nakos, Lilika 1899(?)- .... **CLC 29**
Narayan, R(asipuram) K(rishnaswami) 1906-
CLC 7, 28, 47; DAM NOV; SSC 25
See also CA 81-84; CANR 33, 61; MTCW 1;
SATA 62
Nash, (Frediric) Ogden 1902-1971 . **CLC 23;**
DAM POET; PC 21
See also CA 13-14; 29-32R; CANR 34, 61; CAP
1; DLB 11; MAICYA; MTCW 1; SATA 2,
46
Nashe, Thomas 1567-1601(?) .... **LC 41**
See also DLB 167
Nashe, Thomas 1567-1601 .... **LC 41**
Nathan, Daniel
See Dannay, Frederic
Nathan, George Jean 1882-1958 ... **TCLC 18**
See also Hatteras, Owen
See also CA 114; 169; DLB 137
Natsume, Kinnosuke 1867-1916
See Natsume, Soseki
See also CA 104
Natsume, Soseki 1867-1916 .... **TCLC 2, 10**
See also Natsume, Kinnosuke
See also DLB 180
Natti, (Mary) Lee 1919-
See Kingman, Lee
See also CA 5-8R; CANR 2
Naylor, Gloria 1950-**CLC 28, 52; BLC 3; DA;**
DAC; DAM MST, MULT, NOV, POP;
WLCS
See also AAYA 6; BW 2; CA 107; CANR 27,
51, 74; DLB 173; MTCW 1
Neihardt, John Gneisenau 1881-1973**CLC 32**
See also CA 13-14; CANR 65; CAP 1; DLB 9,
54
Nekrasov, Nikolai Alekseevich 1821-1878
NCLC 11

Nelligan, Emile 1879-1941 .... **TCLC 14**
See also CA 114; DLB 92
Nelson, Willie 1933- .... **CLC 17**
See also CA 107
Nemerov, Howard (Stanley) 1920-1991**CLC 2,**
6, 9, 36; DAM POET; PC 24
See also CA 1-4R; 134; CABS 2; CANR 1, 27,
53; DLB 5, 6; DLBY 83; INT CANR-27;
MTCW 1
Neruda, Pablo 1904-1973**CLC 1, 2, 5, 7, 9, 28,**
62; DA; DAB; DAC; DAM MST, MULT,
POET; HLC; PC 4; WLC
See also CA 19-20; 45-48; CAP 2; HW; MTCW
1
Nerval, Gerard de 1808-1855**NCLC 1, 67; PC**
13; SSC 18
Nervo, (Jose) Amado (Ruiz de) 1870-1919
TCLC 11
See also CA 109; 131; HW
Nessi, Pio Baroja y
See Baroja (y Nessi), Pio
Nestroy, Johann 1801-1862 .... **NCLC 42**
See also DLB 133
Netterville, Luke
See O'Grady, Standish (James)
Neufeld, John (Arthur) 1938- .... **CLC 17**
See also AAYA 11; CA 25-28R; CANR 11, 37,
56; CLR 52; MAICYA; SAAS 3; SATA 6,
81
Neville, Emily Cheney 1919- .... **CLC 12**
See also CA 5-8R; CANR 3, 37; JRDA;
MAICYA; SAAS 2; SATA 1
Newbound, Bernard Slade 1930-
See Slade, Bernard
See also CA 81-84; CANR 49; DAM DRAM
Newby, P(ercy) H(oward) 1918-1997 **CLC 2,**
13; DAM NOV
See also CA 5-8R; 161; CANR 32, 67; DLB
15; MTCW 1
Newlove, Donald 1928- .... **CLC 6**
See also CA 29-32R; CANR 25
Newlove, John (Herbert) 1938- .... **CLC 14**
See also CA 21-24R; CANR 9, 25
Newman, Charles 1938- .... **CLC 2, 8**
See also CA 21-24R
Newman, Edwin (Harold) 1919- .... **CLC 14**
See also AITN 1; CA 69-72; CANR 5
Newman, John Henry 1801-1890 ..**NCLC 38**
See also DLB 18, 32, 55
Newton, (Sir)Isaac 1642-1727 .... **LC 35**
Newton, Suzanne 1936- .... **CLC 35**
See also CA 41-44R; CANR 14; JRDA; SATA
5, 77
Nexo, Martin Andersen 1869-1954 **TCLC 43**
Nezval, Vitezslav 1900-1958 .... **TCLC 44**
See also CA 123
Ng, Fae Myenne 1957(?)- .... **CLC 81**
See also CA 146
Ngema, Mbongeni 1955- .... **CLC 57**
See also BW 2; CA 143
Ngugi, James T(hiong'o) .... **CLC 3, 7, 13**
See also Ngugi wa Thiong'o
Ngugi wa Thiong'o 1938- .. **CLC 36; BLC 3;**
DAM MULT, NOV
See also Ngugi, James T(hiong'o)
See also BW 2; CA 81-84; CANR 27, 58; DLB
125; MTCW 1
Nichol, B(arrie) P(hillip) 1944-1988 **CLC 18**
See also CA 53-56; DLB 53; SATA 66
Nichols, John (Treadwell) 1940- .... **CLC 38**
See also CA 9-12R; CAAS 2; CANR 6, 70;
DLBY 82
Nichols, Leigh
See Koontz, Dean R(ay)
Nichols, Peter (Richard) 1927- **CLC 5, 36, 65**
See also CA 104; CANR 33; DLB 13; MTCW
1

Nicolas, F. R. E.
See Freeling, Nicolas
Niedecker, Lorine 1903-1970 .... **CLC 10, 42;**
DAM POET
See also CA 25-28; CAP 2; DLB 48
Nietzsche, Friedrich (Wilhelm) 1844-1900
TCLC 10, 18, 55
See also CA 107; 121; DLB 129
Nievo, Ippolito 1831-1861 .... **NCLC 22**
Nightingale, Anne Redmon 1943-
See Redmon, Anne
See also CA 103
Nightingale, Florence 1820-1910 ... **TCLC 85**
See also DLB 166
Nik. T. O.
See Annensky, Innokenty (Fyodorovich)
Nin, Anais 1903-1977**CLC 1, 4, 8, 11, 14, 60;**
DAM NOV, POP; SSC 10
See also AITN 2; CA 13-16R; 69-72; CANR
22, 53; DLB 2, 4, 152; MTCW 1
Nishida, Kitaro 1870-1945 .... **TCLC 83**
Nishiwaki, Junzaburo 1894-1982 .... **PC 15**
See also CA 107
Nissenson, Hugh 1933- .... **CLC 4, 9**
See also CA 17-20R; CANR 27; DLB 28
Niven, Larry .... **CLC 8**
See also Niven, Laurence Van Cott
See also AAYA 27; DLB 8
Niven, Laurence Van Cott 1938-
See Niven, Larry
See also CA 21-24R; CAAS 12; CANR 14, 44,
66; DAM POP; MTCW 1; SATA 95
Nixon, Agnes Eckhardt 1927- .... **CLC 21**
See also CA 110
Nizan, Paul 1905-1940 .... **TCLC 40**
See also CA 161; DLB 72
Nkosi, Lewis 1936- .... **CLC 45; BLC 3; DAM**
MULT
See also BW 1; CA 65-68; CANR 27; DLB 157
Nodier, (Jean) Charles (Emmanuel) 1780-1844
NCLC 19
See also DLB 119
Noguchi, Yone 1875-1947 .... **TCLC 80**
Nolan, Christopher 1965- .... **CLC 58**
See also CA 111
Noon, Jeff 1957- .... **CLC 91**
See also CA 148
Norden, Charles
See Durrell, Lawrence (George)
Nordhoff, Charles (Bernard) 1887-1947
TCLC 23
See also CA 108; DLB 9; SATA 23
Norfolk, Lawrence 1963- .... **CLC 76**
See also CA 144
Norman, Marsha 1947-**CLC 28; DAM DRAM;**
DC 8
See also CA 105; CABS 3; CANR 41; DLBY
84
Normyx
See Douglas, (George) Norman
Norris, Frank 1870-1902 .... **SSC 28**
See also Norris, (Benjamin) Frank(lin, Jr.)
See also CDALB 1865-1917; DLB 12, 71, 186
Norris, (Benjamin) Frank(lin, Jr.) 1870-1902
TCLC 24
See also Norris, Frank
See also CA 110; 160
Norris, Leslie 1921- .... **CLC 14**
See also CA 11-12; CANR 14; CAP 1; DLB 27
North, Andrew
See Norton, Andre
North, Anthony
See Koontz, Dean R(ay)
North, Captain George
See Stevenson, Robert Louis (Balfour)
North, Milou
See Erdrich, Louise

DRAM; MTCW 1
Orwell, George . TCLC 2, 6, 15, 31, 51; DAB; WLC
See also Blair, Eric (Arthur)
See also CDBLB 1945-1960; DLB 15, 98, 195
Osborne, David
See Silverberg, Robert
Osborne, George
See Silverberg, Robert
Osborne, John (James) 1929-1994 CLC 1, 2, 5, 11, 45; DA; DAB; DAC; DAM DRAM, MST; WLC
See also CA 13-16R; 147; CANR 21, 56; CDBLB 1945-1960; DLB 13; MTCW 1
Osborne, Lawrence 1958- .... CLC 50
Oshima, Nagisa 1932- .... CLC 20
See also CA 116; 121
Oskison, John Milton 1874-1947 .. TCLC 35; DAM MULT
See also CA 144; DLB 175; NNAL
Ossian c. 3rd cent. - .... CMLC 28
See also Macpherson, James
Ossoli, Sarah Margaret (Fuller marchesa d') 1810-1850
See Fuller, Margaret
See also SATA 25
Ostrovsky, Alexander 1823-1886 NCLC 30, 57
Otero, Blas de 1916-1979 .... CLC 11
See also CA 89-92; DLB 134
Otto, Rudolf 1869-1937 .... TCLC 85
Otto, Whitney 1955- .... CLC 70
See also CA 140
Ouida .... TCLC 43
See also De La Ramee, (Marie) Louise
See also DLB 18, 156
Ousmane, Sembene 1923- .... CLC 66; BLC 3
See also BW 1; CA 117; 125; MTCW 1
Ovid 43B.C.-18(?) CMLC 7; DAM POET; PC 2
Owen, Hugh
See Faust, Frederick (Schiller)
Owen, Wilfred (Edward Salter) 1893-1918 TCLC 5, 27; DA; DAB; DAC; DAM MST, POET; PC 19; WLC
See also CA 104; 141; CDBLB 1914-1945; DLB 20
Owens, Rochelle 1936- .... CLC 8
See also CA 17-20R; CAAS 2; CANR 39
Oz, Amos 1939- CLC 5, 8, 11, 27, 33, 54; DAM NOV
See also CA 53-56; CANR 27, 47, 65; MTCW 1
Ozick, Cynthia 1928- CLC 3, 7, 28, 62; DAM NOV, POP; SSC 15
See also BEST 90:1; CA 17-20R; CANR 23, 58; DLB 28, 152; DLBY 82; INT CANR-23; MTCW 1
Ozu, Yasujiro 1903-1963 .... CLC 16
See also CA 112
Pacheco, C.
See Pessoa, Fernando (Antonio Nogueira)
Pa Chin .... CLC 18
See also Li Fei-kan
Pack, Robert 1929- .... CLC 13
See also CA 1-4R; CANR 3, 44; DLB 5
Padgett, Lewis
See Kuttner, Henry
Padilla (Lorenzo), Heberto 1932- ..... CLC 38
See also AITN 1; CA 123; 131; HW
Page, Jimmy 1944- .... CLC 12
Page, Louise 1955- .... CLC 40
See also CA 140; CANR 76
Page, P(atricia) K(athleen) 1916- CLC 7, 18; DAC; DAM MST; PC 12
See also CA 53-56; CANR 4, 22, 65; DLB 68; MTCW 1
Page, Thomas Nelson 1853-1922 .... SSC 23

See also CA 118; DLB 12, 78; DLBD 13
Pagels, Elaine Hiesey 1943- .... CLC 104
See also CA 45-48; CANR 2, 24, 51
Paget, Violet 1856-1935
See Lee, Vernon
See also CA 104; 166
Paget-Lowe, Henry
See Lovecraft, H(oward) P(hillips)
Paglia, Camille (Anna) 1947- .... CLC 68
See also CA 140; CANR 72
Paige, Richard
See Koontz, Dean R(ay)
Paine, Thomas 1737-1809 .... NCLC 62
See also CDALB 1640-1865; DLB 31, 43, 73, 158
Pakenham, Antonia
See Fraser, (Lady) Antonia (Pakenham)
Palamas, Kostes 1859-1943 .... TCLC 5
See also CA 105
Palazzeschi, Aldo 1885-1974 .... CLC 11
See also CA 89-92; 53-56; DLB 114
Paley, Grace 1922- CLC 4, 6, 37; DAM POP; SSC 8
See also CA 25-28R; CANR 13, 46, 74; DLB 28; INT CANR-13; MTCW 1
Palin, Michael (Edward) 1943- .... CLC 21
See also Monty Python
See also CA 107; CANR 35; SATA 67
Palliser, Charles 1947- .... CLC 65
See also CA 136; CANR 76
Palma, Ricardo 1833-1919 .... TCLC 29
See also CA 168
Pancake, Breece Dexter 1952-1979
See Pancake, Breece D'J
See also CA 123; 109
Pancake, Breece D'J .... CLC 29
See also Pancake, Breece Dexter
See also DLB 130
Panko, Rudy
See Gogol, Nikolai (Vasilyevich)
Papadiamantis, Alexandros 1851-1911 TCLC 29
See also CA 168
Papadiamantopoulos, Johannes 1856-1910
See Moreas, Jean
See also CA 117
Papini, Giovanni 1881-1956 .... TCLC 22
See also CA 121
Paracelsus 1493-1541 .... LC 14
See also DLB 179
Parasol, Peter
See Stevens, Wallace
Pardo Bazan, Emilia 1851-1921 .... SSC 30
Pareto, Vilfredo 1848-1923 .... TCLC 69
Parfenie, Maria
See Codrescu, Andrei
Parini, Jay (Lee) 1948- .... CLC 54
See also CA 97-100; CAAS 16; CANR 32
Park, Jordan
See Kornbluth, C(yril) M.; Pohl, Frederik
Park, Robert E(zra) 1864-1944 ...... TCLC 73
See also CA 122; 165
Parker, Bert
See Ellison, Harlan (Jay)
Parker, Dorothy (Rothschild) 1893-1967 CLC 15, 68; DAM POET; SSC 2
See also CA 19-20; 25-28R; CAP 2; DLB 11, 45, 86; MTCW 1
Parker, Robert B(rown) 1932- CLC 27; DAM NOV, POP
See also BEST 89:4; CA 49-52; CANR 1, 26, 52; INT CANR-26; MTCW 1
Parkin, Frank 1940- .... CLC 43
See also CA 147
Parkman, Francis, Jr. 1823-1893 .. NCLC 12
See also DLB 1, 30, 186
Parks, Gordon (Alexander Buchanan) 1912-

CLC 1, 16; BLC 3; DAM MULT
See also AITN 2; BW 2; CA 41-44R; CANR 26, 66; DLB 33; SATA 8
Parmenides c. 515B.C.-c. 450B.C. CMLC 22
See also DLB 176
Parnell, Thomas 1679-1718 .... LC 3
See also DLB 94
Parra, Nicanor 1914- ...... CLC 2, 102; DAM MULT; HLC
See also CA 85-88; CANR 32; HW; MTCW 1
Parrish, Mary Frances
See Fisher, M(ary) F(rances) K(ennedy)
Parson
See Coleridge, Samuel Taylor
Parson Lot
See Kingsley, Charles
Partridge, Anthony
See Oppenheim, E(dward) Phillips
Pascal, Blaise 1623-1662 .... LC 35
Pascoli, Giovanni 1855-1912 .... TCLC 45
See also CA 170
Pasolini, Pier Paolo 1922-1975 . CLC 20, 37, 106; PC 17
See also CA 93-96; 61-64; CANR 63; DLB 128, 177; MTCW 1
Pasquini
See Silone, Ignazio
Pastan, Linda (Olenik) 1932- CLC 27; DAM POET
See also CA 61-64; CANR 18, 40, 61; DLB 5
Pasternak, Boris (Leonidovich) 1890-1960 CLC 7, 10, 18, 63; DA; DAB; DAC; DAM MST, NOV, POET; PC 6; SSC 31; WLC
See also CA 127; 116; MTCW 1
Patchen, Kenneth 1911-1972 ... CLC 1, 2, 18; DAM POET
See also CA 1-4R; 33-36R; CANR 3, 35; DLB 16, 48; MTCW 1
Pater, Walter (Horatio) 1839-1894 .. NCLC 7
See also CDBLB 1832-1890; DLB 57, 156
Paterson, A(ndrew) B(arton) 1864-1941 TCLC 32
See also CA 155; SATA 97
Paterson, Katherine (Womeldorf) 1932- CLC 12, 30
See also AAYA 1; CA 21-24R; CANR 28, 59; CLR 7, 50; DLB 52; JRDA; MAICYA; MTCW 1; SATA 13, 53, 92
Patmore, Coventry Kersey Dighton 1823-1896 NCLC 9
See also DLB 35, 98
Paton, Alan (Stewart) 1903-1988 CLC 4, 10, 25, 55, 106; DA; DAB; DAC; DAM MST, NOV; WLC
See also AAYA 26; CA 13-16; 125; CANR 22; CAP 1; DLBD 17; MTCW 1; SATA 11; SATA-Obit 56
Paton Walsh, Gillian 1937-
See Walsh, Jill Paton
See also CANR 38; JRDA; MAICYA; SAAS 3; SATA 4, 72
Patton, George S. 1885-1945 .... TCLC 79
Paulding, James Kirke 1778-1860 ... NCLC 2
See also DLB 3, 59, 74
Paulin, Thomas Neilson 1949-
See Paulin, Tom
See also CA 123; 128
Paulin, Tom .... CLC 37
See also Paulin, Thomas Neilson
See also DLB 40
Paustovsky, Konstantin (Georgievich) 1892-1968 .... CLC 40
See also CA 93-96; 25-28R
Pavese, Cesare 1908-1950 ... TCLC 3; PC 13; SSC 19
See also CA 104; 169; DLB 128, 177
Pavic, Milorad 1929- .... CLC 60

5, 6

Slesinger, Tess 1905-1945 .... **TCLC 10**
See also CA 107; DLB 102

Slessor, Kenneth 1901-1971 .... **CLC 14**
See also CA 102; 89-92

Slowacki, Juliusz 1809-1849 .... **NCLC 15**

Smart, Christopher 1722-1771 ..**LC 3; DAM POET; PC 13**
See also DLB 109

Smart, Elizabeth 1913-1986 .... **CLC 54**
See also CA 81-84; 118; DLB 88

Smiley, Jane (Graves) 1949-**CLC 53, 76; DAM POP**
See also CA 104; CANR 30, 50, 74; INT CANR-30

Smith, A(rthur) J(ames) M(arshall) 1902-1980 **CLC 15; DAC**
See also CA 1-4R; 102; CANR 4; DLB 88

Smith, Adam 1723-1790 .... **LC 36**
See also DLB 104

Smith, Alexander 1829-1867 .... **NCLC 59**
See also DLB 32, 55

Smith, Anna Deavere 1950- .... **CLC 86**
See also CA 133

Smith, Betty (Wehner) 1896-1972 .... **CLC 19**
See also CA 5-8R; 33-36R; DLBY 82; SATA 6

Smith, Charlotte (Turner) 1749-1806 **N C L C 23**
See also DLB 39, 109

Smith, Clark Ashton 1893-1961 .... **CLC 43**
See also CA 143

Smith, Dave .... **CLC 22, 42**
See also Smith, David (Jeddie)
See also CAAS 7; DLB 5

Smith, David (Jeddie) 1942-
See Smith, Dave
See also CA 49-52; CANR 1, 59; DAM POET

Smith, Florence Margaret 1902-1971
See Smith, Stevie
See also CA 17-18; 29-32R; CANR 35; CAP 2; DAM POET; MTCW 1

Smith, Iain Crichton 1928-1998 .... **CLC 64**
See also CA 21-24R; 171; DLB 40, 139

Smith, John 1580(?)-1631 .... **LC 9**
See also DLB 24, 30

Smith, Johnston
See Crane, Stephen (Townley)

Smith, Joseph, Jr. 1805-1844 .... **NCLC 53**

Smith, Lee 1944- .... **CLC 25, 73**
See also CA 114; 119; CANR 46; DLB 143; DLBY 83; INT 119

Smith, Martin
See Smith, Martin Cruz

Smith, Martin Cruz 1942- ..... **CLC 25; DAM MULT, POP**
See also BEST 89:4; CA 85-88; CANR 6, 23, 43, 65; INT CANR-23; NNAL

Smith, Mary-Ann Tirone 1944- .... **CLC 39**
See also CA 118; 136

Smith, Patti 1946- .... **CLC 12**
See also CA 93-96; CANR 63

Smith, Pauline (Urmson) 1882-1959**TCLC 25**

Smith, Rosamond
See Oates, Joyce Carol

Smith, Sheila Kaye
See Kaye-Smith, Sheila

Smith, Stevie .... **CLC 3, 8, 25, 44; PC 12**
See also Smith, Florence Margaret
See also DLB 20

Smith, Wilbur (Addison) 1933- .... **CLC 33**
See also CA 13-16R; CANR 7, 46, 66; MTCW 1

Smith, William Jay 1918- .... **CLC 6**
See also CA 5-8R; CANR 44; DLB 5; MAICYA; SAAS 22; SATA 2, 68

Smith, Woodrow Wilson
See Kuttner, Henry

Smolenskin, Peretz 1842-1885 .... **NCLC 30**

Smollett, Tobias (George) 1721-1771**LC 2, 46**
See also CDBLB 1660-1789; DLB 39, 104

Snodgrass, W(illiam) D(e Witt) 1926-**CLC 2, 6, 10, 18, 68; DAM POET**
See also CA 1-4R; CANR 6, 36, 65; DLB 5; MTCW 1

Snow, C(harles) P(ercy) 1905-1980**CLC 1, 4, 6, 9, 13, 19; DAM NOV**
See also CA 5-8R; 101; CANR 28; CDBLB 1945-1960; DLB 15, 77; DLBD 17; MTCW 1

Snow, Frances Compton
See Adams, Henry (Brooks)

Snyder, Gary (Sherman) 1930-**CLC 1, 2, 5, 9, 32; DAM POET; PC 21**
See also CA 17-20R; CANR 30, 60; DLB 5, 16, 165

Snyder, Zilpha Keatley 1927- .... **CLC 17**
See also AAYA 15; CA 9-12R; CANR 38; CLR 31; JRDA; MAICYA; SAAS 2; SATA 1, 28, 75

Soares, Bernardo
See Pessoa, Fernando (Antonio Nogueira)

Sobh, A.
See Shamlu, Ahmad

Sobol, Joshua .... **CLC 60**

Socrates 469B.C.-399B.C. .... **CMLC 27**

Soderberg, Hjalmar 1869-1941 ..... **TCLC 39**

Sodergran, Edith (Irene)
See Soedergran, Edith (Irene)

Soedergran, Edith (Irene) 1892-1923 **T C L C 31**

Softly, Edgar
See Lovecraft, H(oward) P(hillips)

Softly, Edward
See Lovecraft, H(oward) P(hillips)

Sokolov, Raymond 1941- .... **CLC 7**
See also CA 85-88

Solo, Jay
See Ellison, Harlan (Jay)

Sologub, Fyodor .... **TCLC 9**
See also Teternikov, Fyodor Kuzmich

Solomons, Ikey Esquir
See Thackeray, William Makepeace

Solomos, Dionysios 1798-1857 .... **NCLC 15**

Solwoska, Mara
See French, Marilyn

Solzhenitsyn, Aleksandr I(sayevich) 1918-**CLC 1, 2, 4, 7, 9, 10, 18, 26, 34, 78; DA; DAB; DAC; DAM MST, NOV; SSC 32; WLC**
See also AITN 1; CA 69-72; CANR 40, 65; MTCW 1

Somers, Jane
See Lessing, Doris (May)

Somerville, Edith 1858-1949 .... **TCLC 51**
See also DLB 135

Somerville & Ross
See Martin, Violet Florence; Somerville, Edith

Sommer, Scott 1951- .... **CLC 25**
See also CA 106

Sondheim, Stephen (Joshua) 1930- .**CLC 30, 39; DAM DRAM**
See also AAYA 11; CA 103; CANR 47, 68

Song, Cathy 1955- .... **PC 21**
See also CA 154; DLB 169

Sontag, Susan 1933-**CLC 1, 2, 10, 13, 31, 105; DAM POP**
See also CA 17-20R; CANR 25, 51, 74; DLB 2, 67; MTCW 1

Sophocles 496(?)B.C.-406(?)B.C. ... **CMLC 2; DA; DAB; DAC; DAM DRAM, MST; DC 1; WLCS**
See also DLB 176

Sordello 1189-1269 .... **CMLC 15**

Sorel, Georges 1847-1922 .... **TCLC 91**

See also CA 118

Sorel, Julia
See Drexler, Rosalyn

Sorrentino, Gilbert 1929-**CLC 3, 7, 14, 22, 40**
See also CA 77-80; CANR 14, 33; DLB 5, 173; DLBY 80; INT CANR-14

Soto, Gary 1952- **CLC 32, 80; DAM MULT; HLC**
See also AAYA 10; CA 119; 125; CANR 50, 74; CLR 38; DLB 82; HW; INT 125; JRDA; SATA 80

Soupault, Philippe 1897-1990 .... **CLC 68**
See also CA 116; 147; 131

Souster, (Holmes) Raymond 1921-**CLC 5, 14; DAC; DAM POET**
See also CA 13-16R; CAAS 14; CANR 13, 29, 53; DLB 88; SATA 63

Southern, Terry 1924(?)-1995 .... **CLC 7**
See also CA 1-4R; 150; CANR 1, 55; DLB 2

Southey, Robert 1774-1843 .... **NCLC 8**
See also DLB 93, 107, 142; SATA 54

Southworth, Emma Dorothy Eliza Nevitte 1819-1899 ....
NCLC 26

Souza, Ernest
See Scott, Evelyn

Soyinka, Wole 1934-**CLC 3, 5, 14, 36, 44; BLC 3; DA; DAB; DAC; DAM DRAM, MST, MULT; DC 2; WLC**
See also BW 2; CA 13-16R; CANR 27, 39; DLB 125; MTCW 1

Spackman, W(illiam) M(ode) 1905-1990**C L C 46**
See also CA 81-84; 132

Spacks, Barry (Bernard) 1931- .... **CLC 14**
See also CA 154; CANR 33; DLB 105

Spanidou, Irini 1946- .... **CLC 44**

Spark, Muriel (Sarah) 1918-**CLC 2, 3, 5, 8, 13, 18, 40, 94; DAB; DAC; DAM MST, NOV; SSC 10**
See also CA 5-8R; CANR 12, 36, 76; CDBLB 1945-1960; DLB 15, 139; INT CANR-12; MTCW 1

Spaulding, Douglas
See Bradbury, Ray (Douglas)

Spaulding, Leonard
See Bradbury, Ray (Douglas)

Spence, J. A. D.
See Eliot, T(homas) S(tearns)

Spencer, Elizabeth 1921- .... **CLC 22**
See also CA 13-16R; CANR 32, 65; DLB 6; MTCW 1; SATA 14

Spencer, Leonard G.
See Silverberg, Robert

Spencer, Scott 1945- .... **CLC 30**
See also CA 113; CANR 51; DLBY 86

Spender, Stephen (Harold) 1909-1995**CLC 1, 2, 5, 10, 41, 91; DAM POET**
See also CA 9-12R; 149; CANR 31, 54; CDBLB 1945-1960; DLB 20; MTCW 1

Spengler, Oswald (Arnold Gottfried) 1880-1936 **TCLC 25**
See also CA 118

Spenser, Edmund 1552(?)-1599**LC 5, 39; DA; DAB; DAC; DAM MST, POET; PC 8; WLC**
See also CDBLB Before 1660; DLB 167

Spicer, Jack 1925-1965 **CLC 8, 18, 72; DAM POET**
See also CA 85-88; DLB 5, 16, 193

Spiegelman, Art 1948- .... **CLC 76**
See also AAYA 10; CA 125; CANR 41, 55, 74

Spielberg, Peter 1929- .... **CLC 6**
See also CA 5-8R; CANR 4, 48; DLBY 81

Spielberg, Steven 1947- .... **CLC 20**
See also AAYA 8, 24; CA 77-80; CANR 32; SATA 32

Tate, (John Orley) Allen 1899-1979**CLC 2, 4, 6, 9, 11, 14, 24**
　　See also CA 5-8R; 85-88; CANR 32; DLB 4, 45, 63; DLBD 17; MTCW 1
Tate, Ellalice
　　See Hibbert, Eleanor Alice Burford
Tate, James (Vincent) 1943- ..... **CLC 2, 6, 25**
　　See also CA 21-24R; CANR 29, 57; DLB 5, 169
Tavel, Ronald 1940-............................ **CLC 6**
　　See also CA 21-24R; CANR 33
Taylor, C(ecil) P(hilip) 1929-1981 .... **CLC 27**
　　See also CA 25-28R; 105; CANR 47
Taylor, Edward 1642(?)-1729 ..... **LC 11; DA; DAB; DAC; DAM MST, POET**
　　See also DLB 24
Taylor, Eleanor Ross 1920- .... **CLC 5**
　　See also CA 81-84; CANR 70
Taylor, Elizabeth 1912-1975..... **CLC 2, 4, 29**
　　See also CA 13-16R; CANR 9, 70; DLB 139; MTCW 1; SATA 13
Taylor, Frederick Winslow 1856-1915 **T C L C 76**
Taylor, Henry (Splawn) 1942-........... **CLC 44**
　　See also CA 33-36R; CAAS 7; CANR 31; DLB 5
Taylor, Kamala (Purnaiya) 1924-
　　See Markandaya, Kamala
　　See also CA 77-80
Taylor, Mildred D. .... **CLC 21**
　　See also AAYA 10; BW 1; CA 85-88; CANR 25; CLR 9; DLB 52; JRDA; MAICYA; SAAS 5; SATA 15, 70
Taylor, Peter (Hillsman) 1917-1994**CLC 1, 4, 18, 37, 44, 50, 71; SSC 10**
　　See also CA 13-16R; 147; CANR 9, 50; DLBY 81, 94; INT CANR-9; MTCW 1
Taylor, Robert Lewis 1912-1998 .... **CLC 14**
　　See also CA 1-4R; 170; CANR 3, 64; SATA 10
Tchekhov, Anton
　　See Chekhov, Anton (Pavlovich)
Tchicaya, Gerald Felix 1931-1988 .. **CLC 101**
　　See also CA 129; 125
Tchicaya U Tam'si
　　See Tchicaya, Gerald Felix
Teasdale, Sara 1884-1933 .... **TCLC 4**
　　See also CA 104; 163; DLB 45; SATA 32
Tegner, Esaias 1782-1846.................. **NCLC 2**
Teilhard de Chardin, (Marie Joseph) Pierre 1881-1955 ....

TCLC 9
　　See also CA 105
Temple, Ann
　　See Mortimer, Penelope (Ruth)
Tennant, Emma (Christina) 1937-**CLC 13, 52**
　　See also CA 65-68; CAAS 9; CANR 10, 38, 59; DLB 14
Tenneshaw, S. M.
　　See Silverberg, Robert
Tennyson, Alfred 1809-1892... **NCLC 30, 65; DA; DAB; DAC; DAM MST, POET; PC 6; WLC**
　　See also CDBLB 1832-1890; DLB 32
Teran, Lisa St. Aubin de .... **CLC 36**
　　See also St. Aubin de Teran, Lisa
Terence 195(?)B.C.-159B.C. **CMLC 14; DC 7**
Teresa de Jesus, St. 1515-1582 .... **LC 18**
Terkel, Louis 1912-
　　See Terkel, Studs
　　See also CA 57-60; CANR 18, 45, 67; MTCW 1
Terkel, Studs .... **CLC 38**
　　See also Terkel, Louis
　　See also AITN 1
Terry, C. V.
　　See Slaughter, Frank G(ill)
Terry, Megan 1932- .... **CLC 19**

　　See also CA 77-80; CABS 3; CANR 43; DLB 7
Tertullian c. 155-c. 245 .... **CMLC 29**
Tertz, Abram
　　See Sinyavsky, Andrei (Donatevich)
Tesich, Steve 1943(?)-1996 .... **CLC 40, 69**
　　See also CA 105; 152; DLBY 83
Tesla, Nikola 1856-1943 .... **TCLC 88**
Teternikov, Fyodor Kuzmich 1863-1927
　　See Sologub, Fyodor
　　See also CA 104
Tevis, Walter 1928-1984 .... **CLC 42**
　　See also CA 113
Tey, Josephine .... **TCLC 14**
　　See also Mackintosh, Elizabeth
　　See also DLB 77
Thackeray, William Makepeace 1811-1863
NCLC 5, 14, 22, 43; DA; DAB; DAC; DAM MST, NOV; WLC
　　See also CDBLB 1832-1890; DLB 21, 55, 159, 163; SATA 23
Thakura, Ravindranatha
　　See Tagore, Rabindranath
Tharoor, Shashi 1956- .... **CLC 70**
　　See also CA 141
Thelwell, Michael Miles 1939- .... **CLC 22**
　　See also BW 2; CA 101
Theobald, Lewis, Jr.
　　See Lovecraft, H(oward) P(hillips)
Theodorescu, Ion N. 1880-1967
　　See Arghezi, Tudor
　　See also CA 116
Theriault, Yves 1915-1983 .... **CLC 79; DAC; DAM MST**
　　See also CA 102; DLB 88
Theroux, Alexander (Louis) 1939-**CLC 2, 25**
　　See also CA 85-88; CANR 20, 63
Theroux, Paul (Edward) 1941- **CLC 5, 8, 11, 15, 28, 46; DAM POP**
　　See also BEST 89:4; CA 33-36R; CANR 20, 45, 74; DLB 2; MTCW 1; SATA 44
Thesen, Sharon 1946- .... **CLC 56**
　　See also CA 163
Thevenin, Denis
　　See Duhamel, Georges
Thibault, Jacques Anatole Francois 1844-1924
　　See France, Anatole
　　See also CA 106; 127; DAM NOV; MTCW 1
Thiele, Colin (Milton) 1920- .... **CLC 17**
　　See also CA 29-32R; CANR 12, 28, 53; CLR 27; MAICYA; SAAS 2; SATA 14, 72
Thomas, Audrey (Callahan) 1935-**CLC 7, 13, 37, 107; SSC 20**
　　See also AITN 2; CA 21-24R; CAAS 19; CANR 36, 58; DLB 60; MTCW 1
Thomas, D(onald) M(ichael) 1935- . **CLC 13, 22, 31**
　　See also CA 61-64; CAAS 11; CANR 17, 45, 75; CDBLB 1960 to Present; DLB 40, 207; INT CANR-17; MTCW 1
Thomas, Dylan (Marlais) 1914-1953**TCLC 1, 8, 45; DA; DAB; DAC; DAM DRAM, MST, POET; PC 2; SSC 3; WLC**
　　See also CA 104; 120; CANR 65; CDBLB 1945-1960; DLB 13, 20, 139; MTCW 1; SATA 60
Thomas, (Philip) Edward 1878-1917 . **T C L C 10; DAM POET**
　　See also CA 106; 153; DLB 98
Thomas, Joyce Carol 1938- .... **CLC 35**
　　See also AAYA 12; BW 2; CA 113; 116; CANR 48; CLR 19; DLB 33; INT 116; JRDA; MAICYA; MTCW 1; SAAS 7; SATA 40, 78
Thomas, Lewis 1913-1993 .... **CLC 35**
　　See also CA 85-88; 143; CANR 38, 60; MTCW 1
Thomas, M. Carey 1857-1935 .... **TCLC 89**
Thomas, Paul

　　See Mann, (Paul) Thomas
Thomas, Piri 1928- .... **CLC 17**
　　See also CA 73-76; HW
Thomas, R(onald) S(tuart) 1913- **CLC 6, 13, 48; DAB; DAM POET**
　　See also CA 89-92; CAAS 4; CANR 30; CDBLB 1960 to Present; DLB 27; MTCW 1
Thomas, Ross (Elmore) 1926-1995 ... **CLC 39**
　　See also CA 33-36R; 150; CANR 22, 63
Thompson, Francis Clegg
　　See Mencken, H(enry) L(ouis)
Thompson, Francis Joseph 1859-1907**TCLC 4**
　　See also CA 104; CDBLB 1890-1914; DLB 19
Thompson, Hunter S(tockton) 1939- **CLC 9, 17, 40, 104; DAM POP**
　　See also BEST 89:1; CA 17-20R; CANR 23, 46, 74; DLB 185; MTCW 1
Thompson, James Myers
　　See Thompson, Jim (Myers)
Thompson, Jim (Myers) 1906-1977(?)**CLC 69**
　　See also CA 140
Thompson, Judith .... **CLC 39**
Thomson, James 1700-1748 ... **LC 16, 29, 40; DAM POET**
　　See also DLB 95
Thomson, James 1834-1882 **NCLC 18; DAM POET**
　　See also DLB 35
Thoreau, Henry David 1817-1862**NCLC 7, 21, 61; DA; DAB; DAC; DAM MST; WLC**
　　See also CDALB 1640-1865; DLB 1
Thornton, Hall
　　See Silverberg, Robert
Thucydides c. 455B.C.-399B.C. .... **CMLC 17**
　　See also DLB 176
Thurber, James (Grover) 1894-1961 . **CLC 5, 11, 25; DA; DAB; DAC; DAM DRAM, MST, NOV; SSC 1**
　　See also CA 73-76; CANR 17, 39; CDALB 1929-1941; DLB 4, 11, 22, 102; MAICYA; MTCW 1; SATA 13
Thurman, Wallace (Henry) 1902-1934**T C L C 6; BLC 3; DAM MULT**
　　See also BW 1; CA 104; 124; DLB 51
Ticheburn, Cheviot
　　See Ainsworth, William Harrison
Tieck, (Johann) Ludwig 1773-1853 **NCLC 5, 46; SSC 31**
　　See also DLB 90
Tiger, Derry
　　See Ellison, Harlan (Jay)
Tilghman, Christopher 1948(?)- .... **CLC 65**
　　See also CA 159
Tillinghast, Richard (Williford) 1940-**CLC 29**
　　See also CA 29-32R; CAAS 23; CANR 26, 51
Timrod, Henry 1828-1867 .... **NCLC 25**
　　See also DLB 3
Tindall, Gillian (Elizabeth) 1938- ...... **CLC 7**
　　See also CA 21-24R; CANR 11, 65
Tiptree, James, Jr. .... **CLC 48, 50**
　　See also Sheldon, Alice Hastings Bradley
　　See also DLB 8
Titmarsh, Michael Angelo
　　See Thackeray, William Makepeace
Tocqueville, Alexis (Charles Henri Maurice Clerel, Comte) de 1805-1859**NCLC 7, 63**
Tolkien, J(ohn) R(onald) R(euel) 1892-1973 **CLC 1, 2, 3, 8, 12, 38; DA; DAB; DAC; DAM MST, NOV, POP; WLC**
　　See also AAYA 10; AITN 1; CA 17-18; 45-48; CANR 36; CAP 2; CDBLB 1914-1945; DLB 15, 160; JRDA; MAICYA; MTCW 1; SATA 2, 32, 100; SATA-Obit 24
Toller, Ernst 1893-1939 .... **TCLC 10**
　　See also CA 107; DLB 124
Tolson, M. B.
　　See Tolson, Melvin B(eaunorus)

Tolson, Melvin B(eaunorus) 1898(?)-1966 **CLC 36, 105; BLC 3; DAM MULT, POET**
See also BW 1; CA 124; 89-92; DLB 48, 76

Tolstoi, Aleksei Nikolaevich
See Tolstoy, Alexey Nikolaevich

Tolstoy, Alexey Nikolaevich 1882-1945**T C L C 18**
See also CA 107; 158

Tolstoy, Count Leo
See Tolstoy, Leo (Nikolaevich)

Tolstoy, Leo (Nikolaevich) 1828-1910**TCLC 4, 11, 17, 28, 44, 79; DA; DAB; DAC; DAM MST, NOV; SSC 9, 30; WLC**
See also CA 104; 123; SATA 26

Tomasi di Lampedusa, Giuseppe 1896-1957
See Lampedusa, Giuseppe (Tomasi) di
See also CA 111

Tomlin, Lily .... **CLC 17**
See also Tomlin, Mary Jean

Tomlin, Mary Jean 1939(?)-
See Tomlin, Lily
See also CA 117

Tomlinson, (Alfred) Charles 1927-**CLC 2, 4, 6, 13, 45; DAM POET; PC 17**
See also CA 5-8R; CANR 33; DLB 40

Tomlinson, H(enry) M(ajor) 1873-1958**TCLC 71**
See also CA 118; 161; DLB 36, 100, 195

Tonson, Jacob
See Bennett, (Enoch) Arnold

Toole, John Kennedy 1937-1969 **CLC 19, 64**
See also CA 104; DLBY 81

Toomer, Jean 1894-1967**CLC 1, 4, 13, 22; BLC 3; DAM MULT; PC 7; SSC 1; WLCS**
See also BW 1; CA 85-88; CDALB 1917-1929; DLB 45, 51; MTCW 1

Torley, Luke
See Blish, James (Benjamin)

Tornimparte, Alessandra
See Ginzburg, Natalia

Torre, Raoul della
See Mencken, H(enry) L(ouis)

Torrey, E(dwin) Fuller 1937- .... **CLC 34**
See also CA 119; CANR 71

Torsvan, Ben Traven
See Traven, B.

Torsvan, Benno Traven
See Traven, B.

Torsvan, Berick Traven
See Traven, B.

Torsvan, Berwick Traven
See Traven, B.

Torsvan, Bruno Traven
See Traven, B.

Torsvan, Traven
See Traven, B.

Tournier, Michel (Edouard) 1924-**CLC 6, 23, 36, 95**
See also CA 49-52; CANR 3, 36, 74; DLB 83; MTCW 1; SATA 23

Tournimparte, Alessandra
See Ginzburg, Natalia

Towers, Ivar
See Kornbluth, C(yril) M.

Towne, Robert (Burton) 1936(?)- ..... **CLC 87**
See also CA 108; DLB 44

Townsend, Sue .... **CLC 61**
See also Townsend, Susan Elaine
See also SATA 55, 93; SATA-Brief 48

Townsend, Susan Elaine 1946-
See Townsend, Sue
See also CA 119; 127; CANR 65; DAB; DAC; DAM MST

Townshend, Peter (Dennis Blandford) 1945-
CLC 17, 42
See also CA 107

Tozzi, Federigo 1883-1920 .... **TCLC 31**

See also CA 160

Traill, Catharine Parr 1802-1899 .. **NCLC 31**
See also DLB 99

Trakl, Georg 1887-1914 .... **TCLC 5; PC 20**
See also CA 104; 165

Transtroemer, Tomas (Goesta) 1931-**CLC 52, 65; DAM POET**
See also CA 117; 129; CAAS 17

Transtromer, Tomas Gosta
See Transtroemer, Tomas (Goesta)

Traven, B. (?)-1969 .... **CLC 8, 11**
See also CA 19-20; 25-28R; CAP 2; DLB 9, 56; MTCW 1

Treitel, Jonathan 1959- .... **CLC 70**

Tremain, Rose 1943- .... **CLC 42**
See also CA 97-100; CANR 44; DLB 14

Tremblay, Michel 1942- **CLC 29, 102; DAC; DAM MST**
See also CA 116; 128; DLB 60; MTCW 1

Trevanian .... **CLC 29**
See also Whitaker, Rod(ney)

Trevor, Glen
See Hilton, James

Trevor, William 1928-**CLC 7, 9, 14, 25, 71, 116; SSC 21**
See also Cox, William Trevor
See also DLB 14, 139

Trifonov, Yuri (Valentinovich) 1925-1981 **CLC 45**
See also CA 126; 103; MTCW 1

Trilling, Lionel 1905-1975 ...... **CLC 9, 11, 24**
See also CA 9-12R; 61-64; CANR 10; DLB 28, 63; INT CANR-10; MTCW 1

Trimball, W. H.
See Mencken, H(enry) L(ouis)

Tristan
See Gomez de la Serna, Ramon

Tristram
See Housman, A(lfred) E(dward)

Trogdon, William (Lewis) 1939-
See Heat-Moon, William Least
See also CA 115; 119; CANR 47; INT 119

Trollope, Anthony 1815-1882**NCLC 6, 33; DA; DAB; DAC; DAM MST, NOV; SSC 28; WLC**
See also CDBLB 1832-1890; DLB 21, 57, 159; SATA 22

Trollope, Frances 1779-1863 .... **NCLC 30**
See also DLB 21, 166

Trotsky, Leon 1879-1940 .... **TCLC 22**
See also CA 118; 167

Trotter (Cockburn), Catharine 1679-1749**L C 8**
See also DLB 84

Trout, Kilgore
See Farmer, Philip Jose

Trow, George W. S. 1943- .... **CLC 52**
See also CA 126

Troyat, Henri 1911- .... **CLC 23**
See also CA 45-48; CANR 2, 33, 67; MTCW 1

Trudeau, G(arretson) B(eekman) 1948-
See Trudeau, Garry B.
See also CA 81-84; CANR 31; SATA 35

Trudeau, Garry B. .... **CLC 12**
See also Trudeau, G(arretson) B(eekman)
See also AAYA 10; AITN 2

Truffaut, Francois 1932-1984 .. **CLC 20, 101**
See also CA 81-84; 113; CANR 34

Trumbo, Dalton 1905-1976 .... **CLC 19**
See also CA 21-24R; 69-72; CANR 10; DLB 26

Trumbull, John 1750-1831 .... **NCLC 30**
See also DLB 31

Trundlett, Helen B.
See Eliot, T(homas) S(tearns)

Tryon, Thomas 1926-1991 .**CLC 3, 11; DAM POP**

See also AITN 1; CA 29-32R; 135; CANR 32; MTCW 1

Tryon, Tom
See Tryon, Thomas

Ts'ao Hsueh-ch'in 1715(?)-1763 .... **LC 1**

Tsushima, Shuji 1909-1948
See Dazai Osamu
See also CA 107

Tsvetaeva (Efron), Marina (Ivanovna) 1892-1941 .... **TCLC 7, 35; PC 14**
See also CA 104; 128; CANR 73; MTCW 1

Tuck, Lily 1938- .... **CLC 70**
See also CA 139

Tu Fu 712-770 .... **PC 9**
See also DAM MULT

Tunis, John R(oberts) 1889-1975 ...... **CLC 12**
See also CA 61-64; CANR 62; DLB 22, 171; JRDA; MAICYA; SATA 37; SATA-Brief 30

Tuohy, Frank .... **CLC 37**
See also Tuohy, John Francis
See also DLB 14, 139

Tuohy, John Francis 1925-
See Tuohy, Frank
See also CA 5-8R; CANR 3, 47

Turco, Lewis (Putnam) 1934- ...... **CLC 11, 63**
See also CA 13-16R; CAAS 22; CANR 24, 51; DLBY 84

Turgenev, Ivan 1818-1883 .... **NCLC 21; DA; DAB; DAC; DAM MST, NOV; DC 7; SSC 7; WLC**

Turgot, Anne-Robert-Jacques 1727-1781 **L C 26**

Turner, Frederick 1943- .... **CLC 48**
See also CA 73-76; CAAS 10; CANR 12, 30, 56; DLB 40

Tutu, Desmond M(pilo) 1931-**CLC 80; BLC 3; DAM MULT**
See also BW 1; CA 125; CANR 67

Tutuola, Amos 1920-1997**CLC 5, 14, 29; BLC 3; DAM MULT**
See also BW 2; CA 9-12R; 159; CANR 27, 66; DLB 125; MTCW 1

Twain, MarkTCLC 6, 12, 19, 36, 48, 59; SSC 6, 26; WLC**
See also Clemens, Samuel Langhorne
See also AAYA 20; DLB 11, 12, 23, 64, 74

Tyler, Anne 1941- . **CLC 7, 11, 18, 28, 44, 59, 103; DAM NOV, POP**
See also AAYA 18; BEST 89:1; CA 9-12R; CANR 11, 33, 53; DLB 6, 143; DLBY 82; MTCW 1; SATA 7, 90

Tyler, Royall 1757-1826 .... **NCLC 3**
See also DLB 37

Tynan, Katharine 1861-1931 .... **TCLC 3**
See also CA 104; 167; DLB 153

Tyutchev, Fyodor 1803-1873 .... **NCLC 34**

Tzara, Tristan 1896-1963 ...... **CLC 47; DAM POET**
See also CA 153; 89-92

Uhry, Alfred 1936- ... **CLC 55; DAM DRAM, POP**
See also CA 127; 133; INT 133

Ulf, Haerved
See Strindberg, (Johan) August

Ulf, Harved
See Strindberg, (Johan) August

Ulibarri, Sabine R(eyes) 1919-**CLC 83; DAM MULT**
See also CA 131; DLB 82; HW

Unamuno (y Jugo), Miguel de 1864-1936 **TCLC 2, 9; DAM MULT, NOV; HLC; SSC 11**
See also CA 104; 131; DLB 108; HW; MTCW 1

Undercliffe, Errol
See Campbell, (John) Ramsey

Underwood, Miles

See also CA 13-16R; CAAS 22; CANR 5, 21, 44, 67; DLB 175; NNAL
Vizinczey, Stephen 1933- .... **CLC 40**
See also CA 128; INT 128
Vliet, R(ussell) G(ordon) 1929-1984 **CLC 22**
See also CA 37-40R; 112; CANR 18
Vogau, Boris Andreyevich 1894-1937(?)
See Pilnyak, Boris
See also CA 123
Vogel, Paula A(nne) 1951- .... **CLC 76**
See also CA 108
Voigt, Cynthia 1942-.......................... **CLC 30**
See also AAYA 3; CA 106; CANR 18, 37, 40; CLR 13, 48; INT CANR-18; JRDA; MAICYA; SATA 48, 79; SATA-Brief 33
Voigt, Ellen Bryant 1943- .... **CLC 54**
See also CA 69-72; CANR 11, 29, 55; DLB 120
Voinovich, Vladimir (Nikolaevich) 1932-**CLC 10, 49**
See also CA 81-84; CAAS 12; CANR 33, 67; MTCW 1
Vollmann, William T. 1959- ..**CLC 89; DAM NOV, POP**
See also CA 134; CANR 67
Voloshinov, V. N.
See Bakhtin, Mikhail Mikhailovich
Voltaire 1694-1778. **LC 14; DA; DAB; DAC; DAM DRAM, MST; SSC 12; WLC**
von Aschendrof, BaronIgnatz
See Ford, Ford Madox
von Daeniken, Erich 1935- .... **CLC 30**
See also AITN 1; CA 37-40R; CANR 17, 44
von Daniken, Erich
See von Daeniken, Erich
von Heidenstam, (Carl Gustaf) Verner
See Heidenstam, (Carl Gustaf) Verner von
von Heyse, Paul (Johann Ludwig)
See Heyse, Paul (Johann Ludwig von)
von Hofmannsthal, Hugo
See Hofmannsthal, Hugo von
von Horvath, Odon
See Horvath, Oedoen von
von Horvath, Oedoen
See Horvath, Oedoen von
von Liliencron, (Friedrich Adolf Axel) Detlev
See Liliencron, (Friedrich Adolf Axel) Detlev von
Vonnegut, Kurt, Jr. 1922-**CLC 1, 2, 3, 4, 5, 8, 12, 22, 40, 60, 111; DA; DAB; DAC; DAM MST, NOV, POP; SSC 8; WLC**
See also AAYA 6; AITN 1; BEST 90:4; CA 1-4R; CANR 1, 25, 49, 75; CDALB 1968-1988; DLB 2, 8, 152; DLBD 3; DLBY 80; MTCW 1
Von Rachen, Kurt
See Hubbard, L(afayette) Ron(ald)
von Rezzori (d'Arezzo), Gregor
See Rezzori (d'Arezzo), Gregor von
von Sternberg, Josef
See Sternberg, Josef von
Vorster, Gordon 1924-......................... **CLC 34**
See also CA 133
Vosce, Trudie
See Ozick, Cynthia
Voznesensky, Andrei (Andreievich) 1933- **CLC 1, 15, 57; DAM POET**
See also CA 89-92; CANR 37; MTCW 1
Waddington, Miriam 1917-.................... **CLC 28**
See also CA 21-24R; CANR 12, 30; DLB 68
Wagman, Fredrica 1937- .... **CLC 7**
See also CA 97-100; INT 97-100
Wagner, Linda W.
See Wagner-Martin, Linda (C.)
Wagner, Linda Welshimer
See Wagner-Martin, Linda (C.)
Wagner, Richard 1813-1883 .... **NCLC 9**
See also DLB 129

Wagner-Martin, Linda (C.) 1936- .... **CLC 50**
See also CA 159
Wagoner, David (Russell) 1926- **CLC 3, 5, 15**
See also CA 1-4R; CAAS 3; CANR 2, 71; DLB 5; SATA 14
Wah, Fred(erick James) 1939- .... **CLC 44**
See also CA 107; 141; DLB 60
Wahloo, Per 1926-1975 .... **CLC 7**
See also CA 61-64; CANR 73
Wahloo, Peter
See Wahloo, Per
Wain, John (Barrington) 1925-1994 . **CLC 2, 11, 15, 46**
See also CA 5-8R; 145; CAAS 4; CANR 23, 54; CDBLB 1960 to Present; DLB 15, 27, 139, 155; MTCW 1
Wajda, Andrzej 1926- .... **CLC 16**
See also CA 102
Wakefield, Dan 1932- .... **CLC 7**
See also CA 21-24R; CAAS 7
Wakoski, Diane 1937- **CLC 2, 4, 7, 9, 11, 40; DAM POET; PC 15**
See also CA 13-16R; CAAS 1; CANR 9, 60; DLB 5; INT CANR-9
Wakoski-Sherbell, Diane
See Wakoski, Diane
Walcott, Derek (Alton) 1930-**CLC 2, 4, 9, 14, 25, 42, 67, 76; BLC 3; DAB; DAC; DAM MST, MULT, POET; DC 7**
See also BW 2; CA 89-92; CANR 26, 47, 75; DLB 117; DLBY 81; MTCW 1
Waldman, Anne (Lesley) 1945- .... **CLC 7**
See also CA 37-40R; CAAS 17; CANR 34, 69; DLB 16
Waldo, E. Hunter
See Sturgeon, Theodore (Hamilton)
Waldo, Edward Hamilton
See Sturgeon, Theodore (Hamilton)
Walker, Alice (Malsenior) 1944- **CLC 5, 6, 9, 19, 27, 46, 58, 103; BLC 3; DA; DAB; DAC; DAM MST, MULT, NOV, POET, POP; SSC 5; WLCS**
See also AAYA 3; BEST 89:4; BW 2; CA 37-40R; CANR 9, 27, 49, 66; CDALB 1968-1988; DLB 6, 33, 143; INT CANR-27; MTCW 1; SATA 31
Walker, David Harry 1911-1992 .... **CLC 14**
See also CA 1-4R; 137; CANR 1; SATA 8; SATA-Obit 71
Walker, Edward Joseph 1934-
See Walker, Ted
See also CA 21-24R; CANR 12, 28, 53
Walker, George F. 1947- . **CLC 44, 61; DAB; DAC; DAM MST**
See also CA 103; CANR 21, 43, 59; DLB 60
Walker, Joseph A. 1935- .... **CLC 19; DAM DRAM, MST**
See also BW 1; CA 89-92; CANR 26; DLB 38
Walker, Margaret (Abigail) 1915-1998**CLC 1, 6; BLC; DAM MULT; PC 20**
See also BW 2; CA 73-76; 172; CANR 26, 54, 76; DLB 76, 152; MTCW 1
Walker, Ted .... **CLC 13**
See also Walker, Edward Joseph
See also DLB 40
Wallace, David Foster 1962- ..... **CLC 50, 114**
See also CA 132; CANR 59
Wallace, Dexter
See Masters, Edgar Lee
Wallace, (Richard Horatio) Edgar 1875-1932 **TCLC 57**
See also CA 115; DLB 70
Wallace, Irving 1916-1990 **CLC 7, 13; DAM NOV, POP**
See also AITN 1; CA 1-4R; 132; CAAS 1; CANR 1, 27; INT CANR-27; MTCW 1
Wallant, Edward Lewis 1926-1962**CLC 5, 10**

See also CA 1-4R; CANR 22; DLB 2, 28, 143; MTCW 1
Wallas, Graham 1858-1932 .... **TCLC 91**
Walley, Byron
See Card, Orson Scott
Walpole, Horace 1717-1797 ....**LC 49**
See also DLB 39, 104
Walpole, Hugh (Seymour) 1884-1941**TCLC 5**
See also CA 104; 165; DLB 34
Walser, Martin 1927-.......................... **CLC 27**
See also CA 57-60; CANR 8, 46; DLB 75, 124
Walser, Robert 1878-1956 **TCLC 18; SSC 20**
See also CA 118; 165; DLB 66
Walsh, Jill Paton .... **CLC 35**
See also Paton Walsh, Gillian
See also AAYA 11; CLR 2; DLB 161; SAAS 3
Walter, Villiam Christian
See Andersen, Hans Christian
Wambaugh, Joseph (Aloysius, Jr.) 1937-**CLC 3, 18; DAM NOV, POP**
See also AITN 1; BEST 89:3; CA 33-36R; CANR 42, 65; DLB 6; DLBY 83; MTCW 1
Wang Wei 699(?)-761(?) .... **PC 18**
Ward, Arthur Henry Sarsfield 1883-1959
See Rohmer, Sax
See also CA 108
Ward, Douglas Turner 1930- .... **CLC 19**
See also BW 1; CA 81-84; CANR 27; DLB 7, 38
Ward, Mary Augusta
See Ward, Mrs. Humphry
Ward, Mrs. Humphry 1851-1920 .. **TCLC 55**
See also DLB 18
Ward, Peter
See Faust, Frederick (Schiller)
Warhol, Andy 1928(?)-1987 .... **CLC 20**
See also AAYA 12; BEST 89:4; CA 89-92; 121; CANR 34
Warner, Francis (Robert le Plastrier) 1937- **CLC 14**
See also CA 53-56; CANR 11
Warner, Marina 1946- .... **CLC 59**
See also CA 65-68; CANR 21, 55; DLB 194
Warner, Rex (Ernest) 1905-1986 ...... **CLC 45**
See also CA 89-92; 119; DLB 15
Warner, Susan (Bogert) 1819-1885 **NCLC 31**
See also DLB 3, 42
Warner, Sylvia (Constance) Ashton
See Ashton-Warner, Sylvia (Constance)
Warner, Sylvia Townsend 1893-1978 **CLC 7, 19; SSC 23**
See also CA 61-64; 77-80; CANR 16, 60; DLB 34, 139; MTCW 1
Warren, Mercy Otis 1728-1814 ..... **NCLC 13**
See also DLB 31, 200
Warren, Robert Penn 1905-1989**CLC 1, 4, 6, 8, 10, 13, 18, 39, 53, 59; DA; DAB; DAC; DAM MST, NOV, POET; SSC 4; WLC**
See also AITN 1; CA 13-16R; 129; CANR 10, 47; CDALB 1968-1988; DLB 2, 48, 152; DLBY 80, 89; INT CANR-10; MTCW 1; SATA 46; SATA-Obit 63
Warshofsky, Isaac
See Singer, Isaac Bashevis
Warton, Thomas 1728-1790 .....**LC 15; DAM POET**
See also DLB 104, 109
Waruk, Kona
See Harris, (Theodore) Wilson
Warung, Price 1855-1911 .... **TCLC 45**
Warwick, Jarvis
See Garner, Hugh
Washington, Alex
See Harris, Mark
Washington, Booker T(aliaferro) 1856-1915 **TCLC 10; BLC 3; DAM MULT**
See also BW 1; CA 114; 125; SATA 28

Wilson, Robert M. 1944- .... CLC 7, 9
  See also CA 49-52; CANR 2, 41; MTCW 1
Wilson, Robert McLiam 1964- .... CLC 59
  See also CA 132
Wilson, Sloan 1920- .... CLC 32
  See also CA 1-4R; CANR 1, 44
Wilson, Snoo 1948- .... CLC 33
  See also CA 69-72
Wilson, William S(mith) 1932- .... CLC 49
  See also CA 81-84
Wilson, (Thomas) Woodrow 1856-1924TCLC 79
  See also CA 166; DLB 47
Winchilsea, Anne (Kingsmill) Finch Counte
  1661-1720
  See Finch, Anne
Windham, Basil
  See Wodehouse, P(elham) G(renville)
Wingrove, David (John) 1954- .... CLC 68
  See also CA 133
Wintergreen, Jane
  See Duncan, Sara Jeannette
Winters, Janet Lewis .... CLC 41
  See also Lewis, Janet
  See also DLBY 87
Winters, (Arthur) Yvor 1900-1968 CLC 4, 8, 32
  See also CA 11-12; 25-28R; CAP 1; DLB 48; MTCW 1
Winterson, Jeanette 1959-CLC 64; DAM POP
  See also CA 136; CANR 58; DLB 207
Winthrop, John 1588-1649 .... LC 31
  See also DLB 24, 30
Wiseman, Frederick 1930- .... CLC 20
  See also CA 159
Wister, Owen 1860-1938 .... TCLC 21
  See also CA 108; 162; DLB 9, 78, 186; SATA 62
Witkacy
  See Witkiewicz, Stanislaw Ignacy
Witkiewicz, Stanislaw Ignacy 1885-1939 TCLC 8
  See also CA 105; 162
Wittgenstein, Ludwig (Josef Johann) 1889-1951 TCLC 59
  See also CA 113; 164
Wittig, Monique 1935(?)- .... CLC 22
  See also CA 116; 135; DLB 83
Wittlin, Jozef 1896-1976 .... CLC 25
  See also CA 49-52; 65-68; CANR 3
Wodehouse, P(elham) G(renville) 1881-1975 CLC 1, 2, 5, 10, 22; DAB; DAC; DAM NOV; SSC 2
  See also AITN 2; CA 45-48; 57-60; CANR 3, 33; CDBLB 1914-1945; DLB 34, 162; MTCW 1; SATA 22
Woiwode, L.
  See Woiwode, Larry (Alfred)
Woiwode, Larry (Alfred) 1941- .... CLC 6, 10
  See also CA 73-76; CANR 16; DLB 6; INT CANR-16
Wojciechowska, Maia (Teresa) 1927-CLC 26
  See also AAYA 8; CA 9-12R; CANR 4, 41; CLR 1; JRDA; MAICYA; SAAS 1; SATA 1, 28, 83; SATA-Essay 104
Wolf, Christa 1929- .... CLC 14, 29, 58
  See also CA 85-88; CANR 45; DLB 75; MTCW 1
Wolfe, Gene (Rodman) 1931- CLC 25; DAM POP
  See also CA 57-60; CAAS 9; CANR 6, 32, 60; DLB 8
Wolfe, George C. 1954- .... CLC 49; BLCS
  See also CA 149
Wolfe, Thomas (Clayton) 1900-1938TCLC 4, 13, 29, 61; DA; DAB; DAC; DAM MST, NOV; SSC 33; WLC

See also CA 104; 132; CDALB 1929-1941; DLB 9, 102; DLBD 2, 16; DLBY 85, 97; MTCW 1
Wolfe, Thomas Kennerly, Jr. 1930-
  See Wolfe, Tom
  See also CA 13-16R; CANR 9, 33, 70; DAM POP; DLB 185; INT CANR-9; MTCW 1
Wolfe, Tom .... CLC 1, 2, 9, 15, 35, 51
  See also Wolfe, Thomas Kennerly, Jr.
  See also AAYA 8; AITN 2; BEST 89:1; DLB 152
Wolff, Geoffrey (Ansell) 1937- ....CLC 41
  See also CA 29-32R; CANR 29, 43
Wolff, Sonia
  See Levitin, Sonia (Wolff)
Wolff, Tobias (Jonathan Ansell) 1945- . C L C 39, 64
  See also AAYA 16; BEST 90:2; CA 114; 117; CAAS 22; CANR 54, 76; DLB 130; INT 117
Wolfram von Eschenbach c. 1170-c. 1220 CMLC 5
  See also DLB 138
Wolitzer, Hilma 1930- .... CLC 17
  See also CA 65-68; CANR 18, 40; INT CANR-18; SATA 31
Wollstonecraft, Mary 1759-1797 .... LC 5
  See also CDBLB 1789-1832; DLB 39, 104, 158
Wonder, Stevie .... CLC 12
  See also Morris, Steveland Judkins
Wong, Jade Snow 1922- .... CLC 17
  See also CA 109
Woodberry, George Edward 1855-1930 TCLC 73
  See also CA 165; DLB 71, 103
Woodcott, Keith
  See Brunner, John (Kilian Houston)
Woodruff, Robert W.
  See Mencken, H(enry) L(ouis)
Woolf, (Adeline) Virginia 1882-1941TCLC 1, 5, 20, 43, 56; DA; DAB; DAC; DAM MST, NOV; SSC 7; WLC
  See also CA 104; 130; CANR 64; CDBLB 1914-1945; DLB 36, 100, 162; DLBD 10; MTCW 1
Woolf, Virginia Adeline
  See Woolf, (Adeline) Virginia
Woollcott, Alexander (Humphreys) 1887-1943 TCLC 5
  See also CA 105; 161; DLB 29
Woolrich, Cornell 1903-1968 .... CLC 77
  See also Hopley-Woolrich, Cornell George
Wordsworth, Dorothy 1771-1855 .. NCLC 25
  See also DLB 107
Wordsworth, William 1770-1850..NCLC 12, 38; DA; DAB; DAC; DAM MST, POET; PC 4; WLC
  See also CDBLB 1789-1832; DLB 93, 107
Wouk, Herman 1915-CLC 1, 9, 38; DAM NOV, POP
  See also CA 5-8R; CANR 6, 33, 67; DLBY 82; INT CANR-6; MTCW 1
Wright, Charles (Penzel, Jr.) 1935-CLC 6, 13, 28
  See also CA 29-32R; CAAS 7; CANR 23, 36, 62; DLB 165; DLBY 82; MTCW 1
Wright, Charles Stevenson 1932- ... CLC 49; BLC 3; DAM MULT; POET
  See also BW 1; CA 9-12R; CANR 26; DLB 33
Wright, Frances 1795-1852 .... NCLC 74
  See also DLB 73
Wright, Jack R.
  See Harris, Mark
Wright, James (Arlington) 1927-1980CLC 3, 5, 10, 28; DAM POET
  See also AITN 2; CA 49-52; 97-100; CANR 4, 34, 64; DLB 5, 169; MTCW 1
Wright, Judith (Arandell) 1915- CLC 11, 53;

PC 14
  See also CA 13-16R; CANR 31, 76; MTCW 1; SATA 14
Wright, L(aurali) R. 1939- .... CLC 44
  See also CA 138
Wright, Richard (Nathaniel) 1908-1960 C L C 1, 3, 4, 9, 14, 21, 48, 74; BLC 3; DA; DAB; DAC; DAM MST, MULT, NOV; SSC 2; WLC
  See also AAYA 5; BW 1; CA 108; CANR 64; CDALB 1929-1941; DLB 76, 102; DLBD 2; MTCW 1
Wright, Richard B(ruce) 1937- .... CLC 6
  See also CA 85-88; DLB 53
Wright, Rick 1945- .... CLC 35
Wright, Rowland
  See Wells, Carolyn
Wright, Stephen 1946- .... CLC 33
Wright, Willard Huntington 1888-1939
  See Van Dine, S. S.
  See also CA 115; DLBD 16
Wright, William 1930- .... CLC 44
  See also CA 53-56; CANR 7, 23
Wroth, LadyMary 1587-1653(?) .... LC 30
  See also DLB 121
Wu Ch'eng-en 1500(?)-1582(?) .... LC 7
Wu Ching-tzu 1701-1754 .... LC 2
Wurlitzer, Rudolph 1938(?)- .... CLC 2, 4, 15
  See also CA 85-88; DLB 173
Wycherley, William 1641-1715LC 8, 21; DAM DRAM
  See also CDBLB 1660-1789; DLB 80
Wylie, Elinor (Morton Hoyt) 1885-1928 TCLC 8; PC 23
  See also CA 105; 162; DLB 9, 45
Wylie, Philip (Gordon) 1902-1971 ... CLC 43
  See also CA 21-22; 33-36R; CAP 2; DLB 9
Wyndham, John .... CLC 19
  See also Harris, John (Wyndham Parkes Lucas) Beynon
Wyss, Johann David Von 1743-1818NCLC 10
  See also JRDA; MAICYA; SATA 29; SATA-Brief 27
Xenophon c. 430B.C.-c. 354B.C. ... CMLC 17
  See also DLB 176
Yakumo Koizumi
  See Hearn, (Patricio) Lafcadio (Tessima Carlos)
Yanez, Jose Donoso
  See Donoso (Yanez), Jose
Yanovsky, Basile S.
  See Yanovsky, V(assily) S(emenovich)
Yanovsky, V(assily) S(emenovich) 1906-1989 CLC 2, 18
  See also CA 97-100; 129
Yates, Richard 1926-1992 .... CLC 7, 8, 23
  See also CA 5-8R; 139; CANR 10, 43; DLB 2; DLBY 81, 92; INT CANR-10
Yeats, W. B.
  See Yeats, William Butler
Yeats, William Butler 1865-1939TCLC 1, 11, 18, 31; DA; DAB; DAC; DAM DRAM, MST, POET; PC 20; WLC
  See also CA 104; 127; CANR 45; CDBLB 1890-1914; DLB 10, 19, 98, 156; MTCW 1
Yehoshua, A(braham) B. 1936-.. CLC 13, 31
  See also CA 33-36R; CANR 43
Yep, Laurence Michael 1948- .... CLC 35
  See also AAYA 5; CA 49-52; CANR 1, 46; CLR 3, 17, 54; DLB 52; JRDA; MAICYA; SATA 7, 69
Yerby, Frank G(arvin) 1916-1991 .CLC 1, 7, 22; BLC 3; DAM MULT
  See also BW 1; CA 9-12R; 136; CANR 16, 52; DLB 76; INT CANR-16; MTCW 1
Yesenin, Sergei Alexandrovich
  See Esenin, Sergei (Alexandrovich)
Yevtushenko, Yevgeny (Alexandrovich) 1933-

CLC 1, 3, 13, 26, 51; DAM POET
See also CA 81-84; CANR 33, 54; MTCW 1
Yezierska, Anzia 1885(?)-1970 .... **CLC 46**
See also CA 126; 89-92; DLB 28; MTCW 1
Yglesias, Helen 1915- .... **CLC 7, 22**
See also CA 37-40R; CAAS 20; CANR 15, 65;
INT CANR-15; MTCW 1
Yokomitsu Riichi 1898-1947 .... **TCLC 47**
See also CA 170
Yonge, Charlotte (Mary) 1823-1901 **TCLC 48**
See also CA 109; 163; DLB 18, 163; SATA 17
York, Jeremy
See Creasey, John
York, Simon
See Heinlein, Robert A(nson)
Yorke, Henry Vincent 1905-1974 ...... **CLC 13**
See also Green, Henry
See also CA 85-88; 49-52
Yosano Akiko 1878-1942 .... **TCLC 59; PC 11**
See also CA 161
Yoshimoto, Banana .... **CLC 84**
See also Yoshimoto, Mahoko
Yoshimoto, Mahoko 1964-
See Yoshimoto, Banana
See also CA 144
Young, Al(bert James) 1939- **CLC 19; BLC 3;
DAM MULT**
See also BW 2; CA 29-32R; CANR 26, 65; DLB
33
Young, Andrew (John) 1885-1971 ...... **CLC 5**
See also CA 5-8R; CANR 7, 29
Young, Collier
See Bloch, Robert (Albert)
Young, Edward 1683-1765 .... **LC 3, 40**
See also DLB 95
Young, Marguerite (Vivian) 1909-1995 **C L C
82**
See also CA 13-16; 150; CAP 1
Young, Neil 1945- .... **CLC 17**
See also CA 110
Young Bear, Ray A. 1950- ...... **CLC 94; DAM
MULT**
See also CA 146; DLB 175; NNAL
Yourcenar, Marguerite 1903-1987 **CLC 19, 38,
50, 87; DAM NOV**
See also CA 69-72; CANR 23, 60; DLB 72;
DLBY 88; MTCW 1
Yurick, Sol 1925- .... **CLC 6**
See also CA 13-16R; CANR 25
Zabolotsky, Nikolai Alekseevich 1903-1958
TCLC 52
See also CA 116; 164
Zamiatin, Yevgenii
See Zamyatin, Evgeny Ivanovich
Zamora, Bernice (B. Ortiz) 1938- .. **CLC 89;
DAM MULT; HLC**
See also CA 151; DLB 82; HW
Zamyatin, Evgeny Ivanovich 1884-1937
TCLC 8, 37
See also CA 105; 166
Zangwill, Israel 1864-1926 .... **TCLC 16**
See also CA 109; 167; DLB 10, 135, 197
Zappa, Francis Vincent, Jr. 1940-1993
See Zappa, Frank
See also CA 108; 143; CANR 57
Zappa, Frank .... **CLC 17**
See also Zappa, Francis Vincent, Jr.
Zaturenska, Marya 1902-1982 ...... **CLC 6, 11**
See also CA 13-16R; 105; CANR 22
Zeami 1363-1443 .... **DC 7**
Zelazny, Roger (Joseph) 1937-1995 . **CLC 21**
See also AAYA 7; CA 21-24R; 148; CANR 26,
60; DLB 8; MTCW 1; SATA 57; SATA-Brief
39
Zhdanov, Andrei Alexandrovich 1896-1948
TCLC 18
See also CA 117; 167

Zhukovsky, Vasily (Andreevich) 1783-1852
NCLC 35
See also DLB 205
Ziegenhagen, Eric .... **CLC 55**
Zimmer, Jill Schary
See Robinson, Jill
Zimmerman, Robert
See Dylan, Bob
Zindel, Paul 1936- **CLC 6, 26; DA; DAB; DAC;
DAM DRAM, MST, NOV; DC 5**
See also AAYA 2; CA 73-76; CANR 31, 65;
CLR 3, 45; DLB 7, 52; JRDA; MAICYA;
MTCW 1; SATA 16, 58, 102
Zinov'Ev, A. A.
See Zinoviev, Alexander (Aleksandrovich)
Zinoviev, Alexander (Aleksandrovich) 1922-
CLC 19
See also CA 116; 133; CAAS 10
Zoilus
See Lovecraft, H(oward) P(hillips)
Zola, Emile (Edouard Charles Antoine) 1840-
1902 **TCLC 1, 6, 21, 41; DA; DAB; DAC;
DAM MST, NOV; WLC**
See also CA 104; 138; DLB 123
Zoline, Pamela 1941- .... **CLC 62**
See also CA 161
Zorrilla y Moral, Jose 1817-1893 .... **NCLC 6**
Zoshchenko, Mikhail (Mikhailovich) 1895-1958
TCLC 15; SSC 15
See also CA 115; 160
Zuckmayer, Carl 1896-1977 .... **CLC 18**
See also CA 69-72; DLB 56, 124
Zuk, Georges
See Skelton, Robin
Zukofsky, Louis 1904-1978 **CLC 1, 2, 4, 7, 11,
18; DAM POET; PC 11**
See also CA 9-12R; 77-80; CANR 39; DLB 5,
165; MTCW 1
Zweig, Paul 1935-1984 .... **CLC 34, 42**
See also CA 85-88; 113
Zweig, Stefan 1881-1942 .... **TCLC 17**
See also CA 112; 170; DLB 81, 118
Zwingli, Huldreich 1484-1531 .... **LC 37**
See also DLB 179

Literary Criticism Series
Cumulative Topic Index

This index lists all topic entries in Gale's *Classical and Medieval Literature Criticism, Contemporary Literary Criticism, Literature Criticism from 1400 to 1800, Nineteenth-Century Literature Criticism,* and *Twentieth-Century Literary Criticism.*

Topic Index

Topic Index

Topic Index

Twentieth-Century Literary Criticism
Cumulative Nationality Index

Hardy, Thomas **4, 10, 18, 32, 48, 53, 72**
Henley, William Ernest **8**
Hilton, James **21**
Hodgson, William Hope **13**
Hope, Anthony **83**
Housman, A(lfred) E(dward) **1, 10**
Housman, Laurence **7**
Hudson, W(illiam) H(enry) **29**
Hulme, T(homas) E(rnest) **21**
Hunt, Violet **53**
Jacobs, W(illiam) W(ymark) **22**
James, Montague (Rhodes) **6**
Jerome, Jerome K(lapka) **23**
Johnson, Lionel (Pigot) **19**
Kaye-Smith, Sheila **20**
Keynes, John Maynard **64**
Kipling, (Joseph) Rudyard **8, 17**
Laski, Harold **79**
Lawrence, D(avid) H(erbert Richards) **2, 9, 16, 33, 48, 61**
Lawrence, T(homas) E(dward) **18**
Lee, Vernon **5**
Lee-Hamilton, Eugene (Jacob) **22**
Leverson, Ada **18**
Lewis, (Percy) Wyndham **2, 9**
Lindsay, David **15**
Lowndes, Marie Adelaide (Belloc) **12**
Lowry, (Clarence) Malcolm **6, 40**
Lucas, E(dward) V(errall) **73**
Macaulay, Rose **7, 44**
MacCarthy, (Charles Otto) Desmond **36**
Maitland, Frederic **65**
Manning, Frederic **25**
Meredith, George **17, 43**
Mew, Charlotte (Mary) **8**
Meynell, Alice (Christina Gertrude Thompson) **6**
Middleton, Richard (Barham) **56**
Milne, A(lan) A(lexander) **6, 88**
Moore, G. E. **89**
Morrison, Arthur **72**
Murry, John Middleton **16**
Nightingale, Florence **85**
Noyes, Alfred **7**
Oppenheim, E(dward) Phillips **45**
Orwell, George **2, 6, 15, 31, 51**
Ouida **43**
Owen, Wilfred (Edward Salter) **5, 27**
Pinero, Arthur Wing **32**
Powys, T(heodore) F(rancis) **9**
Quiller-Couch, Arthur (Thomas) **53**
Richardson, Dorothy Miller **3**
Rohmer, Sax **28**
Rolfe, Frederick (William Serafino Austin Lewis Mary) **12**
Rosenberg, Isaac **12**
Ruskin, John **20**
Rutherford, Mark **25**
Sabatini, Rafael **47**
Saintsbury, George (Edward Bateman) **31**
Saki **3**
Sapper **44**
Sayers, Dorothy L(eigh) **2, 15**
Shiel, M(atthew) P(hipps) **8**
Sinclair, May **3, 11**
Stapledon, (William) Olaf **22**
Stead, William Thomas **48**
Stephen, Leslie **23**
Strachey, (Giles) Lytton **12**
Summers, (Alphonsus Joseph-Mary Augustus) Montague **16**
Sutro, Alfred **6**
Swinburne, Algernon Charles **8, 36**
Symons, Arthur **11**

Thomas, (Philip) Edward **10**
Thompson, Francis Joseph **4**
Tomlinson, H(enry) M(ajor) **71**
Upward, Allen **85**
Van Druten, John (William) **2**
Wallace, (Richard Horatio) Edgar **57**
Wallas, Graham **91**
Walpole, Hugh (Seymour) **5**
Ward, Mrs. Humphry **55**
Warung, Price **45**
Webb, (Martha) Beatrice (Potter) **22**
Webb, Mary (Gladys Meredith) **24**
Webb, Sidney (James) **22**
Welch, (Maurice) Denton **22**
Wells, H(erbert) G(eorge) **6, 12, 19**
Williams, Charles (Walter Stansby) **1, 11**
Woolf, (Adeline) Virginia **1, 5, 20, 43, 56**
Yonge, Charlotte (Mary) **48**
Zangwill, Israel **16**

ESTONIAN

Talvik, Heiti **87**
Tammsaare, A(nton) H(ansen) **27**

FINNISH

Leino, Eino **24**
Soedergran, Edith (Irene) **31**
Westermarck, Edward **87**

FRENCH

Alain **41**
Alain-Fournier **6**
Apollinaire, Guillaume **3, 8, 51**
Artaud, Antonin (Marie Joseph) **3, 36**
Barbusse, Henri **5**
Barres, (Auguste-) Maurice **47**
Benda, Julien **60**
Bergson, Henri(-Louis) **32**
Bernanos, (Paul Louis) Georges **3**
Bernhardt, Sarah (Henriette Rosine) **75**
Bloy, Leon **22**
Bourget, Paul (Charles Joseph) **12**
Claudel, Paul (Louis Charles Marie) **2, 10**
Colette, (Sidonie-Gabrielle) **1, 5, 16**
Coppee, Francois **25**
Daumal, Rene **14**
Desnos, Robert **22**
Drieu la Rochelle, Pierre(-Eugene) **21**
Dujardin, Edouard (Emile Louis) **13**
Durkheim, Emile **55**
Eluard, Paul **7, 41**
Fargue, Leon-Paul **11**
Feydeau, Georges (Leon Jules Marie) **22**
France, Anatole **9**
Gide, Andre (Paul Guillaume) **5, 12, 36**
Giraudoux, (Hippolyte) Jean **2, 7**
Gourmont, Remy (-Marie-Charles) de **17**
Huysmans, Joris-Karl **7, 69**
Jacob, (Cyprien-)Max **6**
Jammes, Francis **75**
Jarry, Alfred **2, 14**
Larbaud, Valery (Nicolas) **9**
Leautaud, Paul **83**
Leblanc, Maurice (Marie Emile) **49**
Leroux, Gaston **25**
Loti, Pierre **11**
Martin du Gard, Roger **24**
Melies, Georges **81**
Mirbeau, Octave **55**
Mistral, Frederic **51**
Moreas, Jean **18**
Nizan, Paul **40**
Peguy, Charles Pierre **10**

Peret, Benjamin **20**
Proust, (Valentin-Louis-George-Eugene-) Marcel **7, 13, 33**
Rachilde **67**
Radiguet, Raymond **29**
Renard, Jules **17**
Rolland, Romain **23**
Rostand, Edmond (Eugene Alexis) **6, 37**
Roussel, Raymond **20**
Saint-Exupery, Antoine (Jean Baptiste Marie Roger) de **2, 56**
Schwob, Marcel (Mayer Andre) **20**
Sorel, Georges **91**
Sully Prudhomme **31**
Teilhard de Chardin, (Marie Joseph) Pierre **9**
Valery, (Ambroise) Paul (Toussaint Jules) **4, 15**
Verne, Jules (Gabriel) **6, 52**
Vian, Boris **9**
Weil, Simone (Adolphine) **23**
Zola, Emile (Edouard Charles Antoine) **1, 6, 21, 41**

GERMAN

Andreas-Salome, Lou **56**
Auerbach, Erich **43**
Barlach, Ernst **84**
Benjamin, Walter **39**
Benn, Gottfried **3**
Borchert, Wolfgang **5**
Brecht, (Eugen) Bertolt (Friedrich) **1, 6, 13, 35**
Carossa, Hans **48**
Cassirer, Ernst **61**
Doblin, Alfred **13**
Doeblin, Alfred **13**
Einstein, Albert **65**
Ewers, Hanns Heinz **12**
Feuchtwanger, Lion **3**
Frank, Bruno **81**
George, Stefan (Anton) **2, 14**
Goebbels, (Paul) Joseph **68**
Haeckel, Ernst Heinrich (Philipp August) **83**
Hauptmann, Gerhart (Johann Robert) **4**
Heym, Georg (Theodor Franz Arthur) **9**
Heyse, Paul (Johann Ludwig von) **8**
Hitler, Adolf **53**
Horney, Karen (Clementine Theodore Danielsen) **71**
Huch, Ricarda (Octavia) **13**
Kaiser, Georg **9**
Klabund **44**
Kolmar, Gertrud **40**
Lasker-Schueler, Else **57**
Liliencron, (Friedrich Adolf Axel) Detlev von **18**
Luxemburg, Rosa **63**
Mann, (Luiz) Heinrich **9**
Mann, (Paul) Thomas **2, 8, 14, 21, 35, 44, 60**
Mannheim, Karl **65**
Michels, Robert **88**
Morgenstern, Christian **8**
Nietzsche, Friedrich (Wilhelm) **10, 18, 55**
Ophuls, Max **79**
Otto, Rudolf **85**
Plumpe, Friedrich Wilhelm **53**
Raabe, Wilhelm (Karl) **45**
Rilke, Rainer Maria **1, 6, 19**
Simmel, Georg **64**
Spengler, Oswald (Arnold Gottfried) **25**
Sternheim, (William Adolf) Carl **8**
Sudermann, Hermann **15**
Toller, Ernst **10**
Vaihinger, Hans **71**
Wassermann, (Karl) Jakob **6**
Weber, Max **69**

Esenin, Sergei (Alexandrovich) **4**
Fadeyev, Alexander **53**
Gladkov, Fyodor (Vasilyevich) **27**
Gorky, Maxim **8**
Gumilev, Nikolai (Stepanovich) **60**
Gurdjieff, G(eorgei) I(vanovich) **71**
Guro, Elena **56**
Hippius, Zinaida **9**
Ilf, Ilya **21**
Ivanov, Vyacheslav Ivanovich **33**
Khlebnikov, Velimir **20**
Khodasevich, Vladislav (Felitsianovich) **15**
Korolenko, Vladimir Galaktionovich **22**
Kropotkin, Peter (Aleksieevich) **36**
Kuprin, Aleksandr Ivanovich **5**
Kuzmin, Mikhail **40**
Lenin, V. I. **67**
Mandelstam, Osip (Emilievich) **2, 6**
Mayakovski, Vladimir (Vladimirovich) **4, 18**
Merezhkovsky, Dmitry Sergeyevich **29**
Pavlov, Ivan Petrovich **91**
Petrov, Evgeny **21**
Pilnyak, Boris **23**
Platonov, Andrei **14**
Prishvin, Mikhail **75**
Remizov, Aleksei (Mikhailovich) **27**
Shestov, Lev **56**
Sologub, Fyodor **9**
Tolstoy, Alexey Nikolaevich **18**
Tolstoy, Leo (Nikolaevich) **4, 11, 17, 28, 44, 79**
Trotsky, Leon **22**
Tsvetaeva (Efron), Marina (Ivanovna) **7, 35**
Zabolotsky, Nikolai Alekseevich **52**
Zamyatin, Evgeny Ivanovich **8, 37**
Zhdanov, Andrei Alexandrovich **18**
Zoshchenko, Mikhail (Mikhailovich) **15**

SCOTTISH

Barrie, J(ames) M(atthew) **2**
Bridie, James **3**
Brown, George Douglas **28**
Buchan, John **41**
Cunninghame Graham, R(obert) B(ontine) **19**
Davidson, John **24**
Frazer, J(ames) G(eorge) **32**
Gibbon, Lewis Grassic **4**
Lang, Andrew **16**
MacDonald, George **9**
Muir, Edwin **2, 87**
Sharp, William **39**
Tey, Josephine **14**

SOUTH AFRICAN

Bosman, Herman Charles **49**
Campbell, (Ignatius) Roy (Dunnachie) **5**
Mqhayi, S(amuel) E(dward) K(rune Loliwe) **25**
Plaatje, Sol(omon) T(shekisho) **73**
Schreiner, Olive (Emilie Albertina) **9**
Smith, Pauline (Urmson) **25**
Vilakazi, Benedict Wallet **37**

SPANISH

Alas (y Urena), Leopoldo (Enrique Garcia) **29**
Barea, Arturo **14**
Baroja (y Nessi), Pio **8**
Benavente (y Martinez), Jacinto **3**
Blasco Ibanez, Vicente **12**
Echegaray (y Eizaguirre), Jose (Maria Waldo) **4**
Garcia Lorca, Federico **1, 7, 49**
Jimenez (Mantecon), Juan Ramon **4**
Machado (y Ruiz), Antonio **3**
Martinez Sierra, Gregorio **6**
Martinez Sierra, Maria (de la O'LeJarraga) **6**

Miro (Ferrer), Gabriel (Francisco Victor) **5**
Ortega y Gasset, Jose **9**
Pereda (y Sanchez de Porrua), Jose Maria de **16**
Perez Galdos, Benito **27**
Salinas (y Serrano), Pedro **17**
Unamuno (y Jugo), Miguel de **2, 9**
Valera y Alcala-Galiano, Juan **10**
Valle-Inclan, Ramon (Maria) del **5**

SWEDISH

Bengtsson, Frans (Gunnar) **48**
Dagerman, Stig (Halvard) **17**
Ekelund, Vilhelm **75**
Heidenstam, (Carl Gustaf) Verner von **5**
Key, Ellen **65**
Lagerloef, Selma (Ottiliana Lovisa) **4, 36**
Soderberg, Hjalmar **39**
Strindberg, (Johan) August **1, 8, 21, 47**

SWISS

Ramuz, Charles-Ferdinand **33**
Rod, Edouard **52**
Saussure, Ferdinand de **49**
Spitteler, Carl (Friedrich Georg) **12**
Walser, Robert **18**

SYRIAN

Gibran, Kahlil **1, 9**

TURKISH

Sait Faik **23**

UKRAINIAN

Aleichem, Sholom **1, 35**
Bialik, Chaim Nachman **25**

URUGUAYAN

Quiroga, Horacio (Sylvestre) **20**
Sanchez, Florencio **37**

WELSH

Davies, W(illiam) H(enry) **5**
Evans, Caradoc **85**
Lewis, Alun **3**
Machen, Arthur **4**
Thomas, Dylan (Marlais) **1, 8, 45**

TCLC-87 Title Index

Title Index

ISBN 0-7876-2739-9

90000

9 780787 627393